The CIVIL WAR YEARS

A Day-by-Day Chronicle of the Life of a Nation

ROBERT E. DENNEY

Foreword by Gregory J.W. Urwin

Sterling Publishing Co., Inc. New York

Acknowledgments

First, I would like to express my thanks to my wife, Frances, and our youngest son, Bruce, for their patience and effort in reading the manuscript for content.

Next, I would like to express my thanks to that "grand old man" Eldon "Josh" Billings, Civil War book expert and gentleman. Josh was kind enough to provide not only many of the diaries from his collection, but words of advice and encouragement which were deeply appreciated.

Further thanks for encouragement go to my friends and fellow members of the Civil War Round Table of the District of Columbia and the Lincoln Group of the District of Columbia. Special thanks go to Gayle Harris, my friend and magician at the Library of Congress, for her assistance. I wish also to thank Virginia Cherwek and Wendy Swanson for their welcome boost.

Finally, I wish to thank my editor, Keith L. Schiffman, for his seemingly endless patience in dealing with this project.

Library of Congress Cataloging-in-Publication Data

Denney, Robert E.
The Civil War Years : A Day-by-Day Chronicle of the Life of a Nation / Robert E. Denney ; foreword by Gregory J.W. Urwin.
p. cm.
Includes index.
ISBN 0-8069-8519-4
1. United States—History—Civil War, 1861-1865—Chronology.
2. United States—History—Civil War, 1861-1865—Sources.
I. Title.
E468.3.D44 1992
973.7'02'02—dc20 92-28956

CIP

10 9 8 7 6 5 4 3 2 1

First paperback edition published in 1994 by
Sterling Publishing Company, Inc.
387 Park Avenue South, New York, N.Y. 10016

Distributed in Canada by Sterling Publishing
c/o Canadian Manda Group, P.O.Box 920, Station U
Toronto, Ontario, Canada M8Z 5P9
Distributed in Great Britain and Europe by Cassell PLC
Villiers House, 41/47 Strand, London WC2N 5JE, England
Distributed in Australia by Capricorn Link (Australia) Pty Ltd.
P.O. Box 6651, Baulkham Hills, Business Centre, NSW 2153, Australia
Manufactured in the United States of America

Sterling ISBN 0-8069-8519-4 Trade
0-8069-8515-1 Paper

To my old high school history teacher

Arthur Pope

whose relating of the many stories and tales as told him by the Civil War veterans who were alive when he was a young man did much to inspire my interest in THE WAR.

May he rest in peace.

CONTENTS

FOREWORD

Gregory J. W. Urwin

The Civil War claimed more American lives than any other war in history. It is also the most written-about of America's wars. Though the Confederacy fell nearly 130 years ago, interest in the conflict that swept away the Old South remains high. The best-selling status achieved by such recent titles as *Battle Cry of Freedom* by James M. McPherson and *The Civil War* by Geoffrey Ward, Ric Burns, and Ken Burns attests to the public's enduring fascination with a period in which the United States nearly destroyed herself.

The elements that account for the Civil War's undying appeal are the same that go into the making of great drama. What other era in American history is so teeming with noble heroes and outright villains, military geniuses and bunglers, unspotted idealism and base corruption, miraculous battlefield victories and tragic defeats? And what single event so changed the nature of this nation or molded the character of her people? Anyone who wishes to understand what the United States is today cannot afford to ignore the Civil War.

In *The Civil War Years,* Robert E. Denney has prepared a rare treat for devotees of what the Lincoln Administration called the War of Rebellion. More than an authoritative reference tool, this is a book to be read from cover to cover, for it allows the reader to experience the Civil War as that struggle unfolded to the people caught up in it. Unlike E. B. Long's straightforward chronology, *The Civil War Day by Day,* Denney augments his daily entries with generous doses of eyewitness testimony. Here are the words of the soldiers, sailors, and civilians of the North and South, woven together in a narrative that is both moving and informative.

Perhaps the two most praiseworthy features of *The Civil War Years* are its comprehensiveness and balance. Far too many overviews of the Civil War are written by authors infatuated with Robert E. Lee and his brilliant exploits in the Eastern Theater. Instead of giving proper coverage to the campaigns waged in Western Theater, where hard-marching Union armies under Grant, Sherman, and Thomas scored the breakthroughs that actually decided the conflict, acolytes of the "Lee Cult" devote a disproportionate amount of their attention to the seesaw struggle in northern Virginia. Consequently, too many Americans still tend to view Johnny Reb as a superman and find it difficult to understand how he lost the war. Furthermore, Denney does not neglect the North's massive naval effort, which turned the South's navigable rivers into invasion routes and steadily inhibited the Confederacy's attempts to sustain her outnumbered armies.

Finally, Denney avoids the common pitfall of depicting the Civil War as some intricate chess game played by politicians and generals. It was a people's contest, demanding an unprecedented level of sacrifice from the opposing masses. It was the people of the North and South black and white alike, who shaped the war's outcome as much as their leaders. To his credit, Denney lets the men in the ranks tell much of the story. These were the men who did the killing and the dying, the men who upheld the causes defined by the politicians and carried out the decisions made by the generals, and their accounts lead us to an intimate familiarity with the real Civil War.

Denney acquired his sympathy for the lowly G.I.s of the Civil War—the Billy Yanks and the Johnny Rebs—through hard experience. A decorated combat veteran who saw action both in Korea and Vietnam, he served for three years in the U.S. Marine Corps, followed by seventeen years in the Army. He understands what truly matters to the men who fight wars, which is readily apparent on every page of *The Civil War Years.* He has assembled a haunting chorus of soldier voices to guide us on an unforgettable journey through four years of nightmare and glory.

The Civil War Years possesses a timeless quality, which makes it a worthy addition to our long canon of distinguished Civil War literature. A work of this size and scope demands a considerable amount of a reader's time, but those who make that investment will reap tremendous dividends in both entertainment and increased insight.

PROLOGUE

The American Civil War has probably been written about more than any other war in history. During the actual conflict, many writers, diarists, and magazines contributed millions of words (representing many man-hours of effort) to the description of people, places, and events. Today, countless scholars and buffs write articles, pamphlets, and books explaining the most minute events of the war. During the centennial celebration, a great surge of literature was published and this flood has scarcely abated.

This book doesn't attempt to prove a point, establish guilt (or innocence) for any action, political or military, that occurred during that period. It uses actual diaries and books of soldiers who participated in the conflict and records their daily lives. No attempt is made to analyze strategy, tactics, or troop movements.

The characters described within this book are real. Every attempt has been made to breathe life into their stories by providing a perspective of the overall event—the war.

THE MILITARY FORCES AT THE BEGINNING OF THE WAR

At the beginning of 1861, the United States Army and Navy were small indeed for so vast a country. The Army consisted of less than 16,000 officers and men. These were scattered over the entire country, with most of them in the west guarding settlers against Indians.

General Winfield Scott, a native Virginian, the senior officer in the service, was born in 1786. He was 75 at the beginning of the war. A veteran of every war since 1812, he had never commanded more than a few thousand troops in a single mass. Before the war, he was partial to the enlistment of Southern "gentlemen" into the Army, and took great pains to groom them for command. He would eventually be replaced by Major General George B. McClellan (whose ego was larger than Scott's own) and fade from public view. He refused an offer to head the Confederate Army, and chose instead to stay with the Union he had served for more than 40 years.

At the outset of the war there were 1,108 officers in the Army, counting all grades and ranks. Of these, 387 either resigned to join the Confederacy or were dismissed for sympathy with the South. The place of birth wasn't always a factor in where the individual officer placed his loyalty. Many Northerners went with the Confederacy, many Southern-born officers stayed with the North. There were 162 officers of slave-state origin who stayed with the Union. Of the 308 Army officers who listed their birthplaces within the 11 Confederate states, not counting the border states, 222 resigned in 1861, the remaining 86 staying with the Union. Eighty-one Virginia-born officers resigned, 47 remained;

from Tennessee, 18 resigned, 7 remained; 24 sons of North Carolina resigned while 8 stayed with the Union; and 6 of 34 South Carolinians fought in Union blue.

Within the United States Navy, in December 1860, there were 1554 officers present for duty. Of these, 373 "went South," 157 of that number were dismissed for Southern sympathies.

Much has been made of the resignation of the officers and little is heard of the common soldier or sailor and his beliefs. In the service of 1861 there was little room for regional preferences among the enlisted personnel. They did not have the option of resigning, as did the officers. If they left their duty station to go to the South, they were classed as deserters, and subject to execution if caught. In addition, the army of that day consisted mostly of the dregs of society—foreigners, misfits, malcontents, romantics, illiterates, wanderers, and adventurers. Few had regional ties to family or group. Life was hard on the frontier for the common soldier. He could hope for little more than long treks in pursuit of Indians, sleeping on the ground in all kinds of weather and a diet of hardtack and beans. He might become a "pincushion" for some Native American's arrows.

The sailors of the Navy were much like sailors anywhere, at any time, footloose and satisfied if their ship was decently operated. Life at sea in the mid-1800s was no picnic. Discipline was harsh, punishment swift and often cruel, and life expectancy not long. Due to the nature of the sea tradition, there were some black sailors in the Navy at the beginning of the war.

Many of the officers serving in the armies had been classmates at West Point; others never met during their years of service. Although both Lee and Grant served in Mexico during that war, Lee did not remember Grant. Many strong friendships developed before the war and would survive, although some friends would become antagonists. Joe Johnston, the only General Officer to resign and go South, did not meet Sherman until after the Battle of Bentonsville in 1865. These two would become good friends and Joe Johnston would attend Sherman's funeral in 1890, where he caught pneumonia from standing in the rain without his hat. Johnston died two weeks later.

Many of the officers, in or out of the service in 1861, were in rather unusual roles at the time the war started. Pierre G.T. Beauregard was Superintendent of West Point. William T. Sherman was head of a school in Baton Rouge, Louisiana, which later became Louisiana State University. McClellan was President of the Ohio and Mississippi Railroad in 1860. Grant was down on his luck after resigning in 1854, and he was "rescued" by the war. Joe Hooker was a farmer in California in 1861, after resigning from the Army in 1853. "Stonewall" Jackson was a professor of Artillery and Natural Philosophy (an unusual combination) at Virginia Military Institute (VMI) after resigning his Army commission in 1851. Leonidas Polk resigned his commission soon after graduation and entered the Virginia Theological Seminary in Alexandria, Virginia. By 1860, he was a bishop in the Episcopal Church in Louisiana.

POPULATION AS SHOWN IN THE 1860 CENSUS

The best picture we can get of the available manpower for the opposing sides in the war is that derived from the census of 1860. The figures are revealing in that it shows a *very* wide disparity between the North and South in available *white* manpower.

The total population for the country was 34,399,301, which included 29,257,471 whites and 4,441,830 blacks (slave and free) in *all* the states and the District of Columbia.

Of the white population, 20,010,771 lived outside the fifteen slave states, 5,447,220 within the eleven seceding slave states, and 1,499,480 in the four nonseceding slave states.

Blacks living in the eleven seceding slave states numbered 3,521,130 slaves and only 132,760 free, while those in the four nonseceding slave states had a population of 429,401 slaves and 118,027 free. Blacks living *outside* the slave states numbered 240,512.

The *white* population of the eleven seceding states was only 27 percent of the Northern white population—not much of a manpower pool.

The *black* population of the eleven seceding states was 60 percent of their white population. Of their black population, *free blacks* were only 3.6 percent of the white population (and most of these blacks were in Virginia, North Carolina, and Louisiana).

During the period of the Civil War, immigration to the Union never ceased, but it was stopped to the Southern states. During this period, about 233,000 Germans, 196,000 Irish, and 85,000 English immigrated to the United States.

THE SOCIETY AND ECONOMIES OF THE NORTH VERSUS THE SOUTH

By 1860, American society was largely concentrated in the few major cities of the North and the South. Southern ladies travelled to New York and Philadelphia on shopping trips and their men bought the latest in mechanical innovations there. Little manufacture was done in the South.

The United States was largely agricultural in 1860. Large cities were few. In that census year, only nine cities had a population of over 100,000, and only seven other cities had a population of over 50,000, none of the latter being in the South. The 1860 census shows the following population for the major cities involved in the war:

The nine cities in the United States with a population of over 100,000 were: New York (805,651), Philadelphia (562,529), Brooklyn (266,661), Baltimore (212,418), Boston (177,812), New Orleans (168,675), Cincinnati (161,044), St. Louis (160,773), and Chicago (109,260).

The seven cities with more than 50,000 but fewer than 100,000 included the largest, Buffalo (81,129), and the smallest, Providence, R.I. (50,666). Washington D.C. (61,122) ranked fifth in this category. The others were Newark (71,914), Louisville (68,033), Albany (62,367), and San Francisco (56,802).

Major southern cities, other than New Orleans, all had fewer than 50,000 inhabitants. These included Charleston, S.C. (40,578), Richmond (37,190), Montgomery (35,967), Mobile (29,508), Memphis (22,623), and Savannah (22,292). Other cities smaller than those just mentioned also played a prominent part in the war. These included Nashville, Natchez, Vicksburg, Chattanooga, Atlanta, Raleigh, and Columbia, S.C.

The amount of land under cultivation, the value of the products produced by that land, the livestock supported and used, and the use of products also varied greatly between North and South. The generalized figures, taken from the 1860 census, show the wide disparity.

Improved farmland accounted for more than 106 million acres in the North and a little over 57 million acres in the South. The cash value of the land in the North was in excess of 4.7 billion dollars, as opposed to 1.8 billion dollars in the South.

The North had nearly three times as many horses, and nearly twice the number of working oxen. In milk and beef cattle, sheep and swine, the North far outweighed the South. Only in the production of peas, beans, sweet potatoes, cotton and rice did the South exceed the North. The production of "truck garden" products for sale and preserving was much greater in the North than it was in the South. This category of food production had considerable impact in feeding both the civilian and military population.

The North far exceeded the South in exports and imports in 1860. With incomplete returns for the South, the North exceeded the South by about $195 million in exports and $321 million in imports. The largest ports were New York and New Orleans.

It is obvious from the above figures that the North was in better shape economically at the beginning of the war.

THE ISSUE OF STATES' RIGHTS

In 1798 the four Alien and Sedition Acts were passed by Congress to give then-President John Adams the authority to banish or imprison any foreigner he thought to be dangerous to the government. These acts were never used by President Adams; they were meant to embarrass and defeat Thomas Jefferson, who was running for the Presidency. Jefferson and his friend James Madison instigated legislation in the states of Virginia and Kentucky to proclaim the Alien and Sedition Acts unconstitutional, essentially stating that any act passed by Congress with which the individual state did not agree could be nullified within that state. The concepts of "states' rights" and "nullification" were born.

One major problem was that the Constitution did not provide a means for a law passed by Congress to be declared unconstitutional after it had been signed by the President. During the framing of the Constitution it was assumed that the courts would assume this function, but this did not occur until 1803, when the U.S. Supreme Court stated that the courts had the right to pass on the constitutionality of any act passed by Congress.

This situation simmered during the settlement of the Northwest Territories (later to become the states of Ohio, Indiana, Illinois, Michigan and Wisconsin). There was much sentiment in the Territories for nullification, partly as a resentment against the New England states, which were strongly represented in Congress and, in some cases, laid claim to land in the Territories. Unpopular laws were being passed, as the "westerners" saw it, without due consideration for their own situation. From this area came most of the "western" armies of the Civil War; more than 90 percent of Sherman's army was composed of westerners. Paradoxically, although the western states often wished to counter New England's policies, they were strongly in favor of a central government, which they felt would best protect their interests.

No further overt action was proposed on nullification until 1828, when Congress passed a tariff law, and Senator John C. Calhoun of South Carolina wrote a document called the "South Carolina Exposition," in which was discussed the problem caused by the rising industrial strength of the Northeast influencing Congress to pass protective tariffs that greatly cut the availability of goods in the South. South Carolina even talked of secession. Calhoun's reason for recommending nullification was as an alternative to secession. His argument was that the states had given certain powers to Congress, and that the states alone had the right to say if Congress had exceeded its powers. The "states' rights" were being violated. The great Hayne-Webster debate of 1830 on the floor of Congress was the direct result of Calhoun's document.

Feelings were running very high in the South, and, in particular, in South Carolina. By 1831 the question of states' rights so preyed on the mind of one South Carolinian that he named his son States Rights Gist. Born on September 3, 1831, States Rights attended South Carolina College and went on to Harvard University Law School before setting up a law practice and becoming very active in the militia in his home state. He would later be one of six Confederate generals to die at the Battle of Franklin, Tenn., on November 30, 1864.

Congress again passed a protective tariff in 1832. This prompted South Carolina to declare both the 1828 and 1832 Acts null and void within its boundaries. It even stated its intention of leaving the Union if the laws were enforced. President Andrew Jackson replied with a proclamation to the effect that the tariffs would be collected and the laws would be enforced. After Congress passed a Force Bill to uphold the President, South Carolina backed off. The concept of nullification died at this time. The concept of states' rights did not die so readily.

MEDICAL PRACTICES AND SERVICES AVAILABLE IN 1861:

Union Medical Service and the U.S. Sanitary Commission

Prior to the firing on Ft. Sumter in 1861, the U. S. Army lacked good medical services. The Chief Medical Officer of the Army was a veteran of the War of 1812, fought 47 years previously. He was a martinet who was extremely harsh on his staff and on the doctors serving throughout the country. He is reported to have flown into a rage when he learned that one post actually had two sets of surgical instruments.

The overall medical staff at the beginning of the war consisted of the Surgeon General, 30 surgeons, and 83 assistant surgeons. Of these, 3 surgeons and 21 assistant surgeons resigned to go with the Southern forces. This was somewhat balanced by the fact that 5 surgeons and 8 assistant surgeons who were from the South chose to remain in the Union Army.

The Union Medical Service was tradition-bound, bureaucratic, and slow to respond. Fortunately for the common soldier, this was not to last long. The United States Sanitary Commission was formed early in the war, and took an immediate active interest in the welfare of the troops.

The mobilization of the Union Army in 1861 led to many immediate problems, not the least of which was the availability of doctors for the combat units. The Regular Army Medical Service used its normal procedure of inducting doctors who had recently completed medical school. The states, responsible for the mobilization of the regiments, appointed their own doctors to the various regiments. In many cases the doctor was appointed, like the colonel commanding the regiment, because of political favoritism and not necessarily his qualifications. Some of the governors of the states required examinations, some did not. Among those from the western states (Indiana, Ohio, Iowa, Wisconsin, Minnesota, Kansas, etc.), the doctors from Ohio were among the best. In New England, those from Vermont and Massachusetts were well screened.

One of the major duties of the regimental doctors was the examination of enlistees from their states before their muster into service. Of the first-call volunteers, about 20 percent were discharged for disabilities incurred prior to entering the Army—syphilitics, men over 60 years old, those with hernias, those with no teeth, some with missing fingers. One instance was reported where a doctor "examined" over 90 recruits in one hour. In one Chicago regiment the doctor had recruits parade past him and he passed the entire group *en masse.* Most often, these unfit men clogged the hospitals and took needed facilities from the troops who were sick or injured after coming into the service. One state, New York, conducted a reexamination of the troops furnished to the Federal service. Of the 47,417 men initially "accepted" for service, a special board of doctors weeded out 5,554. It was unfortunate that more states did not emulate New York.

By May 1861, around 30 percent of all the troops mustered had been on the sick list at least once. Mostly the complaint was "acute diarrhoea." The health of the troops from the eastern states was better than that of those from the western states, especially concerning communicable diseases such as measles, chicken pox, mumps, and smallpox. Because of the rural environments of the western states, where cities were small, towns and villages even smaller, and most of the population lived on farms in isolated or semi-isolated areas, the men came into contact with few people, and with even fewer strangers. The eastern states, with their larger cities, provided a more fertile bed for "childhood" diseases to immunize the citizenry. Many soldiers, east and west, were very sick, and often mortally so, with viral-type diseases that the doctors knew little about.

A major problem in the initial stages of the war was training the troops in field sanitation. Because most of the western troops, and Southern as well, were from farms, their idea of personal hygiene and the use of toilets was somewhat lacking. The problem was less in those units which were officered by current or former Regular Army officers. Sherman, upon taking command of a regiment early in the war, immediately indoctrinated his junior officers in the use of field latrines and demanded enforcement of good sanitation measures. His personal inspections of his troops' living and mess conditions brought home the message loud and clear. As a consequence, the sick rate in his units was low.

Intestinal infections increased dramatically during the first two years of war. Typhoid fever, caused by polluted water (polluted usually by human feces) caused 17 percent of the deaths in 1861. By 1865, the mortality rate from typhoid had reached 56 percent of those ill with the disease. Diarrhoea and dysentery caused a high sick rate of 64 percent (of all the forces) in the first year of the war, and this increased to 99.5 percent in 1862. Improved field-sanitation conditions brought this rate down dramatically later in the war.

When French military observers visited Union Army troop sites during the period 1861-1862, the drawings and instructions on how to construct a pit latrine were among the more popular items taken back to France.

The Sanitary Commission prepared pamphlets for issue to the troops on the preparation and use of latrines, as well as on personal hygiene items such as bathing. The commission believed that field sanitation was the responsibility of the line officer, from the colonel down through the lieutenant.

Other major contributors to poor health were the clothing and food issued to the troops. Initially, the states were responsible for the "outfitting" of the regiments. This included providing them with proper uniforms (including undergarments), blankets, eating utensils, and weapons. When a regiment was equipped and mustered into Federal service, the state would then present a bill to the Federal government for the cost. Governments being what they are, this worked well in some cases, but not so well in others. Some troops were provided shoddy uniforms, and the state "contractors" were paid in full for the equipment.

Food was a major problem once the troops went into camp. Rather than use a common kitchen for an entire company, usually about 100 men, the men formed themselves into informal "messes," where resources were "pooled" and the individual who knew how to boil water was appointed cook. If no one knew how to boil water, they drew straws. The results of this arrangement can be imagined. The food, in most cases, was almost inedible after being cooked. The type of food was somewhat limited; usually it was a hard-baked (water, salt and flour) cracker, salt pork in various stages of preservation, beans, and coffee. The hardtack crackers had to be soaked in water, coffee, or some other liquid to make them even chewable. Sometimes the hardtack was ground using stones (or one-half of an old mess kit with nail holes in it to make a grater), and then added to other items or combined with water, formed into cakes and fried in bacon fat. The troops fried rice and beans, they fried beef, they fried everything they could get into their skillets. The doctors often referred to their ailments as "death from the frying pan."

Seldom were fresh vegetables issued. If they were available locally, the price was usually much higher than normal, due to price-gouging by local farmers. Late in 1862, the Union Army tried a new dried-vegetable mixture called "desiccated vegetables" (referred to by the troops as "decimated vegetables"). It was described variously as "not fit for the hogs," "tasteless to the extreme," and these were some of the nicer descriptions. It did have one advantage in that it stored well, and thousands of tons of it were issued from Virginia to Georgia for the Union troops. The results of this diet could be easily predicted—stomach ailments, scurvy, and general ill health.

Another problem was that several days' rations were issued at one time, and the soldier would eat his three days of food in one day. He then went hungry for the following two days. There were numerous instances where soldiers in formation would faint from weakness because they had not eaten for two or three days.

Confederate Medical Service

The Confederate government had an entirely different problem. There were neither established offices nor channels for the army medical profession in 1861. These had to be created, using what personnel they had gained from the U.S. Army, and from the volunteers available.

While rapid progress was made in most areas of organization and administration, the greatest advance was in the organization of the hospital system throughout the South. By the end of 1863, approximately 18 months after the First Battle of Bull Run (Manassas), the medical service had organized military hospitals in many locations. Among these were Virginia (39), North Carolina (21), South Carolina (12), Georgia (50), Alabama (23), Mississippi (3), Florida (4) and Tennessee (2).

The number of men flowing in and out of Confederate hospitals equalled the number in the Northern hospitals, and surpassed it in many ways. The South's largest hospital, the Chimborazo in Richmond, had a very impressive record in treatment and humanity. Always working with limited resources, during the period from Nov. 1, 1861, to1863, that hospital admitted 47,176 patients, of whom 17,384 were transferred, 17,845 returned to duty, 4,378 were furloughed, 635 were discharged, 846 deserted, and 3031 died. This was a very low mortality rate, a little over 6%, considering the conditions. The number of desertions is surprising. The number returned to duty during this two-year period represents two Confederate corps, or more.

Within the Department of Virginia during the period Sept. 1862-Dec. 1863, the 39 hospitals in service processed 293,165 patients, as if all of Lee's army had been admitted to the hospital three times. Of this number, 95,875 were returned to duty, 2807 were discharged as unfit for duty, 4446 deserted, and 19,248 died. The toll in human suffering was vast and far-reaching.

UNITED STATES SANITARY COMMISSION

The origin of the Sanitary Commission and its growth during the early part of the war presents a study in organizational capabilities. Originally just one of several organizations that provided much needed succor to the troops, it grew rapidly, and, as its organization was superior to that of other groups, it rapidly, became the controlling force that coordinated relief efforts.

The original groups were formed by women, usually mothers, sisters or wives of soldiers, who felt that they should do "their part" for the Union. The initial efforts were to manufacture and organize the supply of hospital necessities, such as bandages and lint. This further spread to the making of shirts, drawers, hospital gowns, bedding kits, etc., as well as the collection of money to furnish such items as sewing kits, writing paper, and stamped envelopes.

At the beginning, there was much duplicated effort, resulting in a glut of some items and an extreme shortage of others. Too, the packing of the items was somewhat less than efficient, and many packages were spoiled when food (packed with clothing) turned rancid or rotted. The Commission eventually organized depots where local support groups sent their contributions. At these places *all* packages were opened, examined, and repackaged. Like items were packed together—shirts with shirts, drawers with drawers, etc.—and all items were clearly stamped with indelible ink stating they were from the Commission. Packages were clearly labelled with their contents, and with Commission markings. This prevented the looting of the supplies by transportation handlers, etc., who might sell the items to the soldiers for their own profit.

The object of the Sanitary Commission was to cut the government red tape, and to provide the necessary support in a flexible and efficient manner, something no government had ever achieved. The Commission began with a Doctor Bellows, who visited Washington in 1861 and went back to New York with a plan of organization and the blessings of the President and the Secretary of War. The highest officials of the government felt that the Commission "could do no harm."

All major officials of the Commission were medical professionals who devoted much time and money to the effort. The Commission doctors were sent to inspect the camps and the mess facilities to garner information on which to base recommendations. Their primary concern was the health of the troops. Early in the war, the Commission published 18 pamphlets dealing with field sanitation in the camps, handling of the sick and wounded, the use and storage of medicines, etc. These pamphlets proved invaluable to the government in the control of disease and the alleviation of suffering.

Several innovations were instituted by the Commission. Among these were the development and use of wheeled kettles in which soup was prepared in the rear areas of the battlefield to be served to the wounded or injured, even while the battle was raging.

The Commission also established a series of "Soldiers' Homes" or "Soldiers' Rests" along the routes the soldiers followed going to and from the fighting areas. A forerunner of the USO as we know it, these "rest stops" furnished dormitories, good food, libraries, bathing and laundry facilities, etc., to all who needed them. During the war, over 800,000 soldiers availed themselves of these services, eating over 4,500,000 meals and lodging for 1,000,000 nights. All of this was furnished to the troops free. The cost was paid by the communities and by donations of food and services.

There was no Federal allotment of money to the families of the troops during the war. Some states did provide a small allowance, but this was not common. The Commission established a "Claim Agency" to help the soldiers obtain their "bounty" payments when they were in arrears. A "Pension Agency" was also established to aid the soldier who was discharged for disability (often because of an amputation) to get his pension from laggard government agencies. It also had a "Back Pay Agency," which helped the soldier whose paybook was lost (or otherwise not usable) to gain his pay. This was a very useful service in an army where many were illiterate.

A locator service, called the "Hospital Directory," was established where information on patients and invalids in the 233 general hospitals could be found. These directories were established in Washington, Philadelphia, New York, and Louisville, where the names of more than 600,000 men were registered.

During a battle or engagement the Commission was always on the battlefield to care for the wounded and to relieve suffering.

GENERAL TACTICS AND STRATEGY IN 1861

The military tactics used by both sides were identical in most cases. There were very few surprises in the way the troops were handled, and in the way the logistics problems were solved. Depending upon the individual commander (some being stronger in defense than offense), the formations were alike, and artillery was handled similarly. Several of the general officers on both sides had spent time in Europe during the Crimean War or visiting the old Napoleonic battlefields such as Waterloo (Jackson had visited the latter, McClellan the Crimea). Frontal assaults were in vogue, and if a flank attack could be developed, so much the better. Infantry formations were elbow to elbow. The belief was that mutual support could be gained by the physical presence of one's comrades. Such formations also provided easier control of the troops by the company line officers. Since all communication was by voice (with the exception of some drums), the proximity of the commander to those being commanded was essential.

Artillery was used aggressively by both sides, the guns being placed as far forward as possible in direct support of the infantry. Both sides used identical guns. As opposed to modern American military designations of millimetres of diameter (105 mm, 155 mm, etc.), the guns were measured in "inches of bore" or by the weight of the missile, such as the "22-pounder," etc. The guns were usually of bronze- or cast-iron-based metal. Ranges for the weapons varied with the size and temperature of the gun tube at the time of firing. Massed guns were desired, but seldom achieved. Gettysburg was one of the exceptions, where over 100 guns were brought to bear on a single target.

Cavalry, as a combat arm, was not widely developed. There were few battles where cavalry action was *the* major factor in a win or loss. In general the terrain over which the battles were fought was not suitable for large cavalry formations, unlike the terrain in Europe. Some commanders, such as Nathan Bedford Forrest, used the cavalry effectively by mounting Confederate infantry for transportation to the battle site in order to rapidly close with the enemy—an effective stratagem, but not widely used by either side. In general, cavalry was used for scouting and for protecting the flanks of troops during a battle.

LOGISTICS

There has never been a war won without a major effort made in logistics. The glory goes to the infantry or to other combat arms, but the real battle is fought with rations, shelter, ammunition, transportation, and medical support. Of the commanders, North and South, going to war in 1861, there were few who had any experience in the logistics of waging a long campaign. For starters, the governments had never fielded such large armies.

Considering the transportation available at the beginning of the war and its vulnerability to attack, there were some very rude lessons to be learned by some very senior commanders. Think about the feeding of the men and animals in McDowell's army that fought at 1st Manassas. How would *you* start to feed 35,000 men three times a day and provide forage for over 1000 animals? With poorly developed food storage capabilities (the preservation of vegetables, etc., in metal cans was not widely developed), the rations had to be salt-cured or fresh. This led to maintaining large herds of cattle on the hoof, and using cured bacon and hams (generally referred to as salt horse). Few advances were made in this area (except in the drying of vegetables) during the war.

Road transportation was always a major problem. Roads that could support troops and artillery in large numbers, in all weather, were few. Both armies were disadvantaged by the use of long wagon trains carrying war matériel. Grant's trains leaving the Wilderness were more than 25 miles long, and they moved extremely slowly.

Railroads were used for the first time tactically (for the movement of troops to a battle) and strategically (such as Sherman's movement of supply bases forward to support his Atlanta campaign). This was done at a very high cost in manpower to guard the railroad lines from guerrilla or other attack. The Union developed the most efficient means of replacing destroyed track or laying new track. At the beginning of the war, the North was far better equipped to move large volumes of matériel and troops than was the South. In 1860 the South had about 8500 miles of track (over 1700 of these were in Virginia) compared to over 22,000 miles in the North. The North had more connecting lines, facilitating the movement of traffic. Before the war was over, the Northern U.S. military railroads alone would have 2105 miles of track with over 400 locomotives and 6000 railway cars.

The South had only one direct route from Richmond to Memphis (via Chattanooga). Many of the

Southern tracks were of different gauge (the measured distance between the rails) and this meant changing trains often during a journey. The South had fewer locomotive construction resources to call on, and, consequently, it was faced with an ever increasing problem of repair and maintenance.

Some innovations were made in the outfitting of railcars for the transportation of wounded by slinging litters in leather straps within the cars. Little of this was done, however; the wounded were laid on straw in boxcars that had previously carried supplies or animals.

COMMUNICATIONS

The United States Mail was the primary means of communication between the various parts of the country in 1861. Mail was still being delivered to South Carolina and the other Confederate states as late as April 1861. The Confederate mail service was adapted directly from the U.S. Mail, using the same facilities and personnel. There was a system devised in late 1863 between the opposing governments whereby mail could be delivered under a "flag of truce." The troops of the Kentucky "Orphan Brigade" used this method to communicate with their families in Union-held Kentucky. U.S. postage was required, however.

The telegraph was much more widely used in the North than it was in the South, even before the war. The more industrialized North had installed over 15,000 miles of lines for the operation of the U.S. Military Telegraph, used by the Union forces during the war. The South, short of trained operators and equipment, never reached the capacity of the North, and it even lost ground as the Union occupied Southern territory. The wires usually followed railroad tracks from city to city, and the lack of track in the South was a real handicap.

The steam riverboat had not been around for very many years before the war began, but in a span of about 30 years the number of steamboats available had steadily proliferated. The boats were generally of shallow draft and could navigate most of the rivers, North and South. The larger boats, of course, ran the Mississippi, Ohio, and Missouri Rivers. Some of the larger and many of the medium-size boats navigated the Cumberland and Tennessee Rivers in Kentucky and Tennessee, as well as the other rivers of the South. The smaller boats, of which there were hundreds, were used as "local" transportation to service the smaller towns along the waterways for both passenger and freight traffic. Boat transportation was both cheap and reliable.

Railroads were much more prominent in the North even at the beginning of the war. The North used a common gauge of track (something the South failed to do) and had many more connecting lines between major railroad trunks. Each line built its own railway stations, some cities having as many as three stations. The concept of bringing all tracks into a common "Union" station had not been developed. In the early stages of the war, troops from Massachusetts marching from one station to another in Baltimore were set upon by a pro-Southern mob, resulting in the death of some of the demonstrators.

1861

Terrible agony afflicted those of the North and South who wished to find some way of reconciling the differences between the regions. South Carolina, with fire-eaters in control, had dealt the fatal blow by seceding from the Union. These same people blamed the Federal government and the Republican Party for their own departure, ignoring Lincoln's message at the Cooper Union in February 1860 on South Carolina's excuses for dissolving the Union. At that time, Lincoln reminded the South:

> Under all these circumstances, do you really feel yourself justified to break up this Government, unless such a court decision as yours is shall be at once submitted to as a conclusive and final rule of political action?
>
> But you will not abide the election of a Republican President! In that supposed event, you say, you will destroy the Union; and then, you say, the great crime of having destroyed it will be upon us?
>
> This is cool. A highwayman holds a pistol to my ear, and mutters through his teeth, "Stand and deliver, or I shall kill you, and then you will be a murderer!"
>
> To be sure, what the robber demanded of me—my money—was my own, and I had a clear right to keep it; but it was no more my own than my vote is my own; and the threat of death to me, to extort my money, and the threat of destruction to the Union to extort my vote, can scarcely be distinguished in principle.

Among the officers of the United States Army and Navy located around the country, it was a time for soul-searching and heart-wrenching decisions. For those of Southern birth it was especially difficult: Having served the Union for so long, where did their loyalty lie? Many others were faced with the separation of business and personal ties. In Louisiana, where William T. Sherman was the head of the Louisiana State Seminary of Learning and Military Academy (later to become Louisiana State University at Baton Rouge), the decision had been made. In late December of the previous year he stated his position clearly:

> If Louisiana assumes a position of hostility toward the government, then this Seminary becomes an arsenal and a fort, and I quit.... I will do no act, breathe no word, think no thought hostile to the government of the United States.... You may assert that in no event will I forego my allegiance as long as a single state is true to the old Constitution.

When Christmas Eve of 1860 arrived, and Sherman was nearly alone in the Seminary in Baton Rouge, the newspapers brought news of South Carolina's secession. Sherman, in the depths of despair, addressed his friend David F. Boyd, who was Professor of Ancient History at the Seminary, on the effects of this secession:

> You, you the people of the South, believe there can be such a thing as peaceable secession. You don't know what you are doing. I know there can be no such thing... If you will have it, the North must fight you for its own preservation. Yes, South Carolina has by this act precipitated war.... This country will be

drenched in blood. God only knows how it will end. Perhaps the liberties of the whole country, of every section and every man will be destroyed, and yet you know that within the Union no man's liberty or property in all the South is endangered....

You people speak so lightly of war. You don't know what you are talking about. War is a terrible thing. I know you are a brave, fighting people, but for every day of actual fighting, there are months of marching, exposure and suffering. More men die in war from sickness than are killed in battle. At best war is a frightful loss of life and property, and worse still is the demoralization of the people....

You mistake, too, the people of the North. They are a peaceable people, but an earnest people and will fight too, and they are not going to let this country be destroyed without a mighty effort to save it.

Besides, where are your men and appliances of war to contend against them? The Northern people not only greatly outnumber the whites at the South, but they are a mechanical people with manufactures of every kind, while you are only agriculturists—a sparse population covering a large extent of territory, and in all history no nation of mere agriculturists ever made successful war against a nation of mechanics.....

The North can make steam-engine, locomotive or railway car; hardly a yard of cloth or a pair of shoes can you make. You are rushing into war with one of the most powerful, ingeniously mechanical and determined people on earth—right at your doors. You are bound to fail. Only in your spirit and determination are you prepared for war. In all else you are totally unprepared, with a bad cause to start with.

At first you will make headway, but as your limited resources begin to fail, and shut out from the markets of Europe by blockade, as you will be, your cause will begin to wane... if your people would but stop and think, they must see that in the end you will surely fail....

Braxton Bragg, an old friend of Sherman's from Army service and West Point, was out of the Army and in business in Louisiana. He had been appointed by the Governor of Louisiana to "organize the Commonwealth against the danger of war." Realizing that Sherman was going North, he wrote his thoughts on secession to Sherman late in December 1860:

You are acting on a conviction of duty to yourself and to your family and friends. A similar duty on my part may throw us into an apparent hostile attitude, but it is too terrible to contemplate and I will not discuss it.

You see the course of events—South Carolina is gone, nothing can recall her. The Union is already dissolved.... The only question is: can we reconstruct any government without bloodshed? I do not think we can—a few old political hacks and barroom bullies are leading public opinion.... They can easily pull down a government, but when another is to be built who will confide in them? Yet no one seems to reflect that anything more is necessary than to secede.

Major Robert Anderson, USMA class of '25, was 56 years old in 1861, and a veteran of the Black Hawk, Seminole, and Mexican wars. A native Kentuckian, he would remain with the Union. Since November 1860, Anderson had been commanding the Army garrison at Ft. Moultrie, S.C., at the mouth of Charleston Harbor. When seriously threatened after South Carolina seceded, he moved his entire garrison to the island of Ft. Sumter under the cover of darkness. The South Carolinians were outraged at having been tricked. A delegation from Charleston met with no success in getting Anderson to remove himself from Sumter.

January 1 (Tuesday)

A gloomy day in Washington. The White House held its usual New Year's Levee, but the holiday cheer was somewhat forced. A very arrogant letter was en route from South Carolina to President Buchanan about Anderson's move to Sumter. The governor of South Carolina was of the opinion that an agreement had been reached with the President to leave Anderson at Ft. Moultrie, and that his move was a breach of confidence. The state also seized Ft. Johnson in Charleston Harbor. The fort had been abondoned previously.

At a Cabinet meeting, Gen. Scott favored sending a fast steamer with resupply to Anderson as soon as possible.

January 3 (Thursday)

The War Department cancelled plans to ship guns from Pittsburgh to the forts in the South. Former Secretary of War Floyd, who resigned and went South, had been shipping weapons and large guns South for the past several months to help build up the Southern arsenal. Delaware rejected a proposal that it join the South in seceding.

January 5 (Saturday)

The Secretary of the Navy ordered Capt. Algernon S. Taylor, USMC, with 40 marines to Ft. Washington on the Potomac, south of the capital, to garrison the fort.

In New York, the merchant vessel *Star of the West* sailed with supplies and 250 troops for Ft. Sumter in Charleston. While it was supposed to be a secret, official Washington was as leaky as a sieve even then, and the officials in Charleston were notified immediately by their Washington representatives.

Alabama seized Forts Morgan and Gaines, which protected the harbor at Mobile, with no resistance, after seizing the U.S. Arsenal at Mt. Vernon, Ala., on January 4.

January 6 (Sunday)

The U.S. Arsenal at Apalachicola, Fla., was seized by the state with no resistance.

In New York, the Mayor declared that if the Southern states could secede, then New York City should also become a free city, to trade with both North and South. No action was taken.

The Governor of Maryland sent a message to the people strongly opposing Maryland's secession from the Union.

January 8 (Tuesday)

Secretary of the Interior Jacob Thompson of Mississippi, the last Southerner in Buchanan's Cabinet, resigned because he believed that he should have been told about Anderson's move to Sumter. To prove that he could act in good faith and keep a secret, Thompson telegraphed the authorities in Charleston that the *Star of the West* was coming with reinforcements and supplies for Anderson.

At Ft. Barrancas, guarding the entrance to Pensacola Harbor, Federal troops fired on a raiding party of about 20 men, who then fled. Florida seized the Federal fort at St. Augustine on January 7, with no resistance.

January 9 (Wednesday)

First Lt. Andrew J. Hays, USMC, was dispatched with thirty marines from the Washington Navy Yard to garrison Ft. McHenry in Baltimore until further notice.

On this day, Senators Judah P. Benjamin and John Slidell of Louisiana telegraphed Gov. Moore of that state that Federal gunboats were secretly bringing supplies to the forts at the mouth of the Mississippi River. Here was another pair who were secretly betraying a government to which they still swore allegiance. Gov. Moore, in a panic, ordered Braxton Bragg and 500 militiamen to seize the forts and the United States Arsenal at Baton Rouge.

In Jackson, Miss., the State Convention met and voted 84 to 15 to secede. As the vote was concluded, an immense shout went up that set off waves of cheering when it was heard outside the State House. Mississippi was the second state to leave the Union.

In Charleston, the *Star of the West* arrived shortly after midnight, and at daylight the vessel crossed the bar and steamed up the main channel towards Sumter. A Southern steamer ahead of it fired rockets as signals. About a mile and three quarters from the fort, a masked battery opened fire on the Federal vessel. A single shot struck the forechains on the bow of the vessel, all others missed. Lt. Charles R. Woods, commanding the troops aboard the vessel, later said that they had to turn around before they were cut off. The vessel left the harbor undamaged and without further action, heading back to New York.

The flag on the *Star of the West* was answered by raising the Union flag at Ft. Sumter; the guns and parapets on the fort were manned and ready for action. The officers on the island fort were angry because Anderson would not let them reply to the Southern fire, and they were further incensed that the vessel left with no attempt to land supplies or troops. To add to the incongruity, Anderson sent officers ashore *to use the telegraph in Charleston to inform Washington of the situation.* Charleston was in an uproar.

January 10 (Thursday)

Bragg and the militia seized the United States forts and arsenals in Louisiana. Sherman spurred his horse to Alexandria and resigned. His agreement had been to serve until Louisiana seceded, but the state was making war before it seceded. Sherman frankly stated that Bragg's action was "an act of war and a breach of common decency." Yielding to pressure from the school authorities, Sherman agreed to remain for a few days to turn over the Seminary funds, etc., to his successor.

At Tallahassee, the Florida Convention voted for secession 62 to 7, making it the third state to secede. In Pensacola, the Federals abandoned Ft. Barrancas, moving all the troops and munitions to Ft. Pickens, on Santa Rosa Island.

In North Carolina, citizens of Smithville and Wilmington occupied Forts Johnson and Caswell. The state government at Raleigh later repudiated this move.

William H. Seward, Lincoln's old opponent for the Republican presidential nomination, accepted the post of Secretary of State, which he would hold for the duration of the war.

In the United States Senate, Jefferson Davis called upon the Senate to act. This call came from a senator representing a state that had already seceded from the Union. In his call he stated:

> Senators, we are rapidly drifting into a position in which this is to become a Government of the Army and Navy in which the authority of the United States is to be maintained, not by law, not by constitutional agreement between the States, but by physical force; and you will stand still and see this policy consummated?

According to Davis, "If secession was necessary, it was a quarrel not of the South's making and if allowed to separate peacefully, there need be no difficulty."

January 11 (Friday)

By a vote of 61 to 39, the State of Alabama left the Union. The vote against secession was higher here than it was in the preceding three states. In northern Alabama, as in eastern Tennessee, there were pockets of strong pro-Union forces who were not happy with the vote. In Montgomery, as in Jackson, the crowds cheered and set off fireworks when the news was announced. In Charleston, the surrender of Sumter was again demanded and was again refused by the dauntless Anderson.

Mass meetings and demonstrations continued in the North and South. In Richmond, former Secretary of War Floyd, having furnished the South with tons of munitions and guns, urged opposition to coercion in the settlement of the dispute.

January 12 (Saturday)

The State of Mississippi, having left the Union, withdrew its Representatives from the House. At the same time, artillery seized from the Federal arsenals was ordered to Vicksburg in order to stop shipping on the Mississippi.

In Florida, state troops took over all of the forts and the Navy Yard around Pensacola Bay, except Ft. Pickens. The commander of Pickens refused a demand for surrender by state troops.

In New York, the *Star of the West* arrived from Charleston, still loaded with supplies and troops.

January 13 (Sunday)

Gov. Francis W. Pickens of South Carolina, late Minister to Russia, dunned the United States for the $3000 due him from his tour to Russia. Washington sent him a draft (check) drawn on the Treasury office (in Charleston), which had already been taken over by the state.

In other happenings, Lt. J. Norman Hall carried messages by train from Charleston to Washington to President Buchanan, looking for instructions for Major Anderson. He was accompanied by one J. W. Hayne, the Attorney General of South Carolina. Some sort of deal had been hatched between Anderson and Pickens to allow peace while Anderson asked for directions. The whole arrangement embarrassed Buchanan, who later claimed that the "truce" lasted only until February 5th, when he informed the South Carolina representative that Sumter would not be surrendered under any circumstance.

January 18 (Friday)

Off Key West, Fla., the Federal Army garrisoned Ft. Jefferson on Dry Tortugas. While not much use as a fort, it made a good prison for political prisoners during the war. Florida again demanded the surrender of Ft. Pickens; it was still refused.

Massachusetts, the first state to do so, offered the President men and money to support the present emergency and to maintain the authority of the nation.

In the United States House of Representatives, John Sherman, brother of William T. Sherman, rose to reply to his Ohio colleague, Pendleton, that the North should be conciliatory towards the

South. Sherman, in a highly emotional speech, said that it was not the North that should be conciliatory, it was the South; were they not the ones who had fired on the flag and seized government property? Was not Mississippi stopping all traffic at Vicksburg for search?

> This touched the unwritten law that the Mississippi River, gathering all the rivulets of the Northwest into one current, must be permitted to float our commerce, uninterrupted and untrammeled, to the sea, or thousands of men will float down upon its waters and make it free. You and I see already rising in the West, where military feeling is rife, a spirit which will not brook much longer the insults already cast upon the flag of the country.... if you have any misapprehension about the Northern people—if you suppose that because they are cold, because they are not fired by your hot blood, they will not perform their duty everywhere, you are very much mistaken. We are the equals of each other; we are of the same blood, the same parentage, the same character; your warm sun has quickened your blood, but our cold climate has steadied our intellects and braced our energies.

January 19 (Saturday)

In a State Convention at Milledgeville, Georgia became the fifth state to secede by a vote of 208 to 89—a large majority. This was a turnaround from the sentiment before the 1860 national elections. Before Lincoln was elected, a majority of the Georgians were pro-Union. Celebrations occurred as in Montgomery and Jackson, but in the upper highlands of the state a strong Union sentiment still prevailed.

Virginia, in an attempt to settle matters peacefully, called for a convention of all the Southern states in Richmond to "discuss the problem."

January 21 (Monday)

Mississippi troops seized Ft. Massachusetts off the coast, in the Gulf. Its loss deprived the Union Navy of a refueling point in the Gulf. Ship Island, located at the mouth of the Mississippi River in the Gulf of Mexico, is seized by Rebels. Ship Island is a key point in the defense of New Orleans.

Today, five Senators from the South took their leave of Washington. The most moving speech came from Jefferson Davis, saying goodbye to the nation and government he had served as an Army officer, Secretary of War, and as U.S. Senator. His voice faltering with emotion, his eyes awash with unshed tears, he bid his friends "a final adieu." His speech was heard in deep, respectful silence, followed by applause. His wife, Varina, later reported that he prayed for peace that night.

January 23 (Wednesday)

New York authorities raided private warehouses and seized guns destined for Georgia. Throughout the North rumors flew. Southern agents were reported everywhere and up to all sorts of mischief. In New York the Brooklyn Navy Yard was to be burned; railroads at many points were to be destroyed; general havoc and mayhem were the order of the day.

Commander John A. Dahlgren at the Washington Navy Yard moved cannon and ammunition to the attic of the main building to be used in case of attack.

John Adolph Bernard Dahlgren was born in Philadelphia, on November 13, 1809, the son of the Swedish Consul. He was denied an appointment as a midshipman and served as a common sailor until 1842, when he became an acting midshipman. He came to the Washington Navy Yard, where he established the Navy's ordnance department. At the beginning of the war he came in close contact with Lincoln, and they formed a solid friendship. He was promoted to Captain in the summer of 1862, and then to Rear Admiral the following summer. He was then assigned as commander of the South Blockading Squadron, based at Port Royal, S.C. He was heavily involved in the capture of Savannah and Charleston. At the end of the war he returned to the Washington Navy Yard as Commandant, where he died on July 12, 1877.

January 25 (Friday)

Yesterday, Georgia troops occupied the U.S. Arsenal at Augusta with no resistance. In Ft. Monroe, Hampton Roads, Va., Federal reinforcements sailed for Ft. Pickens on Santa Rosa Island off Pensacola. North Carolina first voted to hold a state convention, but then instead submitted the secession issue to the people.

Many naval officers resigned their commissions and joined the Confederate Navy. This was very upsetting to Capt. Samuel F. Du Pont (of the

Delaware Du Ponts) who wrote Commander (later Admiral) Andrew Hull Foote:

> What made me most sick at heart, is the resignations from the Navy.... I [have been] nurtured, fed and clothed by the general government for over forty years, paid whether employed or not, and for what—why to stand by the country, whether assailed by enemies from without or foes within—my oath declared "allegiance to the United States" as well as to support the Constitution.... I stick by the *flag* and the national government as long as we have one, whether my state does or not and she knows it.

Samuel Francis Du Pont was born in New Jersey on September 27, 1803. He entered the Navy as a midshipman on December 15, 1815, and rose to the rank of Captain by 1855. Secretary of the Navy Gideon Welles named him to head the Strategy Board which organized the blockade, and then assigned him as the commander of the South Blockading Squadron which captured Port Royal and Beaufort, S.C. as an operating base in November 1861. He was one of the first three Rear Admirals in the Navy, promoted to that rank on July 31, 1862. He attempted an assault on Charleston Harbor that was repulsed. He got into a squabble with Welles over the effectiveness of the mortar boats used against the defenses of Charleston and asked to be relieved of command. He was replaced by Rear Admiral Dahlgren on July 6, 1863, at which time Du Pont returned to his home near Wilmington, Del. He died while visiting Philadelphia on June 23, 1865.

January 26 (Saturday)

At Savannah, Ga., Ft. Jackson and the Oglethorpe Barracks were seized by state troops.

Louisiana voted for secession 113 to 17. Business in New Orleans was almost at a standstill because the Mississippi was closed both to Northern river traffic and to foreign ships coming in from the Gulf.

While Sherman waited for his successor to arrive, the Louisiana authorities sent to the Seminary the guns Louisiana had seized at Baton Rouge, in the old boxes with just the "U.S." scratched off. It was a wicked blow to Sherman.

January 29 (Tuesday)

Yesterday, in Louisiana, state troops took possession of Ft. Macomb, outside of New Orleans.

Kansas was admitted to the Union as the thirty-fourth state. Largely pro-Union, it would be racked by guerrilla warfare and border raids from Missouri.

The marines and soldiers aboard the U.S.S. *Brooklyn* were not to be landed to support Ft. Pickens at Pensacola unless the fort was attacked.

The revenue cutter *Robert McClelland* was surrendered to the Louisiana state authorities by Capt. John G. Breshwood, despite directions not to do so given by the Secretary of the Treasury.

January 30 (Wednesday)

Lincoln left Springfield, Ill. to visit his stepmother, Sarah Bush Lincoln, in Coles County, Illinois, prior to his departure for Washington. Although he had not attended his father's funeral there in 1852, he went back for a final visit. Then he returned to Springfield, said goodbye to his law partner Herndon and went home to Mary at the Chenery House.

In Mobile Bay the U.S. Revenue Schooner *Lewis Cass* was surrendered to Alabama state authorities by its commander, Capt. James J. Morrison.

January 31 (Thursday)

In New Orleans, the U.S. Branch Mint, located on the waterfront of the Mississippi River, was seized by the state troops, as was the Revenue Schooner *Washington.*

FEBRUARY 1861

The month would bring more changes to the once indivisible Union. A new government would be formed in Alabama which would assume the responsibilities of creating a new nation during the turmoil of a civil war. In Washington, many were still trying for compromise—a hopeless undertaking. Where were the leaders who could mend the broken fences and again bring the North and South into some sort of harmony? Obviously, there were more hotheads than conciliators.

February 1 (Friday)

A convention in Texas voted for secession 166 to 7 and set the date for departure at February 23rd.

Lt. Col. Robert E. Lee, a veteran of nearly 32 years of service in the U.S. Army, departed Texas for Virginia upon the secession of Texas from the Union.

Robert Edward Lee, a native Virginian, born in

1807, son of "Light Horse Harry" Lee, the Revolutionary War cavalry hero, was graduated second in his class from West Point in 1829. A veteran of the Mexican War of 1849, he served as the Engineering Officer for that expedition. He was later Superintendent of West Point during a three-year period, 1852-1855. Lee served with the cavalry in Texas in 1856-57 and was on leave visiting his wife's home, "Arlington," in 1859 when he was assigned to command a detachment of marines to capture John Brown at Harpers Ferry. He returned to Texas in 1860 to rejoin his regiment and was there when Texas seceded from the Union. He returned to "Arlington" to await developments.

February 3 (Sunday)

Much stir and bustle was going on in Montgomery, Ala., as the State House was prepared for the Convention to be held on Monday. The final touches were applied to the main meeting room and the celebrants were crowding the hotels and inns. The following day, the Convention of the seceded states met to form the Confederacy and elect their officials.

In Washington, the two Senators from Louisiana, Benjamin and Slidell, left for Baton Rouge. Their state was already represented in the Confederate Congressional Convention. The Convention would adopt the Constitution on the 8th. In Virginia the Peace Convention met, eventually having representatives from 21 states, totalling 131 members. Nothing firm came from the meeting, but at least a try was made.

The Choctaw Indian Nation declared for the Confederacy on the 7th.

February 9 (Saturday)

Jefferson Davis was elected President for six years with no option for reelection. Alexander Stephens of Georgia was elected Vice President, same term, same conditions. In a little twist, the Convention declared all United States laws to remain in force unless they conflicted with the new Confederate Constitution.

In Tennessee, voters rejected the proposal to call a convention to consider secession by nearly 10,000 votes. It would remain for the state politicians to finagle the State of Tennessee out of the Union.

Off Pensacola, the U.S.S. *Brooklyn* arrived with supplies and reinforcements for Ft. Pickens. These were not landed because of a deal struck with the State of Florida that no changes would be made on either side regarding the fort. The U.S.S. *Brooklyn*, *Sabine*, *Macedonia*, and *St. Louis* remained off Pensacola but did not land troops.

The United States Mail continued to be delivered everywhere, North and South. Commerce went on almost as it had before, with some slowdown on river traffic in the west.

The Southern Congress, in an attempt to court the old Northwestern states (Indiana, Ohio, Michigan, Illinois, and Wisconsin) voted to keep the Mississippi open for navigation of commerce. Some optimists in the South believed that the Northwest would secede and join the South, feeling that they had received unfair treatment from the Eastern monied interests on Wall Street. They did not understand that the Northwest still considered itself the first child of the central government and its loyalty to that government would not be shaken.

February 11 (Monday)

Yesterday in Mississippi, Jefferson Davis was in the garden with his wife, Varina, pruning rosebushes. A courier arrived and Davis learned he was the new President of the Confederacy.

The train was leaving Springfield at 8 o'clock on this drizzly morning for Washington. Aboard would be the President-elect and his party of 15. The train consisted only of an engine with tender and a single passenger car. Lincoln, on the morrow, would be fifty-two years old, the youngest man to yet fill the job of President of the United States. With saddened face, Lincoln addressed his hometown crowd for the last time:

> My friends, no one not in my situation can appreciate my feeling of sadness at this parting. To this place and the kindness of these people I owe everything. Here I have lived for a quarter of a century, and have passed from a young man to an old man. Here my children have been born, and one is buried. I now leave, not knowing when, or whether ever, I may return, with a task before me greater than that which rested upon Washington. Without the assistance of that Divine Being who ever attended him, I cannot succeed. With that assistance I cannot fail. Trusting in Him who can go with me and remain

with you and be everywhere for good, let us confidently hope that all will yet be well. To His care commending you, as I hope in your prayers you will commend me, I bid you an affectionate farewell.

Four years and a few weeks later, Sally Bush Lincoln said, "I knowed when he went away he wasn't ever coming back alive."

Commander Dahlgren at the Washington Navy Yard urged Congress to approve the building of more gun-sloops and an "iron-cased" ship.

February 15 (Friday)

Lincoln addressed a crowd in Pittsburgh, showing a puzzling aspect of his concept of the current "problem." Lincoln continued to Cleveland.

In Washington, Raphael Semmes resigned his naval commission to join the Confederate Navy. He will later command both the C.S.S. *Sumter* and *Alabama*.

Raphael Semmes was born in Charles County, Md., on September 27, 1809. He was appointed a midshipman on April 1, 1826, and Commander in 1855. He served off Mexico during the Mexican War. When the war started, he resigned his commission and became a Commander in the Confederate Navy. He convinced Confederate Secretary of the Navy Mallory that commerce raiders were a good method of warfare against the United States and was given command of the C.S.S. *Alabama*, which was finally sunk off the coast of France June 19, 1864, by the U.S.S. *Kearsarge*. He returned to the Confederacy where he was promoted to Rear Admiral. At the end of the war he was arrested and taken to Washington, D.C. to be tried for treason and violation of the rules of war, but he was released after three months. He returned to Mobile, Ala., where he practised law. He died there on August 30, 1877.

February 16 (Saturday)

In Montgomery, Davis arrived to serve as President of the Confederacy. He exclaimed, "We ask nothing; we want nothing; we have no complications." William L. Yancey proclaimed "The man and the hour have met."

Lincoln left Cleveland for New York State. At San Antonio, Tex. the local arsenal was seized by state troops.

February 17 (Sunday)

Lincoln was in Buffalo, and in Montgomery, Davis awaited his inauguration on the morrow.

Sherman finally booked passage up the river for February 25. His friend and fellow academician, Boyd, witnessed his farewell to the cadets at the Seminary. The cadets wept, Sherman wept. Sherman finally said he could not make the speech he had intended and, placing his hand over his heart, said "You are all here," turned quickly and left.

With his accounts up to date, Sherman obtained receipts from the state for all the records "being in good order" and prepared to leave. Former U.S. Major Pierre G.T. Beauregard thanked him for the care he had given his two sons and a nephew at the Seminary. Beauregard was starting for Montgomery, Ala., where Jefferson Davis was waiting to make him commander of all Confederate armies.

Braxton Bragg complained about Beauregard's assignment, believing his old rank in the U.S. Army entitled him to the honor of commanding the Confederate forces.

Sherman had a farewell tea in New Orleans with Braxton and Mrs. Bragg, during which the latter remarked, "You know, my husband is not a favorite with the new President." To this Sherman replied, "I didn't know Bragg knew Mr. Lincoln." Mrs. Bragg responded, "I didn't mean *your* President, but *our* President."

February 18 (Monday)

This day saw the inauguration of Jefferson Davis, amid much fanfare and highly emotional speeches. Davis, in a letter to his wife, described the event.

> The audience was large and brilliant. Upon my weary heart was showered smiles, plaudits, and flowers; but, beyond them, I saw troubles and thorns innumerable. We are without machinery, without means, and threatened by a powerful opposition; but I do not despond, and will not shrink from the task imposed upon me.

Lincoln travelled from Buffalo to Albany to address a joint session of the New York Legislature. In his speech, he remarked, "It is true that while I hold myself, without mock modesty, the humblest of all individuals that have ever been elevated to the

Presidency, I have a more difficult task to perform than any one of them."

In Washington, the surrender of all U.S. military posts in Texas by Brevet Major Gen. David E. Twiggs was considered treason, although he insisted it was done under threat of larger forces.

February 19 (Tuesday)

Lincoln travelled from Albany to New York City, accompanied by local and state politicians. Many brief stops and speeches were the order of the day, until they reached the city, where an estimated 250,000 people met the train. To the crowd he admitted that he had avoided taking a stand on the current issues until such time as he could speak officially. The entourage stayed at the Astor House.

In the South, Davis completed his Cabinet selections. Many of those appointed had previously held government offices, elected or appointed, in the U.S. Government. Of those appointed, only two would remain until the end of the war: Secretary of the Navy S.R. Mallory of Florida and Postmaster General J. H. Reagan of Texas.

In New Orleans, the U.S. Paymaster's office was seized by state troops. In Texas, although David E. Twiggs had surrendered all U.S. military posts to the local troops, U.S. Col. Carlos A. Waite took over nominal command of them. All would soon be in the hands of state troops.

February 20 (Wednesday)

In Montgomery, the Confederate Navy was officially established. Davis was busily getting his government organized and finding the facilities a bit cramped for the multitude of offices needed. The city overflowed with office seekers and general sightseers.

In New York City, the Lincolns were joined by Vice President-elect Hannibal Hamlin of Maine. Lincoln met the Mayor and attended the opera.

February 21 (Thursday)

Lincoln left New York for Philadelphia this morning with a short stop in Trenton, New Jersey, for a brief talk to the state's General Assembly. Arriving in Philadelphia in the late afternoon, Lincoln met the Mayor and was later warned about an assassination plot in Baltimore. He refused to change his plans.

In Montgomery, Davis continued his work on the Cabinet appointments, naming Stephen R. Mallory of Florida as the Secretary of the Confederate Navy. The Confederate Congress declared the Mississippi open for navigation.

February 22 (Friday)

In Philadelphia, on the anniversary of George Washington's birth, Lincoln spoke at Independence Hall. In his remarks, he said,

> I have never had a feeling politically that did not spring from the sentiments embodied in the Declaration of Independence. It was that which gave promise that in due time the weights should be lifted from the shoulders of all men, and that all men should have an equal chance.

Lincoln travelled on to Harrisburg, where he learned that plans for the trip to Washington had been revised in an attempt to avoid any possible difficulty in pro-Southern Baltimore. Leaving the remainder of the party to follow, Lincoln and Ward H. Lamon, an old-time friend, boarded a special train for Washington.

The residents of Charleston, S.C., celebrated the birthday of Washington with a speech by Gov. Pickens. In San Francisco, a mass meeting declared California for the Union.

February 23 (Saturday)

After travelling all night from Harrisburg via Philadelphia and Baltimore, Lincoln arrived in Washington at 6 A.M. in the company of Ward Lamon and Allan Pinkerton. Initially greeted by Elihu Washburne, an Illinois Representative, Lincoln visited William Seward at the Willard Hotel on Pennsylvania Avenue and then called upon the President and his Cabinet at the White House.

In Texas the voters approved secession by a vote of 34,794 to 11,235.

February 26 (Tuesday)

"A lady's thimble will hold all the blood that will be shed. The Yankee traders and mudsills will never fight." was a oft-repeated phrase in the South at this time. Coming through Illinois, Indiana, and Ohio, Sherman began to wonder if it were not true. Life seemed to be plodding along much as usual, with little attention being paid to the overall national situation.

Sherman, in Lancaster, Ohio, fretted over the political situation and was torn about what to do on a personal level. Lincoln continued meetings over Cabinet appointments.

February 27 (Wednesday)

In Washington, Congress was vainly attempting to arrive at some solution to the problem of slavery and states' rights. Amendment followed amendment in an attempt to reach a compromise. Most amendments dealt with "non-interference" by the Federal government with the slaves in the South and the border states. All amendments failed and the end of compromise drew closer.

Gov. Pickens of South Carolina wrote President Davis that "we feel that our honor and safety require that Ft. Sumter should be in our possession at the very earliest moment."

In Washington, Lincoln met with Senator Stephen Douglas of Illinois and others who felt that conciliation or compromise could be accomplished.

The United States Congress authorized the construction of seven steam sloops to augment existing naval forces. Gideon Welles notes "… for steam, as well as heavy ordnance, has become an indispensable element of the most efficient naval power."

February 28 (Thursday)

In Washington, Congress voted to form the Territory of Colorado as a part of the Union. In Congress also, the House passed an amendment, approved by the President-elect, stating that slavery could not be interfered with in those states where it already existed.

In Raleigh, N.C., a majority of 651 votes showed the state rejecting a state convention on secession and a very strong pro-Union sentiment emerging. The same sentiment was present in eastern Tennessee, where the request for a similar convention was defeated by more than 10,000 votes. This sentiment was also present in western South Carolina, and in northwestern Georgia. Most of these areas were not slaveholding.

At Montgomery, Ala., the Confederate Congress decided to borrow $15,000,000 to support the government. More would be asked for.

From Charleston, Major Robert Anderson, commander of Ft. Sumter, stayed in almost daily contact with Washington by telegraph. This was an incongruity that would last for several weeks.

MARCH 1861

In the South, tension was building to a fever pitch. So far, seven states had left the Union and set up their own government. Would it last? Would the North demand the price for secession in blood? In Washington, President Buchanan's administration awaited the inauguration of the new President, doing nothing in the meantime. This somewhat rural city was flooded with newcomers seeking office and appointments. In just a few days, the destiny of the nation would be in the hands of a new leader and no one knew to what pressure he would bow.

March 1 (Friday)

At Charleston, S.C., Gen. Pierre G.T. Beauregard was assigned command of the area for the Confederacy. Major Robert Anderson still held Ft. Sumter and maintained such friendly relations with the Charlestonians that rations were supplied to the fort from the city. The Confederates were, however, building forts themselves to threaten Sumter.

Pierre Gustave Toutant Beauregard was born in St. Bernard Parish, La., on May 28, 1819. Of Creole parentage, he spoke French before he spoke English. He was graduated from West Point, class of '38, ranking second in a class of 45. He served as an engineer in the Mexican War, receiving two wounds and two brevets for gallantry. Appointed as Commandant of West Point as a Major in January 1861, he shortly resigned his commission and joined the Confederate Army as a Brigadier General. At the end of the war he returned to New Orleans, where he served as the supervisor of the state lottery and as the state Adjutant General. He died in New Orleans on February 20, 1893.

Lt. Col. Robert E. Lee arrived at "Arlington" from Texas after that state had seceded from the Union. The dismissal of Brigadier Gen. Twiggs from the U.S. Army for having handed over all Federal property in Texas without a struggle came as no real surprise.

In Washington, Lincoln offered the position of Secretary of War to Simon Cameron, who readily accepted. Cameron was a major political force in

Pennsylvania and the appointment was not unexpected.

Simon Cameron was born in Lancaster County, Pa., on March 8, 1799. A printer by trade, he bought the Harrisburg *Republican* in 1826 and used its influence to control state politics. For his assistance to Buchanan in the senatorial elections of 1833, he was named Indian Claims Adjustor and immediately became involved in graft and corruption. He served in the U.S. Senate for one term in 1845, but he was not reelected until 1858, as a Republican. He delivered Pennsylvania to Lincoln in 1860 and expected to be named Secretary of War, which was done. Cameron's use of patronage and shady contracting practices finally caused his downfall. Lincoln accepted his resignation in January 1862 and named him Minister to Russia. He returned from Moscow in 1863. He was again elected to the Senate in 1864 and remained there until 1874, when he retired and had his son appointed in his place. He died in Lancaster on June 26, 1889.

In Richmond, tension mounted as the decision to secede came closer and more pressure was placed on the state government to act.

March 2 (Saturday)

In Washington, Lincoln awaited his inaugural. Seward, having been appointed Secretary of State, requested relief from the appointment, and Salmon P. Chase's appointment as Secretary of the Treasury was running into opposition. Chase would later prove to be a thorn in Lincoln's side.

Congress was busy. The Territory of Nevada was added to the Union on this day. The Dakota Territory, which contained what would become both North and South Dakota and most of Wyoming and Montana, was also added. In a bald-faced attempt to appease the Southern states, Congress offered an amendment to the Constitution to provide that "... no amendment shall be made to the Constitution which will authorize or give Congress the power to abolish or interfere within any State with the domestic institutions thereof, including that of persons held to labor or service by said State." While this was never approved by the several States, it was indicative of the mood of the times and the reconciliation attempts being made.

In the U.S. Senate, John J. Crittenden of Kentucky proposed the adoption of the Peace Convention of February 27, 1861. The Senate rejected the proposal and Crittenden gave it all up. Returning to Kentucky, he devoted his energies to keeping Kentucky a neutral state. This, too, failed, and he had the agony of seeing his two sons face each other as adversaries in the Civil War, both as Major Generals.

In Montgomery, Ala., the Confederacy admitted Texas into its new government, and kept a watchful eye on the events in Charleston. With Texas departing the Union, the U.S. Revenue Schooner *Henry Dodge* was seized at Galveston.

March 3 (Sunday)

In Washington, the troops ordered into the city to provide security for the inaugural activities were being organized and assigned their respective duties. The old soldier Winfield Scott informed Secretary of State William Seward that he thought it impractical to defend Ft. Sumter. Confederate Gen. Pierre G.T. Beauregard arrived in Charleston and took command of the military there.

Major Anderson at Ft. Sumter was still sending daily telegrams to the Secretary of War and Gen. Scott through the telegraph offices in Charleston.

March 4 (Monday)

Inauguration Day in Washington. Lincoln would become the 16th President of the United States and would preside over one of the deadliest wars in history. At the Willard Hotel on Pennsylvania Avenue, Lincoln met with William Seward and obtained his agreement to remain in the Cabinet. Along the streets of the capital, troops lined the curbs and watched from windows and rooftops; people were out in the mid-fifty-degree weather expecting to enjoy themselves and to be present at a historic event. Artillery and troops were posted on the grounds of the Capitol, where a throng of nearly thirty thousand awaited the arrival of the present and future Presidents.

Shortly after noon, President Buchanan and President-elect Lincoln left the Willard Hotel by carriage, under partly cloudy skies, for the ride to the Capitol. In the Senate, the full house was called to order and Vice President John Cabell Breckenridge, soon to be a Brigadier General in the Confederate forces, swore in Vice President-elect Hannibal Hamlin of Maine as Buchanan and

Lincoln watched. At about 1 o'clock, Buchanan and Lincoln emerged from the Capitol to find clear skies. Advancing to the special platform on the portico, Lincoln was inaugurated and then he gave the address he had prepared weeks before in Springfield, Illinois; some changes had been made in the speech due to recent events.

Lincoln's address was clear and simple. The Southern people need not fear because of the election of a Republican President; he had no intention of interfering with the institution of slavery where it currently existed, and each state had the right to control its domestic institutions. It seemed a moot point, since several of the states had already seceded. Lincoln went on to stress that "the Union of these States is perpetual" and that that Union could not be dissolved. He considered acts of violence against the central authority of the United States to be "insurrectionary or revolutionary." Lincoln stated further, "To the extent of my ability, I shall take care, as the Constitution itself expressly enjoins me, that the laws of the Union be faithfully executed in all the States."

Lincoln added that there need be no bloodshed or violence and that there would be none "unless forced upon the national authority." Driving the point further, Lincoln said,

> In your hands, my dissatisfied fellow countrymen, and not in mine, is the momentous issue of civil war. The government shall not assail you. You can have no conflict, without being yourselves the aggressors. You have no oath registered in Heaven to destroy the government, while I have the most solemn one to "preserve, protect and defend" it.

Appealing to the past relationships, Lincoln further reminded the South,

> Though passion may have strained, it must not break our bonds of affection. The mystic chords of memory, stretching from every battlefield and patriot grave to every living heart and hearthstone, all over this broad land, will yet swell the chorus of the Union, when again touched, as surely they will be, by the better angels of our nature.

The poetry was lost on those who now were gathered in Montgomery to build their own government. The Union had a new President, and the changing of the guard was accomplished. The Federal government began recalling ships stationed in foreign ports to add to those available for immediate use. In all, only 42 ships were in commission at this time.

In Montgomery, the "Stars and Bars," the first official Confederate flag, was raised for the first time over the Alabama State House, which was being used as the Confederate Capitol. The flag, designed in early 1861 by Nicola Marschall, contained two wide red bars separated by a wide white bar, with 7 white stars in a field of blue in the upper left corner. The resemblance of this flag to the Union Stars and Stripes caused much confusion on the battlefield, and this confusion led to the adoption of the Confederate Battle Flag, with the starred St. Andrew's Cross.

March 6 (Wednesday)

In Montgomery, the Confederate Congress, meeting mostly in secret, hammered out the bills and acts which authorized the new government's work. Provisions were made for postage, rail transport, etc.

In the North, military and naval officials met to discuss the problem of Ft. Sumter. At this point, Gen. Scott informed all that the problem now belonged to the Navy, and that he could do no more.

The three commissioners sent by Jefferson Davis to open a dialogue with the Federal government cooled their heels.

March 8 (Friday)

Yesterday, the Missouri Convention was leaning more towards the Union. In Washington, Lincoln held Cabinet discussions about Ft. Sumter, but no consensus was reached. Gideon Welles of Connecticut took office as Secretary of the Navy.

The Lincolns held a public reception. The three Confederate commissioners tried to reach Secretary of State Seward to open an official dialogue.

March 11 (Monday)

The Confederate Congress in Montgomery adopted the Constitution of the Confederacy, which would be ratified by the end of April 1861.

Brigadier Gen. Braxton Bragg of North Carolina assumed command of all Confederate forces in Florida.

Gen. Scott replied to Lincoln that it was uncertain how long Major Anderson could hold out at Sumter. He also said that it would require a large fleet of warships with troops to relieve the fort, including 5000 regulars and about 20,000 volunteer troops. Quite a large order for an army that had contained fewer than 16,000 officers and men only six months previously!

March 13 (Wednesday)

Lincoln instructed Secretary of State Seward not to meet with the Confederate commissioners. Meeting with them would be a tacit recognition of their status as representatives of a foreign nation and Lincoln would not accept the fact that the Confederate States were no longer a part of the Union. Meanwhile, in England, the newspapers were in an uproar, taking sides on the question of recognizing the Confederacy.

Gustavus Vasa Fox, a former naval officer, conferred with Lincoln on the possible resupply of Ft. Sumter.

Gustavus Vasa Fox was born in Saugus, Mass., on June 13, 1821. He was graduated from the Naval Academy in 1838. He resigned as a Lieutenant in 1856, and became an agent for the Bay State Mills in Massachusetts. He was married to the sister of the politically powerful Montgomery Blair. Blair managed to get him appointed to do some work for Lincoln in the negotiations over Ft. Sumter. He was an excellent diplomatic administrator and he earned the respect and cooperation of both career naval officers and politicians. He was a major influence in the adoption of ironclads in the Navy. At the end of the war he returned to the textile business. He died in New York City on October 29, 1883. His personal papers were later published by the Naval Historical Society. These papers contained valuable information on the conduct of business within the Navy during the war years.

March 16 (Saturday)

Yesterday, the State of Louisiana transferred over $536,000 in money taken from the U.S. Mint in New Orleans to the Confederate government.

In Montgomery, the Confederate Congress recommended that William L. Yancey, Pierre A. Rost and A. Dudley Mann be appointed commissioners to Britain to negotiate recognition.

Out west, the Territory of Arizona declared itself out of the Union.

Lt. Col. Robert E. Lee, United States Army, was promoted to Colonel of the 1st U.S. Cavalry. The commission was signed by Lincoln on March 28.

March 18 (Monday)

In Texas, old Sam Houston, now Governor, refused to take an oath of allegiance to the Confederacy. He didn't think that just because Texas had seceded from the Union it owed any allegiance to the Confederacy. At Montgomery, Davis told Pickens in South Carolina that he would prefer that Major Anderson leave Sumter peacefully.

In the Florida panhandle, Gen. Braxton Bragg refused to permit further supply of Ft. Pickens, the cork to the bottle of Pensacola Bay. A Federal fleet off the coast awaited developments.

March 20 (Wednesday)

While events quickened in Charleston and Pensacola, Texas gained three more Federal forts, surrendered by their commanders. At Mobile, a Federal supply ship, the U.S. sloop *Isabella*, was seized before it could sail with supplies for Pensacola.

In Washington, an uproar was created when some of the correspondence between Seward and the Confederate commissioners was released to the press. Lincoln was informed that his two sons had the measles.

March 25 (Monday)

G.V. Fox visited Charleston and Ft. Sumter to discuss the situation with Anderson and the Southern leaders. After observation, he recommended that Sumter be resupplied by sea. Tensions were mounting hourly in Charleston. Col. Ward H. Lamon (the one who accompanied Lincoln by train from Harrisburg) visited Charleston and conferred with both Gov. Pickens and Gen. Beauregard.

March 29 (Friday)

Having been deposed as Governor of Texas, Sam Houston refused an offer of the Federal government to reestablish him in that post. He quietly retired, this being his last official act of a public life spanning several decades.

Lincoln made his decision to hold both Sumter

and Pickens, ordering an expedition to accomplish this to be ready to sail by April 6th. The Cabinet was still split on the decision: three-to-two in favor.

APRIL 1861

This month arrived with a feeling of dread for some, elation for others. The elation was in the South, where the hot-blooded zealots believed that the war would be short-lived and they would soon be left to their own devices. That not all so believed was shown by the opposing votes of the various state conventions; there were still strong ties to the Union.

In the North, the abolitionists felt that their chance had finally come to free the country of the stain of slavery. Not all felt the same way. Many would prefer to let well enough alone and let the "peculiar institution" die a natural death.

The storm clouds of war were gathering.

April 1 (Monday)

In Washington, Secretary of State Seward wrote the President several "suggestions" which were really statements informing Lincoln that he, Seward, should be the one to direct the effort against the Confederacy by acting as a prime minister in all matters. In fact, Seward suggested that he would start a war with Spain or France to help reunite the country.

Lincoln, in his gentle way, reminded the Secretary that *he* was President, not Seward. This would not be the last reminder from Lincoln to Seward.

April 3 (Wednesday)

The Cabinet met with Lincoln to further discuss the state of affairs at Sumter and Pickens. Lincoln sent Allan B. Magruder as his emissary to Richmond to contact the Unionists in Virginia.

On a previous visit to the Washington Navy Yard, Lincoln had conferred with Capt. Buchanan and, in the hope of dissuading the Captain from resigning and going South, Lincoln had agreed to give away the bride at Buchanan's daughter's wedding. Well, the President was late, the wedding was held without him, and Buchanan eventually went South. There was, however, a first meeting between Lincoln and Commander John A. Dahlgren that would develop into a lasting mutual trust that would carry them through the next four years.

In the South, a battery placed on Morris Island in Charleston Harbor fired at the Federal schooner *Rhoda H. Shannon*, further inflaming the situation. The South Carolina State Convention met and approved the Constitution of the Confederate States by a margin of 114 to 16; there were some who would not give up the old government easily.

In Virginia, William Edmondson "Grumble" Jones was elected Captain of the Washington City, Va. "Washington Rifles" which he had organized. "Grumble," a native Virginian, 37 years old in 1861, was a graduate of West Point, class of '48. He served on the frontier until 1857, when he resigned and returned to his farm in Virginia. He served as Colonel of the 1st Virginia before assuming command of the 7th Virginia in March 1862.

John Sherman, brother to William T. (called "Cump" by his family and friends) and a U.S. Senator, had been trying to get "Cump" to take a position in the government in Washington. Sherman, then in St. Louis, Mo., had recently taken a job there and was somewhat settled. He also had some resentment against the powerful Blair family, which was very prominent in Missouri and national politics. John told William that he should look to his future and forget his feelings against the Blairs, further stating that several of the Cabinet members have "high appreciation of your merits and you will find they will readily and cheerfully accord to you anything in their power in a military way."

April 4 (Thursday)

In Richmond, the Virginia State Convention rejected by a vote of 89 to 45 a motion to pass an ordinance of secession and have it voted on by state residents.

At Washington, Lincoln met with John B. Baldwin, a Virginia Unionist, in the hope of gaining support for Virginia to remain in the Union.

The former naval officer G.V. Fox was informed that the expedition to relieve Sumter would go on or about April 11th or 12th. A letter was sent to Major Anderson at Sumter asking that he hold on until the expedition arrived, if that was possible. The follow-

Harpers Ferry, Va., on the Potomac, as it appeared in June 1861. This strategic town guarded the entrance to the Shenandoah Valley.

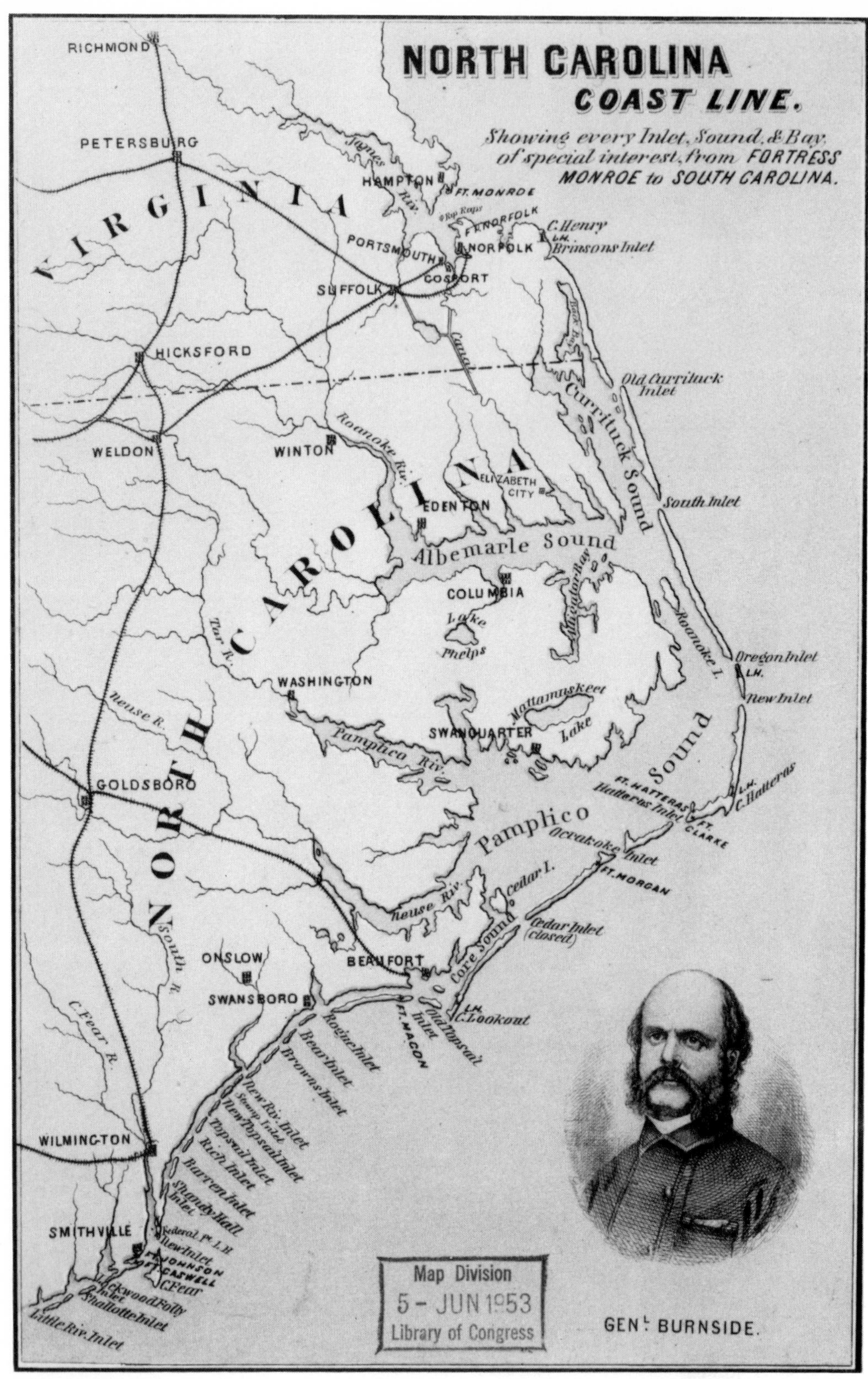

A map of the North Carolina coast, showing the conquests of Union forces under Gen. Ambrose Burnside in January 1862

The U.S.S. Monitor, *in March 1862*

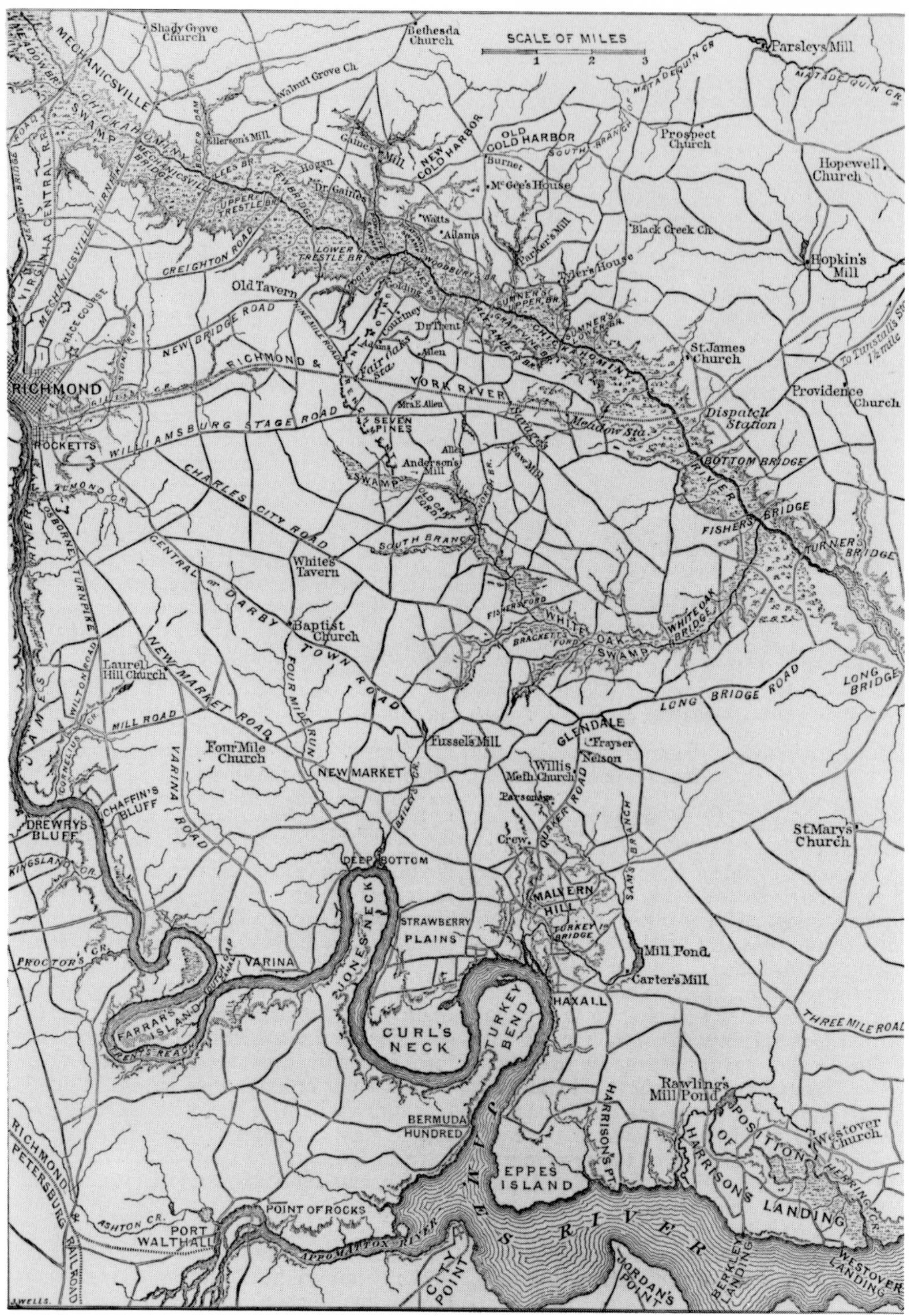

A map of the region of the Seven Days' Battle outside of Richmond, Va., June 1862

Aboard a Federal mortar schooner, March 1862

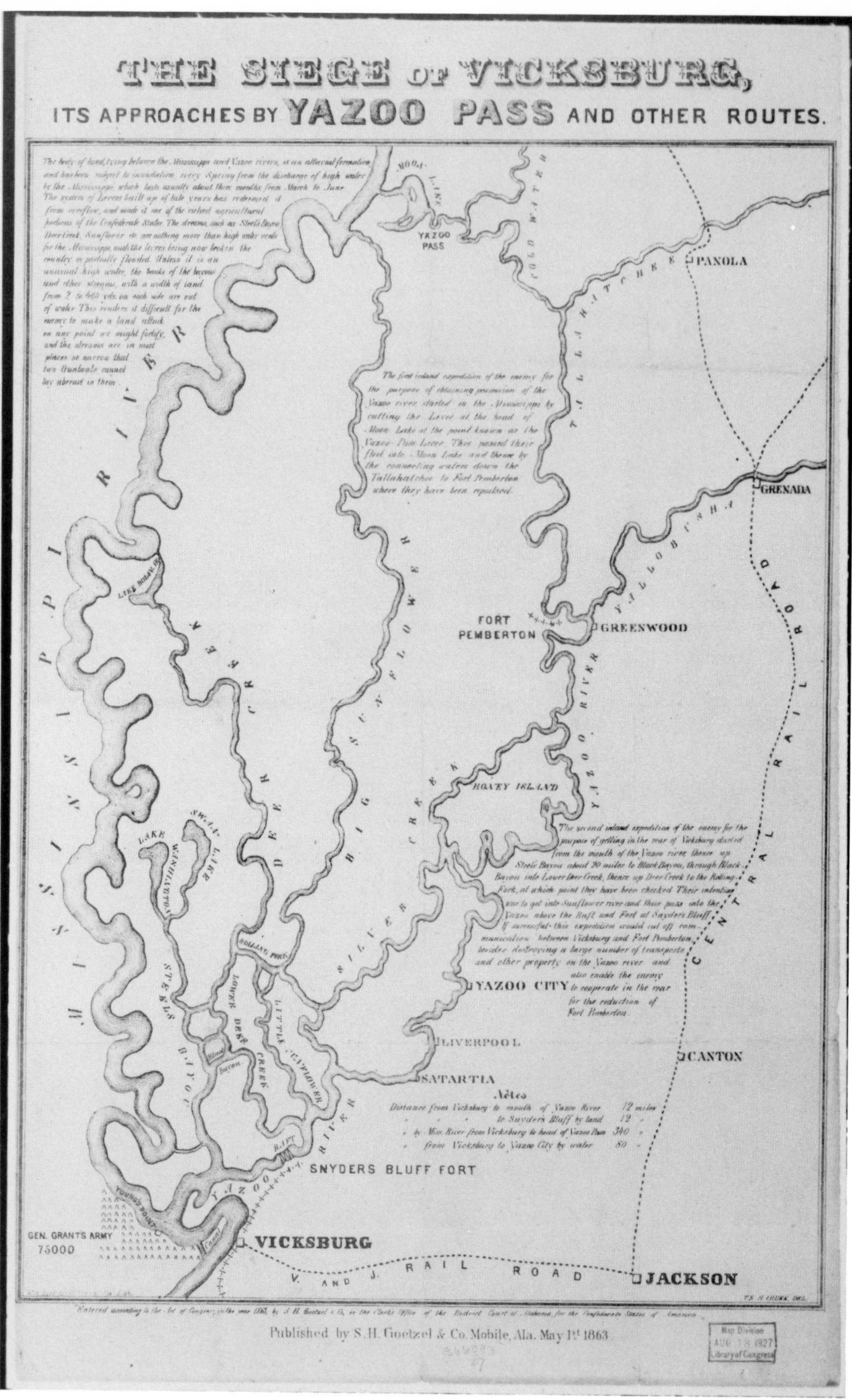

A map of the Vicksburg, Miss., area, May 1863

The Old Capital Prison in Washington, D.C., as it appeared in July 1862

A map of Port Hudson, La., a town that figured prominently in the siege of Vicksburg, May 1863

H

ing day, Secretary of the Navy Gideon Welles ordered ships to Charleston to provision Sumter. The *Powhatan*, previously secretly dispatched by Lincoln, was en route to Ft. Pickens and would miss the show at Charleston.

April 6 (Saturday)

Lincoln, in Washington, sent an emissary to Gov. Pickens in Columbia, S.C., to inform the Governor that Ft. Sumter would be supplied with provisions only, no reinforcements of men or guns. The plan to relieve Ft. Pickens was foiled by the Federal naval commander, who decided that he did not have the authority to cancel an agreement made by the Buchanan administration about the supply of the fort.

April 7 (Sunday)

Gen. Beauregard today notified Major Robert Anderson that no further interaction would be allowed between Ft. Sumter and Charleston. The fort was now essentially cut off and could only be reached by sea.

Naval Lt. John L. Worden was dispatched to Ft. Pickens with specific orders for the landing of troops by the Navy. Gen. Braxton Bragg, the local Confederate commander, requested permission from his Secretary of War to fire on any attempt to land troops at Pickens.

John Lorimer Worden was born in Westchester County, N.Y., on March 12, 1818. He entered the Navy as a midshipman at age 15 and served for the remainder of his life. He was the commander of the U.S.S. *Monitor* during the battle at Hampton Roads in March 1862 that changed naval warfare forever. He later commanded ships in the South Atlantic Blockading Squadron, ending the war with the rank of Captain. He served as Superintendent of the Naval Academy from 1869 to 1874, being promoted to Rear Admiral. He died in Washington, D.C., on October 18, 1897.

Braxton Bragg was born at Warrenton, N.C., on March 22, 1817. Graduating from West Point in 1837, he served in the Mexican War, and was promoted to Lieutenant Colonel before resigning to become a Louisiana planter in 1856. He entered the Confederate Army as a Brigadier General in March 1861, and was promoted to Major General a year later. He served at the Battles of Shiloh and Corinth. A close friend of President Davis, Bragg was promoted to full General and given command of the Army of Tennessee. He led his army into Kentucky in 1862 and was forced back into Tennessee by a superior Federal force. He attacked Rosecrans at Stones River in December 1862, losing that battle. Rosecrans then forced Bragg out of Tennessee. The Battle of Chickamauga was fought in September 1863, which Bragg won, forcing Rosecrans back to Chattanooga. When he was beaten by Grant at Missionary Ridge, he resigned his command. He was made Chief of Staff to Davis, a position he filled admirably, and was with Johnston when the surrender was made in North Carolina in 1865. He died at Galveston, Tex., on September 27, 1876.

April 8 (Monday)

Lincoln's emissary, R.S. Chew of the State Department, arrived at Columbia, S.C., and delivered his message to Gov. Pickens. Pickens read the message to Gen. Beauregard. Beauregard placed all Confederate forces in the area on alert. No one was taking a backward step at this challenge, and the Confederate Secretary of War, Leroy P. Walker, gave Bragg permission to resist any attempt to reinforce Ft. Pickens, while from New York, the *Harriet Lane* departed for Sumter, loaded with supplies.

Sherman replied to Montgomery Blair's offer of employment in the War Department by saying, "I cannot accept." This led several Cabinet members to believe that Sherman planned to join the Confederacy if war came.

April 9 (Tuesday)

In Charleston, S.C., the *Mercury* newspaper declared that the resupply of the fort meant war. On Sumter, the supplies dwindled further and lookouts were scanning the sea for ships to relieve them.

The Confederate government was in a quandary. If it allowed the resupply of the forts at Charleston and Pensacola, it was tacitly agreeing that they belonged to the Union government, and that the secession movement was meaningless. If it repelled the resupply and reinforcement, it meant that it, the Confederacy, would be branded the aggressor. Confederate Secretary of State Robert Toombs told Davis that to fire on the national flag would be "suicide, murder and will lose us every friend at the

North. You will wantonly strike a hornet's nest which extends from mountain to ocean, and legions now quiet will swarm out and sting us to death. It is unnecessary; it puts us in the wrong; it is fatal."

April 10 (Wednesday)

The Confederate Secretary of War informed Beauregard that if he was sure that the attempt would be made to resupply the fort, he should demand its immediate surrender and evacuation. If refused, Beauregard was to take whatever action he deemed necessary to reduce the fort. Beauregard moved a floating battery to near Sullivan's Island, and the other earthworks surrounding Sumter were manned.

From Hampton Roads, Va., the Federal ship U.S.S. *Pawnee* sailed for the relief of Sumter.

In Pensacola, Lt. Worden arrived with his message about landing troops at Ft. Pickens. Gen. Bragg gave the Lieutenant permission to visit the fort.

April 11 (Thursday)

Today, Col. James Chesnut (a former U.S. Senator and the husband of the famed Civil War diarist Mary Chesnut), Capt. Stephen D. Lee (late of the U.S. Army), and Lt. Col. A. R. Chisolm, a representative of Gov. Pickens, left the dock at Charleston and went to Ft. Sumter to demand its immediate surrender. There they met with Major Robert Anderson and discussed the demand. After a consultation, Anderson declined to surrender, but stated that he would probably be starved out in a few days anyway, if not battered to pieces by artillery. Beauregard, not wishing to create more bloodshed than necessary, asked Walker, the (Confederate) Secretary of War if he could outwait Anderson. Walker replied that Beauregard should seek to get a definite time for the evacuation of the fort.

In Washington, Lincoln conferred with the Governor of Maryland about the uncertain loyalties of that state. The three Confederate commissioners left the city convinced that they had been gulled by Seward and the Lincoln administration.

At the direction of Secretary of the Navy Gideon Welles, Commander James Alden reported to the Norfolk Navy Yard to take command of the U.S.S. *Merrimack*, then under construction.

A steamer from Texas arrived in New York with U.S. troops returning from that state after secession.

April 12 (Friday)

Shortly past midnight, Roger Pryor and three men were sent out in a boat flying a white flag to Ft. Sumter to again confer with Major Robert Anderson about the surrender of the fort. To these men Anderson replied that he would evacuate the fort on the 15th unless he received additional instructions or supplies, not realizing that a relief fleet was lying just outside the harbor, awaiting daylight to enter. To the men in the boat, anything less than immediate surrender was not acceptable. They then informed Anderson that firing would commence within one hour if he did not surrender. Anderson, realizing what was coming, shook the hands of the four men and told them, "If we do not meet again in this world, I hope we may meet in the better one." The boat left for Cummings Point about 3:20 A.M., arriving there at 4 A.M.

At Cummings Point, Roger Pryor, a Virginian, was offered the honor of firing the first shot and he declined. Another Virginian, a 67-year-old fire-eater and avid secessionist, Edmund Ruffin, gladly accepted the honor, and at 4:30 A.M. pulled the lanyard on the gun. Sumter was fired upon. The war had begun.

In Charleston, people gathered on the rooftops to watch the display of artillery as Beauregard's 47 guns began the bombardment. The crowd, in a holiday mood, cheered as the shells struck home and the fort was battered. Beauregard's gunners threw over 4000 rounds at the fort, tearing up the earthworks, dismantling guns, and making life miserable for the defenders. The flag was shot from its staff only to be nailed up again by a courageous Sergeant. There could be no doubt of the outcome. Anderson was outgunned and beyond hope of help from the outside. The firing continued all day Friday and through the night.

At Pensacola, Federal troops were landed on Santa Rosa Island to reinforce Ft. Pickens. The Confederates were unable to prevent the landings and the fort would remain in Federal hands throughout the war, thereby denying the use of the harbor to the Confederates.

April 13 (Saturday)

The firing on Sumter continued into this day, the defenders now down to few rations and little water. At last, honor satisfied, Anderson capitulated to his former artillery student and agreed to the surrender terms offered on Thursday, the 11th. Roger Pryor returned to Sumter to participate in the ceremonies which took place in the fort hospital. No casualties had occurred on either side in spite of all the weight of iron thrown about. The surrender was signed and Anderson was permitted to fire a fifty gun salute to his flag. During the firing a burning ember fell in some powder and the resulting explosion killed Private Daniel Hough and wounded five other Federal soldiers—the first real casualties of the war. The flag was lowered and given to Anderson, who packed it with his personal effects. This same flag was hoisted over Sumter after four long years of blood and agony. When the battered Federal artillerymen left the harbor, the Confederate gunners removed their caps in salute to them. Sumter was lost.

In a bizarre twist, Lt. Worden, who had carried the message to Pensacola to reinforce Ft. Pickens, was arrested while travelling by train at Montgomery, Ala.

April 14 (Sunday)

The evacuation of Sumter was complete, and Charleston was in a festive mood. Large crowds on boats gathered in the harbor to see the Federals leave the island fort and board boats to take them North. The news spread rapidly throughout the South, uplifting spirits and firming decisions for those who were wavering on the subject of secession.

In Washington, Senator Stephen Douglas, Lincoln's old political adversary, called upon the President to offer his support in the coming conflict.

April 15 (Monday)

In Washington, Lincoln issued a call for 75,000 volunteers to serve for three months and called for a special session of Congress for July 4th. While the Northern states quickly affirmed their commitment to supply troops, North Carolina and Kentucky just as quickly refused. Seventeen ships from Southern ports were seized in New York because they lacked clearances.

April 16 (Tuesday)

Throughout the North, the firing on Sumter was a unifying experience, awakening the strong bonds of Union within the people. Even in some parts of the South, the Union spirit was rampant. William G. Brownlow, a local newspaper editor in Knoxville, Tenn., declared that he would "fight the Secessionist leaders till Hell froze over, and then fight them on the ice." One hardy soul in Knoxville placed a Union flag atop a 125-foot pole and dared anyone to remove it.

The calls to the then-border states of Virginia, North Carolina, Tennessee and Arkansas for troops led to action to join the South, in most cases. In Tennessee, Gov. Isham Harris, who had already started raising a "State Militia," declared, "Tennessee will furnish not a single man for the purpose of coercion, but fifty thousand if necessary for the defense of our rights and those of our Southern brothers." This furnished a prime excuse for Harris to "ask the Confederacy for protection" and take the State into the Southern camp, although the voters had refused such a move by a majority of 10,000 votes.

Isham Green Harris, born in Franklin County, Tenn., on February 10, 1818, was educated locally and moved to Paris, Tenn. in 1832. He studied law with a local attorney and passed the bar in 1841, and then went into politics and was elected to the state legislature in 1847. When Lincoln was elected, he urged the people of Tennessee to pass a secession ordinance and refused Lincoln's call for troops. After the Federal occupation of Nashville, in 1862, he haunted the camps of the various Confederate commanders until he was elected to the Confederate Congress towards the end of the war. He was essentially a Governor without a state, having the title only. At the end of the war he went to England, returned in 1867, and was elected U.S. Senator for three terms. He died in Washington on July 8, 1897.

April 17 (Wednesday)

Kentucky also refused to send troops. The Governor of Missouri called the requisition "illegal, unconstitutional, revolutionary, inhuman, diabolical and cannot be complied with."

Virginia, upon receiving the call for troops, replied that since Lincoln had chosen to "inaugurate the war," Virginia would send no troops. The Governor declared that "the people of this Commonwealth are free men, not slaves." So, in a secret ballot, a Secession Convention, by a majority of 88 to 55, voted to join the Confederacy.

More Federal troops were landed at Pensacola to support Ft. Pickens. The *Star of the West*, the ship that was to have relieved Ft. Sumter, was captured off the coast of Texas by Confederates.

Jefferson Davis issued a proclamation inviting all interested in "service in private armed vessels on the high seas" to apply for Letters of Marque and Reprisal—an accepted method at the time to set up legalized piracy.

April 18 (Thursday)

In Washington, five companies of troops arrived from Pennsylvania for the defense of the capital. Coming through Baltimore, they met with cold stares and ugly looks. They arrived unarmed, untrained and wholly unprepared.

The Army Arsenal at Harpers Ferry was abandoned by its garrison and many of the buildings burned. Col. Robert E. Lee, recently returned to his home, "Arlington," met with Francis P. Blair, Sr. at the latter's home across from the White House. Blair, acting on behalf of the President, offered Lee the command of all Union forces being raised to fight the Confederacy. Lee declined, later recalling that he told Blair, "as candidly and courteously as I could that though opposed to secession and deprecating war, I could take no part in an invasion of the Southern states." Leaving Blair, he visited Gen. Winfield Scott and informed his old friend about the situation. Lee was not aware at this time that Virginia, in a secret ballot, had already seceded from the Union. He returned to "Arlington" for the last time.

In New York, Major Robert Anderson and the garrison from Ft. Sumter arrived as heroes.

Capt. Hiram Paulding was directed by Secretary of the Navy Welles to proceed to Norfolk and "take command of all naval forces there afloat... and should it finally become necessary, you will... destroy the property."

April 19 (Friday)

The 6th Massachusetts Volunteer Infantry Regiment arrived in Baltimore and was marching from one station to another, en route to Washington, when a large crowd of Southern sympathizers began to throw rocks and bricks and fired into the ranks of the troops. These troops, unlike those of the day before, were armed, and returned the fire, killing twelve civilians and wounding several more. The troops picked up their four dead, packed them in ice and sent them home, and then came to the capital with their 17 wounded.

In Washington, Lincoln declared a blockade of the Southern ports. With the trouble in Baltimore, the troops coming to the capital were embarked on naval vessels at Philadelphia for transport to Annapolis and then to Washington by rail. In Norfolk, Va., Navy Capt. David G. Farragut left his home for New York; he would remain in the Federal service.

Col. Robert E. Lee learned of the secession action of the Virginia Convention. While friends and relatives gathered at "Arlington" to discuss the situation, Lee walked alone in the garden, trying to make his decision. He later returned to his room and paced the floor for several hours. Shortly after midnight, he emerged with his resignation from the United States Army after 32 years of service. His decision cost him his career and "Arlington." The decision had to be made quickly before he received orders from the Federal War Department to act against the South.

April 20 (Saturday)

Robert E. Lee forwarded his resignation to the United States War Department.

In Louisville, Ky., former Vice President John Cabell Breckenridge addressed a large gathering, where he denounced Lincoln's call for troops as illegal.

In Norfolk, Va., the Gosport Navy Yard was abandoned, several ships were burned, some were saved, and the Navy Yard was handed over to the Confederacy. One of the ships, the U.S.S. *Merrimack*, was sunk after burning. It was, however, refloated by the Confederacy and came back as the C.S.S. *Virginia.*

Out in the Shenandoah Valley at Lexington, the Virginia Military Institute cadets were ordered to Richmond by the governor. Thomas J. Jackson, the senior military officer present, was to command the cadets.

Thomas Jonathan "Stonewall' Jackson was born in Clarksburg, Va. (now W.Va.) on January 21, 1824. His parents died when he was quite young and he was raised by his uncle. He entered West Point in 1842 and was graduated in 1846. He served in Mexico during that war and resigned in 1851 to become a professor of artillery and natural philosophy at Virginia Military Institute (VMI). At the onset of war, he was sent to Richmond with the cadets from VMI and assimilated into the Confederate Army as a Colonel. He served brilliantly in the Valley Campaign of 1862 and at Chancellorsville in May 1863, where he was accidentally killed by his own troops. He died on May 10, 1863, and was buried at Lexington, Va.

April 21 (Sunday)

A delegation from Baltimore called upon Lincoln to protest the killings of citizens in Baltimore the previous Friday (the 19th), calling it "a pollution" of Maryland soil. Lincoln replied that he must have troops to defend the capital. Dissatisfied, the Marylanders returned to Baltimore and cut the telegraph wires, burned bridges, and tore up miles of track. The city of Washington was now cut off from any rail support, Harpers Ferry being held by Confederate militia.

Washington began to look like a beleaguered city. Public buildings were barricaded with sandbags, troops were quartered under the unfinished Capitol dome. The Willard Hotel had fewer than 100 guests. Many of the residents, expecting the Confederate troops to enter the city at any time, wore secessionist badges and talked openly of the occupation of the city.

Today, the Governor of Virginia asked Robert E. Lee to take command of Virginia's defenses. Lee, at this point, still did *not* command the Confederate Army of Northern Virginia. Lee accepted and departed for Richmond.

At Lexington, Va., Thomas J. Jackson got his cadets organized for church, then marched them off to stagecoaches for the connection to the railroad. It was shortly after noon, and it would be the last time Jackson saw Lexington alive. (He would be buried there.) The first night was spent in Staunton, just a few miles away.

At the Philadelphia Navy Yard, the Commandant, Capt. Du Pont, was directed to "procure five staunch steamers from ten to twelve feet draught... for coast service." Like orders went to the navy yards in New York and Boston.

April 22 (Monday)

The Federal troops to defend the Capital were coming, albeit slowly. In Washington, Lincoln told a YWCA delegation from Baltimore to "keep your rowdies in Baltimore and there will be no bloodshed." At the Navy Yard, Capt. John A. Dahlgren assumed command after the previous Commandant, Capt. Franklin Buchanan, resigned and "went South." The Chief of Navy Ordnance, Capt. George A. Magruder, resigned and went to Canada, where he would sit out the war. When Magruder left, so did everyone else, stripping the department of all but a messenger, some draftsmen, and a young Lieutenant named Henry Wise. The departure of the Navy Yard personnel left only about 150 officers and men with whom to defend this vital installation.

Jackson arrived in Richmond with his charges and turned them over to State authorities. For the next few days he was put to work at the new Camp Lee, organizing the training of recruits.

April 23 (Tuesday)

Robert E. Lee, having gone to Richmond and now formally a Major General in the Virginia forces, assumed command of all State troops.

In Washington, Lincoln was still awaiting more troops to defend the Capital. Troops were moving down Chesapeake Bay to Annapolis and would be transshipped from there to Washington. The Capital could feel less threatened now; the U.S.S. *Pawnee* had arrived up the Potomac from Norfolk.

In Montgomery, President Jefferson Davis was assuring Gov. Claiborne Jackson of Missouri that he would support an attack on the U.S. Arsenal at St. Louis. Davis wanted desperately to get Missouri into the Southern camp.

April 24 (Wednesday)

Lincoln still awaited troops from Rhode Island to protect the Capital. At Hampton Roads, near Norfolk, Flag Officer Pendergrast captured the Confederate tug *Young America* and the schooner *George M. Smith*, which was loaded with a cargo of arms and ammunition. At Annapolis, the U.S.S. *Constitution* ("Old Ironsides") departed for Rhode Island with the midshipmen from the Naval Academy aboard, to remain there during the war at the site of the displaced Naval Academy.

April 25 (Thursday)

The troops finally arrived in Washington. First it was the 7th New York, followed by the Rhode

Island Militiamen, and a group of 1200 from Massachusetts, who had repaired a damaged engine and relaid the rails torn up by the "rowdies" of Baltimore between Annapolis and Washington.

In the west, one Capt. Stokes of Illinois was given orders to obtain rifles from the St. Louis Arsenal to equip the Illinois troops. He took a steamer with a few troops and landed at the Arsenal late at night and loaded over 10,000 muskets and other stores before the secessionists knew what was going on. All returned safely. Further west, Brigadier Gen. Edwin V. Sumner replaced Col. Albert Sidney Johnston as Commander in the West. Johnston would begin his long ride east to become a General in the Confederate forces and meet his fate at the Battle of Shiloh in less than one year.

In Richmond, Thomas J. Jackson was commissioned a Major of Engineers. He had been more than slighted, considering the West Point diploma, the Mexican War, and his experience in training. Needless to say, Jackson was a very unhappy man; he'd been given a desk job!

April 26 (Friday)

In Virginia, Major Gen. Joseph E. Johnston, of the Virginia Volunteers, was assigned to command all Virginia State forces in and around Richmond. On this day, Jackson's friend J.M. Bennett, discovering Jackson's fate, called on the Governor of Virginia and told him that this was a terrible waste of talent. The Governor agreed and promoted Jackson to Colonel and sent him to Harpers Ferry to see what mischief he could do there.

Joseph Eggleston Johnston was born in Farmville, Va., on February 3, 1807. He was graduated from West Point in 1829, 13th in a class of 46, a classmate of Robert E. Lee (who was graduated second). Like Lee, Johnston was assigned to the Engineers, spending time in the Topographical Engineers. He served with distinction in Mexico. He was promoted to Brigadier General in 1860, and assigned as the Quartermaster General of the U.S. Army. He was the only general officer to resign and join the Confederacy. He served in many capacities during the war, ultimately surrendering the army in North Carolina to Sherman in 1865. After the war, he was involved in several enterprises, including insurance companies, and served in the U.S. House of Representatives for two terms. On March 21, 1891, he died in Washington, two weeks after attending Sherman's funeral, where he had caught pneumonia.

Both North and South, the people felt that the war would not last long. War fever ran high, and volunteers in both areas were fast pouring in. At the top of Chesapeake Bay, Lt. G.W. Rodgers, commanding the U.S.S. *Commerce*, captured the steamer *Lancaster* at Havre de Grace, Md. He also chased a steam tug, but couldn't catch her.

In Georgia, the Governor issued an order repudiating all debts owed Northern interests.

April 27 (Saturday)

The blockade, previously covering only the southern tier of states, was extended to Virginia and North Carolina by Lincoln. He also suspended the writ of *habeas corpus*, for reasons of public safety. Many civil servants were resigning from the Federal government and "going South," as well as many officers of the Army and Navy. At Annapolis, Brigadier Gen. Benjamin F. Butler, was assigned control of the local area.

In Harpers Ferry, Col. Thomas J. Jackson was assigned command of the lower Shenandoah Valley and the city. Richmond extended an invitation to the Confederate government to make it the capital of the Confederacy because of limited facilities in Montgomery.

Gideon Welles issued orders for all United States ships to seize Confederate privateers on the high seas. The steamer *Helmick* was seized at Cairo, Illinois, loaded with powder and munitions.

April 28 (Sunday)

Lincoln visited the 7th New York Infantry, which was quartered in the House of Representatives chamber in the Capitol. The volunteer troops in the west were arriving at their first posts and becoming indoctrinated into the Federal Army.

Charles W. Wills was 21 years old in April 1861, a native of Illinois and a graduate of the State Normal School at Bloomington. When the first call came for volunteers to serve for three months, he joined Company E, 8th Illinois Infantry, on April 26, 1861. The organization was sent to Cairo, Illinois, to protect the confluence of the Ohio and

Mississippi rivers. His experience leaving his hometown is typical of the time.

Wills, Pvt., 8th Illinois Infantry, Cairo, Illinois:

> This is the twilight of our first day here. We started from Peoria last Wednesday at 11 A.M. amid such a scene as I never saw before. Shouting, crying, praying, and shaking hands were the exercises. Along the whole line from Peoria to Springfield, from every house we had cheers and waving of handkerchiefs. Got to Springfield at dark and marched out to Camp Brick (it is a brick kiln) by moonlight. Our beds were of hay, scattered on the earthen floor of the dry shed. We had to sleep very close together, being cramped for room. Our eatables are bread, bacon, beef, coffee, beans, rice, potatoes, and sugar and molasses and pickles.

In the haste of getting the volunteers to the various strategic points around the area, quite often the numbers required for a unit to be mustered in were ignored. Another factor was the political appointment of the regimental commander, which depended upon the successful enlistment of 1000 officers and men before that officer could officially be named. This led to some real infighting among some politicians to get their commissions.

Reorganization of the newly recruited units was not uncommon, because some were over-recruited, while others barely filled the quotas. Wills records, "We were trimmed to 77 rank and file each. This created considerable dissatisfaction and made a deal of very wicked swearing. Some of the men who were turned out of our company threatened to shoot our captain, but he is still living."

The war fever in the South was as virulent as in the North, if not more so. Even prior to 1861, during the very heated political campaigns of 1860, military units were formed as a part of "social activities." These units later became active units in the Confederate forces. Quite often, the fervor was greater in the female population than it was in the male. There was one case in Alabama where a young man was somewhat reluctant to join the Army and his girlfriend sent him one of her sets of pantaloons and a dress with the message, "Wear these or enlist!" He enlisted.

Julius D. Allen was born in Salisbury, N.C., on October 22, 1837. Sixteen days after Sumter was fired upon, Allen was in Asheville, N.C. He wrote his parents:

> There has been a great deal of excitement in this place since I came here. There were two military companies here some time ago—the Buncombe Riflemen and a light-horse company of volunteers. On Saturday, the 20th, the citizens of Buncombe county held a meeting and organized a company of volunteers, called the Rough and Ready Guards, which number about eighty men. The Hon. J.B. Vance has also organized a company of about 100 men. Since these companies were organized, they have been drilled twice a day and once at night. They drilled this evening for the first time on Sunday. The Riflemen have been called out by the Governor and will leave on to-morrow. They go from here to Raleigh, and from there they know not where. All the Union men here have become Secessionists, and the flag of the Southern Confederacy floats in triumph over this place. In East Tennessee many still stick to the Union. Among them Parson Brownlow and Andy Johnson are the most prominent men.
>
> Mr. Shackleford received a letter from his brother in Greenville, Tenn., yesterday which says that they have raised a Union flag 105 feet high over the place, and were going to "stick up to the Union until hell froze over so they could skate on ice."
>
> The people here held a meeting on Sunday last, and appointed another on Thursday, for the purpose of getting more volunteers. Then they sent men all over the county to notify the people. One fellow went out in the country to a church where there was preaching, rode up to the house full speed, jumped off his horse, walked into the church and up the aisle, hat in hand, and accosted the preacher thus: "Mr. Preacher, by request of the citizens of Asheville, I have a letter for you to read to this congregation." The preacher took the notice, reproved the man for interrupting him in the middle of his discourse, and refused to read it. It was finally read, however, by one of the members, and the patriotic messenger went on his way.
>
> No one deplores the state of affairs in this county more deeply than I do, but it is the work of fire-eaters, and I can do nothing to save my country, or I would do it gladly. I have no sympathy for secession, and am still for the Union for which our fathers fought, bled and died; but I cannot express myself here. I do not think I shall ever fight under the banner of the Southern Confederacy. Please give me your

sentiments, and tell me what are the views of the people of Davidson in the present crisis.

... We have buttermilk every day since I have been at Shackleford's, and I have begun to think that some of their cows give buttermilk, or there must be a spring of it somewhere about here. I have a great many things to tell you if I ever see you again, which I have not the time to write.

April 29 (Monday)

In Annapolis, the Maryland House of Delegates voted 53 to 13 against secession. This would not settle matters from a practical viewpoint, since much of Maryland's Eastern Shore was pro-South and they would cooperate with the South whenever possible.

President Davis addressed a session of the Confederate Congress, blaming Lincoln for starting the war and declaring that "all we ask is to be let alone."

April 30 (Tuesday)

Col. Thomas J. Jackson arrived in Harpers Ferry and issued his first command. The action was not popular with the militia troops already there.

By the end of this month, the crisis had eased considerably in Washington. There were enough troops present to provide at least a modicum of protection while others arrived. The command structure of the newly formed Army was slowly being sorted out, and at least Maryland was not leaving the Union.

The "Hero of Sumter," Major Robert Anderson, was promoted to Brigadier General and sent to his native Kentucky to help keep that state in the Union. Kentucky being neutral, he established headquarters in Cincinnati.

MAY 1861

The dangerous game of war began, albeit slowly. On both sides there was a feeling of unreality that was hard to describe and even harder to deal with. Suddenly, this argument was getting serious, much more serious than some had bargained for. The hotheads on both sides had won the day, at least for a while, and the fever built.

The border states presented Lincoln with a special problem, Kentucky in particular. The proximity to Tennessee made it easy for pro-Confederate Kentuckians to leave the state and form military units in Tennessee, where they were welcomed by that Governor, and supported. Lincoln, desirous of furnishing arms to the Kentucky Unionists without providing them to the State government, finally found a means of doing this "unofficially." The answer was found in one William Nelson.

May 1 (Wednesday)

At Harpers Ferry, Col. Thomas J. Jackson was ordered to remove most of the weapon-making machinery from the arsenal and have it shipped to Winchester and Strasburg. It would later be moved again to Richmond and Fayetteville, N.C., for the manufacture of Confederate rifles and cannon.

In Boston, the soldiers killed by the mob in Baltimore were afforded full military honors at their burial. The city that had seen much of the Revolutionary War now buried the first dead of the Civil War. On the York peninsula, the Federal Navy blockaded the James River and the Hampton Roads access to the Naval Yard at Norfolk.

The Governor of Tennessee was authorized to enter into league with the Confederacy by the State Legislature.

The U.S.S. *Hatteras*, commanded by George F. Emmons, captured the Confederate schooner *Magnolia*, loaded with a cargo of cotton.

May 2 (Thursday)

More troops were arriving in Washington daily. The New York Fire Zouaves, with their short jackets and bloused trousers, arrived. Col. Elmer E. Ellsworth, their commander, was to be among the first casualties of the war.

The aging Gen. Winfield Scott had not lost his eye for strategic operations. In a letter to Major Gen. George B. McClellan, he cited his views:

> We rely greatly on the sure operation of a complete blockade of the Atlantic and Gulf ports soon to commence. In connection with such a blockade, we propose a powerful movement down the Mississippi to the ocean, with a cordon of posts at proper points... the object being to clear out and keep open this great line of communication in connection with the strict blockade of the seaboard, so as to envelop the insurgent States and bring them to terms with less bloodshed than by any other plan.

May 3 (Friday)

Expanding his troop requirements beyond the 75,000 in the first call, Lincoln now called for an additional 42,000 volunteers to serve for three years. Lincoln also expanded the regular Army to nearly 23,000 and authorized enlistment of naval personnel to 18,000. All of this was done without the approval of Congress.

A new Department of the Ohio was formed, covering Ohio, Indiana and Illinois. The order also placed 34-year-old George Brinton McClellan in command of the new Department. In Kentucky, 14 companies offered their services to the Confederacy and went into camp in the southern part of the state for training and organization. The Governor of Missouri, Claiborne Jackson, declared that State to be for the South. This would cause an immediate reaction from Washington.

Commander Dahlgren, now Commandant of the Washington Navy Yard, notes:

> Besides the Yard, I have to hold the bridge next above, so some howitzers and a guard are there. It is from this direction that the rebels of the eastern shore [of the Anacostia] may come. This Yard is of great importance, not only because of its furnishing the Navy so largely with various stores, but also as a position in the general defenses of the city.

May 4 (Saturday)

In western Virginia, several pro-Union groups were meeting to discuss possible secession from Virginia.

In Missouri, the United States ordnance stores located in Kansas City were seized by the pro-South State government. At Gretna, La., near New Orleans, one of the first guns for the Confederate Navy was cast at the Phoenix Iron Works. The *Star of the West* of Ft. Sumter fame, was now in the hands of the rebels, and was used as a receiving ship in New Orleans.

May 5 (Sunday)

In Maryland, Major Gen. Benjamin F. Butler took over the Railroad Relay House on the B&O Railroad running between Washington, Baltimore and Annapolis, securing the line for the present.

Benjamin Franklin Butler was born in Deerfield, N.H., on November 5, 1818. He studied law and became a power in state politics. In 1860, he was a delegate to the Democratic Convention, held in Charleston, S.C., and voted for Jefferson Davis as the Presidential candidate 57 times. After Ft. Sumter was fired upon, he formed a regiment and took it to Washington, D.C., and was appointed the first Major General of Volunteers by Lincoln. He would prove to be one of the worst choices for this position. Almost everything he touched went sour, until finally, in January 1865, Grant relieved him of command, and Butler resigned his commission in November 1865. Serving as a U.S. Representative, he was very active in the impeachment of Andrew Johnson. He also ran, unsuccessfully, for President. He died on January 11, 1893, in Washington.

May 6 (Monday)

On this date, the states of Tennessee and Arkansas passed Secession Ordinances and left the Union officially, the 9th and 10th states to join the Confederacy. In Montgomery, Ala., President Davis approved a bill of May 3rd, declaring that a state of war existed between the two governments. In London, the government recognized the Confederacy as a belligerent, but not as a separate nation.

In St. Louis, there resided one Capt. Nathaniel Lyon, a hard-bitten New Englander, and a graduate of West Point, class of '41. A red-headed, hot-tempered Unionist, he believed that anything was legal to keep the pro-Southern Governor of Missouri from getting the arms stored in the local arsenal. When Gov. Jackson called out the local state militia, Lyon disguised himself as a farm woman, complete with veil to hide his red hair and beard, and toured the local militia camps in a horse-drawn vehicle. He carried a wicker basket with two loaded revolvers in it. Using the intelligence he gathered (which was probably already available elsewhere), he planned his attack.

May 7 (Tuesday)

Isham Harris, Governor of Tennessee, took action within the Legislature to join the state to the Confederacy; this was done without a vote by the citizens of the state. In Knoxville, Tenn., there was a riot between the pro-Union and secessionist factions. One man was mortally wounded during the fracas. Eastern Tennessee was very strong for the Union, and would remain so for the duration of the war.

U.S.S. *Yankee*, Lt. Thomas O. Selfridge, was fired upon by Confederate batteries at Gloucester Point, Va., just north of Yorktown.

Barber, Pvt., Co. D, 15th Illinois Volunteer Infantry, Marengo, Illinois:

> After organization of the Company, we held ourselves subject to orders and in readiness to march when called upon. In the meantime, some of the boys returned to their homes and pursued their usual avocations, while some stayed in town and were boarded and lodged by the generosity of the people of Marengo; but soon an order came from Gov. Yates ordering us to report at Freeport, Illinois, on the 11th of May and go into Camp of Instruction.

May 8 (Wednesday)

The Richmond *Examiner* agreed *not* to publish information on military movements. This agreement would last only so long as it took a paper to go to press. On both sides the "leaking" of information via the press was a serious problem. At one time, a New York paper published diagrams of all the fortifications of Washington, D.C..

Secretary of the Navy Gideon Welles appointed Gustavus Fox as Chief Clerk of the Navy, and requested that he take up his new duties as soon as possible.

May 9 (Thursday)

The Lincolns attended a concert by the 71st New York Regimental Band encamped at the Washington Navy Yard. After the concert, Lincoln asked to see Dahlgren's new 11-inch smoothbore gun fired. Dahlgren, happy to oblige, put on a demonstration in the nearby Anacostia River.

The Confederate Congress authorized the President to accept into volunteer service those forces deemed necessary for the duration of the war. The South, like the North, initially accepted volunteers for one year. This changed rapidly in the South, and soon all troops were in "for the duration."

Across the York River from Yorktown, Va., the Federal blockade vessels traded shots with the Confederate batteries located at Gloucester Point. The blockade of Chesapeake Bay and its tributaries was increasing in scope.

The U.S. Naval Academy arrived at its new home in Newport, Rhode Island, along with "Old Ironsides," the U.S.S. *Constitution*.

May 10 (Friday)

After assessing the information gained on the 8th, Capt. Lyon decided that the militia was really meant to seize the arsenal, so he took it upon himself to surround the camp with his own troops and those of Frank Blair's Home Guards, and capture it. The odds were definitely lopsided: Lyon's nearly 7000 to his opponent's 700. He marched the would-be rebel soldiers off to prison through the streets of the city, causing a disturbance. Lyon's troops, many of them of German descent, were met with cries of "Damn the Dutch" and some drunk fired into the troops as they marched. The regiments turned and fired into the crowd, killing twenty-eight men, women, and children.

There were two observers in St. Louis that day. W.T. Sherman was walking on the streets with his son and his brother-in-law when the shots cut the leaves from the trees above them. These were the first shots Sherman ever heard fired in anger. He grabbed his son Willy, and, dropping down into a gully, raced for home. The other observer was Ulysses S. Grant, now a Colonel of the 21st Illinois Volunteer Infantry.

Francis (Frank) Preston Blair, Jr. was born in Lexington, Ky., on February 19, 1821. He was the brother of Lincoln's first Postmaster General, Montgomery Blair, and the son of Francis P. Blair, Senior, who had been an advisor to Presidents since Andrew Jackson. As Attorney General in New Mexico Territory in 1847, he had a serious clash with Gov. Sterling Price. In Missouri in 1861, Blair and Nathaniel Lyons captured the St. Louis Arsenal's contents from Sterling Price's State militia. Blair recruited seven regiments of Union troops in Missouri in the summer of 1862, and was appointed a Brigadier General on August 7th. In November, he was appointed Major General and served under Sherman during the Yazoo River expedition. He became a corps commander under Grant and later served Sherman in the same capacity. An able general, he was one of the few political generals who understood his role in the army. After the war he served in the U.S. Senate. He died in St. Louis on July 9, 1875.

The U.S.S. *Niagara* began the first of many blockade patrols off Charleston, S.C.

In a Secret Act of the Confederate Congress, President Davis authorized "the Navy Department to send an agent abroad to purchase six steam propellers, in addition to those heretofore authorized, together with rifled cannon, small arms, and other ordnance stores and munitions of war."

May 11 (Saturday)

After a stormy night of mob action in St. Louis that closed the saloons, the mob still roamed the streets. Another clash caused the death of more citizens. Slowly the people calmed down and the interminable discussions began about which way Missouri should go—North or South. Large pro-Union meetings were held in San Francisco and Wheeling, Va.

The U.S.S. *Pawnee* was ordered from the Washington Navy Yard to Alexandria, Va., to protect Federal vessels from attack.

Wills, 8th Illinois, Cairo, Illinois:

> One of the boys has just come in with a report that there are "to a dead certainty" 5000 men now at Columbus (20 miles below) who have just arrived this morning. They are after Cairo. The boys are all rumor proof, though, and the above didn't get a comment. One of the boys has just expressed my feelings by saying: "I don't believe anything, only that Cairo is a damned mud hole."... A general order was given last night for every man to bathe at least twice a week. Most of us do it every day. The Ohio is warm enough and I swim every night now. There were over 2000 of us in at once last night. We had a candy pulling this P.M. There was an extra gallon of molasses in to-day's rations, and we boiled it and had a gay time. Our company is, I believe, the orderly one here. We have lots of beer sent us from Peoria, and drink a half barrel a day while it lasts.

Barber, Pvt., Co. D, 15th Illinois Volunteer Infantry, Freeport, Illinois:

> ...the usually quiet streets of Marengo were thronged with spectators, friends and relatives of the soldiers who had come to witness their departure. A few hours before leaving, the ladies of Marengo presented the Company with a fine flag and 'neath its folds we took a solemn vow never to disgrace it or bring it back until our flag could wave in triumph over all our land.
>
> The shrill snort of the iron horse now told us that the hour had come to sever home associations and take the tented field. Amidst the tears and benedictions of our friends, the train moved on. Smothering the pent-up emotions which were surging in my soul, I looked forward to the time when I could greet them all again, when peace had folded her mantle over a rescued country. We arrived at Freeport at 11 A.M. and went into camp on the fair grounds south of the city. We immediately went to work fitting up our quarters to make them so that we could use them for the night. Rows of sheds were built on the outer edge, straw thrown in and on this we made our first bed in camp, each soldier having brought a quilt with him..... We went into camp with no provision made for rations and cooking utensils. Our supper the first night consisted of raw beef, which we cooked by holding it on a sharp stick over a poor fire; but nevertheless, we enjoyed our supper well and bore our privations in good humor, considering it a good initiation into the beauties of camp life.

May 13 (Monday)

In Kentucky, there lived a family named Nelson who produced a son, named William, who grew to be a very large man. His six-foot, four-inch, 300-pound frame contained a steel-trap mind and a prodigious memory. After completing two years at Norwich University, he was appointed a midshipman in the U.S. Navy in 1840, and spent 21 years in the naval service, rising to the rank of Lieutenant.

In early 1861 Nelson contacted Lincoln (an old family friend) to discuss Nelson's recent trip to Kentucky. Lincoln, ever mindful of the sensitive local issues in Kentucky, was seeking a means to supply the pro-Unionists with arms without funnelling the arms through the State government, which was pro-Confederate (supposedly neutral). Nelson volunteered for the job of distributing the weapons. Lincoln ordered 5,000 muskets and had them shipped to Cincinnati. Nelson went to Ohio, and shortly thereafter the guns found their way into the hands of the pro-Union forces.

From St. Louis, where he was awaiting developments, Sherman wrote his friend Boyd one last letter. In this letter he said,

> Already Missouri is humbled. I have witnessed it; my personal friends here, many of them Southern,

admit that Missouri's fate is sealed. I have no doubt 100,000 disciplined men will be in Louisiana by Christmas next. The Mississippi River will be a grand theater of war.... It is horrible to contemplate but it cannot be avoided. I know that I individually would not do any human being a wrong, take from him a cent or molest any of his rights or property, yet I admit fully the fact that Lincoln was bound to call on the country to rally and save our constitution and government. Had I responded to his call for volunteers I know that I would now be a Major-General. But my feelings prompted me to forbear and the consequence is my family and friends are almost cold to me and they feel and say that I have failed at the critical moment of my life. It may be I am but a chip on the whirling tide of time destined to be cast on the shore as a worthless weed.

Barber, Pvt., Co. D, 15th Illinois Volunteer Infantry, Freeport, Illinois:

> ... the camp was put under strict military rules, no one being allowed to pass in or out without a pass from a commanding officer. Company B came provided with muskets and they were used for guard duty. Happy indeed was the fellow who was lucky enough to get on guard, and one would imagine, to see him strutting back and forth, that the "fate of the empire" depended upon his vigilance; but time and service took the "primp" out of us. Soon the guard duty ceased to be a novelty and some of the boys became as anxious to evade the duty as they had been to perform it. Their main energies were devoted now to see how they could evade the guard and get down town and have a time. Many stratagems were employed and many tricks were played to accomplish what they wanted, but a large majority of the soldiers lived up to the rules and conducted themselves as properly as they would were they at their own firesides. Drilling soon became the order of the day.... We had company drill two hours in the morning, rested one hour and then had battalion drill until dinner. The same order was observed in the afternoon...

In London, Queen Victoria announced England's stance of strict neutrality—no recognition of the South as a nation.

Major Gen. Benjamin Butler occupied Baltimore. This was unsettling to some and gratifying to others. It had one effect: it kept down the noise against the Union.

May 14 (Tuesday)

William T. Sherman returned to the Army, accepting a commission as the commander of the newly formed 13th Infantry (Regulars).

The trains at Harpers Ferry had been running between Washington and points west since hostilities first opened. Col. Thomas J. Jackson decreed that the trains might not run at night; then he confiscated several of the trains the following morning, and sent them south into the Shenandoah Valley.

Back in St. Louis, the Federal general commanding the area issued a proclamation to the citizens telling them to ignore a bill passed by the State Legislature to raise troops for the South.

May 15 (Wednesday)

Stalwart Nathaniel Lyon in St. Louis dispatched troops to Potosi, Mo., to help pro-Union citizens. Gen. Ben Butler was sent from Annapolis and Baltimore to Ft. Monroe to command that area.

The U.S.S. *Bainbridge* was ordered to sail to Panama to protect the California steamers hauling gold from the mines in California to New York. The Southern privateers desperately sought these ships, for their specie was needed for Confederate coffers.

May 17 (Friday)

Yesterday Gov. Isham Harris of Tennessee finally achieved his purpose: Tennessee was admitted to the Confederacy on May 16.

Nathaniel Lyon, captain of militia, was promoted to Brigadier General in the Union Army. He mounted a campaign to drive the pro-Southern forces from Missouri. He would die leading his troops at the Battle of Wilson's Creek on August 10th.

Joseph Hooker, 49 years old, West Point, class of '37, veteran of the Mexican War, where he won a Brevet Lt. Colonelcy at Chapultepec, had been farming in California. After the Mexican War, he had fallen into disfavor with Gen. Winfield Scott, and he resigned from the Army in 1853. At the outset of the war he volunteered, but was rejected, by Scott, who had a long memory. However, on this date, he was appointed Brigadier General of Volunteers and assigned to the Washington defenses.

North Carolina was admitted to the Confederacy, contingent upon ratification of the Constitution.

May 18 (Saturday)

Arkansas was admitted to the Confederacy. The political leader in St. Louis, Francis P. Blair, Jr., received a letter from Lincoln asking that he watch Gen. Harney a little longer before having him relieved of command. Both Lincoln and Blair felt Harney was too pro-South.

Along Virginia's shore, the mouth of the Rappahannock River was blockaded, sealing a major supply and communication artery.

Barber, Pvt., Co. D, 15th Illinois Volunteer Infantry, Freeport, Illinois:

> On the 18th we were sworn into the State service. Here some were rejected on account of height and physical disability, five feet and six inches being the shortest to insure acceptance. So eager were some of the boys to be accepted they would attempt to conceal their deformities and would appear as tall as possible when passing before the mustering officer. Some felt so bad as to shed tears at their rejection....

May 19 (Sunday)

At Sewell's Point, near Hampton Roads, Va., the blockading ships and shore batteries mixed it up for the second day in a row.

Allen, Co. K, 10th Illinois Cavalry, Asheville, N.C.:

> I have been well since I wrote before, and begin to like Buncombe pretty well. My employer is a very clever man and has a very pretty daughter.
>
> The excitement here is not as great as it has been, but one can hear nothing but war yet. The Buncombe Riflemen left town on the 29th ult., and the Rough and Ready Guards on the 3rd inst. I witnessed the departure of both companies. That of the first was the most affecting scene I ever beheld. They were placed in single file, and their relatives and friends passed along the rank and bade them farewell. Strong men shed tears, and women cried aloud.
>
> Buncombe has raised two other companies besides those that have gone off. These mountaineers are a stout, hardy set of men—Vance's averaged 165 pounds. A few days ago there were five companies of volunteers quartered in town, numbering over 450 men, but none of them were armed or uniformed. On yesterday the Madison and Haywood companies left, and the Macon companies came in, so there are still four here.
>
> I do not read the papers much, as there are so many false reports in circulation, that one does not know what to believe. I think this State will certainly secede, and as I am not a secessionist, and do not think I ever will be, I do not like to stay where I dare not express my opinion without being regarded as a Tory. For your sake I will remain in North Carolina if I can get into business in Catawba or Davidson that will pay; if not, I will go to Tennessee, and from there to Illinois, and then go on to my journey's end, as I can not be satisfied to make North Carolina my home if she secedes. Please write immediately when you get this, otherwise I may not be here when your letter reaches Asheville.
>
> The companies that left here yesterday took a parcel of free negroes with them that had been overheard talking about the war and taking sides with Lincoln. When I came to this place there were two papers published here—the Asheville *News* and the Asheville *Spectator*, but the editor of the latter stopped his. Each of the companies that have gone from Buncombe had a doctor with them and Vance's had a Methodist preacher, one of the professors of the Female College of this place.
>
> I was out in the country yesterday, on the top of a mountain, about five miles from here by the road (of course not so far in the straight course), where I could see town plainly; and on every side as far as the eye could reach I could see nothing but hill and mountain, with fields scattered here and there over them....
>
> I have had buttermilk every day since I have been at Shackleford's, but there is not a spring of it as I supposed at first. They churn every day and that accounts for their having so much of it.

May 20 (Monday)

Throughout the North on this day, U.S. Marshals "raided" the telegraph offices and confiscated all files of telegrams sent during the past calendar year. It was hoped that this would reveal spy sources and personnel. In some cases this was successful.

North Carolina officially seceded from the Union. This made the 11th state to leave the Union, and the last. While North Carolina may have been the last to leave, she furnished more troops and suffered more casualties than any other Southern state during the war.

Kentucky declared her neutrality and forbade the movement of any troops on state soil. This would be a very difficult position to maintain and would not last long before being violated by both sides.

The Confederate Congress voted to move the capital of the Confederacy to Richmond. This not only gave them more room, it ensured Virginia's involvement.

May 23 (Thursday)

Virginia completed her vote for secession. The vote went 3-to-1 in the eastern and central parts of the state. There was still much pro-Union sentiment in the mountains to the west.

Wills, Pvt., 8th Illinois Infantry, Cairo, Illinois:

> Lots of men come through here with their backs blue and bloody from beatings; and nine in ten of them got their marks in Memphis. A man from St. Louis was in camp a few days since with one-half of his head shaved, one-half of a heavy beard taken off, two teeth knocked out and his lips all cut with blows from a club. This was done in Memphis the day before I saw him.... I never enjoyed anything in the world as I do this life, and as for its spoiling me, you'll see if I don't come out a better man than when I went in.... I commenced this about 12 last night in the hospital, but I had so much to do and there were so infernal many bugs that I concluded to postpone it. We do have the richest assortment of bugs here imaginable, from the size of a pin-head up to big black fellows as large as bats. I was sitting up with an old schoolmate from Bloomington, whose company have gone up to Big Muddy and left him to the tender care of our surgeons. The poor devil would die in a week but for the care he gets from a dozen of us here that used to go to school with him. There are about 50 men in our regiment's hospital, and save the few that go up to care for their friends unasked, the poor fellows have no attendance nights. I gave medicine to four beside my friend last night, two of who are crazy with fever. One of the latter insisted on getting up all the time, and twice he got down stairs while I was attending the others. Not one of our company is here, thank heavens.... The companies here with inexperienced officers have worlds of trouble, and five captains and one lieutenant, though good men at home, have resigned at the wish of their companies. Four of these companies tried to get our first lieutenant for captain, but he won't leave us....

May 24 (Friday)

Federal troops crossed the Potomac River near Washington and captured Alexandria, Va., before dawn. It would remain a Federal city for the duration of the war. A sad note of the affair was the death of Col. Elmer Ellsworth. At the age of 24, he had organized the First Fire Zouaves (11th New York), and brought them to Washington for the defense of the capital. He was killed by hotel owner James Jackson, after Ellsworth had removed a Confederate flag from the roof of the hotel. Ellsworth would be given a lavish funeral and become a martyr, as would Jackson.

At Ft. Monroe, Ben Butler stirred the pot by refusing to release three Negro slaves who had entered his lines, stating that they were "contraband of war," thus giving a new twist to the slave issue.

Barber, Pvt., Co. D, 15th Illinois Volunteer Infantry, Freeport, Illinois:

> On the 24th of May we were transferred and sworn into the U.S. service for three years, or during the war, by Capt. Pope, afterwards Major-General. Our oath simply consisted in swearing allegiance to our Government and obeying all legal orders of our superior officers. On the same day we were sworn in, William and Rollin Mallory, of Riley, and James Barber, of Java, New York, joined the Company. James came for the sole purpose of enlisting and being in the same Company with his brother and myself....

May 26 (Sunday)

Yesterday Col. Ellsworth lay in state in the East Room of the White House. His funeral was attended by both the President and Mrs. Lincoln. He was among the first to die in this bloody struggle.

The Baltimore and Ohio Railroad was a vital link

between Washington and the west and had to be protected to keep communications open. In Cincinnati, Major Gen. George B. McClellan ordered three Federal regiments into western Virginia for this purpose; the focus was to be on the major terminus of Grafton.

Postmaster General Montgomery Blair ruled that no further postal service would be provided to the Southern states after May 31st. Troops under Ben Butler occupied Newport News, Va., on Monday, the 27th.

May 30 (Thursday)

Yesterday, in Washington, Miss Dorothea Dix was finally authorized by Simon Cameron to organize and establish military hospitals.

Federal troops commanded by Col. R. F. Kelley occupied Grafton, in western Virginia. A further blow to the South came when Secretary of War Simon Cameron notified Ben Butler in Ft. Monroe, Va., that he should retain any slaves entering his lines, employ them and keep records of their service.

At Norfolk, the Confederates raised the U.S.S. *Merrimack*, which had been burned when the Navy Yard was evacuated.

May 31 (Friday)

Federal troops arrived in Ft. Leavenworth, Kansas, from the abandoned posts in Indian Territory, led by Jesse Chisholm along the Chisholm Trail.

The Confederacy named Gen. Pierre Gustave Toutant Beauregard to command their forces on the "Alexandria Line," which included all of northern Virginia.

In Missouri, Gen. Harney was finally relieved by Lyon and Blair, using authority given them by Lincoln earlier in the month.

JUNE 1861

There was a flurry of activity both North and South as young men flocked to the colors. In both areas there were many who had been no further than to the local county seat, and the glamour of the uniform, the drums, and the adventure was an all-powerful incentive. In both North and South there was a severe shortage of rifles for the infantry. Many of the state arsenals were equipped with old flintlock muskets, last used in the Mexican War, and few rifled wepons were available. The two main arms manufacturing sites were at Springfield, Mass., and Harpers Ferry, Va.; the latter site was now lost and the equipment shipped south by Col. Thomas J. Jackson.

June 1 (Saturday)

Federal cavalry moved into Fairfax Court House, Va., about 20 miles south of Washington, entering the town on a north road. Confederate military forces consisting of a cavalry company from Prince William County, another company of cavalry from Rappahannock County, and the Warrenton Rifles, commanded by Capt. John Q. Marr, were in the town at the time. The cavalry was composed of raw recruits who soon bolted and left the Warrenton Rifles holding the bag. There were only about 40 Confederate soldiers engaged in the melee that followed. The Rifles made a good accounting of themselves, sending the Union cavalry back with several empty saddles. Capt. Marr could not be found initially, some believing he had been cut off from his troops by the Union cavalry. A search of the area found his body in a clover patch, shot through the heart. His body was taken back to Warrenton, where he was interred with honors. Capt. Marr became one of the first Southern casualties of the war. His *alma mater*, Virginia Military Institute, listed him as one of the fallen.

At the confluence of the Ohio and Mississippi rivers, the town of Cairo, Ill., was a strategic defense point for both North and South. Large batteries were installed to prevent boats from passing upriver without authority. Today, the first gun was test-fired.

The blockade of the Southern ports and the use of privateers gained immediate foreign attention, especially in England, one of the major consumers of Southern cotton. England's attitude raised some consternation in the United States, although Britain, with other nations, had established a policy of preventing the belligerents from carrying prizes into any British port. Capt. Du Pont at the Philadelphia Navy Yard wrote:

> I do not like the tone of things in England.... Lord Derby and Granville, etc., talk of two thousand miles of coast to be blockaded! They seem to forget so far as their rights and international interests are concerned we have only to blockade the *ports of entry*—

from Chesapeake to Galveston—any... venture into any other harbors or inlets of any kind is liable to capture as a smuggler....

Barber, Pvt., Co. D, 15th Illinois Volunteer Infantry, Freeport, Illinois:

> Elon, James, Rollin, William, Harvey Huntington and myself received three days' leave of absence to go home and make our final adieux. It was the last time I saw home for nearly three years. Ere that time had elapsed, the fire blaze of battle had swept over me. Toil, hunger and sickness had left their marks upon me. Death, too, had made its mark in the family circle and took a loved sister to her spirit home....

June 2 (Sunday)

Gen. Pierre Gustav Toutant Beauregard, often called "the Creole," took command of the Confederate forces in northern Virginia. Among other names, this collection of units would be referred to as the Army of Northern Virginia, a name which would see much glory.

In western Virginia, Col. R. F. Kelley sent his troops south from Grafton in a driving rain. The area was extremely hilly and the roads of this era were seldom all-weather-capable. The narrow valleys tended to channel the runoff and create unexpected torrents in the many small streams. Marching was not easy in this terrain, especially at night. To add to Kelley's woes, the troops were green, unused to march discipline, and barely trained in marching.

June 3 (Monday)

Stephen Arnold Douglas, the "Little Giant" from Illinois, was best known for his debates with Lincoln during the campaign of 1860. The split in the Democratic Party during that election year virtually assured Lincoln's election. In spite of his defeat, at the outset of the war he worked very hard for the Union and strongly defended Lincoln's war measures. His hard efforts took their toll, however, and he died on this day in Springfield, Illinois, where he was later interred.

About daylight, Col. Kelley's troops entered the town of Philippi, just south of Grafton, after marching all night in a pouring rain. Two columns, under the overall command of Brigadier Gen. T. A. Morris, struck the Confederates of Col. G. A. Porterfield completely by surprise, and the Rebels fled south with the Federals in hot pursuit. The chase became known as the "Philippi Races" in the Northern papers, and as "disgraceful" in the Southern press. This minor action did much to enhance the reputation of Major Gen. George B. McClellan, and although he had little to do with the actual action, he took full advantage of the publicity.

In a strange turnabout of captures, the brig *Joseph* was captured by the Confederate privateer *Savannah*, which was then captured in turn by the U.S.S. *Perry*.

Barber, Pvt., Co. D, 15th Illinois Volunteer Infantry, Freeport, Illinois:

> When we got back to camp, we found it dressed in habiliments of mourning in memory of the lamented Douglas. His funeral obsequies were observed in Freeport and the regiment attended en masse.

June 4 (Tuesday)

At Philippi, in western Virginia, the Union troops consolidated their gains, got some sleep, and prepared to move on Beverly, to the south. Beauregard inspected his organization in preparation for the defense of northern Virginia. More troops were being brought into this area, some from as far away as Louisiana.

In Kentucky, naval Lt. William Nelson was receiving more guns from Lincoln to be distributed among the loyalists of Kentucky and eastern Tennessee—5,000 to Nelson and 1,000 to be distributed by ex-Congressman Emerson Etheridge of Tennessee. The pro-Confederate forces dubbed these weapons as "Lincoln guns," a name taken up immediately by the loyalists to be used with pride. Meanwhile, the pro-Southern governor of Kentucky, Beriah Magoffin, paid $60,000 for weapons to give to the secessionists, only to find that the guns were unserviceable and (worst of all) had been sold to him by some wily Yankee trader.

June 5 (Wednesday)

Near Hampton Roads, Va., is a spit of land called Pig Point. The Confederates installed a shore battery early in the game, and today they were trading shots with the Revenue Cutter *Harriet Lane*, Capt. Faunce.

The U.S.S. *Niagara*, blockading Mobile, Ala., captured the schooner *Aid*. In more captures, Flag Officer Pendergrast reported the taking of the bark *General Green* by Commander Overton Carr on the U.S.S. *Quaker City* at the Capes of the Chesapeake.

Beauregard, consolidating his Army of Northern Virginia at Manassas, issued a proclamation to the people of northern Virginia:

> A reckless and unprincipled tyrant has invaded your soil. Abraham Lincoln, regardless of all moral, legal, and constitutional restraints, has thrown his abolition hosts among you, who are murdering and imprisoning your citizens, confiscating and destroying your property, and committing other acts of violence and outrage too shocking and revolting to humanity to be enumerated.

June 6 (Thursday)

The former governor of Virginia, Henry A. Wise, now a Brigadier General in the Confederate Army, was directed to command the Rebel forces in western Virginia. Appointed only the day before as a Confederate officer, Wise had no military training and would prove to be a failure in this role. He was a noted Virginia politician and a strong advocate of slavery. He was governor during John Brown's Harpers Ferry raid and he ordered Brown's execution after the trial. At the end of the war he never applied for the pardon which would restore his citizenship, preferring to practise law in Richmond quietly. He died in 1876, at the age of 70.

June 7 (Friday)

The "Little Giant," Stephen Douglas, was buried today in Chicago, Illinois. In remembrance, Lincoln ordered the White House draped in black and received no visitors. Many schools and businesses closed throughout the North.

In Washington there was a spit of land called Greenleaf's Point that projected into the Potomac at what is now known as Buzzards Point. This was the site of the Washington Arsenal and also the Federal Penitentiary. Later in the war, the prisoners would be removed and the entire block of buildings would be turned over to the arsenal. But this early in the war, the buildings of the arsenal were mostly occupied by repair shops and ammunition-manufacturing facilities. In June 1861, one building was occupied by over two hundred boys, from twelve to sixteen years of age, who manufactured about 130,000 cartridges per day, each boy being paid from sixty to eighty cents per day. Adults were also employed at the arsenal. One of the workers, trying to cut a defective fuse from a spherical case shot, hit the fuse with a cold chisel, causing a spark to ignite the shell. That shell exploded, along with several others, killing only one man, but seriously wounding several others. The explosion lifted the ceiling of the room, blew out the doors, damaged the walls, and set ammunition boxes afire. The building contained in excess of 36,000 artillery rounds and almost 7,000,000 small-arms cartridges. Fortunately, the manager kept his head, and the fires were quickly extinguished.

June 8 (Saturday)

By a margin of slightly over 2-to-1, the voters in western Tennessee approved secession. The same ratio in reverse was voted in eastern Tennessee. In any case, the vote was a little late, since the state had already joined the Confederacy as a result of actions by Gov. Isham Harris.

The United States Sanitary Commission was authorized by Lincoln and Secretary of War Simon Cameron on this day.

The blockade of Key West, Fla., was established by the U.S.S. *Mississippi*, Flag Officer Mervine. In other naval action, Acting Master W. Budd of the U.S.S. *Resolute* captured the schooner *Somerset*, towed her close to the Virginia shore and burned her. It is not known why the ship wasn't taken to port.

Robert E. Lee was unemployed today after the Governor of Virginia transferred all State troops to Confederate Government control. Lee remained as an advisor to Gov. Letcher and President Davis.

A command change took place in northwestern Virginia, when Brigadier Gen. Robert S. Garnett took command of the disorganized forces that participated in the "Philippi Races" earlier in the month.

June 9 (Sunday)

British-owned ships had entered the blockade-running business and took their chances getting caught by the blockading U. S. fleet. One such incident was the capture of the *Perthshire* by the U.S.S. *Massachusetts* near Pensacola. The ship was loaded with cotton and bound for England.

In the worst nightmare that a commander could imagine, the Federal troops moving from Newport News and Ft. Monroe became confused in the dark and began firing into their neighboring units. This was not uncommon when green troops were placed in a frightening situation and lacked the discipline that only comes with long campaigning.

June 10 (Monday)

The first serious battle of the war was fought today at Big Bethel, Va., between 2,500 Federals from Ft. Monroe and 1,200 Confederates. The Federals got their noses bloodied, losing 18 dead. The Confederates lost 1 man.

Off Savannah, Georgia, the U.S.S. *Union* captured the brig *Hallie Jackson*, carrying a cargo of molasses. At the Norfolk Navy Yard, now a Confederate facility, the raised U.S.S. *Merrimack* was renamed the C.S.S. *Virginia* and would be redesigned for service as an ironclad.

June 11 (Tuesday)

At Wheeling, in western Virginia, pro-Unionists met to organize a separate state government which would be loyal to the Union. This eventually became the basis for the West Virginia government.

Col. E.R.S. Canby assumed command of all Federal forces in the Southwest Department of New Mexico after Col. William W. Loring resigned and "went South." Canby would later become a Major General commanding the siege of Mobile.

Edward Richard Sprigg Canby was born at Platt's Landing, Ky., on November 9, 1817. He moved with his family to Indiana and entered West Point from that state, and was graduated in 1835. He was assigned to the New Mexico Territory to fight Indians he and was there when the war started. He did well in the west and was promoted to Brigadier General after the Battle of Glorieta Pass, March 26-28, 1862, after which he was assigned as assistant adjutant general in Washington, D.C. In July 1863, he commanded the troops during the draft riots in New York City. He was promoted to Major General in May 1864, and was assigned to command the Military Division of West Mississippi. He captured Mobile, Ala., on April 12, 1865, and on May 26th accepted the surrender of Confederate Gen. E. Kirby Smith. He was given the permanent rank of Brigadier General and was sent to the Pacific Northwest in 1870. He was murdered by hostile Modoc Indians at Siskiyou, Calif. on April 11, 1873.

In a meeting among Nathaniel Lyon, now a general, Francis P. Blair, Jr., and the pro-Confederate Governor of Missouri, accompanied by Gen. Sterling Price, Lyon declared that he would not tolerate the State government dictating where Federal troops would be moved. The meeting having ended, the governor ordered the destruction of bridges over strategic rivers and Lyon started dictating troop movements.

June 13 (Thursday)

Col. Lew Wallace, later the author of *Ben Hur*, entered Romney, western Virginia, after a long march from Cumberland, Md. Romney, like Grafton, was a major rail terminus and an important link in communications to the west. After a brief skirmish with Confederate forces, Wallace returned to his base in Maryland.

Lewis Wallace was born in Brookville, Ind., on April 10, 1827. Wallace, a political general, served in the Mexican War and then returned to his legal and political careers. When the Civil War started, he organized the 11th Indiana Infantry Regiment and was appointed Colonel of that regiment. He was appointed Brigadier General of Volunteers on September 3, 1861. He served with Grant during the Ft. Donelson campaign and was promoted to Major General on March 21, 1862. During the Battle of Shiloh his performance was less than satisfactory, and he was removed from command of troops. He would end the war in an administrative post after his failure at Shiloh. After the war, he served as Governor of New Mexico and Minister to Turkey. He died at Crawfordsville, Ind., on February 15, 1905.

Confederate Gen. Joseph E. Johnston, former Brigadier General of the United States Army and the highest ranking army officer to "go South," now commanded the troops around Harpers Ferry. He expressed doubts about holding the area without reinforcements.

June 15 (Saturday)

After setting fire to the bridge across the Potomac, Gen. Joe E. Johnston evacuated Harpers Ferry and moved south towards Winchester. Federal Gen. Robert Patterson, a 69-year-old Irish immigrant, veteran of the War of 1812 and the Mexican War, and in general slow to react, cautiously moved into the space vacated by Johnston. Slow and timid, Patterson would make a poor showing. Winfield Scott would remove him from command on July 19th.

The installation of shore batteries along the major rivers of the Eastern Shore moved apace in Virginia. Gen. Robert E. Lee reported to Gov. John Letcher:

> Six batteries have been erected on the Elizabeth River, to guard the approaches to Norfolk and the Navy Yard… to prevent ascent of the Nansemond River and the occupation of the railroad from Norfolk to Richmond, three batteries have been constructed.… Sites for batteries on the Potomac have also been selected, and arrangements were in progress for their construction, but the entire command of that river being in the possession of the U.S. Government, a larger force is required for their security than could be devoted to that purpose. The batteries at Aquia Creek have only been prepared.… On the Rappahannock River a 4-gun battery… has been erected.

Army Engineers removed a rock weighing 100 tons from the tracks of the Baltimore and Ohio Railroad near Point of Rocks, Md. Supposedly, Confederate troops had pushed the rock down on the tracks; there were no explanations as to how this was done.

Jefferson City, Mo., was occupied by Federal forces under Gen. Nathaniel Lyon, the Missouri militia having departed the city, heading west towards Boonville. The type of warfare to prevail in Missouri was beginning to surface, with guerrilla raids increasing.

June 17 (Monday)

Gen. Lyon, after occupying Jefferson City, Mo., moved about 1700 men by boat to Boonville. After a short fight, the forces of Gov. Jackson departed the area and left Lyon with the town. This was a minor action that had far-reaching consequences; the Federals now controlled most of the northern part of the state and the Missouri River.

At Vienna, Va., a party of Ohio troops was repairing the Loudoun and Hampshire Railroad about 15 miles west of Alexandria when they were ambushed by a group of Confederates led by Col. Maxcy Gregg and the 1st South Carolina Regiment. Not much damage was done, except to the ego of the Federal troop commander.

As a first, "Professor" Thaddeus S. C. Lowe and a small group ascended in a tethered balloon to demonstrate the effectiveness of using the device for aerial observation. Communication was made with Lincoln from the balloon by telegraph. Lowe had just completed a 9-hour, 900-mile balloon flight from Cincinnati, Ohio, to Unionville, S.C., 19-20 April, 1861, a week after the firing on Ft. Sumter. Lowe used balloons to an advantage, being the first to provide artillery direction from an aerial platform.

The citizens of Greeneville in eastern Tennessee gathered to show their pro-Union sentiment and to discuss action to remain in the Union.

June 18 (Tuesday)

The supply of small arms for the Union forces was becoming very crucial. The old arsenals were inadequate to meet the demand, and it took time to gear up new ones and get them into production. As a stopgap measure, arms were bought from commercial manufacturers, such as Colt in Massachusetts. Col. James W. Ripley, now Chief of Ordnance, had been promoted to Brigadier General and he was repeatedly berated for nondelivery of requested arms. Ripley had 47 years of active service when the war broke out in 1861, having fought the Seminole and Creek Indians under Andrew Jackson, and in the Mexican War. He was a dyed-in-the-wool bureaucrat, and he tended to be a stumbling block in all that he did. He was rude, short-tempered, and imperious with all he met, even the President.

Gen. Lee, showing his concept of cooperation between land and sea forces, wrote the commander of C.S.S. *Teaser*, Lt. Robert Randolph Carter:

> It is desired that the C.S. steam tender *Teaser* shall unite with the batteries at Jamestown Island in defense of James River, and be employed in obtaining intelligence of the movements of hostile vessels and

the landing of troops either side of the river.... It is suggested that you establish a system of signals as a means of communication with the troop, and take every precaution not to jeopardize the safety of your boat by proceeding too far beyond the protection of the guns of the batteries....

Barber, Pvt., Co. D, 15th Illinois Volunteer Infantry, en route to Alton, Illinois:

> ... we were ordered to move camp to Alton, Illinois. At this time we had more baggage in one company than would be allowed in a whole brigade in one of Sherman's campaigns. It took two heavy trains to remove the regiment. We were vociferously cheered all along the route, the fair sex singing patriotic songs wherever we stopped and expressing their sympathy in various other ways.

June 19 (Wednesday)

In Wheeling, western Virginia, Francis H. Pierpont was named as the provisional governor of what would eventually become West Virginia. Pierpont, born in western Virginia in 1814, amassed quite a fortune as a lawyer for the B&O Railroad and in investments in coal mines before the war. He had never held elective office before this appointment. By 1860, Pierpont was a strong Unionist, antislavery, and a supporter of Lincoln. When the new State of West Virginia was admitted to the Union in 1863, a new governor was elected, and Pierpont went to Alexandria, Va. After the war he returned to his law practice. He died in Pittsburgh, Pa.

Barber, Pvt., Co. D, 15th Illinois Volunteer Infantry, Alton, Illinois:

> We arrived at Alton... and went into camp one mile north of the city. The Seventeenth, Twentieth and Hecker's German Regiment, Twenty-fourth, were camped with us, forming a brigade commanded by Brigadier-Gen. John Pope, late Capt. Pope. Col. Turner assumed command of the camp and it was soon placed in a state of rigid discipline..... We now had a reorganization in our culinary department. Heretofore the men formed in messes to suit their convenience; now the whole company was put into one mess. A company cook was detailed (John Bliss) and five more were detailed daily to assist him. We bought a large coffee boiler, holding ten gallons, and camp kettles to match. This arrangement gave general satisfaction, but the captain was inexorable and would not change.

June 20 (Thursday)

Kansas, admitted to the Union on January 29, 1861, was becoming embroiled in the border dispute with Missouri. With only about 100,000 citizens in mostly rural communities (only 10 towns had more than 500 inhabitants), Kansas would provide over 20,000 troops by the end of the war, suffering nearly 8,500 casualties—the highest rate per capita of any Northern state. On this day the Governor of Kansas issued a proclamation calling on the citizens to organize military companies to repel attacks from Missouri's pro-South element. This would continue throughout the war, with the worst slaughter at Lawrence, Kansas, on August 21, 1863.

June 22 (Saturday)

The pro-Union session in Greeneville, Tenn., declared its preference for the Union. Although this part of the state remained under Confederate control until late in the war, it furnished more troops for the Federal forces than it did for the South.

In western Virginia, Major Gen. George B. McClellan trumpeted the success of the Union forces there and, of course, took all credit for that success. "Professor" Lowe was readying his balloon for another ascent near Washington.

June 23 (Sunday)

"Professor" Lowe and an artist ascended in Lowe's balloon to observe the Confederate forces in the area of Falls Church, Va. This was probably the first example of aerial "photography."

Gen. McClellan proclaimed that he would now "prosecute the war vigorously," a promise that never came true.

At the Confederate-held Norfolk Navy Yard, construction began on the C.S.S. *Virginia* to convert the ship to an ironclad.

June 24 (Monday)

In Washington, J.D. Mills of New York became the world's first machine-gun salesman. Mills called it "the Union Repeating Gun.... An Army in six feet square." Lincoln, being fascinated with gadgets, had to see this one. In the hayloft of Hall's carriage shop across Pennsylvania Avenue from the Willard Hotel the device was displayed for Lincoln, and he was allowed to operate it.

The device was ingenious. Mounted on a light, two-wheeled artillery carriage, it had a single barrel which was fed by a revolving mechanism designed to hold regular .58 calibre paper cartridges in specially made steel jackets. Lincoln turned the crank and watched the cartridges move through the mechanism, into the barrel of the gun, be extracted and dropped into another hopper for reloading. Lincoln called it what it reminded him of—a coffee mill—and the name stuck for the rest of the war.

The next day the gun was fired on the Washington Arsenal grounds for an audience of three Cabinet members, five generals, the Governor of Connecticut, and the President. Major Gen. Joseph K.F. Mansfield, who commanded the defenses of Washington, immediately requested a number of the guns.

The next steps faltered in a bureaucratic maze of stupidity. Gen. Ripley, Chief of Ordnance for the War Department, refused to take any steps to order the "coffee mills," citing the need for more testing. In reality, Ripley was afraid to take a chance on new weapons, so the idea almost died in infancy. J.D. Mills turned up again in October and sold Lincoln ten of the guns at $1300 each. Lincoln was elated and tried to get Gen. McClellan interested in using them. "Little Mac" was too preoccupied with other matters at that time.

Gen. Ben Butler in Massachusetts did buy two of the guns, one of which had a part break shortly after it was received. The part cost $172.91 on a gun that cost $1300—an early example of defense-weapon price gouging.

Later in the year, McClellan wanted to buy 50 of these guns but, as usual, did not want to be responsible for ordering them. He was offered the guns at a "quantity discount" of $1200 each. Not willing to take the risk, McClellan tried to get Lincoln to authorize the purchase. Lincoln threw the ball back in the General's court. Finally McClellan ordered 50 at cost plus 20%, and paid $735 each. The first real test would come in January 1862.

One cannot but wonder what a few well-placed "coffee mills" would have done to Pickett's famous charge at Gettysburg. With firepower like that, the Confederate troops would never have made it across the field. The slaughter on many battlefields would have been devastating.

June 27 (Thursday)

Major Gen. Nathaniel Banks, Gen. Ben Butler's successor, arrested the Baltimore Chief of Police as a Southern sympathizer.

In an early example of a "Joint Staff," the Blockade Strategy Board met under the chairmanship of Capt. Du Pont to consider and report on the major problems of the blockade and to plan amphibious operations for the coastal areas. The Board contained members of the Navy, Army Corps of Engineers, and the U.S. Coast Survey.

Secretary of the Navy Gideon Welles received a report that:

> ... the rebels in New Orleans are constructing an infernal submarine vessel to destroy the *Brooklyn*, or any vessel blockading at the mouth of the Mississippi... a projectile with a sharp iron or steel pointed prow to perforate the bottom of the vessel and then explode.

June 29 (Saturday)

Gen. Irvin McDowell outlined his plans for attacking the Confederate force at Manassas Junction at a staff meeting with the Cabinet. McDowell, West Point class of '38, was a major in the Adjutant General's office in Washington when the war started. He was promoted to brigadier general on May 14, 1861 and had the misfortune to command the Union troops at the first Battle of Bull Run (Manassas). He served as a corps commander in the Army of the Potomac under McClellan, and was left with his corps to protect Washington when McClellan started the Peninsula campaign. He was sent to the Shenandoah Valley in early 1862 during Jackson's Valley Campaign, and returned to the Army of the Potomac when McClellan came back north. He spent the remainder of the war in administrative posts. He died in San Francisco in 1885.

The side-wheel steamer *St. Nicholas* was making its scheduled run between Baltimore and the Georgetown piers in the District of Columbia when it was captured by Confederates, who had boarded the boat as passengers at the various stops along the Potomac. The Confederates were led by Capt. George N. Hollins, CSN, who boarded disguised as a woman, and Col. Richard Thomas, CSA. The ship began a search for the U.S.S. *Pawnee*, a Federal gunboat operating near Alexandria, Va., and, failing to find her, went down Chesapeake Bay, where the *St. Nicholas* seized the schooners *Margaret* and *Mary Pierce* and the brig *Monticello*.

June 30 (Sunday)

The warship C.S.S. *Sumter*, Commander Semmes, ran the blockade at the mouth of the Mississippi River and escaped to the high seas. Thus began a distinguished career for Semmes as a commerce raider for the Confederacy.

Allen, Co. K, 10th Illinois Cavalry, Asheville, N.C.:

> I expect to leave here shortly, but whether I leave here or not you shall hear from me again soon. You need not write again until you receive another letter from me. Although I have not written to you for some time I have not forgotten home, as you might suppose. I may never be permitted to see you again in this world, but you may rest assured that my parents and the home of my youth will never be forgotten by me. Since I have been here, the storm of disunion has swept everything before it. Our beloved State has been taken out of the Union at last. No one could be more attached to the Union than I always have been and always will be. I never have bowed the knee to the storm of disunion, and so help me God, I never will. I want to live where I can express my opinion freely, and were I to do so here, I should be hung without judge or jury. I expect to make some Western State my home that has not gone, nor will go, out of the Union. [Neither] North Carolina nor any other [seceded] State can be my home. My body has been out of the Union since the 20th of May, but my spirit has never been, nor will it ever be, while I live. The fire-eaters were determined to rule or ruin the country. They could not do the first, but I am afraid they will succeed in doing the last. I hope you will all leave this State as soon as you can do so safely, for I will not live under "Tycoon Davis's" government, and I hope none of the rest of you will. The people of North Carolina may call me a Tory, traitor, or anything else they please after I have left, but never a secessionist.
>
> I do not read the papers much, as there are so many lies in them that I do not know what to believe. I saw in a paper that I was reading last night that northwest Virginia had declared her independence and had elected a Governor and other State officers, and that the people of Missouri were fighting among themselves. The rebels are going to carry on the war like Indians, I suppose, as I see in a late paper that some of them had killed some United States soldiers and sent their scalps to one of the rebel officers. Some of the volunteers from this place have been here since the skirmish at Bethel Church, Va., who were there when it took place. They say that the United States soldiers, or "Yankees" as they call them, are the poorest marksmen and the greatest cowards in the world, and that there is no fight in them. The object of all these lies that are told and published is to keep up the spirits of the people and secure more volunteers..... Some things are getting to be very dear here. Coffee is selling at the rate of three pounds to the dollar. If the war lasts long, times will be very hard....

JULY 1861

The fever for war was burning both North and South. No major engagements had as yet been fought and the bravado on both sides was sometimes amusing—deadly, but amusing. It was obvious that the two armies at Manassas Junction and Washington, so close to each other, would collide soon, but no one could really predict the results.

July 1 (Monday)

The raising of troops in the border states of Kentucky and Tennessee was approved by the War Department in Washington.

In Baltimore, members of the Police Board were arrested as Southern sympathizers.

The Confederate privateer *Petrel*, using some sort of sleight-of-hand, evaded the blockading Federal ships and put to sea from Charleston, S.C.

July 2 (Tuesday)

Lincoln authorized Gen. Winfield Scott to suspend the writ of *habeas corpus* on, or near, any military line between Washington and New York.

Federal troops under Brigadier Gen. Robert Patterson, a sixty-nine-year-old veteran of the War of

1812, crossed the Potomac at Williamsport, Md., into the Shenandoah Valley. Patterson was to keep the Confederate forces under Gen. Joseph E. Johnston occupied while McDowell moved against Manassas. Johnston and Beauregard had similar plans: to hold Patterson in the Valley and then quickly shift Johnston's troops to the aid of "the Creole" at Manassas. Moving briskly, Patterson advanced towards Martinsburg, western Virginia.

In Washington, Lincoln conferred with Major Gen. John C. Frémont, "the Pathfinder," before Frémont departed for St. Louis to command in Missouri. Frémont, age 48, was already a national figure and was one of the four Major Generals appointed by Lincoln at the beginning of the war. The appointment to command the Western Department was given at the urging of Frémont's friends. Lincoln would long regret this action.

Off Galveston, Tex., the U.S.S. *South Carolina*, Commander James Alden, set up a blockade of that port.

July 4 (Thursday)

On Independence Day, celebrations were held both North and South, the colonial forefathers being venerated equally in both places. At a special session of Congress, Lincoln requested "at least four hundred thousand men and four hundred million dollars" to pursue the war to a speedy conclusion.

Barber, Pvt., Co. D, 15th Illinois Volunteer Infantry, Alton, Illinois:

> The Fourth of July was duly observed and celebrated in an appropriate manner. The boys were all allowed a day of freedom and were put upon their honor as men and soldiers to conduct themselves properly.... A novel mode of punishment was now inaugurated for very fractious soldiers, which consisted in drumming them out of camp, by two men walking behind the offender with fixed bayonets pressing pretty close to his rear, and two musicians in front playing the rogues' march, passing between two lines of soldiers drawn up for the occasion, his head shaved clean on one side, his clothes turned wrong side out, hooted and jeered at by his companions as he passed along, until he was out of camp. Such cases received very little sympathy from good soldiers, as they were always bringing trouble. Degrading as this kind of punishment was, its moral had very little effect. There is no doubt but that, if it had continued, we would have got rid of all of our hard cases, but it would have woefully decimated our ranks. Too many were too anxious to get out of the army to care in what manner they effected their designs. Another mode of punishment was setting the offender to digging stumps and cleaning camp with a guard stationed over him to see that he kept at work. In this manner, our camp was cleared of stumps which thickly covered one hundred acres.

July 5 (Friday)

Missouri Gov. Claiborne Jackson, pro-Confederate, got a little nervous about Gen. Nathaniel Lyon in his rear, only to find out that Brigadier Gen. Franz Sigel was in front of him. Jackson's force waited for Sigel's attack, then assaulted both ends of his line. Sigel retired and retreated through Carthage, Mo., giving the Federal advance a serious setback. Jackson moved to link up with Sterling Price and his force.

Franz Sigel, born in Baden in 1824, was graduated from Karlsruhe Military Academy before immigrating to the United States in 1852. Fleeing Europe, he came to St. Louis, where he taught school until 1861, when he was commissioned a Brigadier General. His popularity among the large German-speaking population in eastern Missouri gave him considerable political clout, which he used to his advantage. After being promoted to Major General in March 1862, he came east and faced "Stonewall" Jackson in the Valley Campaign. He fought at Second Manassas and was sent back to the Valley, where he was defeated at the Battle of New Market in May 1864, after which he was relieved of command. He resigned in May 1865, and died in New York on August 21, 1902.

July 6 (Saturday)

Commander Semmes, C.S.S. *Sumter*, arrived at Cienfuegos, Cuba, with seven prizes-of-war: the Union ships *Cuba*, *Machia*, *Ben Dunning*, *Albert Adams*, *Niad*, *West Wind*, and *Lewis Kilham*. Appointing a Cuban agent to dispose of the prizes, Semmes explained to the Spanish governor of the port that he entered "with the expectation that Spain will extend to cruisers of the Confederate States the same friendly reception that in similar circumstances he would extend to the cruisers of the enemy… " The ships were later released, the Spanish colonial government refusing to recognize the Confederacy as a legitimate government.

Another Confederate privateer, the *Jefferson Davis*, operating east of Cape Hatteras, captured the brig *John Welsh* and the schooner *Enchantress*.

July 7 (Sunday)

Clement L. Vallandigham, of Ohio, later identified with the peace Democrats (Copperheads), visited the Ohio regiments in Virginia to be met with catcalls, stones, and a near-riot. A prominent New Lisbon, Ohio, lawyer, he had run for a seat in the U.S. House of Representatives. He had held meetings with John Brown in 1859, and, in general, had been a strong abolitionist. He would be exiled to the Confederacy in May 1863.

The Confederate privateer *Jefferson Davis* ranged further north and captured the schooner *S. J. Waring* about 150 miles east of Sandy Hook, New Jersey.

Two torpedoes (mines) were picked up in the Potomac River by the U.S.S. *Resolute*, Acting Master W. Budd. This was the first record of such deployment.

July 10 (Wednesday)

In western Virginia, McClellan placed three brigades at Buckhannon and another at Philippi, ready to move against Confederate Gen. Robert S. Garnett's smaller forces at Rich Mountain and Laurel Hill. A general who would become prominent later, William Stark Rosecrans, attacked at Rich Mountain. Rich Mountain was not much of a battle, but it demonstrated Rosecrans's initiative and drive.

Rosecrans, USMA '38, was commissioned a 2nd Lt. of Engineers in 1842, resigning his commission 12 years later to enter business. He was appointed Brigadier General in the Regular Army on May 16, 1861, and was assigned to the Department of the Ohio under McClellan.

The Tsar of All the Russias informed Washington of Russia's policy of neutrality towards the belligerents.

Barber, Pvt., Co. D, 15th Illinois Volunteer Infantry, Alton, Illinois:

> Sickness now began to prevail to a considerable extent, over two hundred being on the sick list at one time. Several deaths occurred while we camped here. A considerable number were being discharged. Surgeons at this time would make out discharges for slight causes, and, if an order from the War Department had not put a stop to it, our army would soon have become badly decimated.
>
> Our camp life at Alton was nothing but a severe routine of military duty; occasionally some little incident would transpire to vary the monotony. The sale of ardent spirits soon got to be a growing evil in our camp, and Col. Turner took measures to suppress it, but one man more bold than the others defied him. He moved his shop outside the camp, supposing that he was out of reach of the Colonel's authority, and continued to sell his hellish fires. Whereupon, Col. Turner gave permission for a squad of soldiers to go and arrest him and spill his whiskey. These proceedings completely broke up the whiskey ring….

July 11 (Thursday)

At Rich Mountain, Rosecrans successfully moved his 2000 troops over very rough terrain and attacked the rear of Confederate Lt. Col. Pegram's force of 1300, cutting off their retreat. McClellan was supposed to attack at the same time that Rosecrans did, but held his position. Nonetheless, McClellan took credit for the victory, not unusual for McClellan. Federal losses were only 12 killed and 49 wounded; no reliable record of Confederate losses is available.

John Pegram was born at Petersburg, Va., on January 24, 1832. An 1854 graduate of West Point, he was assigned to the 2nd U.S. Dragoons. At the beginning of the war he resigned his commission and was appointed Lieutenant Colonel of the 20th Virginia Infantry, with which he fought at Rich Mountain. He later served with Beauregard and Bragg, and then became Chief of Staff to Gen. E. Kirby Smith. Promoted to Brigadier on November 7, 1862, he led a cavalry brigade at Stones River in December of that year. He returned to Virginia, where he served in Lee's army and was wounded at the Wilderness in 1863. He served with Jubal Early during the Valley Campaign of 1864. In January 1865, his marriage to Hetty Cary was the social event of the year. Three weeks later, on February 6th, he was killed at Hatcher's Run, south of Petersburg. His bride returned to St. Paul's Church, the site of their vows, for the funeral.

North of Rich Mountain at Laurel Hill, Federal Gen. T.A. Morris's troops demonstrated against Gen. Robert S. Garnett's Rebel force, causing Garnett to evacuate his positions. The road to Beverly was now open.

At the confluence of the Kanawha and Ohio rivers, a Federal force commanded by Brigadier Gen. Jacob Dolson Cox began its ascent up the Great Kanawha Valley by boat. Cox, born in 1828, was a graduate of Oberlin College and had served as a superintendent of schools in Warren, Ohio, before entering the practice of law. Volunteering at the first call for troops, he was appointed a Brigadier of Volunteers on May 17, 1861, and was assigned to the Department of the Ohio under McClellan.

In Washington, the Senate expelled the Senators from Virginia, North Carolina, Arkansas, and Texas, plus one from Tennessee. This was a mere formality, since they had already departed for home.

July 12 (Friday)

Confederate Brigadier Gen. Robert Selden Garnett was retreating into the Cheat River valley. Part of the troops from Rich Mountain escaped to Staunton, Va. McClellan came into Beverly, western Virginia, about noon.

Robert Selden Garnett, born in Essex Co., Va., December 16, 1819, was graduated (with his cousin Richard Brooke Garnett, also of Essex, Co.), from West Point, class of '41. He fought in the Seminole and Mexican wars with distinction. He returned to West Point as an instructor for three years. At the beginning of the war, he was on leave in Europe. He returned, resigned his commission and accepted a commission as a Brigadier General in the CSA on June 6, 1861.

Cox's Federal force was well into the Great Kanawha Valley, and its meeting with Brigadier Gen. Henry Wise's Confederate force was nearing.

July 13 (Saturday)

Garnett's troops crossed Cheat Mountain in the rain and entered the Cheat River valley. About noon the Federals caught up, and there was a fight at Corrick's Ford in which Garnett was killed, giving him the dubious honor of being the first general to be killed, North or South. His body was recovered by Federal troops, who returned it to his family. Pegram was forced to surrender 555 of his troops.

The northern part of western Virginia was now clear of Confederate troops and the railroad lines running through to the northwest were kept open. Later, a staunch native western Virginian would be back into this same area to threaten communications—Thomas Jonathan "Stonewall" Jackson.

July 14 (Sunday)

In New York, Horace Greeley was shouting, with banner headlines, "FORWARD TO RICHMOND." The point was to get McDowell, headquartered at the home of Robert E. Lee across the Potomac, to take some aggressive action against Beauregard at Manassas. Federal troops scouted from Alexandria, Va. In the Shenandoah Valley, Patterson was stalled just south of Harpers Ferry.

McDowell, with the largest American army ever assembled (even Winfield Scott had only about 14,000 men during the Mexican War), considered leaving his stinking camps around Alexandria and Washington for Manassas. With 35,000 men, McDowell outnumbered Beauregard by at least 10,000, but the addition of Johnston's Valley troops would make the odds even. Both North and South, the troops lacked combat experience. McDowell asked for more time to train his men and Lincoln told him, "You are green, it is true; but they are green also. You are all green alike."

Off Wilmington, N.C., the U.S.S. *Daylight* took station and initiated the blockade of that port.

July 15 (Monday)

In the Valley, Patterson's pickets skirmished with Confederate cavalry as the cavalry advanced towards Bunker Hill, north of Winchester. Gen. Patterson had vowed to attack if the occasion presented itself.

As the news spread of the victories along the Cheat River in western Virginia, the name McClellan became a household word. The first real "hero" had arrived! The campaign, well planned by McClellan, was better executed by his subordinates, with "Little Mac" getting the lion's share of the credit. His ego, already large, soared to new heights.

Confederate privateers, ranging all along the coast from Maine to Galveston, were a subject of much concern to commercial shipping. The blockade was ever tightening, and as it improved, the losses to these predators would diminish.

July 16 (Tuesday)

Out from the camps around Alexandria and Washington moved McDowell's over 1400 officers and 30,000 men. All five of the division commanders and eight of the 11 brigade commanders were Regular Army officers, some with much field experience. The march to Manassas (Centreville) was a nightmare.

The troops had little training in marching and water discipline. The long lines of troops and artillery would snake down a road, stop for a while, move for a short distance, stop for a longer while, and move again. This was done in a hot sun, and with troops that drank all their water in the first three hours and had no place to get more.

There was much breaking of ranks to sit in the shade or to pick blackberries. Equipment that seemed light enough in Alexandria now weighed tons, and was discarded along the road.

The schooner *S. J. Waring*, taken as a prize by the Confederates, was retaken at sea by its original crew, led by a Negro named William Tilghman, and sailed for New York, where it docked on July 22nd.

July 17 (Wednesday)

McDowell's army finally reached Fairfax C.H. McDowell found large quantities of supplies left by the retreating Rebels. Discipline on the march had not improved. Among the brigades en route to Manassas was one commanded by Col. William T. Sherman, until recently assigned as an inspector for Gen. Scott. Sherman described his brigade:

> I selected for the field the Thirteenth New York, Col. Quimby; the Sixty-Ninth New York, Col. Corcoran; the Seventy-Ninth New York, Col. Cameron; and the Second Wisconsin, Lt.-Col. Peck. These were all good strong volunteer regiments, pretty well commanded; and I had reason to believe that I had one of the best brigades in the whole army. Captain Ayres's battery of the Third Regular Artillery was also attached to my brigade. The other regiment, the Twenty-Ninth New York, Col. Bennett, was destined to be left behind in charge of the forts and camps during our absence, which was expected to be short....

Meanwhile, President Davis had ordered Joseph E. Johnston to shake loose from Gen. Patterson in the lower Shenandoah Valley and to join Beauregard at Manassas. This was no problem because Patterson, in defiance of his orders, had withdrawn from the Winchester area to Charles Town, leaving Johnston to go where he would. Johnston headed his troops to the nearest railhead to shuttle them to Manassas Junction.

In the Great Kanawha Valley of western Virginia, Gen. Cox's force was still en route to Charleston, using the Kanawha River for transportation. There was some delay caused by Gen. Wise's harassing tactics.

July 18 (Thursday)

At about noon McDowell's army approached Centreville, 22 miles and two and one-half days after leaving his camps around Alexandria. The temperature was nearing 90°, the men were out of water and did not have the cooked rations they were to have had before they left Alexandria. Johnston was hurrying from the Valley.

McDowell decided to reconnoitre the area and sent a brigade-size force from Brigadier Gen. Daniel Tyler's division to Blackburn Ford, where Col. I.B. Richardson took the brigade further than it was supposed to go and met Beauregard's troops in a bloody clash which accomplished little or nothing, but caused the Federals to retreat.

Sherman, commanding a regiment of Tyler's division, described the action, his first actual combat on any field :

> From our camp, at Centreville, we heard the cannonading, and then a sharp musketry-fire. I received orders from Gen. Tyler to send forward Ayres's battery, and very soon another order came for me to advance with my whole brigade. We marched the three miles at the double-quick, arrived in time to relieve Richardson's brigade, which was just drawing back from the ford, worsted, and stood for half an hour or so under fire of artillery, which killed four or five of my men....

At Richmond, Confederate Secretary of the Navy Mallory provided a report on the status and cost of converting the U.S.S. *Merrimack*, soon to become the C.S.S. *Virginia*, to an ironclad:

The frigate *Merrimack* has been raised and docked at an expense of $6000, and the necessary repairs to hull and machinery to place her in her former condition is estimated by experts at $450,000. The vessel would then be in the river, and by the blockade of the enemy's fleets and batteries rendered comparatively useless. It has therefore been determined to shield her completely with 3-inch iron placed at such angles as to render her ball-proof, to complete her at the earliest moment, to arm her with the heaviest ordnance, and to send her at once against the enemy's fleet. It is believed that thus prepared she will be able to contend successfully against the heaviest of the enemy's ships and to drive them from Hampton Roads and the ports of Virginia. The cost of this work is estimated... at $172,523, and as time is of the first consequence in this enterprise I have not hesitated to commence the work and to ask Congress for the necessary appropriation.

July 19 (Friday)

In Missouri, Brigadier Gen. John Pope declared that anyone taking up arms against the government would be dealt with immediately. John Pope, appointed a Brigadier General of volunteers at the beginning of the war, was not a popular figure among his contemporaries. One fellow general was given to remark, "I don't care for John Pope one pinch of owl dung." Pope was a very large man, loudmouthed, and abrasive. A graduate of West Point, class of '42, he was a veteran of the Mexican War, where he had served with distinction, being brevetted a captain. His career would be somewhat checkered during the war.

At Centreville, Va., all day was used to get McDowell's army fed and regrouped. Stragglers came in at all hours. At Manassas Junction nearby, Gen. Thomas J. Jackson arrived with his Confederate brigade in advance of Joe Johnston's force moving from Winchester. The battle loomed.

Major Gen. McClellan issued congratulations to his army, and to himself, on their conduct in the western Virginia campaign.

Barber, Pvt., Co. D, 15th Illinois Volunteer Infantry, en route to Missouri:

> Early the next morning the steamer "Alton" arrived and we embarked and proceeded down to the mouth of the Missouri River. We then turned our course up that stream. Just as we turned our course, a soldier from Company H fell overboard, and just as assistance was within reach, he sank to rise no more.

July 20 (Saturday)

McDowell's officers did reconnaissance of the proposed battlefield, assigning approaches to the enemy works, etc. Beauregard had been planning and working on his troop alignments for two additional days. Gen. Joe Johnston arrived from the Valley at about noon, having left Patterson north of Winchester, doing nothing. The rest of the troops would arrive as fast as they could be transported by rail from camps south of Winchester.

McDowell started his troops in motion after dark, and they were all moving by about 2:30 the following morning. Both commanders planned a strike against the enemy's left flank.

Barber, Pvt., Co. D, 15th Illinois Volunteer Infantry, St. Charles, Mo.:

> We proceeded up the river as far as St. Charles, Mo., where we arrived the next evening (July 20th), and we immediately disembarked and went into camp one mile above the city. We apprehended some trouble on landing, as the rebels were rampant, but no serious difficulty occurred. We were now for the first time in what we considered an enemy's country.

July 21 (Sunday)

Both Davis and Lincoln were "toughing it out," waiting until Sunday afternoon, when Davis could wait no longer. He took a train to Manassas from Richmond to find out what was going on, arriving in midafternoon while the battle was in progress.

Knowing that the battle would be on this day, several U.S. Congressmen and their ladies travelled to Centreville by carriage to see it. Picnics and wine were the menu for most. Their traffic and constant jockeying for position on the field interfered with the troop movements and control.

Each general attempted to outflank the other's left flank. The end result was almost a disaster for both sides. The Confederates were in trouble until Johnston's main force arrived from the Valley. This made the difference and gave enough weight to the line to start the Union rout.

Jackson, who had spent a year in Europe studying

the battlefields of the Napoleonic Wars, remembered the Battle of Waterloo and used the same tactic by screening his men just below the crest of the hill where they could fire over it without the risk of being fired into. Not being in too much danger, his troops were holding steady when Gen. Bee, attempting to rally his own men, cried, "There is Jackson standing like a stone wall. Rally on the Virginians."

As the battle progressed, the Federal troops became confused, and finally a retreat turned into a rout. The fleeing troops mingled with the sightseeing civilians from Washington, and the scene quickly became one of bedlam, with everyone trying to get away. Not all Federal troops ran. The regulars held and did well, a result of better discipline and trained officers. The U.S. Marines serving at the battle, commanded by Major Reynolds, did well also, losing 9 killed, 19 wounded, and 16 missing in action.

No pursuit was made by the Confederates, primarily because none would have been possible. Their forces were almost as confused as the Federals.

The Federals' speed in fleeing was such that they covered the same ground inbound in less than one day that had taken two and one-half days outbound. The wounded straggled badly, with all the ambulances having fled pell-mell back to Washington, and it took some of the wounded three days to return on their own. Some walked the distance with half their jaws shot away, legs badly mauled, broken arms, head wounds, and many other injuries. Even when they arrived in Washington, they found that the medical service was not prepared to handle such a large group of wounded, and chaos reigned.

Edmonds, S. Emma E., Union Field Nurse, Georgetown Hospital, Washington, D.C.:

> Washington at that time presented a picture striking illustrative of military life in its most depressing form. To use the words of Captain Noyes, "There were stragglers sneaking along through the mud inquiring for their regiments, wanderers driven in by the pickets, some with guns and some without, while every one you met had a sleepy, downcast appearance, and looked as if he would like to hide his head from all the world." Every bar-room and groggery seemed filled to overflowing with officers and men, and military discipline was nearly, or quite, forgotten for a time in the Army of the Potomac.... The hospitals in Washington, Alexandria and Georgetown were crowded with wounded, sick, discouraged soldiers. That extraordinary march from Bull Run, through rain, mud, chagrin, did more towards filling the hospitals than did the battle itself.... Measels, dysentery and typhoid fever were the prevailing diseases after the retreat....

July 22 (Monday)

Gloom and surprise spread over the North as the results of Bull Run were learned. Where was the invincible army that contained those who could "lick two Rebels with one hand?" Recriminations were passed around wholesale, with McDowell getting the lion's share of blame. For all the failure, his was a good plan, and his actions during the battle were correct. The army was ill trained and disciplined, and was beaten by circumstance more than generalship or valor.

The "Crittenden Resolution," passed by the House of Representatives, stated that the war was being waged "to defend and maintain the supremacy of the Constitution and to preserve the Union," and *not to interfere with slavery or subjugate the South.*

Lincoln sent for Major Gen. George Brinton McClellan in western Virginia to take command of the Federal forces around Washington, leaving Major Gen. Rosecrans to assume command of the Department of the Ohio.

Barber, Pvt., Co. D, 15th Illinois Volunteer Infantry, St. Charles, Mo.:

> We could say now that our actual military life had just begun. I was placed on picket the first night at St. Charles, and well I remember my feelings on that occasion.... Every noise was noticed and every dark object turned into imaginary rebels. I could plainly hear the pulsations of my own heart.... The fellow that was with me was completely demoralized, hence it required greater vigilance on my part. He deserted the same night and nothing have I heard of him since.
>
> Here we heard of the terrible and disastrous battle of Bull Run, and a deep, burning shame crimsoned our cheeks at the defeat and disgrace of our

arms. The first reports were favorable but the sad sequel soon came and our Government learned a lesson which they did not soon forget....

The following day (the 24th), after reaching the Charleston, western Virginia, area, Gen. Jacob D. Cox's soldiers attacked the Confederates of Gen. Henry A. Wise, only to see the Confederates quit the field and retreat towards Gauley Bridge to the east, while the Federals took over the city.

July 25 (Thursday)

By a vote of 30 to 5, the U.S. Senate passed the Crittenden Resolution. Senator Andrew Johnson of Tennessee moved for adoption. The House had previously approved the Resolution on the 22nd.

In the Shenandoah Valley, Maj. Gen. Banks assumed command from Brig. Gen. Patterson. Patterson had been slow to attack in the Valley and retreated to Charles Town, western Virginia, allowing Confederate troops under Gen. Joseph E. Johnston to leave the Valley and support Beauregard at Manassas.

In St. Louis, Maj. Gen. John Charles Frémont assumed command in the Western Department of Missouri. At Ft. Monroe, Va., John LaMountain began balloon ascents for reconnaissance of enemy areas.

July 28 (Sunday)

Yesterday, Major Gen. George B. McClellan assumed command of the newly formed Army of the Potomac. The Seventh U.S. Infantry, all ten companies, surrendered to the Confederate force led by Capt. John R. Baylor at St. Augustine Springs, New Mexico Territory, without a shot. New Madrid, Mo., just across the Mississippi from the Kentucky/Tennessee line, was occupied by Confederate forces.

July 30 (Tuesday)

At Ft. Monroe, Hampton Roads, Va., Maj. Gen. Ben Butler wrote to Secretary of War Simon Cameron on the continuing problem of Negroes entering his lines to seek freedom. At this time he had about nine hundred former slaves in his care, and he didn't know what to do with them. May they be treated as property, and if so, were they now contraband? The real problem involved the Fugitive Slave Law, which required the return of "runaway" slaves to their masters. Could this be enforced in the present set of circumstances? While waiting for a reply, Butler put the Negro men to work building fortifications around the area.

Gen. Cox moved his forces from Charleston up the Kanawha River to the Gauley Bridge to face the Confederates under Gen. Henry A. Wise.

Barber, Pvt., Co. D, 15th Illinois Volunteer Infantry, Mexico, Mo.:

> We now practiced target-shooting daily. We had drawn our full complement of guns, tents, and other equipment before we left Alton. We now began to get a foretaste of army fare. Our bacon was so maggoty that it could almost walk, and our hard-tack so hard we could hardly break it. We were not sorry when the order came for us to move camp to Mexico, Mo., which was about two hundred miles from St. Charles.
>
> The road was infested with guerrillas and bushwhackers. A detachment of the 21st Illinois came from Mexico and guarded a railroad train which was to move us. They had a skirmish on the way down, without anything serious occurring except two or three breakdowns and smashups on the road.

July 31 (Wednesday)

The State Convention in Missouri formally elected Hamilton R. Gamble as governor. Gamble was pro-Union and replaced pro-Southern Claiborne Jackson.

Lincoln nominated Col. Ulysses S. Grant, among others, to be Brigadier General of Volunteers. When Grant's father learned of the promotion, he wrote to Grant saying, "Ulyss, this is a good job, don't lose it."

AUGUST 1861

August was confused, both North and South. The South, obviously, had won the Battle of Manassas, but the Federal Capital still held, and Gen. Joe Johnston's army was being berated by various Southern newspapers for inactivity.

It was obvious that the war was going to last much longer than expected. In the North and South, stockpiling of supplies and materials began. Considerations were given to the future strength of the forces. In the initial fervor, many of the best young men had volunteered, and many more were waiting for their turn to serve. Lincoln would issue another call for volunteers shortly. Davis would consider conscription.

A major problem was arming the troops. The capacity of the Springfield (Mass.) Arsenal was insufficient to meet the demand, so action was taken to obtain arms in Europe. At Springfield, the output was only 4000 muskets per month, despite a doubling of the the work force. The Chief of Ordnance finally replaced the civilian heading the Arsenal with Major Alexander B. Dyer, who increased production to over 10,000 by January 1862, still not enough to equip an army of 500,000.

Not much activity had taken place in the Ohio and Mississippi valleys up to this time. Kentucky was still "on the fence." Forces for both South and North were actively trying to sway events there. State. Missouri was in a state of disarray. Armed forces, North and South, jockeyed for position and would soon clash.

August 1 (Thursday)

Confederate Gen. Robert E. Lee, advisor to President Davis, arrived in western Virginia on a mission to "inspect and coordinate" the Southern forces in Virginia's western counties. He shortly took command from Gen. W.W. Loring and began developing a strategy to hold the area for the Confederacy.

William Wing Loring was born in Wilmington, N.C., on December 4, 1818. At age 14, he fought in the Seminole War in Florida, and later in the Mexican War. He was a lawyer, planter, sugar-mill owner, and a politician. In the Mexican War, he lost an arm. He remained in the army, reaching the rank of colonel before resigning his commission on May 13, 1861. He was appointed Brigadier General in the Confederate Army and served, not too willingly, with Jackson during the winter campaign of 1861. Loring complained bitterly about the treatment of his troops by Jackson, taking his complaints to Richmond. Jackson was ordered to remove Loring's unit from Romney in western Virginia, and Jackson never forgave Loring for "going over his head." Loring was transferred to the west, where he faced Grant during the Vicksburg campaign. He served with Polk in northern Mississippi and took over Polk's corps when that general was killed at Pine Mountain, Ga., in 1864. At the end of the war he fled the country, becoming a general for the Khedive of Egypt. In 1879, he returned to the States and published a book in 1884. He died in New York on December 30, 1886.

In the far west, John Baylor and his crew of "buffalo hunters" proclaimed that the New Mexico Territory was a part of the Confederacy.

Brazil recognized the Confederate States as a belligerent, giving them some status.

Lincoln appointed ex-naval officer Gustavus Vasa Fox as Assistant Secretary of the Navy, a promotion from Chief Clerk of the Navy Department. One of his major strengths was the network of acquaintances he had throughout the Navy. He could, and did, use these contacts to get things done, and to smooth ruffled feathers. He would serve the Navy and the Union well.

In Mexico, Mo., an incident was reported by Pvt. Julius Barber, which has not been substantiated in any other known document and most likely did not occur. It was not the manner nor temper of Grant to play such childish games.

Barber, Pvt., Co. D, 15th Illinois Volunteer Infantry, Mexico, Mo.:

> We found the 21st Illinois Regiment Volunteer Infantry here, commanded by Col. Ulysses S. Grant, afterward the great hero of the War. There was a sharp strife between Colonels Turner and Grant as to which outranked. Turner claimed superiority on account of the date of commission. Grant claimed it on account of having belonged to the Regular Army, and with his usual pertinacity and Pope's order, gained his point and assumed command of the camp.
>
> The first order he issued was for a detail from the 15th to clean up his regiment's quarters. It was needed bad enough, but the order did not set well on our stomachs. We had just put our own camp in splendid order and we did not feel like doing the dirty work of his regiment. Luckily for us, Col. Turner was away when the order came and Lieut-Col. Ellis was in command. He took the order, read it, his face burning with anger, and sent word to Col. Ulysses S. Grant that his regiment did not enlist as "niggers" to do the dirty work of his or any other regiment. This emphatic protest brought Col. Grant over at once. High words ensued, which resulted in Lieut-Col. Ellis

tendering Col. Grant his sword, but as for obeying that order, he should never do it.

I think Grant must have admired his spirit, as he refused to receive his sword and did not enforce the order. As a natural consequence, the 15th Regiment Illinois Volunteer Infantry did not fall in love with Grant then, but we surely did with Lieut-Col. Ellis. We saw the stuff he was made of and the bold stand he took for his own and our rights and we would have followed him to the death if he had so ordered. It was not until Grant had showed great courage, indomitable perseverance and lofty patriotism that we could regard him with any degree of favor.

August 2 (Friday)

Major Gen. Ben Butler, at Ft. Monroe on Hampton Roads, banned the sale of all intoxicating beverages to the soldiers. This type of action has never, in history, been effective. Whiskey was found stored in the barrels of the big guns, canteens and gun barrels of the pickets, and any other container imaginable.

Gen. Frémont went down the Mississippi to Cairo, Illinois, with eight boats and reinforcements for Gen. Nathaniel Lyon, who was expecting some action on the part of the Confederate forces.

John Charles Frémont was born in Savannah, Ga., on January 21, 1813. He was appointed a Major General on May 14, 1861. Very political, he often took matters into his own hands, causing embarrassment to Lincoln's administration. His premature emancipation of slaves in Missouri and his lack of military activity led to his removal from command in St. Louis, Mo., three months after his arrival. His second, and last, chance came in western Virginia, when he faced Jackson during the Valley Campaign. Refusing to serve under John Pope, who outranked him, he resigned from the Army. In 1864, his personal fortunes failed with the loss of his property in California. He served as the territorial governor of Arizona between 1878 and 1883. He died in New York on July 13, 1890.

Col. William T. Sherman, already commanding a brigade, was promoted to Brigadier General of Volunteers, with date of rank to May 17, 1861. He was transferred to Kentucky as second-in-command to the ailing Robert Anderson.

Wills, Pvt., 8th Illinois Infantry, Cairo, Illinois:

Hot! You don't know what that word means. I feel that I have always been ignorant of its true meaning till this week, but am posted now, sure. The (supposed-to-be) "never failing cool, delicious breeze" that I have talked about so much, seems to be at "parade rest" now and—I can't do justice to the subject. The health of the camp is much better now than at any time before, since we have been here. There is not a sick man in our company. My health remains gorgeous. We drill now five hours a day, under a sun that cooks eggs in 13 minutes, but we think we feel the heat no more walking than lying around the quarters.... Yesterday 12 men from the Pekin company and 12 men from ours with some artillerymen went 30 miles up the Mississippi to collect all the boats we could find on the Missouri shore. We found three large flats tied up to trees along the shore which we confiscated. One of them wasn't very good so we sunk it. The object was to prevent marauders from visiting Illinois. I had charge of the men from our company.

August 3 (Saturday)

Napoleon III of France visited Lincoln at the White House and remarked on the notable lack of ceremony at the official residence of the President. He later dined with the President and Mrs. Lincoln at a state dinner.

The ladies in upstate New York sent Lincoln 1300 havelocks. Named after the British general who originally devised it in India, it was a cloth device that attached to the military kepi, or hat, and draped down the back of the head onto the shoulders of the wearer. Its intent was to keep the sun from the back of the neck and prevent sunstroke. While it was effective, it never gained much favor with the troops and soon faded from use.

At Hampton Roads, Va., John LaMountain made the first ascent in history in a balloon from the deck of a ship. The Union ship *Fanny* had been specially fitted for this experiment. The purpose was to observe the Confederate battery on Sewell's Point, near Hampton Roads. The aircraft carrier of the future was born!

August 5 (Monday)

Congress voted to impose an income tax of 3 percent, effective January 1, 1862. This was never enforced. It also authorized Lincoln to enlist seamen in the Federal Navy for the duration of the war.

In Missouri, Gen. Lyon retreated towards Springfield from Dug Springs, in the face of a larger Confederate force.

Barber, Pvt., Co. D, 15th Illinois Volunteer Infantry, Mexico, Mo.:

> Some of the boys began to get sick here on account of the poor water we had to use, and our rations grew no better very fast. Some of the boys positively asserted that our bacon had followed us from St. Charles, and our hard-tack was harder still... we hailed the advent of a barrel of flour with great joy, although we had no convenience for cooking it. But, "necessity is the mother of invention," so we hatched up a plan whereby we could get pancakes for supper, though "Biddy," the cook, would have been horrified at the idea of calling them pancakes; but in the absence of anything better, we voted them excellent, but the stomachs refused to sanction our decision.
>
> We now concocted a plan to get rid of our old defunct rations. The boys gathered all of the hard-tack together, placed it upon the back of the bacon, and proceeded to "drum them out of camp," the bacon carrying the hard-tack; but what was our surprise, the next morning, to find that the bacon had come back during the night... It was again expelled and the last we heard of it [was from] some fellow who said he saw it wandering about the country inquiring for the 15th.

August 6 (Tuesday)

Lincoln was at the Capitol to sign bills. One such concerned the freeing of slaves employed or used by Confederates in arms or labor against the United States. Another increased the pay of the private soldier. Reluctantly, he also signed a bill authorizing the confiscation of property "used for purposes of insurrection."

In Kentucky, a pro-Union assembly point and training camp named "Dick Robinson" was established against the wishes of the secessionists. Those in favor of neutrality were also upset by this action. This camp would be used by hundreds of Union soldiers during the war and it became a rallying point for the mountaineers of southeastern Kentucky and eastern Tennessee to join the Union forces.

August 7 (Wednesday)

Confederate Gen. John B. Magruder burned Hampton, Va., because he said that he had learned that Gen. Ben Butler intended to use the village as a holding point for "runaway slaves" whom he considered as "contraband of war." According to Butler, Magruder only gave the residents fifteen minutes to leave before the fires were lit, and Butler declared it a "wanton act of war." Butler previously had made suggestions that the Negroes entering Union lines looking for freedom were "contraband", much as any other property of the secessionists. Based on this, he "freed" them, and provided them shelter and employment among the Union forces. This would become a bone of contention with Lincoln and his plans to hold the emancipation issue at bay for the present.

"Prince John" Magruder, USMA '30, was commander of an artillery battery in Washington at the beginning of the war. Resigning his commission, he returned to Virginia and was commissioned a Colonel in June 1861. He commanded the Confederate force at the "battle" of Big Bethel, and his name became a household word in his home state. His sense of theatrics would prove both useful and devastating for his career. After the war, he refused to apply for a parole, and he went to Mexico for a period of time, finally returning to Houston, Tex., where he died in February 1871.

The War Department issued a contract with J. B. Eads of St. Louis for the construction of seven shallow-draft, ironclad river gunboats. These boats, the *Cairo*, *Carondolet*, *Cincinnati*, *Louisville*, *Mound City*, *Pittsburg*, and *St. Louis*, were to become the backbone of Grant's western river operations.

August 8 (Thursday)

Secretary of the Navy Gideon Welles appointed Commodore Joseph Smith, Capt. Hiram Paulding, and Commander Charles H. Davis to "a board of skillful naval officers to investigate the plans and specifications that may be submitted for the construction or completing of iron- or steel-clad steamships or steam batteries..." Congress appropriated a sum of $1,500,000 for this purpose.

The Confederate government recognized the states of Kentucky, Missouri, Maryland and Delaware as being part of the Confederacy, and authorized the raising of troops in those states. This meant that local military units could be organized and then mustered into the Southern forces, much the same as the Northern States' system. The big difference, of course, was that the Confederate government did not physically control these states.

The editor of a New Hampshire newspaper made demeaning remarks about the locally raised Federal troops, the 1st New Hampshire Volunteers. The troops, taking exception, mobbed and wrecked the *Democratic Standard* in Concord.

Gen. Butler, in Hampton, Va., had asked the Secretary of War, Simon Cameron, for clarification on what to do with Negroes entering Union lines to escape slavery. He, Butler, being an avid abolitionist, had devised a way around the old federal Fugitive Slave Laws which required the return of all "runaway" slaves, by treating them as "property," and as such classifying them as "contraband of war." Cameron, ever the sly fox, said the Fugitive Slave Laws must be respected in the states of the Union; however, for the states in insurrection the situation was different. In essence, if a slave in Kentucky, Maryland, Missouri, the District of Columbia, or elsewhere in the North ran away, that slave must be returned to the master, but in the Southern states different rules were to be applied. Cameron did concede, however, that those slaves now classed as "contraband" could not be returned to their masters.

Barber, Pvt., Co. D, 15th Illinois Volunteer Infantry, Fulton, Mo.:

> Elon and Harvey, two of my tent mates, were taken sick here, Harvey with very sore eyes. The dull monotony of camp life was now broken by an order to march, the left to Hannibal, Mo., and the right to Fulton, Mo. The march was to be performed afoot, consequently, all the sick had to be left, Elon and Harvey among them. The weather was extremely hot and I came very near "bushing" the first day, but being too proud to show symptoms of distress, I struggled on, although I could scarcely put one foot before the other. It was ten o'clock that night before we went into camp, and I was about used up and immediately retired, supperless and sick. We had marched twenty miles since noon.
>
> Our camp was situated near where was fought one of the first battles in Missouri for the Union, and there was great danger of being attacked during the night.... We were on the move before daylight the next morning. I was feeling some better but I had no appetite for breakfast. We had fifteen miles to march and we made it before ten o'clock.... Some of the time we made four miles per hour. We halted at one of the churches in Fulton and rested. A collection was taken up to procure a dinner, and we had the satisfaction of soon sitting down to a nice, warm meal. My appetite had now returned and I ate heartily and felt much refreshed....
>
> Our situation here was a dangerous one. We had only four hundred men and were isolated from any other command, and out of reach of assistance if overpowered, in an enemy's country, with spies lurking all around us.... We were always on the alert and prepared for emergencies.... Our position was admirably situated for defensive operations....
>
> About the 12th of August we received an order to march. A squad of men was sent out to press teams to move our baggage, and early the next morning we were on the march. Our destination was St. Aubert on the Missouri river, forty miles from Fulton. We marched twenty-five miles the first day....

August 9 (Friday)

In Missouri, Confederate Gen. Ben McCulloch led the Southern forces; the ill-equipped Missouri state troops were led by Sterling Price. They neared Springfield with a combined force of nearly 11,000 men. Concentration would be made around an area filled with underbrush and thickets of stunted oaks.

In Springfield, Union Gen. Nathaniel Lyon gathered his 5400 men and set off to find the secessionist army. The odds were greater than two-to-one.

Sterling Price was born in Prince Edward County, Va., on September 20, 1809, and migrated to the Missouri frontier, where he became a slaveowner and a tobacco farmer. He served as military governor of New Mexico Territory during the Mexican War. He served in state and national offices, and as Governor of Missouri. He initially opposed secession in Missouri, but was so angered by the takeover of the State's Camp Jackson by Francis (Frank) P. Blair, Jr. and Nathaniel Lyon that he offered to command the State troops for the Confederacy. He won the Battle of Wilson's Creek, but lost all his other engagements. In late 1864, he led a raid through Missouri, hoping the citizens would rise and join him. When the support did not materialize, he was driven back to Arkansas. At the end of the war, he went to Mexico, returning to Missouri in 1867, broke and in poor health. He died on September 29, 1867, in St. Louis.

The American schooner *George G. Baker* was captured by the Confederate privateer *York* only to be retaken by the U.S.S. *Union* in this continuing game of "Who owns the ship now?" The *York* was set ablaze by her crew to prevent capture off Cape Hatteras, North Carolina by the *Union.*

August 10 (Saturday)

Today, the second major battle of the Civil War was fought, the first in the western theater, in the rolling hills and brush-choked gullies around Wilson's Creek, Mo. Headstrong but capable, Lyon began the attack by dividing his inferior force, sending Franz Sigel to make a rear attack on the opposing force. Sigel, 37, a native German and graduate of Karlsruhe Military Academy, had been commissioned a Brigadier only three days before the battle and was not familiar with American military practices. Independent command was not one of his strong points.

Sigel's attack came to nothing: His troops were routed and he was out of the battle without having contributed much except confusion. Lyon drove the Confederates back at first but they rallied, and, with their superior numbers, eventually won the day. Lyon was killed leading his men—a stupid Civil War practice that cost both North and South many able generals. With Lyon dead, the Federals withdrew and the Confederates were too worn out to follow. The Federals left 1317 of their force dead along Bloody Ridge, nearly 25 percent of their original force. No other battle in the state would be as heavy during the war.

The Federals withdrew all the way to Rolla, southwest of St. Louis, conceding a large part of the state to the secessionist forces. A Confederate victory was claimed, and morale soared in the South. Two victories in a row did much to boost the pride of the fledgling nation.

In Washington, Lincoln met with Gen. Winfield Scott to possibly smooth the friction between Scott and McClellan. Scott, having commanded the Army for so many years, felt that he could do no wrong. "Little Mac," a legend in his own mind, felt that he was the savior of the Union. A clash was inevitable.

August 11 (Sunday)

In the mountains of east Tennessee and Kentucky, always areas of strong Federal support, the distinction between "Yankee" and "Rebel" was becoming clearer. While some Union supporters were slaveholders, their loyalty was not in question on the point of secession. Wayne County in southeastern Kentucky was fairly typical of the area. Settled mostly by English or Scots-Irish immigrants in the late 1700s, there were few foreigners in the county. While there was some Southern sympathy among the slaveholders, being a slaveholder did not automatically place the individual with the South. In 1860, there were 203 slaveholders who owned nearly 1000 slaves, about 10 percent of the total population of the county. During the war about 9.4 percent of the white male population fought, not to end slavery, but to preserve the Union.

In late July, throughout eastern Kentucky and northeastern Tennessee, a trickle of "mountain men" began to flow towards central Kentucky, looking for a place to join the Union forces. Their journey has been described:

> Under cover of the night's darkness and guided by the sound of a cowbell in the hands of an old hunter, they had been led through the difficult defiles of the mountains along the border and enabled to escape the vigilance of their rebel persecutors. There were few coats or shoes among them. When not in their shirt sleeves and barefoot, they commonly wore old-time hunting shirts and moccasins. They were nearly all ragged either from ordinary wear of their apparel or from the lacerations of the brambles and briers through which they had passed in their exodus, or both. Some of them carried their trusty flint-lock hunting rifles and most of them had long sabre-like hunting knives swung to their belts. They had left their homes, their families, and their all at the mercy of an unscrupulous foe and had come forth to fight under the flag they loved. While somewhat outré in dress, they were at the same time hardy and of manly form and a more thoroughly incensed and vindictive crew never sallied out on the war-path. They were enthusiastically received, bountifully fed, and kindly cared for by the citizens along their route.

August 12 (Monday)

In the aftermath of the Battle of Wilson's Creek and the Federal retreat, the Confederate commander, Gen. Ben McCulloch, said that the Union people in Missouri would be protected, but that the time had come for them to choose sides, North or South.

At Cairo, Illinois, three new wooden gunboats, *Tyler*, *Conestoga*, and *Lexington*, arrived to cover operations until such time as ironclads could be built.

August 13 (Tuesday)

In Washington, President Lincoln dined with the newly promoted Brigadier Gen. Robert Anderson, hero of Ft. Sumter. The discussion surely included the assignment of Anderson to Kentucky.

Barber, Pvt., Co. D, 15th Illinois Volunteer Infantry, St. Aubert, Mo.:

> ... resumed the march early. The day was very hot. Before two hours had elapsed, I had a touch of sunstroke and I had to "wilt." I was placed in a wagon. One of our officers had his wife along and she pillowed my head in her lap. I thought if this was the treatment for sunstroke, I would not object to being struck a little every day, but Dr. Buck soon came around and gave me some brandy and water which revived me a great deal. We arrived at St. Aubert about nine o'clock the next morning, having marched fifteen miles in four hours. Some of the boys were now guilty of great imprudence by going into the river when their blood was so hot. Rollin Mallory and Sidney Babcock swam across the river and poor Sid paid the penalty with his life soon after. He was taken sick and died at Keokuk, Ia. The regiment remained here overnight. I recovered sufficiently to be able to go on picket....

Confederate Secretary of the Navy Mallory had sent CSN Commander Bulloch to England to purchase, if possible, ships for the Confederate Navy. The pickings were slim for the type of ship needed for use in coastal waters. Bulloch reported from London:

> After careful examination of the shipping lists of England, and inspecting many vessels, I failed to find a single wooden steamer fit for war purposes.... Wood as a material for ships has almost entirely gone out of use in the British merchant service, and their iron ships, though fast, well built, and staunch enough for voyages of traffic, were too thin in the plates and light in the deck frames and stanchions to carry guns of much weight. I therefore made arrangements to contract with two eminent builders for a gun vessel each....

August 14 (Wednesday)

In Richmond, President Davis proclaimed the banishment of foreigners who did not recognize the government of the Confederacy. In St. Louis, Major Gen. Charles Frémont declared martial law and suppressed two local newspapers for Southern sympathies.

Barber, Pvt., Co. D, 15th Illinois Volunteer Infantry, en route to St. Louis, Mo.:

> This morning a steamer hauled up and we embarked on it and we were soon borne on the sluggish current of the Missouri towards St. Louis. The channel of this river is so changeable that it requires a most skillful pilot to run. The sand bars change every few days. We soon ran afoul of one of them but we soon succeeded in sparring off. Soon after we ran into a snag which detained us for several hours.

Outside Washington, the entire Seventy-Ninth New York Volunteer Regiment was placed under guard after it mutinied when its request for furloughs was denied. Several of the ringleaders were arrested.

August 15 (Thursday)

Brigadier Gen. Robert Anderson was named the new commander of the Department of the Cumberland, which consisted of Kentucky and Tennessee. To spare his native state the embarrassment of setting up headquarters there, he moved his headquarters to Cincinnati, Ohio.

A little mutiny in the Second Maine Regiment resulted in 60 members being sent to perform fatigue duty on the Dry Tortugas off Key West, Fla.

Frémont, in Missouri, called for reinforcements, fearing that Confederate Generals McCulloch and Price would again advance.

Barber, Pvt., Co. D, 15th Illinois Volunteer Infantry, Jefferson Barracks, St. Louis, Mo.:

> ... we passed St. Louis and landed twelve miles below at Jefferson Barracks, where we found the left

wing of the regiment waiting for us. The sick were also here. Elon had nearly got well, but Harvey's eyes were so bad that he was discharged, as were also John Burst and Charlie Pierce.... Tidings of the bloody battle of Wilson Creek began to reach us and we were hastened forward to reinforce that gallant little army contending against such fearful odds. Soon the news of the death of the brave Lyon reached us and that his shattered little army under Sigel was retreating. On arriving in St. Louis, I was again detailed to help transfer the baggage to the cars and it was midnight before our task was done. In the meantime, the boys had been behaving badly and having lots of fun. They had been deprived of their dinner and supper and as they were passing along Market St. and noticed its richly laden viands, etc., they pitched in and helped themselves, much to the indignation of the proprietors and the amusement of the bystanders. While they were trying to catch one thief, a dozen would steal still more. The police, for some unknown cause, did not interfere.... Most of the boys got their fill. I was kindly remembered. I was too hungry to inquire how they got it.... The train left at one o'clock A.M. and the next morning we arrived in camp at Rolla (August 18th).

August 16 (Friday)

Charges of disloyalty were brought against the New York newspapers *Journal of Commerce, Daily News, Day Book, Freeman's Journal,* and the Brooklyn *Eagle* for pro-Southern sympathies. The Federal government was taking a less liberal view of dissent.

Lincoln, at long last, declared the Southern states in a state of rebellion and forbade all commerce with them. This ended, at least legally, the trade in cotton, etc. in the sub-rosa marketplace.

August 17 (Saturday)

The main army of the eastern area was formed this day with the merger of the Departments of Northeastern Virginia, Washington, and the Shenandoah into the Army of the Potomac. This army would carry the brunt of the war in the east and be much maligned, poorly led, and much bloodied. Major Gen. Henry W. "Old Brains" Halleck was appointed a Major General in the Regular Army.

Major Gen. Benjamin F. Butler, later of New Orleans fame, began to organize forces to capture the Cape Hatteras, N.C., area, after turning over his Department of Virginia to Major Gen. John E. Wool.

Wool, a veteran of the War of 1812 and the Mexican War, was 77 at the beginning of the Civil War. He had served, in a somewhat lackluster manner, in California during 1854-57, and commanded the Department of the East from 1857 to 1861. In 1861, he was the Army's senior Brigadier General and fully expected to be appointed as Army Commander when Winfield Scott retired. This was not to be. McClellan was appointed Major General ahead of him. Wool was given several appointments during the early years of the war, and was finally promoted to Major General in 1862. His performance was poor, and he retired in July 1863, after more than 50 years of service. He retired to Troy, N.Y., where he died in November 1869, at age 85.

The Union Army issued orders to provide for 40 cents and one ration a day for nurses.

August 18 (Sunday)

Union and Confederate cavalry skirmished at Pohick Church, Va., about 10 miles south of Alexandria.

The Federal Assistant Secretary of the Navy, Fox, had received information from Lt. Reigart B. Lowry, USN, that the "stone fleet" to block the inlets of the rivers in Albemarle Sound in North Carolina was ready for deployment.

> We have nineteen schooners properly loaded with stone, and all our preparations are complete to divide them in two divisions and place them in tow of this steamer [*Adelaide*] and of the *Governor Peabody*. I think all arrangements are complete, as far as being prepared to "sink and obstruct"... the obstructing party could place their vessels in position, secure them as we propose, by binding chains, spars on end in the sand to settle by action of the tide, anchors down, and finally sink them in such a way as to block the channels so effectively that there could be no navigation through them for several months to come, at least till by the aid of our new gunboats the outside blockade could be effectual.

At the entry of St. Augustine, Fla., the Confederate privateer *Jefferson Davis* met its untimely end by running aground on the bar. This privateer had led a quite successful career to date along the east coast as far north as New York. Her demise led the Charleston *Mercury* to comment, "The name of the privateer *Jefferson Davis* has become a word of terror to the Yankees. The number of her prizes and the amount of merchandise which she captured have no parallel since the days of the *Saucy Jack* [a privateer during the War of 1812]."

August 19 (Monday)

George H. Thomas, one of the native-born Virginians who stayed with the Union, was promoted to Brigadier General by Lincoln. Major Gen. Henry W. Halleck was ordered to Washington from California; it was expected that he would be named to head the Army.

George Henry Thomas was born in Southampton County, Va., July 31, 1816. He graduated from West Point and later served there as an instructor. At the beginning of the war he chose to remain with the Union, an action which alienated him from his family. He served with distinction at First Manassas and was then transferred to Kentucky. In the west he served under Halleck, Buell, and Rosecrans. His action at Chickamauga led to his name "The Rock of Chickamauga." He served with Grant at Chattanooga and was sent to Nashville to protect that city when Sherman began his drive to the sea. His performance at Nashville almost cost him his career, but his victory over Confederate John B. Hood was brilliant. He was promoted to Major General in the Regular Army and assigned to California in 1869. He died in San Francisco on March 28, 1870.

In Richmond, the Confederate Congress virtually admitted Missouri into the Confederacy, giving the state two governments; this would later happen with Kentucky. The planters of the South were also asked for a loan of 100 million dollars to finance the war.

Pro-Unionists raided newspaper offices in Easton and West Chester, Pa., and a publisher of a paper in Haverhill, Mass., was tarred and feathered by a mob for his supposed Southern sympathies.

There was some light skirmishing across the river from Cairo, Illinois, at Bird's Point.

Wills, Pvt., 8th Illinois Infantry, Cairo, Illinois:

> The boys are writing today for some butter and things from home. The expense by express from Peoria is not worth speaking of and the other boys have things sent them often. We have made up our minds to lying here six weeks longer at least, and conclude that time will pass better with a few home extras to grace our table.

August 20 (Tuesday)

Major Gen. George Brinton McClellan assumed command of the Army of the Potomac.

A convention was held in Wheeling, western Virginia, to consider the separation of the western counties from the Old Dominion. The name of Kanawha was suggested for the new entity.

President Davis wrote Confederate Gen. Joseph E. Johnston, now at Manassas Junction, about complaints he had received on the lack of proper food and care of the sick in the local military hospitals.

Barber, Pvt., Co. D, 15th Illinois Volunteer Infantry, Rolla, Mo.:

> Rolla at this time... contained but two or three hundred inhabitants.... We found in camp here the 13th Illinois Volunteer Infantry... Maj-Gen John C. Frémont was in command of the Western Department and he now advanced out of his own pocket $10.00 to each man on our wages, an act of generosity on his part which we never forgot. We had not been in camp but a few days before Sigel's brave and shattered army came straggling in. It was sorrowful to look at them. Some were sorely wounded and it must have been very painful for them to march, but they seemed to be cheerful, though all looked nearly worn out. Their clothes were in tatters. Footsore and weary, they struggled on. Brave men! They deserved a better fate. The most of these soldiers' time (three months) had expired before the battle, but rather than leave with a foe at their backs without punishing them, they voluntarily went into the fight, and on that bloody field many of them voluntarily gave up their lives.... We now have another reorganization in our cooking department by being divided off into five messes. A cook is appointed for each mess, who was excused from all camp duties. This arrangement gave general satisfaction and was ever after continued.

Allen, Pvt., Co. K, 1st Bn., 10th Illinois Cavalry, Versailles, Illinois:

> Dear Father and Mother: I left Overton county, Tenn., on the 20th of July and got over into Clinton county, Ky., the same day. I felt perfectly safe as soon

as I crossed the Tennessee line. I passed through Albany on the next day. From there I went to Burkesville and Glasgow. I took the cars at Glasgow Junction, some nine or ten miles from that place, and came on to Louisville, Ky., a distance of ninety miles.... I crossed the Ohio and visited Camp Jo. Holt opposite Louisville where there were over 1800 U.S. Volunteers that had been raised in Kentucky. They had Jefferson Davis hung in effigy on a locust tree on the bank of the river. I passed the Indiana State Prison at Jeffersonville, and saw the convicts working in a brick yard outside the walls, but did not visit the establishment.

I came from New Albany to Vincennes, Ind., by way of Paoli, Washington, and some smaller places. I there crossed the Wabash... I came to Versailles and then to William Boss's about five miles from Versailles.... I reached Boss's on Thursday, the 25th inst., having walked all the way from Overton county, Tennessee, except the ninety miles I came on the L & N Railroad in Kentucky.... This is a very good country, but Morgan is the richest part of this State I have seen. Times are hard and money scarce. Corn sells at from 10c. to 15c., and wheat at from 55c. to 60c. per bushel.... Write soon and give me all the news.

August 24 (Saturday)

Today, President Jefferson Davis named Pierre A. Rost as commissioner to Spain. He also named James M. Mason to Great Britain and John Slidell to France. Their mission was to gain recognition for the Confederacy and to act as purchasing agents for arms, materials, etc.

In Washington, the spy Mrs. Rose Greenhow was arrested, along with Mrs. Philip Phillips, on charges of corresponding with the Confederates.

In Kentucky, Gov. Beriah Magoffin was informed by Lincoln that he could not, and would not, remove the pro-Union forces from neutral Kentucky. This was expected in all quarters.

August 26 (Monday)

On the western rivers, Navy Capt. Andrew Foote assumed command of the river forces, relieving John Rodgers. Foote turned out to be an excellent choice, working well with the Army commanders.

The operations against Hatteras began with the departure of the combined forces from Hampton Roads, Va., where Flag Officer Stringham sailed with the U.S.S. *Minnesota, Wabash, Monticello, Pawnee,* the Revenue Cutter *Harriet Lane,* and the tug *Fanny.* They would be later joined by the *Susquehanna* and the *Cumberland.* The *Susquehanna* escorted two transports carrying about 900 troops under Maj. Gen. Ben Butler's command to perform the first combined amphibious operation of the war at Hatteras Inlet, N.C. The Confederates had erected two "forts," Hatteras and Clark, constructed of sand and logs, to guard the entrance to the bay at Hatteras Inlet, a vital entry for the blockade runners. The following day, Gen. Ben Butler, with eight ships and nine hundred men, arrived off Hatteras, and the Navy began bombardment of the forts. Clark was abandoned early with little or no opposition. Hatteras resisted. Butler got some troops ashore, but with great difficulty, due to wind and seas.

August 28 (Wednesday)

More shelling on Ft. Hatteras. The fort suffered severe damage and surrendered with light casualties. This, in effect, sealed off a very important port for bringing in supplies for the Confederacy. The effect on morale in the South was devastating. It was the first successful invasion of Southern territory.

In St. Louis, Gen. Nathaniel Lyon, killed at Wilson's Creek, was buried with appropriate ceremony.

Barber, Pvt., Co. D, 15th Illinois Volunteer Infantry, Rolla, Mo.:

We are now set to work building forts and fortifications.... Soon several strong forts were built with heavy abatis to each with rifle pits connecting the forts.... Our duty was very heavy.... Our hospitals were overflowing. Over two hundred were on the sick list in our regiment alone at one time and deaths were quite frequent, and we soon became accustomed to the slow and solemn dirge of the soldier's obsequies. Elon began to get worse and was getting quite homesick. It was evident that he would not live long if he remained in the army so the doctor concluded to discharge him. About a dozen from our company were discharged from this camp and we also had three or four deaths.... One day a peddler came into camp who had pies and cider for sale, and James and I bought some. Soon after I was taken violently ill, but a thorough purging set me on my feet again.... James soon commenced joking me about the cider and pie.... In a few days he was taken sick, never more to rise....

There was a light skirmish at Bailey's Cross Roads, Va., just south of Washington. Commander Dahlgren, commander of the Washington Navy Yard, sent 400 seamen on the steamboat *Philadelphia* to Ft. Ellsworth in Alexandria to bolster that city's defenses. The reinforcements were heartily received by Brigadier Gen. William B. Franklin at Alexandria.

August 30 (Friday)

From his luxurious headquarters in St. Louis, Mo., Major Gen. John Charles Frémont, late of California and more politician than general, issued his own emancipation proclamation and order of confiscation. This, of course, was entirely unauthorized, and would create endless headaches for the Lincoln.

Frémont thought big. He declared martial law throughout Missouri, and confiscated the property of "those who shall take up arms against the United States," and stated that "their slaves, if any they have, are hereby declared free men." Anyone found in the Union-controlled areas with guns in their hands would be tried by military courts-martial and shot, if found guilty. This also applied to all those who were "proven to have taken an active part with their enemies in the field".

The outrage at this order was immediate and nearly unanimous. Lincoln termed it "dictatorial."

August 31 (Saturday)

In Richmond, the government announced the appointment of five full generals. This was somewhat unprecedented in American military procedures. There had been few full generals (four-star rank) in American history. Washington was the only one of the Revolutionary War. Others had been appointed briefly, but the only other major figure was Winfield Scott. The Union Army had no General Officers above the rank of Major General during the war until Grant was appointed Lieutenant General in March 1864. The South would have several Lieutenant Generals, including Longstreet, A.P. Hill, and T. J. Jackson.

The appointments were made, in order of seniority, as follows: Samuel Cooper, a Colonel and Adjutant General of the U.S. Army before the war, once based in Washington; Albert Sidney Johnston, a Colonel before the war, once based in California; Robert Edward Lee, a Colonel before the war, once based in Texas; Joseph Eggleston Johnston, a Brigadier General before the war, once assigned as the Quartermaster General of the U.S. Army in Washington; Pierre Gustav Toutant Beauregard, a Major before the war, and once Superintendent of West Point.

Samuel Cooper, born in New Jersey in 1798, was graduated from West Point in 1815. After serving 30 years in the artillery, he was appointed Adjutant General in 1852 because of his proficiency in administration. His close relationship with Jefferson Davis during Davis's tenure as U.S. Secretary of War, his home in Virginia, and his wife's family (she was the great-granddaughter of George Mason) led him to cast his lot with the Confederacy, after more than 45 years of service to the Union. He was immediately appointed CSA Adjutant General on March 8, 1861, and would be the ranking general in that army (a situation not appreciated by Gen. Beauregard). Perhaps Cooper's greatest contribution to history was that he turned over the records of the Confederate forces intact at the end of the war. This has been a great boon to generations of historians doing research on that era. Cooper died on December 3, 1876.

There was a light skirmish of cavalry at Munsons Hill near Annandale, Va.

SEPTEMBER 1861

September 1861 was a time for soul-searching. The Battle of Manassas (Bull Run) was sobering to both North and South. The North found their leaders to be lacking, and had assigned Major Gen. George B. McClellan to command the Army of the Potomac. He had begun his task of reorganization and training. Not the least of the problems was the question of weapons for the troops. This problem, still unresolved, would plague the military for two years.

In the South, the government agencies and

departments were finding that their resources were limited. The seceding states, so eager to leave the Federal "yoke," were also rather restive under their new "yoke."

September 1 (Sunday)

Brigadier Gen. U. S. Grant assumed command in the area of Cape Girardeau, in southeast Missouri.

Wills, Pvt., 8th Illinois Infantry, Cairo, Illinois:

> We had blankets given us this last week and new accoutrements throughout. If they would only change our guns now we would have nothing but a move to ask for. A uniform was also furnished us last week. It is of excellent all-wool goods, and not so heavy as to be uncomfortable. The color is very fine grey, the pants are fashionably cut and equal to such as would cost six dollars in Peoria. The coats have short skirts and are rather fancifully trimmed with blue. It is much the best uniform I have seen yet, although it costs but $13.... There are wagons and mules here now by the hundreds, and when our tents are ready (they are here now) we will be ready to move. I think there must be near 10,000 men here now.... Gen. McClernand is here now. Every one thinks we will move in a very few days.... Our cook is a jewel, and by trading off rations keeps us in clover all the time. He sets a better table for us than the Peoria house boarders eat from, honestly. An old schoolmate of mine in our mess furnishes us with milk. He and John Wallace go out every night about 2 or 3 o'clock and—somebody's cow don't milk well the next morning....
>
> I have been visiting Col. Raritan's and Hick's Camp this P.M. They have no guns yet and their sentinels stand guard with sticks. Looks funny. We have about 50 prisoners here now. They think they are treated splendidly and say that if any of our boys fall into their hands they will remember it. Several of them are very intelligent-appearing men. One of them is about as big as a house with a foot like a cooking stove....
>
> We have had some fighting in camp lately. An artillery man stabbed one of the 9th and got knocked, kicked, and bayoneted for it.... One of our company got drunk to-day, got to fighting, was sent to the guardhouse, tried to break out, guard knocked him down with a gun, cut his cheek open, etc. He then got into a fight with four men in the guard house and of all the bunged eyes and bloody faces they beat the record.

The news arrived in Washington about the successful operations at Hatteras in North Carolina. This was a major morale booster to the North, considering the low morale following the defeat at Manassas.

September 2 (Monday)

On August 30th, Major Gen. Frémont issued an unauthorized proclamation freeing the slaves of owners who fought for the South, confiscating the owner's property, and assigning death sentences to the owners. Lincoln notified Frémont to "modify" (essentially rescind) this order because of the effect on border states such as Kentucky.

Maj. Gen. Leonidas Polk, CSA, lately Bishop of the Episcopal Church in Louisiana, was assigned command and control of Arkansas and Missouri. Polk, age 55, was a 1827 graduate of West Point, where he had established a friendship with Jefferson Davis. Polk had also been Davis's roommate at the Point. When he was graduated, he left the Army about three months later to enter the Virginia Theological Seminary in Alexandria, Va. Ordained a deacon in the Episcopal Church in 1830, in 1841 he was named Bishop of Louisiana. He entered the Confederate Army on June 25, 1861 as a Major General, having only three months' army service since his graduation from the Academy. His commission was based primarily on his friendship with Jefferson Davis, not his military and leadership ability. Somewhat contentious, he was arbitrary in command and a fomenter of unrest among the senior officers of the western armies.

September 3 (Tuesday)

Confederate forces commanded by Major Gen. Gideon Pillow marched into Kentucky en route to Columbus, Ky., on the Mississippi River. Kentucky was no longer neutral. The Confederate Secretary of War notified Maj. Gen. Polk, who had ordered the "invasion," to withdraw, but the Secretary was overruled by President Davis.

This movement brought howls of protest from the pro-Union forces in Kentucky, and a flurry of enlistments in the Union forces, as well as departures for the Confederate Army. The pro-Southern factor within the state was overjoyed that the issue was finally decided one way or the other, after many months of tension.

September 4 (Wednesday)

Grant arrived at Cairo, Illinois, to establish his headquarters, and to try to sort out the fast-moving military situation. The Confederate shore batteries at Hickman, Ky., teamed up with the C.S.S. *Jackson* and fired on the Federal gunboats U.S.S. *Tyler* and *Lexington* on the Mississippi.

Off Georgia, Commander Green of the U.S.S. *Jamestown* captured the schooner *Col.Long* and scuttled her, after removing her cargo.

Polk got into the propaganda business by asserting that Federal forces were conducting a buildup across the river from Columbus; therefore he had to take the city to "protect it."

September 5 (Thursday)

At Cairo, Grant realized the importance of the invasion of Kentucky and the taking of Columbus. Feeling Paducah to be important, Grant moved to form an expedition to take this city at the junction of the Tennessee and Ohio rivers, upriver from Cairo. The troops, including the 8th Illinois Infantry, left this night.

In South Carolina, the Charleston *Mercury* opened with a charge of "inactivity" on the part of the Confederate forces in Virginia at Manassas. The newspaper claimed that nothing was being done, with the Federal Capitol within sight. This would be one of many criticisms from that newspaper.

Lincoln met with Gen. Winfield Scott to discuss what could be done with Frémont, who was becoming more of a liability every day. In St. Louis, Capt. A. H. Foote, USN, reported to relieve Commander J. Rodgers as overall commander of naval operations on the western rivers. Andrew Hull Foote, age 55, left West Point in 1822, after several months, to accept an appointment as a midshipman at Annapolis. His record was that of a fighter. In 1856-58, while stationed in China, he personally led a party of over 300 sailors and marines against several thousand Chinese after the American flag had been fired upon. His work, and especially his eager support of land forces, during his tenure as commander in the west was a major factor in Grant's success at Forts Henry and Donelson, and the capture of Island No. 10 on the Mississippi River. Wounded in the action at Donelson by shell splinters, ill health finally resulted in his being sent back to Washington to a desk job. Dissatisfied, he finally won command of the South Atlantic Blockading Squadron, but died en route to his new command on June 26, 1863.

September 6 (Friday)

Grant landed Federal troops from transports, protected by gunboats, at Paducah, Ky., to prevent the Confederates from occupying the city. The city was captured without a shot. The later capture of Smithland at the junction of the Ohio and the Cumberland prevented the South from claiming Kentucky by planting the Confederate flag on the Ohio River. Both rivers, the Tennessee and Cumberland, would play prominent roles in later campaigns.

Brigadier Gen. Charles Ferguson (C.F.) Smith was assigned to command western Kentucky. Grant went back to Cairo. Smith, at age 54, was a veteran of the Mexican War, having reached the rank of Lieutenant Colonel during that conflict. He served on the frontier in the 1850s and was with Col. Albert Sydney Johnston in the campaign to suppress the Mormons in 1857. At the beginning of the war, he returned to Washington and got involved in politics; he was relegated to recruiting duty in New York. Rescued by Frémont, he was assigned to St. Louis and promoted to Brigadier General of Volunteers. He served with distinction at Forts Henry and Donelson, and was promoted to Major General in March of '62. At Pittsburg Landing he slipped and badly scraped his shin while entering a small boat. The wound refused to heal, and he died at Savannah, Tenn., on April 25, 1862. His body was returned to Philadelphia for burial.

September 7 (Saturday)

The furor over Frémont in Missouri reached new heights when reports arrived about the lavish expenditures he and his staff had made in St. Louis. He had spent nearly $12 million dollars for steamboats, fortifications, uniforms, food, and parties, in a spending spree that seemed to have no end. Most of this was blamed on his staff of "California robbers and scoundrels." Lincoln asked Gen. David Hunter to go to St. Louis and "assist" Frémont in the administration of the Department.

Things got worse in Missouri, with bushwhackers running rampant in the countryside. Confederate Sterling Price was refitting his troops, largely with arms picked up from the Wilson's Creek battlefield, and preparing to move on Lexington, Mo.

September 9 (Monday)

Lincoln was still concerned about Frémont's activities in Missouri. Frémont sat in St. Louis and Sterling Price advanced on Lexington.

Wills, Pvt., 8th Illinois Infantry, Cairo, Illinois:

> The refreshments and drygoods from home arrived Saturday. We were at Paducah then and they were taken care of by two or three of the lame and halt, that were not in traveling order and were left behind. We returned this morning and after acknowledging the excellence, profusion, variety, gorgeousness, and confiscarity of your benevolent appropriation to our temporal wants, I will particularize by saying that you needn't worry about your picture, as it is in my possession; that the cakes are both numerous and excellent, that the pickles are prodigious in quantity, beautiful in quality and remarkably acceptable. That the butter and cheese are *non ad com valorum.* The tobacco and Hostetter, the boys say, are very fine. To Mrs. Dewey and Mrs. Heald we all return thanks and send our kind respects and love. We have sent a share of the eatables to the Canton boys of the 17th which is again encamped near us; this time on the Kentucky shore.... We have just received orders to get ready to start in five minutes.
>
> Time extended a little. We had 1,500 troops in Paducah, Ky., and received information that they would be attacked Saturday, so Friday night 350 of us were sent up as an advance. Now we go.

September 10 (Tuesday)

In the west, Gen. Albert Sidney Johnston was appointed head of Tennessee, Missouri, Arkansas and Kentucky for the Confederate government.

Albert Sidney Johnston was born at Washington, Ky., on February 2, 1803. A graduate of West Point in 1826, he served in the Black Hawk and Mexican Wars with distinction. He was a close personal friend of Jefferson Davis. He was commander of the U.S. 2nd Cavalry in 1855, when he led the expedition to punish the Mormons in Utah. When the war began, he was a brevet Brigadier General and commanding the Department of the Pacific. He resigned his commission and rode all the way across country to Richmond, where he was commissioned a general in the Confederate Army and sent to command in Kentucky and Tennessee. The fall of Forts Donelson and Henry led to the Battle of Shiloh April 6-7, 1862. During this battle, he was wounded in the leg and bled to death before anyone realized he was wounded.

In St. Louis Frémont waited six days to respond that he would not rescind the emancipation order. However, if the President so ordered, he would do it. The antislavery radicals in the North were ecstatic. Further, Frémont sent his reply in care of Mrs. Frémont, who was something of a fire-eater herself. Lincoln, not pleased with the letter, showed his displeasure, and Mrs. Frémont showed her temper and explained that Frémont was "above and beyond" the ordinary run of soldiers. She left the White House in a huff to return to Missouri.

In Kentucky, Brigadier Gen. George H. Thomas was assigned to command Camp Dick Robinson, the major Federal training camp in that state. Camp Robinson, located on 3200 acres of the estate of Dick Robinson, Esq., remained in service during the entire war.

Barber, Pvt., Co. D, 15th Illinois Volunteer Infantry, Rolla, Mo.:

> Up to this time, James had remained in our tent, as the hospital was somewhat crowded, but he had gotten so bad that it was necessary to have him removed where he could be more quiet and get more care. I had spoken to Dr. McKim, the surgeon, several times about it, but he kept putting it off. I finally determined that I would not be put off any longer, and I importuned the doctor so much that he got angry and gave me a terrible raking, interspersed with a variety of choice oaths. I waited until he had spent his wrath and then told him that I did not feel guilty of anything wrong in this matter. It was only my intense anxiety for my cousin that induced me to endeavor to procure him better treatment and I supposed that it was his duty as surgeon of the regiment to see that the sick were well cared for. He cooled down and prepared a place for him and had James removed. Ever after, Dr. McKim was a friend to me. He did all he could to save

James, but human aid was unavailing. While not on duty, I was by his bedside. He was not content to have me away a moment. I once began to flatter myself that he would get well, but one day, while I was on duty, a summons came for me from Dr. McKim to repair immediately to the bedside of James. I was released from duty and thereafter remained with James as long as he lived. I found him suffering a terrible relapse and in the agonies of a congestive chill. He did not know me and was raving terribly.

Hope sank within me now. I knew that I must lose one of my nearest and dearest friends. A brother's love could not have been greater than that I bore for James, and I know that love was reciprocated. The closest confidence existed between us. In his wild delirium he would throw his arms around my neck and call me "brother." All that affection could prompt and skill perform were done to save him. On the 18th of September, at two o'clock A.M. he breathed his last, under the influence of ether. It was a sad blow to his kindred and friends....

In western Virginia, Federal Gen. Rosecrans attacked the Confederates at Carnifix Ferry, but was unable to break their lines. The Rebels, however, withdrew, leaving the field to the Union forces. A little to the north, Gen. Robert E. Lee was planning his assault on Cheat Mountain, near the Pennsylvania line.

September 11 (Wednesday)

President Lincoln wrote Frémont that he would order that the clause in Frémont's proclamation regarding confiscation of property and the emancipation of slaves be modified to conform with current law and established Acts of Congress.

In Kentucky, the legislature called for the Governor to expel all Confederate troops from the state. A resolution for the expulsion of all troops from the state was defeated.

In western Virginia, Lee commenced his five-pronged attack against the Union forces. The weather was stormy with heavy rains, slowing movement in the heavily wooded, mountainous area.

September 12 (Thursday)

The Federal government ordered the arrest for disloyalty of Maryland legislators who were scheduled to convene in Frederick on Sept. 17th. Arrests began on this day and continued through the 17th. The prisoners were sent to Ft. Warren in Boston Harbor. Maryland remained loyal to the Union.

Surgeon General of the Army Finley had become more than a thorn in the side of the Sanitary Commission. In its view, the "old guard" was so used to doing without that they had no idea what was required for the massive work confronting them. As stated by Adams:

> An attempt by the reformers to influence members of Congress to a more realistic view came to nothing. Feeling that Finley's "devotion to routine" and his "undisguised hostility" would wreck their plans for a healthier Army, the commission, at its meeting on September 12, 1861, voted to ask for the removal or retirement of the Surgeon General and to press for remedial legislation.

In western Kentucky, the 8th Illinois Infantry marched to Paducah to "relieve" an expected attack on Federals in that location.

Wills, Pvt., 8th Illinois Infantry, Camp Norfolk, Ky.:

> Agreeable to our very short notice, we packed our knapsacks, put three days' rations in our haversacks, were carried across the river to Bird's Point in two boats, and just at dark, started out through the woods. 'Twas a confounded, dark, dirty, narrow road and I was right glad when the word "halt" was given and preparations made for bunking in for the night. The next morning we started again along down the river, the gunboats, two of them, keeping a couple of miles ahead of us. We started with a couple of pieces of field artillery, but the road got so bad that we had to leave it after about three miles. We advanced about 5 miles when the gunboats, which were about a mile and one-half ahead of us, opened mouth, and thunder! what a rumpus they did keep up. We could not see them for the thick brush between us and the river, but we thought sure our little fight had come at last. We were drawn up in the front yard of some secesher's deserted house (a fine one), and the colonel with a small party went ahead to reconnoiter.
>
> While they were gone we ate our dinners and made ready for the expected march and fight. But the colonel, on his return, scooted us back to our morning's starting place. Whew, but that was a sweating

old march. About an hour after we started back, 15 of our cavalry scouts were run in, through the place where we took dinner, by 60 or 70 secesh cavalry. Three or four were wounded and our boys say that they killed several of the Rebels.... We have had it sweet the last day and two nights. Rained like sixty and we have no tents. There is no shelter but a few trees and you know they amount to nothing in heavy rains. It is amusing to see the boys figure at night for dry beds. Every thing, gates, cordwood, rails, cornstalks, weeds and panels of fence and boards are confiscated and genius is taxed to utmost to make the sleeping as comfortable as possible. Milo Farewell, Hy Johnson and myself sleep on an armful of cornstalks thrown on a floor of rails....

I fell in love with Paducah while I was there and I think I will settle there when the war is over. I never saw so many pretty women in my life. All fat, smooth-skinned, small-boned, highbred-looking women. They hollered "Hurrah for Jeff" at us, some of them, but that's all right. I could write until tomorrow about Paducah, but I must go confiscate some corn for dinner.

In Missouri, Sterling Price began his assault on Lexington by besieging Mulligan's Irish Guard, a 2800-man force in trenches on the campus of the Masonic College. The Confederates used a form of "rolling breastworks" in their advance which cut down on their casualties. In St. Louis, Frémont was startled and decided to act.

In Kentucky, after the Legislature passed the resolution for all Confederate forces to leave the State, Confederate Gen. Simon Bolivar Buckner called upon all Kentuckians to "defend their homes against the invasion of the North."

Buckner, age 38, graduated from USMA, class of '44, and later served in Mexico with Winfield Scott. He left the Army in 1855 to go into business. In 1860, he became the head of the Kentucky State Guard. He refused a commission in the Union Army, and in July 1861 he resigned from the Kentucky Guard and went further south to avoid arrest as a traitor. Commissioned a Brigadier General in the Confederate Army in September 1861, he was assigned to Gen. Albert S. Johnston's army to occupy Bowling Green, Kentucky. Later, when all other senior officers had left Ft. Donelson, he surrendered the fort to his former Academy classmate U.S. Grant on February 16, 1862. Surviving the war, he was elected Governor of Kentucky in 1887 and was very active in Confederate veterans' organizations. He died at his home in Munfordsville, Ky., on January 8, 1914, the last survivor of the top three general ranks of the Confederacy.

September 14 (Saturday)

In the predawn darkness at Pensacola, sailors and marines of the U.S.S. *Colorado* swarmed aboard the privateering schooner *Judah* from small boats at the same time as they landed at the Pensacola Navy Yard. The schooner was burned, and the guns at the Navy Yard were spiked. At the mouth of the Potomac River, the U.S.S. *Albatross*, Commander Prentiss, captured the Confederate schooner *Alabama*.

In St. Louis, there was much stirring about in Frémont's camps. He was organizing 38,000 troops to relieve Mulligan at Lexington, Mo.

In Richmond, President Davis had received a complaint from Gen. Joseph E. Johnston about the ranking of the Confederate generals. Johnston felt he had been slighted and should be ranked ahead of some of those who now outranked him. He was the only one of General Officer rank to leave the United States Army to join the Confederate Army. Lee was a recently promoted Colonel and Beauregard was only a Major at the time of secession. This would be one of several sore points between Johnston and Davis during the war.

September 15 (Sunday)

Frémont ordered the arrest of political powerhouse Frank Blair. Frémont continued to "get ready" for his relief of Lexington. In Washington, Lincoln met with his Cabinet to discuss the dismissal of Frémont. Lincoln was under attack for the arrest of the Maryland lawmakers, but he largely ignored the charges.

Lee closed his campaign in western Virginia. He would be severely criticized for his handling of the campaign.

In the west, Gen. Albert Sydney Johnston assumed direct command from Gen. Leonidas Polk.

September 16 (Monday)

William Nelson, the huge Kentuckian who was so instrumental in getting guns to the Unionists in

Kentucky earlier in the year, was promoted to Brigadier General. He would serve at Shiloh, Corinth, and Chattanooga before being promoted to Major General in July 1862.

Federal troops, now over 2000 strong, including the 8th Illinois Infantry, moved towards Columbus, Ky., from Paducah. Confederate gunboats opposed the move and shelled the Union positions, usually unsuccessfully.

Wills, Sgt., 8th Illinois Infantry, Camp Norfolk, Ky.:

> Yesterday (Sunday) the *Yankee* came up and shelled the woods where we were the day before. She tried to throw some shells into our camp but they didn't reach us by a mile and a half. One of our gunboats has to lay here all the time or the *Yankee* would make us skedaddle out of this on double quick.
>
> Don't talk about furloughs. They are played out. A dispatch came this last week to Col. Oglesby that his wife was dying. He went up to Cairo but Gen. McClernand showed him an order from McClellan vetoing furloughs, no matter for what. So the colonel had to return here. I'd like very much to go home but I'll enjoy it all the more when this business is finished. My office is sergeant, two grades above private. Our company goes on picket to-night.

September 17 (Tuesday)

At Ocracoke Inlet, N.C., the Federal Navy destroyed the fort defending the inlet and thus closed another port for blockade runners.

Grant's campaign to hold Paducah, Ky., was successful. The troops brought from Cairo, Illinois, were finding the wilderness a little rough.

Wills, Sgt., 8th Illinois Infantry, Camp Norfolk, Ky.:

> Well, I've slept half of this day and feel sleepy yet. I had a tough time on picket last night. We were divided into four squads, and owing to the small number of men we had out (only 50), the corporals had to stand guard as privates; so I had all the stationing of reliefs to do myself and did not get a minute's sleep all night. We were not troubled any by the enemy but the mosquitoes and fleas gave us the devil.
>
> A coon came sliding down the tree Sam Nutt was stationed under and he thought he was taken sure. The people here say that there are lots of bears and tiger cats killed here every winter.... Our cook has been sick for several days and we have been just about half living on account of our being too lazy to cook. I don't mean to be disrespectful when I say I was about as glad to see him cooking again this [morning] as I would be to see you. He is a splendid nigger, seems to think the world of the boys. He buys a great many little things for us with his own money, which, as we are all out, is a good institution. We are to get our pay next week, the officers say. My pay is some $18 or $20 a month now. I am entitled to a straight sword, but as I have to carry a musket also, I'll trade it off for gingerbread if they'll let me, and if they won't, I'll lose it for sure, for I have enough to carry without it. I can hear the tattoo now before the colonel's quarters at the other end of the camp and our boys are singing, "Home Again" as they lie around me in our tent.... We are rapidly learning to appropriate and confiscate. On our last scout one of our boys rode a stray horse back and another came in with a female jackass and her child. Chickens are very scarce here now and the natives complain that sweet potato hills have turned into holes since we have been here. Our mess have this P.M. confiscated the roof of a man's barn to cover our cook house with.

The Union Navy took possession of Ship Island, Miss., with the landing party from the U.S.S. *Massachusetts.* The island would become an important staging and refueling site for the blockading squadrons.

September 20 (Friday)

At Lexington, Mo., the siege that began on the 12th was ended with the surrender of Col. James A. Mulligan's Irish Guard command of 2800 Federals. The Confederate commander, Maj. Gen. Sterling Price (former Governor of Missouri), delayed assaulting for five days while Mulligan waited for relief from Union forces under Gen. John Frémont that never came. On the 18th, Price assaulted the works to no avail. An attempt was made again on the 19th with more success; this time the Confederates used dampened bales of hemp, rolling them forward as they advanced to protect the assaulting troops. Finally, Mulligan capitulated. Price, with an additional 2800 muskets available, called for the people of Missouri to join him. This was a great morale boost for the South, and very disheartening for the North. The victory was a great show, but the

Confederates did not stay long. Retreating south, their new-found recruits began dropping off at home, as the army went towards Arkansas.

Barber, Pvt., Co. D, 15th Illinois Volunteer Infantry, Rolla, Mo.:

> Rumors of an attack now became rife in camp. Price and McCulloch were reported to be near with a large army. This just served to keep up excitement enough to destroy the ennui of army life. Maj. Gen. Hunter was in command of the post now. He received a wound at the battle of Bull Run. We made several forced marches out to meet the enemy, but each time failed to bring them to an engagement; as soon as our backs were turned, they would commence bushwhacking. A great many of the citizens adopted the role of being friends to our face and foes to our back.

September 22 (Sunday)

In St. Louis, the lack of energy on the part of Frémont in the relief of Lexington brought down a storm of criticism on his head. He was now looked upon with less favor by many of his supporters.

Kansas Jayhawkers, led by James H. Lane, raided, looted and burned the town of Osceola, Mo., in yet another example of terror on the Kansas-Missouri border. No military advantage was gained in this senseless act.

Barber, Pvt., Co. D, 15th Illinois Volunteer Infantry, Rolla, Mo.:

> A difficulty occurring at this time between Lt. Curtis and Capt. Wayne was settled by the former resigning. We now prepared for a long campaign. We were furnished with fifteen six-mule teams, and well supplied with clothing, etc. We were expecting orders to move every day.

Wills, Sgt., 8th Illinois Infantry, Camp Norfolk, Ky.:

> We are all again bored to death with lying still, but patience and we'll get what we want in time. We have the report here to-day that Col. Mulligan has capitulated to Price, Jackson & Co. at Lexington. This, if true, will certainly retard our movement down the Mississippi. I'm getting perfectly indifferent about Frémont's being superseded or as to who has the command. It seems to me that none of our commanders are doing anything. With at least 75,000 troops at Paducah, Cairo and in Missouri, to allow the gallant Mulligan to be forced to surrender is perfectly shameful. It's disheartening to a soldier, I tell you. Let them go on; if this war goes against us 'twill be the fault of our commanders, and not of the men, sure....

September 25 (Wednesday)

Secretary of the Navy Welles, in a historic command, instructed Flag Officer Du Pont, Commander of the South Atlantic Blockading Squadron:

> The Department finds it necessary to adopt a regulation with respect to the large and increasing number of persons of color, commonly known as "contrabands," now subsisted at the navy yards and on board ships-of-war. These can neither be expelled from the service, to which they have resorted, nor can they be maintained unemployed, and it is not proper that they should be compelled to render necessary and regular services without compensation. You are therefore authorized, when their services can be made useful, to enlist them for the naval service, under the same forms and regulations as apply to other enlistments. They will be allowed, however, no higher rating than "boys" at a compensation of ten dollars per month and one ration a day.

September 26 (Thursday)

John S. Jackman, a native Kentuckian, born in December 1841, began one of the most important periods of his life when he left Kentucky for service in the 1st Kentucky Brigade, later to be known as the "Orphan Brigade," of the Confederate Army. He was to serve until the end of the war as a private. His story, in this chronicle, begins here:

> The first six months of my "soldier life" I let pass without making notes of any kind. To make my Journal more complete, I shall write up that period from memory. I shall use no dates but those positively known to be correct.
>
> Late in the afternoon left home with the intention of making my way to Green River, where the advance of the Confederate Army was then

encamped. My mind was made up to undertake this journey almost instantly. On the evening mentioned I walked down to the Depot, about car time, to get the daily papers, and as I was passing in, W.S. said to me, "Let us go to Bloomfield to-night and join the party going through to Dixie!" or something to that effect. I had scarcely thought of such a thing before, but in an instant my mind was made up, and I answered, "All right." I immediately returned home and put on a heavy suit of clothes, and tried to slip off from the folks, but they divined my purpose. I told them I would only be gone a few days—that I was going to see Bro and would be back. (My mind was not fully made up to join the army when I left home—was not satisfied my health would permit me). Taking nothing with me but a traveling shawl, I mounted my horse and joined W.S. at his home. We were soon in the road, two modern Don Quixotes starting to seek adventure.

They were then rendezvousing at Camp "Charity"—so called because the people furnished us rations while there encamped—several companies from different counties, and among them was one from Bardstown, the "Allsin Greys." To this company we purposed to attach ourselves during the trip, under temporary organization.

Though nearly four years have passed, the incidents of the journey to Camp "Charity," and my first experience as a soldier, are still fresh in memory. The stirring scenes through which I have passed in nearly four years of warfare have not dimmed from memory the most trifling occurrence.

There were several recruits from Samuel's Depot neighborhoods going to Camp "Charity" that night, and arrangements had been made for all to meet at Mr. P's. W.S. and I took supper there. Shortly after dark all were ready and my brother Don Quixote took leave of his Dulcinea. We rode off in high spirits. A short distance from P's, our party was augmented by three more boys. For fear of being molested by the home guards we went on by-roads, leaving Bardstown [on] our right. The night was beautiful. Nearly a full moon gave us light. Just before coming out on the main Bloomfield road beyond Bardstown, Capt. G. and I rode forward as a reconnoitering party, to see that the road was clear. Finding all clear, we signaled the troops on and met with no further delay until near camp. There, we were riding along in high glee, and were suddenly challenged "Who goes there?" Silence came over our party immediately and Capt. G., who was at the head, answered promptly, "Recruits for the Rebel Army." We were then commanded to halt, and a picket came forward to inspect. This was something novel to me—this was soldiering in reality. As the picket advanced, I caught a glimpse of his polished bayonet as it gleamed in the moonlight. That was the first bayonet I had seen in actual use, to overturn the "best government the world ever saw." I shall never forget my feelings at first beholding that polished steel glittering in the moon beams.

After being satisfied that we were all right, the picket conducted us to the stand, and another one set out with us, to show us the way to camp. Being then midnight, and all the fires having burnt down, we were very close to the camp before we knew it. A sentinel on post challenged us, and I distinctly heard the clicking of his lock, as he drew the hammer back. I thought this extreme vigilance. After parlaying sometime with the sentinel, who was green, we were taken in by Capt. W., afterward Lieut. Col., and conducted to the bivouac of his company. A fire was "recruited," and we sat around chatting awhile with James H. and others hailing from about Samuel's who had preceded us the day before. Being weary I soon rolled myself up in my shawl, and tumbled down under a large beech tree to sleep. I lay a moment watching the "lamps of heaven" as they twinkled through the foliage of the old tree, my thoughts busy contemplating the *sublimeness* of soldiering; then I sank into a restless slumber.

September 27 (Friday)

In Washington, a rather heated discussion developed when the lack of aggressive activity on McClellan's part was brought into a discussion at a Cabinet meeting attended by McClellan.

In Kentucky, Jackman began to get a taste of his future life in the Confederate Army.

Jackman, Pvt., "The Orphan Brigade," Camp Charity, Ky.:

At daylight, woke with the rain pattering down in my face. I broiled a piece of fat bacon on the end of a stick, and with a fragment of corn-bread, made my breakfast. I then looked around to see what I could see. Camp "Charity" I found to be three miles from Bloomfield, and on no very public road. There was an old log church in the centre of the bivouac, which was used for an arsenal and commissary depot. The men (who were mostly dressed in gay uniforms) were sheltered by rude arbors made of tree branches. There were then between two and three hundred men in camp. The "Lexington Rifles," a company commanded by Capt. John H. Morgan, afterwards a noted cavalry General in the Confederate service, was present. Morgan was commander-in-chief of the forces.

At 9 A.M. was placed on guard, and for the first time "buckled on my armor." How proud I felt as I paced to and fro in my beat, with a long sabre bayonet on my gun which glittered not a little in the sun beams. There was no rain after daylight and the sun came out bright and clear. Had a good dinner. James H., who was in the commissary department, fed me on pies and such things. That was the best commissariat we ever had. That night until the moon came up, was black as Erebus, and my beat was back of the camp in a dense wood. I could hardly "keep on the track." I was delighted at hearing my brother sentinels challenging and calling for the Corporal. They generally used their lungs pretty freely and I imagined they could be heard for miles. I longed for an opportunity to try my lungs, *à la militaire,* but I had almost despaired of finding a pretext when one suddenly offered. The hour was after midnight, and all quiet as death. I heard two fellows coming to the spring which was just inside my beat. I walked to one extremity and kept still, hoping they would miss their way and wander over. Sure enough, they did. They soon found out their mistake and started again for the spring, but I halted them "instanter." They commenced begging me to let them in, but I pompously told them *my duty* kept me from letting anyone pass my post unless first giving the countersign, which they did not have. The next moment "Corporal of the guard, post no. 8" was bawled out by me in my best military manner. It was passed from sentinel to sentinel to my entire satisfaction. Even the owls stopped hooting, either through respect, or being terror-stricken. Presently I heard the Corporal coming, tumbling over logs, and swearing true trooper style. The "Corp" let the water-hunters in, and I was left to pace my beat, "solitary and alone." Two years after, I met the Corporal—then a Lieutenant—at Dalton, Ga., and I told him how I played off on him. He laughed heartily.

September 28 (Saturday)

Things were relatively quiet on all fronts this day. The Confederates evacuated Munson's Hill, near the present location of Bailey's Crossroads, Va.

Jackman, Pvt., "The Orphan Brigade," to Green River, Ky.:

At 2 o'clock P.M. our little army took up its line of march for Green River. We had been recruited to upwards of 400—about equally divided foot and horse. Our departure was amid tears of the gentler sex, who were present to bid relatives farewell. The column moved off, nearly all joining in singing a war-song. Many who then marched away with buoyant step were doomed never to return. They found graves far from home—far from kindred!

We presented quite a formidable appearance—we "night-hunters." All well armed, and all, save those who had old muskets, had forty rounds of ammunition. Our course lay in four miles of Bardstown, where, we had learned, a force had been sent to intercept us. Morgan rode at the head of the column unperturbed. We passed all the roads without interruption. Night overtook us just beyond the Springfield pike, and was very dark. Our course led mostly through the woods and often we followed by-paths. The infantry marched in front, in two ranks, and the cavalry brought up the rear. Our wagon train consisted of a small spring-wagon used for hauling ordnance, etc., and a buggy in which was the Rev. Dr. Ford and his wife. It has always been a mystery how our "train" got over such a rough road. There was also a trader along, with a small drove of mules. A lantern was carried at the head of the column which those in the rear could occasionally see, as we wended our way through the dark woods. The infantry were "ferried" over the Beech Fork mounted behind the cavalry. When over, all the cavalry were requested to dismount and let the infantry ride awhile, but many refused to dismount. In the confusion, part of us took the wrong road. We got righted at last, after much trouble, and moved on rapidly to overtake the advance. I had to help James H. along. (Someone had promised to give him a horse if he would ride it. He mounted... but was barely seated when the horse ran off with him, and threw him against a tree, hurting him so he could scarcely walk.) Camp fires were seen ahead of us and the report got started that the enemy was in front. Capt. M. swore he would not lead his men into action unless there was an equal distribution of cartridges! Some even leveled their guns to shoot in [the] direction of the fires. I now saw what I had considered a body of *veteran* troops turned into a mob. I knew that if we did meet with any resistance—I was certain the enemy was not encamped there—such conduct [as] was then exhibited would cause us to "go up." James H. and I thought seriously of forsaking the crowd and shifting for ourselves. The fires had been kindled by those in advance who were waiting for us to come up.

September 29 (Sunday)

Gov. Oliver P. Morton of Indiana was complaining that Lincoln was not paying enough attention to Kentucky. Morton, at age 38, was a hard-headed fire-eater. Early in the war, getting no immediate support from the Federal government, he suspended the State Legislature and directed State funds to the arming and outfitting of Union regiments. He established his own arms factory when rifles were not forthcoming, keeping this going throughout the war. Mostly through his efforts, Indiana furnished nearly 150,000 troops during the war, with little resort to the draft.

Oliver Hazard Perry Throck Morton spent his boyhood with two staunch Presbyterian aunts, after the death of his mother. He had some formal elementary education, getting most of his knowledge from reading. He attended Miami University (Oxford, Ohio) for two years and then read for the law, becoming a very successful lawyer, with the railroads as major clients. He ran unsuccessfully for prosecuting attorney on the Democratic ticket in 1848, at age 25. In 1854, he took a firm stand on the Kansas-Nebraska Act and supported the People's Party, a forerunner of the Republican Party. The Republicans nominated him for governor in 1856, but he lost the election. In 1860, he was nominated for lieutenant governor, and won the election. The elected governor, Henry S. Lane, was named to the U.S. Senate, and Morton became governor. He was reelected in 1864 by a wide margin, mostly by arranging to have over 9000 soldiers brought back home to vote. In 1865 he suffered a stroke that left him paralyzed for a time. He was elected to the U.S. Senate in 1867, where he led the movement to pass the 14th Amendment to the Constitution providing for black suffrage. He suffered a second stroke in August 1877, in Washington. He returned to Indiana, where he died on November 1, 1877.

Jackman, Pvt., "The Orphan Brigade," en route south:

> At daylight we crossed the Lebanon Branch Railroad. After crossing a long rocky hill, we stopped [by] a creek to breakfast. I had walked 40 miles without hardly resting, carrying my gun and 40 rounds—also some articles of clothing. My breakfast was a piece of beef, broiled on the end of a stick, without salt. After waiting about an hour we pushed on. I thought to ride awhile, but we had scarcely got in the road before a report came that the enemy was in front. I took my place in the company on foot. We waded a deep creek without breaking ranks—it would not have been *soldierly* to have done otherwise—and my boots drew to my feet so when in the sun that I could not walk. I then rode until we got to the top of Muldraugh Hill. The day was beautiful and the scenery in the road was often picturesque. Sometimes our road led under rocky steeps where we could have been destroyed by a handful of men with ease. I was too tired to admire the scenery much. After dismounting on top of the Hill, I had not crippled far before the infantry was ordered to mount behind the cavalry. It fell to my lot to be mounted behind a very large man on a very small horse. Just before coming out in the Elizabethtown pike a fight seemed imminent and the big "man" on the little horse put me down to shift for myself. I had not gone far, however, when a Don Quixotic–looking individual took me up. We passed out in the pike without molestation. Our march was continued until long after dark. I was so sleepy I could scarcely sit on the horse. I reeled about so my "Don" often threatened to put me down. At last we got to "Sandy Hollow" where we camped. I tumbled off the horse, down by a big oak tree, not even taking time to wrap up in my shawl, and went to sleep. It was broad daylight when I awoke. Hill lay down near me across some rails that were on fire and he slept so soundly that his coat was burned off without breaking his slumbers.

September 30 (Monday)

In Washington, Lincoln was still wrestling with the problem of Frémont. Meanwhile, McClellan was sitting in Virginia doing little except admiring himself and "his" army. Lincoln was getting testy.

Jackman, Pvt., The "Orphan Brigade":

We moved out early. I mounted O's horse. Had not proceeded far when a drum commenced to rattle out in the bushes and firing of small arms commenced in front. I thought the ball had opened and unslung my gun. The drum was beat by a body of home-guards and they also soon "beat a retreat" further into the woods and the firing in front came from the advance, killing turkeys for breakfast. At a little town, just before we left the pike, the United States flag was floating quietly in the breeze at the top of a high pole. It was not molested by us. We halted at noon to rest, not to dine, for we had nothing to eat. That afternoon I could not walk and our Captain mounted me on his horse. At last we came to the top of a high range of hills, where we could survey the Green River valley. Far away we could see the river threading its way among the blue hills; and looking more narrowly, could see the tents of the confederates dotting the valley. The day was beautiful—such as we generally have during the indian-summer. The smoke from the camps hazed the landscape, giving additional beauty. We had yet to travel several miles and it was dark when we arrived at the camp of the 2nd Ky. which was at the south end of the railroad bridge. We were welcomed by music and the firing of cannon. Being on horseback I went with the balance of the cavalry to a cavalry camp close by. I was so exhausted from travel that I could not dismount and was taken from my horse and placed in the tent of H. who gave me a pint of coffee and a piece of camp-baked bread. I slept well that night. This was the first time I ever slept in a tent.

Wills, Sgt., 8th Illinois Infantry, Camp Norfolk, Ky.:

Since my last, we had had some more fun here. Our company was out a few miles the other day to capture an old cuss we thought was peddling news from our camp down to Columbus. He had skedaddled though before we got to his house. We gobbled up all the loose plunder we could find lying around, it wasn't much, and marched back.

We had a mighty good time on picket a few nights ago. It was confounded cold, [and] bushwhackers or no bushwackers, we concluded to have a fire. A couple of the boys volunteered to go back to camp for kettles and coffee, and we found lots of nice roasting ears in the field we were camped in, and a kind of pumpkin that ate very well after a little roast before the fire. Then there were splendid pawpaws, lots of nuts of all kinds which a little fire made ripe, and we sat and cooked and ate all night....

The month came to a quiet and not very successful end for either side of the struggle.

OCTOBER 1861

The Army of the Potomac lay idle and nothing seemed to move McClellan into action. The golden days of autumn were fast slipping away and the rains of fall approached. McClellan was organizing and training "his" army into one of the finest and best organized armies ever seen on the continent. All he needed to do now was to use it for its intended purpose. McClellan was also having his problems with both Winfield Scott and the President. They were, after all, either too old or too uninitiated to "understand" his overall designs.

In Richmond, and elsewhere in the South, the puzzlement over the "nonevents" at Manassas was the talk of the town. Just why was Gen. Joseph E. Johnston sitting on his hands and not taking the offensive? Materials were being stockpiled throughout the South, to the chagrin of many consumers, for use by the army. Richmond was also concerned about the recognition of the Confederacy by foreign governments. This act would place the stamp of legitimacy on secession in the eyes of the world.

Kentucky had lost its neutrality and was being somewhat "occupied" by the Northern armies. All key cities were firmly in control of Federal troops. In eastern Tennessee, western North Carolina and southeastern Kentucky the "mountain men" loyal to the Union were making their way to places to enlist in the Federal forces.

In the west, Missouri still needed attention with Frémont in command. His "order of emancipation and confiscation" still rankled the administration.

October 1 (Tuesday)

At Centreville, Va., President Jefferson Davis and Generals Joe Johnston, Pierre Beauregard, and G.W.

Smith held a council of war and strategy. The sentiment was to concentrate the armies in the east and to await Union attack in the spring. This recommendation, of course, would not satisfy the fire-eaters of the South, but it was most practical, considering the manpower and matériel available.

The War Department in Washington created a whole new Department of New England so that Major Gen. Benjamin Butler could recruit troops for the New Orleans expedition.

Pamlico Sound in North Carolina was the scene of a lopsided battle and victory for the Confederacy when the C.S.S. *Curlew*, *Raleigh*, and *Junaluska* under Flag Officer William F. Lynch, CSN, captured the steamer *Fanny*, which was loaded with arms and troops. This gave the South a boost in morale and provided some much needed supplies and arms.

The question of issuing "letters of marque" which allowed privateering on the high seas was finally settled for the Union when Secretary of the Navy Gideon Welles refused to issue such letters on the grounds that they would be "a recognition of the assumption of the insurgents that they were a distinct and independent nationality."

Jackman, Pvt., "The Orphan Brigade," "Camp Charity":

> We commenced camp life—learning how to cook, pitch tents, drill, etc., etc. I could not walk about much, my feet were so sore. Afterwards all the nails came off my toes. Saw my brother Jo and several old acquaintances in the 2d. I had expected to see the soldiers better clad than I found them—they were very ragged and dirty. Our camp was a short distance from the 2d Reg't.

October 2 (Wednesday)

There was a brief cavalry skirmish at Springfield Station, Va., about 12 miles south of Washington.

In a move to somewhat control wartime profiteering, Gov. A.B. Moore of Alabama issued a proclamation against tradesmen and government suppliers overcharging for services and materials.

In Richmond, a list of enemy aliens was being prepared for publication in the local papers. This caused quite a stir in the community.

Jackman, Pvt., "The Orphan Brigade," Mumfordville, Ky.:

> The company held a council of war in the morning and resolved to go into the service under old organization. That evening we fell in and marched to the headquarters of the 2d Ky., where we were sworn into the service of the Confederate States by Maj. Hewitt. We were to serve for three years or during the war. When we started back, the soldiers standing about who then considered themselves veterans, but who had, in fact, seen no service, commenced bawling out: "Sold to the Dutch—sold to the Dutch" in order to make us feel bad.
>
> Just before sundown the company fell in under arms and we marched out beyond Mumfordsville to do picket duty. There was a company of the "veterans" with us. They guarded the dirt road—we the pike. Our base, though, was the same place, in an old orchard near town. That night one of our boys, while out on vidette, shot at an old sow, thinking her an enemy—one of the "vets" shot at a rock in the road, thinking it a sneaking foe. Just before daylight my time came to go on vidette and had not been on past long before I heard many hoofs clattering on the pike, advancing with the rattling of sabres, and loud talk. My hair at first went "on end" but soon the horsemen were close up and I could see through the gray light of morning their still grayer uniforms. They were scouts returning to camp.

Wills, Pvt., 8th Illinois Infantry, Bird's Point, opposite Cairo, Illinois:

> Just at noon yesterday orders came to strike tents and in an hour we were under way and have come to a halt in this forsaken hole. It seems the 8th can't get out of hearing of the Cairo morning and evening gun anyway. Our major says they are talking of chucking us into Cairo and making us garrison it this winter. I'll be tempted to desert if 'tis so. The 22d call us the featherbed regiment now, and if they keep us this way much longer we will be tender as women. It was late and we were tired when we pitched our tents last night and we didn't "ditch round" as usual, trusting to providence for a dry night. But 'twas confidence misplaced and some of the boys found the ground slightly damp under them this morning. It has been raining like the devil all A.M. and the mud is quite

salubrious.... I have disposed of all my surplus baggage and now have two shirts, two pair socks, one blanket, one pair pants, one coat, one pair shoes, one hat, toothbrush, and one pocket comb. That's all I am worth.... You scout the idea of one's liking such a life as this. I tell you that I never was so well satisfied in my life as I have been since I joined the army. I do really enjoy it all the time, and if our boys here write the truth home they will say the same. Nobody ever heard me grumble a word about soldiering and never will if they don't station us in Cairo.

October 3 (Thursday)

Because of the lack of storage space in New Orleans, Gov. Thomas O. Moore of Louisiana banned the shipment of cotton to that city "during the existence of the blockade." This was a two-pronged effort. It was also meant to force the recognition of the Confederacy by England and France by withholding cotton from their industries. While England was not, as yet, in trouble on this point, such trouble would be reached shortly.

Federal troops from the Alexandria, Va., area occupied the area around Pohick Church just south of Alexandria. There was more cavalry skirmishing around Springfield Station, Va.

October 4 (Friday)

President Lincoln watched a balloon ascent in Washington and conferred with officials from Frémont's Department of the West. In the west, the Confederate government signed treaties with the Shawnee and Seneca Indians and would sign another with the Cherokees on the 7th of October.

The U.S.S. *South Carolina* captured 4000 to 5000 stands of arms when the Confederate schooners *Ezilda* and *Joseph H. Toone* were taken near South Pass of the Mississippi River, south of New Orleans.

On August 17, 1861, President Davis had issued a proclamation, based on an act of the Confederate Congress of August 8th, ordering all enemy aliens to leave the Confederacy within forty days. The War Office clerk in Richmond recorded that several applications had been received from "aliens" to leave the country, provided their names would not be published in the local papers. Some applicants hinted at bribery to keep their names undisclosed. When this was refused, the applicants withdrew their papers.

October 5 (Saturday)

In England, the London *Post* published an editorial backing the Confederacy, while the London *Times* leaned towards the Union.

Jackman, Pvt., "The Orphan Brigade," Bowling Green, Ky.:

> In the evening two companies took the train for Bowling Green and arrived there just after dark. When we saw the camp fires in the suburbs, all said the world was there encamped. We knew little about armies then. The two companies immediately marched out 2 miles N.W. from town where two other companies, [purported] to be in the same regiment, were encamped. They had guard on, and Leander Washington Applegate was Corporal of said guard. Leander talked wonderfully through his nose and offered us no little amusement. I afterwards found him to be a "bully fellow." He at last let us in and we pitched tents, dark as it was. We had no straw and I came near freezing or as much as one of the boys wound my shawl around himself leaving me on the ground without covering. When I awoke my teeth were chattering. I then placed my friend in a freezing condition by unwinding him.

Barber, Pvt., Co. D, 15th Illinois Volunteer Infantry, Jefferson City, Mo.:

> It rained all night and continued to rain all day. We were in open cars and got thoroughly drenched. When we arrived at Jefferson City, we were ordered to keep on the train in the pelting storm until further orders, but those orders came right speedily. Lt. Col. Ellis defied the authority of the commander of the post and told his men to seek shelter, which they were not slow in doing. Col. Ellis was immediately put under arrest, and there was a fair prospect for a general row. The boys were determined to see Ellis all right if they had to fight for him, but he was soon released and marched us up to the State Capitol, within whose walls we took shelter.
>
> Our company took up their quarters in the Senate Chamber, where only a few months before the

traitor Governor of Missouri, Jackson, and his confederates were plotting treason and endeavoring to drag Missouri into the whirlpool of secession. On the walls hung life-sized portraits of Benton and Jackson. Though dumb, they seemed to speak to us in burning words of eloquence to drive the traitorous foe from the soil of Missouri.

The streets of the city wore a desolate aspect. War's rude finger had left its mark. Traitors and patriots met on the street with set teeth and blazing eyes, brother against brother, and father against son. Missouri at this time was in a terrible state of anarchy....

October 6 (Sunday)

The pony express across the western plains was officially discontinued after a brief but spectacular 18 months in business. The legend of those brave men who withstood the elements and Indian attacks would live long after they were all gone.

Barber, Pvt., Co. D, 15th Illinois Volunteer Infantry, Tipton, Mo.:

> Tipton is a nice village, containing one thousand inhabitants, surrounded by as splendid a country as the eye ever looked upon. Here Frémont's grand army was concentrating preparatory to that grand campaign which was to sweep the rebel horde from Missouri, but strange to say, Frémont permitted Price and his army which had been up to Lexington and captured Mulligan and his command, to pass back across his flank without molesting him. While we were camped here, we received a visit from the Secretary of War—Cameron. The weather soon set in very rainy and we were in danger of being flooded. In this emergency, the boys commenced tearing down several old buildings near camp to get lumber to protect us from the wet, but our proceedings were summarily stopped by an order from Col. Turner, who declared we should pay for every board and stick we had taken; but Col. Ellis was standing by and he gave the boys one of his peculiar winks and then we knew we had a strong advocate in our behalf. Gen. Frémont soon issued an order for us to go to the lumber yard and get what lumber was necessary to build floors in our tents, but we did not stay long to enjoy it.

Jackman, Pvt., "The Orphan Brigade," Bowling Green, Ky.:

> The next day we established Camp Warren on the spot. Col. H. came out and commenced organizing the regt. There were already four companies in camp—a company from Owensboro, the Citizen Guards, The "Portland Roughs" from Portland, and our company. A camp guard was established and drilling commenced. We soon after got a kettle drum which was rattled to perfection by Mon. or Prof. Francois Gevers. While there we had good rations issued and we learned how to cook them. After being in camp a week or so I was detailed to work in a bake oven in town and on the first day lost my shawl. A day or two afterwards the regiment moved over nearer town to Camp "Dismal." The next day the rain poured down incessantly. My brother Don Quixote was in police pulling up the tall ragweeds about camp.... "Bro. Don" was not in a good humor and I shall not attempt to say what he said on that occasion. That night I went to a hotel but I had been used to sleeping on the ground and could not sleep in a good bed—I rested badly.
>
> The next morning we took train for Russellville but did not leave Bowling Green until nearly night. When we got to R. it was dark as pitch and the rain pouring down in torrents. We got off the cars and marched to the Court House where we quartered for the night. The following day... we went regularly into camp....
>
> While at Camp "Magruder," the people treated us well. Many ladies visited our camp and often brought us baskets of nice provisions. Here we first drilled in battalion, our regiment being of pretty good size. Our drums were increased to at least a dozen, small and great, and the band at reveille had to march (drumming) through all the streets. The noise was sufficient to wake the Seven Sleepers.

October 7 (Monday)

In Missouri, Frémont, late and slow, left St. Louis for Springfield to command the chase after Sterling Price, who was withdrawing towards Lexington.

Secretary of War Simon Cameron left for an "inspection" trip of the western area, carrying with him a letter from Lincoln to Brig. Gen. Samuel R. Curtis, asking Curtis's opinion on whether Frémont should be relieved. In Washington, Lincoln conferred with the Cabinet about Frémont and other things military.

Day, Pvt., Co. B, 25th Massachusetts Volunteer Infantry, Worcester, Mass.:

We were today mustered into the service of the United States by Capt. John M. Goodhue, U.S.A. The company is designated as Company B, and the regiment as the 25th Massachusetts volunteers. I suppose we are now stuck for three years unless sooner shot.... Most of the officers and many of the enlisted men have done military duty either in the state militia, or as three-months men around Washington. See we are not an entirely green crowd. The officers are a fine looking body of young men, and I think, with a little flattery and catering to their vanity, we shall get along nicely with them.

October 8 (Tuesday)

The Union Department of the Cumberland changed commanders. Brig. Gen. Robert Anderson, the hero of Sumter, was in ill health and suffered a breakdown. Brig. Gen. William T. Sherman, his second-in-command, assumed command of the Department, with headquarters in Louisville. Anderson would never return to active service. After a period of recovery, he lived in New York, where he took evening strolls, wearing a long cloak to hide his general's stars; he became something of a local celebrity. Sherman aggressively assumed command, and he soon made such demands for troops and expressed so much concern for his command that he, too, seemed to be on the verge of collapse.

October 9 (Wednesday)

Confederate Gen. Richard H. Anderson landed one thousand troops on Santa Rosa Island near Pensacola, to attack Ft. Pickens. His goal was the Federal batteries commanding the entrance to Pensacola Bay. After some fighting around one of the batteries, they were forced to withdraw by Union reinforcements from the fort itself.

October 10 (Thursday)

There was little activity this day. Troops, both North and South, were moving into new quarters, setting up winter camps, and enduring the dull monotony of camp life.

Wills, 3rd Sgt., 8th Illinois Infantry, Bird's Point, opposite Cairo, Illinois:

I have just finished a dinner of cider, cake, bread, butter, etc. We have just been paid off and of course have to indulge in a few delicacies for a while. Last Tuesday we were ordered to strike tents and pack for a march. It wasn't much of a march though, for we were put on the cars and rolled out to Charleston, 12 miles from here, where we camped on a beautiful little prairie adjoining town. The 11th Illinois, Taylor's artillery, and two companies of cavalry and our regiment formed the party....

We came down from Charleston Thursday. We marched about 10 miles of the way through an immense (it seemed so to me) cypress swamp. I think Mrs. Stowe's "Dred" would have enjoyed that swamp hugely. It was a rather interesting piece of scenery for a first view, but I don't think I should enjoy living in sight of it. The 18th, Col. Lawler, worked six or eight weeks in this swamp repairing bridges the secesh had burnt, and it put half their men on the sick list. We got our pay in treasury notes, but they are as good as the gold. Lots of the boys have traded them off for gold "even up." I get $21 this time for two months and five days, our other boys got $14 or $15. I am third sergeant now, our second having been appointed sergeant major. I think I would rather be sergeant, for the field officers make a kind of servant of the sergeant major.

I send you a couple of daguerreotypes to let you see what a "skeleton" I have become. Our boys are all very well. The 17th is in pretty bad condition, nearly half of them sick and as a regiment pretty badly used up....

Barber, Pvt., Co. D, 15th Illinois Volunteer Infantry, Camp Hunter, near Tipton, Mo.:

We were now paid two months' wages, less the $10.00 received from Gen. Frémont, and moved camp three miles south of town to Camp Hunter. We now commenced preparations to march. The army was divided into three divisions. Gen. Hunter commanded the first, McKinstry the second and Gen. Asboth the third. The 15th was in the first brigade, Grand Army of the West. Lt. Col. Ellis now put us through a very thorough course of drilling and we soon had the name of being one of the best drilled regiments in the army. Col. Turner lacked the necessary qualifications for drill-master, and he made bungling work whenever he attempted to drill the regiment, but he was a strict disciplinarian—so strict that he got the ill-will of most of his men—and he soon became unpopular. He felt it and kept aloof from the regiment a great deal....

October 12 (Saturday)

At Charleston, S.C., Mason and Slidell, Commissioners to England and France respectively, slipped past the blockading ships aboard the Confederate ship *Theodora* bound for Cuba.

James Murray Mason was almost 63 years old. A Virginia aristocrat, he was educated at the College of William and Mary, and practised law in Winchester, Va., until he entered politics in 1826. Elected to the U.S. Senate in 1847, he was a avid supporter of slavery, advocating the counting of only whites for representation in the U.S. Congress, and he drafted the Fugitive Slave Act of 1850. His attitude was arrogant and domineering in almost all meetings with his fellow legislators. At the outbreak of war Mason offered his services to President Davis, who appointed him Commissioner to England because of Mason's experience in the Senate Foreign Relations Committee. Mason would have little success in England for the South. Returning to Canada in 1866, he waited until President Johnson's second amnesty proclamation to return to Virginia in 1868. He died in Alexandria, Va., on April 28, 1871.

John Slidell, 68, a native New Yorker, moved to New Orleans in 1819 and practised law. He was elected to the U.S. House of Representatives in 1843, and to the U.S. Senate in 1853. He worked with other Southern legislators to repeal the Missouri Compromise and to get Kansas admitted to the Union as a slave state. Staying with the South, he was appointed by Davis as Commissioner to France, where Slidell failed in most of his dealings with the French government. At the end of the war he remained in Paris for a period of time, never seeking pardon from the Federal government. He died in London on July 29, 1871.

In a historic engagement, three Confederate ships, the metal-sheathed ram *Manassas* leading the armed steamers *Ivy* and *James L. Day*, attacked five Federal ships near Head of Passes, south of New Orleans in the Mississippi delta. The *Manassas* rammed the U.S.S. *Richmond* and forced her and the U.S.S. *Vincennes* aground under heavy fire before the Confederate ram withdrew. Acting Master Edward F. Devens of the *Vincennes* reported:

> From the appearance of the *Richmond's* side in the vicinity of the hole, I should say that the ram had claws or hooks attached to her... for the purpose of tearing out the plank from the ship's side. It is a most destructive invention... [*Manassas*] resembles in shape a cigar cut lengthwise, and [is] very low in the water. She must be covered with railroad iron as all the shells which struck her glanced off, some directly at right angles. You could hear the shot strike quite plainly. They did not appear to trouble her much as she ran up the river at a very fast rate.

Another historic event took place at Carondelet, Mo., when the first Federal ironclad, the *St. Louis*, was launched.

Day, Pvt., Co. B, 25th Massachusetts Volunteer Infantry, Worcester, Mass.:

> The boys are settling down to the routine of military duty, and getting accustomed to camp life. They take kindly to discipline, and seem anxious to learn the drill. Presentations are the order of the day. The adjutant has had a horse presented to him by his firemen friends. A great stout, clumsy, good-natured horse. I should think he was better adapted for hauling a fire engine than for a parade horse, but perhaps will answer the purpose well enough. The major's friends have also presented him with a horse. A good kind of horse enough. Nothing very stylish or dashy about him for a war charger, but perhaps he can smell the battle as far as any horse. The major, in a clever little speech, assured his friends that they would never hear of the nag's striking his best gait to the rear. The major being a man of immense rotundity, I imagine that the horse, after carrying him a couple of hours, would feel willing to give boot to go into the ranks rather than remain on the staff.
>
> The Worcester ladies, with commendable patriotism, have presented us with a splendid silk banner (the national colors), and have enjoined us to carry it with us in our wanderings, and return it again to them without dishonor. And we have sworn by a thousand stout hearts and bright bayonets, that

banner shall float above the battlements of secession and be again returned to them, crowned with the laurel wreaths of victory. And when amid the flame and thunder of the battle, we look on its bright folds, remembering its fair donors, [we] rush to victory and glory.

After hearing several candidates for the office of chaplain, they have finally settled on Rev. Horace James, pastor of the old South church, Worcester. I think they have shown good judgment in selecting a chaplain of the orthodox faith, as no one visiting our camp for an hour could doubt their belief in the existence of the burning lake by the way they consign each other to that locality. The pretty girls, God bless their souls, are always first and foremost in every good work, and they are now in session at the Agricultural Hall, busily at work for the soldiers. They are making repairs and alterations to our uniforms, sewing on chevrons and doing whatever small jobs of needlework we may desire. They have also furnished us with needles, thread, wax, buttons, pincushions, pins and other small articles which we may need. For all of which they will please accept the warmest emotions of grateful hearts.

October 15 (Tuesday)

In Missouri, self-promoted Gen. Merriwether Jeff Thompson, normally called "Jeff," burned the Big River Bridge near Potosi and captured some Federal troops. This followed by one day his announcement to the local citizens to "drive the invaders from your soil or die among your native hills." Thompson, a native of Harpers Ferry, western Virginia, at age 35 had been involved in many things since leaving his native state. He was rejected by both West Point and the Virginia Military Institute, but still aspired to a military career. At the beginning of the war, he organized a battalion of volunteers and offered their services to the Governor. This was rejected, so he began his own war on the Union, operating in the swampy areas and raiding the countryside. He became known as the "Swamp Fox of the Confederacy," operating both as a part of other Confederate forces and as an independent command. He surrendered his command on May 9, 1865, finally moved to Memphis and then to New Orleans, where he died on September 5, 1876.

October 18 (Friday)

In Missouri, Federal forces moved against "General" Jeff Thompson from Cape Girardeau.

Wills, 3rd Sgt., 8th Illinois Infantry, Bird's Point, opposite Cairo, Illinois:

> We yesterday drew our overcoats, and splendid ones they are. The cloth is light blue and they reach nearly to our feet. They have capes on them that come over a fellow's head nicely nights. The weather is about like you have I expect, but I know we will be very comfortable with the clothing we have in any weather. I wouldn't have the war end before next spring for anything, for I want to try a winter out of doors.... They are just burying some poor fellow. We have had several deaths in the regiment lately. They do not play the prettiest dead marches here.
>
> I have been detached from the company for a week acting as sheriff of a court martial.... I have four men a day to guard the prisoners and two orderlies to send errands for me, so I play big injun strongly. The prisoner murdered a comrade while we were down at Norfolk. Smote him on the head with a club. He is from Company B of our regiment. That company, besides this case, had a man shot dead the other day by one of their own company. An accident. This morning they had a man stabbed, and day before yesterday they confined one of their men for trying to kill two others. For all this, they are really a good company of men....

October 20 (Sunday)

A lady visited the Confederate War Office in Richmond and left a "programme of the enemy's contemplated movements." The lady in question, not identified, had recently reached Richmond from Washington, where she had attended a dinner party with Gen. John A. Dix, at which the deployment strategy was discussed. The movements included Bank's advance on Manassas after crossing the Potomac near Leesburg, and the expeditions of Generals Burnside (into North Carolina) and Butler (into Louisiana).

Brigadier Gen. Charles P. Stone crossed some troops at Edwards Ferry–Ball's Bluff on a short reconnaissance and then withdrew them after a short time. Reconnaissances were also made to

Hunter's Mill and Thornton Station in northern Virginia.

October 21 (Monday)

At Ball's Bluff on the Potomac, a disaster awaited Union forces. Brig. Gen. Charles P. Stone ferried his troops across the river in wholly inadequate boats to the base of the bluff and downstream of Edwards Ferry. The immediate commander at Ball's Bluff was one Col. Edward D. Baker, U.S. Senator from Oregon and a personal friend of Lincoln's. After light skirmishing in the morning, the Confederates drove the Federals back to the edge of the bluff in the afternoon. A mass exodus began. Col. Baker was killed, the boats got swamped in the water, men drowned, were captured, or fled on foot. Each side had about 1700 troops committed during the battle. The Union lost 49 killed, 158 wounded, and 714 missing—a total of 921 casualties. The South lost only 36 killed, 117 wounded and 2 missing. The blame was placed on Stone, and he was accused of treason. Later imprisoned, he was released and restored to duty, but his career was ruined. McClellan, who ordered this debacle, escaped criticism.

October 23 (Wednesday)

The officers and men of the Confederate privateer *Savannah* went on trial in New York for piracy, in a move to discourage this type of activity.

Barber, Pvt., Co. D, 15th Illinois Volunteer Infantry, opposite Warsaw, Mo.:

> The next morning we were early on the move; marched twenty miles, and on the 23rd we camped on the south side of the Osage opposite the ruined city of Warsaw. We laid over here one day—for what purpose I do not know. Price was reported only twenty-five miles off. We gave him an opportunity to disband that portion of his army who lived in the country through which he passed and rest the remainder. Then we started after him again. We got as far as Mt. Au Revoir and halted again. We were pressing Price too hard. It would never do. We must wait and let him get farther ahead. So we waited a week.

October 24 (Thursday)

Western Union announced that the transcontinental telegraph was finally complete, with the last segment from Denver to Sacramento finished. In western Virginia, the people voted overwhelmingly to form a new state.

Colonel and Senator Baker had his funeral today in Washington, attended by the President and many members of Congress. Lincoln also informed Brigadier Gen. R.S. Curtis that he should deliver enclosed orders to Major Gen. Frémont and Gen. David Hunter. The orders were to relieve Frémont of command and place Hunter in his stead. If, however, Frémont had won a battle, or a battle was pending in the interim, the orders were not to be delivered.

October 25 (Friday)

The charge of Frémont's cavalry into Springfield, Mo., was a gallant affair, even if the opposition was almost nonexistent. Much was made of this by Frémont's supporters, but he knew the game was up and was making sure that no one could reach him with reassignment orders. His actions did little to halt the retreat of Price from Lexington, and nothing to affect the overall military situation.

At Greenpoint, N.Y., the keel was laid for the U.S.S. *Monitor*, a historic ship that would make the existing navies of the world obsolete.

The concept of amphibious operations in coastal warfare was supported by Flag Officer Du Pont in his letter to Assistant Secretary of the Navy Fox: "Landing a brigade today to exercise Ferry boats and Surf boats—reaping immense advantages from the experiment by seeing the defects."

October 27 (Sunday)

In the Atlantic, the C.S.S. *Sumter*, the scourge of Union shipping, captured and burned the schooner *Trowbridge* after removing five months' provisions from the schooner's holds.

In Springfield, Mo., Frémont stated he would pursue Price, who was believed to be advancing on the city. Actually, Price was in full retreat in the opposite direction.

A boat expedition from the U.S.S. *Louisiana*, led by Lt. Alfred Hopkins, surprised and burned three Confederate ships at Chincoteaque Inlet, Va. This was where the citizens had taken an oath of allegiance to the Union government and presented a petition on October 14th, stating their "abhorrence of the secession heresy."

Wills, 3rd Sgt., 8th Illinois Infantry, Bird's Point, opposite Cairo, Illinois:

Although soldiering is a hugely lazy life, yet these short days we seem to have but little spare time. We are up nearly an hour before sun up, have breakfast about sunrise, drill (company) from 8 to 10. Cards until dinner time, 12; lounge or read until 2; battalion drill until 4:30 or 5, supper, and then dress parade at 4:45; from candle lighting until bedtime (taps), 10, we have cards mixed with singing or some awful noises from Sam Nutt and Fred Norcott. Those two boys can make more noise than three threshing machines.... That gunboat, *New Era* that the papers blow so much about is of no account as a gunboat. She is laid up at Mound City for a battery. The men on her have told me that she wouldn't half stand before a land battery that amounted to anything. . .

The sickly season is over now and the health is improving very much. We had 18 on the sick list in our company three weeks ago and now we have but three, and they are only diarrhoea or the like. I tell you I feel as strong as two mules and am improving. I haven't been the least unwell yet....

October 28 (Monday)

In a command change in the west, Gen. Albert Sydney Johnston assumed command of the Army of Central Kentucky at Bowling Green, where Gen. Simon Bolivar Buckner was holding the fort.

October 29 (Tuesday)

A fleet of 77 vessels, the largest Federal fleet assembled to date, sailed from Ft. Monroe on Hampton Roads for Port Royal, S.C. The fleet was commanded by Flag Officer Du Pont, and was carrying over 16,000 troops, commanded by Brigadier Gen. Thomas W. Sherman. The intent of this massive array of armament was to take Port Royal for a refuelling and servicing station for the blockading squadrons. This would not be an easy task, since Port Royal was one of the first locations heavily fortified by the Confederacy. To add to the problems, heavy gales were awaiting the fleet off Cape Hatteras in North Carolina.

October 30 (Wednesday)

Downriver from Ft. Donelson, the Confederates sank stone-filled boats to discourage Union gunboats from coming upriver. They didn't do much good when the river rose.

Barber, Pvt., Co. D, 15th Illinois Volunteer Infantry, Mt. Au Revoir, Mo.:

While we were in camp at Mt. Au Revoir, numerous peddlers frequented our camp, peddling apples, peaches, etc. and we had good reasons for believing that these very peddlers were a portion of the rebel army, and as these came to their homes, they were permitted to remain, attend to their farms, gather in their harvest, etc., and at a call from Price, again take to the field.

It was a very common sight to see three or four able-bodied young men at the different farm houses along the route, eyeing us with a look of triumph. They all professed to be peaceful citizens and perfectly neutral. I never had a doubt in my own mind but what Price disbanded a large part of his army in this way. He knew perfectly well that he could not cope with us in battle and so he adopted that plan as the most feasible way of saving his army and annoying us. He succeeded but too well.

October 31 (Thursday)

Day, Pvt., Co. B, 25th Massachusetts Volunteer Infantry, Worcester, Mass.:

It seems that at last we have been ordered from these cold, frosty climes, to a warmer and more genial one—the Sunny South. After partaking of a collation furnished by the ladies at the hall, at 3 P.M. we broke camp, and taking all our worldly effects upon our backs, preceded by our band, marched through Highland and Main Streets to the common, where we took cars for New York. At the common we were met by a large concourse of citizens, friends and relatives of the regiment, who took us by the hand, giving us words of encouragement and a hearty God bless you.

Here were leave takings that required some nerve to suppress the rising tear. Probably some of us have seen our friends for the last time on earth, and bade them the last good-bye. But we will go forward to duty, trusting in God, and hoping for the best.

NOVEMBER 1861

This month found both North and South having gained no advantage in the seven months since

Sumter was fired upon. There had been some battles in the east and west, but nothing very decisive that could break the stalemate. Both presidents were urging their respective field commanders to "do something," but this came to naught. Neither Johnston in Virginia or Frémont in Missouri were advancing their causes. Many of the troops were looking towards winter quarters.

November 1 (Friday)

As he went into voluntary retirement, Gen. Winfield Scott received a farewell visit from Lincoln and the Cabinet. Scott left for West Point somewhat disheartened. His replacement, 34-year-old George B. McClellan, had been carping about Scott for months, both in the press and at public gatherings. No doubt "Little Mac" had done a grand job organizing the Army of the Potomac, but he had done little else to endear him to officialdom. He seemed to talk incessantly about his "grand strategy", but did little to implement it.

The 77-ship fleet that sailed from Hampton Roads on October 29th was struck by a violent storm off Cape Hatteras. The ships were scattered, and one transport, *Governor*, sank, but Major John G. Reynolds and his battalion of marines on board were saved the following day by the U.S.S. *Sabine.*

At Springfield, Mo., Frémont had learned that the order removing him from command had been sent from Washington. He immediately closed off access to himself so that the order could not be delivered. Gen. Curtis, who was sent by Lincoln to deliver the order, had the order sent by a captain disguised as a local farmer who said he had to see Frémont about a local problem. When the captain gained his audience, he handed Frémont the order and the captain was immediately placed under arrest to keep the news quiet. Frémont then finally set out to attack Sterling Price, only to find that Price had fallen back sixty miles and was beyond his immediate reach.

Jackman, Pvt., "The Orphan Brigade," Bowling Green, Ky.:

> Camped at Russellville until the latter part of November when we moved by rail to Bowling Green. Many ladies were present at our departure to bid relatives farewell which was fine amid friends weeping on the part of the ladies. We went into Camp (Price) in the suburbs of town. Here we were regularly mustered into the service and drew our first uniforms.

Barber, Pvt., Co. D, 15th Illinois Volunteer Infantry, Mt. Au Revoir, Mo.:

> One day one of these neutral rebs came into camp with a load of apples to sell. He inadvertently betrayed his sentiments and, with the permission of Col. Ellis, the boys relieved him of his apples in less time than it takes to write it. Rollin and Milton, who were always on hand at such a time, managed to secure two bushels for tent No. 6. The fellow was lucky in getting off as well as he did. We soon resumed our march.... We had a splendid country to march through. It was well watered and timbered.... The last day but one before reaching Springfield, we had marched twenty-seven miles and had just eaten our supper and were preparing to lie down when an order came for us to reach Springfield by daylight, if possible, as a battle was expected the next day.

Day, Pvt., Co. B, 25th Massachusetts Volunteer Infantry, New York, N.Y.:

> We left Worcester about 5 o'clock last evening. Arriving at Norwich, we went aboard the large and splendid steamer *Connecticut,* the regiment numbering one thousand and thirty, with all our horses, wagons and camp equipage.... landing us in New York about 9 o'clock this morning. After disembarking and forming the regiment, we marched amid a perfect storm of applause and the New Yorkers' peculiar "Hi! hi!" to the City Hall park. A guard was then posted and the regiment dismissed until drum call. A committee of gentlemen waited on the colonel, inviting him, his officers and the band, to a dinner at the Astor House. After they had gone, we fellows, by invitation, marched into the park barracks, to regale ourselves on mutton soup. And in all fairness, I must say that a worse soup or dirtier surroundings never came under my observation. I didn't hanker for any and beat a hasty retreat. If that soup didn't smell to heaven, it must have achieved a high altitude above the city.... I suppose the evening papers will have it that the 25th Massachusetts regiment dined at the Astor House. So we shall get the name, if we missed the turkey.... With an easy, swinging gait, in column

of platoons, we marched down Broadway looking the very soul of soldiery, and were greeted with a perfect ovation all along the route... we crossed to Jersey City and took cars for Philadelphia....

November 2 (Saturday)

Today the British steamer *Bermuda*, a blockade runner loaded with 2000 bales of cotton, escaped from Charleston.

After being in command for 100 days, spending in excess of $12 million, issuing an unauthorized emancipation declaration, and refusing to bow to the commands of the President of the United States, John C. Frémont sent a farewell address to his command and returned to his wife in St. Louis, Mo. There were some protests about his removal but these soon died.

"General" Jeff Thompson was active in Missouri and expeditions were being sent against him daily. The Atlantic coast Confederate papers were warning the populace about an impending Federal landing "somewhere" south of North Carolina. The Federal fleet was approaching South Carolina and Port Royal.

In Tennessee, the governor who took the State into the Confederacy now asked the citizens to furnish rifles and shotguns for the troops. The shortage of weapons was very acute in the South at this stage.

Barber, Pvt., Co. D, 15th Illinois Volunteer Infantry, Springfield, Mo.:

> The other divisions had taken different routes and reached Springfield first. We had twenty-seven miles to go yet, but the roads were so muddy and the country so rough that it was long past daylight before our division came in sight of the city, and then only about one-third of the command came in together. The rest were worn out for want of sleep and rest and stopped on the road.... We had marched nearly sixty miles without sleep and very little rest, and to our mortification there was no prospect of a battle at that time.... A few days before, Frémont's body guard, under command of Maj. Zagonyi, had had a severe battle at Springfield. With this small body of men, he charged twenty times his number and drove the enemy from town, but over one-half of his command perished in the fight. This charge was one of the most brilliant and bravest on record....
>
> Gen. Frémont is now relieved of his command and Gen. Hunter assumed temporary command. Springfield is a beautiful young city, but like many other places in Missouri, war had left its blighting marks there. The bloody battle field of Wilson's Creek was only twelve miles from here. After resting for a few days, we were ordered to counter-march, this leaving all southern Missouri open again to the ravages of the enemy, besides having the miserable consciousness that our campaign had been a miserable failure. Our march back was easy and slow, making from ten to fifteen miles per day. Our ox team proved to be of great good to us.... We halted at Warsaw a few days and then went back to our old Camp Hunter.
>
> We had a considerable quantity of fruit and vegetables and a good deal of fresh meat. The latter article the boys procured mostly by confiscating such unlucky porkers as happened to come in their way. We had fresh beef issued to us two or three times a week.... We did not remain in Camp Hunter but a few days, but moved camp one and one-half miles north of Tipton.

Day, Pvt., Co. B, 25th Massachusetts Volunteer Infantry, Philadelphia, Pa.:

> Arrived in Philadelphia at 1 A.M.; were met at the depot by a committee of the citizens, and escorted to the old cooper-shop saloon, where we took breakfast. Our reception here was in striking contrast with that in New York yesterday. Instead of dark, gloomy, dirty barracks, with dirty, insolent attendants, we were taken to a large, clean, well-lighted hall where we were met by a corps of neat, well-dressed and courteous attendants, both ladies and gentlemen, who seemed to vie with each other in their attentions to our wants. The tables were neatly spread and contained even more than reasonably hungry men could desire. We had boiled corned beef, tongue, ham, brown and white bread, butter, pies, cake, fruit, tea, coffee, milk, etc. Not satisfied with our eating all we wanted, they emptied our haversacks and filled them with ham, tongue, bread, cake and apples, remarking at the same time that soldiers couldn't carry salt mule and hard tack through Philadelphia.
>
> The regiment now reformed for a march across the city to take the cars for Baltimore. As our band struck up the music, waking the echoes of the early morning, the windows on either side flew up and out

peered hundreds of heads, in their scantily arranged toilets, and with wild hurrahs and waving handkerchiefs, cheered us on our way. At 4 A.M. we were aboard the cars and moving towards Baltimore....

November 3 (Sunday)

Major Gen. David Hunter was now in command, relieving Frémont on this day. Hunter, at age 59, had been on active service since graduating from West Point in 1822. Promoted to Colonel and assigned to the 3rd U.S. Cavalry, he was again promoted, to Brigadier General, three days later and commanded the 2d Division at Bull Run, where he was severely wounded. Promoted to Major General in August, he was later sent to Missouri to command a division in Frémont's army. His later claim to fame would be as the "scourge" of the Shenandoah Valley, and as the head of the committee that tried the Lincoln assassination conspirators. He died in Washington in February 1866.

At Fairfax Court House, Va., Gen. Thomas J. "Stonewall" Jackson readied to leave for Winchester to begin his Valley Campaign.

Day, Pvt., Co. B, 25th Massachusetts Volunteer Infantry, Baltimore, Md.:

> We reached Havre de Grace about noon. A heavy storm has set in. It is raining hard and the wind blows a gale. We crossed the Susquehanna river at this place on a big steam ferry boat and I must confess to some fears, as I looked from the car windows down to the water, a distance of nearly fifty feet, and wondered why we did not capsize. Here I saw a government mule pen. Several acres were enclosed, and I was told that the pen contained about 10,000 mules. A large number of negroes are employed taking care of them.... An hour's ride brought us to the famous gunpowder bridge, which crosses an arm of the Chesapeake bay not far from Baltimore. This bridge the rebels attempted to burn and partially succeeded. Many of the charred timbers are still to be seen on the bridge. We reached Baltimore about 3 P.M. and left the cars in the midst of a drenching rain and marched about a mile through the rain and wind to the steamboat landing, the band playing "The Campbells are Coming." No boat being in readiness to take us to Annapolis, Col. Upton told the captains of companies that they must find quarters for their men and be ready for an early start in the morning. Capt. Clark obtained a loft in a grain store for his company, where we passed the night very comfortably.

November 4 (Monday)

At Fairfax Court House, "Stonewall" Jackson bid a temporary farewell to his old brigade, now called the Stonewall Brigade, a name it would carry for the war. He was headed towards a part of Virginia that he knew intimately, and he would make good use of that knowledge.

At Port Royal, S.C., the Coast Survey Ship *Vixen*, escorted by the U.S.S. *Ottawa* and *Seneca*, entered the Sound to take depth readings in the channel. This was not done without protest by the Confederate Navy, which fired upon the Union survey ships commanded by Commodore Tattnall.

Day, Pvt., Co. B, 25th Massachusetts Volunteer Infantry, Annapolis, Md.:

> ... morning in Baltimore, and a stiller or more quiet place I never saw.... It looks like a deserted city. We took a hurried glance at a portion of the city, visiting Pratt street where the assault on the 6th Massachusetts took place. The bullet holes and scars on the walls of the buildings gave proof that the boys got a good deal interested while passing through the street. We embarked on the steamer Louisiana about 9 A.M. for Annapolis. As we steamed past old Ft. McHenry, I was reminded of an interesting scrap of history connected with this fort. When the British fleet bombarded this fort during the last war with England, there was aboard one of the ships an American prisoner, a Mr. Key, I think his name was, who watched with the most intense anxiety the result of the bombardment, and during its progress, wrote the song that has since become famous as one of our national anthems, The Star Spangled Banner.... Arrived at Annapolis about noon and marched up to the Naval Academy where we quartered and took dinner with the 21st Massachusetts, now doing garrison duty at this post....

November 7 (Thursday)

At Port Royal, S.C., the fleet under the command of Flag Officer Du Pont entered Port Royal Sound and engaged the Confederate squadron (not much opposition) and Forts Walker (located on Hilton

Head) and Beauregard (located on Bay Point). Commander Tattnall used his small Confederate flotilla to rescue troops from the forts but could do little else. The troops abandoned the forts readily enough under the accurate and withering fire of the Federal fleet. Gen. Thomas Sherman's 12,000 Union troops were soon ashore and the occupation of Hilton Head and Port Royal began, and would last for the remainder of the war. Du Pont wrote later, "It is not my temper to rejoice over fallen foes, but this must be a gloomy night in Charleston." Indeed it was.

Brigadier Gen. U.S. Grant fought his first battle, capturing a Confederate fortified position near Belmont, Mo.: The Confederate General Polk sent troops across the river to counterattack and Grant was forced to retreat. As a battle, Belmont amounted to little. Neither side gained an advantage, but Grant learned some lessons here that would do him good later.

November 8 (Friday)

Mason and Slidell left Havana, Cuba, on the British mail ship *Trent*, bound for London. The *Trent* met the Union ship *San Jacinto* in the Bahamas Passage. When the two ships parted, Mason, Slidell and their aides were aboard the Union ship and bound for Northern waters. The *Trent* sailed on to England. This set off a major international incident which would take some time to resolve.

Lt. James E. Jouett of the U.S.S. *Santee* organized a "cutting out" expedition of small boats near Galveston, Tex., where the schooner *Royal Yacht* was captured and burned. These types of expedition were very popular in naval warfare during this period. Usually they consisted of two or more ship's boats loaded with sailors and marines who used the cover of darkness and muffled oars to approach the target ship.

Lee arrived in Savannah to take command of a very large territory which was blockaded and poorly manned. The news about the capture of Port Royal sent tremors through the city of Savannah, prompting many of the people to pack up and head inland for safety. At Hilton Head, S.C., Federal troops pushed out from their beachhead into the area around Beaufort.

The pro-Union population in east Tennessee tired of waiting for Federal help, and they began their own campaign against the Confederacy by burning bridges and generally harassing the local Confederate commander, Brig. Gen. Felix Zollicoffer, who called for reinforcements. This part of Tennessee would never be completely dominated by the Confederacy. Zollicoffer, a native of Tennessee, was 49 in the fall of 1861. A former editor of several newspapers in eastern Tennessee, a member of the U.S. House of Representatives, and a duellist with the editor of the Nashville *Union*, he was appointed a Brigadier General of state troops by Gov. Harris. He was killed at Mill Springs in January 1862.

The Stonewall Brigade left Fairfax C.H. for Manassas to entrain for Winchester in a pouring rain.

November 9 (Saturday)

More heavy rain today as the trains carrying the Stonewall Brigade headed for Winchester, Va.

The Federal force in South Carolina captured Beaufort without a fight and blocked the Broad River, effectively cutting water communications between Charleston and Savannah. Lee, at his headquarters at Coosawhatchie, S.C., wrote to Confederate Secretary of War Judah P. Benjamin,

> The enemy having complete possession of the water and inland navigation, commands all the islands on the coast and threatens both Savannah and Charleston, and can come in his boats, within 4 miles of this place. His sloops of war and large steamers can come up Broad River to Mackay's Point, the mouth of the Pocotaligo, and his gunboats can ascend some distance up the Coosawhatchie and Tulifinny. We have no guns that can resist their batteries, and have no resources to meet them in the field.

In the west there were some command changes which would do much to shape later events. One major change was that Major Gen. Henry W. Halleck was assigned command of the Department of the Missouri, which encompassed Missouri, Arkansas, Illinois, and Kentucky west of the Cumberland River, and included Grant's command. Gen. William T. Sherman was also replaced in command by Gen. Don Carlos Buell, with Sherman leaving under a cloud.

Halleck, born in Westernville, N.Y., on January 16, 1815, was a great advocate of spit and polish.

He graduated from West Point, class of '39, three years ahead of Grant and Thomas, ranking third in his class. Without doubt one of the most brilliant officers in the Army at the beginning of the war, he was not one to make friends easily, and his aloof manner caused much resentment among his fellow officers, who often referred to him as "Old Brains" because of his intellect, and a "cold, calculating owl" because of his personality. He was no friend of either Grant or Sherman during his stay in the west, and he tried, unsuccessfully, to have Grant branded as a drunk and Sherman as a lunatic. Sherman said of Halleck that he "plans nothing, suggests nothing, is good for nothing." Before the war he had published many books on military subjects and was well regarded for his mental capacities. He, however, was not a good field general because of his cautious attitudes and his fear of doing something wrong. After his fiasco in May 1862 at Corinth, he was assigned to Washington to be the General-in-Chief (in reality a chief of staff) for the Army. In this position he caused only confusion and problems. When Grant became head of all the Union armies in March 1864, Halleck was reduced to little more than a message passer, and he often did that badly. After the war, he served briefly in California and then in Kentucky. He died in Louisville on January 9, 1872.

Buell began the war held in high esteem by Scott, and he showed great promise. A graduate of USMA, class of '41, he served with distinction in the Mexican War and later in several positions. He remained in the Army at a time when many were leaving for civilian careers. Promoted to Brigadier General in May 1861, he commanded a division in the Army of the Potomac until he replaced Sherman in Kentucky. Promoted to Major General, he brought his troops to the relief of Grant at Pittsburg Landing after the Battle of Shiloh in April 1862, and became the hero of the hour. But by September 30, 1862, he was notified that because of his performance in command since April, he would be replaced in command by Major Gen. George H. Thomas. Thomas, insisting that Buell was on the verge of attacking the Confederates, requested a delay until after the impending battle was settled, so the replacement order was cancelled. Buell led his forces against Bragg on October 8, 1862, at the Battle of Perryville with some success, but he failed to pursue the retreating Bragg, enraging both his superiors and the general public. On October 24, 1862, he was removed from command and never led troops again. He would be "investigated" until he was mustered out of the Army in May 1864. He lived much longer than many of his contemporaries, dying in Kentucky in 1898, at age 70.

November 10 (Sunday)

Federal troops expanded their hold on Port Royal, S.C., by carrying out an expedition against Braddock's Point. The last train carrying the Stonewall Brigade to Winchester left Manassas at 8:30 A.M. and arrived at Strasburg about sundown.

Allen, Pvt., Co. K, 1st Battalion, 10th Illinois Cavalry, Camp Butler, Illinois:

> When we reached this place, about midnight on the 28th ult., we found no quarters prepared for our reception and spent the remainder of the night by fires which we built in the woods near our present camp. John Hill was so much discouraged that he left next morning after breakfast. On Tuesday we put up our tents and since then we have had as comfortable quarters as any soldiers at Camp Butler.... All of our boys have been sworn into service except Thomas Whitesides, who backed out and went home because he lacked the spunk of a soldier.... We were examined by the Surgeon, which made some of our modest boys blush.... There are nearly 6000 soldiers here at present. Most of them are Cavalry. Our regiment numbers about 700.... There is a Company in this Regiment from Chicago, nearly all of whom are sailors. If they are not a wild set, there never was one. The Company next to ours in the camp has a good many Germans in it and is known as the Dutch Company.... I have not been to Springfield since I came out here, but expect to pay our Capital a visit soon, as I wish to see the President Lincoln's home and the public buildings....

November 11 (Monday)

Near Ft. Monroe, Professor Thaddeus Lowe was making history by raising the balloon from the deck of the balloon-boat *G.W. Parke Custis.* The boat, purchased for $150, had been specially fitted for this purpose at the Washington Navy Yard and sent to Ft. Monroe. Lowe reported,

> I left the navy-yard early Sunday morning, the 10th instant... towed out by the steamer *Coeur de Lion*, having on board competent assistant aeronauts, together with my new gas generating apparatus, which, though used for the first time, worked admirably. We located at the mouth of Mattawoman Creek, about three miles from the opposite Virginia shore. Yesterday [November 11] proceeded to make observations accompanied in my ascensions by Gen. Sickles and others. We had a fine view of the enemy's camp-fires during the evening, and saw the rebels constructing new batteries at Freestone Point.

The Stonewall Brigade marched from the railhead at Strasburg to Winchester, Va., in a bright sun. This helped to dry them out somewhat, after two days on the move in heavy rain.

An accidental gun explosion at Columbus, Ky., killed seven Confederate soldiers, and it also wounded Gen. Leonidas Polk, though not seriously.

November 13 (Wednesday)

McClellan had assumed an imperious attitude in his dealings with everyone. He firmly believed he was the "Savior of the Union," and he acted the part. On one occasion, Lincoln, Seward, and Lincoln's secretary John Hays visited McClellan's house. When informed by a servant that McClellan was out at a wedding, they decided to wait. When McClellan arrived about an hour later, he was informed that the President and the Secretary of State were awaiting him. He smiled, went past the room where they were waiting, and into another room. Half an hour later, the servant went looking for McClellan to remind him that his guests were still waiting, only to find that McClellan had gone to bed! Lincoln, humiliated, later commented that he would hold McClellan's horse if only he would bring success. However, from that time on, Lincoln summoned McClellan to the White House when he wanted to see him.

November 15 (Friday)

Capt. John Wilkes, aboard the *San Jacinto*, arrived at Hampton Roads, Va., for a fuel stop and informed the port authorities of his cargo of passengers: Mason, Slidell, et al. He refuelled and steamed north in accordance with his instructions to deliver his cargo to the Federal prison at Ft. Warren in Boston Harbor.

The Young Men's Christian Association (YMCA) organized the U.S. Christian Commission to serve the Federal troops. This organization would serve well for the duration of the war.

November 16 (Saturday)

Confederate Secretary of the Navy Mallory advertised for bids to build ironclad ships for the Confederate Navy. Four ships were to be built, each carrying four guns.

Cooler heads were beginning to appear over the "*Trent* affair," when both Senator Charles Sumner of Massachusetts and Postmaster Gen. Montgomery Blair urged the release of Mason and Slidell at once.

Day, Pvt., Co. B, 25th Massachusetts Volunteer Infantry, near Annapolis, Md.:

> Here it is the middle of November and the weather is most delightful. No frosts, but a warm, mellow atmosphere like our Indian summer in October.... While our farmers in New England are putting up and feeding their cattle in barns, the cattle here are luxuriating in white clover, young, sweet and tender enough to suit the most fastidious taste of any of the cattle on a thousand hills.... Some of the boys brought in some egg plants which grow about here. I never saw any before but am told they are very good when properly cooked. I am not disposed to doubt it, never having eaten any of them, but I cannot believe they would make good egg nog.
>
> We begin to see a little something of the peculiar institution—slavery. There are a great many negroes strolling around the camps, most of them runaways, and as Maryland is supposed to be a loyal state, we have no right to take sides and afford them protection.... The masters and hunters are frequently here looking up their boys, as they call them, and we generally manage to put them on the wrong track and then run the boys into other camps, and they run into the woods....

November 20 (Wednesday)

Two days ago in Kentucky, a convention at Russellville passed an ordinance of secession and formed a Confederate government for the state. A convention held in Hatteras, N.C., repudiated the secession of the state from the Union and established a provisional government for that state. This made three states with two governments: Missouri, North Carolina and Kentucky.

Day, Pvt., Co. B, 25th Massachusetts Volunteer Infantry, near Annapolis, Md.:

> Yesterday, having a day to myself, I visited Annapolis. I was greatly interested in visiting the old State House on account of the historic memories that cluster around it. I was shown up in the hall where Washington, in December, 1783, resigned his commission in the army to the Continental congress, then in session at this place. His resignation was a very solemn and formal affair, and as I stood in this venerable hall, my thoughts went back to those grand old days when our fathers struggled for independence....
>
> To the eye of the stranger, the antique, moss-covered and vine-clad houses, with their deep embrasured windows and peculiar architecture, present a singular appearance. The Naval academy and Episcopal college present a striking contrast to the rest of the town. The buildings are large and of modern style, the grounds around them spacious and tastefully laid out....

November 21 (Thursday)

Judah P. Benjamin was named Confederate Secretary of War by President Davis. The brother of Gen. Braxton Bragg was named Attorney General to fill Benjamin's vacated post.

Confederate Gen. Albert S. Johnston called for 10,000 volunteers and militia from Tennessee to help defend the area from the Federal advance.

November 24 (Sunday)

Capt. Wilkes arrived at Ft. Warren, Boston, with his celebrated prisoners, Mason and Slidell. Wilkes was toasted as a hero, a medal was struck in his honor, and he was praised from pulpit to barroom for his actions.

The U.S.S. *Flag*, Commander J. Rodgers, along with the U.S.S. *August*, *Pocahontas*, *Seneca*, and *Savannah* took possession of Tybee Island in Savannah Harbor. Flag Officer Du Pont reported, "This abandonment of Tybee Island is due to the terror inspired by the bombardment of Forts Walker and Beauregard, and is a direct fruit of the victory of the 7th [capture of Port Royal]."

Today an almost obscure Confederate undertook an expedition into Kentucky from Tennessee. Nathan Bedford Forrest was beginning his career as one of the cavalry geniuses of the war. Forrest was to become a legend during the war and certainly had something heroic in his personality. Born in Tennessee in 1821, the son of a poverty-stricken, backwoods blacksmith, he had to take over the entire support of his large family at age 16, when his father died. By 1861, he had become a successful merchant and slave trader in Memphis. Nearly illiterate, he enlisted in the Confederate cavalry at the age of 40, along with his oldest son. He was soon released to form his own cavalry unit, which he equipped at his own expense. His exploits during the war and his capability as a cavalry commander made his tactics memorable, and they were studied for generations thereafter. He rightfully was called a "wizard of the saddle."

November 25 (Monday)

The first load of armor plate for the C.S.S. *Virginia* was delivered to and accepted by Confederate Secretary of the Navy Mallory. It was then given to Lt. Catesby ap Roger Jones at the Norfolk Navy Yard for use on the ship.

Catesby ap Roger Jones was born in Fairfield, Va., on April 15, 1821. He entered the Navy as a midshipman and was ultimately promoted to lieutenant in 1849. In 1853, he worked with Lt. John Dahlgren at the Washington Navy Yard on the improved version of the Dahlgren gun, which was later heavily used in the war. When the war began, he resigned and joined the Confederate Navy as a lieutenant, and later he was assigned as the head of the Naval Foundry and Ordnance facility at Selma, Ala. After the war, he entered business, buying surplus government armaments and selling them to foreign governments. He was shot by a neighbor because of a quarrel between their children, and he died in Selma on June 20, 1877.

November 27 (Wednesday)

The British registry ship *Trent* arrived in England with news of the American boarding in the Bahamas Passage and the removal of Mason, Slidell and their aides from the ship. The British Parliament was in an uproar. The reaction was immediate. Eight thousand troops boarded ships for Canada. New fortifications were to be constructed along the border between Canada and the northern States. Shipyards in England received orders for new ships in quantities not seen since the Napoleonic Wars.

In Washington, Seward believed that if England declared war on the United States, the Southern states would stop their quarrel over states' rights and reunite to fight England. While the South, hoping to gain England's support for her cause, would be eager to draw England into the war on her side, there was still strong feeling against England left over from the War of 1812.

Lincoln, the cooler head in this case, played down heated reaction and cautioned, "One war at a time." In his address on December 1st to Congress, Lincoln omitted any mention of the "*Trent* affair," and the excitement over the situation slowly died.

November 29 (Friday)

Along the coast of South Carolina and Georgia, fires could be seen where planters were burning cotton to prevent it falling into the hands of the North. The Charleston *Mercury* exclaimed, "Let the torch be applied whenever the invader pollutes our soil."

The future commander of the U.S.S. *Monitor*, Lt. John Lorimer Worden, arrived in Washington after seven months as a prisoner of war in the South. Born in New York in 1818, he began his career in the Navy as a midshipman in 1833. In 1861, he was sent on a secret mission to the U.S.S. *Sabine*, then off Ft. Pickens, Fla. After delivering the message, he was captured by the Confederates and held at a prison in Montgomery, Ala. In March 1862, he returned to the South as the commander of the ironclad *Monitor* to participate in the famous duel in Hampton Roads. He would serve with distinction during the war, and later as superintendent of the Naval Academy from 1869 to 1874. He died in Washington in October 1897.

November 30 (Saturday)

Lord Russell, British Foreign Secretary, informed Lord Lyons, Minister to the United States, that the "*Trent* affair" constituted aggression against England; Mason and Slidell must be released and an apology given for their seizure. If no action were taken within seven days, Lyons was to depart Washington and return to England with all his personnel.

Day, Pvt., Co. B, 25th Massachusettss Volunteer Infantry, near Annapolis, Md.:

> According to the customs of our Puritan Fathers, last Thursday was observed in Massachusetts and other states as a day of thanksgiving to God for his manifold mercies and bounties to the erring children of men. The day was observed here throughout all the camps as a holiday. All drills were suspended, and in our camp religious services were held, after which the boys engaged in ball playing and other amusements to which their inclinations might lead....

DECEMBER 1861

Along the Atlantic seaboard smoke columns rose from the pyres of burning cotton set ablaze by the planters to prevent it being seized by the Yankees. Lincoln was readying his address to Congress and puzzling over what to do about the "*Trent* affair." In both North and South, the soldiers were settling into winter camps and long sessions of drill, drill, and more drill. Most were learning to cope with living outdoors, using inadequate shelter for the first time.

December 1 (Sunday)

Lincoln, becoming impatient, sent a memorandum to McClellan inquiring "just *how long* would it require to actually get in motion?" Off the coast of Georgia, the U.S.S. *Seminole*, Commander John S. Missroon, with a small group of other ships, captured the sloop *Lida*, with a cargo of coffee, lead, and sugar. The noose of the blockade was tightening.

Jackman, Pvt., "The Orphan Brigade," Russellville, Ky.:

> About the 1st of December I took the camp fever and was sent to regimental hospital in town. Our regiment had two very nice buildings for that purpose. I was pretty sick for a while. The day after Christmas I was sent in charge of a party of convalescents to Camp "Recovery" which was at some winter quarters four or five miles from town on the Nashville pike. The cabins had been put up by part of the brigade and left. There were eight or ten of us and we had a cabin all to ourselves but no cooking utensils. The first night at a late hour the pickets commenced firing

on the road and we were all turned out under arms. Capt S., commander, gave me charge of thirty or forty men and ordered me to defend the part of camp most exposed to the attack. I divided my ammunition, which made one round to the man, some of the cartridges wouldn't fit, and marched to the position assigned me. We waited patiently for the enemy to appear. While changing my front a little, making considerable noise, someone out on the field challenged us. We asked who it was but received no answer. We heard several guns cocked out front. We made ready. But instead of firing, we commenced questioning and I found the army opposing us was a scout unit out to reconnoiter and now returning with the report that no enemy could be found. We disbanded and went to bed.

The next day, walked to Bowling Green. Felt strong. The following day offered to go to my command and walked to town in time for the train. Soon ran up to Oakland, 12 miles, and there found the regiment encamped. Was glad to be with the boys again. The brigade commander, Brig. Gen. Breckinridge, had just returned from what they always termed the "Merry Oaks March." They represented it as a very hard march—disagreeable—and since, have always spoken of that as being one of their *hard* times. I believe the next day we were mustered for pay. Then I saw Genl. John C. Breckinridge for the first time—he inspected us. Our regiment was then considerably reduced from sickness. Here Billie S-N. first complained of sickness.

December 2 (Monday)

Lincoln authorized Major Gen. Henry Halleck in the Department of Missouri to suspend the writ of *habeas corpus* in areas where he found it necessary. This was a considerable widening of the original suspension, which covered only an area along the eastern seaboard.

Lt. Robert D. Minor, CSN, reported a laboratory having been established in New Orleans for "the supply of ordnance stores for the vessels fitting out at this station." This facility was not destined to be in business very long.

Secretary of the Navy Gideon Welles sent his first annual report to the President containing an upbeat note. Things were looking fairly well for the Union, as regarded the Navy:

Since the institution of the blockade one hundred and fifty-three vessels have been captured... most of which were attempting to violate the blockade.... When the vessels now building and purchased are... ready for service, the condition of the navy will be... a total of 264 vessels, 2557 guns, and 218,016 tons. The aggregate number of seamen in the service... is now not less than 22,000.... The amount appropriated in the last regular session of Congress for the naval service for the current year was $13,168,675.86. To this was added at the special session in July last $30,446,875.91—making for the fiscal year ending June 30, 1862, an aggregate of $43,615,551.77. This sum will not be sufficient....

December 4 (Wednesday)

The United States Senate voted 36 to 0 to expel Senator John C. Breckinridge of Kentucky. Breckinridge, having served as Buchanan's Vice President, was elected to the Senate in 1860. He remained in the Senate hoping to find some peaceful solution to the problem, but, seeing this as an impossible task, joined the Confederate Army in November. He was appointed Commander of the 1st Kentucky Brigade, which became known as "the Orphan Brigade."

John Cabell Breckinridge had just turned 40 in January 1861, and he was in the prime of his life. A very handsome man, he practised law in his native city of Lexington, Ky., before being elected to the State Legislature in 1849, to be followed by two terms in the U.S. House of Representatives from 1851 to 1855. He was the youngest man ever to serve as Vice President, age 35 in 1856. He was not a secessionist, and he worked hard to reverse the trend in the South for secession. Serving with distinction in the Confederate Army, he was appointed Confederate Secretary of War in February 1865. He fled south with President Davis and the Cabinet when Richmond was evacuated in April 1865, and he was in Georgia when the war ended. Escaping to Cuba, he remained there for three years in exile before returning to Kentucky to resume his law practice. He died at age 54, on May 17, 1875. His integrity was never in question.

There were minor skirmishes near Burke Station, Va., just south of Washington, and in the Mississippi Sound the Confederate steamers *Florida* and

Pamlico attacked the U.S.S. *Montgomery*, Commander Thompson D. Shaw.

December 5 (Thursday)

The Confederate Central Army of Kentucky had a new commander, Major Gen. William J. Hardee. Hardee, USMA class of '38, was 45 years old and a Lt. Colonel in the U.S. Army in 1861. He resigned his commission on June 17th and was appointed a Brigadier General in the Confederate Army on that date and was promoted to Major General on October 7, 1861. A native Georgian, he had served with distinction in the Army before the war, developing a textbook on tactics which was adopted as the standard manual for all the U.S. Army. This book was used by the Confederate Army for their training, as well. He was promoted to Lieutenant General on October 10, 1862, and he would remain in that rank for the remainder of the war. He served with distinction throughout the campaigns in Tennessee, Georgia, and the Carolinas, finally surrendering to Sherman on April 25, 1865, at Greensborough, N.C. After the war, he settled in Selma, Ala., and became a planter. While travelling in Virginia, he died on November 6, 1873.

The Federal Navy had collected wooden ships which were of little service and loaded them with stones. These ships were sent to Flag Officer Du Pont at Savannah, Ga., to be used to block the rivers and entrances to the ports in that area. Du Pont, writing about his expedition to Wassaw Sound, Ga., stated:

> *Ottawa*, *Pembina*, and *Seneca* penetrated into Wassaw… the stone fleet are all at Savannah, and I hardly know what to do with them—for with Wassaw that city is more effectively closed than a bottle with wire over the cork…. I am sending to [Capt. James L.] Lardner to know if he can plant them on the Charleston bar…. One good thing they [the stone fleet's appearance at Savannah] did, I have not a doubt they were taken for men-of-war, and led to giving up the Wassaw defenses . .

Day, Pvt., Co. B, 25th Massachusetts Volunteer Infantry, near Annapolis, Md.:

> Courts martial seem to be a prominent feature in camp affairs just at present, and almost every night at dress parade the charges and specifications are read against some unlucky wight. The burden of the song seems to be too drunk to perform the duties of a soldier; but as this is a camp of instruction, I presume these courts are really more for practice than any thing else.

December 6 (Friday)

Brigadier Gen. George G. Meade led a foraging expedition into northern Virginia in the area of Dranesville. George Gordon Meade was born in Cádiz, Spain, where his father was stationed as a naval agent for the U.S. Upon returning to the United States, the family fell upon hard times, and his father died, forcing George to leave his school in Philadelphia and attend one in Washington headed by Salmon P. Chase. He entered the USMA in September 1831, graduating 19th in a class of 56 in 1835. He resigned from the Army in 1836 to work on the survey of a railroad in the South, rejoining the Army in 1842, where he remained. He served at various posts until the beginning of the Civil War, when he was appointed Brigadier General of Volunteers on August 31, 1861. All of his service would be with the Army of the Potomac. He was appointed commander on the eve of the Battle of Gettysburg, in July 1863, and served as Commander of the Army of the Potomac for the remainder of the war. After the war, he returned to Philadelphia, where he died on November 6, 1872, as a result of old war wounds complicated by pneumonia. While not a brilliant soldier, he was steady and a good administrator.

December 7 (Saturday)

To further complicate the "*Trent* affair," the British schooner *Eugenia Smith*, outbound from the mouth of the Rio Grande River, was stopped by the U.S.S. *Santiago de Cuba*, and passenger J.W. Zacharie, a Confederate purchasing agent from New Orleans, was removed.

December 9 (Monday)

The first of the "oversight" committees to be set up by Congress over the years, the Joint Committee on the Conduct of the War was authorized on this date. The Committee would highly criticize and also give much approval to the Northern commanders during the war. Little would escape its attention and investigations. Probably many millions of man-hours were wasted in testimony to this committee.

December 10 (Tuesday)

In Richmond, the State of Kentucky was admitted to the Confederacy, making the 13th, and final, state. The Confederate government of Kentucky had no permanent home, and it moved around frequently.

Lt. James W. A. Nicholson took the U.S.S. *Isaac Smith* up the Ashepoo River in South Carolina. He landed part of his crew on abandoned Otter Island and took possession of a Confederate fort, which he later turned over to the Federal Army.

Barber, Pvt., Co. D, 15th Illinois Volunteer Infantry, Otterville, Mo.:

There were about twenty thousand troops stationed here.... This place was now used as a depot of supplies. The weather soon became intensely cold and some of the boys froze their hands and feet... a heavy guard was kept around the camp. Col. Hovey being absent for a few days, the command devolved on Ellis, and one bitter cold and stormy night, he took off the guard. We had pickets out and men up to alarm the regiment in case of danger, so he was perfectly safe in doing so.

When Col. Hovey returned, he had him placed under arrest for taking off the guard. Ellis demanded a trial, pled his own cause and was acquitted. This affair created a sort of ill-feeling between the Indiana and Illinois regiments. One day the 15th and 24th got to snow-balling, and the sport soon began to wax pretty warm. Something harder than snow began to fly. The Lieut-Col. of the 24th came out to stop it and was hit by a chunk of ice and knocked down. A general melee seemed inevitable, but at this moment Col. Ellis appeared and the 15th boys desisted and returned to their quarters.

The 26th Indiana were a very inferior looking set of men, and they were certainly the most filthy looking set of men I ever saw. Some of our boys caught one of the dirtiest of them down at the river one day, and they stripped him and soused him in. He came out looking more like a white man. This affair had a wholesome effect on the whole regiment.

We made frequent forays out into the country and confiscated corn, etc., from the rebels; on such occasions, there was usually a scrambling to see who would go. Almost invariably the boys would come in loaded down with the best that the country afforded. The weather became so intensely cold that we had to adopt some plan to keep from freezing. We pegged our tent as close to the ground as possible, and covered over the lap with dirt. We then built a sort of fire-place at the foot, with the chimney just outside the tent, and got a good bed of twigs and straw to lie on; had the opening of the tent so arranged that we could fasten it tight, and at night, beneath our heavy covering, we nestled together like a litter of young pigs. Though the thermometer was ten below zero, we slept warm and comfortable....

We were now set to work building winter quarters. I shouldered my ax and went into the woods and felled nine trees, from eighteen inches to two feet in diameter, and cut them into the right length for building. I was so lame the next day I could hardly stir.... The boys all worked with energy. The prospect of having comfortable houses during such cold weather was very comforting, but oh, the fallacy of human hopes. The very next day we were ordered to march.... After traveling for ten days through sleet and snow, we surprised and captured thirteen hundred prisoners. There was scarcely any fighting; and [we] went into camp at Sedalia.... While we were at Sedalia, a very severe snow storm occurred, after which it turned very cold, and on one of these cold days we were ordered to march.

Outside of Annapolis, Md., Private D.L. Day took a stroll through the countryside and found that the local philosophy of farming didn't agree with his New England Yankee idea of tidiness and thrift. His entry for this day made it clear that he didn't think much of the Maryland farmers.

Day, Pvt., Co. B, 25th Massachusetts Volunteer Infantry, near Annapolis, Md.:

The weather holds warm and springlike.... I took a walk of a few miles into the country yesterday on a tour of observation. I noticed what appeared to be a great extent of good land, but very badly improved. Occasionally I saw a farm where things seemed to be kept up snug and showed some evidences of thrift, but more of them looked as though the owners studied to see how shiftless they could be and still manage to live. Buildings and fences are going to decay; fields of corn are yet unharvested, the cattle and hogs running through and destroying them. I asked one man why he didn't harvest his corn. "Oh" he said, "there is no hurry about that, I have got all winter to do it in and the corn is just as well off in the field as anywhere." I came to the conclusion that his plan of harvesting was about as fast as he wanted it to eat.... I made up my mind that a man with an ordinary degree of enterprise, with our improved implements for farming and with hired labor, might take this land and make money on it. I am unable to see any profits from slave labor in Maryland; it is poor help at the best; besides they have to be clothed and fed several months in a year during which time they are not earning much, and there is always on a farm, employing a dozen or more field hands, a lot of old men and women and small children who are not earning anything, but still have to be supported.

December 13 (Friday)

Two days ago in Charleston, S.C., a raging fire swept the business district east of King Street and near the Cooper River. Coupled with the shortages created by the blockade and providing food to the Confederate Army, this was a new, and unwanted, blow to the economy.

Not a lucky day for either Confederates or Federals on Buffalo Mountain in western Virginia. Brigadier Gen. R.H. Milroy led the Federals against the Rebels and after a severe fight fell back, suffering 137 casualties. The Southerners didn't fare much better, taking 146 casualties. Both sides retreated, the Confederates to Staunton in the Shenandoah Valley.

Robert Huston Milroy would be an unlucky general. A native of Salem, Ind., he was 45 at the beginning of the war, and a lawyer in his hometown. He graduated from Norwich Academy in 1843, and served in the Mexican War as a Captain in the 1st Indiana Volunteers. Mustered into service as the Colonel of the 9th Indiana Regiment on April 27, 1861, he participated in the operations in western Virginia, and was promoted to Brigadier General on September 3, 1861. After service in western Virginia, he served at Second Bull Run and the Shenandoah Valley Campaign, being promoted to Major General on November 29, 1862. His greatest loss was at Winchester, Va., which resulted in his investigation after losing 3400 captured, along with 23 cannon. He was eventually cleared of charges and was assigned other duties in Tennessee. He resigned from the Army in July 1865, and he returned to Indiana for a period. He finally became the Indian Agent at Olympia, Wash., where he died on March 29, 1890, at age 74.

December 14 (Saturday)

In England, one of the Union's strongest advocates, Prince Albert, consort to Queen Victoria, died. Shortly before his death he had been instrumental in drafting some of the diplomatic correspondence relating to the "*Trent* affair," counselling moderation in the dealings with the United States.

December 16 (Monday)

Clement Vallandigham of Ohio introduced a resolution in the U.S. House of Representatives commending Capt. Wilkes on his conduct during the "*Trent* affair." The resolution, somewhat embarrassing, was sent to committee for study.

Today the Stonewall Brigade left camp at Winchester, Va., and marched 15 miles to Martinsburg, and another 13 miles to the bluffs overlooking Dam No. 5 of the Chesapeake and Ohio Canal, paralleling the Potomac. It was bitterly cold and all baggage had been left at Big Springs.

December 17 (Tuesday)

In England, the country was still in an uproar over the "*Trent* affair." Mason, Slidell and their aides were in Ft. Warren prison in Boston Harbor, awaiting events. Lord Russell had drafted his message to the United States on the affair and presented it to the Queen.

The *Times* of London declared,

> By Capt. Wilkes let the Yankee breed be judged. Swagger and ferocity, built on a foundation of vulgarity and cowardice, these are the characteristics, and these are the most prominent marks by which his countrymen, generally speaking, are known all over the world.

Near Dam No. 5 of the C&O Canal, the Stonewall Brigade huddled in the bitter cold all day waiting for darkness to begin their destruction of the dam. At darkness, thirty members of the group went to the dam and began to dismantle it.

At the entrance to Savannah Harbor, Flag Officer Du Pont ordered the sinking of seven of the "stone fleet" vessels.

December 18 (Wednesday)

Lord John Russell was given the task of writing a reply to be delivered to the American ambassador. It was an ultimatum: either an abject apology, with the return of the two emissaries, or war. The original statement was toned down to asking for an explanation and apology, because the British government did not believe that the act was done with the approval or instructions of the United States government.

At daylight, the Federals discovered the Stonewall Brigade's presence at Dam No. 5 of the C&O Canal and began firing at the soldiers working on the destruction of the dam. Jackson brought his artillery to bear, but this was replied to by Federal artillery, so operations were suspended until dark. Jackson's men were hiding in the old mill on the Virginia side of the Potomac when this building was brought under fire by Federal artillery, causing a sudden evacuation of Confederates.

Private D.L. Day had his New England Yankee thrift working overtime again on this day.

Day, Pvt., Co. B, 25th Massachusetts Volunteer Infantry, near Annapolis, Md.:

> I have been looking through the camp around here and am astonished at the amount of offal and swill that is buried up and lost instead of being turned into valuable account. An enterprising farmer could collect from these camps manure and swill to the value of $100 a day, costing nothing but simply carting it off, thus enriching his land and fattening hundreds of hogs and cattle; but this lack of energy and enterprise prevents these people from turning anything to account. They content themselves with sitting down and finding fault with the government and their more enterprising and energetic neighbors of the north.

December 20 (Friday)

In England, troop transports loaded with 8000 troops sailed for Canada so that troops would be available if the "*Trent* affair" was not settled without war.

Flag Officer Du Pont ordered Capt. C. H. Davis to sink some of the "stone fleet" vessels at the mouth of Charleston Harbor to restrict movement. The steamer *Gordon* had a good run and made it into harbor at Wilmington, N.C.

After waiting out the long, cold day yesterday to get back to the destruction of Dam No. 5 on the C & O Canal, Jackson moved some of his men upriver and the Federals followed, thinking he was headed for Dam No. 4. Immediately, the destroyers returned to Dam No. 5 and fell to with vigor in the icy water. The Federals did not return to Dam No. 5. The Brigade completed their work of destruction on Dam No. 5 and prepared to depart. The final work had been free of Federal interference.

Day, Pvt., Co. B, 25th Massachusetts Volunteer Infantry, near Annapolis, Md.:

> We are having cold weather; freezing quite hard at night, and making our lodgings in these little rag houses anything but comfortable. I have been on a detail of men down to the wharf unloading and storing army supplies. Annapolis is a depot of supplies and immense quantities are landed here and sent by rail to Washington. A person never having given the subject of army preparation and supplies much thought, would be astonished at the immense quantities he would see here and would begin to calculate how long it would be before Uncle Sam would be bankrupt. Large warehouses are filled and breaking down under the weight of flour, beef, pork, bread, sugar, coffee, clothing, ammunition, etc., while the wharves and adjacent grounds are filled with hay, oats, lumber, coal, guns, mortars, gun-carriages, pontoons, and other appendages of an army. I presume the cost of feeding and clothing an army of half a million of men is not really so much as the same number of men would cost at home, but the army being consumers instead of producers, the balance will eventually be found on the debit page of the ledger.

December 21 (Saturday)

The Stonewall Brigade left for its camps at Winchester, arriving there on the 23rd. The weather was bitter cold and the troops suffered terribly.

The British Minister, Lord Lyons, again met with Secretary of State Seward over the "*Trent* affair." The pressure was on Lincoln's government to release Mason and Slidell and to apologize for the incident to the British government. The Southern newspapers were wild with the possibility of war between England and the United States, hoping that this would lead to Southern independence.

In western Virginia, Brigadier Gen. Henry A. Wise had fumbled enough. He was relieved of his command and sent to North Carolina.

December 24 (Tuesday)

A good Christmas Eve for Lt. Irvin B. Baxter and the crew of the U.S.S. *Gem of the Sea* who caused a bad holiday eve for the crew of the British blockade runner *Prince of Wales* off Georgetown, S.C., when the English ship was taken and destroyed.

Day, Pvt., Co. B, 25th Massachusetts Volunteer Infantry, near Annapolis, Md.:

> Tomorrow will be Christmas and the boys in all the camps are making great preparations for the coming event. The camps are being put in order and decorated with evergreens. Some of them trimmed in good taste and look very neat and pretty.... Santa Claus is expected here tonight with our Christmas dinners but he may be delayed and not get here for a week to come.

December 25 (Wednesday)

The Cabinet met in Washington for lengthy discussion on the fate of Mason and Slidell. A decision was to be made on the morrow. President Lincoln and family entertained guests for dinner at the White House, and at Winchester, Va., Thomas J. "Stonewall" Jackson spent the day with his wife. This was to be their last Christmas together.

No time for Christmas aboard the U.S.S. *Fernandina*, Acting Lt. George W. Browne, when it captured the schooner *William H. Northrup* off Cape Fear, N.C.

December 26 (Thursday)

Today, a Cabinet meeting decided that the seizure of Mason and Slidell was illegal and they would be released. The British Ambassador, Lord Lyons, was so notified. They were more trouble in prison than they would be in England and France.

Martial law was declared in St. Louis, and along all railroads operating in the state of Missouri.

Day, Pvt., Co. B, 25th Massachusetts Volunteer Infantry, near Annapolis, Md.:

> Christmas went off very pleasantly and apparently to the satisfaction of all. Drills were suspended and all went in for a good time. The Irishmen had their Christmas box, the Germans their song and lager, while ball playing and other athletic sports used up the day and music and dancing were the order of the evening. Santa Claus came with a Christmas dinner for a few, but more of us he passed by; however, I think the old gentleman has got a store for us somewhere on the way. Our camp was visited by a number of ladies and gentlemen from the city who were guests at headquarters, Chaplain James doing the polite, and entertaining them as best he could. No farther south than this, I was surprised to hear the chaplain tell of the ignorance of these people in regard to northern people and their institutions. One lady, noticing a box of letters in the chaplain's tent, said she thought he must have a very large correspondence to have so many letters. He told her those were soldiers' letters going home to their friends. "Why," she asked, "are there many of your soldiers who can write?" He informed her that there were not half a dozen men in the regiment [who] could not read and write. He told her that free schools were an institution in the north. No man was so poor that he could not educate his children, and the man who neglected their education was regarded as little better than the brutes. The lady appeared quite astonished and said she thought our free schools were only for the rich.

December 30 (Monday)

Banks in the United States suspended the practice of redeeming paper money for metal currency, a practice that would continue until 1879.

Flag Officer Foote on the western rivers wrote Assistant Secretary of the Navy Fox stating the pay scale he was using for his officers:

> In the case of Masters, and Pilots, I have been obliged, in order to secure the services of efficient Men, to pay 1st Masters $150 per month, 2nd Masters $125, 3rd Masters $100 and 4th Masters $80 per month, while Pilots are paid $175 per month. These prices are much less than the incumbents received in ordinary times, while they have before been provided with table furniture and stores, bedding, etc. which I have not allowed them.

December 31 (Tuesday)

Things were not going at all well for Lincoln or his cause. He tried to sort some sense out of the command structure in the west by asking both Buell and Halleck if they were doing any joint planning. The replies he got were not encouraging. Buell replied that he had no provision for concerted action, and Halleck said he didn't know what Buell was doing and couldn't cooperate in any case. Lincoln wired both generals to do some cooperating and then visited the Quartermaster General of the Army, Montgomery C. Meigs. During his visit he asked,

> General, what shall I do? The people are impatient; Chase has no money, and tells me he can raise no more; the General of the Army has typhoid fever. The bottom is out of the tub. What shall I do?

There would be no Happy New Year for the schooner *Island Belle* that attempted to run the blockade near Bull's Bay, S.C. She was captured by the U.S.S. *Augusta*, Commander Parrot. Meanwhile, up the coast near Wilmington, N.C., a lightship that had been fitted out as a gunboat by the Confederates was destroyed by a boat party from the U.S.S. *Mount Vernon*, headed by Acting Masters A. Allen and H.L. Sturges.

Barber, Pvt., Co. D, 15th Illinois Volunteer Infantry, Otterville, Mo.:

> We took the old road back towards Otterville, at which place we arrived after two days' hard marching. On the second day I gave out. I had long been suffering from a severe cold, and I had neuralgia in my hip, and the traveling being very difficult on account of the snow and ice, made it very painful for me to travel. Dr. Buck kindly gave me his horse to ride....
>
> When we got back to our old camp, we found that some rascals had destroyed our fireplace, and our situation that night was anything but pleasant, but soldier-like, we did not despond. We scraped the snow off the ground and put up our tent. It was nine o'clock before we got our supper. Many went to bed supperless, with the frozen earth for a couch. The inmates of tent No. 6 slept close that night, but Roll and Charlie, whose turn came to sleep on the outside, suffered from the cold.
>
> As nothing more was said about building winter quarters, the inmates of tent No. 6 went to work and built some of their own. We first built a fire-place. In this we patterned after the southern style. They generally build their chimney first and then match their house to it. So we built our chimney and one door, which occupied the front. Then we laid up small logs, house style, some four feet high, and then fastened our tent on top of it for a roof. We built our beds so that our feet came together, and the sides served as a seat before the fire-place. We had plenty of room and cooked all our grub inside. When the other boys came to see how much more comfortable we were, they went and did likewise.

In a three-day action, a naval squadron under Commander C.R.P. Rodgers, including the gunboats *Ottawa*, *Pembina*, and *Seneca* and four armed boats carrying howitzers, joined in an amphibious attack on Confederate positions at Port Royal Ferry and on the Coosaw River. In this joint operation, gunboat fire covered the landing and troop advance while guns and naval gunners were landed to provide artillery support. In an unusual move, Army signal officers accompanied the troops ashore to act as gunfire observers, relaying the fire adjustments to the fleet using signal flags. This action disrupted the Confederate attempt to erect shore batteries and build troop strength in the area. The Rebels intended to close the Coosaw River and isolate the Federal troops on Port Royal Island. Gen. Stevens in his report wrote,

> I would do great injustice to my own feelings did I fail to express my satisfaction and delight with the recent cooperation of the command of Capt. Rodgers in our celebration of New Year's Day. Whether regard be had to his beautiful working of the gunboats in the narrow channel of Port Royal, the thorough concert of action established through the signal officers, or the masterly handling of the guns against the enemy, nothing remained to be desired. Such a cooperation... augurs everything propitious for the welfare of our cause in this quarter of the country.

1862

January 1, 1862, was bright with promise for some, and looked upon with dread by others. It was a cold, bitter winter for the soldiers. Most of the soldiers in the armies were not psychologically prepared for a long war. Many, especially in the South, were just settling in after enlistments, which were for the duration of the war. They could not easily adapt to camp life without some hardship.

The seized emissaries, Mason and Slidell, had been turned over to the British minister at Provincetown, Mass. Capt. Wilkes, bedecked with laurels and medals, continued his sailing business, more closely supervised than before. The general feeling was that the United States had done what was expedient, not necessarily what was desirable.

January 1 (Wednesday)

The New Year was celebrated in Florida with the Federals bombarding Ft. Barrancas and the Confederates doing the same to Ft. Pickens, near Pensacola.

On the Ohio River, Flag Officer Foote sent the U.S.S. *Lexington*, Lt. Shirk, to provide support to the "Union people" along that river. She would be joined by the U.S.S. *Conestoga*, Lt. S.L. Phelps, in this endeavor.

John Jackman began the year moving into new quarters and setting up housekeeping.

Jackman, Pvt., "The Orphan Brigade," in camp, Tennessee:

> We moved camp to "Clear Water," two or three miles off the railroad, and near the pike. We were near a church which was used as regtl. hospital. No other troops were camped near us. The first thing I did after the tent was pitched, was adding a good chimney which answered us a good purpose while there encamped. We had a little A tent and seven in the group—two being very large men. There was a great deal of rain fell and about camp was very muddy. The colonel had old tan bark hauled to pave the streets and had it piled on all the beats. Sometimes on a dark night a sentinel could not keep on the little ridge of bark and would get off into the mud knee deep.

In Massachusetts, the imprisoned Confederates, Mason and Slidell, and their secretaries were released due to British demands, and the "*Trent* affair" was finished. They continued on to England aboard the British warship H.M.S. *Rinaldo*.

Lincoln and his Cabinet held the traditional New Year's reception. The entire diplomatic corps was in attendance. General George McClellan, who had not made an aggressive move for five months, was ill.

President Davis hosted a reception line in which thousands paraded past. His hand was very sore at the end of the day.

In the Shenandoah Valley, Gen. Thomas J. Jackson began his movement towards Romney in western Virginia. His ultimate goal was the Baltimore and Ohio Railroad and the locks of the Chesapeake and Ohio Canal—an attempt to cut communications with the west. The Stonewall Brigade began the march in fairly nice weather, but as the day progressed, the weather turned windy and cold, and then the snow and ice came. A thoroughly miserable day for marching; only eight miles were covered this day.

January 2 (Thursday)

Gen. McClellan reported that he was feeling better, but that he was still unable to take active command of the army again.

After much confusion and delay on the part of Gen. Ripley, Chief of Ordnance, the Union finally received a quantity of machine guns. These were the "coffee mill" guns first demonstrated to Lincoln on June 24, 1861, in Washington. Col. John W. Geary, commanding the 28th Pennsylvania Infantry, a unit guarding the approaches to Washington on the upper Potomac, had the dubious honor of receiving these guns for use in the field.

John White Geary, at 42, had already seen a distinguished career. Enlisted as a private during the Mexican War, he rose to the rank of Colonel of Volunteers and became the Governor of Mexico City under Gen. Winfield Scott. Leaving the Army, he organized the postal service in California, and served as Mayor of San Francisco and Governor of Kansas Territory. At the beginning of the war he returned to his native Pennsylvania and raised the oversize 28th Pennsylvania Infantry Regiment, being elected colonel. In April he was promoted to Brigadier General. At Cedar Mountain, in the Valley, he was wounded in the foot and shoulder, but he recovered rapidly and returned to command a division in the XII Corps. He fought at Chancellorsville and Gettysburg with the Army of the Potomac, and then went west to participate in the Battle of Lookout Mountain. He went with Sherman to Atlanta, and then to Savannah, where Sherman appointed him military governor of the city. After the war he was twice elected Governor of Pennsylvania. On February 8, 1873, he died of a stroke at Harrisburg, Pa.

On the western rivers, Flag Officer Foote was having a hard time getting gunboats completed by the contractor and into service. Things were further complicated by the lack of crews. He wrote Secretary of the Navy Gideon Welles, "I hope to be able to send 60 men on board of each gunboat within the week. We are waiting for the 1000 men to fill up our complement… The carpenters and engineers are behindhand in their work." While pushing as rapidly as possible, Foote was having more demands placed on his existing gunboats with requests received from Gen. Grant, such as, "Will you please direct a gunboat to drop down the river… to protect a steamer I am sending down to bring up produce for some loyal citizens of Kentucky?"

The Stonewall Brigade made another eight miles today, as far as Unger's Store, over very rough mountain roads in extreme conditions.

January 3 (Friday)

The diseases that ravaged many of the new camps left few untouched. It was not uncommon for a company that began with 100 or more men to lose 20 or more during the first few months to disease, accident or disability.

Statistics were to show that during the first year and half of the war the Union lost 2.01 percent of its force to disease. The figures for the Confederate forces were higher, at 3.81 percent. Nearly half again as many Rebels died of diarrhea and dysentery as the Yanks. Nearly five times as many Rebels died of pulmonary diseases.

Jackman, Pvt., "The Orphan Brigade," in a Kentucky camp:

> We had been in camp but a few days when Billie S.N. was sent to the hospital with the typhoid fever and soon after died. A week or two afterward three others of the mess were sent off—"Bro Don," H.O. and "Capt." G.—Billie A.G.P. and myself were all that remained. Four of the company died in hospital while encamped at "Clear Water" and retreating, left A.O. at Gallatin, Tenn who died.

The Stonewall Brigade, on its way to Romney, headed north and reached the area around the town of Bath (present-day Berkeley Springs), noted for its mineral-water springs. Jackson hoped to surprise the Union troops here, but a Union outpost discovered the Confederate force. The Brigade went into camp amid the snow for the night.

January 5 (Sunday)

Flag Officer L.M. Goldsborough wired Brigadier Gen. Ambrose E. Burnside to start his ships for the Hatteras Inlet as early as possible, especially those which had to be towed. These were destined for the Roanoke Island expedition.

Early yesterday morning, Jackson captured Bath, chasing the Federals to the Potomac. The town of Hancock refused to surrender, and, after giving time to remove the women and children, a few shells were lobbed into the town. The Arkansas troops with Jackson burned the railroad bridge over the Great Cacapon River in western Virginia. In addition, damage was done to a dam on the C&O Canal along the Potomac. More snow was falling and the pickets almost froze.

Barber, Pvt., Co. D, 15th Illinois Volunteer Infantry, Otterville, Mo.:

> We now received another installment of pay. A good many of the boys had acquired the habit of gambling. "Chuck Luck" was their favorite game... Many a soldier would venture all his hard earnings on the throw of the dice, and thus lose in a few hours what it had taken him months to earn. This species of gaming was carried on to such an extent that an order was issued prohibiting it. If anyone was caught at it, he was arrested and his money confiscated, but this did not stop the practice.... Gaming engendered other vices and too many of the boys gave free rein to their passions and indulged in all manner of excesses of the grossest nature.

Day, Pvt., Co. B, 25th Massachusetts Volunteer Infantry, near Annapolis, Md.:

> Orders have been issued to break camp and go aboard the transports tomorrow morning. The boys are now breaking the frozen ground around the tent pins, packing their knapsacks, and getting ready for a start. We have been here so long it seems almost like leaving home to break up and go out on untried scenes.

January 6 (Monday)

Flag Officer Foote on the western rivers was having a hard time manning his river gunboats, the Navy supplying him only 500 of the required 1000 men. The Navy Department informed him that he would have to obtain the rest of the crew from the Army. Gen. Grant's letter to Gen. Halleck suggests that men currently in the guardhouse for various offenses be supplied to the Navy for their gunboats.

The Union force near Hancock, in western Virginia, got reinforcements and Jackson withdrew his men, abandoning any chance of crossing the Potomac and raiding north.

Gen. McClellan was feeling well enough to talk to Lincoln, who again rejected suggestions from some of the senators that McClellan be removed for inaction. Lincoln also was after Buell again on the east Tennessee situation.

Day, Pvt., Co. B, 25th Massachusetts Volunteer Infantry, aboard the steamer *New York*, Annapolis Harbor:

> Reveille beat at 6 o'clock this morning and all hands turned out in the midst of a driving snow storm.... The companies were formed in their company streets, the rolls called, and we marched out on the parade ground and formed the regimental line.... We then marched to the Naval Academy where seven companies, with the field and staff, their horses, and all the camp equipage went aboard the steamer *New York*.... All aboard, the *New York* steamed out into the harbor a short distance and anchored till further orders.

January 7 (Tuesday)

A severe ice storm developed, making the ground very dangerous walking for Jackson's column, now heading south. The column reached Unger's Store after a surprise skirmish at Hanging Rock Pass, which caused much consternation.

The U.S.S. *Conestoga*, Lt. S.L. Phelps, ran up the Tennessee and Cumberland rivers in Kentucky and gained valuable information on the defenses of Forts Donelson and Henry. Phelps reported to Flag Officer Foote:

> The rebels are industriously perfecting their means of defense both at Dover and Ft. Henry. At Ft. Donelson (near Dover) they have placed obstructions in the river, 1½ miles below their battery, on the left bank and in the bend where the battery comes in sight.... The fire of gunboats here [at Donelson] would be at a bad angle.... The forts are placed, especially on the Cumberland, where no great range can be had, and they can only be attacked in one narrow and fixed line.... It is too late now to move against the works on either river, except with a well-appointed and powerful naval force.

Day, Pvt., Co. B, 25th Massachusetts Volunteer Infantry, aboard the steamer *New York*, Annapolis Harbor:

> Here we are, packed like sardines in a box.... The officers and band occupy the saloon and state rooms on the upper deck, the other companies fill the

cabin on the forward deck, the ladies' saloon and gangway amidships. The horses are forward and the baggage is piled forward and on the guards. Altogether, we are settled in here pretty thick....

January 8 (Wednesday)

President Davis was still badgering the various governors of the Confederate States for more support and troops. The reluctance of the governors was growing. Jackson's men remained at Unger's Store for the day, getting some rest in the bitter cold. The sick list was very long and many men were absent. Jackson had water heated so the troops could bathe.

January 9 (Thursday)

Lincoln complained to McClellan, supposed General-in-Chief, about the inactivity and nonresponse of both Buell and Halleck to his requests for action. Lincoln was talking to the wrong man on this subject. "Little Mac" was the greatest "nonmover" of them all.

In Cairo, Illinois, Grant was preparing to conduct a reconnaissance-in-force towards Columbus, Kentucky, on the Mississippi.

In New Orleans, the blockade was causing considerable concern. The *Commercial Bulletin*, a local New Orleans paper, reported:

> The situation of this port makes it a matter of vast moment to the whole Confederate State that it should be opened to the commerce of the world within the least possible period.... We believe the blockading vessels of the enemy might have been driven away and kept away months ago, if the requisite energy had been put forth.... The blockade has remained and the great port of New Orleans has been hermetically sealed.

Unbeknownst to the Editor of the *Commercial Bulletin*, things were going to get worse in the very near future. In Philadelphia, orders reached Flag Officer Farragut assigning him to command the Western Gulf Blockading Squadron to cover an area from west Florida to the Rio Grande. His primary mission, however, was to gain access to the Mississippi and to capture New Orleans, and then go upriver to connect with Grant coming downriver.

Day, Pvt., Co. B, 25th Massachusetts Volunteer Infantry, aboard the steamer *New York*, Chesapeake Bay:

> As bright and lovely a morning as ever dawned on Chesapeake bay. The expedition sails today. The harbor is full of life, tugboats are running in all directions, vessels are getting themselves in their order of line, the anchors are all up and waiting the signal gun to start. 10 A.M. The signal gun announces that all is ready for the departure of the expedition. Slowly the flag-boat containing Gen. Burnside and staff moves off, followed by other boats as fast as they get ready to sail.... We passed the mouth of the Potomac river a little before sunset and shortly after dropped anchor for the night.

January 10 (Friday)

There were increasing charges against the War Department for corruption, and murmurs were rising for the resignation of Simon Cameron, the Secretary of War.

Grant moved his troops on a cold, wet, and miserable march towards Columbus, Ky. While little was gained of military importance, the lessons learned in winter marching would be of great value later for both the troops and the commander.

The cooperation between the Union Army and Navy was paying off in the Port Royal area of South Carolina on the Coosaw River. Confederate Brigadier Gen. John C. Pemberton described the effectiveness of this teamwork:

> Although the enemy did not land in force at Page's Point or Cunningham's Bluff, it was entirely practicable for him to have done so under the cover of his gunboats.... At no time during his occupation of the river bank did he leave their [the gunboats,] protection, and, finally, when withdrawing to the island, did so under a fire from his vessels almost as heavy as that under which he had landed... by far the larger proportion of the [Confederate] casualties being from the shells of the fleet.

John Clifford Pemberton, a native Philadelphian, developed a love for the South during his days at West Point, where he graduated in 1837. He served as a cavalry officer in the Mexican War with distinction. In 1848 he married Martha Thompson of Norfolk, Virginia. On April 24, 1861, he resigned to join the Confederate Army, his two brothers remaining with the Union. He was appointed a Brigadier General initially, promoted to Major General in Jan 1862, and to Lt. General in October

1862. He commanded the Confederate forces during the siege of Vicksburg, and surrendered 29,000 men to Gen. U.S. Grant on July 4, 1863. Exchanged, he could find no job as a Lt. General, so he resigned and became a Colonel of Artillery, a rank he served in to the end of the war. He died in Pennsylvania in 1881.

Day, Pvt., Co. B, 25th Massachusetts Volunteer Infantry, aboard the steamer *New York*, Chesapeake Bay:

> A thick heavy fog envelopes the bay this morning, so thick we cannot see half the boat's length. In a little while the fog began to settle and it looked curious to see the topmasts of the boats and schooners above the fog as they passed us, their hulls being hidden entirely from view. 9 A.M. Weighed anchor and proceeded on our journey.... A little before noon we sighted Fortress Monroe and as we passed the *Minnesota* and other men-of-war lying in the roads, the sailors sprung into the rigging and cheered lustily to which the boys responded heartily from the boats, the bands playing as each boat passed. At 12 m., our boat dropped anchor between the rip raps and the fort....

January 11 (Saturday)

In Washington, Simon Cameron resigned as Secretary of War. Lincoln accepted with alacrity.

Day, Pvt., Co. B, 25th Massachusetts Volunteer Infantry, steamer *New York*, Hampton Roads, Va.:

> As I look out on the Old Dominion, the Mother of presidents, statesmen and heroes, my mind is filled with historical reminiscences of its past greatness and glory. Alas! that Virginia, a state that bore such a proud record in the history of our country... should now be sunk is the mire and slough of rebellion. There is no appearance of leaving here today....

January 12 (Sunday)

The fleet to conduct the amphibious operations against Roanoke Island sailed today from Hampton Roads, Va., headed by Flag Officer L. M. Goldsborough and Gen. Ambrose Burnside. The seizure of Hatteras Inlet in August '61 gave partial control to the Federals, but the Confederate control of Roanoke Island between Pamlico and Albemarle sounds still permitted Albemarle to be used for blockade running. The capture of Roanoke Island would also provide control of the many rivers flowing from the interior of North Carolina.

Day, Pvt., Co. B, 25th Massachusetts Volunteer Infantry, aboard the steamer *New York*, Hampton Roads, Va.:

> The big expedition, with colors flying and bands playing, sailed this afternoon, leading seaward. No one on board will know our destination until we round Cape Henry, when the seals are to be broken. A little before night we passed Cape Henry and headed south. We are now fairly at sea; the wind is blowing hard and the schooners are going past us as though we were anchored. Night has settled down on us and darkness covers the face of the deep....

January 13 (Monday)

In Washington, Lincoln indicated he would nominate Edwin M. Stanton as the new Secretary of War, replacing Cameron. Lincoln also held a meeting of the Cabinet and a council of generals, including McClellan, to discuss the plans for the war. McClellan refused to discuss his operational plans, resenting the interference of Lincoln and the other generals. Lincoln let this slide for the time being, hoping "Little Mac" did, indeed, have a plan.

"Stonewall" Jackson resumed his march south after remaining at Unger's Store in western Virginia since January 7th. The day began sunny, again, but a storm developed in the late afternoon. The march continued towards Romney.

Naval Lt. Worden was today ordered to New York to take command of the U.S.S. *Monitor*, now in the building process. On the western rivers, Flag Officer Foote ordered gunboats up both the Cumberland and Tennessee rivers in a demonstration of power.

The Federal fleet arrived off Hatteras Inlet and began the crossing of the bar into Pamlico Sound, N.C. Brigadier Gen. Burnside assumed command of the Department of North Carolina.

Day, Pvt., Co. B, 25th Massachusetts Volunteer Infantry, aboard the steamer *New York*, Hatteras Lighthouse, N.C.:

> Going on deck this morning, I found we were riding at anchor in sight of Hatteras light.... As they

weighed anchor, the boat rose and fell with the swells. I rather enjoyed this and thought it very nice. After a few moments I began to experience a peculiar sensation around the waistband, and it occurred to me that I had better go and lie down. After half an hour I was all right again and went on deck. Mr. Mulligan said, "We are going to have a great storm and Hatteras is a bad place to be caught in a storm." But by way of encouragement, he tells us we are safer with him aboard the *New York* than we should be home in bed. At 1 P.M. we dropped anchor in front of the battery at Hatteras inlet, in the midst of a terrific southeast storm. Our fleet comprising nearly 100 sail are making the inlet as fast as possible; but it is feared that some of them will not be able to get in and will either be lost or have to put back. This is indeed the grandest, wildest scene I ever beheld! As far as the eye can reach, the water is rolling, foaming and dashing over the shoals, throwing its white spray far into the air, as though the sea and sky met. This is no time for man to war against man. The forces of Heaven are loose and in all their fury, the wind howls, the sea rages, the eternal is here in all his majesty....

A large steamer, attempting to run in this afternoon ran on the shoals and will probably prove a wreck. As she came in sight and attempted the passage of the inlet, we watched her with breathless anxiety until she seemed to have passed her greatest danger and all were hopefully looking for her safe arrival, when suddenly she struck the shoal and turned broadside towards us, the sea breaking over her. A shudder ran through the crowd and disappointment was on every countenance. Tugs were immediately dispatched to her assistance, but returned unable to render her any. Capt. Clark thinks if she does not break up during the night, and the wind lulls, that perhaps in the morning she can be got off, or at least those on board of her can. It is not known whether she contains troops or stores. If she should go to pieces during the night, God help those on board of her, as there is no one here that can.

January 14 (Tuesday)

Jackson's men were on the road all day heading towards Romney, marching in a rain-and-sleet storm which made things more than a little difficult.

Barber, Pvt., Co. D, 15th Illinois Volunteer Infantry, Otterville, Mo.:

The doctor examined me and told me that he would make out my discharge papers. I told him that I did not want a discharge, but would be glad of a furlough, and he put me down for a sixty days' furlough, and I supposed that I would get one without doubt. Great was my astonishment when the furloughs were made out, to learn that I did not get one....

Day, Pvt., Co. B, 25th Massachusetts Volunteer Infantry, Hatteras Lighthouse, N.C.:

This morning presents a scene of terror and wildest grandeur. The wrecked steamer has not broken up, but has settled down in the sand, the sea breaking over her, and her rigging is full of men. Boats that have been sent to her assistance are returning, having been unable to render any. We learn from the returning boats that she is the *City of New York*, loaded with stores. Another tug, with Gen. Burnside and a crew of picked men has just gone to their assistance and it is hoped will be able to take them off. The general is not one to see his men perish and make no effort to rescue them. I reckon our friends at home, when they hear of the loss of this boat, will confound it with our own and will experience the greatest anxiety until they get our letters, or get righted through the papers. The tug returned this afternoon, bringing off the officers and crew of the wrecked steamer who report that she is breaking up and will soon go to pieces.

The wind is blowing a gale. Many of our boats and vessels which have arrived are parting their cables and dragging their anchors, are being driven ashore or sinking or fouling with each other. The saloon and upper works of our boat are stove in from gunboats and schooners fouling with us. One of our anchor cables has parted and the engine is slowly working, helping the other one. Many of our vessels are still outside and fears are entertained that some of them will be lost. Capt. Clark says no boat can get in here today without the most skillful pilot, and then at great risk of being lost. The gunboat *Zouave*, with companies D and H of our regiment aboard is in a sinking condition. Tugs are alongside of her and the boys are scratching for their lives to get aboard of them. This is the kind of soldiering that makes the boys think of home and of their mothers. I cannot help laughing just a little when a boat or schooner fouls with us and the timber and planks begin to crack, to see the boys come out of their bunks, their eyes sticking out of their heads, and rush up the stairs to see what the matter is. Well, it is not strange that these young boys should feel a little nervous, as it takes a man of pretty strong nerve to keep his fears down. We are here and have got to make the best of it....

January 15 (Wednesday)

Stanton was confirmed by the Senate as the new Secretary of War. This would prove to be a mixed blessing. He was a friend of McClellan's, and not so friendly with Lincoln. Edwin McMasters Stanton was 57 years old at this time, a native of Steubenville, Ohio, a former Attorney General in the Buchanan Administration, and an avid believer in saving the Union at any cost. He would draw much criticism during his tenure as Secretary of War, much of it deserved. He stayed in the Cabinet after Lincoln's death, resigning in 1868. Grant offered him a seat on the U.S. Supreme Court, which he accepted. He died on Christmas Eve, 1869, four days after being confirmed by the Senate.

Jackson's column finally reached Romney, western Virginia, after two weeks on the march.

Day, Pvt., Co. B, 25th Massachusetts Volunteer Infantry, Hatteras Inlet, N.C.:

Rough weather still continues and we are out of rations, subsisting entirely on hardtack and a short ration of that. Unless it calms down so a tug can get alongside, we shall be entirely out in a day or two more. Three more boats dragged their anchors and went ashore this morning and other boats with their flags union down, are calling for help. In fact, things are beginning to look gloomy, but amidst all the trouble and discouragements, Gen. Burnside is everywhere to be seen, flying about among the boats and vessels, encouraging his men and looking as cheerful as though everything was going to suit him. Today a rebel boat came down the sound to take a look at us. One of our boats went out to meet her, but the rebel, not caring for an interview, hauled off. The colonel, surgeon, and one other man of the 9th New Jersey regiment were drowned today by the upsetting of a small boat they were in. And so we go, trouble and dangers by sea, and I suppose there will be more by land, if we ever get there.

January 16 (Thursday)

At Romney, Jackson wanted to attack Cumberland, Md., which was a major terminus of the Baltimore and Ohio Railroad, and capture the storehouses there, but he could not get enough men together for the attack. It was deferred for the day.

Lt. Worden reported to New York to command the U.S.S. *Monitor*, and wrote Secretary of the Navy Gideon Welles, "... I have this day reported for duty for the command of the U.S.S. *Steamer*, building for Capt. Ericsson." In two months, Worden's name would be forever inscribed in naval history after the battle of the ironclads in Hampton Roads.

Day, Pvt., Co. B, 25th Massachusetts Volunteer Infantry, Hatteras Inlet, N.C.:

Three small boats ashore and leaking, one of them is the U.S. mail-boat *Suwanee* from Fortress Monroe for Hilton Head. She ran in here this morning to leave mails and dispatches for this fleet, intending to sail this afternoon, but owing to the high winds and heavy sea, she parted her cable and drifted on an anchor fluke, breaking a hole in her bottom and sunk. She lies on the sand with her deck about four feet out of water. It is said she can be pumped out and raised when it calms, of which time, however, there seems to be a very dim prospect. We have just heard from the old steamer *Pocahontas*. She went ashore below Hatteras light. She had our team horses aboard and nearly all of them were lost. The men who were aboard of her got ashore and are now coming down the island. The schooner on which the signal corps were aboard has not been seen or heard from and there is much anxiety for her safety. We have kept alive on hardtack thus far, but on account of the storm no tug has been able to get alongside with rations, and we going it with half a ration of hardtack and coffee once a day. Five cents apiece are freely offered for hardtack with no takers.

Amid a naval bombardment, boat crews from the U.S.S. *Hatteras* landed at Cedar Keys, Fla., and destroyed a Confederate battery, seven small ships loaded and ready to run the blockade, the railroad depot, a wharf, and the telegraph office. Community services were disrupted for a period of time.

Flag Officer Foote, on the western rivers, reported that seven of the gunboats being built by Eads were placed into commission on this day. Although all were of wooden construction, they would play a decisive role in the war.

January 17 (Friday)

Today, Jackson ordered the attack on Cumberland, Md., but had to cancel it for lack of troops, for the second time. One of his units had but 15 men able to walk.

Operations were beginning against Ft. Henry on the Tennessee River. About 20 miles below St. Louis, the Mississippi was blocked solid with large ice floes, disrupting all river navigation.

Day, Pvt., Co. B, 25th Massachusetts Volunteer Infantry, Hatteras Inlet, N.C.:

> The great storm has at last subsided and the sun once more shines out. All the bands are out playing, everything is putting on a more cheerful appearance and we can now look around and see the result of the storm. Boats and vessels are ashore all around us, in a partially wrecked or damaged condition. The upper works of our boat are little better than a wreck, from the bowsprits of schooners and catheads of other craft that have fouled with us. Our accommodations are rather limited as is also the fare, but by practicing forbearance and great good nature, the harmony is as perfect as could be expected. A tug is alongside with rations, so at last the long fast is broken. I think the boys will not be over nice about their dinners when they get them. I have sometimes thought I could relish a dinner from that soup I saw at the park barracks. Our dinner today was served about 2 P.M.; bill of fare, pea soup and coffee. I have always persuaded myself that I didn't like pea soup and wouldn't eat it, but today I changed my mind and thought I never ate anything that tasted quite so good as pea soup. I voted it a great luxury.

January 18 (Saturday)

John Tyler, former President of the United States, was buried today at Hollywood Cemetery in Richmond, near the James River. He would have some very distinguished company there before the end of this bloody conflict.

In Kentucky, the Virginian who had remained loyal to the Union, George H. Thomas, brought his troops closer to the confrontation with Brigadier Gen. George B. Crittenden, CSA, on the Cumberland River. Crittenden had his back to the river and was in a poorly defined position.

Jackson finally ordered his troops into winter quarters at Bath (Berkeley Springs) and Moorefield. Loring's Brigade, a recent newcomer to Jackson's command, was at Romney, which they referred to as a "pig pen."

The long chase after the C.S.S. *Sumter*, Commander Semmes, took on a new look. The U.S.S. *Kearsarge* had been ordered to Cadiz, Spain, to track Semmes down. The chase would be a long one.

January 19 (Sunday)

The Battle of Mill Springs was fought near the banks of the Cumberland River in Kentucky, between Federal forces under Brigadier Gen. George H. Thomas, and Confederate generals Crittenden and Zollicoffer. Crittenden escaped the Federals and left the area in a pouring rain. Zollicoffer wore a white raincoat during the engagement and was killed. The Rebels escaped across the river, leaving only discarded equipment and supplies. The Confederate defense line in Kentucky had been broken and would never be repaired—a demoralizing effect on all, except for the Federals, who gained support in eastern Kentucky and Tennessee.

Day, Pvt., Co. B, 25th Massachusetts Volunteer Infantry, Hatteras Inlet, N.C.:

> Witnessing boat collisions and wrecks is getting old and the boys are amusing themselves by writing letters, making up their diaries, playing cards, reading old magazines and newspapers which they have read half a dozen times before; and some of them are actually reading their Bibles. Of all the lonely, God-forsaken looking places I ever saw, this Hatteras island takes the premium. It is simply a sandbar rising a little above the water, and the shoals extend nearly 100 miles out to sea. The water is never still and fair weather is never known; storms and sea gulls are the only productions. Sometimes there is a break in the clouds when the sun can get a shine through for a few moments, but this very rarely happens. The island extends from Cape Henry, Virginia to Cape Lookout, North Carolina, with occasional holes washed through it, which are called inlets. It is from one-half to two miles wide, and the only things which make

any attempt to grow are a few shrub pines and fishermen. I don't think there is a bird or any kind of animal, unless it is a dog, on the island, not even a grasshopper, as one would have to prospect the whole island to find a blade of grass, and in the event of his finding one would sing himself to death.... It is the key, or gate-way, to nearly all of eastern North Carolina and places us directly in the rear of Norfolk, Va....

January 20 (Monday)

At Hatteras Inlet, N.C., the amphibious operations fleet had arrived on the 13th and was preparing for the assault on Roanoke Island. The C.S.S. *Sea Bird*, Flag Officer Lynch, reported that he had visited the Hatteras Inlet and "there saw a large fleet of steamers and transports." He further wrote to Confederate Secretary of the Navy Mallory of the importance of the area which Roanoke Island controlled, "Here is the great thoroughfare from Albemarle Sound and its tributaries, and if the enemy obtain lodgements or succeed in passing here he will cut off a very rich country from Norfolk market."

With the arrival of Flag Officer Farragut in the Gulf of Mexico, the operational areas were split, giving Farragut the area from west Florida to Mexico. His main mission, however, was to capture New Orleans.

David Glasgow Farragut was born at Campbell's Station, Tenn., on July 5, 1801. He was adopted by Commander David D. Porter. Farragut was raised with Porter's son, also named David D. Through the elder Porter's influence Farragut was appointed a midshipman on December 17, 1810, and served under Porter during the War of 1812. He was promoted to Captain in 1855. He was living in Norfolk, Va., at the beginning of the war, going north because of his loyalty to the Union. He commanded the Gulf Squadron that captured New Orleans and Mobile Bay. He was appointed the first Rear Admiral and Vice Admiral in U.S. naval history and was promoted to full Admiral after the war. He died at Portsmouth, N.H., on August 14, 1870.

Wills, 3rd Sgt., Co. E, 8th Illinois Infantry, near Columbus, Ky.:

It goes confounded good once more to stand on boards, and be able to sit down without wet coming through a fellow's pants.... We got on the steamer *Aleck Scott* last Tuesday morning with five days' rations and started down the river through very heavy floating ice. 'Twas a very cold day and full three inches of snow lay on the ground. We landed at Ft. Jefferson and camped for the night. By some mismanagement our tents and equipage failed to come and we had to cook the bacon we had in our haversacks on sticks over the fire, for supper, and sleep out on the snow, without tents to protect us from the wind. That was a sweet old night! Next day we shouldered our knapsacks, blankets all wet by a rain from 2 to 5 in the morning... and tramped about 10 miles in a southeast direction... and camped on Mayville Creek. Again we lay on the snow and frozen ground with feather beds of brush, and at 9 next morning started on the road to Columbus.

We went out to Little Meadows which is about eight or nine miles from Columbus and halted. Taylor's battery... now unlimbered and planted their guns.... We waited here two hours and then formed again and returned to our camp of the previous night. It had turned warm by this time and the slush was six inches deep on our backward march. Slept in the mud that night and remained in camp all next day, during which it rained every hour. Friday night it rained in a small way all the time....

Saturday we got out of "provish" and at 1 P.M. we struck tents, and thought we were off for home sure. But we only marched back a few miles and camped at Elliott's Mills. Here, by orders from the colonel, we killed two hogs for the company, and we took what cornmeal we wanted from the mill, and we supped sumptuously.

Sunday we started for the river and of all the marches, that beats! We waded through at least eight streams from one to two feet deep and five to ten yards wide. I had shoes, and after wading the first stream, I cut all the front upper off to let the water out handier. It made it gay and festive after that. Object of expedish, don't know, don't care, only know that it did me good. I feel 100 percent better than I did when I started.

Col. Pitt Kellogg has brought me my commission as 1st Lieutenant in his regiment, and I am adjutant in the 3d battalion, Major Rawalts. I go to Cape Girardeau the last of this week.

January 21 (Tuesday)

After remaining in Romney, western Virginia,

since the 16th, Jackson ordered Garnett and the Stonewall Brigade back to Winchester. Jackson went with his old brigade. It was Jackson's 38th birthday.

Lt. S.L. Phelps, USN, had completed a reconnaissance of the area around Ft. Donelson, and was recommending the use of mortar boats. Flag Officer Foote, however, had no boats which could become available to meet the Army's schedule for assault of Donelson.

Day, Pvt., Co. B, 25th Massachusetts Volunteer Infantry, Hatteras Inlet, N.C.:

> The weather still continues in an unsettled state. Although not so rough as it was, it is still too rough to attempt to do much. All the vessels of our fleet are now here, except those that were lost and the schooner with the signal corps. Nothing has been heard from her and we are beginning to think that she too may be lost. Albert Tucker of company B died this morning and his body was taken ashore and buried on the beach this afternoon. It is a sad sight to see men die and be buried here on this low, lonely sand-bar.

January 22 (Wednesday)

In New York, Lt. Worden reported good progress on the U.S.S. *Monitor.* He was awaiting delivery of the 11-inch guns which made up the main armament.

On the Tennessee River, Lt. Shirk and Brigadier Gen. Charles F. Smith were aboard the U.S.S. *Lexington* making an assessment of the defenses of Ft. Henry. The snows in the mountains and the rain of the fall had the river running full. Shirk reports, "The river is so full at present (and is still rising) that whenever there is water there is a channel."

Day, Pvt., Co. B, 25th Massachusetts Volunteer Infantry, Hatteras Inlet, N.C.:

> The light-draught boats are engaged in finding and making a channel across the bar, or swash as it is called, of sufficient depth of water to enable the large steamers to cross into the sound. One great trouble about that is if they find one today it will all be filled up tomorrow. We shall have to wait till calmer weather before we can cross.
>
> A schooner came alongside today and left us rations of steamed pork, hardtack and condensed sea water. This was a very timely arrival as we have been very short of water for two or three days and pretty much everything else. Rattlesnake pork will taste pretty good again after a few days fast. Condensed sea water is rather a disagreeable beverage, but still is a little ahead of no water at all. I think, however, it might be made palatable by adding about nine parts whiskey to one of water. This water and pork is all manufactured here on the spot. They have a sort of rendering establishment where they make it, but I cannot believe that the pork would take a premium in any fair in the country unless it was for meanness....
>
> Old Dan is having a terrible fit of the blues. He cannot understand why we were sent to this God-forsaken place. I tell him that God has not forsaken it, but has sent us here to save it; and Dan, with a big oath swore that it was not worth saving....

January 23 (Thursday)

In Missouri, Major Gen. Henry Halleck ordered the seizure of pro-Southerners who had failed to pay assessments for the aid to pro-Northern refugees.

Jackson arrived back in Winchester, where he was reunited with his wife, who had stayed at the home of Rev. Graham.

Day, Pvt., Co. B, 25th Massachusetts Volunteer Infantry, Hatteras Inlet, N.C.:

> Another great storm. The wind is blowing a gale and the sea is dashing, foaming and threatening everything with destruction. The camps on shore are flooded, the soldiers driven into the fort or up the island; more vessels ashore and the fleet going to the devil. A great many of the men are beginning to despond and in fact the success of the expedition begins to look gloomy enough. Nothing but hardship and disaster has attended us since we left Fortress Monroe, and God only knows when it will end.... I have always had rather a desire for a sea voyage, but I am willing to confess that that wish is fully gratified. This being "rocked in the cradle of the deep" sounds all very pretty in song and romance, but the romance is played out with me, and I think the person who wrote the song, "A Life on the Ocean Wave" must have been a proper subject for a lunatic asylum.

January 24 (Friday)

Probing operations continued up the Cumberland and Tennessee rivers in the west and the troops were busy in the Pamlico Sound area.

Day, Pvt., Co. B, 25th Massachusetts Volunteer Infantry, Hatteras Inlet, N.C.:

The storm has subsided somewhat, but is still rough enough for all practical purposes. Mr. Milligan says fair weather *has been known here*, and taking that as a precedent, we may naturally conclude it perhaps *may* be again. This is certainly the longest storm I ever remember of and never read of but one that exceeded it. That was the one Old Noah got caught out in, but he had the advantage of us, as his was the only craft afloat and had plenty of sea room; besides his style of navigation was ahead of ours, as he let her drift around where she pleased and trusted to luck for a landing. That kind of navigation might have answered for those times, but would never do for Hatteras....

January 25 (Saturday)

The struggle continued to move the troop transports across the sandbar at Hatteras Inlet into Pamlico Sound. This had to be done before operations against Roanoke Island could be accomplished.

Day, Pvt., Co. B, 25th Massachusetts Volunteer Infantry, Hatteras Inlet, N.C.:

The storm is at last over, for to-day at least. It has cleared off warm and pleasant and is the first bright day since we came here.... Our attention is taken up watching the operations going on in the harbor among the shipping. Steamers are being towed across the swash into the sound and steamers and tugs are at work straining every nerve to pull off the boats that are ashore.... The big steamer *Northerner* attempted to cross the sound at flood tide this morning and stuck in the middle. She carries the 21st Massachusetts and I think they will have to be taken off before she can get across....

The horses do not appear to stand hardships and privations as well as the men. On short feed, condensed sea water, with no exercise, they grow sick and debilitated. A schooner is lying but a short distance from us with a deck-load of horses belonging to a Rhode Island battery and they are jumping them overboard and swimming them ashore. It is curious to observe the horses as they are led up to the gangway; to see them brace themselves back and shudder to take the fearful leap.... The *Northerner* has crossed into the sound and anchored. As she got off and moved into the sound, cheer after cheer went up from all the fleet....

January 26 (Sunday)

The "Creole," Gen. Pierre G.T. Beauregard, was ordered to Tennessee to be second-in-command to Gen. Albert Sidney Johnston. Beauregard, the hero of Sumter and Manassas, previously served with Gen. Joseph E. Johnston, commanding the Confederates in Virginia.

Day, Pvt., Co. B, 25th Massachusetts Volunteer Infantry, Hatteras Inlet, N.C.:

Quite a number of boats have been hauled off and are now lying in the sound.... The steamer *Louisiana* with the 6th New Hampshire aboard lies high and dry on the shoal and it will be a job to get her off, but I reckon she will have to come or come to pieces. When half a dozen big steamers get hold they make a pretty strong team and something has got to come or break. I learn she is hogged, whatever that is. I shouldn't be surprised if she was, if she has been well supplied with this gull bait they call pork....

Allen, Pvt., Co. K, 1st Battalion, 10th Illinois Cavalry, Quincy, Illinois:

...hope you will excuse me for not writing soon this time.... The health of our regiment continues good. While at Camp Butler there was very little sickness in the 10th Cavalry except measles, of which there were many cases, but no deaths. We had fine weather for a long time after we went to Camp Butler, but for a while before we left that place, there was some colder weather than I ever felt in North Carolina, but I did not mind it.... Muddy, sloppy weather was more disagreeable to us than cold weather and cooking out of doors over a log fire in bad weather was the most disagreeable duty we had to perform, much more so than standing guard. We left Camp Butler on last Tuesday evening on the cars, and were detained so that we did not reach Versailles until about sunrise next morning. We passed quite a disagreeable night, crowded in the box cars on top of our baggage without any fire or blankets.... We reached Quincy safe and sound on Wednesday evening. Our regiment is quartered at Camp Flagg in the fair grounds, but Company K is quartered in the third story of a large brick building on the river. Our house was formerly used as a cotton factory.... We have good quarters and a large cooking stove.... I bought a horse of our captain for $115, payable in two, four and six months. Our regiment was paid off on January 11th and 13th. Each private in Company K who went to Camp Butler at first, received $52.90. I paid $35 on my horse and sent $6 by our captain to Ravenscroft for your father, which he has no doubt received before this time.... Give my respects to my friends and to all good Union men. As to the Secessionists, they may all go to hell....

January 27 (Monday)

President Lincoln, finally weary of McClellan's inactivity, issued General War Order No. 1, which declared that on February 22, 1862, all land and sea forces would attack the insurgents. It was, in fact, an act of desperation on Lincoln's part. No one seemed eager to get moving, in particular McClellan.

Confederate Secretary of War Judah Benjamin issued an order to Gen. Wise, who was commanding the troops at Roanoke Island, to hold the island at all costs. The odds were 5-to-1 in favor of the Federals.

Day, Pvt., Co. B, 25th Massachusetts Volunteer Infantry, Hatteras Inlet, N.C.:

...We were transferred to the steam ferry-boat *Curlew* and are now anchored in the sound. The *New York* is to be lightened of everything on board and it is thought that with a full sea and some help, she may be able to cross.... We are packed in here as thick as bees with scarcely standing room and the old craft is open at both ends, admitting the cold winds and rains, besides being wet and dirty as a stable.... I should think the water casks were a cemetery for dead rats by the way the water tastes; condensed sea water is a luxury to it and by way of encouragement we are told that we are to have some tomorrow....

January 28 (Tuesday)

Flag Officer Foote notified Gen. Henry Halleck that he and Gen. Grant were of the opinion that Ft. Henry might be taken with four gunboats and the troops available. Halleck considered the condition of the river and notified Grant that the order would be issued as soon as he determined the conditions of the roads. Foote, impatient, told Halleck that the river was at flood stage and *this* was the time to make the attack using the river. Halleck waited.

In Hampton Roads, the presence of the C.S.S. *Virginia* kept the blockading ships in a constant state of alert and worry.

Day, Pvt., Co. B, 25th Massachusetts Volunteer Infantry, Hatteras Inlet, N.C.:

Work is still going on getting the boats off and getting them across the bar.... The little steamer *Pilot Boy* with Generals Burnside and Foster aboard is flying around among the vessels of the fleet giving orders to the boat commanders and commanders of the troops. The sutler came aboard today.... He brought with him a small stock of fruit and other notions which went off like hot cakes at any price which he chose to ask. Some of the boys thought the prices pretty high but they should consider that it is with great difficulty and expense that things are got here at all....

January 29 (Wednesday)

At Occoquan, south of Washington, a dance was being held by a group of Confederates when some Federals dropped in, uninvited. A brief skirmish ensued, and the party broke up.

At Hatteras Inlet, the troop ships were still not all over the sandbar. Supplying fresh water to the troops on the ships was a real problem, and it got worse daily.

Day, Pvt., Co. B, 25th Massachusetts Volunteer Infantry, Hatteras Inlet, N.C.:

The long lost signal corps arrived today.... They have had a hard time of it, having been fourteen days on the passage from Fortress Monroe. They ran out to sea in the first great storm and the succession of storms has prevented them from getting in. They were well nigh famished when they arrived.

We are today luxuriating on good water, the first we have had for many days.... We are thriving on a half ration of steamed pork and hardtack, with condensed sea water. The half ration of pork is a bountiful supply; it is so strong and oily a very little answers the purpose and hardtack is the chief dependence.... Coffee is entirely out of the question for on this craft there is no chance for the cooks to make it in great quantities although they do manage to make a small amount for the officers....

January 30 (Thursday)

A landmark in history was reached today when the U.S.S. *Monitor* was launched at Greenpoint, Long Island.

Mason and Slidell finally landed at Southampton, England, after their interrupted journey from Charleston.

Loring's Brigade of Jackson's force had been in Romney since January 15th, and today Loring and his officers signed a petition asking for relief. This petition was sent over Jackson's head directly to Secretary of War Judah Benjamin, because Loring believed he could get no satisfaction from Jackson directly. Benjamin, in an immediate action, sent a directive to Jackson to remove Loring's command from Romney to Winchester. This ended one of the toughest campaigns attempted during the war by either army.

Major Gen. Henry Halleck ordered the advance up the Cumberland and Tennessee rivers in Kentucky, warning Grant that the roads would be quagmires. Grant moved his men and supplies by gunboat.

Day, Pvt., Co. B, 25th Massachusetts Volunteer Infantry, Hatteras Inlet, N.C.:

> Our canteens are again filled with contraband water so we shall be alright today as far as that is concerned. Some of the boys made a raid last night on the sutler's stuff and appropriated to themselves pretty much what he had. I cannot approve of that, as the sutler is at a good deal of trouble and expense to get a few notions for us and probably sells them as cheap as he can afford.... This afternoon a small boat was seen coming down flying a white flag. The boat contained one darkey who had risked the perils of the sound to escape from the land of Jeff, the house of bondage.

January 31 (Friday)

Lincoln, to supplement his General War Order No. 1, issued Special War Order No. 1, which was directed specifically at Major Gen. George B. McClellan. In this order, Lincoln directed that action be taken against Manassas *before* February 22nd. "Little Mac" ignored the whole thing.

Day, Pvt., Co. B, 25th Massachusetts Volunteer Infantry, Hatteras Inlet, N.C.:

> This morning a small schooner was seen coming down the sound. A boat went over and met her; she contained seven darkies who said they stole the schooner and left in her from Roanoke island.... They can probably give some valuable information in regard to the affairs on the island.... We got a big mail today; any quantity of letters and newspapers and the boys are cheered up wonderfully to hear from home.

FEBRUARY 1862

In the wintering armies, the troops sickened with the usual colds, flu, and other maladies common to large groups of people. The Southern coast, already in peril, braced itself for more troubles as the Union advanced towards Roanoke Island and Savannah. Few Southern ports were open for even the occasional blockade runner. The noose tightened.

In the west, especially on the Tennessee and Cumberland rivers, the Federal gunboats reigned supreme. The Confederate Navy was nonexistent on these waters, and Flag Officer Foote was having things his way. The February *Atlantic Monthly* published the latest poem by Julia Ward Howe which was almost immediately translated into song as "The Battle Hymn of the Republic."

February 1 (Saturday)

The assault on Forts Henry and Donelson was getting underway, Flag Officer Foote telegraphed Washington, "I leave early to-morrow with four armored gunboats on an expedition cooperating with the Army. Senior officer will telegraph you during my absence...." This represented a continuation of the good working relationships between the Army and Navy on the western rivers.

Barber, Pvt., Co. D, 15th Illinois Volunteer Infantry, Jefferson City, Mo.:

> Orders now came for us to march to Jefferson City. Not being able to travel, I was sent with the sick by rail.... On arriving at Jefferson City, I took up my quarters at a private boarding house, and one week later when the regiment arrived, I reported for duty.

The regiment rested here for a few days and then took the cars for St. Louis.

Day, Pvt., Co. B, 25th Massachusetts Volunteer Infantry, Hatteras Sound, N.C.:

A very heavy rain set in last night and continued until 9 o'clock this morning. The old *Curlew* looks as though she had been down cruising for mermaids and came back disappointed. She is all afloat, fore, aft and amidships; the rain drove in at the ends, the deck leaked and altogether we had a pretty rough night of it. I cannot say how the others slept, but my sleep was anything but balmy. I did not, in fact, dream of dwelling in marble halls.

The *New York* has crossed the bar and we are again aboard of her; thank our lucky stars. Good-bye, old *Curlew*! and may you find a sweet and lasting repose at the bottom of the sound before you are many days older....

February 2 (Sunday)

The U.S.S. *Hartford*, flagship of Flag Officer Farragut, hoisted anchor at Hampton Roads near Ft. Monroe, and sailed for Ship Island, Mississippi, today. Farragut was to take command of the Western Gulf Blockading Squadron with the primary mission of capturing New Orleans.

On the western rivers, Flag Officer Foote, just before sailing, exhorted his command on coolness under fire with the following order to his four gunboats:

Let it be also distinctly impressed upon the mind of every man firing a gun that, while the first shot may be either of too much elevation or too little, there is no excuse for a second wild fire, as the first will indicate the inaccuracy of the aim of the gun, which must be elevated or depressed, or trained, as circumstances require. Let it be reiterated that random firing is not only a mere waste of ammunition, but, what is far worse, it encourages the enemy when he sees shot and shell falling harmlessly about and beyond him....

Day, Pvt., Co. B, 25th Massachusetts Volunteer Infantry, Hatteras Sound, N.C.:

A high wind prevailed this morning and the sea was somewhat rough; the boat had considerable motion, but the boys had their sea legs on, so it caused them very little trouble. Our company cooks, with commendable enterprise and industry and with an eye to our present well being, furnished us with baked beans and hot coffee for breakfast. This was a great treat and every man had all he wanted; a vote of thanks was given the cooks. For dinner, boiled beef was served, the first we have had since leaving Fortress Monroe. I hope this kind of fare will hold out, but fear we shall have a relapse of the worst kind....

February 3 (Monday)

In Washington, President Lincoln declined the offer of war elephants from the King of Siam stating that the weather "does not reach a latitude so low as to favor the multiplication of the elephant."

In a good move, the Washington government deemed that the crews of captured privateers were to be considered "prisoners of war" and not pirates.

In Richmond, reports from intelligence sources told of the departure of the river fleet for Ft. Henry on the Tennessee River. The reports were certainly true. Grant, embarking his troops on transports at Cairo and Paducah, advised Halleck, "Will be off up the Tennessee at 6 o'clock. Command, 23 regiments in all."

Day, Pvt., Co. B, 25th Massachusetts Volunteer Infantry, Hatteras Sound, N.C.:

The winds have ceased and the sea is as calm as an honest man's conscience.... Business is brisk today; all the boats are in the sound and the schooners are alongside of them supplying them with coal, water, and rations, preparatory to a trip up the sound. Everything now seems to be nearly ready, and I expect that some fine morning we will make a call on our southern friends.... I would much rather they welcome us to a good dinner of fishballs than cannon balls; but I suppose they will have their own choice of reception and we must reciprocate the best we can. Merchandise brings a right smart price in this market, and a man needs a heavy purse to purchase very extensively. I paid $1 for the same quantity of tobacco I bought at home for forty cents.

In Southampton, England the C.S.S. *Nashville*, Lt. Robert B. Pegram, sailed. The H.M.S. *Shannon* stood by to prevent the U.S.S. *Tuscarora* from sailing in pursuit. International agreements required a 24-hour period between sailings of ships of belligerent nations from a neutral port.

February 4 (Tuesday)

At Ft. Henry on the Tennessee River, Brigadier Gen. Lloyd Tilghman informed Gen. John B. Floyd that an enemy force had landed five miles below the fort. While the troops were landing, Flag Officer Foote and Gen. Grant aboard the U.S.S. *Cincinnati* led the four gunboats up the river to reconnoitre and trade some ammunition with the Confederate gunners. Torpedoes, torn loose from their moorings, floated past, and Foote had one taken aboard for inspection. The story goes that while Foote and Grant were watching the disassembling of the mine, a strange hiss was heard. The deck was cleared very fast with Grant getting to the top of the ladder first. When Foote asked Grant what the hurry was, Grant replied that "the Army did not believe in letting the Navy get ahead of it." The landing went well and the approach march was set amid the pouring rain.

In Richmond, the Virginia House of Delegates discussed enlisting free Negroes in the Confederate forces. In many Southern units the terms of enlistment were about to expire, and the commanders were appealing to the troops to stay on.

February 5 (Wednesday)

At Ft. Henry, the river had flooded a good portion of the lower fort, and Gen. Tilghman's troops were having a hard time with morale. They had only 3000 or so men to defend the fort.

In England, Queen Victoria lifted all restrictions against shipping gunpowder, arms and ammunition from Britain. This threw the door wide open for profiteers.

Day, Pvt., Co. B, 25th Massachusetts Volunteer Infantry, Albemarle Sound, N.C.:

> The clink of the windlass is heard on all the boats hoisting up their anchors, so here we go for a trip up the sound, probably for Roanoke island. This island holds the Albemarle sound and all that part of North Carolina lying on it and also Southeast Virginia. It is quite an important point and we learn is strongly defended. Our fleet consists of about seventy sail of all kinds and makes an imposing appearance.... After a few hours sail, the low, pine-covered shore of the old North state presented itself to view. We were in sight of the shore all day and not a house was to be seen or any visible signs of life, excepting huge columns of smoke rising above the tree-tops. These were probably signal fires as they could be seen along the shore as far as the eye could reach. We sailed today to within ten miles of the lighthouse at the western end of the Pamlico sound, the entrance to Croatan sound, in which is situated the coveted island. Here we dropped anchor for the night....

February 6 (Thursday)

The Navy stole the march on the Army today when Flag Officer Foote and his gunboat armada captured Ft. Henry with ground troops. Using four armored and three wooden gunboats, the fire from the fleet was sufficient to cause Brigadier Gen. Tilghman to surrender his reduced strength command, Tilghman having sent most of his men cross-country to Ft. Donelson. The gunboats opened fire on the open fort at about 11 A.M. and Tilghman, after striking the flotilla with 59 shots, lowered the flag at about 2 P.M. and gave up his command of 12 officers, 66 men and 16 patients. Heavy rains had prevented Grant's 15,000 troops from reaching the fort in time for the assault. Foote departed with most of the fleet for Cairo to repair his ships and prepare for the assault on Ft. Donelson. The Confederate gunners had used their guns well, but Gen. Albert S. Johnston, CSA, noted:

> The capture of that Fort [Henry] by the enemy gives them the control of the navigation of the Tennessee River, and their gunboats are now ascending the river to Florence [Alabama].... Should Ft. Donelson be taken it will open the route to the enemy to Nashville, giving them the means of breaking the bridges and destroying the ferryboats on the river as far as navigable.

In North Carolina, the transports were all across the sandbar and preparations for the assault on Roanoke Island proceeded.

Day, Pvt., Co. B, 25th Massachusetts Volunteer Infantry, near Roanoke Island, N.C.:

> Hoisted anchor and steamed to within a short distance of the light house and in full view of the

island. Here we again dropped anchor and the day was spent in prospecting by the gunboats. They went up near the island and after a few hours returned, reporting three forts and a number of armed boats and schooners.... One would have supposed to have heard the boys talk last night that we were all Napoleons. They talked of booming guns, the rattle of infantry, of splendid bayonet charges... On the principle, I suppose, of those who know nothing, fear nothing, but then it is a good plan not to get our tails down until we are obliged to.... Ammunition was dealt out today and our cartridge boxes now contain forty rounds of the death-dealing missiles....

At Jefferson City, La., the C.S.S. *Louisiana* was finally launched after much delay. It still required fitting with guns before it would see service.

February 7 (Friday)

At the White House, Willie Lincoln, the President's youngest son, lay critically ill with typhoid fever. Mrs. Lincoln was beside herself with grief and worry.

In western Virginia the Confederates abandoned Romney, and it was occupied by Federal troops again. The Confederates moved back towards Winchester.

On the Tennessee River Lt. S.L. Phelps, commanding the U.S.S. *Conestoga*, forced the Confederates to abandon and burn the steamers *Samuel Orr*, *Appleton Belle*, and *Lynn Boyd* to prevent their capture by the Federals. The *Samuel Orr* was loaded with torpedoes, and as Phelps reported:

> ...very soon exploded; the second one was freighted with powder, cannon, shot, grape, balls, etc. Fearing an explosion from the fired boats (there were two together), I had stopped at a distance of 1,000 yards; but even there our skylights were broken by the concussion; the light upper deck was raised bodily, doors were forced open, and locks and fastenings everywhere broken. The whole river for half a mile around about was completely beaten up by the falling fragments and the shower of shot, grape, balls, etc.

Brigadier Gen. John A. McClernand took this opportunity to rename the newly captured Ft. Henry. It was to be called Ft. Foote in honor of the Flag Officer.

John A. McClernand was a political general through and through. Born in Kentucky on May 30, 1812, his family moved to Illinois, where he grew up and studied law. Eventually he became the Democratic Representative from Lincoln's home district. Like Lincoln, his only military experience Was during the Black Hawk War. When the Civil War started, he was appointed a Brigadier General on May 17, 1861. He was ambitious, selfish, and pompous, and he irritated just about everyone he met in the military. He was appointed Major General on March 21, 1862, and he outranked all the generals in Grant's army except Grant himself. He held a bitter resentment towards West Pointers, and he made no bones about it. Later, he would be given permission by Lincoln to raise an expedition to capture Vicksburg. Grant, however, appropriated McClernand's troops when he wasn't present and gave them to Sherman for an assault. This led to many bitter and lengthy battles between Grant and McClernand. The argument finally culminated after the fall of Vicksburg, when Grant relieved McCernand of command. He did badly in the Red River Campaign, fell ill, and resigned his commission. He returned to politics in Illinois, and died there on September 20th, 1890.

The Governor of Tennessee, Isham G. Harris, advised Secretary of War Judah Benjamin that the door to Nashville, and all of Tennessee, was almost open. Only Ft. Donelson remained. Gen. Albert S. Johnston ordered reinforcements to Ft. Donelson from Clarksville, Tenn., and from Russellville, Ky. At Bowling Green, Ky., Johnston, Beauregard and Hardee held a council of war to discuss the tragic breach of the line.

The assault on Roanoke Island finally got underway today. The gunboats leading, the assault force headed into the battle with the heavy bombardment of Ft. Barrow at Pork Point. An eyewitness on a troop ship told the story.

Day, Pvt., Co. B, 25th Massachusetts Volunteer Infantry, Bombardment of Roanoke Island, N.C.:

> A thick fog prevailed this morning and continued until about 9 o'clock when it lifted and the gunboats got under way. Slowly they steamed towards the island and took their positions before the forts but at a sufficient distance not to incur much damage from them. We were all eagerly watching the movements

of the boats when at about 10 o'clock we saw a white cloud rise from one of the boats and the next moment a huge column of dirt and sand rose from the enemy's works, showing the effect of the shot. The fort replied from all its guns, but their shots fell short as the boats lay beyond their range. The bombardment now commenced in earnest, the boats sailing in a circle and delivering their fire as they passed the fort. Their firing was not rapid, but well directed.... At noon the transports commenced the passage of the narrow channel into Croatan sound. From here we had a much nearer and better view of the bombardment. The boats were sailing much nearer the fort and firing more rapidly. They had driven the men from the guns on the fort and their fire was feebly replied to. At this time the shells from the boats had set the barracks and other buildings near the fort on fire. Great clouds of smoke and flame rose from the burning buildings and the boats belched forth their fire more furiously than ever, the shots tearing up the parapet of the fort or burying themselves in the mound of sand covering the magazine. It was truly a grand and fearful exhibition! Thousands looked on with breathless suspense, expecting every moment to see the magazine blow up or the rebels strike their colors.

The enemy's gunboats which had been idle spectators behind the blockade now came to the rescue; but a few well directed shots from 100-pounder rifles sent them reeling back to their places.... During the bombardment a small sloop or yacht attracted a good deal of attention. She carried one 100-pounder gun. She lay low in the water, below the range of the enemy's guns and was skillfully handled. She sailed in a circle, running close up to the fort and delivering her fire with telling effect. With every shot she was cheered by the fleet....

About 2 P.M.... I was standing near Col. Upton at the gangway forward of the wheelhouse as the *Pilot Boy* ran alongside and heard Gen. Foster tell the colonel to order his men to load with ball cartridge, take three days rations and come aboard his boat and the barges as soon as possible. This loading with ball cartridge was a new order to me; it implied that our holiday soldiering was over. A peculiar feeling such as I had never before experienced came over me; I felt it to the very taps of my brogans and thought I would rather be excused.... In quick time we left the *New York* and were going towards the shore, followed by other boats containing the balance of our brigade. The intention was to land about four miles above the fort in a little nook called Ashby bay, near Ashby house; but as we neared the bay, a line of bayonets seen above the bushes going double quick in that direction changed the general's mind and we turned our course towards a marsh a mile or more nearer the fort. As we ran alongside the marsh where we were to land, Capt Pickett of company A made a leap for the land, going half way to his neck in mud and water. He was the first man on the island.

At this time the line of bayonets above the bushes was seen coming back. The little gunboat *Delaware* now came up and commenced shelling the bushes and woods to cover our landing. In a few minutes we were all on the marsh and wading through the mud and water for the hard land, a distance of some forty rods. On reaching this, we soon came out to a small clearing on which was a house, barn and outbuildings, the occupants of which had suddenly taken their leave. Here we found things as the occupants had left them, the cat quietly sitting in the corner and the teakettle singing over the fire. Adjutant Harkness and Lieutenant Richter of company G climbed to the top of the house and nailed thereon a small flag in honor, I suppose, of our landing....

5 P.M. Foster's brigade had all landed and by dark nearly the whole division was ashore. Now commenced the work of carrying rails and planks to build a road across the marsh to get the howitzers of the marine artillery ashore. Soon after dark, Gen. Foster with the 21st Massachusetts and a section of the marine artillery, hauling their howitzers, went past us into the woods to establish his picket line. After a while the general returned and said we might build fires and make ourselves comfortable. Fires were kindled and we began to look around for places to sleep, but a rain setting in put an end to that. In the rain we stood around the camp-fires through the long night while an occasional shot out in the woods served to keep up a little excitement and prevent us from getting sleepy.

February 8 (Saturday)

The battle for Roanoke Island resumed about 9 A.M.. By 4 P.M. the obstructions sunk by the Confederates had been cleared sufficiently for the Federal gunboats to enter Albemarle Sound. The Confederate gunboats offered only token resistance, being overwhelmed by the Federal fleet.

The back door to Norfolk was now open.

Day, Pvt., Co. B, 25th Massachusetts Volunteer Infantry, Battle of Roanoke Island, N.C.:

At daylight, the order to fall in was heard on all sides. Putting on my equipment and taking Spitfire and a big sweet potato which I had, with much labor, succeeded in baking, I took my place in my company. The brigade all ready, Gen. Foster gave the order to march.... We soon came out to the pickets and the road that runs through the island. Here we filed to the left, marching up the road. Company A, Capt. Pickett, was thrown out as skirmishers. They soon fell in with the enemy's pickets and drove them in. The column moved up the road to within a short distance of the clearing in front of the rebel works. On the right of the road the ground was hard and free from brush, but on the left was an almost impenetrable swamp covered with dense growth of tangle-brush and horse briars. The right wing of the regiment filed to the right, while the left plunged into the swamp and with swords and jack-knives succeeded in cutting a path until they had penetrated the swamp far enough to form our line. The regiment was now nearly all in the swamp, the right resting just across the road. The howitzer battery had taken position in the road, in front of our right wing....

We were now in line in the swamp and, facing to the front, commenced firing. The battery had already opened the ball and were receiving the attention of the enemy in front. We could see nothing to shoot at, but taking our range by the smoke of the enemy's guns, we blazed away. We fired high, low, and obliquely, thinking if we covered a wide range of ground we might possibly lame somebody and it seemed our shots must have proved troublesome for they turned their attention to us, pouring musketry and canister shot without stint into the swamp. We were up to our knees in mud and water so their shot passed over us without doing much damage.

We were now ordered to cease firing and advance, but how to advance was the question. We could stand on a bog and cut away the briars in front of us and jump to another one; where they were not too large we could crawl through them, tearing not only our clothes, but our hides as well. The officers rendered good service in cutting away the briars with their swords. In this way we could advance a few steps at a time and then fire a few rounds; the enemy all this time showing us marked attention.

Capt. Foster of company D was the first man I saw hit. I was watching him as he stood on a bog, cutting away the briars with his sword and thinking of him as colonel of the old 8th regiment Massachusetts volunteer militia, in which I used to muster. The shot struck him in the eye. He whirled round on the bog and would have fallen had not three of his men caught him and led him to the rear....

By cutting and crowding ourselves through the briars, we advanced to within about 300 yards of the enemy. Our ammunition being now exhausted and having been in the swamp about three hours, we were ordered out.... Seeing that all was now lost, the rebels took to their heels for the head of the island, followed by Reno and Foster's brigades. At the head of the island, near the enemy's camp, was Gen. Burnside with the 24th Massachusetts regiment to whom Col. Shaw, in command of the Confederate forces, surrendered. By this, about 3000 prisoners, with their arms, ammunition and stores, fell into our hands. But the greatest prize of all, old ex-Governor Wise, slipped through our fingers....

During the action I had seen quite a number hit and led back to the rear, but I had little time to think much about it. After the chase commenced and we marched through the little redoubt and over the ground held by the enemy and I began to see the mangled forms of dead and dying men, I was filled with an indescribable horror and wanted to go right home. I now began to realize what we had been doing, and thought that if in this age of the world, with all our boasted civilization and education, men could not settle their differences short of cutting each other's throats, we were not far removed from barbarism. But I suppose as long as the nature of man is ambitious and selfish, he will try to obtain by force what he cannot attain by other means....

The impact of the loss of Ft. Henry reverberated about the South. While a Confederate gunner at the fort was providing accolades for the gunnery of the U.S.S. *Carondelet* and giving her a large share of the credit for the dismantling of guns at the fort, Gen. Albert S. Johnston, CSA, wrote to the Confederate War Department:

The slight resistance at Fort Henry indicates that the best open earthworks are not reliable to meet successfully a vigorous attack of ironclad gunboats.... [Concluding that Ft. Donelson would fall] the way to

Nashville will be open. The occurrence of the misfortune of losing the fort will cut off the communication of the force here under General Hardee from the south bank of the Cumberland. To avoid the disastrous consequences of such an event, I ordered General Hardee yesterday to make, as promptly as it could be done, preparations to fall back to Nashville and cross the river. The movements of the enemy on my right flank would have made a retrograde in that direction to confront the enemy indispensable in a short time. But the probability of having the ferriage of this army corps across the Cumberland intercepted by the gunboats of the enemy admits of no delay in making the movement. Generals Beauregard and Hardee are, equally with myself, impressed with the necessity of withdrawing our force from this line at once.

As if to reinforce Johnston's decision, Lt. Phelps and the U.S.S. *Conestoga* had proceeded upriver to Chickasaw, Ala., where the steamers *Sallie Wood* and *Muscle* were taken. The Confederates burned three other steamers to prevent their capture.

February 9 (Sunday)

Confederate Brig. Gen. Gideon J. Pillow assumed command of Ft. Donelson. Pillow, 55 when the war began, had been a law partner of James K. Polk in Columbia, Tenn., and had done much to get Polk elected President in 1844. In 1846, Polk appointed Pillow a Brigadier General of Volunteers and later promoted him to Major General, the rank at which he served during the Mexican War. He argued much with Gen. Winfield Scott and kept up a steady correspondence with Polk during that war. He was appointed senior general of Isham Harris's provisional army, and he later became a Brigadier General in the Confederate Army. He was sent to Donelson as second-in-command to Brigadier Gen. Floyd. Leading an attack on the Federals on February 15, he lost his nerve, gave up the initiative, and recalled his troops. Floyd gave up the command to Pillow, who, in turn, gave it to Brigadier General Simon B. Buckner. Pillow later led a brigade at Stone's River and then was given minor assignments until the end of the war, when he entered law practice with former Governor Harris in Memphis. He died in Helena, Ark., on October 8, 1878.

Barber, Pvt., Co. D, 15th Illinois Volunteer Infantry, St. Louis, Mo.:

The captain now offered to assist me in getting a furlough. I rejected his proffered services and told him I did not want one then as my health was much improved and I did not care about leaving the regiment then. It was cold and stormy when we arrived in St. Louis. We halted on the levee and were ordered to remain there until further orders by Col. Turner, but it required something more than his order to keep the men there exposed to the cold, pelting storm.

Day, Pvt., Co. B, 25th Massachusetts Volunteer Infantry, Battle of Roanoke Island, N.C.:

A hard looking lot this morning and no doubt feeling as hard as we looked. Tired, hungry, ragged, covered with mud, and sore from our flesh being torn and scratched with the tangle-brush and briars through which we forced ourselves yesterday. After a good ration of whiskey and a breakfast of fried bacon, with hot coffee, we began to limber up and feel a little more natural. We can now look over the field and see the results of yesterday's work. Our regiment lost six killed and 47 wounded, some them probably fatally.... Our march up from the battle-ground yesterday afternoon was rather an interesting one, if men nearly dying from exhaustion can be said to get interested. The trees for a mile in front of our line are marked and scarred by our shot, showing the terrible effectiveness of our rifles. The road was strewn with guns, knapsacks, equipments, blankets and everything that impeded their retreat or which they thought they had no further use for.

Passing a little brown house by the wayside, I noticed quite a crowd of surgeons and officers standing around. Crowding my way up to the little window, I saw the pale, quivering form of a young man lying on a cot, with a slight covering over him, apparently in a dying condition. I inquired if anyone knew who he was, and was told it was Capt. O. Jennings Wise, son of ex-Governor Wise. He had received a mortal wound and could not possibly survive many minutes. He was editor of one of the Richmond papers and captain of the Richmond Light Infantry Blues, the crack company of that city. He was a brave young fellow and his was the last company to leave the redoubt, and then only when he fell mortally wounded.

February 10 (Monday)

With Roanoke Island taken, Commander Rowan in the U.S.S. *Delaware*, loaded with Marines, dashed after the retiring Confederate naval force led by Flag Officer Lynch, CSN, up the Pasquotank River. Engaging the Confederates at Elizabeth City, N.C., Rowan captured the C.S.S. *Ellis* and sank the *Seabird*. The Confederates burned the C.S.S. *Black Warrior*, *Fanny*, and *Forrest* to prevent capture. The Federals destroyed the fort and batteries at Cobb's Point, completely shattering the defenses of the city. Commander Rowan, commended for the "dash" with which he led the attack, recommended Quarter Gunner John Davis as one with even more daring and coolness. Rowan told Flag Officer Goldsborough:

> I would respectfully call your attention to one incident of the engagement which reflects much credit upon a quarter gunner of the *Valley City* and for which Congress has provided rewards in the shape of medals. A shot passed through her magazine and exploded in a locker beyond containing fireworks. The commander, Lieutenant Commander Chaplain, went there to aid in suppressing the fire, where he found John Davis, quarter gunner, seated with commendable coolness on an open barrel of powder as the only means to keep the fire out, all the while passing powder to provide the division on the upper deck while under fierce enemy fire.

Davis was awarded the Medal of Honor by General Order 11 on April 3, 1863, for this action.

Day, Pvt., Co. B, 25th Massachusetts Volunteer Infantry, Roanoke Island, N.C.:

> The prisoners are a motley looking set, all clothed (I can hardly say uniformed) in a dirty looking homespun gray cloth. I should think every man's suit was cut from a design of his own. Some wore what was probably meant for a frock coat, others wore jackets or roundabouts; some of the coats were long skirted, others short; some tight fitting, others loose; and no two men were dressed alike. Their head covering was in unison with the rest of their rig; of all kinds, from stovepipe hats to coon-skin caps; with everything for blankets, from old bedquilts, cotton bagging, strips of carpet to Buffalo robes. The Wise legion are a more soldierly looking set; they wear gray cloth caps of the same pattern, and long sheep's gray overcoats with capes. Most of the officers are smart, good looking young men, wearing well-fitting gray uniforms, not unlike those of our own officers.
>
> It is not dress altogether that makes the man or the soldier. I find among these chaps some pretty good fellows. I came across one young man from Richmond; he was smart appearing and very loquacious. In some talk I had with him he said: "This has turned out not as I wished, but not different than what I expected when we saw the force you had. In fact we had no business staying here after seeing your strength. We have met the enemy and we are theirs. I accept the situation and am glad it is no worse. I am Secesh clear through, and after I am exchanged, shall be at you again. We are now enemies, but in peace friends, and when this little dispute is settled, if any of you fellows ever come to Richmond, hunt me up. If alive, you will be welcome as long as you choose to stay, and when you leave, if you don't say you have had as right smart a time as you ever had, call me a liar and I will call you gentlemen." The fellow gave me his card and said his father owned a plantation just out of the city.
>
> These fellows threw away a good many pistols and knives which they carried, many of which our boys have found. The knives are large, coarse, ugly looking things, forged at some country blacksmith shop, by a bungling workman, out of old rasps, scythe-points and anything containing steel.... The boys are mixing in among the prisoners, talking over the fight, trading jack-knives, buttons and such small notions as they happen to have and getting acquainted with each other.... Our gunboats have wiped from the face of the earth that part of the Confederate navy which prowled around these waters. They chased them up the Pasquotunk river to Elizabeth City where, after less than an hour's engagement, the enemy set their boats on fire and fled.

In the west, Gen. Halleck was sending urgent messages to Flag Officer Foote to provide gunboats for the troops on the Cumberland River who would soon assault Ft. Donelson. Meanwhile, Foote was trying mightily to repair battle damage to his small fleet of gunboats.

Down in the Gulf of Mexico, Flag Officer Farragut was assembling the ships and mortar boats which would comprise the fleet attempting to capture New Orleans. His progress was watched keenly by the Confederate spies in the area.

The Confederates occupying the St. Simon's and Jekyll Island fortifications were coming under increasingly heavy fire and pressure from the Federal fleet in the area. Gen. R. E. Lee gave the local commanders authority to withdraw if it would save their commands. The South's access to the sea was disappearing.

February 11 (Tuesday)

The gunboats of Flag Officer Foote went upriver to assist Grant in the assault on Ft. Donelson. Federal Gen. McClernand approached from Ft. Henry, and Grant approached from downriver. Federal gunboats raced up the Cumberland to support the assault on the fort, as Brigadier Gen. Simon Bolivar Buckner, CSA, arrived. The Confederates departed Bowling Green, Ky., leaving only Columbus on the Mississippi on the empty Kentucky Line of defense.

In South Carolina, Federal troops occupied Edisto Island immediately following the evacuation of Confederate troops.

February 12 (Wednesday)

In the area around Ft. Donelson, Grant now had his troops in a ring around the fort, which was anchored on the river. He awaited the arrival of Foote and his gunboats, which were on the way.

Flag Officer Foote left Cairo last night after notifying Secretary of War Gideon Welles:

> I leave Cairo again to-night with the *Louisville, Pittsburg,* and *St. Louis* for the Cumberland River to cooperate with the army in the attack on Ft. Donelson.... I shall do all in my power to render the gunboats effective in the fight, although they are not properly manned.... If we could wait ten days, and I had men, I would go with eight mortar boats and six armored boats and conquer.

Julius Barber's diary becomes disconnected at this point. The days referred to do not agree in fact with those written in his diary.

Barber, Pvt., Co. D, 15th Illinois Volunteer Infantry, St. Louis, Mo.:

> Though I regret to say it, a good many of the boys took refuge in beer saloons and got tight, or in other words "dead drunk." You never saw the boys before or since get on such a spree as they did here. Col. Turner did not seem to have much control over them. It was a humiliating sight.... By night everything was on board and we were soon sailing down the Mississippi.

Day, Pvt., Co. B, 25th Massachusetts Volunteer Infantry, Roanoke Island, N.C.:

> The Confederate Officers have been paroled and sent to Elizabeth City.... The 25th had the distinguished *honor* of escorting them and carrying a part of their baggage to the wharf where they took the boat.... Those officers had with them their colored servants, but after they were all captured, officers and servants were a good deal mixed as to who they belonged to. When the officers were about leaving, Gen. Burnside settled the question. He told the darkies they could decide for themselves; they could go with their masters or stop here, just as they liked. A few of them went with their masters, the rest staid back to take their chances with the Yankees.

February 13 (Thursday)

In a little twist, the West Virginia Constitutional Convention, meeting at Wheeling, adopted a provision that *no slave or free person of color should come into the state for permanent residence.*

On the Savannah River, Lt. John P. Bankhead, U.S.S. *Pembina,* found several mines known as "tin-can" torpedoes which had been moored to the bed of the river. These mines were only visible at low tide. He had one of these "infernal machines" removed for examination and decided that the easiest way to clear the passage was to destroy the remainder with rifle fire. Many of the mines did not explode but, losing their buoyancy, sank to the river bed.

At Ft. Donelson, Gen. Floyd arrived and assumed command from Gen. Pillow. There had been some skirmishing between the forces, and the gunboat U.S.S. *Carondelet* bombarded the fort in the morning. The fair weather of the morning turned into freezing rain and sleet in the afternoon, and the temperature fell to only ten degrees at night.

John Buchanan Floyd was born in Montgomery County, Va., on June 1, 1806. He attended South Carolina College and then pursued a political career, becoming a member of the House of Delegates and then Governor of Virginia. President Buchanan appointed him Secretary of War in 1857, and he filled the arsenals in the South with weapons and munitions until he resigned on December 29, 1860, at which time all remaining weapons shipments were halted. He was appointed Brigadier General in May 1861, and he was involved in several small battles in western Virginia. His brigade was sent to Kentucky to serve with Albert S. Johnston in late 1861, and he was further assigned to Ft. Donelson as commander. Grant, assaulting the fort, demanded surrender. Floyd, after an abortive breakout attempt, turned the command over to Simon B. Buckner and went to Nashville. He was relieved on March 11, 1862, for deserting his command. He died at Abington, Va., on August 26, 1863.

February 14 (Friday)

At Mystic Harbor, Conn., the U.S.S. *Galena*, an experimental ironclad, was launched.

The assault on Ft. Donelson was made by Gen. Grant and Flag Officer Foote. The fort, being situated on high ground, could subject the fleet to plunging fire (i.e., the shells falling nearly vertically) into areas on the gunboats which were lightly protected. Despite this, Foote ordered his boats into the battle. The U.S.S. *St. Louis*, Foote's flagship, was hit 59 times, lost her steering and began to drift downriver. The *Louisville*, although not hit as many times, also lost steerage and drifted out of the conflict. Foote, injured during the melee, would have to give up command of the flotilla later because of the injury. The gunboat attack was broken off for the time being.

Grant, disappointed that the gunboat bombardment did not cause an easier victory, gathered his forces for further fighting in very cold weather. The front door to Nashville was being knocked upon *very* hard!

Barber, Pvt., Co. D, 15th Illinois Volunteer Infantry, Cairo, Illinois:

> ... (February 14th) we arrived at Cairo where we halted for orders. We now turned our course up the Ohio. When we arrived at Paducah, we learned that a fierce and bloody battle was in progress at Ft. Donelson on the Cumberland river. We soon came to the mouth of the Cumberland and turned our course up that stream. We had no doubt now of our destination. We were all eager to get to the scene of action in time to participate in the fight, but the captain of the boat was a rank rebel and he refused to run nights, and to the shame of Col. Turner, he refused to use his authority and compel him to run.

February 15 (Saturday)

Commodore Tartnall, CSN, tried to free a passage for the steamer *Ida* from Ft. Pulaski to Savannah with no luck. His attack on the Federal batteries at Venus Point failed, and he was forced back to Savannah.

The gunboats of Flag Officer Foote were back on the Cumberland River in support of the assault of Ft. Donelson. Major Gen. Lew Wallace summed up the role of the Navy in this engagement:

> I recollect yet the positive pleasure the sounds [naval gunfire] gave me... the obstinacy and courage of the Commodore.... Was the attack of assistance to us? I don't think there is room to question it. It distracted the enemy's attention, and I fully believe it was the gunboats... that operated to prevent a general movement of the rebels up the river or across it, the night before the surrender.

The gunboats may have been back, but the Confederates were far from finished. Gen. Pillow organized an assault on McClernand's line, aided by Gen. Buckner's troops. After a hot fight, McClernand's line was broken and the road to Nashville was open, but nobody did anything about it immediately. An argument developed, and Pillow ordered the troops back into the fort. McClernand, with the help of Gen. Lew Wallace, advanced and the troops occupied their old positions by nightfall. The Federals almost lost this one. Floyd, after a council, decided to surrender and took the opportunity to flee the fort, turning his command over to Pillow. Pillow followed Floyd, leaving the command to Gen. Buckner.

One commander within the fort was thinking of everything but surrender. Tonight, Nathan Bedford Forrest would lead his cavalry out of Donelson, through a freezing swamp, and to safety. His would be the only organized body of troops to escape. Both

A view of Gettysburg, Pa., June 1863

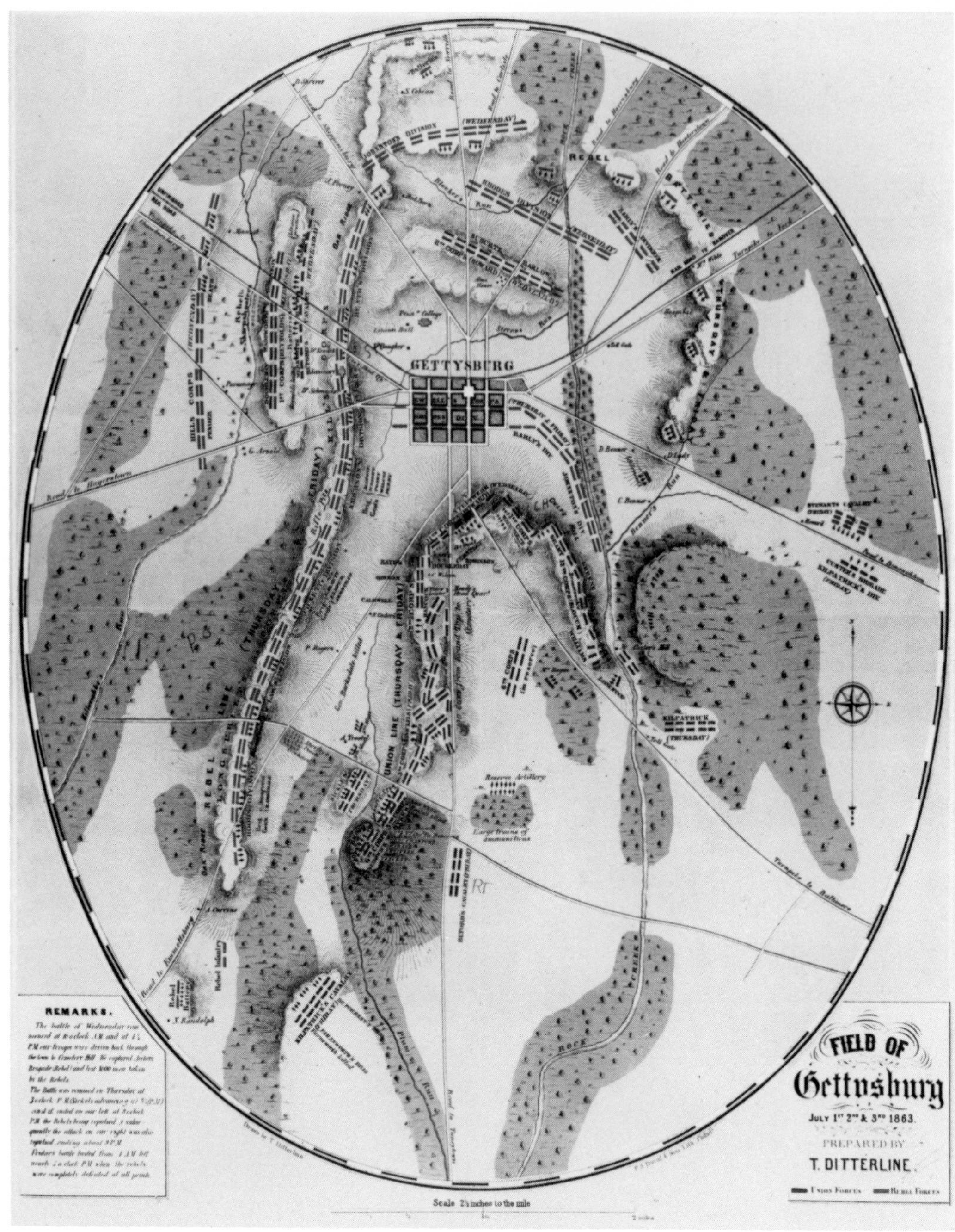

A map of Gettysburg Battlefield, July 1863

Gettysburg, Pa., July 1863

A view of Chattanooga, Tenn., with Lookout Mountain in the distance

The infamous Confederate prison camp at Andersonville, Ga., in 1864

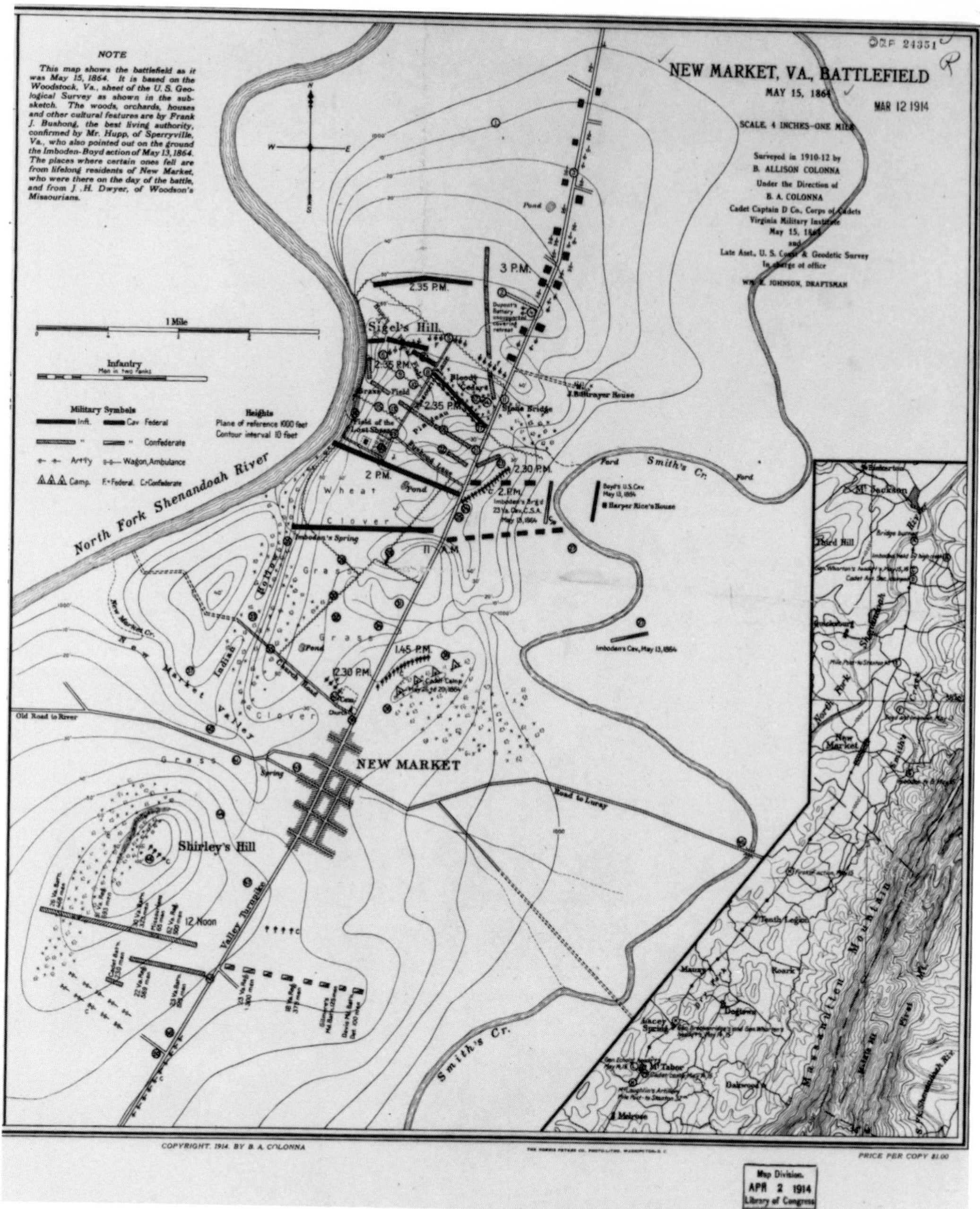

A map of New Market, Va., Battlefield, May 1864

Ft. Sumter, Charleston Harbor, S.C., destroyed by Federal bombardment, March 1865

A view of the destruction caused by the Federal bombardment of Charleston, S.C. The Circular Church was almost completely destroyed.

Floyd and Pillow rowed across the Cumberland River and slunk away in the night.

Jackman, Pvt., "The Orphan Brigade," in hospital, Bowling Green, Ky.:

> I had not been well since my return to the regiment and about the middle of February was sent to the regimental hospital still being kept up in Bowling Green. There had been a great deal of sickness in camp. All of one company from Texas which had been attached to our regiment were sent to the hospital save one little boy—a drummer. I found "Bro Don" and A.O. very sick and staying at a private house in town. Capt. G. (unwell) was giving them attention. I also went to see Capt. W. who was very sick at a private house.

In St. Louis, Mo., Brigadier Gen. John M. Schofield assumed command of the Department of St. Louis. John McAllister Schofield was born at Gerry, N.Y., on September 29, 1831. He graduated from West Point in 1853, and served for two years with the artillery in Florida before being sent back to West Point, where he taught philosophy until 1860. At the outbreak of war he was in St. Louis teaching at Washington University. He was assigned to the staff of Nathaniel Lyon and fought at Wilson's Creek, where Lyon was killed. He suggested retreat, but was not listened to, and the result was heavy casualties. On November 21, 1861, he was promoted to Brigadier General and was assigned administrative duties in Missouri. Promoted to Major General on May 12, 1863, his campaigning for a more active role was successful when he was assigned to Sherman's army as commander of the Department of the Ohio. After the taking of Atlanta, Hood left the area for northern Alabama, and Schofield was assigned to follow him and assist George Thomas at Nashville. Schofield escaped a trap at Spring Hill, Tenn., and successfully fought Hood at Franklin, Tenn., on November 30, 1864, in a fight that claimed six Confederate generals. Schofield continued on to Nashville and assisted Thomas in the defeat of Hood in December. After the war he served in several capacities, including a stint of five years as Superintendent of West Point. In 1888, he followed Sheridan as head of the Army, and he retired as a Lieutenant General in 1895. He died in St. Augustine, Fla., on March 4, 1906.

February 16 (Sunday)

Gen. Simon B. Buckner in Ft. Donelson asked Grant for terms for surrender. Grant gave his now famous reply: "No terms except unconditional and immediate surrender can be accepted. I propose to move immediately upon your works." Buckner believed and accepted.

The surrender of Ft. Donelson created great confusion, anger, and consternation in New Orleans, where Confederate Secretary of the Navy Mallory was blamed for the loss because he had no effective counter to the Federal gunboats which controlled the river. To add to the failure, Flag Officer Foote sent gunboats upriver to Dover to destroy the Tennessee Iron Works above that town.

Foote's efforts to gain some experienced sailors for his gunboats finally paid off. McClellan wired that "I will send nearly 600 sailors for you to-morrow."

Barber, Pvt., Co. D, 15th Illinois Volunteer Infantry, Ft. Donelson, Tenn.:

> On the morning of the 16th a gunboat passed us which a few moments before left the fort with dispatches. From the officers of the boat we learned that Ft. Donelson, with immense stores of provisions, munitions, ordnance and fifteen thousand troops had just surrendered to General Grant. It was a glorious victory.... After this fight, the General rose amazingly in the estimation of the 15th. At ten o'clock A.M. on the morning of the 16th we rounded a curve in the river and the high battlements and frowning batteries of Ft. Donelson, with the stars and stripes floating on the ramparts met our visions. It was a scene well calculated to thrill the minds of the beholders with enthusiasm. The place had surrendered just one hour before we arrived and had it not been for a secesh captain and an over-prudent colonel, we would have been there in time to have shared in the honors of the victory....
>
> Our troops had to lie two nights on the frozen earth, covered with snow, without fire or shelter. The double-dyed traitor Floyd succeeded in escaping with a portion of his brigade, leaving his subordinate, Gen. Buckner, to his fate. When we arrived at the fort we found everything in a state of confusion. The spoils of war were being gathered. Guns, accoutrements, clothing, ammunition, etc., were scattered around in promiscuous profusion. Some had thrown their arms

in the river. The prisoners were busily embarking on transports, preparatory to going North. As a general thing, the prisoners were a hard looking set of men. Some were quite communicative and disposed to be cheerful. Some were very sullen and spoke only to hail vituperations and abuse on the detested Yankees.

February 17 (Monday)

The Confederate ironclad C.S.S. *Virginia*, formerly the U.S.S. *Merrimack*, was commissioned this day at Norfolk. She was still short of crew, but afloat.

Today, Generals Floyd and Pillow arrived in Nashville to be greeted by Gen. Albert S. Johnston. Forrest would arrive with his cavalry tomorrow. The South was in turmoil, and Nashville in a panic. Many of the citizens were packing to leave for points unknown.

Grant, now known as "Unconditional Surrender" Grant, was promoted to Major General of Volunteers by a grateful government in Washington.

On the western rivers, Flag Officer Foote was still very busy. He informed Secretary of the Navy Gideon Welles:

> I leave immediately with a view of proceeding to Clarksville with eight mortar boats and two ironclad boats, with the *Conestoga*, [a] wooden boat, as the river is rapidly falling. The other ironclad boats are badly cut up and require extensive repairs. I have sent one of the boats already since my return and ordered a second to follow me, which, with eight mortars, [I] hope to carry Clarksville.

Jackman, Pvt., "The Orphan Brigade," in hospital, Franklin, Tenn.:

> Just before daylight the next morning a fire broke out on main street on the public square and caused a great deal of confusion. Walls were battered down by using artillery to stop the spreading flames.
>
> That morning after daylight all the sick were moved to the Depot to be loaded on the cars. I hope never to witness another scene such as was presented there that day. Men at the lowest stage of sickness were not half attended and were thrown around like the commonest freight. Many died from want of attention. There was no official present to direct the removal of the sick—every man for himself. Capt. G. and myself were able to walk about and we had to give all of our attention to the two boys named, also to another of the company very sick. They all had the typhoid fever. We got into a passenger car and it was noon before we moved off.... About sundown we got to Franklin.

February 18 (Tuesday)

The first officially elected Confederate Congress met in Richmond, amid the news of the fall of Forts Donelson and Henry.

In Nashville, there were many discussions about what to do when the Federals arrived. Plans were made for the military to evacuate the city and move southeast towards Chattanooga.

Barber, Pvt., Co. D, 15th Illinois Volunteer Infantry, Ft. Donelson, Tenn.:

> Toward evening we disembarked and went into camp. Volunteers were called for to help attend to the wounded and place them on transports. In company with several others from Company D, I offered my services which were accepted. It was nearly midnight before our task was done.
>
> It was a pitiful and sickening sight to see such a mass of mangled limbs and mutilated bodies, but the patience with which they bore their injuries excited our admiration. Of the twenty which I helped carry on the boat, not one uttered a complaint, even though a leg or an arm were missing. The next day we took a stroll over the battlefield. We saw sights that fairly froze the blood in our veins. The dead lay as they had fallen, in every conceivable shape, some grasping their guns as though they were in the act of firing, while others, with a cartridge in their icy grasp, were in the act of loading. Some of the countenances wore a peaceful, glad smile, while on others rested a fiendish look of hate. It looked as though each countenance was the exact counterpart of the thoughts that were passing through the mind when the death messenger laid them low. Perhaps that noble looking youth, with his smiling up-turned face, with his glossy ringlets matted with his own life-blood, felt a mother's prayer stealing over his senses as his young life went out. Near him lay a young husband with a prayer for his wife and little one yet lingering on his lips. Youth and age, virtue and evil, were represented on those ghastly countenances. Before us lay the

charred and blackened remains of some who had been burnt alive. They were wounded too badly to move and the fierce elements consumed them. We now came to where the rebels made their last desperate effort to break our lines, and in a small cleared field the dead were piled up, friend and foe alike in death struggle.

Jackman, Pvt., "The Orphan Brigade," in hospital, en route to Gallatin, Tenn.:

> ... until daylight the next morning we were on the road to Gallatin. The weather turned cold that night and a snow two or three inches deep fell. The train was so heavy, the engineer said, that he could not pull it. I believe he wanted it captured. I did not sleep a moment that night. The car was crowded to overflowing with sick and I had to stand up a great deal of the time.

Day, Pvt., Co. B, 25th Massachusetts Volunteer Infantry, Roanoke Island, N.C.:

> The prisoners are all paroled, and were sent off to-day. Paroling the prisoners was rather interesting to the lookers on. They were required to affix their autographs to the parole, and it was curious to observe that a large majority of them wrote it the same way, simply making the letter X. Capt. Messenger, the provost marshal, was master of ceremonies....

February 19 (Wednesday)

With Flag Officer Foote's small armada facing them, the Confederates evacuated Clarksville, Tenn., where Federal forces under Gen. C.F. Smith occupied Ft. Defiance and took possession of the town. Col. W.H. Allen, commander of the Confederate force, reported to Gen. Floyd:

> Gunboats are coming; they are just below point; can see steamer here. Will try and see how many troops they have before I leave. Lieutenant Brady set bridge on fire, but it is burning very slowly and will probably go out before it falls.... I will have to go in a hurry when I go.

Jackman, Pvt., "The Orphan Brigade," in hospital, Gallatin, Tenn.:

> At daylight we got to Gallatin and Capt. G. and I went to a hotel and got our breakfast. We brought the boys something to eat. All day long the train was trying to make it over a grade running up from the depot. In the evening late, the engineer and his fireman got drunk and were arrested by the military. Capt. G. took the three boys off the train and moved them to a private house. There N.O. died.
>
> I remained on the train and at sundown a new engine was hitched on and we went flying to Nashville. I could scarcely walk to the hospital near by. There were several of us together and all the bunks being occupied, we had to sleep on the floor by the stove. There were 150 sick men in that room, their bunks all arranged in rows. A cold chill ran over me at seeing so many pale faces by gaslight.

Robert E. Lee, charged with the defenses of the Florida district, was having a very difficult time with this assignment. He had few troops to work with and little artillery for shore batteries, and the rail network in this part of the country was less than satisfactory. He looked long and hard at the defenses on the many islands on the coast and wrote Brigadier Gen. Trapier:

> In looking at the whole defense of Florida, it becomes important to ascertain what points can probably be held and what points had better be relinquished. The force that the enemy can bring against any position where he can concentrate his floating batteries renders it prudent and proper to withdraw from the islands to the main-land and be prepared to contest his advance into the interior. Where an island offers the best point of defense, and is so connected with the main that its communications cannot be cut off, it may be retained. Otherwise, it should be abandoned.

February 20 (Thursday)

In Washington, William Wallace "Willie" Lincoln died at the age of 12 of typhoid fever. The tragedy overwhelmed the President, who tried to console his wife. They were not the only ones suffering from the loss of loved ones. The casualty notices from Ft. Donelson were being posted, both North and South, in all the towns and villages that had sent their men to war.

On the Mississippi River, the forts defending

Columbus, Ky., were ordered evacuated by the Confederate government. With the loss of Forts Henry and Donelson, the fortifications were now useless.

Flag Officer Farragut arrived at Ship Island, Miss., to begin his assault on New Orleans. Earlier, Gen. Braxton Bragg, CSA, had reported to Richmond that large bodies of troops and quantities of supplies were being landed at the island.

At Nashville, Governor Isham Harris abandoned the city by moving the State government to Memphis. Confederate troops left the city, headed for Murfreesboro.

In the Hatteras area, Flag Officer L.M. Goldsborough wrote Asst. Secy. of the Navy Gustavus Fox concerning the obstructions in the local rivers:

> At Washington [North Carolina], and also at New Bern the obstructions in the river are very formidable, and admirably placed. They consist of a double row of piles thoroughly well driven by steam, and sunken vessels. The rows are at right angles to the shore and parallel with each other. One stretches all the way from the right bank nearly over to the left, and the other all the way from the left bank over to the right, and there is a battery of considerable force on either bank between them; so that attacking vessels must first go bows on to one, then after passing it, be raked aft by one and forward by the other at the same time.

Jackman, Pvt., "The Orphan Brigade," Nashville, Tenn.:

> The next day looking in all the hospitals for brother Jo, but did not find him. That morning, or the next, I have forgotten which, the news came of the fall of Ft. Donelson and the whole city was thrown into consternation. Excited crowds collected on the corners and were harangued by prominent citizens. Commissary and Quartermaster Depots were thrown open to the populace, citizens commenced packing up and moving off; and the hospital rats commenced bundling up and "shoving out"—in fact there was great confusion. The evening of the same day the startling news came, my regiment passed through in the march and I slung my knapsack, shouldered my gun, and fell into ranks. I could scarcely walk though. We camped four or five miles from town that night.

February 21 (Friday)

In Nashville, the bureaucrats were having a hard time dealing with reality. The city was loaded with mountains of supplies awaiting shipment east to troops in Georgia and Virginia. The military could only carry so much on their marches and the railroads were jammed with fleeing citizens. The solution seemed to be to destroy the supplies rather than give them out to the local population. Orders went out for guards to prevent citizens from taking any of the food from the warehouses for their personal use; after all, it was government property and the common citizen had no right to it.

Some, including Col. Nathan Bedford Forrest, took exception to this policy and assisted the citizens in loading the food in wagons at the depots. There were entirely too few citizens and wagons, so most of the tons of food was destroyed. Approximately 30,000 pounds of bacon and ham were set ablaze, forming a river of grease and a fantastic odor for days.

Jackman, Pvt., "The Orphan Brigade," en route to Murfreesboro, Tenn.:

> ... we marched four or five miles farther towards Murfreesboro and camped. The weather looked favorable that evening. We neglected to ditch our tent and were well paid for our negligence. That night, at a late hour, a heavy rainstorm came up and perfect rivers were running under us from that till morning. Of course, rested badly.

February 22 (Saturday)

President Davis was inaugurated today in Richmond as the first President of the Confederacy. His would be a short tenure.

Flag Officer Farragut lost no time in his preparations. Today he ordered the coast survey team to sound the Mississippi passes and mark out the safest channel for his approach to New Orleans.

In Georgia, Union gunboats entered the Savannah River through Wall's Cut, thus isolating Ft. Pulaski from the rest of the Confederate defenses.

Jackman, Pvt., "The Orphan Brigade," en route to Murfreesboro, Tenn.:

> ... the rain pounds down incessantly. We made a fire in our tent and by night my eyes were nearly out

from smoke. Here we received a lot of overcoats, hats, and gloves. A present to the regiment from the merchants of New Orleans.

February 23 (Sunday)

In Nashville, the citizens were in a panic to leave the city, as Federal gunboats drew closer. In Washington, President Lincoln named Andrew Johnson, a native of Knoxville, as Military Governor of Tennessee.

On the Tennessee River, Lt. Gwin, commanding the U.S.S. *Tyler*, proceeded upriver to Eastport, Miss. At Clifton, Gwin seized 1100 sacks and barrels of flour and about 6000 bushels of wheat at the river docks.

Flag Officer Foote, active again, reconnoitred the Mississippi River down to Columbus, Ky. His reported force consisted of four ironclad boats, two mortar boats, and three transports containing 1000 troops.

Jackman, Pvt., "The Orphan Brigade," en route to Murfreesboro, Tenn.:

> The day after, our company wagon was sent to the city for clothing; but before it got back in the evening the regiment had moved. I was left to load in our baggage. We had to tumble the boxes off in the road to make room for our camp equippage. After we were loaded I took an axe and bursted some of the boxes and heaped clothing on top of our load as long as it would stay—the balance was burned. We marched about 10 miles and bivouacked.

Day, Pvt., Co. B, 25th Massachusetts Volunteer Infantry, Roanoke Island, N.C.:

> The boys are amusing themselves making pipes from briar roots and fixing long stems of cane to them. Some of them are carved very handsomely and show much artistic skill. Washington's birthday was celebrated by salutes from the forts and a holiday in the camp....

February 24 (Monday)

Federal troops under Don Carlos Buell reached the bank of the Cumberland River opposite Nashville, as the troop transports from Grant's army arrived at the docks and unloaded. Forrest's cavalry acted as the rear guard for the retreat of Confederate forces towards Murfreesboro.

Funeral services were held for Willie Lincoln in Washington, and his brother Tad, ailing, showed some improvement. Only one of the Lincolns' children would reach adulthood.

At Norfolk, Capt. Buchanan, CSN, readied his small fleet, the centerpiece to be the new ironclad C.S.S. *Virginia*. Confederate Secretary of the Navy Mallory wrote to Buchanan:

> The *Virginia* is a novelty in naval construction, is untried, and her powers unknown; and hence the department will not give specific orders as to her attack upon the enemy. Her powers as a ram are regarded as very formidable, and it is hoped you will be able to test them. Like the bayonet charge of infantry, this mode of attack, while it is most destructive, will commend itself to you in the present scarcity of ammunition. It is one also that may be rendered destructive at night against the enemy at anchor. Even without guns the ship would, it is believed, be formidable as a ram. Could you pass Old Point and make a dashing cruise in the Potomac as far as Washington, its effect upon the public mind would be important to our cause. The condition of our country, and the painful reverses we have just suffered, demand our utmost exertions; and convinced as I am that the opportunity and the means for striking a decisive blow for our navy are now, for the first time, presented, I congratulate you upon it, and know that your judgment and gallantry will meet all just expectations. Action, prompt and successful just now, would be of serious importance to our cause.

Off the coast of Florida, the U.S.S. *Harriet Lane*, commanded by Lt. Jonathan M. Wainwright, the grandfather of the Gen. Jonathan M. Wainwright who surrendered Bataan during World War II and participated later in the surrender of Japan, captured the schooner *Joanna Ward*.

February 25 (Tuesday)

Federal troops in large numbers were now in Nashville, and the city remained in Federal hands for the duration of the war.

Capt. Dahlgren, commander of the Washington Navy Yard, was present at the commissioning of the

U.S.S. *Monitor* at Greenpoint, Long Island. Dahlgren described the appearance of the *Monitor* as "a mere speck, like a hat on the surface." The ship had some problems in her steering mechanism and other mechanical parts, but these were corrected.

Nashville, with its colonnaded buildings, was occupied by Union troops without a struggle. The U.S.S. *Cairo,* Lt. Nathaniel Bryant, convoyed seven troop transports to the city. The troops, under the command of Brigadier Gen. William Nelson, occupied the state capitol and assumed control of the city. The loss of the city was more than a moral loss: Huge quantities of supplies had been stockpiled there for distribution to the Confederate forces in Virginia and elsewhere.

Jackman, Pvt., "The Orphan Brigade," Murfreesboro, Tenn.:

> The day following, raining hard all day long. I lay in the tent with a high fever. Dr. P. came to see me and gave me medicine. That evening Col. H. gave me a pass, approved by Genl. Breckinridge, to go to a private house—I objected going to hospital. I got into an ambulance to be taken to town but it got stuck in the mud and I slept in it all night.

February 26 (Wednesday)

In Washington, Lincoln signed historic legislation creating a national currency of United States notes, and providing for the sale of stock to finance the currency. Prior to this time, all federal monies had been in specie (metal coins). The states and some cities had issued monies on the "state banks" which were redeemable only in that locality.

The New Orleans "Committee of Safety" reported to President Davis the "most deplorable condition" of the Navy Department finances in that city. They stated that the lack of money was preventing the enlistment of men and that the "outstanding indebtedness... can not be less than $600,000 or $800,000" owing to foundries and machine shops, draymen, and other suppliers, and that for months "a sign has been hanging over the paymaster's office of that department, 'No funds'... unless the proper remedy was at once applied, workmen can no longer be had."

Jackman, Pvt., "The Orphan Brigade," Murfreesboro, Tenn.:

> Next morning "Capt. G." placed me in a large wagon and we were nearly all day finding a place to stop. At last "Prof" Francois took me to a family where he was staying. The accommodations were poor, but it was the best we could do. I had to sleep on the floor the first night; after that though had a bed provided. The "Pro" staid with me and was very kind. I was out of my head a great deal—bad off. Dr. P. and G. visited me daily.

February 27 (Thursday)

In Richmond, the Confederate Congress gave President Davis the right to suspend *habeas corpus,* something that Lincoln had already done. Davis, unlike Lincoln, would use this power very little during the war.

Lt. Worden, USN, was having problems with the U.S.S. *Monitor.* He had to wait for a day for ammunition for his guns, and then when he sailed he had to turn back to the Navy Yard because the steering mechanism failed again. At Norfolk, the *Virginia* was delayed because of a lack of gunpowder.

February 28 (Friday)

On the Mississippi River, Gen. John Pope moved his force down the west bank of the river towards New Madrid, Mo. Island No. 10 was the main bastion of the Confederates at this point on the river, and it was the daily target of Federal gunboats.

In all, this had not been a good month for the Confederacy. Forts Henry and Donelson had been lost and one of the major cities, Nashville, had been occupied.

MARCH 1862

There had been many changes since March 1861. One year previously, the first blush of war had not been dimmed by the battle casualties of Bull Run and Forts Henry and Donelson. At that time, troops were gaily preparing for a war that no one believed would last long. Now, the outlook was much more grim and realistic. The casualty lists had been posted, a major city of the Confederacy had been lost and, for all practical purposes, Tennessee had been lost as well. North Carolina was almost sealed from the sea, and South Carolina's major harbors were either blockaded or occupied. In the North, little seemed right. McClellan was still waiting for an opportune time to move. It was clear that the war would not be won overnight.

March 1 (Saturday)

In the west, the Confederates concentrated their forces at Island No. 10, at Ft. Pillow on the Mississippi, and in Corinth, Miss., Gen. Albert S. Johnston was moving his troops that he had evacuated from Nashville to the southwest, towards Corinth. Grant was moving up the Tennessee River towards Eastport, Miss., with his gunboats and troops.

After the fall of Ft. Henry, the Federal gunboats had moved upriver and captured a ship in drydock which the Confederates were fitting out. This ship, the *Eastport*, was over 100 feet longer than the Federal gunboats and would be very fast. Flag Officer Foote had requested permission, and money, to complete the ship as a Federal vessel. Today, he exhorted the Secretary of the Navy again:

> I have applied to the Secretary of the Navy to have the rebel gunboat, *Eastport*, lately captured in the Tennessee River, fitted up as a gunboat.... She can be fitted out for about $20,000, and in three weeks. We want such a fast and powerful boat. Do telegraph about her, as we now have carpenters and cargo ahead on her and she is just what we want. I should run about in her and save time and do good service. Our other ironclad boats are too slow. The *Eastport* was a steamer on the river, and she, being a good boat, would please the West. No reply yet from the Secretary and time is precious.

At Pittsburg Landing (Shiloh), the U.S.S. *Tyler*, the aggressive Lt. Gwin commanding, and the U.S.S. *Lexington*, Lt. Shirk, landed a party of sailors and army sharpshooters under the cover of naval gunfire to determine the strength of the Confederate forces. Although Flag Officer Foote commended Gwin for his initiative, he admonished him:

> But I must give a general order that no commander will land men to make an attack on shore. Our gunboats are to be used as forts, and as they have no more men than necessary to man the guns, and as the Army must do the shore work, and as the enemy want nothing better than to entice our men on shore and overpower them with superior numbers, the commanders must not operate on shore, but confine themselves to their vessels.

Barber, Pvt., Co. D, 15th Illinois Volunteer Infantry, Ft. Donelson, Tenn.:

> This was an unhealthy place and quite a number were taken sick; amongst them were William and Samuel. We were ordered to march about the 1st of March. The sick and surplus baggage were sent around by water. William and Sam were left, but came up the next day.

March 2 (Sunday)

The last of the Kentucky Line of the Confederate defenses was gone as Gen. Leonidas Polk completed the evacuation of Columbus, Ky., leaving it open to Federal occupation. The advance units of the Federals were not far away.

Barber, Pvt., Co. D, 15th Illinois Volunteer Infantry, Ft. Donelson, Tenn.:

> Our route lay towards Ft. Henry on the Tennessee river. It was a mountainous, wild and sterile region. I saw the first pine and beech trees on this march that I had seen in the south.... It was only fifteen miles between the two rivers at this point, and yet it took two days hard marching. We traveled twelve miles the first day and camped eight miles from our starting point. The teams did not come up that night, they were fast in the mud two miles back. We went to bed supperless and without shelter. During the night it stormed hard and we awoke in the morning and found ourselves covered with snow. It was so late when the teams came up that we did not move that day—in fact, Colonel Ellis refused to march an inch until his men got something to eat.

March 3 (Monday)

At Fernandina, Fla., Flag Officer Du Pont reported to the Secretary of the Navy that his force was in full possession of Cumberland Island and Sound, Amelia Island and the town of St. Mary's, which was located immediately south of the Georgia line. Commander Drayton, U.S.S. *Ottawa*, chased a train with the guns on his gunboat for one and one-half miles. The train escaped with little damage, but the passengers fled into the woods.

Union general John Pope began his assault on New Madrid, Mo., today while Federal troops occupied Columbus, Ky., to the north. Gen. Halleck, in a snit because Grant got the glory for the capture of Forts Henry and Donelson, accused Grant of not reporting properly during those operations and other, largely unspecified, misconduct (a rumored charge of drunkenness). Halleck got authorization from Washington, and placed Brig. Gen. C.F. Smith in charge of the Union forces going up the Tennessee River.

Barber, Pvt., Co. D, 15th Illinois Volunteer Infantry, near Pittsburg Landing, Tenn.:

> ...we marched to a landing four miles above Ft. Henry. Here we found some of our sick and the Captain just from home.... Here an immense fleet of transports had collected, which was to convey the army up to a point near Corinth, to operate against the rebel army which was concentrating all its available forces at the latter place. The river was so high that it was almost impossible to get to the landing....

March 4 (Tuesday)

In Richmond, Confederate Secretary of the Navy Mallory completed his *wish list* to President Davis with a summary:

> ...fifty light-draft and powerful steam propellers, plated with 5-inch hard iron, armed and equipped for service in our own waters, four iron or steel-clad single deck, ten gun frigates of about 2,000 tons, and ten clipper propellers with superior marine engines, both classes of ships designed for deep-sea cruising, 3,000 tons of first-class boiler-plate iron, and 1,000 tons of rod, bolt, and bar iron are means which this Department could immediately employ. We could use with equal advantage 3,000 instructed seamen, and 4,000 ordinary seamen and landsmen, and 2,000 first rate mechanics.

In the west, Halleck directed that Grant stay at Ft. Henry, while Grant's troops, under C.F. Smith, went upriver. Andrew Johnson was confirmed as Brigadier General by the U.S. Congress, as well as Military Governor of Tennessee.

President Davis was having his problems. Gen. Joseph E. Johnston was giving Davis a hard time about the reenlistment of troops in his (Johnston's) army, while the Congressmen from the western states of the Confederacy were yelling for more guns to defend the river.

Barber, Pvt., Co. D, 15th Illinois Volunteer Infantry, near Pittsburg Landing, Tenn.:

> I worked all night. I stepped on shore a few minutes in the morning and before I returned the fleet had loosed its moorings and sailed. If I had had my knapsack and gun with me I should not have cared, but I was in time to get onto the *City of Memphis.* It was a grand sight to see that magnificent fleet of fifty steamers sweep around in line, with colors flying and drums beating. It seemed as though the grand old forests looked on with awe and admiration at the sight... The fleet halted at Savannah for a short time, and I was glad to rejoin my comrades. I found my things all right. The boys had taken good care of them.

March 5 (Wednesday)

In the Shenandoah Valley, Union Gen. Nathaniel Banks moved his troops south, *up* the Valley, towards Winchester, where "Stonewall" Jackson waited.

Nathaniel Prentiss Banks was born in poverty in Waltham, Mass., on January 30, 1816. He was head of the Democratic Party in Massachusetts, and then joined the new Republican Party, and was elected Governor in 1858. He was a political general who quickly ran into trouble with things military when he opposed Jackson in the Shenandoah Valley in the early part of 1862. He was outclassed completely by Jackson, and after the Battle of Cedar Mountain, before Second Manassas, Banks was relieved of command and sent to replace Major Gen. Benjamin Butler (another inept political general) in New Orleans. Banks's troops assaulted Port Hudson at the same time that Grant was attacking Vicksburg. His star began its descent with the unauthorized Red River campaign, which was a complete failure. He was subsequently relieved from direct combat command, and he left the Army. He returned to Massachusetts in August 1865, and was elected to six terms in the U.S. House of Representatives. He died in Waltham, Mass., on September 1, 1894.

The first of Gen. C.F. Smith's forces reached Savannah, Tenn., just northeast of Corinth, Miss. Another 80 troop transports, escorted by gunboats, soon followed. The buildup was increasing rapidly.

Flag Officer Foote's gunboats needed repair badly after their service at Forts Henry and Donelson. While Halleck urged him to immediately attack Island No. 10, he declined because

> The gunboats have been so much cut up in the late engagements at Forts Henry and Donelson in the pilot houses, hulls, and disabled machinery, that I could not induce the pilots to go in them again in a fight until they are repaired. I regret this, as we ought to move in the quickest possible time, but I have declined doing it, being utterly unprepared, although General Halleck says go, and not wait for repairs; but that can not be done without creating a stampede amongst the pilots and most of the newly made officers, to say nothing of the disasters which must follow if the rebels fight as they have done of late.

In northern Arkansas, Confederate Gen. Earl Van Dorn had joined former Missouri Governor, now General, Sterling Price. Price had been chased from Missouri by Federal Gen. Samuel R. Curtis's superior forces.

Van Dorn, graduate of USMA, class of '42, served in the Mexican War with distinction and later served in Texas, where he won a name fighting the Comanche Indians. He resigned his commission in the Union Army on January 3, 1861, to return to his native South, where he became a Colonel. He was promoted rapidly, to Brigadier General on June 5th and to Major General on September 19, 1861. A glory seeker and a poor tactician, he lost two major battles, Pea Ridge in Arkansas and Corinth in Mississippi, due to poor staff work. At Corinth, he was charged with being drunk on the battlefield, but this was not proven; the charge did, however, wreck his career as far as commanding armies was concerned. Given a cavalry command, he was successful in raiding Grant's supply depots and lines of communication during the Vicksburg campaign. Quite the lady's man, he was killed by an irate husband at his own headquarters in Spring Hill, Tenn., on May 7, 1863.

Barber, Pvt., Co. D, 15th Illinois Volunteer Infantry, Pittsburg Landing, Tenn.:

> Four divisions of the army now proceeded up the river twenty miles and disembarked at Pittsburg Landing. A gunboat had had a fight here a few days before with a land battery on the river bank. The place was almost a wilderness. A few log shanties were the only signs of human habitation . . The fourth division was the first to land. Our camp was situated one and a half miles from the landing and in the center of the military position of the army. On our right were Sherman and Prentiss, on the left, McClernand. Wallace's division landed at Crump Landing a few miles below. The landing of the army on this side of the river was a bold move in Grant as it placed him between the rebel army and the river, thus cutting off his retreat in case of disaster.

Jackman, Pvt., "The Orphan Brigade," to Chattanooga, Tenn.:

> When the troops left about a week after, I was still sick but I had "Capt." G. to take me to the depot and was placed in a passenger coach. I was again fated to be packed, like a sardine, in a sick car. Dr. V., of the 6th Ky., was aboard and if it had not been for him I don't believe I could have kept up. The train ran down as far as Tullahoma by dark and laid over for daylight.

March 6 (Thursday)

The U.S.S. *Monitor* left New York Harbor in the company of the U.S.S. *Currituck* and *Sachem.* The *Monitor* was being towed by the tug *Seth Law.* All were on the way to Hampton Roads, Virginia.

North of Fayetteville, Ark., four blue-clad divisions under the command of Brigadier Gen. Samuel R. Curtis were dug in along Sugar Creek, awaiting an assault by the Confederate forces of Earl Van Dorn. Van Dorn, not liking the odds, decided to move around the flank of the Federals during the night and attack their rear at Pea Ridge.

Samuel Ryan Curtis was 56 years old at the beginning of the war and had not served since the Mexican War. A graduate of USMA, class of '31, he served on the frontier for a period of time and resigned his commission to go to Ohio and study law and engineering. After the Mexican War, he moved to Iowa, where he practised law. He served in the U.S. Congress for three terms. A formidable-looking man, he presented a very stern appearance and was considered aloof. He resigned his seat in

Congress to accept a commission as a Brigadier General of Volunteers on May 17, 1861. He commanded well at Pea Ridge and was promoted to Major General on March 21, 1862. He left the Army at the end of the war and died in Council Bluffs, Iowa, on December 26, 1866.

Jackman, Pvt., "The Orphan Brigade," en route to Chattanooga, Tenn.:

> ... the next day we were running to Chattanooga. I was burning with fever all the time and often I looked out the window at the clear mountain streams dashing over the rocks and wished to be bathing in them—the weather was cold then.

The U.S.S. *Monitor*, after several problems, sailed from Long Island for Hampton Roads, Va., where destiny awaited.

March 7 (Friday)

Flag Officer Foote, still trying to get his gunboats in shape to attack Island No. 10 on the Mississippi River, wrote to the Secretary of the Navy of his continuing difficulties:

> The *Benton* is underway and barely stems the strong current of the Ohio, which is 5 knots in this rise of water, but hope, by putting her between two ironclad steamers to-morrow, she will stem the current and work comparatively well.... I hope on Wednesday [March 12] to take down seven ironclad gunboats and ten mortar boats to attack Island No. 10 and New Madrid. As the current in the Mississippi is in some places 7 knots, the ironclad boats can hardly return here, therefore we must go well prepared, which detains us longer than even you would imagine necessary from your navy-yard and smoothwater standpoint.... We are doing our best, but our difficulties and trials are legion.

In northwest Arkansas, Gen. Earl Van Dorn's columns had passed around the flank and attacked Brigadier Gen. Curtis's Federal force from the rear. The Federals reacted quickly and fought strongly all day. Brigadier Gen. Benjamin McCulloch was killed by a sharpshooter during the fight, causing much confusion in the Confederate ranks. Confederate Brigadier Gen. James McIntosh was also killed. Curtis concentrated his forces at nightfall and awaited the attack by Van Dorn on Saturday.

Ben McCulloch was no stranger to fighting. He went to Texas at about the same time as Davy Crockett, fighting at the Battle of San Jacinto. He was later a commander of the famed Texas Rangers. Commissioned a Brigadier General on May 11, 1861, by President Davis, he was sent to the Indian Territories to deal with the Cherokees. He fought at Wilson's Creek in Missouri with distinction, but developed a strong dislike for Sterling Price. He was shot at about 10:30 A.M. on March 7th, during the Battle of Pea Ridge.

In Virginia, McClellan finally got moving south amid bands blaring and drums beating. Joe Johnston, not really looking for a fight, retreated ahead of "Little Mac." At Winchester, Nathaniel Banks's troops skirmished with Jackson's smaller force.

Jackman, Pvt., "The Orphan Brigade," Chattanooga, Tenn.:

> We were in the car shed at Chattanooga until the next evening at 6 o'clock. I could get nothing which I could eat. Coffee was given me but it made me sick. A.W.—who belonged to the same company, was very kind to me. He afterwards died in the hospital.

March 8 (Saturday)

The Battle of Pea Ridge ended today, with the Confederates retreating hastily towards the Arkansas River. Gen. Curtis wrote his brother:

> The enemy is again far away in the Boston Mountains. The scene is silent and sad—the vulture and the wolf now have the dominion and the dead friends and foes sleep in the same lonely graves.

Jackman, Pvt., "The Orphan Brigade," en route to Atlanta, Ga.:

> The night we were on the train for Atlanta was very disagreeable. The water gave out and I sat by a window and caught the rain in a cup drop-by-drop as it fell off the car. I was glad of its raining that night.
>
> The train arrived at Atlanta about daylight and we were taken to the old City Hotel which was being fitted up for a hospital. So many sick were being brought to the city that they could be but poorly accommodated. We had to lie down on the hard floor. A doctor came to me just in the nick of time and had mustard plasters put on my chest. I was in great pain.

At Hampton Roads, Va., the C.S.S. *Virginia* steamed out of Norfolk under command of Flag Officer Buchanan, and created havoc among the Federal fleet. Her opponents were mostly wooden ships that could not withstand a ram from the *Virginia* or the weight of her guns. After a time the ironclad returned to Norfolk the victor. Like the cavalry arriving too late, the U.S.S. *Monitor* steamed into the Roads in early evening, after a hard trip from New York.

March 9 (Sunday)

Today began a new age in naval warfare. In an engagement that began at about 9 A.M. and lasted nearly four hours, the ironclads U.S.S. *Monitor* and C.S.S. *Virginia* stood toe to toe and slugged it out on the waters of Hampton Roads, Va. Neither won the contest, but the reverberations of this battle were felt worldwide. As Capt. Dahlgren phrased it, "Now comes the reign of iron—and cased sloops are to take the place of wooden ships."

South of Charleston, S.C., a naval force under Commander Godon, consisting of the U.S.S. *Mohican*, *Pocahontas*, and *Potomska*, took possession of St. Simon's and Jekyll islands, and continued on to land at Brunswick, Ga. All fortifications had been abandoned by the Confederates.

Gen. Joe Johnston's Confederate troops withdrew slowly south towards Rappahannock Station. McClellan's army stopped its southward progress and returned to its bases around Alexandria, Va.

Jackman, Pvt., "The Orphan Brigade," Atlanta, Ga.:

> The next morning I felt better and A.W. got me some soup which was the first nourishment I had taken for days. That day a gentlemen from Louisville, Mr. S., came and took four of us, belonging to the same company, to the Washington Hall, a first class hotel. I commenced improving and in two weeks could walk about the streets. I then reported to go to my command—which I afterwards regretted—for the exposure came near "fixing" me again—I went before I was entirely recovered.

Barber, Pvt., Co. D, 15th Illinois Volunteer Infantry, Pittsburg Landing, Tenn.:

> The rebels were concentrating all their available forces at Corinth, only twenty miles from us, and the two armies lay watching each other for several weeks, like ferocious bull dogs eager for a fight. Grant was waiting for Buell to come to his assistance before he commenced offensive operations, but all the while threatening the rebel army. Our camp was a very pleasant one and had been selected with some care....

Day, Pvt., Co. B, 25th Massachusetts Volunteer Infantry, aboard the *New York*, Pamlico Sound, N.C.:

> A beautiful Sabbath morning, not a ripple disturbs the smooth surface of the sound.... All the troops except one or two regiments, left to garrison the island, are again afloat, and the talk now is that New Bern is the next point of attack.

March 11 (Tuesday)

In Washington there was a new order of command. McClellan was relieved as General-in-Chief, but was retained as Commander of the Army of the Potomac. Other similar command changes occurred. All Department Commanders now reported directly to the Secretary of War.

At Winchester, Jackson withdrew his 4600 men southward, followed closely by Banks.

In Richmond, President Davis refused to accept or acknowledge the reports sent by Generals Floyd and Pillow, who had fled Ft. Donelson. Both were relieved from command.

Day, Pvt., Co. B, 25th Massachusetts Volunteer Infantry, aboard the *New York*, Pamlico Sound, N.C.:

> This morning the clink of the windlass is again heard from all the boats hoisting their anchors. We steam out of Croatan into Pamlico sound, so here we go for new conquests.... About 11 A.M. the *New York* went on to a shoal and came to a dead halt. Here was a pretty fix, stuck in the middle of Pamlico sound.... Three large steamers hitched on to us, to pull us off. After a good deal of hard work, lots of swearing and breaking hawsers, they finally succeeded about 4 P.M. in hauling us off. We again started and dropped anchor at Hatteras inlet at 10 P.M.

March 12 (Wednesday)

Landing parties from the U.S.S. *Ottawa*, Lt. Thomas F. Stevens, occupied Jacksonville, Fla., today without opposition.

Federal troops occupied Winchester, on the heels of Jackson's retreating men. This town would change hands many times during the war, almost like a seesaw.

There was a degree of panic in Richmond as the citizens learned that McClellan was going to York Peninsula. The proximity to Richmond caused a rush on the "passport" office of those wanting to leave the city. Gen. Winder, in charge of this business, moved the office so that it could accommodate more people.

Day, Pvt., Co. B, 25th Massachusetts Volunteer Infantry, aboard the *New York*, Pamlico Sound, N.C.:

> This morning weighed anchor and our fleet, comprising upwards of 50 sail, steamed up Pamlico sound for New Bern.... About 3 P.M. we enter the Neuse river, which is here about two miles wide. Situated on the left bank, thirty miles up the river, is the city of New Bern. Slowly we steam up the river, seeing nothing but the low, piney shores, and the smoke of the enemy's signal fires. About 8 P.M., when 15 miles up the river, in a wide place forming a kind of bay, we dropped anchor for the night. The transports lay huddled together in the middle of the river, while a cordon of gunboats surrounds us as a picket. A dark, black night has settled down on us, and all is still and silent as the tomb.... It is really oppressive, and seems as though it has remained unbroken since the morning of creation....

March 13 (Thursday)

Commander D.D. Porter reported the arrival of the mortar fleet at Ship Island, Miss. In five days they would be over the bar and into the Mississippi River, ready to support the assault on New Orleans.

David Dixon Porter was born at Chester, Pa., on June 8, 1813, the son of Commander David D. Porter, a distinguished naval officer and diplomat. He went to sea with his father at the age of ten. At the outset of war he was a Commander and giving serious thought to leaving the Navy for other opportunities. He was given command of the U.S.S. *Powhatan* and sent to the relief of Ft. Pickens, Fla., in 1861 and was assigned as the commander of the Mississippi Squadron in 1862. He worked extremely well with Grant and Sherman in the western campaigns. After the abortive Red River campaign, he was assigned as commander of the North Atlantic Blockading Squadron, which attacked Ft. Fisher at Wilmington, N.C., in January 1865. He was promoted to Rear Admiral in 1863, and he became Superintendent of the Naval Academy at the close of the war. Promoted to Admiral, he remained active in the Navy until his death at Washington, D.C., on February 13, 1891.

At a conference at Fairfax Court House, Va., McClellan pressed his plan to move the Army of the Potomac to the York Peninsula and James River , for an assault on Richmond. Lincoln reminded McClellan that the city of Washington must be kept covered by adequate troops at all times.

In New Bern, N.C., Gen. Burnside's troops landed under cover of naval bombardment on the west bank of the Neuse River and began to advance on the city.

Gen. Lee returned to Richmond today after his assignment as Commander of the Department of Florida.

Day, Pvt., Co. B, 25th Massachusetts Volunteer Infantry, ashore at New Bern, N.C.:

> The morning of the 13th was dark and rainy, and we made preparations to land. It always rains where we go; first at Hatteras, then at Roanoke, and now here. I think we are rightly named a *water* division. We landed in a mudhole at the mouth of Slocum's creek. Before noon the troops were all landed, and the march commenced. The 25th taking the advance, we marched up the river bank about a mile, the gun-boats shelling the woods in advance of us. We then struck into the woods which presented a novel appearance. There was no undergrowth, but a short grass covered the ground while masses of long, gray moss hung in festoons from the branches of the trees, giving them a weird and somber appearance. We soon came out to a cart road, or horse path, along which we followed for a couple of miles, when we came to a deserted cavalry camp. I reckon when they heard the sounds of revelry on the river, there was

mountings in hot haste, and they sped away to some safer locality. The clouds now broke and the sun shone out hot, which, together with the mud, made the march a toilsome one. A little further on, we came to the carriage road....

As Parke's brigade marched past us, we saw at the right of one of the companies in the 5th Rhode Island regiment, marching by the side of the orderly, a lady, dressed in a natty suit, with high boots and jockey hat, surmounted by a big ostrich feather. She was observed of our whole brigade, and cheer after cheer went up along the line for the pretty woman.... The deep mud in the road, together with the heat, began to tell on the boys, and many of them were obliged to fall out by the way. Our march began to grow slower, and when about dusk it commenced raining again, we turned into the woods at the right of the road, where we were to bivouac for the night.... Here in the soft mud of the swamp, with the rain pouring down on us, was our hotel... too tired for supper, the boys laid themselves down in the mud to sleep and bitterly thought of the morrow.

On the Mississippi River, Major General John P. McCown, CSA, ordered the evacuation of New Madrid, Mo.. to Island No. 10 or to the east bank of the river. The evacuation took place under the guns of the Confederate ships *Livingston, Polk* and *Pontchartrain.*

March 14 (Friday)

The advancing Federals at New Madrid, Mo., found their enemy had evacuated to Island No. 10 or across the river, to the eastern bank of the Mississippi. Gen. John Pope still did not have Island No. 10 in his possession, but he was plugging away at it.

Flag Officer Foote at Cairo, Illinois, departed with seven gunboats and ten mortar boats to attack Island No. 10.

At New Bern, N.C., Burnside's 11,000 men moved on the town and captured it, after some minor fighting, from a force of about 4000 Confederates. The attack had been carried out through pouring rain and over muddy roads. With this city taken, another port and useful supply point was established.

Day, Pvt., Co. B, 25th Massachusetts Volunteer Infantry, Battle of New Bern, N.C.:

...The boys slept well, but woke up cold and wet. There was no time to make a cup of coffee, for we were close on the enemy, and the order was again for battle. We caught a few hasty mouthfuls of cold meat and hardtack, and quietly fell into our places in line... it took a great amount of swearing and hurrying to and fro of aides and hoarse shoutings of officers to get us around where we were wanted. We were within a half mile of the enemy's line, and Reno's and Parke's brigades were deploying in front of them, on the centre and left of our line.... We soon came in sight of the enemy's works which were only a short rifle-shot from us.... We filed out of the road to the right, moving towards the river. As we moved out we were honored with a salute from one of the enemy's batteries, but the shots passed harmlessly over our heads. The boys looked a little wild, but with steady step, moved on.... The howitzer battery now came up, took position in the road between the 24th and 27th Massachusetts, and commenced firing.... We were on the extreme right and well towards the river, seeing nothing in front of us to draw our fire.... We were ordered, if possible, to turn the enemy's left. We advanced nearly to the edge of the woods, and only a short distance from the enemy's line. I was running my eye along it to see where and how it ended, expecting every moment to hear the order to charge, but just then the boats commenced throwing shell over us towards the Confederate line. They had got a low range and the shells were coming dangerously near, splintering and cutting off the trees, and ploughing great furrows in the ground directly in front of us. In this condition of affairs, we were compelled to fall back. The boats, however, were soon notified of their mistake and ceased firing.

We again advanced, going over and beyond where we fell back, when all at once we received a galling flank fire from an unseen battery. We again fell back a few rods, dressing the line, and again cautiously advanced. We now discovered that their works curved and connected with a large water battery situated just in the edge of the woods and concealed by the trees. In the rear of this battery were mounted old 32-pounder marine guns, which gave them an enfilading fire of the clearing in front of their works. From these guns they fired grape shot, which weighed about four pounds each. To charge was hopeless, and in falling back we received another fire from this battery. From these we lost quite a number of men, killed and wounded. I had the honor of stopping one ball myself; it struck a tree, however, before it did me. Having got back from under the guns of this battery, Col. Upton reported the situation to Gen. Foster, who ordered him to move his regiment to the left of the 24th Massachusetts and support the howitzer battery.

During all this time, however, the battle was raging furiously along the centre and left. In front of our battery the enemy had a large gun which commanded the road, and which proved rather troublesome. This gun, after each discharge, was hauled around, and again back into position by a pair of mules. After each discharge, a young dare-devil of a marine lieutenant would run down the road almost to the gun to see what they were up to. On one of these excursions he discovered one of the mules down, probably from a stray shot. He came running back up the road like a wild man swinging his cap and shouting at the top of his voice: "Come on, come on! for God's sake, come on. Now is your time." The 25th, without any other order, sprang forward, followed by the 24th Massachusetts and all the line. On the charge, they received a heavy fire from the enfilading battery, but on they went, scaling the ditch and parapet like blackbirds, but no enemy was there. Seeing us coming, they took that as a notice to leave, and acted on it immediately. Inside the works, I heard Gen. Burnside ask Gen. Foster who gave the order to charge. Foster replied he didn't know, but it made no difference so long as it was done.

The 25th reformed and marching a short distance to the rear charged across the railroad into the swamp, capturing Col. Avery and his South Carolina regiment who were covering the retreat. Thus, after five hours hard fighting, ended the battle of New Bern. Victory had again perched upon our banners, and the cheers of the victors were ringing out on every side. Although the battle resulted as I wished, I certainly did not feel like glorying for who can compute the woe, anguish, and sorrow of this day's work? I cannot get over my horror of a battle....

Foster's brigade starts up the railroad for town.... Cautiously we moved along, thinking perhaps the enemy may have formed a second line and are awaiting our approach. It soon became apparent, however, that they were making the distance between them and us as long as possible. We then hurried along, arriving at the river where the railroad bridge was burned which crossed into the town. The view from here was an appalling one. The railroad bridge, a fine structure upwards of 1500 feet in length, was in ruins and the town was on fire in several places. Dense clouds of smoke of inky blackness settled like a pall over the town, while every few moments the lurid flames, with their forked tongues, would leap above the clouds, and the bellowing of the gunboats on the river, throwing their large shells over the town after the retreating enemy, conspired to make a most hideous scene.

It was near the middle of the afternoon when the old ferry boat *Curlew* (which a few weeks before I had wished sunk) arrived. On board this, Major McCafferty, with a mixed company of about 100 men, with the colors, crossed the river and landed on the wharf at the foot of Craven street. These were the first troops and colors in the city. After landing, we marched up Craven street nearly to Pollock street, when we halted. The major did not appear to have any business on hand or instructions to make any, so we waited for further orders or for the regiment to join us.

Here was presented an indescribable scene. A town on fire, an invading army entering its gates, the terror-stricken inhabitants fleeing in every direction. The negroes were holding a grand jubilee, some of them praying and in their rude way, thanking God for their deliverance; others, in their wild delight, were dancing and singing, while others with an eye to the main chance, were pillaging the stores and dwellings. But in the midst of all this appalling tumult and confusion, the boys, true to the natural instincts of the soldier, were looking around to see what could be found in the line of trophies and fresh rations. They soon begin to come in with their plunder, which the major told them to carry back, as he should allow no pillaging while he was in command. Presently Stokes comes along bringing a little package. The major asked, "What have you there?" "Sausages, sir!" "Go, carry them back where you got them from." "I reckon not," replied Stokes, "a lady out here gave them to me." The major was incredulous, but Stokes offered to show him the lady and let her tell it, whereupon, the former subsides, and Stokes, with a roguish twinkle of his eye, jams the package into my haversack, saying "Sausage for breakfast." I was proud of the boy, to see how well he was observing instructions, as I have told him from the start that to stand any sort of a chance as a soldier, he must learn to do a right smart job of stealing, and be able to lie the hair right off a man's head. He has certainly shown some smartness, and I doubt if a commissioned officer could have done any better.

The regiment landed at the north side of the city and about night rejoined us. Our hard day's work was at last finished, the regiment was dismissed and the companies quartered in any unoccupied buildings they might find. Generals Burnside and Foster, with soldiers, citizens, and negroes, were putting out the fires and bring order out of confusion. Company B was quartered in a small house on Craven street, and the boys, although hungry, tired, and worn down by the fatigues of the day, made frolic of the evening and celebrated their victory.

March 15 (Saturday)

Flag Officer Foote's flotilla of gunboats and mortar boats reached the area above Island No. 10, but dense fog and rain prevented any action.

The divisions of Sherman and Hurlbut arrived at the landing docks of Pittsburg Landing on the Tennessee River. Major Gen. Don Carlos Buell was ordered from Nashville to the area around Savannah, Tenn., which was close by. Halleck, on one of his better days, dismissed the rather superficial charges against Grant, and restored him to command in Tennessee. Grant replaced Gen. C.F. Smith, who had injured his leg getting into a boat. Forces were concentrating around Pittsburg Landing.

Day, Pvt., Co. B, 25th Massachusetts Volunteer Infantry, battle aftermath, New Bern, N.C.:

> The boys came out this morning looking a little the worse for wear, lame, sore and stiff; but with a good bumper of whiskey to lubricate their stiffened joints, and a little stirring around to take the kinks out of their legs, a good breakfast, hot coffee, etc., they soon resumed their normal condition.... Negroes are coming in by the hundred, and the city is full of soldiers and marines traveling about and having things pretty much their own way. Guards are sent out to patrol the streets and assist Capt. Dan, the provost marshal, in preserving order preparatory to putting on a provost guard and bring the city under law and order. Some enterprising party has hoisted the old flag on the spire of the church on Pollock street. There let it proudly wave...

March 17 (Monday)

Grant arrived at Pittsburg Landing and assumed command, placing his headquarters at Savannah, north of the Landing.

In Alexandria, Va., long blue lines of soldiers marched through the streets to board waiting transports to carry them to York Peninsula for the assault on Richmond.

Day, Pvt., Co. B, 25th Massachusetts Volunteer Infantry, New Bern, N.C.:

> It would seem that the people had no thought of evacuating the city until the very last moment. When they saw that the Philistines were upon them, they hastily gathered up their valuables and what light articles they could carry on their persons, and fled, leaving their houses, stores and property, just as they stood. Today the several companies of our regiment moved into the deserted mansions of the Confederate martyrs, which will be our quarters during our stay. Company B went into a two-story brick house on East Front street. It has a pretty flower garden in front, with an orchard, vegetable garden, and servant's quarters in the rear. The house is nicely furnished throughout; the floors, halls and stairs are carpeted, as are the chambers. The front parlor has upholstered furniture, center table, piano, lace curtains, ornaments, gas fixtures, etc. The back parlor is furnished similar to the front, excepting the piano. The basement contains all the necessary culinary utensils. I don't see but we are pretty well fixed, but this is only one of the occasional sunny spots in a soldier's life. Some of the other companies are quartered in more pretentious and better furnished houses on Pollock, Craven, and Broad streets....

At Island No. 10, the U.S.S. *Benton*, with Flag Officer Foote aboard, was lashed between two other gunboats to provide a stable platform for gunnery. The *Benton* was hit several times and the other gunboats were damaged.

March 18 (Tuesday)

In Richmond, President Davis named Secretary of War Judah Benjamin to be the new Secretary of State. George W. Randolph was to be the new Secretary of War.

At Corinth, Miss., Gen. Albert Sidney Johnston's

troops began arriving from Murfreesboro. Due to shortage of transportation and bad roads, it would take more than a week for all the troops to close up.

March 19 (Wednesday)

The defenders of Island No. 10 on the Mississippi River still provided strong resistance to Flag Officer Foote's floating artillery. Foote said this place "is harder to conquer than Columbus, as the island shores are lined with forts, each fort commanding the one above it."

Flag Officer Farragut commented, " I sent over to Biloxi yesterday, and robbed the post-office of a few papers. They speak volumes of discontent. It is no use—the cord is pulling tighter, and I hope I shall be able to tie it. God alone decides the contest; but we must put our shoulders to the wheel."

March 20 (Thursday)

At Ship Island, Miss., Major Gen. Benjamin F. Butler assumed command of the troops that would make the assault on New Orleans and southern Louisiana.

In Richmond, President Davis wrote regarding the defense of the James River approach to the city:

> The position of Drewry's Bluff, seven or eight miles below Richmond... was chosen to obstruct the river against such vessels as the *Monitor*. The work is being rapidly completed. Either Ft. Powhatan or Kennon's Marsh, if found to be the proper positions, will be fortified and obstructed as at Drewry's Bluff, to prevent the ascent of the river by ironclad vessels....

Drewry's Bluff remained in business until April 1865, when it was abandoned by the Confederates after Richmond fell.

Federals near Strasburg, threatened by Ashby's cavalry, moved back towards Winchester. "Stonewall" rested his infantry near Mt. Jackson, Va.

In North Carolina, Burnside's troops moved from New Bern towards Washington, N.C., without opposition.

Day, Pvt., Co. B, 25th Massachusetts Volunteer Infantry, New Bern, N.C.:

> New Bern, situated at the north confluence of the Trent and Neuse rivers, was, I think, first settled by colonists from Berne, Switzerland, and in honor of the old town was named New Berne, but for short is now written as pronounced. The chivalry, in their hasty flight, thought to make a Moscow of it, and fired it in several places, destroying the long and expensive railroad bridge across the Trent river, all the turpentine distilleries (save one) of which there was quite a number, and three squares of the town in one of which was the large Planter's hotel.
>
> The city has a fine waterfront on the south and east sides, furnishing ample wharfage for shipping and warehouses. It contains a population of about 8000. The streets cross at right angles thus forming squares which are compactly built over. The area of the city is much less than many northern towns of 2000 inhabitants, but land is scarce here and it doesn't do to waste it for building purposes. There are, however, several fine residences with ample surroundings.
>
> There are four churches, several halls, one academy, one hotel, court house, jail, post office, printing office, and many large wholesale stores and warehouses. There is a small cotton mill, manufacturing cotton yarn, a lumber mill, one turpentine distillery, tannery, gas works, and a large machine shop and foundry connected with the railroad depot at the north side of the city. There are two banks here, but at present they do not seem to be doing a regular banking business. Capt. Dan, the provost marshal, occupies the Merchant's, while the master of transportation occupies the Bank of North Carolina. Whether the latter bank discounts or not, I am unable to say, but I know that Capt. Dan does when there is anything in the bottle.
>
> The streets are wide and level, set on either side with handsome shade trees. Altogether, it is a rather pretty city. This has been a town of some commercial importance, having had a large inland and coastwise trade, exporting shingles, staves, and other lumber to the West Indies, cotton and naval stores to northern ports, and bringing return cargoes of such goods as the market here demanded.

March 21 (Friday)

Distilled beverages such as whiskey and brandy, were very scarce in Richmond. Brandy, in particular, was imported and rare. Usually it was only dispensed through the local "drug stores" of the day by prescriptions signed by a physician. There was a large bootleg market in this commodity.

On the Mississippi, Flag Officer Foote's guns still

pounded Island No. 10, which still held out. Halleck expressed his appreciation to Foote for his efforts.

March 22 (Saturday)

Jackson left his camp at Mt. Jackson for Strasburg, twenty-six miles away. His famed "foot cavalry" covered the twenty-six miles and camped outside the town that night. Hard work, and it was just beginning. The advance of Jackson's small army collided with Shields's Federals outside Kernstown, and a skirmish developed.

In New Orleans, the Confederate officials sent six steamers of the River Defense Fleet upriver, soon to be followed by 14 more, much to the consternation of the local populace. The officials believed that the real threat was from the north, not from Farragut's fleet in the Gulf of Mexico.

The C.S.S. *Florida* donned false colors and departed Liverpool, England, as the British ship *Oreto* for Nassau, Bahamas Islands. A small ship, she was the first to be built in England for the Confederacy. Her guns, four 7-inchers, were sent to Nassau by separate ship.

March 23 (Sunday)

Early in the morning, the cooking fires had done their duty and were being extinguished as Jackson's "Stonewall Brigade" got back on the road. At about 2 P.M. they approached the village of Kernstown, about three miles from Winchester. Jackson immediately went into battle with 2700 men against 11,000 (some reports say Jackson had 3500 and Shields 9000). He lost, but said that if he had had another 2000 men he would have won. The battle was a complete success in that it caused the officials in Washington to send over 60,000 men after him, thus tying up resources that could have been used on the Peninsula. Jackson's men fell back to Newton (Stephens City). This marked the beginning of the famous Shenandoah Valley campaign.

In the vicinity of Beaufort, N.C., the Federals besieged old Ft. Macon after the local Confederate commander refused to surrender.

Jackman, Pvt., "The Orphan Brigade," to Chattanooga, Tenn.:

> About 30 of us were placed under the charge of a Lt. Whetstone and locked up in a car for Chattanooga. The commander of the post made us a little speech before he fastened us up hoping we would be orderly, *keep on train*, etc. We left at 7 P.M. and arrived at C. about the same time the next morning. We got off the train and I never again saw the Lt. He was such a "Goober." I don't believe he knew which road to take. Here I spent the last money for breakfast—a piece of fat pork and a bit of corn bread.

March 24 (Monday)

Jackson ordered his command back to the vicinity of Mt. Jackson, Va.

At Ship Island, the U.S.S. *Pensacola* sailed towing a chartered schooner loaded with guns and stores for the Mississippi River, where the *Pensacola* ran aground at high tide. She failed to get over the bar, even with four steamboats towing her through the mud. An accidental parting of a hawser killed two men and injured others.

At Corinth, Miss., the last of Gen. Albert S. Johnston's men from Murfreesboro arrived.

Jackman, Pvt., "The Orphan Brigade," to Huntsville, Ala.:

> Left C. at 8 A.M. and arrived at Huntsville that afternoon. Lay over at H. until 2 the next morning when we ran down to Decatur. I had nothing to buy my breakfast and tried to trade my pocket knife to an old negro for a piece of gingerbread but we couldn't come to terms. I then went to a camp close by and got my breakfast gratis. Sometime in the forenoon the train left for Corinth. I got into the same car with two soldiers from the 6th Ky. who had their wives along, which wives had a very large basket of provisions. I soon ingratiated myself with the ladies and as a consequence, "lived high" the balance of the trip.

March 25 (Tuesday)

There was a stiff little fight between two Confederate ships and one Federal at Pass Christian, Miss.. Neither side was damaged in the engagement. Gen. Butler had arrived at Ship Island with his troop transports and dined with Flag Officer Farragut, who wrote:

> I am now packed and ready for my departure to the mouth of the Mississippi River.... I spent last

evening very pleasantly with General Butler. He does not appear to have any very difficult plan of operations, but simply to follow in my wake and hold what I can take. God grant that may be all that we attempt… victory. If I die in the attempt, it will only be what every officer has to expect. He who dies in doing his duty to his country, and at peace with his God, has played out the drama of life to the best advantage.

Day, Pvt., Co. B, 25th Massachusetts Volunteer Infantry, New Bern, N.C.:

There are swarms of negroes here. They are of all sexes, ages, sizes and conditions. They sit along the streets and fences, staring and grinning at every thing they see, laughing and chattering together like so many black-birds. They have very exaggerated notions of freedom, thinking it means freedom from work and a license to do about as they please. There is no use trying to get them to work, for if they can get their hoe-cake and bacon, it is all they want, and they are contented and happy. When a party of them is wanted to unload a vessel or do any job of work, the commissary or quartermaster requests the colonel to send along the men. The colonel orders one of the companies to go out and pick them up and report with them where they are wanted. A patrol is detailed and put in charge of a non-commissioned officer who starts out to pick up his party. On seeing a good, stout looking fellow, the officer halts his squad, and calling the darky's attention, says, "Come here, boy!" The unsuspecting darky comes grinning along up and asks, "Wat 'er want 'er me?" "Fall in here, I want you," "Wat I don' 'er want me?" "Well, I want you to do something; fall in here," "O, lor' a gorra, boss, i'se so busy today i'se couldn't go nohow, i's go tomorrer suah." "Never mind that, fall in here," and the darky falls in, his eyes rolling around and his thick lips sticking out, feeling about as mad as the well can, doubtless thinking that freedom is no great thing after all.

In that way the whole party is picked up in a few minutes and marched off to where they are wanted. They are set to work, and at night will all promise to be on hand the next morning, "suah." The next morning perhaps a few of them will put in an appearance, but the most of them will keep away, and another patrol will be sent out to pick up another lot. But I think, after a little while, they will learn that freedom means something besides idleness and they will feel a willingness to work. They have a curious custom of carrying everything on their heads, toting they call it, and will tote large or small bundles along the street or through a crowd as unconcernedly and safely as though it were a basket slung on their arm. They will tote a brimming pitcher or tumbler of water without spilling scarcely a drop. These darkies are a curious institution.

March 26 (Wednesday)

Flag Officer Foote warned his fleet captain at Cairo:

You will inform the commanders of the gunboats *Cairo, Tyler* and *Lexington* not to be caught up the river with too little water to return to Cairo. They, of course, before leaving, will consult with the generals with whom they are cooperating. As it is reported on the authority of different persons from New Orleans that the rebels have thirteen gunboats finished and ready to move up the Mississippi, besides the four or five below New Madrid, and the *Manassas*, or ram, at Memphis, the boats now up the rivers and at Columbus or Hickman, should be ready to protect Cairo or Columbus in case disaster overtakes us in our flotilla.

Jackman, Pvt., "The Orphan Brigade," Burnsville, Miss.:

The train got to Burnsville, Miss. late at night and finding our brigade was encamped there, I got off. Some of the boys were in town on detail and I stayed with them till morning. Early I went to camp and found all the boys " *in status quo.*"

The brigade had marched all the way from Bowling Green to Decatur, Ala. having been transported by rail from the latter place to Burnsville. I missed nearly all of this march but I would rather have gone through it than suffered as I did.

March 29 (Saturday)

Along an old road leading to the Shenandoah Valley was the little town of Middleburg. The whole town had only three churches, seven stores of various kinds, a local academy, a tobacco factory and about 80 houses. The 28th Pennsylvania Infantry, commanded by Col. John W. Geary, reached Middleburg, and its passage was contested by a group of

Confederate cavalry and infantry based in the town. With a swirl of street fighting, the Rebels broke and their cavalry covered the evacuation of the infantry. The cavalry regrouped in a hollow west of the town where they were fired upon by the Federals, resulting in the Confederates retreating.

The interesting thing about this action was that for the first time a machine gun (Lincoln's "coffee mill") was employed against enemy troops. One Capt. Bartlett, describing the action about a month later, said, "One of these guns was brought to bear on a squadron of cavalry at 800 yards, and it cut them to pieces terribly, quickly forcing them to fly." One of the deadliest weapons invented had had its first field trial in combat.

At Corinth, Miss., the Confederate Army of the Kentucky and that of the Mississippi were consolidated under one command, that of Gen. Albert Sydney Johnston.

In western Virginia, Frémont took command from William S. Rosecrans, who would depart for the west and a new command.

March 30 (Sunday)

Flag Officer Foote directed Commander Henry Walke, U.S.S. *Carondelet,* one of his more adventuresome commanders:

> You will avail yourself of the first fog or rainy night and drift your steamer down past the batteries, on the Tennessee shore, and Island No. 10... for the purpose of covering General Pope's army while he crosses that point to the opposite, or to the Tennessee side of the river, that he may move his army up to Island No. 10 and attack the rebels in the rear while we attack them in front.

Jackman, Pvt., "The Orphan Brigade," Burnsville, Miss.:

> Being Sunday morning, the boys are rubbing up for inspection to be at 2 o'clock P.M.. Drill in camp. Am not well.
>
> *Evening*—Heavy firing of artillery in the direction of the Tennessee. First hostile guns heard. The firing lasted some time and made me feel "devilish" as the deep thunder came rolling over the hills. All on the *qui vive* to know the cause. The company ordered to be ready to march at 5, morning.

APRIL 1862

At last the Northern armies were moving. Long columns of troops were departing Alexandria, Va., for York Peninsula around Norfolk and Yorktown. McClellan was finally doing something with the thousands of men he had been training for the past several months.

In the west, Island No. 10 on the Mississippi was under siege, and Federal gunboats were slipping past the island to the broad stretches of river previously under Confederate control. Memphis was threatened. If Grant could succeed in his bid for control of the Tennessee and Cumberland rivers, the western part of Tennessee would be lost to the South, and Mississippi would be threatened from above. On the coastal areas, Maj. Gen. Burnside's troops were besieging Ft. Macon and already a large piece of the Pamlico Sound area was in Federal hands.

April 1 (Tuesday)

The Army of the Potomac, "Little Mac's" army, boarded steamers in seemingly continuous streams and headed for the wharfs and piers of the Peninsula. The army was strong, well-equipped, and itching for battle.

Jackson, at his headquarters near Hawkinsville in the Shenandoah Valley, had his troops fall back up the Valley in the face of Hunter's reinforced troops, who pushed through Strasburg and on to Edinburg. Col. Ashby's cavalry had already been driven up the Valley beyond Edinburg. Ashby's troops burned the bridge at Edinburg and held the high ground above the town.

On the western rivers, Federal gunboats pushed up the Tennessee River as far as Eastport, Miss., and Chickasaw, Ala. At Island No. 10, a small Federal raiding party sneaked in, spiked six guns, and escaped without loss. Col. Roberts, USA, gave high praise to the boat crews for their conduct during the raid.

In Richmond, the congregation of the Second Baptist Church donated their bronze bell to be cast into cannon, and also promised to donate enough money to raise a battery of artillery to be called the Second Baptist Church Battery. So much for beating swords into plowshares.

Day, Pvt., Co. B, 25th Massachusetts Volunteer Infantry, New Bern, N.C.:

> I learn that Major McCafferty has resigned and is going to leave us. I am sorry to learn that his ambition for fame is so soon gratified.... We are now living in clover, having little else to do but to keep ourselves, clothes, arms and equipments clean and in good order... Our rations are of good quality and variety. We now have our fresh beef three times a week, and with all the soft bread we want. With our government rations, and what we can buy, such as oysters, fresh fish, chickens, eggs, sweet potatoes, etc., we are running at a high rate of speed. We often contrast this with our life at the inlet.

April 2 (Wednesday)

Confederate Gen. Albert Sidney Johnston, the darling of the Confederacy, was commanding the newly reorganized army at Corinth, Miss. Johnston decided that he would attack the Federals at Pittsburg Landing and drive them into the river. The troops were to move early on April 3rd.

Gen. McClellan and his staff arrived at Ft. Monroe aboard the steamer *Commodore.* "Little Mac" intended to outflank the Confederates, using his naval superiority on the James River. Federal gunboats began a bombardment of Yorktown which would continue until the Confederates evacuated the city early in May.

At Pittsburg Landing, near the meeting house at Shiloh, Grant awaited reinforcements prior to moving on the Confederates at Corinth. Sherman, Prentiss, Hurlbut, and McClernand commanded divisions within the army.

April 3 (Thursday)

Confederate forces under Johnston were to begin their march on Pittsburg Landing early this day, but as usual, one delay caused another and there was no chance to launch an attack on the following day as planned.

Flag Officer Du Pont and Brigadier Gen. Henry W. Benham planned to cut off Ft. Pulaski from Savannah, on the Georgia coast.

Jackman, Pvt., "The Orphan Brigade," Burnsville, Miss.:

> Through the day drew and cooked up three days rations; and forty rounds issued to the man. After dark, the regiment was drawn up before the Colonel's tent and a battle order given.

Grant's army was still unaware of the approaching Confederate force although there had been some skirmishing around Shiloh Church. Reinforcements were arriving and being placed as rapidly as possible. Sherman was placid, believing the Confederates would not attack.

Lincoln, disturbed because only twenty thousand troops had been left to guard Washington when McClellan moved the Army of the Potomac south, ordered the Secretary of War, Stanton, to keep in northern Virginia one of the corps destined for the Peninsula. McDowell's Corps was retained. McClellan, protesting, as he always would, that he would not have enough troops for the coming battle, was left with only 100,000 troops to fulfill his battle plan. He was initially opposed by Confederate Gen. Magruder with 20,000. Lincoln directed McClellan to advance at once.

The United States Senate voted to abolish slavery in the District of Columbia by a vote of 29 to 14.

April 4 (Friday)

More delays for the Confederate forces around Shiloh. Nothing seemed to be working right for Gen. A.S. Johnston in getting his attack on Grant moving. The amount of skirmishing increased between the opposing armies. Johnston believed that any real chance of surprise was gone. Still, the Union forces didn't realize what was happening.

Barber, Pvt., Co. D, 15th Illinois Volunteer Infantry, Shiloh, Tenn.:

> ... we were soon awakened from our repose by a spirited dash of the enemy into our very midst making a reconnaissance. This was the Friday before the battle. The 15th was called upon to repulse this attack from the enemy. Promptly and quietly they obeyed the order and [were] the first regiment on hand from the fourth division. We received great credit for our behavior on this occasion....

Jackman, Pvt., "The Orphan Brigade," en route to Shiloh, Tenn.:

> Had reveille at 4 and marched at daylight. Nearly all the baggage was sent to Corinth by direct road. We had to strike tents and load baggage in a pelting

rain. Being weak and debilitated and feeling like a "snort," I picked up a bottle in which I thought was whiskey, but upon turning it up and taking a "big horn," I found it to be alcohol and camphor mixed—medicine for the "Prof's" inflammation. I thought the stuff would burn me up—it cut blood out of my throat. That taught me a lesson.

At the outset our road led through a swamp where, in some places, the mud and water was knee deep every step. The rain continued to pour down all the forenoon. I soon regretted that I had started. For a time I kept up but soon the column commenced continuing past me. While the troops would be resting, I would be walking to overtake them. About noon our road led over piny ridges and the sun came out very hot. Once I stopped off on the side of the road at a spring to rest. While resting some soldier took my new minnie rifle which I had left leaning against a tree, and left his old flint-lock in the place. I was vexed. When I got back on the road I found the division, commanded by Genl. Breckinridge, the only troops on that road, had all past and the wagon trains moving by. I gave up walking any farther and got into our surgeon's wagon. At sundown we passed through Farmington, 4 miles of Corinth. Night soon overtook us and as the road often led over creeks, which were swampy, the train had to stop before coming up with the columns. That night it rained and James H. and I slept in a wagon. I had a high fever that night.

On York Peninsula, McClellan moved his 100,000 against Magruder's less than 20,000, and still called for more reinforcements. He believed the Confederate forces vastly outnumbered his available force. McClellan failed to make a crossing of the Warwick River, giving Confederate Gen. Joseph E. Johnston time to shift his forces from the Manassas and Richmond areas to the Peninsula. All available Confederate forces were concentrating in the Peninsula to defend Richmond.

In the west, a canal was cut through the swamps so that small boats could move around Island No. 10. During the night, and during a storm, the Federal gunboat *Carondelet*, Commander Walke, ran past the Confederate batteries on the island and gained the open river below. The Confederates spotted the gunboat from the island and the night turned into a hellish scene with the storm, lightning, roar of the thunder and naval guns. Walke had strengthened his gunboat by piling cord-wood around the boilers, adding extra deck planking and anchor chains for armor protection.

Wills, 1st Lt., Adj., HQ, 3rd Battalion, 7th Illinois Cavalry, near Pt. Pleasant, Mo.:

... Our regiment has had a run of bad luck since we've been here. Two men killed on the plank road, two wounded at same place, two killed by falling trees in a storm of night of April 1st, and dozen wounded, and yesterday one drowned while watering his horse in a swamp, and our horses are dying off very fast of horse cholera. This latter is a serious thing in a regiment where the men own the horses themselves. For they (or nearly all of them) cannot buy others. Most of them are still owing for the horses they have....

Between here and Madrid we have batteries every three miles and the Rebels have rather more on the opposite side. Both are right on their respective banks and have their flags fluttering their mutual hatred in each others faces.... This fuss about "Island 10" I think is all humbug. Don't believe they have attacked it yet. It don't sound like Foote's fighting. Look on the map and see what a nice pen there is between the rivers Tennessee and Mississippi. Don't it look that if Grant and company can whip them out at Corinth, that we'll have all the forces at Memphis and intermediate points to "Island 10" in a bag that they'll have trouble in getting through?... I firmly believe the summer will see the war ended. But it will also see a host of us upended if we have to fight over such ground as this....

Things were not rosy on the home front in Alabama. Governor John Gill Shorter was having problems getting the state's quota of regiments filled. The problems seemed not one of a scarcity of recruits, it was more about intramural squabbling. He explained it to an unknown Colonel:

I only received your dispatches, I have also your letter by Captain Sanford—I sent word immediately to all the Macon County companies you mentioned—and told Mayor of Tuskeegee to go and see them, & to try & prevail on them to go & join your regiment. But there are so many officer hunters among them and they are so anxious to make [bargaining] in the organizations of the new regiments, & so much disgusting [deal] making & electioneering going on that it is impossible to raise companies for the public advantage. I regret this very much. Stewart told me today that the new companies objected to going into the 3rd Regt because it was so well filled, and they feared they would be put to extra hard work etc.—this is all stuff—If you or Bather could get a furlough & come to Alabama & visit these companies I think you could succeed—otherwise I don't believe any will go....

The Confederate gunboat U.S.S. *Carondelet*, Lt. Washington Gwathmey, was also in action. Accompanied by the C.S.S. *Pamlico* and *Oregon*, Gwathmey engaged the Federal gunboats *J. P. Jackson, New London*, and *Hatteras*, and the troops on board the transport *Lewis*, but could not prevent the landing of the troops at Pass Christian, Mississippi. Once ashore, the troops destroyed the Confederate camp there. The way to New Orleans was partially open.

April 5 (Saturday)

McClellan, in front of Yorktown, Va., had been held at bay by Magruder, who marched his men around in circles, letting the Federals see the long columns of troops through a gap in the fortifications. McClellan believed what he saw and thought that Magruder was being reinforced by thousands more troops. Meanwhile Joe Johnston was shifting his troops as rapidly as possible to help Magruder.

In the west, Albert Sidney Johnston again failed to attack. He didn't get his troops aligned until late in the day, and decided to wait until tomorrow. The Federals still did not realize that the Rebels were nearly on them. Some pickets reported large troop movements, but no one, including Sherman, believed them.

Barber, Pvt., Co. D, 15th Illinois Volunteer Infantry, Shiloh, Tenn.:

> ... Let your thoughts wander along the spring-decked shore of the Tennessee, girded by dense forests just blossoming into life, until they rest on Shiloh's field, then pause, and take a sweeping glance at the magnificent scene spread out before you. The day is one of the loveliest of spring-time; the golden rays of the sun are gilding the tree-tops with their last expiring light, and reflection on the camp of the patriot army whose tents so thickly dot the plain. It is a quiet evening—an almost dread silence prevails —a silence which, ere the morning rays of the sun gild the eastern horizon, will be broken by the flash of arms which will make the earth tremble, and the grand old forests echo and re-echo with the crash of artillery, bowing and shivering the giant monarchs of the forest with the fiery blast; but how quiet the scene now! How unconscious are we that the morrow will be ushered in by a blood-red sun and the echoing notes of the deep-toned artillery, and that thousands who are now all unconscious of danger will, ere another sun sets, be sleeping that last long sleep that know no waking!...

Jackman, Pvt., "The Orphan Brigade," en route to Shiloh, Tenn.:

> This morning felt completely broken down. The wagon was so heavily loaded and behind too. I had to try it afoot again. The train rolled past me and I was left a complete straggler. A staff officer in charge of the rear ordered me back to Corinth but as soon as he was gone, I kept ahead. The next house I came to I stopped. The lady gave me some milk and bread to eat. I felt so bad I thought I would go no further. Soldiers were straggling along all day. That evening, there was some artillery firing towards Shiloh. Again had fever that night.

In the west, the news of the gunboat running past Island No. 10 had electrified the local troops. The Northern papers, including Greeley's *Tribune*, made light of the announcement at first.

Andrew Johnson, the appointed Federal Military Governor of Tennessee, suspended the mayor and other city officials of Nashville for refusing to take the oath to the Union.

Wills, 1st Lt., Adj., HQ, 3rd Battalion, 7th Illinois Cavalry, near Pt. Pleasant, Mo.:

> One of our boys has just returned from Madrid and says he saw our gunboat *Cairo* there. She slipped by the batteries at "Island No. 10" in the storm last night. Mosquitoes here already.

On the Mississippi approach to New Orleans, Flag Officer Farragut took a personal look at the defenses of Forts Jackson and St. Philip. The forts opened fire on his ship but Farragut, up the mast for a clear view, paid no attention to the firing.

April 6 (Sunday)

In the early morning hours, Confederate Gen. Albert Sidney Johnston finally got all his troops together and sent them screaming into the still unsuspecting Union lines around Shiloh Church. As the picket firing increased dramatically, some Union troops reacted but most did not and were unprepared for the charge that burst upon them. Grant, at his headquarters in Savannah, Tenn., several miles north, was alerted and immediately went to Pittsburg Landing. He also ordered Maj. Gen. Lew Wallace at Crump's Landing to march immediately to Shiloh Church. The first units of Maj. Gen. Don Carlos Buell's army were at Savannah, Tenn., under Brig. Gen. William Nelson. Most of Buell's troops were still en route.

Barber, Pvt., Co. D, 15th Illinois Volunteer Infantry, Shiloh, Tenn.:

...The camp was alarmed Sunday morning just as the streaks of red begin to tinge the eastern sky, by the rapid firing of the pickets, who soon came in with the report that the enemy was marching on us in overwhelming numbers and were even now in sight, as a shower of bullets which fell around too plainly indicated. There was no time to give orders then. It was life or death. The enemy was in camp before it had time to arouse and form a line. Some were shot in their sleep, never knowing what hurt them. Terrible and complete was the surprise. Our boys fought as only those can fight who are fighting for the right. Rally[ing] amidst a perfect storm of bullets, shot and shell, they tried to form a new line, and as the infuriated enemy, made mad with whisky and gunpowder, hurled themselves against the line, it gradually fell back, step by step, forming new and stronger lines and leaving their track strewn with the dead and dying. The onset of the foe was terrific, but instead of the easy victory that had been promised them, they were met with a valor superior to their own, as the cool aim of our boys which strewed the ground with dead amply testified. Our camp was situated three miles from where the fighting began, and it was not until after sunrise that the tide of battle surged upon us. I heard the distant rattling of musketry and first thought it was something else. I was writing a letter home at the time. But soon the long roll was sounded and then I knew that there was work for us to do. Throwing my unfinished letter to Milton, who was sick, I told him to finish it and tell where I was, then hastily putting on my accoutrements, gun in hand, took my place in the company. In less than five minutes from the time the bugle was sounded, the regiment was on the march to the scene of conflict. Milton, the brave boy, unable to endure the suspense, though so weak from the effects of fever he could hardly stand, with blood now on fire and with artificial strength, followed us to the field. No remonstrance of mine or the captain could make him stay back....

We had not proceeded far before we met crowds of stragglers skulking to the rear. It was a humiliating sight, and our boys heaped curses, bitter and cutting, on their cowardly heads. They tried to excuse their conduct by innumerable excuses, not one of which would weigh a farthing in this crisis. Some had received only a slight scratch and two or three would be supporting him as though his life depended upon their care.... Long trains of ambulances now passed us going to the rear, loaded with the wounded. We saw two long lines of troops engaged in terrific fighting—long sheets of fire and smoke from one end of the line to the other; shot answering shot; charge meeting charge; and the wild shouts of the combatants at each successive turn of the battle presented to us a scene terribly sublime. We halted here to receive orders and to learn in what position we would be placed in the line. My eye wandered eagerly and anxiously along the line of battle, watching the effect of each discharge....

...our unlimited confidence in our commanders, Ellis and Goddard, went a great way towards *schooling* our nerves for the fiery ordeal through which we were about to pass. The clear tones of Colonel Ellis now recalled our wandering minds, and the word, "Forward" was given. The music fell back to the rear, still playing. We marched forward and took our position in line. Just then there was a short lull in the fight. We took our position a little forward of a rise of ground, while a few rods in front, just beyond the brow of a hill, the rebels were effectually concealed from our sight, gathering their energies for a fresh onset. We had, as our support, the 53rd Ohio.

We had hardly gotten our line formed before the enemy opened on us with grape and canister. At first it fell short of its mark, but nearer and nearer the death-dealing missiles strike, tearing up the earth and filling the eyes with dust. Soon they come crashing through our ranks. We were commanded to lie down. Thick and fast the iron hail comes. Groans reach us as the soldiers, wounded and mangled, crawl to the rear. The emboldened enemy now advanced in solid column, having ten to our one. The 53rd Ohio, appalled at the sight, broke and ran without firing a gun and we were left single-handed to contend against these fearful odds. We were now ordered to rise and commence firing. Rapidly and coolly we poured our deadly fire into the advancing column. Now a rebel sergeant, in front of us, performed a brave act worthy of a better cause. He advanced in front of his command and with his own hands planted the rebel flag on a piece of our artillery that they had captured; but this act sealed his doom. He fell, pierced and riddled with bullets. I shot at him, but I hope that it was not my bullet that sealed his eyes in death. The enemy now opened a fire upon us so terrific that our little band seemed likely to be annihilated. Our brave boys were dropping by scores. A ball struck the stock of my musket, shivering it and nearly knocking it from my grasp. Another ball passed through my canteen, while another cut the straps to my haversack. Thick as hailstones the bullets whistled through my hair and around my cheek, still I remained unhurt. The bushes and trees around would writhe, twist and fall before this blast.

Early in the action as Col. Ellis was standing on a log watching with eager eyes the motions of the enemy, a ball passed through his wrist. Lieut. Smith tied a handkerchief around it and Col Ellis continued giving his orders as coolly as though nothing had happened, but soon an unerring shot pierced his noble heart.... Soon I saw Major Goddard receive his death wound while standing a few feet from me.... Capt. Wayne now came to me and called my attention to the rebel soldier concealed behind a root. He turned and immediately received his death wound. Lieut. Fred A. Smith was now in command. He was struck by a ball while standing by my side and knocked to the ground. As he was falling, he reached his hands out to me for assistance; almost involuntarily I bore him to the rear over the brow of the hill, took his handkerchief and bound up his wound as well as I could, then gave him in charge of Lieut. Bradley, of Company C, who was passing. I then hastened back to rejoin my company, but what was my astonishment to find not one living member of the 15th Regiment. It seems that as soon as Fred was wounded, our boys, to prevent being surrounded and taken prisoners, broke and retreated in disorder and in the tumult, I had not noticed it, so instead of finding our regiment where I left it, I found the ground swarming with rebels. Something said to me, "This is not a safe place for Luke Barber," and that if I wanted to live to fight another day, I must retreat out of that, and retreat I did, very rapidly too....

I tried hard to find where the regiment was.... Failing in this, I found an Iowa regiment belonging to our division and fought with them until two o'clock P.M. Here I had the satisfaction of seeing the rebels run. Back and forth the tide surged. I had now expended all of my ammunition and there being a lull in the fight, I determined to again seek for what was left of the 15th regiment. I went to Gen. Hurlbut and asked where they were and stated the circumstances which separated me from it. He thought that it was down at the landing, but did not know. He told me I had better fall in there for the present. So I did. Gen. Hurlbut was forming a new line, the strongest that had yet been formed, and all attempts of the enemy to force it back were fruitless. He had a large number of siege guns planted where they were protected by heavy works and it was impossible for the enemy to face the fire of these monsters. In their last attack they were handsomely repulsed. Their line was formed within half a mile of the landing. The enemy had spent their strength and their best efforts could not move us now. Our cause began to brighten. Gen. Grant had made every disposition to take the offensive in the morning and it is my unshaken belief that if Buell had not arrived during the night the result would have been the same. During the afternoon the rebel General A. Sidney Johnson was killed, and much of the life of the rebel army went out with his death. He was a brave man and an able officer. After his death, it was plainly seen that the rebel army was not handled as skillfully as before and the remark that Gen. Beauregard made, that he would water his horse in the Tennessee or in hell was not realized. The enemy occupied our camp that night and the thought was not very consoling, as all our things were left lying around in the tent in a very loose manner, which did not look very well to receive company.

I started out again to look for the regiment, and this time I had the unspeakable pleasure of being successful. I found them down at the landing.... In the morning we mustered five hundred and fifty men. Now scarcely two hundred answered to their names. Company D had only thirteen men out of fifty that were mustered in the morning. I now learned of the movements of the regiment after I became separated from it. The men had rallied again in camp and were under the direction of Charles F. Barber, adjutant of the regiment. They again took the field but were kept in reserve. All our line officers were killed or wounded excepting three or four. The regiment was now in command of Captain Kelly.... Our regiment camped that night on the hill by the landing. The night was dark and stormy. The rain came in perfect torrents and we had neither food nor shelter. Through the long dismal night our rest was broken by the deep reverberating tones of the guns from the gunboat which kept up an incessant roar all night.... the close of the first day's fight witnessed the two armies lying within a few rods of each other, each confident of victory on the morrow.

During the night General Buell crossed over a portion of his army and marched to the front. Our success now seemed almost certain....

Lew Wallace's division was lost somewhere in the tangled tracks and lanes of the area between Crump's and Pittsburg Landings. He would not arrive on this day to aid Grant in any way at all.

Hurlbut, with a greatly reduced command, organized a new line around Pittsburg Landing and the resistance to the Confederate advance stiffened, troops who had been hiding under the bluffs next to the river joining in the defense. Prentiss, with his gallant division, held the Rebels at the Hornet's Nest until finally overcome by superior numbers, and he surrendered the remnants of his division. The reinforcements of Gen. Nelson also organized a supporting line.

Sometime around 3 o'clock in the afternoon, Gen. Albert S. Johnston, commanding the Confederate forces, was wounded in the leg. At first it did not seem serious, and he continued to direct the battle. He slowly bled to death, his boot filling with blood. Falling from his horse, he died shortly thereafter, and the command of the troops passed to Gen. Pierre G.T. Beauregard. "The Creole" attempted to gather the scattered army and get it into some fighting shape, but time was against him, and he would have to wait for the morrow.

Taylor, Surgeon, U.S. Army, attached to Buell's Army, Shiloh, Tenn.:

Heard the firing early Sunday morning at Pittsburg and knew the fight had become general. Waited on orders to march from Genl. Grant—did not receive any up to one o'clock. Genl. Nelson started the column—when within 2 miles of the battle field, Genl. Grant's aide overtook us with orders to hurry up in double quick or the day was lost. Arrived at the river at 3. Genl. Ammon crossed the river in time to save the day, but for it the whole army would have gone up.

Jackman, Pvt., "The Orphan Brigade," Shiloh, Tenn.:

This day will long be remembered. Soon after the sun had risen, the firing of artillery became so general and the roar of musketry could be heard as distinctly, I knew the battle had commenced. I wished to be on the field but was not able to walk so far. The gentleman with whom I was staying had his only remaining horse caught, which I mounted. When I bade "mine hostess" goodbye, she looked very sorrowful which affected me not a little and I never knew why she took such an interest in me. The gentleman walked and kept up. Four miles brought us to Monterry and just beyond we met some of the wounded on foot with arms and heads bound up in bloody bandages and I felt then that I was getting in the vicinity of warfare. Soon we met ambulances and wagons loaded with wounded and could hear the poor fellows groaning and shrieking as they were being jolted over the rough road. Met a man on horseback with a stand of captured colors. We were now in proximity of the fighting and we met crowds of men, some crippling along wounded in the legs or about the body, others no blood could be seen about them yet all seemed bent on getting away. I now "dismounted" and started on foot. I never saw the gentleman afterwards who had kindly brought me so far on the road. Being in so much excitement, I became stronger. I met a fellow dressed in a suit of "butternut" jeans who was limping but I don't believe was scratched. He asked me in that whining way: "Has youns been in the fight yet?" I thought he must be some general and asked my "brown" interrogator what troops General "Youns" commanded. He seemed astounded and at last made me understand him. I told him "no" and went on. I afterwards got quite familiar with the "youns" and "weens" vernacular of "Brown Jeans."

While passing a hospital in the roadside, I happened to see one of our company lying by a tent wounded. I went out to see him and there found the brigade hospital established. There were heaps of wounded lying about, many of them I knew and first one then another would ask me to give him water or some other favor for him. While thus occupied, Dr. P. told me to stay with him, that I was not able to go on the field, that I would be captured. There was no one to help him and I turned surgeon, *pro tempore.* I was not able to do much but rendered all the assistance in my power. Part of my duties was to put patients under the influence of chloroform. I kept my handkerchief saturated all the time and was often dizzy from the effects of it myself. It was about one o`clock in the day when I got there.

All day long the battle raged. Occasionally there would be a lull for a short time, but the cannon were never completely hushed. They would break out in increased thunder and the roar of musketry would roll up and down the lines vibrating almost regularly from one extreme to the other. All day long the ambulances continued to discharge their loads of wounded. At last, night set in and the musketry ceased, but the Federal gunboats continued shelling awhile after dusk. Nearly midnight when we got through with the wounded. A heavy rain set in. I was tired, sick and all covered with blood. But I was in far better fix than many that were there. I sat on a medicine chest in the surgeon's tent and "nodded" the long night through.

During the night, in a raging storm, Gen. Buell landed more of his troops at Pittsburg Landing. The Confederates had lost the battle from this point. Grant had been surprised, but not beaten. Tomorrow would be another bloody day, but the conflict would be settled.

On the Mississippi, Gen. John Pope finalized his plans for the assault on Island No. 10. He would also attack the Rebel troops at Tiptonville, Tenn.

Meanwhile, at Yorktown, Va., McClellan was still preparing his siege lines. Lincoln, impatient with the inactivity of the Army of the Potomac, urged "Little Mac" to move. As usual, McClellan called for more troops and supplies. Confederate Joe Johnston was hurrying his troops to Magruder's aid.

April 7 (Monday)

On this morning, Gen. Lew Wallace's division finally arrived at Pittsburg Landing after a long, wearying march. Gen. Don Carlos Buell had also arrived with the remainder of his troops. Grant now had the hammer to beat the Confederate anvil. Grant assaulted early, and quickly regained his old camps and most of the ground lost on the previous day. Some snags, however, developed. At the Peach Orchard, a deadly and furious fight ensued when the Confederates rallied.

Barber, Pvt., Co. D, 15th Illinois Volunteer Infantry, Shiloh, Tenn.:

The army was astir early Monday morning. In consideration of our disorganized state, we were held in reserve for the greater portion of the day. Company D could only muster thirteen men this morning. We were commanded by Corporal Handy. Lieutenant-Colonel Cam was assigned to command the regiment. As we filed along to our place in line, Gen. Hurlbut gazed on our decimated ranks with watery eyes.... Now the rattling of musketry, increasing in volume every moment, tell us that the ball has been opened by General Grant. The now discouraged rebels begin to yield before our resistless advance. Soon the action became general, and deafening discharges sweep along the whole line.... By noon we had passed our camp. Faster and faster the enemy begin to yield. Harder and harder now press on our victorious troops.... Occasionally the line would halt for a few moments and our tired boys would instantly fall into a doze.... A heavy battery of Parrott guns was placed in our rear and fired over our heads. Even this would fail to arouse us, but when the shouts of victory from our boys rent the air as the rebs were once more hurled back, then we would start up and again advance.

About three o'clock P.M. we received an order which effectually banished sleep from our eyelids. We were ordered to the front to prepare for a charge.... Soon the line was formed. Before us was an open field, skirted on the farther side by underbrush. In this brush the rebels lay concealed. General Grant was here in person to superintend the charge and as he rode to the front of the line, he was greeted with tremendous cheers. Soon the brave McCook rode to the front, drew his sword, waved it over his head and shouted: "Now give them a touch of Illinois! Forward! Charge!" and with one wild shout, we sprang forward, making the earth tremble beneath our feet. The rebels shrank back dismayed before this charge.

In wild panic and confusion they broke and ran. The defeat had now turned into a perfect rout. Through woods and swamps, over hills and through valleys, we pursued the flying foe until sheer exhaustion compelled us to stop. ... Our poor and insufficient cavalry followed them a short distance. If we had had good cavalry, the rebel army would have been completely destroyed.... Thus ended the memorable battle of Shiloh.

We now turned our weary steps towards camp, and just as the evening shades began to fall, we reached it. Our camp showed plainly the marks of war. Our tents were riddled by shot and shell and everything was turned upside down. The rebs had stayed there the night before and the uncivil rascals had helped themselves to what they wanted. I could stand in camp and count two hundred dead rebels. There had been a sharp fight on this very ground.... An unbroken stillness reigned where a short time before echoed the peals of battle. How changed the scene! Out in the darkness lay thousands sleeping their last long sleep.... Their tired spirits are at rest.

Beauregard, hoping for reinforcements from Van Dorn, finally got word that Van Dorn could not make it from Arkansas to give him the needed support. The Rebels were widely scattered, tired, and generally played out. Beauregard decided to break off the battle and retreat towards Corinth.

Jackman, Pvt., "The Orphan Brigade," Shiloh, Tenn.:

With the dawn came the roar of battle; but the combat did not wax very warm until later in the day. Early, all the wounded that could walk were given passes to go to the rear, and those not able to walk were placed in wagons and started for Corinth. Many poor fellows were not able to be moved at all. Once that morning a body of Federal cavalry came close enough to fire on us, tearing up the tents but fortunately hurting no one. Dr. P. and I were standing close together talking when a ball passed between our noses which instantly stopped our conversation. We soon hung up strips of red flannel to prevent further accidents of the kind. A little after the middle of the day, the battle raged terribly—it was the last struggle of the confederates, ending in defeat. Soon after I saw Genl. Beauregard, accompanied by one or two of his staff, ride leisurely back to the rear as cool and unperturbed as if nothing had happened. A line was being formed in the rear of us and we had to move. Jim B. and I put the only remaining wounded of our regiment who could be moved into a large spring wagon and started back. We had to leave some that it would have been death to put them in wagons. We hated to do so but we could not do otherwise. The wagon was heavy, the horses were balky, and the roads were rough and muddy—besides the driver was inexperienced—all combined, we came near not getting out. B. was strong and would tug at the wheels—I would plan, abuse the driver, and try to stir up the horses. At last we came up with brother Jo who was slightly wounded and he assisted us. I believe if it had not been for him, we never would have gotten out. Night overtook us before we got far and we drove off to the side of the road to wait till morning. The rain commenced pouring down and continued all night. The road was in a perfect slush and the shattered columns were [plodding] over it all night. As luck would have it, a tent fly was in the wagon and we cut bows and stretched it over the wagon bed. I crept in and with my feet propt up managed to sleep a little.

In the bloodiest battle fought to date, the losses were staggering. Union forces lost 13,047, of which 1,754 were killed. Rebel losses were 10,694, a total of 1,723 killed. Combined, nearly 24,000 Americans had been killed, wounded, or were missing in two days. This total was larger than the population of most cities in Indiana or Illinois. There were more casualties here than at the Battle of Waterloo, where Napoleon met his fate. Unfortunately, there would be many Waterloos to come.

As the battlefield became quiet, the cleanup began. The wounded were collected and removed for treatment. The dead were identified, where possible, and buried where they fell. Medical supplies and equipment were at a premium. The Sanitary Commission began bringing in supplies for the relief of the wounded, and before the last man was removed from the battle area they would have dispensed over 11,400 shirts; nearly 3700 pairs of drawers; almost 3600 pairs of socks; about 2800 bedding kits; 543 pillows; nearly 1100 bottles of brandy, whiskey and wine; 800 bottles of porter; about 950 lemons; over ten tons of dried fruit; almost 7600 cans of fruit; and over seven tons of farinaceous food (ground corn for making mush).

On the Mississippi, opposite Island No. 10, Gen.

John Pope got his floating artillery. The U.S.S. *Carondelet* had now been joined by the U.S.S. *Pittsburg*, Lt. Egbert Thompson, south of the island and was now in a position to assault Tiptonville on the Tennessee side of the river. Pope wasted no time in using his gunboats to hammer the Rebel gun positions, driving the crews from their guns. Landing under the cover of the gunboats, the troops quickly cut off the escape of the Rebels. The Rebels, after a not-too-outstanding defense, surrendered both at Tiptonville and at Island No. 10. The Mississippi was open to Memphis.

Island No. 10, the "key" to the Mississippi, surrendered to the naval forces of Flag Officer Foote. Tons of munitions and four steamers were taken. Congress tendered Foote a vote of thanks for his actions. A part of the haul was the *Red Rover*, a steamer that had been damaged by mortar fire. This ship was moved to Cairo and converted into the Navy's first hospital ship. By June 10th she was back in service and, shortly thereafter, received her first patients. Sisters of the Holy Cross volunteered and served as nurses aboard the ship—pioneers of the U.S. Navy Nurse Corps.

Wills, 1st Lt., Adj., HQ, 3rd Battalion, 7th Illinois Cavalry, near Pt. Pleasant, Mo.:

In a very fine house. If this isn't fine, your brother is incapable of judging. Cozy brick house, damask curtains, legged bedsteads, splendid tables and chairs, big looking glass, and everything just as fine as a peacock's tail.... During the storm of Saturday night, the 5th instant, one of the gunboats ran by "Island 10." I heard of it Sunday morning and got out a pass for Andy Hulit and myself to look for forage, intending, of course, to ride down to the river and watch the gunboat as we knew there'd be fun if she attempted to run below Madrid.

We rode up the river about six miles (half way) to a point that extends into the river on our side, and got there just as the boat did. 'Twas the *Carondelet*, and indeed she looked like an old friend. The sight of her did me more good than any amount of furloughs could. At this point I spoke of, we have three batteries within a half-mile, and there were two Rebel batteries visible right at the water's edge, opposite. We just got there in time to see the ball open. Besides the two secesh batteries visible, they opened from four others masked by the brush and trees, and hitherto unknown to us. Their six, our three, the gunboats, all firing together made by far the grandest thing I ever witnessed. I suppose there were from 30 to 40 guns used, and at least a half thousand shots fired. Andy and I were on a little rise of ground a couple of hundred yards from our main battery and where we could see every shot fired and its effect. There were lots of shots fell around that battery, but none near enough us to be disagreeable. About an hour's fighting silenced the Rebel batteries, and that fun was over. Our boat didn't go over to them at that time, but came into our shore and laid up. She was not struck once, nor was there a man hurt on our side.

Andy and I rode out in the country and got our dinners with a friend of mine, and about 3 P.M. started home. We just got here as the gunboat was preparing to attack the batteries immediately opposite here. She ran down the river on our side, a mile below their guns, and then turning her bow square towards the enemy, started for them and commenced firing. We could see every motion of the Rebel gunners plainly, and they worked like men, until the boat got within about 300 yards of them, when they broke, and I tell you they used their legs to advantage; all but one and he walked away with his arms folded, perfectly at ease.... I saw another fight this morning, but 'twas too far off for interest, after what I saw yesterday. Two more gunboats came down last night in the rain and darkness past the island. This fight this morning was commenced by the *Carondelet*, on a five-gun battery, only four miles below and across from Madrid. She called the *Louisville* to her aid, and then one walked up on the battery from below and the other from above. It is grand to see these gunboats walk into the enemy. They go at them as though they were going right on land, if the Rebels would stay there.

... an artillery captain came dashing up through the door, just from Madrid, and wanted to know where the gunboats were. He said that the Rebel floating battery, that has been lying at Island 10, was floating down and the transports were afraid to try and bring her into land, and he wanted to notify the gunboats so they could catch her. We told him they had gone down to Palmer's division, six miles below, and away he went. I've been waiting to see her pass, but she hasn't arrived yet.... All such items help to make soldiering interesting. Our three transports have taken 20,000 troops over into Tennessee since 9:30 this A.M. I call that good work....

Forty of the Rebels deserted and came to our gunboats to-day. Sergeant Wells, who while over there is a spy, was taken prisoner the other day, escaped to our gunboats. It saved his neck.

In Virginia, McClellan was still digging trenches around Yorktown, still believed he was outnumbered, still crying for more troops and supplies.

On the Mississippi River approaches, the U.S.S. *Pensacola* and *Mississippi* were successfully brought over the sandbar and into the Mississippi River after several previous attempts had failed. These were the heaviest ships ever to enter the river and would do much to help in the assault on New Orleans. Flag Officer Farragut's comment was, "Now, we are all right."

April 8 (Tuesday)

At Corinth, Miss., Beauregard collected his battered units and organized a defense. The double blow of Shiloh and Island No. 10 caused much mourning and consternation in the South. The Union forces cleaned up their camps, buried the dead and cared for the wounded left on the battlefield. The heavy rains had left the area drenched, muddy, and miserable.

Jackman, Pvt., "The Orphan Brigade," Shiloh, Tenn.:

Still raining awhile in the morning. On starting we came to a little branch across the road in which were sticking fast in the ground several pieces of artillery. We knew we could not cross and had to cut out a new road thru the bushes. All the army and wagons had now passed by us save our brigade which was covering the retreat. We got a mile or two but at last got stuck in the mud and immovable. I went off to camp nearby to see if I could not get assistance. The camp was deserted. Went on a little further, hoping to find some loose horse or mule, but wearied and came back. While gone, our Q.M. had come up and put new horses on the wagon. They were in camp eating breakfast, hardtack and bacon being plentiful. On setting out I mounted one of the old horses barebacked and with an old rope for a bridle. I looked Quixotic then indeed and felt worse than the original after his fight with the wind-mill. We got within six miles of Corinth that night. Our Q.M. who was a doctor by profession dressed all the wounds. I slept in a corn crib that night. Bro. Jo had gone on to Corinth. The day ended clear and warm.

Taylor, Surgeon, U.S. Army, attached to Buell's Army, Shiloh, Tenn.:

The fight on Monday was a terrible one. I was in many places where the balls flew thick. Sometimes leading a squad of men, and ever and anon, cheering them in the lines where ever I went. I now shudder to think how foolish I was—and the risk taken.

Genl Nelson, Genl Ammon & me will never get credit for the part we played in the fight.

Barber, Pvt., Co. D, 15th Illinois Volunteer Infantry, Shiloh, Tenn.:

The morning succeeding the battle dawned bright and beautiful, and over that bloody field the sun cast its smiling rays upon the faces of silent sleepers, reflecting its beams upon the bright-green foliage, kissing the dew-drops from the flowerets and tingeing all nature with the golden hue of liveliness. What a contrast from the dark picture of the past two days! We busied ourselves that morning putting things to rights and purifying [the] camp. Scarcely was this accomplished before the sharp rattling of musketry caused every soldier to spring for his arms and take his place in line before there was time for orders to be given. We marched out towards the spot from whence the firing proceeded and threw out skirmishers, but to our chagrin, we found that we had been fooled. The alarm was occasioned by the pickets discharging their guns after being relieved. This event, trivial as it was, produced a panic amongst the teamsters. They came rushing in headlong flight to the rear.

We now had a painful task before us in burying the dead. In the first place, I sat down and wrote a letter home apprising them of my safety and giving a brief account of the fight. Then I got permission to go and see Samuel. I found him on the *Blackhawk* and after much difficulty, succeeded in getting on board. I found him cheerful and much better than I expected. His wound, though severe, was not dangerous.... During the day our regimental dead were brought in. We dug a long, deep trench near our camp and buried them in one grave.

On the Mississippi, the Confederates at Island No. 10 formally surrendered to the Federal forces under Gen. John Pope.

April 9 (Wednesday)

Throughout the Northwest, the people not only responded with cheers for the victory at Shiloh, they began gathering food and medicine for the fallen at Shiloh. In some cases after a battle, the relatives of the fallen would journey to the battle area and recover the body of their son, or husband, who had been killed and transport it to their home for burial. The trip would be arduous, considering the priority for transportation being given the wounded and the fresh troops going to the front. The various relief organizations rushed food and help to Shiloh to assist in the evacuation of the over 16,000 wounded, North and South. The Confederate evacuation to Corinth was still in progress. The mixup of units had been so great that some were not united for several days after the battle.

Jackman, Pvt., "The Orphan Brigade," Corinth, Miss.:

> Cool and cloudy. Started with a new teamster. In trying to cross a stream the wagon got stuck but was finally engineered out. Soon after another soldier and myself stopped at a house and got some milk and bread for the wounded, but the wagon left us so far behind we did not overtake it. I walked to town—the camp was just beyond. I was about played out when we got into camp—found nearly all of our wounded in the tents. Of those brought in the wagon, all died of their wounds but two.

In Richmond, not yet a year into the war, the Confederate Congress passed a conscription bill to get the necessary manpower for the army. Many Confederates objected to this draft law, claiming it infringed upon the liberties of the individual. It seemed those people who left the Union for "liberty infringement" were having no better luck with their new government.

There was some scrambling around Jackson, Mo., as the opposing forces collided on the fringes.

In Washington, the President was trying to explain to McClellan that he had held McDowell's corps behind for the defense of the city. McClellan was turning a deaf ear and calling for more men. Lincoln was also beginning to wonder about the rather large "discrepancy" between the count of the enemy as stated by McClellan and as shown by the intelligence gathered by other sources.

In New Orleans, the threat of Farragut and his fleet was becoming more real every day, suggesting that the armed steamers sent north should be returned for the defense of the city. However, Confederate Secretary of the Navy Mallory was still convinced that Foote's gunboats north of Memphis were the real threat and refused to allow the boats to return to New Orleans. This would be a costly decision.

April 10 (Thursday)

The Federal Congress passed a joint resolution calling for the gradual emancipation of the slaves in all the states. Lincoln approved the measure and signed it.

At Shiloh, the cleanup continued. Most of the dead soldiers were buried by now, and the wounded who could be moved were long gone down the Tennessee River to hospitals in the North. Private Barber reported a theme recurring among the Union troops about the Confederate dead.

Barber, Pvt., Co. D, 15th Illinois Volunteer Infantry, Shiloh, Tenn.:

> It was a painful task. Months passed before I recovered from the effects of it. Now we turned our attention to the rebel dead. We noticed that the faces of all of them had turned black. On examination, we found that their canteens contained whiskey and gunpowder which was, no doubt, the cause of it. It seems that this had been given to them just before going into battle to make them fight. This was the cause of the rebels fighting so like demons the first day. It took two days to bury all of them. I will not attempt to give much of a description of this battle-field. It was Ft. Donelson on a larger scale.... On one spot of ground, where we generally had our reviews, an artillery duel was fought and the ground was so thickly strewed with dead horses that you could walk nearly all over it on the carcasses.... The official report of Grant showed upwards of thirteen thousand killed, wounded and prisoners. Nearly all of General Prentiss' division, with himself, were taken prisoners. Lew Wallace's division suffered the least. He was at Crump Landing when the fight began and did not

arrive in season to participate in the first day's fight.... Our loss footed up two hundred and fifty-two, killed and wounded, and there was only one man... not accounted for. We had in our camp about thirty wounded prisoners, and they received every attention from us that we could bestow. They were Louisiana troops and gloried in the name of "Louisiana Tigers." Judging from their looks and the arms they carried, they did not belie the name.

In the west, to meet Beauregard's call for more troops, Davis telegraphed each of the Southern governors to send more troops to Corinth.

At Cockspur Island, off the coast of Georgia, a Federal force under the command of Col. Quincy Adams Gillmore prepared to attack Ft. Pulaski, near the entrance to Savannah Harbor. Gillmore, the top graduate of USMA, class of '49, was commissioned in the Corps of Engineers and spent his time until the start of the war building fortifications. What better expert to send to destroy one?

At Ft. Pulaski, Gillmore used rifled guns to batter the masonry outer walls of the fort—a first. For his success, he was appointed Brigadier General on April 28, and sent to Kentucky, where his talents would be wasted for a year.

April 11 (Friday)

In the west, Beauregard's army recovered at Corinth, Miss. The redoubtable Kentucky "Orphan Brigade" which had covered the retreat from Shiloh, finally arrived at Corinth with Breckenridge.

In Georgia, Ft. Pulaski surrendered. Only one Federal and Rebel each were killed during the siege, although the Federals had fired more than 5000 rounds of rifled artillery at the fort. Savannah was effectively lost as a Confederate port for the remainder of the war.

At Hampton Roads, Va., the ironclad C.S.S. *Virginia* (*Merrimack*) was loose. From Norfolk, the ship approached the harbor, captured three merchant vessels, and retired with its escort of gunboats. The *Monitor*, though present, took no action although she had been challenged by the other ironclad.

At Pittsburg Landing, Tenn., Maj. Gen. Henry W. Halleck arrived to assume direct command of the troops. This relegated Grant to number two position. Tongues wagged about Grant's supposed "drinking problem." Grant considered resigning. In a concentration of troops, Gen. Pope's army would soon join the forces at Shiloh in preparation for the drive on Corinth.

April 12 (Saturday)

At Gibraltar, the C.S.S. *Sumter* was abandoned by her crew and commander, Capt. Raphael Semmes. Serious boiler problems that could not be resolved were the primary cause. This commerce raider had caused serious damage to Union shipping throughout the Atlantic. The crew was given permission to find their way home as best they could.

Smoke from the coal used to fire the boilers was a matter of concern. Secretary of the Navy Gideon Welles wrote President Lincoln:

> It is of the greatest importance that the exportation of anthracite coal from ports of the United States to any and all foreign ports should be absolutely prohibited. The rebels obtain the coal for their steamers from Nassau and Havana, and the fact that it burns without smoke enables them to approach blockaded ports with greater security, as all other coals throw out so much smoke as to render their presence visible a great distance at sea.

Wills, 1st Lt. Adj., HQ, 3rd Battalion, 7th Illinois Cavalry, Camp New Madrid, Mo.:

> I have the extreme happiness to inform you that there is at last a hope of my dating the next letter from Memphis or vicinity. Our regiment has for several days been alone at Point Pleasant and we enjoyed it very much.... Yesterday we were ordered to report here immediately to General Granger, commanding cavalry division which numbers full 4,000. There are two brigades in this division; Colonel Kellogg commands the 1st brigade and therefore is now a brigadier general. There have been about 25 steamboats arrived here since 4 P.M. yesterday and the army will probably commence embarking to-day. It will take full 60 boats to hold us all. The rain has been falling in torrents ever since we started...
>
> We hardly think the Rebels will make a stand at Pillow, Randolph or Memphis if the news from Corinth is correct. I'm almost afraid to look over the list of dead that fight has made.... I know as many people here as in Fulton, almost, and I have yet to hear the first insulting speech or word to me. "What

are they going to do with Island No. 10 I wonder; I am afraid that Commander Foote and his gunboats are a humbug." Aren't you ashamed of that speech? Damn the New York *Tribune.* I do believe in McClellan and nearly all the rest of our leaders. If those *Tribunes,* big and little, were where any regiment in this army could get at them they wouldn't stand fifteen minutes.... Orders have just arrived for embarking this P.M. Will be under way down the river to-night. Wish us a pleasant voyage.

In Georgia, the scene was set for one of the great adventures of the war, the Great Locomotive Chase, later to be immortalized in a 20th-century movie. A party of twenty-two Union volunteers under James J. Andrews boarded a train at Marietta, Ga., and rode it as passengers to Big Shanty. There the train stopped for breakfast, and everyone, including the crew, got off to eat. Andrews and his band detached the locomotive "General" and three freight cars and took off northward. The train crew, not even finishing their grits, started the chase in another engine, the "Texas." North of Ringgold, Ga., the hijackers ran out of fuel, abandoned the train and took off into the woods; they were later captured. Andrews and seven others were executed, eight escaped prison, and six were paroled. The daring of Andrews captured the imagination and admiration of both the North and South.

In Ft. Pulaski, Ga., David Hunter declared all slaves to be confiscated and freed, an order later rescinded by Lincoln.

Around Yorktown, Va., McClellan was still digging. Magruder was getting more troops; he now had about 30,000 to match Little Mac's 100,000. McClellan complained, still, about McDowell's corps being left at Washington, and he asked for reinforcements.

April 14 (Monday)

More reconnaissance by Halleck towards Corinth. Generally quiet in northern Mississippi. On the Mississippi River, Federal gunboats shelled Ft. Pillow.

Day, Pvt., Co. B, 25th Massachusetts Volunteer Infantry, New Bern, N.C.:

... another change has occurred, Capt. Clark of company B has resigned. If this thing becomes chronic, I am not quite sure but I shall resign and go home, and then, perhaps, I shall be given a sutler's or horse doctor's commission and be sent back.... The vernal season is now upon us and nature is arraying herself in her most beautiful robes. The trees are in leafage, while the yards and gardens attract the eye with their almost endless variety of plants and flowers. Roses are in great variety.... Beautiful flowering vines clamber the verandas and porticos of the houses, sending out their sweet perfume...

April 16 (Wednesday)

In Richmond, President Davis signed the bill authorizing conscription of every white male between eighteen and thirty-five years of age. This bill provided for substitutions of draftees, a pattern to be followed by the North later. In this act there was no provision for exemptions.

In Washington, President Lincoln signed the bill abolishing slavery in the District of Columbia. Lincoln also inquired of McClellan, again, as to progress. On the Peninsula, McClellan was still digging trenches, and asked for reinforcements.

In the west, there was a gathering of forces across the Mississippi to reinforce the army at Shiloh. As Lt. Wills could testify, things do not always work the way they were planned.

Wills, 1st Lt. Adj., HQ, 3rd Battalion, 7th Illinois Cavalry, *Henry Clay,* off New Madrid, Mo.:

I finished my last in a great hurry, helped strike and load our tents and equipage and started for the levee, confident we would be off for Memphis, [New] Orleans and intermediate landings, before the world would gain 12 hours at farthest in age. That day over 30 steamers arrived, received their loads of soldiers and departed, all down stream, preceded by six or eight gunboats and 16 mortar boats. Word came at nightfall that there were not enough boats for all and the cavalry would have to wait the morrow for more transports. We lay on the river banks that night, and the next day all the cavalry got off except our brigade and two regiments. Another night on the banks without tents, managed to get transportation for two battalions, one from each regiment. They started down yesterday at about 10 A.M. and more boats coming we loaded two more battalions, but at 9 P.M. a dispatch came up with orders for us to stop loading and await further orders. The same boat turned back all the cavalry of our brigade that had started and landed them at Tiptonville; we are at 6 this P.M. lying around loose on the bank here awaiting orders.... What the devil we are going to do is more than three men like me can guess. It's awful confounded dull here. Nothing even half interesting. Saw a cuss, trying to drown himself yesterday, and saw a fellow's leg taken off last night. These are better than no show at all, but still there's not much fun about either case. I'm bored considerably by some of my Canton friends wanting me to help them get their niggers out of camp. Now, I don't care a damn for the darkies, and know that they are better off with their masters 50 times over than with us, but of course you know I couldn't help to send a runaway nigger back. I'm blamed if I could. I honestly believe that this army has taken 500 niggers away with them. Many men have lost from 15 to 30 each. The owners were pretty well contented while the army stayed here, for all the generals assured them that when we left the negroes would not be allowed to go with us, and they could easily get them back; but they have found out that was a "gull" and they are some bitter on us now. There will be two Indiana regiments left here to guard the country from Island 10 to Tiptonville, and if you don't hear of some fun from this quarter after the army all leaves but them, I'm mistaken. They'll have their hands full if not fuller....

That Pittsburg battle was one awful affair, but it don't hurt us any. Grant will whip them the next time completely.... Yesterday it was reported and believed that the *Monitor* had sunk the *Merrimac*, that Yorktown was taken, and that another big fight had taken place at Corinth and we held the town. That was very bully but it lacks confirmation....

On the lower Mississippi, Flag Officer Farragut moved his fleet upriver to just below Forts Jackson and St. Philip. Although these forts mounted over 100 guns, they were currently flooded by high water, despite the efforts of the crews working round-the-clock to keep the water out. The Confederate defenses included a huge chain supported by empty ship hulks, one unfinished ironclad, the *Louisiana*, an array of fire rafts, and some makeshift gunboats. Against this, Farragut had 17 ships carrying 154 guns and 20 mortar boats.

April 18 (Friday)

A hellish nightmare became reality at Forts Jackson and St. Philip below New Orleans when Commander David Dixon Porter's mortar boats opened fire. Farragut, Porter's adopted brother, doubted the effect of using mortars on ships until this action, where these doubts were generally confirmed. For six days the mortars pounded the forts with little effect except to keep the defenders' heads down.

McDowell left the Washington area and arrived at Falmouth, Va., across the river from Fredericksburg. He was still fulfilling his mission to keep between the Confederate army and Washington. In Yorktown, McClellan was still digging trenches and still asking for more troops, while not using the 100,000 he had on hand.

April 20 (Sunday)

Southeast of New Orleans, Farragut sent parties from the U.S.S. *Itasca* and *Pinola* to blow up the river obstructions in the Mississippi near Forts Jackson and St. Philip. The powder failed to explode, but there was enough damage to the obstructions to force a break in the barricade.

At Aquia Creek, Va., near Falmouth, Gen. McDowell played host to President Lincoln and Cabinet members Stanton and Chase. In the same area, the Potomac flotilla had been very busy. Lt. Wyman, commanding the flotilla, reported the capture of the *Eureka*, *Monterey*, *Lookout*, *Sarah Ann*, *Sydney Jones*, *Reindeer*, *Falcon*, *Sea Flower*, and *Roundout* at the mouth of the Rappahannock River.

In western Tennessee, Halleck gathered his force for the assault.

Jackman, Pvt., "The Orphan Brigade," Corinth, Miss.:

Raining—evening sent in ambulance to depot with other sick to be sent to Castillian Springs, Miss. We had hay put down on the floor of a box car to lie down on. Rested better than usual that night.

Barber, Pvt., Co. D, 15th Illinois Volunteer Infantry, Shiloh, Tenn.:

Colonel Turner now arrived and assumed command of the regiment.... We now began to prepare for an active campaign. We were reviewed and we knew that the ball would open again soon. Gen.

Pope's army, the heroes of Island No. Ten, had now arrived, and, with Buell's army, our numbers were increased to one hundred thousand men. The enemy was also receiving large re-inforcements and were busily fortifying at Corinth.

In North Carolina, the Union forces were settled into a tedious routine.

Day, Pvt., Co. B, 25th Massachusetts Volunteer Infantry, New Bern, N.C.:

Not caring to trouble the captain all the time for passes, I have got in the habit of going about town on my sagacity and I have not yet [been] discovered, but it answers the purpose as well as a pass, but I was brought up a day or two ago when I ran against Charley of Company D, who was standing sentinel on the corner of Broad and Middle streets. I was walking leisurely along, when coming to Charley's post, he halted me and demanded my pass. I said I had not got any. He replied if that was the case, it was his duty to march me to the provost's office. Rather than have trouble with him, and to have it military in form, I handed him an old pass I happened to have in my pocket. He looked at it and, tearing it up, took the position of a soldier saying, "You non-coms are getting too big for your clothes, you are putting on altogether too many airs, but I will let you know that you can't put them on over me." I said, "Perhaps there is a shadow of truth in what you say. It is possible that they may be somewhat afflicted with inflation, but you know I am one of the meek and lowly kind." "You? You are the worst pill in the box, you never have a pass, but are all over town, in the back rooms of all the sutler's stores and taking more liberties and putting on more style than half the commissioned officers." "Now, Charley, that is a sad state of affairs indeed; but you are the first one that has found any fault with it, but if you desire the honor of escorting me to the provost's office, you can have the job. After you get me there, Old Dan will give you the biggest setting up you have had recently."

He marched me over, and as we entered, Old Dan looked up and, addressing my escort, asked, "What are you here for? What do you want?" "I found this man running at large without a pass and thought it was my duty to bring him here." "Without a pass? Was he making any disturbance?" "No sir." "And so you arrest one of your own regiment because he happens to be without a pass and then come in here to interrupt me. If you come here again on such an errand, I will put you in the guard house. Go to your post." After my escort had gone out with a flea in his ear, Capt. Dan removed his spectacles, and wiping his eyes, which a good deal resembled gashes cut in ripe tomatoes, pointed to the table saying, "I reckon there is something left in the bottle, help yourself." I did as the captain requested. After chatting a little with him, a couple of officers came in, and I touched my cap, bade the captain good-day and made my escape.

Among the white people here are very few who would be ranked among the first, or even second class. Nearly all of them are what is called the poor white trash or clay-eaters. I am told they actually do eat clay, a habit they contract like any other bad habit. Now I cannot vouch for the truth of this, never having seen them eating it, but some of them look as though that was about all they had to eat. They are an utterly ignorant set, scarcely able to make themselves intelligible, and in many ways, they are below the negroes in intelligence and manner of living, but perhaps they are not wholly to blame for it, the same principle that will oppress a black man, will a white one. They are entirely cut off from the means of acquiring land or an education, even though they wished to. Public schools are unknown here and land can only be purchased by the plantation. That leaves them in a rather bad fix; poor, shiftless, and ignorant. Their highest ambition is to hunt, fish, drink whiskey, and toady to their masters. You speak to one of them and he will look at you in a listless sort of way as though unable or undecided whether to answer or not. Ask one of them the distance across the river and he will either say he don't know, or "it is right smart."... They do not seem to have any intelligent idea about anything, and in talking with the cusses, one scarcely knows whether to pity them or be amused.

The women here have a filthy habit of snuff chewing, or dipping as they call it, and I am told it is practiced more or less by all classes of women. The manner of doing it is simple enough; they take a small stick or twig about two inches long, of a certain kind of bush, and chew one end of it until it becomes like a brush. This they dip into the snuff and then put it in their mouths. After chewing a while, they remove the stick and expectorate about a gill, then repeat the operation. Many of the women among the clay-eaters chew plug tobacco and can squirt the juice through their teeth as far and as straight as the most accomplished chewer among the lords of creation.

April 21 (Monday)

In Richmond, another scene relative to the conscription of troops was enacted. This listed the exemptions for such trades and professions as: government officials, ferrymen, pilots of boats, employees in iron mines and foundries, telegraph operators, ministers, printers, educators, hospital employees, and druggists, among others. There would be more exemptions announced later.

Barber, Pvt., Co. D, 15th Illinois Volunteer Infantry, Shiloh, Tenn.:

> Everything betokened an active and bloody campaign. Gen. Halleck, Commander of the Department, now arrived and assumed command in person. In the meantime, important changes had taken place in our Company. Fred, now promoted to Captain, had gone home, and Col. Turner had nominated a private for the office of 2nd Lieutenant, who was on detached duty and was not with the regiment in the fight. Our indignation knew no bounds at this gross outrage. Our new Lieutenant's authority was respected just about as much as we respected him. We knew how he had figured around headquarters to obtain the position, and the boys could hardly keep their hands off from him. Our Captain, hearing how matters stood, came back long before his wound was healed. Sergeant Waldock was the one entitled to the position.

Flag Officer Farragut was delayed in his approach to New Orleans. The chains barring the river were still a problem, so he did something about them:

> We have been bombarding the forts for three or four days, but the current is running so strong that we cannot stem it sufficiently to do anything with our ships, so that I am now waiting a change of wind, which brings a slacker tide, and we shall be enabled to run up.... Captain Bell went last night to cut the chain across the river. I never felt such anxiety in my life as I did until his return. One of his vessels got on shore, and I was fearful she would be captured. They kept up a tremendous fire on him; but Porter diverted their fire with a heavy cannonade. They let the chain go, but the men sent to explode the petard did not succeed; his wires broke. Bell would have burned the hulks, but the illumination would have given the enemy a chance to destroy his gunboat, which got aground. However, the chain was divided, and it gives us space enough to go through.

April 22 (Tuesday)

A real fracas developed near Aransas Pass, Tex., when two boats from the U.S.S. *Arthur*, Acting Lt. Kitteridge, captured a schooner and two sloops and were attacked in turn by Confederate vessels and troops. A little water ballet.

Barber, Pvt., Co. D, 15th Illinois Volunteer Infantry, Shiloh, Tenn.:

> I was agreeably surprised one morning when I awoke to find Uncle Washington in my tent. My friends had sent him down to see if anything was needed. Although his services were not required, his company was very acceptable. He stayed a couple of weeks with us and then returned home. The roads were in an awful condition at this time and it was impossible for the army to move....

April 23 (Wednesday)

Col. John W. Geary, of the 28th Pennsylvania Infantry, had used the "coffee mill" machine gun successfully at Middleburg, Va., on March 29th, although not much publicity was given to the event. Today Col. Geary returned the two guns to the Washington Arsenal, reporting that they had been found "inefficient, and unsafe to the operators." These two came from the lot of 10 purchased by Lincoln, not the 50 later bought by McClellan. Gen. Ripley, who had opposed the whole idea at the beginning, found vindication in Geary's report. Using this report, with a few of his own embellishments, he plotted to prevent the purchase of any additional guns, even deliberately lying to Lincoln by substituting Geary's report for another, more favorable. The NIH (Not Invented Here) syndrome was going full tilt. The machine gun would have to wait for a few more years when Ripley was gone and Gatling had solved some of the mechanical problems before it came into its own.

Jackman, Pvt., "The Orphan Brigade," Castillian Springs, Miss.:

> Early went out in town, a small village, and looking

> cadaverous, a lady called me in and gave me a nice breakfast of milk and bread. While out in this expedition, many ladies had assembled at the cars with provisions for the sick and wounded. The Springs are three miles from town and the soldiers were brought out in carriages. About the middle of the forenoon, J.H., D.P. and myself came out in a carriage. The boys had a bottle of "Hoostetter" and were quite merry. I am in a room on the 2nd floor, occupied by "Morgan's Men," the boys I came with belonging to that "lay out." Morgan's Men are quite a curiosity to the people down here.
>
> The building is a two story frame with "wings," "ells," etc. and is accommodating nearly three hundred sick and wounded—nearly all Kentuckians. The grounds are tastefully arranged about the springs and the scenery in the vicinity is romantic. There was lately a female school kept in this place—was broken up to convert the building into a hospital. The principal is our steward. The water of the Springs is chalybeate. This evening had some pleasant conversation with ladies.

Below New Orleans, Farragut decided that the mortar boats bombarding the forts protecting New Orleans were not doing the job. He couldn't land troops because of the swampy terrain. The solution was to run his deep-sea vessels past the forts early in the morning to gain New Orleans.

In the Virginia/North Carolina border area, Union forces blocked the Chesapeake and Albemarle Canal, cutting off an easy supply route for the Confederates.

April 24 (Thursday)

At 2 A.M. the U.S.S. *Hartford*, Farragut's flagship, signaled the fleet to begin passing the forts below New Orleans. This would entail passing the barricade of chains and sunken ships. An hour later on this chill morning, the first ships were under way and passing the barrier. At 3:40 A.M., when the moon rose, the ships following were discovered and Forts Jackson and St. Philip opened fire. The second division, including Farragut's flagship, came under heavy fire from the forts. The mortar boats added to the hellish confusion by opening on the forts, doing little damage but creating mental stress on the Confederate gunners. The Confederates used fire-rafts in an attempt to block the Federal fleet, but to no avail. All the Federal ships made it through except for three small vessels, which were too badly damaged. Farragut left the forts to their own devices; they were soon abandoned.

Once past the barricades, the Federal fleet faced the Confederate gunboats, including the ram *Manassas.* The ram struck both the U.S.S. *Mississippi* and *Brooklyn*, but with little damage. Most of the Confederate fleet fled upriver.

Farragut had now captured the South's largest city and its major port. With the taking of this port the Union had a base of operations to control the economy of most of the southern tier of the South.

Around Corinth, Halleck kept probing for Rebels.

April 25 (Friday)

Farragut moved up the Mississippi to New Orleans. The local people had set the waterfront afire, and Farragut anchored his fleet in the river away from the flames. A rude, nearly violent, and noisy throng met Farragut's officers when they landed to meet the mayor of New Orleans. The mayor claimed no authority to surrender the city. It didn't really matter much who surrendered it. It was fairly taken. It would never be taken from Federal authority again during the war.

At Ft. Macon near Beaufort, N.C., the Federal troops of John G. Parke opened fire and dismounted half the guns of the fort. With gunboats bombarding the fort from the water side, it surrendered late in the afternoon of this day.

In Savannah, Tenn., Major Gen. C.F. Smith died of a scraped shin which had become infected. His body was returned to Philadelphia, Pa., for burial.

April 28 (Monday)

South of New Orleans, Fts. Jackson and St. Philip formally surrendered to Federal forces. The Mississippi River was now open for navigation—at least as far as New Orleans. At the city, Farragut threatened to bombard the city if the Rebels didn't show some respect for the Union flag.

Allen, Pvt., Co. K, 1st Battalion., 10th Illinois Cavalry, Springfield, Mo.:

> We left Quincy on March 10th and reached St. Louis on the evening of the next day. Our quarters were in Camp Benton, which is the liveliest place I

have ever seen. While we were there, there were 10,000 to 12,000 soldiers there—infantry, cavalry and artillery. Hundreds of them were drilling every day, some on foot and some on horseback; some drilled with guns, some with sabers and others with cannon. Some were leaving almost every day for the South, and others coming in. Camp Benton is a perfect mudhole in wet weather and a very dusty place in dry weather, but I liked it pretty well and thought it was not such a bad place after all. We left St. Louis on the cars on April 5th, and reached Rolla on the same evening about midnight. We slept in the cars until morning and then took our horses off, saddled them and rode out to Camp Lyon, about three miles. We pitched our tents there for a few days when we moved about a mile nearer town.

... On the 15th we left Rolla for Lebanon on horseback and traveled six miles. We encamped on an island in the Little Piney, remained there two days, when we again set out on our journey. We reached Lebanon on the 21st and remained there until the 25th. We had rather a rough trip to Lebanon, as the roads were bad and our team stuck in the mud occasionally, besides we had to travel in the rain all day on Easter Sunday.... While we were at Lebanon, three of our men deserted and have not been heard from yet.... They took their horses and revolvers, but left their sabers.

I must tell you something about the country we have come through. From St. Louis to Rolla is about 130 miles. The country is rough and broken and rather poor. The railroad passes through two tunnels. From Rolla to Lebanon is 60 miles and the country is still worse. I had no idea that Missouri was such a poor country. Rolla is in Phelps county, which adjoins Dent on the north. If Dent is as poor as Phelps, Dave Headrick did not better himself much by coming to Missouri.... The country from Lebanon to this place, 50 miles, is pretty good, but sadly desolated by the ravages of war. Many houses along the road are deserted and many others have been burnt, fine fields are turned out and the whole country has a desolate appearance.... Springfield is a pretty town, but has a desolate appearance as many houses have been deserted and many burned. The battle of Wilson's Creek was fought about ten miles from here, and there have been some skirmishes about town since the war broke out. There are more soldiers than citizens here and no doubt many of the latter are rebels at heart.... I have been in good health and spirits since I wrote and like soldiering as well as ever. I had my likeness taken at Rolla and sent it to you by mail. I want you to keep it, and if I die or get killed before the war is over, send it to my folks in North Carolina. Of course you cannot do this until peace is made, but you can then, and I beg this favor of you as a friend and old neighbor....

April 29 (Tuesday)

Major Gen. Halleck, with over 100,000 men, prepared to attack Beauregard's nearly 65,000. Halleck would march from Pittsburg Landing for Corinth. Grant, named second-in-command, was very upset at what he considered a demotion. In all events, Halleck was not looking for a hero who would outshine him in the coming campaign.

In New Orleans, Federal officers raised the flag at the New Orleans Custom House near the waterfront, and over the City Hall, much to the chagrin of the natives.

April 30 (Wednesday)

Stonewall Jackson left Elk Run in the Blue Ridge Mountains, headed for Staunton. Federal Gen. Banks was in for a rough time over the next several weeks.

Halleck continued towards Corinth, slowly.

MAY 1862

Things were looking grim. Tennessee had been lost for all practical purposes, most of the Atlantic coast was either occupied or blockaded, the Gulf of Mexico ports were mostly sealed, and the South's largest city, New Orleans, was occupied by the blue-coats. The drastic reverses within the past 90 days offset the euphoria of the fall of '61, when the Confederacy basked in the glory of the victory at Manassas. Richmond was threatened from the Peninsula by McClellan's Army of the Potomac. Banks was in the Shenandoah Valley, and McDowell was in the vicinity of Fredericksburg, also threats to Richmond. In the west, the bloody battlefield of Shiloh had been cleaned up, but not forgotten. The forces there awaited action at Corinth. The North had to keep up the momentum.

May 1 (Thursday)

Union Major Gen. Benjamin F. Butler and his troops assumed control of New Orleans.

Siege guns were mounted opposite the Confederate fortifications in Yorktown, Va., increasing the pressure against Gen. Joseph Johnston. The U.S.S. *Marblehead,* Lt. Sommerville Nicholson, shelled Yorktown from the James River. If Yorktown were evacuated, the city of Norfolk, the Norfolk Navy Yard, and other peninsular assets would be abandoned.

President Lincoln was concerned that McClellan had not attacked Johnston, but seemed to be preparing for a lengthy siege. He asked McClellan, one of many times, "Is anything to be done?"

Barber, Pvt., Co. D, 15th Illinois Volunteer Infantry, near Corinth, Miss.:

> We left Pittsburg Landing about the 1st of May.... We marched five miles the first day but it took all day, the roads were so bad. We halted for several days. During the time, we drew new Enfield muskets. The 53rd Illinois was here added to our brigade. We were called out one morning to prepare for a fight. We formed a line but the enemy did not make its appearance. It was probably a scouting party of rebel cavalry.

Day, Pvt., Co. B, 25th Massachusetts Volunteer Infantry, New Bern, N.C.:

> Martial law not being a very favorable institution for pleasure parties, I presume the usual May day festival is dispensed with here... the woods abound with wild flowers in great variety and beauty. Ft. Macon surrendered to Gen. Burnside last Friday evening, after a bombardment of eleven hours. The general succeeded in getting his siege guns in battery behind some sand ridges about half a mile in rear of the fort, unobserved by the garrison, and the first notice they had of this presence was a shot from one of the guns. After holding out for eleven hours... they hauled down their colors... 65 guns and 450 prisoners, with stores and ammunition, have fallen into our hands....

It was a miserable day in the Shenandoah Valley—rain by the bucket. Jackson was moving from Conrad's Store towards Staunton, but didn't make more than five miles due to the roads.

May 3 (Saturday)

The Confederate forces around Yorktown withdrew from their fortifications before McClellan started his bombardment. Richmond was alarmed about rumors that Norfolk and Portsmouth were to be abandoned. Confederate forces numbered about 55,000, versus Union forces of over 100,000. McClellan was still calling for more manpower, even as the Rebels retreated.

There was skirmishing in the Corinth area between Beauregard's and Halleck's forces, but nothing major.

Jackson's troops crossed Brown's Gap and headed for the railhead at Mechum River. The troops washed out their muddy clothes in the cold mountain streams.

May 4 (Sunday)

The Army of the Potomac entered Yorktown and continued towards Williamsburg. Advance Union units clashed with Confederate Generals Longstreet and D.H. Hill's troops outside of town. Boat crews from the U.S.S. *Wachusett,* Commander W. Smith, raised the United States flag at Gloucester Point, opposite Yorktown. Two Confederate schooners were captured.

In the Valley, Jackson's men boarded trains and headed for Staunton, where they arrived about 5 P.M. to counter the advance of Milroy from western Virginia. Jackson took quarters at the Virginia Hotel.

Barber, Pvt., Co. D, 15th Illinois Volunteer Infantry, near Corinth, Miss.:

> We kept hitching along now from one-fourth to two miles a day, generally marching it in the evening. Before going to rest, we built earth-works in front of the regiment. Each regiment was required to do this before going into camp. Two hours was sufficient for us to throw up breast-works that would stand the test of light artillery. We were required to be up at three o'clock A.M. and form in line for battle and remain with accoutrements on until daylight. The General usually rode along the lines every morning, accompanied by his staff. General Halleck made a poor appearance as a military man. He usually wore a slouched hat, pulled low down over his eyebrows. His general appearance was ungainly and unprepossessing.

May 5 (Monday)

Lincoln decided to really play the role of Commander-in-Chief. He went to Ft. Monroe aboard the steamer *Miami*, accompanied by Secretaries Stanton and Chase. The following day he directed the gunboat operations against Sewell's Point on the James River. The Confederates had abandoned the sloop *Water Witch* above Gloucester Point, Va., and she was boarded by a crew from the U.S.S. *Corwin*, Lt. T.S. Phelps.

Heavy fighting took place around Williamsburg, the old capital of Virginia, when McClellan's forces collided with those of Joseph Johnston. Longstreet and D.H. Hill led their Confederates well in the rearguard action that brought on more casualties than would have been expected for this type of fighting. Johnston continued his retreat up the Peninsula.

During the fighting at Williamsburg, Joseph Hooker was accidentally "tabbed" with the name "Fighting Joe Hooker" by a newspaper reporter who began his story, "At the fighting. Gen. Joe Hooker..." The period was omitted in the final print, making the text read as if the reporter was referring to "Fighting Joe Hooker."

Stonewall Jackson finally got his new Confederate uniform in Staunton, Va. Up to this time he had been wearing his old major's uniform from Virginia Military Institute, where he had taught before the war.

May 6 (Tuesday)

Federal troops occupied Williamsburg, Va., on the heels of the retreating Confederates. Joe Johnston continued his retreat towards Richmond. Federal troop transports were escorted up the York River by the U.S.S. *Wachusett*, Commander W. Smith, and the *Chocura* and *Sebago* to make a landing at West Point. Acting Master William F. Shankland of the U.S.S. *Currituck* reported that some twenty schooners had been sunk and two gunboats burned by the Confederates above West Point.

At Corinth, Halleck's advance turned into more of a snail's crawl. Halleck was not the most aggressive general in the world, but he still was not as bad as McClellan.

May 8 (Thursday)

The Battle of McDowell took place in western Virginia today, as Jackson's 10,000 men were attacked by about 6000 from Frémont's command under Gen. Schenck. The Federals retreated towards Franklin and Jackson pursued. His "foot-cavalry" was making its mark.

Around Corinth, more probing was being done by Halleck's forces.

Barber, Pvt., Co. D, 15th Illinois Volunteer Infantry, near Corinth, Miss.:

> When the army came to a strong position, they would throw up strong works, irregular in shape, and commanding every possible position. These fortifications were considered secure places to fall back upon in case of disaster. The whole intervening space between us and the Landing was one continual series of fortifications. General Halleck was one of those old fogy commanders with more caution than spirit. We will admit that the enemy had taught us to respect their bravery, but with the army that Halleck had, he should have marched right up to their stronghold and sat down before it and expended labor in besieging the place instead of so much in the rear to provide for contingencies.

Day, Pvt., Co. B, 25th Massachusetts Volunteer Infantry, New Bern, N.C.:

> Our city life is about over; we have orders to break up housekeeping here tomorrow and go on a rusticating tour in the country....

Rumors of the evacuation of Norfolk seemed to be well founded. A tug deserting from Norfolk brought the news that the evacuation was well under way and that the C.S.S. *Virginia* and her escort of gunboats was to proceed up the James or York River.

At Baton Rouge, La., a landing party from the U.S.S. *Iroquois*, Commander James S. Palmer, took possession of the arsenal.

May 9 (Friday)

On the western rivers, Flag Officer Foote was relieved of command due to injuries received at Ft. Donelson. Foote had done yeoman service for his country as the commander of the river fleet, and he deserved his country's gratitude. At Corinth, Miss., the forces clashed with heavy skirmish lines in Halleck's advance against Beauregard.

At Hampton Roads, the President was aboard the *Miami* "directing" the naval operations. Learning that the Norfolk Navy Yard might be abandoned, he ordered the *Monitor* to see if the batteries at Sewell's Point were still manned. Finding them abandoned, Lincoln ordered Gen. Wool to occupy Norfolk.

Major Gen. David Hunter, now at Hilton Head, S.C., ordered the emancipation of the slaves in Florida, Georgia, and South Carolina. He further authorized the arming of all able-bodied blacks in those states. The order was immediately denounced by Congress and by the President on May 19th.

After the Battle of McDowell in western Virginia, Jackson pursued the fleeing Milroy on the road to Franklin for about 10 miles, and then went into a blocking position against Frémont.

Day, Pvt., Co. B, 25th Massachusetts Volunteer Infantry, picket duty, N.C.:

> After nearly two months of scrubbing and cleaning, with new camps and pants, the 25th regiment stands in columns of platoons on Pollock street, as tony a looking regiment as there is in the service.... Leaving the city, we soon enter the woods, and after marching about three miles, come out to a cotton plantation. Here we make a short halt and look over the place. It looks rather run down, the house is old and out of repair, the negro quarters are built of logs and look as though they were hardly habitable. But I presume everything on a plantation has to correspond. The gentlemanly proprietor, whoever he was, has left, taking with him the best of his servants, leaving here a few old ones to shift for themselves.
>
> A few miles further on, we came to another cotton plantation. This presented a better appearance, a neat cottage house, painted white with green blinds, good barns and surroundings. The negro quarters were comfortable looking houses, built of boards, with glass windows and whitewashed. This gentleman with his servants had also gone up the country... a road branched to the right leading into the woods, which we took, following it about four miles, coming out at a small clearing where was a little red house and log barn, with a few negro cabins. This is known as the Red house and we relieve the 23rd Massachusetts which is doing picket duty. And this then is to be our home for a while. It certainly is retired and rural, not another house within four miles of us. The clearing is not over twelve or fifteen acres in extent, with a small creek running through it. The tents up, the pickets out, dress parade and supper over, I reckon the country must be safe for one night at least...

May 10 (Saturday)

The Confederates set fire to the Norfolk Navy Yard before evacuating it and moved west towards Richmond. Union troops under Major Gen. Wool crossed Hampton Roads and occupied the city. While many of the supplies were destroyed, much remained. The loss of the naval base was a great blow to the Confederacy and left the C.S.S. *Virginia* without a home. In Richmond, the departure of President Davis's family for Raleigh, along with the families of most of the Cabinet members, was reported.

Confederate forces began evacuating Pensacola yesterday after the fall of both Island No. 10 and New Orleans. They fired the Navy Yard and destroyed all the ships under construction. Today, the Union Army and Navy occupied the city, and Commander David D. Porter reported, "The Rebels have done their work well. The yard is a ruin."

The Confederate River Defense Fleet made an attack on Union gunboats and the mortar flotilla at Plum Point Bend, Tenn. Several boats were rammed and sank in shallow water. Several of the Confederate gunboats were severely damaged and the fleet withdrew downriver.

In New Orleans, Gen. Benjamin Butler, later immortalized as "Spoons" Butler, seized $80,000 in gold from the Netherlands Consulate. An odd move, even for him.

Jackson continued his advance towards Franklin in western Virginia. Frémont was effectively blocked from joining Milroy.

Barber, Pvt., Co. D, 15th Illinois Volunteer Infantry, near Corinth, Miss.:

> Gen. Beauregard knew what kind of man he had to deal with and shaped his plans so as to completely fool Halleck. If Sherman, Grant, or Thomas had had command of the army, Beauregard would not have gotten away as slickly as he did. The nearer we approached the enemy, the more cautious he was—so cautious, that it seemed more like cowardice than prudence.

May 11 (Sunday)

The C.S.S. *Virginia,* née U.S.S. *Merrimack,* was gone. She was blown up by her crew after leaving Norfolk and discovering that she had too deep a draft to go up the James River. Thus died many hopes of success and glory for the Confederacy. A further advantage: The Union fleet now had free access up the James River towards Richmond, at least as far as the formidable defenses of Drewry's Bluff.

Being told by Lincoln about the fall of Norfolk and the destruction of the Confederate ironclad, Halleck was further admonished to "... sustain no reverse in your Department." This would not likely happen since the Union forces at Corinth were moving so slowly that a yard was a cause for celebration.

Jackson sat near Franklin in western Virginia.

Day, Pvt., Co. B, 25th Massachusetts Volunteer Infantry, picket duty, N.C.:

> This place is what is called a turpentine plantation, where they get the pitch from which turpentine is distilled. The owner, Mr. Bogey, a harmless, inoffensive old gentleman, claims to be a Union man, and I reckon he is, because he does not run away or seem to be afraid of us. He tells me he owns 2000 acres of land, nearly all turpentine forest, and has 10,000 trees running pitch. He said the war had ruined him and thinks it has the whole south. He said the rebels had taken all but one of his horses and about everything else he had that they wanted. His niggers had all left him and gone down town. He expected that when we came, but cared very little about it, as he had only a few and they were about as much trouble and expense to him as they were worth.... I asked him if all those pigs running about in the woods were his. He reckoned they were. I inquired if he knew how many he had. He couldn't tell exactly, but reckoned there was right smart. The thought occurred to me that if that was as near as he could tell, if a few of them were gobbled they would never be missed, provided the squeal could be shut off quick enough. I learn that Gen. Burnside has given Mr. Bogey a protection whatever that is. That perhaps may do well enough for him, but I should not want to warrant it a sure thing for all these pigs and sheep running about here....

May 12 (Monday)

Natchez, Miss., surrendered to Farragut's fleet today. Farragut was pushing his way upriver to see how far he can go towards Foote's river fleet. The stranglehold on Memphis was tightening.

At Nashville, a meeting of those loyal to the Union got under way, supported by the military government of Andrew Johnson.

In Richmond, those who could afford to do so, left. There was much arguing about what stores and supplies were to be destroyed, especially the valuable tobacco crop. Many of the tobacco traders were looking for ways to save their stock from destruction and fell upon the device of "selling" it to foreign government representatives then in Richmond.

Barber, Pvt., Co. D, 15th Illinois Volunteer Infantry, near Corinth, Miss.:

> We got very poor water now and the consequence was that some of the boys were taken sick. Charlie and myself amongst the number. Milton had cut his foot badly and he was put on the sick list. A sick and convalescent camp was established and we three were left behind, much to our disappointment. The army had got so far advanced that there was skirmishing daily. Our situation in our sick camp was anything but pleasant. Those whose business it was to draw rations for us, sold half of them, thus making money out of sick men's necessities, but we had the satisfaction of seeing some of them brought to grief by this outrage.

May 13 (Tuesday)

In the Shenandoah Valley, Jackson departed Franklin and headed back towards the main valley. Frémont and Milroy were taken care of for the moment. There was still terrible dread in Richmond. More families, at least those who could afford it, were leaving the city for western Virginia or North Carolina.

In Charleston, S.C., the all-Negro crew of the steamer *Planter* was left on board while its captain was ashore. Under the leadership of Robert Smalls, the ship sailed out of the harbor and was surrendered to the U.S.S. *Onward,* Acting Lt. Nickels. Flag Officer Du Pont reported the incident:

> At 4 in the morning she left her wharf close to the Government office and headquarters, with pal-

metto and Confederate flag flying, passed the successive forts, saluting as usual by blowing her steam whistle. After getting beyond the range of the last gun she quickly hauled down the rebel flags and hoisted a white one.... The steamer is quite a valuable acquisition to the squadron.... You should have heard his [Smalls's] modest reply when I asked him what was said of the carry away of General Ripley's barge sometime ago. He said they made a great fuss but perhaps they would make more 'to do' when they heard of the steamer being brought out.

On the Mississippi, Natchez was occupied by forces from the U.S.S. *Iroquois*, Commander Palmer, and the U.S.S. *Oneida*, Commander S.P. Lee, while Flag Officer Farragut steamed upriver. In Bayou Bonfuca, La., the U.S.S. *Calhoun*, Lt. DeHaven, sent a boat crew to capture the Confederate gunboat *Corypheus*, moored in the bayou.

May 14 (Wednesday)

Around Corinth, Miss., the skirmishing was fairly light. Halleck had a bad case of the "slows" on this campaign. It would prove to be the only time he commanded a force in battle.

The James River flotilla, under Commander John Rodgers, was advancing up the James River towards Richmond. This caused even more panic in Richmond, since the army under Gen. Joseph E. Johnston was also falling back.

Jackman, Pvt., "The Orphan Brigade," Castillian Springs, Miss.:

Brown died in our room this morning. How little feeling soldiers have sometimes! While willing to help a comrade while living, when dead, there is never much shedding of tears for them. We were all standing around Brown's bed and when he drew his last breath one of the boys bent over him, observed him for a moment, and said: "He never will draw another breath *so long as he lives*." This was said so simply the whole room rang out in laughter. We buried B. in the evening. Many are dying here. Intend to go to the front in a few days.

Day, Pvt., Co. B, 25th Massachusetts Volunteer Infantry, picket duty, N.C.:

I was out in the woods yesterday and last night on picket duty and picket duty is simply lying around in the brush watching the approach of outside parties. Parties approaching in the night time and failing to promptly respond to the hail of the picket are given an instantaneous passport to a land that is fairer than this. A picket is composed of three or more men stationed at convenient distances from each other along the roads, horse paths, and anywhere an enemy might be supposed to come. One keeps watch while the others sleep, but with the hooting of the owls, sand-fleas, woodticks, lizards, and mosquitoes, their repose is a good deal disturbed.

... with a strong scouting party went out to Tuscarora, a little hamlet about five miles distant, where is the enemy's outpost and where is kept a post of observation. On the approach of the colonel and his party they left, but before doing so set fire to a new steam saw and grain mill which was destroyed. Mr. Bogey was a good deal vexed at the destruction of this mill. He said it was built only two years ago at a cost of $5000 and was a great accommodation to the people here abouts, and he, with other farmers, put in their money to help build it. These people have a great notion of burning their property on our approach. I really cannot understand it. They ought to know that it is of no use to us, and in the end will be a sore loss to them.

Barber, Pvt., Co. D, 15th Illinois Volunteer Infantry, near Corinth, Miss.:

As Milton and Charlie were wandering away from camp one day, they discovered where a dairy was kept. Our mess, five in number, conceived the idea of having new milk added to our scanty fare, so three of us arose before daylight, sent out and milked, and got back to camp before it was astir, thus keeping others off the scent. We hid our milk after we brought it into camp. After a few days the owners of the dairy discovered that someone had kindly milked their cows for them, so they laid in watch for us one night and caught us at it. High words followed but they knew better than to meddle with us. After that, they would set their dogs on us, but as we went armed, a few shots put a quietus on them. Milk we wanted, and milk we would have. We were sick and it was a military necessity and they had to submit.

May 15 (Thursday)

The James River flotilla consisting of the U.S.S. *Monitor*, *Galena*, *Aroostook*, *Port Royal*, and *Nau-*

gatuck, approached to within eight miles of Richmond on the James River. At this point they found obstructions across the river and strong gun emplacements at Drewry's Bluff. In the action the *Galena* was heavily damaged. Commander John Rodgers ordered the fleet back downriver, stating that if troops had been available to take Drewry's Bluff from the rear, Richmond might have fallen.

The first Medal of Honor awarded to a member of the U.S. Marine Corps was authorized by Department of the Navy General Order 17, dated July 10, 1863, for valor during this action. It was presented to Corp. John B. Mackie, a member of the *Galena's* Marine Guard.

Gen. Joseph E. Johnston's Confederate army withdrew across the Chickahominy River to within three miles of Richmond.

In the west there was some skirmishing around Corinth, as Halleck's snail kept inching along.

At Liverpool, England, the ship destined for fame as a commerce raider was launched: the C.S.S. *Alabama.* She raided American commerce until she met the U.S.S. *Kearsarge* off the coast of France.

In New Orleans, Major Gen. Benjamin F. Butler created a sensation when he issued Order Number 28 to counter the treatment his soldiers had been receiving from the ladies of the city:

> As the officers and soldiers of the United States have been subject to repeated insults from the women (calling themselves ladies) of New Orleans in return for the most scrupulous non-interference and courtesy on our part, it is ordered that hereafter when any female shall by word, gesture, or movement insult or show contempt for any officer or soldier of the United States she shall be regarded and held liable to be treated as a woman of the town plying her avocation.

The ladies' reaction was to have Butler's likeness painted in the bottom of their chamber pots.

The U.S.S. *Sea Foam,* Acting Master Henry E. Williams, and the U.S.S. *Matthew Vassar,* Acting Master Hugh H. Savage, captured sloops *Sarah* and *New Eagle* off Ship Island, Miss. Both were loaded with cotton.

May 16 (Friday)

In New Orleans, Gen. Ben Butler added insult to injury by taking over the offices of the local newspapers, the *Bee* and the *Delta.* On the river heading north, a Union naval squadron led by the U.S.S. *Oneida,* Commander S.P. Lee, shelled Grand Gulf, Miss.

In Richmond, the panic eased and the citizens breathed a little easier. McClellan made his headquarters at White House, one of the old Lee family dwellings.

In the Valley, Jackson's men were observing a "fast day" as prescribed by Gen. Jackson.

In the vicinity of Corinth, skirmishes were the order of the day all along the line, with heavy pickets out on both sides.

Barber, Pvt., Co. D, 15th Illinois Volunteer Infantry, near Corinth, Miss.:

> We were now getting nearly well and requested the doctor to send us to the front but did not succeed at first. We had one of those ignoramuses for a doctor that was a disgrace to the profession. He used quinine in powder or pills for all diseases from a fever down to a sore finger—in fact, he considered it a panacea for all the ills that flesh is heir to. I believe that he did have a little blue mass and calomel which he gave to persons in a dying condition to make them die easier. You need not look incredulous, reader, we had just such men for doctors in the army. One day, our regimental teams came along, having been back for rations. We hastily gathered our things together and "slyed" off and that night we slept in camp. We were now within four miles of Corinth and one-half mile from the enemy's lines. Skirmishing was going on all the time. One-half of the company was on picket every day. The rest helped fortify camp. There was sharp fighting at times, but the enemy seemed to avoid a general engagement. Pope was pitching in very lively on the left. The boys had a lively time on picket. There was just fighting enough to make it interesting.

Day, Pvt., Co. B, 25th Massachusetts Volunteer Infantry, picket duty, N.C.:

> For some time past the pickets of the 17th Massachusetts have been a good deal troubled by being fired on in the night. The enemy's cavalry would come down, a few of them dismount and creeping up would fire on them. They would sometimes have cow bells with them, in order to divert attention and get nearer. But the boys soon learned that dodge and

when they heard a cow bell, would draw their straightest bead on it and let fly. In this state of affairs, it was thought best to make those fellows a call, and if they wanted anything of us to give them an opportunity to take it.

So, yesterday morning, we marched out to the Trent road where we joined the 17th Massachusetts, with five companies of the 3d New York cavalry, and a section of a battery, the whole under command of Col. Amory of the 17th. The cavalry taking the advance, we marched up the road a couple of miles, coming to a deep gully or ravine; crossing this, the advance cavalry guard soon came upon the enemy's pickets, driving them in and beyond their station into a swamp where they formed an ambuscade, thinking there was only a small cavalry force and that they might capture them. By this time the infantry had come up to their rendezvous, which was a large, nice house, with ample barn room for their horses. Thinking this was too good accommodation for them and too near our line, it was set on fire and burned. We now heard firing ahead and hurried on. They had closed around the advance cavalry guard and commenced the fight. The other companies being close by, soon took a hand in it and were giving them about all they wanted when the infantry came up. When they saw the infantry and artillery they took to their heels towards Trenton, a small village a few miles distant.

... In this skirmish the enemy lost eight killed and two prisoners, one of them wounded. Our cavalry had two wounded. The wounded men were brought out and loaded into ambulances. When they brought out the wounded rebel they put down the stretcher on which he was lying near where I was standing. He was a smooth-faced, fair-haired boy, and was moaning piteously with pain from the bullet wound in his head, and asking himself what his mother would say when she heard of it.... We arrived back in camp late in the afternoon, tired, hungry and covered with mud. I reckon they will not disturb our pickets any more at present in the way they have done. Creeping up in the dark and firing on a lone picket is mean and cowardly....

May 18 (Sunday)

Commander S.P. Lee, U.S.S. *Oneida*, submitted a demand on behalf of Flag Officer Farragut and Gen. Butler for the surrender of Vicksburg, Miss. The demand was refused. The city would be placed under siege and would surrender in less than 14 months.

Jackman, Pvt., "The Orphan Brigade," Corinth, Miss.:

> On the move all night. Took breakfast at Holly Springs. Got to G.J. at 10 A.M. and changed cars for Corinth where the train arrived at 1 P.M.. Being Sunday, all quiet. Soon found the regiment which had moved camp. Found the boys all well. The camp is about two miles west of town and about the same distance from the fortifications in the left wing. The boys have been working on the fortifications. Soon after I had left the brigade marched out in the night expecting a battle...

Barber, Pvt., Co. D, 15th Illinois Volunteer Infantry, near Corinth, Miss.:

> The picket lines of the two opposing armies were within hearing distance, but as each side managed to keep pretty well concealed, the firing did but little damage, although occasionally one would get wounded. The night watch was the more dreary and dangerous. We knew not how many secret foes were lurking around to take advantage of every movement. There were no lights to penetrate the gloom and all of our conversation was carried on in whisper. The videttes who were placed in advance had a most trying and responsible position. It was on such occasions that a soldier's thoughts would wander back to home and friends and in the dread silence, his imagination would weave bright pictures of fancy for the future. Thus between watching and waiting, the time passed until the cautious tread of the relief smote on his listening ear and then another dreamer would take his place.

May 19 (Monday)

In Richmond the activity to the east was still in doubt. No one knew if McClellan would make it to the city, but there was much conjecture.

In the Valley, Jackson rousted his troops out at 2 A.M. and they were on the road by 3 A.M. after a very hasty breakfast. The North River was crossed using wagons planked to serve as a bridge. Camp was made just below Harrisonburg.

May 20 (Tuesday)

In Richmond, President Davis, in response to a resolution of the Confederate Congress, announced that Richmond would be defended. This was still early in the war, before the casualties of Seven Days, Second Manassas, Fredericksburg, etc. were brought to Richmond. The spirit would be more subdued a year later.

In Washington, President Lincoln signed the Homestead Law, which guaranteed 160 acres of public land to anyone who would settle on it and make improvements for five years. Many veterans of this war would take advantage of this law to settle in the west.

Jackson went 12 miles towards New Market, pushing his columns hard in the fair weather. He now had 16,000 men and 48 guns, with the addition of Gen. Richard Ewell's force.

Richard Stoddert Ewell was born in Washington, D.C., on February 8, 1817, and moved to Virginia in 1826 with his family. Graduating from West Point in 1840, he was assigned to the dragoons in Oklahoma. He served in the Mexican War, then in Baltimore, before returning to the Southwest. He was on sick leave when the war started. Joining the Confederate forces, he was assigned as Lieutenant Colonel, and then was promoted to Brigadier General in June 1861, and to Major General in January 1862. His leg was amputated after the Battle of Groveton, in August 1862. He returned to duty in May 1863 in time for Gettysburg. Because of his disability, he was assigned to command the defenses of Richmond, evacuating the city in April 1865. He was captured at Saylor's Creek on April 6, 1865. After the war he retired to a farm in Tennessee, where he died on January 25, 1872.

East of Richmond, there was minor contact between Johnston's Confederates and McClellan's Federals.

The Stono River above Cole's Island, S.C., was occupied by Federal gunboats. The Confederates set fire to their barracks and fled inland when the gunboats shelled the base.

Barber, Pvt., Co. D, 15th Illinois Volunteer Infantry, near Corinth, Miss.:

> My health was so far improved now that I reported for duty. Capt. Smith had gotten back and the company now began to assume its old buoyant spirits. There was a log house in front of our picket line and each side had tried to hold possession of it, so one day the General thought that he would decide the matter. The rebels occupied it at the time.

Day, Pvt., Co. B, 25th Massachusetts Volunteer Infantry, picket duty, N.C.:

> Lying around here in the woods, hearing no sound but the moaning of the wind through the tree tops is rather dull business. There is nothing in it that inspires any lofty, rapturous thought, and yet it inspires thought, and already one of Mr. Bogey's sheep has fallen a victim to thoughts inspired by the soughing of the wind through this dark forest shutting out the day; I reckon it will not be necessary to say anything to Mr. Bogey about it, as he is a loyal man, and, as the lawyers say, the presumption is he would be more than glad to contribute a mutton in suppression of this unholy rebellion....

May 22 (Thursday)

Jackson's column crossed the Luray Gap of the Massanutten Mountain yesterday and emerged on the eastern side of the Valley. Federal Gen. Banks was in the main part of the Valley, trying to find out where Jackson went. Today Jackson began his march up the Luray Valley between Massanutten Mountain and the Blue Ridge, with Turner Ashby's cavalry screening his movements. Jackson's famed "foot cavalry" was performing its peculiar brand of magic again.

More skirmishing at Corinth and on the Chickahominy.

Jackman, Pvt., "The Orphan Brigade," Corinth, Miss.:

> Beautiful sunny day. Early the long roll was beat and we fell in with two days rations in haversacks, all equipped for battle. When we moved off a long train of ambulances followed us, each having the red flag "out" which indicated a battle. A long ordnance train also followed us. The infirmary corps marched in the rear of each regiment bearing their white litters which, perhaps, would soon be stained with human gore. Once, while fronted on the road, Genl. Breckinridge rode by. He was dressed in citizen suit with a

broadrimmed felt hat on. He passed our regt. first and the boys cheered him. He said: "Boys, I shall try and be with you more today than before." When asked after the Battle of Shiloh why he was not with his old brigade more during the battle he said that he knew the Kentucky boys would fight without the presence of their Maj. Genl. but that he was needed more on other parts of the field. This was considered quite a compliment. When passing the other regiments—all cheered him loudly. Two or three miles beyond the fortifications on the left wing we formed line of battle. We marched some distance then which was very difficult on account of the under-growth. We were the third line. When close to the evening, hotter, "lounged about" waiting for Van Dorn to open on the right but he failed to accomplish the flank movement intended and we marched back to camp that evening without any battle.

Barber, Pvt., Co. D, 15th Illinois Volunteer Infantry, near Corinth, Miss.:

A large force of our men went and drove the rebels out. In return, the rebels soon returned with large re-inforcements and our boys were compelled to give it up again. Then we had the whole division in line, supported by several batteries, and charged the rebels and again they were compelled to give way. This time they did not renew their attempt to take it as it would likely have brought on a general engagement. The next day we moved our lines forward again, but we had hard fighting. The enemy contested every inch of ground.

May 23 (Friday)

Today the Battle of Front Royal took place. Jackson, approaching from the south, took Banks's troops, about 800 men, by surprise and captured many of them. As a battle it wasn't much, but it created a stir in Washington. The people of that city could see Jackson's "legions" looming in the distance. Jackson's next task was to cut Banks off from Winchester and try to destroy his army piecemeal. An interesting sidelight was the fighting between the First Maryland Infantry, USA, and the First Maryland, *CSA*. This was the second defeat of the Federals by Jackson in about two weeks. Jackson defeated Frémont at McDowell on the 8th, and Banks today.

May 24 (Saturday)

In the Valley, Jackson failed to trap Banks, and most of the Federals escaped towards Winchester. The advance of Turner Ashby's cavalry, supported by Poague's artillery battery, created panic among the Federals, who abandoned large quantities of provisions and equipment. Upon reaching Newtown, Jackson found that Ashby's cavalry had given up the chase to plunder the Union supply wagons. Banks ordered his long supply trains north on the Valley Pike towards Williamsport. Lincoln ordered McDowell to send 20,000 men towards the Shenandoah to capture Jackson. He also ordered Frémont to enter the Valley and to cut off Jackson's retreat south.

Turner Ashby, a native Virginian, was born in Fauquier County on October 23, 1828. Educated at home, he and his brothers managed the family farm, "Rose Hill." In 1859, after John Brown's raid at Harpers Ferry, he raised a company of cavalry that later became a part of the 7th Virginia Cavalry, and he was soon assigned as the commander of the regiment. In June 1861, his brother was murdered by a Union patrol, an act that so filled Turner with a desire for vengeance that he became reckless in battle. He was promoted to Brigadier General on May 23, 1862. He was killed on June 6, 1862, southeast of Harrisonburg, and was buried in Winchester, Va.

The diversion of McDowell's men to the Valley gave McClellan another excuse for not pressing his attack on the Peninsula. He continued to believe he was under strength, although he had over 100,000 men. Skirmishing was still going on at Corinth and on the Chickahominy.

May 25 (Sunday)

At Winchester, Banks held Jackson and Ewell for a period of time before Banks's troops broke and ran for Harpers Ferry. Another great haul of supplies and munitions was garnered for the Confederacy. Jackson's legend grew. He had 16,000 against Banks's 8000. The citizens of Winchester were jubilant, cheering in the streets. Most of the Shenandoah Valley belonged again to the Confederacy, at least for a while.

Lincoln wired McClellan that it was time to make a decision. Either attack Richmond or come back to defend Washington.

May 26 (Monday)

Jackson occupied Winchester, and he prepared to go towards Harpers Ferry. Banks had left quite a haul for the Confederacy. Jackson gathered up 9000 rifles, 500,000 rounds of ammunition, a section of artillery, several small herds of cattle, and wagons of bacon, bread, sugar and salt. Frémont and McDowell were moving to cut his line of retreat.

More skirmishing around Richmond and at Corinth.

At Yazoo City, Miss., one Lt. Isaac Newton Brown, CSN, was about to perform a miracle. Brown had been ordered to take command of the C.S.S. *Arkansas* and get it ready "without regard to expenditure of men or money." A naval captain who inspected the ship reported that "... the iron with which she is covered is worn and indifferent, taken from a railroad track, and is poorly secured to the vessel; boiler iron on stern and counter; her smokestack is sheet iron." Nonetheless, Brown set to, and in five weeks from the day he had arrived, he had a man-of-war, such as she was. Brown had reinforced her bulwarks with cotton bales and mounted a formidable array of 10 guns.

Jackman, Pvt., "The Orphan Brigade," Corinth, Miss.:

> Cooking four days rations. Mystery about the movements. Nearly all the tents taken from us—12 to a tent. Some say retreat—some say fight. Old "Beauré" knows what he is about.

Barber, Pvt., Co. D, 15th Illinois Volunteer Infantry, near Corinth, Miss.:

> We are now in hearing of the rebel camp. We could plainly hear the drums beating, the heavy lumbering of the cars as they came into Corinth. Matters seemed to be approaching a crisis. We advanced our lines a little every day and the enemy slowly and sullenly fell back. We could hear the cars arriving and departing rapidly. It was evident that the rebs were either receiving large re-inforcements or were evacuating the place. The latter seemed the most plausible to us. But still Halleck with that extreme cautiousness, crept slowly up and allowed the wily foe to slip from his grasp. The enemy kept up a heavy skirmish line to make it appear that they were still there in strength, but subsequent events showed that they were rapidly evacuating at this time. We had now began to suffer for want of water and it became absolutely necessary for the army to move forward where they could get water or retreat. The latter was not to be thought of. We were furnished one-half gill of whiskey a day. I mixed it with my drinking water, this partially neutralizing its bad effects. General Pope was now thundering for admittance into the stronghold of Corinth.

May 27 (Tuesday)

Jackson pushed on towards Harpers Ferry, with skirmishing at Loudoun Heights. At Corinth there was more skirmishing.

Barber, Pvt., Co. D, 15th Illinois Volunteer Infantry, near Corinth, Miss.:

> ...after sharp skirmishing, we established our line in sight of the enemy's outer works. We could see that they were strongly surrounded by a heavy abatis and mounted some heavy guns though afterwards some of them proved to be wooden ones. We now set to work to fortify our position, the enemy the meanwhile shelling us, causing us considerable annoyance, yet, we perserveringly kept at work and soon had a formidable line of earth-works in front of us. Our regiment was detailed to support a six-pounder gun rifled battery. The enemy now commenced throwing grape and canister at us. A charge struck the ground in front of us, throwing the dirt in our faces; another passed over our heads, but another dropped in dangerous proximity to us, and some of the boys were wounded. In the meantime, there was sharp fighting on the skirmish line. Companies A and B were out. One from Company B was killed. The rebels suddenly broke cover and charged our men, yelling like demons. Our skirmishers were driven in, but in good order. Our battery had placed their guns in position and as soon as the rebels were in range, six pieces simultaneously opened upon them. The effect was awful. Some of the shells dropped in their very midst and the men were blown into atoms. The rebels suddenly came to a halt, turned and fled in dismay in every direction except towards us. The concussion of the discharge was terrific. We were lying down, but the jar fairly raised us off the ground. The rifled gun had a sharp ringing sound which jarred severely on the nerves. Simultaneous with the discharge, we all

rose up to note its effect. It was all that we could wish. This was the last effort that the rebels made on our part of the line. Pope kept up a continuous cannonading all night. We fell back two or three miles and went into camp and were relieved by another division.

May 28 (Wednesday)

Assistant Secretary of the Navy Fox wrote to Senator Grimes about the regulation permitting the issue of grog (rum) aboard navy ships. This practice was a carryover from the British, who issued their sailors and marines a pint of rum a day. Fox wrote,

> I beg of you for the enduring good of the service, which you have so much at heart, to add a proviso [to the naval bill] abolishing the spirit ration and forbidding any distilled liquors being placed on board any vessel belonging to, or chartered by, the U. States, excepting of course, that in the Medical Department. All insubordination, all misery, every deviltry on board ships can be traced to *rum*. Give the sailor double the value or more, and he will be content.

Fox was successful in his appeal. Congressional Act of July 14, 1862, did abolish the spirit ration in the Navy. Of course, not everyone was happy with this, especially the sailors.

Jackman, Pvt., "The Orphan Brigade," Corinth, Miss.:

> In the morning broke up camp and started the wagon train to the rear, then marched out to the trenches where we lay in reserve all day. Our brigade is the reserve of the division and our regt. the reserve of the brigade. Heavy skirmishing along the whole line today. In the evening the enemy were close enough to throw two solid shot over us. Tonight all quiet. Cannot tell whether we are going to wait for an attack or retreat. Have been suffering for water all day.

Barber, Pvt., Co. D, 15th Illinois Volunteer Infantry, near Corinth, Miss.:

> Early next morning we received ten month's pay, and we immediately started for the front again. On our way there we learned that the enemy had evacuated and that our forces held possession of the place. Soon we heard of a terrible fight in Virginia and that McClellan was defeated. The bulk of Beauregard's army was in the fight, so the campaign against Corinth was a drawn game. The rebels gained the battle in Virginia but lost possession of the stronghold of Corinth. We entered the place about ten o'clock. The rebels had destroyed everything they did not take with them. Huge piles of provision were strewed around, thus confuting the statement that the rebel army was starving. We saw where some of their magazines were that were blown up during the night. Corinth is a small city of about two thousand inhabitants and at this time was a place of considerable military importance, being the junction of the Charleston and Memphis and Mobile & Ohio railroads. The town wore a desolate looking aspect. The fire from our heavy siege-guns had driven all the inhabitants out. Some of our shots had set the depot on fire and it was a smoldering mass of ruins. Several engines and a large number of cars were burnt also. We went into camp about one mile south of Corinth.

Day, Pvt., Co. B, 25th Massachusetts Volunteer Infantry, picket duty, N.C.:

> It has rained almost constantly for the past week and when it rains here in Dixie it is no drizzle, but comes down a perfect waterfall, sometimes for twelve hours together, accompanied with lightning and thunder of the grandest description. There is a grandeur in one of these storms at night, when in the woods among the tall pines, far away from the camp on picket, that no person can form much of an idea of unless they have been there to witness it. On such a night the solitude is awfully impressive, the picket stands concealed behind a tree in the drenching rain, solitary and alone, absorbed only in his own reflections and looking out for the lurking foe. The vivid lightning with almost continuous flashes illumes the grand old woods, while peal after peal of deafening thunder breaks, rolls, and rumbles athwart the sky, sending back echoes, as though a hundred batteries filled the air....

May 29 (Thursday)

At Harpers Ferry, there was quite a gathering in the works. Jackson had about 16,000 troops opposing Banks's 8000. But behind Jackson, up the Valley, Frémont had about 15,000, and McDowell's 20,000 were ready to cut off Jackson's retreat. Jackson was at Halltown, watching.

Near Seven Pines on the Chickahominy there was some light skirmishing, and some further north along the South Anna River.

After all the waiting and watching at Corinth, nothing happened! Beauregard decided to quit the bout before the first bell rang and ordered a pullout. To cover the withdrawal, he had the frontline troops make loud noises to keep the Federals occupied.

Jackman, Pvt., "The Orphan Brigade," Corinth, Miss.:

> Have not moved today. Little skirmishing in front—very quiet. Have been suffering for water all day. The wagon trains have now been gone 2 days. A little after dark all of our troops fell back but we did not know it at the time.

May 30 (Friday)

Halleck sat a few miles north of Corinth, completely oblivious to the fact that Beauregard was moving his entire army towards Tupelo; there was a thin screen between Halleck and the retreating Confederates. Although Halleck called it a victory, some wondered.

In the Valley, Jackson began to fall back from Harpers Ferry to avoid the trap being laid by McDowell's troops (commanded by Gen. Shields), with Frémont's forces at Front Royal.

Heavy rains on the Peninsula deterred any serious engagements. The bottomlands were flooded.

Jackman, Pvt., "The Orphan Brigade," Corinth, Miss.:

> Last night about 12 o'clock the order came around in whispers to fall in—to be silent about it. It was so dark we could not see our file leaders. After much trouble the regiment was formed. All day we had been speculating whether we were to go out of the fortifications and hazard a battle, wait on attack, or retreat. Falling in at that hour we knew that we were going out to fight or retreat, and that we would soon know. We were in suspense—all were silent and anxious. Just as the column started to move, someone set an old tent on fire, which suddenly blazed up, dispersing the darkness for a moment and revealed the head of the column moving towards the trenches. The light shed only a moment on the aslanted guns of the gray column as it wended through the cols of old oaks, then died away leaving inky dark. When we got up to the trenches—had been lying in the rear—we found all the troops had left them. We moved on parallel with the works towards the sally-port—Suspense! Would we go out, or turn off on the road to the left! We moved on the road to the left and [a] hum of subdued voices came from the retreating column. There was no longer suspense. If we had gone out at the sally-port, all would have been as cheerful marching towards the enemy, as they now were retreating from him. The "Orphans" are always cheerful, whether sharing the glories of victory or in the midst of disaster. We soon came up with a section of Cobb's Battery which was to stay with our regiment, now the rear guard.
>
> Our road led from the left wing and a little to the left of town. The night was so dark, the artillery and our two ambulances kept getting against trees and stumps delaying us. We have to cross bridges over swamps and some of the boys fell off into the mud. I could always travel well of night and while others were tumbling over stumps and root, I kept my footing.
>
> When we got on the Kossuth road, in sight of Corinth to the rear, gray morning had come and we halted to rest. Soon the sun came peeping over the hill and no troops were to be seen except a few cavalry scouts. Ever since the signal gun had broken the stillness of the night our troops had been marching away. After daylight the commissary stores that had been left behind were fired and high up rose a black pillow of smoke. All was quiet as death. A few wounded and broken down cavalry horses were quietly cropping grass on the common and were the only animated creatures to be seen. We fell in and marched to the Luscumbia, 5 miles to town and filed off the road and stacked arms in line of battle. The two howitzers were planted on the road. We took some breakfast. In the afternoon moved across the river and our cavalry scouts having come over, the bridge was burned and trees cut across the road. Here we joined the 22d Miss. of the same division. Tonight all quiet. Bivouacking in line of battle. Rations short.

May 31 (Saturday)

McClellan had one corps north of the Chickahominy and two south of that river. Joe Johnston's Confederates attacked the two corps at Fair

Oaks (or Seven Pines). Several mistakes caused delays and the Confederate attack did not pick up momentum until 1 P.M., and even then the contact was spotty. The Rebel drive was stopped when Gen. Sumner, not waiting for McClellan's order, moved his corps into the battle. At this point a chance bullet changed the way the war would be fought from this time forward in the eastern theater.

Gen. Joseph Eggleston Johnston was wounded and Robert E. Lee was given command of the Army of Northern Virginia the next day. During the night, the Federals brought in more troops and strengthened their positions.

Another general officer was wounded this date. Union Brigadier Gen. Oliver O. Howard was wounded twice, forcing the amputation of his right arm. For his actions he was awarded the Medal of Honor.

Oliver Otis Howard was born at Leeds, Me., on November 8, 1830. He graduated from West Point in 1854, and he was teaching mathematics there when the war broke out. He was placed in command of the 3d Maine Regiment, which he led at First Manassas, performing well and getting a promotion to Brigadier General. At Seven Pines he was wounded twice and recuperated fast enough to fight at Antietam and at Fredericksburg, where he was promoted to Major General. At Chancellorsville, he commanded the XI Corps, which suffered the brunt of Jackson's flank attack, and he was blamed for not holding. He served with Meade at Gettysburg, where he did extremely well. Going west, he was assigned to the IV Corps, and then as commander of the Army of the Tennessee during Sherman's March to the Sea. After the war, he headed the Freedman's Bureau, which suffered some scandals caused by his subordinates. A court of inquiry cleared him of all charges in 1874. He was the major force in the founding of Howard University in Washington, D.C. He served again in the west and retired in 1894. He died at Burlington, Vt., on October 26, 1909.

Jackson left the Winchester area in a heavy rain and the "foot cavalry" raced south to avoid the trap, just getting through the gap between Frémont's and McDowell's troops. In addition to all else, Jackson had the captured Federal trains to move south. Jackson made good his escape, much to Lincoln's disgust.

Jackman, Pvt., "The Orphan Brigade," near Luscumbia, Miss.:

> All quiet this morning. A scout from the enemy came to the opposite side of the river but went back. The Luscumbia is a small stream, but a few yards wide, but deep. The swamps on either side impassable. At 4 P.M. fell in to march but the order was countermanded. Late a heavy skirmish at the bridge above us.

Corinth was a victory, of sorts. The Mississippi River above New Orleans to Vicksburg was open. The threat of the C.S.S. *Virginia* was no more; she had been destroyed. McClellan had wasted a golden opportunity, and Jackson had escaped a trap in the Valley.

JUNE 1862

The beginning of June brought Lincoln no answer to his command problems. McClellan was still timorous and crying for more men on the Peninsula. Halleck, after he had relieved Grant and taken charge of the army so that the glory could be his, lacked the stamina and nerve to attack. Banks, McDowell, and Frémont in the Valley failed to trap Stonewall Jackson, although they had more than twice his number of troops. Lincoln pondered his next step, and lived with the command that he had.

In the South, the only bright spot was that Richmond had not fallen. Tennessee was gone, along with New Orleans and most of the Mississippi River. Pensacola was in Federal hands, and much of the southern east coast was under the Stars and Stripes. Many of the residents of Richmond had fled, and Davis looked to Lee to manufacture a miracle.

June 1 (Sunday)

A freshwater expedition up Aucilla River, Fla., ended in disaster for eleven sailors and Acting Master Samuel Curtis, U.S.S. *Kingfisher*, when they were surprised by Confederates. Two Federals were killed and the remainder taken prisoner.

In the Valley, Jackson's "foot cavalry" were racing towards Harrisonburg to escape the closing Federal net. Jackson's legend was growing daily.

East of Richmond, near the Chickahominy River, the last day of the Battle of Seven Pines (Fair Oaks) was fought. Lee was in charge, effective this morning, and was trying to make sense of the confusion. By 3 P.M. Lee had decided to have his troops withdraw to their original lines, having gained nothing except to swell the casualty list on both sides. The South had suffered over 6000 new casualties, about 1000 more than the North. Both sides decided to wait.

Jackman, Pvt., "The Orphan Brigade," Corinth, Miss.:

Early in the afternoon heavy showers of rain. Was detailed on a scout to go down the river and had a muddy tramp—saw nothing. At 4 P.M. fell in and took up our line of march on the Corinth road. Our regiment, the 22d Miss., and a section of Cobb's Battery with a few cavalry composed the rear guard on the road. The command kept closed up and was under the command of Col. H. As the sun was setting, passed through the little town of Kossuth. The night set in dark and we pushed forward, never stopping. Just before midnight I was so tired, not having marched any for a long time, and not feeling well, I had to tumble out into a fence corner to rest—one of the boys fell by the way with me and the column moved on. We were both soon napping. We had fallen out just as the column was turning off the main road on another to the right. In a short time I was waked by a party of cavalry riding by taking the straight road and from the rattling of their sabres I took them to be Federals. As soon as they were gone, I roused my companion and... pushed on. There were several roads branching off, but fortunately the artillery was in the rear of the troop and we could, by stooping low, see the broad track of the wheels in the dust. This guided us on the proper road. We heard the report of a gun and when we caught up found a cavalryman had accidently shot himself through the leg. The scouts reported the enemy half a mile off on the other road. When we caught up, the regt. had just halted to rest and I lay down (12 o'clock). I slept an hour of the best sleep in my life. We were roused at 1 o'clock and pushed on from that until daylight. When we stopped a short time to rest I was tired enough.

Barber, Pvt., Co. D, 15th Illinois Volunteer Infantry, Corinth, Miss.:

Gen. Pope commenced a vigorous pursuit of the enemy on the line of the Mobile & Ohio railroad, but after a few days returned, with poor success. The rebels had destroyed all the bridges in their retreat. We lay in camp a few days and then took up our march on the line of the Charleston & Memphis railway. It was generally supposed that we were going to Grand Junction, a station at the junction of the Charleston & Mississippi railroad, where it was reported that a large force of the rebels were fortifying. This place is forty-seven miles from Corinth and fifty-three from Memphis. We marched one day and went into camp, where we remained over a week, building bridges and scouting. We finally resumed our march and the second day we passed Grand Junction and camped one-half mile beyond, in the wood, between Grand Junction and Lagrange.

Day, Pvt., Co. B, 25th Massachusetts Volunteer Infantry, New Bern, N.C.:

And now something else has turned up, and here we are encamped just outside the city and behind our batteries. The order to move took us by surprise as the first notice we had was to pick up our traps and be ready to march in half an hour. At the time appointed, everything was packed and loaded on the wagons and we were on the march. Dark found us here with our tents up ready for housekeeping.... All the advance regiments are drawn in behind the forts and the whole division, with the exception of the three regiments, are now here. I have heard no reason why the division is concentrated, but perhaps the general expects company and intends to be in readiness to give them a right royal reception.... With 10,000 troops behind the works, with a wide open field in front, it looks as though our position was a pretty safe one...

June 2 (Monday)

At Fair Oaks, east of Richmond, the cleanup of the battlefield began with the burial of the dead and the gathering of scattered equipment.

Near Corinth, Gen. John Pope was following the retreating Confederates when a clash developed near Rienzi, Miss.

Jackman, Pvt., "The Orphan Brigade," withdrawing from Corinth, Miss.:

Marched until noon when we halted to rest an hour. Here the roads came together and we were joined by several other regiments. The Federal cavalry was reported to be in front of us, on the flanks, and, of course, following us. We drew some hardtack and bacon and ate dinner. When our hour was out, ordered to fall in. We saw the field officers riding about looking "blue" but we were too near worn out to pay any attention to impending danger. The enemy was reported closing in around us and Col. H. who was still in comd. of the rear, commenced forming his lines. Lt. Col. Johnson was in command of our regiment. The boys called him "Uncle Bob." Uncle Bob is a clever, brave man but utterly ignorant of military tactics. Uncle Bob ordered us to fall in. Now, he was not at all afraid but a little excited. Not moving off immediately, some of the boys being worn out, sat down in ranks. Uncle Bob seeing it, ripped out an oath and said the regiment didn't know the first principle of drilling. All the boys being brought to their feet, Uncle Bob gave the order "right four"—not a man moved. He grew purple with rage, thinking he had a little mutiny on hand. "Why don't you move?" shouted Uncle Bob. Some one remarked to him that we could not until we "came to shoulder." He "simmered" and said something about all being liable to make mistakes. The boys were full of laugh and knew that he would make other mistakes and resolved to show them to him. After marching us around through the woods awhile, he at last came to where he wished us to seat in line of battle and gave the order to "front." We did so but our *faces were set from the enemy instead* of towards them. Uncle Bob again drew himself up and wanted to know what in the h—l we were doing. "Didn't you order us to front?" asked one of the Captains, dutifully saluting. "Yes, but I wanted you to face this way" cried Uncle Bob. The regiment could hold in no longer and roared in laughter. Col. H., about that time, came up and took command. The regiment moved out in the road and continued the march. Uncle Bob slunk back to the rear of the reg't. looking like he had been doing worse things than teaching us the "first principle of drilling." Before that, it seems the Colonels, in a council of war, had gotten into disputes about something and Col. H. declared he would take his regiment and go on through, enemy or no enemy. The commander of the 22d Miss. said he would follow him with his regiment—I believe all the rest followed. When we got to Black Land, three miles, we found the Federal cavalry had just left. The day was hot and we could get no water fit to drink. Late in the evening had a heavy rainstorm, which rendered the roads so slippery we could hardly march. Just before sundown, we came to our lines and Genl. Breckinridge was surprised to see us—had given us up as lost knowing the Federal cavalry was swarming about our way. At sun set, came to our wagon train near Baldwyn, camped in a low swampy place. We were a tired set of boys. I was in a good condition to sleep in mud and water.

June 4 (Wednesday)

The evacuation of Ft. Pillow was completed tonight; the road was open to Memphis. The evacuation caused cotton planters on the river to burn huge stores of cotton before it could be taken by the Yankees. Long columns of smoke could be seen on the horizon from Memphis and Yazoo City.

In the Valley, Jackson was wet and weary from the rain and the strain of trying to get his trains south on muddy, miserable roads.

June 6 (Friday)

The city of Memphis, Tenn., fell to Union forces. The Federal fleet under command of Commodore Charles Davis sailed down the Mississippi and engaged the Confederate ships below the bluffs of the city. Citizens of Memphis lined the bluffs to watch the Federals be defeated. The fight became a free-for-all with gunboats and rams going in every direction, either running or attacking. After an initial assault by the rams, the gunboats took over the action and blasted the Confederate ships. Few escaped. The Confederates also lost five large transports and other vessels under construction. The battle lasted only two hours, and was completed by 7:30 A.M. Most of the spectators lining the bluff went home, many in tears. At 11 A.M., the mayor surrendered the city. Federal troops that were part of the flotilla occupied the city and mounted guards. The Mississippi was now open all the way to Vicksburg, Miss.

Day, Pvt., Co. B, 25th Massachusetts Volunteer Infantry, New Bern, N.C.:

> We are now in a neatly arranged camp on somewhat elevated ground at the west side of the city, and about a quarter of a mile to the rear of Fort Totten, a large field fortification mounting twenty heavy guns.... We can now brush ourselves up and settle down to the dull routine of camp life—Drills, parades, reviews, inspections.... The Red house is again in enemy's country, but Mr. Bogey is not there; he thought he had rather live under the old flag and take his chances and so moved with us into town.

Jackson continued his retreat towards Port Republic, in the Valley southeast of Harrisonburg. In a skirmish just south of Harrisonburg, Col. Turner Ashby, Jackson's cavalry leader, was killed in a rearguard action. Jackson's pursuers were still coming fast.

June 7 (Saturday)

One William B. Mumford, a stalwart Confederate, decided he would take down and destroy the Stars and Stripes which were flying over the U.S. Mint Building on the lower end of the French Quarter in New Orleans. A dim view was taken of this by Maj. Gen. Benjamin F. Butler, who said that Mumford was to hang.

Federal troops shelled Chattanooga, Tenn., waking the Confederates to the realization that they had better fortify that important rail junction or lose it.

Jackman, Pvt., "The Orphan Brigade," Tupelo, Miss.:

> Fell in at sun rise and marched towards Tupelo. As the division meandered through the long lanes the sun reflecting on thousands of polished guns, I was struck with the scene. There seemed a tide of melted silver flowing on across the green fields. There *was* a good deal of *lead* along but was not melted. Soon the day got hot and dust obscured all such scenery. I had on a new pair of shoes which blistered my feet. Once I pulled them off, but the sand was so hot I could not stand it. I managed to keep up all day. Suffered for water. Marched 20 miles.

June 8 (Sunday)

Memphis was now an occupied city, much to the chagrin of the citizens. The Federals found the city interesting, and did a bit of sightseeing, especially in the area below the bluffs along the river, where the local entertainment and bars are located. Like any other river town of the era, Memphis had its seamy side.

To the east, Beauregard was still moving towards Tupelo; his troops were closing up. Jackman didn't think too much of the town.

Jackman, Pvt., "The Orphan Brigade," Tupelo, Miss.:

> Marched 12 miles to Tupelo, then 5 miles west, and bivouacked. Sore feet, mine. Tupelo is a small dirty-looking town on the Mobile and Ohio railroad. The war, I presume, has given it something of its dirty appearance.

At Port Republic, Va., with McDowell sitting on the sidelines, Jackson faced two Federal columns under Frémont and Shields. The Federals were trying to accomplish a pincer movement on Jackson's small army. Frémont attacked at Cross Keys against the force of Gen. Richard Ewell, who fought him off, causing Frémont to partially retreat. Lincoln decided that since McDowell couldn't catch Jackson, he could just as well go back to threatening Richmond.

June 9 (Monday)

On the Roanoke River in North Carolina, the U.S.S. *Commodore Perry*, Lt. Flusser, together with the *Shawsbeen* and *Ceres*, going upstream loaded with troops, were brought under small arms fire for two hours from the riverbanks. Troops, however, were landed at Hamilton without opposition, where the steamer *Wilson* was captured.

Jackson pulled another one of his magic tricks at Port Republic and brought Ewell across the river in time to help punch Shields's troops in the nose before Frémont realized that he was facing only a skeleton Rebel force. This was the last battle of the Valley Campaign. In the past 38 days Jackson's "foot cavalry" had marched nearly 400 miles and kept tens of thousands of Federal troops tied up and away from the front at Richmond. This campaign, above all others, made Jackson's name legendary.

June 11 (Wednesday)

At Corinth and environs, Grant was getting acquainted with his new command.

Jackman, Pvt., "The Orphan Brigade," Tupelo, Miss.:

> Hot!!! Edibles are running low in camp—bill of fare: corn-bread, pickled beef, fat back—and molasses. Sometimes we get something from the country people. Prices current: Spring chickens, 50 to 75 cts; tough hens, 80 cts to $1; old roosters, $1 to $1.25; turkeys, $1.50 to $2.00; old ganders, $1.50; goose, same; vegetables—50 cts for peeping over the fence into the garden!

Jackson rested his troops near Port Republic while everyone, including his staff, tried to figure out what he would do.

June 12 (Thursday)

At 2 A.M. Confederate Gen. JEB Stuart mounted his 1200 cavalry and began his four-day ride completely around the Army of the Potomac. While it did little in the way of military accomplishment, it was very embarrassing to Gen. McClellan and it gave the South a morale boost. It also added to the Southerners' general conception that they possessed a native talent for horsemanship far exceeding that of the Northerners. It had one other effect: It stirred both North and South to equip and field more cavalry.

James Ewell Brown (JEB) Stuart was born at "Laurel Hill" in Patrick County, Va. He graduated from West Point in 1854, and was appointed a 2nd Lieutenant of Mounted Rifles. Transferred to the 1st U.S. Cavalry, he served in Kansas for the next six years. He was visiting the east when John Brown raided Harpers Ferry in 1859 and served as Lee's aide during that fight. On May 10, 1861, he had just been promoted to Captain, but resigned his commission and was appointed a Colonel in the Confederate Army. He fought through most of the major campaigns, serving as Lee's "eyes." His failure during the Gettysburg campaign was noteworthy. A very flamboyant character, he had many affectations, including that of wearing a plume in his hat. He was mortally wounded in a cavalry battle with Sheridan's Union cavalry at Yellow Tavern, north of Richmond, on May 11, 1864. He died the following day and was mourned by all the South; "the Cavalier of Dixie" was dead.

Barber, Pvt., Co. D, 15th Illinois Volunteer Infantry, Coldwater, near Holly Springs, Miss.:

> We lay in camp some time. It was blackberry season and they were plentiful around our camp and the boys just feasted on them. The tedium of our camp life was now relieved by an order to be ready to march by daylight with three days' cooked rations in our haversacks. Our destination was Holly Springs, a beautiful city just across the State line in Mississippi. It was reported that the rebels were here in force. The second day at noon, we halted for rest and refreshments on the Coldwater, six miles from Holly Springs. Our march had been so rapid that a number of the boys gave out, William and myself amongst the number. It was the first time in one and one-half years' hard service that my feet failed me. Now they were raw and blistered.

Lee, toying with McClellan, sent some troops to reinforce Jackson. The idea was to give the impression that a major thrust would be from that direction. Frémont withdrew from the Harrisonburg area to around Mt. Jackson to the north.

June 13 (Friday)

Stuart's cavalry made a right turn from the South Anna River north of Richmond and moved around the right flank of McClellan's army on the Peninsula, passing through Hanover Court House. There was a brief skirmish at Haw's Shop and Old Church, and the time for a decision had come—go ahead or turn back? Stuart forged ahead. He continued during the night, and by morning he was at Forge Bridge, which crossed the Chickahominy.

Jackman, Pvt., "The Orphan Brigade," Abbeville, Miss.:

> On battalion drill at 2 P.M. Hot work. All the time while encamped at Tupelo had regular drills and the weather could not have been hotter. There was only one small spring to water the brigade, which was guarded, and no one could get water save at regular water calls.

June 15 (Sunday)

Yesterday Stuart's troopers had to rebuild a bridge at Forge Site to get across the Chickahominy. The troops worked like demons, fearful of being cut off behind the lines. They got moving after three long hours and proceeded on around the left flank of the Army of the Potomac. Stuart went on ahead, leaving the troops in the hands of Fitzhugh Lee, son of Robert E. Lee.

Today, Stuart arrived back in Richmond a legend. He had brought back valuable information for Lee concerning terrain, roads, etc., but his excursion may have also had a negative effect, since it alerted McClellan that the Union flanks were vulnerable.

June 16 (Monday)

Near Charleston, S.C., Federal Brigadier Gen. H.W. Benham disregarded both orders and advice and assaulted the Confederate works at Secessionville. The attack failed completely, resulting in 683 unnecessary casualties. Eventually Benham was relieved of this command, and he faded into obscurity.

The Confederates, in an attempt to block the advance of Federal gunboats up the White River, sank two steamers, *Eliza G.* and *Mary Patterson*, along with the C.S.S. *Maurepas.*

Barber, Pvt., Co. D, 15th Illinois Volunteer Infantry, Coldwater, near Holly Springs, Miss.:

> We were left here to recruit. We also answered the purpose of rear guard. Near our camp was a rank old rebel planter. He was very kind and affable while the army was there and one would think, to hear him talk, that he was one of the best Union men in the South. He said that the rebels had taken nearly all of his personal property and he prevailed on the General to grant him a safe guard, but no sooner had the army left than his sneaking, traitorous disposition showed itself. Two of our boys, nearly worn out, stopped at his house and requested a drink of water, which he refused, and then commenced abusing them. He did not know that we were camped just across the river. When the boys told us how they had been used, we vowed to have revenge. Seeing a fine drove of hogs nearby and naturally supposing them to be his, the boys went in and commenced killing them. The old rebel soon saw what was up and in a towering rage came down to stop it, but gun in hand, I stepped upon the bridge and halted him and kept him there until the boys had got what fresh pork they wanted and then I let the old fool go. He was livid with rage. The next evening the command returned to Coldwater. The rebels had evacuated the place the day before and pursuit was deemed impracticable. We got a good joke on Milton here. Just before the army started back, he took some canteens and went for water and before he got back the army left. To lighten his load, he gave the canteens to a cavalryman to carry and he never saw them again. We boys knew better than to loan or give anything to a cavalryman unless he was a friend. It taught Milt a lesson.

Day, Pvt., Co. B, 25th Massachusetts Volunteer Infantry, New Bern, N.C.:

> It is so hot most of the time we are scarcely able to do anything more than keep ourselves as comfortable as possible. All duty is suspended except guard duty and dress parade, and we are getting almost too lazy to eat; in fact, do miss a good many meals unless they happen to have something we like. We lie around in our tents or in the shade of the trees from 9 o'clock in the morning till 4 in the afternoon, brushing away the flies, and trying to keep cool. I thought I had seen some flies at home but they are no comparison to what we have here. I really believe there are more flies in this camp than there are in the whole state of Massachusetts. Besides, they are regular secesh ones... We were visited last evening by a thunder storm which makes it quite comfortable today. For several days past the weather has been very hot, the thermometer ranging about 100 degrees in the shade....

June 17 (Tuesday)

Jackson was leaving the Shenandoah Valley, going to reinforce Lee east of Richmond. As fast as trains could be made available, the troops were loaded and sent east.

In a move of mixed blessings, Major Gen. Charles Frémont resigned his command in protest of having to serve under John Pope, who was being brought east to command the new Army of Virginia, which would consist of Frémont's and Banks's command. Major Gen. Franz Sigel was assigned to replace Frémont.

In the west, Gen. Braxton Bragg, Sherman's old friend, was named to command the Confederates now facing Grant and Buell. Beauregard left the army ill and feeling mistreated.

In a joint expedition, the Navy, under command of Commander Kilty, U.S.S. *Mound City*, with the U.S.S. *Lexington*, *St. Louis*, and *Conestoga*, accompanied by a regiment of troops, engaged the Confederate batteries at St. Charles, Ark. The troops landed under cover of naval bombardment and took the guns, but the *Mound City* was hit, exploding her steam drum and causing many casualties. The capture of the emplacement gave control of the White River to the Federals.

Flag Officer Foote, still recovering from wounds received at Ft. Donelson, was relieved of command of the river fleet. The command went to newly promoted Flag Officer Charles H. Davis, who had been in command since Foote left for the hospital.

June 18 (Wednesday)

A terrain feature that would be repeatedly fought over during the war was taken by Federal troops under Brigadier Gen. George W. Morgan. The Cumberland Gap, that pass through the mountains that had been used for centuries by the Indians and then by Daniel Boone to gain entry to Kentucky, that "Bloody Ground," was again being fought over. This had the side effect of raising the morale of the pro-Northerners in east Tennessee and in the western parts of North Carolina.

On the Mississippi River, Vicksburg was at last paying some attention to her long-neglected defenses. The citizens and the Confederate Army were busy repairing old emplacements and building new ones, for they knew that the Yankees were coming. Just below the city, Flag Officer Farragut was busy assembling his gunboats and mortar boats, preparing to assault the city.

June 19 (Thursday)

Lincoln signed into law legislation prohibiting slavery in the territories of the United States.

Commander Maury of the Confederate Navy planted electric mines (battery-detonated) near Chaffin's Bluff on the James River. These were made of boiler plate encased in watertight wooden casks. One of the batteries used to fire the mines was on loan from the University of Virginia.

Jackman, Pvt., "The Orphan Brigade," Abbeville, Miss.:

> Genl. Breckinridge's division being ordered west marched at an early hour with three days rations in haversacks. At 1 P.M., got to Pintotoc, 15 miles, and bivouacked near town. Though my feet were very sore, went blackberry hunting that evening.

June 20 (Friday)

Commander Semmes, C.S.S. *Alabama*, was in England getting the raider outfitted for sea. There was a problem getting the guns aboard because this was strictly prohibited by the British Parliament. Semmes wrote Confederate Secretary of the Navy Mallory:

> It will doubtless be a matter of delicacy and management to get the *Alabama* safely out of British waters without suspicion, as Mr. [Charles F.] Adams, the Northern envoy, and his numerous satellites are exceedingly vigilant in their espionage. We can not, of course, think of arming her in a British port. This must be done at some concerted rendezvous, to which her battery and most of her crew must be sent in a merchant vessel.... I think well of your suggestion of the East Indies as a cruising ground, and hope to be in the track of the enemy's commerce in those seas as early as October or November next, when I shall doubtless be able to make other rich 'burnt offerings' upon the altar of our country's liberties...

Jackman, Pvt., "The Orphan Brigade," Abbeville, Miss.:

> Mch'd early. Cut my shoes so they did not hurt my feet quite so bad and I marched with greater ease. A very hot and dusty march of 18 miles brought us to La Fayette Springs late in the afternoon. Springs not much improved. I believe a ten-pin alley is all the improvements to be seen with a little stone house over the springs which are chalybeate. Had to cook rations tonight.

June 21 (Saturday)

Slight skirmishing along the Chickahominy east of Richmond. Lee was bringing Jackson from the Valley, and organizing his own forces for an attack on McClellan.

Jackman, Pvt., "The Orphan Brigade," Abbeville, Miss.:

> On the road early. Our course led mostly over pine ridges today. Very hot and dusty. The 4th Ky. marched in front and tried to march us down. About the middle of the day our boys got mad and commenced double-quicking and cheering. Before that my feet were so sore I could scarcely walk, but in the excitement I forgot my feet. We ran over the 4th and went on. At 2 P.M. bivouacked near a nice stream for bathing.

Barber, Pvt., Co. D, 15th Illinois Volunteer Infantry, near La Grange, Tenn.:

> We suffered considerable on this march for want of water. We arrived back in our old camp three and one-half days after we left it, marching sixty miles during the time. We did not remain here in camp long but moved one and one-half miles below Lagrange. This was a very pleasant village and in time of peace contained fifteen hundred inhabitants. The weather was now very hot and the dull monotony of camp life began to be quite irksome.

June 25 (Wednesday)

The Seven Days' Battle began today in a small and mild way when McClellan ordered his forward units to advance on his left flank which, he said, was to be a general movement forward. The troops of Gen. Samuel Heintzelman's corps clashed with the Confederates of Gen. Ben Huger, and a smart little fight began.

Jackman, Pvt., "The Orphan Brigade," to Vicksburg, Miss.:

> Had reveille before daylight and by sunrise our column was on the road. Five miles brought us to Abbeville on the Mississippi Central. The little village looks woebegone now. When I passed it last spring, it was a nice looking little town. Armies, whether friend or foe, desolate a country. The distance from here to Tupelo is 60 miles. We have just gone through a hot and dusty tramp. Bivouacked near town and waiting for transportation on the railroad.

June 26 (Thursday)

The second day of the Seven Days' Battle began with sharp fighting around Mechanicsville, when Gen. A.P. Hill attacked at 3 P.M., after waiting for Jackson to come up. Hill's troops pushed through Mechanicsville, and the Federals fell back into strong prepared positions. Hill threw his men at the position and the attack failed. Jackson was still not on the field. During the night the Federals withdrew to other prepared positions around Gaines Mill, and McClellan ordered supplies moved to the James in the vicinity of Harrison's Landing. McClellan asked for more troops.

On the Mississippi River, the bombardment of Vicksburg began with the mortar boats sending their missiles arching through the sky to their targets.

June 27 (Friday)

The third day of the Seven Days' Battle began with Fitz John Porter holding at Gaines Mill and the Confederates attacking about 3 P.M. and getting their Rebel noses severely bloodied. Jackson was not up again. After dark, the Confederates under Gen. John Bell Hood and George Pickett broke the lines at Gaines Mill, but the force was not sustained, and they had to fall back. Porter, amid the confusion, did a brilliant job of withdrawing his battered corps across the river and back into the folds of the Army of the Potomac. For the day's fighting, Porter lost about 6800 men to Lee's 8700. McClellan began his withdrawal to the James River.

At Vicksburg, the mortars were still beating their deadly tune. The bombardment continued. A canal was dug on the Louisiana side of the river to permit small boats to pass upriver.

In Washington, Lincoln accepted the resignation of Major Gen. Frémont from the Army. Some say it was accepted with alacrity. Frémont was at the end of his military career.

June 28 (Saturday)

On the fourth day of the Seven Days' Battle it was fairly quiet. The long lines of wagons moving towards the James River marked McClellan's retreat. Lee reorganized his forces for yet another attack. McClellan sent a telegram to Lincoln saying the battle was lost because his force was too small. The General blamed the President for the failure.

At Vicksburg, Farragut's fleet moved upriver at 2 A.M. in an attempt to pass the defenses. At 4 A.M., the air between the city and the river was full of flying shells and mortar bombs as the boats raced north and the shore guns tried to sink them. In two hours it was over. All but three of the ships made the passage despite the amount of iron flying around. Something was proven: Gunboats could pass defenses if Union losses could be held to an acceptable level.

Jackman, Pvt., "The Orphan Brigade," to Vicksburg, Miss.:

Late in the evening our regiment marched to the depot to take the cars. A flat car close behind the engine fell to our company. We also had to pile our camp equippage on the same car and when all things were ready for the whistle to blow, it was piled up mountain high, indiscriminately, with men, tents, camp chests, camp kettles, etc.. At 8 P.M. whirled away towards Jackson. We had the benefit of all cinders and sparks from the locomotive and many had their clothing burnt. At midnight, lay over at Grenada for daylight.

June 29 (Sunday)

The fifth day of the Seven Days' Battle. Confederate forces were closely following and attacking McClellan's retreating columns. The Federal rear guard was constantly in action and withstood the repeated assaults. Jackson was late again. Although the Federals safely withdrew, they left more than 2500 sick and wounded at Savage's Station on the Richmond and York Railroad.

Jackman, Pvt., "The Orphan Brigade," to Vicksburg, Miss.:

Got to Canton at noon and lay over one hour or two. I went to a hotel for dinner. You get a ticket, after much crowding, and wait into the dining hall with a jam. Was fortunate enough to get a plate and commenced bawling at a waiter to bring something to eat. Now there were few waiters and many soldiers yelling at them, making the eyes of the said waiters grow large and white from fear and I did not get my roast beef for some time. At last it came and though I always considered my teeth good, yet I could not even make a print in the pieces brought over. Could get nothing else to eat on my plate and seeing all the rest turn waiters for themselves, I took my plate and also went to the cook room. There I found a crowd of soldiers with plates in their hands standing around the cook who was preparing the last thing in the house fit to eat—a beef heart. My heart failed me and I went back to the train and dined out of my haversack. Train arrived at Jackson the middle afternoon and we moved out on Vicksburg road about sundown. Ran as far as Clinton, 18 miles, and the train switched off till morning. During the whole trip the sun was very hot and we had no protection from the heat being on a flat car.

Day, Pvt., Co. B, 25th Massachusetts Volunteer Infantry, New Bern, N.C.:

Companies C and B, together with Capt. Schenck's New York battery company as infantry, returned yesterday afternoon from an expedition across the Neuse river, having been gone three days. We crossed the river Thursday morning... penetrated into the country some four or five miles, coming out at a cross road. There in the shade of the woods we halted for rest and lunch. Put out a few pickets to prevent surprise.... After a little time... there was a stir among the pickets in the rear and it was reported they had made a capture. The authorities went out to see what was up and soon returned with an old horse and cart containing a few bags of meal and driven by a couple of grown-up girls, or more properly speaking, young ladies. They were returning from the mill and were pretty badly frightened on finding themselves prisoners of war. The officers behaved towards them with the utmost gallantry, assuring them that no harm should come to them. On these assurances, they were soon comforted and seemed to regard it as rather a good joke. After holding them close prisoners of war about a couple of hours, they were paroled and allowed to go their way.

We resumed our march and about two miles farther on came out at another cross road. Here we left a few pickets and proceeding a mile or so farther, came out to Latham's plantation. This is the finest plantation I have yet seen, a large two-story modern-built house, with large, nice lawns and surroundings, the road and driveways set with shade and ornamental trees, and everything kept up sleek and nice, showing thrift, wealth and refinement. Here on the lawn in front of the house we bivouacked for the night....

Mrs. Latham was greatly surprised at seeing us, and had made no preparations to receive us. To relieve her embarrassment as much as possible, the boys left her to entertain the officers in the mansion while we took care of ourselves. The boys brought from the barn about two tons of husks and corn leaves, spreading them under the rose-trees on the lawn for beds. They then milked the cows, killed the chickens and pigs, emptied the hives of their honey, and made all necessary preparations for our comfort during our stay. The darky women in the kitchen were kept busy with their fry-pans, hoe-cakes and coffee pots until late hours in the night, and never before were there guests at Latham's whom they were more pleased to see or willing to serve. This was truly the land flowing with milk and honey, and the boys reveled in luxury far into the night, after which they sought rest and repose under the roses.

In the morning, the darky women asked if they might go with us to New Bern. They were told they might and to pick up their traps and follow along. As we were about leaving, Mrs. Latham inquired of Capt. Schenck who was to pay her for the damage we had done. The captain told her to make out her bill and one of these days Uncle Sam and Latham would have a settlement and she could then work it in. As we moved out of the yard we were joined by the darky women, toting big bundles on their heads. Mrs. Latham came running down the lawn shouting after them at the top of her voice, "Here, Kitty, Peggy, Rosa, Dinah, where are you going with those horrid men? Come right back here this minute!" The women, looking back over their shoulders and showing immense rows of ivory, replied to her, "Goo-bye, missus, goo-bye! spec we'es gwine ober to New Bern; goo-bye, missus, goo-bye!" and we marched off down the road, leaving Mrs. Latham alone to reflect on the vicissitudes incident to a state of war. I must needs say, however, that after being so hospitably entertained, it was a rascally, mean trick to run off the servants and leave our sleeping apartments in such a disordered condition. But then, Latham had no business to be away from home. He should have been there, ready to entertain company.

...What the results of this expedition will be, remains for the future historian to record. The trophies were two prisoners of war paroled, four darky women, one horse, a big yellow dog, and lots of fun...

June 30 (Monday)

The sixth day of the Seven Days' Battle. At White Oak Swamp, Lee's Army of Northern Virginia tried to attack McClellan across a swamp. McClellan successfully countered the attack. Longstreet could not break the lines, and, Jackson was late again. By nightfall, McClellan had drawn his lines in around Malvern Hill, where the finale would be played tomorrow.

In any event, McClellan had been beaten, mostly by his own fears, and Richmond had been saved. Some officers of the Army of the Potomac were of the opinion that the army saved itself with little help from "Little Mac."

Jackman, Pvt., "The Orphan Brigade," to Vicksburg, Miss.:

Trains move out to Vicksburg in the morning and the middle of the afternoon running to V. Very hot day. The trees all along the road hung with long gray moss. The train first ran down near town but backed to 4 mile bridge where we dismounted the iron-horse and went into camp. We pitched our tents in beautiful dell under wide-spreading live oaks. After our hot trip it was quite a luxury to extend out on the grass in the cool shade. We lacked water though a brook had run through the valley but now only stagnant pools remained. We had to drink this water which had a sweet, brackish taste. Across the valley, or ravine, was a high trestle work which the iron-horse was continually crossing. Our camp was nearly under the bridges. My friend, J.H.—the *fastidious* gentleman at home, this evening on details today to dig a well near the Col's tent, in the margin of the brook. He looks well. Has off his shoes and his breeches are rolled up nearly to his knees—said breeches have suffered greatly in the rear-end and now that he is in the shade his hat is thrown off and his soiled shirt is open wide at the collar. He is not *very* fastidious now, but is merry withal—is singing and toiling away with pick and spade in quest of water which I hope he will find—that is he and his fellow workers.

Barber, Pvt., Co. D, 15th Illinois Volunteer Infantry, near La Grange, Tenn.:

Picking blackberries was an agreeable pastime and to this luxury we added sweet potatoes. The boys had to get the latter on the sly as General Veatch had forbidden them to forage for them less under proper authority. Some of the boys paid little heed to this order. Two from my mess were out one day and found where there was a large pile of them. They loaded themselves down with them and started for camp, but in order to elude the picket and get into camp, they had to pass the General's headquarters, and in doing so, got caught. Their potatoes were confiscated and they put under guard. The guard proved to be a negligent fellow and they succeeded in slipping away for a few minutes and took their potatoes to camp. Then spying a nice lot that the General had laid up for his own use, they stole every one of them and took them to camp. They did this, they said, in revenge for being arrested, but they went back to their old place and the stupid guard never knew but what they had been there all the time. After awhile the General called them up and gave them a good talking to for disobeying orders. They affected to be very penitent, promised to be good soldiers in the future, and so he let them off, but I imagine that if he had known that the rogues had stolen his "taters," they would not have gotten off so easily. The boys were highly elated with their adventure.

JULY 1862

The month of June had changed things drastically for the South. Jackson had proven more than a match for the Federal generals in the Valley, and Lee had firmly taken over the Army of Northern Virginia. A bloody battle was raging just east of Richmond as the new month began, its outcome uncertain. In the west, Farragut was north of Vicksburg and the Mississippi River was open from Vicksburg to New Orleans and the sea. Much had been gained here but there was still a thorn in the middle—the city of Vicksburg was still in Confederate hands. A full year would go by before that changed.

July 1 (Tuesday)

The seventh day of the Seven Days' Battle. Lee, hoping to destroy the Federals entrenched on Malvern Hill, ordered the attack. With his usual luck lately, nothing seemed to get moving until late afternoon. His artillery proved no match for the Union artillery and, although he tried several assaults, he couldn't get very far. This was one of Lee's costliest mistakes during the war. He would make another exactly a year from now at Gettysburg. His attacks, largely disjointed due to poor coordination, were cut to pieces by the Federal gunners and riflemen. In many cases the Confederate casualties were very heavy, as in a South Carolina regiment that began piling up its dead to serve as breastworks to resist the attack of a Union brigade containing the 83rd Regiment Pennsylvania Volunteers. The Rebel regiment lost its colors in the fracas to Sgt. W.J. Whittrick.

The naval gunboats were providing direct support to the Federals during the Confederate attack. The support was described by the Washington *National Intelligencer*:

> About 5 o'clock in the afternoon the gunboats *Galena*, *Aroostook*, and *Jacob Bell* open from Turkey Island Bend, in the James River, with shot and shell from their immense guns. The previous roar of field artillery seemed as faint as the rattle of musketry in comparison with these monsters of ordnance that literally shook the water and strained the air.... They fired about three times a minute, frequently a broadside at a time, and the immense hull of the *Galena* careened as she delivered her complement of iron and flame. The fire went on... making music to the ears of our tired men.... [Confederate] ranks seemed slow to close up when the naval thunder had torn them apart...

The casualties for both sides for the Seven Days' Battle were heavy, with the South bearing the brunt of them— about 20,000, to 16,000 for the Federals. This represented a much larger percentage for the South of the total number of men engaged—about 88,000, to 115,000 for the Federals.

In the west, the saltwater fleet of Flag Officer Farragut joined the freshwater fleet of Flag Officer Davis north of Vicksburg today. The meeting of the squadrons had a great morale effect in the North, but Vicksburg was still there. Farragut wrote:

> The iron-clads are curious looking things to us salt-water gentlemen; but no doubt they are better calculated for this river than our ships.... They look like great turtles. Davis came on board.... We have made the circuit (since we met at Port Royal) around half the United States and met on the Mississippi.

Jackman, Pvt., "The Orphan Brigade," Vicksburg, Miss.:

> During the forenoon occasionally the boom of cannon would come over the hills from the direction of the river. At 4 P.M., marched into the city, 4 miles, and halted at the court house which is in the centre of town. Here I first saw the "father of waters" and three miles below the city, saw the Federal fleet. Their mortar boats were perhaps closer, having covered the rigging with limbs of trees and crept up along the far banks, but now the leaves had died and they could be plainly seen. I also saw the smoke away up the river where the "Lincunn gun-boats lay." About sundown, detailed for picket duty and was posted upon the river bank above town. Was after dark and very dark before we got to our positions and had great difficulty in marching, the bluffs were so steep and rugged. Though the day had been very hot, yet the wind swept down the river at night cold and disagreeable. Relieved at daylight, or rather we were drawn off, and we returned to the regiment which had bivouacked above town (half a mile) during the night.

South of Corinth, in Mississippi, Col. Philip H. Sheridan, currently commanding a cavalry unit, defeated a force of Confederates. Philip Henry Sheridan was 30 when the war began. Raised in Somerset, Ohio, he falsified his birth certificate so that he could enter the USMA in 1848. Shortly after his arrival at West Point, he became so infuriated with a cadet officer he chased him with a fixed bayonet. This caused his suspension for a year. Returning, he graduated in the Class of '53, and was assigned to an infantry unit on the Rio Grande, and then to the Pacific Northwest. In 1861 he was a captain and served in Missouri and under Halleck during the Shiloh campaign, later moving to Corinth. Hating his staff duty, he became a thorn in the command's side until he was assigned as a colonel in the 2d Michigan Cavalry on May 25, 1862. A victory at Booneville, Miss., gained him his Brigadier's star. Within the year he distinguished himself at Perryville, where he commanded an infantry division, and at Stone's River. In March 1863, he was promoted to Major General with rank to December 31, 1862. At Chickamauga in September 1863, he proved himself as commander of the XX Corps and brought himself to the attention of Grant. When Grant went east in March 1864, he brought Sheridan with him to command the cavalry of the Army of the Potomac. "Little Phil's" aggressive nature led to a string of victories over the Confederates, notably in the Shenandoah Valley, where he adopted a "scorched earth" policy to drive Jubal Early from the Valley. He commanded the Federal cavalry at the Battle of Brandy Station, south of Culpeper C.H., Va. In April 1865, he led the cavalry that broke Lee's line around Petersburg and helped cause the Confederate retreat towards Lynchburg. Driving his troops hard, Sheridan gained a position in front of Lee's army and effectively blocked the escape, leading to the surrender at Appomattox. After the war he served in several capacities, and he was promoted to full general on June 1, 1888. He completed his memoirs three days before his death in Nosquit, Mass., on August 5, 1888, at the age of 57.

Barber, Pvt., Co. D, 15th Illinois Volunteer Infantry, La Grange, Tenn.:

> ... we received orders to make another descent upon Holly Springs. The boys received the order in no enviable frame of mind. The weather was extremely hot and there was a great scarcity of water on that route. After the first six miles we had to travel fifteen miles before we came to a pure stream of water; besides, we had little hopes of our march amounting to anything, and like its predecessor, proving a weary and fruitless one.

In Washington, President Lincoln recommended that Congress give Flag Officer Foote a vote of thanks for his work on the western rivers. Lincoln also approved a federal income tax which provided for a 3% tax on incomes $600 to $10,000 and 5% over $10,000. This one was collected. Another bill approved provided for the railroads to be built across the west.

July 2 (Wednesday)

On the James River in Virginia, McClellan retreated from Malvern Hill to Harrison's Landing in a driving rain. The site had been chosen by Commander Rodgers because it was so situated that gunboats could protect both flanks of the army.

Jackman, Pvt., "The Orphan Brigade," Vicksburg, Miss.:

In the forenoon all quiet. As evening came on, moved down nearer the city in a ravine close to where "Whistling Dick" was mounted. The upper fleet soon after commenced shelling from mortar boats and it seems they knew where we were for most of the shells fell about our ravine. There can be no dodging from mortar shells. One has to stand bolt upright like a duck in the rain. Dr. P. and others got into a sink hole for shelter but came near being buried alive by a shell. First we would hear the mortars go boom, boom, boom away over the bend of the river and soon after could hear the shells whining high up in the air as they came circling over and then they would come shrieking down. If they burst in air, first little tufts of smoke could be seen then the loud reports as they were burst into fragments and immediately the jagged pieces would commence humming down, different sized pieces making the different notes in the demoralizing music. I felt sorry for the inhabitants. Those that were left in the city commenced leaving town. I noticed one lady going out a street with five or six little children about her that were gamboling along unconscious, it seemed, of danger until a bomb burst almost in their midst when they all huddled about their mother for protection. Late in the evening marched to the lower end of the city and after dark went down and bivouacked about the lower water battery. Nearly all night long the lower mortar fleet was throwing shells over us into the city. Could first see the flash, then came the report of the mortar and almost with the thunder came the sound of the screeching shell until it reached the top of the circle and could hear it no longer (but could see the light of the fuse as [if] it were a meteor traveling the heavens) and presently could hear it crashing among the houses up town.

Lincoln today signed the Morrill Act (so named for the Senator from Vermont), which provided for the states to receive thirty thousand acres of land for each senator and representative as an endowment for proposed agricultural and mechanical schools. This was the beginning of the land grant universities.

July 3 (Thursday)

McClellan was safely entrenched at Harrison's Landing, protected by his artillery and the Federal gunboats. Lee probed for a hole to drive his troops through. On both sides, the finger-pointing escalated, as nearly everyone was looking for scapegoats. McClellan chose Lincoln and Congress as his patsies for having failed. After all, they hadn't given him the troops he had asked for (although he outnumbered Lee by 30,000). Lee was silent and was reorganizing his army while thinking of what could be done to John Pope, who was posturing in the Manassas area.

The pundits in Richmond had explanations as to why Lee should have done this or that, although they were safely in the rear when the battle raged. In Richmond, the more gory side of the battle was becoming known.

The mortar boats were giving Vicksburg no peace. Federal gunboats, both north and south of the city, were threatening it.

Barber, Pvt., Co. D, 15th Illinois Volunteer Infantry, Coldwater, Miss.:

> ... we arrived at Coldwater and went into camp. Gen. Lauman, who now commanded the division, sent forward a reconnoitering party which returned and reported no enemy near. We camped on an old cotton field. We were without tents and a heavy storm coming on added greatly to our discomfort. We were also short of rations. William, Rolling, Milton and myself got permission to go out in the country. We soon made a descent upon a large plantation and came down upon the proprietor for dinner, and he knew better than to refuse us. Hungry soldiers will not stand upon ceremony when their inner man is constantly crying "Cupboard." Soon we had the satisfaction of sitting down to a very good meal...

July 4 (Friday)

The celebration of Independence Day was carried on in the North with great enthusiasm, despite the defeat on the Peninsula. Speeches, picnics, more speeches, parades, and more speeches were the order of the day. The South did not celebrate. In fact, Nashville would not celebrate this day for a long time.

On the James River, the C.S.S. *Teaser*, Lt. Davidson, was finally abandoned after a shell from the U.S.S. *Maratanza*, Lt. Stevens, exploded her boiler. The *Teaser* had served the South well. She was adroit at laying mines and other mischief, and today was equipped to launch a balloon, made of old silk frocks, for observation. The balloon, as well as a quantity of insulated wire and mine equipment, were found aboard. Six shells with "peculiar fuzes" were also taken and sent to Capt. Dahlgren at the Washington Navy Yard for examination.

The gunboats supporting McClellan at Harrison's Landing were a formidable force, even to Robert E. Lee, who wrote President Davis:

> The enemy is strongly posted in the neck formed by Herring creek and James River.... The enemy's batteries occupy the ridge along which the Charles City road runs, north to the creek, and his gunboats lying below the mouth of the creek sweep the ground in front of his batteries. Above his encampments which lie on the river, his gunboats also extend; where the ground is more favorable to be searched by their cannon. As far as I can now see there is no way to attack him to advantage; nor do I wish to expose the men to the destructive missiles of his gunboats.... I fear he is too secure under cover of his boats to be driven from his position...

July 5 (Saturday)

An Act to reorganize the U.S. Navy Department, guided through Congress by Senator Grimes of Iowa, increased the number of Bureaus to eight: Yards and Docks, Equipment and Recruiting, Navigation, Ordnance, Construction and Repairs, Steam Engineering, Provisions and Clothing, and Medicine and Surgery.

In Richmond, conscripted soldiers were arriving to fill the ranks of the decimated Army of Northern Virginia. President Davis agreed with Lee that the Confederate armies were not strong enough to begin an offensive at this time.

Day, Pvt., Co. B, 25th Massachusetts Volunteer Infantry, New Bern, N.C.:

> The Fourth was celebrated with salutes from the forts, batteries, and gunboats morning, noon, and night. There were gala times in Camp Oliver last night. A huge bonfire was set from a pyramid of 75 barrels of resin, and when well on fire it lighted up the camp in grand style....

July 6 (Sunday)

At Cape Hatteras, N.C., Gen. Burnside, having accomplished his task of capturing Albemarle Sound and Roanoke Island, sailed with part of his troops to reinforce McClellan on the James River.

Commodore Wilkes was ordered to report to Flag Officer L.M. Goldsborough to support Gen. McClellan on the James River. Secretary of the Navy Gideon Welles instructed Wilkes:

> You will immediately place yourself in communication with Major General McClellan, Commanding the Army of the Potomac, near Harrison's Landing.... It will be your special duty to keep open the navigation of James River and afford protection to all vessels transporting troops or supplies, and generally to cooperate with the army in all military movements.

In Richmond it was reported that "Thousands of fathers, brothers, mothers, and sisters of the wounded are arriving in the city to attend their suffering relations, and to recover the remains of those who were slain."

Barber, Pvt., Co. D, 15th Illinois Volunteer Infantry, Balls Bridge, Tenn.:

> Soon we were ordered to Balls Bridge to guard that. Only the 15th was included in the order. We had a fine camp here. The duty was light and as we were just outside the main army, we had a better chance to forage. I was detailed to go out one day with a forage train, and a squad of us, in charge of Captain Kinyon, was left at a crossing to guard against the approach of the enemy in that direction. Near us was a large farm-house, situated back in the fields. The captain went that way to reconnoiter. He was gone a long time—so long that we became alarmed for his safety.... We crept up cautiously towards the house, and when near we made a charge, but, to our chagrin, we found... that the captain was indeed a prisoner, captured by the bright eyes and handsome face of a young miss whom we found lecturing him soundly on his Yankee principles, while the captain replied in playful good humor. When we broke in upon them, they both seemed surprised. When I told the captain what we came for, he laughed, and we joked him considerably about his heart being captured by a rebel miss.

July 7 (Monday)

The President was coming to Harrison's Landing to visit the Army of the Potomac aboard the U.S.S. *Ariel.* There were several items of some urgency to discuss with "Little Mac," not the least of which was McClellan's idea that he could now advise the President on matters political as well as military. McClellan felt that military operations should not interfere with slavery and should be limited to strictly military forces. Lincoln, an old hand at settling this type of situation, awaited his talks with McClellan.

A convoy system was set up on the James River to move troops and mail. Commander John Rodgers reported to Flag Officer Goldsborough:

> There is to be a convoy of gunboats each day from Harrison's Bar to near the mouth of the Chickahominy, going and returning each day. As there was no better reason for the time than the arrival and departure of the mail from Old Point, it was agreed that at 9 A.M. all the transportation down should sail, convoyed by gunboats—I had selected four for it. And at 3 P.M. all the army transportation to this point should come up, convoyed by the same force.

Jackman, Pvt., "The Orphan Brigade," Vicksburg, Miss.:

> Marched into town again. Troops have to be kept here all the time to support the batteries. We relieved Preston's brigade. Remained until the 10th. Shells falling in the city all the time but fortunately none in range. We had a good time having nothing to do but lie around in the shade, eat five watermelons, etc.. I prefer staying in the city to camp. Here we get good cistern water to drink and are now used to the shells.

July 9 (Wednesday)

In Kentucky, John Hunt Morgan was loose. Driving his cavalry hard, Morgan chased the Federals and captured Tompkinsville, Ky. Morgan, born in Huntsville, Ala., on June 1, 1825, was raised in Kentucky and attended college at Lexington for two years before being expelled. He served as a Lieutenant of Volunteers in the Mexican War. On his return, he purchased a hemp factory and a woolen mill. In 1857, he organized the Lexington Rifles as a local militia unit and took this unit into the Confederate Army in September 1861. He was promoted to colonel of the 2nd Kentucky Cavalry on April 4, 1862. A handsome man, Morgan stood over six feet, was always immaculately dressed, and had the charm and manners of a courtier. His raid into Kentucky during July 1862 caused great alarm among the residents of southern Ohio and Indiana, and caused the diversion of Federal troops for the protection of those localities. He was promoted to Brigadier General on December 11, 1862. His final raid was in July 1863, when, on a wild 24-day exploit, he rampaged through southern Indiana and across Ohio and was captured and imprisoned in Ohio. Escaping, he returned to the Confederate Army and was killed in a surprise cavalry raid at Greeneville, Tenn., on September 3, 1864.

Gen. Lee, opposite McClellan on the James River, tried his hand at using field artillery against the guns of the gunboats in the river:

> After a through reconnaissance of the position taken up by the enemy on James River, I found him strongly posted and effectually flanked by his gunboats.... I caused field batteries to play on his forces, and on his transports, from points on the river below. But they were too light to accomplish much, and were always attacked with superior force by the gunboats....

Three gunboats, the U.S.S. *Commodore Perry, Shawsbeen*, and *Ceres*, used field artillery in a very portable way by landing a field piece from one of the ships, accompanied by soldiers and a party of sailors, at Hamilton, N.C., where the steamer *Wilson* was captured.

July 10 (Thursday)

Continual Confederate concern about the gunboats was noted by a British Army observer, Col. Garnet J. Wolseley, who wrote that he "noted with some interest the superstitious dread of gunboats which possessed the Southern soldiers. These vessels of war, even when they have been comparatively harmless, had several times been the means of saving northern armies."

In Mississippi, near Guntown, the Federals and Confederates got together under a flag of truce to discuss the war and other topics of the day in a friendly fashion.

In Kentucky, Morgan called for the citizens to "rise and arm, and drive the Hessian invaders from [their] soil." Not too much response, although the Federals did capture 90 guerrillas drilling in a field near Gallatin, Tenn.

John Pope was shooting off his mouth again. He now declared that the people would be held responsible for injury to railroads, attacks on trains, etc. In the case of damage by guerrillas, the people would be held financially responsible. If any Federal soldier were fired upon from a house, the house would be razed, and people detected in acts against the army would be shot without due civil process. This same tactic had been tried by Halleck in Missouri. It hadn't worked there, and it wouldn't work here.

July 11 (Friday)

"Old Brains" Halleck was promoted to General-in-Chief of all U.S. land forces. Halleck was a fusspot, a procrastinator, an envious man, and a fairly good administrator. An excellent armchair general, as were some others in this war, he commanded the army at Corinth poorly and showed no aggressiveness. He would remain in this post in Washington until Grant was appointed to it in March 1864.

The Federal Congress passed an act for the relief of relatives of the officers and men who died aboard the U.S.S. *Cumberland* and *Congress* when these vessels were destroyed by the C.S.S. *Virginia* in March.

July 12 (Saturday)

Morgan captured Lebanon, Ky., causing panic in the cities along the Ohio. The citizens of Cincinnati, Evansville, and Louisville asked for protection.

In New Orleans, the city was reported to be cleaner than ever "in the memory of the oldest inhabitant and never more healthy at this time of the year." Although ruling the city with an iron hand, Gen. Benjamin Butler also accomplished many good things. One was the control of the dreaded and deadly yellow fever. Every year since its settlement, the city had been plagued by this fever, which decimated the population every few years. Some years thousands would die, and those who fled to the shores of Lake Pontchartrain were the ones who were lucky. The fever was caused by the pools of stagnant water lying in the streets and empty lots of the city where the mosquitoes bred. Butler took action to have these puddles filled with dirt and sand and, in doing so, unknowingly solved a major part of the problem. The war years showed a great decline in yellow fever.

July 13 (Sunday)

Murfreesboro, Tenn., saw some action when Confederate Nathan Bedford Forrest led his cavalry into the town and captured the Union garrison.

Lee was beginning to move more of his army away from the Peninsula and towards the west. At Gordonsville, Jackson did some skirmishing with the Federals. Union forces burned the railroad bridge over the Rapidan River in central Virginia.

Lincoln was beginning to have serious doubts about McClellan's ability to get results from the Army of the Potomac.

July 14 (Monday)

Well, it finally happened. The worst nightmare of old sailors came true. Congress passed an act stating that

> ... the spirit ration in the Navy of the United States shall forever cease, and... no distilled spirituous liquors shall be admitted on board vessels of war, except as medical stores... there shall be allowed and paid to each person in the Navy now entitled to the ration, five cents per day in commutation and lieu thereof, which shall be in addition to their present pay.

Gen. John Pope's loudmouth posturing was getting worse all the time.

Jackman, Pvt., "The Orphan Brigade," Vicksburg, Miss.:

> Struck tents, loaded the wagons, and moved camp to the suburbs of town. Established in a grassy ravine, a few trees standing about to lend us shade. The day has been very hot. We shall have cistern water hauled to us all the time now. Regiment came in at dark.

Gen. John Hunt Morgan had now reached Cynthiana, Ky., with his raiding cavalry. The citizens of southern Indiana and Ohio were in an uproar.

July 15 (Tuesday)

The C.S.S. *Arkansas*, Lt. Isaac Brown, was lying up the Yazoo River, more or less minding her own business, when the U.S.S. *Carondelet*, Commander Walke, and the U.S.S. *Tyler*, Lt. Gwin, engaged her. Both Walke and Gwin had Army sharpshooters aboard to fend off the Rebels who fired from the river bank. In the fight that followed, Brown partially disabled both Union ships and entered the Mississippi River above Vicksburg, much to the surprise of the Union river fleet. Brown took the

Arkansas through heavy fire to refuge under the guns of Vicksburg, arriving badly damaged and with many wounded and dead aboard. Farragut commented that nothing could be seen in the night except the flashes of the guns. Brown's daring brought him thanks from President Davis and the Confederate Congress and high praise from the Confederate commander at Vicksburg, Gen. Earl Van Dorn. It also brought him promotion to the rank of Commander.

Farragut took his fleet past the Confederate guns at Vicksburg but with heavy damage to two ships, the *Winona*, and the *Sumter*.

Jackman, Pvt., "The Orphan Brigade," Vicksburg, Miss.:

> At 9 A.M. heard firing up the river and went up on the bluff to see the cause. Could see a commotion in the upper fleet which was sending up a dark cloud of smoke and firing. Presently we saw the C.S. ram *Arkansas* coming around the bend and soon after landed at the levee under our batteries where there was an enthusiastic crowd assembled to welcome her. Late in the evening marched to our old positions—about the railroad cut, below the depot, or rather the engine house. The air was full of shells. Just as we were filing off the railroad up a street where there was a high bluff that would protect us in a measure from the shells, all the upper batteries opened and were replied to by the upper fleet dropping down before the city. The first intimation we had of this movement was of long conical shells—2 feet in length and 10 inches in diameter, [which] came shrieking just over our heads making something [of] the noise of a man screaming in agony. Soon the fight became general. The mortar fleet above and below filled the air with bursting shells; the fleet vomited forth iron and flame; our batteries thundered, making the very earth tremble; hot shot from the fleet were flying through the air mimicking the forked-tongued lightning and the flash of artillery made the night as light as day. To heighten the grand scene, some buildings up town took fire from the hot missiles and a pillar of flame pierced the very heavens. As the storm-cloud passes, so did this. Soon a perfect silence brooded over the city and we went to sleep. I hardly think the firing lasted an hour.

July 16 (Wednesday)

In Paris, Napoleon III received Confederate Commissioner John Slidell, who requested France's formal recognition of the Confederacy and the aid of French warships in breaking the blockade, in exchange for cotton. France declined.

Today a precedent was set. The first (by date of rank) Rear Admiral in the history of the United States was appointed: Flag Officer David G. Farragut.

The Navy's overall officer rank structure was reformed to include the ranks of Commodore and Lt. Commander. Three Rear Admirals were to fly a square blue flag at the mainmast head: Farragut, L.M. Goldsborough, and Du Pont. Rear Admirals were to rank with Army Major Generals, the highest rank in the Army at that time.

July 17 (Thursday)

Lincoln signed several bills today. Among them was a bill authorizing the use of postage stamps as money, due to the lack of metal coins in small denominations. Another bill authorized the call-up of men between the ages of 18 and 45 for nine months' militia service. This bill was interpreted as a draft, and it was never put into effect. Grant assumed command of all western troops.

The Confederacy suffered from an institution that would adversely affect the North in the future: the purchase of substitutes for those conscripted. The conscription laws, never popular, led to much evasion and subterfuge by those eligible but not willing to go. Eligible males were enrolled much the same way in both North and South. Geographic areas were "surveyed" by local officials, who listed all those of the proper age for conscription. These lists were then used as the basis for calling up the men. Many people, learning that an "enrollment" was to be held, would visit relatives in other places during the enrollment to avoid being listed.

Another precedent was set on this day. Congress passed an act which established that

> ... every officer, seaman, or marine, disabled in the line of duty, shall be entitled to receive for life, or during his disability, a pension from the United States, according to the nature and degree of his disability, not exceeding in any case his monthly pay.

July 18 (Friday)

Morgan's raiders crossed the Ohio River and raided the town of Newburg, Ind., located near Evansville.

In England, a motion in the House of Commons to mediate the struggle between the warring factions was discussed and withdrawn from consideration.

In the North at this time, it was still relatively easy for a citizen to travel within the Union without restriction. The South, however, had imposed rather severe travel restrictions on all its citizens, requiring them to have "passports" to travel from place to place within the Confederacy. In essence, a person had to have a "passport" to travel from Richmond to Petersburg, Chattanooga, Knoxville, or Atlanta. The granting of these documents was usually the purview of the War Department, and was supervised by the Provost Marshal of each locality. Richmond, the capital, was most concerned about "spies" carrying information across the lines to the Federals.

Jackman, Pvt., "The Orphan Brigade," Vicksburg, Miss.:

> About 12 m. a piece of a shell wounded one of Co. G badly while lying in his tent. Many of our tents have been cut up but no one hurt until today. One night, a party was in the Q.M.'s tent playing "poker" and while piling up the "chips" a piece of shell came through the tent scattering the "tea party" as well as the "chips." Nobody hurt. In the evening regiment in town on duty. The mortar fleets keep up shelling. They have regular hours: commence at 10 A.M. and continue until 12 when they knock off for dinner; then commence at 2 P.M. and continue shelling until night. One day "Mc" said when they had stopped for dinner that he hoped they would have "bony fish" to eat so they would be a long time getting them down.

July 19 (Saturday)

Morgan's men and Union troops clashed near Paris, Ky.

Yesterday, Secretary of the Navy Gideon Welles informed the Fleet that the President, by act of Congress, now might appoint three enlisted men per year as midshipmen to the Naval Academy. Each of the three new Admirals was requested to nominate one man from his command, not over 18 years of age and

> ...they must be of good moral character, able to read and write well, writing from dictation and spelling with correctness, and to perform with accuracy the various operations of the primary rules of arithmetic, viz, numeration, and the addition, subtraction, multiplication, and division of whole numbers.

Barber, Pvt., Co. D, 15th Illinois Volunteer Infantry, en route to Memphis, Tenn.:

> ... the hottest day we had yet experienced. The army moved very slowly, resting ten minutes every half hour, in the shade, when we could find it, but notwithstanding, scores of men would drop down, some dying instantly, others so far gone as not to be able to move. It was a common sight that day to see dead soldiers by the roadside. I came very near going under, but by exerting every nerve, I managed to get along, but it injured me.

A naval court-martial meeting in Richmond acquitted Flag Officer Tattnall with honor for ordering the destruction of C.S.S. *Virginia*, née *Merrimack*, on May 11th, after the evacuation of Norfolk. The court found that "the only alternative... was to abandon and burn the ship then and there, which in the judgment of the court, was deliberately and wisely done..."

July 20 (Sunday)

Barber, Pvt., Co. D, 15th Illinois Volunteer Infantry, entry into Memphis, Tenn.:

> ... when within but six miles of the city, I had a touch of sunstroke. The doctor was near me and put me in an ambulance, so I did not experience its worst effects. The army halted within a few miles of the city to clean up as much as possible, so as to make as decent an appearance as they could while passing through.
>
> A large number of the boys had become so immodest as not to care for appearances. Indeed, the whole army was in a deplorable condition for want of clothing. If a soldier had a sound seat in his pants, it was immediately noticed, it being an exception to the general rule, and not a few of the soldiers marched through the city with pocket handkerchiefs hanging out behind, but despite our appearance, we were greeted with cheers and laughter. Many a fair damsel came out to see us pass, and if they wondered at the manner in which some carried their handkerchiefs,

they did not say much, but occasionally we could see a smile lurking around their dimpled cheeks as they noticed some who were more conspicuous than others. The boys felt rather proud of their rags. It caused so much notice to be taken of them. We went into camp one and one-half miles south of the city....

July 21 (Monday)

Confederate raiders were busy around the Union-held city of Nashville, Tenn., burning bridges on the road to Chattanooga. This type of activity would continue during much of the war.

On the Ohio River at Evansville, Ind., the U.S. steamers *Clara Dolsen* and *Rob Roy*, and the tug *Restless*, all under the command of Commander Alexander M. Pennock, arrived with a load of troops to protect the city from Confederate guerrillas. The ships landed the troops and retook Henderson, Ky., across the river, burned several boats, and began patrolling the river against attack. This action, requested by Indiana's Governor Oliver P. Morton, brought kudos from Major Gen. John Love, who wrote Commander Pennock expressing "the gratitude with which the citizens of Indiana and of this locality will regard the prompt cooperation of yourself and your officers in this emergency, which threatened their security."

Jackman, Pvt., "The Orphan Brigade," Vicksburg, Miss.:

> Reg't. in town on duty. At night our company deployed on the river bank with Co. G to picket. While in camp the mosquitoes never bothered us on account of the camp fires but when we would get out on duty like this where we were not even allowed to smoke a pipe, the mosquitoes would give us "fits." I had often heard of their being so large in Texas that they carried a brick-bat under their wings with which to whet their bills but I never believed the story until I came to Vicksburg.

Barber, Pvt., Co. D, 15th Illinois Volunteer Infantry, entry into Memphis, Tenn.:

> The first thing we did after being settled in camp was to draw clothing and then Gen. Hurlbut, in consideration of our having so long been deprived of the luxuries and associations of civilization, granted five passes a day from each company to go to the city, said pass lasting 24 hours to be returned to division headquarters when the holder returned.... Each soldier was required to go armed with a bayonet or revolver. The rebel citizens were very violent yet, and the soldiers would not brook insult or hear our flag spoken lightly of.... The evil disposed now began to plunge into all kinds of dissipation, frequenting drinking saloons and other places of infamous resort....

July 22 (Tuesday)

President Davis was trying to help Isaac Brown get crewmen for the C.S.S. *Arkansas*. Davis wired Gov. John J. Pettus of Mississippi:

> Captain Brown of the *Arkansas* requires boatmen, and reports himself doomed to inactivity by the inability to get them. We have a large class of river boatmen and some ordinary seamen on our Gulf Coast who must now be unemployed. Can you help Captain Brown to get an adequate crew?

Davis's plea came at an opportune time. Today the U.S.S. *Essex*, Commander W.D. Porter, and the Union ram *Queen of the West*, Lt. Col. Ellet, attacked the C.S.S. *Arkansas*, Lt. Brown, while she was at anchor with a disabled engine and lying under the guns of Vicksburg. Although many of Brown's crew were ashore sick or wounded, Brown fought gallantly. The *Essex* got into a close, stiff fight with Brown's ship but finally the Union ship broke contact and went downriver amid a hail of shot from shore batteries to join Farragut's fleet below the city. The *Queen of the West* attempted to ram the *Arkansas*, but with little effect. The Union ram then went back upriver in a badly beaten condition.

Brown, now thoroughly irate, fired the steam engine and steered his ship up and down the river in a show of defiance, but under cover of the shore batteries at Vicksburg. A member of the *Arkansas* crew, Dabney M. Scales, described the action in a letter to his father:

> At 4 o'clock on the morning of the 22nd, I was awakened by the call to quarters. Hurrying to our stations, with not even a full complement of men for 3 guns, our soldiers having left just the night before, we discovered the enemy coming right down on us.... We did not have men enough to heave the anchor up and get underway, before the enemy got to us, even if

we had had steam ready. So we had to lay in to the bank, and couldn't meet him on anything like equal terms.... The *Essex* came first, firing on us with her three bow guns. We replied with our two bow guns as long as they could be brought to bear, which was not a very long time, as our vessel being stationary, the enemy soon came too much on our broadside for these guns, and their crews had to be shifted to the broadside guns. In the meantime, the *Essex* ranged up alongside us, and at the distance of 20 feet poured in a broads[ide] which crashed against our sides like nothing that I ever heard before.... We were so close that our men were burnt by the powder of the enemy's guns....

All this time the Ram [*Queen of the West*] was not idle, but came close down on the heels of his consort.... We welcomed him as warmly as we could with our scanty crew. Just before he got to us, we managed by the helm and with the aid of the starboard propellor, to turn our bow outstream a little, which prevented him from getting a fair lick at us. As it was, he glanced round our side and ran aground just astern of us.

On the bluffs above the river, John Jackman was on sentry duty and had a ringside view of the action between the gunboats.

Jackman, Pvt., "The Orphan Brigade," Vicksburg, Miss.:

Companies withdrawn before daylight but a few of us were left until after sun up to watch the river to see that no one crossed. We were stationed about 60 yards apart and ordered to secrete ourselves but watch vigilantly. I hid away "neath a rosy bower" by a little white cottage, now tenantless, and waited for morn. Soon the gray light of morning came—then came the "powerful king of day, rejoicing in the East." The landscape was beautiful and I was admiring it, peeping out from my "rosy bower"—and occasionally out of the corner of my eye at two large frigates just below me, their sides bristling with guns and wondering what would be the consequence were they to give us a broadside—when "Whistling Dick" & Co. commenced thundering up the river and I forsook my "bower" to see what was going on. I saw the *Essex** coming down and give the *Arkansas* a broadside. After that, she closed all her ports. About that time, the Corporal came along withdrawing us and we started up town. Before we got up the bank a heavy water-battery commenced firing over our heads at the *Essex* and the concussion was so great from the balls passing over that we were almost lifted off the ground. The *Essex* kept on her way, our guns peppering her but the balls would bounce off as raindrops from a duck's back. Today our regiment lounged about the grounds of Prentiss' Castle. The place shows him to have been a man of great taste as well as orator. We were conspicuous here and were shelled away in the evening about the time we were starting for camp.

* Reported at the time to be the *Essex* but afterwards it was stated that it was the *Queen of the West*.

In Livingston, Tenn., Gen. John Hunt Morgan's raiders arrived from their foray into Kentucky and Indiana.

July 23 (Wednesday)

Major Gen. Henry Halleck assumed command of all Union Army forces today. At Carmel Church, just south of Fredericksburg, Va., Federal cavalry raided a Southern supply depot, destroying supplies.

In northern Virginia, John Pope was at it again. This time he declared that any male who refused to take the oath of allegiance to the Union would be sent south. If he was caught again in the area, he would be considered a spy. Any person violating his oath would be shot and his property confiscated.

There seemed to be a surplus of mortar boats on the Mississippi River at the moment, so some were transferred to the James River to support the Army of the Potomac. Asst. Secy. of the Navy Fox wrote Major Gen. John G. Barnard:

Part of the mortar fleet are ordered to James River and should be there by the 1st proximo. There is no army to cooperate at Vicksburg where we have been lying two months, and the keeping open James River up to McClellan's position is the first duty of the Navy, so we ordered twelve of the vessels there.

If a fort is erected below you on the right bank of the James (and I see no obstacle) or if offensive or defensive operations are undertaken I think the mortar will not come amiss.... The iron boats are progressing.... We have forty underweigh, and are putting others in hand as fast as contracts for engines shall be made. The machinery for manufacturing marine engines is limited.

The rapidity with which the North could build ironclads far outclassed the South's, causing a wide disparity of naval forces.

The Confederate Army in the west was also on the move. Bragg was moving his troops from Tupelo, Miss., south to Mobile, then to Montgomery, and finally to Chattanooga. This trip of 776 miles was carried out using six railroads. The situation of railroads in the South was disastrous. Most of the lines were local, most were of different gauges, and all were in poor repair. This was in contrast with the North, where Gen. Herman Haupt could build railroads almost as fast as shovels could turn dirt.

July 24 (Thursday)

Admiral Farragut's river fleet departed the area around Vicksburg today for Baton Rouge and New Orleans, leaving five gunboats to guard the river. The falling water level, his saltwater ships requiring a deeper draft, and his sick crews necessitated a move. The Confederacy still could get limited supplies from the west, which were brought over under cover of the guns of Vicksburg or at night. To counter this, Flag Officer Davis, with Army support, patrolled the river from Helena, Ark., to Vicksburg. This not only cut the flow of supplies, it prevented the South from building forts along this stretch of river.

Jackman, Pvt., "The Orphan Brigade," Vicksburg, Miss.:

> In town again. Not well—have been feeling badly several days. At night a detail was made to report to the *Arkansas* for duty and I had to go from our company. Twas first thought we were to make up the crew and one fellow objected so loudly that he ran off. We all objected to such a fate and Lieut. McC. in charge of the whole detail from the brigade said that if such was the case, he would resist. We had to wait until morning for all the detail to get together.

July 25 (Friday)

Jackman, Pvt., "The Orphan Brigade," Vicksburg, Miss.:

> The Lt. found out that we were to do some work at the *Arkansaw* and as I did not feel well enough to work, tried to get off, but of course no. Went down to the boat and reported. The Captain told us that we would not be wanted until dark so we went up town and took up quarters in a large mansion then vacated. There were fifty on the detail. The boys had piano music and dancing with plenty of books to read.... The ram had gone up the river and did not get back until 9 P.M.. We went down then and found out our job was to coal the boat which had to be done by carrying the coal some distance in bags. I didn't work much. Got through by midnight and went back to our house. All day two mortars had been at work which was the last shelling done that season.

Day, Pvt., Co. B, 25th Massachusetts Volunteer Infantry, New Bern, N.C.:

> The colonel, thinking that guard duty and dress parade are not quite exercise enough for us, has ordered company drills in the forenoon. The company officers do not take very kindly to this, and thinking it a good opportunity to give the sergeants a little practice in drilling the companies, they shirk out of it every time they can invent an excuse to do so. The companies are sent out under command of the orderlies or some other of the sergeants frequently. B company moved out of the company street on to the parade ground, and after executing a few brilliant maneuvers, starts off across the fields to the Trent road, a little out of sight of the camp, and here in the shade of the trees we sit down and await the recall, when we march back into camp with all the pomp and circumstance of glorious war. The duty has been performed, and everybody seems well enough satisfied, except perhaps the performers.
>
> Gen. Foster has his wife and daughter with him here, which must make it very agreeable for him. Mrs. Foster is engaged in works of love and mercy around the hospitals, while Miss Foster, a young lady of some 16 or 17 years, is pretty much engaged in horseback riding and having a good time generally. She is quite a military character, as we notice that when she and the general ride past here, she always returns the salutes from the sentinels as gracefully as the general. She frequently rides past here alone, and the sentinels along the street take great pride in honoring her with a present arms, a compliment which she never fails to acknowledge by a graceful wave of her hand and her face wreathed with smiles.

July 28 (Monday)

In Liverpool, England, the steamer *Enrica*, soon to be called the C.S.S. *Alabama*, was to sail soon for the Azores, where it would rendezvous with the bark

Agrippina, Capt. Alexander McQueen, for the purpose of transferring guns, ammunition, coal, and other cargo to the *Alabama*. Capt. Raphael Semmes was getting his job done speedily.

Jackman, Pvt., "The Orphan Brigade," Vicksburg, Miss.:

> Reg't. got off this morning. This evening I learn a car in the train on which our regiment was moving broke down but no one seriously hurt. I hope to follow the troops in a few days. Remained in this camp until I left for my command Aug 6th. I only had to take medicine two or three days as the fever did not get a good hold upon my system. I then applied to follow the regiment but could not get transportation. Went to Vicksburg one day and J.B. and I went out a short way into the country the day before I left, after peaches, the only time I was out of camp. That camp was like all—monotonous. The evening before I left J.B. and I got some reeds and made a nice bunk to sleep on at 2 o'clock A.M.

July 29 (Tuesday)

A woman accused of being a Confederate spy was captured near Warrenton, Va., by the Federals. Belle Boyd was accused of being a spy and mail courier and sent to the Old Capital Prison in Washington (the current site of Ft. McNair). Released on August 28th for lack of evidence, she would return to her chosen work with zeal.

July 30 (Wednesday)

Halleck ordered McClellan to move all his sick and wounded to Harrison's Landing for evacuation. This would relieve the Army of the Potomac of the burden of moving so many men later.

Ben Butler, in New Orleans, had confiscated the church bells which had been donated to be smelted down into cannon and sent them to Boston. Today, they were sold at auction in Boston.

Generals Stuart and Jackson visited the Confederate War Department today, much to the delight of the employees and visitors.

July 31 (Thursday)

President Davis informed Gen. Lee that on July 22nd a cartel for exchange of prisoners had been signed with the Federal government. He also informed Lee that because of Gen. John Pope's declarations about treatment of citizens, any commissioned officers captured from Pope's army were to be treated as felons rather than as prisoners of war. This was a drastic step and one that Lee would invoke but sparingly.

AUGUST 1862

The hospitals in Richmond and the North were still fairly crowded with wounded from the Seven Days' Battle east of Richmond. Many who were badly wounded or suffered amputation had died. The crowd in Richmond of relatives who came to collect their dead or wounded was thinning out. In the west, Vicksburg still held strong against the river gunboats and Grant's army. Buell was shuffling along from Corinth to Chattanooga at a slow pace. Bragg, at Chattanooga, was getting ready for a campaign into Kentucky to rouse the state and get volunteers. He might have better luck than John Hunt Morgan did, but it was doubtful.

August 1 (Friday)

President Davis was upset about supposed actions against civilians and the arming of Negroes in the North. Primarily, he was concerned about John Pope's actions in the Manassas area and the arming of the slaves in the parts of South Carolina under Union control. He wrote to Lee with his grievances.

Some in Richmond believed that because Vicksburg successfully withstood the gunboat assault, New Orleans should not have been surrendered without a battle. No comparison between terrain was taken into account. Vicksburg was on a bluff and hard to assault. New Orleans was flat and had no defense against attack from the river.

August 2 (Saturday)

A minor bureaucratic breakthrough occurred when Jonathan Letterman, Medical Director for the Army of the Potomac, had his plan approved for the establishment of the Army Ambulance Corps. In effect, this transferred the control of ambulances from the Quartermaster Corps to the Medical Director and permitted the ambulances to carry medical supplies. This innovation was to have a major impact on the treatment and care of the wounded in future battles.

The modern torpedo was being invented. William H. Aspinwall, a merchant, wrote Assistant Secretary of the Navy Fox:

> I have been thinking for some time about the probability that a properly shaped cylindrical shot fired 6 or 8 feet under water will be the next improvement on iron clad vessels. At short range great effect could be attained below the iron plating.... I have the plan for firing a gun projecting 6 or 10 feet below the water line of a vessel, which I think would work well, if it is found that shot can be relied on to do the intended injury—under water.

August 4 (Monday)

After over a year of trial and error, Lincoln told the military to get rid of the deadwood officers and incompetents and make an effort to promote more worthy officers. This had been a continuing problem because most of the original units elected their officers. Many of these officers were political hacks who were hard to get rid of.

At Aquia Creek, north of Fredericksburg, Gen. Burnside's troops from North Carolina unloaded from their steamer transports and got ready to defend Washington against Lee's projected advance into northern Virginia.

In New Orleans, Gen. Benjamin Butler began his version of a social program by collecting a total of $341,916 from local "secessionists" for the benefit of the poor in the city.

Lincoln, offered two Negro regiments from Indiana for the Union Army, declined, suggesting they be used as laborers.

August 5 (Tuesday)

Recruiting for troops in the North was going well, both to fill the old regiments and to create new ones. The problem was this: Now that some of the older regiments were decimated, were the survivors to be assigned to new units, or to fill up the old regiments? In both armies, "regimental identity" was quite often the thing that held units together. Some men, when consolidated with other regiments (which had also been decimated), deserted rather than serve under a new regimental flag.

There was skirmishing at Malvern Hill and elsewhere east and north of Richmond, as the two armies sparred.

August 6 (Wednesday)

Within gunboat range of the Mississippi River, north of Baton Rouge, Major Gen. John Cabell Breckinridge led about 2600 Confederates through the fog and into a fight with about 2500 Union troops commanded by Brigadier Gen. Thomas Williams. Even with limited visibility, the Rebel attack was turned aside, and the Federals ended the battle by 10 A.M. with the aid of the gunboats U.S.S. *Sumter*, *Cayuga*, *Kineo*, and *Katahdin*. Losses were reasonably heavy for the numbers engaged. The Confederates pulled back north and began to fortify Port Hudson. The C.S.S. *Arkansas* dropped down from Vicksburg to lend a hand and got into trouble.

C.S.S. *Arkansas*, Lt. Henry Stevens temporarily in command, having become unmanageable due to engine failure while advancing to support a Confederate attack on Baton Rouge, was engaged by her old enemy, the U.S.S. *Essex*, Commander W.D. Porter. Lt. Stevens recognized the hopeless condition of the ship, shotted his guns, and ordered her destroyed to prevent her capture. He later reported: "It was beautiful to see her, when abandoned by Commander and crew, and dedicated to sacrifice, fighting the battle on her own hook." Her creator, Lt. Brown, now a Commander, had taken leave to recover from an illness. Gen. Van Dorn, commander at Vicksburg, ordered the ship to support the ground attack. Stevens tried his best, but the odds were against the battered old lady making it. Had the *Arkansas* been serviceable, Baton Rouge might have been retaken and the Red River supply route reopened for the Confederacy. For want of boiler parts the battle may have been lost.

It was hardly safe anywhere now, even in an ambulance. Brigadier Gen. Robert L. McCook of Ohio was not feeling well and was riding in an ambulance from Athens, Ala., going north, when he was attacked and wounded by a band of guerrillas. He later died from his wounds.

Jackman, Pvt., "The Orphan Brigade," Jackson, Miss.:

> All that were able had to get up and prepare to start for the regiment. I did not object to rising from my reed bed which was almost equal [to] a spring mattress for I wanted to be off—my friend was not able to go and could use it. After daylight about 60

from the reg't. able to go went to the railroad but we could not immediately get a train so we came back to camp about noon and drew new uniforms and other clothing—the first we had drawn for a long time. We got started in time to reach Jackson a little after dark. There were 200 or 400 men from Breckinridge's division in transition. Left Jackson at 8 P.M. on the G.N. & W.R.R.. Lay down on the floor of a box car and went to sleep.

August 7 (Thursday)

President Lincoln, accompanied by Secretaries Seward and Stanton, went to the Navy Yard today in Washington to see a demonstration of the "Rafael" repeating cannon. Later, Capt. Dahlgren took them aboard a steamer to cool off and rest a bit.

The Federals left Malvern Hill to the Confederates again today. This was the second time the bluecoats abandoned this defense position. This time it was voluntary.

Jackman, Pvt., "The Orphan Brigade," Camp Moore, La.:

> Waked up just as day was dawning and found that we were going lightning speed towards New Orleans. Dense pine forests were on either side of the road. Soon passed through Brook Haven, a nice little town. Summit and Hazelhurst are also pretty towns. At 9 A.M. arrived at Tangipahoa, 80 miles from New Orleans and 100 miles from Jackson, Miss. We were now in Louisiana. Camp Moore is a short distance from the station and we disembarked and took up quarters in the camp. Camp nicely arranged, "shanties" and tents. There is a stream circling the camp of the clearest water I ever saw. I believe it is called a river, but I don't know the name.* This is where all the Louisiana troops met to organize before starting for the seat of war. Tangipahoa is a small village, built since the railroad.

August 8 (Friday)

In northern Alabama there was a very serious problem of guerrillas firing into trains as they went along the tracks through the forests. To counter this, the Union commander ordered the arrest of local ministers and other leading churchmen and placed one of them a day on the trains—a rather harsh remedy, and there was no indication that it worked.

In Baltimore those avoiding the draft by leaving the area were arrested. This practice was so widespread that the War Department issued orders to prevent draft evasion throughout the rest of the North.

The Confederacy was attempting to maintain its credit with England by placing funds in the hands of British brokers located in the South. The inflation rate for Southern currency on the foreign market was high, and it made the rate of exchange, 200 to 210 percent, disadvantageous to the South.

August 9 (Saturday)

Gen. John Pope was in the vicinity of Culpeper, Va., advancing towards Orange C.H. and Gordonsville. Jackson's corps of troops was just south of Culpeper on the north bank of the Rapidan, waiting to attack Pope's troops. However, Gen. Nathaniel Banks got in the first lick at Cedar Mountain when his corps successfully attacked two of Jackson's divisions. Banks was beating them pretty badly when A. P. Hill piled into the fracas in a counterattack. Banks pulled back, still with his force intact.

In Richmond, the news of McClellan's departure from the Peninsula was greeted with joy. There was skirmishing going on in Missouri and Louisiana.

August 10 (Sunday)

More skirmishing around Cedar Run, near Culpeper, Va. Jackson's and Pope's men were too close not to clash occasionally.

On the Mississippi River south of Baton Rouge, Admiral Farragut carried out his threat to retaliate against the town of Donaldsonville if the local citizens didn't quit firing on the ships as they passed:

> ...[I] sent a message to the inhabitants that if they did not discontinue this practice, I would destroy the town. The last time I passed up to Baton Rouge to the support of the army, I... heard them firing upon the vessels coming up, first upon the *Sallie Robinson* and next upon the *Brooklyn.* In the latter case they made a mistake, and it was so quickly returned that they ran away. The next night they fired again upon the *St. Charles.* I therefore ordered them to send their women and children out of the town, as

* The Tangipahoa River.

I certainly intended to destroy it on my way down the river, and I fulfilled my promise to a certain extent. I burned down the hotels and wharf buildings, also the dwelling houses and other buildings of a Mr. Phillips Landry, who is said to be a captain of guerrillas.

Jackman, Pvt., "The Orphan Brigade," en route to Baton Rouge, La.:

Early started on the march for the division encamped near Baton Rouge. There are 2 to 300 of the division along (some that started from Vicksburg are left at Camp Moore), under the command of Lt. Col. Crump, and old "yellow hammer," I believe. Hot day. Our march led through a pine forest. Just before we stopped for the night passed through Greensburg, the parish-town of St. Helena. Marched 10 miles today.

August 11 (Monday)

Jackson withdrew for a time from Cedar Run to south of the Rapidan near Gordonsville, a major rail junction between the Valley and Richmond.

Grant, near Corinth, reorganized and refitted his army. He ordered that slaves entering his lines be used for labor and paid either in wages or in kind.

August in Louisiana was not really the time for a march through the woods, but Jackman had little choice in the matter. The idea was to be as comfortable as possible in the circumstances.

Jackman, Pvt., "The Orphan Brigade," en route to Baton Rouge, La.:

The old Colonel tried to get us to fall in and march in order but such a dusty arrangement didn't suit us; so we divided off in squads to please ourselves. Been another hot day. Our road led through an interminable pine forest. The country is perfectly level and there is no undergrowth to obstruct the view—can see a long way through to the woods, the pines standing not very thick—straight and beautiful. The ground is covered by a carpet of green wire grass. The country is pretty to look at, but the sand wouldn't suit an old farmer. What stillness in these pineries! You never see a bird or ever hear a grasshopper chirp. While marching today—and a very hot one it has been—we could always see a shade ahead of us in the road but could never make it. The foliage of the pines only partially breaks the sunshine and it also suffered for water. At night bivouacked at an old schoolhouse. Had nothing to eat but sweet potatoes for supper.

August 12 (Tuesday)

Things were quiet around Cedar Run in Virginia. Both Pope and Jackson awaited Lee's arrival from the Peninsula. McClellan was withdrawing towards Alexandria and Aquia, Va.

Gallatin, Tenn., was in for a surprise when Gen. John Hunt Morgan and his cavalry swept into town on another of their raids. He captured the town and the Union garrison. A little hot for all this activity.

Jackman and his cronies killed a "bear" today. For "bear," read "hog."

Jackman, Pvt., "The Orphan Brigade," en route to Baton Rouge, La.:

This morning Charlie A. of our company and Sam S. of the 4th killed a "bear" in the swamp and Billie A. and Gus M. having gone to a house and had bread cooked, we had a feast. There were five of the company along—also Sam S., and this morning we concluded to journey by ourselves—let the old Col. go on. Marched all day through the same character of country—hot and water scarce. At night our little party spread their blankets under an old oak on the roadside, true gipsy style.

Barber, Pvt., Co. D, 15th Illinois Volunteer Infantry, Memphis, Tenn.:

We now shifted camp to a more eligible situation, on a high bluff by the river; opposite from camp the bed of the river made an abrupt bend, running west for several miles and then gradually resuming its natural course. A small channel kept straight on and joined the other miles below, forming a beautiful island, which was the favorite resort of the boys. Plenty of melons, tomatoes and other vegetables grew there and nearly every day some of us would go over and get a fresh supply. 'Neath the shade of a large tree overhanging the bluff was a favorite resort of mine. I have sat there for hours in the heat of the day and in the twilight hours, watching the noble steamers plowing the dancing waves of the river for miles each way.... Closely hugging the Arkansas shore was the rebel gunboat *Beauregard*, about half submerged in water. A little above and farther in the stream was the *Van Dorn.*

August 15 (Friday)

On the James River in Virginia, Commodore Wilkes sent three gunboats, the U.S.S. *Galena, Port Royal,* and *Satellite,* to cover McClellan's left wing as it withdrew across the Chickahominy River.

Major Gen. Breckinridge was anxious to get troops into Port Hudson, La., for the defense of the city and to hold a crossing of the Mississippi River. The former was possible, the latter was not. Regardless, night marches were made to hurry the troops along.

Jackman, Pvt., "The Orphan Brigade," Port Hudson, La.:

> The commands are so reduced from sickness, today companies and regiments consolidated. Our regiment joins with the 4th and Lt. Col. Hines of that regiment is in command, being the ranking officer, Gen'l. Helms being wounded. Col. Traber of the 4th Ky. is in com'd of brigade. Col. Hunt commanded the brigade during the last battle and was wounded.
>
> At 5 P.M. fell in to march. At the time, a heavy rain storm was passing over—never saw it rain harder. We marched towards Baton Rouge. Soon the sun came out and the evening was very warm. In five miles of the city we filed to the night towards Port Hudson. Dark set in soon after leaving the main road and the sky became clouded. Dark is not the word to express the blackness of the night. Occasionally a flash of lightning would reveal our file leaders so that we could keep closed up. At bridges, too, fires were kindled by the citizens so we could see how to cross. The dusky column would pass these lights, again into utter darkness. The road was uneven and in places, muddy. At last we halted and tumbled down on the wet grass, being already drenched to the skin, and slept till morning. I believe this was the darkest night I ever saw. Have been on more uncomfortable marches though.

August 16 (Saturday)

McClellan was finally free of the Peninsula with many of his troops now at Alexandria and Aquia Creek. He was supposed to support Pope's Army of Virginia, which was now heading into a major clash with Lee near Manassas. Lee's army, now consolidated, was moving north from Gordonsville towards Culpeper and Manassas.

Confederate forces under Major Gen. E. Kirby Smith crossed the Cumberland Mountains into Kentucky in what would prove to be more of a nuisance than a real threat, at least for a time.

Edmund Kirby Smith was born in St. Augustine, Fla., on May 16, 1824. He attended preparatory school in Alexandria, Va., and then graduated from West Point in 1845. He served in the Mexican War and was a captain in the 2nd U.S. Cavalry regiment in 1855. In 1861 he accepted a commission as a Brigadier Gen. in the Confederate Army and fought at First Manassas, where he was wounded. After the Kentucky Campaign in 1863, he was promoted to Lieutenant General and sent to command the Trans-Mississippi Department in the west. He surrendered to Canby on May 26, 1865. He later served as president of the University of Nashville, and he taught at the University of the South, Sewanee, Tenn., where he died on March 28, 1893.

On the Mississippi, a fleet of gunboats convoyed and covered Army troops under Col. Charles R. Woods in a joint expedition upriver from Helena, Ark., as far as the Yazoo River. The troops landed at several points, capturing the steamer *Fairplay* above Vicksburg, with a cargo of arms, dispersing Confederate troop encampments, and destroying a new gun emplacement about 20 miles up the Yazoo River.

Jackman, Pvt., "The Orphan Brigade," Port Hudson, La.:

> Very hot day. When the brigade stopped at 12, Lt. H. and I were the only ones of the company up and there were not more than 30 of both regiments together. All the balance had fallen by the wayside. Sometimes we would march through lanes a mile in length and not a shade near. Our course led through large sugar plantations and the country looked better than usual.

August 18 (Monday)

Pope, pressed by Lee's advance, withdrew north of the Rappahannock River and waited for reinforcements from McClellan's idle legions. It would be a long wait.

Clarksville, Tenn., was recaptured today by the Confederates without a fight. This small city had been captured by Flag Officer Foote's gunboats and a small unit of Union troops without a fight just a few months previously. The commander of the Union garrison, Col. R. Mason of the 71st Ohio, would later be court-martialed for "cowardice in the face of the enemy."

Jackman, Pvt., "The Orphan Brigade," Port Hudson, La.:

Moved two miles off the road and camped in a grove of magnolia and beech trees. A "babbling brook" was near and we had an abundance of pure water. At night when silence had come over the camp an order came in for us to cook rations preparatory to a move for Kentucky. Soon hundreds of campfires blazed up and cheer upon cheer rose from the noisy thousands. After a moment the bands all commenced playing "Old Kentucky Home" and cheers went up with a will. After we had cooked the rations, we sat around the campfires talking until morning. Nobody could sleep.

August 19 (Tuesday)

An uprising of the Sioux Indians that began on the 17th was still in progress. The Indians, facing starvation on their reservations, rebelled and began a bloodbath in which nearly 600 people would be killed in Minnesota. They rampaged through the countryside, killing and burning as they went.

Jackman, Pvt., "The Orphan Brigade," en route to Kentucky:

At an early hour all the Kentucky troops, with Breckinridge at the head, took up line of march for Tangipahoa, a distance of 60 or 70 miles. We moved off with a light and buoyant step, the bands playing "Get Out of the Wilderness." At noon, halted for dinner and made time to help get the wagon train over a creek. A heavy rain set in and continued all evening. After marching 18 miles, we stopped for the night. Blanket and clothing wet and could get no wood, hardly, to make fires.

Allen, Pvt., Co. K, 1st Battalion, 10th Illinois Cavalry, Old Town Landing, near Helena, Ark.:

Friend Hillery: I wrote you a short letter on the 14th of July, but as I have not received an answer, I suppose you did not get my letter. I will now give you a more full account of our march from Springfield to Helena, and tell you how I am getting on in this land of canebrakes, cypress swamps and mosquitoes.

We left Springfield on the 14th of June with one Battalion of our Regiment, two of the 2nd Wisconsin Cavalry, and ninety wagons to join Gen. Curtis. The rebels had heard of our coming and boasted they would capture the train before it reached Curtis's army; but they did not make the attempt although they were in our neighborhood a good part of the time before we reached the army. On the 30th of June they fired on Co. L of the 2d Wisconsin Cavalry when it was out from camp, wounding one of the Lieutenants. We marched out to attack them, but they fled, as they usually do unless attacked by greatly inferior numbers. On the 4th of July we reached Curtis's army at Jacksonport. From there we came with the whole army, numbering about 30,000, to Helena. We came through the towns of Augusta, Cotton Plant and Clarendon. On the 9th the troops in the advance were attacked by rebels from this State and Texas, at a place called Bayou de Cache or Round Hill, near Cotton Plant. The rebels were defeated after a severe fight with a loss of over 150 killed and wounded. Our loss was forty… of whom eight were killed. We were near enough to hear the cannon. Next morning a large force, of which our Battalion formed a part, went out to renew the fight but the enemy was satisfied and had fled during the night. Our men were burying the dead, who were scattered along the roadside in the bushes. I noticed one poor butternut lying on his face in the road under a tree, looking like a man asleep but on coming closer I saw that a musket ball had passed through his body and his sleep was that of death.

The army was nearly out of provisions and we had to make a forced march to Helena, on the Mississippi river, in order to get them, as our supplies were cut off by way of White river. Our march was a very hard one all the way from Springfield. The weather was hot and dry and we marched day after day through dust so thick we could scarcely see our horses' heads. Most of the time our horses had nothing but grass to eat and sometimes that was scarce. Occasionally our teams did not reach camp at night and consequently we sometimes were nearly two days without food. The water in this State is very bad and very scarce. We have had to drink creek, river and swamp water in Arkansas. Notwithstanding our dangers and hardships, we reached Helena on the 12th of July. Helena is about 100 miles below Memphis on the river. We remained at Helena four weeks. While there the Company was out on three scouts, two in this State and one in Missouri. We came to this place a week ago. It is twenty miles below Helena on the river, and is the meanest hole I ever was in. There are so many mosquitoes that one can not sleep without mosquito bars. The weather this month has been very hot, but the last few days have been cooler, and the nights and mornings now feel like Fall. My health has been rather poor since we came to Helena but I have been able to be about all the time, though not fit for duty part of the time. I feel better now than I have for some time.... There is considerable sickness in our Company at present.... I fear there will be more....

August 20 (Wednesday)

Skirmishing between Pope and Jackson was becoming more frequent and widespread. As Lee advanced, Pope withdrew, still waiting for reinforcements from McClellan's idle thousands.

The Sioux were still killing and burning in Minnesota. However, their attack on Ft. Ridgley failed, and they withdrew.

Jackman, Pvt., "The Orphan Brigade," en route to Kentucky:

On the road at 4 A.M. Marched through Clinton, in order. Quite a crowd of ladies assembled to see us. Marched 16 miles and camped on the Comite. At noon, while resting, the brigade Q.M. came along having a lot of flour, and the boys cheered at the sight of the barrels. We were used to musty corn meal, ground in corncrackers, baked without sifting, and poor blue beef. Rained again this evening.

Day, Pvt., Co. B, 25th Massachusetts Volunteer Infantry, New Bern, N.C.:

Until recently I have been quite a popular commander of Sunday church parties. The boys would get up their parties and get me a pass to take them into town to church. I would take them in and halting on some convenient corner, would deliver myself of a little speech. I would say, "Boys, I have always believed in the largest tolerance in matters of religion and politics, and as much as I would like to have you attend church with me, if you have any preferences you are at liberty to enjoy them; far be it from me to impose my authority on your feelings or conscience. I shall expect you on the corner at the appointed time that we may report back in camp in season for dress parade."

Now, if they couldn't have had a tolerably good time under those conditions, it certainly was no fault of mine. But this, like every other good thing, could not always last. One Sunday afternoon when we gathered on the corner, one of the party failed to put in an appearance. After waiting beyond a reasonable time, he was defaulted and we returned to camp. About night he came in, showing unmistakable signs of having been on the hardest kind of fatigue duty. Instead of going to his quarters as he was told to, he thought it was his duty to interview the captain. That interview resulted in a court martial, before which I was ordered to appear. I was asked numerous questions, all of which I answered to the best of my knowledge and belief, and my evidence not only convicted the prisoner but reflected somewhat on myself, for in summing it up, they somehow fixed it up in such a way as to make it appear that I was in the practice of taking parties into town on Sundays, ostensibly to church, and then letting them go wherever they pleased, and inquired of me if that was not about the true solution of the problem. Wishing to avoid controversy, I assented. I was then told that I could retire from that august presence, a privilege of which I availed myself immediately, but what I noticed as being rather singular, after that interview I was in command of no more Sunday parties.

Barber, Pvt., Co. D, 15th Illinois Volunteer Infantry, Memphis, Tenn.:

Our duty was light. Col. Turner now undertook to put the regiment through a course of drill, but he made such bungling work of it that he soon became the laughing stock of the whole regiment. This galled his proud spirit deeply. There were plenty of privates who could beat him manoeuvering the regiment.... We now made quite an improvement in our camp by raising the tents about four feet from the ground and making sleeping bunks. This arrangement made it cool and nice. Every morning before the sun rose I used to get up and go down to the river and bathe, and hundreds did the same. A good many waited until the heat of the day and then they would stay in the water for hours. The consequence was that many were taken sick.... We drew the best kind of rations and plenty of them. To these we added extras, such as hens' eggs, potatoes, fresh fish, etc. There was not a meal but what some of these articles were in.... For the good of the regiment it was necessary that it should move. Too many of the boys were becoming too dissipated to attend their ordinary duties. So foul had the pestilential breath of the city become that decent ladies were not seen on the streets. The city itself was beautiful but it harbored more vice and was steeped in [more] degradation and filth than any city I had yet seen, but we will draw a veil over this scene....

August 21 (Thursday)

At the Kelly's, Beverly, and Freeman's ford crossings of the Rappahannock River, Confederate cavalry clashed with Federal pickets as Lee moved further north.

Federal troops evacuated Baton Rouge today, at least for a while. More troops were needed to hold the large area between Vicksburg and New Orleans.

In the Chattanooga area, Gen. Braxton Bragg moved north of the Tennessee River to begin his campaign into Kentucky.

Two Federal generals, Major Gen. David Hunter and Brig. Gen. John W. Phelps, were declared felons by President Davis in Richmond for organizing slaves for the Union Army. Davis decreed that they should be treated as outlaws if captured. Davis wouldn't have to worry about one of them: Phelps resigned from the U.S. Army in protest, because the Union government would not honor his actions.

Admiral Farragut commented on press reports of the intervention of foreign powers in the civil war, "I don't believe it, and, if it does come, you will find the United States not so easy a nut to crack as they imagine. We have no dread of 'rams' or 'he-goats,' and, if our Editors had less, the country would be better off. Now they scare everybody to death."

August 22 (Friday)

Still more skirmishing along the Rappahannock between Lee and Pope. Pope was a little embarrassed when JEB Stuart raided Catlett's Station and captured all of Pope's baggage and papers. Now he had no clean shirts, and no reinforcements.

After burning, looting, and mutilating corpses around Ft. Ridgley, Minn., and being driven off, the Sioux Indians were back again, only to be repulsed again.

More of McClellan's Army of the Potomac arrived at Alexandria and Aquia Creek. It took a long time and many ships to move over 100,000 men and their equipment.

After President Davis's declaration condemning two Federal generals for organizing slaves for the Union Army, Davis now had a third: Ben Butler in New Orleans had started enlisting Negroes.

Jackman, Pvt., "The Orphan Brigade," en route to Kentucky:

> Marched at 1 A.M. and arrived at Tangipahoa 6 A.M. Stacked arms on the sides of railroad and waited for cars. At 9, got on the train and moved off for Jackson, Miss., where we arrived after dark. All the way up the ladies were waving their handkerchiefs. We slept at the fair grounds.

August 23 (Saturday)

There was minor fighting all over today. Skirmishes were reported in Missouri, Louisiana, Kentucky, and Virginia. No major clashes as yet, but one was coming.

The citizens around Bayou Sara, La., made a mistake when they fired on a boat crew from the U.S.S. *Essex*. The ship immediately shelled the town.

Jackman, Pvt., "The Orphan Brigade," en route to Kentucky:

> Marched 6 miles out on the Brandon road where we found our camp already established, the wagon train having arrived from Vicksburg a day or two before. While marching out to camp, the weather was so hot, Col. Hines disbanded the regts on the road and let every fellow take care of himself. All did not get into camp until late in the evening.

August 24 (Sunday)

At Waterloo Bridge in Virginia, the opposing forces clashed in a brief skirmish, casualties light. Other activity occurred in Missouri and Louisiana.

Jackman, Pvt., "The Orphan Brigade," en route to Kentucky:

> On fatigue all day. My health is improving some. This regular camp does not look much like going to Kentucky soon. Our camp is on the side of a hill grown up with stunted oaks and tall pines. We have plenty of good water close at hand. The weather is very hot and sultry. Our provisions are abundant and we can get fruit and melon every day from citizens.

Off the island of Terceira, Azores, the C.S.S. *Alabama* was commissioned today amid cheers from the crew and the band playing "Dixie." Finally equipped, she would begin her two-year career raiding the commercial vessels of the United States.

August 26 (Tuesday)

The inevitable happened. Lee and Pope were beginning a battle which would be known as the Second Battle of Bull Run (or Second Manassas.)

The opening action was taken by cavalry under Fitzhugh Lee, one of Robert E. Lee's sons, when he entered Manassas Junction and captured the rail depot and cut off the communication to Washington. Jackson, on the move since the previous day, had come through the Bull Run Mountains at Thoroughfare Gap and was now positioned at Bristoe Station. The Confederates captured tons of supplies at the Manassas Junction rail depot, and begin moving much of it south.

Meanwhile, Pope didn't know where Jackson, Lee, or anyone was at the moment. McClellan was at Alexandria awaiting the remainder of his army from the Peninsula.

In Richmond, a well-deserved promotion came to Capt. Franklin Buchanan, CSN, when he was promoted to the rank of Admiral. Buchanan had commanded the C.S.S. *Virginia* before it was destroyed.

August 27 (Wednesday)

Pope, already outflanked by Jackson, left his lines and moved north towards the old Manassas battlefield. Jackson, now at Manassas Junction rail depot, was destroying everything that couldn't be carried off. Longstreet was coming up in support of Jackson. Pope was in trouble, but didn't realize it.

Lincoln, in Washington and cut off from any communication with Pope, felt he was in a vacuum. About half of the Confederate Army of Northern Virginia was now between Pope and Washington. Supposedly, some of McClellan's troops which had landed at Aquia Creek were en route to support Pope.

In southeastern Kentucky, Major Gen. E. Kirby Smith was moving his Confederate troops further north into the central part of the state preparatory to Bragg's autumn campaign to retake the state.

August 28 (Thursday)

At Manassas, Pope arrived at about noon to find that Jackson had withdrawn. Pope had no idea where Jackson had gone. Jackson was sitting along the Warrenton Turnpike just west of the old Bull Run battlefield. Pope hurried towards Centreville, where he thought Jackson had gone, and slammed into that force at Brawner's Farm without knowing that they were there. Intelligence in this battle was very poor. Longstreet and Lee proceeded through Thoroughfare Gap and passed to the north of Pope undetected. The stage was set for defeat.

The female spy (or so accused), Belle Boyd, was released from the Old Capital Prison in Washington for lack of evidence.

In the mountains north of Chattanooga, Braxton Bragg's troops crossed Walden's Ridge, and entered central Tennessee on their way into Kentucky.

August 29 (Friday)

At Manassas, Pope was trying to make sense of the tactical situation. He believed that he had Jackson trapped, and he ordered attacks against Jackson's positions. Jackson had a strong position in a railroad cut at Sudley Springs and held without difficulty. Meanwhile, Longstreet and Lee arrived about noon and took positions near the old Confederate line of July 1861.

As night settled, the fighting quieted down. Halleck, in Washington, was urging McClellan to send troops immediately to support Pope. McClellan, having a strong dislike for Pope, "tried his best" to comply but little was done. Many believed that "Little Mac's" ego would not stand having to play second fiddle to anyone, let alone John Pope.

In Washington, Lincoln was cut off from all telegraphic communication and was pacing the floor.

In Kentucky, Confederate Major Gen. E. Kirby Smith's troops fought the Federal garrison at Richmond, Ky., in the beginning of the campaign.

At Eunice, Ark., the U.S.S. *Pittsburg*, Lt. Thompson, landed troops under the cover of the ship's guns. The troops seized a large wharf boat fitted out as a hotel.

August 30 (Saturday)

At Manassas, Pope believed that the Confederates had retreated. Pope attacked Jackson's line, the Confederate left flank. Longstreet attacked from the Confederate right flank and rolled up Pope's army, sending them into retreat towards Centreville. Pope had been beaten, but the army did not panic and go into a rout. While Lee won the battle, he hadn't destroyed the Union Army on the field.

It was finally over. There was enough glory (Confederate) and blame (Federal) to share. Pope had been humiliated after his bombastic pronouncements before the campaign, and he would be sent west to command an administrative district. McClellan would deny any blame for not reinforcing Pope. Halleck had proven, once again, that he was not forceful enough in a crisis.

The Union had suffered over 16,000 casualties, and the South over 9000. For relieving the pressure on Richmond, over 25,000 men were killed, wounded, or missing.

At Richmond, Ky., E. Kirby Smith attacked the Federal garrison, which put up a stiff fight before retreating towards Louisville.

August 31 (Sunday)

At Manassas, the cleanup began. The wounded were gathered for evacuation, the dead were buried, the discarded equipment recovered for later use, and the battered units rested. A little late, two corps from the Army of the Potomac arrived to reinforce Pope. Lee, using information gathered by Stuart's cavalry scouts, got ready to attack Pope again by turning the Union right flank. He moved Jackson to a position just west of Chantilly, with Longstreet following along. The game was not over just yet.

Kirby Smith basked in the glow of his victory at Richmond, Ky., and awaited developments on the Union side.

At Fredericksburg, Va., the Federals evacuated the city, leaving behind considerable quantities of supplies.

Barber, Pvt., Co. D, 15th Illinois Volunteer Infantry, Memphis, Tenn.:

> My health was quite poor now. William was also quite feeble. A great number of the boys were sick. Near our picket line was a large farm house where a dairy was kept. It was my usual custom to go there for my meals when on picket and get fresh milk. We also had plenty of fruit. Peaches were just in their prime. Under this diet I soon recovered my usual health....

SEPTEMBER 1862

It seemed that Richmond was safe for the time being. McClellan was back in northern Virginia strutting like a peacock about his "victory" on the Peninsula, and complaining that he hadn't received the support he had needed. Pope, thoroughly defeated at Second Manassas, was licking his wounds and awaiting Lee's further action. Washington was threatened, and Lincoln was worried.

In the west, Vicksburg was safe for the moment. Grant was east of Corinth, Miss. Bragg was to begin his campaign into Kentucky within days and some of the people in that state would welcome a return of the Confederates.

September 1 (Monday)

After Manassas, Lee was not yet finished. Lee sent Jackson around the Federal right, where Stonewall ran into Federal Generals I.I. Stevens and Kearny. In the midst of a heavy rainstorm the fighting swirled around Chantilly until evening. During this scrap both Stevens and Kearny were killed, a real blow to the North. Pope held on and withdrew towards Centreville, pressured by Lee. As night fell, Washington was safe, but Lee was very close.

In Richmond, Davis was exchanging hot words about conscription with some of the Confederate States who felt that it was a violation of rights; this time South Carolina was complaining the loudest.

At Holly Springs, Miss., John Jackman was detailed to the regimental adjutant's office as a clerk.

At Havana, Cuba, the C.S.S. *Florida*, Lt. Maffitt, entered port after suffering an epidemic of yellow fever on board that killed several crew members.

Rear Adm. L.M. Goldsborough was relieved as Commander, North Atlantic Blockading Squadron by Rear Adm. S.P. Lee. Goldsborough had served with distinction at Hatteras.

September 2 (Tuesday)

South of Washington, Pope pulled back into the entrenchments around the city and was pressured by Lee with skirmishing at Fairfax C.H., Vienna, Falls Church, and Flint Hill. Lincoln, reluctantly, returned McClellan to command of all the armies in northern Virginia, a move hotly opposed by Secretaries Stanton and Chase. Pope was now without a command. Lee gathered his army near Chantilly and rested the men while he thought of what to do next. The Federals evacuated Winchester, much to the delight of Richmond, leaving enough ordnance stores for a campaign. Sometimes one wondered whom the United States Quartermaster Corps was serving, the North or the South.

In Kentucky, Gen. Kirby Smith occupied Lexington and awaited Bragg's army coming north from Chattanooga. The people of southern Ohio and Indiana were in a state of high alarm because of the approaching Southern armies. Militia were called out to begin drilling, and the governors of both States asked for assistance.

September 3 (Wednesday)

Lee withdrew a few miles to around Leesburg, but there was still skirmishing around Falls Church, Fairfax C.H., and other places in northern Virginia. Lee was now close to the ferries crossing the Potomac, and there were actions west of Washington, near Harpers Ferry. Gen. Richard Ewell had his leg amputated and would be absent from the army for nearly a year.

Pope, now without a command, wrote his report to Gen. Halleck in which he accused Gen. Porter of disobeying orders in the face of the enemy, and Gen. McClellan of not sending troops in a timely fashion.

In Kentucky, Kirby Smith's troops were in Frankfort and occupied the State Capitol.

On the Mississippi, Federal troops had evacuated Natchez on July 25th, and things had been fairly peaceful. Today, the U.S.S. *Essex*, Commodore W.D. Porter, was chasing the C.S.S. *Webb* when one of the *Essex*'s boats was fired upon from the city. The *Essex* bombarded the city for an hour until the Mayor surrendered it again.

September 4 (Thursday)

The South's position in the outside world was not promising. Neither France nor England had recognized Southern independence, and no other nation had either. Something was needed to prove that the Confederacy was a viable power and deserving of a place in the community of nations. Lee felt that he had a solution. An invasion of the North would prove to anyone that the Confederacy had sufficient strength to stand on its own feet. With this in mind, Lee headed his troops to the crossings of the Potomac and into Maryland, where he hoped the people would rise for the South.

The movement of the Army of Northern Virginia into Maryland caused fighting at all the major fords of the Potomac. Federals evacuated Frederick, Md., just a few miles north.

John Hunt Morgan and his band of cavalry raiders were back in Kentucky, joining Kirby Smith at Lexington.

The C.S.S. *Florida*, Lt. Maffitt, ran the blockade into Mobile Bay with many of her crew suffering from yellow fever. She took a broadside from the U.S.S. *Oneida*, and managed to run past the U.S.S. *Winona* and *Rachel Seaman* before gaining the protection of the guns of Ft. Morgan. She suffered several hits during the run.

September 5 (Friday)

Pope was notified that the Army of Virginia would be merged into the Army of the Potomac; he no longer had a command. His role in the war would be greatly reduced and he would loudly complain for years about the support given to him at Second Manassas. McClellan, back in full command, said, "I will save the country."

Meanwhile, Lee approached Frederick, Md., and the citizens of Baltimore and other cities were in a panic. Armed men roamed the streets to "protect" against the invaders.

In the west, Buell was withdrawing from Alabama towards Murfreesboro, Tenn. Bragg, at Sparta, Tenn., was prematurely proclaiming the State to be free.

Off the Azores in the eastern Atlantic, the commerce raider C.S.S. *Alabama* seized and burned her first victim, the *Ocmulgee*. Many more were to follow.

September 6 (Saturday)

Stonewall Jackson entered Frederick, Md. The Rebels expected a warm greeting and some recruits but received closed doors, locked stores and mostly a cold shoulder. There would be heavy skirmishing in the forefront of the Confederate army for several days as they pushed north. Some Southerners, believing it wrong to invade the North, refused to cross the Potomac into Maryland. Others did not cross because of illness, lack of shoes or other equipment, or just plain malingering.

Pope was given command of a new Department of the Northwest and was sent to Minnesota to cope with the Indians who were rampaging and destroying the countryside. McClellan left Aquia Creek and headed towards Washington, destroying enough supplies and equipment at Aquia to outfit several regiments rather than move it.

At Washington, N.C., the U.S.S. *Louisiana*, Acting Lt. Richard T. Renshaw, used her guns on the town during an engagement. She "rendered most efficient aid, throwing her shells with great precision, and clearing the streets...."

September 7 (Sunday)

McClellan was moving his vast army northwest at a snail's pace, protecting the capital and not having the foggiest notion where Lee was or where he was going. Stuart was providing effective screening.

Bragg was moving across Tennessee at a steady pace towards Kentucky, avoiding Buell's forces at Murfreesboro and Nashville. Clarksville, Tenn., so ignominiously surrendered to the Confederates by Col. Mason, was retaken.

Port Hudson, Miss., was getting to be a dangerous place for Federal boats. The U.S.S. *Essex*, Commodore W.D. Porter, ran past the town and was hit with heavy shot 14 times. He noted that this "would seriously interrupt the free navigation of the Lower Mississippi."

September 8 (Monday)

With Lee getting deeper into Maryland, Lincoln asked McClellan, who was at Rockville, "How does it look now?" Lee, issued a proclamation citing the South's sympathy with the people of Maryland who were pro-Southern and offered to provide protection for those who chose to go with the Confederacy. The choice, however, was to be the individual's.

There was heavy skirmishing around Poolesville, Md., just west of Washington. McClellan still did not know where Lee was.

September 9 (Tuesday)

At Frederick, Md., Lee issued his famous Special Order 191, which defined his campaign strategy. He then divided his forces, and continued on the move. He sent troops to Harpers Ferry, Boonsborough, Md., and Crampton's Gap. None of these forces was large.

The raider C.S.S. *Alabama*, Capt. Semmes, had burned four Union ships off the Azores in the past three days: the cargo ship *Starlight* and the three whalers *Ocean Rover*, *Alert*, and *Weather Gauge*.

September 10 (Wednesday)

In Maryland west of Washington, McClellan learned that Lee had evacuated Frederick. McClellan rushed his long blue lines to the northwest.

The people of Indiana and Ohio were very nervous about the presence of Kirby Smith and John Hunt Morgan, and Bragg's approach.

Barber, Pvt., Co. D, 15th Illinois Volunteer Infantry, en route to La Grange, Tenn.:

> Our march lay through a swampy country, threaded by muddy creeks and rivers. The rebels had destroyed most of the bridges, hence our progress was very slow. We were obliged to take a circuitous route to avoid the enemy.... Guerrillas lurked in our track, picking up stragglers. Lon Howe and Emory Hiner of our company were captured within one mile of camp.

Jackman, Pvt., "The Orphan Brigade," en route to Kentucky; Holly Springs, Miss.:

> Broke up camp and marched to the city. At noon took train on the Mississippi Central for Holly Springs. Got as far up as Goodman at sundown. Here the engineer took water and as the train moved on past the tank, some fellows on the first car pulled the water-pipe down which caused a perfect flood of water to drench the train as it paraded slowly along. Just in front of us was a flat car on which was Co. "H" and the water had plenty of fall. The boys rolled up in their blankets and took it. The train stopped as

the spout was over our car and the field band being on top, soon a shower of drums, fifes, drum-sticks, etc. came pouring down with the flood. This was great sport to all save a Captain on the front part of the train who jumped off to avoid the water and had both his legs crushed off by the wheels.

September 11 (Thursday)

Kirby Smith's troops were within seven miles of Cincinnati, causing panic there. Smith had already occupied Maysville, Ky., just southwest of the city.

Lee's men were in Hagerstown, Md. There were more skirmishes as the armies drew closer together. Lee's exact whereabouts and intentions were still not known to McClellan.

Jackman, Pvt., "The Orphan Brigade," en route to Kentucky; Holly Springs, Miss.:

> During the morning arrived at Holly Springs and I tried to get my breakfast at the hotel, but failed. The train took us 16 miles above and we got off at what we called "Cold-Water." We lived well while in this camp, a few "bears" being killed during the time. Waiting all the time—Lt. O'C. acting as Adjt.—I made a Monthly Return—a very complicated report for a new-beginner to make.

September 12 (Friday)

McClellan's men moved into Frederick, Md., as Jackson was converging on Harpers Ferry. In Richmond, a debate went on about the advisability of invading the North. Harrisburg, the capital of Pennsylvania, had moved the public records, and Philadelphia was in an uproar.

In Kentucky, Kirby Smith's men occupied Glasgow, only about 55 miles from Louisville, while Bragg's columns drew nearer to Lexington. Much consternation in Ohio and Indiana.

September 13 (Saturday)

The Union Army entered the town of Frederick, Md., almost as soon as the Confederates left the other side of town. In the Federal ranks of the 27th Indiana Volunteer Regiment one Billy W. Mitchell found three cigars wrapped in paper lying in a fence corner. Being a frugal sort, and not having had a good smoke in a while, Mitchell picked up the packet and discovered that he had Gen. Robert E. Lee's Special Order No. 191 in his hand. This order contained all the details of the Confederate invasion. Lee's order was rapidly transmitted to McClellan, who was jubilant over the discovery. By evening, McClellan had his long blue columns hurrying west of Frederick towards South Mountain, that long hogback dividing the valleys. Stuart and his cavalry awaited them.

Charleston, in western Virginia, was evacuated by the Federals today after they were confronted by a larger Confederate force under Gen. W.W. Loring—a setback in the Kanawha Valley.

September 14 (Sunday)

A whole series of blunders began today. Major Gen. William B. Franklin had been sent with his corps to reinforce Harpers Ferry, which had been lightly held by a Federal force. He went through Crampton's Gap easily, brushing aside the troops of Confederate Lafayette McLaws, but then he got nervous and decided he was outnumbered, and he dug in. McLaws, keeping part of his troops to hold Franklin, sent the rest to Jackson, who was approaching Harpers Ferry, and who would attack in the evening.

Meanwhile, the Federal cavalry, under Gen. Pleasanton, engaged D.H. Hill's troops at Fox's Gap and Turner's Gap. Both gaps provided crossing of South Mountain. By evening, Hill's men had been outflanked and the passes were in Federal hands.

Miller, Pvt., 87th Ohio Infantry, Harpers Ferry, western Virginia:

> During the bombardment of Harpers Ferry.... I was sent down with a dollar to get some tobacco for the men. You will understand that men compelled to stand in line and be shot at, and the shots being large oblong shells that screamed through the air with a peculiar noise and made the hair stand on end and the heart get a way up in the throat, and the men unable to fight back at the fellows who were shooting from the top of a mountain, across a river—only stand and take it—such men get very nervous, and they chew a great deal of tobacco, or at least they seek an excuse to get out of line to go after tobacco, and get out of danger. Well, the Captain, wishing to hold men in line, detailed me to take an Indiana

paper dollar and go down to the sutler and get tobacco to supply the men who were asking for it.

While I was parleying with the sutler, who had refused to accept the Indiana money, which was below par at that time, a wounded Indiana soldier came in from Maryland heights, his hand being shot and a handkerchief tied around it. As soon as he learned what the controversy was about, he ordered the sutler to take the money—and take it p.d.q. The sutler refused. The soldier said "I am an Indiana soldier, and you refuse to take Indiana money of Indiana soldiers in line fighting for your protection. I'll see about it." And he quietly began loading his gun, against his wounded hand. Then he took a cartridge and tore off the end with his teeth and inserted the charge of powder and ball in the muzzle of his gun; then taking hold of the ramrod he drew it up, and turned it into his gun barrel. By this time the sutler began to explain that, of course, I could have the tobacco, but the money was of no use to him. "Indiana money is good enough for any damned sutler" said the soldier, and he proceeded to put a cap on his gun. The sutler wilted and proposed to accept the money for 10 plugs of black strap tobacco and never again under the circumstances refuse the money of any loyal state.

As we started out together, the soldier smiled and remarked that he was wanting a chaw of tobacco himself pretty bad. I handed him a plug, and thanked him for helping me out of a tight place, and we separated, he saying, "You were not in as tight a place as that d— sutler."

In Kentucky, Gen. Buell had been rushing north from Tennessee and today reached Bowling Green. Gen. Braxton Bragg's columns had been approaching Munfordville, but they had been repulsed by the Federal force there.

The expected recruits for three regiments would require about 3000 able-bodied men. There certainly were not that many in Lexington at this time, nor hardly any in the surrounding countryside. Bragg had carried wagonloads of muskets to Kentucky for new recruits and carried most of them back with him to Tennessee. Many in the South believed that Kentucky would rise up, but most of her men who were to volunteer for the Confederate armies were already gone.

September 15 (Monday)

Harpers Ferry went into the hands of Stonewall Jackson today. This was not the first time he had been here. He had stripped the arsenal of weapons-making machinery over a year ago and had sent it south. There wasn't much of a battle. The Federal commander, mortally wounded, offered little resistance. Lee, now alarmed by McClellan's movements because his own army was so scattered, began to concentrate his forces at Sharpsburg, thinking seriously about withdrawing across the Potomac, just a few miles south. However, with the troops from South Mountain and Harpers Ferry in hand, he decided to stay at Sharpsburg and see what McClellan would do. McClellan was bringing his troops forward as fast as possible.

In Kentucky, Kirby Smith gave the people of Cincinnati a bad scare when he briefly appeared at Covington, just across the river. Bragg was in a battle at Munfordville trying to clear that town of Federals.

In Mississippi, Gen. Sterling Price had occupied the little town of Iuka, located near the old Corinth battlefield.

Day, Pvt., Co. B, 25th Massachusetts Volunteer Infantry, en route to Plymouth, N.C.:

... the 25th, Major Pickett in command, with the 17th Massachusetts and the 10th Connecticut regiments, the whole under the command of Col. Upton, embarked on steamers bound for Plymouth, on the Roanoke river which empties into the Albemarle sound at its extreme western end.

Barber, Pvt., Co. D, 15th Illinois Volunteer Infantry, Bolivar, Tenn.:

As we approached Bolivar, the country became more open and beautiful. We found Bolivar to be a fine looking village of two thousand or more inhabitants, surrounded by a fertile country, watered by the Hatchie river which flows within one mile of that city.... We stayed here one night then we went to Dunlap Springs, five miles from Bolivar. There had been a fierce cavalry fight here and Col. Hogg left a glorious record to his country. He fell while leading a saber charge on the rebel cavalry. A hospital was situated here so that the people could enjoy the medicinal properties of the Springs.... The grounds were tastefully laid out, being dotted with fine covered arbors and shady walks. There were several springs, and it is a curious fact that no two springs had the same medicinal properties.

September 16 (Tuesday)

In the pre-battle lull in Pleasant Valley, Md., Jonathan Letterman, Medical Director of the Army of the Potomac, continued riding the local area looking for hospital sites. Sites at Boonsboro; Keedysville; Hoffman; the Samuel Poffenberger farm where Clara Barton worked; the Pry farm; the barn on Henry Rohrbach's farm; the buildings at the Jacob Miller farm; the Grove farm; and the Smoketown Hospital were all selected and readied for the slaughter to come. Most of the civilians had abandoned the area and left their homes and possessions to the opposing armies.

Many problems remained for Letterman. There was a shortage of medical supplies, many having been captured or destroyed during the Peninsular Campaign just completed. Many of the ambulances for the army had been left at Ft. Monroe, near Norfolk, Va., due to lack of transportation and time to move them. A severe shortage of hospital tents created further problems. A good many men would die in the next two weeks because of lack of treatment.

Lee gathered his troops at Sharpsburg, leaving Gen. A.P. Hill at Harpers Ferry, but bringing Jackson and the rest of his corps to Antietam. McClellan moved cautiously, as usual, and lost a good opportunity to crush Lee while the Rebel army was still somewhat scattered.

Ambrose Powell Hill was born in Culpeper, Va., on November 9, 1825. Graduating from West Point in 1847, he served in the Mexican War and in the third Seminole War. In 1861 he resigned his commission and joined the Confederate Army as a Colonel of the 13th Virginia. Promoted to Brigadier on February 26, 1862, he fought at Williamsburg with distinction, which brought him a promotion to Major General in May 1862. He fought in the Seven Days' Battle and with Jackson in the Valley. He fought in all the major battles of 1863, taking command of the newly formed III Corps after Jackson's death in May 1863. He was lackluster as a corps commander and generally avoided further battles by reporting sick. He was killed south of Petersburg in the opening phases of the spring campaign on April 2, 1865 . He was buried in Richmond.

E. Kirby Smith withdrew from Covington, Ky., back towards Lexington, while Bragg had the town of Munfordville surrounded, with some 4200 Federal troops in the bag.

Day, Pvt., Co. B, 25th Massachusetts Volunteer Infantry, en route to Plymouth, N.C.:

> ... we passed Roanoke island and our attention was attracted towards it as being the scene of our first conflict and success. We soon afterward entered the Albemarle sound, a beautiful sheet of water running east and west, about 70 miles long with an average width of some 20 miles. It was a beautiful day and the sail, as we slowly steamed along, was delightful, affording us a fine view of the shores. The shores were in striking contrast; the south shore is low and swampy, rising scarcely out of the water, while the north is bold with a gently rising slope and shows many handsome farms. The scenery here is the first that has reminded us of home, and looks as though it was inhabited by a better class of people than we have yet seen.
>
> About dusk we reach the upper end of the sound, and turning sharply to the left enter the woods, where the overhanging branches of the tall trees seem almost to embrace each other. We are now in the Roanoke river, which is here quite narrow. In the dusk of the evening, as we grope our way along the narrow channel through the trees, the scenery is grandly wild. Some five or six miles through the woods brought us to the little town of Plymouth, situated on the left, or south, bank of the river. Here we drop anchor for the night and wait until morning to learn more of our excursion.

September 17 (Wednesday)

The day dawned foggy and misty at Sharpsburg, Md. Dawn found the Army of Northern Virginia nearly assembled and ready for battle, outnumbered two to one. McClellan, as usual, delayed the attack for some hours, until about 6 A.M., awaiting the alignment of his troops. Jackson and Stuart were on the left of the Rebel forces, with Longstreet's corps holding the right wing. A.P. Hill was not up from Harpers Ferry yet.

On this day 23,110 Americans would be reported as killed, wounded, or missing in action: 12,410 Union and 10,700 Confederate. They would fall at the rate of about 2000 per hour, or about 35 per minute, from 6 A.M. to 6 P.M. If laid end to end, the dead and wounded would have lined a road for 25 miles. This was the bloodiest single day in American history.

At the stone bridge over Antietam Creek, forever after known as Burnside Bridge, Color Sgt. George E. Bailey, carrying the national colors, was to lead the 11th Connecticut Volunteers storming the bridge, but another sergeant, carrying the state colors, refused to advance without a full color guard. An officer slashed Bailey's arm for refusing to advance, whereupon Corp. Henry A. Eastman took the colors from him, and carried them into battle. Corp. Eastman would survive the battle, later being promoted to Captain. The 11th would lose 181 men during this battle.

The regiment suffering the most casualties of either army this day was the 15th Massachusetts.

Sgt. Jonathan Stowe, Co. G, wrote entries for this day:

> Battle Oh horrid battle. What sights I have seen. I am wounded! And am afraid shall be again as shells fly past me every few seconds carrying away limbs from the trees.... Am in severe pain. How the shells fly. I do sincerely hope I shall not be wounded again.

As evening shadows filled the hollows throughout the battlefield, cries of the wounded could be heard. The few women left in the area went to the fields looking for the soldiers, Yank and Reb, who needed aid and comfort. The stretcher-bearers continued their gruesome task of carrying the wounded to the aid stations and hospitals. The hospitals had become carnage houses where the wounded were treated on doors ripped from their hinges or on window shutters which happened to be nearby. Hot water was readied to sluice the "operating table" after each operation but, in the heat of the activity, the fires were neglected, the water became merely warm, not hot, and finally even the washing was forgotten. The surgeons had no time to wash their hands or instruments; the coats of the orderlies and doctors become smeared, then caked, with blood from too many men. As the daylight faded, candles were stuck in bottles or musket barrels to provide a feeble light to amputate arms and legs. Little was available to alleviate pain. The shrieks of the patients filled the air.

Where did they put the wounded? A report by a member of the Sanitary Commission after the battle stated:

> Indeed there is not a barn, or farmhouse, or store, or church, or schoolhouse, between Boonesville, Sharpsburg, and Smoketown that is not gorged with wounded—Rebel and Union. Even the corn-cribs, and in many cases the cow stable, and in one place the mangers, were filled. Several thousands lie in open air upon straw, and all are receiving the kind services of farmers' families and the surgeons.

Day, Pvt., Co. B, 25th Massachusetts Volunteer Infantry, Plymouth, N.C.:

> ... we learned the expedition had been given up, and we steamed back down the river on our return trip, without scarcely getting a glimpse of Plymouth. On coming out into the sound, we could see the little town of Edenton on the north shore, hid away in a little nook of the sound, and almost buried in trees. From our standpoint it looked like a charming little town. It is occasionally occupied by our troops and the gunboats make frequent calls there. The only setback to the pleasure of the trip down the sound was the annoyance caused the officers by the hilarity of the boys who entered into the spirit of fun and seemed to be bent on having a general good time. The officers occupied the saloon and were greatly disturbed by the noise and racket on deck over their heads. They would often send up and order the boys to keep more quiet as the noise disturbed them. The boys of course would respect their wishes, and for a time all would be quiet, but soon another party would come on deck from some other part of the boat and bedlam would again break loose.
>
> The officers had my commiseration; I exercised all my authority to preserve order and would willingly have done anything that lay in my power to have alleviated their sufferings, for it is not surprising that men brought up in machine shops, rolling mills, foundries and like places should be possessed of rather sensitive nerves.

The Federal garrison at Munfordville, Ky., finally surrendered to Braxton Bragg's butternut columns. Kirby Smith was near Lexington.

September 18 (Thursday)

With dawn on this day the terrible slaughter of Antietam was more apparent. Thousands of dead were still lying in the fields and along the fence rows. Nearly 12,000 lay in Miller's cornfield. The Bloody Lane was filled with Confederate dead, in some places four deep. Lee awaited McClellan. "Little

Mac" was loath to act, as usual. The wounded suffered and the dead awaited burial.

Stowe, Sgt., Co. G, 15th Massachusetts, hospital at Sharpsburg [Antietam], Md.:

> Misery acute, painful misery. How I suffered last night. It was the most painful of anything have ever experienced. My leg must be broken for I cannot help myself scarcely any. I remember talking and groaning all night. Many died in calling for help.... Sergt Johnson who lies on the other side of the log is calling for water.
>
> Carried off the field at 10 A.M. by the Rebs who show much kindness but devote much time to plundering the dead bodies of our men.... Water very short. We suffer very much.

Day, Pvt., Co. B, 25th Massachusetts Volunteer Infantry, New Bern, N.C.:

> We arrived back at New Bern... having had a pleasant excursion of about 400 miles and if we could have had our band with us, the thing would have been complete. It seems the object of our visit to Plymouth was for the officers of the expedition to consult with the military and naval officers at that station in regard to the expediency of dislodging the enemy's forces at Rainbow bluff, a point some 30 miles up the river, which prevents our boats from ascending higher up and which they cannot shell out. At the council of officers, it was decided that if we should succeed in capturing it, it would be without results, as it is of no military consequence to us and that it would be unwise to risk men in an enterprise that would be barren in results. Hence our return to New Bern.

Off the Azores in the eastern Atlantic, the C.S.S. *Alabama*, Capt. Semmes, destroyed five whaling ships, the *Altahama*, *Benjamin Tucker*, *Courser*, *Virginia*, and *Elisha Dunbar*, since the 13th of the month. Semmes wrote, "The whaling season at the Azores being at an end... I resolved to change my cruising-ground, and stretch over to the Banks of New Foundland..." The season was over because all the ships were gone!

September 19 (Friday)

At Sharpsburg, Lee began his retreat across the Potomac, and McClellan crowed about his victory although he went through the battle without committing over 30,000 of his soldiers, who could have overwhelmingly defeated the Confederate force. He allowed Lee to disengage and to escape with no pursuit. The news getting to Richmond was garbled.

The wounded on the battlefield had mostly been picked up and given some attention. Sgt. Stowe reported in his diary of his treatment.

Stowe, Sgt., Co. G, 15th Massachusetts, hospital at Sharpsburg [Antietam], Md.:

> Rained only a little. I had a rubber blanket & overcoat. Rebs retreat. Another painful night.
>
> Oh good good a whole line of our skirmishers are coming.... There are lots of us here lain out.... By and by our boys come along. What lots of the 15th. Captain comes down to get the names and has coffee furnished us—Twas the best cup I ever tasted. Dr. looks at my wound and calls it doubtful case. Get me on ambulance at 3 P.M. but do not get to hospital till nearly dark. Plenty of water which gives us a chance to take down inflammation. Nurses worn out by fatigue. Placed on straw near the barn.

The Sanitary Commission reacted to the carnage of Antietam by bringing in supplies, as well as food, to treat the wounded. Before the last hospital was closed and the last wounded man sent from the area, the Commission would have distributed over 28,700 pieces of dry goods, shirts, towels, bed-ticks, pillows, etc.; 30 barrels of old linen, bandages, and lint for dressing of wounds; nearly 3200 pounds of farina; over 2600 pounds of condensed milk; over 5000 pounds of beef-stock and canned meats; over 4000 sets of hospital clothing; 3000 bottles of wine and cordials; several tons of lemons and other fruit; crackers, tea, sugar, coffee, rubber cloths, tin cups, chloroform, opiates, surgical instruments, etc. All of these supplies were donated by volunteers in Northern communities or bought with donated money.

Near Corinth, Miss., the Confederates, under Sterling Price, had moved to Iuka earlier, where they awaited Grant's response. They had only a little while to wait. Grant and Rosecrans drove towards Price at Iuka, Rosecrans leading the way. It was hardly a contest, although the fighting was sharp for a while. Rosecrans forced Price to withdraw south in the face of the blue assault.

September 20 (Saturday)

Lee moved his divisions across the Potomac unopposed. This was McClellan's major blunder; he could have trapped Lee's army against the flooding river. Instead, he sent his cavalry to harass the gray columns and sat in Antietam. This would be McClellan's last battle.

Throughout the countryside around Sharpsburg the wounded lay in the open. The weather had been reasonably mild, but this was September, and fall came early in this part of Maryland. Those that could be evacuated were moving. The more seriously wounded awaited their fate.

Stowe, Sgt., Co. G, 15th Massachusetts, hospital at Sharpsburg [Antietam], Md.:

> Fearful it will rain. How cheerful the boys appear. Many must lose their arms or legs but they do not murmur.... Leg amputated about noon. What sensations—used chloroform hope to have no bad effects. There are some dozen or more stumps near me. Placed in barn beside J. Hughes...

Day, Pvt., Co. B, 25th Massachusetts Volunteer Infantry, New Bern, N.C.:

> All the regimental bands have been mustered out and have gone home. Ours left the first of this month, and it seems quite lonely to have them gone. They were the solace of many a weary hour. I understand that this is in the interest of economy, the bands costing so much it was thought best to let them go. I also learn that the officers' pay has been raised, so just where the savings comes in does not appear. As I am only an enlisted man I am not supposed to see things quite so clearly, so I presume it is all right any way, but we think it is rather sharp economy.

Barber, Pvt., Co. D, 15th Illinois Volunteer Infantry, Bolivar, Tenn.:

> We supposed that this was to be our permanent camp... but the very next day we were ordered back to Bolivar.... We went into camp in the suburbs of the town and went to doing provost guard duty. This was very heavy and it required all the men that were able for duty. Some of the most prominent southerners had lived here. There was a splendid cemetery, and on some of he monuments were carved the names of prominent men, amongst which was that of James K. Polk. The ravages of war had dealt lightly with this place. Merchants still continued to trade and other branches of business were still open. Our 1st Lieutenant, Shapley, now resigned and there was an exciting contest for the vacancy. The aspirants for the position were 1st Sergeant Mike Schoonmaker, and 2d Lieutenant John Waldock. We were all well aware that Mike would be the choice of the company. It was well-known that I would cast my vote for Waldock. Not because I did not like Mike, but because I thought it rightly belonged to Waldock. Mike received all the votes but six, but notwithstanding, Gov. Yates gave the position to Waldock. The same day the non-commission ranks were filled up and I was surprised to find my name heading the list of newly-appointed corporals. Lieut. Waldock had before asked me if I would accept of a corporalship. The captain wanted him to recommend one. I told him I did not desire it and so I supposed that the matter was settled. The greatest objection that the boys had to Waldock was on account of his John Bull proclivities, he being an Englishman. We were now relieved of provost duty and we removed our camp one and a half miles out of town into a cotton field.... We now had battalion drill every day. We were reviewed several times by Veatch and Hurlbut.

September 21 (Sunday)

More wounded leaving today at Antietam. Slowly, ever so slowly, the dead were buried and the dying given their final solace. Many wounded, especially amputees, would die from infections caused by the unsanitary "operating room" conditions.

McClellan sat, while Lee withdrew into Virginia.

Stowe, Sgt., Co. G, 15th Massachusetts, hospital at Sharpsburg [Antietam], Md.:

> Very weak and sore.... Hot weather by day cool at night. Hard to get nurses. Men come in and stare at us but detailed men clear out & leave us. How pitiously do they beg for water. People come in from all parts of the country. Stare at us but do not find time to do anything.

Barber, Cpl., Co. D, 15th Illinois Volunteer Infantry, Bolivar, Tenn.:

Our picket duty was quite heavy. Our regiment had a certain place to picket and the companies took turns. It required two companies a day. About this time, a little twelve-year old boy ran away from his rebel uncle and joined us. He was a bright and staunch union boy. He remained with us all through the war. His name was George King.

Jackman, Pvt., "The Orphan Brigade," en route to Kentucky; Jackson, Miss.:

Had an excellent breakfast at the hotel. Our train staid on the switch until late in the evening when we ran down below town and disembarked. Established camp on a nice grassy plot, immediately on the railroad. We are here waiting orders from Breckinridge whether to go *via* Mobile or Demopolis.

Braxton Bragg moved his columns towards Lexington to join up with Kirby Smith and left the roads open for Gen. Buell to move his troops around Bragg's left and go to the relief of Louisville. Bragg's victory at Munfordville was short-lived; Federal troops were back in town today.

September 22 (Monday)

Lincoln issued his "preliminary" Emancipation Proclamation today. It did little except free the slaves in the states not held by the Union.

Federal troops returned to Harpers Ferry after the Confederates had departed south with Lee. At Antietam, the wounded were still dying at a tremendous rate.

Stowe, Sgt., Co. G, 15th Massachusetts, hospital at Sharpsburg [Antietam], Md.:

Two men died last night.... How painful my stump is. I did not know [I] was capable of enduring so much pain. How very meager are accommodations—no chamber pots & nobody to find or rig up one. How ludicrous for 2 score amputated men to help themselves with diarrhea.

Jackman, Pvt., "The Orphan Brigade," en route to Kentucky; Meridian, Miss.:

This morning Companies "A" and "C" stacked arms stating their time was out and declaring the "C.A. Government" had no right to conscript them. Col. C.—Col. H. still being away wounded—had them all put under guard, Co B being detailed to guard them. This evening Col. H. came in camp on crutches and talked to the "mutineers" awhile. They all returned to duty being promised the War Department would be consulted as to whether they could be held in service or not. Got on cars in the evening, late, and remained on side-track all night.

During a storm in the Gulf of Mexico, Admiral Farragut noted that "... these are the times that try the commander of a squadron. I could not sleep last night, thinking of the blockaders. It is rough work lying off a port month in and month out.... I have 6 vessels off Mobile, so that one can always come in for coal. They are all the time breaking down and coming in for repairs."

September 23 (Tuesday)

McClellan's men had almost finished cleaning up the battlefield at Antietam. More wounded had been evacuated and the Sanitary Commission was still active in providing supplies and aid to the wounded.

Stowe, Sgt., Co. G, 15th Massachusetts, hospital at Sharpsburg [Antietam], Md.:

Oh what long fearful horrid nights. What difficulties we have to contend.... Relief can hardly be found. I have at length got my limb dressed by volunteer surgeon. But never was so nearly exhausted for want of refreshment.

Jackman, Pvt., "The Orphan Brigade," en route to Kentucky; Demopolis, Miss.:

Left Meridian at daylight on new road being constructed to Demopolis. The road being new, the train ran very slowly taking nearly all day to run out to York Station the terminus of the road. Once the car in front of the Col.'s ran off and went bouncing over the ties. I looked out to see what was the matter and saw the men, even in front of the car, jumping off. Expecting every moment our car would run off. We commenced "rolling out"—the Col. first, to show the balance how to jump; then followed the staff, not questioning rank. The car kept running over the ties for several hundred yards before the train was stopped. Looking back, the road was littered with soldiers, some sitting up, feeling their heads and limbs to see that no bones were broken, others were still lying on the ground; and a crowd came following the train, some limping, some laughing. The car was then put on the track and we moved on. Went into camp near York Station, 30 miles from Meridian. [We were] waiting for wagons to haul our camp equippage to Demopolis, 20 or 30 miles distant.

September 25 (Thursday)

Don Carlos Buell arrived in Louisville before Bragg's columns could reach the city. A bad move on Bragg's part. The occupation of Louisville would have been a big blow to the morale of the region.

Stowe, Sgt., Co. G, 15th Massachusetts, hospital at Sharpsburg [Antietam], Md.:

> Such nights! Why they seem infinitely longer than days. The nervous pains are killing 2 or 3 every night. All sorts of groans & pleadings ... Many patients are leaving daily. Some have gone today to H. Ferry. I watch over J. Hughes nightly. Has had fever. Very cold last night & we are very short for clothing. Sundown just Recd. Blankets and beds.

Jackman, Pvt., "The Orphan Brigade," en route to Kentucky; Meridian, Miss.:

> Train started early and we got to Meridian by noon. Our car was on the passenger train. The train on which the regiment was transported was delayed until nearly dark by engine running off the track.

September 26 (Friday)

Stowe, Sgt., Co. G, 15th Massachusetts, hospital at Sharpsburg [Antietam], Md.:

> Very cold last night. J. Hughes had shakes again last night.... This cold weather may all come for best, certainly maggots do not trouble so much and air is some purer. 4 P.M. J. Hughes died.... O there comes Mrs. Gray with refreshments. Such a treat...I got tomatoes...just what I wanted. Have since forgotten my stump first hemorrhage—It was very copious and tho I had stoutly affirmed that I would not use Brandy was now plainly told that if not should be dead in 3 days.

Jackman, Pvt., "The Orphan Brigade," en route to Kentucky; Mobile, Ala.:

> Left Meridian at 9 A.M. and on the road all day running to Mobile. At noon a rain set in and kept up all through the day and night. The road to Mobile is through one interminable pine forest—almost a wilderness. When we got to the city—a little after dark—the train was put on a side-track. All the officers and men near by immediately went out in the city to "have a time." I preferred staying at home and passed a very disagreeable night, the car leaking badly.

In Charleston, S.C., Admiral Du Pont had developed an new method of refueling his ships. A large coal hulk, fitted with hoisting equipment and a capacity of 1000 tons of coal, has been "parked" in the area. Schooners hauling coal from the North unload into it and his ships refuel from it, using the machinery—a novel approach.

September 27 (Saturday)

The South raised the age limit for the conscription of troops to 45.

Lincoln was becoming annoyed with McClellan, who sat and crowed about his "victory."

A first: A regiment of free Negroes was mustered in at New Orleans as the First Regiment Louisiana Native Guards.

Stowe, Sgt., Co. G, 15th Massachusetts, hospital at Sharpsburg [Antietam], Md.:

> Commence taking brandy none too soon. Dr. tells me I am dangerously ill and must take his prescription in order to change condition of blood. He is earnest & too good a man. Mr. L. Sloan a kind hearted chaplain telegraphs for me. Suffer continuously from position in bed. Have to elevate my stump to prevent bleeding and be very still...

Jackman, Pvt., "The Orphan Brigade," en route to Kentucky; Mobile, Ala.:

> A murky man was "Old Trib" as the boys called Col. Trabue, tried to keep us all at the depot but soon the whole brigade was scattered over the city. All bent on having a spree. I went down on the quay, first place, to see the bay. The fog was just lifting and had a very pretty view. Feeling like breakfast, I stopped into an oyster saloon and took a few dozen standards.

When I got back to the depot, I found the drays and wagons ready to transport our baggage to the wharf. The rain commenced pouring down, again and kept up all the time we were moving. Our regiment embarked on an old cotton boat, the "Waverly"—the 4th and 6th on a fine passenger steamer, the *R.B. Taney.* We lay at the wharf all day after we had embarked. The day turned out beautiful. The boys kept coming aboard in squads, many in a condition, "how come you so." Just as the sun was disappearing "behind the western waters," the good steamer *Waverly* cast loose and steamed up the Alabama. Soon the *Taney* followed and a race was inevitable. Our steam was down and they soon past us cheering and giving us "music" on the waters from brass bands, mixed with a screaming calliope. Company "H" of our regiment, being nearly all steamboatmen, took charge of affairs and soon the *Waverly* mounted the waves like a "thing of life." It seemed every man in the regiment turned fireman, *pro tempore.* When we overtook the *Taney,* she was turned across the channel to keep us from passing, but we ran around her and went on. The night was dark and misty.

September 28 (Sunday)

Stowe, Sgt., Co. G, 15th Massachusetts, hospital at Sharpsburg [Antietam], Md.:

> Oh what lengths to the nights. The horrid smell from mortifying limbs is nearly as bad as the whole we have to contend. Mrs. Lee and another lady are here daily dispensing cooked broths.... They seem to employ their whole time for us. Move outdoors in P.M. Excessively hot.

Jackman, Pvt., "The Orphan Brigade," en route to Kentucky; on the Alabama River:

> When morning came our "antagonist" was nowhere to be seen. We stopped at a wood yard and cooked two days rations. Just as we were getting through, the *Taney* passes us. We hurried on board and soon left them behind again. Cloudy all day but no rain fell.

September 29 (Monday)

In a hotel lobby in Louisville, Ky., Brigadier Gen. Jefferson C. Davis shot Brigadier Gen. William Nelson to death in front of several witnesses. The quarrel between the two was recent. Davis had been assigned to assist Nelson in recruiting soldiers around Louisville. After two days, Nelson was not satisfied with Davis's performance and told him so. Davis, a West Point graduate, resented this and demanded more respect from Nelson, who thereupon relieved him of his duties. The morning of this day, Davis confronted Nelson in the lobby of the Galt House Hotel, where Nelson had his headquarters, and demanded an apology, which demand was refused. Davis then threw a wad of paper in Nelson's face, and Nelson slapped him and started upstairs. Davis borrowed a pistol, followed Nelson, and called his name. When Nelson turned, Davis shot him in the chest from about three feet away. Nelson died within the hour. Davis was never tried, the affair being treated as a "matter of honor."

Stowe, Sgt., Co. G, 15th Massachusetts, hospital at Sharpsburg [Antietam], Md.:

> Slept little more comfortable last night. Got nice soups and nice light biscuit and tart also nice butter from Mrs. Lee. Also she gets me milk again this morning. How the quinine keeps me parched for water and so sleepy and foolish. Am much better off here than in barn. 10 A.M. my comrade died from 18th Minn. Regt. I recd 4 letters from friends at home but am so boozy it takes the whole A.M. to read them. Mr. Dr. Kelsey dressed my stump admirably and am quite comfortable if the quinine does not choke me to death. It is far more quiet here but begins to rain.

At 7:54 this evening, Stowe had a telegram sent to J.W. Stowe as follows: "Dangerously wounded at Hoffmans hospital near Sharpsburg. Come instantly."

It was too late. On October 1, Stowe died of his wounds and the amputation. He had lain on the battlefield for a day without food or water and then was taken to the Nicodemus farm by the Rebels and remained there without treatment for 24 hours. The cumulative effects were too much.

Jackman, Pvt., "The Orphan Brigade," en route to Kentucky; on the Alabama River:

> Clouds broke away at noon. The boys amused themselves by shooting alligators lying out on the

sandbars and banks sunning themselves. The scenery all up the river is monotonous. The banks are generally low and the country seen from the boat not much improved; sometimes fine plantations could be seen skirting the river. Passed two towns today—Catalpa and Selma—the latter quite a place. Saw two ironclads being built at Selma; and formidable looking craft too. Soon after passing Selma, darkness again came over the water.

September 30 (Tuesday)

Jackman, Pvt., "The Orphan Brigade," en route to Kentucky; West Point, Ga.:

> At noon arrived at Montgomery having traveled 450 miles by water. Our baggage was moved to the depot by 3 P.M. and we took train for West Point, Ga. I did not have time to look over Montgomery much. The train sped away between 3 and 4 P.M. and until dark set in we were rushing through pine forests. Goodness! Shall we ever get out of the pines! Took supper at the Talladega Junction. Arrived at West Point midnight.

OCTOBER 1862

September was over and the aftermath of Antietam was still with both sides in the form of the wounded and dying. It would be months before many of these men could shoulder a musket, and for some it would be a long trip home—minus an arm or a leg. The long wagon trains of wounded coming back into Virginia had unloaded their cargo at train depots, and the wounded who could travel were sent on to Richmond and other military hospitals for better care. Those who were native to the Valley were taken home to recuperate. Many Union soldiers went home, others to the large hospitals around Washington, and slowly, ever so slowly, the wounded were shipped out during the cooler days and crisp nights.

October 1 (Wednesday)

The gunboats on the western rivers, heretofore operating under the Army, were transferred to the Navy and placed under command of Acting Rear Admiral David Dixon Porter, then a Commander. Secy. of the Navy Gideon Welles defended the two-grade promotion on the grounds of Porter's specialty.

Major Gen. John C. Pemberton was given command of the defense at Vicksburg, replacing Van Dorn. The people of southern Indiana, Ohio and northern Kentucky were now free of Bragg's columns as they withdrew. The South's hope of a popular uprising was unfulfilled.

Jackman, Pvt., "The Orphan Brigade," en route to Kentucky; Atlanta, Ga.:

> Changed cars for Atlanta at 8 A.M.—until 2 P.M. reaching Atlanta. At La Grange, Newnan and other towns, a throng of ladies at the depot to give us a cheer. By the time we got to Atlanta the cars were piled up with bouquets. In Atlanta all the people were scared having heard that Breckinridge's "Wild Kentuckians" were coming through. At 7 P.M. whirled off on the Western & Atlanta road. Having heard we were coming, the Kentucky refugees at Marietta were at the depot to see us. I was asleep at the time and did not see any of the "bright eyes" from the "promised land."

October 2 (Thursday)

Science was introduced to the Secretary of War's office in Richmond with the installation of telegraphic equipment. It seemed that the line went all the way to Warrenton. During a Federal foray into that area, one Yankee telegrapher sent a message to Richmond saying all was quiet and asking how things were in Richmond.

North of the Potomac in the vicinity of Antietam, Gen. McClellan was visited by the President. Lincoln had come to see what "Little Mac" was doing with his army.

Jackman, Pvt., "The Orphan Brigade," en route to Kentucky; Knoxville, Tenn.:

> At Dalton by daylight. Here Genl. Breckinridge came in our car for the balance of the trip. At 10 A.M. left on the Ga. & East Tenn. road for Knoxville. At every station the train stopped the people found out that Breckinridge was on board and would crowd around the car to see him. Often he was requested to speak, but he always declined. Up in East Tennessee—out of the pines at last! The country begins to look natural—see stacks of grain, fields of heavy corn, fat cattle, hogs, etc. Once a crowd came to see

the General, who was out at the time, and Dr. P., our surgeon, was pointed out to them as the General and they went off as well satisfied as if they had seen the *rara avis* sure enough. Got to Knoxville at 10 P.M.. Slept in the cars all night.

October 3 (Friday)

At Headquarters of the Army of the Potomac, McClellan regaled Lincoln with parades and demonstrations. Lincoln, not entirely taken in, called the troops "Gen. McClellan's bodyguard."

Gunboats U.S.S. *Commodore Perry*, *Hunchback*, and *Whitehead*, under the overall command of Lt. Cmdr. Flusser, went up the Blackwater River in Virginia to support troops in an assault on Franklin. Finding the stream full of obstacles, they turned to go back, only to find the Confederates felling trees behind them trying to fence them in. Escape was narrow.

Jackman, Pvt., "The Orphan Brigade," en route to Kentucky; Knoxville, Tenn.:

> Went into camp a short distance from town. While here we lived off the "fat of the land." We had very good rations issued to us and there was a plentiful and cheap market at hand. Was very busy in the office all the time making reports and recording orders which had gotten behind before I came with the office. The troops were being thoroughly organized and equipped for a march into Kentucky. While this was going on the time of some of the 6th Ky. expired and they refused to do duty longer. Genl. B. came out and had the brigade drawn up about him. He made a little speech to the boys giving all a little raking over for being so wild and having made too free with other folks' property during the late trip; and then, he addressed himself to our boys that had stacked arms at Meridian. He told them he was surprised at their having acted so. That though he had since been told the action was to raise the question whether the government had a right to hold them in the service or not, which he said, would take some of the edge off the crime—yet, if he had been there he would have had either unconditional surrender or unconditional mutiny. He then said that as an investigation had been promised them he would see that they received an answer from the War Department. He wound up by giving the "mutineers" in the 6th fifteen minutes to return to duty and they all did so before the time expired. Our company having heard Bragg's army was at Bardstown all in a glee thinking they would soon be home. Alas! they knew not then how many hard marches were before them—how many battles had to be fought, and yet, never march into Kentucky. In ten or twelve days, everything was put in order for a long march. The greatest trouble was in getting transportation.

Near Corinth, Miss., the Confederates attacked Rosecrans's lines and drove them in towards the town. The attack, led by Van Dorn and Sterling Price, was made to force the Federals to withdraw into Tennessee.

Barber, Cpl., Co. D, 15th Illinois Volunteer Infantry, Bolivar, Tenn.:

> ... we were ordered to march in light marching order with no train except an ammunition and ambulance train. It was very evident that we were going on a forced march and that something of unusual moment was afoot. To our division was added the 12th Michigan and 68th Ohio Infantry regiments making in all a fighting force of a little less than four thousand men. General Hurlbut starting in command of the expedition.... We marched twenty-eight miles the first day and camped near the Hatchie river. Tired out, we soon went to rest...

October 4 (Saturday)

A landing party from the U.S.S. *Thomas Freeborn*, Lt. Cmdr. Magaw, raided Dumfries, Va. (just north of the current site of Quantico Marine Base), and destroyed the telegraph office and wires of the line from Occoquan to Richmond.

Another saltworks was destroyed in Florida by a landing party from the U.S.S. *Tahoma*, Cmdr. John C. Howell.

The second day of battle near Corinth saw Van Dorn renewing his attacks on Rosecrans. The battle swayed back and forth with attack and counterattack until midafternoon, when Van Dorn withdrew to the northwest around the town of Chewalla. So far the Union had lost about 2500 and the Confederates a little over 4200. The result of the battle was a draw—no reinforcements were sent to Buell, but Grant did not pull back into Tennessee. The rail center of Corinth was still in Federal hands.

Barber, Cpl., Co. D, 15th Illinois Voluntary Infantry, on the Hatchie River, Battle of Corinth, Miss.:

Just as the streaks of day began to tinge the east, we were on the move. We had not proceeded far before we met the rebel picket. After a slight skirmish, they hastily retreated. Our brigade was immediately deployed in line of battle and slowly and steadily advanced, our skirmishers feeling our way for us. The enemy was prepared to receive us. They were strongly posted along the river to dispute our passage. Soon the shells were screaming through the air, bursting over our heads. We rushed like the speed of the wind to the high hill beyond and soon the crest was gained. The enemy in rapid succession was pouring in their shot and shell, but they generally flew wide of the mark, passing over our heads. Soon Bolton and Burnap planted their artillery on the crest of the hill and its hoarse notes replied to the rebel thunder. For fifteen minutes a furious cannonading was kept up. With rapid precision and deadly aim, our well-trained battery men poured in their death-dealing charges upon the enemy. Gradually their fire slackened as one after another their guns were dismounted and most of their horses slain. During a temporary lull in the fight, the second brigade was ordered forward, marching in echelon, with the 14th Illinois in advance. We swept across the field towards the river. This was a thrilling military sight, such as one seldom sees. With colors flying, with well-dressed ranks and measured tread, our gallant lines moved on.... Our firm, undaunted bearing struck terror to the hearts of the enemy. After a few irregular volleys, they broke and ran. We poured in our fire at short range and with a fierce yell rushed forward to the charge. Some threw down their arms and plunged into the river and escaped to the other side. Some were drowned while attempting to cross. Some threw themselves before us and pled for mercy. Yes, the boasted Southern chivalry knelt at the feet of the despised Northern mud-sills and pled for mercy. A guard was detailed to take them to the rear and we again moved on.

... On one narrow bridge, in face of a terrible fire of grape and canister with which the rebels were raking it, our troops were to cross and form on the other side. Maj.-Gen. E.O.C. Ord had arrived on the ground and took command and he, being ignorant of the nature of the ground on the other side, got the troops mixed up and thrown into confusion. At this point the river makes an abrupt bend and the regiments were ordered to cross and form on each side of the road, but the bend in the river prevented them forming on the right. Gen. Ord was now wounded and taken off from the field and Gen. Hurlbut was again in command and he, understanding the situation, ordered the troops to deploy to the left. We were the third regiment to cross. The 53d Ohio preceded us but being met by a withering volley of grape and canister, they fell back in some confusion. Our regiment was then ordered to cross. We trailed arms and at a double quick we swept across the bridge without the loss of a man. The 53d made another attempt and succeeded, though they suffered severely during the time. The enemy's shots were mowing down our men with fearful rapidity. During the confusion, our regiment became entangled with others and a portion of Company D was left on the bank near the bridge, William, Rollin, Milton and myself among the number. The grape shot and canister were tearing up the ground in front of us, making general havoc amongst us. In order to reach the regiment, we had to cross an open field, raked by the enemy's fire. It was our only hope, so we made the attempt, and strange to say, only one man, James Eagan, was wounded and he succeeded in getting across.... At or near the bridge four hundred and fifty of our boys lay weltering in their blood. Gen. Veatch was struck by a spent ball and forced to leave the field.

The rebels were now strongly posted behind a rail fence, a few rods in front of us, but so thick was the underbrush that we could not see them. They poured in withering volleys through the brush but the thickness of the copse saved us many lives. Our regiment was protected by a long log behind which we lay.... The bullets pelted against the log like hailstones. ... Soon our batteries were across the bridge and their well-directed shots soon put the enemy in rapid retreat.... we now marched forward, pursuing the flying foe. In front of us was a large open field... in the edge of the field and running parallel with it was a road with an embankment of four or five feet on which was a rail fence. Behind this... the rebels had concentrated their entire force and made their last desperate stand. Our skirmishers were thrown forward and kept up a galling fire on the rebel artillery, while our artillery was being planted on the crest of the hill. We had twenty-four pieces in all and they were extended along the whole length of the line, the muzzles of the guns just clearing the top of the hill so that the recoil would put them back out of range of the enemy's fire.... peering over the brow of the hill, we saw a long, dense line of rebels evidently preparing for a charge.... Cautiously the rebels began to advance.... Our artillery men stand ready and at a given signal, a sheet of fire and flame burst forth from the muzzles.... It was impossible for the rebel officers to make their men face the music. They broke and sought the cover of the woods.

A rapid and continual cannonading was now kept up on each side for nearly an hour. That hill seemed to be ablaze with fire and glory.... From our position we could see the effect of every shot. It was truly a grand sight.... Before us was a veteran army of twenty-five thousand men, commanded by their ablest Generals—Price and Van Dorn. Opposed to them was our own little, gallant division, numbering scarcely four thousand men, henceforth to be known as the "Fighting Fourth." ...They soon were in rapid retreat but we did not pursue them any farther.... There was but one road for them to escape by, and leaving their baggage train and throwing away everything, the terror-stricken enemy broke up in squads and ran for dear life. Thus ended the memorable battle of Corinth and Matamora.... We never ascertained the rebel loss in this engagement, as they succeeded in carrying off all of their wounded and burying most of their dead....

We now busied ourselves taking care of our wounded and burying our dead, which took us until nearly dark. Rollin, Milton, and Simon Smith came in with a good porker for supper.... One day a citizen asked Hurlbut what name he was going to give the late battle. "Hell on the Hatchie" was his prompt reply, and Col. Rogers had it inscribed on the battle flag of the 15th and although it did not show good taste, it suited a majority of the regiment....

October 5 (Sunday)

Van Dorn, while not hotly pursued by Rosecrans, was ambushed by Federal troops under General E.O.C. Ord at the Hatchie River, where a stiff fight took place. The Federals paused to regroup and the Rebels took off towards Holly Springs, ending this campaign, which accomplished little except for more casualties.

Edward Otho Cresap Ord was born in Cumberland, Md., on October 18, 1818, but was raised in Washington, D.C. Graduating from West Point, class of '39, he served in the Mexican War and was a part of the expedition that captured John Brown at Harpers Ferry, Va., in 1859. Appointed Brigadier General in September 1861, he was assigned to the defense of Washington. Promoted to Major General in May 1862, he served in the west at Iuka and at Corinth, where he was severely wounded. He returned to duty in time to serve with Grant at the siege of Vicksburg, and he commanded the XIII Corps after Grant relieved Gen. John A. McClernand during the siege of Jackson, Miss., after the fall of Vicksburg. When Grant went east, Ord followed and was assigned commander of the XVIII Corps in the Army of the Potomac, and was again wounded during the assault on Ft. Harrison (Signal Hill). As noted, he relieved Butler as commander of the Army of the James. Ord was present at the surrender of Lee at Appomattox C.H. He remained in the Regular Army as a Brigadier General. He died in Havana, Cuba, on July 22, 1883.

In Kentucky, Bragg was slowing pulling back to Bardstown, his long wagon trains ahead of him headed for Tennessee.

October 6 (Monday)

Lincoln, having departed McClellan's headquarters on the 4th, now directed McClellan to take some action. He sent a message through Gen. Halleck: "The President directs that you cross the Potomac and give battle to the enemy or drive him south. Your army must move while the roads are good."

In Kentucky, Bragg's main force was withdrawing towards Harrodsburg, as Buell entered Bardstown. Neither side was moving very fast.

October 7 (Tuesday)

In Kentucky, Bragg's columns were moving on two different roads and were therefore divided. Buell, hoping to take advantage of this, approached the column near Perryville, hoping to defeat that Confederate column before the other column could come up.

The Confederate Congress passed a bill increasing the pay of the soldiers by $4 per month. It did not increase the pay of other government workers.

October 8 (Wednesday)

The only major battle fought on Kentucky soil was fought today at Perryville. Major Gen. Don Carlos Buell's Union army clashed with Gen. Braxton Bragg's Confederates. Not all of Buell's troops were engaged. A strange atmospheric condition prevented the sound of the guns from being heard in the rear and Buell did not know that his forward elements were engaged until late in the afternoon. Much of the heavy fighting was done by a unit commanded by Philip H. Sheridan. Bragg's forces managed to disengage and withdraw to the southeast. In total forces, the Union outnumbered the Confederates by more than 2 to 1. However, neither side had its total force engaged at any time. It was a partial victory for the North, and in one way a total victory, in that no major invasion of Kentucky was attempted again by the South.

October 11 (Saturday)

The C.S.S. *Alabama*, Capt. Semmes, captured and burned her fourth ship this month off Nova Scotia. Semmes noted, "...the *Manchester* brought us a batch of late New York papers.... I learned from them where all the enemy's gun boats were, and what they were doing.... Perhaps this was the only war in which the newspapers ever explained, beforehand, all the movements of armies and fleets, to the enemy."

JEB Stuart entered Chambersburg, Pa., where he cut the telegraph lines, seized horses, wrecked everything in sight that looked useful and couldn't be carried away, and left in the afternoon, going south towards Emmitsburg, Md.

October 14 (Tuesday)

Today, elections held in several of the midwestern states elected Democrats to Congress, except in Iowa, which was solidly Republican.

Brigadier Gen. James Birdseye McPherson today became a Division Commander in Grant's army. He would distinguish himself many times before he was killed outside Atlanta.

Barber, Cpl., Co. D, 15th Illinois Volunteer Infantry, after Corinth, Tenn.:

> Gen. Hurlbut was now relieved of command and ordered to report to Jackson, Miss., to assume command of the military district.... Brevet Brigadier-General James B. McPherson to assume command of the division.... When he assumed command the boys were nearly all prejudiced against him as they were against all West Point graduates, but...our dislike changed into esteem...amounted to almost veneration, and soon McPherson's name became synonymous with all that was good and noble....
>
> Troops begin to concentrate here and active preparations were being made for a fall campaign.... Our decimated ranks were being filled up by new troops under the five hundred thousand called in July. We now marched to La Grange.... We had not proceeded far...before Col. Turner received a dispatch announcing that his resignation had been accepted. The regiment halted and with visible emotion he bade farewell to it.... The boys on this march committed those acts of lawlessness which wanton soldiers indulge in. Amongst others, they burned the fences all along the route. All the efforts of the officers to find the incendiaries proved unavailing. On the third day the regiment was back again in its old quarters. The 15th regiment was soon detailed to guard Ball's Bridge, a place one and one-half miles from camp.

October 15 (Wednesday)

Barber, Cpl., Co. D, 15th Illinois Volunteer Infantry, La Grange, Tenn.:

> This was an agreeable duty as it enabled the boys to forage without being subject to the restraints of picket and camp rules. A good number of the boys went into a private speculation by confiscating cotton and then selling it on the sly. About this time the 95th Illinois joined the army. Seven companies of this regiment were raised in McHenry County and three in Boone, and many of our friends and acquaintances were in it, amongst whom I will mention Asahel Eddy, Wif. Mallory, Dan Mitchell and Jimmie Williams. The 72nd Illinois Infantry was now added to our brigade, making in all five regiments still under command of Gen. Veatch, whom the boys had learned to love as a father, but they had not yet gotten over the disposition to play off jokes on him....
>
> Preparations were now made for a forward movement and soon Grant's army was on the move. The enemy retreated in great haste as we advanced. Near Holly Springs we got a slight skirmish out of their rear guard. When we arrived at that place, Col.

Rogers was offered the position to command the post and garrison it with his regiment, but he preferred to accompany the army and that traitor, Murphy, of the 109th Illinois was left in command.

Jackman, Pvt., "The Orphan Brigade," en route to Kentucky; to Cumberland Gap:

> All things being ready, broke up camp and marched 12 miles towards Cumberland Gap. All marched with a buoyant step. There was no straggling and the column kept well closed up. Col. Hanson in command of the brigade. We went into camp before sundown and pitched our tents in regular order. We are going to Kentucky in grand style!

October 17 (Friday)

Jackman, Pvt., "The Orphan Brigade," en route to Kentucky; to Cumberland Gap:

> When the column got fairly out on the road this morning a courier came dashing up to Genl. Breckinridge and handed him a dispatch. We were ordered back and pitched our tents on old grounds. Various rumors are afloat about camp as to the cause of our delay. Some say that Bragg has been whipped and is retreating from Kentucky; others say he has captured a large lot of supplies and is sending a large wagon train through the Gap, that we shall have to wait until it passes; and various other rumors are going the rounds.

October 19 (Sunday)

Yesterday near Lexington, Ky., the cavalry of John Hunt Morgan defeated a Union cavalry force, entered the city, captured the garrison, paroled the prisoners, and went away.

Bragg's columns reached the Cumberland Gap and began moving through. This would take several days with the long wagon trains of confiscated grain, herds of cattle, etc. he was moving.

Jackman, Pvt., "The Orphan Brigade," return to Knoxville, Tenn.:

> Early struck tents and with "heads all lowly bending" marched 15 miles towards Knoxville. Camped where we did the first night out. Going to Kentucky "played out." The boys not so cheerful today as when going on the road the other way. They didn't keep up so well.

October 21 (Tuesday)

Lincoln ordered Major Gen. John A. McClernand, one of Illinois's political generals, to organize a force in Illinois, Indiana, and Iowa to assault Vicksburg. McClernand went to work with a will, believing that he would have a free hand in this campaign and make his name. He organized the units and sent them south to Grant's army. There they were assigned to Sherman's corps, which was to assault Vicksburg via the Yazoo River. The acrimony over the assignment would last for many years after the war, but the immediate result was dissension in Grant's army.

The mail steamer *Gladiator* had been attacked by guerrillas early on October 19th. Today, the U.S.S. *Louisville*, Lt. Commander Meade, in company with the steamer *Meteor*, landed Army troops at Bledsoe's Landing and Hamblin's Landing, Ark. The towns were burned in reprisal. Meade reported to Adm. D.D. Porter that "the people along the river bank were duly informed that every outrage by the guerrillas upon packers would be similarly dealt with."

October 22 (Wednesday)

Three 12-pounders were mounted in boats from the U.S.S. *Wabash* to take part in an assault in the Battle of Pocotaligo, S.C. Ordinary Seaman Oscar W. Farenholt, the first Navy enlisted man to reach flag rank, was wounded in the action.

At Cumberland Gap, Bragg's long trains had moved through, and his troops were now passing into Tennessee.

Jackman, Pvt., "The Orphan Brigade," Shell Mound, Tenn.:

> Left Chattanooga in the forenoon and got off the train near Shell Mound. Camped regularly on the side of the road. The Tennessee "rolls her crystal waters" in sight of camp. The mountain scenery about us is grand—picturesque. Shell Mound is nothing more than a station on the Nashville and Chattanooga railroad 16 miles distant from the latter place.

October 24 (Friday)

The C.S.S. *Alabama*, Capt. Semmes, captured and burned the whaling ship *Lafayette* south of Halifax, Nova Scotia. Semmes, it seemed, took no rest.

A landing party from the U.S.S. *Baron de Kalb*,

Capt. Winslow, "impressed" horses to pursue a small Confederate scouting party. The chase lasted nine miles and resulted in the capture of the Rebels.

Don Carlos Buell was removed from command in Kentucky and replaced by Major Gen. William S. Rosecrans. Rosecrans had a little over two months before his major battle at Stone's River.

October 25 (Saturday)

Lincoln, irked by McClellan's inactivity, had just read a telegram in which McClellan was complaining about sick horses. Lincoln responded, "I have just read your despatch about sore tongued and fatigued horses. Will you pardon me for asking what the horses of your army have done since the battle of Antietam that fatigue anything?"

In the west, Major Gen. Grant assumed command of the Thirteenth Army Corps and the Department of the Tennessee.

The Confederacy was building ironclads in the rivers throughout the South in an attempt to break the Union's blockade. Admiral Du Pont, South Atlantic Blockading Squadron, was trying to get the two seagoing ironclads currently being commissioned in the North, for his own area of operations. He remarked:

> The idea seems to be to open the Savannah river, then come to Port Royal, and thence off Charleston, and raise the blockade.... I submit that the *Ironsides* and *Passaic* be dispatched at an early day.

Jackman, Pvt., "The Orphan Brigade," en route to Bridgeport, Ala.:

> In the evening struck tents and loaded our baggage on the train to be run down to the river opposite Bridgeport. We then marched down on the railroad, being 5 miles. Dark was setting in when we unloaded our baggage on the side of the railroad and bivouacked among the drift. Looking like rain, we pitched our tent and well we did for when morning came the ground was covered with snow. A very sudden change—yesterday being too hot for comfortable marching.

October 26 (Sunday)

The Army of the Potomac began crossing the river and into Virginia. This was its first major move in more than two months. The movement was not rapid.

Jackman, Pvt., "The Orphan Brigade," en route to Bridgeport, Ala.:

> The Tennessee is here divided by an island nearly half a mile in width and a bridge spans each arm of the river, the island being the centre span. The old bridges were burned during last summer and the new ones, now up, are not far enough advanced for trains to cross.—Whew! wintry this morning and had to carry all of our baggage 200 yards to the landing. Here a company at a time got on board of a small steamboat and ferried over to the island—then lugged across to another boat and was put over on the Bridge Port side. By 3 P.M. our regiment was packed away on a train of cars like sardines. I believe we never were before so crowded on a train. I stood up nearly all the time, the train having left at 4 P.M. and running all night.

October 27 (Monday)

Jackman, Pvt., "The Orphan Brigade," Murfreesboro, Tenn.:

> About noon arrived at Murfreesboro and the first man I saw was Bro. who was in company with "Capt" G. Took dinner with them. In the evening established camp half a mile from town on the Shelbyville Pike. Camped nearly on the same ground we occupied on retreat from Kentucky.
>
> Now commenced a long siege of monotonous camp life. However, I was kept busy writing all the time and did not have an opportunity of watching how the heavy hours went by. The boys too were kept pretty busy drilling and standing guard. Col. Hanson, soon after promotion to Brigadier General, now took command of the brigade and had everything done up in military order. He was the best disciplinarian we ever had. The brigade was all under the same guard line and at dress parade the whole brigade would be in a perfect line of battle, on the color line. Guard duty had to be done to the letter. "Old Roger" as we called the General—most of his own regiment called him "Flintlock"—was going the rounds at all hours of the night to see that all was well. The boys had many adventures with him.
>
> We lived well all the time we were encamped at Murfreesboro. Good rations were issued us, and we

always could buy butter, chickens, eggs, turkeys, sweet potatoes, apples, etc. from the country people at the old rates, paying "Confederate."....

Late in the fall, when the weather got cool, the boys built brick chimneys to their tents which made them quite comfortable. We had an army stove in the office made of sheet iron. By keeping it full of wood all the time our tent was kept very warm and cozy.

October 28 (Tuesday)

In Richmond, Braxton Bragg had returned to report directly to President Davis, an old friend, on the status of his army after Perryville.

McClellan continued to move the Army of the Potomac across the river and in the direction of Warrenton, Va. Lee shifted his forces to cover his flanks.

A boarding party led by Lt. John Taylor Wood, CSN, boarded the Federal steamer *Alleghanian*, which was anchored at the mouth of the Rappahannock River waiting to sail to London with a cargo of guano. The ship was burned.

October 29 (Wednesday)

A landing party from the U.S.S. *Ellis*, Lt. Cushing, destroyed a large Confederate saltworks at New Topsail Inlet, N.C. Cushing commented that "it could have furnished all Wilmington with salt."

South of Nova Scotia, Capt. Semmes, on the raider C.S.S. *Alabama*, seized the brig *Baron de Castina*. Semmes released the ship, sending her on her way along with the crews of the last three ships he had burned.

Day, Pvt., Co. B, 25th Massachusetts Volunteer Infantry, New Bern, N.C.:

Our regiment is now left with only one field officer, Major Pickett. Col. Upton left us yesterday and Lieut. Col. Sprague and Adjutant Harkness left us two weeks ago. Lieut. Col. Sprague left to take command of a nine-months regiment already recruited in the city of Worcester. Adjutant Harkness is commissioned major of the same regiment. Col. Upton resigned on account of failing health, which I hope he may speedily recover after reaching home.... As a slight token of their regard for Col. Upton, the enlisted men are having manufactured a $1000 sword, which they intend to present to him. Major Pickett will succeed to the colonelcy and, according to military usage, Capt. Moulton of company H will be Lieut. Col. and Capt. Atwood of company C will be major.... I reckon if I was of an ambitious turn of mind, I should aspire to some of these places of honor and emolument, but remembering the promise that whoever humbleth himself shall be exalted, I will continue to wait on.

Massachusetts boys are getting thick as blueberries about here, and we are glad to see them. Three regiments of nine months troops have just arrived...more are coming.... I learn that Gen. Foster leaves tomorrow on an expedition, taking with him nearly all the force here, including the three new regiments. That will be breaking them in pretty quick after getting here. They, of course, have not had much drill and probably half of them never fired a gun. But to us, a little trip up the country is cheering news....

October 30 (Thursday)

The United States Navy Department had offered a reward of $500,000 for the capture of the C.S.S. *Alabama*, or $300,000 if she were destroyed. A dozen ships were chasing her.

Day, Pvt., Co. B, 25th Massachusetts Volunteer Infantry, New Bern, N.C.:

... Major Pickett, with six companies (the other four being on picket up the Trent road), left New Bern, embarking on the steamer Highlander for Washington on the Pamlico river. Here we joined Gen. Foster's expedition for a raid up the country. The force consisted of the 17th, 23rd, 24th and 25th Massachusetts and 10th Connecticut regiments of three-years troops, and the 3d, 5th and 44th Massachusetts regiments of nine-months troops, with five batteries of the 3d New York Artillery, Capt. Belgers's Rhode Island battery and seven companies of the 3d New York cavalry, besides a heavy wagon and ambulance train.

October 31 (Friday)

The Confederate Congress authorized a Torpedo Bureau under Brigadier Gen. Gabriel J. Rains and a Naval Submarine Battery Service under Lt. Hunter Davidson. The purpose was to organize and improve methods of torpedo (mine) warfare.

NOVEMBER 1862

October had been a month of healing and trying to forget. The ranks of the armies, North and South, were missing messmates who were left at Antietam's Stone Bridge or Bloody Lane, some field near Corinth, or a fence corner at Perryville. Soldiers, through the ages, have remembered their comrades and pondered their own fate.

McClellan had finally started moving again, albeit slowly. Lincoln kept urging him on, but to little avail. Lee sat at Winchester and considered a move to Gordonsville, where he could protect Richmond better. Bragg and his battered and weary legions were back in Tennessee after a long and arduous campaign that had gained little. Rosecrans had beaten Van Dorn at Corinth, and the Confederate Army in that area retreated. Vicksburg was under siege, but lightly.

November 1 (Saturday)

In Kentucky, the new Federal commander, Major Gen. William S. Rosecrans, prepared his troops for the move back into Tennessee and the search for Braxton Bragg. On the Mississippi River, Grant was preparing an overland campaign against Vicksburg, despite the political machinations being carried on by Major Gen. John McClernand in Illinois.

A naval task force, under the overall command of Commander Davenport, was formed yesterday to support the Army in its assault on Plymouth and Hamilton, N.C. The force consisted of the U.S.S. *Hetzel*, *Commodore Perry*, *Hunchback*, *Valley City*, and the Army gunboat *Vidette*. Today, the task force opened fire on a Confederate encampment near Plymouth, causing the Rebels to flee. Davenport had now been ordered to meet Gen. John G. Foster at Williamston on Monday to support the assault on Hamilton. Davenport responded "that we would begin our advance on Hamilton that night...."

Barber, Cpl., Co. D, 15th Illinois Volunteer Infantry, Oxford, Miss.:

> We continued to push the enemy until they crossed the Tallahatchie. Here they seemed disposed to make a stand, and well they might. The place was impregnable against a direct assault; bound on three sides by a broad and impassable swamp, with a deep, muddy river, backed by the strongest fortifications I had ever seen, but the invincible Sherman soon flanked them with his division and they beat a precipitate retreat. So rapidly now did we press them that their rear guard and our advance guard were constantly skirmishing. Soon the beautiful city of Oxford was reached and we marched triumphantly through its streets. We were now within twenty-five miles of Grenada, where it was supposed that the rebels would make a stand. ...about this time, the news of the surrender of Holly Springs reached us. This put a stop to further operations for the present.

November 2 (Sunday)

Capt. Semmes, C.S.S. *Alabama*, had run out of whaling boats to burn off Nova Scotia, so he has shifted his operations to the seas off Bermuda. Today, he caught another whaler, the *Levi Starbuck*, which he burned.

Day, Pvt., Co. B, 25th Massachusetts Volunteer Infantry, on a raid, N.C.:

> ...the expedition left Washington for a march across the country to the Roanoke river. The 23rd and 25th were detailed as guard over the wagon and ambulance train. We marched through a poor and sparsely populated section of country without interruption or anything to create excitement until about the middle of the afternoon when we heard firing on the advance. They had reached a swamp of considerable width, with a small creek running across and overflowing the road for quite a distance. At this point, two regiments of the enemy disputed the passage of the swamp and a brisk infantry and artillery fire commenced which lasted, with short intervals, for an hour or more, when the cavalry and two batteries charged across. The enemy beat a precipitate retreat, greatly accelerated by shells from the batteries. Our loss was small, not over a dozen killed and wounded, and most of these were from the 44th Massachusetts, which behaved nobly.
>
> During this skirmish the wagon train made slow progress, advancing a short distance and then halting. It was late in the evening when we reached the swamp. All the troops were on the other side, but we got orders to halt where we were over night. The mules were fed and we made a supper of cold meat, hardtack and coffee, after which we lay down by the side of the fence to sleep.

November 3 (Monday)

Longstreet arrived with his corps at Culpeper C.H., Va., moving in from the Valley to get in front of McClellan, who was now at Warrenton. No contact had been made yet.

James Longstreet was born in Edgefield District, S.C., on January 8, 1821. He attended West Point in the same class ('42) with U.S. Grant, Henry Halleck, Irvin McDowell, George H. Thomas, and William Sherman. He served in the Mexican War, where he was wounded and brevetted major. On June 1, 1861, he resigned to join the Confederate Army where he was commissioned Brigadier General on June 17th. He fought at First Manassas with distinction and was promoted to Major General on October 8, 1861. He fought at the Seven Day's Battle and at Malvern Hill. His reputation was badly damaged at Gettysburg when he was slow to react to Lee's orders to attack. He went to assist Bragg at the Battle of Chickamauga and fought at Knoxville, Tenn. He returned to Lee's army and surrendered at Appomattox in April 1865. After the war he would be blamed for the defeat at Gettysburg, primarily by Jubal Early, who was trying to remove the blame for that battle from Lee. After the war he was involved in an insurance agency and also supervised the Louisiana State Lottery. He died at Gainesville, Ga., on January 2, 1904.

Task Force "Davenport" moved upriver towards Hamilton, on schedule, to support the attack. One more gunboat, the U.S.S. *Seymour*, had been added to the force.

Day, Pvt., Co. B, 25th Massachusetts Volunteer Infantry, on a raid, N.C.:

> ...the mule teams commenced the passage of the swamp and mudhole. Hearing a great noise and shouting, I went down to see what was up. I mounted a rude foot bridge at the side, improvised for the benefit of pedestrians, and walked along until I was near the middle of the mudhole and where the creek crossed the road.
>
> Here was a line of men on each side of the road, armed with hoop-poles and standing in mud and water from six inches to three feet deep. When a team was driven in, it received all necessary encouragement from the hoop-poles and strong lungs of the men while running the gauntlet. If the pilot was skilful and kept on the corduroy, the passage would be made before the mules would get discouraged. Sometimes the mules would get off the corduroy, but if the wagon kept on, the mules would manage to flounder back and go on. After a spell, a careless driver ran his wagon off the corduroy and down it went to the axle. Here was a pretty fix. The mules couldn't haul it out and no other team could get by. It was decided to unload the wagon so the mules could pull it out. The load, consisting of beef and hardtack, was dumped into the creek, but the mules knew nothing of this arrangement, they only knew they were hopelessly stuck and when they were appealed to to haul out the wagon, they obstinately refused; bracing out their forelegs and sticking their ears straight up in the air, they seemed to proclaim themselves a fixture. No amount of swearing and belaboring them with hoop-poles had the slightest effect.
>
> Capt. Schenck, who was standing by watching the fun, told them he would hitch on one of his teams and haul them out. The captain had a battery of 20-pounder Napoleon guns with teams of eight heavy horses. He ordered in one of the teams and told them to hitch on to the mules, and when all was ready, he would give the order. When all was ready, the captain yelled, "Forward march!" The horses understanding the order, stepped smartly off; while the mules, not understanding it, did not step with the horses, but standing there braced out, the heels of three or four of them went up in the air, and they came down on their heads; in this way, sometimes under the water and sometimes out, kicking and floundering, trying to gain their feet, they were dragged out through the mudhole, to the great delight and amusement of the captain and all other spectators.
>
> This place is known as Rawls' Mills creek.... All the teams across, the march was resumed through a much better country, and we reached Williamston on the Roanoke river about noon. Our teams are four horse and six mule teams. Some of the mule teams are driven by darkies who sit on the nigh hind mule and pilot the craft by means of a single line running to the leaders, called a jerk line. With this line and their peculiar mule dialect, they handle the team admirably. Darkies and mules work together naturally; they understand each other perfectly and have the same dialect. Take a mule team that a white man can do nothing with and let a darky come along and

speak to them; in a minute they are entirely different animals and as docile as a kitten. They seem to have a love for him and are perfectly cognizant of all his actions and movements. If a darky, while driving, falls asleep, the mules know it in a minute and will stop. The leaders will face about and commence tangling themselves up in the chains and gearing of the next pair, and that will go on until some one hits the nigger on his head with a pine knot or lump of clay, waking him up. He will give the line a few jerks and call out to the mules in their language, and they will untangle themselves, straighten out and go on as though nothing had happened. Niggers and mules are a great institution.

Williamston is a pretty little town of about 1200 or 1500 inhabitants, nearly all of who had left, leaving it to the tender mercies of an army; of course what was left lying around loose was gobbled up. When the wagon train marched through, the boys were frying the chickens and pigs in the streets and probably the houses and stores contributed to their wants.... we again resumed the march, going up the Hamilton road. We went up this road for about 10 miles and bivouacked in a large field of corn about 10 P.M.... A great quantity of corn was yet unharvested and a few barnsful of harvested corn which we found was set on fire, as being the best and quickest way to market it.

Soon after we got into camp, a few darkies were seen lurking around not knowing exactly whether it would do to come too near. But their fears were soon dispelled by a few darkies who were with us.... They soon began to flock into camp, and in a little while a hundred or more had come in.

After the boys had their suppers, large fires were kindled, around which 200 or 300 of the boys formed a ring and getting thirty or forty of these darkies, men and women, inside, set them to dancing.... Three or four of them would pat the time and the rest would dance...men and women were dressed in well-worn garments of gunny cloth or Kentucky jeans, with enormous brogan shoes of russet leather, some of them looking as though they had a whole tannery on their feet....

In Berwick Bay, La., the C.S.S. *Cotton*, Capt. Edward W. Fuller, and the shore batteries took on four Union ships in a gun battle. Fuller did himself and his ship proud, doing considerable damage to the U.S.S. *Calhoun*, *Kinsman*, *Estella*, and *Diana* before he ran out of cartridges. To extend the battle, and to take a few parting shots, he had the men cut the legs off their trousers to make powder bags.

November 4 (Tuesday)

In the North, the Democrats won the elections in some states, notably New York, New Jersey, Illinois and Wisconsin. This raised the hopes of the Southerners, who believed that the Democrats would be able to contain the hated Lincoln and bring peace, especially on their terms. Not all was good news for the Democrats however. The control of the House of Representatives remained with the Republicans.

Task Force "Davenport," at 11 A.M., having failed to get any signal from the Army, proceeded up the Roanoke River. Hamilton was evacuated by the Confederates, and Union troops took possession of the town while the gunboats proceeded further upriver. The troops then proceeded on their march to Tarboro.

Day, Pvt., Co. B, 25th Massachusetts Volunteer Infantry, on a raid at Hamilton, N.C.:

> On the march at sunrise; just before noon we came out of the woods into an open country and in full view of the famous Rainbow bluff of which we had heard so much. The batteries were soon in position and skirmishers were sent out to examine the situation. After a time word came back that no enemy was near, the batteries limbered up and the march resumed.
>
> We were soon on the bluff, which was well fortified on the river and east sides but quite defenseless in the rear; it would have been an easy matter to have shelled out an enemy had there been one there. Here we found our gunboat fleet which had come up and was going to keep us company higher up the river. After destroying the works, we moved on, reaching the little town of Hamilton about 2 P.M. and halted just outside. Here we were to stop three or four hours for rest and dinner.
>
> I suggested to Doctor Ben that it would be a good plan to forage our dinner; to this he assented...we separated, each one to obtain his share of the dinner.... I soon filled my haversack and returning to the corner, waited for the doctor. Great was my surprise to soon see him coming down the street with a

hen dangling by the legs and in charge of the officer of the guard, going in the direction of the general's headquarters.... Being an interested party, I thought I would attend the conference. The officer preferred his charges, and Capt. Dan, the provost marshal, commenced the trial. ...the doctor was getting along nicely with it until the general began to a cross-examination by asking if he had not heard the order in regard to foraging? The doctor admitted that he had. "How then does it happen that you do not observe it?" This was a pretty close question and I began to tremble for him but he proved equal to the emergency; after waiting a moment, he looked up and said, "General, this rebellion has got to be crushed if it takes every hen in North Carolina." A smile lit up the face of the general, who asked, "Where is your regiment?" "Just beyond here, sir." "Go to it, my boy, and get your dinner and be ready to march in a couple of hours or so." We started, congratulating each other over the fortunate turn of events... the order came to march about 6 P.M.

This was a small town about half as large as Williamston, and like all other southern towns I have seen was built all in a heap. The inhabitants all left on our approach and exhibited a bad feeling by cutting their well ropes and filling the wells with rubbish. This so incensed the boys that on leaving they set the town on fire, and we marched away by the light of it. A tramp of five or six miles up the Weldon road brought us to a plantation on which was a big cornfield. Into this we filed and put up for the night. Here again was forage for the team and cavalry horses...our force of darkies was greatly augmented, they came in by hundreds....

The gunboats had come up the river, and were now working their way towards Halifax, causing, I presume, the people of that town a terrible fright. They would fire an occasional shot as an advance notice of their coming, and on the still night air the boom of the big guns far up the river was wafted back to our camp.

Jackman, Pvt., "The Orphan Brigade," Manchester, Tenn.:

Brigade marched with three days' rations in haversacks towards Nashville. The camp was left standing. Am left behind making Monthly Return and so on. Col. Hunt having requested me to sleep in his tent at night, I do so, sleeping magnificently on the Col.'s feather bed.

The brigade returned to camp the next day, or the day after, I have forgotten which. The movement was first on Nashville, going within five miles of the city. Morgan came into Edgefield opposite the city at the same time.

Barber, Cpl., Co. D, 15th Illinois Volunteer Infantry, Oxford, Miss.:

For a week we lay undecided what to do. The boys were getting discontented. Nothing will annoy a soldier more than to have his ration line cut off, and Gen. Lauman, who now commanded our division, gave strict orders against foraging, but of little use were his orders. Some of the boys, to show their appreciation of his orders, stole him blind one night while on guard at his headquarters. He never again called for a detail from the 15th to guard his quarters. From that time a strong dislike sprang up between Lauman and the regiment. Gen. McPherson had been appointed to command one wing of the army. We had marched fifty miles south of Holly Springs and twelve on the direct route to Grenada and Vicksburg.

Shallotte Inlet and New Topsail Inlet, which provided approaches to Wilmington, N.C., had both been effectively blockaded.

November 5 (Wednesday)

In what would be a shock to McClellan, President Lincoln ordered him replaced, assigning Major Gen. Ambrose E. Burnside as the commander of the Army of the Potomac. Burnside, an able general at some levels, realized his shortcomings and told Lincoln that he did not want the command and that he was unfit for it. This brought an end to McClellan's military career. McClellan's departure created much controversy in the ranks of the Army of the Potomac, which venerated him. He had been their father and protector almost since the army was formed. At the same time, Major Gen. Fitz John Porter was relieved from command and was replaced by Major Gen. Joseph Hooker.

Fitz John Porter was born to a naval captain and his wife at Portsmouth, N.H., on August 31, 1822. He graduated from West Point in 1845 and served in the Mexican War. He was an artillery instructor at

West Point for six years before joining Col. A.S. Johnston on the Mormon Expedition in 1857. In August 1861, he was appointed a Brigadier of Volunteers and served with McClellan through the Peninsula Campaign, where he fought with distinction, being promoted to Major Gen. on July 4, 1862. He was transferred to Pope's army when McClellan was in trouble. Porter didn't get along well with Pope, but then no one did. After Second Manassas, Pope relieved Porter, charging him with disloyalty and misconduct in the face of the enemy. Porter served again with McClellan at Antietam in September 1862. Relieved of command in November 1862 by Burnside, his career was ruined by political vendettas waged by Hooker and Stanton, who sat on the courts-martial board. He was cashiered from the army on January 21, 1863, and he spent the remainder of his life trying to clear his name. In 1878, a board headed by Gen. John Schofield exonerated Porter, and in 1886 President Grover Cleveland signed a bill restoring him to the rank of Colonel, with no back pay. He died at Morristown, N.J., on May 21, 1901.

Task Force "Davenport," still in support of the Army on the Roanoke River, sent the *Seymour* back downriver to destroy the guns at Rainbow Bluff, which posed a threat to the fleet. The remainder of the gunboats supported the Army's raid on Tarboro.

Day, Pvt., Co. B, 25th Massachusetts Volunteer Infantry, on a raid at Tarboro, N.C.:

> They were expecting us at Halifax and Weldon and were making preparations to receive us, but the general was not up in that part of the country looking for a fight. A battle up there would have been without results to us, unless it was the loss of men.... The general, not caring to go where they were expecting him...turned his course across the country towards Tarboro, a town on the Tar river, some twenty miles west, hoping to reach there before the enemy could concentrate their forces against him. This day's march was through a rich and fertile section of country, abounding in large, rich plantations, affording plenty of luxuries for the boys and a great many horses and mules for the use of the army. The contrabands flocked in droves to our standard, and were very useful in carrying our blankets, filling canteens, foraging chickens and pigs, toting rails for the fires, and in many other ways.... A heavy northeast rain storm set in during the night and we could hear the cars running, bringing troops into Tarboro. Scouting parties were sent out...and reported they were in force and fortified between us and the town. As the general's errand up through this part of the country was more for observation than fight... the next morning ordered a retreat.

In the west, Grant probed towards Somerset, Tenn., feeling out the Confederate forces between his position and Vicksburg.

November 6 (Thursday)

In Richmond, the promotions of James Longstreet and Stonewall Jackson from Major Gen. to Lieutenant Gen. were announced, as were their assignments to the First and Second Army Corps.

Task Force "Davenport" was waiting on the Roanoke River for news of the raid on Tarboro, N.C.

Day, Pvt., Co. B, 25th Massachusetts Volunteer Infantry, retreat from Tarboro, N.C.:

> The morning was dark and dreary. With a heavy northeast rain storm blowing, the enemy in force.... Quietly the order was given for the wagons to start and make the time as short as possible back some eight miles to an old church and crossroads past which we had come the day before.... Three companies of cavalry preceded us as an advance guard. The road was very muddy and the traveling hard, but that made no difference.... Their whole souls seemed centered on the old church, and they were thoroughly absorbed in their efforts to reach it. I don't believe they ever took half so much interest before in going to a church. The old church and crossroads were reached before noon.... The cavalry informed us that the bridge [that] we crossed the day before, was taken up and things looked as though somebody might be waiting for us on the other side.
>
> The troops were now coming up, and a couple of batteries dashed past us down the road into the swamp.... Two roads branched from the one we were on, one taking a north-easterly direction, the other north-westerly. Up these roads the cavalry were sent.... The pioneer corps were ordered down to the creek over which the bridge had been taken up and commenced felling trees as though they intended to

> rebuild it. ...the cavalry returned and reported everything all right. A part of the infantry and artillery now took the advance going up the north-easterly road, followed by the wagon train.... the sharp ring of the axes could be heard out in the swamp as though that was the intended route, but after the column had got well under way, the pioneers abandoned their job and followed along.... About night we reached the site where two days before stood the town of Hamilton. Nothing remained but a few scattered rookeries on the outskirts occupied by negroes.... The night was cold and stormy, snowing quite heavily, and the little army was obliged to stand it or find shelter as best they could. I reckon the boys who set the fires bitterly regretted their acts as they must have suffered much, and a good many of them were worn down and sick from the long march.

November 7 (Friday)

At nearly midnight on this date an officer appeared at the headquarters of the Army of the Potomac bearing the orders of November 5th that replaced McClellan as head of that army. "Little Mac" was surprised, stunned, and hurt. However, it was probably the best thing for the Union at this time.

In the west, Bragg assigned the two corps of his army to Major Gen. Leonidas Polk and William Hardee. In Kentucky, Rosecrans was moving his army to Nashville.

Union forces were withdrawing from Tarboro, N.C., with over 300 sick and wounded. Upon reaching Hamilton, these men were loaded aboard the gunboats for transport downriver to Williamston.

Day, Pvt., Co. B, 25th Massachusetts Volunteer Infantry, retreat from Tarboro, N.C.:

> By morning the storm had abated but there were about two inches of soft snow or slush and some of the boys were barefoot, having worn out their shoes and a good many were nearly, or quite sick. The surgeons looked over their regiments, sending the sick and bare-footed aboard the gunboats for Plymouth, for which place the troops were bound. The order of exercises for today was a march back to Williamston...but I had been a little under the weather for a day or two and I was sent with the others aboard the little gunboat Hetzel where we were greatly sympathized with by the marines who seemed to think we had had a pretty hard time of it and who showed us every favor.... The boat steamed slowly down the river, keeping along with the army, and arriving at Plymouth on the afternoon of the 10th, having made a two weeks excursion.
>
> I reckon the landed nobility up the country through which we traveled will never care to see another excursion of the same kind.... The Confederate commissariat can mourn the loss of many thousand bushels of corn.... We cleaned up pretty much everything there was, bringing back with us upward of 1000 negroes and several hundred horses and mules.

The resourceful Acting Lt. W. Budd, U.S.S. *Potomska*, did yeoman service today in support of the Army transport *Darlington*. Escorting the transport up the Sapelo River in Georgia, Budd found that his gunboat had too deep a draft to continue so he transferred to the *Darlington* and continued. At Spaulding the ship was fired upon from the shore, but it was undamaged. She continued to Fairhope, where Budd destroyed a saltworks and other buildings. Returning downriver, they were again fired upon at Spaulding. The *Potomska* being close by, she provided gun support by covering the landing party, which destroyed much public property and captured some small arms.

November 8 (Saturday)

Capt. Semmes, C.S.S. *Alabama*, still off Bermuda, burned the *T.B. Wales* after removing the crew.

In New Orleans, Major Gen. Benjamin F. Butler ordered all the breweries and distilleries in the city closed. Butler, who had been accused of almost everything imaginable, was a fading star. In Washington, the President appointed Major Gen. Nathaniel Banks, late of the Shenandoah Valley, to replace Butler. Banks was given specific instructions that his job was to open the Mississippi River, not to worry about breweries.

November 9 (Sunday)

Major Gen. Ambrose E. Burnside today assumed command of the Army of the Potomac, then at Warrenton, Va., about 40 miles southwest of Washington.

Ambrose Everett Burnside was born in Liberty, Ind., on May 23, 1824. He was the son of a former South Carolina slaveowner who moved to Indiana after freeing his slaves. He graduated from West Point in 1847 as a lieutenant of artillery. He served in the Mexican War and was later slightly wounded while fighting Apaches in the Southwest. He resigned in 1853 to open his own factory to produce a breech-loading rifle of his own design. He was forced into bankruptcy when an expected government contract did not materialize. Until the war began, Burnside worked for George B. McClellan, who was chief engineer of the Illinois Central Railroad. Burnside then accepted an appointment as Major General of Volunteers in the Rhode Island Militia. He came back into the Union Army as a colonel and fought at First Manassas as a brigade commander. He was promoted to Brigadier General and commanded the Hatteras campaign in early 1862. He commanded the IX Corps in McClellan's army and fought at Antietam. He had no illusions about his own capabilities and refused the command of the Army of the Potomac when it was offered by Lincoln. Lincoln ignored Burnside's refusal and appointed him anyway. The debacle at Fredericksburg proved Burnside right: he was not suited to army command. He was then sent to Ohio, where he became involved in political scrapes. He was relieved of his command after the Battle of the Crater in 1864. He resigned on April 15, 1865, and went to Rhode Island, where he was elected governor three times. He later served in the U.S. Senate until his death on September 13, 1881.

The town of Greenville, N.C., surrendered to a joint Army-Navy landing party commanded by Second Assistant Engineer J.L. Lay of the U.S.S. *Louisiana.*

November 10 (Monday)

Major Gen. George B. McClellan, at age 36, had commanded more men than any other general in American history. He took a dispirited army and, with his unique organizational skills, built it into a magnificent body of men, the like of which had never been seen on the continent. For all his virtues, and there were many, he had a failing that could not be tolerated in a general: he would not commit his men to battle with a will to win. For this reason, today he left his beloved Army of the Potomac forever. His farewell parade set the men to cheering as long as he was in sight. They would not soon forget this man, even if for the wrong reasons.

Commander Maury, CSN, arrived in Halifax, Nova Scotia, from Bermuda after five and one-half days on a very uncomfortable ship. He wrote his wife: "This is a place of 25 or 30,000 inhabitants. They are strongly 'secesh' here. The Confederate flag has been flying from the top of the hotel all day, in honor, I am told 'of our arrival.' "

Barber, Cpl., Co. D, 15th Illinois Volunteer Infantry, Oxford, Miss.:

> The former was the objective [Grenada] point.... Gen. Sherman's division did not march any farther than the Tallahatchie, but went back to Memphis and took transports and went down the river to cooperate with Grant from that quarter.

November 14 (Friday)

Admiral Farragut arrived in New Orleans to find a French admiral with two vessels and one British Navy corvette off the city.

Burnside, at Warrenton, reorganized his army and prepared for an offensive against Lee.

Barber, Cpl., Co. D, 15th Illinois Volunteer Infantry, Oxford, Miss.:

> We now kept shifting position and performing those uncertain movements so perplexing to a soldier. Some of the boys became almost desperate. Restricted on our rations, all communications cut off, and with no prospects of getting any more very soon, and surrounded by a relentless horde of rebel cavalry, our situation was anything but pleasant. The boys commenced an indiscriminate foraging with an avidity that knew no limits. In many places gold was found which the rebels had buried before leaving for the war to prevent its falling into the hands of the Yankees, but a little coaxing would induce the head darkey on the plantation to divulge its hiding place.

November 15 (Saturday)

In Virginia, Burnside shook the Army of the Potomac out of its camps at Warrenton and put them on the road towards Fredericksburg.

In Washington, President Lincoln, accompanied

by Secretaries Seward and Chase, drove to the Navy Yard to view the trial of the Hyde rocket. It blew up in its perforated launching tube. Capt. Dahlgren was horrified when he realized that the President might have been killed.

Barber, Cpl., Co. D, 15th Illinois Volunteer Infantry, to Abbeyville, Miss.:

> On the 15th the whole army was countermarching and the 15th was rear guard. We were harassed a good deal by the rebel cavalry who were watching for an opportunity to capture our baggage train. Our knapsacks were carried and we were in light marching order and the rebs would have had hard work to have gotten the start of us. Our route lay through a splendid country, the best in the state. It was well watered and timbered. On the streams were numerous mills which we made use of in grinding corn. In this way our army was enabled to subsist without drawing heavily on our commissary.
>
> One morning, just before marching, a very serious affray occurred in Company F. Two men, Ser. Hill and Ser. ________, got into a dispute about some trifling matter. Words led to blows and _______ drew his knife and, before any of us could interfere, stabbed Hill through the abdomen. The wound was supposed to be mortal and the surgeon left him at a plantation near Springdale. One of his comrades volunteered to stay and nurse him. It was a noble act. The would-be murderer was arrested on the spot. A double guard was placed around him, but notwithstanding, he made his escape. He went back to his wounded victim, asked and received his pardon for his rash act; nursed him until he was nearly well and then left for the rebel army. The other two men were made prisoners, paroled and eventually got back to the regiment.
>
> We halted when within ten miles of Abbeyville, and camped for several days in order to repair the bridge across the Tallahatchie. Our men were reduced to one-quarter rations. Indeed some were entirely without hard bread and the pangs of hunger actually began to gnaw at our vitals. The country round about was poor and barren. All we could find was the small pea-beans, but luckily some of our boys made a raise of some meal. So we got along much better than some of the others. The line and field officers shared our privations.

November 19 (Wednesday)

Lt. Gen. James Longstreet brought his corps onto Marye's Heights near Fredericksburg today after a march from Culpeper. Burnside arrived at Falmouth, across the river.

Yesterday, Capt. Semmes, C.S.S. *Alabama*, arrived in Martinique and was blockaded by the U.S.S. *San Jacinto*, Commander William Ronckendorff, who must have thought that he had finally caught the big fish. Today, during foul weather, the C.S.S. *Alabama* slipped past the U.S.S. *San Jacinto*, and got away.

In Richmond, the Hon. James A. Seddon (Va.) was appointed Secretary of War.

Shore batteries at Ft. McAllister, on the Ogeechee River in Georgia, entered into a gunfight with the U.S.S. *Dawn*, Acting Lt. John S. Barnes, and the U.S.S. *Wissahickon*, Lt. Cmdr. John L. Davis. Davis was temporarily disabled during the fight.

November 20 (Thursday)

Jackson's corps was at Winchester getting ready to move to Fredericksburg. Lee arrived at Fredericksburg today, resuming command.

A party from the U.S. mortar boat *Henry James*, Acting Master Pennington, went ashore at Matagorda Bay, Tex., to buy fresh meat for the crew, but the party was captured.

Day, Pvt., Co. B, 25th Massachusetts Volunteer Infantry, afloat at Plymouth, N.C.:

> All the troops, with the batteries, wagons, horses, mules, and negroes have been sent around to New Bern by boats and we alone are left to garrison the town till further orders. In the meantime it would be agreeable to have a change of clothing.... The major seems to take a great pride in his regiment, but I really cannot see why he should take much in such a ragged, dirty, lousy set of vagabonds as we are, but anyway he does, and naturally likes to take us out for dress parade and show up to the naval officers, of whom there are quite a number stationed here. In this he sometimes gets a little set back when about half the boys appear without any shirts on. At this he will mildly remonstrate, but will be told their shirts are out being washed and they appear out with their blouses for shirts, with their pants and suspenders outside.
>
> This thing continued for a few nights until the

major became so disgusted he swore a big swear that he wouldn't have another dress parade until we had some shirts. That, of course, made the boys feel properly bad, and they said, if that was the case, they would vote never to have any. Plymouth is a small but rather pretty town, situated on the south bank of the Roanoke river, about five miles up from the sound. It is a half shire town of Washington county, and contains two churches, two hotels, U.S. custom house, court house and jail, but no school-house. It has been a place of considerable trade, doing a good coasting business and exporting large quantities of cotton, corn, shingles, lumber, fish, and naval stores. There are some Union people about here, who appear to be nice sort of folks but nearly all of secesh proclivities are away.

November 21 (Friday)

Gen. Nathan Bedford Forrest was sent to western Tennessee by Bragg to cut the communications of both Grant's and Rosecrans's armies. He would do a good job of it, being a constant fly in the ointment.

On the Rappahannock, Burnside asked that the city of Fredericksburg surrender; it refused. The bombardment of the town was threatened, and the Mayor requested time to remove the sick, wounded, women, and children. Jackson was hurrying from the Valley.

Barber, Cpl., Co. D, 15th Illinois Volunteer Infantry, Watertown, Miss.:

> We were soon enabled to cross the river. The cars ran up as far as the bridge. We now got a scant supply of rations, but a good many had eaten their last mouthful before the supply came. We camped that night on an open plain and we had to go a mile for wood to cook our suppers. Soon a train came along. It was a glad sight for us. Visions of plenty now began to float before our eyes and we were content. We now proceeded as far as Watertown, where our regiment was left as a garrison. We found comfortable quarters that the regiment before us had occupied and soon we were comfortably established.
>
> This place was now used as a kind of depot for supplies and in addition to guarding this, we had heavy picket duty to perform and it required every man who was able to do duty. Our orders were very strict. Rebel cavalry were prowling about. Every non-commissioned officer in charge of posts received written instructions. The boys foraged here on a pretty extensive scale and they ran great risk of being captured.... A great many of the boys adopted a new style. Instead of asking, now they demanded, or went right in without saying a word. They would slaughter a man's hogs right before his eyes and if he made a fuss, cold steel would soon put a quietus on him.... If this practice had been carried out only on that kind of characters, it would not have looked so bad, but there were unprincipled soldiers who had not the least particle of humanity about them. They would rob rich and poor, old age and youth, widows and orphans, and weak and helpless alike. I have time and again seen a poor, lonely woman with a house full of little ones, on her knees, begging these wretches not to take the last mouthful from her starving children, and perhaps when they left, she would be houseless and homeless, left with her little ones to starve, unless some kind hand would succor them....

November 25 (Tuesday)

Lt. Cushing, U.S.S. *Ellis*, had been aground for two days and couldn't get the vessel refloated. He ordered fires set to keep her from the enemy. Cushing reported, " I fired the *Ellis* in five places and having seen that the battle flag was still flying, trained the gun on the enemy so that the vessel might fight herself after we had left her."

November 27 (Thursday)

President Lincoln arrived at Aquia Creek yesterday. He conferred with Gen. Burnside on the plans for a new offensive. Their plans differed.

Rear Admiral Farragut wrote from New Orleans:

> I am still doing nothing, but waiting for the tide of events and doing all I can to hold what I have, & blockade Mobile. So soon as the river rises, we will have Porter down from above, who now commands the upper squadron, and then I shall probably go outside.... We shall spoil unless we have a fight occasionally.

November 29 (Saturday)

The steamships providing the blockade required a large amount of coal to keep them on station. As a measure of the amount needed, Admiral Du Pont reported during this time that his ships required 950 tons per week, requiring many ships to move it.

The type of coal was also a problem. All coal used in the U.S. Navy at this time was anthracite from the eastern part of Pennsylvania. It was sent to Philadelphia by rail, or by barge down the Schuylkill River. It was then loaded into coal schooners and sent to the various squadrons. The ships in the squadrons often had to borrow from the Army when they ran short of coal, which was a problem.

November 30 (Sunday)

The C.S.S. *Alabama*, Capt. Semmes, had moved its base of operations to the Leeward Islands, where he burned the *Parker Cook*.

Barber, Cpl., Co. D, 15th Illinois Volunteer Infantry, Watertown, Miss.:

> While we were at Watertown Lieut-Col. Rogers received his commission as Colonel of the regiment and feeling pretty well over it, he thought, to use an army phrase, "he would wet it," that is, treat his friends. So gathering a few choice friends about him, they had a regular "time," and to use a common expression, "got pretty well sprung." Soon after, while returning from a visit to one of his particular friends and feeling pretty well, he thought that he would "cut a swell." He mounted his horse and rode at a furious rate down the railroad, never stopping for bridges or culverts. He would make his horse jump them or walk the stringers, but he came to one place which more than taxed the gallant steed's power. He just cleared the culvert and fell headlong, throwing the Colonel over his head, striking his head on a railroad iron, gashing it horribly. He was picked up for dead, but it is an old saying that "a drunken man was never known to be killed by accident." So it proved in this case. He recovered, but it left a long scar on his face.

The month ended on a quiet note. This month saw much jockeying for position, both east and west, in both armies. A time of rest before the storm.

DECEMBER 1862

December arrived almost without anyone prepared for it. In Richmond, Vicksburg, and Mobile, the citizens were short of many of the commodities they had taken for granted just a short year ago. Clothing was getting to be in short supply. Cooking fuel was very expensive, and often so expensive that it could not be spared for heating a parlor. Meat was expensive, as was cornmeal, butter, and flour. The value of Confederate money shrank as inflationary pressures ate away at the currency. The North was in better shape economically. While inflation had some effect, food was still plentiful, as were clothing and other necessities. Those ingenious Yankees could make anything out of almost nothing.

On the war front, Bragg was at Murfreesboro, Tenn., and planning an operation to drive the Union forces out of the state. Rosecrans, in Nashville, had other ideas. Grant was near Holly Springs and working on his plans for Vicksburg. Burnside and Lee faced each other over the Rappahannock in Fredericksburg. The battles were building.

December 1 (Monday)

Near Fredericksburg, Jackson arrived from the Valley with his corps ready for a fight. Lee awaited Burnside's actions.

In Washington, Secretary of the Navy Gideon Welles reported to the President that the United States Navy now consisted of 427 vessels, armed with 1577 guns and having a combined capacity of 240,028 tons.

December 2 (Tuesday)

There was minor skirmishing along the Rappahannock between Lee's and Burnside's forces, but nothing major. Civilians evacuated Fredericksburg as fast as they could. Many took trains to Richmond. Many sent their slaves to points south to prevent them from either escaping into the Federal lines or being freed by the Federals. Once within the blue lines, they were usually gone forever.

The Confederate steamer *Queen of the Bay*, H. Willke, CSA, was taking soundings of Corpus Christi Pass, Tex., when it was chased by boats from the U.S.S. *Sachem*. Willke ran his ship aground, landed his men and fired upon the *Sachem*'s boats. One boat escaped, the other was beached; and the crew, including a wounded officer, escaped by going thirty miles overland, where they were picked up.

December 4 (Thursday)

Gen. Joseph Eggleston Johnston assumed command of the Confederate armies in the west today. Near Port Royal, on the Rappahannock River east of

Fredericksburg, there was a clash between patrols of the two armies. The same was true on the Stone's River near Murfreesboro, Tenn.

Allen, Pvt., Co. K, 1st Battalion., 10th Illinois Cavalry, St. Louis, Mo.:

> It has been so long since I wrote you that you probably think I am no longer in the land of the living. After I wrote to you in August, my health improved very much and I became quite hearty, but I went to the hospital of the 33rd Illinois at Old Town and remained until the fever had broken. I then lay in camp for some time without proper food or medical attendance. I was then sent up the river in a boat to this hospital. I have now been here two months. When I came here my system was so out of order that I recovered my health and strength slowly. With the best of treatment which I have had all the time at this hospital, I am happy to inform you that I am now quite restored to health again and will return to my Company soon.
>
> This hospital is about five miles west of the city. The building is a large, three-story one, built of brick and is warmed up with heaters, which make the rooms quite comfortable in the coldest of weather. There are about 900 sick and wounded men here. Many are quite well and are going to their Regiments all the time but newcomers fill their places as fast as they leave. We have good physicians and nurses here, and get plenty of good wholesome food. Many a poor soldier is restored to health here who would die if left in the camp. I believe that I would never have recovered if I had been left in camp....
>
> The sickly season down in Arkansas is now over, and a letter from one of our Company received a few days ago states that the health of the men is much improved. The place where I was taken sick—Old Town Landing—is the meanest, sickliest place I have ever been in my travels. Nearly all the boys were sick, but few of them died.... I wish I could spend the Christmas holidays with you; but it cannot be, so I will not think about it....

Admiral Farragut reported that he was so busy trying to keep his ships repaired and fueled that it took all of his energy just to keep up with them.

December 5 (Friday)

Boats from the U.S.S. *Mahaska*, Commander F. A. Parker, and the U.S.S. *Gen. Putnam*, under Lt. Blake, captured and destroyed "several fine boats," and a schooner and two sloops in branches of the Severn River near Annapolis and brought back the schooners *Seven Brothers* and *Galena*.

A large number of the recruits who signed up during Bragg's excursion into Kentucky deserted and returned to their homes.

Jackman, Pvt., "The Orphan Brigade," on a raid, southern Tenn.:

> Early the brigade fell in equipped for a campaign, and marched away leaving the camp standing. I was left behind again. A heavy snow storm was passing and soon the gray column was lost to view in the whirling snow. The brigade marched 18 miles and bivouacked at Beard's Mills. Here, the next day, 6th, at 2 P.M. a force was organized for the expedition to Hartsville, composed of the 9th and 2d Ky. infantry under Col. Hunt and two of Morgan's Regiments of cavalry. The whole force was commanded by Morgan. A section of Cobb's Battery was also along. The expedition got to the Cumberland river, 25 miles, by midnight and the infantry immediately commenced crossing over in an old leaky ferry boat which had to be kept afloat by constant bailing. The cavalry, and I believe the artillery, forded the river.

December 7 (Sunday)

About 12 miles from Fayetteville, Ark., two evenly matched armies got into a fight in freezing weather in what later became known as the Battle of Prairie Grove. Gen. Thomas C. Hindman's 10,000 Confederates attacked the combined Union force of Generals James Blunt and Francis J. Herron, also with 10,000. Herron, coming to Blunt's support, arrived in time to thwart Hindman's attack. Hindman had hoped to fight the Federals piecemeal. During the night the Rebels withdrew and sought shelter. The casualties were about even: 1251 Federals and 1317 Confederates.

At Hartsville, Tenn., John Hunt Morgan and his cavalrymen waged a small battle with Col. A. B. Moore's garrison and took them lock, stock, and barrel. Moore lost over 2000 men, 1800 of them captured.

Jackman, Pvt., "The Orphan Brigade," Beard's Mill, Tenn.:

> By daylight all were over and the column pushed

on to the camps, yet five miles off. The enemy was attacked at sunrise and an engagement of three fourths of an hour caused him to surrender his whole force, 2000 strong. By noon, the confederates were back across the river—the rear being shelled some by the Federal reinforcements coming up—and by 9 P.M. were back at Beard's Mills with the balance of the brigade. On the evening of the 8th, all returned to camp well loaded down with booty. Had three stands of colors; the prisoners were left in town.

December 9 (Tuesday)

There was increased activity at Falmouth just across the river from Fredericksburg. Burnside issued orders for his Grand Division commanders to issue 60 rounds per man, prepare three days' cooked rations, and be prepared for an assault on the Rebels across the river. Pontoon bridges were coming up to span the Rappahannock for the crossing.

December 10 (Wednesday)

The U.S. House of Representatives passed a bill creating the new state of West Virginia; the same bill had passed a Senate vote the previous July.

All day the officers of the Union army scrambled to ensure that everything was in order for the assault tomorrow on Fredericksburg. Details were checked, rechecked, and checked again.

Day, Pvt., Co. B, 25th Massachusetts Volunteer Infantry, New Bern, N.C.:

> We were right glad to once more get back to camp, where we could clean ourselves up and get a change of clothing, but were much more glad to find mail and express matter from home. We were not, however, overjoyed to find an order awaiting us to be ready early in the morning to start on a long and rapid march, but having become accustomed to adapting ourselves to circumstances, the order was soon forgotten and we were absorbed in our letters and papers, after which the contents of the boxes were attended to. There was a generous quantity of goodies from the loved ones at home, some of which are of a perishable nature; what shall we do with them?... There are no taps tonight, and the candles burn long and well, so we sit down and gorge ourselves until we can eat no more, putting aside what we think will keep until we get back and crowding as much as we can that remains into our haversacks. ...by morning we are ready. I wear my best clothes, thinking if I should happen to become a guest at the Hotel de Libby, I should like to appear respectable.
>
> During our stay at Plymouth, large reinforcements of troops arrived at New Bern. These troops consisted of Gen. Wessell's brigade of six regiments of New York and Pennsylvania troops, and the 8th, 43d, 45th, 46th and 51st Massachusetts regiments of nine-months troops. They were to join in an expedition under Gen. Foster, against Goldsboro and the Wilmington and Weldon railroad; the object being to destroy that road, thus preventing reinforcements reaching Gen. Lee at Fredericksburg, where Gen. Burnside was about to make an assault. This part of the plan was successfully carried out, but too late to be of any use to Burnside, as he made his attack three days before we reached and destroyed the road. Although Gen. Foster started the moment his troops arrived, it was about a week too late. The division consisted of four brigades.... The whole made a force of about 20,000 men and when the procession was in line of march, it covered a distance of about seven miles.

Barber, Cpl., Co. D, 15th Illinois Volunteer Infantry, Holly Springs, Miss.:

> We now rejoined our division and marched to Holly Springs. The rebels had burned the best part of the place, but there was still enough left to make a splendid looking place. It was now filled with a set of regular sharpers, hangers-on of the army. There were a large number of sutler stands and stores put up in anticipation of the army soon arriving. The 26th Illinois Volunteers, commanded by Col. Loomis, was garrisoning the town. A few of the roguishly inclined boys in our brigade were bent on a spree. They had been to Holly Springs so many times on a "tom fool" errand that they were determined on revenge now. So one night they went to town and raised the deuce generally. The patrol of the town could not do anything with them. Col. Loomis was sent for and he attempted to awe them into submission, but ingloriously failed. He drew his revolver and threatened to shoot into the crowd and struck one of the soldiers with the flat of his sword. The boys could not stand this, so they pitched in and cleaned out the guard and brick-batted Col. Loomis back to his quarters. In a towering rage, he now called out his whole regiment and was going to arrest everyone, at the same time

sending word to our brigade commander how his men were acting.

In the meantime, some of the boys in camp had learned how matters stood and went down and informed the boys in town, so they all hurried up to their quarters. Orders were issued to have a roll-call all through the brigade, and report to brigade headquarters all absentees. The men were all there to answer to their names, and so Col. Hall reported to Col. Loomis that all his men were in camp. Loomis hated our brigade after that. He gave us the name of "Lauman's mob." Of course, all good soldiers were deeply mortified at the conduct of these men.... We had men from all walks of life in the ranks...but there were about a dozen in the regiment that were a pest and curse to us and they were continually getting into scrapes....

These rascals, the night before we left Holly Springs, set it on fire, notwithstanding the watchfulness of the guard, and in the confusion occasioned by the fire, they stole everything valuable that they could lay their hands on....

The next day, on the march, one of the staff officers caught one of our boys with a plug hat on. He rode up to him, snatched it off and threw it into the mud. The fellow belonged to our company and not relishing such treatment, he sprang for the officer and would have thrashed him on the spot if someone had not interfered. The officer drew his revolver and was going to shoot. This act of his aroused the ire of the other boys and they compelled him to put it up. A general melee now seemed inevitable, but our officers finally succeeded in quieting the men.

December 11 (Thursday)

In the predawn darkness at 4:45 A.M. the alert was given to the Confederates that the Yankees were building their bridges for the assault. The Confederates came up to their positions. Barksdale's Mississippians were placed in the brick buildings whose blank rear walls faced the river to the west. Loopholes were knocked in the brick and firing posts assigned. They looked directly out on the bridges. At daylight, the firing began and it became downright dangerous to be on the bridges. The engineers left their positions to scamper back out of the fire only to be driven back to work by their officers. Finally at 10 A.M., Burnside had enough of this. He ordered his artillery to demolish those houses, and they certainly did. Over 140 guns poured nearly 5000 rounds of heavy artillery into the city. Barksdale's men came back, however, and shot a few more of the engineers. Eventually, a bridgehead was established and the Yanks poured over the bridges and into the city. The Confederates withdrew and it was nearly 7:30 P.M. by the time the last of the Mississippians were back into their own lines. It would be a long night for everyone.

Day, Pvt., Co. B, 25th Massachusetts Volunteer Infantry, en route to Goldsboro, N.C.:

> The expedition started... about noon Col. Lee's brigade fell in on the left, the 25th being in this brigade.... We marched this day about 12 miles, getting into camp late in the evening. This bivouac was on an extensive plain and was covered with troops, horses, mules and wagons, and in the dim moonlight, its thousand camp fires made a grand illumination. It was not long after supper before the men were all rolled up in their blankets asleep, and on that cold December night, as I looked over that field and saw by the glare of its many camp fires, those thousands of brave, self-sacrificing men lie stretched upon the ground, I could but think that the bright spirits of the immortal band of American patriots hovered over that camp and looked down approvingly upon our efforts to sustain that government and these institutions for which they had sacrificed and suffered so much to establish.

December 12 (Friday)

This morning a dense fog blanketed Fredericksburg, and limited visibility to just a few yards. Burnside's men came to the bridges and crossed and headed for the heights above the town, where Lee's formidable entrenchments had been waiting for weeks. Artillery had been sited and fields of fire had been laid for the infantry. The fog didn't lift until noon, and by then it was too late to organize the assault; it would be done tomorrow. Lee sent for Jackson's two divisions to come up from downriver where they were covering Skinker's Neck crossing.

Day, Pvt., Co. B, 25th Massachusetts Volunteer Infantry, en route to Goldsboro, N.C.:

> On the morning...the march was resumed, but was necessarily slow as the roads were badly obstruct-

ed. In one swamp, for a distance of three miles the trees were thickly felled across the road making a forenoon's job for Capt. Wilson and his pioneer corps to clear away. They had no sooner finished this job when another presented itself in building a bridge across a creek which took nearly all afternoon. The 25th crossed this bridge about dark, and a little farther on, saw lights ahead. We now thought we were nearing camp and we began to cheer up, thinking our day's work nearly over, but on coming to the camp fires, we found only the 51st Massachusetts, Col. Sprague, and a battery left here at the junction of the main road leading to Kinston, with orders to hold it until noon the next day, while the column moved up the old or back road towards Southwest creek.

Finding this was not our hotel, we took fresh courage and pushed on. A few miles farther brought us into camp. It was a cold night, and being nearly the last in, we found the rails and wood had all been appropriated; we must either go without fires or go half a mile for fuel. We went for it, and after a hard scramble, succeeded in getting a partial supply, enough however with prudence, to go through the night and make our morning's coffee. Our march this day was only about ten miles.

Today, the Union lost the first ship to torpedoes (mines). The U.S.S. *Cairo*, Lt. Cmdr. Thomas O. Selfridge, on an expedition up the Yazoo River to destroy torpedoes, struck one and, as Selfridge reported, "The *Cairo* sunk in about 12 minutes after the explosion, going totally out of sight, except for the top of her chimneys, in 6 fathoms of water." She was the first of about 40 to be destroyed in this way during the war.

December 13 (Saturday)

Another foggy morning. Sunrise was at 7:17 A.M., but it couldn't be seen. Longstreet, on the left flank, waited in his entrenchments. Jackson held the right, with Stuart to Jackson's right, covering the flank. All was ready. At ten o'clock the fog thinned and the artillery began to roar. On Marye's Heights, the Confederates watched as the Federals aligned their ranks and prepared for the charge up the hill. It finally came at 11:30 A.M. when the assault began and the Yankees assaulted Longstreet's men who were positioned behind a stone wall and at a higher elevation. It was slaughter of the worst kind. Wave after wave of blue-clad troops lined up and went up the hill only to be shot down. This lasted until nearly 3:30 P.M. when there was a lull. An assessment was made and the assault was resumed. Five charges had been made by sunset, about 4:15 P.M., and all had been repulsed. A sixth was ordered and went dutifully forward, only to meet the fate of the first five. By 6 P.M. the fighting was over in the darkness. Burnside would recross the river in the early hours of the next day. It had been a futile exercise that killed nearly 1300 Union troops, wounded about 9600, and left almost 1800 as prisoners. The South lost about 600 killed, 4100 wounded, and 650 missing.

In the west, President Davis reviewed Braxton Bragg's troops at Murfreesboro, Tenn., during his visit and inspection trip.

Day, Pvt., Co. B, 25th Massachusetts Volunteer Infantry, en route to Goldsboro, N.C.:

> ... we took an early start. A mile or two up the road, another road branched to the right, leading to Kinston.... About the middle of the forenoon firing was heard in the advance; Col. Heckman had got a job. He found the enemy in considerable force at Southwest creek, and with his own and one or two other regiments, succeeded in driving them out, capturing one gun.... We halted early in the afternoon, to let the teams, which were stuck all along the road, come up. We were not about five miles from Kinston. The infantry bivouacked on the left side of the road, on which was a growth of small pines, making a nice, clean camp-ground. The batteries and teams, as fast as they came up, were parked in the open field on the right. The cavalry, which we had not seen for two days, were playing a lone hand, and were scouting around over the country, making feints and bothering the enemy. Under the pines we make soft beds, and at dark, kindle the fires, make coffee, eat our suppers, and go to bed, expecting in the morning our further progress up the country will be vigorously disputed. All was quiet during the night....

Jackman, Pvt., "The Orphan Brigade," Beard's Mill, Tenn.:

> "Jeff" reviewing the troops. First reviewed our brigade and was well pleased with the "Orphans."

They conducted themselves "every inch the soldier." They passed in review, marching perfectly. Hanson was made Brigadier General on the spot. First time I even saw "old Jeff."

December 14 (Sunday)

Burnside was ready to order another assault on Lee but was dissuaded by his commanders. Lee rightly declined to leave his prepared position and attack Burnside. He had no pontoons to cross the river and, besides, there was a mighty array of cannon to face. The cleanup of the battlefield began with the searching for the wounded and the burying of the dead.

A skirmish was fought at the little Quaker village of Waterford, Va.

Day, Pvt., Co. B, 25th Massachusetts Volunteer Infantry, battle at Kinston, N.C.:

> ...early in the morning...the camp was astir. The general ordered that in order to lighten our teams, every man take three days' rations and 60 rounds of extra ammunition. While this was being dealt out, someone suggested that the teams could be still further lightened by issuing a ration of whiskey. Acting on that suggestion, the liquor was ordered and there was far less complaint about taking it than there was in taking the extra ammunition. Breakfast over, the chaplain offered prayer, after which a hymn was sung; we then filed into the road and commenced the march. The advance was well up the road, and we began to hear firing ahead. As we drew nearer, it became more distinct and there was more of it. Wessell's and Amory's brigades were hotly engaged and the roar of artillery gave notice that the batteries were not silent spectators.
>
> We hurried on and soon met the stretcher corps bringing out the dead and wounded men. This to me was a sickening sight, to see men with pallid faces, writhing with pain and blood dripping from the stretchers. I know not how it is with others, but there is nothing that so completely takes the pith out of me when going into action as this. I want to get engaged before seeing the dead and wounded; after that I do not mind so much about it.
>
> The enemy, under command of Gen. Evans, was in strong force and posted on the south side of the river near Kinston, commanding the road that led through a thick wet swamp some half a mile wide. This swamp prevented our batteries from working with much accuracy, consequently, the fight became an infantry one. Wessell's and Amory's brigades pushed into the swamp and engaged them in front, while the other regiments, as they came up, were posted on the right, to prevent a flank movement, or to make one ourselves if necessary. The 25th, with Morrison's battery, were drawn up in line of battle on an open field near the river, to the left of the swamp. As the battle was confined to the swamp in front, we were not under fire at all. The battle lasted about three hours when our troops got through the swamp and charged on them. The 9th New Jersey led the charge, followed by Wessells' and Stevenson's brigades. They charged them across the river and through the town, capturing eleven pieces of artillery and 300 prisoners. After which they shelled them, driving them up the country, out of sight and hearing. In this battle the enemy numbered about 8000, with several batteries of artillery. We had no means of knowing their loss, but it must have been considerable; they got off most of their wounded and probably some of their dead.
>
> When Lee's brigade got on the battle-ground, it was halted, and burying parties were detailed to bury the enemy's dead which here covered the ground. This ground was hard and considerably higher than the swamp; in the midst of a pretty grove of trees stood an old church. The boys did not take very kindly to this burying business, as they were in a hurry to get into town and secure their share of the spoils, but the job had to be done and they went about it with a will. They dug trenches a little more than two feet deep, and in these the dead were placed with the capes of their overcoats wound around their heads; over those not having overcoats, pine boughs were thrown and all were covered over with earth. Our loss in this battle was about 200, some 50 of whom were killed.... About dark, we marched into a field a short distance south of the town where we were to bivouac. Now commenced the destruction of fences and old buildings for fires, and after supper, parties went up town to look over the prize, and late in the evening began to return, bringing back their plunder. One party had been very successful; they came in hauling an express wagon loaded with tobacco, cigars, apple-jack, scuppernong wine, pigs, etc. Of course a dividend was struck, and all that wanted, had

a share in the tobacco and cigars, with a drink or two of the wine and apple-jack. This was a pretty good Sunday's job.

December 15 (Monday)

While the rest of Burnside's men withdrew across the Rappahannock, the recriminations began. Hooker would be one of the most vocal of Burnside's critics, a fact that would be remembered by Lincoln in the days to come.

In the west, Nathan B. Forrest crossed the Tennessee River at Clifton with 2500 men to raid the communications around Vicksburg. In New Orleans, Major Gen. Benjamin F. Butler said farewell to his troops and turned the command over to Nathaniel Banks. The citizens of New Orleans, especially the ladies, held their own farewell parties for Butler, but only after he left.

Day, Pvt., Co. B, 25th Massachusetts Volunteer Infantry, en route to Goldsboro, N.C.:

> ...the division was again on the move, destroying the road and railroad bridges over the Neuse river as we left. We marched up the river road about 18 miles, getting into camp late in the evening, having met with no obstacles during the day. Here again was a scramble for rails and wood for fires; all the rails nearby were gone, and we had to tote ours about a quarter of a mile. The fires kindled, making coffee was in order... If there is any one thing more than another that will draw the cuss-words out of them, it is when a dozen cups of coffee are sitting along a burning rail boiling, and some careless fellow comes along, hits the end of the rail, dumping it all over. It is not the loss of the coffee they care so much about, but it is going perhaps half a mile for water to make more. It is of no sort of use to send a darky for it in the night, as he would not find his way back before morning.

Assistant Secretary of the Navy Fox thought that the capture of Wilmington, N.C., was of more importance than that of Charleston, S.C. However, the guns at Ft. Fisher prevented an easy capture.

December 16 (Tuesday)

The Army of the Potomac was licking its wounds at Falmouth and at Stafford Heights near Fredericksburg. The army would winter here, denuding the countryside for miles around for firewood. The soil, lacking the living vegetation to hold it, would become a quagmire and erosion would strip the land of its rich topsoil. Many years would pass before the land returned to its 1861 condition.

Day, Pvt., Co. B, 25th Massachusetts Volunteer Infantry, en route to Goldsboro, N.C.:

> ...Morning...it was reported that the enemy was in force across the river at a place called Whitehall, about three or four miles from where we were, and where they were building a steam ram. Of course that must be attended to, and when we left our bivouac, the ball had opened and heavy firing was heard ahead. Lee's brigade hurried on and an hour's march brought us to the scene of conflict. A road turned to the right, leading down to the river, where our batteries were at work. The 25th was ordered down this road, but when about halfway down, and only a short distance in rear of the batteries, were ordered to halt and wait further orders.
>
> An artillery duel was being fought, our batteries on the south side of the river, the enemy's on the north, with the bridge up that here crossed the river. We had ten batteries engaged and the enemy had what we had not captured at Kinston. The roar of artillery, screaming shot and bursting shell, was fearful. The enemy had sharpshooters along the river bank who were rather troublesome to our artillerists and to meet them men were called for from our regiments; Major Pickett was called on for 100. He asked for volunteers and more than half the regiment stepped forward for the service. I didn't volunteer; I never do; I rather pride myself on not committing a great amount of foolishness in this business. The 100 were soon off to the river where they took available positions and did good service.... After nearly three hours, the fire began to slacken and the enemy drew off. The steam ram on the river, which was said to be quite a formidable craft, was then blown up and destroyed....getting into camp about night, some seven or eight miles from Goldsboro.

December 17 (Wednesday)

Grant, out in Holly Springs, Miss., was plagued with cotton speculators who roamed his lines looking for plantation owners who wanted to sell their cotton. There was also the usual plague of peddlers, unauthorized sutlers, and just plain sharks who travelled over the area taking advantage of the troops. Finally, Grant reached his limit of endurance and issued his famous General Order No. 11, which stated, "The Jews, as a class violating every regulation of trade established by the Treasury Department and also department orders, are hereby expelled from the department within twenty-four hours from the receipt of this order." A strong statement that would be rescinded by both Lincoln and Halleck on the 4th of the next month. This would follow Grant for years, well into his Presidency.

In Washington, Lincoln had more troubles than Grant. Salmon P. Chase was constantly intriguing with members of Congress to gain the upper hand over Seward. This came to a head when Seward offered to resign from the Cabinet. The resignation was declined by Lincoln.

Day, Pvt., Co. B, 25th Massachusetts Volunteer Infantry, en route to Goldsboro, N.C.:

> Early in the morning...Lee's brigade took the advance, and after a march of five or six miles, the scouts reported the enemy in the woods near the railroad and bridge which crosses the river about two miles below Goldsboro.... The column was halted, a regiment sent out as skirmishers and a battery advanced and took position on a knoll of ground a little to the left and front of the column and commenced shelling the woods. This had the effect of stirring them up so we knew where they were. The infantry and batteries were ordered forward...after some skirmishing, at about 10 A.M., the battle commenced and continued with short intermissions until the middle of the afternoon at which time we had silenced the enemy's guns and driven them from the field. We burned the railroad bridge, and with the help of the cavalry tore up and burned ten or twelve miles of track and tressel work of the Wilmington and Weldon railroad. Gen. Foster said the object had been accomplished and ordered a retreat, Lee's brigade being ordered to cover it. It was near sunset when we left the field....
>
> We halted at a farm house a little way off to load our dead and wounded men into ambulances. While doing it, a battery officer dashed up exclaiming, "For God's sake, send us an old regiment! The enemy are charging our batteries! Quick! hurry up!" The 27th and 25th Massachusetts were on the left or rear of the column and immediately faced about and started on the double quick for the batteries. ...the enemy had been reinforced and seeing our batteries alone and perhaps thinking they might be out of ammunition, thought it would be a nice little trick to capture them. In going to the relief of the batteries we had to run a gauntlet of shot and shell from a six-pounder battery out in the woods a little to the left and front of our batteries, who were supporting their [Confederate] charging brigade. We went to Belger's support and the 27th to Morrison's.
>
> In the meantime, the batteries had opened fire on the charging columns but without checking them. When we came up they were coming close across the railroad; but another discharge from the guns and seeing their support, the enemy thought they had taken too much of a job and facing about, they put for the woods. That little battery out in the woods was wonderfully active, shying their shot and shell thick and fast. Fortunately their guns had a high elevation.... They soon corrected that, however, and the shot began to come lower. Capt. Belger ordered us to lie down, I am always quick to hear that order and was the first man down. They now got our range well down, the shot just skimming over us.... They had a splendid range on me.... About once a minute a shot would come directly over me... they kept getting them lower, until I had flatted out as thin as a sheet of tissue paper. I could stand this no longer...I pushed along about ten feet to the left and would have liked to have pushed about ten miles to the rear.... But that was their last shot, for after the charging column had turned, the guns were turned on that battery...we heard nothing more from it. It was now after sunset and peace reigned once more in Warsaw.
>
> ...we again drew off the field. On coming to the little creek which we had crossed dry shod an hour before, we now found a roaring torrent running bankfull, with barrels, rails and pieces of timber borne on the surface of its swift current. We had got to go through it and the boys... waded in. The water was waist deep and when my company went in, I waited on the bank, thinking I would step into the rear as they passed by, but I made a wrong calculation of the bank. When I stepped in, I went in all over and in trying to recover myself, I let go my cartridge box, blanket and Spitfire, but caught the last between my knees and commenced ducking to get it. The major was standing on the bank, cautioning the boys to

keep their powder dry. When he happened to observe me going through my aquatic performances he yelled vociferously: "What in hell are you doing there? Why don't you keep your powder up out of the water?" I paid no attention to him, but kept reaching for Spitfire, and every time I reached for it, the current would nearly take me off my feet. After I had succeeded in fishing it out, I turned my attention to the major and answered his little conundrum by asking him what in hell powder was good for with out Spitfire? The major laughed and jumping on a gun carriage, was ferried across....

The night was freezing cold and in our wet clothes we felt it very sensibly. A mile march brought us to the woods which were some four or five miles through and on the other side was our last night's bivouac. The advance troops had set the woods on fire and when we went through it was a roaring mass of flame. This served us a good turn as it lighted up the road and kept us warm. We reached our bivouac late in the evening, wet, cold, tired and hungry.... Our wagons were bare of meat and whiskey, and our supper consisted of coffee and hardtack. Through the long, weary night, wet, cold and hungry we stood shivering over the fires....

December 18 (Thursday)

To follow up the attempted resignation of Seward, a delegation of nine Congressmen came to the White House to urge the President to reorganize his Cabinet more in line with their thinking, that is, to give Chase a larger role in decision making. They felt that Seward had too big a voice in the proceedings. Lincoln heard them out and rescheduled a meeting for tomorrow, when he would bring in the Cabinet members to face their critics.

In Tennessee, Nathan B. Forrest engaged and defeated a Federal cavalry force near Lexington in his continuing efforts to disrupt supply lines.

Grant announced the organization of his army. Sherman, Hurlbut, McPherson, and McClernand were to be corps commanders. McClernand was satisfied, at least temporarily, with his new assignment.

James Birdseye McPherson was born near Clyde, Ohio, on November 14, 1828. Although he grew up in extreme poverty, a merchant friend got him an appointment to West Point, from which he was graduated in 1853, first in his class. Assigned to the Engineers, he served at several ports and harbors around the country prior to the war, at one time sharing rooms with Sherman in New York. He initially served in the war as an aide to Major Gen. Halleck and then as Chief Engineer for Grant at Ft. Donelson and at the Battle of Shiloh. Recommended by both Grant and Halleck, he was promoted to Brigadier General on August 19, 1862, and to Major General two months later. In January 1863, he became commander of the XVII Corps in Grant's army during the Vicksburg campaign. He served with Sherman during the Meridian expedition, and then in the Atlanta campaign. He was killed in action on July 22, 1864, outside Atlanta. This was a great loss, and he was universally mourned.

At Chattanooga, Jefferson Davis reported that Bragg's troops at Murfreesboro were in fine shape and were ready for the coming campaign.

Day, Pvt., Co. B, 25th Massachusetts Volunteer Infantry, retreat from Goldsboro, N.C.:

> ...we hailed the first grey streaks of dawn and took fresh courage, knowing we should soon be on the road for home. At sunrise the whole army was in motion on the road for New Bern....

December 19 (Friday)

Today the Congressmen who came to the White House to complain about the Cabinet organization got their chance, albeit unexpectedly, to face those they were criticizing. Chase, a major instigator in the plot, was squirming because he had been placed in an awkward position. All of Chase's backdoor carping came back to haunt him. It finally ended with Lincoln dismissing the meeting.

Forrest is tearing up the railroads in Grant and Rosecrans's rear, causing delays in the movement of supplies.

December 20 (Saturday)

The Cabinet crisis ended today when Chase offered his resignation. To Chase's great surprise and discomfort, Lincoln accepted it. Chase had presidential ambitions and had been plotting to discredit Lincoln almost from the time he had joined the Cabinet. While Lincoln accepted the paper, he declined to put it into force. Lincoln had, however, a sword to hold over Chase's head, since he could accept the resignation at any time.

The great raid on Holly Springs, Miss., took place today. Van Dorn, unexpectedly, attacked the huge depot and it was shamefully surrendered almost without a fight. Eighteen hundred men were taken prisoner and over $1,500,000 worth of matériel was destroyed. This effectively cancelled Grant's plans for a drive on Vicksburg and he withdrew to LaGrange, Tenn. Meanwhile, on the Mississippi, Sherman left Memphis, attempting to take Vicksburg from the north, through the swamps. This was doomed to failure.

December 21 (Sunday)

Today, the U.S. Congress authorized the Medal of Honor, the nation's highest award, to be awarded to such Navy personnel as distinguished themselves by their gallantry in action. During the war, a total of 327 sailors and marines were awarded the Medal of Honor.

Both Forrest and Morgan were busy raiding supply lines, Forrest in Tennessee, and Morgan on a raid into Kentucky. Jefferson Davis was visiting Vicksburg.

On the Rappahannock, things were quiet. Both armies were settling into winter quarters. Burnside visited Washington at Lincoln's request.

Day, Pvt., Co. B, 25th Massachusetts Volunteer Infantry, Arrival at New Bern, N.C.:

> ...we arrived a little after noon, nearly dying from hunger and exhaustion. When we started on this expedition it was thought the wagons contained an ample supply of rations, but our march up the country was so impeded by blockaded roads and so vigorously contested that it was prolonged beyond what was anticipated; besides it was an awful poor section of the country for pigs, chickens, and apple-jack....
>
> Our little major since the two last tramps has become very popular in his regiment and I expect when the eagles light on his shoulders we shall feel pretty proud of him. He is a good fellow, and in a fight is always on the lead, inspiring the men with courage by his coolness and daring. On the road he is equally good, letting the boys have it pretty much their own way, never troubling himself about how they came by their chickens and apple-jack, and is often seen trudging along on foot, letting some sick or footsore soldier ride his giraffe.

December 24 (Wednesday)

Christmas Eve of the first full year of war. Around many campfires the soldiers were feeling homesick, lonely, and discouraged, no matter which uniform they wore.

A Christmas present in the form of artillery arrived at Columbus, Ky., aboard the U.S.S. *New Era*, Acting Master Frank W. Flanner. The guns arrived in the nick of time, as the local troops were threatened by a large Confederate force.

December 25 (Thursday)

President and Mrs. Lincoln visited hospitals in Washington today.

The holiday meant little to John Hunt Morgan's men as they continued their Kentucky raid, with fighting at Green's Chapel and Bear Wallow.

Sherman's corps was operating around Milliken's Bend on its way to Vicksburg.

December 27 (Saturday)

Sherman's men were approaching Vicksburg's defenses on the north, while Pemberton was bringing in more troops for the defense of the city. A stalemate would soon develop.

Rosecrans's army was moving slowly towards Bragg at Murfreesboro. Contact had been made and there was some skirmishing between the forces.

Morgan's men were as far north as Elizabethtown, Ky., on their current raid. Tomorrow he would destroy a bridge near Muldraugh's Hill (near the site of the present Ft. Knox), and then run for Tennessee.

December 28 (Sunday)

The advance men under Rosecrans were at Murfreesboro, Tenn. Sherman was approaching the bluffs at Vicksburg, coming from the Yazoo River.

Jackman, Pvt., "The Orphan Brigade," Battle of Murfreesboro, Tenn.:

> This morning moved out on Stone River; the camp is left standing. Adj't. C. ordered me to stay with the office. He seems to have a presentiment something is going to happen to him. Left word with me for Maj. W. who is away on special duty. A beautiful sunny day

and a stream of glittering bayonets has been passing through town all day long—troops marching out to their respective positions in the line of battle. In the evening a detail came from the regiment and struck tents, loaded the wagons. While thus occupied, Col. H. came into camp, having started away the evening before on a leave of absence but had now come back to participate in the battle. Feeling like I would have some adventure, as well as the other boys, I asked the Col. to let me go with the regiment. He seldom refuses a fellow the privilege of trying his hand in a fight and told me to come out, after seeing that everything was packed away in the wagon properly. One of our company had been left in camp, too sick to walk and after dark went to the College hospital to get him admitted which I did after a good deal of talk—came back and sent him away on horseback. The wagon train moved out on the Manchester Pike about 9 P.M. Looked desolate enough about the old camp, the numbers of brick chimneys left standing alone made it appear a city that had been destroyed on the spot. Billie A. who was sick and going out with my load concluded to stay then until morning. We tried to sleep but without much success as the wagon trains were rumbling and roaring over the pike all night—the teamsters popping their whips and yelling.

December 29 (Monday)

Sherman's troops fought the Battle of Chickasaw Bayou to gain the bluffs on the north side of Vicksburg. The terrain was not friendly and all the work of the campaign went for nothing. The positions were too strong to take by frontal assault. Sherman awaited developments.

Outside Murfreesboro, Tenn., the contact between Bragg and Rosecrans was heavier and the fighting became more frequent between the pickets. In one case, General Joseph Wheeler's cavalry, having completed the screening of the Confederate flank, swept down on a Federal brigade and captured 20 wagons loaded with supplies for Crittenden's men. Morgan was fighting his way back into Tennessee at Springfield and New Haven, Ky.

Barber, Cpl., Co. D, 15th Illinois Volunteer Infantry, Moscow, Miss.:

We camped near Holly Springs for several days longer and then took up a line of march for Moscow. The 4th division was ordered to guard the Memphis & Charleston railroad between Lagrange and Memphis. We supposed that our quarters would be at Moscow, but there was a misunderstanding and we were ordered to Lafayette, twenty miles farther towards Memphis, and when within a few miles of that place, we were ordered to countermarch back to Moscow. It was late when we pitched our camp and we got into a mudhole and could not get out until morning.

Jackman, Pvt., "The Orphan Brigade," Battle of Murfreesboro, Tenn.:

When morning came we got up, shook off the drowsiness, ate our breakfast, then started for the regiment lying in line of battle. The morning was beautiful being the commencement of one of those lovely Indian summer days, which sometimes come even in the winter season down south. Though the day was beautiful, a storm was brewing. The deep resonance of cannon came rolling over the hills from towards Nashville and we could smell saltpeter in the air. Two miles from town, came up with the regiment, the boys lying lazily about on a rocky hill waiting the coming of events. A wagon came out with rations and cooking utensils and we cooked rations. The thunder of cannon kept coming nearer. As the gloom of evening set in, a large brick mansion (Cowan's house) across the river from us and in front of Wither's division was set on fire, to be burned out of the way and high up leaped the flames, mingled with an inky column of smoke which pierced the very heavens. Gloomy sight at such a time as this. Soon after, our cavalry which had been falling back in front of the Federal Army burst out of the cedars in front of Withers and also came dashing back from our side of the river. We immediately fell in and advanced in line of battle over a rocky ravine and through an old field where the weeds were up to our shoulders and so thick we could hardly march. The evening was warm and I had a heavy overcoat on, which, with tugging through the weeds, caused me to nearly suffocate. I pulled it off once with the intention of abandoning it, but again picked it up and buckled it under my belt. Well I did so, for afterwards it came in good place. We halted and sent forward Co. D as skirmishers. They moved forward to a cornfield and were soon engaged, Lt. B. in command being wounded. The field named being on a hill, which, if taken possession of by the enemy would have been disastrous to us, for it was the key to our position. I don't know why we were not ordered to take position on this hill in the beginning. We moved forward to support our skirmishers and lay down just under the crest of the hill. Cobb's battery was placed in position on top. Darkness had now come on. The enemy advanced and drove our skirmishers in. They fired pretty briskly for a time, making the cornstalks rattle about us. In the darkness the Federal skirmish line came right up among the battery which was being unlimbered and a little in advance of us. One of the "Feds" hollered out "Boys, here is a cannon, let us get away from here" and they all skidaddled. Two of our regiments then advanced and the Federal force, whatever it was, withdrew over the river. A strong skirmish line was then established on the margin of the river and the brigade fell back into the old weed field where they slept on their arms. I went back to the rocky hill to stay by a fire. About midnight a rain set in and I adjourned to a neighboring corn crib and slept in the shucks.

December 30 (Tuesday)

Lincoln finished his draft of the Emancipation Proclamation. He circulated it to the Cabinet for comment. The document stated that all slaves in *Confederate-held* territory were free, but *not* those in Union territory. This, in effect, did not free a single slave. It did, however, have the very far-reaching effect of preventing France and England from recognizing the Confederate government; to have done so would have meant recognition of a slave-holding government.

Sherman remained in position near Chickasaw Bayou at Vicksburg hoping for a break so that he could capture the city. His plans for withdrawal were still in effect.

At Murfreesboro, it was obvious that a major battle was taking place. Fighting began with an unexpected assault on the Federal lines which drove the Union forces back through the woods. Things might have been different if Sheridan had not been there with his division. He held, although he would lose his three brigade commanders before the day was over. At night the firing faded and the commanders prohibited the troops from building fires to warm themselves. In the bitter cold, everyone had a miserable night.

Jackman, Pvt., "The Orphan Brigade," Battle of Murfreesboro, Tenn.:

> A murky morning—misting rain. Started for the regiment and found it had moved. I then went back to where Billie A. was having some coffee made by his boy—Billie was not able to be with the regiment but was in the field. Stayed with him until the afternoon when I went to the regiment. The enemy shelling our lines during the day. Our army kept quiet. We did see a little fighting in front of Withers. We had a tent fly which we put up temporarily to shield us from the rain. Sometimes the shell would make us seek shelter behind a big rock. In the afternoon the rain having slackened a little, I sought out the regiment which I found lying about in a cedar thicket, grumbling at the weather. Sometimes, too, shells would come tearing through the cedars making a fellow feel uncomfortable. At last, night came on and we moved back into the ravine in rear of the line near where Billie and I had been all day. Here the boys had fires. Rain ceased at dark. I slept with Billie A. under our fly.

December 31 (Wednesday)

Not long after midnight, the U.S.S. *Monitor* foundered in heavy seas off Cape Hatteras, N.C., and sank with a loss of 16 officers and men. The U.S.S. *Rhode Island* rescued 47 officers and men.

At Murfreesboro, Hardee's corps made an attack in a wheeling motion and the Federals retreated, also in a wheeling motion. At last Rosecrans's men were pinned against Stone's River and they went no further. The Confederates made several assaults against the line until late afternoon. The Confederates won the day, but at a very heavy cost. Bragg's casualties were in excess of 9000. A few more victories like this one and he would have no army.

Jackman, Pvt., "The Orphan Brigade," Battle of Murfreesboro, Tenn.:

> The sun came up clear. The regiment had moved off before I waked up. Had breakfast. The ambulances and caissons are sheltered in our ravine. Just as the sun was coming up I heard a yelling over towards Wither's division and ran up on the hill to see the

cause. That division was charging across a big field in perfect line of battle, the men yelling and cheering. Soon the Federal batteries opened on them [with] the musketry and I could see his [Wither's] men falling. Presently they opened fire and the line was obscured in smoke. That was, I believe, the grandest scene I ever witnessed in the military line. I stood a moment watching the battle and a stray shell came near cutting me down. Thinking the ball had now opened in earnest, I "buckled on my armor" and started for the regiment. One of the boys was with me. We had to pass over a long field in the rear of a battery which was then being subject to a heavy fire. First a shell would tear up the ground in front of us; then we would be a little slow; then a ball would plow up the ground in rear of us; then we would quicken our pace. When we got to the regiment it was falling in to march out in rear of the battery which was composed of twelve guns and on the hill where we skirmished on the first evening. As soon as the regiment got to this position about equal distance from the guns, ordered to lie down. Our battery, for there were more than three parked together, opened fire on the advancing columns and the Federal guns replied, firing over the heads of their troops. I believe there were 38 cannon playing on us at once. The hill protected us a little, yet I saw from my position on the extreme left of the regiment numbers of cannon balls strike just in front of the lines and skip over. We were not behind the battery more than five minutes before seeing the numbers that were being hurt. Genl. Hanson had the regiment moved off a little to the right, out of range. In this we lost about 20 or 30 wounded but luckily no one killed. We did not move again during the day. Our company went to get in the trenches by the guns in the evening but the order was corrected and it came back. Just before sundown, a cannon ball passed through Adjt. G. killing him instantly. I had just left his side having been to get some tobacco. The day was cool though the sun shone out all the time—cold wind from the north. Lying on the cold ground a good deal during the day, was chilled, and when darkness put a stop to the stirring scenes, I went back to the ambulance station to get by the fire. Dr. P. gave me a "drink" and we spread down blankets together—slept well.

Sherman, placing his withdrawal plans on hold, stuck to Chickasaw Bayou, hoping for a chance to take Vicksburg.

Forrest almost got snagged after raiding Grant's lines. He lost about 300 men, his guns, ammunition, and captured matériel, but managed to get most of the cavalrymen away.

1863

New Year's Day saw more fighting in the Battle of Murfreesboro (Stone's River). The dead and wounded were still lying on the field. Fredericksburg had been a blow to the Union and there were recriminations among the generals and Lincoln's Cabinet.

January 1 (Thursday)

As the new year began, the Battle of Murfreesboro (Stone's River) continued. Lincoln's Emancipation Proclamation went into effect. It did nothing to free the slaves in the Northern states, but it was a major moral force in the South, and in France and England, where support for the South would be to support slavery—not a thing the common man would tolerate.

Jackman, Pvt., "The Orphan Brigade," Murfreesboro, Tenn.:

> All quiet today. Both armies seem to be taking a "blowing spell" after the hard fighting yesterday. Turned my gun over to one of the infirmary corps, they having to take arms.

The blockading ships off Galveston Harbor, Tex., were dealt a blow today by a force led by a Confederate Army Major, Leon Smith, using *cotton-clad* gunboats with sharpshooters aboard. The gunboats, the C.S.S. *Bayou City* and *Neptune*, were accompanied by the tenders *John F. Carr* and *Lady Gwin*. The Union fleet was taken by surprise. The Union command ship, the *Harriet Lane*, Commander Jonathan M. Wainwright, was rammed, and, in turn, rammed another ship. Finally, Wainwright's ship was boarded and he was killed in the hand-to-hand fighting that ensued. Another Union ship, the U.S.S. *Westfield*, Commander Renshaw, ran aground and was blown up to prevent her capture, Renshaw being killed during the explosion. The remaining Union ships ran through heavy fire from Confederate shore batteries and went out to sea.

Barber, Cpl., Co. D, 15th Illinois Volunteer Infantry, en route to Lafayette, Miss.:

> I never saw it rain harder in my life than it did that morning, and it continued to rain the most part of the day. Ravines and gulches that we passed over dry-shod the day before, were now filled with water rushing in torrents from down the hillsides and valleys, and, in some places, the mules had to swim in order to cross. We had heavy knapsacks to carry, and that, in addition to our guns and other accoutrements and thoroughly soaked clothing, made our load quite heavy, but, for all that, the boys jogged along as happy as larks. The harder it rained the louder would we sing and shout and crack our jokes.
>
> ...The river was so swollen that we could not cross to Moscow, so we camped two miles west of

that place. We got in camp about an hour before sundown. Near us was a large plantation with a number of outhouses, and no sooner had we stacked arms than the boys made for these buildings, and, as if by magic, they disappeared in a twinkling, before the officers could interfere. My mess got a goodly share, and William and I made us a bunk to sleep on. The officers did not attempt to interfere. They were too glad to get a share themselves, and if any fuss was made about it, the regiment would pay for it. Soon we had a rousing fire built and our wet garments were steaming before its ruddy blaze. Our tents now came up and soon our camp was formed.

While we were standing about the fire we spied a fine drove of shoats, about a half mile off, which we thought would make good roasters. So dispatching our most expert foragers, Roll and Milt, from our mess, they sallied out and soon every one of those pigs were slain. Our mess secured four of them, and in less than thirty minutes they were in our bake ovens, stewing before a hot fire. It was an excellent dish… our mess of fifteen devoured them. Our cook, William Underwood, surpassed himself that night. He always could get a good meal on short notice, and this was our New Year's feast. By the time our supper was dispatched, our garments were dry and we were spending a short time around the camp fire cracking jokes and telling stories as the time flew by.… Finally we retired to rest well.…

The Confederacy had laced the Yazoo River with a collection of torpedoes (mines) and Col. Charles R. Ellet, USA, had an idea for a "mine sweeper":

My plan was to attach to the bow of a swift and powerful steamboat a strong framework, consisting of two heavy spars, 65 feet in length, firmly secured by transverse and diagonal braces extending 50 feet forward of the steamer's bow. A crosspiece, 35 feet in length, was to be bolted to the forward extremities of these spars. Through each end of this crosspiece and through the center a heavy iron rod, 1½ inches in diameter and 10 feet long, descended into the river, terminating in a hook. An intermediate hook was attached to each bar 3 feet from the bottom.… My belief was that the curved hooks of the rake would catch these cords, and driven by the powerful boat, would either explode the torpedoes or tear them to pieces and break the ropes, thus rendering them harmless.…

January 2 (Friday)

More fighting at Stone's River this day. Breckinridge's "Orphan Brigade" managed to take a small hill but were driven from it with heavy losses. Everyone took another breather. Bragg announced to Richmond that he had a great victory.

Both Morgan and Forrest were back in reasonably safe territory. Forrest crossed the Tennessee River at Clifton, the same point he used outbound on his raid. Sherman aborted his attack up the Yazoo River on Vicksburg. His troops were placed under the command of McClernand as they emerged from the river.

Jackman, Pvt., "The Orphan Brigade," Murfreesboro, Tenn.:

Raining in the morning. Back at the ambulance train nearly all the time. All quiet until about 3 P.M. when Bragg ordered Breckinridge's division to charge *over Stones River* at Rosecran's army! All the brigade went into the charge, save our regiment which was left to support the batteries and hold the hill heretofore mentioned. The rain stopped just before the charge was made. Hanson killed.

Barber, Cpl., Co. D, 15th Illinois Volunteer Infantry, Lafayette, Miss.:

On awakening the next morning we found six inches of snow on the ground, and scarcely were our preparations for breakfast made before we received marching orders back to Lafayette. To say that there was some pretty rough swearing when this order was received would but faintly express the truth.… We arrived at Lafayette about sundown, and now, as if to add to our already overcharged patience, a portion of the regiment was ordered to go on picket, supperless and worn out. Some of the boys invented a new string of oaths expressly for this occasion. Lieut. Paxton, Ser. Sedam of Company C and myself were sent out in charge of one company. We relieved Logan's men and they marched that very night for Memphis.

Just in front of our line was a large cotton gin and other buildings, and our Lieutenant, with a perfect recklessness which was inexcusable under any circumstances, ordered his men to take possession of them, which brought his videttes in rear of the reserve. If any picket officer had happened around that night, or I had chosen to report him, it would have been the last picket he would ever have stood. As if to add still deeper to his disgrace, he permitted his men to go out foraging, leaving only a very few on post, and finally to cap the climax, the men soon returned with a large quantity of old cider—so strong that one good drink would make a person dizzy. Although it almost scorches my pen to write it, yet truth compels me to say that every person except two on that post got drunk and all night long reveled in a drunken spree. The two sober persons were Charlie Mitchell and myself, and on us alone the safety of that part of the line depended. Sleep was far from my eyelids. Any small force could have come in and captured the whole of us. It would have been utterly impossible to have rallied the men in case of an attack. Had it not been for some extenuating circumstances, I would have reported the conduct of the men, but it seems that the picket officer himself was negligent of his duty for he never made his appearance. It was a good thing for us that he did not.

I went the rounds at midnight and found a fire at every post except one and all asleep except Charlie. I had a hard job of it to wake up the next relief—all were in a drunken stupor. I finally got them up but they were no better than dead men. I don't think that there was ever a more disgraceful picket duty performed....

January 3 (Saturday)

Gen. Braxton Bragg determined that he could not hold the positions at Murfreesboro, and he retreated to Manchester, leaving Rosecrans in possession of the field. The cleanup began. Jackman found a good meal and began the march:

Jackman, Pvt., "The Orphan Brigade," Murfreesboro, Tenn.:

> Rain pouring down all day long. At the regiment part of the time helping dig in the entrenchments. Late in the evening having "got word" that the army was going to fall back that night, I went into town to see Bro. W. at Dr. P.'s. Soon after getting in town, the rain came down in torrents and continued all night long. Went to the Medical Purveyor's office and there found Bro. W., Dr. S. and Dr. P., medical director of the division. They had been in the field and had gotten things nice to eat and still have some on hand. Not having eaten anything but "dough" for a week I enjoyed a good supper. Wrote home, giving the letter to Dr. P. to mail as he was to be left with the wounded. Troops marching back through town all night. Slept with Bro. W before a large fire in the office.

January 4 (Sunday)

Major Gen. McClernand, with Sherman's corps, and Rear Admiral D.D. Porter joined forces this day for an expedition up the White River, Ark., for the purpose of capturing Ft. Hindman. The fort, which mounted 11 guns, was not going to be easy to take. To conserve fuel, Porter had 11 gunboats towed upriver by the troop transports.

There was scattered skirmishing between Murfreesboro and Manchester, Tenn., as Bragg withdrew to Manchester.

Gen. Halleck, by direction of the President, ordered Grant to revoke his infamous General Order No. 11 that expelled all Jews from his operational area.

Jackman, Pvt., "The Orphan Brigade," retreat from Murfreesboro, Tenn.:

> Up before daylight. The Dr. having a spare horse, I was to ride. We mounted just at daylight and made off through a pelting rain. All had left before the dawn. We overtook our regiment 5 miles from town on the Manchester pike acting as rear guard. Being mounted, Col. H. sent me ahead to turn back an ordnance wagon.... In the after part of the day the sun came out hot. Evening, came up with the wagon train, camped near Manchester. Not having been on horseback for so long, this ride of 30 miles tired me almost as much as if I had walked.

January 5 (Monday)

Boat crews, sent by Commander Earl English of the U.S.S. *Sagamore*, captured the British sloop *Avenger* in Jupiter Inlet, Fla., with a cargo of coffee, gin, salt, and baled goods.

Bragg's army started towards Tullahoma, but returned to Manchester. President Lincoln thanked Rosecrans for the latter's victory at Stone's River.

Barber, Cpl., Co. D, 15th Illinois Volunteer Infantry, Lafayette, Miss.:

> ...The 2d brigade now became fairly established

at Lafayette, as garrison and railroad guard. We built as comfortable quarters as possible and then went to work and built several forts and put the place in a complete state of defense. We now had a long season of rest and the boys were in a condition to fully appreciate it. Our picket duty was pretty heavy, especially on the non-commissioned officers....

We were camped in a very rich country and the boys had great times foraging. When a forage train started out, it was a signal for the boys to go out with it, and under its protection, load themselves down with the product of the country, such as sweet potatoes, other vegetables and fresh pork. Very often a whole wagon load of fresh pork would come. Our mess got several weeks supply which we salted down in boxes. At the same time we drew our regular rations of bacon, but this we burned for fuel. We had made a little stove for our tent out of an old iron kettle and our bacon furnished us with all the fuel we needed. At one time our company had about a cord piled up. Afterward we would have given a great deal if we could have had that bacon which we burned at Lafayette.

January 6 (Tuesday)

Jackman, Pvt., "The Orphan Brigade," retreat from Murfreesboro, Tenn.:

> In the morning the regiment came up. The trains being again ordered towards Tullahoma. I kept with it on "my horse." When we got as far as we did before, the wagons of our regiment were ordered back to Manchester.... That night my mess did not put up the tent—we slept on it. Late at night I waked up with something heavy on my face. I found it to be an old gander, quietly roosting on my head....I presume he saw that I had no feathers under my head and concluded to put some on top instead of underneath. I thanked him by flinging him against a stump hardby.

Jackman and the "Orphans" went into winter quarters at Manchester. The pace was slow, the duty dull, the recreation better than average:

> Now commences a long siege of inaction. Nothing much to vary one day from another.... I made no entries in my journal from Jan. 6th to April 23d.
>
> Manchester, the county-town of Coffee, is a small place on the branch railroad running to McMinnville. At the time we sojourned in its vicinity, the town was very much torn up, both armies having had a turn at the place. The boys, however, found enough society to keep up amusement and all the winter were flirting with the young ladies. Balls were frequent. I attended two—one at the hotel in town—the other, at an unfinished paper mill below town on Drock river. When the latter came off, a rain poured down all night so no one could go home. At this ball, Geo M. Hes. played Bombasti Furavso a stage having been arranged for the purpose. The boys would defray all expenses in getting the refreshments, etc. When they would go to invite the "girls" the old dames would be informed an abundance of *pure* coffee would be on hand then all objections to their "girls" going to the ball would cease—"You may look for *me* and my 'gals' to be thar, shore." The boys knew the proper cord to touch to bring the "gals." The "gals" would dance and the old ladies would sip coffee....

January 7 (Wednesday)

In Washington, the Federal government gave permission for 450 women and children (Southern refugees) to leave for Petersburg, Va. Their final destination would be the Richmond area, but the rivers were blockaded by Union gunboats.

A joint Army-Navy foray up the Pamunkey River to destroy boats, barges, and stores at West Point and White House, Va., was largely successful. The U.S.S. *Mahaska* and *Commodore Morris*, under command of Commander Foxhall A. Parker, convoyed the transport *May Queen* and provided gun support.

In Tennessee, Grant rescinded his General Order No. 11 which had expelled the Jews.

Since the Emancipation Proclamation was issued on January 1st, slaves in the South had been celebrating as best they could. For many years, even into the 20th century, that day was celebrated as "Freedom Day." The custom, unhappily, has died out in recent times. Many of the slaves, especially those in proximity to Union forces, left their homes and entered the Federal lines, where they were freed and usually employed in one capacity or another.

January 9 (Friday)

Florida was a very large salt-manufacturing area. Today, boat crews of the U.S.S. *Ethan Allen*, Acting Master Isaac A. Pennell, destroyed "a very large salt manufactory... capable of making 75 bushels of salt per day" south of St. Joseph's, Fla. This was the fourth manufactory he had destroyed in his area.

At Arkansas Post on the Arkansas River, Major Gen. McClernand's troops were landed under the cover of naval gunfire, which drove the enemy from their rifle pits. This enabled McClernand's men to approach Ft. Hindman unseen. Grant evacuated Holly Springs, Miss.

January 10 (Saturday)

At Ft. Hindman, on the Arkansas River, Gen. McClernand's troops were not in position for the attack as yet, so the gunboats plied the river, bombarding the fort to prepare for the assault on the 11th. The gunboats, moving to within 60 yards of the fort, were raked by the fort's eleven guns. The boats, the U.S.S. *Baron de Kalb, Louisville, Cincinnati, Lexington, Rattler*, and *Black Hawk*, sustained little damage from the fort.

The Union Navy returned to the Galveston area to try to retake control of the harbor. Commodore Henry H. Bell and his squadron bombarded the city but did not try to enter the harbor, due to the narrow channel and low water. He finally gave up and left it for another time.

The 450 women and children who left Washington on the 7th arrived in Petersburg on the 10th.

January 11 (Sunday)

On this morning the bombardment of Ft. Hindman was continued from the gunboats and "after a well directed fire of about two and one-half hours every gun in the fort was dismounted or disabled and the fort knocked to pieces... "Brig. Gen. Thomas J. Churchill, CSA, surrendered the fort after a gallant resistance. The Confederates surrendering included 36 naval officers and men. Admiral Porter wrote later,

> The fight at Ft. Hindman was one of the prettiest little affairs of the war, not so little either, for a very important post fell into our hands with 6,500 prisoners, and the destruction of a powerful ram at Little Rock, which could have caused the Federal Navy in the west a great deal of trouble....

Not all things went well that day. The C.S.S. *Alabama*, Capt. Raphael Semmes, was now in the Gulf of Mexico and it took on the U.S.S. *Hatteras*, Lt. Commander Homer C. Blake, thirty miles off Galveston. A stiff fight resulted in the sinking of the *Hatteras*, all hands being saved by Semmes. The other Union ships in the area gave Semmes chase, but all they saw were his heels.

January 13 (Tuesday)

Out of Memphis, the U.S.S. *General Bragg*, Lt. Joshua Bishop, went to Mound City, Ark., looking for guerrillas who had been attacking steamers on the river. Bishop reported:

> Ascertained that there was quite a force of guerrillas in the neighborhood, who intended destroying steamers; that their rendezvous was at Mound City, Marion and Hopefield.... At 9 A.M. left Bradley's Landing and proceeded to Mound City, firing shells at intervals into the woods, as it was supposed there were guerrillas thereabouts. At 10 landed at Mound City and disembarked the troops. The infantry made prisoners of several citizens, who had been harboring guerrillas....

January 14 (Wednesday)

Back in the Ft. Hindman area, the U.S.S. *Baron de Kalb* and the *Cincinnati*, with two Army transports in tow, were a part of a force commanded by Lt. Cmdr. John G. Walker and Brig. Gen. Willis A. Gorman to follow up the Hindman victory. They found that the remaining Confederates had left their positions and had headed upriver on the *Blue Wing*. The *Baron de Kalb* went off in pursuit.

The U.S.S. *Columbia*, Lt. Joseph P. Couthouy, ran aground on the coast of North Carolina, due to high seas and winds. The weather prevented the crew from freeing her, so she was set on fire and the crew surrendered to the Confederates three days later.

January 16 (Friday)

The C.S.S. *Florida*, Lt. John N. Maffitt, after four months in Mobile for repairs, ran the blockade. Going past the blockading ships, passing within 300 yards of the U.S.S. *R.R. Cuyler*, Commander George F. Emmons. *Florida* cleared the blockade and went on to capture a prize before entering Havana to unload the crew from the sunken ship. At Havana, U.S. Consul-General Robert W. Shufeldt described the raider:

> The *Florida* is a bark-rigged propeller, quite fast under steam and canvas; has two smoke-stacks fore

and aft of each other, close together; has a battery of four 42's or 68's of a side and two large pivot guns. Her crew consists of 135 men... is a wooden vessel of about 1,500 tons.

At Devall's Bluff, Ark., on the White River, Lt. Commander J.G. Walker of the U.S.S. *Baron de Kalb* sent a landing party ashore and "took possession of all public property," including guns and munitions. When Gen. Gorman arrived with his troops, Walker turned everything over to the Army and prepared to depart the following morning in pursuit of the Confederate steamer *Blue Wing*.

January 17 (Saturday)

On this day, the U.S.S. *Baron de Kalb* arrived at Des Arc, Ark., in company with the U.S.S. *Forest Rose* and *Romeo*, along with an Army transport still chasing the Confederate steamer *Blue Wing*. Lt. Commander Walker reported:

> At that place I found 39 rebel soldiers in the hospital, whom I paroled. I also found and brought away 171 rounds of fixed ammunition, 72 cartridges, and 47 shot for 12-pounder rifled gun. I took possession of the post-office.... The troops reached Des Arc about an hour after me, and searched the town for arms and public property.

January 19 (Monday)

At Fredericksburg, Burnside had convinced Lincoln that a new attack across the Rappahannock was possible. This day, the troops of the Army of the Potomac started upriver towards the U.S. Ford in good weather. By nightfall, two of the Grand Divisions were near the ford.

A letter, intercepted coming out of Nassau, Bahamas, showed the effect of the blockade on the South:

> There are men here who are making immense fortunes by shipping goods to Dixie.... Salt, for example, is one of the most paying things to send in. Here in Nassau it is only worth 60 cents a bushel, but in Charleston brings at auction from $80 to $100 in Confederate money, but as Confederate money is no good out of the Confederacy, they send back cotton or turpentine, which, if it reaches here is worth proportionally as much here as the salt is there.... It is a speculation by which one makes either 600 to 800 percent or loses all.

January 20 (Tuesday)

On the Rappahannock River crossing at U.S. Ford, Burnside delayed crossing while he reorganized his plans. The rains began late in the evening.

In Havana, Cuba, a correspondent for the New York *Herald* described Lt. John N. Maffitt, commander of the raider C.S.S. *Florida* that had just come into port:

> Captain Maffitt is no ordinary character. He is vigorous, energetic, bold, quick and dashing, and the sooner he is caught and hung the better it will be for the interest of our commercial community. He is decidedly popular here, and you can scarcely imagine the anxiety evinced to get a glance at him.... Nobody, unless informed, would have imagined the small, black-eyed, poetic-looking gentleman, with his romantic appearance, to be a second Semmes, probably in time to be a more celebrated and more dangerous pirate.

Barber, Cpl., Co. D, 15th Illinois Volunteer Infantry, Lafayette, Miss.:

> Two members of Company D, whom I will not name, performed an act here which in a law-abiding land would have consigned them to prison. The persons referred to succeeded in eluding our pickets and went daily to a farm house within two miles of camp. Here lived a poor and respectable couple with a daughter, a young lady, who soon became the dupe of the rascals. One of them paid his addresses to her, won her affections and she consented to marry him. One day he brought a comrade with him whom he introduced as a chaplain and a mock ceremony of marriage was performed (January 24th). It was not until the regiment moved that treachery was suspected. The outraged father followed the regiment in hopes of finding the destroyer of his daughter's happiness, but by using disguises and keeping out of sight, they eluded his search. I did not know who the persons were that committed this vile act until the father of the girl had left and to the disgrace of the officers of our regiment, nothing was ever said or done to bring the rascals to justice....

January 21 (Wednesday)

Along the Rappahannock in Virginia, the famous "Mud March" of the Army of the Potomac was about to begin. The Army having gone to U.S. Ford to effect a crossing, the rains swelled the river to prevent any such activity and created mud, mud, and more mud.

President Davis ordered Gen. Joseph E. Johnston to Manchester, Tenn., to investigate the withdrawal from Murfreesboro. Since Bragg and Johnston did not get along well, this would not be a good trip.

January 22 (Thursday)

Along the Rappahannock, the scene was one of complete misery. Burnside's Army of the Potomac was stuck in colossal mud. Gun carriages and supply wagons were axle-deep and the horses and mules were dropping dead trying to pull them out. The troops were slogging through mud nearly knee-deep in places and the rain still fell. This march would be the subject of many campfire chats during and long after the war.

Grant, finally tired of McClernand's grandstand plays, assumed command of all troops in Arkansas; this reduced McClernand from commander of the expedition to a corps commander. McClernand was furious and went to Lincoln with his problem. Lincoln told him to calm himself.

Lt. Maffitt, leaving Havana, captured and burned the brigs *Windward* and *Corris* off the coast of Cuba. The C.S.S. *Florida* sailed on.

Iron was getting so short in the South that President Davis contemplated destroying railroads to get iron for ironclads.

January 23 (Friday)

On the Rappahannock, the Army of the Potomac was finally back in its old camps at Falmouth. There had been much bickering and backbiting among the Grand Division commanders, both among themselves and against Burnside. Burnside, angry, issued orders, subject to approval by Lincoln, that removed Hooker, W.B. Franklin, and W.F. Smith from command of their Grand Divisions, with Hooker to be dismissed from the service completely. These were not approved by Lincoln nor were they ever carried out.

January 24 (Saturday)

Having trapped 11 Confederate steamers loaded with supplies for Port Hudson up the Yazoo River, Rear Admiral D.D. Porter wrote to Secretary of the Navy Welles:

> The army is landing on the neck of land opposite Vicksburg. What they expect to do I don't know, but presume it is a temporary arrangement. I am covering their landing and guarding the Yazoo River. The front of Vicksburg is heavily fortified, and unless we can get troops in the rear of the city I see no chance of taking it at present, though we cut off all their supplies from Texas and Louisiana.

January 25 (Sunday)

Lincoln met with Burnside, who argued, unsuccessfully, for the removal of the generals. If this was not done, said Burnside, he would resign from the Army of the Potomac. Lincoln appointed Hooker the new commander and relieved Generals E.V. Sumner and W.B. Franklin. Burnside, who never wanted the command to begin with, settled for this.

January 26 (Monday)

The U.S. brig *Bainbridge*, sitting in Panama waiting for masts and spars to replace those lost at sea in a storm, would have to wait a while longer. Capt. Semmes, C.S.S. *Alabama*, off Haiti, captured and burned the *Golden Rule*, which was transporting the replacement masts and spars.

At Fredericksburg (actually across the river at Falmouth), Major Gen. Joseph Hooker took command of the Army of the Potomac, a job for which he had been angling for months. Lincoln wrote a letter to Hooker regarding his assignment:

> Jan 26, 1863.
> Major-General Hooker.
>
> General: I have placed you at the head of the Army of the Potomac. Of course, I have done this upon what appears to me to be sufficient reasons, and yet I think it best for you to know that there are some things in regard to which I am not quite satisfied with you.
>
> I believe you to be a brave and skillful soldier, which, of course, I like. I also believe you do not mix politics with your profession, in which you are right. You have confidence in yourself, which is a valuable,

if not indispensable quality. You are ambitious, which, within reasonable bounds, does good rather than harm. But I think that, during General Burnside's command of the Army, you have taken counsel of your ambitions, and thwarted his as much as you could, in which you did a great wrong, both to the country, and a most meritorious and honorable brother officer.

I have heard, in such a way as to believe it, of your recently saying that both the army and the Government needed a dictator. Of course, it was not for this, but in spite of it, that I have given you a command.

Only those generals who gain success can set up as dictators. What I ask of you is military success, and I will risk the dictatorship. The Government will support you to the utmost of its ability, which is neither more nor less than it has done and will do for all commanders. I much fear that the spirit that you have aided to infuse into the army, of criticizing their commander, and withholding confidence from him, will now turn upon you. I shall assist you as far as I can to put it down. Neither you nor Napoleon, if he were alive again, could get any good out of an army while such a spirit prevails in it.

And now, beware of rashness! Beware of rashness! But with energy and sleepless vigilance, go forward and give us victories.

Yours very truly,
A. Lincoln

January 27 (Tuesday)

Commander John L. Worden, lately of the ironclad U.S.S. *Monitor*, now commanding another ironclad, the U.S.S. *Montauk*, accompanied by the wooden ships U.S.S. *Seneca*, *Wissahickon*, *Dawn*, and the mortar schooner *C.P. Williams*, took on the batteries at Ft. McAllister, Ga., on the Ogeechee River. Worden was giving the *Montauk* a little battle test preparatory to the assault on Charleston, S.C. Worden, unable to get close due to obstructions sunk in the river, engaged for four hours before withdrawing. Du Pont reported that the *Montauk* was struck thirteen or fourteen times with no injury. He did wonder, however, if one ironclad could not silence eight guns, how were five ironclads to take the 147 guns that defended Charleston Harbor.

January 30 (Friday)

The Richmond *Dispatch* printed a listing showing the price of groceries had increased tenfold since the war had started.

Grant assumed command of all operations against Vicksburg and he informed Admiral D.D. Porter that he [Grant] intended to cut a canal through Lake Providence, La., to get the troops south of Vicksburg so a landing could be effected and the city taken from the rear.

January 31 (Saturday)

Two Confederate rams, the C.S.S. *Chicora*, Cmdr. John R. Tucker, and *Palmetto State*, Lt. John Rutledge, under the overall command of Flag Officer Duncan N. Ingraham, left Charleston Harbor in an early-morning fog and attacked the blockading fleet. The rams successfully destroyed the U.S.S. *Mercedita*, Capt. Stellwagen, and the *Keystone State*, Cmdr. William E. LeRoy. Gen. P.T.G. Beauregard, commander of the Charleston district, claimed that the blockade had been lifted. More Federal ships arrived.

FEBRUARY 1863

There was little activity as the armies lay in their respective camps, trying to stay warm and outwait the weather until the spring campaigns could begin. The blockade vessels on the coasts continued their endless patrols, occasionally catching a blockade runner. The Army of Tennessee huddled in its tents at Manchester, Tenn. and tried to build a social life in the town. Grant was constantly probing for a way to get into Vicksburg. A quiet time in the war.

February 1 (Sunday)

In late January, Commander Worden had taken the ironclad U.S.S. *Montauk* against Ft. McAllister on the Ogeechee River, in Georgia, near Savannah. He had been repelled, not by the guns, although they were formidable enough, but by obstacles placed in the river. Now, having knowledge of the location of the obstacles and the mines, he tried again, this time getting closer to the fort with the mortar schooner *C.P. Williams* and the gunboats U.S.S. *Seneca*, *Wissahickon*, and *Dawn* in support.

Early that morning Worden moved to within 600 yards of the fort and opened fire at 7:45 A.M. The first of 48 rounds from the shore batteries hit his turret at 7:53 A.M., the rest coming during the four-hour engagement. Col. Robert H. Anderson, commanding the fort, said of the attacking flotilla:

> The enemy fired steadily and with remarkable precision. Their fire was terrible. Their mortar fire was unusually fine, a large number of their shells bursting directly over the battery. The ironclad's fire was principally directed at the VIII-inch columbiad, and... the parapet in front of this gun was so badly breached as to leave the gun entirely exposed.

February 2 (Monday)

Col. C.R. Ellet, commander of the ram U.S.S. *Queen of the West* had her decks covered with confiscated cotton bales for protection, and her paddle wheels boarded over with heavy planks. She, in effect, looked like a floating box with a long snout. Ellet intended to take the ship under the guns of Vicksburg to ram and sink the steamer *City of Vicksburg* early that morning. However, he was delayed and didn't get ready until after daylight. This was no deterrent to Ellet; he took the *Queen* in anyway. The shore batteries opened fire but hit her only three times before she reached her target. Ellet reported:

> Her position was such that if we had run obliquely into her as we came down, the bow of the *Queen* would inevitably have glanced. We were compelled to partially round to in order to strike. The consequence was that at the very moment of collision the current, very strong and rapid at this point, caught the stern of my boat, and, acting on her bow as a pivot, swung her around so rapidly that nearly all momentum was lost.

Ellet had ordered the starboard gun loaded with incendiary shell. Firing this set the Confederate steamer aflame. The fire was quickly extinguished by the Confederate crew. The *City of Vicksburg* fired into the cotton bales on the *Queen*, setting them on fire, in turn. The firing of Ellet's gun had set his own vessel on fire and the drifting smoke from the burning cotton almost killed the crew in the engine room. They finally put out the fire by cutting loose some bales of cotton and pushing them overboard. By this time they were beyond the *Vicksburg*, so they went downriver.

The C.S.S. *Alabama*, Capt. Semmes, had a fire aboard at night that was quickly extinguished by the crew. A fire aboard a wooden warship was a dangerous thing. A misplaced spark could blow the ship sky high.

February 3 (Tuesday)

On this date, Ellet, on the U.S.S. *Queen of the West*, was below the mouth of the Red River, south of Vicksburg, where he met the Confederate steamer *A. W. Baker* coming upriver. The *Baker* ran ashore, but she was captured. Empty, she had just delivered her cargo to the Confederate troops at Port Hudson and was returning for another load. Just about the time Ellet put a crew aboard the *Baker*, the Confederate steamer *Moro* appeared, coming downstream. A shot across her bow stopped her, and Ellet had gained 55 *tons* of pork, almost 500 live hogs, and a large quantity of salt, all bound for Port Hudson. Running back upriver to get more coal, he stopped and destroyed about 12 tons of cornmeal waiting to go to Port Hudson, and he also seized the steamer *Berwick Bay*, loaded with 200 barrels of molasses, 10 hogsheads of sugar, 15 tons of four, and 40 bales of cotton, all bound for Port Hudson. Ellet ordered all of the steamers burned, along with their cargo.

North of Vicksburg, the Federals blew up the levee, creating a gap almost 75 yards wide. The Mississippi River gushed through, flooding the Yazoo Pass. It was hoped that gunboats and transports could go over this flood to attack Vicksburg from the rear.

A small flotilla of gunboats under the overall command of Lt. Commander Fitch went to the support of the garrison at Ft. Donelson, which was under attack by a larger force of Confederates. The Rebels, not expecting the gunboats, were surprised out in the open and taken under heavy fire. They retreated, leaving the field to the Union.

In Washington, the French minister, M. Mercier, hoping to get a mediation going between North and South, made his offer to "chair" such a meeting to Secretary of State Seward. Seward was more than a little offended by what he called "interference by a foreign power in a family dispute," and turned down the offer. Congress, when it learned of the offer, was also highly incensed.

February 4 (Wednesday)

Admiral Du Pont found that the construction of the ironclads presented a problem of communications between ships. The older wooden ships, with their masts and spars, signalled by "running up" the mast strings of flags (each of which had a different meaning), which were readily seen by the other ships. Since the new ironclads had no masts, the problem presented itself. Du Pont wrote Major Gen. David Hunter, his counterpart, and suggested that the Army Signal Codes be used by the Navy, since these relied on fewer flags, and in some cases, used light. Hunter agreed that this was a good idea, and Du Pont sent several young officers to learn the system. It would also make it easier for the two services to communicate with each other during joint operations.

February 5 (Thursday)

At Falmouth, Va., Hooker was busy reorganizing the Army of the Potomac into corps, eliminating Burnside's Grand Divisions. Eight corps were formed, and the cavalry was placed in a separate command under Stoneman. This command arrangement would remain essentially the same for the remainder of the war.

February 9 (Monday)

On the 6th, the Army of the Potomac detached one corps, the Ninth, to Newport News, Va. This corps was commanded by Major Gen. William F. Smith.

The convoys of supply steamers going to Nashville were increasing in both number and frequency. Lt. Commander Fitch, U.S.S. *Fairplay*, reported from Smithfield, Ky., that "... my return from Nashville, having landed in safety at that place with some 45 steamers. This makes 73 steamers and 16 barges we have convoyed safely to Nashville...."

The South Atlantic Blockading Squadron, Admiral Du Pont, was constantly having supply problems, and he was not alone in this situation. He reported:

> Our requisitions for general stores, I have reason to believe, are immediately attended to by the bureaus in the Department... but there seem to be unaccountable obstacles to our receiving them.... We have been out of oil for machinery. Coal is not more essential.... We were purchasing from transports or wherever it could be found, two or three barrels at a time. Finally the *Union* came with some, but it was stored under her cargo.... The vessel was to have brought important parts of the ration, such as sugar, coffee, flour, butter, beans and dried fruit with clothing but she did not.... My commanding officers complain their wants are not supplied....

February 11 (Wednesday)

On the Mississippi, Admiral D.D. Porter was also having supply problems, mostly with coal for the steamers. He directed Commander Pennock at Cairo:

> As circumstances occur I have to change the quantity of coal required here.... I want a stock of 160,000 bushels sent to the Yazoo River, besides the monthly allowance already required, viz, 70,000 bushels here, 40,000 at White River, and 20,000 at Memphis.... You will also have the *Abraham* filled up with three months' provisions and stores for the squadron, or as much as she can carry, and keep her ready at all times... to move at a moment's notice to such point as I may designate.

February 12 (Thursday)

In the Gulf of Mexico, Admiral Farragut was having supply problems as well as an increasing demand on his few ships. He travelled between Mobile and New Orleans like a commuter.

The commander of the U.S.S. *Queen of the West*, Col. C.R. Ellet, ran up the Red River and ascended the Atchafalaya, with a landing party, where he destroyed a train of twelve Confederate Army wagons. Coming back down, he was fired upon near Simmesport, La.

The C.S.S. *Florida*, Lt. Maffitt, captured the clipper ship *Jacob Bell* in the West Indies. The clipper was inbound from China with a cargo of tea, firecrackers, matting and camphor, valued in excess of $2,000,000. The clipper was burned the next day.

February 13 (Friday)

The U.S.S. *Queen of the West*, Col. C.R. Ellet, returned to Simmesport, La., the scene of the attack the previous day, and in reprisal, destroyed all the buildings in the town and three adjoining plantations.

Ellet got some help today. Lt. Commander George Brown ran past the batteries at Vicksburg with the U.S.S. *Indianola*, towing a barge loaded with coal, going past the upper batteries unseen. The lower batteries, however, opened on him with heavy fire but did no damage. Admiral Porter had told Brown to: "Go to Jeff Davis' plantation, load up with all the cotton you can find and the best single male negroes."

Reports from Wilmington, N.C., indicated that the fortifications of that port were being heavily reinforced. From Glasgow, Scotland, Commander James H. North, CSN, wrote to Confederate Secretary of the Navy Mallory:

> I can see no prospect of recognition from this country.... If they will let us get our ships out when they are ready, we shall feel ourselves most fortunate. It is now almost impossible to make the slightest move or do the smallest thing, that the Lincoln spies do not know of it....

February 14 (Saturday)

The U.S.S. *Queen of the West* met her fate today when she came under heavy fire from the shore batteries at Gordon's Landing on the Black River. Attempting to back down the river, she ran aground directly under the guns of the shore batteries, which poured shot into the ship with every broadside. The ram was abandoned and fell into Confederate hands. The crew escaped primarily by floating downriver on cotton bales; they were picked up by the *De Soto*, an Army steamer.

Off the Cape Fear River, N.C., a blockade runner successfully eluded three Union ships and picket boats and made it into port. The run was made along the coast in the early-morning hours; the ship relied upon blending in with the shore to make her escape. It worked.

February 16 (Monday)

In a landmark decision that would cause much turmoil, the U.S. Senate passed the Conscription Act. The South had been conscripting men for more than a year at this time.

February 17 (Tuesday)

Admiral D.D. Porter optimistically told Secretary of the Navy Gideon Welles about the conditions at Port Hudson, a Confederate bastion below Vicksburg:

> I have reason to believe that the enemy's troops at Port Hudson are in a strait for want of provisions, and if pushed by Gen. Banks' troops that fort will fall into our hands. It is situated in a swampy, muddy region 60 miles from any railroad, and the rains, which have exceeded anything I ever saw in my life, have rendered hauling by wagon impossible. Our vessels above them cut off all hope of supply or aid....

The U.S. tug *Hercules* had seven coal barges in tow when she was taken by the Confederates opposite Memphis. The tug was burned and the Rebels attempted to take off the barges, but this was thwarted by heavy fire from the gunboats across the river at Memphis.

February 19 (Thursday)

On station with the South Atlantic Blockading Squadron, Port Royal, S.C., Admiral Du Pont talked of his problems in keeping ships running:

> No vessel has ever attempted to run the blockade except by stealth at night—which fully established internationally the effectiveness of the blockade—but it is not sufficient for our purpose, to keep out arms and keep in cotton—unfortunately our people have considered a total exclusion possible and the government at one time seemed to think so. A cordon of ships—some twenty-one miles moored together head and stern—would do it easy.... I have forty ships of all classes, sometimes more—never reaching fifty—a considerable number are incapable of keeping at sea or at outside anchorage—the wear and tear and ceaseless breaking of American machinery compared with English or even French now, keep a portion of the above always in here repairing. If I had not induced the Department to establish a floating machine shop, which I had seen the French have in China, the blockade would have been a total failure....

There was heavy skirmishing along the Yazoo River where Grant was trying to get at the Vicksburg defenses.

There were mass rallies in support of the Emancipation Proclamation at Liverpool and Carlisle, England. Because of popular support for the freedom of the slaves, if the British government endorsed the South, it would be against the will of the people. Britain hereafter stayed neutral.

February 21 (Saturday)

Capt. Semmes, C.S.S. *Alabama*, told of the capture, burning, and sinking of the ship *Golden Eagle*, inbound from the Pacific:

> I had overhauled her near the termination of a long voyage. She had sailed from San Francisco, in ballast, for Howland's Island, in the Pacific; a guano island of which some adventurous Yankees had taken possession. There she had taken in a cargo of guano, for Cork.... This ship had buffeted the gales of the frozen latitudes of Cape Horn, threaded her pathway among its ice-bergs, been parched with the heats of the tropic, and drenched with the rains of the equator, to fall into the hands of her enemy, only a few hundred miles from her port. But such is the fortune of war....

Jackson, at Moss Neck, Va., worked on more court-martial proceedings for deserters.

Gen. Pickett's division passed through Richmond on the 19th, and today Hood's division marched through the city. Both were headed towards the Peninsula to counter the corps sent there by Hooker from the Army of the Potomac.

February 22 (Sunday)

Along the Manchester Pike between Murfreesboro and Manchester, Tenn.,the pickets of Bragg's Army of Tennessee and Rosecrans's Union forces exchanged a few rounds a day.

Allen, Pvt., Co. K, 1st Batallion, 10th Illinois Cavalry, Helena, Ark.:

> I wrote you a letter while I was in the hospital at St. Louis and have waited long and patiently for an answer, but none has yet come. I left St. Louis on Dec. 24th on the steamboat Sunnyside and had a very pleasant trip down to this place, which I reached on the 29th. I felt pretty well when I came down, but was not stout. About two weeks afterwards, exposure made me sick again and I was in our Battalion hospital for some time. I came back into camp as soon as I was able and have been slowly improving, but am not able to do duty yet.... I was down town the other day and got stuck fast in the mud. Being weak, I was unable to get out until I was helped out by a comrade.
>
> As no one speaks or writes without saying something about the war, I will give my humble opinion in as few words as possible: I believe that with proper management the accursed rebellion can be put down and could have been put down long ago; but that with management like the past, it will never be put down. I approve of the acts of the Administration, except the Emancipation Proclamation which virtually amounts to nothing, as the act for freeing the slaves and confiscating the property of rebels accomplishes all that the Proclamation can do, besides the latter excites some discontent in the army, and more among the people of loyal States. In regard to the arming of the blacks, I have no very great objection to that if the white and black soldiers are kept distinct and separate; but I think we have plenty of white men to whip the damned rebels....
>
> ...I ate the first mess of eggs this morning that I have had in Arkansas. Eggs cost 35c., butter 35c., dried apples 15c. per lb., dried peaches 20c. per lb., Irish potatoes $3 per bushel, milk 20c. per qt.
>
> I send you three Confederate Treasury notes, so you can see what sort of money they have in Dixie....

February 23 (Monday)

Floating and sunken logs were always a hazard on the rivers and bayous of Louisiana. The U.S.S. *Kinsman*, Acting Lt. Wiggen, transporting a body of troops, struck a log and sank in Berwick Bay, La. Six men were reported missing.

Simon Cameron, former governor of Pennsylvania, political boss of a corrupt machine, Secretary of War who was (essentially) fired by Lincoln, today resigned his post as Ambassador to Russia, which post had been given to him as a sop. Cameron's tour as Secretary of War initiated one of the most corrupt eras ever seen in this country of wholesale bilking of the government for war matériel.

February 24 (Tuesday)

The Confederates had raised the ram *Queen of the West* and put her to work on the Mississippi chasing the U.S.S. *Indianola*, the ram being in consort with the C.S.S. *William H. Webb* and *Beatty*. The Confederates, overtaking the *Indianola* about 10 P.M., started the attack. The *Queen* tried to ram the *Indianola* but hit a coal barge being towed alongside the *Indianola* for protection. The *Indianola* then was struck by the *Webb*, swung around from the blow and was hit by the *Queen* again, but with no great damage. Next, the *Queen* got in behind the *Indianola* and rammed her, shattering the starboard wheelhouse framework. The *Webb*, having gone upstream, returned and rammed the *Indianola* in the port wheelhouse, disabling the ship. Lt. Commander Brown of the *Indianola* let the ship fill with water while he got to the shore, where he surrendered to the commander of the *Beatty*, Col. Frederick B. Brand.

In perhaps one of the most poignant diary entries ever written in the war, James K. Boswell, who had served as an aide-de-camp to Jackson for one year, recorded:

> How long it seems since that day; it appears more like ten years than one; the truth is that I have thought, felt and acted more in the last year than in all the rest of my life. During the year I have been present in ten hard-fought and bloody battles, besides a number of skirmishes. I have been once with Gen. Jackson when he was defeated, and nine times when he was victorious; in some of these battles I have been exposed to death in all its forms, and in others I have been exposed but little. I have heard the wild cry of victory as it rose above the roar of cannon and musket. I have seen the field strewn with thousands of corpses, both of friend and foe. I have heard the groans of the wounded and dying. I have seen the fairest portions of the Old Dominion desolated by the ravages of war. I have seen towns ransacked, and hundreds, nay thousands, of helpless women and children thrown homeless upon the world. I have seen our noble leader, Gen. Lee, again and again on the field of battle. O war, why art thou called glorious when such are thy fruits? How long must our dear land be desolated by the ravages and our bravest sacrificed upon thy altars? One year ago I was full of life and animation, hope dressed the future in "couleur de rose," all my dreams were cherished as though I were sure of their realization.

James K. Boswell would have his rendezvous with death in early May at the Battle of Chancellorsville, just west of Fredericksburg, Va.

The U.S. Congress organized Arizona Territory today, separating it from New Mexico Territory.

February 25 (Wednesday)

In Washington, Lincoln signed the act authorizing the national bank and national currency system.

The Confederates were working madly to get the U.S.S. *Indianola* raised. The *Queen of the West* was sent upriver to Vicksburg to get pumps to help raise the sunken ship, but she returned within a short time with news that a large Union "gunboat" was passing the Vicksburg batteries and approaching the squadron. All the Confederate ships took off without delay downriver, leaving the work crew aboard the sunken ship. The Federal "gunboat" did not approach within 2½ miles of the sunken ship. The next evening, the work crew decided that the *Indianola* could not be raised, so they fired the heavy XI-inch Dahlgren guns into each other, and burned the ship to the water line. It later was learned that the "gunboat" was a large barge fitted to look like a gunboat; it fooled the Confederates for a while at least.

The U.S.S. *Vanderbilt*, Acting Lt. Charles H. Baldwin, captured the British blockade runner *Peterhoff* off St. Thomas in the Virgin Islands. A large quantity of mail, bound for England, was taken, along with the ship. The British demanded the mail be returned unopened. This was done eventually but it almost caused an international incident.

February 26 (Thursday)

Confederate guerrillas made a haul near Woodburn, Tenn., today when they stopped a Union train and unloaded over 200 mules and commercial and military stores. The train was burned, the mules and cargo taken away.

February 27 (Friday)

The C.S.S. *Alabama*, Capt. Semmes, captured the ship *Washington* after he "wet the people on her poop, by the spray of a shot..." and then released the ship on bond.

Confederate General Joseph E. Johnston was unhappy with the command arrangements in the west. He said his armies were too scattered for offensive operations, and were too small for good defensive operations. He asked to be relieved and assigned some other command.

February 28 (Saturday)

Commander Worden, U.S.S. *Montauk*, shelled and destroyed the blockade runner *Rattlesnake*, formerly the C.S.S. *Nashville*, while the RATTLESNAKE was lying under the guns of Ft. McAllister on the Ogeechee River, Ga. Having noticed that she had run aground the day before, Worden took the opportunity to attack this morning and destroy her. Amid shelling from the fort, Worden set the *Rattlesnake* on fire within 20 minutes. About 9:30 A.M., the fire reached her magazines and she blew up. Meanwhile, the *Montauk* struck a torpedo at about 8:30 A.M., while withdrawing and had to be run onto a mudbank to effect repairs.

For several days the expedition through the Yazoo Pass to attack Vicksburg from the rear had been underway. The Rebels had cut trees across the path of the gunboats and, the passages being so narrow, the progress was usually measured in yards per day rather than in miles.

MARCH 1863

Even in the "sunny" South there was bitter cold and deep snows to contend with. The food distribution system was still in need of repair and there was near famine in the larger cities, such as Richmond. Vicksburg still stood, as did Port Hudson. Little progress had been made over the winter. In the camps, the soldiers still outwaited the weather and hoped for dry roads.

March 1 (Sunday)

On this date a new national color was presented to the colonel of the 11th Connecticut Volunteers by a Miss Julia A. Beach of Wallingford, Conn. It was to replace the old flag, presented to the regiment in 1861, which had been carried through many battles. The new flag, and what remained of the old one, were placed on the same staff and carried until the end of the war.

March 2 (Monday)

It was amazing that people travelled around between the North and South so much and so easily. Frequently, reports were read of visitors from places you would think out of reach. A case in point is a comment by Admiral Farragut in New Orleans:

> I have recently seen persons from Mobile, and they all concur in the statement that provisions are very high, and very scarce even at those high figures. Flour, $100 per barrel; bacon and meat of every kind, $1 per pound; meal, $20 per sack.... At present, I am all ready to make an attack on or run the batteries at Port Hudson, so as to form a junction with the army and navy above Vicksburg.... The army of General Banks will attack by land or make a reconnaissance in force at the same time that we run the batteries.... My first objective will be destroy the boats and cut off the supplies from the Red River. We expect to move in less than a week....

Amid the trials of war there was often a chance to do good for someone. Admiral D.D. Porter sent instructions to Lt. Commander Selfridge, U.S.S. *Conestoga*:

> Mrs. Twiddy, at Wilson and Mitchell's Landing, Bolivar, has 130 bales of cotton which she is desirous to sending to Cairo. This cotton must be seized the same as all other cotton and turned over to the civil authorities at Cairo, and, after it has been sold, Mrs. Twiddy can, by proving her loyalty to the Government, receive the value for it. She has also permission to go up to Cairo herself and take all her effects. If it is necessary, a gunboat will protect her self and property. When she is ready to go she will hoist a white flag, but you had better run down there occasionally and see how she is getting on. You will make a full report to me of all the particulars of this case....

Three weeks later, the U.S.S. *Bragg* took Mrs. Twiddy, her cotton, and her personal effects to Cairo.

March 3 (Tuesday)

Lincoln signed a national conscription act imposing a liability on all male citizens between 20 and 45 years of age. The cooperation between the Army and Navy on the western rivers continued in good form. Admiral D.D. Porter informed Assistant Secretary of the Navy Fox that

> There is delightful concert here between the Army and Navy. Grant and Sherman are on board almost every day... we agree in everything, and they are disposed to do everything for us they can, they are both able men, and I hope sincerely for the sake of the Union that nothing may occur to make a change here.

Lt. Commander W. Smith, Navy commander of the Yazoo Pass expedition, reported that progress was not more than 1½ miles per hour, if that fast, due to the heavily treed area they were moving through.

On the Ogeechee River in Georgia, Admiral Du Pont set his three ironclads U.S.S. *Passaic*, *Nahant*, and *Patapsco*, with three mortar boats and the wooden gunboats U.S.S. *Seneca*, *Dawn*, and *Wissahickon* against Ft. McAllister again for six hours. This was as much a training exercise as anything to toughen the crews to the stress of combat and give to them target practice.

March 5 (Thursday)

The Union Army finally acknowledged that the practice of the men doing their own cooking was both bad for their digestion and for their morale. Cooking was a major problem in both Northern and Southern armies. Most of the men were not familiar with the preparation of food (their mothers or their wives did this for them), and the consequent product was often inedible and generally very greasy.

Another real problem, just being dealt with, was the conduct of the officers who commanded the regiments. Most of these officers were 'rewarded' for forming the regiments (sometimes at their own expense) by being appointed colonel of the regiment. In all too many cases they had no experience in military matters, and, in some cases, no desire to learn. This was true, unfortunately, both for North and South.

A Confederate ironclad made her appearance at New Inlet on the Cape Fear River in North Carolina, a new development. There were no opposing Union ironclads in the vicinity, but the Rebel ship withdrew upriver because she could not take the ocean currents.

March 7 (Saturday)

The officer shortage in the North Atlantic Blockading Squadron was getting serious. Admiral S.P. Lee, commander of the Squadron, requested:

> Owing to the increase of blockade runners off the coast of North Carolina, and frequent captures made of them, I would request that six officers capable of taking charge of prizes may be ordered to this squadron. The vessels blockading off Cape Fear are greatly in want of them, owing to the number they have heretofore sent away in prizes, which leaves our vessels very deficient in officers.

March 8 (Sunday)

The sloop *Enterprise*, living up to her name, loaded with cotton, made a run for the Bahamas from Mosquito Inlet, Fla., only to be captured near Nassau by the U.S.S. *Sagamore*, Lt. Commander English.

In Richmond, Judge Samuel A. Meredith had stated an opinion that foreigners, Marylanders, and others, who had served in the Army had become domiciled, and were thus liable for conscription. There was a rush for passports to leave the Confederacy.

March 9 (Monday)

In Tennessee, Rosecrans braced for a Confederate attack. The riverbanks were "filled with guerrillas" who attempted to stop the supply boats on the Tennessee and Cumberland Rivers. The big problem seemed to be with crewing the boats. As Admiral Porter said, "The only trouble is want of men. We can get the vessels faster than we can get crews."

Grant, just having a little fun on the Mississippi, sent a second fake ironclad past the batteries of Vicksburg, drawing a tremendous amount of fire. The "gunboat" was made of logs with barrels for smokestacks.

This evening at Fairfax C.H., south of Washington, Union Gen. Edwin H. Stoughton and his staff were captured in their beds by Confederate John S. Mosby and his band. This was most embarrassing for the general since he was supposed to be out to capture Mosby. The officers were taken to Confederate lines and turned over as prisoners-of-war. They were later exchanged.

March 11 (Wednesday)

The U.S.S. *Chillicothe*, Lt. Cmdr. J.P. Foster, engaged the batteries at Ft. Pemberton at a range of about 800 yards. Foster had one gun crew "rendered perfectly useless, 3 men being killed outright, 1 mortally wounded, and 10 others seriously wounded, while the other 5 of the gun's crew had their eyes filled with powder." A shell from the enemy's emplacements penetrated the port slide (3 inches thick) and struck the tulip of the port gun, exploding, and igniting her (the port gun's) shell just after it was in the muzzle. The shell in the muzzle exploded, carrying away the two forward port slides, weighing 3,200 pounds, tearing out part of the turret backing, plus setting fire to the cotton which had been providing some protection. Since he couldn't get more than one gun to bear on the fort, Foster moved a 30-pound Parrot gun onshore to shell the fort's emplacements while he effected repairs.

Conscription was getting tighter in the Confederacy. Heretofore, many people had been exempt due to their jobs or connections. Now the Bureau of Conscription in Richmond decided that all clerks in the departments, appointed later than October 11, 1862, were eligible for the draft.

March 12 (Thursday)

Admiral Farragut arrived at Baton Rouge aboard his flagship, the U.S.S. *Hartford*, to finalize the plans for the assault on Port Hudson. The U.S.S. *Richmond*, Capt. James Alden, was at Baton Rouge awaiting Farragut's arrival.

There was no shortage of newspapers in Richmond, even if all of them were printing only half sheets. A new paper, *The Sentinel*, was published for the first time on March 11.

March 13 (Friday)

At the Richmond Arsenal, located near the James River, at the foot of 7th Street in Richmond, the building was shaken when the Confederate States Laboratory on nearby Brown's Island exploded. Forty-five women and children were killed in the explosion.

On the Yazoo River, where the assault on Ft. Pemberton was taking place, the U.S.S. *Chillicothe*, previously damaged, sustained another 38 hits before running out of ammunition and withdrawing. The U.S.S. *Baron de Kalb* engaged for another three hours before retiring, its ammunition exhausted.

Admiral Du Pont wrote about the upcoming assault on Charleston:

> We are steadily preparing for the great experiment, to see whether 20 guns, counting one broadside of the *Ironsides*, can silence or overcome some hundreds.... I did a very wise thing... in trying the ironclads, four of them at least, against a live target in the shape of Fort McAllister. The experience has been invaluable, for they were wholly unfit to go into action.... Then Dahlgren writes the life of his fifteen inch [gun] is 300 [firings]! This is about the worst thing yet—for I look for such pounding as done to the *Montauk*, today, by the torpedo—it is bad and hard to mend.... Our papers instructed the rebels at what spot to aim at and they did *exactly* but I have sent for more iron....

March 14 (Saturday)

At Ft. Anderson on the Neuse River, N.C., the Confederates launched a surprise night attack which was driven off by naval gunfire provided by the U.S.S. *Hunchback*, *Hetzel*, *Ceres*, and *Shawsheen*.

On the Mississippi River, Admiral Farragut sent his squadron of seven ships against the shore batteries of Port Hudson, attempting to run past them. At 10 P.M., the fleet sailed upriver, the heavier ships on the fort side, the lighter ships farther away from the guns. The flagship U.S.S. *Hartford* made it past the guns but the *Richmond* took a round in her steam plant and was disabled. With the aid of the *Genesee*, which was lashed alongside, the *Richmond* made it out of range with little more damage. The next ship, the *Monongahela*, ran aground under the guns of the lower fort and took a pounding for 30 minutes before getting off with the aid of the *Kineo*. The *Monongahela* had at least eight shots pass entirely through the ship. The bridge was shot from underneath Capt. James P. McKinstry, injuring him and killing three others. An attempt was made to continue upriver but with no luck. She drifted downstream and anchored out of range of the guns.

The U.S.S. *Mississippi*, Capt. Melancthon Smith, with Lt. George Dewey aboard, saw the *Richmond* coming back downriver and tried to close the gap. The *Mississippi* ran aground and could not be brought off the mudbar. She was set afire and abandoned. At 3 A.M. the next morning she blew up while floating downriver; the blast could be heard for miles. George Dewey escaped and became the hero of Manila Bay 35 years later, during the Spanish-American War.

On the Yazoo, another group of gunboats tried a different direction to get to Vicksburg. This time the U.S.S. *Louisville*, *Cincinnati*, *Carondelet*, *Pittsburg*, *Mound City*, and four mortar boats with four tugs made their way to Black Bayou. Beyond that point, the trees were cleared by pulling them out or pushing them over with the gunboats to clear the channel. It took 24 hours to go four miles to Deer Creek.

March 15 (Sunday)

In a little side action in San Francisco, the U.S.S. *Cyane*, Lt. Commander Paul Shirley, sent boats to board and seize the schooner *J.P. Chapman*, getting ready to sail. The ship, suspected of being fitted as a commerce raider for the Confederacy, was found to have a crew of four on deck and another 17 concealed below decks along with guns, ammunition, and other military stores. The cargo was offloaded and the crew confined on the island of Alcatraz.

March 16 (Monday)

Commander J.P. Foster, U.S.S. *Chillicothe*, renewed his attack on Ft. Pemberton, and in the brief encounter the ship was hit eight times, rendering her guns inoperative and forcing her to retire from the fight. So far, in three days of engagement, the ship had lost 22 killed, wounded, and drowned.

South of Vicksburg, Farragut had the flagship U.S.S. *Hartford* and one gunboat north of Port Hudson. The remainder of his ships being struck and disabled, floated downriver to safety except for the *Mississippi*, which had blown up.

March 17 (Tuesday)

At Kelly's Ford on the Rappahannock, Federal cavalry under Gen. William W. Averell crossed the river and ran into a nasty group of Confederates who gave them a stiff fight in brushy and second-growth timber country. The South lost one of its favorite sons, young John Pelham, age 25, known as "the gallant Pelham," who was killed while observing the fight.

March 18 (Wednesday)

The U.S.S. *Wissahickon*, Lt. Commander John L. Davis, captured and destroyed the steamer *Georgiana* when she attempted to run the blockade into Charleston, S.C., with a cargo which included rifled guns. This ship, observed in other ports by United States consuls, was reported to have been pierced for 14 guns and was intended to be a commerce raider, like the C.S.S. *Florida* or *Alabama*. Secretary Welles wrote Admiral Du Pont when he heard of the *Georgiana's* destruction that

> ...it would have been better would she have been captured but the fact that she is disposed of is a relief. We had serious apprehensions in regard to her. In disposing of both her and the *Nashville* you have rendered great service to our commerce, for had they got abroad they would have made sad havoc with our shipping....

Day, Pvt., Co. B, 25th Massachusetts Volunteer Infantry, New Bern, N.C.:

> After months of idleness in camp, at last comes a change. At 4 o'clock P.M. orders came to break camp, pick up our traps and be ready to march in half an hour. Dark found seven companies of us on board the steamer *Escort*, bound for Plymouth.... The night being dark and stormy, we waited till morning before leaving.

In Richmond, Hood's Texans were marching through the city, going back north to join Lee's army, south of Fredericksburg.

March 19 (Thursday)

Farragut, undaunted that he was almost alone on the Mississippi, having only the U.S.S. *Albatross* for company, engaged the shore batteries at Grand Gulf, Miss., and proceeded on to the mouth of the Red River. Two days earlier, he went farther north towards Natchez, tearing down the telegraph lines to Port Hudson. The night of March 18, he had anchored below Grand Gulf, and on the 19th he ran past the guns, coming to anchor just below Warrenton, Miss.

Day, Pvt., Co. B, 25th Massachusetts Volunteer Infantry, on the steamer *Escort*, for Plymouth, N.C.:

> Heavy northeast storm blowing this morning. Steamer starts down the river and enters the sound about 10 o'clock, wind increases, the sound grows rough, the boat rolls, the boys grow sick, the water breaks on deck and many of them get wet; altogether the passage is rather unpleasant. We arrive at the north end of the sound, near the entrance to Croaton sound, about 9 P.M. and anchor for the night.

March 20 (Friday)

Farragut, below Warrenton, Miss., sent a message to Grant and Admiral Porter offering his assistance in stopping the supplies from crossing at the mouth of the Red River. He also asked for coal to resupply his two ships. Grant floated a coal barge down past the guns of Vicksburg for the resupply.

Day, Pvt., Co. B, 25th Massachusetts Volunteer Infantry, Plymouth, N.C.:

> This morning finds the storm unabated. The boat starts at daylight, passing Roanoke island, and enters the Albemarle, arriving at Plymouth late in the afternoon, where we make our quarters in a large warehouse on the wharf.

Snow was eight inches deep in Richmond that day and the Texans who were stopped from going to Fredericksburg were having snowball fights on Main Street.

March 22 (Sunday)

The water-borne expeditions to attack Vicksburg from the rear had now been cancelled. Admiral D.D. Porter described them as "a most novel expedition. Never did those people expect to see ironclads floating where the keel of a flat boat never passed." Some good, if that can be said, came out of the whole mess. A large quantity of corn was destroyed and many horses, mules, and cattle were taken. An estimated 20,000 bales of cotton were destroyed and enough was taken to pay for a gunboat. A great many able-bodied Negroes left with the gunboats when they withdrew, most carrying with them the stores of their former masters.

Day, Pvt., Co. B, 25th Massachusetts Volunteer Infantry, Plymouth, N.C.:

> The garrison here consists of companies G, Capt Swift, and H, Capt Sanford, of the 27th Massachusetts; company D, Capt Howard, of the 5th Massachusetts; company C, Capt Cliff, of the 1st North Carolina Union volunteers, and part of a company of the 1st North Carolina cavalry. The fellows here are telling us bear stories about one rebel General Garnett (whoever he is) and his brigade which is hovering around here. I think he must be quite a harmless character to let so small a garrison as this go undisturbed but it is possible he has a wholesome fear of Captain Flusser and his gunboats.
>
> This town has undergone quite a change since we were here last fall. During the winter the enemy made a dash in here, setting the town on fire, burning up the central and business portion of it. These people have singular ideas; they seem to think that by destroying their property, they are in some way damaging us, but if we destroy any property, it is a great piece of vandalism....

Food distribution was badly disrupted by the snow, although the day had warmed up and the snow was melting.

March 23 (Monday)

Admiral Farragut wrote his wife from his flagship below Vicksburg. In this letter he clearly stated the credo of every good military leader in history:

> I passed the batteries of Port Hudson with my chicken (U.S.S. *Albatross*) under my wing. We came through in safety.... Would to God I only knew that our friends on the other ships were as well as we are! We are all in the same hands, and He disposes of us as He thinks best.... You know my creed: I never send others in advance when there is a doubt, and, being one on whom the country has bestowed its greatest honors, I thought I ought to take the risks which belong to them. So I took the lead....

March 24 (Tuesday)

Brig. Gen. Alfred W. Ellet informed Capt. Walke that he intended to send the rams *Lancaster* and *Switzerland* past the guns at Vicksburg to support Farragut on the Red River. Brig. Gen. A.W. Ellet ordered Col. C.R. Ellet (a relative), commander of the ram fleet:

> You will not, in the event that either boat is disabled, attempt, under fire of the batteries, to help her off with the other boat, but will run on down, it being of primary importance that one boat at least should get safely by.

Day, Pvt., Co. B, 25th Massachusetts Volunteer Infantry, Plymouth, N.C.:

> Gen. Foster arrived this morning and went to work laying out a fort and other defenses which we

are to build. That job done, he took companies F, I and K of the 25th and H of the 27th Massachusetts with a party of marines, and a boat howitzer (on board his boat the *John Ferrin*) and set out on some sort of an excursion up the Chowan river. The general is no idler, he is always on the move and seeing that everybody else is....

March 25 (Wednesday)

Up and stirring before daybreak, the Union rams *Lancaster* and *Switzerland* started their run past the guns at Vicksburg to join Admiral Farragut. Col. C.R. Ellet, a relative of Brig. Gen. Alfred W. Ellet, on *Switzerland*, later reported:

> The wind was extremely unfavorable, and notwithstanding the caution with which the boats put out into the middle of the stream, the puff of their escape pipes could be heard with fatal distinctness below. The flashing of the enemy's signal lights from battery to battery as we neared the city showed me that concealment was useless.... Shot after shot struck my boat, tearing everything to pieces before them.

Directly in front of the Vicksburg batteries, a shell plunged into *Switzerland*'s boiler, stopping the engines. The pilots kept the ram in the river and she floated down, still under a hail of shot, to safety.

The *Lancaster*, commanded by another relative of Brig. Gen. Ellet, meanwhile, received a fatal shot that pierced her steam drum, and a heavy plunging shot struck her in the frailest part of her stern, passing through and piercing the hull in the center near the bow, causing an enormous leak. She sank almost immediately.

Farragut, below Vicksburg, was having maintenance problems with his ships, although Grant was floating coal barges down the river to him.

Barber, Cpl., Co. D, 15th Illinois Volunteer Infantry, Memphis, Tenn.:

> Col. Richardson, a noted guerrilla, now began to harass us. Several regiments of the 4th division were sent out to disperse this band. They were strongly posted in a low, swampy ground, accessible only on one side by the artillery. A sharp fight ensued. We lost several killed and wounded. A Major in an Iowa regiment was killed.

March 26 (Thursday)

A Frenchman named Brutus de Villeroy designed a semi-submarine boat and sold it to the government in Washington. This contraption was 46 feet long, 4½ feet wide, and carried a crew of 17. It originally was propelled by oars, but these were replaced at the Washington Navy Yard by a hand-operated screw propeller. This "ship," called the *Alligator*, was sent to Admiral Du Pont to be used as a reconnaissance craft.

March 27 (Friday)

Farragut's flagship, U.S.S. *Hartford*, sailed past the guns at Warrenton on the Mississippi. Two days later, the U.S.S. *Albatross* joined Farragut after waiting to refuel from the coal barges that had been floated down the river.

Day, Pvt., Co. B, 25th Massachusetts Volunteer Infantry, Plymouth, N.C.:

> We have cleared off the debris from a portion of the burnt district and pitched our camp there. The colonel might take a little more pride in showing us up to the naval officers at dress parade than he did when we were here last fall, but he is in command of the post; Lieut. Col. Moulton is in command of the regiment and he will do the honors. The 46th Massachusetts has arrived....
>
> Work commenced today on the defenses.... I was detailed to take command of a working party from my company. Now this was all new business to me. I knew nothing about building forts so I stood with my men and looked on. This was not very hard work, but after a spell a captain said, "Bring your men this way." The order was promptly responded to and the boys set to work. I thought they worked well enough, although I noticed that the bank in front of them did not rise very fast, but I supposed that was owing to the hardness of the soil. After a while they complained of feeling tired; I told them to rest and they squatted. After that they seemed to be tired pretty much of the time. The captain would come along and ask me why my men were not working. I would answer him that they were tired, and after resting, would handle their spades right smart. At night we had a bank thrown up about a rod long and nearly a foot high, but the boys worked well and I know they will sleep well after it....

March 29 (Sunday)

Commander Duncan, U.S.S. *Norwich*, reported the evacuation of Jacksonville, Fla., by Union forces after they destroyed the greater part of the city.

On the Mississippi, Grant asked Admiral D.D. Porter if Porter could get gunboats south of Vicksburg to support a landing of troops on the east bank at Grand Gulf. Porter agreed, but wanted to wait until his gunboats from the Yazoo expedition were back with him. Grant, meanwhile, ordered Gen. McClernand to move his troops south from Milliken's Bend to the vicinity of New Carthage, on the west bank of the river.

Day, Pvt., Co. B, 25th Massachusetts Volunteer Infantry, Plymouth, N.C.:

> Church service today for the first time in several weeks; we occupied the Methodist church. Chaplain James discoursed on neutrality. He said there could be no such thing as neutrality; a man must be one thing or the other, and those who do not declare for the government should be treated as its enemies. The house was well filled with soldiers and the galleries running around three sides of the house were filled with darkies, who somewhat resembled an approaching thunder squall.

March 30 (Monday)

In the words of Lt. Maffitt, C.S.S. *Florida*, the crew were "living like lords on Yankee plunder" from the provisions taken from the seized bark *M.J. Colcord*. The ship, loaded with provisions and bound for Cape Town, South Africa, was taken, the provisions transferred to the *Florida*, the crew to a Danish brig, *Christian*, and the *Colcord* destroyed.

March 31 (Tuesday)

The Confederate Army forces launched a large attack on the Union garrison at Washington, N.C. The Confederate forces were supported by large numbers of artillery to cope with Union gunboats. This siege would last till mid-April with the garrison being supplied by gunboats running past the artillery batteries of Gen. A.P. Hill.

Below Vicksburg, the Union ram *Switzerland* had been repaired and joined Farragut near Warrenton. This night, the three ships would run past Grand Gulf and then continue downriver to the mouth of the Red River. Many boats, barges, and skiffs carrying supplies across the river were destroyed during the next couple of days.

Meanwhile, Gen. McClernand's troops had left Milliken's Bend and were en route to New Carthage, on the west bank of the Mississippi.

APRIL 1863

Spring crept through the South, greening the laurel bushes, setting the woods ablaze with blooming dogwood trees, and lifting the heart of civilian and soldier alike. The runoff of the snows into the streams made the larger rivers, like the Mississippi, Ohio, Cumberland, and Tennessee, flood and fill with hazards to navigation. In the camps, the soldiers stretched their aching muscles, long stiffened from winter's inactivity, and prepared for the coming campaigns. In the distance, the summer bugles called the men to arms.

April 1 (Wednesday)

A day earlier, March 31st, Lt. Commander Gillis, U.S.S. *Commodore Morris*, proceeded up the Ware River in Virginia, with a load of soldiers, looking for a large quantity of grain that was reported to be stored in the area. At Patterson Smith's plantation, grain was found in excess of 22,000 bushels. On April 1, as the soldiers and sailors from the ship prepared to remove the grain to the ship, the landing party was attacked by Confederate cavalry. The landing party immediately formed into ranks, the guns from the ship fired on the cavalry, the Union men charged, and the Confederates were routed. What grain could not be removed to the ship was burned.

In the Hilton Head area of South Carolina, Admiral Du Pont was in the final stages of preparation for the assault on Charleston. He sent the ironclads U.S.S. *Passaic*, *Montauk*, *Patapsco*, and *Keokuk* to the North Edisto River to pre-position themselves for the attack. Other gunboats were also positioned for the assault.

On the Yazoo River north of Vicksburg, Generals Grant and Sherman, in the company of Admiral D.D. Porter, used the gunboat U.S.S. *Tuscumbia* to reconnoitre the area around Haynes Bluff to determine whether it could be assaulted. The decision was negative. The Grand Gulf plan seemed to be the best hope.

Barber, Cpl., Co. D, 15th Illinois Volunteer Infantry, Memphis, Tenn.:

> Our picket duty here required the utmost vigilance. Rank rebels of both sexes, under the guise of peaceful citizens, obtained passes to go beyond the lines, and citizens outside of the lines obtained passes to go into the city to purchase groceries, etc. The passes lasting one month and subject to renewal by the Commander, Gen. Veatch. It was soon discovered that these persons carried on a regular system of smuggling through contraband articles. It became necessary to form a chain picket. Even then, some would succeed in eluding the guard. Things, calling themselves ladies, were caught with quinine and other articles secreted in their crinolines. Gen. Veatch now issued an order that all ladies of suspicious character should be searched before passing out. Of course, these women were highly indignant at this, but their unladylike conduct begged the necessity of the order.

April 3 (Friday)

There was no mention of yesterday's "food riot" in the Richmond papers this day. Crowds of women and other "non-draftable" individuals still gathered on street corners asking for food. The City Battalion, charged with keeping the peace, was finally called in, and the crowds dispersed.

In a letter to the Confederate War Department, Gen. D.H. Hill complained about the enforcement of the conscription law in North Carolina. The law was ineffective and existed only to line the pockets of those running the system.

Lt. Commander Fitch took a fleet of gunboats up the Cumberland River to Palmyra, Tenn., and destroyed the town in retaliation for its firing on the Federal convoy the day before. Included in the fleet were the U.S.S. *Lexington, Brilliant, Robb, Silver Lake,* and *Springfield.*

April 4 (Saturday)

In Washington, D.C., Lincoln boarded a steamer to visit Gen. Joseph Hooker at Fredericksburg.

Capt. Semmes, C.S.S. *Alabama,* captured the coal-laden ship *Louisa* off the coast of Brazil. Semmes, always foresighted, took the ship with him in the event he missed his next rendezvous with his supply ship. Sure enough, there was no supply ship. Semmes refueled from his prize and burned it on the 17th.

Admiral Du Pont issued his order of battle for the attack on Charleston:

> ...The Squadron will pass up the main channel without returning the fire of the batteries on Morris Island, unless signal should be made to commence action. The ships will open fire on Fort Sumter when within easy range, and will take up position to the northward and westward of that fortification, engaging its left or northeast face at a distance of from 600 to 800 yards firing low and aiming at the center embrasure.... Each ship will be prepared to render every assistance possible to vessels that may require it.... After the reduction of Fort Sumter it is probable that the next point of attack will be the batteries on Morris Island. The order of battle will be line ahead....

April 5 (Sunday)

Admiral Du Pont left North Edisto for Charleston, arriving in the afternoon. The channel off the Stono bar was buoyed to mark the safe channel, and two gunboats, the U.S.S. *Catskill,* Commander George Rodgers, and U.S.S. *Patapsco,* Commander Ammen, remained inside the bar to protect the buoys from being destroyed or moved. As a precaution, Du Pont had brought along enough steamers to tow off any of the gunboats that were disabled.

At New Carthage, Grant's troops were preparing to cross the Mississippi south of Grand Gulf, in the attack to take Vicksburg in the rear.

Barber, Cpl., Co. D, 15th Illinois Volunteer Infantry, Memphis, Tenn.:

> This summary proceeding of Gen. Veatch soon put a stop to this kind of smuggling. Then another queer expedient was resorted to, which was no less than secreting contraband goods in the carcasses of dead horses. Under the plea of removing them out of the way, they got permission to have them taken beyond our lines. This mode of proceeding was soon found out and then smuggling became a dangerous enterprise in Memphis.

We probably lived better at this time than we did at any other time during our term in the army. Provisions were cheap and every day our table was covered with delicacies such as eggs, ham, pies, sausages, etc. Our lyceum was still in operation, considerably enlarged, numbering over eighty active members. The society did me the honor to elect me its president for one month. It was our custom to invite speakers to deliver addresses before our society and Dr. Mc Kim and the chaplain of the 14th Illinois favored us with lectures.

Day, Pvt., Co. B, 25th Massachusetts Volunteer Infantry, Plymouth, N.C.:

I fear I was not appreciated on the fort, as I was superseded after my first day's effort and have since been assigned to other duty; but I nobly served my country, and I know that history will do me justice. Yesterday I was out in the country among the wild flowers. I went out with a picket guard, about three miles in a southeasterly direction, to what is called Mills cross-roads, relieving the old picket. After spreading our blankets on the grass beside the fence, we entered vigorously on our duty of waiting and watching for the rebel Gen. Garnett and listening to the sweet warbling of the singing birds.... About the middle of the afternoon, we heard the approach of horses, and looking up the road, saw two ladies coming at a swift gallop towards us. My first impulse was to charge cavalry, but I refrained from doing so, as I saw they were not enemies. As they came up, I recognized Mesdames Bartholomew and Cliff. I turned out the guard and extended to them the customary civilities. They said they were out for an afternoon's ride and supposed it was as far as they could go in that direction. I told them they might go further if they wished, and I should be pleased to furnish them an escort, only it would weaken my lines. They laughed and thanked me for my gallantry, but thought they had better not venture farther. I inquired if there were any news stirring in town, and they answered, "All quiet on the Roanoke." They then bade us good afternoon and started on the retreat....

April 6 (Monday)

Lincoln, visiting Hooker at Fredericksburg, expressed his opinion that "our prime object is the enemies' army in front of us, and is not with, or about, Richmond...." This would be his constant message and it would not be understood until Grant took command eleven months later.

Admiral Du Pont moved his gunboats inside the Stono bar off Charleston, planning to attack this day. However, the weather became so hazy that the pilots doubted that they could estimate ranges effectively, so the attack was delayed.

The Confederacy was building ironclad gunboats in North Carolina. Capt. William F. Lynch reported from Wilmington that:

One ironclad, the *North Carolina*, building here, is very nearly ready for her crew.... The other, the *Raleigh*, is now ready for her iron shield, and can in eight weeks be prepared for service, as far as the material is concerned. At Whitehall, upon the Neuse, we have a gunboat in nearly the same state of forwardness as the *Raleigh*; at Tarboro we have one with the frame up, the keel of one is laid near Scotland Neck....

Charles W. Wills commented on the railroads in Tennessee from the Board of Survey Office in LaGrange:

I was in Memphis a few days since.... The city is full of butternut refugees from North Mississippi and some from Arkansas but I could find none from the vicinity of Madison. The M&C R.R. is almost classical. From Memphis to Decatur, Ala. (that is as much as I've seen of it) you are rarely out of sight of fortifications, and on almost every mile, lay the remains of a burned train of cars. Hardly a bridge, culbert or cattle guard but has been burned from three to ten times and rebuilt as often. Night before last I had just retired (12 o'clock) when an order came to have the regiment in line and ready for action at a moment's notice. We got up, stacked arms on the color line, and—went back to bed again.

April 7 (Tuesday)

On this day, Charleston was attacked. Du Pont, unable to get underway before noon because of the tides, was delayed again because the torpedo raft became fouled in the ship that was pushing it. Finally, at about 3 P.M., the attack got under way as the ships got to within range of Forts Moultrie and Sumter. The U.S.S. *Weehawken*, Capt. John Rodgers, was in the van and had the ship lifted a little with a torpedo, but no other damage from the mine. The big problem was the line of obstructions stretching from Forts Moultrie to Sumter. Thinking the ship would be caught and entangled, Rodgers swung his bow towards the sea, and against the strong flood tide that was sweeping into the harbor. After the turn, he moved a few hundred feet south to give the other ships a chance to make their turn. In a hot 40-minute firefight, the ship was struck 53 times.

The ships following Rodgers had as difficult a time. The U.S.S. *Passaic*, Capt. Drayton, had her main gun disabled and was unable to turn the turret for several hours. Her pilot house was badly dented, having taken 35 hits. The U.S.S. *Montauk*, Capt. Worden, was hit 14 times with little effect. The U.S.S. *Patapsco*, Commander Ammen, lost headway and became a drifting target which was hit 47 times before gaining her steerage and turning away.

The flagship, U.S.S. *New Ironsides*, became unmanageable and lay directly over an electric torpedo of some 2,000 pounds for a period of time. The Confederates tried in vain to fire the torpedo, finding later that a wagon had broken one of the wires. Meanwhile, the U.S.S. *Catskill*, Commander George Rodgers, went past the flagship, took 20 hits, and had her forward deck plating torn loose, and she started taking water. The U.S.S. *Nantucket*, Commander Donald McD. Fairfax, also went past the flagship and got 51 hits, one jamming her turret. The U.S.S. *Nahant*, Commander John Downes, took 36 hits, three of which disabled the turret.

The U.S.S. *Keokuk*, Commander Alexander C. Rhind, drove past the crippled *Nahant* and was the last ship to come within less than 600 yards of Ft. Sumter. For thirty minutes she fought it out and took 90 hits. Eighteen of them pierced the ship at or below the waterline. She managed to escape and get out to sea, where, in heavier seas, she sank the next day.

The flagship withdrew from the battle due to failing light, and the battle was over. Du Pont abandoned his attack on Charleston and told Gen. David Hunter that he now believed that the port could not be taken by a sea assault.

April 8 (Wednesday)

On the Mississippi River below Port Hudson a strange craft approached the U.S.S. *Richmond*. It turned out to be a disguised canoe containing Mr. Edward C. Gabaudan, secretary to Admiral Farragut, who had a message from the Admiral. Gabaudan's adventure was one for the books. A small canoe was covered with branches and twigs to make it resemble a floating log, a common sight on the river. At nightfall, Gabaudan lay down in the bottom of the canoe with a small paddle and a loaded revolver. The canoe drifted past Port Hudson and got in towards the riverbank, where some Confederates put out in a boat to investigate. Gabaudan, thinking this was the end, clutched his pistol and prepared to make a fight of it. The Rebs, however, didn't come close enough to get a good look, and the danger passed. At ten o'clock that evening a rocket was seen from Farragut's flagship, signalling a successful trip.

Gen. McClernand's corps continued operations around New Carthage on the river. Grant's plans for crossing proceeded.

April 10 (Friday)

In Richmond, President Davis called for the people to plant "truck gardens" to grow vegetables for the army's use. This effort was very successful. After all, the South couldn't sell cotton at this time.

The captor was captured when a boat crew from the U.S.S. *New London*, Lt. Benjamin F. Day, captured a small sloop and four prisoners in the Sabine City area of Texas. Among the prisoners was Confederate naval Captain Charles Fowler, former skipper of the C.S.S. *Josiah Bell*, who had captured the U.S.S. *Morning Light* and *Velocity* the previous January.

Barber, Cpl., Co. D, 15th Illinois Volunteer Infantry, Memphis, Tenn.:

> In addition to our lyceum, a reading-room was established and a small tax of five cents a week, for each member, furnished us with all the wholesome reading matter we could digest. A class in bookkeeping was also established; also a sort of normal school for reviewing the common branches of learning. These exercises, with my usual duties, kept my time pretty well occupied and the time glided swiftly and silently by.
>
> While we were thus occupied, many were spend-

ing the days and nights in the foul atmosphere of the city, frequenting haunts of vice and dissipation. Not satisfied with that, the atmosphere of camp must needs be corrupted with poor degraded women.

April 11 (Saturday)

At Charleston, S.C., Gen. P.T.G. Beauregard commanded the defenses of the harbor. He believed that Du Pont would attack again and wanted two spar-torpedo boats to attack the Federal ships remaining inside the Stono bar. These boats, oar-driven, held a large mine in front on a boom (spar) which was rammed against the ship at the waterline, hoping to blow a hole in the side. Du Pont withdrew the fleet before the attack could take place.

In the Suffolk and York river areas of Virginia, the Union commanders requested gunboats as added protection against threatening Confederate forces. Gen. Lee informed the Secretary of War that he was sending a cavalry brigade into Loudoun County, Va., to bring back stored supplies to his army at Fredericksburg.

Col. A.D. Streight moved out from Nashville with 1,700 Federal cavalry mounted on mules, for a raid into Georgia.

April 12 (Sunday)

Gen. Hooker, at Falmouth, Va., evidently was not listening to Lincoln about what the real objective was for the Army of the Potomac—Lee's army. He wrote Lincoln with a plan to go around Lee's left flank and cut him off from Richmond. What he intended to do with Lee after he cut him off was not stated.

On the Mississippi River above Vicksburg, Admiral D.D. Porter got ready to move most of his gunboats past the Vicksburg guns to support Grant's attack from New Carthage (on the west bank) to Grand Gulf (on the east bank). Porter wrote to Secretary of the Navy Welles:

> ...[Major Gen. Grant] proposes to embark his army at Carthage, seize Grand Gulf under fire of the gunboats, and make it the base of his operations.... The squadron will pass the batteries and engage them while the transports go by in the smoke, passing down, of course, at night....

This was not the only effort Porter was making with his gunboats. Eight were ordered to the mouths of the Arkansas and White rivers. There were 23 vessels, including a Marine brigade, in the Tennessee River for support, and more going to the Cumberland. Porter was having trouble manning all of his boats. He reported to Welles that Grant had provided about 800 soldiers and they were using about 600 Negro contrabands to man the guns.

An enterprising young Confederate, Acting Master George C. Andrews, took a crew and a launch and captured the steamboat *Fox* while she was tied up in the coal yard at Pass l'Outre, Miss. He ran the ship into Mobile past the blockade on April 15.

April 14 (Tuesday)

Two days of heavy fighting near Suffolk, Va., resulted in the U.S.S. *Mount Washington* being disabled and grounded. She was brought off by the U.S.S. *Stepping Stones.* The Union gunboats repeatedly drove the Confederates from their rifle pits, but they kept coming back. The attack by the gunboats prevented the Rebels from crossing the river to attack the Federal troops.

The former Federal ram, now a Confederate ram, *Queen of the West,* was sunk this day in Grand Lake, La. She was engaged by the U.S.S. *Estrella,* Lt. Commander Augustus P. Cooke, the U.S.S. *Arizona,* Acting Lt. Upton, and the U.S.S. *Calhoun,* Acting Master Meltiah Jordan.

On board the C.S.S. *Georgia* at Savannah, Commander Charles F.M. Spotswood wrote Commander Mitchell:

> ...*anything* that floats at sea will suit me... for being shut up in an Iron Box (for she is not a vessel) is horrible, and with no steam power to move her, in fact she is made fast here to a pile pier.... She is not a fit command for a Sargent of Marines....

At Shreveport, La., the C.S.S. *Missouri* was launched on the Red River. She would never see action, staying above the obstructions until after the war.

Conscription in the South was not gaining too much for the armies. It was reported that only 700 per month were being obtained in Virginia, the most populous state in the Confederacy.

April 15 (Wednesday)

In the west, Grant's forces continued to concentrate at, or near, New Carthage, La., getting ready for the crossing. The Confederates withdrew from the assault on Washington, N.C., which had been going on since the end of the previous month. A relief expedition of Union gunboats and troops was coming up and it would overpower Confederate strength.

Barber, Cpl., Co. D, 15th Illinois Volunteer Infantry, Memphis, Tenn.:

> So foul had the morals of the city become that Gen. Veatch issued an order expelling two boat loads of fallen humanity. Indeed, matters had come to such a pass that a decent lady was ashamed to be seen on the street, and stringent measures had to be resorted to to remedy the evil. All the bad passions of the naturally dissipated in our division were brought to light here, and too often were the young and noble drawn into this whirlpool of vice.

April 16 (Thursday)

Day, Pvt., Co. B, 25th Massachusetts Volunteer Infantry, Plymouth, N.C.:

> Work goes bravely on at the fort; one gun mounted today and if we can have two or three days more we shall be ready to receive company.... We heard that Gen. Spinola left New Bern with quite a force, going overland to the relief of Gen. Foster, but when about half way there he got scared and turned back. Gen. Foster will not compliment him very highly for that feat. I have heard a rumor that we have had an invitation to surrender.... Col Pickett... thought it wouldn't look hardly military to surrender without first burning a little powder over it. He then dismissed the flag. Bravo, Colonel, bravo!

Around April 16, 1863, the Army of the Potomac was preparing for the move to Chancellorsville. The paymaster visited many of the units and paid all that was due through February 28, 1863. Pay at this time was *only* 45 days behind.

One of "Fighting Joe" Hooker's better accomplishments was to establish a system of corps "badges" for the Army of the Potomac—a forerunner of the modern Division insignia.

April 17 (Friday)

On this day, Col. Benjamin H. Grierson led 1,700 Union cavalry from LaGrange, Tenn., on a raid through Mississippi and Louisiana. This raid was later immortalized in the movie *Horse Soldiers*. The raid, which lasted 16 days, covered 600 miles.

At about 11 P.M. last night eight gunboats began running interference for Army transports, past the guns of Vicksburg. One transport was sunk, without loss of life, and another was temporarily disabled. The passage lasted for two and one-half hours and all ships were ready for further service within 30 minutes after passing the guns. Each of the vessels had a coal barge with 10,000 bushels of coal in tow. Something new had been tried. The ships were covered with heavy logs, and bales of wet hay to absorb the shock of the shore battery shells. It worked extremely well. Now the way was open for the landing at New Carthage and the assault on Grand Gulf.

Off the coast of Brazil, Lt. Maffitt, C.S.S. *Florida*, captured the ship *Commonwealth*, bound from New York to San Francisco, and destroyed her.

April 18 (Saturday)

The schooner *Alabama* must have been expecting good profits that never materialized from its cargo of wine, coffee, nails, and dry goods. She was taken by the U.S.S. *Susquehanna*, Commodore Hitchcock, off the Gulf coast of Florida. Many of the privately owned blockade runners, which most of them were, made enormous profits from luxury goods brought in through the blockade.

Grierson's cavalry raid was skirmishing already, the first full day into the ride. The South would mobilize as much force as possible to trap this band of adventurers.

April 19 (Sunday)

Grierson's cavalry was in trouble again near Pontotoc, Miss., where some stiff skirmishing took place.

On this day a Union soldier recorded in his diary that "Mr. Howe is now visiting us. His son has been discharged, the old gent, I believe, also." This was in reference to Elias Howe, the inventor of the sewing machine. The editor of the diary, Edward Marcus, footnotes the entry with:

Although he was clubfooted and in his forties, Elias Howe, inventor of the sewing machine, served with the 17th Connecticut Regiment but was never officially mustered in. His son, Elias, Jr., enlisted in Company D on August 28, 1862, serving to the end of the war. Elias Howe, then a wealthy man, made himself responsible for many of the expenses of the 17th. When the regiment had gone three months without pay early in 1863, he gave the paymaster his personal check to cover what was due all officers and men. Then, the story goes, he went back into line and drew $39, his pay for three months as a private.

Day, Pvt., Co. B, 25th Massachusetts Volunteer Infantry, Plymouth, N.C.:

> The steamer *Thomas Collyer* arrived last night, bringing dispatches.... This morning... the 12th New York battery was on the wharf, the 46th Massachusetts and the other detached companies were breaking camp, preparatory to going aboard the boat. This meant evacuation and going to the relief of Foster.... Just as the troops were aboard, the old *Massasoit* comes puffing up the river, bringing the welcome news that Foster has run the blockade and the order of evacuation is countermanded. Cheer after cheer rends the air, smiles light up every countenance.... It seems that after Spinola's abortion and the troops' return to New Bern, the brave Col. Sisson of the 5th Rhode Island was so disgusted with the whole thing that he proposed going with his regiment alone to Foster's relief. He and his regiment went aboard the steamer *Escort* and on the evening of the 13th, under cover of a heavy fire from the gunboats on the batteries at Hill's Point, seven miles below Washington, he successfully ran the blockade, arriving at Washington with his troops and supplies. The next evening, with Gen. Foster aboard, he again ran the gauntlet, landing the general safely in New Bern. But it is said that the *Escort* looked like a pepperbox from the shot holes made in her while running the gauntlet. On this perilous trip only one man (the pilot) was killed. The little garrison at Washington held out bravely. It consisted only of eight companies of the 27th and the 44th Massachusetts regiments, two companies of the 1st North Carolina, one company of the 3d New York Cavalry and one New York battery, aided by two or three gunboats on the river. Against this small force was opposed some 12,000 of the enemy as near as we can learn....

April 20 (Monday)

Lincoln declared that the new State of West Virginia would join the Union on June 20th of this year.

At New Carthage, La., Admiral D.D. Porter informed Grant that the Confederates at Grand Gulf, Miss.:

> ...are at work fortifying. Three guns mounted on a bluff 100 feet high, pointed upriver. Two deep excavations are made into the side of the hill (fresh earth); it can not be seen whether guns are mounted on them or not.... My opinion is that they will move heaven and earth to stop us if we don't go ahead. I could go down and settle the batteries, but if disabled would not be in condition to cover the landing when it takes place, and I think it should be done together. If the troops just leave their tents behind and take only provisions, we can be in Grand Gulf in four days....

Barber, Cpl., Co. D, 15th Illinois Volunteer Infantry, Memphis, Tenn.:

> There was one, in whom I felt more than a common interest, who was one day thrown into the company of roughs who were bound to get him drunk. Too well they succeeded! Late at night he came to camp partially intoxicated. To say that I was shocked, would be too feeble an expression. I knew that it would be useless to talk to him. So I sat down and wrote him an appeal, directed as though it came from home, and handed it to one of my comrades, William Mallory, to hand to him as a letter from home. I had the consciousness of knowing that my appeal was not in vain. He was never known to be intemperate after that.
>
> An order from the Secretary of War now permitted the enlistment of colored troops and the appointment of white officers to command them. I was offered a recommendation by the adjutant of the regiment for a commission, but I preferred my present position to any in a Negro company. Several members of the 15th did receive commissions....

If imitation is the sincerest form of flattery, Admiral Farragut should have been well pleased with the action of the U.S.S. *Estrella*, Lt. Commander Cooke, in company with the U.S.S. *Clifton*, *Arizona*, and *Calhoun*, which attacked and accepted the surrender of Ft. Burton, Butte à la Rose, La. A member of the party, Third Assistant Engineer George W. Baird, noted in his diary:

The fight was short, sharp and decisive. It was done after the style of Daddy Farragut: we rush in.... We rushed right up to it and the four black vessels all firing made a savage appearance.

April 21 (Tuesday)

Secretary of the Navy Mallory reported that the Confederate experimental triple-banded Brooke naval gun drove a 140-pound wrought-iron bolt through 8 inches of iron and 18 inches of wood, using 16 pounds of powder, at a range of 260 yards.

At Grand Gulf on the Mississippi, Admiral D.D. Porter took the U.S.S. *Lafayette* on a personal recon of the fortifications of that place. He reported a "strong fort" under construction and shelled the workers out of the site. The Confederate steamer *Charm* attempted to land supplies at Grand Gulf while Porter was in the area, and the steamer was chased back up the Big Black River.

In the gamble to get boats past the guns at Vicksburg, six tried the run and three were either sunk or badly damaged.

Gen. Lee reported to the Confederate War Department today that his men subsisted on a daily ration of one-quarter pound of meat and a pound of flour. In addition, they received a pound of rice for every ten men, two to three times a week. Scurvy and typhoid fever were breaking out among the men.

Confederate Gen. Marmaduke's cavalry were raiding in Missouri, near Patterson.

April 22 (Wednesday)

Admiral Farragut expressed his view on the new Admiral's uniforms to Assistant Secretary of the Navy Fox:

Pray do not let those officers at Washington be changing our uniform every week or two.... I wish that uniform [for Rear Admiral] had been simply a broad stripe of lace on the cuff—say an inch and a quarter wide—with a narrow stripe of a quarter of an inch above it, and a little rosette with a silver star in the centre. The star is the designation of the Admiral and therefore should be visible... but this adding stripes until they reach a man's elbow, appears to me to be a great error... you must count the stripes to ascertain the officer's rank, which at any distance is almost impossible.... [The practical uniform should be] well suited to the necessities of the service—easy to procure—not expensive—easily preserved—and the grades distinctly marked.

April 23 (Thursday)

After a long absence, John S. Jackman began entries in his diary. It had been a long winter at Manchester, Tenn., for "The Orphan Brigade."

Jackman, Pvt., "The Orphan Brigade," Bush Grove, Tenn.:

Broke up camp at Manchester & marched to Bush Grove, 12 miles toward Murfreesboro. Camped in a clover field. The hills about here remind me of Kentucky. They are covered with rich pastures and beautiful groves of beech trees which are now leaving out. Springtime is again coming over the hills with "gayety and song." The brigade is commanded temporarily by Col. H., Genl. Helms being in command of ours and Brown's brigade. Bush Grove, in other days, had a country grocery and post office; there is a nice church which is still used as a place of worship.

April 24 (Friday)

General Grierson's cavalry were deeper into Mississippi and skirmishing at Garlandville and Birmingham. Marmaduke's Confederate cavalry were at Mill Creek, Mo.

Day, Pvt., Co. B, 25th Massachusetts Volunteer Infantry, Plymouth, N.C.:

The noise of the battle is over and we are no longer harassed by war's dread alarms, but can now sit down, eat our fresh shad and herring and drink our peach and honey in peace and quiet. Our provost marshal, Major Bartholomew of the 27th Massachusetts, has opened a broker's office where he is exchanging salt and amnesty for allegiance oaths, and as this is the fishing season, he is driving a right smart business. The natives for miles around come in droves, take the oath, get their amnesty papers and an order for salt, and after being cautioned not to be found breaking their allegiance they go away happy. There are probably some honest men among them who would like to do about right if they dared to, but the whole thing looks ludicrous, for there is evidently not one in a hundred of them who would ever think of taking the oath were it not for the hope of obtaining a little salt. The boys call it the salt oath.

April 25 (Saturday)

News of Grierson's raid into Mississippi had reached Richmond, causing much consternation among the people.

Jackman, Pvt., "The Orphan Brigade," Bush Grove, Tenn.:

Moved camp two miles down the creek and pitched our tents on a ridge in a grove of beech trees. Beautiful prospect from camp—can see for miles over gently undulating fields and green pastures on the one hand—on the other is stern mountain scenery. The musicians are at work. The merry whistle which the farmer boy sends up from the field does not accord with our shrill fifes—neither do our ministrations. This evening ordered to be ready to march at daylight tomorrow morning.

April 26 (Sunday)

Grierson was in central Mississippi now, on his route from LaGrange, Tenn., to Baton Rouge, La. Streight and his mule-borne cavalry left Tuscumbia, Ala., and headed for Rome, Ga. Meanwhile, Grant was continuing his preparations to cross the Mississippi to the east bank for the expedition against Vicksburg. Confederate Major Gen. John C. Pemberton, inside this beleaguered city, waited and watched developments as best he could.

Allen, Pvt., Co. K, 1st Battalion, 10th Illinois Cavalry, Helena, Ark.:

Your very welcome letter was duly received.... I commenced doing duty on the last of February. About two weeks after that I took the whooping cough which rendered me unfit for standing guard for a month. I have been on guard again for some time; am nearly well of the cough; am getting about and feel better than I have since I took the fever last Fall down at Old Town.... Whilst our Company was on picket on Saturday, the 18th inst., Dan Barker and two others went to a house about a mile outside the post to buy milk, when nine mounted guerrillas, armed with rifles and double-barreled shotguns, came up and fired on them. Barker was wounded in the thigh and arm and his horse was shot down, but the other two escaped unhurt. The Rebels took Barker's revolver and fled. Our men pursued them but they made good their escape. Barker's leg had to be taken off as the bone was badly shattered. He has been doing well ever since and will be able to be sent up home soon. The Company received four months pay on Wednesday last and the boys made up about $300 to get Barker a cork leg. Since Barker was shot, we have had to keep out a strong picket and keep our eyes and ears wide open while on duty. Some of Co. G were fired on last Sunday while on picket but no one was hurt. We burned down the house where Barker was shot and took all their horses and cattle and other property that would be of any use to us.

You ask what I do with my money. In reply I can inform you that I keep it with me except when I am on a scout or on picket. I then leave it with Lt. Curry, or someone else that I can rely on who is not exposed to danger.... I owe nothing and if I get killed I wish my money to be sent to my folks when the war is over. We received orders on Friday to be in readiness to march, or rather to go on a boat, for Milliken's Bend, Louisiana, at a moment's notice.... The soldiers are all in favor of the Conscrip Law, having no objection to it but the $300 clause. A large number of black soldiers have been raised and are being drilled here. They do remarkably well and although I was not in favor of using them as soldiers, I sincerely hope that they will be useful to us in crushing the rebellion....

April 27 (Monday)

The Army of the Potomac was on the move from its winter quarters at Falmouth. They marched up the Rappahannock towards the fords which would take them to Lee's rear.

Admiral D.D. Porter gave specific instructions to his gunboat commanders prior to the assault on Grand Gulf, Miss.:

...it is desirable that all four places should be engaged at the same time. The *Louisville, Carondelet, Mound City*, and *Pittsburg* will proceed in advance, going down slowly, firing their bow guns at the guns in the first battery on the bluff, passing 100 yards from it, and 150 yards apart from each. As they pass the battery on the bluff they will fire grape, canister, and shrapnel, cut at one-half second, and percussion shell from rifled guns.... The *Lafayette* will drop

> down... stern foremost, until within 600 yards, firing her rifled guns with percussion shells at the upper battery. The *Tuscumbia* will round to outside the *Benton,* not firing over her while so doing; after rounding to, she will keep astern and inside of the *Benton,* using her bow guns while the *Benton* fires her broadside guns. The *Tuscumbia* and *Benton* will also fire their stern guns at the forts below them whenever they will bear, using shell together.

Marmaduke's cavalry were at Jackson and near White Water Bridge, Mo., on their latest raid. This cavalry was getting worn down from the hard riding.

April 28 (Tuesday)

Hooker's Army of the Potomac began crossing the Rappahannock upstream from Fredericksburg, leaving Major Gen. John "Uncle John" Sedgwick facing Lee. At Fredericksburg the bells of the Episcopal Church rang out the alarm for the Confederates.

Grierson's cavalry were skirmishing near Union Church, Miss., on their way to Baton Rouge, La.

April 29 (Wednesday)

On the Mississippi at Grand Gulf, Admiral D.D. Porter's gunboats engaged the fortifications at that city for five and one-half hours while Grant's troop transports passed the guns at night. The gunboats U.S.S. *Benton, Tuscumbia,* and *Pittsburg* were, in Porter's words, "pretty cut up," but the expedition was successful and the army was below Grand Gulf on the eastern bank of the river.

The majority of Hooker's army was across the river at Kelly's and U.S. Fords beyond the left flank of Lee's Army of Northern Virginia. Movement was made through the Wilderness area into the clearings around the Chancellor home.

In western Virginia, Confederate Gen. William Edmondson "Grumble" Jones fought a skirmish with Federals at Fairmont, about 15 miles south of Morgantown.

April 30 (Thursday)

At Chancellorsville, Hooker, in his exuberance, prepared a message to be read to the troops on May 1st, in which he informed his army that "the operations of the last three days have determined that our enemy must ingloriously fly, or come out from behind their defenses and give us battle on our ground, where certain destruction awaits him."

Grant's first landing of troops on the east bank of the Mississippi River near Bruinsburg met with success. The final stages of the Vicksburg campaign were set.

On the Yazoo River north of Vicksburg, Sherman's troops led a diversionary attack on Hayne's Bluff to prevent troops from Vicksburg being sent to Grand Gulf.

In violation of Gen. Burnside's General Order 38, which forbade expression of sympathy for the South, Clement L. Vallandingham spoke to a large audience in Columbus, Ohio, in which he made many derogatory remarks about Lincoln and the war effort. His hope was to be arrested, thereby gaining popular support for his peace movement.

MAY 1863

At the beginning of May 1863, major actions were pending in Virginia and Mississippi. The Army of the Potomac had left its muddy, sprawling camps in the denuded countryside around Falmouth and had moved to the fords of the Rappahannock and Rapidan, poised for an assault on Lee. Grant, in the west, was across the Mississippi at Grand Gulf, tightening the noose around Vicksburg.

May 1 (Friday)

Hooker, with 70,000 men, crossed the fords and began the Battle of Chancellorsville. Lee hurriedly withdrew all but Jubal Early and 10,000 Confederates, whom he left facing Major Gen. Sedgwick's 40,000, and with 47,000 men turned to face Hooker.

The Army of the Potomac moved forward, and then in the afternoon Hooker stunned his own officers *and* Lee by withdrawing and concentrating in a small area near Chancellorsville. With little or no fighting, "Fighting Joe" Hooker went on the defensive.

That night Lee and Jackson talked in the now famous "cracker barrel" conference which resulted in Jackson taking 26,000 of the 47,000 available forces around the left flank to attack Hooker's right flank.

As Grant's forces gained the east side of the Mississippi, they pushed inland towards Port Gibson as rapidly as possible. Troops from the Confederate force at Grand Gulf, now having been outflanked, raced to head off McClernand's Federals, and there was much skirmishing throughout the day. Gen. John S. Bowen's Confederates occupied Port Gibson briefly and then evacuated the town.

In this same area, Col. Grierson's Union cavalry were having a brisk firefight with pursuing Confederate cavalry at Wall's Bridge, north of Baton Rouge, on the Amite River. Grierson had been out since April 17th, but his ride was about over.

In northern Alabama, Col. Streight's mule-borne raiders were in the area of Blountsville.

Barber, Cpl., Co. D, 15th Illinois Volunteer Infantry, Vicksburg, Miss.:

> It was with some regret, but no reluctance, that I bade adieu to Memphis.... Our brave comrades, in their grapple with the rebel "Gibraltar of the West"—Vicksburg, needed our assistance....

Confederate Secretary of the Navy Mallory solved a sticky problem by getting the Congress to create a Provisional Navy. This allowed him to transfer the better young men from the Regular Navy to this new category and promote them without offending the older Regular Navy officers. Mallory also got Congress to pass legislation permitting men in the other services to transfer to the Navy, but this didn't always work too well. Many requested the transfer, but few got it.

May 2 (Saturday)

Early in the morning, Jackson's corps was moving deeper into the Wilderness, going past Catherine Furnace at a rapid pace. The columns were seen from the Union lines but it was believed that the Rebels were withdrawing. Jackson reached the Orange Turnpike late in the afternoon and at 6 P.M. gave the order which opened the assault against the unsuspecting Federals' right flank. Crashing through the brush and second-growth timber and screaming the Rebel Yell at the top of their lungs, the gray-clad soldiers must have looked like demons from hell. On the Federal left flank, Lee opened fire against George Meade's men to draw attention from Jackson.

The Federal right flank fell back in confusion and panic and rolled up like a carpet. Few of the units fought well, most fleeing back towards the main body of the army at Chancellorsville.

In the twilight, Jackson and some of this staff were riding on a recon when they were mistaken for Federals and fired upon by their own troops. Jackson, struck twice in the left arm and once through the palm of the right hand, was taken to a nearby farmhouse, where his arm was amputated later that evening.

Jackson's senior subordinate, Gen. Ambrose Powell (A.P.) Hill had been wounded earlier, struck in both legs by shell fragments, and command of Jackson's troops fell to JEB Stuart.

On this night Hooker ordered Sedgwick to assault Lee from the rear; this action brought on the Second Battle of Fredericksburg.

Jackman, Pvt., "The Orphan Brigade," Hoover's Gap, Tenn.:

> Our regiment thrown forward as advanced infantry and camped one mile in the Gap. Our camp is in a pleasant place. On either side of the pike are hills mountain high. Our division is to defend the pass.

In the west, Grant's corps was moving rapidly eastward towards Jackson. Col. Grierson's raiding party, now reduced to about 900 very tired troopers, was being chased by a Confederate cavalry force; they met in a stiff fight at Robert's Ford on the Comite River. Shortly after noon, the Union cavalry rode into Baton Rouge on a road lined with cheering crowds. In 16 days of hard riding over 600 miles, Grierson's men fought four engagements, destroyed nearly 60 miles of railroad, captured over 1000 horse and mules, and lost only 24 men killed, wounded, or missing. They accomplished their mission of creating confusion behind the Confederate lines during Grant's move across the river.

May 3 (Sunday)

This was not a happy day for President Lincoln. Haunting the telegraph office at the War Department, he could get little or no news from the Army of the Potomac.

At dawn, Stuart moved artillery to a low hill called Hazel Grove, from which he shelled the Federal emplacements. One shell struck the house where Hooker was headquartered and some falling debris struck him on the head, temporarily disabling him. Hooker ordered a retreat, and Gen. Darius Couch organized the movement across the Rapidan.

Sedgwick twice attacked Marye's Heights and finally drove Early off the Heights, but with tremendous casualties. Lee's line finally gave way, and Early retreated. Lee, using some of the troops awaiting Hooker's assault, turned and stopped Sedgwick at Salem Church late in the afternoon.

Day, Pvt., Co. B, 25th Massachusetts Volunteer Infantry, Plymouth, N.C.:

> Attended church this morning. Steamer *Thomas Collyer* arrived this afternoon with orders for the regiment to report at New Bern. All was bustle and hurrah.... At dark we were aboard the boat.... We had a beautiful moonlight and a splendid sail down the Albemarle; arriving at New Bern in the afternoon of the 4th....

In the west, Lt. Commander Selfridge was operating in the vicinity of Greenville, Miss., where Confederate guerrillas were using artillery to harass the steamers on the river. The day before, the steamer *Era* was fired on, and then the *Minnesota* was destroyed by the shore guns. Both the U.S.S. *Cricket* and *Conestoga* were involved in the attempt to destroy the shore batteries, but to no avail. Finally, on May 7th, Selfridge sent the U.S.S. *General Bragg* to destroy all the property in the area—houses, barns, etc.—bringing an end to annoyances from the guerrillas.

Admiral Porter told Secretary of the Navy Welles, "... it is with great pleasure that I report that the Navy holds the door to Vicksburg." With Grant across the Mississippi and behind the fortifications of Grand Gulf, the Confederates evacuated Grand Gulf so that when Porter sent his gunboats back they found the city nearly empty. Porter took his gunboats downriver and met with Farragut at the mouth of the Red River.

In northern Alabama, Nathan Bedford Forrest had been chasing Col. Streight's raiders for several days and this day obtained their surrender. Much controversy would result from this surrender, many saying it was too easy, and that Streight could have resisted more.

May 4 (Monday)

Things were a mess for the Union forces in the area west of Fredericksburg. Hooker, losing his nerve and the initiative, ordered his Army of the Potomac back across U.S. Ford on the Rapidan River, disengaging from Lee's Army of Northern Virginia. Lee took some of the troops from his front and reinforced Early near Salem Church. Late in the afternoon, the Rebels attacked, but failed to cut off Union Major Gen. "Uncle John" Sedgwick from Bank's Ford over the Rappahannock. Sedgwick crossed the river on pontoons during the night.

Grant was still pulling his troops across the river at Bruinsburg and pushing them east towards Jackson, Miss., as rapidly as possible. Speed was of the essence to keep the Confederates off balance.

Admiral Porter, having refueled at the mouth of the Red River on the Mississippi, took his flotilla upriver. The ships included the gunboats U.S.S. *Benton*, *Lafayette*, *Pittsburg*, *Sterling Price*, *Estrella*, and *Arizona*, the ram *Switzerland*, and the tug *Ivy*. Quite a formidable array of power.

Admiral Farragut wrote Secretary Welles:

> Feeling now that my instructions of October 2, 1862, have been carried out by my maintenance of the blockade of Red River until the arrival of Admiral Porter.... I shall return to New Orleans as soon as practicable, leaving the *Hartford* and *Albatross* at the mouth of the Red River to await the results of the combined attack upon Alexandria....

May 5 (Tuesday)

At 2 A.M., Clement L. Vallandigham was arrested at his home by Federal troops. He was taken to Gen. Ambrose E. Burnside's Department of the Ohio headquarters in Cincinnati, and jailed.

Lee prepared his forces to attack Hooker but found that the Federals were moving back across the Rappahannock in defeat. The Battle of Chancellorsville was over, as was the Second Battle of Fredericksburg. The Union fielded nearly 134,000 men, suffering almost 17,300 casualties. Confederate losses were about 12,800 from an effective force of nearly 60,000 (nearly 20%), a loss that they could ill afford. But perhaps the greatest loss to the Confederacy in this battle was "Stonewall" Jackson; there was no replacement for him.

The long lines of springless wagons began their trip to the rear, both North and South. The Union wounded would be taken to Aquia Creek, where they would be loaded on steamers for the hospitals in Washington. The Confederates would be taken by train from Fredericksburg to Richmond, as they could be moved. In both cases, the agonizing trip from the battlefield to the hospital would cause many deaths, and the cries of the wounded jolting over the rutted roads would stay with the survivors for as long as they had memory.

Jackman, Pvt., "The Orphan Brigade," Hoover's Gap, Tenn.:

> Climbed a high hill near camp and could see Murfreesboro 17 miles off; also the smoke rising from the camps of the "Army of the Cumberland" about the place. Far beyond could see the blue hills bordering the Cumberland river. I remained nearly all day admiring the grand scenery about me.

On this day Porter's flotilla arrived at Ft. De Russy, La. This strong fortification, which the day before had given the U.S.S. *Albatross* such a problem, had been evacuated by the Confederates in the face of the Union naval threat. The place was deserted. The boats went on upriver.

May 6 (Wednesday)

An anxious Lincoln got news of the defeat at Chancellorsville from Hooker *and* the Richmond newspapers, adding more to his sorrow.

Confederate General Ambrose Powell (A.P.) Hill was assigned Jackson's old corps. Jackson was lying in a house at Guiney's Station. His wife would join him there and remain with him until his death.

Clement L. Vallandigham was taken before a military tribunal in Cincinnati and tried for treason. Denied the writ of *habeas corpus*, he was sentenced to two years' confinement in a military prison.

Admiral Porter, on the Red River, pushed past the obstructions placed there and proceeded to Alexandria, La., which surrendered without resistance. Low water prevented him from going any further, so he prepared to send his fleet back to the Mississippi.

There had been some controversy about making another attack on Charleston. Even Lincoln felt that it should be done. On May 6, Capt. Drayton, commander of the U.S.S. *Passaic*, which had taken 35 hits during that first engagement, visited Rear Admiral Dahlgren at the Washington Navy Yard. Later, Dahlgren noted in his private journal:

> Capt. Drayton came in about suppertime from New York, where he had brought the *Passaic* from Port Royal. He says it would be madness to go into Charleston again, and all the Captains who were in the action so agree fully. He thinks Dupont intended to renew the attack, but when the Captains of the iron-clads assembled on his ship, and made their reports, he gave it up.

May 7 (Thursday)

At Falmouth, Va., Lincoln and Gen. Halleck concluded their meeting with Hooker and returned to Washington. Lincoln was very concerned about the effect of the defeat on the people of the North.

The U.S.S. *Keokuk*, which sank on April 8th after taking more than 90 hits during the battle for Charleston Harbor, had had her guns salvaged by the Confederates. The Charleston *Mercury* reported:

> The guns of this famous ironclad now lie on the South Commercial wharf. They consist of two long XI-inch columbiads, and will be mounted for our defense, valuable acquisitions, no less than handsome trophies of the battle of Charleston Harbor.... The turret had to be unbolted, or unscrewed, and taken off before the guns could be slung for removal. This was an unpleasant job of some difficulty, the labor being performed under water, when the sea was smooth, and in the night time only. Those engaged in the undertaking, going in the small boat of the fort, were sometimes protected from the enemy by the presence of our gunboats; at other times not. One gun was raised last week, being removed by the old lightboat. General Ripley himself, night before last, went down to superintend the removal of the second gun. Enterprise, even with scant means, can accomplish much.

At Alexandria, La., Admiral D.D. Porter turned the town over to the Army, sent part of the flotilla on a recon up the Black River, and took the remaining boats down to Ft. De Russy, where he partially destroyed the fortifications. On the Black River, Porter's gunboats met stiff resistance from shore batteries located on a high bluff near Harrisonburg. The boats returned to the Red River.

Sherman was now across the river from Milliken's Bend with his large corps and started moving towards Jackson, Miss., directly east of Vicksburg to cut the rail lines of supply. In an early lesson on foraging, Grant's orders were to "live off the country" and this was exactly what the Federals did. Foragers fanned out daily to raid farms and plantations for their food. The countryside was soon stripped.

Major Gen. Earl Van Dorn, CSA, was shot today by a Dr. Peters, who accused the General of philandering with his wife.

May 8 (Friday)

In the North, as well as the South, aliens were exempt from the draft laws. Many used this exemption for a period of time, but on May 8, Lincoln issued a proclamation that if an alien had applied for citizenship, he was eligible for the draft.

Secretary of the Navy Gideon Welles, having received the message from Admiral Porter about the fall of Grand Gulf, informed the President. Lincoln was quite pleased.

At Port Hudson, La., the Union Mortar Flotilla, Commander Charles H. B. Caldwell, and supported by the U.S.S. *Richmond*, Capt. Alden, began bombarding the fortifications of that city.

May 9 (Saturday)

With Charleston more and more bottled up, and New Orleans gone, the blockade runners were concentrating more on Wilmington, N.C., which would become the principal port for such activity. To protect the port, the Confederates spent much time on the defenses of the approaches. The emplacements were made but large-calibre guns were lacking.

Grant was now at Utica, about 20 miles southwest of Jackson, Miss., and driving hard. Confederate Gen. Joseph E. Johnston was assigned overall command of all troops in Mississippi, but there was little he could do with his limited resources.

May 10 (Sunday)

On this Sunday in a small house south of Fredericksburg, near Guiney's Station, the mighty "Stonewall" Jackson died, his last words being "Let us cross over the river and rest under the shade of the trees."

The Army of the Potomac settled back into its old camp at Falmouth, Va., and the usual duties of picket, railroad guard, wood details, etc., resumed. The northern papers blamed nearly everyone for the defeat at Chancellorsville.

Grant drove towards Jackson, sending Union cavalry east towards Crystal Springs, Miss.

May 12 (Tuesday)

In Massachusetts, Col. Robert Shaw had exceeded his 1000-man limit in recruiting the first all-black regiment in the Union army—the 54th Massachusetts. The spillover in manpower was used to form the second black regiment—the 55th Massachusetts.

Grant's army was at Raymond, Miss., barely 10 miles from Jackson, when Gen. John Logan's division of McPherson's corps ran head-on into a brigade of Confederates commanded by Brig. Gen. John Gregg. A stiff fight ensued, but the outnumbered Rebels were forced to withdraw to Jackson. Meanwhile, Sherman and McClernand found that they had skirmish lines to their fronts. Grant decided to handle the city of Jackson first and then go on to Vicksburg. Gen. Johnston tried to encourage Pemberton to stiffen Vicksburg's resistance.

Barber, Cpl., Co. D, 15th Illinois Volunteer Infantry, Vicksburg, Miss.:

> The weather was delightful. Spring had on its richest dress. All was life and animation.... The first day we passed Helena with its rocky crags and frowning precipices, made glorious and historic by the thrilling deeds of valor performed on its crest by freemen beating back traitors.... About noon on the second day, while passing Greenville, one of our boats was fired into by a band of guerrillas. Our troops immediately landed and laid everything waste on the shore. This mode of retaliation may look barbarous to some, but it was the only way in which we could check these lawless villains in their murderous schemes.
>
> By night we arrived at Lake Providence, La., where a short time before Grant's army was camped. Halting but a short time here, we pressed on, and on the third day at noon, Milliken's Bend was reached.

> We passed four miles farther down to where the river makes an abrupt bend, circling around a point toward Vicksburg, and we disembarked. In the distance, the towers and steeples of Vicksburg were plainly discernable, and a cloud of dust rising over the city indicated that some great excitement was existing....

There had been, thus far in the war, many instances where infantry was loaded on gunboats and a joint "hunting expedition" was undertaken. Lt. Commander S.L. Phelps, USN, and Col. K.M. Breckenridge, Federal cavalry, teamed up in a different way. The horses were loaded aboard a transport and taken to a point near Linden, Tenn., on the Tennessee River, where they were unloaded. The troops set up an ambush. The accompanying gunboat then went to Linden, and fired on the Confederate cavalry detachment. The Rebels, fleeing the naval guns, ran into the Union cavalry ambush. Good tactics on the part of both parties.

In Richmond, Jackson's body arrived and was taken to the Capitol for viewing. The funeral would be on the morrow.

May 13 (Wednesday)

Beleaguered Vicksburg was calling for more support, and the Confederate Secretary of War was pulling troops from Charleston and other areas to help. Beauregard, commander at Charleston, warned that this would drastically weaken that port's defenses.

Grant sent Sherman and McPherson towards Jackson, and diverted McClernand north to Clinton, Miss., about 10 miles northwest of Jackson and an important rail center. Johnston, with only about 12,000 men, tried his best to stall Grant until more could arrive.

Gen. Banks asked that the gunboat support of his army not be withdrawn from above Port Hudson. He felt that the absence of the gunboats would reopen the traffic of supplies coming from the west and going to Vicksburg and points east.

The remains of Lt. Gen. Thomas Jonathan "Stonewall" Jackson were honored in Richmond by a mourning Confederacy. Many other soldiers who had lost their lives in the severe fighting at Chancellorsville were being interred in Richmond or sent to their homes for burial. Col. J.C.S. McDowell, commander of the 54th North Carolina, was one of these. Private Benjamin H. Freeman, Co. K, 44th North Carolina Infantry, was a part of the guard of honor:

> Dear Farther and Mother
>
> I this evening take the opportunity of writing you a few lines to inform you that I am well and getting on well as common. General Jackson is dead. He was shot in the arm and it had to be amputated[;] also Col Macdowall [is dead]. Our regiment had to hold an escort over his corps[e]. Also over General Jackson's corpse. His coffin was wrap[p]ed up in the flag of the Confederacy with fine [w]reaths of flowers and vines... all along it. I never saw as many Ladies and Children in my life. I thought I had see[n] a great man[y]. I sure saw as ma[n]y. The Capitol Square was full of men and women [gazing] upon our Regiment. General Elgin said it was the finest Regiment he ever saw. We was dressed in our new uniform Dress. It looked very nice. You aught to have been here to look at us march on the Capitol Square. It is the finest Square of grass I ever saw. General George Washington was on his Monument sitting on his horse. Also Henry [George] Mason and Jefferson. They are a great deal larger than a man. Washington was sitting on his great big horse. We Escorted Col Mcdowall's Corps[e] to [the] RR Road. Yesterday evening it was to be sent to Raleigh. The late Col J C S McDowell. The remains of the gallant officer who fell at the head of his regiment (The 54th North Carolina) in the charge on Mary[e] heights Monday last, are now sent to Raleigh to be buried. I do not know where Stonewall Jackson will be sent. We have been expecting to have to salute his corpse to day but have not been called on yet....

After the funeral services, Jackson's body, accompanied by his family, was placed on a canal barge and sent to Lynchburg, Va.

May 14 (Thursday)

Lincoln wrote to Hooker that he had heard that "some of your corps and Divisions Commanders are not giving you their entire confidence." The shoe was now on the other foot for Hooker. During Burnside's tenure as commander of the Army of the Potomac, Hooker wasted no time in trying to undermine Burnside's position.

Gen. Nathaniel Banks had now embarked on his

mission to capture Port Hudson, the Confederate fortification south of Vicksburg.

Sherman's and McPherson's corps neared Jackson, Miss., in midmorning. Sheets of rain were restricting visibility and making the march soggy. Joe Johnston, knowing he had little hope against Grant's superior force, evacuated as much of the vital supplies as he could and sent two brigades to delay the Yankees until he could get safely away with the remainder of his troops. These two brigades were ineffective against the Union troops, and by midafternoon the Union was in control of Jackson. Meanwhile, McClernand was solidly astride the railroad at Clinton, the only link to Vicksburg. Grant prepared to move west.

The U.S.S. *Currituck*, Acting Master Linnekin, sent a boat crew to capture the schooner *Ladies' Delight* near Urbanna, Va. Most of the boats taken in the Potomac and Rappahannock rivers were unarmed sail, light schooners and sloops, which plied between points on the rivers. Few, if any, had any armed men on board, so it was not too difficult to capture them. They had little defense against the steam gunboats.

At Lynchburg, Va., "Stonewall" Jackson's remains were taken by an escort of Virginia Military Institute cadets to Lexington, where his body was placed in his old lecture hall.

May 15 (Friday)

Leaving Sherman in Jackson to dismantle the place, Grant moved in several columns to about 15 miles east of Clinton to Edward's Station, where Pemberton's main force was located. By nightfall, Grant was within four miles of Pemberton.

Admiral Du Pont's floating machine shop, now in operation for several months at Port Royal, S.C., required some additional support. Du Pont wrote the chief of the Bureau of Steam Engineering, Benjamin F. Isherwood:

> This establishment is a most essential and important accession to the efficiency of this squadron, turning out an amount of work highly creditable to all concerned with it.... In this connection I would call the attention of the Bureau to the necessity of sending out a small store vessel in which the materials required for work at the machine shop, now constantly increasing since the arrival of the ironclads, could be stored, and that some person be carefully selected to take charge thereof. The machine shop, as the Bureau is aware, is in two old hulks, one of which is taken up entirely as a workshop and for quarters; and the other is in too decayed a condition to be suitable for the purpose of stowage.

At Lexington, Va., Jackson's body was taken to the Presbyterian Church for a brief funeral service. The casket, covered with the first Confederate flag ever made, was then taken to the cemetery south of town for burial.

May 16 (Saturday)

Today, the Battle of Champion's Hill was fought. Grant, moving fast towards Edward's Station, blocked a move by Pemberton to join Johnston, and the two forces collided at Champion's Hill. By midafternoon the hill had changed hands three times, and the Confederates had had enough, beginning their withdrawal towards Vicksburg and towards the bridge crossing the Big Black River. The Confederates had lost about 3850 men at Champion's Hill as opposed to 2440 Union lost. Pemberton could not afford such losses for long. Johnston never got into the fight.

The South, lacking money in Europe, was using cotton certificates for credit. Not having fantastic luck in England with getting ships built on credit, it was believed that the French would provide ships without money or certificates upfront. This did not seem to be the case, as Commander Bullock wrote Secretary Mallory from London:

> ...I had understood, and Mr. Slidell was under the impression, that French builders, being anxious to establish business connections with the South and to compete with England for the custom of the Confederate States after the war, would be willing to deal with us largely on credit.... I found that French builders, like the English, wanted money, and were not willing to lay down the ships unless I could give them security in the shape of cotton certificates....

May 17 (Sunday)

The Confederates under Pemberton had their backs to the Big Black River and were facing Grant's Union corps with some misgivings. One of Pemberton's divisions had been cut off and went to join Johnston, thereby missing the final surrender in July at Vicksburg. Grant attacked, and the Rebels retreated across the bridge and burned it. Grant was stopped temporarily and Pemberton went into Vicksburg—minus about 1700 prisoners. Starting with about 20,000 men, in two days Pemberton had lost nearly 5550. Grant, stymied, began building bridges to cross the Big Black. Gen. Banks was gathering his troops and supplies on the west bank of the Mississippi in preparation for the assault on Port Hudson.

May 18 (Monday)

Things were heating up in the Vicksburg area. Grant was back from Jackson and the Battle of Champion's Hill was over. On this day, Grant invested Vicksburg. The fortifications were completely surrounded on the land side, and the gunboats were on the river. No escape now for Pemberton's army.

Barber, Cpl., Co. D, 15th Illinois Volunteer Infantry, Vicksburg, Miss.:

> We stopped in camp but a few days, then crossed the neck of land opposite Vicksburg. We took transports for Grand Gulf, but the army was so far advanced toward Jackson that we received orders to return to Young's Point and join the army by the way of Haines Bluff on Yazoo. About midnight on the day of our arrival at Grand Gulf, we again embarked and were speeding on our way back to Vicksburg. We approached within four miles of the city, nearly opposite Ft. Warren, but the enemy commenced shelling us and we were forced to disembark farther down the river. Before sundown, we were back at Young's Point and again on transports. Soon we passed into the mouth of the Yazoo which empties into the Mississippi at this point. We received a large mail that night.... We arrived at the Landing about nine o'clock P.M. Our regiment was detailed to guard five thousand prisoners captured the day before. The prisoners were ragged, dirty and disheartened, still they were called the "flower of the rebel army." The next day we went into camp on the bluff....

Also on the Mississippi, Acting Lt. T.E. Smith, U.S.S. *Linden*, was escorting five Army transports down the river when the lead ship, a transport named *Crescent City*, was fired into by a masked battery at Island No. 82. Some of the soldiers on the transport were wounded. Smith immediately opened fire, and under cover of the guns, infantry was landed and the buildings in the area were destroyed, along with the gun emplacement.

In Massachusetts, the 54th Massachusetts Volunteer Infantry Regiment, the first all-black regiment in the Union Army, received orders to depart on May 28th for an assignment to the Department of the South.

May 19 (Tuesday)

President Lincoln, following a Cabinet meeting, commuted the May 7th sentence of Clement L. Vallandigham for treason to banishment to the Confederacy.

At Vicksburg, Grant made his first assault on the entrenchments, sending Sherman, McPherson, and McClernand against the Confederates in a quick rush he hoped would gain a quick victory. This was not to be. The Union forces were repulsed. The Union fleet of mortar boats began their deadly barrages, supported by the gunboats on the flanks of the city.

May 20 (Wednesday)

Admiral Farragut wrote to Secretary Gideon Welles:

> We are again about to attack Port Hudson. General Banks, supported by the *Hartford, Albatross* and some of the small gunboats, will attack from above, landing probably at Bayou Sara, while General Augur will march up from Baton Rouge and will attack the place from below... my vessels are pretty well used up, but they must work as long as they can.

May 22 (Friday)

At Vicksburg, Grant lost almost 3200 of his total force of 45,000 in a large-scale attack on the Confederate defenses. The attack began at 10 A.M. and extended over a three-mile segment of the line. The Confederate losses were less than 500. Sherman's troops briefly held the top of one trench line but were beaten back. Grant went into a siege mode.

Braxton Bragg, now at Tullahoma, Tenn., was

awaiting action by Rosecrans. Jefferson Davis asked if any help could be sent to Gen. Joe Johnston, who was trying to relieve Vicksburg. "The Orphan Brigade" was alerted for Mississippi.

Barber, Cpl., Co. D, 15th Illinois Volunteer Infantry, Vicksburg, Miss.:

> It was fifteen miles to Vicksburg and we could plainly hear the heavy notes of artillery. On the 18th and 22d, when the charges were made, the hills fairly shook with the shock of artillery. Grant saw what a sacrifice of life it would cost to take the place by storm, so he waited the slow and surer operations of a siege....

May 24 (Sunday)

Jackman, Pvt., "The Orphan Brigade," en route to Miss.:

> Had reveille early, loaded baggage and moved out. Very hot day and we had to march 12 miles to Wartrace on the Nashville and Chattanooga railroad where we arrived shortly after 12 m. and bivouacked near the town in a wood. All the boys suspected that the brigade was ordered to Mississippi and were grumbling a great deal, not liking to make another summer campaign in that state.
>
> Shortly after we stacked arms, Genl. Breckinridge sent around an order for all the brigade to assemble at brigade HdQrs at a given signal that he wished to speak to the boys. Many said that if the brigade was ordered to reinforce Johnston and if left with them to vote whether to stay or go, they would vote to stay in Tennessee. We fell in without arms and the regiments were drawn up about the Genl. He got upon a stump and commenced by telling them that he had received orders from Genl. Bragg to report at Wartrace with all of his division save that portion composed of Tennessee militia and hold himself in readiness to move on the cars. He said that he was not to receive further orders until he reached Atlanta but that he had a pretty good idea where they were going and that he supposed the boys could also guess at their destination. He said knowing they would object to making a campaign in a climate as deleterious to health, especially in the summer season, he had, through Genl. Hardee, sent a communication to Genl. Bragg requesting that the Kentucky troops of his division be also permitted to remain with the Army of Tennessee and Mississippi troops be given him instead who would be glad to get back to their native state. He said that in reply to this communication Genl. Bragg left it to his (Breckinridge's) options whether the Ky. troops should go or stay. This, he said, left him in a dilemma and that he intended to leave the question with them to decide. Bragg and Breckinridge had been at "loggerheads" since the battle of Murfreesboro and the boys felt that if they did not vote to follow their Maj. Genl. outsiders would think they also condemned him as well as Bragg; so when the vote was put, they not only held up their right hands to a man, but cheered loudly—the Genl. then thanked them in a little, but eloquent speech. He is the most eloquent speaker I ever heard....

Barber, Cpl., Co. D, 15th Illinois Volunteer Infantry, Vicksburg, Miss.:

> Our officers now asked and were granted permission to take their commands to the front, and on the 24th of May, we took up our position on the extreme left of the line, near Ft. Warren, below Vicksburg. The rebels were now completely hemmed in....

Above Austin, Miss., the Confederates made a very serious mistake when they fired on the commissary and quartermaster boat of the Marine Brigade, commanded by Marine Brig. Gen. A.W. Ellet, the evening of May 23. Before dawn on May 24, Ellet landed some of the Marines, who engaged the Confederate cavalry eight miles outside of Austin and made them withdraw. Finding evidence of smuggling, and in reprisal for the firing on the boats, Ellet ordered the town burned. He reported:

> As the fire progressed, the discharge of firearms was rapid and frequent in the burning buildings, showing that fire is more penetrating in its search [for hidden weapons] than my men had been; two heavy explosions of powder also occurred during the conflagration.

May 25 (Monday)

Lt. Commander J.G. Walker had gone up the Yazoo River with the gunboats U.S.S. *Baron de Kalb, Forest Rose, Linden, Signal,* and *Petrel* to see what could be done to destroy things in general, shipping in particular. About 15 miles below Ft. Pemberton, four steamers which had been sunk on a bar as obstructions were burned. A large sawmill was burned and a large quantity of iron was taken from the Navy Yard at Yazoo City. Walker then proceeded up the Sunflower River for about 150 miles, destroying boats of all sizes and burning grain before returning. Walker reported destruction of shipping to a value of $700,000 on the trip, which ended on the 30th.

Jackman, Pvt., "The Orphan Brigade," on a fast train en route to Miss.:

> At 6 P.M. all of our regiment got on the trains (save one or two companies) on which the 6th Ky. was "stored." Col. G. and the Col. of the 6th had to take a car in partnership and we were very much crowded. The train ran away with the engineer while coming down the mountain this side of the terminal. The grade is steep and 7 miles long and we ran the 7 miles in 4 minutes and a half. I was sitting on a camp stove in the center of the car and could hardly keep my seat. The moon was just sinking behind the mountains and as I watched it, as it were, skipping from crag to crag, I thought farewell "old Mom," I'll never see you again! We thought every moment the car would be dashed to pieces against the rocks or be pitched off some of the cliffs and ground into dust. At last the train was stopped and word came forward that the hindmost car, on which was Company "C," had smashed up or was missing at least. We all expected to find the last men killed or badly hurt, and our surgeons started back to find them. I went back also. The car flew to pieces just as the train was at the bottom of the grade. No two pieces of it were left together; but fortunately, though some of the boys were hurt, not a man killed or a limb broken. One little fellow that was on top of the car was thrown clear over the telegraph wires into a bramble of briars, receiving no other injury than being "powerfully" scratched.

May 26 (Tuesday)

Clement L. Vallandigham, sentenced to two years in a military prison for treason, had had his sentence commuted by President Lincoln to banishment to the Confederacy. Today, he arrived at the Confederate lines outside Murfreesboro, Tenn., and was told to head south. The Ohio Democrats, angry over the treatment of one of their number, voted 411-11 to nominate him for Governor of Ohio at the June convention.

Today, gold was discovered at Alder Gulch, Montana Territory, providing a major boost to the Federal war coffers.

At Port Hudson, Gen. Banks requested that Admiral Farragut drop a few mortar rounds into the fortifications at odd times during the night to keep the defenders awake. Farragut complied.

Barber, Cpl., Co. D, 15th Illinois Volunteer Infantry, Vicksburg, Miss.:

> ...We were now within one and one-half miles of the rebel line and two and one-half miles from Vicksburg. In our immediate front was a strong fort, a little isolated from the others, mounting heavy siege guns.

May 27 (Wednesday)

Major Gen. Nathaniel Banks today launched his long-awaited attack on Port Hudson, La., with little result other than nearly 2000 killed, wounded or missing, out of a force of 13,000. The attack, poorly coordinated, was made through rough terrain, heavily wooded and cut with deep ravines, which caused troop alignment problems. Admiral Farragut's gunboats provided close support where possible, and continued firing on the fortifications after the attack faltered.

At Vicksburg, the U.S.S. *Cincinnati*, Lt. Bache, moved into position to enfilade some Confederate rifle works when the Rebel shore batteries took her in plunging fire and sank her despite her protection of logs and soaked bales of hay. The ship lost about 30 men, but went down with the colors nailed to the mast.

The C.S.S. *Chattahoochee* had her boilers explode today while at anchor in the Georgia river of the same name. The accident killed 18 men and injured others. She was raised later but never went to sea, and she was then destroyed at the end of the war.

May 28 (Thursday)

The 54th Massachusetts Volunteer Infantry left Boston for Hilton Head, S.C., the first all-black regiment to be ordered south.

Admiral Porter made sure that his crews understood their responsibilities:

> ...it will be the duty of the commander of every vessel to fire on people working on the enemy's batteries, to have officers on shore examining the heights, and not to have it said that the enemy put up batteries in sight of them and they did nothing to prevent it.

Jackman, Pvt., "The Orphan Brigade," Hoover's Gap, Tenn.:

> The regiment left at 10 A.M. on a train of flat cars. Dr. B. and I, *with a barrel of whiskey in charge*, left at 1 P.M. on passenger train. Rain commenced pouring down about 11 A.M. and continued until next morning. Our train passed the regiment just before we got to Montgomery and the boys looked like drowned rats. At the depot, the whiskey was issued out by the buckets full. Though dark as pitch and raining, we had to move on board the *R.B. Taney*. I slept on a chair in the cabin the remainder of the night.

May 29 (Friday)

There was a lot of negative political feedback on the banishment of Vallandigham of Ohio. Gov. Morton, the fire-eater from Indiana, was upset. Gen. Burnside, who directed the banishment, offered to resign, but Lincoln refused to accept.

At Vicksburg, Grant asked Porter for gunboats to support Major Gen. Frank P. Blair, Jr., who was trying to clear the Rebels between the Big Black and the Yazoo rivers. Blair was after the Mississippi Central Railroad bridge that could bring in troops to relieve Vicksburg. Grant wanted the boats up as high as Yazoo City if possible. Porter complied.

In a second request, Grant asked for heavy naval guns to be taken ashore for firing on Vicksburg, and the crews to man them. This would be complied with in a few days.

Jackman, Pvt., "The Orphan Brigade," en route to Miss.:

> Left Montgomery wharf at daylight and arrived at Selma 5 P.M.. Immediately disembarked and moved our baggage to the railroad and at 8 P.M. were whirled off toward Demopolis. A passenger car was attached to the train on which our regiment was being transported for Genl. Helm and Col. C. I "guided" myself on a cushioned seat and slept until we got to D. at 2 A.M.. I there missed the good things the people had at the station for the boys to eat.

May 30 (Saturday)

President Davis's hopes of getting enough troops to aid Pemberton were still alive, but dying rapidly. The famed "Orphan Brigade" was coming to help.

Jackman, Pvt., "The Orphan Brigade," en route to Miss.:

> Before midnight, commenced moving on board a small steamer on the Tom Bigbee and at sunrise we dropped down the river 3 miles where we disembarked again meeting with railroad connection. When the road is completed a bridge will save all this trouble. At 11 A.M. the train moved off for Meridian where we arrived at 5 P.M. Laid over on a switch for daylight.

Lee's Army of Northern Virginia, lying quiet for the present, was reorganized into three corps under Generals Ewell, A.P. Hill, and James Longstreet. This organization would remain until the end of the war.

May 31 (Sunday)

Jackman, Pvt., "The Orphan Brigade," en route to Miss.:

> At 7 A.M. train moved off for Jackson. In the evening, got off the train 6 miles from Jackson the road having been torn up by the Federals that far out from the city and went into camp. Suffered greatly for water.

At Perkins Landing, just below Vicksburg, an Army force was cut off from its parent unit and was in danger of being captured by a larger group of Confederates. The U.S.S. *Carondelet*, Lt. Murphy, came to the rescue, shelling the woods and keeping the Confederates at bay until a troop transport could get the Union forces off. The *Forest Queen* arrived, and as the troops began to board, the Confederates made a concerted effort to press the attack, which was broken up by the *Carondelet*'s guns. After the troop transport left, Murphy kept his ship at the landing long enough to load as many of the supplies as could safely be taken on board; then he fired the remainder, gave a couple of parting shots, and left Perkins Landing to the Confederates.

Admiral Porter and some of his staff officers went ashore and rode to Sherman's headquarters to see if there was more they could do. The result was that two naval 8-inch howitzers, complete with crews, were installed in embrasures built by the Army early in June.

The defenses of Charleston seemed a little less threatening after an Army reconnaissance party landed at James Island and then was taken off with no casualties. One Confederate officer remarked that the exercise "... removes all [their] fear of our supposed batteries... no doubt we will have visits from them often." He was right.

JUNE 1863

Throughout the South, the June heat had a telling effect on the protagonists. The ironclads operating on the rivers and along the coast were like ovens most of the time, the boilers heating things up internally, the sun externally. The soldiers around Vicksburg and Port Hudson were also steaming, realizing that the worst of the summer was yet to come. In the South the prices of goods were increasing, not only from scarcity, but also due to the decreased value of the Confederate dollar. Both sides had their woes this summer.

June 1 (Monday)

Ambrose E. Burnside, Major Gen., USA, closed the Chicago *Times* for publishing disloyal statements. This created a furor throughout the North among the defenders of the First Amendment.

Barber, Cpl., Co. D, 15th Illinois Volunteer Infantry, Vicksburg, Miss.:

> We now received orders to move farther to the right. We kept changing position every few days, gradually drawing nearer the rebel lines, fortifying as we advanced. One day we were on the skirmish line and the next in the trenches. There was no rest for us, but labor, fight and dig was the order.... Perhaps while lying concealed in some thicket or copse watching for the foe, the dull thud of a bullet striking a bush or log near you would apprise you that in the same thicket lay concealed rebels.
>
> Our rifle pits were built in the night. So noiselessly did we work that the enemy, perhaps not more than ten rods off, would not know what we were about until the next morning when perhaps a new line of works, nearer than the others, would extend around the line.... The ground was cut up by deep ravines, winding around in such a manner that we could march almost to their lines without being seen.... Sometimes for amusement, we would fire at the men on the fort from one-half to one mile distant.

In Selma, Ala., the local Iron Works was taken over by the Confederate government to cast naval guns. Commander Catesby ap R. Jones, CSN, was put in charge, and between this month and April of next year he would cast nearly 200 guns of 6.4- and 7-inch Brooke rifles.

June 2 (Tuesday)

Vallandigham, previously sent South from Murfreesboro, Tenn., from the Union lines, was now sent to Wilmington, N.C., by President Davis, where the Ohioan was held as an "alien enemy." No one wanted this man who had so stirred up the Midwest.

The South was having a hard time filling its ranks with conscripts—so many had disappeared about the time they were due to report, and there were still many exemptions from the draft—and the harvest season was beginning in the deep South. Concerned with this, the Davis administration attempted to ease the burden on the farmers a little by issuing a circular from the Bureau of Conscription suggesting that overseers and managers on farms be disturbed as little as possible just at this time, for the benefit of the crops.

In the South Atlantic, off Montevideo, the C.S.S. *Alabama*, Capt. Semmes, chased the bark *Amazonian* for eight hours before capturing and burning the ship. She was outbound from New York with a commercial cargo, including mail.

June 3 (Wednesday)

The Gettysburg campaign began with the movement of Lee's legions from the Fredericksburg area to the west. The long gray columns quit their camps and began the trek to the Shenandoah Valley, where they would turn north for Pennsylvania. In Hooker's camps, no movement was yet to be seen. The Yankee commander was unaware that his adversary was moving.

Rear Admiral Porter, feeling generous, wrote to Lt. Commander Greer, of the U.S.S. *Benton*, urging a continual fire from the gunboats into the Vicksburg positions. He wrote, "The town will soon fall now, and we can afford to expend a little more ammunition." Grant, looking for as much muscle as he could get, ordered the Ninth Army Corps from Kentucky to the Vicksburg area to add more weight to the siege.

Jackman, Pvt., "The Orphan Brigade," Jackson, Miss.:

> Moved camp near the city in an old field east of town on the margin of a small lake and not very far from Pearl river... this was more healthy than camping in the woods. In the evening walked through the city which presented quite a desolate appearance, a great deal of it having been lately burned down by Genl. Grant's army. This improved the feelings of the inhabitants though towards the "Rebels" for now they bring water out on the streets for the soldiers marching through when before they would refuse a Rebel soldier a drink from their cistern or wells. Now commences a month of monotonous camp life. When we started for Miss. we thought we would jump off the cars and start immediately for the relief of Vicksburg. Our delay was caused for want of field transportation and artillery horses. Our division remained camped about Jackson—Loring's, Walker's and French's about Canton. The weather kept very hot all the time. We had a good place to bathe in Pearl river. The boys caught a great many fish out of the lake and river. One way of catching them was rather novel; two men would go into the lake where the water was not very deep and hold a blanket spread out down close to the water, then others would commence lashing the water about making it muddy and the fish would commence skipping above the surface of the lake and fall on the blanket, thus being caught by hundreds....

Col. Robert G. Shaw and the 54th Massachusetts Volunteers arrived at Port Royal, S.C., where the Negro Union troops become a curiosity to the natives as well as to the other Union soldiers.

June 4 (Thursday)

The day before, Longstreet's corps had left Fredericksburg for Culpeper C.H. On June 4, Ewell's corps took to the road, leaving only A.P. Hill's corps to face Hooker, who, on the other side of the Rappahannock at Falmouth, was trying to guess whether Lee had decamped for good or was just moving to greener pastures.

Out in Tennessee, Rosecrans's Federals and Bragg's Confederates mixed it up a little south and east of Murfreesboro, at Franklin, and at Snow Hill. Nothing heavy as yet.

On June 4 and 5, the U.S.S. *Commodore Morris*, Lt. Commander Gillis, U.S.S. *Commodore Jones*, Lt. Commander John. G. Mitchell, with the Army gunboat *Smith Briggs* and the transport *Winnissimet* with 400 troops aboard went up the Mattaponi River to Walterton, Va., to destroy a foundry where Confederate ordnance was being made. The troops were landed and marched to the Ayletts area, where they destroyed the foundry machinery, a flour mill, and a large quantity of grain. Meanwhile, the gunboat *Commodore Morris* was keeping the river open to the south so the flotilla could get back to Chesapeake Bay. The troops arrived back at Walterton with captured livestock, and all boarded and returned downriver with the gunboats blasting everything in sight that might house a Rebel.

Barber, Cpl., Co. D, 15th Illinois Volunteer Infantry, Vicksburg, Miss.:

> One day General Grant rode along the line and told the boys that he had plenty of ammunition and not to be afraid to use it. This was the signal for firing. Some of the boys expended over two hundred rounds that day. The rebs lay in their trenches, quiet as mice, not daring to show their heads.
>
> Some evenings when not on duty, we would crawl to the top of the hill near camp and watch the gunboats shell the city. From the instant the shell left the gun, we could trace its progress through the air. The shell had a rapid rotary motion and the burning fuse with its red glare showed its course, describing a semicircle in traveling four miles. When at its highest altitude, we would hear the report of the gun. When it

neared the earth, we could see the flash as it exploded, and after several seconds, we could hear the report.

Sometimes the rebels would make a charge on our picket line in the night and try to force it back. In one of these charges, they surprised the 14th Illinois, killed and wounded seven and took twenty prisoners, Lieut. Col. Cam amongst the number, and filled up their rifle pits. All this was done so quickly that we, only a short distance from them, were unable to render them any assistance....

In Washington, Lincoln requested that Secretary of War Stanton revoke Gen. Burnside's order suspending publication of the Chicago *Times.*

Bluffton, S.C., was visited today by the U.S.S. *Commodore McDonough,* Lt. Commander Bacon, accompanied by the steamer *Island City,* the transport *Cossack,* and the Army gunboat *Mayflower.* The troops disembarked without opposition, but ran into strong Confederate resistance in Bluffton. The gunboats opened fire on the town, the buildings were destroyed, and the troops loaded back on the transport.

June 5 (Friday)

Hooker, trying to find where Lee's army had gone, probed the crossings at Franklin's Crossing and Deep Run, only to find them screened with pickets from A.P. Hill's corps. Lincoln suggested to Hooker that he might attack the moving Confederates, but Hooker delayed until it was too late. Lee's last corps, A.P. Hill's, was set in motion for Culpeper.

The C.S.S. *Alabama,* Capt. Semmes, captured the ship *Talisman,* which was in mid-Atlantic, taking the eastern route to Shanghai. Semmes recorded in his log:

> Received on board from this ship during the day some beef and pork and bread, etc., and a couple of brass 12-pounders, mounted on ship carriages. There were four of these pieces on board, and a quantity of powder and shot, two steam boilers, etc., for fitting up a steam gunboat.... At nightfall set fire to the ship, a beautiful craft of 1,100 tons.

June 6 (Saturday)

In the sun-dappled fields of Brandy Station, Va., were over 8000 horsemen on parade, with sabres sparkling in the June sunlight. Gen. JEB Stuart's famed cavalrymen put on a show for the ladies, and themselves, which would be long remembered by the viewers.

At Berryville, Va., the advance pickets of Longstreet's corps were skirmishing with Union troops guarding the crossings of the Potomac. Lee's pace was leisurely, but steadily north.

Lt. Maffitt, C.S.S. *Florida,* captured and burned the *Southern Cross,* bound from Mexico to New York with a load of wood, perhaps some exotic wood for furniture.

The two entrances to Wilmington Harbor in North Carolina made it very difficult to catch the blockade runners going in or out. To add to the confusion and difficulty, the blockade runners ran in pairs, so that at least one could escape. Admiral Lee asked Secretary Welles for more blockade ships, especially fast schooners, to help catch these "rascals."

June 7 (Sunday)

At Milliken's Bend on the Mississippi, Union troops were assaulted by a larger force of Confederates. The Federals withdrew to the riverbank, putting the Rebels within range of the U.S.S. *Choctaw,* Lt. Cmdr. Ramsay, and the U.S.S. *Lexington,* Lt. Cmdr. Bache, who used their guns, firing shell, grape, and canister into the Confederates, who withdrew.

At Brierfield Plantation, Miss., the home of Confederate President Jefferson Davis was burned by Federal troops. The plantation was owned jointly by Davis and his brother.

June 8 (Monday)

At Passe à l'Outre, Mississippi River, on April 12th, a ship was taken by a Confederate naval boat crew and run into Mobile Bay past the blockade. The boat crew, commanded by Master James Duke, CSN, boarded and captured the steam tug *Boston* and then put to sea, where Duke then captured and burned the Union barks *Lenox* and *Texana.* Three days later he sailed past the blockading fleet off Mobile right into the bay. Admiral Farragut was less than pleased with such success.

At Culpeper C.H., Va., Stuart held another review of his cavalry, this time for Generals Lee and Longstreet and Hood's entire division. To the north, the pickets were still out, screening the Army's movement.

There was skirmishing again between Rosecrans's and Bragg's armies in Tennessee.

Grant and Admiral Porter were giving Vicksburg no rest. Twenty-four hours a day the mortar boats lobbed their deadly missiles into the city. Many of the residents now lived in caves to escape the danger.

June 9 (Tuesday)

The "northern neck" of Virginia is an area along the Rappahannock River that extends to where that river enters Chesapeake Bay. Many of the residents of this area relied on the river for transportation and for their livelihood. The Union forces, attempting to cut down on smuggling, had been operating in this area clandestinely for a period of time. One local newspaper, the *Whig*, reported the harassment of the people:

> Nearly every house was visited, and by deceptive artifices, such as disguising themselves in Confederate gray clothes, stolen, or otherwise surreptitiously obtained, they imposed themselves upon our credulous and unsuspecting people; excited their sympathies by pretending to be wounded Confederate soldiers—won their confidence, and offered to hide their horses and take care of them for them to prevent the Yankees from taking them, who, they said, were coming on. They thus succeeded in making many of our people an easy prey to their rapacity and cunning. In this foray, they abducted about 1000 negroes, captured from 500 to 700 horses and mules, a large number of oxen, carriages, buggies and wagons—stole meat, destroyed grain, and robbed gentlemen, in the public road, of gold watches and other property. There are some instances related of personal indignity and violence. They returned with their spoils to camp, after a week devoted by them in the Northern Neck, among our unhappy people, to the highly civilized, brave, and chivalrous exploits of theft, robbery, and almost every species of felony committed upon a defenseless, unarmed, and helpless population—chiefly consisting of women and children! It was an easy achievement—a proud conquest—the more glorious to the noble and heroic Yankee, because stained with crime and won without danger to his beastly carcass.

At Beverly and Kelly's Ford on the Rappahannock, west of Fredericksburg, Union cavalry galloped across the fords, driving in the Confederate pickets, and went looking for Lee. Stuart, at Brandy Station, was caught by surprise, and was rapidly engaged in the largest cavalry battle ever fought on the North American continent. Almost 20,000 horsemen, evenly divided, swirled and clashed at Stevenburg and Fleetwood Hill for about 12 hours. The Confederates held the ground at the end of the day, but it was a close thing indeed. Gen. Alfred Pleasanton's Federal cavalry had reversed the image of the North's cavalry, and had given Southern cavalry a bloody nose. Jokes about "Who ever saw a dead cavalryman?" would no longer be in vogue in either army.

Union mortar boats were bombarding Vicksburg almost every hour. From dawn till noon, a total of 175 shells were fired into the city. The pounding the city was taking was severe. Rear Admiral Porter wrote Secretary Welles:

> The mortars keep constantly playing on the city and works, and the gunboats throw in their shell whenever they see any work going on at the batteries, or new batteries being put up. Not a soul is to be seen moving in the city, the soldiers lying in their trenches or pits, and the inhabitants being stowed in caves or holes dug out in the cliffs. If the city is not relieved by a much superior force from the outside, Vicksburg must fall without anything more being done to it. I only wonder it has held out so long....

Jackman, Pvt., "The Orphan Brigade," Jackson, Miss.:

> Was waked up by the fire bells in the city and opening my eyes saw that the light of a fire was shining into the office—the walls of the tent being up—making it light as day. Could see the Bowman House, a large hotel near the Capitol, wrapped in flames which roared not a little in the stillness of the night. Heavy cannonading all night at Vicksburg.

June 10 (Wednesday)

Hooker finally found out in which direction Lee was headed but Hooker had this "target fixation" on Richmond. He suggested to Lincoln that now was a good time to take that city. Lincoln replied that the target was Lee's army, not the Confederate capital. Lee left Culpeper C.H., Ewell's corps leading and heading northwest towards the Potomac fords. The citizens of Maryland and Pennsylvania were already alarmed.

One group of Confederate prisoners would not make it to their Union prison camp. Being transported to Ft. Delaware on the steamer *Maple Leaf,* they overpowered the guards, captured the ship, and forced it to land below Cape Henry, Va., where they escaped.

June 11 (Thursday)

In Ohio, C.L. Vallandigham, currently in Wilmington, N.C., was nominated for governor by the Peace Democrats.

On this day, the 54th Massachusetts Volunteer Infantry Regiment received its first combat experience. This, the first all-black regiment in the Union Army, went on an amphibious raid on Darien, Ga., with the 2nd South Carolina. The commander of the expedition, one Col. James Montgomery, had the town sacked and burned for no apparent reason. A somewhat startling introduction to the war.

At Port Hudson on the Mississippi, Admiral Farragut informed Gen. Nathaniel Banks, "...we have been bombarding this place five weeks, and we are now upon our last 500 shells, so that it will not be in my power to bombard more than three or four hours each night, at intervals of five minutes...."

June 12 (Friday)

The Army of Northern Virginia, led by Ewell's corps, streamed through the Blue Ridge Mountains of Virginia today, headed towards Winchester and the Potomac crossings. Skirmishing was increasingly heavy on the march route as Union troops resisted the advance. Hooker was slow to move from Falmouth, just now stirring.

In the South, the old battle over "states' rights" was being fought again between President Davis and Vice President Alexander Stephens. The states which joined the Confederacy left the Union because they felt the Union was interfering with their basic rights to self-determination. Now the Confederate government, in Stephens's view, was taking away the rights from the Confederate states. It was felt by many that the Confederacy would have fallen from its own political mistakes, if it hadn't fallen from military intervention.

June 13 (Saturday)

Ewell's corps was still leading Lee's army northwest. At Winchester, the Confederates drove in the Union pickets at that city and moved on to occupy Berryville. Hooker started the blue columns north by northwest from Falmouth about three days behind Lee.

June 14 (Sunday)

Major Gen. Milroy was with his Union troops, 6,900 strong, at Winchester, directly in line with Lee's oncoming army. Washington suggested that it might be prudent to move over to Harper's Ferry, but, too late, Milroy was caught between two Confederate forces. That night he decided he would try to get away after burning his supplies and wagons. Meanwhile, Lee moved another Rebel force in between him and Harper's Ferry. Milroy was neatly trapped. With Hooker gone from Falmouth, Gen. A.P. Hill moved his Confederate corps onto the roads taken by Lee's army and hurried them along northwest.

At Port Hudson on the Mississippi, Gen. Nathaniel Banks called on the Confederate commander to surrender. He declined, and Banks ordered a dawn assault. The Union troops failed to break the Confederate line and the siege went on.

Confederate guerrillas fired into the transport *Nebraska* from the same area that they had fired on the U.S.S. *Marmora* on June 13. Acting Lt. Getty had had enough of this action. He sent a landing party ashore, where it destroyed the town of Eunice, "including the railroad depot, with locomotive and car inside, also a large warehouse...."

June 15 (Monday)

About one o'clock in the morning, Gen. Milroy started his troops toward Harper's Ferry, only to run into Gen. Edward Johnson's Confederate division at Stephenson's Depot, about four miles up the road. A brisk fight followed in which some of Milroy's men got away, but not many. The Confederates captured over 4000 men and tons of supplies and equipment. Gen. Rodes crossed the Potomac with three brigades of Ewell's corps into Maryland, at Williamsport.

In Washington, Lincoln called for 100,000 militia from Pennsylvania, Ohio, Maryland, and West Virginia to meet the threat of invasion.

The new Confederate ironclad C.S.S. *Atlanta*, Commander Webb, sailed in the early evening for an attack on the Union ships at Wassaw Sound, Ga. Webb passed over the obstructions in the Wilmington River and dropped anchor for the remainder of the night to fuel the craft.

June 16 (Tuesday)

The C.S.S. *Atlanta*, having fueled, lay in the broiling Georgia sun all day waiting to sail on down to position to attack the Union gunboats. About dark, she sailed to a point about five or six miles from the Union craft and dropped anchor until morning.

Lee's gray columns were strung out all over western Virginia and into Maryland. Hooker reached Fairfax C.H., about 20 miles from the capital, and between Lee and Washington. Hooker got into a telegraphic fight with Halleck in Washington about what to do next. Lincoln told Hooker he must deal with Halleck, for his orders. Hooker, of course, disliked this idea.

June 17 (Wednesday)

In Wassaw Sound, Ga., the C.S.S. *Atlanta*, Commander Webb, in company with the wooden steamers *Isondiga* and *Resolute*, attacked the Federal ironclads U.S.S. *Weehawken*, Capt. John Rodgers, and *Nahant*, Commander Downes. The *Atlanta* was fitted with a percussion torpedo extending from the bow with which Webb hoped to sink the *Weehawken*. Unfortunately, the *Atlanta* ran aground, was gotten off, but thereafter couldn't be steered—her rudder being damaged somehow. The *Weehawken* poured five rounds from her heavy guns into the helpless ship while the *Nahant* moved into firing position. The two wooden Confederate ships took off upriver and Webb surrendered his ship with two gun crews out of action, two of the three pilots injured, and the ship hard aground—she had never fired a shot. The surrendered crew contained 21 officers, 96 sailors, and 28 Marines. For this action, among earlier ones, Capt. John Rodgers was recommended for promotion to Commodore in the United States Navy.

June 18 (Thursday)

At Vicksburg, Gen. McClernand, the political general from Illinois, finally reached the end of his rope when he issued a message to his troops praising them for their conduct in the latest round of assaults and casting doubts on the bravery of the other units involved. Grant, who was convinced that all McClernand wanted was to make political headway, relieved him of command and sent him north.

Stuart was doing a good screening job for Lee at the present time, keeping the Union troops out of the passes in the Blue Ridge Mountains where the Federals could observe what Lee was doing.

June 20 (Saturday)

The mountain counties of Virginia, having voted for separation from their parent state, were admitted into the Union as the new State of West Virginia.

Barber, Cpl., Co. D, 15th Illinois Volunteer Infantry, Vicksburg, Miss.:

> We had now got so close to the enemy that in several places along the line we were at work undermining their forts with the intention of blowing them up, by digging a deep trench from our works to theirs. Our boys protected themselves in their work by placing cotton bales before them, shoving them along as fast as they dug. When up to the fort the rebs attempted to stop our work by throwing hand grenades over at our boys, but generally they would get out of the way before they burst. Some of the boldest would grab one and hurl it back before it burst, exploding it in the rebel ranks. The chief engineers were bent on undermining Ft. Hill, the strongest works that the rebels had. Finally everything was in readiness, the troops were under arms, ready to make the charge if a breach was made and our boys went in.
>
> The concussion was terrific. Rebels were thrown twenty feet into the air and buried in the ruins, but so strong were the works that the explosion failed to make a breach. A fierce hand-to-hand encounter ensued over the parapet, bayonets crossed over the works and thrusts and stabs were made. Our boys finally retired, confident that victory would soon crown our efforts. The 45th Illinois stood the brunt of this engagement.

June 23 (Tuesday)

Lincoln finally stirred Rosecrans enough to get him moving towards Braxton Bragg at Tullahoma,

Tenn. Rosecrans did well in this campaign, outflanking Bragg and forcing him to fall back towards Chattanooga. Rosecrans's activity would be largely overshadowed by Gettysburg and Vicksburg when the campaign for middle Tennessee ended in early July. Perhaps if greater events had not occurred, his star would have appeared brighter.

June 24 (Wednesday)

At the Potomac crossings near Harper's Ferry, the gray columns of Longstreet and A.P. Hill began going into Maryland. There was a short, brisk skirmish in the vicinity of the old Antietam battlefield.

Rosecrans was doing well in his attack on Bragg in middle Tennessee and Grant was receiving reinforcements and putting more pressure on Pemberton inside Vicksburg.

In Washington, Rear Admiral Dahlgren at the Navy Yard was ordered to sea to replace Admiral Du Pont at Port Royal, S.C., as commander of the South Atlantic Blockading Squadron.

June 25 (Thursday)

Gen. Lee made a big mistake today. He gave JEB Stuart permission to leave the Army of Northern Virginia, giving up his role of being the "eyes of the commander," and to join Lee on the other side of the Potomac. Stuart went on his way and Lee would not see him until the middle of the Battle of Gettysburg.

In middle Tennessee, Bragg had his hands full with Rosecrans. President Davis tried to get Bragg to send troops to Gen. Joe Johnston, who was trying to relieve Vicksburg. Bragg declined, citing his own problems.

Barber, Cpl., Co. D, 15th Illinois Volunteer Infantry, Vicksburg, Miss.:

> The next day we were ordered to hold ourselves in readiness for action. The artillery received orders to look to their ammunition. On the morrow, at four o'clock A.M., a general cannonading along the whole line was ordered and to be kept up until ten o'clock A.M. The 15th lay just in the rear, supporting several heavy siege-guns and some twenty-pound Parrott guns. We waited with impatience for the ball to open.
>
> Soon the signal gun was fired; then, as if by magic, the hoarse notes of hundreds of pieces of artillery shook the ground. It seemed as though the very earth was going to open and swallow us up.... We lay where we could note the effect of this cannonading. Our solid shot would strike the rebel works, filling the air with a cloud of dirt. The air was full of screeching shells, crossing each other's track and finally bursting in town or in the rebel camp. For six hours this terrible cannonading was kept up but it failed to elicit a response from the rebels. They remained quiet as the grave.
>
> While our regiment was on picket one day, Company I caught eleven rebs trying to steal through our lines. They had two hundred thousand percussion caps and a dispatch from Johnston to Pemberton in cipher.... Occasionally we would succeed in getting hold of a paper printed in Vicksburg. It was printed on wall paper and with a miserable type, fit emblems of the waning fortunes of the Confederacy. This paper would have flaming editorials telling about Johnston, how that, at the proper moment, he would attack and annihilate Grant.... Desertions became quite frequent from the rebel lines. They would have deserted by regiments if they could have gotten away....

June 26 (Friday)

This day saw the passing of Rear Admiral Andrew Hull Foote, at age 57, in New York City. He died of the wounds received at Ft. Donelson in the spring of 1862. He was a great innovator of river warfare on the western rivers, and a great supporter of joint-service actions. He would be sorely missed.

Confederate Gen. Jubal Early passed through Gettysburg, Pa., for the first time today on his way to York, Pa. Gov. Curtin of Pennsylvania called for 60,000 volunteers to serve for 90 days to repel the invaders. Just how these raw troops were supposed to stand up to Lee's battle-hardened veterans has always remained a mystery.

Jubal Anderson Early was born in Franklin City, Va., on November 3, 1816, into a prominent family. He attended West Point, class of 1837, and was assigned to the artillery. He fought in the Seminole Wars and then resigned to practice law in Rocky Mount, Va. He voted against secession, but when Virginia left the Union he volunteered, and he was assigned as a colonel of state troops. He commanded the 6th Brigade at First Manassas and so impressed

Beauregard that he was appointed a brigadier general. He fought with Joe Johnston in the Seven Day's campaign and then with Jackson in the Valley campaign, returning in time for Malvern Hill. His greatest battles were in the Valley in 1864, when he defeated several Union generals and threatened Washington. He was finally defeated by Sheridan in late 1864. When Lee surrendered, Early travelled to Texas, to Havana, and then to Ontario, Canada. He returned to Lynchburg, Va., in 1869 and reestablished his law practice. He later supervised the Louisiana State Lottery, and he was the first president of the Southern Historical Society. He died at Lynchburg on March 2, 1894.

Lt. Read, CSN, the commerce raider who switched ships about as often as shirts, was off the light at Portland, Me., when he picked up two fishermen who, thinking the C.S.S. *Archer* was a pleasure party, offered to lead them into the harbor. From these fishermen Read learned that there were two ships in harbor that would remain overnight—the revenue cutter *Caleb Cushing* and the passenger steamer *Chesapeake.* Read made a hasty plan to seize both the cutter and steamer that night.

Read sailed into Portland Harbor in the evening and anchored as if he belonged there. Setting the fishermen ashore, he discussed the problems with his crew. The engineer felt that he would need more help than what was available to get the passenger steamer going, so Read decided to concentrate on the revenue cutter.

June 27 (Saturday)

In Washington, Lincoln did something rarely done in the annals of military history. He relieved the commander of a major army on the eve of battle. "Fighting Joe" Hooker was relieved by George Gordon Meade, Major Gen., USA, as commander of the Army of the Potomac. Meade was now expected to take on the legendary Robert E. Lee and beat him. Quite a task for a newcomer to so large a command.

Longstreet and Hill were at Chambersburg, Pa,. and Early was at York, with other Confederate units near Harrisburg. Stuart's cavalry were still in Virginia, skirmishing near Fairfax C.H..

At 1:30 in the morning, Lt. Read's boarding crew went on the revenue cutter *Caleb Cushing,* "without noise or resistance," slipped the lines and started out to sea. However, their luck failed this time. The tide was incoming and they couldn't make the distance beyond the fort's guns before daybreak. By midmorning the alarm had been given and although the cutter was 20 miles out to sea, she was chased by two large steamers and three tugs. Read cleared the cutter for action, fired five rounds and found that he was out of ammunition. About to be pounded in a crossfire, he set the cutter on fire and took to the boats to surrender. The cutter blew up at noon, an explosive ending to Read's career as a commerce raider. In his relatively short fling, he had captured 22 prizes and created enough havoc for a lifetime.

June 28 (Sunday)

At 7 A.M., Gen. Meade received word that he was to relieve Hooker. He now had over 100,000 men in his command scattered widely between the Potomac (and points south), and Frederick, Md.

In Pennsylvania, Lee started to concentrate his forces at Gettysburg, recalling Early from York.

Rosecrans's troops were busy with Bragg, trying to chase him back to eastern Tennessee. Grant and Banks, on the Mississippi River, battered their respective targets and awaited results.

June 29 (Monday)

Meade wasted no time ordering the Army of the Potomac towards Gettysburg. Gen. Buford's cavalrymen were in Gettysburg already and more troops were coming up fast. Lee was calling his men in as fast as possible.

In Tennessee, Rosecrans was mixing it up with Bragg at Tullahoma, with heavy skirmishing in other points nearby.

June 30 (Tuesday)

The Confederates under Bragg evacuated Tullahoma, Tenn., today and withdrew towards Chattanooga. This would be a very rough campaign on Bragg, and one he would not live down.

In Pennsylvania, Early's men left York for Gettysburg, and Gen. Meade ordered Gen. Reynolds to occupy the city. Buford's cavalry was scouting the area, looking for Lee's main force. They were about to find it. In Washington, Lincoln ignored the demands that McClellan be put back in command.

JULY 1863

The broiling heat of July baked the land from Vicksburg to Gettysburg. In Pennsylvania, the blue and gray columns about to collide at Gettysburg marched down the dusty roads in sweltering sun. Water was in short supply and the troops suffered. In Vicksburg and Port Hudson, the heat was even more intense. At those places, the fortifications were bombarded incessantly, the defenders waiting with stoic patience for the outcome. In Tennessee, the elevation made the heat more tolerable but to those on the roads, no less a problem. Rosecrans drove for Chattanooga, moving Bragg into Georgia.

July 1 (Wednesday)

At dawn the Confederates moved towards Gettysburg along the Chambersburg Pike, A.P. Hill's skirmishers looking for Union troops. They found them about four miles west of town in the form of Company E, 9th New York Cavalry of John Buford's cavalry division, armed with repeating rifles. By 8 A.M. the contact had reached a point where Buford's men were opposing two Confederate brigades, but Major Gen. John F. Reynolds's corps of infantry was coming up fast. By midmorning, the fighting was getting heavy and in the midst of battle Reynolds was killed at the edge of McPherson's Woods. The Union lines held the Confederates, and by afternoon, with Abner Doubleday leading Reynolds's corps, the fighting was still heavy and spreading as more troops from both sides came into the area. The Federals, for a time, were outnumbered and almost outflanked, this being prevented by their pulling back to Cemetery Hill and Cemetery Ridge. The famed "fishhook" line was established on Cemetery Ridge, with the Confederates occupying Seminary Ridge across the way. All day long the Federals streamed into Gettysburg and were placed in defensive positions. There was a lot of confusion and milling about until things settled down about dark. Meade arrived on the field about midnight.

The 24th Michigan Volunteer Regiment, a part of the famed "Iron Brigade," began this day with 496 officers and men in its ranks. The Iron Brigade was the first infantry to engage the Rebels; before the day ended with their retreat to Culp's Hill, the 24th Michigan would lose 316 killed and wounded. The 24th carried only a state flag into battle, a gift from the citizens of Detroit. At least seven color-bearers were killed or wounded that day. The colors were so badly riddled with shot and shell that only a few pieces remained after the battle. The men of the regiment agreed to cut the remainder to pieces, which were distributed among the survivors.

At Vicksburg the end was clear—surrender or starvation. Grant's army encircled the city with a death grip, and Gen. Joseph E. Johnston's small force to the east around Clinton, Miss., was vastly outnumbered and had little or no means to transport itself beyond the railroad line from Jackson. The mortar boats kept up a constant bombardment of the city.

Just south, along the Mississippi, Port Hudson was also in dire straits. The commander of the mortar flotilla at Port Hudson reported to Admiral Farragut: "From the 23 of May to the 26 of June… we have fired from this vessel [the U.S.S. *Essex*] 738 shells and from the mortar vessels an aggregate of 2800 XIII-inch shells." That was a lot of flying hardware to absorb in so small an area. Like Vicksburg, it was only a matter of time before surrender.

Jackman, Pvt., "The Orphan Brigade," Clinton, Miss.:

> Have marched today 14 miles. Bivouacking 2 miles west of Clinton. The hottest march we have ever made. Many soldiers tumbled down in the road from sunstroke. Water very scarce. I had nothing to carry but in helping the other boys along wore myself out.

Barber, Cpl., Co. D, 15th Illinois Volunteer Infantry, Vicksburg, Miss.:

> One day I saw some of Herron's pickets march up and surprise and capture a rebel picket post, right in face of the enemy's big guns. Before the astonished rebs could recover their senses, our boys were well on their way back, but a sweeping discharge of grape and canister laid some of the brave fellows low. The siege of Vicksburg was noted for such daring and bravery on our part. We had a splendid signal corps camped on the highest point of observation in our lines and not a movement the rebels could make of any importance but what was signaled to headquarters. Grant

had high towers or lookouts built where he could look down into the city. It seemed now as if the decisive moment must soon arrive.... We now had several of their forts undermined and about ready to be blown up, but General Grant thought proper to demand a surrender before proceeding to extremities.

...So sharp was our target shooting that a rebel could not even show his head above the works, but a dozen bullets would speed after him. There was not a spot in the sand-banks which formed their loopholes but what was pierced with bullets. The rebels lay in their trenches forty-eight hours without scarcely stirring. They dared not attempt to leave.... They showed a perseverance and valor worthy of a better cause, but it was not possible for human flesh to hold out much longer. The last ration was nearly consumed before the rebel general asked for an armistice to arrange terms of capitulation.

July 2 (Thursday)

Things were stirring early at Gettysburg. Not all the Union troops had arrived as yet, the long columns still pouring in. Gen. Dan Sickles took things into his own hands and moved his Third Corps out of the assigned positions on the Union left and forward to the area of the Peach Orchard and Devil's Den to an exposed position. Lee wanted Longstreet to attack this salient of the Union left and Longstreet opposed the plan. Fortunately, Major Gen. Gouverneur K. Warren, the Chief Engineer of the Army of the Potomac, rode to the Little Round Top, recognized that disaster was awaiting for the left flank unless something was done, and sent his aides to pull any troops off the road and send them to the hill. Meanwhile, Longstreet sent his Confederates against Sickles's exposed men and drove them from the Peach Orchard and Devil's Den to the crest of Cemetery Ridge. Gen. John Bell Hood's Texans got into a stiff fight with the 20th Maine of Col. Chamberlain on Little Round Top and the fighting was hand-to-hand and rock-to-rock. Chamberlain's men ran out of ammunition, so he ordered a bayonet charge that so demoralized the Rebels that they fled. The left flank was saved for the Union.

Gen. Jubal Early was to have attacked Culp's Hill at the same time Longstreet began his attack, but delays occurred and the charge up East Cemetery Hill did not begin until dusk. It went on until 10 P.M. and ended with Early back down the hill and where he started from. The day ended with many casualties, including Dan Sickles, who would lose a leg from his wounds, many deaths, but no real advantage gained by either side. Meade was fighting a defensive battle and handling it well, so far.

During the fighting, the 150th Regiment Pennsylvania Volunteers, the "Bucktails," lost their colors when they fell back to Cemetery Ridge. The defense of the colors was so gallant that Confederate Gen. D.H. Hill remarked that he "was sorry to see such a gallant Yankee meet his fate." The colors were later presented to President Davis and were found in his trunk when he was captured at the close of the war. Eventually they were returned to the State of Pennsylvania.

During the fighting, JEB Stuart arrived back at the Army of Northern Virginia, quite pleased that he had brought Gen. Lee a wagon train of supplies. Lee was angry with Stuart for his grandstand ride around Meade's army when Stuart should have been available to provide scouts for intelligence purposes. Quickly taking advantage of the situation, Lee ordered Stuart to use his cavalry to cut Meade's retreat route to the east. Stuart rested his horses and got ready.

In the area of Vicksburg, the tension was growing. Surely the city could not hold much longer. Joe Johnston's Confederates waited the outcome of the battle, knowing that when Grant was finished with Vicksburg, he would turn on the Confederate force to destroy it. At Port Hudson, the bombardment continued.

Jackman, Pvt., "The Orphan Brigade," Bottom Station, Miss.:

Reveille at 2 A.M.. Had scarcely a wink of sleep last night. Dr. B. on a bender and kept me awake by pulling my blanket and bothering me generally. Marched at 3 A.M. and arrived at Bottom Station, 9 miles, on the Vicksburg and Jackson railroad before the sun got hot. Bivouacked near the station. The boys have been getting green corn out of "Jeff's" fields; and this evening I went blackberry hunting on his plantation—"Briar Field," I believe it is called; I know there were an abundance of briars and blackberries in some old fields that have been "turned out."

A Confederate cavalry force, 2500 strong, crossed the Cumberland River near Burkesville, Ky., and headed north, led by John Hunt Morgan.

In Richmond, President Davis sent Vice President Alexander Stephens to Hampton Roads, and possibly Washington, under a flag of truce to negotiate prisoner exchange. However, in case the subject came up, he was to be ready to discuss an end to the war. The plan was discarded when Lincoln replied: "The request is inadmissible."

July 3 (Friday)

A little after midnight, a council of war was held at Gettysburg, behind the Union lines by Gen. George G. Meade and his generals. It was decided to stay and fight. The entrenchments began and the artillery rolled forward into place. By dawn the place known as Cemetery Ridge fairly bristled with muskets and artillery.

Across the little valley on Seminary Ridge, Lee pondered his next move. He had tried assaults on both flanks of Meade's army and been repulsed. Now he would try the middle. He would send 15,000 men in three divisions against the Union center in a charge that would forever be known as "Pickett's Charge," but that would be made up of troops from the divisions of Henry Heth (commanded on the field this day by Gen. James J. Pettigrew), Dorsey Pender (commanded by Gen. Isaac Trimble), as well as Pickett's Virginians.

There were delays. Longstreet again advised against the attack, feeling that it would mean nothing but slaughter. Lee was adamant and the attack was ordered, beginning with a tremendous 100-gun artillery barrage against the Union lines that started at 1 P.M., to be answered by about 80 guns from the Federal line. The uproar was deafening for two hours. Then, as the Union gunners slacked off to save their ammunition for the charge they knew was coming, the Rebel guns went silent.

Across the field from the Union position, the Confederates emerged from the woods and formed into lines for the attack. With flags waving, the neat files of gray-clad men began their journey to fame and death. It was a supreme example of raw courage and one of the most heart-stopping spectacles of the war. The Union gunners waited until the gray lines were within range and then pounded them with shot and shell in a seemingly unending stream. The ranks developed wide gaps where the artillery fire took its toll and the men closed ranks, still advancing. As they came within range of the Union muskets, the Federals, behind the cemetery wall and the entrenchments, poured a rain of lead into the gray ranks. Gen. Armistead, an old friend of Gen. Hancock's from prewar days, led his men to the little copse of trees and briefly broke the Union line, where he was killed. All had been to no avail. The charge had failed and the Confederates retreated across the field to be met by Lee, who kept repeating, "All this has been my fault."

By now it was late afternoon and both sides were bloodied and weary. The Union had no taste for an attack, and the Confederates were in no shape to make one. Both sides began sorting out the wounded and getting them to shelter. This battle would cost both sides dearly. The total casualties amounted to about 43,500—23,049 Union and 20,451 Confederate—of whom over 27,000 were wounded. When the cleanup was being done, the burial squads picked up the muskets left on the field by the dead and wounded, affixed the bayonet, and stuck the bayonet in the ground so that the butt of the rifle was up. The 26,000 muskets thus recovered made the battlefield look like a forest of rifles.

Stuart, meantime, was three miles east of town, fighting the Union cavalry under Pleasanton, including the 9th New York Cavalry. This battle raged for about three hours, and Stuart withdrew back to Lee's lines, nothing having been gained.

Early that same morning in Vicksburg, the white truce flags appeared on the defenses of the city. Gen. Pemberton had bowed to a superior force and six weeks of siege after nearly a year of Union operations against him. The two generals, Grant and Pemberton, met under an oak tree to discuss the terms of surrender which would take place the next day, the Fourth of July.

Barber, Cpl., Co. D, 15th Illinois Volunteer Infantry, Vicksburg, Miss.:

> The two generals met beneath the wide spreading branches of a stately oak between the lines.... General Grant gave him until the next morning to accede to his unconditional terms of surrender.... While the truce was being held, the pickets of the two armies

met and conversed on friendly terms on neutral ground between the lines. Blackberries were very thick there and friend and foe picked from the same bush and vied with each other in acts of civility.... Pemberton did not at once accede to Grant's unconditional terms. He was given until ten o'clock the next day to consider.

Jackman, Pvt., "The Orphan Brigade," Bottom Station, Miss.:

> Light shower. Some cannonading [the last guns fired] at Vicksburg. The guns were heard quite plain as we are only 15 miles from the place.

In Tennessee, near Tullahoma and Winchester, the Confederates under Bragg were forced back by Rosecrans's Union forces and withdrew further towards Chattanooga. John Hunt Morgan continued his raid into Kentucky, creating confusion.

Day, Pvt., Co. B, 25th Massachusetts Volunteer Infantry, New Bern, N.C.:

> Received orders for the right wing... to break camp and be ready to march.... At noon the baggage was all on the wagons and we awaited orders. At 1 P.M. we were ordered into town, and... went aboard the little steamer *Mystic*... bound for Washington on the Pamlico river. Left New Bern at 4 P.M.... turning into the Pamlico about dark and running up to within a few miles of Washington where we anchored for the night.

July 4 (Saturday)

Gen. John Pemberton and about 29,000 Confederates surrendered to Gen. Grant at Vicksburg by laying down their arms and marching out of the battered city. Grant watched the flag-raising at the Court House, and on the river the boats shrilled their whistles. The Mississippi was now open, save for Port Hudson, which could not hold out much longer. The citizens of Vicksburg wept with sorrow as the surrender was completed. Grant could now turn his attention to Johnston's army to the east.

Grant also acknowledged the support of the Navy gunboats under the command of Admiral D.D. Porter, saying, "The navy, under Porter, was all it could be during the entire campaign. Without its assistance the campaign could not have been successfully made with twice the number of men engaged."

Barber, Cpl., Co. D, 15th Illinois Volunteer Infantry, Vicksburg, Miss.:

> The morning hours of the Fourth of July were slowly dragging toward ten o'clock and still our strained visions could detect no signs of surrender. A deep silence prevailed. Finally the order came for the troops to be under arms, but just then a white flag was seen to flutter from the rebel works, which proclaimed that the finale had been reached. Then one long, joyous shout echoed and re-echoed along our lines. Its cadence rang long and deep over hill and valley until we caught the glad anthem and swelled the chorus with our voices in one glad shout of joy. It was a glorious opening for the Fourth of July....
>
> On the wings of the wind, the glad news was borne to anxious waiting hearts at our firesides in the North, until every hamlet, town and city pealed forth its notes of joy at the great victory.... This great victory gave us thirty-one thousand prisoners, three hundred pieces of artillery and fifty thousand stands of small arms, and an immense amount of ordnance stores. General Grant paroled the prisoners and they were permitted to go home. They left singly and in groups and by companies and battalions.... We hoped now to enjoy a short season of rest, but scarcely had the excitement begun to abate, consequent upon the surrender of the city, before we received orders to be ready to march immediately.

Raphael Semmes, the famed Confederate commerce raider, wrote later, with keen insight, about the fall of Vicksburg and the loss at Gettysburg:

> ...Vicksburg and Gettysburg mark an era in the war.... We need no better evidence of the shock which had been given to public confidence in the South, by those two disasters, than the simple fact, that our currency depreciated almost immediately a thousand per cent!

In Gettysburg, Lee had decided to retreat into Virginia. Late in the afternoon, in a heavy downpour the wagons filled with wounded began their slow, agonizing journey south. The wounded had days of riding in springless wagons before they could reach safety and proper care. Many would not make it, but would be buried along the road. As the long wagon trains cleared the camps, they would be followed by the infantry and artillery, covered by Stuart's cavalry. Meade, left in possession of the field, had no plans to follow Lee, although he was urged to do so by Lincoln. This would be another opportunity lost to the Army of the Potomac.

Day, Pvt., Co. B, 25th Massachusetts Volunteer Infantry, Washington, N.C.:

> ...we reached our destination. Soon after we were ordered back down the river and companies K and I landed at Rodman's point, four miles below town, while the *Mystic* kept on and landed F, C and B at Hill's Point, three miles lower down, relieving a New York battery company which was on duty there.
>
> Our first business was to tote our baggage and camp equipment up the bluff and under a broiling sun we worked hard, at least I thought it was hard. I carried my knapsack up and was so exhausted I thought I had better celebrate the rest of the day. I started out to explore the surroundings and soon my eye rested on a board shanty at the foot of the bluff. I entered and found a noble scion of African descent; he was running a restaurant, his whole stock consisting of corn meal, with which he made hoe-cakes for the boys on the bluff.
>
> I inquired if he intended remaining here or going with the company we had just relieved. He said he should stay if he met with sufficient encouragement from the boys. I gave him a great deal of encouragement, telling him I thought he would have right smart of business and would do well, that I would give him my patronage and that he might commence now by making me one of his best hoe-cakes for dinner. He said it would be ready in half an hour. I went out and worked hard during that time watching the boys get the freight up the bluff. I went for the cake and was shown one of about fifteen inches across and of good thickness. I began mentally to size my pile, thinking I had been a little indiscreet. I inquired the price of that monstrosity, and was told it was ten cents. I felt relieved and handing out the dime, took the cake and went up the bluff. Here I met Spencer and asked him if he had any meat. He replied, "just a little." I showed him the hoe cake and said I thought we had better dine together; he thought so too. Getting a cup of water, we sat down on a log and ate our Fourth of July dinner. The afternoon was used up pitching tents and mounting picket guard. Thus was spent the Fourth of July, 1863.

At Hampton Roads, Va., Confederate Vice President Alexander Stephens arrived in the C.S.S. *Torpedo*, hoping to meet with Federal officials to discuss prisoner exchange and, possibly, the end of the war. Permission for the negotiations was refused by the Federal government.

July 5 (Sunday)

From Gettysburg, Lee's army had moved south towards Hagerstown, Md., and Meade sat in Gettysburg—an act somewhat reminiscent of those of McClellan.

Day, Pvt., Co. B, 25th Massachusetts Volunteer Infantry, Hill's Point artillery emplacement, N.C.:

> Like most other Sabbaths in the army, so was this; all day busy cleaning up the camp ground.... We had our Fourth of July dinner today; bean soup, hoe cake and lemonade.... Hill's Point is not a point in the river.... It is the terminus of a table-land beyond, and is formed by wide deep ravines on either side which run back and soon ascend to the level of the table-land.... During the siege last spring, they had a powerful battery here which caused General Foster a heap of trouble. Since then, he has occupied it himself. This is an intrenched camp, sporting three brass six-pounder field pieces....

Vicksburg was in Federal hands, supplies came in for the relief of the citizens of the city, and troops occupied the public buildings. The Federals began to parole the Confederates. Sherman stirred his men out of their entrenchments and prepared for an attack towards the city of Jackson, and Joe Johnston, to the east.

Barber, Cpl., Co. D, 15th Illinois Volunteer Infantry, Vicksburg, Miss.:

> The indomitable Grant, never easy when any armed traitors were within striking distance, immediately upon the surrender of Vicksburg, turned upon Johnston, hoping to give him a blow before he heard

of the fall of Vicksburg, but that wary General had no desire to measure swords with Grant just then and so he beat a precipitate retreat, closely followed by our victorious army.... Early on the morning of the 5th we were on the move. The weather was excessively hot. I came very near giving out the first day, but I got permission to fall out from the ranks and take my own time. In this manner, I got along quite well. We camped near Black River the first night, having made only nine miles. Here we had to wait until other troops crossed, and it was not until the morning of the sixth that we crossed.

Jackman, Pvt., "The Orphan Brigade," towards Vicksburg, Miss.:

> At 4 P.M. moved out and marched 6 miles towards Vicksburg, moving on the railroad which is the hardest marching. The evening very hot. Division bivouacked in line of battle on the battle field of "Champion Hill" or Baker's Creek. All are expecting hot work tomorrow. We are close to the Big Black and have pontoons ready to put down.

July 6 (Monday)

Rear Admiral John A. Dahlgren, former commander of the Washington Navy Yard and a friend of President Lincoln, arrived in Port Royal, S.C., as the new commander of the South Atlantic Blockading Squadron, replacing Rear Admiral Samuel F. Du Pont. There had been a lot of finger-pointing about the failure of the assault on Charleston, S.C., and it appeared that the scapegoat was to be Du Pont, who had been widely criticized for his failure to take Charleston. Du Pont sought to explain his failure to the nation. Secretary Welles feared that such an explanation might shake public confidence in the ironclad ships and the mortars which Porter considered to be the source of the problem. Du Pont had argued hotly with Secretary of the Navy Gideon Welles about this and had been admonished. He now retired from the naval service, the end of a brilliant career for a brilliant man.

Sherman had begun his move towards Jackson, Miss., and this move was being countered by Confederate Joe Johnston with his inferior forces. There was a lull while the players got into position.

Barber, Cpl., Co. D, 15th Illinois Volunteer Infantry, towards Jackson, Miss.:

> ...we halted at five o'clock P.M. on the battle ground of Champion Hill and supposed that we were going into camp. Our regiment was detailed for picket duty. We had scarcely been posted before orders came to resume the march. The night set in dark and stormy. The rain came down in torrents. We were soon wet to the skin. The water in the road was ankle deep, and we had to pick our way by the flash of the lightning. In this way we continued on until after midnight, when we halted on a high hill to seek rest and sleep.

Jackman, Pvt., "The Orphan Brigade," Clinton, Miss.:

> Fell in early and lo! instead of marching toward Vicksburg, the head of the column turned back toward Jackson. We are confident Johnston secured the intelligence of the fall of Vicksburg last night. A hot and dusty march of 10 miles brought us to Clinton. We are bivouacked near town by a good spring. Heavy rain in the morning.

There was light skirmishing between the cavalry forces of Lee and Meade as Lee withdrew through Maryland to Virginia. Meade still sat in Gettysburg, despite Lincoln's urging.

John Hunt Morgan's Rebel cavalry had run through Bardstown, Ky., and other points, and now occupied Garnettsville as he moved towards the Ohio River. Panic was in the streets of the cities along the river.

July 7 (Tuesday)

The forces gather for the Union assault on Joe Johnston and Jackson, Miss. While the generals shuffled the maps and symbols, the troops waited.

Barber, Cpl., Co. D, 15th Illinois Volunteer Infantry, towards Jackson, Miss.:

> A huge fire of rails was soon built, and stretching ourselves on a few rails before the fire, we soon fell into a profound slumber, from which the rain beating upon our faces failed to arouse us.... At daylight we were on the march again, but the roads were so bad we only made fifteen miles that day.

Jackman, Pvt., "The Orphan Brigade," Battle of Jackson, Miss.:

> Marched by the Raymond road to Jackson and bivouacked 2 miles below the city on Pearl river. This march of 15 miles has been about as disagreeable as we generally have. Water very scarce on the road. I had to straggle a little today.

At Port Hudson, south of Vicksburg, the last remaining Confederate bastion held out despite short rations and incessant pounding by mortar boats.

Browning, Pvt., 53d Massachusetts Volunteers, Port Hudson, Miss.:

> My Dear Wife The band has just ben playing a lively tune and the men of the different Regts have ben cheering this morning the reason for it is General Banks has sent word round that Vixburg has surrenderd the report is that it surrenderd on the 4th of July I hope that the report will prove true it is said that a gun boat came down from there and brought the news it puts the pluck into our men it is better than a dose of Epsom Salts for the sick. This is the most important news that we herd so that I have to write. I presume you have herd of it before this time and of corse it will be not the news to you. I thougt I must shout it it was so cheering to us. My health is very good and I am in hopes that we shall be able to get inside the Fortifications so that the men will have rest but from present appearances I think it will be severl days before the attempt is made. There has just commenced a heavy cannonade there is a constant rattle of guns and the bursting of shells what it means I dont know. Gen B has had the Sappers & Miners to work ever since the last fight diging approaches to their works. These are made by diging in a zigzag form by turning at short angles in the room of diging in a stright line in his form so that we can approach their works without danger from their guns it is this that makes me think that it will be severl days before the attack will be made Were so near to them yesterday that they could talk with them which they did by cracking jokes at each other. I trust that it will be so arrenged that the mens lives and limbs may be saved I have herd that the firing is a salut in honor of the fall of Vixburg it said that Grant has taken 27000 prisoners & 180 pieces of cannon. The steward has ben cutting my hair and triming my whiskers and they all say that it has improved my looks very much I told Mr Gould the other day that we looked more like bears than like men and if we had not got trimed up I did not believe that our wifes would own us he thought that his wife ould own him no matter how bad he looked what do you think about it. Mr. Eaton is here he has got a very bad leg. I believe that I spoke of it in my last letter. Only one month from today the Regt will be off duty and sent home

Day, Pvt., Co. B, 25th Massachusetts Volunteer Infantry, Hill's Point, N.C.:

> Today a sergeant, corporal and eight privates from each company have been detailed to manipulate the big guns. I had the honor of being selected from my company, and was assigned the left gun, a most dangerous and hazardous position. I feel proud of my promotion and am sure I shall sustain the honor of the artillery service. For a day or two we shall be under the instructions of a battery sergeant who will instruct us in loadings and firings.... My gun on the left occupies a very commanding position, being some ten feet higher than the other guns. From the top of the parapet to the bottom of the ravine it is some 30 or 40 feet, and a part of the way nearly perpendicular. I have a range of the whole clearing and covering both the other guns; because of its great natural strength and commanding position, I have dubbed it the Malakoff. I, being the senior sergeant, am styled on all hands, both by officers and men, as the chief of artillery, a rank I accept and have assumed all the privileges which the rank implies. The little steamer *Undine* plies between town and this port, making her trips mornings and afternoons, giving us frequent and easy transit to town....

Lee, in Hagerstown, Md., notified President Davis of his retreat from Gettysburg and his decision to withdraw further south. Davis was not joyous at the news, but understanding. Lincoln received the news of Vicksburg's surrender and wrote Halleck, "Now, if General Meade can complete his work, so gloriously prosecuted thus far, by the literal or substantial destruction of Lee's army, the rebellion will be over." Lincoln was right again, but he couldn't get his commander of the Army of the Potomac to see this.

July 8 (Wednesday)

The battle for Jackson, Miss,. drew nearer, as Sherman moved east. The news of the surrender of Vicksburg was officially given to the defenders of Jackson and the gloom spread like molasses. There was skirmishing between the forces at Clinton and Bolton Depot, east of Vicksburg.

Jackman, Pvt., "The Orphan Brigade," Battle of Jackson, Miss.:

> The news had not been positively known to the troops of the fall of Vicksburg until today. The news cast a gloom over most of the troops but did not seem to affect the "Orphans" much.

As the news of Vicksburg reached Port Hudson it seemed to be the last straw. Gen. Franklin Gardner, commanding the garrison, asked Gen. Nathaniel Banks for surrender terms, and then surrendered unconditionally after six weeks of siege. Gardner surrendered about 7000 men to Banks, and the Mississippi was open all the way to the sea.

Browning, Pvt., 53d Massachusetts Volunteers, Port Hudson, Miss.:

> As I have a few spar moments I will improve them by writting you. I will give you a history of my morning Dark I got [up] at 4 A.M. and swep the cround off clean round our establishment and set our things to rights by that I was ready for breakfast after which I took care of Mr Eaton I then went down whare Comp B. are encamped on my way back cut a lot of small cane of which I made out of them a bed for my personal use. Out of the sticks I made a broom. Then I went to 2 or 3 sutlers to see if I could get some pater for Mr Eaton but was not succesfull so you see that I have ben bussey until now 10 o'clock A.M.. Now for the news I am in hopes to have the privalage of writting before I close this that Port Hudson has surrenderd for they had had a Flag of Truce out evercince 4 o'clock and it is said that they are making arrengements to surrender at 12 m. if they can be sattisfied that Vixburg has surrenderd. Now if this proves true I shall exspect to see the inside of their works soon. Large numbers of our men have ben up and talked with the Rebels they treated our men to corn cake and corn beer. They seemed to be very freandly. There is a goodeal of anziety to get information as to the result. I must tell you about our coullard cook. We have ben living in good stile for the last few days. As we were all out of money we borrowed some and bought some flower and dried apple the cook manufacterd apple turne overs and sold them 2 for 15 cts so we have money to buye sugar and flower or anything else that we nead and can get so you see we turn our nigger cook to good advantage. Now how should you like to have me bring home with me a cook to help you there is plenty of them here I think I had not better write much more till after we get the result of deliberations in relation to the surrender of Port. There is every appearance of a shower there is heavy thunder over Port Hudson or rather in that direction. It is much said that they have surrenderd and that they are going to stack there arms at 5 o'clock.
>
> Port Hudson is over they have surrenderd without any more fighting how thankful we should be. I tell you that I feel like rejouesing for I exspected there would be a good many lives lost before they would give up

John Hunt Morgan and his cavalry raiders crossed the Ohio River at Cumming's Ferry and Brandenburg, Ky., and entered southern Indiana. It was hoped that the Copperhead movement, reasonably strong in Indiana and Ohio, would provide support to Morgan. This was to be only a raid, but the effect on Southern morale was exhilarating, just at a time when the news of Gettysburg, Vicksburg, and Port Hudson seemed to crush the Southern spirit.

As Lee withdrew into Virginia, there was heavy fighting at Boonsborough, east of Antietam, and at the crossing at Williamsport, Md.

July 9 (Thursday)

As Sherman drew near the Mississippi capital, there was light fighting near Clinton and the approaches to the city. President Davis, wholly out of touch with the situation there, wired Johnston that he hoped Johnston might yet "attack and crush the enemy."

Admiral Farragut wrote Admiral D.D. Porter informing him that the command of the entire Mississippi River was his responsibility from this time. Farragut was leaving to go back to his blockading squadron off Mobile to solve that problem, after a side trip to New York.

Barber, Cpl., Co. D, 15th Illinois Volunteer Infantry, Battle of Jackson, Miss.:

> On the 9th, when within six miles of Jackson, our brigade was ordered to halt and guard a large train which was left here. Our provisions now failed us and we subsisted for three days on green corn. Salt was very scarce and it set a good many of the boys into a diarrhea. I was lucky enough to have some salt with me.... Jeff Davis' plantation was only a few miles from our camp. Some of the boys visited it and brought away relics. Some went to his library and brought away some of his books. Others would bring away a piece of a carpet for a blanket....

Jackman, Pvt., "The Orphan Brigade," Battle of Jackson, Miss.:

> Before daylight news came in that the enemy was approaching and ordered to be ready to move. At daylight, marched to the suburbs of the city. Our division being on the left wing, the Ky. brigade rested on the river below the city and Adam's brigade on the right extended around to the Clinton road. As soon as our line was established, a party was sent into the city to press negroes to work on the fortifications and brought out quite a crowd to our regiment among them a few dandy barbers who did not fancy wielding the pick and shoving the spade much but they had to go to work. After completion, we lay around loose, waiting the coming of events. Our line ran through a dutchman's garden and we took his grape arbor for headquarters. I had to write part of the day, making out field returns, etc.

Port Hudson formally surrendered, clearing the last obstacle for navigation on the Mississippi from Cairo to New Orleans and the sea. There would be minor guerrilla harassment for the remainder of the war.

Browning, Pvt., 53d Massachusetts Volunteers, Port Hudson, Miss.:

> I exspect to be very bussey to day I want to go and see the rebel works this morning and we exspect to move as the Regt have gon down to Banks Head Quaters so that I cannot write much more this morning. I am well with the exception of 2 or 3 sores on my feet My love to all I will write again the first oppitunity this will cure a large number of the sick that we left behind so that I think we shall [ ] a Regt by the time we get ready to come home. We are exspecting a mail just as soon as there is a boat comes up. The Rebs have got a battery between hear & N. Orleans so that it is troubled our boats to get by I shall exspect 2 letters from you by this mail good by for this time my best love
>
> S. M. Browning.

Confederate Morgan was loose in southern Indiana and raiding near Croydon, looting homes and businesses. The raid continued for several more days.

Lee's wagons with the wounded were waiting to cross the Potomac, delayed due to high water.

July 10 (Friday)

At Jackson, Miss., Sherman had his men surround the city and outflank Joe Johnston in the hope of capturing the Rebels entire. Not much fighting today; much moving and milling around.

Jackman, Pvt., "The Orphan Brigade," Battle of Jackson, Miss.:

> Early the enemy came in front which was known by the pop, pop, popping of the sharpshooters. They did not come in front of our brigade but in front of Adam's on the right and Stovall in the centre. Nothing further than sharpshooting with a very little cannonading on the line today.

At Port Hudson the city and fortifications were becoming a tourist attraction for the Union troops who had worked so hard to get inside for so long. The parole process was set in motion to get the Rebel troops out and on their way home.

Browning, Pvt., 53d Massachusetts Volunteers, Port Hudson, Miss.:

> My Dear Wife (we have had orders to move this morning I think not far)
>
> Yesterday morning I went into Port Hudson to see the Rebels lay down their arms and surrender themselves prisoners of war. It was at 9 o'clock A.M. They were a very good looking set of men if they had ben dressed as well I think they would make as good appearing as our own army. They will fight well we have plenty of profe of that and they were looking healthy more so than our own men they were formed in a line our men forming in front they were ordered to ground arms which they did taking off at the same

there belts and carttridge boxs & belts. The sun shone so hot that I did not stop to see the conclusion I watched and they were marched on transports and are to be sent to New Orleans I dont know when they will be able to get them there for it is said that the Rebels have got a battery at Blaquemine a place about half way to New Orleans so that they stop our boats from passing so that we have no communications with New Orleans unless they run by in the night. I think our gun boats will soon clear them out. You must not be surprised if you dont get letters from me very regular Our Regt have gon to do guard duty near Genl Banks Headquaters so they did not have the privalage of going into the fort I think that after they had dun to say the lest as much hard fighting and have ben kept in front all of the time with the exception of the hard march to Clinton they should have had the privalage of being present at surrender of the place in the room of Regts that have dun but little hard duty but have lain back in the woods as reserve force. Some of the men will feel it. I presume that it would have ben differnt if boath of our Gen had not been absent at the time Now that Port Hudson has surrenderd our men think that they shall be relieved & sent home but I think that we shall be kept just as long as they can keep us as Gen Banks will nead all the help he can get to hold all the places he has taken I understand that the whole country through wich we passed before we came here has got to be reconkerd as the Rebels have taken possession. I dont know whether Gen Banks cares to hold that part of the state but if he does he has got to garrison them with soldiers. It is said that Gen Auggies division left yesterday to look after the Rebels that are troubling us in that country. Now how are you getting along at home I wish I was there to see for I dont worry much about it I cannot help thinking that you nead me at home and that you are short of the one thing neadful to make yourselves comfortable. I wish the Government would pay us off so that you could get a little from me. I suppose now that you have no garden you will have all of your vegitables to by and that will make some differance in your expences. I should like to have you keep an acct of the amount of money that you out for such vegitables as we usaley raise in the garden so that we can judge something of the cost and whether it pays to plant a garden. I have got a large ledger or acct book that I got out of the Reb camp to keep our accounts in if I can get it home As I write so often lately I will write short letters so that it will not bother you to read so much poor spelling Tell Azubah that I will amuse her next letter as soon as I can conveniently and not make her wait so long for an annser. My love to them all. I am in hopes that by the time you receive this that my time will be so near out that it will not be necissary for you to annser at any rate I will write you as soon as I find out when we are coming home. Till then accept the best wishes and love from your absent husband

S. M. Browning

Day, Pvt., Co. B, 25th Massachusetts Volunteer Infantry, Hill's Point, N.C.:

This being an isolated post and several miles from any commissary or sutler, the officers feared it would be terribly infected with malaria; having regard for the health and welfare of the men, they prevailed on our assistant surgeon, Doctor Flagg, to order whiskey rations. Up went the order and down came the whiskey, and now the order is to drink no more river water, but take a little whiskey as a preventive. This will prove a terrible hardship to the boys, but the surgeon's order is imperative. The boys in camp get their whiskey at night, and the pickets in the morning when they come in. After a barrel of whiskey has stood out all day in the sun and got about milk warm, it is curious to observe the boys while drinking it. Some of them with rather tender gullets will make up all manner of contortions of face trying to swallow it, but will manage to get it down and then run about fifteen rods to catch their breath. Commanders of companies deal out the whiskey to their men, consequently, I deal out to mine, and when I wish to reward any of my braves for gallant and meritorious conduct, I manage to slop a little extra into their cups. That keeps them vigilant and interested and gallant. Meritorious conduct consists of bringing in watermelons, peaches and other subsistence, of which they *somehow* become possessed.

Lee, waiting for the Potomac River to fall so he could ford it, was at Williamsport, Md., wondering how long it would be before Meade decided to attack. This same situation had occurred after the Battle of Sharpsburg (Antietam). Lee had his back to the river and the Union commander let him get back into Virginia.

Morgan's raiders, leaving Croydon, Ind., headed for New Salem, and then turned towards southern Ohio.

Near Charleston Harbor, Federal troops landed on Morris Island for the assault on Ft. Wagner, under cover of fire from the ironclads U.S.S. *Catskill*, Commander G.W. Rodgers; the *Montauk*, Commander Fairfax; *Nahant*, Commander Downes; and *Weehawken*, Commander Colhoun, all from the South Atlantic Blockading Squadron. During the landings, the enemy poured 60 shots into the *Catskill*, six into the *Nahant*, and two into the *Montauk*.

July 11 (Saturday)

Sherman had invested the city of Jackson, Miss., and the waiting began. Things remained reasonably quiet in the lines.

Jackman, Pvt., "The Orphan Brigade," Battle of Jackson, Miss.:

> In the morning skirmishing all around the line save in front of our brigade. Not much cannonading from either side. Early in the forenoon Buford's Ky. brigade had a pretty lively little fight on the extreme right of the army. At noon the brigade ordered across to the right to support Loring, an assault being expected on that part of the line. Our position was immediately in the rear of Col. Wither's fine mansion, the rifle pits running through his yard. The old Col., who was not in the service, had a musket on his shoulder ready to defend, or help defend, the works in front of his house. His mansion being exposed to artillery fire, he had moved all of his furniture out of the house into the back yard. A rain coming up soon after we got there, myself with others volunteered to help him get his furniture into the house again. We got it all in at the back door save a large mahogany bedstead which we had to carry to the front door where the Federal sharpshooters had full view of us and gave us several rounds but fortunately, no one was hurt. I mention this as it was the only adventure I had during the battle. Several of the brigade were wounded during the evening by sharpshooters. The enemy not assaulting, we returned to our old position late in the afternoon. The next day Col. Withers was killed and when our army evacuated, his house was burned.

At Gettysburg, Meade finally got off his posterior and mounted a halfhearted general offensive against Lee's forces, which had their back to the Potomac. Lincoln, in the wings, cheered Meade on, hoping that he would attack and destroy Lee's army.

On Morris Island, Charleston Harbor, Brig. Gen. Quincy A. Gillmore made a futile assault on Ft. Wagner; a larger attacking force was needed.

July 12 (Sunday)

Sherman practised economy of force and used his troops to hold Joe Johnston in a siege position while Sherman planned other action.

Jackman, Pvt., "The Orphan Brigade," Battle of Jackson, Miss.:

> Early this morning Gen'l. Hovey's division charged in front of Stovall's and the right of our brigade. He was repulsed with heavy loss, mostly inflicted by Cobb's Battery of our brigade and Slocum's Washington Artillery of Adam's brigade. They came up square in front of these two batteries. We captured 3 stands of colors and about a hundred prisoners that I saw. In the evening our regiment and the 2d moved to the rear of Cobb's and Slocum's batteries as a support but late in the evening our regiment came back to old position, leaving the 2d.

Lee, still with his back to the river, awaited either Meade's attack or the falling of the river so he could cross with his main force, which he hoped he could do the next day. Lincoln hoped Meade would be in time to stop Lee, but this was not to be.

In Tennessee, Bragg was now in Chattanooga, having lost the state to Rosecrans. Both commanders were reorganizing and fitting up for the next campaign.

Morgan's raiders were now at Vernon, Ind., with Confederate cavalry troopers straggled all along his route of march as they fell out with broken-down horses and were captured by the aroused Hoosiers.

July 13 (Monday)

The opposition to the Draft Law reached its culmination today with riots in New York City, Boston, Portsmouth, N.H., Rutland, Vt., Wooster, Ohio, and Troy, N.Y. The largest, of course, was in New York, where a mob stormed the draft headquarters, burned houses, and looted stores. Fires broke out, and a Negro church and orphanage were burned as Negroes became the prime target for the mob, made up mostly of working-class Irish. Property losses were estimated at $1,500,000, and it was estimated that 100 people were killed or wounded during the period, which ended July 16th.

As a follow-up to the Vicksburg campaign, Union forces took Yazoo City, Miss., with the aid of gunboats. They also occupied Natchez, which had been occupied off and on for some period of time.

Morgan's raiders left Indiana and crossed into Ohio at Harrison, heading for Hamilton and Cincinnati, where Federal authorities declared martial law.

July 14 (Tuesday)

Things were moving slowly at Jackson, Miss. Sherman was playing a waiting game rather than making a direct assault on Johnston's lines.

Barber, Cpl., Co. D, 15th Illinois Volunteer Infantry, Battle of Jackson, Miss.:

> Much to our satisfaction, we now received orders to march to the front and join our division. Before night we had taken our position in line of battle. Johnston had made a stand at Jackson. General Sherman concluded not to sacrifice the lives of his men by assaulting their works when a safer and surer method was open to him. So we commenced fortifying and gradually extending our lines toward the rear of the enemy with the purpose of surrounding him and cutting off his retreat. Our division General Lauman, now made a blunder which lost him his command. In his strong desire for popularity and promotion, he overdid the thing. He misinterpreted an order to move forward our line for a charge on the rebel works. The charge was made and the rebels finding it unsupported, concentrated their whole available force against us. Unfalteringly we swept up to within a few rods of their works, but their fire was too terrific for flesh and blood to stand. We were forced to retire with fully one-fourth of the boys placed hors de combat. A flag of truce was sent in asking permission to bury our dead. It was refused. They lay where they had fallen until the stench became so offensive to the rebels that they were forced to do something with them. So without any regard to decency, they scooped out shallow holes and rolled them in and left a great many arms and legs in sight.

In New York, the draft riots continued, although they abated in the other cities. In Washington, Lincoln wrote Meade of his appreciation for the job Meade had done, but expressed disappointment that Meade had not attacked Lee when the opportunity presented itself. Many thousands of men would die or be wounded because of this mistake and inertia. Lee crossed the Potomac and was safe, for the time being, in Virginia.

July 15 (Wednesday)

New York became a little quieter as the draft riots abated and things returned to normal.

South of the Potomac, along Lee's route of march up the Shenandoah Valley, Federal cavalry harassed the Confederate columns moving through Halltown and Shepherdstown.

Morgan had now headed east from Cincinnati towards the Ohio River, hotly pursued by Federal troops and local militia.

Sherman began to press Joe Johnston to take some action at Jackson, Miss.

Barber, Cpl., Co. D, 15th Illinois Volunteer Infantry, Battle of Jackson, Miss.:

> By the 15th, we had them nearly surrounded. One more day would have cut off their retreat, but that wary General Johnston, was not to be caught napping. Silently and in a masterly manner, he effected a retreat and our troops took quiet possession of the place and at once proceeded to gather up the spoils of war. Tobacco seemed to be the greatest spoil, but some succeeded in getting the genuine "yellow dogs" (gold). We pursued the foe as far as Brandon, ten miles from Jackson, and then returned.
>
> My health, which had for some time been poor, now entirely failed me. I had a run of fever. I was sent out one day in charge of a fatigue party, to clear the ground in front of our works, but before it was finished, I was forced to give up and go to camp. I found Dr. Myron Underwood there looking for me. He was Assistant Surgeon of a regiment camped near by. He advised me to take medicine

immediately and try and break my fever. I was sent back to Vicksburg in a sick train and started one day in advance of the army. We went by way of Raymond and the army took the old route.... The weather was extremely hot and our wagon being uncovered, I suffered excruciating tortures from the burning rays of the sun.

July 16 (Thursday)

Gen. Joseph E. Johnston decided to abandon Jackson, Miss., to its fate at Sherman's hands. Johnston pulled his men out of the city about midnight.

Jackman, Pvt., "The Orphan Brigade," Battle of Jackson, Miss.:

> Heavy firing of small arms and cannon on the right about noon. Have not learned the cause. I can tell from the looks of affairs we are going to retreat soon—no doubt tonight. As yet there have been no Federals in front of us. They are in front of the 6th on the right.

Barber, Cpl., Co. D, 15th Illinois Volunteer Infantry, return to Vicksburg, Miss.:

> Within ten miles of Vicksburg I left my hot bed and went the rest of the way afoot, though so weak I could scarcely walk. I got into camp about six hours before the regiment.... We now moved camp inside the rebel works, one mile south of the city. The ground was still strewn with the filth of the rebel camp and the air was pregnant with noxious odors. The water was very poor.... As a consequence of our foul camp and the impure water, the sick list increased rapidly, endangering the organization of the regiment. It became necessary to move camp to a more healthy position in order to preserve the organization. Every day the solemn strokes of the muffled drums told the requiem of departed comrades.

Lee wrote President Davis that his men were in good spirits, but that they needed shoes and clothing. These needs satisfied, they could begin operations immediately.

July 17 (Friday)

Amid the darkness of a hot, humid night, the Confederate defenders of Jackson, Miss., defended no more, but decamped and fled.

Jackman, Pvt., "The Orphan Brigade," retreat to Morton, Miss.:

> Last night, 16th, at 12 o'clock, fell in silently and moved through the city across the pontoon bridge over Pearl river and marched out on the Brandon road. We were the last troops to cross the river and the brigade moved in such good order that it excited the admiration of the commanding Gen'l. It has covered so many retreats the boys know just how such things have to be done. When daylight came, we were 4 miles from the city. Marched 14 miles during the day and bivouacked 2 miles of Brandon. A very hot day and dusty marching. All the troops having to move on the same road, we were delayed greatly.

Barber, Cpl., Co. D, 15th Illinois Volunteer Infantry, Vicksburg, Miss.:

> I was attacked with a dysentery but by being very careful, I managed to keep around. One day I went to the city and called on John Eddy, who was clerk in the purveyor's department and he got me up a dinner which did me good.... Much to our satisfaction, we now received orders to take transports and go down the river to Natchez. We were transferred from Logan's command, 15th corps, to the 16th corps, Maj. General E.O.C. Ord, commanding....

Things were looking gloomy all around with Vicksburg and Port Hudson gone, Gettysburg a costly defeat, and now the attack on Morris Island near Charleston.

July 18 (Saturday)

In Ohio the chase after John Hunt Morgan was coming to a close. His weary and saddle-sore men were riding slower and slower as they passed through Pomeroy and Chester, Ohio, attempting to make it to Bluffington, where they hoped to cross into Kentucky. A Federal fort guarding the crossing blocked the escape that night and Morgan had to wait until dawn.

On Morris Island in Charleston Harbor, another assault was made on Ft. Wagner after a heavy pounding by mortar boats and ironclads. The gunboats began their fire shortly after noon, when the tide permitted them to get within 300 yards of the fort. This close-range firing effectively silenced the fort's guns and kept them from firing on the fleet. The assault by Brig. Gen. Truman Seymour's men was led by the 54th Massachusetts Volunteer Infantry, the first of the Negro regiments to enter the war. Of the 6000 men in the assault, 1515 of them would be casualties, including Col. Robert Gould Shaw, who organized and commanded the 54th Massachusetts. He would be buried in the trenches with his men. Later, when his father came to claim the body and asked where it was, he would be told, "He is buried in the trench with his niggers."

The failure of the assault would cause a change in the Federal plan of attack on Charleston from a frontal assault to a siege. For a siege more heavy guns were brought up, including one monster called the "Swamp Angel" that threw a 200-pound projectile. The Confederate defenders also shifted guns from Sumter to other points in the defense positions.

Jackman, Pvt., "The Orphan Brigade," retreat to Morton, Miss.:

> Fooling along in the rear of the wagon train all day. In the evening, the rain pounds down in torrents. After dark, when we went into camp, or rather when we stopped for the night, everything wet and disagreeable. I was too tired to go to the wagons for my blankets and Col. W. loaned me a blanket for the night. Have marched 16 miles today. We remained at this place two or three days, having to cook rations nearly every day. We were on Dead River—and a lifeless looking place it is.

July 19 (Sunday)

At Bluffington, Ohio, daylight found Morgan's raiders embroiled in a stiff fight with Union forces and gunboats guarding the crossing. The U.S.S. *Moose* and steamer *Allegheny Belle* repeatedly prevented Morgan from crossing the river. Caught from behind by militia and Federal troops, Morgan came out second best in this scrape, or at least his command did. He lost about 700 captured and 120 killed, but escaped with the remaining 400 and turned north and east towards Pennsylvania.

Meade's Army of the Potomac *finally* crossed the Potomac after Lee, at Harper's Ferry and other fords, and moved rapidly south towards the Blue Ridge passes, which were being screened by Stuart's cavalry.

July 20 (Monday)

Having eluded capture the day before with about 400 of his men, John Hunt Morgan got into another scrape with Union forces at Hockingport, Ohio, before turning away from the Ohio River.

In the Blue Ridge passes, Federal and Rebel cavalry got into stiff fights with each other as Lee moved through the Shenandoah, and Meade paralleled Lee's route further east.

Day, Pvt., Co. B, 25th Massachusetts Volunteer Infantry, Hill's Point, N.C.:

> There is among army officers a constant jealousy and strife for promotion and rank, watching and looking after each other, fearful lest someone may be assuming some rank or taking some privileges that do not belong to him. I have been giving my men passes out of camp, and these passes have been honored at headquarters. In consequence of that, a spirit of envy and jealousy entered the breasts of the infantry officers; it made them feel sore and uneasy, so they consulted together and decided that that could no longer be allowed. They informed me that I was exceeding my authority in passing men out of camp. Being in a minority and not caring to exhibit any stubbornness over so trifling a matter, I magnanimously waived my authority to issue the passes, but it was a big come down for the chief of artillery. When I wish to leave, I simply look in at headquarters and say to the captain, "I propose going out." If there is anything in the *pitcher* he always says, "You had better come in and take something before going." The captain is as generous as he is brave, and brave men are always generous.

July 21 (Tuesday)

Fighting became heavy at times between opposing cavalry at Manassas Gap, Chester Gap, and the other passes in the Blue Ridge, as Meade's cavalry looked for Lee and were rebuffed by Stuart's hard-riding troops.

Jackman, Pvt., "The Orphan Brigade," Morton, Miss.:

> Marched 9 miles and bivouacked 4 miles east of Morton, a little town on the Southern RR. Looking like rain, we put up our fly and just as we drove the

last pin, a heavy storm of rain came patting down. The companies have neither flies nor tents and the boys have to weather the storm as best they can. They generally, though, stretch their blankets up in the manner of a "dog-tent," which shelters them very well from the inclement weather. Here we remained in camp, or bivouacked, a few days, the time passing monotonously. We had rain nearly every day. Water to drink was very scarce. The country perfectly level about camp and inclined to be swampy.

Barber, Cpl., Co. D, 15th Illinois Volunteer Infantry, Natchez, Miss.:

We hardly got established in camp before an order came for our brigade to guard a train of wagons to Kingston, twenty miles east of Natchez, to secure twenty thousand bales of cotton. Our troops had captured the place, but fearing an attack from overwhelming numbers, sent back for re-inforcements. I had been left back at Natchez sick when my regiment went out. I went out with the re-inforcements. I found the boys having a jolly time and living on the top shelf. We were in rich country. Our tables were loaded with fruits, jellies, vegetables, etc. A company of the 95th got a keg of beer, and of course, they had to treat their friends in the 15th, and together, some of them had rather a jolly time, and some of their heads got so heavy that they could not walk straight. It rained a great deal of the time we were out here, and having no tents with us, we got wet. I took cold.

Finally the last load of cotton was secured and we started for Natchez and it rained hard all day. I got thoroughly drenched. I now had to give up. A fever set in, commencing with ague and terminating with intermittent fever. For two weeks I did not leave my bed.... The doctor considered my case doubtful, but not liking the idea of a doctor getting seven dollars for burying me, I determined to disappoint him, but it was a long time before I was well enough to resume my duties....

July 23 (Thursday)

Morgan's tired, tag-end force was almost caught again at Rockville, Ohio, but, again, Morgan slipped away after losing a few men and horses.

French's Third Corps of the Army of the Potomac pushed on through Manassas Gap into the Valley, only to run into a brigade of Confederates that kept them entangled for hours. During this time, Longstreet's and Ewell's corps moved past the Gap and south to safety. Meade had failed to put enough weight behind the move to make it work. Another golden opportunity was lost.

July 24 (Friday)

Morgan was forced into another skirmish; each skirmish weakened his force by loss of men, horses, and ammunition. This one occurred near Athens, Ohio. Morgan was moving north and east.

Longstreet's corps arrived back at Culpeper C.H. The remainder of the Army of Northern Virginia would follow. Meade started concentrating forces near Warrenton, Va. Both of the armies moved into old camps.

July 26 (Sunday)

Morgan was finally run to ground near the Pennsylvania line. At Salineville, Ohio, he and his spent command surrendered. He had 364 officers and men remaining. The officers were sent to the state prison at Columbus, and the enlisted men to prison camps. Morgan's raid was daring, spectacular, and caused much consternation but did little else. Nothing of great military value was destroyed nor were many people killed. In many ways the raid was a great grandstand play.

The famed Texas patriot Sam Houston died this day at Huntsville, Tex. Although he had opposed secession, he felt that once started on that course, it must be carried through.

John Crittenden, whose long career in public life included many terms in Congress, died in Frankfort, Ky. He had tried several times to achieve a compromise on the war, but he had failed. He had two sons; one fought for the Union, the other for the Confederacy, both general officers.

July 27 (Monday)

In Charleston, Gen. Beauregard had many problems, not the least of which was the coal supply for the few ironclads in the defense fleet. Capt. Tucker, commanding the Confederate naval forces at Charleston, informed Beauregard:

> ...Flag Officer Ingraham, commanding station, Charleston, has informed me officially that he has but 80 tons of coal to meet all demands, including the ironclads, and has admonished me of the necessity of economy of consumption.

The commerce raider C.S.S. *Florida*, Commander Maffitt, sailed from Bermuda, and three weeks later put into harbor at Brest, France, for extensive repairs. The raider was out of service for six months, and during this time Maffitt, in poor health, would ask to be relieved of his command.

A prominent Southerner died this day. William Lowndes Yancey, a man who had much to do with the secession movement, died at his home in Montgomery, Ala.

William Lowndes Yancey was born a Southern aristocrat at "The Aviary," Warren County, Ga., on August 10, 1814. His mother, widowed, had married an antislavery minister from the North and the family moved to Troy, N.Y., in 1822. Yancy returned to the South without completing his studies at Williams College (Mass.), reading law under an old friend of his father's at Greenville, S.C. He moved to Alabama, where he served in the state legislature in 1841 and 1843. He was elected to the U.S. House of Representatives in 1844, resigning before his term was completed. Yancey was an accomplished orator of some note and he used this talent effectively for the Southern cause. He became a radical, advocating secession. Once secession was accomplished, he hoped to become President of the Confederacy, but his radicalism was too much for the conservative element in the government. He became a member of the Confederate Senate in 1862, and a leader of the opposition, attempting to limit Davis's power wherever he could. His health failed rapidly in early 1863.

AUGUST 1863

Considering the events of July, for the North things looked better. The Mississippi was open to the sea and Lee was out of Pennsylvania. The South had a different perspective. The country had been cut in two, with the trans-Mississippi area isolated and the supplies from that region no longer available for the armies in the east. Both North and South, towns and villages counted their dead and mourned for the fallen at Gettysburg, Vicksburg, Port Hudson, Tullahoma, and a thousand other skirmishes. The war continued.

August 1 (Saturday)

There was another melee at Brandy Station, Va., but certainly nothing like the previous cavalry battle at the same site in early June. Opposing cavalry clashed briefly on the old battlefield, the Union looking for Lee.

Belle Boyd, an oft-arrested spy suspect, was again in custody for similar activities at the Old Capital Prison in Washington.

Jackman, Pvt., "The Orphan Brigade," Morton, Miss.:

> Now commences another long term of camp life, nothing going on to break the monotony from one week to another.
>
> "Camp Hurricane" was situated among hills covered with pine. Our regiment camped on a hill nearly to itself, at the base of which was a large spring of excellent water which supplied the division. The spring fed a mill-pond of considerable size and under the mill, which was the smallest affair I ever saw, was a very excellent place for bathing. Our camp was on the margin of a small field on the edge of which was a small cabin made of pine logs the only evidence of civilization to be seen; all else around was an interminable forest of pines, the only growth these sterile hills can produce.
>
> The boys built arbors of pine branches which shielded them from the sun and in a great measure kept off the rain. We pitched the office in a pleasant place and I was kept pretty busy at times writing. Lt. B. left on a leave of absence and willed me his hammock while he remained away. I often tumbled out of it at night while sleeping.
>
> There was no field handy in which to drill and the boys were glad of it. A great deal of rain fell during our stay at "Hurricane" which mostly came of evenings.
>
> The spring was made a kind of market-place for the division where soldiers would speculate on fresh vegetables, etc. Large watermelons would go for $40. The neighborhood of the spring was also being made a resort for gambling when Maj. "Hap" Graves of

Breckinridge's staff made a "descent" upon the sporting gentlemen and broke up such amusement.

Barber, Cpl., Co. D, 15th Illinois Volunteer Infantry, Natchez, Miss.:

> Our division again received marching orders. They crossed the Mississippi into Louisiana and proceeded as far as Washita river and captured Ft. Beauregard. The fort was six miles from Natchez and our boys made the trip there and back in five days.

August 2 (Sunday)

The weather was warm and fair over Richmond but the pall of gloom was everywhere; the people were disheartened. After Gettysburg and Vicksburg came the loss of Port Hudson and now the major threat to Charleston. The hospitals around the city were still full of the wounded from Gettysburg and the Peninsula operations. Food was still scarce and costly. Perhaps things would get better soon.

Admiral D.D. Porter had assumed command of the Mississippi River and was in New Orleans:

> ...The wharves of New Orleans have a most desolate appearance, and the city looks less thriving than it did when I was last here, a year since. It is hoped that facilities will be afforded for the transportation of produce from above. Almost everything is wanted, and provisions are very high.... I think we have arrived at a stage... when trade and commerce should be encouraged. With trade, prosperity will again commence to enter this once flourishing city, and a better state of feeling be brought about.

August 3 (Monday)

In Mississippi, the baked earth gave no relief to Sherman and his men. They were now in camps awaiting dispersal to various installations in western Mississippi and eastern Louisiana as occupation troops. This was directly contrary to Grant's wishes. His plan was to keep the army together and aim for Mobile (not all that far away) and assault that place from the land side while the Navy came from the sea. Halleck, ever the defensive thinker, had other plans, and he was the senior officer in the Army.

President Davis issued what was, in effect, an act of amnesty by requesting that all absentees return to their regiments. Desertion in Lee's army was reaching dramatic proportions. One man, living along the James River east of Richmond, reported more than one thousand, mostly North Carolinian, soldiers crossing there heading for home.

August 5 (Wednesday)

In the west, Sherman's Fifteenth Corps was still intact, but perhaps not for long. The Ninth Corps had been ordered to Kentucky for garrison duty, effectively dismantling the corps as a fighting unit. Sherman was more concerned about the use of Negroes in the army at this time. He did not believe that the Negro would make a good soldier. He was skeptical about the value of the Negro to the army and in a letter to his wife Ellen he said, "... I cannot trust them yet." Although the countryside was alive with freed Negroes who had left their old homes and now wandered about stealing food and causing mischief, Sherman would have nothing to do with the problem.

On the James River above Dutch Gap, Va., an electrically detonated torpedo was set off a few seconds too early by an overeager Confederate of the Submarine Battery Service. Had he waited, he would surely have blown the bottom out of the U.S.S. *Commodore Barney*, commanded by Acting Lt. Samuel Huse. In the words of one observer, the explosion produced "a lively concussion" and washed the decks "with agitated water." About 20 men were either swept or jumped overboard, two of whom were not found and presumed drowned. The explosion stopped the Federals' progress upriver for the time being.

At Charleston Harbor, a detachment of Marines, sent down by Secretary of the Navy Gideon Welles to Admiral Dahlgren, arrived. This detachment was rapidly augmented with Marines from the fleet at Charleston and Port Royal and the command was given to Maj. Jacob Zeilin, USMC, and the detachment was sent ashore on Morris Island.

Off Table Bay, Cape of Good Hope, South Africa, the C.S.S. *Alabama*, Capt. Semmes, captured the bark *Sea Bride* with a load of provisions. The capture was watched by a cheering crowd ashore who cheered for the skill, pluck and daring of the *Alabama* and her crew. The ship was later sold to an English merchant—after Semmes had restocked his larder (of course).

August 6 (Thursday)

At Fairfax C.H., Va., John S. Mosby captured a Union wagon train, getting off scot-free with the goods, leaving the Union troops behind.

John Singleton Mosby was born near Richmond, Va., on December 6, 1833. He attended the University of Virginia until he was imprisoned for shooting another student. While incarcerated, he became interested in the law, and he pursued a legal career. At the beginning of the war he was practicing law in Bristol, Va., where he joined a local cavalry company. He served at First Manassas and was then assigned to Stuart's cavalry as a scout. He later became a famous partisan ranger, creating havoc in northern Virginia and on the "northern neck" of Virginia. He was wounded seven times during the war and was mentioned in Lee's reports more often than any other officer in the army. He surrendered 12 days after Lee and began a law practice in Warrenton, Va. He later supported Reconstruction and was declared an outcast and turncoat by the South. His law practice fell off, and he was often found on the streets of Washington, D.C., in need of food and money. He died in Warrenton on May 30, 1916.

August 7 (Friday)

Confederate Secretary of the Navy Mallory sent notification of promotion to Commander to Lt. Maffitt of the C.S.S. *Florida*, with date of rank to April 29, 1863. Maffitt had been a very successful commerce raider so far, but he was in ill health.

At Charleston, Gen. P.G.T. Beauregard asked that the *H.L. Hunley*, a true submersible fashioned from a cylindrical iron steam boiler, be sent to him from Mobile. The *Hunley*, with tapered ends front and back, was 40 feet long, 3½ feet wide, and 4 feet deep. She carried a crew of nine—one to steer and eight to work the hand-cranked propeller.

August 8 (Saturday)

In Virginia, President Davis rejected an offer by Gen. Robert E. Lee to resign as commander of the Army of Northern Virginia. Lee cited the criticism on his defeat at Gettysburg. He wrote Davis: "... in all sincerity, request your excellency to take measures to supply my place." Many cited Lee's general health and depression for his offer to resign.

August 10 (Monday)

Admiral Farragut arrived in New York City from his squadron off Mobile Bay. He was welcomed back by Secretary of the Navy Gideon Welles. Welles's accolades were followed by those of a group of New York businessmen who also sent a letter of tribute to Farragut:

> The whole country, but especially this commercial metropolis, owes you a large debt of gratitude for the skill and dauntless bravery with which, during a long life of public duty, you have illustrated and maintained the maritime rights of the nation, and also for the signal ability, judgment, and courtesy with which, in concert with other branches of the loyal national forces, you have sustained the authority of the government, and recovered and defended national territory.

In the west, Grant's army was being broken up even more. Sherman's Fifteenth Corps was being sent to Louisiana, where it would perform garrison duty. Neither Grant nor Sherman was happy.

Barber, Cpl., Co. D, 15th Illinois Volunteer Infantry, Natchez, Miss.:

> My health still continued poor. I went back to the company, but was still kept on the sick list. I reported for duty but was not accepted and all the while I was at Natchez, I did not do any military duty except voluntarily.

While many suppliers were gouging the Confederate government for supplies, the state of South Carolina froze the prices paid for state supplies at about 30 percent of the market price.

August 11 (Tuesday)

In one big blast, the Confederate guns at Ft. Sumter, James Island, and Battery Wagner near Charleston opened fire on the Union entrenchments on Morris Island. The firing stopped work for a period of time, but not for long. Also at Charleston, Admiral Dahlgren was becoming frustrated with the harbor defenses, which were formidable. He described them as a "continuous line of works" extending from Ft. Moultrie on the right to Ft. Johnson on the left. Ft. Ripley, supported by C.S.S. *Chicora*, *Charleston*, and *Palmetto State*, and

Castle Pinckney were to the right beyond Moultrie. A line of piles had been driven into the harbor in front of Ft. Ripley, with rope obstructions and anchored torpedoes.

August 12 (Wednesday)

Quite a haul was taken by the U.S.S. *Princess Royal*, Commander Woolsey, when the British schooner *Flying Scud* was taken at Brazos, Tex. The *Flying Scud* had run the blockade with 65,000 pounds of powder, 7 tons of horseshoes, and many medical supplies.

On Morris Island near Charleston, the Union had installed heavy-calibre Parrott rifled guns for the assault on Charleston and Ft. Sumter. The calibration (determining the ranges for firing) began on August 12 with firing on Ft. Sumter, causing damage to the fort's brick outer walls.

The first contingent of the Union Ninth Corps arrived at Covington, Ky., across the Ohio from Cincinnati, where it was loaded on trains bound for eastern Tennessee.

In one of the greater justices of the war, Lincoln refused to give Major Gen. John A. McClernand a new command. McClernand, a political general, had been relieved from command by Grant during the siege of Vicksburg.

Day, Pvt., Co. B, 25th Massachusetts Volunteer Infantry, Hill's Point, N.C.:

> A few days ago orders came to get ready for inspection the next afternoon. ... The artillerists worked like beavers, cleaning up the gun carriages and limbers, using all the grease in the kitchen to brighten them up. The old brass guns were polished up and shone like mirrors....
>
> At the appointed time, Lieut. Col. Moulton and Capt. Rawlston, of somebody's staff, put in an appearance. The captain was the inspecting officer; a very airy, pompous young gentlemen, with a remarkable faculty of making his weak points conspicuous. When the companies fell in, he noticed the artillery detail did not fall in and inquired the reason. Col. Moulton replied that they were expecting to be inspected as artillery. The captain said he knew nothing about that, he was sent here to inspect this detachment as infantry and every man must fall in....
>
> We were marched out and paraded, and after the inspecting officer had "sassed" Col. Moulton and nearly all the other officers, he commenced his job. He found right smart of fault, but didn't find a really good subject until he came to me. He looked me over, and taking Spitfire, gave it a very careful and thorough inspection. Handing it back he gravely informed me that he had inspected the whole army of the Potomac and never before seen a rifle looking so bad as Spitfire, and further complimented me by saying I was about the roughest looking sergeant he had ever seen. I nodded assent, venturing the remark that I had been in the artillery detail while here and my rifle had been somewhat neglected, but I had a gun on the Malakoff that could knock the spots off the sun. He allowed that that was insolence and any more of it would subject me to arrest. Imagine the indignation of the chief of artillery on being threatened with arrest by an infantry captain. My first impulse was to call my command, lash him to the muzzle of the gun on the Malakoff and give him rapid transit over the tops of the pines, but better thoughts soon succeeded and I forgave him, thinking that perhaps he was doing as well as he knew how.
>
> The inspection over, he had not long to stay, as the boat was waiting for him. I noticed the officers didn't pet him very much and I don't believe he got more than one drink....

August 15 (Saturday)

At Charleston, the submarine *H.L. Hunley* arrived at the harbor on two covered railroad flatcars. Gen. Beauregard, in charge of the Charleston defenses, believed that he had the most formidable weapon he could get to destroy the Union fleet. Brig. Gen. Jordan announced that a reward of $100,000 would be paid by John Fraser and Co. for the destruction of the new U.S.S. *Ironsides*, or for the wooden frigate U.S.S. *Wabash*. Half that amount would be paid for the sinking of any *Monitor*-type gunboat.

A five-day Federal search for Mosby began towards Aldie and Centreville, Va.

August 16 (Sunday)

The big Union Parrott rifled guns on Morris Island kept up a bombardment of Ft. Sumter in the harbor, destroying more of the fort's outer works.

On the Stono River near Charleston, the Confederates floated torpedoes down into the Union fleet blockading the harbor. One such torpedo exploded about midnight when it hit a launch being towed by the U.S.S. *Pawnee*, Commander Balch, barely missing the ship. About 4 A.M., another exploded within 30 yards of the ship and another two shortly thereafter. Two torpedoes were retrieved by a Federal mortar schooner, and the *Pawnee* captured a boat that could hold ten of these devices. Admiral Dahlgren took immediate action, and within ten days a net was placed across the river to catch the torpedoes.

Rosecrans finally moved from the vicinity of Tullahoma, Tenn., towards Chattanooga at about the same time that Burnside left Louisville for eastern Tennessee. Rosecrans had delayed, citing the need to gather the crops into his commissary from the surrounding countryside before leaving.

August 17 (Monday)

Admiral Dahlgren renewed the attack on Charleston's defenses using both ironclads and the Union guns on Morris Island. A naval battery previously placed ashore on Mossie Island fired some 300 rounds, mostly at Ft. Sumter, striking the Fort's face or parapet. In all, more than 930 shells were fired at Sumter. Dahlgren's Chief of Staff, Capt. G.W. Rodgers, was killed during the engagement by a shot from Ft. Wagner.

The Chickamauga campaign opened with its first skirmish at Calfkiller Creek, near Sparta, Tenn. Rosecrans moved slowly towards Chattanooga.

Nothing ever seemed to be done right. The Chief Ordnance Officer for Gen. Lee wrote that the ammunition received from Richmond must always be tested before it could be distributed, since some of the artillery shells would not fit the guns.

August 19 (Wednesday)

In New York City the draft was resumed without much difficulty, after the disastrous and deadly riots last month that killed or wounded almost 100 people.

A Confederate signal station near Jacksonville, Fla., was destroyed by boat crews from the U.S.S. *Norwich* and *Hale*, under the command of Acting Master Charles F. Mitchell. The commander of the *Norwich*, Acting Master Frank B. Meriam, reported:

> The capture of this signal station will either break up this end of the line or it will detain here to protect the troops, five small companies (about 200 men) of infantry, two full companies of cavalry, and one company of artillery, that I learn are about being forwarded to Richmond.

August 20 (Thursday)

The guns on Morris Island and the blockading fleet were pounding Sumter again, the fourth straight day of bombardment. The mayor of Charleston requested that the Confederate government send the South Carolinian troops in Lee's army back to the state to "defend their native soil" and that Jenkin's Brigade of South Carolinians also be sent to Charleston for defense of the city. The states' rights issue was not dead. The Southern states would resist their central government to the last breath.

Rosecrans's Army of the Cumberland had reached the Tennessee River east of Chattanooga, where Bragg was holed up awaiting action. Bragg was reluctant to go on the offensive, since he had only 40,000 effectives, according to him, and Rosecrans had nearly 60,000, with Burnside coming down with about 30,000 more. The 2.5-to-1 odds didn't look too good. In Richmond, Samuel Cooper, the former Adjutant General of the U.S. Army, now the senior general in the Confederate Army, suggested to President Davis that Bragg be *ordered* to attack. Davis declined.

Barber, Cpl., Co. D, 15th Illinois Volunteer Infantry, Natchez, Miss.:

> We built a square frame four or five feet high, boarded it up and set our tent on top. On one side we built our bunks, one above the other. This left over half of the tent for spare room. We had a writing table and several camp stools. In one corner was a door and in the other a cozy fire-place with the chimney built on the outside. Just as we had got the chimney built, Captain Smith notified me that my name had been sent in for a furlough, but perhaps it would be several weeks before it got around.

August 21 (Friday)

During the night, in the channel near Morris Island at Charleston, Pilot James Carlin, a former blockade runner, took a small steamer (built of the hulk of an unfinished gunboat), painted it gray, and with engines of dubious worth, burning anthracite coal so no smoke would be seen, sailed out to torpedo the U.S.S. *New Ironsides*, which was anchored in the channel. About 40 yards away from the ironclad, Carlin ordered the engines cut off and pointed the steamer at the ironclad. However, the steamer's helm would not answer, and as the ironclad swung at anchor, Carlin's torpedo failed to make contact, and Carlin came alongside the Federal ship. Finding that his engines wouldn't start, Carlin carried on a conversation with the Officer of the Deck on the *New Ironsides*, while that officer was fuming that he couldn't depress his guns enough to fire on Carlin. About this time the contrary engines started. Carlin made all speed away from the Union gunboat, followed by two shots from the Federal ship that hit the water 20 feet on either side of the little steamer.

Brig. Gen. Q.A. Gilmore on Morris Island demanded the surrender of Charleston or he would continue the bombardment and next time include the city. The Confederates refused to surrender and the firing went on for the fifth straight day.

In one of the more tragic and senseless acts of the war, William C. Quantrill, an outlaw and self-appointed Southern officer, raided Lawrence, Kans., burning the town, looting the stores and people's purses, and murdering many of the men in a wanton slaughter that served no useful purpose. Quantrill's raiders murdered about 150 men and boys and destroyed about $1,500,000 worth of property.

In Tennessee, Union troops were close enough to throw artillery shells into Chattanooga. There was skirmishing between the forces in eastern Tennessee near the city.

August 22 (Saturday)

After five days of intense bombardment of Forts Wagner, Sumter, and Gregg, Admiral Dahlgren ordered an assault on Sumter at night. Unfortunately, the U.S.S. *Passaic* grounded near the fort, and it took so much time to get her off and afloat that the attack was called off before daylight.

At about 1:30 that morning a shell landed in the city of Charleston, S.C., terrifying the residents. This was a present from Maj. Gen. Quincy A. Gillmore's "Swamp Angel," a large siege gun mounted on Morris Island. A total of 16 shells were fired during the morning, 12 filled with "greek fire." St. Michael's Church steeple was used as the aiming point for the gun, and the church was hit several times, but the steeple still stood. Confederate Gen. Pierre G.T. Beauregard, currently in command of the city, sent an angry message to Gillmore, castigating him for firing on innocent civilians. The British and Spanish consuls in the city also sent messages asking that the bombardment be stopped. Gillmore declined.

In the Hatteras area of North Carolina, Acting Ensign Joseph S. Cony showed his leadership qualities while leading two boat crews on a raid in New Topsail Inlet. About August 12th, Lt. Cushing, U.S.S. *Shokoken*, spotted the schooner *Alexander Cooper* in the harbor of the Inlet. He decided to destroy the schooner using a little strategy. He sent two boats ashore, Cony in command, where they carried one of the boats across the neck of land to the inlet. They then assaulted the *Alexander Cooper* while she was at anchor and burned her to the waterline. They also destroyed extensive saltworks in the area and took three prisoners back to the ship.

In Tennessee, Rosecrans's Army of the Cumberland drew closer to Chattanooga as President Davis tried to round up some reinforcements for Bragg.

In Richmond, all of the clerks in the city post office had resigned in a wage dispute with the government. No mail was being delivered, some of which might have been important to the war effort.

August 23 (Sunday)

Admiral Dahlgren bombarded the Confederate batteries on Ft. Moultrie early in the morning after those batteries fired on the fleet that was firing on Ft. Sumter. A fog set in, obscuring the targets for both protagonists, so firing was stopped. The firing on Ft. Sumter had taken its toll. The outer walls of the fort were a shambles, and only one gun was capable of being fired. All told, over 5000 artillery shells had been fired at the defenses of the city in seven days.

Down on Morris Island, near Charleston, S.C., the "Swamp Angel" fired again on the city. Another 20 of the "greek fire" shells were fired, some of them exploding inside the gun. On the 36th round, the breech was blown out of the gun and it was rendered inoperable. The gun was buried in sandbags at the site until after the war, when it was moved to Trenton, N.J., and placed on display.

On August 12th, Lt. Wood, CSN, had departed Richmond with 4 boats on wheels and 80 Confederate volunteers. Four days later, the boats were launched 25 miles up the Piankatank River and were then rowed downriver to the Bay. For a week Wood played hide-and-seek with Union ships, trying to find any such ship in an exposed position. About 1 A.M., on August 23, two ships were found anchored close to each other, the *Reliance* and the *Satellite.* Wood quickly boarded and captured the two ships and took them up the Rappahannock River to Urbanna, Va. Both ships were low on coal and bad weather prevented Wood from doing anything for two days.

August 24 (Monday)

The Confederate submarine *H.L. Hunley* used a unique approach to torpedo a ship. The sub would dive beneath the ship while towing a floating copper-cylinder torpedo some 200 feet astern. When the submarine was safely under the ship, she would surface and go forward until the torpedo struck the target and exploded. A problem arose concerning her attack on the U.S.S. *New Ironsides.* There was not enough water beneath the target for the submarine to safely pass. The new plan was to affix a 90-pound spar torpedo to the bow of the submarine which would explode when it hit the ship.

August 25 (Tuesday)

Lt. Wood, the Confederate officer who had captured the two steamers on the 23d and had taken them to Urbanna, Va., now used the captured *Satellite* to seize the schooners *Golden Rod* (loaded with coal), and the *Coquette* and *Two Brothers,* both loaded with cargoes of anchors and anchor chain, at the mouth of the Rappahannock River. The *Golden Rod* drew too much water to go upriver, so she was burned after the coal was removed and the schooner stripped. The other two were taken to Port Royal, where all three of the ships were stripped and burned.

There was considerable skirmishing in Missouri and Arkansas. As a result of the raid on Lawrence, Kans., on the 21st, Union Brig. Gen. Thomas Ewing, son of the U.S. Senator from Ohio and adopted brother of Gen. W.T. Sherman, issued an order for the people living in Jackson, Cass and Bates counties, Mo., to leave their homes and the area. Those who could prove loyalty to the Union could remain at military posts, all others must leave. About 20,000 people around Kansas City lost their homes as the houses, barns, and crops were destroyed. This had little effect on Quantrill, but it caused deep bitterness against the Union for decades after.

August 26 (Wednesday)

Secretary of the Navy Gideon Welles requested that Admiral Dahlgren send weekly status reports along with sketches of the damage done by the Confederate guns on the ironclads. He wrote:

> These reports and sketches are important to the Bureau and others concerned to enable them to understand correctly and provide promptly for repairing the damages; and frequently measures for improving the ironclads are suggested by them.

Again the Federals assaulted the rifle pits in front of Battery Wagner, this time capturing them. Now the Union was directly outside the fort.

August 27 (Thursday)

Gen. John Buchanan Floyd, CSA, died this day. The defender of Ft. Donelson, who had escaped from that place on a steamer with most of his brigade (leaving Gen. Simon Bolivar Buckner to surrender the post), went on to Nashville, which he also abandoned. For deserting his command in the face of the enemy, he was relieved by President Davis. He then became a major general in the Virginia militia and served in southwestern Virginia, where he tried to raise a band of guerrillas (he called them partisans). He also spent time harassing both the Union forces in the area and the Confederate recruiting officers who were trying to get men into the Confederate Army. His health finally gave out, and he died near Abingdon at the age of 57.

Very little firing was done at Morris Island on August 27. A previous act of the Confederate Congress decreed that any Union officer who was captured by the Confederacy who had commanded Negro troops would be executed. President Davis declined to order the execution of some of the captives, and, instead, ordered them held indefinitely, without exchange.

Jackman, Pvt., "The Orphan Brigade," en route to Mobile, Ala.:

> All on the train by 10 A.M. and moved off for Meridian where we arrived—the train ran very slowly—at 8 P.M.. Immediately changed cars for Mobile. Train running all night.

August 28 (Friday)

In the shipyard above Mobile Bay, the Confederacy was building two ships, the C.S.S. *Tennessee* and *Nashville*. Lt. George W. Gift, CSN, wrote of his visit to the shipyard and his observations:

> She [the *Nashville*] is of immense proportions and will be able to ship any Yankee craft afloat—when she is finished.... She is tremendous! Her officer's quarters are completed. The wardroom, in which I am most interested, is six staterooms and a pantry long, and about as broad between the rooms as the whole *Chattahoochee*. Her engines are tremendous, and it requires all her width, fifty feet, to place her boilers. She is to have side wheels. The *Tennessee* is insignificant alongside her. She... will mount fourteen guns....

Jackman, Pvt., "The Orphan Brigade," Mobile, Ala.:

> Just as the sun was coming up could look down the long vista of pines and see the tall chimneys of manufactories in the city sending up their inky columns of smoke. Soon we were at the depot and immediately moved to the steamer *Natchez*. Though we did not stay long in the city, yet some of the boys had time enough to get on a "bender." Mobile looks about the same as it did a year ago when we passed through. The steamer have us out and on the Bay and up the Tensaw where we landed at the terminus of the Montgomery railroad. Disembarked and bivouacked half a mile from the landing. The day pleasant and the scenery on the Bay beautiful. Right where we are camped there are no pine trees which is quite a relief. The land is a little hilly and looks to be productive.

August 29 (Saturday)

In Charleston Harbor, the submarine *H.L. Hunley* had taken several practice dives and was tied up alongside the steamer *Etiwan* at the dock at Ft. Johnson when the steamer pulled away from the dock unexpectedly, turning the *Hunley* on her side. She filled with water immediately and sank, drowning five of the crewmen. Two escaped, including the commander, Lt. Payne. Five crewmen volunteered immediately to man the submarine when it was raised.

Jackman, Pvt., "The Orphan Brigade," en route to Montgomery, Ala.:

> Took cars for Montgomery at 3 P.M.. Got to Pollard, touching a corner of Florida, at sundown. Have been in the pines again for miles. Dark setting in, swung my hammock across the car and went to sleep.

August 30 (Sunday)

The Confederates at Ft. Moultrie in Charleston Harbor fired on and sank one of their own transports, a case of mistaken identity. The Union batteries on Morris Island opened bombardment again today while the Confederates dug the guns out of the rubble at Ft. Sumter and moved them to Charleston.

Jackman, Pvt., "The Orphan Brigade," en route to Atlanta, Ga.:

> Waked up at daylight and looking out the car saw we were still being whirled through the pine forests. I judge from this that nothing but pines grow by the road its entire length. At sunrise got into Montgomery, having been transported 162 miles by rail since leaving Mobile. Immediately got off the cars and moved through the city to the West Point Depot and bivouacked in a pine grove on the common waiting for transportation. Sunday and the church bells are ringing merrily—reminds me of peaceful days.... Tonight all the boys are in the city [to] have a general spree, Johnnie G. and all that are left in camp.

August 31 (Monday)

Jackman, Pvt., "The Orphan Brigade," en route to Atlanta, Ga.:

> At 8 A.M. moved off on a train for West Point where we arrived without incident at 4 P.M. At 7, changed cars and arrived at La Grange where we had to lay over from 10 until 1 o'clock. The depot at L.

was thronged with ladies with nice provisions for us. I was asleep when the train stopped and was waked up by a boy shoving a broiled chicken into my face with other nice things to eat. I looked out at the platform in front of the depot where there was such a jam of white crinoline and such a chattering of women I thought at first I was in another world. We had a fine time as the ladies staid at the depot until midnight. We found refugees from Ky. and all parts of the south among them.

SEPTEMBER 1863

The war in eastern Tennessee was beginning to warm up considerably. Bragg, in the Chattanooga area, was facing Rosecrans's Army of the Cumberland, currently in eastern Alabama and coming up slowly. The great natural amphitheatre around Chattanooga, the next arena of war, had an interesting history.

Prior to 1838, the city was called Ross's Landing. During that year a meeting was held to rename the town and the names "Lookout City" and "Chattanooga" were proposed. The name finally chosen was taken from the little Indian village situated at the base of the mountain. In the Creek Indian language the name "Chatto-to-noo-gee" meant "Rock coming to a point" or "End of the Mountain," which perfectly described the Point of Lookout Mountain. In 1838, the town supported three hotels and there was a large body of U.S. soldiers in town managing more than 2000 Cherokee Indians who were being quartered in the area. By 1853, the city had subscribed to a railroad to be built to the area to the sum of $600,000—quite a sum in those times. In June 1857, the first hotel opened on Lookout Mountain, a structure of four stories with wide verandas and surrounding cottages for guests who stayed the summer with their servants. The 1860 census shows Chattanooga with a population of 2546, of whom 451 were Negroes.

The first newspaper, *The Hamilton County Gazette*, was established in 1838 when the equipment was brought to town on a flatboat. The first paper was printed on the boat, which was moored under the shade of a great oak tree on the riverbank. The paper later evolved its name to *The Chattanooga Gazette*, and finally, just *The Gazette*. In 1861 *The Gazette* was published by James Hood, and the content was violently partisan against secession.

In 1862 *The Chattanooga Daily Rebel*, a strongly pro-Southern newspaper, came into being, but lasted for only two years. While it lived it enjoyed a great circulation, printing several thousand copies a day, which were sent to places like Tullahoma, where the Confederate Army was encamped.

Other than in Charleston, things were fairly quiet. Grant's army was being taken apart by Halleck and scattered to the winds, sent to garrison duty in Louisiana, Mississippi, Tennessee, and Kentucky. A good part of the Ninth Corps was sent to Burnside, who now was on his way to the Chattanooga area to lend a little weight to Rosecrans's assault. Meade was sitting quietly near Warrenton, Va., occasionally swatting at pesky guerrillas such as Mosby, who persisted in nibbling at him. The Confederacy lived.

September 1 (Tuesday)

Major Gen. Steele's Union forces continued operations against Little Rock, Ark., while in the western part of the state, Ft. Smith was occupied by another Federal force after being abandoned by Confederate Brig. Gen. William L. Cabell. This station would remain in Federal hands for the remainder of the war.

With the defense of Mobile, Ala., in mind, Commander Catesby ap R. Jones, CSN, who was in charge of the naval gun foundry and ordnance works at Selma, Ala., ordered a quantity of munitions sent to Admiral Franklin Buchanan. The quantity was small because most supplies were destined for the defense of Charleston.

Off Wilmington, N.C., Admiral Lee instructed the Federal Blockading Squadron to determine their night positions and to ensure that they were under steam and moving one hour before daylight so that the blockade runners couldn't determine where the blockaders had anchored during the night. Most of the blockade runners made their run at dusk or just at dawn, when visibility was bad.

Late at night, Admiral Dahlgren took the ironclads of the South Blockading Squadron, led by his flagship U.S.S. *Weehawken*, against Ft. Sumter. The bombardment lasted for five hours into the morning of the 2d. The Confederate guns on Ft. Moultrie kept up a constant fire on the fleet, scoring over 70 hits on the ironclads. One hit on the *Weehawken* struck the turret, and drove a piece of iron into the leg of Capt. Oscar C. Badger, severely wounding him. This was the third Flag Capt. Dahlgren had lost in two months.

Near Chattanooga, Rosecrans's Army of the Cumberland was crossing the Tennessee River to prepare for the assault on Bragg's army at Chattanooga. Gov. Isham Harris, a governor without a state, was informed by President Davis that reinforcements were being sent to Bragg.

Jackman, Pvt., "The Orphan Brigade," Atlanta, Ga.:

> Arrived at Atlanta 9 A.M. and without changing cars left for Chattanooga at 11 A.M.. Got off the train 13 miles from Chattanooga 11 o'clock at night and slept until morning on the side of the railroad.

September 2 (Wednesday)

Union Gen. Ambrose E. Burnside easily took Knoxville, Tenn., thus blocking any direct communications between Tennessee and Virginia. His presence in the area was in support of Rosecrans's operations against Chattanooga.

In Charleston Harbor the guns were almost silent, with the Union troops entrenched only eighty yards from the outer works of Battery Wagner. The Union troops had taken the Confederate rifle pits after a second try, the first being repulsed. Brig. Gen. G.J. Rains wrote to Richmond from Charleston that the grenades reported by the enemy to have been so destructive in their first repulse at Battery Wagner were his subterra shells, there being no hand grenades used.

Gabriel James Rains was an interesting individual. An 1827 graduate of West Point, he was brevetted for gallantry in Mexico and was a lieutenant colonel of the 5th Infantry when the war started. He resigned from the U.S. Army a few days after the first Bull Run in July 1861, after 34 years of service. He was appointed a brigadier general in the Confederate forces on September 23, 1861, at the age of 58. He was the inventor of land mines, burying 8- or 10-inch Columbiad shells underground set to detonate when stepped on or moved. Neither army, North or South, liked these "subterra shells" as they were called, considering them unethical weapons. Over the protests of the local commanders, Rains received permission to plant his mines in the approaches to fortifications in Richmond, Mobile, Charleston, and the James River. He survived the war and died in Aiken, S.C., on August 6, 1881.

September 3 (Thursday)

There were problems with some of the 27,000 men paroled from Vicksburg. After having been given a thirty-day furlough by Gen. Pemberton to go home, many of them had not returned to the control of the Confederate Army. Nor had they been exchanged, and therefore they could not legally be used in combat. Gen. Joseph E. Johnston proposed to keep the paroled men in eastern Mississippi for use when their paroles were accomplished.

In England there had been much controversy about British shipbuilders providing ships to the Confederacy, an act the United States government felt was a violation of the neutrality which England proclaimed. There were two ironclad rams being constructed at Birkenhead, and Lord Russell finally came down on the side of the Union by ordering the rams to be kept in port.

September 4 (Friday)

Rosecrans's Army of the Cumberland was across the Tennessee River and forming for the assault on Bragg. The latter was now faced with Union forces from two directions, Burnside coming from Knoxville.

Gen. Grant, an excellent horseman, was riding in New Orleans when his horse shied and fell on him. His injuries would keep him incapacitated for some time, and on crutches for several weeks.

In New Orleans also, an expedition to capture and hold Sabine Pass, Tex., was getting underway. The Navy would supply the gunboats U.S.S. *Clifton*, *Arizona*, and *Granite City* with the steamer *Sachem*, all under the command of Acting Volunteer Lt. Amos Johnson. The gunboats, with about 180 Army sharpshooters aboard, would make the assault and drive the defenders from their positions with their guns. Sabine Pass in Federal hands would go far to strengthen the Union position in that area.

Confederate Major Gen. Jeremy F. Gilmer asked Secretary of the Navy Mallory for as many sailors as Mallory could get to help man the oars to convey troops and matériel to and from Morris Island. The Union batteries and gunboats had been pounding Ft. Wagner and Cumming's Point so badly that the crews had to be exchanged every three days.

It was reported that defection was spreading in North Carolina. In Wilkes County, Gideon Smoot, commander of the insurgents, was reported to have raised the United States flag at the county courthouse.

September 5 (Saturday)

In England a crisis developed when the U.S. Minister to England, Charles Francis Adams, told Lord Russell that if the "Laird Rams" were released to the Confederacy, "it would be superfluous for me to point out to your Lordship that this is war." Russell, anticipating this and hoping to avoid the confrontation, had told the shipbuilders they could not release the ships two days earlier. The matter was closed.

In the early morning hours, small boats carrying Union troops were sent against Ft. Gregg at Cumming's Point, on Morris Island near Charleston. The troops were to have assaulted the fort and spiked the guns, thus permitting the gunboats to get close enough to reduce the fort. At the mouth of Vincent's Creek a boat containing a wounded Confederate was taken but the musket fire alerted the defenders at Ft. Gregg, so the attack was called off. Another attempt was made at dark, but the defenders were now alerted, so the idea was abandoned.

In eastern Alabama, Rosecrans moved into the mountains of northwestern Georgia, skirmishing at Lebanon and other points, on his way to Bragg at Chattanooga. Coming out of Knoxville, Burnside's troops were on the way to the Cumberland Gap, skirmishing near Tazewell, Tenn.

September 6 (Sunday)

During the night, Confederate forces secretly abandoned Morris Island by boat. The previous day, the 5th, one hundred of the nine hundred Confederate defenders of Ft. Wagner were killed in the bombardment by shore batteries and naval gunboats, in particular the U.S.S. *New Ironsides.* Wagner had been under assault for more than 60 days and it had been the subject of a terrible pounding for the past 36 hours. Nearly all the guns were disabled, the men exhausted, and the defenses were mostly destroyed. Beauregard, the commander of the Charleston defenses, ordered the evacuation. The Union attackers now had a full view of the city of Charleston.

At Sabine Pass, Tex., the supposedly secret mission to capture the place became an open secret, the Confederates being warned two days in advance that the Federals were coming.

At Chattanooga, Bragg was hoping his forces, which include the "Orphan Brigade," would be able to hold against both Rosecrans and Burnside.

September 7 (Monday)

With Morris Island evacuated, Admiral Dahlgren demanded the surrender of Ft. Sumter, which by that time was a pile of rubble. Dahlgren described its appearance as "from seaward was rather that of a steep, sandy island than that of a fort." Beauregard declined to surrender the fort and replied for him to "... take it if he could." Dahlgren then ordered the U.S.S. *Weehawken,* Commander Colhoun, to a position between Cumming's Point on Morris Island and Sumter, where the Weehawken ran aground. Soon after, as evening came, the U.S.S. *New Ironsides, Nahant, Lehigh, Montauk,* and *Patapsco* heavily engaged the guns at Ft. Moultrie, drawing fire away from the *Weehawken.* Darkness closed the contest.

Below Chattanooga, Rosecrans advanced on Bragg's lines, bringing contact at Stevenson, Ala.

Jackman, Pvt., "The Orphan Brigade," Chickamauga Station, Ga.:

> At noon today Col. C. came back with orders to move the baggage of the division to Chickamauga station to be shipped to the rear. We had to be in a hurry too for our army having left Chattanooga early this morning there is danger of being "gobbled." We had no wagons to move with and had to "press" some in the country. Being appointed by the Col. to take charge of the affairs, I sent two good fellows from our regiment out to press wagons and had the other regiments to do likewise. Soon our boys came back with an old ox wagon which we kept busy hauling to the station, 2 miles, until dark. By that time all the "sick, lame, halt and blind" of the division were at the depot and mountains of baggage. Had to telegraph for a train of cars to come up for us while it may not come until tomorrow evening, or next day. This place is now uncovered and in all probability we'll

be "gobbled" yet. When the last load was hauled we honorably discharged "Pompey" and his ox team.

September 8 (Tuesday)

Early in the morning, the U.S.S. *Weehawken*, stranded on a sandbar between Cumming's Point on Morris Island and Ft. Sumter, was taken under heavy fire from Ft. Moultrie and the guns on James and Sullivan's Islands. *Weehawken* replied as best she could. The U.S.S. *New Ironsides* came to the rescue, positioning herself between the stranded ship and Ft. Moultrie, firing furiously at the fort. While tugs pulled the *Weehawken* off, the *New Ironsides* was struck over 50 times, finally retiring because she ran out of ammunition. A gallant fight.

The operation at Sabine Pass, Tex., was a disaster. The attack was led by the U.S.S. *Clifton*, which had her wheel rope shot away and was disabled under the defenders' guns. After having 10 men killed, the captain surrendered the vessel. The *Sachem* was totally disabled by a shot through her boilers. The other gunships recrossed the bar and headed back to New Orleans.

The Chickamauga Campaign opened with fighting at Winston's Gap, Ala., and at Alpine, Ga. In Virginia, Longstreet's corps was moving to the relief of Bragg at Chattanooga.

September 9 (Wednesday)

Beginning the night before, an assault by boat was made on Ft. Sumter, led by Commander Stevens. The attack comprised more than 30 boats with some 400 sailors and Marines. The defenders, having recovered a code book from the wreck of U.S.S. *Keokuk*, had read the signals and were ready for the attack. Holding their fire until the boats were nearly ashore, the defenders opened with a heavy fire and hand grenades. The C.S.S. *Chicora* provided a sweeping enfilading fire and, in the words of Admiral Dahlgren, "Moultrie fired like the devil, the shells breaking around us and screaming in chorus." That, effectively, destroyed the attack. More than 100 men were captured, and Ft. Sumter was still safe in Confederate hands.

Outflanked, Gen. Bragg evacuated Chattanooga, Tenn., without a struggle. Rosecrans's Army of the Cumberland immediately occupied the city, with part of his force probing into Georgia, looking for Bragg. Rosecrans had to get his troops collected, they being scattered over forty miles of roads coming into Chattanooga, and Bragg was only a few miles away.

Longstreet, on his way to assist Bragg, had to move his troops through North and South Carolina to Atlanta and then to northwest Georgia. The occupation of Knoxville by Burnside precluded a more direct route being used.

Jackman, Pvt., "The Orphan Brigade," Dalton, Ga.:

> All the troops gone this morning. At sunrise our train started down the road but being so heavy, when we got to Graysville—5 miles—the cars in which our brigade baggage is loaded left on the switch. Here Col. C. left me to "engineer" down the road as best I could. Late in the evening the last engine was passing and I got our cars on. We waited at Ringgold for the passenger train to leave, which was crowded with refugees. That night we ran down to Dalton.

September 10 (Thursday)

Ft. Sumter was not bombarded today. Things were not so quiet in northeast Alabama, northwest Georgia, and eastern Tennessee, as contact between Rosecrans's and Bragg's armies became more frequent, and the skirmishing heavier.

The editor of the Raleigh, N.C., *Standard* had been printing pro-Union and pro-peace articles that incensed the local Confederate troops, so they took his business apart. The soldiers were dispersed after they heard a speech from Gov. Vance, but shortly thereafter, a mob of *citizens* broke into the *Journal*, another Raleigh newspaper, which was ultra-secession, and partially destroyed that place. They were also spoken to by the governor. Seems that middle-of-the-road was the only safe position to take in Raleigh.

Major Gen. Frederick Steele and his Union troops took Little Rock, Ark., as the Confederates evacuated the city. Sterling Price's force withdrew towards Rockport and Arkadelphia, leaving Gen. Kirby Smith to face the Federals by himself. The gunboat support, the U.S.S. *Hastings*, Lt. Commander S.L. Phelps, arrived at Devall's Bluff on the White River, which was falling rapidly. Phelps thought about going over to Little Rock to congratulate Steele, but the horseback ride was a little more than he wanted to take. He went back downriver.

Jackman, Pvt., "The Orphan Brigade," Dalton, Ga.:

> At Dalton all day. Very hot and dusty. Sick—have something like a fever. There are so many cars here no telling when we shall get off. Dull. A man got his head shot off in a row during the evening which was a little variety. Slept on top of a car at night.

September 13 (Sunday)

In Rodney, Miss., twenty members of the crew of the U.S.S. *Rattler*, Acting Master Walter E.H. Fentress, were attending church when the service was interrupted by Confederate cavalry. The Yankee sailors were taken prisoner.

In Virginia, Lee had pulled back from Culpeper C.H. to the town of Orange and immediately the Union forces of Gen. Meade occupied Culpeper. Lee's withdrawal was linked to the movement of Longstreet's corps to Georgia to assist Bragg. There was skirmishing at Brandy Station, around Culpeper C.H., and other points in the area.

Grant was ordered to send all available men to the area around Chattanooga to assist Rosecrans, who was dealing with fighting around Lee and Gordon's Mills, and points from Henderson's Gap to La Fayette, Ga. Bragg had ordered Gen. Polk to attack Crittenden's corps at Lee and Gordon's Mills, but Polk failed to move.

September 16 (Wednesday)

In Georgia, Rosecrans concentrated his troops in the vicinity of Lee and Gordon's Mills, on the Chickamauga Creek, some 12 miles south of Chattanooga. The positions taken placed Crittenden at Gordon's Mills, Gen. Thomas to his right (further south), and Gen. Alexander McDowell on the right flank, near Alpine, Ga.

The Indian name *Tsikamagi* was the name given to two creeks, South and North Chickamauga. The South Chickamauga rises in Georgia and empties into the Tennessee River near the Brainerd section. Two battles were fought on this creek—the Chickamauga Expedition in April 1779, and the Battle of Chickamauga, which would be fought here three days hence. The tradition that "Chickamauga" in Indian means "River of Death" is unfounded. The name derived from a Chickasaw word, "Chucama," meaning good, and a Cherokee word, "Kah," meaning place, therefore "good place," and the name was probably applied to the area by a tribe of Indians called Chitimauca, who settled there sometime in 1721.

September 17 (Thursday)

Secretary of the Navy Gideon Welles wrote Secretary of War Stanton and requested a joint action to locate and destroy an ironclad said to be in the building stage on the Roanoke River. The ship, the C.S.S. *Albemarle*, was said to be nearing completion and it could present a hazard to shipping in the Albemarle Sound.

Rosecrans pulled his corps together from the right flank and now had his units in positions where they could support each other. Bragg had missed his chance to attack the isolated units and beat them piecemeal; now he had to deal with an entire army. As usual, now and later, Bragg blamed his corps commanders for the lapse and they, of course, blamed him. He would never have a good relationship with his subordinate officers. Bragg's intention was to turn Rosecrans's right flank and cut off the Union retreat to Chattanooga. Rosecrans understood the tactic and moved to counter it.

Jackman, Pvt., "The Orphan Brigade," Resaca, Ga.:

> To our great joy, Capt. W. of our regiment came down for all the officer's baggage and all that were able to go the regiment. This evening we came up to Resaca on the cars and loaded the baggage on a wagon in waiting and have footed it out 7 miles in the La Fayette road. We have a walk of 40 miles before us.

September 18 (Friday)

James Longstreet and his corps from the Army of Northern Virginia arrived at Bragg's location in Georgia early this morning, and Bragg wasted no time. He drove all but three of his divisions across West Chickamauga Creek from Ringgold with a part of Longstreet's corps. Heavy fighting broke out with Rosecrans's cavalry at Pea Vine Ridge, Dyer's Ford, Spring Creek, Stephen's Gap, and the bridges at Alexander and Reed.

Rosecrans moved Thomas's corps northeast around Crittenden to protect Rosecrans's flank on the left. All night the troops moved through temperatures that were almost freezing, down a dry, waterless road lined with fires to light the way, and to provide a little heat at the halts. They would not reach their new positions until dawn of the 19th, when Thomas reached the Kelly house. The Chickamauga wandered a lot, moving sluggishly and deep between steep, rocky banks that made the stream impossible to cross except at one of the many bridges.

Much of the area was a low growth of scrub oak, pine, cedar and dogwood, with an underbrush of honeysuckle, poison oak, briars, and other vines. Occasionally there was a clearing, or large trees with little or no brush. Farms were dotted throughout the area, although most of them were at bare subsistence level.

Going into battle, Rosecrans was outnumbered by about 7,000 men, the balance being Confederates, with the arrival of Longstreet.

In eastern Tennessee, Burnside's movements caused skirmishing at Calhoun, Cleveland, Kingsport, and Bristol, Tenn., on the border with Virginia.

Jackman, Pvt., "The Orphan Brigade," en route to Glass' Mill, Ga.:

> About noon came to the road leading off to where the wagon train is encamped we left the wagon and started for the regiment. Part of the time our road led over steep hills and had a very tiresome walk. In the evening a party of us left the main road to make a "near cut." There were 4 of us—Capt. W, 1st Seg't J.F. of his company, Dr. G., our Ass't Surg., and myself. We could hear the cannon booming occasionally. At night we stopped at a cabin on the road side and got a good supper then adjourned to a neighboring pine thicket where we passed the night nearly freezing as blankets were scarce.

September 19 (Saturday)

At Mobile, the inventor and builder of the submarine *H.L. Hunley*, Mr. Horace L. Hunley himself, wrote Gen. Beauregard at Charleston and requested that the submarine be turned over to his command:

> ...ose, if you will place the boat in my hands ...n a crew (in whole or in part) from Mobile who are well acquainted with its management & make the attempt to destroy a vessel of the enemy as early as practicable.

The orders were given and Mr. Hunley brought his crew from Mobile, and in a short time was ready for the attack.

Like two fighters stumbling around the ring blindfolded, Rosecrans and Bragg were unaware of the exact position of the opponent. Thomas was in position on the Union left, guarding the route to Chattanooga. Thomas sent part of his corps up to find the Confederates and the Union forces ran into the dismounted cavalry of Nathan Bedford Forrest, a poor choice of opponent, if you had a choice. The fighting became general, and by 2 P.M. the entire three-mile front was engaged. Bragg, attempting to cut the lines to Chattanooga, couldn't make any progress and casualties were heavy on both sides, but at dark the lines were in about the same location. As darkness settled and the fighting ceased, the troops on both sides were out looking for the wounded, for this was to be a cold night.

Jackman, Pvt., "The Orphan Brigade," Glass' Mill, Ga.:

> On the road early. Stopped at a well to wash and breakfast—a lady seeing us sent out some butter and milk. Five miles brought us to the regiment near Glass' Mill. The brigade had just crossed Chickamauga River at Glass' ford to support Cobb's and Slocum's batteries and the wickedest artillery duel ensued I ever saw. Slocum and Cobb had to "limber to the rear" and move their batteries back across the river. There were several of our regiment wounded—three afterwards died of their wounds. About the middle of the afternoon moved a mile or two further to the right and halted in line of battle sending out skirmish lines. While here we could hear the battle raging further to the right. Just before sundown our division again commenced moving to the right. At sundown and a little after dark the musketry rattled incessantly. I don't believe I ever heard heavier volleys of small arms. The word came back that Cleburn was driving the enemy on the right. Having to move 5 or 6 miles we continued our march until sometime after dark and the night being black we had a deal of trouble. We at last crossed the Chickamauga at Alexander's bridge and not far from the bridge we stopped

in an old field for the night. We built a large fire and yet not having any blankets with me I did not sleep any. The night was very cold and my large overcoat came in good place.

September 20 (Sunday)

Bragg, having placed Polk in command of the left flank of the army, and Longstreet the right, ordered an attack for dawn by Polk on the Union right. Dawn came and went and Polk didn't move until almost 8 A.M.; the attack didn't really get under way until about 9:30 A.M., when Breckinridge's division lunged forward with one of his brigades overlapping Thomas's exposed left flank. This was corrected with the arrival of more Union troops. The Union left fell back, but held. About noon, Longstreet came up opposite the Federal center and found a hole in the line. Union troops under Thomas J. Wood had been pulled out of the line and shifted to the left, leaving a wide gap that Longstreet immediately filled with Confederates, sending them howling into the Union rear, where units fled in panic. The only intact units remaining were controlled by Thomas, who formed a new line around a rise known locally as Snodgrass Hill. There Thomas held throughout the afternoon, repelling assault upon assault by the Confederates. The "Rock of Chickamauga" earned his nickname this day, fighting all afternoon against desperate men who were attacking his position. However, the Confederates could not bring enough troops to bear at any one time to take the hill, and as darkness came, the fighting ceased and the Confederates withdrew.

That night, Thomas, under orders, disengaged and withdrew towards Rossville on the way to Chattanooga, where he set up new defensive lines. The casualty rate for both sides was high—about 28 percent of the forces engaged. The Union casualties were 16,170, the Confederate slightly higher at 18,454. Bragg won the battle, but Rosecrans held Chattanooga.

The "Orphan Brigade" had made one last charge towards the end of the day that drove some of Thomas's men back, and the Brigade held the Union line. After playing the role of rear guard on retreats at Shiloh, Baton Rouge, Murfreesboro, and then Jackson, Miss., it felt good for a change. Breckinridge, ever fond of his old Brigade, exulted in its actions.

Jackman, Pvt., "The Orphan Brigade," Battle of Chickamauga, Ga.:

Before daylight the division moved to take position in line of battle. After we had stopped for the night the field band had been sent to the rear with the horses, and was not back in time so the Col. etc. had to "foot it." The Col. left me at the fire to tell the musicians where to bring the horses. Daylight came and a heavy frost was on the ground. I waited until long after sunup yet the drummers did not come; so I shouldered a long bundle of blankets—intended to put on the horses, and started for the regiment. I had to pass over the ground where Cleburn had fought the evening before. The dead of both sides were lying thick over the ground. I saw where six Federal soldiers had been killed from behind one small tree and where eight horses were lying dead—harnessed to a Napoleon gun. Men and horses were lying so thick over the field one could hardly walk for them. I even saw a large black dog that had been mangled by grape. In the rear of the brigade I found our ambulance and put the blankets in it then went on to the regiment. The boys were lying in line of battle and cracking jokes as usual. Many of them I noticed to be in the finest spirits were a few minutes afterwards numbered with the slain. All the time the skirmishers about two hundred yards in advance were very noisy. About 10 o'clock A.M. Maj. Wilson rode up to Gen'l. Helm, who was sitting against a tree in rear of our regiment talking to Col. C. and gave him the verbal order from Breckinridge to advance in fifteen minutes and adjust his movements to the brigade on the right. The General got up and mounted his horse, laughing and talking as though he was going on parade. I had intended to go along with the infirmary corps but as the drummers had not come up with the horses, Col. C. told me to go back and see if I could find them. I had not gone far before I came to a crowd of our boys that had been wounded on the skirmish line and as the shells were tearing up the ground about them, which makes a helpless man feel very uncomfortable, I helped put them in an ambulance and sent them to a hospital. I went a little further in hopes of finding the drummers but they were nowhere to be found. I then started back for the regiment. The rattle of musketry was kept up pretty lively. As I passed along over the field could see all the little gullies were packed full of straggling soldiers (but I saw none of our brigade among them) avoiding the shells. When I got to the regiment it was just falling back under a heavy fire having charged three times unsuccessfully. The regiment was greatly reduced—by half at least—Col. G. had been wounded. Out of our company my old friend J. H. had fallen with others and many had been wounded. Gen'l. Helm had received a mortal would and had to be borne to the hospital on a litter. Col. W., in command of the regiment, had me ride the Gen'l.'s horse back to the hospital. Our brigade hospital was more than a mile from the field, across the Chickamauga. The wounded I found scattered over a half acre of ground—all out of our brigade too. Here I found one of the refugee drummers on Col. W.'s horse which I immediately rode to the regiment, piloting Maj. Hope and others to the brigade. The sun was then getting low and Col. W. immediately dispatched me on his horse to the wagon train, or cook wagons, to hurry up the rations, the boys not having much to eat for two or three days. I had not been long gone when our troops advanced again on the extreme right and this time our brigade went over the enemy's works. The loss, though, was nothing compared to that of the morning fighting. When I got to the cook train, our wagon had gone to the regiment with rations. I then rode back to the hospital and stayed until morning.

Day, Pvt., Co. B, 25th Massachusetts Volunteer Infantry, Hill's Point, N.C.:

Our last furloughed men have returned and I have the promise of one next week and am congratulating myself on the prospect of once more seeing home. I am anticipating a great deal when I get home; among other things, the pleasure of once more sitting down to a clean, well-spread table, with a good square dinner before me. In anticipation of such an event, I send by this mail a small bill of fare of such dishes as I think I shall relish, and have ordered them to be ready and smoking hot on my arrival:

Roast—Sirloin of beef, spare rib of pork, breast of veal, turkey with cranberry sauce, chicken.

Baked—Bluefish, oyster dressing. Chicken pie.

Boiled—Halibut. Fried—Pouts.

Chicken salad. Lobster salad.

[illegible]ters—Stewed, fried, escalloped. Clam chowder.

[illegible]zen Providence river oysters on the half shell.

Mashed potatoes, boiled onions, beets, turnips, squash, sweet corn, string beans, succotash, stewed tomatoes, tomatoes sliced with vinegar or sugar, apple dumplings with sugar sauce; mince, apple, berry, lemon, cream and custard pie.

Also one moderately sized pumpkin pie, say about thirty-six inches across and not less than eight inches deep; that is as small a pumpkin pie as I care to bother with.

Oranges, apples, pears, grapes, chestnuts, walnuts, cider.

N.B. No boiled salt pork, beef soup or rice and molasses. I don't hanker for that.

With that bill of fare, and such other things as my folks will naturally think of, I reckon I can make a tolerable dinner.

September 21 (Monday)

Dawn found Gen. Thomas at Rossville in good defensive positions which he would hold all day, retiring to Chattanooga after dark. Rosecrans had occupied good defensive positions around Chattanooga and with Thomas inside the perimeter, the Union army was safe, at least for the time. Bragg had ordered a new offensive and then cancelled it, missing a chance to severely damage the Union forces.

The defeat had a sobering effect on the North, and the South celebrated. It was the only bright spot this year! Lincoln ordered Burnside to reinforce Rosecrans.

Jackman, Pvt., "The Orphan Brigade," Battle of Chickamauga, Ga.:

As soon as it was light enough to see how to ride, I started for the regiment. I found them lying around loose in line of battle waiting orders. A skirmish line was soon after sent forward to find the enemy but he had withdrawn during the night. The Army of Tennessee for once had beaten the enemy in an open field fight. Gen'l. Bragg rode along the lines and everywhere was loudly cheered. We tried to get tools to bury our boys but could not. Late in the evening was sent with orders to the hospital and remained there all night. After I had left the brigade started towards Chattanooga. A detail was left to bury the dead.

September 22 (Tuesday)

About two or three days earlier, Acting Master David Nichols, CSN, with a crew of 19 seamen left Mobile in the small cutter *Teaser* and sailed to South West Pass on the Mississippi River. Reaching there, they pulled the cutter into the marshes and made their way to the coal wharf where the tug *Leviathan* was moored. Seizing the tug, they put to sea at once, the tug being fitted with provisions and freshly loaded with coal. The alarm was given and about 40 miles off shore the U.S.S. *De Soto*, Capt. W.M. Walker, put three shots across her bow and the tug hove to. All of Nichols's men were captured.

The Union force, while safely within its entrenchments at Chattanooga, was faced with a strong Confederate force on Missionary Ridge and Lookout Mountain. Hemmed in by mountains and the river, their position was uncertain. To provide support, three divisions of the Fifteenth Corps of Grant's army at Vicksburg were entrained and shipped east as fast as possible. At Knoxville, Burnside had been ordered to go to Rosecrans's relief, but he was having a hard time holding his own positions and controlling the extremely mountainous terrain of eastern Tennessee.

In Washington, Lincoln and his wife, Mary, mourned the death of Confederate Brig. Gen. Ben Hardin Helm, Mary's brother, who was killed at Chickamauga. He commanded the division to which the "Orphan Brigade" belonged.

Jackman, Pvt., "The Orphan Brigade," Battle of Chickamauga, Ga.:

> Early, Lieut. B. and myself followed up the regiment on horseback and found it bivouacked on the side of the road 4 or 5 miles from Chattanooga. Here we remained all night.

September 23 (Wednesday)

In Washington, a council of war was held on what to do to relieve Rosecrans at Chattanooga. It was decided that the Eleventh and Twelfth Corps of the Army of the Potomac, commanded by Joseph Hooker, would be sent to Chattanooga immediately. By commandeering every railcar and engine on the lines, and moving with an unheard-of speed, the move was accomplished in an incredibly short time. The first troops of the Eleventh Corps started moving on September 25th, and the last of them arrived in Chattanooga on October 2nd—an incredible seven days! Chattanooga would be held.

Jackman, Pvt., "The Orphan Brigade," before Chattanooga, in Georgia:

> In the forenoon marched over Missionary Ridge and formed line of battle around Chattanooga. We thought an assault was going to be made and seeing the forts bristling with cannon, and the line of works blue with Federals, we had long faces. There were some shells thrown over us in the evening. At last "night drew her noble curtain round" and we lay down upon arms to sleep. Johnnie G. and I having pulled up a pile of dry grass upon which to lay, covered alone by our overcoats, and slept well.

There was skirmishing around the Rapidan River in Virginia, at Liberty Mills and at Robertson's Ford. Gen. George. E. Pickett had moved to North Carolina with one of Longstreet's divisions that had been left behind.

September 25 (Friday)

Cases of yellow fever and pernicious fever had been reported, along with some deaths from the sicknesses, among the crews of the steamers in the New Orleans area.

In Washington, Lincoln was perturbed by Burnside's lack of movement to relieve Rosecrans. Burnside, in Knoxville, Tenn., had his hands full at the moment with other problems, from which he had difficulty disengaging.

In Richmond, the investigation into the reason the Cumberland Gap fortifications were abandoned without a fight had been going on for several days. At last the investigation was finished and President Davis received a report on the surrender of Gen. Frazer at the Gap.

September 28 (Monday)

At Chattanooga, Major Generals Alexander McDowell McCook and T.L. Crittenden were relieved of their corps commands and ordered to Indianapolis, where a court of inquiry would be held on the conduct of the Battle of Chickamauga. Gen. Thomas escaped criticism.

Jackman, Pvt., "The Orphan Brigade," Missionary Ridge, Ga.:

Went to the wagon train—7 miles in the rear—and changed my linen after taking a bath in the "River of Death." The ablution was quite necessary for I had been dirty for sometime past. At noon returned and saw a train of 160 ambulances coming out of Chattanooga under flag of truce for the Federal wounded that had been left on the field.

September 30 (Wednesday)

At Chattanooga, the two corps inbound from the Army of the Potomac with Joe Hooker were two days away. Early in the morning, Confederate Gen. Joseph Wheeler took his cavalry out of their camps east of Chattanooga and began an 18-day raid against Rosecrans's communications lines. There would be few Union forces there to stop him.

Barber, Cpl., Co. D, 15th Illinois Volunteer Infantry, Natchez, Miss.:

> There were camped here about twenty thousand negroes. Their condition was distressing in the extreme. The small-pox broke out amongst them carrying off as many as one hundred daily. They just rolled in filth and rags, dependent upon the Government for support. A good many earned a little by washing clothes for the soldiers. Most of the able bodied males enlisted and several regiments were formed here. Some of our boys went in as officers of companies.

OCTOBER 1863

Autumn. Throughout the country the trees were ablaze with color, and before the cold rains drove them from the branches, the leaves provided their annual parade of reds, golds, russets, and browns. The armies were in camp mostly, with some activity here and there. Bragg, resting at Chickamauga and Lookout Mountain, watched Rosecrans in Chattanooga, doing nothing to follow up his late victory. Burnside was still busy in Knoxville, sitting astride an important rail link to Virginia. Meade, at Culpeper C.H., was being nibbled at by Mosby and facing Lee, a few miles south at Orange C.H. ... and South had had abundant crops, so ...ood would not be in short supply, ...emained a problem in the South.

October 1 (Thursday)

Joe Wheeler's cavalry was now operating behind Rosecrans, skirmishing with the Federals along the roads and capturing wagon trains of supplies. The entire Eleventh Corps and part of the Twelfth Corps from the Army of the Potomac had passed through Nashville, and were en route to Chattanooga. The Eleventh would arrive the next day.

Jackman, Pvt., "The Orphan Brigade," Missionary Ridge, Ga.:

> Nothing of interest has taken place until today. A very *interesting*, cold autumnal rain has been pouring down all day and I have been crouched under a blanket put up in the manner of a fly all the dreary day. This has certainly been one of Bryant's "Melancholy Days."

In Richmond, John B. Jones, a diarist, recorded a hardly creditable story of a newspaper account (name of the paper is not stated) of sufferings at Gettysburg of the Confederate wounded:

> "A lady from the vicinity of Gettysburg writes: 'July 18th—We have been visiting the battle-field, and have done all we can for the wounded there. Since then we have sent another party, who came upon a camp of wounded Confederates in a wood between the hills. Through this wood quite a large creek runs. This camp contained between 200 and 300 wounded men, in every stage of suffering; two well men among them as nurses. Most of them had frightful wounds. A few evenings ago the rain, sudden and violent, swelled the creek, and 35 of the unfortunates were swept away; 35 died of starvation. No one had been to visit them since they were carried off the battle-field; they had no food of any kind; they were crying all the time "bread, bread! water, water!" One boy without beard was stretched out dead, quite naked, a piece of blanket thrown over his emaciated form, a rag over his face, and his small, thin hands laid over his breast. Of the dead none know their names, and it breaks my heart to think of the mothers waiting and watching for the sons laid in the lonely grave on that fearful battle-field. All of those men in the woods were nearly naked, and when ladies approached they tried to cover themselves with the filthy rags they had cast aside. The wounds themselves, unwashed and untouched, were full of worms. God only knows what they suffered."

It is small wonder that the people of the South, and North, began to distrust their newspapers if this was the type of misinformation that was printed. Upon examination, the whole tale made no sense. Supposedly this happened *14 days* after the battle. As a matter of course, wounded men whose wounds were "unwashed and untouched" for that period of time and who had "no food of any kind" would have died in that span of time and the "two well men among them as nurses" would have been near starvation themselves after 14 days. Can we believe that this many wounded men could remain in an area literally crawling with Union troops for this period of time?

October 2 (Friday)

Joe Wheeler's cavalry was still spreading havoc behind Rosecrans's lines in eastern Tennessee. At Bridgeport, Ala., just south of Chattanooga on the Tennessee River, Gen. Hooker and 20,000 men arrived, having ridden the railroad for 1159 miles in seven days. Quite a feat and the first time the trains had been used to transport a Union force that far in so short a time. The only road open to Chattanooga from Bridgeport was the mountainous trail over Walden's Ridge.

October 4 (Sunday)

Wheeler's cavalry, having taken McMinnville, were raiding the countryside, creating more havoc and disruption—which, of course, was the whole purpose.

Jackman, Pvt., "The Orphan Brigade," Missionary Ridge, Ga.:

> All quiet around the lines. For several days past a truce has ben kept up between the pickets and we don't hear a gun. In the evening moved our lines back up the hill a little and commenced throwing up works. Our corn "dodgers" and blue beef are sent to us daily and in great quantities. We have our tent up and pass the rainy days more comfortably than before.

October 5 (Monday)

In Charleston Harbor a good deal of excitement occurred when the U.S.S. *New Ironsides* was almost blown up by a torpedo. The real excitement, however, occurred aboard the C.S.S. *David*, a 50-foot torpedo boat that mounted a 10-foot spar fixed to the bow. Early in the evening, Lt. Glassell mounted a 60-pound torpedo on the spar and sailed the *David* down the channel towards the *New Ironsides*, getting close to the large ironclad before being spotted. The ironclad hailed the *David* and then opened on her with a barrage of small-arms fire as the torpedo boat plowed full steam towards the *New Ironsides*. The torpedo struck on the Union ship's starboard quarter, shaking the vessel and throwing up an immense column of water which fell on the *David*, putting out her boiler fires and almost swamping her. The *David* now lay completely disabled alongside the Union vessel. Lt. Glassell and Seaman James Sullivan, believing the torpedo boat to be lost, abandoned ship and were picked up by the Union ships. Engineer Tomb, still aboard the *David* because he could not swim, finally got the fires relighted and took the little boat back to Charleston. Although the *New Ironsides* was not seriously damaged, the damage was bad enough to send her to the repair yards. The major effect to this excursion was that now the navies would take heed of this new weapon and develop countermeasures. Union Admiral Dahlgren told Assistant Secretary of the Navy Fox: "By all means let us have a quantity of these torpedoes, and thus turn them against the enemy. We can make them faster than they can."

Barber, Cpl., Co. D, 15th Illinois Volunteer Infantry, Natchez, Miss.:

> Tidings of the bloody battle of Chicamauga now reached us. It came first through rebel sources. There had been a rebel regiment formed from the principal young business men of Natchez which was in the fight and only about thirty escaped unhurt. There was weeping and wailing in the city. These men were the flower of the society here, and although our foes, we could not but sympathize with their friends in their loss.

Confederate Joe Wheeler's cavalry burned an important railroad bridge near Murfreesboro, Tenn., causing an interruption in the flow of supplies and troops to Chattanooga. More Federal troops were being sent from Memphis towards Rosecrans in addition to the two corps coming in with Hooker, and the Fifteenth Corps divisions from Grant's old army.

The possibility of price controls by the Confederate government was being hotly contested by the Richmond newspapers the *Enquirer* and the *Dispatch.*

October 7 (Wednesday)

A landing party under Acting Chief Engineer Thomas Doughty, U.S.S. *Osage,* travelled overland from the Mississippi to the Red River through dense underbrush and vines in an operation against two steamers said to be operating on the river and tied up on the riverbank. Doughty and his men reached the river and captured the steamer *Argus* immediately, and just then the *Robert Fulton* came steaming downriver. Doughty ordered the arriving steamer to come to, and suddenly he was in possession of two steamers and nine prisoners. The *Argus* was burned immediately and the larger *Robert Fulton* was taken downriver. Unable to get the steamer across the bar at the mouth of the Red River, Doughty burned the *Robert Fulton* and returned to the *Osage.*

Off Calcasieu River, La., the steamer *Pushmataha,* loaded with rum, claret, and gunpowder, was chased ashore by the U.S.S. *Cayuga,* Lt. Commander Dana, where she was set afire and abandoned by her crew. A boat crew from the *Cayuga* went aboard the grounded steamer to find that a keg of powder had been opened and a match (fuse) had been inserted in the hole. The fuse was burning when Ordinary Seaman Thomas Morton pulled it out and threw it and the powder overboard. The grounded steamer was destroyed. Shortly after, the *Cayuga* chased another schooner ashore which was carrying gunpowder, but the schooner blew up before she could be boarded.

Wheeler's cavalry was near Shelbyville, Tenn., with skirmishing at Farmington, Blue Springs, and Sim's Farm.

October 9 (Friday)

The commerce raiders of the South ranged far and wide, and any United States ship was a designated target. Off the coast of Morocco, the C.S.S. *Georgia,* Lt. W.L. Maury, captured and burned the *Bold Hunter,* loaded with coal for Calcutta. It hardly seems that the load of coal going to India would hurt the Confederate war effort.

In northern Virginia, Lee was on the move, crossing the Rapidan and moving west, trying to get around Meade's right flank and threaten Washington. Meade, alerted some days before, took immediate action to cover his own flank.

In Tennessee, Wheeler's cavalry continued raiding between Nashville and Chattanooga, as Union troops moved across the State in a steady stream to aid Rosecrans. President Davis had departed Atlanta and passed through Marietta on his way to Bragg's army.

October 10 (Saturday)

In the west the Tennessee River was low and the larger gunboats could not operate upriver in support of Gen. Sherman's activities towards Chattanooga. Admiral D.D. Porter told Grant that he regretted the situation and would get boats up as early as possible. "My intention," Porter wrote, "is to send every gunboat I can spare up the Tennessee. I have also sent below for light-drafts to come up."

At Bragg's headquarters, Jeff Davis arrived and surveyed the scene. He was now talking to Bragg's corp commanders in the hope of quelling the dissention among the officers.

Jackman, Pvt., "The Orphan Brigade," Missionary Ridge, Ga.:

> All quiet until this morning when we had reveille at 2 and the troops kept under arms fearing an advance. Today "Jeff" rode around the lines and was generally loudly cheered. When he and Bragg, with other general officers, passed our line, our boys stood very respectfully on the works but not a man opened his mouth.

Barber, Cpl., Co. D, 15th Illinois Volunteer Infantry, Natchez, Miss.:

> We now commenced fortifying. One of the best houses in the city was pulled down over the rebel owner's head and a fort built on its site. The rebel General Rodney threatened an attack, and for two days our troops were kept under arms. We finally marched out to meet him and he retreated in hot haste.
>
> There is a peculiar feature in the country around Natchez which deserves mention, viz: deep gulches or a sinking away of the earth. These sink-holes are sometimes abrupt and are from eighty to one hundred feet deep and are very irregular in shape. They used to be hiding places for thieves, etc., the thick cane brake and caverns affording good concealment.

Some supposed that these gulches were caused by earthquakes, others by quicksand settling away. The ground is very sandy, and when heavy freshets occur, it caves in. Plantations have been badly injured and the graveyard at Natchez partially destroyed in this manner. Millions of dollars have been expended in building something to prevent this destruction.

Lee was trying hard to get around Meade's right flank and behind the Union army, but Lee had no luck. Meade's cavalry was probing heavily trying to find Lee's main force. For once the armies were well matched in strength. Fighting at Russell's Ford, Germanna, and Morton's Fords, and other points on the Rapidan.

October 13 (Tuesday)

Meade had withdrawn to the vicinity of Manassas and Centreville, closely followed by Lee. The same tactic that was used at Second Bull Run was again successful—a wide flanking movement.

In Ohio, those who had placed Clement L. Vallandigham on the Democratic ticket for Governor (although he had been sent over the lines at Murfreesboro and later went to Canada) were sorely disappointed when he was resoundingly defeated. In Pennsylvania, Gov. Curtin, a staunch Union supporter, was reelected without problem.

The U.S.S. *Queen City*, Acting Lt. G.W. Brown, embarked troops and left Helena, Ark., for Friar's Point, Miss. The Federal troops landed and surrounded the small town late in the evening.

At Bragg's headquarters in northern Georgia, President Davis authorized Bragg to relieve Lt. Gen. D.H. Hill from command. Daniel Harvey Hill, a native South Carolinian, was 40 years old when the war began. An 1842 graduate of West Point, he was a veteran of the Mexican War, and was the Superintendent of the North Carolina Military Academy at the start of the war. He won his first battle, Big Bethel, which earned him a promotion to Brigadier General. He was promoted to Major General in March 1862, and he served with Johnston in the Peninsula campaign. He was always critical of his superiors, making the mistake of criticizing first Robert E. Lee and then Braxton Bragg, the two favorites of President Davis. He had been appointed Lieutenant General in July 1863, but after being relieved from command, the appointment was never confirmed. He would serve in no meaningful capacity for the rest of the war. He died at Charlotte, N.C., in September 1889.

October 14 (Wednesday)

Near Bristoe Station, Va., Lt. Gen. A.P. Hill's Confederates struck Meade's rear guard but not with sufficient strength to dislodge the entrenched Yankees. Meade had time to prepare his lines around Centreville near the old Manassas battlefields. The battle that ensued was fairly matched. Lee found no easy solution, as at Second Manassas, and Meade couldn't find a good opening for an attack. Meade kept falling back to prepared entrenchment, giving Lee no opportunity to disrupt his lines.

At Friar's Point, Miss., the troops which landed the night before from the U.S.S. *Queen City* conducted a search of the town and found more than 200 bales of cotton, which were confiscated. Several prisoners were also taken.

October 15 (Thursday)

Around Manassas and Centreville, Lee and Meade still grappled like two wrestlers looking for a good hold.

In Charleston Harbor a report on the sinking of the submarine *H.L. Hunley* stated:

> The boat left the wharf at 9:25 A.M. and disappeared at 9:35. As soon as she sunk, air bubbles were seen to rise to the surface of the water, and from this fact it is supposed the hole in the top of the boat by which the men entered was not properly closed. It was impossible at the time to make any effort to rescue the unfortunate men, as the water was some 9 fathoms deep.

At the time of the accident, the submarine was under the command of Horace L. Hunley, for whom the boat was named. The submarine was raised again, for the second time, and a third crew volunteered to man her, the new captain to be Lt. George Dixon, CSA. Beauregard ordered that she was not to be used as a submersible again, so she was fitted with a torpedo spar. Over the next several months she would venture out among the blockading vessels at night, hoping for a strike.

October 16 (Friday)

Southern sympathizers were everywhere, it seemed. One Jules David wrote Confederate Secretary of State Judah Benjamin requesting a letter of marque designating him as a privateer so that David and his partners could raid commerce in the Pacific. Mr. David proposed to use a "first-class steamer of 400 tons, strongly built, and of an average speed of 14 miles" for his purposes. The authorization was not forwarded.

In Florida, Admiral Bailey heard that the blockade runners *Scottish Chief* and *Kate Dale* were being loaded with cotton and getting ready to sail from Hillsborough River. Bailey sent the gunboats U.S.S. *Tahoma,* Lt. Commander A.A. Semmes, and the U.S.S. *Adela,* Acting Lt. Louis N. Stodder, to destroy the blockade runners. A diversion tactic was used during the operation. The two gunboats shelled the fort and the town (Tampa) during the day and the landing parties were sent ashore late in the evening to go overland to Hillsborough River. The party of about 100 men went overland about 14 miles and waited for dawn.

A new Military Division of the Mississippi was created, placing Grant in command of the old Departments of the Ohio, the Cumberland, and the Tennessee. Grant was en route from Vicksburg to Cairo, Illinois, to confer with Secretary of War Stanton.

In Virginia, Lee and Meade faced each other without much movement. Neither could seem to find a chink in the other's armor.

Jackman, Pvt., "The Orphan Brigade," Missionary Ridge, Ga.:

> Cloudy and cool—"Novemberish." I have forgotten the date and it was of no little importance at the time. I did not make any note of it but it was along about this time the fact was announced that Chattanooga was to be shelled from Lookout Mountain. That morning I clambered up to the top of the ridge to see the *grand sight.* The guns opened—little field pieces—and first we could see a little tuft of smoke rise out of the trees on the side of the mountain, then presently could hear the feeble report of the gun. Often the shells would fall short and those that did go to the works did no harm.

October 17 (Saturday)

Grant arrived at Cairo and was ordered further to Louisville, Ky. At Indianapolis, he met Secretary Stanton. Riding together on the train, Stanton gave Grant his orders creating the new Military Division and placing Grant in command. Of the two versions offered, Grant selected the one that relieved Rosecrans of command and appointed Gen. George Thomas as commander of the troops at Chattanooga. Sherman was to remain in command, as well as Burnside. Rosecrans's defeat at Chickamauga and his actions afterward led to his downfall. Lincoln and Stanton believed that Grant would be more effective.

In Virginia, Lee began to pull back from Manassas towards the Rappahannock River and its crossings. Lee was not prepared to outwait Meade.

Dawn saw the landing parties from the U.S.S. *Tahoma* and *Adela* at Hillsborough River and boarding the blockade runners *Scottish Chief* and *Kate Dale,* which were loaded with cotton and ready to sail. The two ships were destroyed *posthaste* and the landing party had a running battle to get back to their ships. During the fight, five men from the landing party were killed, ten were wounded, and five were taken prisoner.

At Murrell's Inlet, S.C. (site of today's Myrtle Beach), the schooner *Rover,* loaded with cotton, was destroyed by the U.S.S. *T.A. Ward,* Acting Master William L. Babcock.

October 18 (Sunday)

President Davis left northern Georgia, travelling from Bragg's headquarters southwest towards Mobile, passing through Selma, Ala.

Grant assumed command of the Union forces from the Mississippi River east to the Cumberland Mountains, replacing several "Department" organizations with a leaner, less top-heavy organization. Rosecrans was relieved of his command at Chattanooga, and Gen. George Thomas was placed in command, with the admonition to hold Chattanooga at all costs. In that area the roads were a mess, the rains had been heavy, and getting wagons over Walden's Ridge with supplies for the army was a real problem.

In northern Virginia, Lee was almost back to his old lines at Orange C.H., with Meade following. There were several brisk fights during the withdrawal, but nothing of any weight.

Admiral Dahlgren, South Atlantic Blockading Squadron, based at Port Royal, wrote Secretary of the Navy Gideon Welles that during the attacks on

Charleston over the past two months the Navy had fired more than 8000 rounds of shells and the gunboats had received over 900 hits. The support provided to the Army during the Morris Island operation was such that "its supplies were entirely covered; provisions, arms, cannon, ammunition... were landed as freely as if an enemy were not in sight, while by the same means the enemy was restricted to the least space and action...."

In Charleston Harbor, the *H.L. Hunley*, the submarine that sank on the 15th with all hands, was found in 9 fathoms of water. Efforts were begun to raise the boat.

October 19 (Monday)

The "Buckland Races" were held in northern Virginia between JEB Stuart's and Kilpatrick's cavalry in the vicinity of Buckland Mills, Va. The race ended with the rout of the Union cavalry in what was to be the last major clash of the Bristoe Station campaign. There was light skirmishing elsewhere in Virginia, but otherwise it was quiet.

Grant was in Louisville, talking with Stanton, and preparing to travel to Chattanooga to talk to Rosecrans and to see what needed to be done to move the army out of Chattanooga and back on the offensive.

October 20 (Tuesday)

JEB Stuart took the last of the Confederate forces back across the Rappahannock River and into Lee's lines at Orange C.H., ending a campaign which had accomplished almost nothing for either North or South. Casualties were about equal—Confederate, 1381; Union, 1423.

The rams being built in England known as *294* and *295* were seized by the British government on this day. Commander Bulloch, the Confederate naval agent in London, told Secretary Mallory that this seizure probably stemmed from the fact that:

> ...a large number of Confederate Naval officers have during the past three months arrived in England. The *Florida* came off the Irish coast some six weeks since, and proceeding to Brest, there discharged the greater portion of her crew, who were sent to Liverpool. These circumstances were eagerly seized upon by the United States representative here, and they have so worked on Lord Russell as to make him believe that the presence of these officers and men has a direct reference to the destination of the rams....

Gen. Grant left Louisville for Nashville, en route to Chattanooga and the Army of the Cumberland, which was facing Braxton Bragg in northern Georgia.

Jackman, Pvt., "The Orphan Brigade," Chickamauga, Ga.:

> Brigade moved back across the ridge 2 or 3 miles to the Chickamauga and have gone regularly into camp. The October winds are filling the air with withered leaves and soon the trees will be stripped. To be in camp again makes one feel like he is at home.

There had been several recent "mass meetings" in Richmond to persuade the Confederate Legislature to enact price controls.

October 21 (Wednesday)

Stevenson, Ala., was the meeting point for Grant and Rosecrans to discuss the situation at Chattanooga. Rosecrans, relieved of command, was going to Nashville and then on north, Grant on to Chattanooga. Grant's accident in New Orleans a few weeks ago still had him on crutches, making getting around in the mud (which was everywhere) a real chore.

Jackman, Pvt., "The Orphan Brigade," Chickamauga, Ga.:

> This morning had a slight shower of rain and a very heavy rain has just passed over this evening. A few such rains will entirely strip the trees. A good deal of fuss among the boys about the proper ownership of cooking utensils.... Often the "litigated" property is brought up to the Col's tent for a decision and both parties invariably swear or say they would be willing to "swear on a stack of bibles" as to the ownership of the doubtful property.
>
> At 3 P.M. while a heavy rain was pelting down received orders to strike tents and march. We crossed the Chickamauga on a pontoon bridge and through a swamp two or three miles wide before we got to the solid road. When we marched for Tyner Station (which I have mentioned before) a distance of some 7 or 8 miles the regiment got separated in the swamp and was all night overtaking us, we got lost. At last we

came in sight of the camp fires built by a detail sent forward in the evening for the purpose and soon our troubles were forgotten in slumber.

October 22 (Thursday)

In Tennessee, Grant slopped, slipped, and slid over the muddy roads leading over Walden's Ridge to Chattanooga. Gen. Thomas awaited his arrival.

October 23 (Friday)

President Davis got rid of another of Braxton Bragg's detractors by relieving Lt. Gen. Leonidas Polk of his corps command in the Army of Tennessee. Polk, like Gen. D.H. Hill, who had also been recently relieved, played in the behind-the-scenes criticism of Bragg's actions after Chickamauga. Polk was assigned to an administrative position in Mississippi to replace Gen. Hardee.

Grant arrived at dusk at Thomas's headquarters in Chattanooga, where Grant was briefed immediately on the situation of the Army of the Cumberland and the defenses of the city.

October 24 (Saturday)

In central Tennessee Sherman assumed command of the Army of the Tennessee, replacing Grant. Note that the Confederate army at Chattanooga was named the *Army of Tennessee* while the Federal army, under Sherman, was called the *Army of the Tennessee.* Federal armies were named for rivers—Army of the Potomac, Army of the Tennessee, Army of the Cumberland, etc.—while the Confederate armies were named for geographical locations—Army of Northern Virginia, Army of Tennessee, etc.

Two light-draft Union gunboats arrived at Eastport, Miss., to support Gen. Sherman's operations along the Tennessee River. The support had been delayed due to low water in the river. The captain of the U.S.S. *Hastings*, Lt. Commander S.L. Phelps, was no stranger to these waters, having been one of the first to operate upriver during the Ft. Donelson/Henry campaigns in early 1862.

At Chattanooga, Grant inspected the defenses of the city and the state of the troops. The famous "Cracker Line" was then ordered into effect.

This supply line was suggested by the Army of the Cumberland's Chief Engineer, Major Gen. William F. Smith. Essentially, it involved gaining control of the Tennessee River frontage (below Raccoon Mountain) which was held by the Confederates. This done, supplies could then be brought in by boat.

Jackman, Pvt., "The Orphan Brigade," Chickamauga, Ga.:

> All last night the locomotive kept up a "tooting" over at the station. Longstreet's Corps were shipped towards Knoxville. Today has been cold and cloudy—looks like snow.

October 25 (Sunday)

Arrangements for the expedition to set up the "Cracker Line" were in process. Troop units and equipment were designated and readied for the mission. Grant continued his reorganization and planned his next move.

Barber, Cpl., Co. D, 15th Illinois Volunteer Infantry, Natchez, Miss.:

> My furlough had now gotten around, duly signed and approved by General McPherson. The date was left blank and Col. Rogers gave me permission to fill that but not put it beyond the present month, so I dated it the 29th, thus gaining four days' time. I now felt in excellent spirits at the thought that I would soon be at home.... On the 29th of October, I was on board a steamer with my face set homeward.

October 26 (Monday)

In Charleston Harbor, Ft. Sumter's defenders held on despite heavy bombardment from Union ironclads and shore batteries that fired over 1000 shells in less than 12 hours. Commander Stevens, captain of the U.S.S. *Patapsco*, said the effect of the firing was "hardly describable, throwing bricks and mortar, gun carriages and timber in every direction and high into the air." Sitting through a bombardment of that magnitude could drive men mad.

At 3 A.M. that dark morning 24 pontoon boats were loaded with Brig. Gen. William B. Hazen's Ohioans and a detachment of the 1st Michigan Engineers and, using the current of the Tennessee River, went around Moccasin Point, a dry neck of land opposite Raccoon Mountain which was held by the Confederates, to Brown's Ferry, where Hazen was joined by Brig. Gen. John Basil Turchin, who marched a brigade across Moccasin Point in the dark, undetected.

October 28 (Wednesday)

After seven months at sea raiding United States commerce, the C.S.S. *Georgia*, Lt. W.L. Maury, anchored at Cherbourg, France. During her raids she had destroyed a number of prizes and bonded others to the value of $200,000. However, *Georgia* was now broken down to the point where she could do no more than six knots under a full head of steam. Major repairs were in order.

At Bridgeport, Ala., Gen. Joseph Hooker received orders to move his men up the Tennessee River and to secure the crossing at Brown's Ferry by cleaning out the Confederates at Raccoon Mountain who were threatening the Union forces and their newly created bridgehead. Hooker wasted no time, and during the night he was attacked by Longstreet's men at Wauhatchie in Lookout Valley. The Confederates used larger numbers, but the Union force under Brig. Gen. John W. Geary held, and by 4 A.M. the Confederates withdrew. The "Cracker Line" was not bothered again for the duration of the campaign.

Another round of shelling at Ft. Sumter in Charleston Harbor. Nearly 680 rounds were fired at the heap of rubble that still held out.

October 29 (Thursday)

Admiral D.D. Porter sent more gunboats up the Tennessee River in support of Gen. Sherman. The *Lexington*, *Hastings*, *Key West*, *Cricket*, *Robb*, *Romeo*, and *Peosta* were all detached for duty immediately, and the *Paw Paw*, *Tawah*, *Tyler*, and a few others would go upriver soon. A lot of firepower afloat.

The Union troops of Gen. Hooker, in overwhelming numbers, attacked the Confederates on Raccoon Mountain, and the Union thus secured the route for the "Cracker Line" to begin operations. Supplies would be landed at Brown's Ferry, out of Confederate artillery range, and then shuttled overland into Chattanooga. In two days the first of the supply wagons would arrive in Chattanooga.

President Davis approved a request from Brig. Gen. Nathan Bedford Forrest to separate his forces from Bragg's and to go raiding in northern Mississippi and Tennessee. The devil was loose!

October 30 (Friday)

Jackman, Pvt., "The Orphan Brigade," Chickamauga, Ga.:

> Raining at reveille and continued to pour down all day long. This weather is enough to give one the ennui.

Barber, Cpl., Co. D, 15th Illinois Volunteer Infantry, Cairo, Illinois:

> On the 30th I arrived at Cairo. When my feet again pressed the soil of my adopted State, feelings of joy filled my soul. Every little delay annoyed me exceedingly. My heart filled with pride, viewing as I passed along, the thrift and plenty which prevailed wherever the eye might look. Large fields of golden corn were bending 'neath the weight of their autumnal load. Huge ricks of grain and hay bespoke the plenty with which the country abounded. The villages were teeming with busy life. A stranger, to pass through the State, could not realize that a terrible civil war was raging in our land and that one hundred thousand of the brave yeoman of the soil of Illinois were battling with vehement energy and bravery to save this fair land from disruption and desolation.

October 31 (Saturday)

The training ship of the Confederate Naval Academy, the C.S.S. *Patrick Henry*, saw instruction begin for the 52 cadets of the Academy. The ship, moored at Drewry's Bluff on the James River, would later be moved to Richmond, where it would be moored for the remainder of the war. Lt. William H. Parker, CSN, the Superintendent, would end the war on horseback in South Carolina.

President Davis notified Gen. Bragg that Davis had assigned Gen. Hardee, and possibly two brigades, to Bragg's command and that Hardee was to report without delay. Gen. Polk, previously relieved of corps command in Bragg's army, would replace Hardee in Mississippi.

Firing on Ft. Sumter continued today for the third straight day. A total of 2961 shells were fired at this small dot of landfill in three days, but the Confederate flag still flew.

NOVEMBER 1863

The armies settled fairly well into winter camp along the Rappahannock and Rapidan rivers in Virginia, a time for training and equipment repair. In the west, Grant had relieved the siege of Chattanooga and the "Cracker Line" was in full operation; the Federal troops were eating well again. Bragg, a little crotchety, as usual, was pondering Grant's next move. Ft. Sumter, further reduced to dust, was still defiant. The war ground on.

November 1 (Sunday)

Ft. Sumter was under fire again. Some 780 rounds of artillery and mortar shells would be fired into this crumbling fort, yet the defenders stayed on.

Skirmishing occurred in the vicinity of Eastport and Fayetteville, Tenn., on the outskirts of Grant's lines at Chattanooga.

Jeff Davis, in Savannah, was returning from his trip to Bragg's army and Mobile.

With the relative inactivity of the winter, many of the Union troops were sent home on a rotating basis on furlough. Corp. Barber, an astute observer, contrasted the difference in the countryside, North and South.

Barber, Cpl., Co. D, 15th Illinois Volunteer Infantry, Riley, Illinois:

> I could not help contrasting this busy scene with the desolation which reigned in the South. On the one hand were the friends of freedom and free labor, and thrift and plenty reigned supreme. On the other hand were the friends of slavery and secession, desolating the land which fostered them and seeking to involve the whole in one common ruin.
>
> The next day's light revealed to me the spires of the Golden City. I was just in time to take the morning train. With lightning speed, I passed old familiar objects, and, at noon, I arrived at Marengo. I had hoped to surprise my friends but they were expecting me....

November 2 (Monday)

In Washington, President Lincoln received, and accepted, an invitation to make a "few appropriate remarks" at Gettysburg, Pa., during the dedication of the new National Cemetery.

President Davis, in Charleston, S.C., was greeted with cheers from the general public and a distinguished delegation. This while another 793 shells from mortars and siege guns landed on Ft. Sumter—33 shells per hour, or one every two minutes. One of the observers to the action in the harbor, Lt. Commander Greenleaf Cilley, U.S.S. *Catskill*, reported indications of extensive preparations for a possible assault by the Confederates:

> Two boats under sail were seen moving from Sumter towards Sullivan's Island. About 11 P.M. a balloon with two lights attached rose from Sumter and floated towards Fort Johnson.... At midnight a steamer left Sumter and moved towards Fort Johnson. At sunrise... observed the three rams and the side-wheel steamer anchored in line of battle ahead from Johnson towards Charleston, and each with its torpedo topped up forward of the bows.

Major Gen. Nathaniel Banks had loaded his Union troops aboard transports in New Orleans and the ships were then convoyed to the area of Brazos Santiago, Tex., by the U.S.S. *Monongahela*, *Owasco*, and *Virginia*, all under the command of Commander Strong, USN. Arriving on this date, the landing began late in the afternoon.

November 3 (Tuesday)

Union guns and mortars sent another 661 shells against the walls of Ft. Sumter. Admiral Dahlgren, inspecting the fort from his flagship, commented: "... could plainly observe the further effects of the firing; still, this mass of ruin is capable of harboring a number of the enemy, who may retain their hold until expelled by the bayonet...."

The Union troops of Gen. Banks were all ashore, without opposition, at Brazos Santiago. The Confederates evacuated the town and moved towards Brownsville. In the west the wrangling still went on between Bragg and his generals.

November 4 (Wednesday)

In an action quite uncharacteristic of him, Gen. Bragg detached Gen. Longstreet's corps from the Army of Tennessee and sent it against Burnside at Knoxville. The all-important railroad linking Virginia with the west was the goal. Longstreet moved towards Burnside's position immediately.

In Virginia, Mosby and his Rangers were actively nipping at Meade's backside in northern Virginia. Mosby was a constant pain to the Union commanders in the area.

Brownsville, Tex., was evacuated by the Confederates, as Union troops under Gen. Nathaniel Banks occupied the city. The Mexican border area was now securely in Union hands.

November 5 (Thursday)

Gunboats from the South Atlantic Blockading Squadron, Admiral Dahlgren, joined the chorus of death in shelling the battered remains of Ft. Sumter. Admiral Dahlgren described the condition of the fort: "The only original feature left is the northeast face, the rest is a pile of rubbish."

In Chattanooga, Grant was inspecting the lines and waiting patiently for Sherman to arrive. Sherman was slipping and sliding through the mud and rain, not making too much progress with his long wagon trains containing tons of rations for Grant's army. These rations had been loaded before the "Cracker Line" had been opened, and they were somewhat redundant now. However, Sherman couldn't just leave them in the wilderness. Using every trick in his fertile imagination, Sherman pushed his troops along, even using steamers as bridges to cross swollen streams. It took him 13 days to cover about 115 straight-distance miles—probably nearer to 170 road miles.

November 6 (Friday)

In West Virginia, the Confederates defending Droop Mountain were routed by a two-prong advance of Brig. Gen. William W. Averell's Union troops. This was part of a continuing campaign to clear the Confederates from the important rail links to the southwestern part of that state.

Admiral Dahlgren tried to dislodge the obstructions to Charleston Harbor by using an experimental torpedo that was less than totally satisfactory. The device, a cast-iron shell some 23 feet long and 10 inches in diameter, contained 600 pounds of explosives and was suspended from a raft (attached to the bow of the U.S.S. *Patapsco*) and held in position by two long booms. The contraption seriously interfered with the ship's movements and, when exploded, threw a column of water 40 or 50 feet in the air, some of it coming down on the deck. In the end the idea was sent back to the inventor, John Ericsson, for reconsideration.

The C.S.S. *Alabama*, Capt. Semmes, was now in the Pacific, cruising the East Indies and snapping up United States commercial shipping as it was found. Semmes captured and destroyed the bark *Amanda* with a cargo of hemp and sugar.

November 7 (Saturday)

In Virginia, Meade lunged across the Rappahannock at Rappahannock Station and Kelly's Ford and then stopped. Lee withdrew to the positions he held before his advance on Bristoe Station in October.

In Richmond there was some alarm over the possibility that the 13,000 Union prisoners on Belle Isle might attempt to escape. The Confederates brought out the artillery to surround Belle Isle. The usual conjecture abounded as to whether it was a massive Northern plot or just gossip among the prisoners.

In West Virginia, Gen. Averell's troops made contact with other Union troops under A.N. Duffie and captured Lewisburg, W.Va.

November 8 (Sunday)

Around the Rappahannock Meade's men were not idle. Moving further towards Lee, they skirmished at Warrenton, Brandy Station, Culpeper C.H., and other points.

At Chickamauga, Ga., Major Gen. John Cabell Breckinridge replaced Lt. Gen. Daniel H. Hill as commander of the Second Corps of Bragg's Army of Tennessee. Hill had been relieved of command for his constant carping and back-biting.

November 9 (Monday)

President Davis returned to Richmond amid an early snowstorm, reportedly looking well.

In Washington, President Lincoln, an admirer of the theatre, went to see John Wilkes Booth in *Marble Heart.*

The U.S.S. *Adger*, Commander Thomas H. Patterson, captured the blockade runner *Robert E. Lee* near Cape Lookout Shoals, N.C. The *Lee* had left Bermuda on the 7th with a cargo of shoes, blankets, rifles, saltpeter, and lead. This ended the career of one of the most successful blockade runners yet. Her former captain, Lt. John Wilkinson, CSN, later wrote:

> She had run the blockade twenty-one times while under my command, and had carried abroad between six thousand and seven thousand bales of cotton, worth at that time about two million dollars in gold, and had carried into the Confederacy equally valuable cargoes.

Intelligence concerning the Confederate naval capabilities in the Georgia area was reported as:

> C.S.S. *Savannah*, Commander Robert F. Pinkney, had two 7-inch and two 6-inch Brooke rifled guns and a torpedo mounted on her bow as armament. Two other torpedoes were carried in her hold. Her sides were plated with 4 inches of rolled iron and her speed was about seven knots "in smooth water."
>
> C.S.S. *Isondiga*, a wooden steamer, was reported to have old boilers and "unreliable" machinery.
>
> The frames for two more rams were said to be on the stocks at Savannah, but no iron could be obtained to complete them.
>
> C.S.S. *Resolute*, thought to be awaiting the opportunity to run the blockade, had been converted into a tender, and all the cotton in Savannah was being transferred to Wilmington for shipment through the blockade.
>
> C.S.S. *Georgia*, a floating battery commanded by Lt. Washington Gwathmey, CSN, was at anchor near Ft. Jackson and was reported to be "a failure."

At Mobile, Admiral Buchanan, CSN, sent Acting Midshipman Edward A. Swain to report to Ft. Morgan to take command of the submarine C.S.S. *Gunnison* and proceed off the harbor and destroy, if possible, the U.S.S. *Colorado*, or any other vessel he could reach.

The U.S.S. *Niphon*, Acting Master Breck, ran down and was about to capture the blockade runner *Ella and Annie*, loaded with a cargo of arms and provisions, when the blockade runner tried to ram the naval vessel. The ships swung broadside, so the men of the *Niphon* boarded the runner and captured it.

November 10 (Tuesday)

The clipper ship *Contest*, bound from Japan to New York, was "no-contest" for the C.S.S. *Alabama*, Capt. Semmes, when she was taken and destroyed off Gaspar Strait, East Indies.

Jackman, Pvt., "The Orphan Brigade," Tyner Station, Ga.:

> Froze ice again last night. Cobb's battery joined brig from Missr'y ridge. Saturday the 5th Ky. joined the brigade in place of the 41st Ala. transferred. Our brigade is now composed entirely of Kentuckians.

Barber, Cpl., Co. D, 15th Illinois Volunteer Infantry, Riley, Ill:

> I will pass over briefly my stay at home.... But I cannot omit to again acknowledge the unceasing kindness and care during the illness which succeeded my arrival.... I now learned from letters from the boys that our division had moved up to Vicksburg. After the first glad excitement of being at home began to subside, I began to long for the companionship of old friends and comrades, but my protracted ill health made it necessary for me to stay longer than I anticipated. My furlough had been extended twice. I had been at home over two months. I felt that to remain longer would be a neglect of duty....

November 11 (Wednesday)

Major Gen. Benjamin F. "Beast" Butler returned to active Federal command, replacing Major Gen. John G. Foster in the Department of Virginia and North Carolina.

James Duke, Master, CSN, had developed quite a reputation after his exploits in June when he captured a Union ship near New Orleans. On November 11, he came out of the Perdido River near Pensacola Bay with the *Mary Campbell*, captured earlier the same day. He also had a cutter which he had used to capture the *Mary Campbell* and another vessel named *Norman*, also captured. Seeing the U.S.S. *Bermuda*, Acting Lt. J. W. Smith, come into sight, Duke abandoned the *Mary Campbell* and the cutter and took the *Norman* to shore, where he beached and burned her.

Jackman, Pvt., "The Orphan Brigade," Tyner Station, Ga.:

> Johnnie G. and I commenced building us a house today—tearing down an old out house in the country for the purpose. All the boys are busy as beavers building cabins for winter.

November 12 (Thursday)

The Union guns opened again on Ft. Sumter, beginning a four-day bombardment. The target was already a pile of rubble. In Arkansas, pro-Union delegates met to discuss how they could best arrange to get back into the Union.

At Chattanooga, Grant still waited for Sherman to appear. Grant's problem was really one of morale. The Army of the Cumberland that he inherited from Rosecrans was, he felt, badly demoralized by its defeat at Chickamauga. He also felt that the two corps brought from the Army of the Potomac by Hooker would perform poorly because they had never won a battle. What he wanted was troops that were accustomed to winning and a commander to match them: Sherman and his Fifteenth Corps. The redhead was two days away.

November 13 (Friday)

The Union guns pounded Ft. Sumter again today.

At Chattanooga, Grant prowled the lines, studying the enemy emplacements, cigar smoke billowing behind him.

From Orange C.H., Gen. Robert E. Lee wired President Davis that he was extremely short of corn for the horses, only three pounds per horse, per day, having been received in the last five days. Davis ordered forage to be sent up in preference to other cargo.

November 14 (Saturday)

The bombardment of Ft. Sumter continued. At Charleston, Gen. P.G.T. Beauregard commented on the Confederate gunboats, pointing out their weaknesses:

> Our gunboats are defective in six respects: First. They have no speed, going only from 3 to 5 miles an hour in smooth water and no current. Second. They are of too great a draft to navigate our inland waters. Third. They are unseaworthy by their shape and construction.... Even in the harbor they are at times considered unsafe in a storm. Fourth. They are incapable of resisting the enemy's XV-inch shots at close quarters.... Fifth. they can not fight at long range.... Sixth. They are very costly, warm, uncomfortable, and badly ventilated; consequently sickly.

Brig. Gen. Nathan Bedford Forrest was assigned an "operational area" of western Tennessee for his raiding parties. At Chattanooga, Sherman arrived after leaving his wagon train at Bridgeport and rushing forward to see Grant. Immediately, Grant, Thomas, and Sherman went for a tour of the lines to discuss strategy. What Sherman saw was a huge natural amphitheatre running northeast to southwest with the prominence of Missionary Ridge about three miles distant to the northeast. To the southwest was Lookout Mountain, which overlooked Chattanooga. A grand panorama, filled with the tents and camps of the Confederate army.

November 15 (Sunday)

In early evening the Confederate guns at Ft. Moultrie opened a bombardment of the Union positions at Cumming's Point on Morris Island in Charleston Harbor. Gen. Gilmore, fearing a possible Confederate landing force, requested that Admiral Dahlgren provide a naval screening force to cover the area of Cumming's Point. Dahlgren immediately complied, sending orders to the tugs on patrol to keep a strong watch. During the night, the U.S.S. *Lehigh*, Commander Andrew Bryson, ran aground while covering the Point and was taken under heavy fire from Ft. Moultrie at dawn.

At Chattanooga, Sherman left his divisions at Bridgeport until such time as their deployment could be determined.

November 16 (Monday)

At Campbell's Station, Tenn., Longstreet missed an opportunity to cut off Burnside's line of retreat. Burnside withdrew into Knoxville, which Longstreet immediately besieged. There was other skirmishing and light fighting around Kingston, Tenn.

Gen. Nathaniel Banks's Union troops occupied Corpus Christi, Tex., securing that port for the Union.

At Charleston, the fifth day of bombardment continued with 602 more shells being fired at Ft. Sumter. At dawn in Charleston Harbor, the U.S.S. *Lehigh* was aground and under fire from the Confederate guns at Ft. Moultrie. The U.S.S. *Nahant*, Lt. Commander John J. Cornwell, moved in to assist the *Lehigh* and get her afloat again. All this time the guns at Moultrie were still firing. Finally, landsmen Frank S. Gile and William Williams, together with gunner's mate George W. Leland and Coxswain Thomas Irving carried a line from the *Lehigh* to the *Nahant* while under fire to get the former ship off the bar. These four men were awarded the Medal of Honor for their achievement.

The Union blockade and the loss of Tennessee coal both had a severe effect on the manufacture of goods and the overall economy in Georgia, Alabama, and South Carolina. Commander John K. Mitchell in Richmond wrote Confederate Secretary of the Navy Mallory on the subject:

> The occupation of Chattanooga by the enemy in August has effectually cut off the supply from the mines of that region, upon which the public works in Georgia and South Carolina and the naval vessels in the waters of those States were dependent. Meager supplies have been sent to Charleston from this place and from the Egypt mines in North Carolina.... The prices of almost all articles of prime necessity have advanced from five to ten times above those ruling at the breaking out of the war, and, for many articles, a much greater advance has been reached, so that now the pay of the higher grades of officers, even those with small families, is insufficient for the pay of their board only; how much greater, then, must be the difficulty of living in the case of the lower grades of officers, and, the families of enlisted persons. This difficulty, when the private sources of credit and the limited means of most of the officers become exhausted, must soon, unless relief be extended to them by the Government, reach the point of destitution, or of charitable dependence, a point, in fact, already reached in many instances.

November 17 (Tuesday)

A thousand troops and two batteries of artillery, manned by sailors, were landed on Mustang Island, Aransas Pass, Tex., from troop transports escorted by the U.S.S. *Monongahela*, Commander Strong, to assault the Confederate force on the island. The artillery bombarded the defenders, and combined with the assault by the troops, resulted in a surrender of all Confederate forces.

In Washington, Lincoln worked on his "few remarks" to be made at Gettysburg in two days' time.

Assistant Secretary of the Navy Fox wrote Admiral S.P. Lee, North Atlantic Blockading Squadron, off Wilmington, N.C.:

> I congratulate you upon the captures off Wilmington. Nine steamers have been lost to the rebels in a short time, all due to the "fine spirit" of our people engaged in the blockade. It is a severe duty and well maintained and Jeff Davis pays us a higher compliment than our own people when he declares that there is but one port in 3500 miles (recollect that the whole Atlantic front of Europe is but 2900 miles) through which they can get in supplies.

At Knoxville, Tenn., Longstreet continued his siege of Burnside with little action. At Chattanooga, Grant and the Sherman designed their battle plan to break the siege. The firing on Ft. Sumter continued.

A policy, both North and South, had long existed that permitted soldiers who were wounded to go home to recuperate, providing, of course, they could travel. This served a useful purpose in that it relieved the government of nursing and feeding the wounded. Home care provided the wounded with the tender, loving care that helped in the healing process. The problem arose that there was no one locally, in the various hometowns, who was authorized to determine when the sick or wounded soldier was fit for duty.

November 18 (Wednesday)

At Hog Point, La., Capt. Thomas A. Faries, CSA, got into a duel with a Union ship, the Union naval guns against his artillery. The U.S.S. *Choctaw*, sailing past the redoubt, cut loose with her bow, side, and stern guns, enfilading the artillery pieces for a short time. The other ships, U.S.S. *Franklin* and *Carondelet*, merely watched.

The merchant schooner *Joseph L. Garrity*, loaded with cotton, had sailed from Matamoras, Tex., on the 16th and was headed for New York when five of her passengers, under Thomas E. Hogg, took over the ship and sailed south into the Gulf of Mexico.

In the South the shortage of some commodities was solved by the use of "impressment agents" who had the authority to seize the needed commodity and pay the government price for it in lieu of the market price. Since there was such a disparity between the two prices, the producers objected, some violently, to this practice. Then, of course, there were always the overzealous agents and those who were working more for their own good than for the country's. The citizens of the various areas wrote often to the central government protesting the practices of some of the agents.

In Washington, a depressed President Lincoln

boarded a special train for the trip to Gettysburg, where he would deliver "a few appropriate remarks" at the dedication of the National Cemetery. He was travelling alone: his son Tad was ill and his wife, Mary, was remaining in the White House to tend the boy.

November 19 (Thursday)

At Gettysburg, Edward Everett, a noted orator of the day, talked for two hours, tracing the history of men at war from the earliest times to the present. Beautifully delivered, as always, when his speech was done, hardly anyone remembered what had been said. This was not because his words were not noteworthy, but because of what followed.

Next on the platform was the tall, lanky President. In a few short moments he delivered one of the most eloquent, moving speeches ever written, and one that has become known throughout the world. During the speech, many in the audience paid little attention, expecting the oration to last for some period of time. Others couldn't hear well and were trying to move to positions where this could be corrected. But, then the speech was over and Lincoln was sitting down again. The newspapers, some of them, commented favorably. Others criticized the speech. The President took his train back to Washington that evening to his sick child.

In Chattanooga, Grant and his generals continued to plan their next move. Bragg was sitting at Chickamauga Station arguing with his generals.

November 20 (Friday)

In New York, Admiral Farragut was itchy to get back to sea and his command of the Gulf Blockading Squadron, now operating somewhat short of ships. In a letter to Secretary of the Navy Gideon Welles, Farragut noted that the new ironclads being built on the Mississippi River at St. Louis would be ideal for operating in the coastal waters of Texas. Being light-draft, only drawing six feet of water, they could operate in the smaller rivers, much easier than did his larger gunboats.

Food was ever a problem in Richmond, which had grown from a somewhat sleepy town of less than 40,000 before the war to over 140,000 in about 18 months. Some residents were getting desperate.

At Charleston, the Union gunners fired 1344 rounds onto Ft. Sumter, killing three men and wounding eleven.

In Washington, Lincoln received a note from the orator Edward Everett congratulating the President on how close his remarks were "to the central idea of the occasion" at Gettysburg. Lincoln replied, "I am pleased to know that, in your judgment, the little I did say was not entirely a failure."

November 21 (Saturday)

At Chattanooga, Sherman was on the move, crossing the Tennessee River at Brown's Ferry and heading northeast to the Confederate right flank around Missionary Ridge. Sherman was to attack the north end of the ridge, Thomas the center. Hooker was to attack the Confederate left flank. There were delays, even more than usual, because of the heavy rains, and the roads were quagmires.

Conditions in the South were worsening, especially in those places where large numbers of "non-producers" were located, like Richmond. The depreciation of the currency was appalling and hit those on fixed incomes the hardest.

November 22 (Sunday)

At Missionary Ridge, Ga., Gen. Braxton Bragg detached Gen. Simon Bolivar Buckner from Bragg's Army of Tennessee and sent Buckner to Knoxville, Tenn., to support Gen. James Longstreet, who was besieging Union forces under Gen. Ambrose E. Burnside. Bragg was unaware, of course, that a storm of blue was about to descend upon him in the form of Grant's army. As a part of the Union buildup, Grant ordered Gen. George Thomas to demonstrate in front of Missionary Ridge the following day.

Among the thousands of Confederate soldiers, including John Jackman, at Missionary Ridge wondering what the Union troops were going to do while trying to keep warm, was one James Pleasant Gold, who was a member of the 9th Tennessee Cavalry, Capt. J.D. Kirkpatrick's Cavalry, Morgan's Division. Gold had enlisted, below age, in Company F, 24th Tennessee Volunteers, on July, 19, 1861, at Camp Trousdale. He was put to work hauling flour for about six months and driving cattle from south Georgia to north Georgia (a live ration detail) for a few months before he was discharged for being under age in July 1862. Undaunted, he enlisted again, this time in John Hunt Morgan's cavalry sometime before December 31, 1862. The next day he and John Jackman would face the Yankee onslaught.

Jackman, Pvt., "The Orphan Brigade," Battle of Missionary Ridge, Ga.:

> Have not got off yet. A clear and pleasant day. My personal adventures were few. I saw a hard time the night we got to the ridge, though late, thousands of campfires were sparkling in the valley like a belt of fires encircled Chattanooga showing the lines of the enemy and all around the base of the ridge our fires were gleaming.
>
> When we stopped, Johnnie G. and I made us a bed of brush and tried to sleep having no other covering than our overcoats, we had left our blankets back at the camp. A rain commenced falling, then soon after turned into snow or hail. We had to "nod" around a fire all night.

November 23 (Monday)

Secretary of the Navy Gideon Welles queried Admiral D.D. Porter if he could spare any of the light-draft ironclad gunboats being built at that location for use by Admiral Farragut in the Texas coastal waters.

At Chattanooga, Gen. George Thomas sent the divisions of Maj. Gen. Philip H. Sheridan and Brig. Gen. T.J. Wood forward to demonstrate against the Confederate lines. They moved to about a mile from the Rebel lines, taking Orchard Knob with little opposition, before dark. That night, Sherman sent a brigade across the Tennessee River near South Chickamauga Creek to prepare a bridge.

Jackman, Pvt., "The Orphan Brigade," Battle of Missionary Ridge, Ga.:

> ... night a cold rain was pelting down and while the boys were fortifying I tried to get a little sleep by lying down close to a fire. I did sleep a moment but burnt all the back out of my overcoat—a big hole in it. Afterwards in the campaign I often heard soldiers say, pointing me out, "Golly, didn't a *shell* come near getting that feller, look at the hole in his coat."

November 24 (Tuesday)

Early in the morning the blue-clad troops of Gen. Joseph Hooker crossed Lookout Creek and began the climb up Lookout Mountain to what was to become known as the "Battle Above the Clouds," so named because the top of the mountain was shrouded in mist. Little opposition was met because most of the Confederate troops had withdrawn to Missionary Ridge. By evening the Union held the mountain.

At the other end of the natural amphitheatre, Sherman had captured what he thought was the north end of the ridge, only to find that he was on high ground but that a ravine separated him from the real ridge and Tunnel Hill, one of his main objectives. Things settled down for the night.

Jackman, Pvt., "The Orphan Brigade," Battle of Missionary Ridge, Ga.:

> ...while going to the right I saw Bro. W. who was still in the battery. I tried to get him to go with me but he would not leave. I was standing immediately by Sgt. Young when he was shot and I thought he was killed as the ball knocked him clean off the ground and threw him several feet. When night came on we all commenced piling up leaves and building good fires, well satisfied that "all was well" but we had scarcely laid down before a person came for us to move. When we got back to Chickamauga station the whole army was there in a mess. I got a little sleep during the night between Col. W. and Dr. B. who had blankets.

Further north in eastern Tennessee, Burnside and Longstreet were still at a standoff, with some fighting at Kingston.

November 25 (Wednesday)

In the early dawn light, Sherman's men moved against the north end of Missionary Ridge and Tunnel Hill, the latter being held by Gen. Patrick Cleburne's troops. Heavy fighting continued until about 2 P.M., with little or no progress being made. Hooker, who had been sent to attack the Confederate left and to block any retreat, was also having little luck. Grant then sent Thomas with four divisions against the center. The divisions advanced rapidly from the base of the ridge, overwhelming the Confederate line and driving them up the steep slope of the ridge. The Confederates on top could not fire for fear of hitting their own men and it became a footrace up the steep slopes, the Federals reaching the top in some places before the Rebels. The gray line broke and ran down the back slope of the ridge towards Chickamauga Creek, where some Confederates waded through the icy water rather than going to the bridges.

The continued assault up the ridge had been unplanned, and it seemed that the troops had taken it upon themselves to take the ridge, without direction from their generals. Among the Union men was a newly commissioned second lieutenant named Arthur MacArthur who would one day have a son named Douglas. Lt. MacArthur was awarded the Medal of Honor for action on this day.

Sheridan's division pursued the Confederates, but Hardee's corps held them off and then the Confederates withdrew in the darkness. The battle was over, the siege of Chattanooga was broken, and Bragg's army was intact, but beaten. Grant, with his typical aggressive style, issued orders for a follow-up immediately at first light. The Federal troops, feeling avenged for the defeat at Chickamauga, screamed at the top of their lungs, "Chickamauga! Chickamauga!"

Patrick Ronayne Cleburne was born in County Cork, Ireland, on March 17, 1828. Cleburne was highly intelligent, the son of a prominent doctor. He studied to be a doctor but failed the examinations. In shame, he enlisted in Her Majesty's 41st Regiment of Foot. After serving for three years, he bought his way out and emigrated to America. A naturalized American citizen, he worked for a time as a pharmacist in Cincinnati and then moved to Helena, Ark., where he bought into a drugstore. He studied law, and became a very successful lawyer in Helena. At the beginning of the war, he joined the 15th Arkansas in 1861 as a private, but he was soon elected captain. He was soon colonel of his regiment, and William Hardee appointed him to temporary brigade command in the winter of 1861. On May 4, 1862, the appointment became permanent and he was made Brigadier General. He was a fierce fighter, a solid commander, and one of the best infantry commanders on either side. After many successful periods of combat across Tennessee and down to Atlanta, he was killed leading his men at the Battle of Franklin, after having several horses shot from beneath him. He was one of the six Confederate generals killed on November 30, 1864. A fine soldier, admired by friend and foe.

Jackman, Pvt., "The Orphan Brigade," Ringgold, Ga.:

> The night we got to Ringgold the boys had their choice to wade the stream about waist deep or go 2 miles further by a bridge and many went round by the bridge in preference to washing. Andy C. and myself bargained with a teamster who had a very small mule to take us over for which we were to pay him two dollars each. Andy is a very large man and when we both got on the mule and pushed out into the river, he made demonstrations like he was going to lie down and we had to use our heels with a vengeance to keep him from doing so.

At Knoxville, Burnside and Longstreet sparred for advantage. In Charleston Harbor, the Union gunners threw another 517 rounds against Ft. Sumter.

November 26 (Thursday)

The *Joseph L. Garrity*, a merchant schooner loaded with cotton, had been hijacked at sea by one Thomas E. Hogg and four companions, all Confederate sympathizers, on the 18th, and sailed south. On this day they landed the crew, without injury, on the Yucatan peninsula and sailed for British Honduras (today Belize) in Central America. There the cotton was sold and the ship turned over by the British to the U.S. commercial agent and eventually returned to her owners. Three of the five men were later captured in Liverpool, England, where they were tried for piracy and acquitted. Hogg later became a Master in the Confederate Navy.

The battle for Chattanooga was over. Sherman and Thomas chased Bragg's troops from Chickamauga Station towards Ringgold, Ga., without pause. The Union troops clashed with Pat Cleburne's rear guard near Ringgold and heavy fighting erupted. The Federals finally called a halt, and Bragg had a chance to regroup his army. Both Jackman and Private James Pleasant Gold had survived to fight another day.

Jackman, Pvt., "The Orphan Brigade," Chickamauga Station, Ga.:

> That morning while we were in line over Chickamauga station, I was on the skirmish line with Compa-

ny D and all the troops fell back unobserved but 4 or 5 of us and we were surrounded before we knew it. We got out though by strategy and fast running. I thought for a time "Camp Chase" had me. I was worn out when we stopped at Tunnel Hill for the night.

At Knoxville, Longstreet was preparing an assault, blissfully unaware that Bragg had been defeated and was withdrawing.

In Virginia, on the Rapidan River, Major Gen. George G. Meade's Army of the Potomac crossed the Rapidan in an attempt to turn Lee's right flank near Mine Run. The resultant moves were like a dance with both armies moving to counter each other's movements.

November 27 (Friday)

Admiral D.D. Porter, commanding the river fleet on the Mississippi, responded to Gideon Welles's query about the possibility of supplying some of the new ironclad gunboats (being built at St. Louis) to Admiral Farragut for use in Texas coastal waters. Porter said he could supply eight such ships "in the course of a month" and that "six weeks from to-day I could have ten vessels sent to Admiral Farragut, if I can get the officers and men."

In the Chattanooga area, the Confederates had withdrawn towards Ringgold Gap and Taylor's Ridge, closely followed by Grant's army. At this point it was largely a war of movement. Now that the siege of Chattanooga was broken, Grant sent two divisions under Gen. Gordon Granger to Knoxville, to relieve Burnside.

Jackman, Pvt., "The Orphan Brigade," Ringgold, Ga.:

> We... marched back and forth between Ringgold and Tunnel Hill, 7 miles, two or three times during the day, conforming our movements to Cleburne's. After dark a rain set in and sleep was out of the question.

In Virginia, Meade's sudden offensive of the day before was countered by Lee's move to the east. This caused skirmishing in the old Wilderness Church area and west to the Culpeper area.

At Columbus, Ohio, the prison was short a few prisoners when Gen. John Hunt Morgan and some of his officers escaped and managed to reach Confederate territory. There was a tunnel involved, but rumors persisted that money had changed hands. Either way, he was loose.

November 28 (Saturday)

Sherman was ordered to send more troops, in addition to those sent with Gen. Granger, to the relief of Burnside. Bragg, feeling like the world had fallen in, wired Richmond, "I deem it due to the cause and to myself to ask for relief from command and investigation into the causes of the defeat." Strangely enough, Bragg was little at fault this time. He was defeated by overzealous Union soldiers who refused to stop at the bottom of Missionary Ridge.

Jackman, Pvt., "The Orphan Brigade," en route to Dalton, Ga.:

> ...morning came I did not feel very strong and turned my Enfield, picked up on the ridge, over to a gunless man. We had to stand in line of battle in a pelting rain until noon when Cleburne passed us then we marched for Dalton on the rail road 6 or 7 miles. We stopped for the night in some old hospital building ½ mile from town on the railroad. That night, Nov 28th, I believe was the most disagreeable night I ever spent. The houses were not very tight and I could not sleep on the floor inside so I went out by a fire and hovered around it all night long. I believe the keenest wind was blowing I ever felt. I had not slept any scarcely for 4 or 5 nights and could hardly hold my eyes open; yet I knew if I went to sleep I would freeze.

In Virginia, Meade was sending heavy skirmishers against the Confederate positions at Mine Run. The gray line held without too much trouble and it seemed that Meade's offensive was stalled.

At Charleston, the Union guns were still pounding Ft. Sumter and the other harbor defenses.

November 29 (Sunday)

The area in and around Knoxville, Tenn., had had bad weather. The snow and icy conditions made travel, even walking, difficult. At about dawn, Longstreet sent his Confederates against the defenses of Ft. Sanders, one of the forts guarding the city. With a valiant effort, the gray-clad troops held the parapet for a short period of time but had to retreat. This would be Longstreet's last attempt to take

Knoxville, knowing that Grant had reinforcements on the way. Bragg had settled in at Dalton, Ga., and waited for an answer to his request to be relieved of command.

November 30 (Monday)

Bragg received a telegram from the War Department in Richmond accepting his offer to resign from command. He was directed to turn the army over to Gen. Hardee in the interim. The Army of Tennessee was slowly being pulled together after its near-rout from Missionary Ridge. The troops began to settle in for the winter.

Jackman, Pvt., "The Orphan Brigade," Dalton, Ga.:

> Today our wagons came up from Resaca. Johnnie G. and I immediately fixed up our fly, we had no tent—by weatherboarding the back and building a large fire in front. At night we had our blankets spread down on a bed of leaves and slept "40 miles an hour."

DECEMBER 1863

The last month of the year began with fresh victories at Lookout Mountain and Missionary Ridge for the Union and "non-victories" at Charleston and at Mine Run for the Confederacy. Economically, the South was becoming more desperate, distribution of food being of major concern. The grind of war was also taking its toll, North and South. The casualty lists posted attest to the cost of the war in human terms. The major armies were now settled into their winter quarters fairly well and would remain there until spring, with some eruptions. The South had survived another year.

December 1 (Tuesday)

In Virginia, Major Gen. George G. Meade had decided that he was not going to make it around Lee's flank at Mine Run, so he pulled back across the Rapidan completely and went into winter quarters.

At Knoxville, Longstreet had tried no new major assaults on Burnside's positions, and knowing that more Union troops were on the way, Longstreet prepared to depart.

The bombardment of Ft. Sumter that had begun on November 28th still went on.

In Washington, Confederate spy Belle Boyd, who was ill with typhoid, was released from the Old Capital Prison and was sent to Richmond by flag-of-truce boat, and was told not to come back.

Confederate Gen. Joe Wheeler's cavalry were noted for their raids on the local populace, wherever they were, to obtain rations and mounts. This problem became serious in North Carolina, and the fiery governor of that state, Zebulon B. Vance, wrote to the government in Richmond, "If God Almighty had yet in store another plague for the Egyptians worse than all others, I am sure it must have been a regiment or so of half-armed, half-disciplined Confederate cavalry."

Day, Pvt., Co. B, 25th Massachusetts Volunteer Infantry, on furlough:

> On receipt of my furlough… I, in company with eight others from the three companies, left Hill's Point for Massachusetts. I had 25 days at home, a part of which I used up on the lounge with chills and fever and listening to the expressions of sympathy from callers. After recovering… I enjoyed the balance of my visit very much and reported back in New York the next morning after the expiration of my furlough.
>
> Arriving in New York, I went directly to the New England rooms on Broadway. These rooms are a kind of free hotel for New England soldiers en route through New York, but will accommodate any others when they are not full. The rooms are well fitted up and there is a spacious loft or hall which is used for sleeping with 100 or more single cots, on each of which is a good mattress, pillow, a pair of woolen blankets and white spread. In this room a man is in attendance day and night to attend to the wants of patrons, preserve order and look after things generally.
>
> The dining hall will seat about 200 persons, and the tables are well supplied with plain, substantial, wholesome food. Another room is used for a sick room or hospital and is filled up with a few cots and lounges, and the tables are well supplied with books and newspapers. This room is presided over by a kind-hearted sympathetic lady who was formerly a hospital matron in McClellan's peninsular campaign.
>
> Besides, there is the office and baggage room where one's knapsack or other luggage is put away and checked. The owner takes his check and gives no further thought or care of his baggage until wanted. In addition to these, are all other necessary conve-

niences. These rooms were fitted up and are supported by the patriotic generosity of New Englanders, residents of New York, and many are the thanks and blessings they receive from their beneficiaries.

Here I found Spencer and Lewis, who were furloughed with me, and who had just arrived. The clerk told us we must report to a certain quartermaster up town for instructions. We reported; he examined our papers, endorsed on the backs "reported back all right and on time," and told us we must report at the transportation office down near battery park. We reported and were informed there was no transportation waiting, but we must report every morning in order to avail ourselves of the first boat that left.

There were 100 or more soldiers waiting transportation to New Bern, besides hundreds of others for all parts of the army. The officer in charge would no more than get his coat off and sleeves rolled up, ready for business in the morning, when we would appear to him. He would get rid of us by a wave of his hand and "No boat for New Bern." This continued for several mornings until he became tired of seeing us and hung a card on the door with "No boat for New Bern."

One morning the card was off and all hands made a grand charge inside. He gave us the cheering information that General Foster had moved his old brigade from New Bern to Fortress Monroe and he would give transportation by way of Baltimore to as many of us as belonged to that brigade. No one seemed to know what to do.... I ventured the remark that I had received no official information of the removal of the brigade or of my regiment and until further orders, I thought I had better stick to the order in my furlough and report to North Carolina.... We were soon on the street again. The next morning... the officer said that he had reliable information that the 23d, 25th and 27th Massachusetts and 9th New Jersey regiments together with the 3d New York Cavalry were at Fortress Monroe; he was going to give orders for rations and transportation by way of Baltimore to all those belonging to those regiments and we could come in the afternoon and get them. I inquired if he was authorized to order us to report to Fortress Monroe. That gave him a sort of blind staggers. He said he was not really, but it would be all right enough, especially if we were anxious to join our regiments.

I replied, "We are anxious to join our regiments, but as everything in military has to run in its regular groove, and as one order holds until another is given, it would hardly look military to be acting on our own judgment and hearsay stories, and going off across lots, reporting somewhere else than where our orders say." "You seem to be right on your military. Do you always pay as strict observance to orders?" "That is the way we have been educated, sir." That question settled, we were soon on the pave again.

The outside of Barnum's Museum is always covered with immense show bills and people have become so accustomed to them that they attract but little attention, unless it is some new and curious thing he has got on exhibition. Noticing a picture of an enormous sea lion and reading glowing descriptions of him in the newspapers, I remarked to Spencer: "We had better take that in. "Now Barnum's is a good place to go, as it is a highly moral show, and inexpensive—twenty-five cents giving one the whole range from basement to attic.... One evening we went up.

Exchanging our quarters for tickets, we were admitted... we went down into the basement where is located the aquarium. We soon found the sea lion. He laid on a large platform with his head towards the grating and about three feet from it. At the rear end of the platform was a large tank of water where he could bathe. He was a harmless looking lion enough and resembled a mule as much as a lion.... We tried to start him up, but he seemed to prefer quiet and no motion of our arms and caps had the slightest effect on him. I had an uncontrollable desire to see him go into the tank and looked in vain all around the place for something to stir him up with. Presently a gentlemen came along.... He had an umbrella and I asked him to stir the creature up... he thought he had better not.... A bright thought now struck me; I would fill his eye with tobacco juice and see what effect that would have. I chewed up a large piece of tobacco; filling my mouth with the juice, and getting a beautiful range on his left eye, let drive, covering it completely and, to my utter astonishment, that creature never so much as winked. I was dumbfounded at the result of my experiment as this was the first creature I had ever seen which had eyes that a little tobacco juice in them would not make things lively for a few minutes. I can account for my failure in no other way than that, being a marine animal, there is probably some kind of film or covering over the eye that protects it....

Strolling around up stairs, we came to the mummy cabinet. Now I like mummies and am always interested in them; they have a habit of minding their own business, the steadiest of any class of people I ever met with, besides they are always civil to callers and are free from the disputes, quarrels, gossiping, slanders, and other vices with which our generation is afflicted. They are a very ancient people, and in their time, were doubtless an intelligent and highly respectable class of citizens but they don't amount to much now; they are too far behind the times.... There was a large collection and they looked black and dirty as though they neglected their baths and toilets; they all looked so much alike it was difficult to distinguish their sex. I think if they could be taken out and washed and dressed up in fashionable clothing they would make quite a respectable appearance.... I pointed out the largest one to Spencer and said: "That gentleman was once a soldier and did provost duty in the city of Thebes 3000 years ago." He made no reply but kept looking at it and presently I heard him muttering to himself: "Can that be possible? Brave old fossil!"

After waiting thirteen days, a boat arrived and we were now off.... We arrived at New Bern after a four days' passage and reported to the provost marshal, Capt. Denny of our regiment, who welcomed us back and gave us the liberty of the city. He informed us the regiment was at Fortress Monroe, and if we had only known it while in New York, we could have saved ourselves the trouble of coming here and having to go back. We were somewhat surprised at this intelligence and disappointed at not knowing it while there and saving ourselves all this unnecessary trouble and delay. But, however, we must put up with it and take the next boat back which leaves for Fortress Monroe.

After a four days visit here we went aboard the little steamer Vidette bound for Fortress Monroe. He had aboard about 200 soldiers and about 100 Confederate prisoners. We left in the afternoon and the next morning were at Hatteras inlet. The sea was pretty rough and in crossing the swash we fouled with a schooner, carrying away her bowsprit and losing one of our anchors. The old captain... said he never had such good luck before in getting through the inlet.... The following morning we were at Fortress Monroe and here learned that our regiment was at Newport News at the mouth of the James river. We re-shipped on another boat and an hour after were receiving the ovations and congratulations of our comrades after an absence of nearly two months.

Barber, Cpl., Co. D, 15th Illinois Volunteer Infantry, Riley, Illinois:

Government had offered large inducements for the first three years' men to re-enlist, and by letters from the boys I learned that a good portion of the 15th had re-enlisted for three years longer. Roll, Milt and Charlie Mitchell amongst the number. This produced a feverish state of excitement in my mind. I longed to be with them. I did not say much about it to my folks for I knew that they would oppose me. Perhaps it was foolhardy to think of re-enlisting in my poor state of health, but I believed that one year would see the end of the Rebellion and I thought that I could stand it that length of time....

December 2 (Wednesday)

Commodore H.H. Bell, commander of the West Gulf Blockading Squadron during the absence of Admiral Farragut, wrote Secretary of the Navy Gideon Welles with somewhat of an inventory of the enemy ships in Mobile Bay:

C.S.S. *Gaines* and *Morgan* each mounted ten guns, both sidewheelers; the C.S.S. *Selma* and the nearly completed ironclad C.S.S. *Nashville* mounted four guns each, also both sidewheelers. The ironclad rams C.S.S. *Baltic*, *Huntsville*, and *Tennessee* all mounted four guns each. The C.S.S. *Gunnison* was fitted with a torpedo carrying 150 pounds of powder and another similar boat was being fitted out.

There were also 2 floating batteries mounting 3 guns each and 10 transport steamers operating in the Bay. A large vessel was being built at Selma and three rams being built on the Tombigbee River to be ready this winter.

At Knoxville, Longstreet was threatened by a fast-moving Union force coming up on his rear from Chattanooga to relieve the siege of Knoxville.

At Dalton, Ga., Braxton Bragg was leaving the Army of Tennessee, turning the command over to Lt. Gen. William Hardee. Hardee would command only a short time before Gen. Joseph E. Johnston arrived to assume command. Bragg was a good soldier and a good commander in the technical sense, but he had no facility for dealing with other people over long periods. He would now go to Richmond and report to President Davis.

Jackman, Pvt., "The Orphan Brigade," Dalton, Ga.:

> At night received a letter from home by flag of truce *via* City Point. Bro. W's. battery was fortunately abandoned at the ridge and he is with us.
>
> Two or three days after we move camp over on the railroad about a half mile from town and the boys immediately begin putting up cabins for winter quarters. The nature of the ground does not permit the brigade to be all camped together and the different regiments have selected grounds to suit themselves. I like our "parish" family. Bro. W., the day we moved, went to his command, Carter's Scouts, which is encamped close to Dalton.

A boat expedition reconnoitering Lake Ocala, Fla., found a saltworks that was producing about 130 bushels of salt per day, a considerable amount when you consider the amount of saltwater that had to be boiled down to obtain that result. The boat crews, from the U.S.S. *Restless*, Acting Master William R. Browne, destroyed the boilers, threw a large amount of the salt into the lake, demolished two large flatboats and six ox carts, and captured 17 prisoners.

December 3 (Thursday)

At Charleston Harbor, S.C., Admiral Dahlgren issued specific orders for the deployment of the ironclads of the blockading fleet:

> Picket duty is to be performed by four monitors, two for each night, one of which is to be well advanced up the harbor, in a position suitable for preventing the entrance or departure of any vessel attempting to pass in or out of Charleston Harbor, and for observing Sumter and Moultrie, or movements in and about them, taking care at the same time not to get aground, and also to change the position when the weather appears to render it unsafe. The second monitor is to keep within proper supporting distance of the first, so as to render aid if needed.... The general object of the monitors, tugs, and boats on picket is to enforce the blockade rigorously, and to watch and check the movements of the enemy by water whenever it can be done, particularly to detect and destroy the torpedo boats and the picket boats of the rebels.

At Knoxville, Longstreet began moving his troops away from the city, effectively breaking the siege. He moved north and east to Greeneville, Tenn., where he took up winter quarters. Tennessee was now totally occupied by Union forces.

December 5 (Saturday)

Another boat crew was captured at Murrell's Inlet, S.C., while reconnoitering ashore. This time the crew was from the U.S.S. *Perry*. The last crew lost in the same area was from the U.S.S. *T.A. Ward*.

December 6 (Sunday)

In an unfortunate accident, the U.S.S. *Weehawken*, Commander Duncan, sank when a strong ebb tide washed water down an open hawse pipe and hatch. The ship was loaded with an extra heavy load of ammunition, which reduced the freeboard (space between the water and the deck) to a dangerous level. The ship went down at Charleston Harbor, drowning some two dozen officers and men.

Gen. Sherman and his staff entered Knoxville, Tenn., officially ending the siege. Parts of his old Fifteenth Corps were close behind and coming up fast.

Late last month, the Confederate government in Richmond had "called up the reserve" in the form of units composed of government clerks and sent them to Chaffin's Bluff to guard the eastern approach to the city. They had been there for a week and were finally sent home.

December 7 (Monday)

In quite an impressive display of numbers and statistics, Secretary of the Navy Gideon Welles reported to President Lincoln on the state of the blockade:

> A blockade commencing at Alexandria, in Virginia, and terminating at the Rio Grande, has been effectively maintained. The extent of the blockade... covers a distance of three thousand five hundred and forty-nine statute miles, with one hundred and eighty-nine harbor or pier openings or indentations, and much of the cost presents a double shore to be guarded.... A naval force of more than one hundred vessels has been employed in patrolling the rivers,

cutting off rebel supplies, and cooperating with the armies.... The distance thus traversed and patrolled by the gunboats on the Mississippi and its tributaries is 3615 miles, and the sounds, bayous, rivers and inlets of the States upon the Atlantic and the Gulf, covering an extent of about 2000 miles, have also been... watched with unceasing vigilance.

Welles also reported a naval strength of 34,000 seamen and 588 ships displacing 467,967 tons, and mounting 4443 guns. More than 1000 ships had been captured by the blockaders.

Capt. John Parker, CSN, devised a plot whereby one John C. Braine, in company with 16 other Confederate sympathizers, were sent from New Brunswick, Canada, to New York, where they acquired weapons and boarded the steamer *Chesapeake*, en route to Portland, Me. When the steamer was off Cape Cod, the Confederates took over the ship, killing the second engineer, and took her to the Bay of Fundy in Nova Scotia, where Parker came aboard. The intent was to refuel the ship and go to Wilmington, slipping by the blockade at that port. The capture of the ship caused great alarm in the Northern ports and the U.S. Navy sent ships out to recapture the *Chesapeake* as soon as possible.

December 8 (Tuesday)

Messages from both Presidents Lincoln and Davis went to their respective Congresses, Lincoln's reporting success and hope. Davis's was apprehensive. Lincoln also offered amnesty (with exceptions) to those in the South who would take an oath of allegiance.

In West Virginia, Averell's cavalry went raiding in cold weather to destroy railroads in the southwestern part of that state.

A Confederate shore battery near Morganza, La., picked the wrong time to start shelling a disabled merchant steamer, the *Henry Von Phul*. Hearing the guns, the U.S.S. *Signal*, Acting Ensign William P. Lee, and the U.S.S. *Neosho*, Acting Ensign Edwin F. Brooks, went to the defense of the steamer and silenced the battery.

December 9 (Wednesday)

At Knoxville, Major Gen. John G. Foster replaced Major Gen. Ambrose E. Burnside as commander of the Department of the Ohio.

December 10 (Thursday)

Some skirmishing in West Virginia as Union cavalry raids continued from New Creek and a new raid started from Harper's Ferry.

Day, Pvt., Co. B, 25th Massachusetts Volunteer Infantry, Newport News, Va.:

I am now on the sacred soil of old Virginia and my first care will be to seek an introduction to some of the F.F.V's.... Our camp is near the river and only a few rods from us lie the wrecks of the frigates *Cumberland* and *Congress*, sunk by the rebel ram *Merrimac*. The *Cumberland* lies in deep water out of sight, but the deck of the *Congress* is seen and often visited by the boys at low water. Since the occupation of this place by Federal troops, it has grown into what they call down this way a town, containing quite a collection of rough board store-houses, sutler's shops, Negro shanties, and horse sheds. A boat runs from here to Fortress Monroe every day, and three times a week to Norfolk; the distance to either place is about the same, some twelve miles.

For the first time since the war began the oyster fishing is being prosecuted and Hampton Roads are alive with oyster schooners. The oysters have had a chance to grow and are now abundant and of good size and flavor. Newport News was the first place in Virginia, except Washington, that was occupied by Federal troops and it was from here that a part of old Ben's famous Big Bethel expedition started.

During my absence this military department has gone all wrong. General Foster has been ordered to Knoxville, Tenn. and General Butler has superseded him to this command. I am not pleased with the change. General Foster was a splendid man and fine officer, and I would rather take my chances with a regular army officer than with an amateur. The first year of the war General Butler was the busiest and most successful general we had, but since then he has kind o' taken to niggers and trading. As a military governor he is a nonesuch, and in that role, has gained a great fame, especially in all the rebellious states. He is a lawyer and a man of great executive ability, and can not only make laws but see to it that they are observed, but as a commander of troops in the field, he is not just such a man as I should pick out.

He had a review of our brigade the other day and his style of soldiering caused considerable fun among the boys who had been used to seeing General Foster. He rode on to the field with a great dash, followed by staff enough for two major-generals. He looks very awkward on a horse and wears a soft hat; when he salutes the colors he lifts his hat by the crown clear off his head instead of simply touching the brim. The boys think he is hardly up to their ideas of a general, but as they are not supposed to know anything, they will have to admit that he *is* a great general. He is full of orders and laws (regardless of army regulations) in the government of his department, and his recent order in relation to darkies fills two columns of newspaper print and is all the most fastidious lovers of darkies in all New England could desire. Hunter and Fremont are the merest pigmies beside Ben in their care of darkies.

December 11 (Friday)

Only 220 shells were fired at Ft. Sumter today. One, however, exploded a powder magazine, killing 11 and wounding 41 of the defenders. This would be the last bombardment for the year.

The U.S.S. *Restless*, Acting Master W.R. Browne, in company with the U.S.S. *Bloomer* and tender *Caroline*, entered St. Andrew's Bay, Fla., where the *Restless* began a bombardment of the houses, striking one of the houses, that served as quarters for the Confederates, on the southeast of the group, and setting it afire. The wind was from the southeast and quickly spread the flames through the remaining buildings, burning 32 of them to the ground. Meantime, the *Bloomer* and *Caroline* were at work destroying the saltworks, which was the purpose of the raid. These works, which produced about 400 bushels of salt per day, were described by Browne:

> It was in fact a complete village, covering a space of three-fourths of a square mile, employing many hands and 16 ox and mule teams constantly to haul salt to Eufaula Sound, and from thence conveyed to Montgomery, at which place it is selling at fabulous prices—$40 and $50 per bushel. At this place, were 27 buildings, and 22 large steam boilers, and 300 kettles averaging 200 gallons each, which cost the Government $5 per gallon, all of which were totally destroyed, beside 2,000 bushels of salt, and storehouses filled with cornmeal, bacon, sirup, and other provisions, enough to supply these employed for three months....

Major Gen. D.H. Maury, commander of the defenses of Mobile, Ala., wrote that "I expect the fleet to succeed in running past the outer forts... I shall do all I can to prevent it, and to hold the forts as long as possible."

Confederate Secretary of War Seddon's annual report stated that the reduction in military strength of the army was caused by desertion, straggling, and absenteeism.

December 12 (Saturday)

The United States, until now, had been sending rations to Richmond to feed the 13,000 Union prisoners held there, because the Confederate government did not have the means. This changed today when orders were given in Richmond that no more supplies from the United States should be received by the Federal prisoners.

December 14 (Monday)

Gen. Longstreet attacked Union troops at Bean's Station, Tenn., on his way to Greeneville. He drove back the Federals, under the command of Brig. Gen. James M. Shackelford, in a sharp fight. The Federals held for a while, but withdrew further the following day.

President Lincoln announced that his sister-in-law, Mrs. Benjamin Hardin Helm, who was visiting the White House, had taken the oath of allegiance and had been granted amnesty under his December 8th proclamation.

At Charleston, Gen. Beauregard directed Lt. Dixon, CSA, to take the submarine *H.L. Hunley* to the mouth of the harbor and sink any Union vessel he could reach.

December 15 (Tuesday)

From Paris, France, Secretary of the Navy Mallory was notified by Confederate Capt. Barron that getting ships repaired in European ports was a difficult task. He said that the "spies" of U.S. Ambassador Charles Francis Adams in London "are to be found following the footsteps of any Confederate agent in spite of all the precautions we can adopt...." Mr. Adams constantly frustrated efforts to buy guns and ships for the Confederacy.

Jackman, Pvt., "The Orphan Brigade," Dalton, Ga.:

We have concluded to build a house for winter and have been cutting and hauling pine logs for the purpose today. The troops had four pounds of sweet potatoes issued today in lieu of bread. "Hard up" "Ike" who has been over to the cavalry camp says they are worse off. He says the "spurred" gentry are cutting down old trees and robbing the woodpeckers of their winter store of acorns to the great discomfiture of the red-headed foresters. He says he saw an old woodpecker expostulate in vain with a cavalryman to leave her stores alone.

Admiral Buchanan, CSN, at Mobile, wrote Commander Catesby ap R. Jones at the naval foundry in Selma about the C.S.S. *Tennessee*, currently under construction:

The *Tennessee* will carry a battery of two 7-inch Brooke guns and four broadsides, 6.4 or 9-inch.... There is a great scarcity of officers and I know not where I will get them. I have sent the names of 400 men who wish to be transferred from the Army to the Navy, and have received only about twenty.

December 16 (Wednesday)

It was announced today that Gen. Joseph Eggleston Johnston, CSA, would command the Army of Tennessee, replacing Lt. Gen. William Hardee. Johnston, at Brandon, Miss., left his current command to Lt. Gen. Leonidas Polk.

In Washington, John Buford, who had commanded the cavalry that made the initial contact at Gettysburg, was promoted to Major General, just a few hours before he died of typhoid. Although not a flamboyant fighter like Sheridan and Custer, he was a good, solid soldier.

In Havana, Cuba, the U.S. Consul-General Thomas Savage wrote Commodore H.H. Bell, West Gulf Blockading Squadron, on the status of blockade runners in Havana:

A schooner under rebel colors, called *Roebuck*, 41 tons, with cotton arrived from Mobile yesterday. She left that port, I believe, on the 8th. She is the only vessel that has reached this port from Mobile for a very long time.... The famous steamer *Alice*, which ran the blockade at Mobile successfully so many times, is now on the dry dock here fitting out for another adventure.

December 17 (Thursday)

Lt. Commander Fitch, U.S.S. *Moose*, sent landing parties ashore at Seven Mile Island and Palmyra, on the Tennessee River, to destroy distilleries used by the Confederate guerrilla troops.

Jackman, Pvt., "The Orphan Brigade," Dalton, Ga.:

Had quite a storm of winds and rain last night. Thanks to our "fly" for not leaking much. Looking over Murry's Encyclopedia of Geography, brought into camp by "Paul" for the Col. to read. This old book came to me like a friend of childhood's happy days, to call up pleasing reminiscences of times long ago. When a boy, many of an evening was whiled away scanning over the book. "Paul" made a bad selection for the Col. though, not being a book for the camp. Another time "Paul" was sent out to forage for literature and came into camp with a Patent Office Report and one of Cicero's works in Latin. "Paul" pretended to be one of the *literate*, but I doubt whether he was scarcely able to read. He handed the Col. the large book—the P.O. Report—and said he thought that a "purty" good book; "but this may be" he said, holding out the one in Latin "to much d____d bad print. I don't know whether you can read it or not." It was excellent *print*, but "Paul" didn't understand the [Latin], etc. The Col. never sent him after books again.

The steamer *Chesapeake*, en route from New York to Portland, Me., had been taken over by a party of 17 Confederate sympathizers on the 7th of the month and sailed to the Bay of Fundy, Nova Scotia. The U.S. Navy had instituted a wide search for the vessel and it was retaken today in Sambro Harbor, Nova Scotia, by Acting Lt. J. Frederick Nickels, U.S.S. *Ella and Annie*. The steamer was taken to Halifax, Nova Scotia, where the English Admiralty court restored the ship to its original owners. Most of the Confederates escaped.

December 19 (Saturday)

Back down in Florida at St. Andrew's Bay, the destruction of the saltworks continued. The U.S.S. *Restless*, *Bloomer*, and *Caroline* continued on up the bay, spreading panic and destruction as they went. Acting Master W.R. Browne of the *Restless* reported:

> ...cleared the three arms of this extensive bay of saltworks.... Within the past ten days, 290 saltworks, 33 covered wagons, 12 flatboats, 2 sloops (5 ton each), 6 ox carts, 4,000 bushels of salt, 268 buildings at the different saltworks, 529 iron kettles averaging 150 gallons each, 105 iron boilers for boiling brine [were destroyed], and it is believed that the enemy destroyed as many more to prevent us from doing so.

December 21 (Monday)

At Mobile Bay, Ala., Admiral Buchanan wrote Commander Catesby ap R. Jones in Selma that he had need of ship's crew:

> Have you received any orders from Brooke about the guns for the *Tennessee*? She is all ready for officers, men, and guns, and has been so reported to the Department many weeks since, but none have I received.

Jackman, Pvt., "The Orphan Brigade," Dalton, Ga.:

> Clear all day. At night wrote a letter for G.P. to send home. He cannot write well with his left hand yet (lost his right hand at battle of Hartsville). My *fee* was a dozen oysters. *Paid!*

December 22 (Tuesday)

Capt. Semmes, C.S.S. *Alabama*, moved his base of operations from the East Indies back to the Cape of Good Hope, Africa. He wrote from Singapore:

> The enemy's East India and China trade is nearly broken up. Their ships find it impossible to get freights, there being in this port [Singapore] some nineteen sail, almost all of which are laid up for want of employment.... The more widely our blows are struck, provided they are struck rapidly, the greater will be the consternation and consequent damage to the enemy.

December 23 (Wednesday)

Jackman, Pvt., "The Orphan Brigade," Dalton, Ga.:

> A cold disagreeable day. Had bean soup alone for dinner and for supper had "biled" rice without sugar to sweeten it. Tonight have written another letter for G.P.

December 24 (Thursday)

As somewhat of a Christmas present, Commander Catesby ap R. Jones at the Selma gun foundry wrote Admiral Buchanan in Mobile that the guns for the C.S.S. *Tennessee* would be sent:

> ...as soon as they are ready. We had an accident that might have been very serious. An explosion took place while attempting to cast the bottom section of a gun pit. The foundry took fire, but was promptly extinguished. Fortunately but two of the molds were burned. I had a narrow escape, my hat, coat, and pants were burned. Quite a loss in these times, with our depreciated currency and fixed salaries. As a large casting is never made without my being present, I consider my life in greater danger here than if I were in command of the *Tennessee*, though I should expect hot work in her occasionally. What chance have I for her?

Jackman, Pvt., "The Orphan Brigade," Dalton, Ga.:

> Nothing going on of great interest. In the evening our Q.M. and Capt. G. owing to the proximity of "Christmas Times" & having taken on some "pine top" were singing "The Star Spangled Banner" with a *vim*.

December 25 (Friday)

On John's Island, S.C., the Confederate batteries opened early on the U.S.S. *Marblehead*, Lt. Commander Meade. The Federal ship sustained some 20 hits, while the U.S.S. *Pawnee* and the mortar schooner *C.P. Williams* fired on the shore battery. The firing lasted for about an hour and then the Confederates withdrew, leaving two VIII-inch seacoast howitzers which were taken by Meade.

Jackman, Pvt., "The Orphan Brigade," Dalton, Ga.:

> A cold, cloudy, disagreeable day. Went to church in Dalton in forenoon and to night. Have just written a letter home to send by flag of truce. Set in raining late at night. My Christmas dinner was bean soup without bread. The boys who are out see a great deal of fun—some tipsy.

Many of the two-year regiments mustered in during 1861 were coming up for reenlistment or discharge. The government, of course, preferred to get the soldier to reenlist because it saved training and provided an instant veteran. The bounty was used as an inducement in most cases, part of which would be paid upon reenlistment, the remainder in installments. Capt. Kennedy commanded Company E, 9th New York Volunteer Cavalry, Army of the Potomac, at Culpeper Court House, Va., and on this day witnessed Lt. Hair, one of the company officers, give the oath of allegiance at the swearing-in ceremony for several veterans, including one James Riley who had just reenlisted for three years. Riley, whose age was listed as 21, was, in fact, 17, having been born in 1846 in Morristown, N.J. He had enlisted on September 7, 1861, under age, being only 15. When he reenlisted, he was paid $112 as a part of his bounty, the remaining $290 shown as due. He was also paid $18.25 as a part of his unspent clothing allowance.

Private James Riley had served through most of the campaigns of '61, '62, and '63, including Gettysburg but not Antietam. He would survive the war, being mustered out on July 16, 1865, at Cloud's Mill, Va. He migrated to Jackson, Mich., where he died on January 28, 1920.

December 26 (Saturday)

The C.S.S. *Alabama*, Capt. Semmes, captured and burned the ships *Sonora* and *Highlander*, both in ballast and at anchor in the entrance of the Straits of Malacca. Semmes wrote, "They were monster ships, both of them, being eleven or twelve hundred tons burden." Semmes wrote that one of the ship's masters told him:

> Well, Captain Semmes, I have been expecting every day for the last three years to fall in with you, and here I am at last.... The fact is, I have had constant visions of the *Alabama*, by night and by day; she has been chasing me in my sleep, and riding me like a night-mare, and now that it is all over, I feel quite relieved.

December 31 (Thursday)

Jackman, Pvt., "The Orphan Brigade," Dalton, Ga.:

> Pouring down rain all day. The wind blowing and other disagreeable things. Today, one year ago, we were on "Waynes Hill," Murfreesboro listening to the music of shells.

Secretary of the Navy Gideon Welles wrote in his diary, "The year closes more satisfactorily than it commenced.... The War has been waged with success, although there have been in some instances errors and misfortunes. But the heart of the nation is sounder and its hopes brighter."

In Richmond, the *Examiner* perhaps summed up the totality of the year when it said, "To-day closes the gloomiest year of our struggle."

1864

The third January of the war ended a momentous year and opened one that would prove to be among the bloodiest in our history. Grant had Gen. Joe Johnston stalled at Dalton, Ga., and Meade was watching Lee in Virginia. Economically, the South was in increasingly bad shape. While the blockade runners were getting some material through, many of the ordinary things were gone, or were so costly that only the very rich could afford them. The Confederate currency had depreciated rapidly in 1863, and would worsen in the coming year. The icy wind blowing through the country could be an omen of things to come.

January 1 (Friday)

New Year's Day saw icy winds and extreme cold dampen the spirits of the troops encamped in their winter quarters from the Mississippi River to the east coast. The soldiers, North and South, huddled around their fires in their makeshift tent-covered "cabins" and suffered. Despite the frigid weather, some skirmishing took place at scattered points across the country, accomplishing nothing.

The U.S. Navy turned its attention to the port of Wilmington, N.C., as its next major objective on the east coast. Blockade runners had been entering and leaving the port on the average of two per week. This represented a lot of tonnage going in and much cotton coming out. Joint operations were to be proposed.

Day, Pvt., Co. B, 25th Massachusetts Volunteer Infantry, Newport News, Va.:

> We have now entered on the last year of our soldier service and are looking forward to the end, and may it not only end our service, but the war as well.... About thirty days ago, orders were received from the war department at Washington soliciting re-enlistments from among the soldiers of the old regiments of 1861. Liberal money inducements were offered and in addition the present term of service would end on re-enlistment; the $100 bounty due at the expiration of the three years term could be drawn, together with a thirty day's furlough.... Up to the present time there have been but few enlistments.... The officers have not seemed to take much interest in it and have not used their influence to get the boys to enlist, but have given advice when sought for.... I shall not re-enlist, and my reasons are, first, I have no desire to monopolize all the patriotism there is, but am willing to give others a chance. My second reason is that after I have served three years, my duty to the country has been performed and my next duty is at home with my family.

Jackman, Pvt., "The Orphan Brigade," Dalton, Ga.:

> The new year ushered in a very cold manner. Ground hard frozen this morning. The sun shone bright yet a cool wind blowing in forenoon. Very cold tonight out of doors but the reckless winter winds that come sweeping over the bleak hills, roaring and

> snapping, screaming and shrieking, through the bare branches of the old oak overhanging our abode fail to penetrate the well chinked walls about us. There is a fire kindled in the earthen hearth to convivial glow lending a perfect air of coziness to the little tenement.

January 2 (Saturday)

Secretary of the Navy Gideon Welles proposed to Secretary of War Stanton that a joint Federal effort be made against the defenses of Wilmington, N.C., to close the port. Major Gen. Halleck, the senior general of the Army at this time, vetoed the idea saying that with other campaigns going, the Army could not afford the manpower for this operation.

At Memphis, Major Gen. Stephen A. Hurlbut, the local commander, wired Secretary Welles concerning intelligence received about a new Confederate ironclad: "The *Tennessee* at Mobile will be ready for sea in twenty days. She is a dangerous craft. Buchanan thinks more so than the *Merrimack*...."

The C.S.S. *Tennessee* was the largest ironclad built by the Confederacy. It was 209 feet long, had a beam of 48 feet, and a draft of 14 feet. It had six inches of armor forward and two inches on the decking. She was one of four ships built by Admiral Franklin Buchanan, CSN, at Mobile Bay.

January 5 (Tuesday)

In Washington, Congress passed a resolution prohibiting the payment of the $300 volunteer bounty. Now Lincoln asked them to reconsider to help boost enlistments.

Barber, Cpl., Co. D, 15th Illinois Volunteer Infantry, Riley, Illinois:

> January 5th was the day set for my departure. I felt that the Star of destiny which had so long protected me would still continue to shield me and that when peace dawned upon us, would return me safe home at last. The last good-by had been spoken and I stepped on board....

The price of boots in Charleston, S.C., had reached $250 per pair, according to the latest intelligence.

January 7 (Thursday)

President Lincoln commuted the death sentence of a deserter "because he was trying to evade the butchering business lately." During the war Lincoln commuted many death sentences, especially if the prisoner was young.

One of Major Gen. Benjamin F. Butler's brilliant ideas was to send a commercial steamer into Wilmington, N.C., disguised as a blockade runner, and loaded with troops who would then disembark and play havoc with the shipping in the port and be in a position to attack the rear of the forts guarding the port. This was turned down by the Navy when it was found that the entry to the port was too closely checked.

One tactic used by submarines in the South was to tow a torpedo (mine) behind the submerged boat, go *under* the target with the submarine, and then pull the torpedo into the side of the target. This was the method used by the C.S.S. *H.L. Hunley*, based at Charleston, S.C., and it was the method that was the hardest to detect. Admiral Dahlgren ordered all ships of his Squadron to take precautions against attack by torpedo boats on the surface and warned them of another such attack:

> ...There is also one of another kind, which is nearly submerged and can be entirely so. It is intended to go under the bottoms of vessels and there to operate.... It is also advisable not to anchor in the deepest part of the channel, for by not leaving much space between the bottom of the vessel and the bottom of the channel it will be impossible for the diving torpedo to operate except on the sides, and there will be less difficulty in raising a vessel if sunk.

January 9 (Saturday)

Secretary of the Navy Gideon Welles received notification from Admiral C.H. Bell in California of a Confederate raider being built in Vancouver, British Columbia.

President Davis warned his commanders in Mobile that an attack by Admiral Farragut could be expected soon.

January 10 (Sunday)

Federal cavalry began operations from Memphis to Meridian, Miss., under the command of Brig. Gen. William Sooy Smith. The operation would go well until the 25th, when he would tangle with Nathan Bedford Forrest and be driven back.

Barber, Cpl., Co. D, 15th Illinois Volunteer Infantry, Cairo, Illinois:

> On arriving at Cairo, I found the river so blocked with ice that it would be impossible for a steamer to leave for several days. The first steamer that left, the *Illinois*, bore me as a passenger. We were soon beneath the frowning batteries of the forts at Columbus, Ky. The next day we touched at Memphis. On the same evening we passed Helena, and on the ninth day after leaving home I landed at Vicksburg.... Russell Mallory and Dan Mitchell went to my camp with me. It was situated eight miles from Vicksburg and named Camp Cowan.

January 11 (Monday)

In the U.S. Senate, John B. Henderson of Missouri proposed a joint resolution to abolish slavery throughout the country by amendment to the Constitution. This would be the Thirteenth Amendment.

Confederate Secretary of the Navy Mallory received a letter from Flag Officer Samuel Barron, CSN, in Brest, France, that the original captain of the C.S.S. *Florida*, Commander Joseph N. Barney, was relieved of command due to ill health and that Lt. Charles M. Morris, CSN, had been appointed to command. The *Florida* had completed her repairs and during the trial run had "made 13 knots under steam." The C.S.S. *Rappahannock* and *Georgia* were also in Brest undergoing repairs.

January 13 (Wednesday)

Lincoln directed Major Gen. Nathaniel Banks in New Orleans to "proceed with all possible dispatch" in the construction of a free state government for Louisiana.

Rear Admiral Dahlgren, off Charleston, requested the use of torpedo boats to be used against the Confederate ships and defenses in Charleston Harbor. He recommended a boat of the Confederate "David" type:

> Nothing better could be devised for the security of our own vessels or for the examination of the enemy's position.... The length of these torpedo boats might be about 40 feet, and 5 to 6 feet in diameter, with a high-pressure engine that will drive them 5 knots. It is not necessary to expend much finish on them.

January 14 (Thursday)

Jupiter Inlet, Fla., was a busy place and was fast becoming a boneyard for wrecked ships. The U.S.S. *Roebuck*, Acting Master Sherrill, sent small boats after the British sloop *Young Racer*, which was loaded with salt. She was almost captured before she was burned by her crew.

Day, Pvt., Co. B, 25th Massachusetts Volunteer Infantry, Newport News, Va.:

> Up to this date about 200 of our men have re-enlisted and today the first detachment left for home on their thirty days' furlough.... I hope they will have a good time and enjoy themselves. Orders keep coming from headquarters at the fort to hurry up enlistments and some of them are of a rather threatening character.

Capt. Semmes, C.S.S. *Alabama*, captured and burned the *Emma Jane* off the coast of Malabar, India.

January 15 (Friday)

At Halifax, N.C., the C.S.S. *Albemarle* had been under construction for some period of time. Now, Secretary of the Navy Mallory placed Commander James W. Cooke in command with the instructions to complete her as rapidly as possible. She would be ready for work in April.

Barber, Cpl., Co. D, 15th Illinois Volunteer Infantry, Camp Cowan, Miss.:

> I found the boys all well and in excellent spirits. They were in comfortable quarters. They had log cabins sixteen feet square. I found Mess No. 4 all quartered together, but they had a place left for me. We had a very pleasant camp and we passed three months of contentment here. Soon after getting back, I enrolled my name as a veteran and got my enlistment dated back to the 1st of January. The other boys enlisted the 15th of December. My health was now much improved.

January 16 (Saturday)

The Richmond *Enquirer* reported that there were 26 ships off Wilmington that:

> ...guard all the avenues of approach with the most sleepless vigilance. The consequences are that

the chances of running the blockade have been greatly lessened, and it is apprehended by some that the day is not far distant when it will be an impossibility for a vessel to get into that port without incurring a hazard almost equivalent to positive loss. Having secured nearly every seaport on our coast, the Yankees are enabled to keep a large force off Wilmington.

January 17 (Sunday)

Admiral David Farragut wrote to Admiral D.D. Porter about the availability of ironclad gunboats for use on the assault on Mobile Bay:

> ...I am therefore anxious to know if your monitors, at least two of them, are not completed and ready for service; and if so, can you spare them to assist us? If I had them, I should not hesitate to become the assailant instead of awaiting the attack. I must have ironclads enough to lie in the bay to hold the gunboats and rams in check in the shoal water.

Day, Pvt., Co. B, 25th Massachusetts Volunteer Infantry, Newport News, Va.:

> The balance of the re-enlisted men left for home today, several of the officers going with them. We have now got our ultimatum, either enlist or go into exile. An order was received intimating that as enlistments seemed about through in this regiment, we would be more useful at Yorktown than here, and for us to be ready to march in heavy marching order at any time; but enlistments still drag.

January 18 (Monday)

The pro-Union areas of western North Carolina, northwestern Georgia, and eastern Tennessee were becoming more vocal in their protests about the South's conscription laws. Evasion was becoming more frequent and open meetings were held to protest the draft.

The suppression policy along the Northern Neck of Virginia, the area between the Potomac and Rappahannock rivers, had not been too effective, although the area was occupied by Union troops. Mosby's Confederates were active in the area, stirring up trouble.

Admiral Farragut arrived off Mobile Bay, where he inspected his ships and the Confederate defenses before going on to New Orleans, where he resumed command of the West Gulf Blockading Squadron on the 22nd.

The C.S.S. *Alabama*, Capt. Semmes, had now destroyed more than 60 United States flag commerce vessels and was now the target of yet another Union ship, the U.S.S. *Sacramento*, Capt. Henry Walke. Walke was directed by Secretary of the Navy Gideon Welles to direct all his attention to the *Alabama*.

Day, Pvt., Co. B, 25th Massachusetts Volunteer Infantry, Newport News, Va.:

> The order has arrived and we are under heavy marching orders for Yorktown, which is 30 miles distant and where, it is said, we shall probably all die of malarial fever or other contagious diseases. But there is one redeeming feature to the order; that is, if we will enlist, or three-fourths of those reported for duty will enlist, they can all go home together as a regiment, while those not enlisting will be sent into banishment, the non-coms reduced to the ranks and permanently assigned to other organizations during their terms of enlistment.

Jackman, Pvt., "The Orphan Brigade," Dalton, Ga.:

> Stopped raining at noon and turned cold. Will probably snow. This morning Pro. Pickett spoke to the regiment recommending that they vote for Congressmen to represent us in the Confederate Congress. As Kentucky has never seceded, electing Congressmen to represent the state in the Confederate Congress is all a humbug.

January 19 (Tuesday)

The South was perfecting another infernal device called a "coal torpedo" to be used against the North. This device, made of cast iron and filled with powder, was painted to resemble pieces of coal and was to be placed in the coal depots at the ship refueling stations. The torpedo would be put into the firebox of the ship's boiler where it would explode, seriously damaging the ship, if not sinking it. One such device was used at City Point, Va., later in the war.

In Little Rock, Ark., the pro-Union Constitutional Convention passed an antislavery measure that qualified the state for possible return to the Union.

In Richmond, the furor went on about Commissary-General Northrop, who was almost universally hated by the citizens for being incompetent in his handling of the food distribution.

January 20 (Wednesday)

In Washington, Lincoln proposed an immediate election in Arkansas to bring the state back into the Union.

Unlike the North, which seemed to have the capacity to build miles of railroads at will, the South became more disabled as the war continued. It had little capacity for making track, building engines or cars, and a shortage of manpower for the maintenance of the roadbeds.

Day, Pvt., Co. B, 25th Massachusetts Volunteer Infantry, Newport News, Va.:

> Yesterday and today have been busy days at Camp Upton. The idea of going home as a regiment has found favor with the officers, and as this is the last day of grace, they have been raising heaven and earth to get us to enlist. They have had us out on the parade ground using all their powers of persuasion and eloquence for enlistments, and have succeeded in enlisting nearly the whole regiment. I have reported these speeches and when I get them fixed up with all the necessary embellishments and illustrations, they will make an interesting chapter of literature.

January 21 (Thursday)

The "let's all denounce slavery and rejoin the Union" bandwagon was rolling in Tennessee. The pro-Northern faction met at Nashville and proposed a resolution for the abolition of slavery.

Day, Pvt., Co. B, 25th Massachusetts Volunteer Infantry, Little Bethel, Va.:

> It now appears there are 225 of us who go into exile. We are to take all our earthly effects with us and get them along as best we can, notwithstanding a boat goes around with our camp equipage and might as well take us, but that would be no punishment for our stubbornness. In justice to our officers however, I learn that they endeavored to get transportation for our knapsacks but were not successful. We took our last dinner with the boys at Camp Upton, and at 2 P.M. were in line awaiting marching orders.... As we stand waiting orders, the officers and boys gather around us and a feeling of sadness seems to pervade the whole crowd at the thought that this is the dissolution of the old regiment. Mutual handshakings and best wishes are exchanged, we say good-bye and move off. Leaving Newport News...we made a march of about ten miles, reaching Little Bethel just before dark when we halted and put up in an old church building for the night. Little Bethel contains, besides the church, and old grist and saw mill, a blacksmith shop, and three small houses, all in a rather dilapidated condition. There was no enemy within 100 miles of us, but Capt. Parkhurst, either as a matter of form or through force of habit, put out a few pickets.
>
> The old church had long ago been stripped of its seats and pulpit, if it ever had any, leaving the whole floor unobstructed. After supper and getting a little rested, a dance was proposed. A gallery extended across one end, and on the front of this the candles were thickly set, lighting up the old church in fine style. One of our German comrades of Company G had a violin and furnished the music. Sets were formed and the fun commenced. The pickets outside, hearing the sounds of revelry within, left their posts and came in, and standing their rifles in a corner, threw off their equipments and joined in the dance. The captain remonstrated at such unlawful proceedings, but the cry was "Never mind the pickets! on with the dance! let fun be unrestrained." The dance was kept up until the candles burned low, when we spread our blankets and laid down for rest.

January 22 (Friday)

Major Gen. Rosecrans was named commander of the troops in Missouri, relieving Major Gen. Schofield, who was shifted to the Department of the Ohio. In Arkansas, Isaac Murphy, a new pro-Northern provisional governor was inaugurated.

Acting Ensign James J. Russell, U.S.S. *Restless*, showed bravery and initiative in the capture of the blockade-running schooner *William A. Kain* at St. Andrew's Bay, Fla. The officer and two sailors from the *Restless* had gone on a jaunt to reconnoitre the area when they discovered the captain of the *Kain* and several crew members in the woods near the vessel. Capturing them, Russell then forced them to row him and his men to the schooner, where he captured the remaining crew members and sailed the vessel out of the bay to the protection of the guns of the *Restless.*

Day, Pvt., Co. B, 25th Massachusetts Volunteer Infantry, Yorktown, Va.:

> In the morning we found outside five men with their horses and carts waiting to sell us oysters.... We bought the men's oysters and after breakfast we chartered them to carry our knapsacks to Yorktown, thereby nullifying the order of the great Mogul at Fortress Monroe, and I have not the slightest doubt that if he knew of it he would hang every one of those men for giving aid and comfort to the incorrigible.
>
> Leaving Little Bethel, we marched over McClellan's famous corduroy road through the white oak swamp, coming out at Warwick court house.... We arrived at the forks of the roads, a mile below and in full view of historic old Yorktown about the middle of the afternoon. Here we were met by an officer and commanded to halt till further orders. I thought this was as near as they dared have us come the first day for fear the malaria would strike us too suddenly.
>
> About dusk an orderly rode up, bringing an order for us to proceed to Williamsburg, some fifteen miles further up the country. We tried to get the captain to stop here till morning, and go through the next day, but it was of no use; he had got his orders to march and was going through tonight. I could not see that it was a military necessity to force the march, and after we had gone three or four miles, my knapsack began to grow heavy and I grew tired. I halted by the roadside and said I was going to put up for the night and if any one would like to keep me company, I should be pleased to have them. About twenty rallied to my standard. After the column had passed we stepped through a low hedge of bushes into a small open space, surrounded by high bushes which served as a shelter from the winds. Here we spread our blankets and laid ourselves down to forget in our slumbers the weight of the knapsacks....

January 23 (Saturday)

One of the major problems with freeing the slaves in the Southern states was what to do with them after emancipation. The problem in the South was having an available labor force that could readily be used as the former slaves were used. A solution to this problem was begun (and would go on for several years) that permitted the former slaves to be hired by their former masters at a going wage, based on legal contractual agreements. This solved two problems: the plantation owners got their labor (not necessarily free, but available); and the former slaves got recompense for their labors (not a lot, but it was more than they had before).

Admiral Dahlgren, displaying his appreciation of using economy of force to tie down large numbers of enemy troops, wrote his old friend President Lincoln:

> The city of Charleston is converted into a camp, and 20,000 or 25,000 of their best troops are kept in abeyance in the vicinity, to guard against all possible contingencies, so that 2,000 of our men in the fortifications of Morris and Folly Islands, assisted by a few ironclads, are tendering invaluable service.... No man in the country will be more happy than myself to plant the flag of the Union where you most desire to see it.

Day, Pvt., Co. B, 25th Massachusetts Volunteer Infantry, Williamsburg, Va.:

> ...We awoke in the morning, the rising sun's bright ray was peeping through the bushes.... We made our coffee and started on our journey, and by easy stages came up with the boys in the afternoon. They had pitched the camp and got it all fixed up and named Camp Hancock. I thought the captain was as glad to see us as anyone, but he put on a stern look and inquired where we had been and why we fell out. We told him we were tired and lay down by the side of the road to rest and take a nap. He lectured us on the enormity of such proceedings, telling us we had committed a very flagrant breach of good order and military *despotism.* We assented to all the captain said, but kept thinking all the time that as we were a sort of outcasts, did not belong anywhere and were under no particular command, there wouldn't much come of it.

January 25 (Monday)

After nearly 18 months, Union forces evacuated the area around Corinth, Miss., leaving it to the Confederates. With more troops being drained off towards Chattanooga, a consolidation of forces was necessary.

Jackman, Pvt., "The Orphan Brigade," Dalton, Ga.:

> In the forenoon the brigade was "brigaded" out into an old field near our camp. The attendance was not compulsory and some of the aspirants for Congress spoke to the boys. The old politicians, I see, have not forgotten how to "work the wires."...

Barber, Cpl., Co. D, 15th Illinois Volunteer Infantry, Camp Cowan, Miss.:

> A good many of the boys were engaged in making keepsakes out of "Pemberton oak" as it was called, the wood being gotten from the tree under which Pemberton and Grant sat when the final terms of the surrender of Vicksburg were agreed upon. There was not a root or branch remaining....

January 26 (Tuesday)

In Washington, trade with the South had been a matter of discussion for some time, and now President Lincoln issued new regulations on the subject which clarified the status of those who "traded with the enemy."

Henry Stuart Foote, born in Fauquier County, Va., in 1804, and later transplanted to Tennessee, was largely pro-Union, but the people of Tennessee still elected him to the Confederate Congress in the fall of 1861. His outspoken criticism of the Davis administration made him a constant source of irritation to nearly everyone. He consistently voted against any and all war measures, including conscription, and the suspension of *habeas corpus*. He selected as his favorite target the Commissary-General Col. Northrop. Foote's temper outbursts brought on two physical confrontations with Northrop that led to blows, which was no surprise to any of Foote's friends.

The U.S. Minister to France, William L. Dayton, wrote to Secretary of State Seward:

> I must regret that, of the great number of our ships of war, enough could not have been spared to look after the small rebel cruisers now in French ports. It is a matter of great surprise in Europe that, with our apparent naval force, we permit such miserable craft to chase our commerce from the ocean; it affects seriously our prestige.

January 27 (Wednesday)

In Richmond, President Davis ordered Gen. Braxton Bragg to Richmond, health permitting, at his earliest convenience.

Cavalry, both North and South, were slowly gaining in efficiency but would never be used like the cavalry of the European armies because of the American terrain. In both cases, the cavalry operated in relatively small, independent bands that relied on the local countryside for survival. Cavalry, generally, was held in low esteem by the infantry, as was noted by Sgt. L.G. Sleeper of the 44th Mississippi Infantry regiment, who wrote a compliant to the Secretary of the Army in Richmond to the effect that "The cavalry in Southern Mississippi is almost perfect nuisance, a terror to the people and a disgrace to all civilized warfare. All men who are conscripted join this cavalry and consider themselves out of service."

Day, Pvt., Co. B, 25th Massachusetts Volunteer Infantry, Williamsburg, Va.:

> We had been here only two days when our common sense and judgment were still further imposed upon by three of our former officers from the News, soliciting enlistments. They probably thought that a fifty mile march and being in a strange city had perhaps taken the stiffening out of us somewhat, but they were not long in finding out that that was a delusion. Capt. Parkhurst laughed at them, telling them they had come to the wrong market to peddle their wares; the boys crowded around them, giving them scarcely breathing room, and jokingly told them they had picked some chickens the night before, but had got no tar, but perhaps molasses would answer for a substitute. Finding they had come on a fool's errand, they then wanted Surgeon Hoyt to put as many of us on the sick list as possible, thereby increasing the working force at the News. The surgeon told them that men who could make a fifty mile march, carrying heavy knapsacks, were not supposed to be very seriously indisposed. Finding the leopard hadn't changed his spots, they left, taking with them *two* captives.

Miller, 1st Lt., 1st Ohio Heavy Artillery, Hall's Gap, Ky.:

> Company H was always anxious to distinguish itself. Here at Hall's Gap some of the Co. H boys

got up a scheme. If there was anything good lying around loose, these boys always found it. One of the boys captured a Lieutenant's coat, and assumed command of the squad; they proceeded to the house of a well known citizen and arrested him on charge of moonshining. They also arrested a keg of "apple jack" he had on hand. To the citizen they suggested that he would probably be shot. But to be merciful to him it was hinted that he might make a dash for liberty and they would not make a serious effort to capture him. So he did, and a few shots in the air served to hasten his speed. The program was then carried out. The keg was shouldered, and the march towards camp began. As the keg got empty, the boys got full. This seemed necessary to divide the load so that it would not be a burden to one. A keg, you know, is an unhandy thing to carry.

Upon arriving at camp the whole scheme was given away by acting Lt. Jabez Thomas, who was whooping and yelling like a demon! Berry Steele [who] was also very tired from having carried the keg so far, was called upon for an explanation. He explained by turning over his canteen to Maj. Matthews and Adjutant Martin who analyzed the contents, and passed it around at headquarters until it all had evaporated, and Berry was sorry he had explained. It was now midnight. Jabez was making so much noise that a detail was made to take him over a hill into the next township, out of hearing, and left tied there until morning when he was released to go on the march. He has since joined the Prohibition party.

January 28 (Thursday)

The old "sail Navy" was not placed in mothballs, but deployed where it could best be used. The historic U.S.S. *Constellation*, Capt. Henry S. Stellwagen, was based at Naples, the *St. Louis* west of Gibraltar, and the *Jamestown* in the East Indies. Although steam was faster and more reliable then sail, these old war-horses still did good duty.

It was party time after the U.S. Army steamer *Western Metropolis* captured the blockade-running British steamer *Rosita* off Key West, loaded with a cargo of liquor and cigars. Two U.S. Navy officers, Acting Lt. Lewis W. Pennington and Acting Master Daniel S. Murphy, were on board the Army ship and assisted in the capture, and, presumably, shared in the cargo.

January 29 (Friday)

If one looked for work that had good pay and high adventure in 1864, one should have applied to become the captain of a blockade runner. Lt. Commander James C. Chaplin, USN, wrote Admiral Dahlgren about the arrangements:

> ...They are provided with the best of instruments and charts, and, if the master is ignorant of the channel and inlets of our coast, a good pilot. They are also in possession of the necessary funds (in specie) to bribe, if possible, captors for their release. Such an offer was made to myself...of some 800 pounds sterling. The master of a sailing vessel, before leaving port, receives $1,000 (in coin), and, if successful, $5,000 on his return; those commanding steamers $5,000 on leaving and $15,000 in a successful return to the same port.

Day, Pvt., Co. B, 25th Massachusetts Volunteer Infantry, Williamsburg, Va.:

> Today we were paraded and invited to give our attention to orders. Major Mulcay of the 139th New York volunteers appeared on the ground and read his orders relieving Capt. Parkhurst of the command. He then assumed command, and had a short drill and dress parade. Of course we put the best side out, to give the major a favorable impression. He complimented us on our good drill and neat appearance. Orders were read for a long and rapid march; of course that is one of our kind and we are expected to go on it. The major tells us we shall stay here a few days and then be assigned to his regiment.

January 31 (Sunday)

The month had produced little in the way of "heavy" fighting, the weather being a significant factor. However, the dead from the "light" fighting were just as dead.

The North did not reach a point where those who had paid for substitutes to serve in their stead would be drafted, sufficient manpower being available. In the South, however, the situation was different. By early 1864 the casualties of killed, wounded (those who could not return to the armies), and unexchanged prisoners had mounted considerably, seriously depleting the ranks. Desertion, too, played a role. Many of the Confederates were disheartened and, thinking of their families at home who were in dire straits, left their units, some for a short time, others forever.

The Confederate Congress had passed a law which required even those to serve who had previously paid for a substitute. To some of these men, going to the units they had shunned would be a personal shame they could not bear. Instead, they preferred to form new units. This was disallowed by the central government and caused some furor.

Barber, Cpl., Co. D, 15th Illinois Volunteer Infantry, Camp Cowan, Miss.:

> There was no immediate prospect of either, but instead, a long and arduous campaign was marked out for us. A good many would have backed out if they could, but they had signed their enlistment papers and there was no help for them. We were to receive four hundred dollars government bounty, to be paid, one installment of sixty dollars when sworn in and another two months after, the rest in semi-annual installments of fifty dollars, unless honorably discharged before the expiration of our time, in which case, we were to receive the residue in full.

FEBRUARY 1864

In February the Deep South began to come alive. In Florida and southern Georgia, Alabama, and Mississippi, the people thought more of gardens and the new year's crops. The armies, too, were awakening. At Chattanooga, Grant had sent Sherman home for a well-earned leave. Grant now sent Sherman to Vicksburg to prepare for the Meridian, Miss., campaign. All remained reasonably quiet in Virginia, neither Lee nor Meade stirring. Economically, the state of the South worsened.

February 1 (Monday)

The Federal Congress, after some debate, passed a law reviving the rank of Lieutenant General. The South had initially used the ranks of General (four star) and Lieutenant General (three star) since the time they organized their army. Grant, the hero of Vicksburg and Chattanooga, was the only possible candidate for the new rank. Lincoln called for an additional 500,000 men to be conscripted in March for three years, or for the duration of the war.

At Williamsburg, Va., the Union army was still trying to coerce members of the 25th Massachusetts Infantry into reenlisting at the end of their three-year stretch. Legally, they could, and should be, discharged having served their enlistments honorably. The regimental brass, however, had an idea that they should have a show of solidarity, with the entire regiment volunteering to stay for the duration of the war. The resistance from the ranks continued.

Day, Pvt., Co. B, 25th Massachusetts Volunteer Infantry, Williamsburg, Va.:

> Since being here we have had but little else to do than make up our diaries, write letters and talk over the situation. The last link is broken that bound us to our old regiment. Capt. Parkhurst, Lieuts. Johnson and Saul and Doctor Hoyt left us yesterday and we are now thinking of applying for admission to the orphans' home. The boys are all at sea, without chart or compass, and form no idea of what kind of a landing they will make. The non-coms, of whom there are quite a number, are a good deal exercised over their fate, and are consulting together much of the time.... We can look forward to the end, which is only a few months hence, and during that time we shall probably not be very much worse off than we have been, and certainly can be no worse off than the crowd we are in.
>
> In a talk with Corporal Whipple and a few others, I said I had no fears of our losing our rank, that is if Gen. Sherman is good military authority, which I think he is. Sometime last summer there was some talk at the war department at Washington in regard to consolidating the old regiments. In a letter from Gen. Sherman to the adjutant-general, he said it would be the worst thing for the army that could be done, for in consolidating the old regiments, they would lose a large number of well-trained and efficient soldiers whose places could not easily be filled....

Confederate Gen. Pickett moved his troops from Kinston, N.C., towards New Bern in the latest attempt to recapture the latter. The loss of New Bern to the North could help free the Albemarle Sound for navigation. Pickett attacked along Batchelder's Creek, and when the Union commander withdrew to prepared positions, Pickett withdrew.

Barber, Cpl., Co. D, 15th Illinois Volunteer Infantry, Camp Hebron, Miss.:

> We broke camp at Cowan on the 31st and removed to Camp Hebron, near Black River bridge. The enemy here made a dash at our picket line but was easily repulsed. We now made our final preparations for the campaign. The command comprised the greater portion of the 16th and 17th corps, the former commanded by Maj-Gen. Hurlbut, the latter by Maj-Gen. McPherson. Gen. Sherman was in command of the expedition. Each corps had a train of over five hundred wagons with ammunition and provision. We went in light marching order, carrying only one blanket apiece and no tents.

In Richmond, Commissary-General Northrop was now appointing many ladies to clerkships. Old men, disabled soldiers, and ladies were to be relied on for clerical duty, and all the able-bodied men were to be sent to the Army. There was strong resistance on the part of those who had previously hired substitutes to serving.

February 2 (Tuesday)

Several days ago small boats had been loaded on railcars in Petersburg, Va., and sent to Kinston, N.C., to be launched in the Neuse River. The launched boats contained Confederate Marines and sailors under the command of Commander John Taylor Wood, CSN, grandson of President Zachary Taylor and nephew of Jefferson Davis. Going downriver, the boats, using muffled oars, silently approached the U.S.S. *Underwriter*, a four-gun sidewheel steamer, at about 2:30 in the morning. When within less than 300 feet of the Union vessel, they were sighted and hailed. Forgetting about stealth, the boats raced for the Union ship, where the alarm had been given and the crew was being roused from sleep. Acting Master Jacob Westervelt, captain of the *Underwriter*, came on deck to find the assaulting boats too close for him to fire upon, so he prepared to repel boarders. The Marines and sailors in the Confederate boats clambered aboard and fought hand-to-hand with the crew to capture the Union ship. The fighting moved over the decks, which became slick with blood. Some of that blood belonged to Westervelt, who was killed during the action.

The *Underwriter* had no fires to produce steam, and the shore batteries were now taking the ship under fire, so Commander Wood ordered the ship burned. The assaulting party removed to their boats and returned upriver, under fire from the batteries. The remaining crew of the burned ship escaped overboard and made it to shore. Wood later wrote to Col. Lloyd J. Beall, Commandant of the Confederate Marine Corps, commending the Marines on their performance. Lt. George W. Gift, CSN, one of Wood's officers on the mission, remarked of Wood, "I am all admiration for Wood. He is modesty personified, conceives boldly and executes with skill and courage."

Major Gen. William T. Sherman was back in Vicksburg after his action at Missionary Ridge, Ga., and was ready to begin his campaign against Meridian, Miss. He requested that a diversionary expedition be undertaken up the Yazoo River to confuse the enemy as to intent, and to draw off enemy troops from his front. Admiral D.D. Porter was more than happy to oblige.

At Morris Island, S.C., Major Gen. Quincy A. Gillmore informed Admiral Dahlgren of his intention to place a force ashore for an assault on Jacksonville, Fla. Gillmore requested assistance for transport and gunboats. Dahlgren detailed the screw steamers U.S.S. *Ottawa* and *Norwich* to transport the troops, and the gunboats U.S.S. *Dai Ching*, *Mahaska*, and *Water Witch* to support the operation. Gillmore went to Florida to supervise the naval operations.

February 3 (Wednesday)

Sherman marched today with 26,000 men to wreck the railroads of Mississippi and to disrupt the flow of food to the Confederate armies in the east. With him were 7600 cavalry under Gen. William Sooy Smith and they were late coming up, confirming Sherman's long-held belief that cavalry could not be relied upon. Facing Sherman and Smith were about 20,000 widely scattered Confederate troops under Gen. Leonidas Polk, late of Bragg's Army of Tennessee. Supporting Sherman was an expedition up the Yazoo River to smash things and divert Confederate troops. Part of the troops Sherman would use were at Champion's Hill, on the road to Jackson.

Barber, Cpl., Co. D, 15th Illinois Volunteer Infantry, Champion's Hill, Miss.:

We left camp on the 3d, halted awhile at Black River where Gen. McPherson issued an order which was read to each regiment.... He regretted the necessity that compelled the veterans to go on this march before they had had their furloughs, but he promised them that they should have them as soon as they returned. This satisfied the boys.... We camped near Champion's Hill the first night out and our regiment was detailed to go on picket.

February 4 (Thursday)

Sherman picked up Gen. McPherson's troops in the vicinity of Champion's Hill on his way towards Jackson. Moving over the scenes of fighting for the capture of Vicksburg, fighting broke out at Champion's Hill, Edward's Ferry, and Bolton Depot as Sherman neared Jackson.

Barber, Cpl., Co. D, 15th Illinois Volunteer Infantry, en route to Meridian, Miss.:

The next morning our brigade was in the lead. The cavalry went ahead as skirmishers, but they soon came flying back in disorder. They had met a large force of rebel cavalry and been completely routed. Gen. McPherson ordered Gen. Crocker to send forward his best regiment and deploy them as skirmishers, and the 15th was ordered to perform this duty. Without delay, we proceeded to the front. We advanced one mile uninterrupted and then came upon a brigade of Wirt Adams' rebel cavalry. It was strongly posted in the woods across the open space in front of us. Without any delay, we opened fire upon them, which they returned. They being concealed in the woods had the advantage, but we had good backing and did not hesitate to attack them. The 14th was in line of battle a short distance in our rear as support. Gen. McPherson rode up and took a survey of the field and said that we would soon rout them out of that. Just at this time a rebel officer mounted on a beautiful white charger rode out towards us. We were ordered not to fire, supposing him to be a bearer of dispatches. He rode up to within easy range, coolly drew his revolver and fired several shots at Col. Rogers who was on horseback, then wheeled his horse and fled. A perfect shower of bullets was sent after him, but strange to say, he escaped unhurt. His very boldness insured his safety. We were petrified with astonishment.

Now the order came to advance and we swept across the field in quick time, expecting to meet a withering volley of musketry, but the rebs deemed it prudent to retreat, and just as we gained their first position, we saw them posted in another. The man on the white horse was riding up and down in front of the line, encouraging the men. Shot after shot was fired at him but he still remained unhurt. He seemed to bear a charmed life. A sharp firing was kept up on either side for about fifteen minutes. We took trees for shelter and their firing did us little damage.

We again moved forward and again the rebels retreated. The rider of the white horse rode furiously up and down the line, waving his sword and vainly trying to rally them. As we advanced, we passed seven dead rebels, thus showing that our fire was not without effect, and by the track of blood we knew that many were wounded. The rider of the white horse again succeeded in bringing them to a stand. Again we charged them and again they fled.... The rebs had taken a position just beyond a dwelling house where lived a widow and three small children. She came to the door to see what was going on when a ball struck her, killing her instantly. When our boys got there, they found her form rigid in death.... Her little children were clinging frantically to her, not realizing that she was dead.... About three o'clock the rebels made a determined stand by a stream of water which they supposed we would want to camp by. The stream was bordered by thick underbrush in which the rebels lay concealed. In order to get at them we had to cross an open field two hundred yards in width. The rebels now opened upon us a furious fire from which we took shelter behind a rail fence. They had now brought artillery into play.... At a given signal we trailed arms and with a yell that made the welkin ring, we rushed across the field. The rebels, terrified, hastily retreated, after giving us one volley which passed harmlessly over our heads. Only one man was severely wounded, Lieut. Allison of Company H. The regiments to the rear suffered more than we did, quite a number being killed and wounded. The rebels had planted their artillery so as to rake the bridge, and they commenced pouring in their grape and canister upon us but the thick bushes prevented it from doing any harm. One shell dropped in our midst and exploded, but strange to say, it did not injure any one, although it flew into a hundred pieces. Col. Rogers asked permission to charge the battery but Gen. McPherson was not willing to make the sacrifice of lives which would necessarily follow such a charge. He had a surer and safer method of dislodging them. He sent out our skirmishers and they flanked the battery and poured in so hot a fire that it was forced to retreat. We now quietly crossed the stream. The rebs did not annoy us much more that day. We had marched fourteen miles in line of battle, through swamps and creeks, through dense woods, valleys and over mountains. We had made charge after charge and steadily driven the enemy before us. We were now completely tired out and the 12th Wisconsin took our place for a short time.

We did not march much farther that night.... In the last charge that we made we did not notice the rider of the white horse, but we found the white horse dead by the side of the road and the citizens said it was one that Wirt Adams rode, but whether the rider escaped uninjured, we could not tell. During the night the rebels received large re-inforcements and they boldly resisted our march on the next day. A sharp, severe fight of fifteen or twenty minutes duration in which a number were killed and wounded on both sides, resulted in a total rout of the rebels.

The blockade-running steamer *Nutfield* was chased off New River Inlet, N.C., by the U.S.S. *Sassacus*, Lt. Commander Roe, where the *Nutfield* ran aground. Roe tried for two days to get her off, and when that proved impossible, her cargo of Enfield rifles and quinine was off-loaded and the ship destroyed.

February 5 (Friday)

In Charleston Harbor, the boilers of the C.S.S. *Chicora* wore out, reducing the ship to a floating artillery battery.

Sherman pushed on towards Jackson, Miss., fighting a series of little battles on the way, mainly with Confederate cavalry.

Barber, Cpl., Co. D, 15th Illinois Volunteer Infantry, marching through Mississippi:

Our route lay through a splendid looking country, remarkably level, rich soil and well watered and timbered. The most prominent places we passed through were Brandon, Decatur and Hillsboro. At Decatur, Hurlbut's train was attacked by a band of guerrillas and twenty wagons captured and destroyed. The leader of the assault was a resident of Decatur. His splendid residence and the principal part of the town were burned in retaliation. The country through which we passed was bountifully supplied with bacon and cured hams, and the citizens, in order to put them out of reach of the soldiers, secreted them in swamps, but it was impossible to get them out of the reach of the soldiers. When our keen scent and argus eyes failed us, it did not require much coaxing to get some confidential darkey to reveal the hiding place, and sometimes from some swamp, load after load of the nicest hams was taken. The Southern people surpassed the North in curing hams. I never ate so sweet meat as in the South. They use a great deal of saltpeter and molasses in curing them and smoke them but little. I stood the march very well until one afternoon, about the tenth day out, I had a violent shake of the ague. However I kept on. When my fever was at its height, I lay down in the edge of the woods to rest and fell asleep. I must have slept several hours. When I awoke all the troops had passed and the ammunition train was then passing....

The Federal army was still trying to convince the holdouts of the 25th Massachusetts Infantry to reenlist, with little success.

Day, Pvt., Co. B, 25th Massachusetts Volunteer Infantry, Williamsburg, Va.:

Yesterday afternoon...we marched to the parade ground of the 139th New York during their dress parade and before it was dismissed, the major marched us up and introduced us to Col. Roberts. The colonel received us cordially and complimented us for our soldierly bearing and the good appearance of our arms, equipments, and uniforms. We then listened to the reading of an order, assigning us temporarily for duty to this command. A gleam of light now dawned on us. Col. Roberts again addressed us, saying we were here only during the absence of our own regiment, and would hold the same rank and perform the same duties we had done in our own regiment.... After this another order was read stating that the long expected march would commence tomorrow morning, the 6th. Col. Roberts, after addressing a few remarks to his own regiment, turned to us and said: "To you of the 25th Massachusetts, I have nothing to say. You know your duty and I am satisfied you will perform it."

We were then divided into parties which would equalize the companies of the regiment; the balance, about 25, were sent to Fort Magruder, which is only a short distance away. A dozen others and myself were assigned to company I, Capt. Phillips. The boys were warmly welcomed, and all set about introducing themselves to each other and getting acquainted. This camp is constructed of small log houses, with board floors and glass windows. The houses are furnished with stoves, chairs, stools, table and sleeping bunks. The officers' quarters are built of logs with bark left on, and are large and roomy. Some of them are two stories, others are neat little cottages built in Gothic style, and all present a neat, attractive and artistic appearance. These houses are all supplied and furnished with home comforts, some of them containing cabinet organs. The officers have with them their wives, sisters and other female relatives, who fancy the romance and rough experience of a soldier's camp. This is a Brooklyn regiment; it has been out but little more than a year and has been stationed here all this time, so the men have had the opportunity to fix up their camp to suit them. Their first and only service was with Gen. Dix when he went up the country towards Richmond in the fall of 1862. Since then they have done picket duty around here, and some scouting up in the woods beyond the town.... The Brooklynites are asking our boys a thousand questions, and the latter are telling them blood and thunder stories till the former have come to think we are the veritable heroes of Waterloo.

The mystery which has for so many days hung over us is at last cleared up, and Gen. Butler, after finding we were not to be driven or frightened, has in his order assigning us temporarily for duty, acknowledged he was exceeding his authority in threatening us with permanent assignment and taking our warrants from us. If it had been some other general who didn't know any better I should think he was relenting of his shabby treatment of us, but Gen. Butler *knew* better, and that makes his treatment of us all the more reprehensible. I presume we shall have to get ourselves and knapsacks back to the News the same way we got here, although there are boats running round twice and three times a week.

In the area of northern Georgia, Gen. Joseph Eggleston Johnston rested his army while awaiting further action by Grant. Things had settled into a routine of inspections, drill competitions, and other work to keep the troops occupied.

Jackman, Pvt., "The Orphan Brigade," Dalton, Ga.:

Grand review of the army by Gen'l Johnston today—a beautiful day. For the occasion the review took place in a large field south of town half a mile. The troops were formed in three parallel lines, each nearly, or quite, five miles in length. After the Gen'l rode up and down the line passing in front and rear of each, he took his station at the point for all to see the troops passing in review. A large number of ladies, citizens, and loafing soldiers were assembled, myself being among the latter. I heard the Gen'l tell his wife there were 40 thousand troops in line in the field and thinking it a "story" I thought I would make an estimate. There were 87 regiments and battalions and I put down the infantry at between 23 and 25000. I made no estimate of the artillery. There was one brigade on outpost and Cleburn's division was away. The cavalry was not present. The troops, as a general thing, did not march well....

February 6 (Saturday)

The Union force under Sherman left Jackson for Meridian, Miss., about 100 road miles away. Gen. William Sooy Smith had finally left Memphis, Tenn., on his way to support Sherman, but Smith was many miles away and would be of no immediate help.

With many of the ships of United States registry being attacked by commerce raiders, shipowners were moving their ships' registry to other nations to alleviate this problem. Just as the age of sail was rapidly coming to a close and the age of steam was taking over, so the age of wooden ships was ending as more steel hulls were built. Most of these steel-hull ships were being built in the shipyards of England, where the keels were laid and the ships turned out within months. The mercantile navy of Great Britain was the largest in the world, and growing, as the merchant fleet of the United States, its only competitor, shrunk. This situation would take years to reverse after the war.

Day, Pvt., Co. B, 25th Massachusetts Volunteer Infantry, Williamsburg, Va.:

The morning...found us in line on the parade ground, New York and Massachusetts shoulder to shoulder. Capt. Phillips, wanting a brave and valiant veteran on the left of his company, assigned me to that post of honor. I reckon the reason for it was that two of his sergeants were on the sick list. While standing in line, waiting the order to march, a scene is transpiring which to us of the 25th is altogether new and strange.

The ladies living here in camp are all out, and wetting their handkerchiefs with their tears, are watching the preparations to leave. They are struggling under a fearful burden of anxiety which will not be removed until our return. Groups of men and women are standing around taking each other by the hand and kissing their good-byes. Our Brooklyn friends are visibly affected, while the 25th boys look on stoically. While men and women with streaming eyes are bidding perhaps their last farewell, these roughened, hardened sons of Mars look with unpitying eye on this affecting scene and laugh. I confess I should have taken a greater interest in the thing and my sympathies would have flowed more freely if I could have taken a hand in the kissing.

We marched into town where the brigade line was formed, consisting of the 139th and 118th New York, two regiments of colored troops and one U.S. battery (the 2d I think). The mounted rifles were to follow later. This comprised the whole force under command of Brig. Gen. Wistar, whoever he is. The line of march was taken up the country on the road towards Richmond. Arriving at the woods, about a mile from town, the column was halted and a detail made to act as skirmishers. The 139th being on the advance furnished the detail. In this detail, the 25th was largely represented and was under command of Major Mulcay. The major marched his command a few rods into the woods, formed his skirmish line and ordered them forward, the column following....

After a time the boys started up a rabbit and half a dozen of them gave chase shouting and yelling until they were out of sight in the woods where they waited for the major to come up. The major lectured them a little about charging without orders and warning them of the great danger they were in from bushwhackers.... Capt. Phillips, who had kept up his whistle, suppressed it long enough to say: "Your boys are taking great risks in running off into the woods in that way; some of them will get shot by bushwhackers." I said I thought our boys had very little fear of bushwhackers and would sooner have the fun of chasing them than rabbits, besides I thought there was little danger from bushwhackers for when a force like this was marching through they preferred keeping a safe distance.

A little after noon the cavalry overtook us and we halted to let them go past us. I was surprised to see such a force; there was a whole brigade, numbering between 3000 and 4000 under the command of Col. Spear who had been sent down from the army of the Potomac, landing at Yorktown and had now overtaken us. I could now begin to see through a glass darkly. This is the raid on Richmond of which I had heard some hints before. The cavalry, of course, are the principal actors, and we are simply the supporting column.

The cavalry past us, we again started. The general hurried us up, wishing to keep as near the cavalry as possible, but the major's skirmish line retarded us. It was finally thought that with a large cavalry force in advance, the skirmish line was not absolutely necessary, and it was withdrawn. The march was forced till past the middle of the afternoon, when it began to tell on the Brooklyn boys, some of them giving out. They were unaccustomed to such severe marching and it took hold of them severely.... We pushed along till into the evening; the boys were getting pretty well played out and would make frequent halts without any orders.

There was one of the general's aides who seemed to take a great interest in getting us along, and his interest from some cause or other (probably his canteen) seemed to increase with the evening. The boys would be groping their weary way through the darkness when some one would give a whistle and they would all squat in the road. This aide would ride up in a great passion and order them up, telling them if they didn't get along faster he would put a regiment of colored troops on the advance. The response to that threat would be: "Bring on your niggers!" This officer had another provoking habit which he came well nigh paying dearly for. There were occasional mud holes in the road caused by the rains; some of them two or three rods across. The boys would flank these to keep their feet from getting wet and sore, but this officer attempted to drive them through, saying it took up the time flanking them. At one of these places, he was going to drive them through anyway or it would be the death of some of them. He was swearing at them, wheeling his horse right and left among them, and making himself about as disagreeable as he could. Just then I heard the ominous click of rifle locks and heard some one ask him if he was aware those rifles were loaded. He seemed to catch on to the idea and got himself out of that as quickly as possible and was seen nor heard from no more during the march.

The night wore on, the boys were well nigh exhausted and made frequent halts. The colonel would sympathize with them and encourage them by saying he hoped the day's march was nearly over, telling them to keep up courage.... The major showed some impatience and riding up to the colonel said: "Colonel, I really do not understand the meaning of this." "What's the matter now, major?" "Why, every few moments this entire regiment will simultaneously sit down?" "Oh well, major, the boys are tired; they have come a long way and [are] pretty well played out; change places with some of them, major, and you will understand it better."

We reached the end of our day's tramp at New Kent sometime after midnight, having made a march of thirty miles....

February 7 (Sunday)

After two days at sea, the Union troops under Brig. Gen. Truman Seymour landed under the guns of Admiral Dahlgren's gunboats at Jacksonville, Fla., and moved inland, capturing several pieces of artillery and a large quantity of cotton awaiting shipment by blockade runners. Little resistance was encountered. At McGirt's Creek, just above Jacksonville, the Confederate steamer *St. Mary's* was trapped by the U.S.S. *Norwich*, Acting Master Frank B. Meriam. The Confederates sank their own ship and burned the cotton to prevent it from falling into Union hands.

Gen. Pickett, unable to capture New Bern, N.C., was falling back towards Richmond, where an alarm had been given, later proved false, that Gen. Ben Butler's troops were approaching the city from the Peninsula. Preparations were made to send the "home guards" from Richmond in addition to the regular Confederate troops in the city to positions of defense at Drewry's Bluff. The citizens feared that with the troops gone, the Union prisoners, about 12,000, would escape.

Sherman, moving steadily towards Meridian, Miss., skirmished at Brandon, Morton, and Satartia, as Polk's Confederate forces fell slowly back.

Day, Pvt., Co. B, 25th Massachusetts Volunteer Infantry, New Kent, Va.:

We slept about 3 hours when we were routed up and a little after daylight were again on the march. The boys were pretty stiff and sore, but a mile or two took the kinks out of their legs and limbered them up.... Before noon we reached what is called the Baltimore cross roads, about two miles from Bottom bridge which crosses the Chickahominy river. Here we met the cavalry coming back, and Col. Spear reported to Gen. Wistar that on reaching the river he found all the bridges up and a considerable force of the enemy with infantry and artillery guarding the river. With our small force and only one battery he thought it would be useless to attempt a passage of the river....

Presently an alarm was raised that the enemy was coming up the White House road. The 139th was ordered down the road to meet them. We went about a quarter of a mile and formed a line of battle. A few cavalry went down the road a couple of miles and when they returned, reported no enemy in sight or hearing, a circumstance I did not regret. We then went back and were dismissed for dinner.

This Baltimore is a junction of several roads; the one we came up from New Kent on extends on to Richmond, one runs south to Charles City, one northeast to White House, and another runs north over into Northumberland where once lived a little boy who owned a little hatchet and couldn't tell a lie.... In the little square formed by the intersection of the roads stands an interesting old building—the church in which Gen. Washington was married. It is a log, low, rather narrow building without belfry or ornament of any kind outside or in. It is without paint or even whitewash, and shows the rough marks of age and neglect. It is divested of its seats, having been used for an army hospital....

After waiting here a couple of hours, the column re-formed and marched back over the road. We came nearly to the woods, where we halted to let the cavalry go past us. After passing us, they halted to feed their horses and themselves and while waiting for them an alarm was raised that the enemy were coming through the woods on our flank. Down came the fences and a regiment of darkies filed into the field and deployed as skirmishers. Every few moments they would look back to see where their support was, while their teeth and the whites of their eyes resembled bunches of tallow candles hanging in a dark cellarway. The alarm, of course, was a false one, but the colored troops fought nobly.

We arrived back in New Kent about night and bivouacked on a large field near the village. New Kent is the county seat.... It contains a court house, jail, church, two or three stores, tavern, a small collection of houses and the inevitable blacksmith shop. There is no such thing in Virginia as a school-house; they have no use for such things. All they want is law and gospel, and I have not been able to find out that these give them a great degree of culture and refinement....

Getting into camp, we built fires, made coffee and began to make ourselves comfortable. Some time in the evening the major happened along where a few of us were standing around a fire of burning rails. He began to upbraid us for burning the rails, telling us if we wanted fires we must go into the woods and get our fuel. I said to the major I thought it was all right to burn the rails; as we were sort of guests on the gentleman's place, I presumed he would be entirely willing and glad to contribute a few rails to our personal comfort.... He went off muttering something about destruction of property while the boys added more rails to the fire.

February 8 (Monday)

Sherman pushed on towards Meridian, Miss., skirmishing at Coldwater Ferry, and maintaining almost constant contact with Polk's cavalry.

At the Confederate Naval Gun Factory, Selma, Ala., Commander Catesby ap R. Jones wrote Admiral Buchanan at Mobile concerning the Federal monitors:

> The revolving turret enables the monitor class to bring their guns to bear without reference to the movements or turning of the vessel. You who fought the *Virginia* know well how to appreciate that great advantage. You doubtless recollect how often I reported to you that we could not bring one of her ten guns to bear. In fighting that class, it is very important to prevent the turret from revolving, which I think may be done either with the VII-inch or 6.4-inch rifles or 64-pounder, provided their projectiles strike the turret at or near its base where it joins the deck.... If the turret is prevented from revolving, the vessel is then less efficient than one with the same guns having ordinary ports, as the monitors' ports are so small that the guns can not be trained except by the helm.

Brig. Gen. Truman Seymour's Union troops, which landed at Jacksonville, Fla., two days ago, moved further inland, skirmishing near Point Washington and vicinity.

February 9 (Tuesday)

Major Gen. John M. Schofield, recently replaced as commander in Missouri, assumed command of the Department of the Ohio, replacing Major Gen. John G. Foster.

Among the refugees taken aboard the U.S.S. *Jacob Bell* off Blakistone Island, Va., was an Englishman named Joseph Lenty, who had been working in Richmond for four years. Lenty informed the ship's captain, Acting Master Gerhard C. Schulze, that the Confederates were:

> ...now making a shell which looks exactly like a piece of coal, pieces of which were taken from a coal pile as patterns to imitate. I have made these shells myself. I believe these shells have power enough to burst any boiler. After they are thrown in a coal pile I could not tell the difference between them and the coal itself.

Upon hearing of this device, Admiral D.D. Porter issued warnings to his commanders to place guards over the coal depots and ordered that anyone found attempting to place anything in the coal was to be shot on the spot.

Shore liberty for sailors long at sea had been fabled to be one long binge. This was not the case for the crew of the C.S.S. *Alabama*, the Confederate commerce raider, when she stopped for provisions at the island of Johanna, between Africa and Madagascar. Capt. Semmes related:

> I gave my sailors a run on shore, but this sort of "liberty" was awful hard work for Jack. There was no such thing as a glass of grog to be found in the whole town, and as for a fiddle, and Sal for a partner—all of

which would have been a matter of course in civilized countries—there were no such luxuries to be thought of. They found it a difficult matter to get through with the day, and were all down at the beach long before sunset—the hour appointed for their coming off—waiting for the approach of the welcome boat. I told Kell to let them go on shore as often as they pleased, but no one made a second application.

Day, Pvt., Co. B, 25th Massachusetts Volunteer Infantry, New Kent, Va.:

> ...The march was resumed...we arrived back on the afternoon of the 9th and as we sighted Camp West, the ladies were all out on the parade ground waving their handkerchiefs in greeting of our return. It was like the old Roman armies returning from conquest when fair maidens, with white waving arms, would welcome their coming. Now another scene ensued; fair women and brave men close in fond embraces of love and thanksgiving for their miraculous deliverance. I could but feel that the 25th boys were rather slighted in not receiving a share of the kisses, for who can tell that but for them their friends might not now be dwellers in the Hotel de Libby. On the whole, we have had an interesting excursion, having seen some forty odd miles of the country. It was very woody and I think the poorest I have ever traveled in for chickens, applejack and peach and honey....

In one of the most spectacular escapades of the war, Col. Thomas E. Rose of Pennsylvania led 109 Federal officers, including the elusive Col. A.D. Streight (who had been captured by Forrest), in an escape through a tunnel out of Libby Prison in Richmond. Eventually, 48 were recaptured, two drowned, and the remaining 59, including Col. Streight, made it back to Union lines.

February 10 (Wednesday)

At 2 o'clock in the morning, in a teeming rain, and darkness so thick you could cut it with a knife, the C.S.S. *Florida* slipped out the southern passage of the harbor at Brest, France, and was again free on the seas for the first time since she entered Brest for repairs the previous August. Lt. Morris, her new commander, had received his instructions from Flag Officer Samuel Barron to "...do the enemy's property the greatest injury in the shortest time." Capt. Winslow of the U.S.S. *Kearsarge* noted that the English had also had a hard time blockading Brest. Winslow had been waiting for *Florida* to come out for months.

Another *Florida*, this time one in the United States Navy, chased the blockade runner *Fanny and Jenny* aground near Masonboro Inlet, N.C. Shortly thereafter, Commander Pierce Crosby, the captain of the *Florida*, sighted another blockade-runner, the *Emily*, also aground. Crosby tried to get them both off, while being fired on by shore batteries, but was unable to do so. The ships were searched before being destroyed, and on the *Fanny and Jenny* was found a solid-gold jewel-studded sword with the inscription: "To General Robert E. Lee, from his British sympathizers." Crosby also reported that among the intelligence gathered from the captured crew members, there were ten blockade runners that had sailed from Nassau for Wilmington "...during this dark of the moon. Three had been destroyed, and one put back, broken down, leaving six others to be heard from."

The Union force that landed at Jacksonville, Fla., on the 7th advanced towards Lake City, skirmishing with the Confederate forces in their front.

A fire at the White House stables in Washington destroyed six horses and ponies. Lincoln tried to remove them from the barn but failed, and watched the burning building with tears in his eyes.

Sherman, en route to Meridian, Miss., skirmished with Polk's cavalry at Hillsborough and Morton, Miss.

February 12 (Friday)

The lack of a good transportation network severely troubled the South. Shortages of almost everything were becoming more common, even of cloth to make cartridge bags for the naval guns. Commander John M. Brooke of the Confederate Navy's Office of Ordnance and Hydrography, and the inventor of the Brooke seven-inch banded gun, wrote Flag Officer Barron in France for 22,000 yards of the necessary material for the cartridge bags to be sent to Nassau and then to Wilmington, in 1000-yard lots to prevent it from all being taken at once if the ship were captured.

Sherman and Sooy Smith continued their advances into Mississippi, where resistance was steady, but light.

February 14 (Sunday)

Sherman's soldiers entered Meridian, Miss., today after a march of almost 140 miles from Vicksburg. Gen. Polk continued to withdraw his troops in the face of an overwhelmingly superior force. Sherman rested his men for the night.

The Union troops of Gen. Truman Seymour were divided, and a section of them captured Gainesville, Fla., after a brief skirmish. The main force continued inland.

February 15 (Monday)

After capturing Gainesville yesterday, the Union forces of Brig. Gen. Truman Seymour continued to Fernandina, Woodstock, and King's Ferry Mills, destroying anything that looked useful.

After a good night's rest and feeling chipper, Sherman turned 10,000 of his troops loose on Meridian, Miss., where the force proceeded to take apart railroads, warehouses, shops, supply depots, arsenals, offices, cantonments, hotels, and nearly everything else, in a five-day binge of destruction. The Confederates were worried that Sherman would turn and head for Mobile, Ala., about 150 road miles away. Resistance from Polk's small force was negligible.

February 16 (Tuesday)

Sherman's troops continued their binge of destruction in Meridian, while Confederate Gen. Leonidas Polk watched from outside the city.

Off Mobile, Ala., the U.S.S. *Octorara*, Lt. Commander William W. Low, the converted ferryboat U.S.S. *J.P. Jackson*, Acting Lt. Miner B. Crowell, and six mortar schooners began the bombardment of Ft. Powell. This marked the beginning of the six-month effort to capture Mobile.

Admiral Dahlgren, at Charleston, ordered 100 of the torpedoes designed by Benjamin Maillefert, an engineering specialist. Maillefert had described the torpedoes last November: "Each of these charges will be provided with a clockwork arrangement, which shall determine the exact time of firing; they are to contain 110 to 125 pounds of gunpowder each...." Dahlgren had run tests on the devices and found them satisfactory for use on the obstructions in Charleston Harbor.

February 17 (Wednesday)

Just before 9 P.M., off Charleston, the lookouts aboard the U.S.S. *Housatonic*, Capt. Charles W. Pickering, sighted a strange thing in the water and brought it to the attention of the Officer of the Deck, Acting Master John K. Crosby. Crosby described it. "It...had the appearance of a plank moving in the water." Crosby, however, immediately ordered the anchor cable slipped and the ship began backing full; all hands were called to quarters. Too late, for within two minutes of the first sighting, the Confederate submarine *H.L. Hunley* had rammed her torpedo into the starboard side of the *Housatonic*, forward of the mizzenmast. The ship sank immediately, becoming the first ship ever to be sunk by a submarine in combat.

The *Hunley*, brought to Charleston from Mobile by Gen. P.T.G. Beauregard in 1863, had had its misfortunes, sinking twice and once drowning the crew, plus other mechanical problems. A Confederate Army officer, Lt. George E. Dixon, had been named to command her and, after several months of training, the crew began looking for an opportunity to use the weapon. Their first real attack was a success, but the submarine sank during the attack with all hands and was not recovered for years.

The Charleston *Daily Courier* would report on February 29th:

> The explosion made no noise, and the affair was not known among the fleet until daybreak, when the crew were discovered and released from their uneasy positions in the rigging. They had remained there all night. Two officers and three men were reported missing and were supposed to be drowned. The loss of the *Housatonic* caused great consternation in the fleet. All the wooden vessels are ordered to keep up steam and to go out to sea every night, not being allowed to anchor inside. The picket boats have been doubled and the force in each boat increased.

Day, Pvt., Co. B, 25th Massachusetts Volunteer Infantry, Williamsburg, Va.:

> Our Brooklyn friends left us the 13th. They were ordered to report at Newport News and we to remain here to do guard duty. When they left they expected to return in a few days, but I reckon they have gone for good as they have sent for their ladies and quarter-

master, who have gone, carrying everything with them. That leaves us alone again and we are doing the guard duty up town, which is the outpost....

I reckon we must have given them quite a scare up in Richmond the other day, for in the alarm and confusion which prevailed, quite a number of prisoners escaped and are finding their way in here. Yesterday the cavalry went out to assist any that might be trying to get in.

Corp. Barber's memory is a little off, but essentially correct. Sherman's army continued to destroy Meridian, Miss., with a vengeance.

Barber, Cpl., Co. D, 15th Illinois Volunteer Infantry, marching to Meridian:

The army arrived at Meridian about the 17th. When within twenty miles of there, our provision train was left back and a strong guard with it, also the sick, myself among the number. Rollin, who had a felon on his hand, also remained. Left to our resources, we did just about as we had a mind to. Rollin or I went out foraging nearly every day, but usually Rollin went, as he always had better success than I did.... Rollin seldom came in empty. A porker, some chickens, sweet potatoes, always came within his grasp. We drew plenty of hard bread from the provision wagons nearby, charging the same to Uncle Sam, and for shelter and covering, we appropriated the chaplain's blankets to our use. So, all thing considered, we were faring remarkably well—a great deal better than many of the others....

In the meantime, our boys had arrived at Meridian and were playing havoc with the enemy's lines of communication. Meridian was a central place for railroads from all parts of the South. Each division was assigned a certain portion of the track to destroy, which they effectually did by tearing up the ties, piling them on the rails and then setting them on fire. After the rails were red hot, they would twist them around the trees, utterly unfitting them for further use. In this raid our army destroyed four hundred miles of railroad and burned over twenty engines and a large number of cars. They set fire to Meridian, and Gen. Sherman had his headquarters burned over him. He said that he thought that the boys might have waited until he got out before burning his quarters.

A remarkable instance of revenge was perpetrated here. In Sherman's first disastrous fight at Vicksburg, a federal soldier was taken prisoner. His guard stopped at a residence here for food and refreshments. The woman of the house, after heaping all manner of insults upon the prisoner, finally spit in his face. It happened that the soldier soon after made his escape and rejoined the army. After arriving at Meridian, he proceeded to the house where he had been insulted, piled up the furniture, and told the woman that if she did not want to burn up in her own house, she would have to leave, at the same time reminding her of the insult she had given him. She implored, but to no purpose. Her house and furniture were burned. Thus may it be with all who descend from their high pedestal of womanhood and disgrace themselves by spitting upon helpless prisoners.

February 20 (Saturday)

A Union force under Brig. Gen. Truman Seymour had been ashore in Florida since the 7th when it landed at Jacksonville and moved inland. Along the way they had been tearing up railroads, destroying mills, dams, levees, and anything else that might profit the Confederate war effort. There had been little resistance other than light skirmishing.

On a march from Barber's Plantation towards Lake City, Seymour's men approached Olustee, Fla., where they were met by a Confederate force under Brig. Gen. Joseph Finnegan. The only major battle in the state of Florida began with an attack on the 5500 Federals by about 5000 Confederates. Two of the Union regiments, the Seventh New Hampshire and the Eighth U.S. Colored Troops broke in the confusion of the battle and fell back. The Confederates kept up the pressure until nightfall, when the Federals fell back and withdrew from the field. The retreat to Jacksonville began.

Admiral S.P. Lee, commanding the blockading squadron off Wilmington, N.C., reported 26 ships lost to the blockade runners since July 12, 1863.

Sherman, having destroyed Meridian, Miss., turned his army back towards Vicksburg, moving at a lesiurely pace, destroying the railroad as he went. Once he was clear of Meridian, the Confederates immediately started rebuilding the railroads.

Barber, Cpl., Co. D, 15th Illinois Volunteer Infantry, en route to Jackson, Miss.:

One day the Quartermaster came in and said

that the army had started and that he had orders to break camp and move also. He went as far as Hillsboro and then waited one day for the arrival of the command.... We had only ten days' rations on hand now, but a dispatch had been sent through for a provision train to come out and meet us. Forage was not so plentiful now as on our out trip, but a few days after we left Hillsboro, we took a new road and we found forage in abundance.... Sherman's army left fire and famine in its track. The country was one lurid blaze of fire; burning cotton gins and deserted dwellings were seen on every hand. I regret to say it, but oft-times habitations were burned down over the heads of occupants, but not by orders. Those gangs of ruffians, who always follow in the wake of armies, to pillage and destroy, seemed on the march to give loose reins to their passions. I have seen the cabin of the poor entered and the last mouthful taken from almost starving children. No one, who has a heart that beats in sympathy for the sorrows of others, can look on these things without the strongest feelings of compassion for the victims. The wretches who caused this suffering were brought to punishment as often as caught, but the most vigorous measures could not always stop it.

February 21 (Sunday)

The Union force, retreating after the battle at Olustee, Fla., fought rearguard actions with Confederate General Joseph Finnegan's soldiers. The Confederates repaired the railroads the Federals had destroyed and kept up the pressure. The blue-clad columns continued towards Jacksonville.

In Mississippi, Forrest was after W. Sooy Smith's cavalry with fighting at Ellis' Bridge, West Point, Prairie Station, and near Okolona. Casualties were light on both sides. Smith, having destroyed considerable railroad facilities, cotton and corn, withdrew slowly towards Memphis. Hundreds of Negroes followed the Union column, hoping to be freed.

In Richmond it was reported that several hundred dollars per month was being taken by the persons responsible for forwarding mail through the "flag-of-truce" system, the difference between the actual cost of the postage (3 cents), and what was enclosed for the postage (often 5 to 10 cents), being kept by the mail handler as a "perk."

February 22 (Monday)

Secretary of the Treasury Salmon P. Chase was up to his old tricks again, working behind the scenes to advance himself for the Presidency. This time it was the "Pomeroy Circular" signed by Sen. Samuel C. Pomeroy of Kansas, advocating Chase for President in the 1864 elections. Chase denied he knew of the contents, but did admit that he had talked to the originators of the document. A resignation, previously tendered by Chase, was being considered by Lincoln. Lincoln got good news. The "qualified" voters of Louisiana restored the Union government in that state and elected Michael Hahn governor.

Brig. Gen. Truman Seymour's Union troops reached the port of Jacksonville, Fla., and the protection of the Union gunboats lying in the harbor. This effectively stopped the advance of Brig. Gen. Joseph Finnegan's Confederate troops, who had been pursuing the Federals for two days. The Union troops were loaded on the transports and the force sailed. Much property had been destroyed. Two hundred ninety-six men had been killed and 1993 wounded, North and South, and little else accomplished.

At Dalton, Ga., Major Gen. George H. Thomas decided to probe Confederate Gen. Joe Johnston's lines. The Confederate cavalry videttes were chased away and the Federals moved towards Tunnell Hill, Dalton, and Rocky-Face Ridge.

Jackman, Pvt., "The Orphan Brigade," Dalton, Ga.:

> Just before tattoo I noticed a horse's hoof clattering over the road towards army HdQrs. A courier of course from the front and I remarked that something had "turned up." Sure enough, orders soon came in to be ready to move at a moment's notice and to be prepared for action—to cook two days rations.

Day, Pvt., Co. B, 25th Massachusetts Volunteer Infantry, Williamsburg, Va.:

> William and Mary College...is now a mass of ruins; a company of the 11th Pennsylvania cavalry were the vandals. As this company were returning from a scout, they were fired on with one or two shots from out the college as they were riding past. Instead of surrounding the building and capturing the murderers, they set it on fire and burned it to the

ground. This college was located at the extreme western end of the town, and was a fine brick building over 100 feet in length and three stories high with two tower entrances about 80 feet apart, in one of which was a fine bell....

Confederate Secretary of the Navy Mallory wrote Flag Officer Barron, CSN, in Paris, France, to consider directing the commerce raiders to the New England coast, where the taking of ships from the fishing fleet would create virtual panic among the fishermen. He stated, "Their advent upon the high seas would raise a howl throughout New England, and I trust it may be well founded. The destruction of a few ships off New York and Boston, Bath and Portland would raise insurance upon their coasting trade a hundred percent above its present rates."

Gen. William Sooy Smith's cavalry was moving towards Memphis, when early this morning Gen. Nathan Bedford Forrest's cavalry made a charge against them at Okolona, Miss. During the fight that turned into a five-mile running battle, a Union Tennessee regiment gave way and was routed. The combat was close, often hand-to-hand, and was one of the few purely cavalry battles fought during the war. Forrest's brother, Jeffrey, was killed during the engagement. Smith, starting with about 6000 men, lost a total of 388 during the whole campaign. Forrest claimed that he started with 2500 men, of whom he lost a total of 110.

February 23 (Tuesday)

Gen. Thomas's advance this day and the day before drove in the pickets and caused minor fighting at Catoosa Station and Tunnel Hill. Johnston was not sure whether the advance was an attack or merely a demonstration.

Jackman, Pvt., "The Orphan Brigade," Dalton, Ga.:

> We have again taken the "Warpath"—have left our snug winter quarters and are now only sheltered by the broad canopy of the heavens. At daylight all our baggage was loaded and the trains started for the rear. Everything has the appearance of a retreat. At 3 P.M. our brigade moved up to Mill Spring, or Creek, Gap, 2 miles west of Dalton and formed line on a ridge at the east end of the Gap. This Gap is made through Rocky-Face Ridge by the flow of Mill Creek, a considerable stream, and it is through this Gap the rail road passes leading from Chattanooga to Atlanta. Seeing the troops clambering up the steep hills on either side of the Gap reminded me of pictures seen of Hannibal crossing the Alps. We are held in reserve. The day has been beautiful—springlike. Shall have to sleep on the ground, and no doubt, sadly miss the cozy shantie in which we have been passing the winter.

February 24 (Wednesday)

Braxton Bragg was appointed by Jeff Davis as Chief of Staff of the Confederate forces. He had lost much of the people's confidence by his defeat at Missionary Ridge, and by his never-ending battles with his generals.

For a special man, the Congress of the United States voted to revive the rank of lieutenant general. Grant would be appointed next month.

Fighting continued in the area of Tunnel Hill and Rocky-Face Ridge, Ga., as Thomas pushed at Joe Johnston's lines.

Jackman, Pvt., "The Orphan Brigade," Rocky-Face Ridge, Ga.:

> This morning is one of sunshine. We are quietly resting on arms—not having heard a hostile gun yet. The news from the front is that the enemy is advancing in strong force, slowly, and are about Tunnell Hill, the main body having camped at Ringgold last night. Our troops are still coming up from the rear and are in fine spirits. Things don't look so much like a retreat now—more like a fight.
>
> 9 P.M. I write by the light of a campfire. All was quiet today—save now and then the thunder of cannon would come from the front until about 4 o'clock in the evening. When the skirmishers in front commenced a lively popping, our cavalry coming back to the rear and one of our batteries opened in the gap. The enemy has not fired any "shrieking" shells yet—that is none have come over us: we are some distance in rear of the front line. Just before sundown the brigade moved to the right across the railroad as a support to Steward who was having quite a lively skirmish. A little after dark we moved back to our old position. Clayton's brigade on the right had quite a battle this evening before sundown, the fighting taking place in his old camp. He drove the enemy back—the boys are now sleeping on their arms—

taking a good nights rest, believing the morrow will bring the storm of battle.

February 25 (Thursday)

Thomas sent the Union troops under Major Gen. J.M. Palmer in a probing attack against the Confederate positions at Buzzards Roost. The Rebel position was too strong, and Palmer returned to his old position with the Army of the Cumberland.

Jackman, Pvt., "The Orphan Brigade," Rocky-Face Ridge, Ga.:

> I write at 8 P.M. Contrary to expectations, we have not been engaged today. We moved very little. Late in the evening we clambered about half way up "Buzzards Roost" to our left but at twilight came back to our old stamping ground. In the forenoon all quiet around the lines but as evening advanced considerable cannonading in the Gap and further to the right. We had a few of the "shriekers" to pass over us in the afternoon. Saw a pretty lively skirmish to the right of the railroad this evening. Clayton again drove the enemy back on the right—heavy fighting reported up there—a good deal of "sensational" from the right in fact. All is quiet now though awhile after dark an occasional cannon was heard and the sharpshooters would stir up a fuss. Thousands of campfires are blazing on the hills and in the valleys. Tomorrow, undoubtedly, the "ball" will open in earnest.

February 26 (Friday)

Things had quieted down between Thomas and Joe Johnston. For a while, everyone went back to where they belonged.

Jackman, Pvt., "The Orphan Brigade," Rocky-Face Ridge, Ga.:

> I write at half past 9 A.M. Save an occasional report of a sharpshooters gun, all is now quiet. Just as day was dawning, the skirmishers commenced firing pretty briskly which caused the boys to spring to arms—a good reveille. Cool wind blowing from north east. Sun shining brightly. Rumor says the enemy took Dug Gap, 4 miles to our left, yesterday evening. I had a good nights rest on a "pallet" of boards.
>
> 9 P.M.—Nothing of interest has taken place today. There has not even been any cannonading. The skirmishers also have been kept moderately quiet. Has been a beautiful day. Now the stars are twinkling in cloudless heavens. Nothing is heard save a squeaking violin which some soldier of a musical turn has brought out on the field with him and the hooting of an owl from the neighboring forest. The hills and valley are lit up by thousands of bivouack fires. We moved again today. Our position is on a spur of the main hill which spur juts out into the valley at the east entrance of the Gap. At its terminus on the creek the side is very steep and on the side next the enemy. A few trees stand on top of the ridge, the rest being a cornfield.

Sherman's Meridian campaign is nearly complete. His force had destroyed the city of Meridian, about 115 miles of railroad track, 61 bridges, and 20 locomotives (nearly impossible to replace). The march had totalled between 360 and 450 miles. The count for the campaign was 21 killed, 68 wounded, and 81 missing.

Barber, Cpl., Co. D, 15th Illinois Volunteer Infantry, near Jackson, Miss.:

> We crossed the Pearl River thirty miles above Jackson. We halted here for a few days. After everything had crossed, our company was detailed to go back on the other side to do picket duty. This was a dangerous business, as hordes of rebel cavalry were prowling about, looking for a chance to pounce upon some detachment.... Gen. Sherman had now opened communication with the outside world and the whole country was electrified at the brilliancy of his exploits. We now moved to Canton and camped again for a few days. Canton is twenty-five miles above Jackson, on the Pearly River and forty-five miles from Vicksburg. It is surrounded by a splendid country. Its thrift is more of the Northern style than any city I had yet seen in the South.... We captured fifteen engines and a large number of cars at Canton, all of which were burned....

February 27 (Saturday)

Federal prisoners of war began filing into a new prison camp near Americus, Ga., today. The camp, named Camp Sumter, would become infamous as Andersonville Prison. Many of the prisoners from

Belle Isle in Richmond were transferred there to ease the crowding in Richmond.

The probing demonstration by Thomas ended today with the Federals back in their old lines.

Jackman, Pvt., "The Orphan Brigade," Rocky-Face Ridge, Ga.:

> At 10 A.M. our skirmishers advanced and found the enemy had gone back during the night. I have learned the Federal Army had all passed through Tunnell Hill by 10 P.M. I have been fooled twice in this movement. First I thought we were going to retreat back towards Atlanta—then, later, I thought we were going to have a big battle. We neither retreated nor had to fight much. Pretty day.

Sherman completed his Meridian campaign, closing into the Vicksburg area in a somewhat leisurely manner.

Barber, Cpl., Co. D, 15th Illinois Volunteer Infantry, Canton, Miss.:

> When we left Canton, they hung on our track like blood leeches. Oft-times we would have to turn around and fight them. One afternoon, after we had all gotten into camp, the rascals drew up in a line and showed themselves. This touched the pride of our cavalry and they formed and charged them with drawn sabres. The rebs stood their ground for awhile, but, before our force got to them, they broke and ran in confusion. We had planted artillery so as to rake their flank and help them along in their flight.

February 28 (Sunday)

Gen. Judson Kilpatrick led a force of 3500 Federal cavalry south on a raid to crash through the weakened defenses of Richmond and free the Union prisoners there. He crossed the Rapidan early in the morning accompanied by Col. Ulric Dahlgren.

Brig. Gen. George A. Custer also began a raid in the vicinity of Albemarle County, Va., as a diversionary tactic.

Jackman, Pvt., "The Orphan Brigade," Rocky-Face Ridge, Ga.:

> At 10 A.M. marched back to our old camp which we found in *status quo* and the wagons back. It did not require us long to go to "housekeeping" again.

Confederate Secretary of the Navy Mallory got a progress report on the C.S.S. *Albemarle*, being readied for service:

> ...with the exception of some little connecting work to be completed [she] may be considered as ready. Steam will probably be raised on Friday next. The iron is all on the hull.... Shell room and magazine prepared. Officer quarters arranged and berth deck ready for either hammocks if allowed the ship or bunks if the canvas cannot be obtained.... The ship is now afloat.... The guns, carriages, and equipment have not yet arrived, but are expected on the 4th of March....

February 29 (Monday)

Kilpatrick's cavalry hurried south from the Rapidan towards Richmond, the force splitting, sending 500 men under Col. Ulric Dahlgren to Goochland C.H., the remainder staying with Kilpatrick. Richmond, alerted as to the intent of the raid, was taking defensive measures to counter the attack.

Barber, Cpl., Co. D, 15th Illinois Volunteer Infantry, en route to Vicksburg:

> The next day our regiment was rear guard. The rebs still kept in sight, fighting our cavalry all the time. We were where we could see the whole performance. The only effect these attacks of the enemy had on us was to keep our men from straggling. Towards night they began to lag and finally ceased to annoy us at all. This gave the rebs a chance to give a great puff in their papers that their troops had utterly routed Sherman and driven him back across Black River.

Lt. William B. Cushing, USN, led a landing party from the U.S.S. *Monticello* to Smithville, N.C., in an attempt to capture Confederate Gen. Louis Hebert. In the middle of the night, and within fifty yards of the Confederate barracks, Cushing entered the general's quarters only to find that the general had gone to Wilmington earlier. Cushing later reported to Admiral S.P. Lee: "I send Capt. Kelly, C.S. Army, to you, deeply regretting that the general was not in when I called."

MARCH 1864

Spring was coming, indeed it had arrived in parts of the South, and the campaigns would begin in earnest. Grant, in Chattanooga, prepared for his offensive against Confederate Joe Johnston, but Grant would soon be called to higher command. Banks, in Louisiana, was organizing the Red River expedition with Admiral Porter. In the North, the fall elections were already on people's minds, and the war had much to do with their feelings; the "peace Democrats" looked to former Gen. McClellan as a candidate. Everywhere the armies stirred and became restive—the winter camps had been long and boring.

March 1 (Tuesday)

Major Gen. Ulysses S. Grant was nominated by President Lincoln for promotion to the rank of Lieutenant General.

The Federal cavalry raid led by Gen. Kilpatrick which started on February 28th was now within a few miles of Richmond. The "home guard" in the city was alerted and was out to defend the city in the entrenchments to the north. Kilpatrick, thinking the Rebel entrenchments too heavy to capture, turned east in a driving rain towards Chickahominy and the Peninsula. Col. Ulric Dahlgren, riding strapped to the saddle, had gone more westerly to Goochland C.H., and was within two miles of the Richmond at nightfall. Faced with stiff resistance from Gen. Custis Lee, Dahlgren realized that the raid had failed and attempted to escape with his men.

Prior to beginning the Red River campaign, Admiral D.D. Porter sent a heavy reconnaissance expedition up the Black and Ouachita rivers of Louisiana. The small fleet, under the command of Lt. Commander Ramsay, consisted of the paddle-wheel monitor U.S.S. *Osage* and the gunboats *Ouachita*, *Lexington*, *Fort Hindman*, *Conestoga*, and *Cricket*. The force moved up the Black River without incident until about 4 P.M., when Confederate sharpshooters began sniping from the shoreline below the town of Trinity. The gunboats replied with a hail of grape, canister, and shrapnel, then went above the town, where they anchored for the night.

The C.S.S. *Florida*, Lt. Morris, had slipped past the U.S.S. *Kearsarge*, Capt. Winslow, at Brest, on February 10th, and gained access to the high seas. Within a couple of weeks *Florida* had entered the port of Funchal, Madeira. The U.S.S. *St. Louis*, Commander George H. Preble, was one of the old-line sailing ships and attempted to capture the *Florida*, with no success. Preble reported:

> Nelson said the want of frigates in his squadron would be found impressed on his heart. I am sure the want of steam will be found engraven on mine. Had the *St. Louis* been a steamer, I would have anchored alongside of her, and, unrestricted by the twenty-four hour rule, my old foe could not have escaped me.

March 2 (Wednesday)

The United States Senate confirmed the appointment of Ulysses S. Grant to the rank of Lieutenant General of the United States Army.

East of Richmond, Gen. Fitzhugh Lee's cavalry pursued the remnants of Judson Kilpatrick's cavalrymen through the night and into the morning. Kilpatrick headed on to a junction with Gen. Ben Butler's men on the Peninsula.

Col. Ulric Dahlgren (son of Rear Admiral John Dahlgren), who had already lost a leg in the action at Gettysburg, had insisted on being one of the leaders of a cavalry raid against Richmond. His force of about 500 men was sent on a separate part of the raid to Goochland County, where it reached a point to within two miles of Richmond. Realizing the raid had failed, Dahlgren swung east, hotly pursued by Fitzhugh Lee's cavalry. An ambush at Mantapike Hill between King and Queen C.H. and King William C.H. trapped Col. Ulric Dahlgren and his remaining men. Dahlgren was killed in the action, and about 100 of his men were captured by a force of Confederate infantry and cavalry. A few escaped to the U.S.S. *Morse*, positioned on the York River near Brick House Farm. Admiral Dahlgren, hearing of his son's death, wrote in his diary, "How busy is death—oh, how busy indeed!"

As a result of the raid, which had been an attempt to release the prisoners in Richmond, the fear of the prisoners getting loose in Richmond caused much panic and concern there.

Early in the morning, after a hasty breakfast, the crews of Lt. Commander Ramsay's flotilla hauled anchor upstream from Trinity, La., and entered the Ouachita River. The *Osage* had problems with her turret, effectively putting her gun out of commission. Continuing upriver, the fleet shelled Harrisonburg, La., and then began to pick up artillery fire from shore batteries, most of the fire being directed at the *Fort Hindman*, which took 27 hits, one of which disabled her starboard engine. Ramsay sent the *Hindman* back, transferring his command to the *Ouachita*, which took three hits without serious damage. The gunboats finally silenced the shore batteries. Ramsay went on upriver as far as Catahoula Shoals before turning back.

Admiral D.D. Porter arrived at the mouth of the Red River to coordinate a joint operation which would send 10,000 troops from Sherman's army at Vicksburg upriver as far as Shreveport, La. After establishing a base there, further actions would be taken against Texas. The rendezvous would be on March 17th. Porter, however, found potential problems and wrote to Secretary Welles of his concern: "I came down here anticipating a move on the part of the army up toward Shreveport, but as the river is lower than it has been known for years, I much fear that the combined movement can not come off without interfering with plans formed by General Grant." Grant had committed the troops under Sherman for his spring offensive scheduled for April 10th, and it was unlikely that the Red River campaign would be completed by that time.

Day, Pvt., Co. B, 25th Massachusetts Volunteer Infantry, Williamsburg, Va.:

> The 11th Connecticut regiment arrived here today and we are ordered back to the News where we rejoin a part of our old regiment which has just returned from home. This is good news to our boys who have been impatiently awaiting their return. So far as I am concerned, I shall leave here with some regrets. We have been here several weeks and have got used to the officers and the place. The duty is light and somebody has got to stay here; as we have only a few months long[er] to remain, we might as well be here as anywhere; but the orders are to go and orders must be obeyed....

March 3 (Thursday)

Major Gen. Ulysses S. Grant was ordered to Washington to receive his commission as Lt. General.

Lt. Commander Ramsay, commanding the Union flotilla on the Ouachita River in Louisiana, returned downriver, picking up cotton and artillery pieces along the way. Little or no opposition was encountered. They anchored for the night before reaching the conflux of the Red River.

Barber, Cpl., Co. D, 15th Illinois Volunteer Infantry, Canton, Miss.:

> We arrived back in our old camp March 3d. On this our last day's march of the campaign, we started at six o'clock in the morning and at eleven A.M. we were in camp, having marched twenty miles, or rather ran. It could scarcely be called marching. So eager did we become to get back to camp. Our brigade was in the lead and perhaps we were a little vain of our marching and wished to exult over the rest of the command. We left them far in the rear and it was not until five o'clock P.M. that the rear regiments arrived. Our first thought after arriving was to secure our mail. I found a goodly number of letters awaiting me.... My next move was to doff my travel-stained attire and substitute a clean suit from my knapsack. We had made this march without a change of clothing. We left our knapsacks in our tents. It made us feel almost like new men to once more be clothed in a clean and wholesome suit....

March 4 (Friday)

At Vicksburg, Miss., the greater portion of Sherman's men returned from their expedition to Meridian, Miss., which they destroyed.

At Washington, Admiral John A. Dahlgren called on the President to try and learn the fate of his son, Col. Ulric Dahlgren, who had been killed on Kilpatrick's abortive raid on Richmond. The U.S. Senate confirmed Andrew Johnson as Military Governor of Tennessee, and in Baton Rouge, La., the new pro-Union Gov. Michael Hahn took office.

Longstreet was calling for reinforcements from Lee's army to be sent to him as early as possible, citing that he was facing an overwhelming force.

Lt. Commander Ramsay, and the flotilla on the Ouachita River in Louisiana, continued downriver, picking up more cotton and artillery pieces, and meeting little or no opposition. They reached the mouth of the Red River on the Mississippi late today and anchored for the night.

Capt. Semmes, C.S.S. *Alabama*, wrote in his journal:

> My ship is weary, too, as well as her commander, and will need a general overhauling by the time I can get her into dock. If my poor service shall be deemed of any importance in harassing and weakening the enemy, and thus contributing to the independence of my beloved South, I shall be amply rewarded.

March 5 (Saturday)

The Confederate government ordered that all blockade runners must give half of their cargo space to government items. This would take a lot of the profit out of the business, but it would help bring in much-needed government supplies and weapons. This order applied to both incoming and outgoing vessels, government cotton being taken outbound.

The former Vice President of the United States, John Cabell Breckinridge of Kentucky, now a Major General in the Confederate Army, assumed command of the Confederate Department of West Virginia.

In Richmond there were rumors that Col. Ulric Dahlgren was part of a plot to kill President Davis, and that papers, reported to have been found on his body, proving such facts were now in Richmond.

Commander John Taylor Wood, CSN, led another daring raid against the Federals, this time at Cherrystone Point, Va. Wood, with some 15 men in open barges, crossed the Chesapeake Bay at night and landed early in the morning at the Union telegraph station, which was quickly taken. Shortly thereafter, two small U.S. Army steamers, the *Aeolus* and *Titan*, arrived, unaware that the station was in Confederate hands. These two ships were quickly taken by Wood, who then destroyed the station and the warehouses there, disabled and bonded the *Aeolus*, and then sailed up the Piankatank River on the *Titan*. Two gunboats in the area, the U.S.S. *Currituck* and *Tulip*, gave chase but lost the little *Titan* in the early-morning haze.

At Yazoo City, Miss., a Confederate attack was beaten off by the Federal gunboats U.S.S. *Petrel*, Acting Master Thomas McElroy, and the *Maramora*, Acting Master Thomas Gibson. McElroy wrote of the action:

> I am proud to say that the Navy was well represented [ashore] by 3 sailors, who...stood by their guns through the whole action, fighting hand to hand to save the gun and the reputation of the Navy. The sailors are highly spoken of by the army officers....

March 6 (Sunday)

Another of those "heart in the throat" experiences occurred in the North Edisto River near Charleston when the "David" torpedo boat, commanded by Assistant Engineer Tomb, CSN, attacked the U.S.S. *Memphis*, Acting Master Robert O. Patterson. A spar torpedo weighing 95 pounds was mounted on the "David" and Tombs pointed the little submarine directly at the *Memphis*. The "David" was sighted some 50 yards to port of the ship and a hail of musket fire was directed at her without effect. The torpedo struck squarely against *Memphis*'s port quarter, about eight feet below the waterline, but the torpedo didn't explode. Tomb turned away and came back again, aiming at the starboard quarter of the big ship. Again the torpedo struck, but only a glancing blow, because the *Memphis* was now moving. The two vessels collided, damaging the "David," but Tomb managed to get her away under heavy fire.

In the west, Gen. Sherman sent Brig. Gen. Andrew J. Smith with the portion of Sherman's army going on the Red River expedition. He directed Smith to: "...proceed to the mouth of the Red River and confer with Admiral Porter; confer with him and in all the expedition rely on him implicitly, as he is the approved friend of the Army of the Tennessee, and has been associated with us from the beginning...." Strong praise coming from one such as Sherman!

In Richmond, the clerks, walking wounded, old men, and anyone else who could walk, crawl, or totter, had been called out to defend the city against Kilpatrick's abortive raid.

March 7 (Monday)

President Davis was pressing Gen. James Longstreet at Greeneville, Tenn., to take the initiative by entering Kentucky. Longstreet had already asked for reinforcements, and would not budge without them.

After Commander John Taylor Wood, CSN, had captured the telegraph station at Cherrystone Point, Va., on the 5th, he had also captured two small Union army steamers and then took one of them, the *Titan*, up the Piankatank River as far as possible, eluding two Federal gunboats in the escape. Commander F.A. Parker, USN, followed Wood upriver with a force of five gunboats and found the *Titan* destroyed, as well as a number of large captured Union boats that Wood had prepared for a raid.

Day, Pvt., Co. B, 25th Massachusetts Volunteer Infantry, Newport News, Va.:

> Left Camp West on the 3d, arriving at Yorktown in the afternoon. Here our officers tried to get transportation but were ordered to move on. Went on about six miles below Yorktown and on coming to an old church in the woods, halted for the night. This was a brick building with nothing but bare walls and roof, the floors, windows, and finish having been removed. We gathered what wood we could find and kindled a fire inside; the night was cold and wood scarce, so that we passed a very uncomfortable night, not sleeping a wink. We took an early start in the morning, reaching the News about the middle of the afternoon, where we rejoined about 200 of the boys who first went home. We were glad to once more see each other, and the greetings were cordial among both officers and men. We introduced our new officers to our old ones, and when our new officers were about leaving us, as a slight expression of our regard for them, we shook hands with them and gave them three rousing cheers.

March 8 (Tuesday)

At the Willard Hotel in Washington a rather nondescript Major General, accompanied by a small boy, stepped to the desk and asked if a room was available. The clerk, as befitting an employee of the best hotel in town, almost decided to deny the officer a room. However, he asked that the general sign the register and then turned a couple shades of white with shock. The clerk, reading the name, saw that the general had signed "U.S. Grant & Son—Galena, Illinois" in the book. The new Lieutenant General of the Armies of the United States had arrived in Washington. The guests in the lobby of the hotel were dumfounded in seeing this rather small man who had become such a hero. They were more accustomed to the swaggering Joe Hooker and the grand McClellan than to this unassuming general. Lincoln, hearing that Grant had arrived, sent word that he was to attend the President in the White House that evening, without informing Grant that this was the day of the President's weekly reception, when anyone who was anyone visited the White House. Grant went the short distance to the White House, and wearing his battered uniform he was ushered into a hall filled with people dressed "to the nines." Lincoln greeted his guest warmly and asked that Grant stand on a sofa in the East Room so everyone could see him. The crowd cheered and Grant felt embarrassed, as did Lincoln. A feeling of mutual trust was almost immediate.

Lt. Commander Thomas O. Selfridge seemed to have nothing but bad luck with ships whose name began with the letter "C." He had been a member of the crew of the U.S.S. *Cumberland* at Hampton Roads when she was rammed by the C.S.S. *Virginia* on March 8, 1862 (two years ago to the day); he was in command of the U.S.S. *Cairo* when she hit a torpedo and sank instantly on the Yazoo River on December 12, 1862. Now, as commander of the U.S.S. *Conestoga*, he was rammed by another Union ship, the U.S.S. *General Price* about ten miles south of Grand Gulf on the Mississippi River. The *Conestoga* sank in four minutes, losing two crew members. When Admiral Porter received the report, in person, from Selfridge, he remarked: "Well, Selfridge, you do not seem to have much luck with the top of the alphabet. I think that for your next ship I will try the bottom." Selfridge was then assigned command of the U.S.S. *Osage*, which grounded in the Red River and was destroyed. His next ship was the *Vindicator*, further down in the alphabet.

John Carvel Arnold was the captain of a canal barge named the *Maney Louisa* when he enlisted from Pennsylvania in 1864. He was one of many "bounty" men who entered the war late. Unlike many, he only enlisted once rather than deserting and reenlisting in other units to collect more bounty. The following letter places him at the Pennsylvania "Redistribution" Depot awaiting assignment to a unit.

Arnold, 49th Pennsylvania Volunteers, Camp Curtin, Penn.:

> Harrisburg Camp Curtin
> March 8th 1864
>
> Dear wife and famly I take this preasant oppertunity to write a few lines to informe you that I am well at preasant time and hope dose few lines will find you

in a state of enjoying good health and rather I let you know that wee ware put in camp last eaving last night wee slept in the barrak this morning we went to a tent it is a large tent and we have a stove and can live pirty confordable our boarding is tolerable wee can live by it and I dont know in what Reigement we will be put but I think by all information that I can lern wee will be put in the Fortyninth and the[y] say that Reigement is now a laying at Elexsander and iff it should come to pass that wee will be put in the Fortyninth I do not think we will be here more then a day or two any more at least I dont exspect to come home for a while and it will be of no use for you to write untill I send you a nother letter and give you my address which I cannot do at preasant as I dont know what the name of our company will be and concerning our Government Bounty wee have not drawed any yet but as soon as wee get it I will write to you and lieve you know and I will also lieve you know that I received a letter yesterday from your sister Lizzy she sent it with John Griner and a bout that blanked I guess you may live Issac Shafer have it and give you what he thinks is write I havent learnt yet what the cost and havent got one yet I guess I will bring my letter to a close for this time you must excuse my bad writing I have no table to write on I rote this letter on my lap

So much from your cinsear husband and friend

My love to you all
J. C. Arnold

March 9 (Wednesday)

Grant was commissioned Lt. General on this date, being officially handed the commission by President Lincoln in the presence of the Cabinet. Following the ceremony, Grant and Lincoln held private conversations, before Grant left for the Army of the Potomac and a visit to Major Gen. Meade.

Admiral Porter, eager to get the Red River expedition assembled so he could meet Gen. Nathaniel Banks at Alexandria, La., on March 17th, directed that a close watch be kept for the arrival of transports carrying Sherman's troops downriver. Porter's force included 13 large gunboats, two large steamers, and four small paddle-wheelers.

March 10 (Thursday)

Grant arrived at Gen. Meade's headquarters for a conference that concerned the state of the Army of the Potomac and their working command relationship, since Grant would be in the field with Meade during the coming campaign.

Barber, Cpl., Co. D, 15th Illinois Volunteer Infantry, Canton, Miss.:

...those of us who had not been sworn in our new term of service, duly took the required oath and received our discharge from first term of service, dating back to time of re-enlistment. The non-veterans took a deep interest in these proceedings. No less patriotic than the veterans, home ties had a stronger claim on them. For three years they had served their country faithfully and well. There were thousands yet at the North whose duty it was to enlist and it is no wonder that we thought it was their turn now....

March 12 (Saturday)

Grant had returned to Washington only long enough to catch a train to Nashville, where he had an appointment with Sherman, soon to be the commander of the western armies. Major Gen. Halleck, at his own request, was relieved as General-in-Chief and named Chief of Staff to Grant; Grant was assigned command of *all* the armies; Sherman was named as Grant's replacement in the west, with McPherson moving to Sherman's vacated billet.

The Red River expedition got under way with Admiral Porter's gunboats U.S.S. *Eastport*, *Essex*, *Ozark*, *Osage*, and *Neosho*, and the wooden steamers *Lafayette*, *Choctaw*, *Fort Hindman*, and *Cricket* proceeding up the Red River. Porter took the ironclads U.S.S. *Benton*, *Chillicothe*, *Louisville*, *Pittsburg*, and *Mound City* and the wooden paddle-wheelers *Ouachita*, *Lexington*, and *Gazelle* into the Atchafalaya River to cover the Federal army landing at Simmesport, where an initial landing party from the *Benton*, Lt. Commander Greer, drove in the Confederate pickets before the main landing.

In other naval action, a tug, the U.S.S. *Columbine*, Acting Ensign Francis W. Sanborn, went up the St. John's River in Florida in support of an Army operation, and Sanborn captured the Confederate river steamer *General Sumter*. A prize crew from the U.S.S. *Pawnee* was placed aboard and the two ships proceeded upriver. Two days later, the 14th, the two ships captured another steamer, the *Hattie*, at Deep Creek on Lake Monroe. Several days were spent in the area destroying a sugar refinery and other installations.

March 13 (Sunday)

Grant was en route to Nashville from Washington, Sherman from Vicksburg.

Admiral Porter's gunboats covered the landing of the Union army troops at Simmesport early in the morning. The troops then advanced, driving the Confederates back towards Ft. De Russy. Meanwhile, Lt. Commander Samuel Phelps took the *Eastport* and his other gunboats up to the obstructions on the Red River which had so laboriously been built by the Confederates and were thought to be impassable. Porter observed that: "They supposed it impassable, but our energetic sailors with hard work open a passage in a few hours." As soon as a passage could be gained, the *Eastport* and *Neosho* went upriver and began the bombardment of Ft. De Russy while the Federal troops landed at Simmesport prepared for a land assault.

March 14 (Monday)

The combined weight of the naval bombardment and the land assault on Ft. De Russy on the Red River had the desired results, and the fort surrendered. Porter and Sherman's Brig. Gen. Andrew Jackson Smith cooperated beautifully during the action. Porter wrote of the action:

> The surrender of the forts at Point De Russy is of much more importance than I at first supposed. The rebels had depended on that point to stop any advance of army or navy into rebeldom. Large quantities of ammunition, best engineers and best troops were sent there....

March 15 (Tuesday)

Leaving the ironclads U.S.S. *Benton* and *Essex* at Ft. De Russy where the fort was being destroyed, Admiral Porter convoyed the main body of troops upriver towards Alexandria, La. Porter sent the U.S.S. *Eastport*, *Lexington*, and *Ouachita* racing upriver hoping to capture the Confederate vessels trying to get above the Alexandria rapids. The race was lost, however, the Rebel ships having gone beyond the rapids 30 minutes before the Federal ships arrived. The Confederate steamer *Countess* had run aground and was burned to prevent her capture.

The new pro-Union governor of Louisiana, Michael Hahn, was vested with the powers that formerly belonged to the Military Governor of the state, increasing Hahn's power and transferring more power to the civil authority.

March 16 (Wednesday)

There were nine Union ships at Alexandria, La., by this morning, and a landing party commanded by Lt. Commander Selfridge had occupied the town without resistance. Porter came up during the day and the Union force waited for the arrival of Major Gen. Banks's army, which was slogging through mud and heavy rain to get there.

The Confederate ram, the C.S.S. *Albemarle*, being built on the Roanoke River in North Carolina was becoming a topic of concern for the naval units in Albemarle Sound. The latest intelligence on the vessel was that she was to have two layers of iron and would be ready to sail to Williamston, N.C., on the first of next month. This was a formidable vessel and she would dominate the waters around Plymouth, N.C., until her destruction.

"Devil Forrest" was loose again in western Tennessee on a raid that would last until mid-April. At Tullahoma, Tenn., Confederate raiders struck at the Nashville and Chattanooga rail line, severing service for a while.

The Richmond *Examiner* reported that Gen. Joseph Johnston's report of operations in Mississippi in summer 1863 indicated that the disaster at Vicksburg was caused by Gen. Pemberton's disobedience of orders, Johnston having ordered Pemberton to concentrate his army and give battle before the place was invested, and under no circumstances to allow himself to be besieged, which, of course, would result in disaster. Johnston also said he was about to maneuver in a manner that would probably have resulted in saving a larger proportion of the men, when, to his astonishment, he learned that Pemberton had surrendered! Gen. Joseph Eggleston Johnston's hindsight was always better than his foresight.

Barber, Cpl., Co. D, 15th Illinois Volunteer Infantry, en route home on furlough:

> On the 16th of March, we bade adieu to comrades, marched to Vicksburg and embarked on board a steamer for St. Louis where we were to be paid off. On arriving at St. Louis a grand ovation was given us.

March 17 (Thursday)

Grant, now in Nashville, took time to formally assume command of all the armies of the United States and informed everyone that "Headquarters will be in the field, and, until further orders, will be with the Army of the Potomac." Having settled that, Grant and Sherman boarded a train for Cincinnati, Ohio, to do their planning in private. Sherman would remember forever after the details of what happened in that room—the plan to skin the Confederacy alive.

March 18 (Friday)

In Cincinnati, Grant and Sherman were huddled in a hotel room thick with cigar smoke, plotting the destruction of the Confederacy. Sherman officially assumed command of the armies in the west.

The Sanitary Commission had been holding a fair in Washington, and Lincoln was present at its closing to make a few remarks. His comments included praise for the contribution of the women to the war, saying "... if all that has been said by orators and poets since the creation of the world in praise of woman applied to the women of America, it would not do them justice for their conduct during this war."

Lt. Gen. E. Kirby Smith, CSA, with some foresight, ordered the steamer *New Falls City* to be sent to Scopern's Cut-off below Shreveport, on the Red River, where she was to be sunk as an obstacle to the Union fleet coming upriver. He also ordered torpedoes to be placed in the river below that point.

March 20 (Sunday)

Lt. Charles C. Simmes, CSN, had been assigned as the commander of the C.S.S. *Baltic* and wrote Commander Catesby ap R. Jones, commander of the Naval Ordnance Factory at Selma, Ala., concerning an inspection report on the ship. The inspector, he said,

> ...has made a very unfavorable report on the condition of the ship and recommended that the iron be taken from her and put upon one of the new boats that were built.... Between you and I the *Baltic* is rotten as punk and is about as fit to go into action as a mud scow.

Barber, Cpl., Co. D, 15th Illinois Volunteer Infantry, St. Louis, Mo.:

> A deputation of the citizens presented each soldier with a badge of welcome. We were then marched to a capacious hall where a bountiful feast had been prepared for us. After dinner, we all adjourned to the saloon where all who chose were treated to beer. While we remained in St. Louis, every attention was shown us. It was not until the second day of our arrival that we were paid off. During the interval, we were allowed our liberty and took this occasion to see the sights of the city. I attended the theatre both evenings. We were paid on the 22d.... I received two hundred and eighty-seven dollars.

March 22 (Tuesday)

Major Gen. Lewis Wallace replaced Brig. Gen. Henry H. Lockwood as commander of the Middle Department, which included Maryland and occupied Virginia.

Snow began to fall in the early evening in Richmond.

Jackman, Pvt., "The Orphan Brigade," Dalton, Ga.:

> Last night the snow fell three or four inches deep and continued snowing, not very hard though, through the day. We have seen more fun today that at any one time during the war. Early in the morning the 4th Ky., whose camp is near Tyler's brigade, of our division, got up a snow fight with Tyler's men, and all the other regiments in our brigade went to reinforce the 4th. After fighting awhile, our brigade and Tyler's "made friends" and both went over to Finley's brigade of our division and charged the camp. Finley was soon "cleaned out." Not having enough fun, our division and Bates' marched on Stovall's brigade, Stewart's division, two miles off. We moved in military order and when we got in the neighborhood of the camp sent forward, after

forming lines of battle, a line of skirmishers to develop the enemy. Our skirmishers soon had to fall back before superior numbers and we made a general assault. We took the camp with so little fighting—not having seen near sport enough—our lines fell back and let Stovall's men prepare for defense. By this time Gen'l S. came in person and had his brigade formed. We charged again and took a stand of colors and Gen'l S. himself. Lt. McC. and myself had the honor to capture the flag which we brought to camp. Having entirely demoralized Stovall, we came home—I got several bruises.

In the afternoon a courier came over from Tyler's brigade stating that all of Stewart's division was advancing on our division. Soon our regiments were marching to the half-way grounds which was to be the seat of war. We formed our lines on a range of hills and waited for the enemy after sending out skirmishers. Had not been in line long when we could see the red banner of the advancing hosts contrasting beautifully with the white snow. They came steadily forward and soon the air was full of snow-balls. Before the action commenced, our Q.M. who had the honor to cmd our regiment—and we had the honor to be commanded by him—made us a stirring speech. All of Stewart's men had ten rounds each of snow-balls in their haversacks and we had to fall back. I rece'd a wound in the left eye in the early part of the action. Q.M. came near being captured only saving himself by putting spurs to his horse. As we were driven through Finley's and Tyler's camp, their men deserted us and we still had to retreat before superior numbers. We took advantage of ground occasionally and gave the overpowering columns a check. A detachment of our men captured Gen'l Stewart. At last when they had driven us back to the camp of the 4th Ky., our regiment made a flank movement which so surprised the enemy he was soon put to rout and our camp saved from pillage. The 4th and 2d lost their flags. We took the banner captured from the 47th—perhaps the 41st—and we brought it back with us. Lt. McC. acted as Color Sergeant and I as his guard. After we had routed the enemy, we captured many prisoners among them Maj Austin of La. who occasionally gave us something to laugh at over the name of "Maj. Currycomb." Tonight I felt "terribly" sore.

March 23 (Wednesday)

In Arkansas, Union troops under the command of Major Gen. Frederick Steele moved south to join Banks's expedition coming up the Red River. Steele's purpose was to occupy the Confederate troops to keep them away from Banks's campaign.

The Confederates, while loading cotton at wharves up the rivers, tried a new tactic to keep the Union from capturing steamers. Lt. A.W. Weaver, USN, took a crew up the Santee River, S.C., to where he knew a steamer was loading, intending to cut it loose from the pier and to go downriver. He was surprised to find that the steamer was securely chained to the wharf; shore batteries opened on his crew before he could get the chains loose. He withdrew downriver.

Grant left Cincinnati and returned to Washington, and Sherman headed for Nashville to coordinate his movement into Georgia. The command of the Fifth Corps of the Army of the Potomac shifted from Major Gen. George Sykes to Major Gen. G.K. Warren. Warren was the officer who got the troops to Little Round Top and saved the Union left flank at the Battle of Gettysburg.

Jackman, Pvt., "The Orphan Brigade," Dalton, Ga.:

> The sun shining this morning and the snow is rapidly disappearing. Feel so sore from my sport yesterday I can scarcely move. The boys want me to write an account of the late battle and have it published; but I feel too crippled.

Day, Pvt., Co. B, 25th Massachusetts Volunteer Infantry, Newport News, Va.:

> A snow commenced yesterday and continued through last night with great severity, and as our camp is only a temporary affair it afforded but slight protection; when I awoke this morning I found myself under a blanket of snow about a foot thick; there was quite a depth of snow and it was badly drifted. Before noon it cleared up and the sun shone out warm. Now commenced the snow-ball battles, in which all hands engaged and seemed to take great delight. This afternoon a sleighing party drove into camp and made the rounds of the officers quarters. This was a battery company, which out of some tim-

> bers and boards had improvised a sled about 30 feet long, and had hitched on their whole team of horses, some 80 in number. The battery boys were riding the horses while the sled was covered with officers, both military and naval. Making the rounds of the camps and being entertained at the officers' quarters, they had a high old time. It didn't matter much about the sleighing, whether good or bad, as they had team and whiskey enough to make good sleighing anywhere.

March 24 (Thursday)

Intelligence reports reaching Lt. Commander Flusser, USN, concerning the Confederate ram C.S.S. *Albemarle* indicated that the ram was ready and was now located at Hamilton, N.C. It was further reported that the torpedoes installed in the river below that point were being removed to allow the ships to pass downriver.

High winds and heavy seas thwarted a Union expedition which had sailed from Beaufort, S.C., to capture and destroy two blockade runners at Swansboro, N.C., and to possibly capture a group of Confederates. Sailing from Beaufort on the side-wheel steamer U.S.S. *Britannia*, the force of 200 Army troops under the command of Col. James Jourdan, and about 50 sailors from the various gunboats under the command of Commander Benjamin M. Dove, arrived off Bogue Island Banks late at night but couldn't land because of the weather.

Admiral Porter, heading the naval action on the Red River expedition, reported that since entering the river his boats had captured over 2000 bales of cotton and quantities of molasses and wool, all of which had been sent downriver or destroyed.

March 25 (Friday)

At dawn the heaving seas and gale winds abated and a part of the landing parties from the U.S.S. *Britannia* were put ashore off Bogue Island Banks near Swansboro, N.C., where they had arrived the night before. A party got through to the blockade-running schooners and one of them was burned, but little other damage was inflicted. Returning to the ship, the landing parties went back to Beaufort, S.C., with only part of their mission completed.

Near Paducah, Ky., the Confederates launched a heavy assault on the defense positions of that city and were beaten off by the gunfire of the gunboats U.S.S. *Peosta*, Acting Lt. Thomas E. Smith, and U.S.S. *Paw Paw*, Acting Lt. A. Frank O'Neil. Brig. Gen. Mason Brayman, commander at Paducah, wrote of the action:

> ...shelled the rebels out of the buildings from which their sharpshooters annoyed our troops. A large number took shelter in heavy warehouses near the river and maintained a furious fire upon the gunboats, inflicting some injury, but they were promptly dislodged and the buildings destroyed....

Forrest's cavalry attacked Ft. Anderson, part of the Paducah defenses, but was repulsed. Unable to make much headway with the attack, the Confederates withdrew in the early hours of the next day.

Lt. Commander Babcock, U.S.S. *Morse*, sent a report to Admiral S.P. Lee listing the matériel seized by his ship between February 1st and 12th on the York River. The list contained: a small schooner; a sloop; quantities of corn, wheat, oats, salt, and tobacco; implements such as plows, plow points, plowshares, molding boards and a cultivator. Many of the implements were irreplaceable to the Confederate farmers.

At Alexandria, La., Major Gen. Banks arrived with the main force for the Red River expedition to Shreveport. He was a week late due to heavy rains.

Jackman, Pvt., "The Orphan Brigade," Dalton, Ga.:

> Wind blew very hard last night, bringing up a snow storm. The ground was white again this morning with snow but it soon melted away. The brigade has gone out to the execution of the sentence of a court martial on one Keen of the 2d Fla. reg't who is to be shot for desertion. This is a murky day. I would hate to be shot on such a day—especially for desertion.

March 26 (Saturday)

By dawn, the Confederate forces which had been attacking Paducah, Ky., were gone, and a silence hung over the defenses.

Grant was back in Virginia and had established his permanent headquarters with the Army of the Potomac at Culpeper C.H. McPherson had taken command of the Army of the Tennessee, reporting to Sherman.

Day, Pvt., Co. B, 25th Massachusetts Volunteer Infantry, Portsmouth, Va.:

Broke camp and went over to Portsmouth, opposite Norfolk. Regiment arrived in the afternoon, bringing some 250 recruits. We are once more together and the regiment now numbers about 900 men. Towards night we were ordered out to Getty's Station, about four miles west of Portsmouth.

Barber, Cpl., Co. D, 15th Illinois Volunteer Infantry, Riley, Illinois:

At seven o'clock on the evening of the 26th, we arrived at Marengo. Roll, Milt and I found a load of Riley friends waiting for us and a jolly load of us were soon on our way home.

March 28 (Monday)

The initiative and versatility of the Yankee sailor was shown when crewmen from the U.S.S. *Benton*, Lt. Commander Greer, went ashore on the 27th near Ft. De Russy and removed some 13 bales of cotton from an abandoned plantation back to the ship. Greer reported that today they went back again and "got 18 bales from the same place, which they baled themselves, using up an old awning for the purpose."

In Charleston, Illinois, a group of about 100 Copperheads attacked Union soldiers on leave from their units and visiting the town. By the time the fracas was over, five men were dead and about 20 wounded.

In Louisiana, Gen. Banks's Red River expedition moved into a new phase, with additional fighting on the way to Shreveport.

March 29 (Tuesday)

The rapids at Alexandria, La., gave Admiral D.D. Porter problems in getting all of his gunboats and other vessels up for the advance on Shreveport. Low water in the river was the main problem now and would become a bigger problem later. All the Army transports got safely above the rapids, but several of the gunboats had to remain below. The hospital ship *Woodford* was so battered in the attempt that she sank.

A two-boat expedition under the command of Acting Master James M. Williams, U.S.S. *Commodore Barney*, accompanied by a crew from the U.S.S. *Minnesota*, Acting Master Charles B. Wilder, rowed up Chuckatuck Creek, Va., late at night seeking to capture a party of Confederate troops in the area.

APRIL 1864

The last three weeks had been very busy for the newly promoted Lt. Gen. Ulysses S. Grant. Since he stood on the sofa in the White House on March 8th so that everyone could see him, he had moved to the headquarters of Meade's Army of the Potomac—primarily to escape Washington—and had been organizing and consolidating his grasp of the overall situation. He had much to do.

Things began to heat up during April. The inactivity of the late fall and winter came to a flaming end in both the eastern and western theaters of war. Lee, with the Army of Northern Virginia lying quiet in its camps, awaited Grant's first move.

In the west, the Army of Tennessee watched the Federals at Chattanooga and bided their time. Minor skirmishing was going on throughout.

April 1 (Friday)

Two days ago the Confederates had placed twelve floating torpedoes, each with 70 pounds of powder, in the St. John's River in Florida. The Union army transport *Maple Leaf*, supporting an operation from Palatka to Ft. Gates, struck one of these mines when she returned from a trip upriver to Palatka and was destroyed.

Federal Gen. Banks was still pushing his Red River operation into Louisiana. Major Gen. Frederick Steele, involved in the Camden expedition, was moving south to support Banks and to keep the Rebels occupied while Banks drove for Shreveport.

All was fairly quiet in northwest Georgia, where the famed Kentucky "Orphan Brigade" was awaiting developments around Dalton.

Jackman, Pvt., "The Orphan Brigade," Dalton, Ga.:

Had cornbread "straight" for breakfast—baked beef and irish potatoes for dinner. Cloudy and sometimes raining during the day. Being the first of the month, had to make several reports.... Capt. W. showed me a book this evening which if I ever become again civilized, I shall obtain a copy: The Elementary French reader; or Easy Method for Beginners in translating French, etc. by Norman Pinney, A.M. Capt. W. has been looking over it a week or so and can already read French pretty well.

April 3 (Sunday)

Admiral Porter's array of gunboats convoyed the troop transports from Alexandria, La., to Grand Ecore, where Brig. Gen. Andrew Jackson Smith's troops disembarked, except for one division under Brig. Gen. T. Kilby Smith. A.J. Smith's Federals marched overland towards Nachitoches to join Gen. Banks for the assault on Shreveport. Porter's eight gunboats and three steamers then proceeded upriver.

In western Tennessee, Forrest was raiding near Raleigh. Sumter was being shelled again by mortars.

Day, Pvt., Co. B, 25th Massachusetts Volunteer Infantry, Getty's Station, Va.:

> This is a station on the Seaboard and Roanoke railroad; the camp ground lies between the station and the Nansemond river.... It is the worst ground we have ever camped on, being little else but a mud hole. I have slept out in the woods ever since we came here, but we are getting it drained and the tents stockaded, but by the time we get it habitable, we shall have to leave it.

April 4 (Monday)

Today one tough-minded Major General named Philip Sheridan became the head of the cavalry of the Army of the Potomac. Primarily an infantry commander, Sheridan had seen action in most of the battles in the west and had the full confidence of Grant and a reputation for hard fighting.

April 5 (Tuesday)

There was concern at Plymouth, N.C., that the draft of the Confederate ironclad C.S.S. *Albemarle* would be such that she could easily pass over the obstructions placed by the Union in the Roanoke River. Although the ship had a draft of nearly nine feet, rumors were rampant that the draft was only six to eight feet, making a big difference in her capability.

April 7 (Thursday)

Gen. James Longstreet, who had wintered in Greeneville, Tenn., was ordered back to the Army of Northern Virginia and Lee's command.

On the Red River at Grand Ecore, La., Admiral D.D. Porter, with his usual direct method of command, left Lt. Commander Phelps in charge of the heavier gunboats and proceeded upriver towards Shreveport with the lighter-draft gunboats U.S.S. *Osage, Neosho,* and *Chillicothe* and the steamers *Fort Hindman, Lexington,* and *Cricket.* If the depth of the water improved, Phelps was to join them below Shreveport.

Jackman, Pvt., "The Orphan Brigade," Dalton, Ga.:

> Our corps had another battle today, Cleburne and Bate against Cheatham and Walker, this time using blank cartridges. Many people were on the ground to witness the occasion. Ladies from nearly every city in the south, or in Georgia rather, were present. The spectators were on a hill hard-by where they could see all the manoeuvering. The firing sounded very much like a battle. The cavalry charged our division and we were formed in oblique squares. Our boys shot wads at the spurred gentlemen and wounded one or two pretty badly. In the morning the rain commenced but soon stopped and we had a beautiful day for the occasion. Clouded up again in the evening.

April 8 (Friday)

Gen. Nathaniel Banks had been advancing steadily, with little more than skirmishing, towards Shreveport, La. Now his opponent, Major Gen. Richard Taylor, decided that enough was enough. Taylor had drawn his Confederates up in a defense line at Sabine Crossroads, near Mansfield, and awaited the arrival of Banks. Banks had his blue columns strung out, with his wagons intermixed with the troops in the line of march—a tactical mistake. Banks halted his columns to get them sorted out and Taylor struck late in the afternoon. A full-scale battle was soon going and some of Banks's units withdrew, losing some artillery pieces. Taylor flanked Banks both right and left and the Federals in the middle fled in panic, being slowed by their wagon trains that should not have been there to begin with. Finally, the division of Brig. Gen. William H. Emory made a stand that stiffened the Federals' defense, and Taylor's attack petered out. Banks lost a high percentage of his men to capture—about 1541 out of 12,000. Banks's next problem was to link up with Admiral Porter, who was stalled at Springfield Landing when the water in the river was falling.

The United States Senate passed a joint resolution approving the Thirteenth Amendment, which abolished slavery. The vote was 38 to 6.

April 9 (Saturday)

At Culpeper C.H., Va., U.S. Grant issued his famous campaign order to Major Gen. George G. Meade, stating that Lee's army was Meade's objective: "Wherever Lee goes, there you will go also." Grant intended to maintain contact with Lee's army and wear it down.

Giving Banks no respite, Major Gen. Taylor sent his Confederates against the blue defense line drawn up at Pleasant Hill, La., late in the afternoon, gaining some ground, but the Federals counterattacked and drove the Rebels back, ending the engagement. This was supposedly a win for the North, but Banks's not having reached his objective of Shreveport, it was a no-win also. Gen. Frederick Steele was having his problems in Arkansas, skirmishing for the next four days in the Camden area.

Forrest was operating between the Tennessee and Mississippi rivers in western Tennessee, where he could not be easily reached by Federal gunboats, and where few Union troops were stationed.

About 2 A.M., the Officer of the Deck on the U.S.S. *Minnesota*, Acting Ensign James Birtwistle, saw a small boat 150 to 200 yards off, just forward of the port beam. He hailed the vessel and received the reply, "Roanoke." Birtwistle then ordered the boat to stay clear and received the reply, "Aye." Birtwistle could see no visible means of propulsion, yet the small boat was moving rapidly and still coming straight for the *Minnesota* and was soon too close for the ship's guns to bear. A fifty pound charge of powder was then rammed into the *Minnesota*'s port quarter, and as the ship's log later recorded: "...a tremendous explosion followed."

This was a daring deed carried out by the Confederate torpedo boat *Squib*, commanded by Lt. Hunter Davidson. The boat, described by Acting Master John A. Curtis, second in command, was constructed of wood, "about thirty-five feet long, five feet wide, drew three feet of water, two feet freeboard; designed by Hunter Davidson.... The boiler and engine were encased with iron; forward of the boiler was the cockpit, where the crew stood and from where we steered her." Curtis wrote that he had closed his eyes at the moment of impact; "opening them in about a second, I think, I never beheld such a sight before, nor since. The air was filled with port shutters and water from the explosion, and the heavy ship rolled to starboard, and the officer of the deck giving orders to save yourselves and cried out 'Torpedo, torpedo!' "

The *Squib* almost was lost as the small boat was sucked under the port quarter when the *Minnesota* rolled to starboard. However, Curtis reported, the pressure of the water when the larger ship righted itself pushed the boat away. The *Squib* was still so close that Curtis jumped on the deck and physically pushed against the hull of the *Minnesota* to get the small boat clear. Amid a hail of small-arms fire, the *Squib* withdrew up the James River and escaped. Lt. Davidson was promoted to Commander for his exploit.

April 10 (Sunday)

Gen. Nathaniel Banks was withdrawing from Pleasant Hill towards the Red River and his gunboats and transports. In Arkansas, Gen. Steele disengaged and returned to Little Rock.

Going up the Red River to support Gen. Banks at Shreveport, Admiral D.D. Porter found he was stopped cold at Springfield Landing, La., where the Confederates, with a great deal of ingenuity, had created an obstacle. Porter later described it to Gen. Sherman:

> When I arrived at Springfield Landing I found a sight that made me laugh. It was the smartest thing I ever knew the rebels to do. They had gotten that huge steamer, *New Falls City*, across Red River, 1 mile above Loggy Bayou, 15 feet of her on shore on each side, the boat broken down in the middle, and a sand bar making below her. An invitation in large letters to attend a ball in Shreveport was kindly left stuck up by the rebels, which invitation we were never able to accept.

Word was received at about this time that Gen. Banks had been defeated at the Battle of Sabine

Cross-Roads near Grand Ecore, and was retreating towards Pleasant Hill. The transports with the troops of Brig. Gen. Andrew Jackson Smith were ordered to join Banks at the earliest possible time. The Red River campaign was stalled and effectively done.

April 12 (Tuesday)

At Springfield Landing, La., Admiral D.D. Porter's gunboats and transports turned around and headed back downriver. The Confederates took the Union fleet under fire from the high bluffs overlooking the river and from Blair's Landing. Dismounted Confederate cavalry and artillery attacked the fleet from the riverbanks. The U.S.S. *Lexington*, Lt. Bache, used its guns to silence the artillery but a storm of small-arms fire rained on the ships from the cavalry. This engagement brought to use a unique instrument which had been developed by Chief Engineer Thomas Doughty of the U.S.S. *Osage* and described by Lt. Commander Selfridge as "a method of sighting the turret from the outside, by means of what would now be called a periscope...." The high banks of the river posed a problem for the ship's gunners in aiming their cannon from water level. Engineer Doughty's device helped solve that problem. Selfridge wrote that:

> On first sounding to general quarters...[I] went inside the turret to direct its fire, but the restricted vision from the peep holes rendered it impossible to see what was going on in the threatened quarter, whenever the turret was trained in the loading position. In this extremity I thought of the periscope, and hastily took up station there, well protected by the turret, yet able to survey the whole scene and to direct an accurate fire.

About 50 miles from Memphis, Tenn., Ft. Pillow had been used for some time to protect a small trading post located nearby. On this night, Gen. Bedford Forrest's troopers struck with about 1500 men against 557 defenders. Although the cavalry was driven back by the guns of the gunboat U.S.S. *New Era*, the Confederates mounted an all-out assault by midafternoon and the fort was quickly overrun after its commander, Major William F. Bradford, refused to surrender. There was, and still is, more than a century later, controversy over just how many men surrendered and when. Southern accounts say that about 231 Federals were killed and 100 wounded before the surrender. Federal accounts state that the surrender occurred almost immediately without many casualties. Investigations show that Forrest's men killed nearly 350 of the Union troops at the fort, including most of the 262 Negro troops stationed there. Forrest himself, in a later report to his commander, stated, "We busted the fort at ninerclock and scatered the niggers. The men is a cillanem in the woods." The action resulted in much acrimony on both sides, with a definite revenge motive on the part of Union Negro troops for years to come.

April 13 (Wednesday)

A joint operation went up the Nansemond River, Va., to destroy the Confederate torpedo boat the *Squib*, which had attacked the U.S.S. *Minnesota* on the 9th, and also to capture some Confederate soldiers reported in the area. A handful of prisoners was taken and information obtained that the *Squib* had gone up the James River towards Richmond.

Day, Pvt., Co. B, 25th Massachusetts Volunteer Infantry, Getty's Station, Va.:

> The country above here and that part of it lying between the Suffolk and James rivers is a good deal infected with guerrilla bands. It was thought best to send out in different directions three or four regiments to stir them up.... We left our mud hole early in the morning of the 13th going aboard a big double-ender steamer at Portsmouth. In company with a small gunboat we steamed up the James river some 20 miles, when turning to the left we entered a small creek; following this a few miles we came to a village called Smithfield.
>
> We landed here about noon and marched up into the street. The village seemed to be deserted, scarcely any one in sight. We had not been here many minutes before Col. Pickett was met by a good-looking elderly gentleman, who seemed to be considerably agitated about something. He wished the colonel to send a guard to his house, as he feared the Negroes would take too many liberties with him during our stay. The colonel inquired if there were many Confederates about here. The old gentleman replied that he had seen none recently, and just then the report of rifles was heard up the creek. At this, the colonel, in a

very abrupt and ungentlemanly manner, said: "D—n you and your house! Forward March!" The old gentleman turned away sorrowfully and started for home. This man's name was Atkinson and he was formerly a member of Congress....

Just out the village the road forked. We halted a minute to determine which one to take and while waiting a darky came along driving a pair of bulls hitched to a cart. Not being accustomed to seeing so grand a display, the animals became frightened and balked. The darky, standing in the cart, applied the whip and yelled at them. They began to bellow, and sticking their tails straight up in the air, went bellowing down the road at a gait which would have shamed a locomotive.... We returned to Smithfield and soon after we were joined by the 9th New Jersey who informed us that the 23d Massachusetts had had a brush with a party of guerrillas and had driven them towards Suffolk; those were the troops who were ahead of us when we met the scouts.... We arrived back to Camp Wellington in the afternoon.

April 14 (Thursday)

Forrest's cavalry, reported at Columbus, Ky., yesterday, were now reported at Paducah.

Admiral Porter's gunboats and transports were threatened by the lowering water level in the Red River. He wrote Secretary of the Navy Gideon Welles:

> I found the fleet at Grand Ecore somewhat in an unpleasant situation, two of them being above the bar, and not likely to get away again this season unless there is a rise of a foot.... If nature does not change her laws, there will no doubt be a rise of water, but there was one year—1846—when there was no rise in the Red River, and it may happen again. The rebels are cutting off the supply by diverting different sources of water into other channels, all of which would have been stopped had our Army arrived as far as Shreveport.... Had we not heard of the retreat of the Army, I should still have gone on to the end.

Nashville, Tenn., had become one vast quartermaster depot for the Union army. Sherman, driving to have his army ready to move on Joe Johnston as soon as Grant gave the word that he would be moving on Lee, was in a rage to get his logistics in order. Sherman needed supplies and equipment for three armies and over 35,000 horses and would not be easily dissuaded. On one occasion Sherman stormed at a Quartermaster officer, "I'm going to move on Joe Johnston the day Grant telegraphs me he is to go hit Bobby Lee; and if you don't have my army supplied, and keep it supplied, we'll eat your mules up, sir—eat your mules up!"

Since railroads would play a vital role in supplying his army, Sherman had crews trained to build bridges and lay track as fast as Confederate cavalry could tear it up. He sent for the railroad plans for all bridges on the routes and had bridges precut to replace burned ones. Months later in the Georgia campaign, one Confederate prisoner remarked that Sherman probably carried spare railroad tunnels with him in case one were destroyed!

April 16 (Saturday)

The Army transport *Gen. Hunter* struck a floating mine in the St. John's River in Florida and was destroyed. This was the second victim of twelve floating torpedoes planted in the area on March 30th by the Confederates; the transport *Maple Leaf* was destroyed on April 1st.

Confederate Secretary of the Navy Mallory wrote Commander Bulloch in England to have 12 small marine engines and boilers built for torpedo boats (40 to 50 feet in length, 5 to 6 feet beam, and drawing 3 feet of water). Twenty-five miles of "good" insulated wire and the "best" gun cotton to be used for the torpedoes was also ordered.

Jackman, Pvt., "The Orphan Brigade," Dalton, Ga.:

> Pretty morning. Have not had any newspapers for a week owing to the strike of the printers at Atlanta. I feel at a loss without the daily papers—don't know what is going on in the world. Looking for flag-of-truce letters as ten days have passed since a boat arrived at City Point....

April 17 (Sunday)

In a major change in policy, Lt. Gen. U.S. Grant ordered that no further prisoner exchanges would be permitted until the Confederates balanced Federal releases—in other words, one-for-one. He further directed that "no distinction whatever be made in the exchange between white and colored prisoners." These moves certainly hurt the South more than the

North—the South had fewer men to draw upon. Grant's battle of attrition was beginning.

Confederate troops launched an attack on the Union garrison at Plymouth, N.C., and when the Union gunboats moved up to support the garrison, the boats were promptly taken under attack by shore-based artillery.

April 18 (Monday)

The Confederate attack that began yesterday was continued today on the garrison at Plymouth, N.C. The Union army steamer *Bombshell* was sunk during the engagement, but by late evening the advance of the Confederates had been halted. The two Union gunboats, U.S.S. *Southfield* and *Miami*, supported the defense of the garrison. Lt. Commander Flusser reported that the Confederate ram C.S.S. *Albemarle* would be down at Plymouth tomorrow.

Gibson, S.J., 103rd Pennsylvania Volunteers, Plymouth, N.C.:

> Last night almost continual skirmishing was kept up. The Rebs seem determined to have Ft. Gray but so far have been repulsed with considerable loss & the loss of 1 piece of Arty. They have so damaged the U.S. Gunboat Bombshell that she, after retiring out of action, sunk at her moorings.

At Poison Springs, Ark., the Confederates under the command of John S. Marmaduke attacked a Federal foraging expedition. The Federals withdrew, after a stiff fight, leaving 198 wagons to the Rebels.

April 19 (Tuesday)

At 3:30 in the morning the Confederate ram C.S.S. *Albemarle* attacked the Union gunboats U.S.S. *Southfield* and *Miami*, which had been lashed together for protection and concentration of firepower, at Plymouth, N.C. As the Confederate ironclad approached, Lt. Commander Flusser headed the two wooden ships directly at the *Albemarle*, firing as they went. The Confederate ram struck the *Southfield* a blow with her ram which "tore a hole clear through to the boiler," and the captain of the ram, Commander Cooke, said that his ship plunged ten feet into the side of the wooden gunboat. As the *Southfield* sank after the ram pulled back, the replacement for Flusser (who had been killed during the engagement) had the cables cut that held the two ships together and continued firing into the *Albemarle*. Once the ram was free and turned her attention to the *Miami*, *the Miami* turned and headed downriver in company with the steamer U.S.S. *Ceres* and the tinclad *Whitehead*. The *Albemarle* was left in possession of the sound.

Gibson, S.J., 103rd Pennsylvania Volunteers, Plymouth, N.C.:

> Morning comes after a night of terror. The Rebs are before us, behind us, and on each side of us. They have carried Ft. Wessell on our right & turned its guns on us. their "RAM" has sunk the G.B. Southfield [*U.S.S. Southfield*] and driven off our fleet. Now we are "gone up" unless we get reinforcements, but we will die "game." Bombardment continues all day. Work under a galling crossfire all day & at night Co "B" have to go on pickett. The night is made lively by bursting shells and the sharp rattle of musketry.

At Charleston, S.C., Confederate Engineer Tomb, CSN, tried to sink the U.S.S. *Wabash*, Capt. John DeCamp, using the same "David" boat that he had used in his attack on the U.S.S. *Memphis* on the 6th of March. This time the torpedo boat was seen while still 150 yards off and the Union *Wabash* was under steam. The frigate slipped her cable and rapidly got under way, pouring a hail of musket balls on the "David." Tomb got to within 40 yards before he had to turn back because of heavy swells that almost swamped his small craft.

April 20 (Wednesday)

Facing an overwhelming Confederate force, and with no protection from the gunboats, the garrison at Plymouth, N.C., surrendered at 10 A.M.

Gibson, S.J., 103rd Pennsylvania Volunteers, Plymouth, N.C.:

> Our flag still floats defiantly, but we cannot hold out much longer, the Rebs have got all their artillery in position and have carried the forts on our left. Just at daylight the "ball opens." I am on pickett in front of the works. My chance for getting in looks rather blue. At 7 A.M., the enemy has gained the town & are now in our rear. We form & advance to drive them out. Then commences a most terrific streetfight. At 8 A.M., a parley. Uncon. surr. dem. No surr, come and

take us. At 10 A.M. our flag is lowered. We are prisoners of war.

April 21 (Thursday)

Below Grand Ecore, La., on the Red River, the U.S.S. *Eastport* was finally able to get afloat after carpenters had worked day and night for six days to repair the damage done when she struck a torpedo on the 15th. Lt. Commander Phelps took her downriver, grounding eight times in the next sixty miles.

Jackman, Pvt., "The Orphan Brigade," Dalton, Ga.:

> Cloudy and cool wind from the east. Artillery firing toward Chattanooga again today. We have been living better of late as rations of hams are issued instead of blue beef. Had a shower of rain at 4 P.M. Clear tonight, the moon shining brightly. I hear a whip-poor-will back of our cabin tonight, the first one I have heard this spring.

April 23 (Saturday)

Back in late March Sherman had closed the railroad lines between Nashville and eastern Tennessee to all but military traffic. This brought a storm of protest from residents along the line who relied on the railroad from Nashville. His reply was for them to drive their cattle over the mountains and move the supplies by wagon the way it had been done before the advent of the railroad; "his" line was too important for such things. A Quaker from Pennsylvania tried putting pressure on Sherman from Washington to move himself and food supplies to eastern Tennessee. Sherman let the man go; the supplies stayed in Nashville.

One of Sherman's biggest complaints was the bureaucratic way the trainmen ran the railroads. In the beginning, only about 60 cars a day ran from Nashville east to Chattanooga, and Sherman saw the need to double the number. He proposed laying a double track on the route, but said that even with that the trainmen were so used to timetables that they couldn't cope with the added capacity. To increase the number of cars, Sherman seized all freight cars arriving from Louisville, or other points north, and convinced James Guthrie of the L & N Railroad to seize all cars arriving in Louisville and send them to Nashville. With this pool of cars available, Sherman amazed the railroaders by having 130, then 150, and a maximum of 193 cars per day moving east to Chattanooga.

In Fairfax County, Va., near Hunters Mill, Confederate and Federal patrols clashed in a brief encounter only about 20 miles from the White House.

At sea off the Cape Verde Islands, Capt. Semmes, C.S.S. *Alabama*, captured and destroyed the bark *Rockingham* with a cargo of guano. Semmes wrote of the capture:

> It was the old spectacle of the panting, breathless fawn, and the inexorable stag-hound. A gun brought his colors to the peak, and his main-yard to the mast.... We transferred to the *Alabama* such stores and provisions as we could make room for, and the weather being fine, we made a target of the prize, firing some shot and shell into her with good effect and at five P.M. we burned her and filled away on our course.

Semmes also reported that many of his shots failed to explode, indicating either faulty or aging powder.

April 25 (Monday)

Throughout the month Sherman had been stripping his army of "excess baggage." There would be no "company tents" for marching troops and little of other camp comforts. Even his own headquarters was reduced to one wagon for himself, aides, clerks, and orderlies. This would really be lean living after the past two years of "bloated" headquarters staff arrangements for most corps, division, and regimental staffs. Sherman's intent was to eliminate as many wagons as possible in the trains. During the coming campaign the soldiers would carry "five days' bacon, twenty days' bread, and thirty days' salt, sugar and coffee, nothing else but arms and ammunition." Regiments would be reduced to a single supply wagon.

Sherman also sent a request to Fleet Capt. Pennock in Cairo to protect the General's lines of communications where possible, since Sherman would be going into Georgia and his supply line along the Tennessee River would be exposed.

In Louisiana, the Federals were arriving at Alexandria on their retreat from Sabine Crossroads. Porter was still above the city on the Red River.

April 26 (Tuesday)

The U.S.S. *Eastport*, damaged by a torpedo on the 15th and finally refloated on the 21st, had run aground for the last time. Unable to get the gunboat refloated, Admiral D.D. Porter ordered Lt. Commander Phelps to transfer his men to the steamer U.S.S. *Fort Hindman* and to destroy the *Eastport.* Phelps, the last man to leave the ship, lit fuses that set off 3000 pounds of gunpowder, completely shattering the gunboat.

While arrangements were being made to blow up the *Eastport*, the Confederates attacked the fleet with artillery and infantry, even charging the U.S.S. *Cricket* and trying to capture her by boarding. The *Cricket*, Admiral Porter's flagship, drove the Confederates off with charges of grape and canister. Later in the day, Southern troops again attacked the boats near the mouth of Cane River at Deloach's Bluff, this time with artillery as well as muskets. *Cricket* was hit several times by the artillery, but managed to run around a bend in the river and out of range. Pump Steamer *Champion No. 3* took a direct artillery hit in her boiler, drifted out of control and was captured. The U.S.S. *Juliet* had her engine disabled by artillery but was towed to safety by *Champion No. 5*, which was also badly hit. The wooden gunboat U.S.S. *Fort Hindman* covered the withdrawal of the fleet to a point where repairs could be made.

Confederate Gen. Richard Taylor's stated mission was to "...keep up a constant fight with the gunboats, following them with sharpshooters and killing every man who exposes himself."

The fall of the garrison at Plymouth, N.C., to the Confederates brought about the evacuation of Washington, N.C. The city was now indefensible.

Day, Pvt., Co. B, 25th Massachusetts Volunteer Infantry, Chesapeake and Albemarle Canal, Va.:

> The surrender of Plymouth, N.C., and death of Flusser caused consternation at Roanoke island, lest the dreaded *Albemarle* should make them a visit. On the 22d we were ordered to the succor of that island. Embarking on board a large double-ender boat, we left Portsmouth in the afternoon and proceeded up the river, going past the Gosport navy yard where could be seen the burned and sunken hulks of the U.S. vessels which were destroyed at the surrender of Norfolk and the navy yard at the beginning of the war. We kept on up the river till towards night when we entered the canal. The boat was a little too wide for the canal and our progress was slow.
>
> About midnight we came to a station, having made but a few miles of our journey. There we found our Brooklyn friends who were doing picket duty. There were right glad to see us and kept us busy answering questions about their old home, which they were beginning to despair of ever seeing again. After an hour's stop, we resumed our journey. We had not gone far when the port wheel fouled with a stump so that we could neither go ahead or back off. This caused a delay of about 2 hours as cutting out floats by the light of the lantern is a slow job.... Not until late in the afternoon of the 23d did we come out to a lake, sound, bay, or at any rate, a large sheet of water which we crossed and just before night again entered the canal.
>
> We now enter the eastern edge of the great dismal swamp. I have sometime read a legend of the phantom or witch of the lake of the dismal swamp who all night long by the light of a firefly lamp would paddle her light canoe. On each side of the canal is a cypress swamp and as the officers were about retiring for the night in the house on deck, the colonel charged the boys to keep a sharp lookout for guerrillas and bushwhackers who might be lurking there. About midnight all was still.... Presently the sharp crack of a rifle rang out on the still night air, followed by a general fusillade and a cry that the woods are full of them. The officers came rushing out of the house and the colonel strained his eyes peering into the swamp, but seeing nothing and hearing no return fire, he naturally concluded that the boys were drawing on their imaginations and gave the order to cease firing....
>
> About morning we entered the North river, coming out into Currituck sound and sailing around the head of the island landed at old Fort Huger. The garrison consisted of only the 99th New York, who felt a little nervous about being caught here alone in case the *Albemarle* should make them a visit. On landing, we learned the scare was over. The ram left Plymouth intending to come here, but on getting out into the sound, the old ferry-boats which had been lying in wait, went for her and came well nigh sinking her; at any rate they disabled her so much she put back to Plymouth. Finding we were not needed here, after a few hours rest we re-embarked and started back....

April 27 (Wednesday)

Morning saw a return of the Federal gunboats to run past the artillery batteries on the Red River that had caused so much damage the day before. The U.S.S. *Fort Hindman* took one round that partially disabled her steering and she just drifted past the Confederate guns. *Champion No. 5* was so badly damaged that she grounded and was abandoned and burned. The U.S.S. *Juliet* managed to get past, but was badly damaged. The ironclad U.S.S. *Neosho*, Acting Lt. Samuel Howard, attempting to assist the embattled gunboats, arrived after they had passed the batteries, having endured what Admiral Porter later described as "the heaviest fire I ever witnessed." By the end of the day, Porter had assembled what was left of the fleet at Alexandria and was addressing the next problem—low water on the river and how to get over the rapids at Alexandria.

For the past two weeks the skirmishing between Sherman's army and Joe Johnston's army at Dalton, Ga., had been heating up. A Confederate attack was made on the Union lines at Taylor's Ridge near Ringgold on this date.

Capt. Semmes, C.S.S. *Alabama*, captured and burned the bark *Tycoon* at sea off Salvador, Brazil, with a cargo of merchandise, including some valuable clothing. Semmes described the capture in his diary:

> We now hailed, and ordered him to heave to, whilst we should send aboard of him, hoisting our colors at the same time.... The whole thing was done so quietly, that one would have thought it was two friends meeting.

April 28 (Thursday)

The guns had been periodically bombarding poor Ft. Sumter all month, but not too heavily. That pile of rubble now underwent another seven days of prolonged battering.

At the rapids above Alexandria, La., Admiral D.D. Porter found himself in a very dangerous position due to the falling water in the river and the fact that Gen. Nathaniel Banks had to retreat from his attempt to take Shreveport. Porter advised Secretary Gideon Welles: "...I find myself blockaded by the fall of 3 feet of water, 3 feet 4 inches being the amount now on the falls; 7 feet being required to get over; no amount of lightening will accomplish the object.... In the meantime, the enemy are splitting up into parties of 2000 and bringing in the artillery...to blockade points below here...."

Porter faced the very distinct possibility of having to destroy his squadron to prevent its capture. A solution would, however, be found and a very ingenious one at that. It would require the strenuous efforts of thousands of soldiers and sailors on this ill-fated mission to save them all. Porter realized that: "It has delayed 10,000 troops of Gen. Sherman, on which he depended to open the State of Mississippi; it has drawn Gen. Steele from Arkansas and already given the rebels a foothold in that country; it has forced me to withdraw many light-draft vessels from points on the Mississippi to protect this army...."

April 29 (Friday)

The Confederate commander opposing Admiral Porter at the rapids above Alexandria, La., Major Gen. Richard Taylor, proposed sending one of Porter's disabled boats downriver as a fireboat to create havoc and possibly burn some of the Union ships which were stranded. Meanwhile, the ingenuity of those "Yankee mudsills" was being used to solve the problem. Most of the western armies were composed of men from the Midwest—Ohio, Indiana, Michigan, Wisconsin, Illinois, and Minnesota—among whom were several hundred former lumberjacks and others who knew how to use axes and saws. Added to these people were a couple of regiments of men from Maine who had cut their teeth on axes and saws.

The idea proposed by Lt. Col. Joseph Bailey was to build a dam of logs and debris across the top of the rapids to hold the water until it reached the desired depth of 7 feet. At such time, the dam would be blown and the boats could ride the crest of the water over the rapids to safety, or at least relative safety. Porter wrote of the decision later:

> This proposition looked like madness, and the best engineers ridiculed it, but Col. Bailey was so sanguine of success that I requested Gen. Banks to have it done...two or three regiments of Maine men were set to work felling trees...every man seemed to be working with a vigor seldom seen equalled.... These falls are about a mile in length, filled with rugged rocks, over which at the present stage of water it seemed to be impossible to make a channel.

April 30 (Saturday)

Personal tragedy struck President Davis and his wife, Varina, when their five-year-old son, Joe Davis, fell from the high veranda at the Confederate White House and was killed.

Grant received a letter from President Lincoln expressing his satisfaction with Grant's actions to date.

Jackman, Pvt., "The Orphan Brigade," Dalton, Ga.:

> Bright and clear this morning. The shower last night has freshened things up—showering during the day. At night went to Baptist church and as I was coming back heard a shooting and yelling over at Tyler's (Bates' old) brigade I thought our "blue friends" were paying us a night visit; but before retiring I learn the soldiers were tearing down some pillories which had been erected in the brigade. The boys call this kind of punishment "trying to pass the board." Such things would not be permitted in our brigade and the erection of such "contraptions."

Barber, Cpl., Co. D, 15th Illinois Volunteer Infantry, Cairo, Illinois:

> ...got on board the cars and were soon rapidly whirling toward Dixie. The next day we arrived at Cairo where we found that a regiment of non-veterans had been there, but had left a few days before and had gone up the Tennessee river to Clifton where we expected to join them and then march through the States of Tennessee, Alabama and Mississippi and join Sherman's army in Georgia....

MAY 1864

The South, expecting action on three fronts—Georgia, Northern Virginia, and the Peninsula east of Richmond—waited for the first hammer to strike. Obviously, Grant, now in Virginia, was going to open his summer campaign, but the Confederacy expected much the same from him as from the other Union generals who had faced Robert E. Lee. The economic picture in the South worsened each day. Inflation and currency depreciation had caused near-famine in the larger cities, while the countryside had rations aplenty. Grant and Sherman had made their plans in the hotel room in Cincinnati. The anvil was ready. Which general would swing the first blow?

May 1 (Sunday)

Twenty-five hundred troops of Major Gen. Ben Butler's force on the Peninsula were convoyed up the York River to West Point by the U.S.S. *Morse*, Lt. Commander Babcock, and the U.S.S. *General Putnam*, Acting Master Hugh H. Savage, where they landed under the protection of the ship's guns. Acting Master Henry A. Phelon, U.S.S. *Shawsheen*, joined the *General Putnam* and operated in the Pamunkey River, providing cover for the troops.

In northern Georgia, the contact between Sherman's forces and those of Johnston was picking up. Otherwise it was quiet.

May 2 (Monday)

In Richmond, Va., the Second Confederate Congress met for its first session. President Davis held out little hope for foreign recognition but had hopes for a military victory. He spent some time decrying the "barbarism" of the Federal forces against noncombatants. Yesterday, Davis buried his youngest son.

Jackman, Pvt., "The Orphan Brigade," Dalton, Ga.:

> Cool, though pretty morning. About 10 A.M. received orders to be ready for action at a moments notice—just before the order came, we heard guns at the front. A few minutes after we fell in and marched out through Mill Creek Gap, or nearly through the Gap, and halted in the road.... Soon after, we about-faced and returned to camp. Seeing "Joseph E." on the train going towards Tunnel Hill, the boys gave him a cheer which he acknowledged by taking off his hat....

In Louisiana, the lumberjacks of Maine and the Midwest, working at a feverish pace, had nearly completed the dam across the Red River at Alexandria. Admiral Porter hoped the water would rise high enough to get his marooned gunboat fleet over the rapids and safely downriver. The normal depth of seven feet had been reduced to about four feet due to lack of rain upriver, and to the Confederate diversion of the water to other channels. The fate of the entire fleet and Gen. Nathaniel Banks's army hung in the balance.

At the Confederate prison at Andersonville, Ga., a new batch of prisoners of war arrived to join the others in the stockade. Private S.J. Gibson, 103rd Pennsylvania Volunteers, and most of his unit had been captured at Plymouth, N.C., on Wednesday, April 20, 1864, when the C.S.S. *Albemarle* had left the Roanoke River and sunk, or chased away, the Federal ships supporting the garrison. Held at Plymouth until the 22nd, they were moved to a field near Hamilton, N.C., for three days, following which they were marched to Tarboro and held for another five days before boarding trains for Wilmington, N.C., where they arrived on Saturday, April 30th. Trains took them to Charleston, S.C., arriving on May 1st, and after a brief stop, they were sent on to Andersonville.

May 3 (Tuesday)

In the area of Brandy Station, Va., Grant notified Meade to move the Army of the Potomac out of winter quarters and to cross the Rapidan River on the morning of the 4th. The new offensive was set to go.

In Washington, Lincoln and the Cabinet held long discussions on the events at Ft. Pillow in April, when Negro troops were slain by Forrest's men after the Negroes had surrendered.

Day, Pvt., Co. B, 25th Massachusetts Volunteer Infantry, Yorktown, Va.:

> On the 27th of April we broke camp at Getty's Station, arriving here about dark, and marched up the Williamsburg road about two miles where we bivouacked. On this trip we were furnished transportation. On the morning of the 29th we were ordered into camp about three miles higher up the road. We had not much more than got there when an order came for us to report at the landing immediately. We now had a five mile march before us, with the dust in the road about three inches deep. This was no march, but a race, the companies trying to run past each other and get the advance to shield themselves from the dust. The colonel let them have it their own way and they made the dust fly right smart. We made the distance in less than an hour and on arriving at the landing looked like walking dirt heaps. A guard was placed along the bank of the river to prevent our washing in for fear of creating a sand bar. There didn't appear to be anything wanted of us after we got here and we are now in camp on the bluff just above the landing.

The action began to pick up in northern Georgia with skirmishing at Chickamauga Creek, Catoosa Springs, and Red Clay, where the two forces came in contact.

Joe Johnston telegraphed to Richmond that scouts in the area of Outawah and Cleveland, Ga., reported that the Federals were beginning to mass their troops for movement.

May 4 (Wednesday)

In the early minutes of this day the long-dormant Army of the Potomac moved across the Rapidan River and headed for the Wilderness crossroads. A long, bloody campaign began that would end with the surrender of Lee's army forty-eight weeks later. Grant's army had nearly 122,000 present for duty against Lee's 66,000. Grant moved around Lee's right, forcing Lee to move from Orange C.H. and the Gordonsville area to meet him. Gen. Richard Ewell led the way towards the Wilderness with A.P. Hill following and Longstreet last in the long columns.

On the Peninsula, Major Gen. Ben Butler moved his army, already loaded on transports, towards Richmond.

In Georgia, Sherman prepared to send 98,000 men against Joe Johnston in the area of Dalton, as light skirmishing continued with a brief fight at Varnell's Station.

Jackman, Pvt., "The Orphan Brigade," Dalton, Ga.:

> Warm lazy day. Regiment went out this morning at 8 o'clock to work on fortifications to be back this evening. Such a lazy day. I thought nothing would move; but orders have just come in to be ready in a moments notice to "go in." Our pickets reported driven in on the Cleveland road. Reg't. comes in at 4 P.M.

Near Dunn's Bayou, La., downriver from Alexandria on the Red River, the Confederate infantry attacked the U.S.S. *Covington*, Acting Lt. George P. Lord, and the transport *Warner*. These ships were part of Admiral D.D. Porter's river flotilla which had gone up to support the ill-fated expedition on Shreveport.

May 5 (Thursday)

At the Wilderness in Virginia, Meade's Army of the Potomac collided with Lee's Army of Northern Virginia in the tangled wooded area south of the Rapidan. Warren's Fifth Corps was faced by Ewell's Confederate Second Corps on the Orange Turnpike in the first action between the armies in 1864. By noon they were locked in full-scale combat. Grant would not commit his forces piecemeal—Lee would have to fight the whole army. At the close of the day, both armies entrenched in their positions and awaited the morrow.

On the James River, where the Appomattox merges, Gen. Ben Butler landed his troops at City Point (now Hopewell) to begin his movement to Richmond via Petersburg.

Day, Pvt., Co. B, 25th Massachusetts Volunteer Infantry, City Point, Va.:

> ...morning we started up the James river. The river was alive with boats, schooners, tugs, gunboats, monitors and everything that could float, all loaded to their fullest capacity with troops, horses, artillery and all the paraphernalia of war. We passed Jamestown in the afternoon.... We reached City Point just before night. Gen. Heckman's brigade landed on the Bermuda Hundred side and bivouacked a short distance from the landing, all the other troops remaining aboard the boats. The gunboats and monitors commenced fishing for torpedoes and working their way up the James and Appomattox rivers.

In a three-hour intensive battle, the C.S.S. *Albemarle*, Commander Cooke, successfully fought three Union ships in Albemarle Sound and then returned up the Roanoke River. The action was joined in late afternoon when the *Albemarle*, in company with the *Bombshell*, Lt. Albert G. Hudgins, and the *Cotton Plant* entered the Sound and immediately engaged the U.S.S. *Sassacus*, Lt. Commander Roe, and the sidewheelers U.S.S. *Mattahesett*, Capt. M. Smith, and *Wyalusing*, Lt. Commander Walter W. Queen. Almost immediately the *Bombshell* was captured by the *Sassacus*, and the *Cotton Plant* left the action and withdrew upriver, leaving the *Albemarle* to fight alone. The *Sassacus* took a direct hit in her starboard boiler, knocking her out of action. The two sidewheelers continued the action until darkness forced the contestants to disengage. The *Albemarle* went upriver and two small steamers guarded the mouth of the Roanoke River.

Barber, Cpl., Co. D, 15th Illinois Volunteer Infantry, en route to Huntsville, Ala.:

> We went up as far as Paducah and then waited for the rest of the fleet to come up. We arrived at Clifton on the 6th of May. The boys had left the week before. They drove a large herd of cattle through to Huntsville, Ala.... The scenery on the Tennessee river at this time of the year is very beautiful.... On the 9th of May, we resumed our march, our first point of destination being Pulaski, in Tennessee, on the Coosa river.

Early in the morning, the Confederate army appeared on the Red River banks near Dunn's Bayou, La. with artillery and a large number of infantry. They immediately began an attack on the Federal boats the U.S.S. *Covington*, the transport *Warner*, and the U.S.S. *Signal*, Acting Lt. Edward Morgan. *Warner* almost immediately went out of control, blocking the river at a bend near Pierce's Landing, and she was forced to surrender. *Signal* also became disabled, and although *Covington* tried to tow her upstream, she came loose and soon anchored. The battle continued until *Covington* had run out of ammunition and many of her crew had been killed. *Signal* continued the engagement alone, but finally struck her colors. *Signal* was then sunk in the channel as an obstruction. Hot work for a warm May morning.

May 6 (Friday)

In the Wilderness, the opposing armies awaited daylight to resume fighting. In the early dawn hours the Federals took up the advance and collided heavily with the Rebels. Longstreet made a flank attack that set the Federals back, but temporarily. Late in the afternoon Longstreet tried again, only to be stopped short of the Union lines, and he was severely wounded.

Near Todd's Tavern, Sheridan, in command of the Union cavalry, mixed it up with Stuart's troopers in an indecisive whirl that at least showed Stuart that a "new kid" was on the block. Confederate Gen. John B. Gordon's brigade slammed into the Federal right and made headway, but Gordon found that Ewell would not, or could not, come to Gen. Gordon's support to enlarge the attack.

Grant sat and smoked cigars and whittled sticks while receiving reports. At darkness the fighting tapered off slowly. The next question to be settled was in which direction would the Yankees move. Would they recross the river as they had done before, or would they move on towards Richmond? Casualties were heavy for the North—nearly 17,700 killed, wounded, or missing. The Rebels fared better—somewhere around 7500.

On the James River, within sight of the church spires of Petersburg, Ben Butler's 39,000 troops were opposed by no more than 10,000 Confederates. Butler did some halfhearted scouting and then went into camp. A chance was lost to end the war with one bold stroke.

On the James River, three steamers were dragging for torpedoes when the U.S.S. *Commodore Jones*, a converted ferry boat, was destroyed by a 2000-pound *electric* torpedo. Forty men were killed. Acting Lt. Thomas Wade, captain of the vessel, later reported that the torpedo: "...exploded directly under the ship with terrible effect, causing her destruction instantly, absolutely blowing the vessel to splinters." Other observers reported that the ship was lifted completely out of the water by the explosion. A landing party was immediately sent ashore and captured the two Confederate torpedomen and the galvanic batteries used in the destruction. One of the Confederates, Jeffries Johnson, refused to tell where the other torpedoes were placed until he was placed in the bow of the forward ship dragging for the mines. Johnson then changed his mind and "revealed all."

Day, Pvt., Co. B, 25th Massachusetts Volunteer Infantry, City Point, Va.:

> ...the troops commenced to land and Heckman's brigade was ordered to advance. We marched up the country six or seven miles, getting on to high ground and what is called Cobb's Hill. From here the spires of the churches in Petersburg can be seen, while in front of us is a kind of valley. At this point the Appomatax river turns in a southwesterly direction. On the banks between us and Petersburg was a battery. This is called a good position and here we halted. We sat here under a burning sun, watching the long lines of troops come up and file off to the right into the woods towards the James river until past the middle of the afternoon, at which time the whole of the 18th and 10th corps, comprising the army of the James, under Gen. B.F. Butler, had arrived.
>
> About 4 P.M. Gen. Heckman is ordered to make a reconnaisance towards the Petersburg and Richmond railroad. We moved down the valley in a southwesterly direction and when about three miles out, the 27th Massachusetts were advanced as skirmishers. A mile or two farther on we began to hear scattering shots, indicating that our skirmishers had found game. We hurried on and found the enemy in a shallow cut, on a branch railroad running from Port Walthal to the Petersburg and Richmond road. A sharp skirmish ensued, lasting till near dark, when Heckman withdrew, having accomplished his purpose of finding the enemy. In this skirmish the 25th lost four killed and several wounded.

Jackman, Pvt., "The Orphan Brigade," Dalton, Ga.:

> Beautiful day. All are expecting the "ball to open" soon. There is no telling these times what is going to take place. I don't think there will be much fighting for several days, and I doubt that we fight at all about Dalton. We may go out to "see" our neighbors.

May 7 (Saturday)

Early into the first hour of this day the Army of the Potomac was waiting for a sign that would decide its immediate future in Grant's actions. The fires were burning bright behind the lines as the units collected themselves and recounted what had happened that day. Suddenly, it seemed, long blue lines were moving across their rear to the southeast—not towards the fords across the Rapidan, but towards Richmond. Grant had made his decision. The move would be to dislodge Lee from the woods and get him into the open where the weight of the blue columns could be brought to bear. This army was jubilant; for the first time they were not turning tail and quitting.

Lee realized that Grant was heading for Spottsylvania C.H., and Lee sent cavalry to cut trees to delay the Union advance, while the Confederate general went there and prepared the defenses.

Gen. Ben Butler sat on the Peninsula and waited for something else to happen.

Day, Pvt., Co. B, 25th Massachusetts Volunteer Infantry, Bermuda Hundred, Va.:

...morning...we moved on them in force, Gen. Brook's division moving directly on the Petersburg and Richmond railroad. Heckman's brigade, with a section of a battery, were ordered to occupy the ground of the night before. The enemy were in strong force and opened on us with artillery. Heckman paid no attention to that but moved his battalions into line on the field in columns by division and ordered them to lie down. The 25th were partially covered by a slight roll of ground in our front while the 27th Massachusetts on our left were badly exposed to the enemy's fire and were suffering severely. Heckman saw the situation and ordered Col. Lee to move his regiment to the rear of us. He then ordered forward his artillery, placing them in battery in our front and set them to work. They made the rail fences and dust fly right smart. After a few shots had been fired, a loud explosion was heard followed by a big cloud of smoke, dust, and debris in the enemy line. One of their caissons had blown up and our boys rose up and gave rousing cheers. Our guns continued shelling them but got no return fire, their ammunition was probably exhausted and their guns perhaps disabled.

There was no infantry firing on either side, we simply holding our line and watching events. Heavy firing was heard over on the railroad. Brooks was at them and a fight for the railroad was going on. We were masters of the situation here and able to protect his flank. About noon the enemy got an old gun into position and commenced throwing chunks of railroad iron at us. This caused considerable sport among the boys and they would cheer lustily every time they fired, but a few shots from our guns put a quietus on that sport. I have often read and heard of that kind of practice, but never saw any of it until now.

In the afternoon a battery of four 20-pounder parrott guns drove up, taking position on a roll of ground some 20 rods in our rear and commenced firing. I at first thought they were shelling the enemy in front of us, and was a little surprised at it as all was quiet on both sides. But I soon noticed they were not. I got permission from Capt. Emory and went up there. Here was a signal officer, and nearly half a mile away to the northwest was a group of men signaling to this battery. The guns were at quite an elevation and they would train them a little to the right or left as directed by the signal officer. They were throwing shells over the woods and dropping them among the enemy over on the railroad some two miles away. Those shells were reported to be very annoying to the enemy and of great service to Brooks. It was splendid artillery practice and I was greatly interested in it. While watching them lob those shells over the woods, I wondered where those devils over there thought they came from.

Towards night it was signaled that Brooks had accomplished his purpose, tearing up several miles of road and was drawing back to our line. The day's work was over and we drew back to Cobb's Hill. In this day's fight the 27th Massachusetts sustained the greatest loss.... The heat was intense and the men suffered severely, many of them being prostrated and carried back in ambulances.

Dalton, Ga., had been the site of Gen. Joseph Johnston's winter camp for the Army of Tennessee. It would now become the initial scene for the Battle for Atlanta. Sherman moved his men out of their camps and lunged for the Rebel lines. The Confederates held a good defensive position on and along a high ridge and they had had all winter to improve it. Now there were few gaps in the line. Sherman's army of nearly 100,000 was divided into three armies. North of Dalton was the Army of the Ohio (Schofield); northwest of Dalton, the Army of the Cumberland (Thomas); and west-northwest lay the Army of the Tennessee (McPherson), all in readiness and facing Johnston's 60,000.

Johnston's position on the high ridge was too strong for a frontal attack, so Sherman sent McPherson around the enemy's left flank, cavalry leading, towards Snake Creek Gap. Thomas demonstrated in front of Tunnel Hill and Rocky-Face to provide a diversion.

Jackman, Pvt., "The Orphan Brigade," Dalton, Ga.:

We are again on the "war path.".... Between 9 & 10 A.M. our cavalry driven from Tunnel Hill and soon after we received orders to hold ourselves ready to move at once. At 1 P.M., we moved out and took position on a little ridge just beyond Mill Creek Gap towards Tunnel Hill. Our brigade rested on the railroad on the right and there connected with Stewart's division, our division extending around to the left to the base of Buzzards Roost. Lying around all evening only witnessing a little skirmish among the cavalry in front. Could see blue lines up toward the tunnel 3 miles off. Has been a pleasant spring day. Twelve at night moved back through the Gap and formed as a reserve to Stewart, our left resting on the railroad.

May 8 (Sunday)

As Major Gen. G.K. Warren's Fifth Corps approached Spottsylvania C.H., they found that Anderson's Confederate corps was there and entrenched. It had been somewhat of a footrace for the Rebels to get there first. Warren's troops waded into the Rebels, only to find that the Confederates were in strong defensive positions and wouldn't be shaken. Sedgwick came up and a new attack was made; this failed also. Darkness brought an end to the fighting and both sides formed new lines.

Meanwhile, Grant sent Sheridan to go around Lee and disrupt his rail communications and to keep Stuart off Grant's back. A.P. Hill became ill and was replaced by Jubal Early temporarily. This, however, meant that Lee was without two of his usual corps commanders, since Longstreet was wounded.

In Georgia, there were more demonstrations against Rocky-Face Ridge, Dug Gap, and Buzzards Roost. McPherson was penetrating Snake Creek Gap on Johnston's left flank.

Jackman, Pvt., "The Orphan Brigade," Rocky-Face, Ga.:

> At 11 A.M. our brigade moved to the right and took position on top of Rocky-Face. The day was hot and the hill, or rather mountain, being long and steep, we had quite a hard time getting to our position. Sometimes we would have to clamber up places almost perpendicular. The brigade in single rank was deployed almost as far apart as skirmishers. The position is a strong one. The hill towards the enemy is long and steep and is covered with trees. At the top, however, a wall of solid rock near someplace as high as 40 or 50 feet and in places projects over. These rocks also rise above the top of the hill in such a manner as to form a natural breastwork and this protects us from shells. The valley, or plain, towards Tunnel Hill is "blue" with Federals, Sherman has a large army. The enemy drove back our skirmishers this evening all along the line—this little battle we could plainly see. In the evening, their sharpshooters got close enough to annoy us some. I was sent with an order down the hill to our skirmish line and having passed near an interval came near being "gobbled." Tonight thousands of camp fires are gleaming in the valleys and the Federal bands are giving us a serenade. When our soldiers request they play "Dixie," they readily comply but always start off with "Yankee Doodle."

May 9 (Monday)

Grant and Lee faced off at Spottsylvania C.H. and spent the day sizing each other up and adjusting lines. Burnside moved up closer with his Ninth Corps. Sheridan, drawing Stuart off, began a sixteen-day run around Lee and towards Richmond.

Also at Spottsylvania, Major Gen. John Sedgwick was walking along the line near an artillery unit in full view of the enemy. His troops asked that he not expose himself so carelessly. His reply was that "they couldn't hit an elephant at that distance." A rebel sharpshooter, a few seconds later, placed a bullet through his left eye, killing him instantly His body was placed on a roughly made bier of pine boughs, and he was draped with his headquarters' flag.

In support of Grant's operations, Ben Butler on the Peninsula did one of his usual confused operations. He sent his entire army out to tear up railroad tracks south of the James River, but things got so mixed up and moved so slowly he pulled everyone back in the next day.

Further demonstrations against Joe Johnston's positions at Rocky-Face Gap and Buzzards Roost in Georgia did little to dislodge the Confederates; their lines were too strong. McPherson, who had been sent around Johnston's left flank at Snake Creek Gap, decided that the Confederate positions were too strong for an assault and pulled back, much to Sherman's disappointment.

Jackman, Pvt., "The Orphan Brigade," Rocky-Face, Ga.:

> Before daylight our drums rattled reveille and about the same time our "neighbors" out in front

commenced drumming and bugling making a tremendous noise. Soon the gray light of morning came and presently the sun rose clear and bright. A mist was settled in the valley beneath and out over the plain and it was some time before we could see what was going on. At last the fog broke away and we could see the blue columns marching and taking new positions. We could see for miles up and down the valley; and see as far as Lookout Mountain, nearly 40 miles off! Over this wide expanse of country the fog had settled down in spots and in the light of the morning sun had much the appearance of lakes of water, clear and sparkling. At 8 A.M. Maney's brigade of Cheatham's division came and relieved us and we marched down the hill which we found almost as tiresome as coming up.... Our regiment then clambered up Buzzards Roost and took position...a wing resting on either side of the battery, or "Fort Montgomery" as we called it. We found this position naturally fortified as was the case on Rocky-Face. We could see the fields out in front blue with Federals. They now occupied the little ridge we were on the first evening. Sharpshooting commenced on both sides and the pop, pop, popping was kept up all day. The minies whistled freely over the rocks which protected us. Batteries occasionally opened on the Fort, which was shelling the woods below; and often, the shells would strike against the massive rocks, never jarring them. Received a letter from home by flag-of-truce but could hardly get to read it, an assault being threatened. Seventeen Federal regiments were massed at the base of the hill. As they came marching by the flank across the fields, the sun shining upon their bright guns, the column seemed a stream of molten silver. We had one man mortally wounded today and one had his arm shot off. The night being pleasant, I spread my blanket down on a huge rock and slept soundly till morning.

At the rapids on the Red River near Alexandria, La., Col. Bailey had used stone-filled barges to form a part of the dam to raise the level of the river so that Admiral Porter's fleet could get over the rapids. Two of these barges suddenly gave way under the increasing pressure of the water and formed a chute over the rapids, filled with churning water. Porter immediately ordered his lighter-draft gunboats and steamers to try and get downriver. As the water fell, the ironclads U.S.S. *Osage* and *Neosho*, along with the wooden steamers U.S.S. *Fort Hindman* and *Lexington*, quickly entered the chute and went careening down the spume of water. All made it with little damage. Porter later recalled the incident: "Thirty thousand voices rose in one deafening cheer, and universal joy seemed to pervade the face of every man present."

So far, so good, but not all of the Union ships were over the rapids. The failure of the barges to hold back the water, rather than disheartening Col. Bailey, only spurred him on to greater efforts. Eight days of back-breaking effort had succeeded in saving part of the fleet, so Bailey turned to build another dam.

May 10 (Tuesday)

At Spottsylvania C.H., three corps of the Army of the Potomac assaulted the Confederate "mule shoe" positions late in the afternoon, a very heavy attack being made at about 6 P.M. which temporarily breached the Confederate line; but then the Union forces fell back. Burnside move closer and entrenched facing Early's corps.

Sheridan and Stuart fought skirmishes along the North Anna River near Beaver Dam Station. Sheridan was now within 20 miles of Richmond, with Custer, commanding one of Sheridan's divisions, tearing up track on the Virginia Central railroad. Stuart took a position between Sheridan and Richmond at a place called Yellow Tavern.

Sherman, fuming because McPherson had not succeeded at Snake Creek Gap, continued his demonstrations at Rocky-Face Gap and Buzzards Roost on the Confederate right. He ordered a general movement around the Confederate left to Resaca.

Jackman, Pvt., "The Orphan Brigade," Rocky-Face, Ga.:

> Beautiful morning. With the light of day came the sounds of sharpshooters rifles which have been continuously popping all day. Rained between 10 and 12 o'clock. Cloudy, disagreeable evening. Nothing of any interest occurred. At dark a rain set in and continued until midnight. The "Judge" and I got under a projecting rock and with a blanket over our heads kept dry but could not lie down to sleep. The boys kept up such a yelling, one could not have slept anyway. Passed a most disagreeable night. Too wet to sleep.

Barber, Cpl., Co. D, 15th Illinois Volunteer Infantry, Huntsville, Ala.:

> We drove through a large herd of beef cattle. We had considerable sport. There were numerous rivers to cross and some of the boys who could not bear the thought of stripping and wading would mount a young steer, but the wild and frightened animal would generally land them on all fours in the river. It was amusing to see us crossing these rivers.... Imagine several thousand men, stripped naked, their clothes wadded up in a bundle and held high over their heads, wading the Elkhorn river. At times the water would be too deep for the short ones to wade. They would stretch and walk on their tip toes to keep their heads out of the water. The current being too swift for some, they would be submerged. Those who had crossed would stand on the bank and laugh at the others' mishaps. Two darkies were drowned and some of the boys made sport of the occurrence.
>
> ...We came up with the rest of the command at Huntsville, Ala. We found the boys well, but terribly chafed in spirit, but that did not prevent them from extending to us a cordial welcome. The non-veterans had been shamefully misused. It seemed as though some of the officers wanted to vent their spite on them because they would not re-enlist. The idea of marching them two hundred miles just as their term of service was about to expire, when it was of no earthly use, was an outrageous one. They were treated more like dogs than patriot soldiers, which they were; and, finally, to cap the climax, on the very day that their term expired, they were ordered to drive a drove of cattle through to Chattanooga, a distance of one hundred and fifty miles. This was more than they could bear, and, in their just indignation, they revolted. They had the sympathy of all the veterans, and the officers found that they could not stem the tide of wrath which was setting against them and the order was rescinded. The procuring of this order was attributed to Colonels Hall and Rogers, who represented to headquarters that the boys were willing to go. After Gen. Crocker found out the facts of the case, he declared that the boys should not go.

On the Red River above Alexandria, La., work was proceeding on the wing dams to again block the river and get sufficient water below the hulls to float the river fleet over the rapids. While changing locations, the U.S.S. *Mound City* and *Carondelet* ran aground, but were freed after some effort.

May 11 (Wednesday)

Sheridan's march on Richmond had reached a little crossroads town called Yellow Tavern about six miles north of Richmond when Sheridan was attacked by JEB Stuart's cavalry. In the swirling fight that ensued, a dismounted Federal cavalryman shot Stuart as he rode past, mortally wounding him. He was taken from the field for treatment. When told of the loss of his cavalry leader, Lee stood alone for several minutes in his sorrow and remarked to one of his staff, "I can scarcely think of him without weeping."

At Spottsylvania C.H., Grant and Lee still were in a face-off, awaiting developments. Grant, obviously, had the next move. Lee could not afford to attack the larger army and hope to survive long. He could not stand the casualties.

In Georgia, Sherman ordered a swing towards Resaca to the southeast and completely behind the Confederate army now at Rocky-Face Gap and at Buzzards Roost. Johnston was to be outflanked. Sherman would not waste his men on a frontal assault.

Jackman, Pvt., "The Orphan Brigade," Rocky-Face, Ga.:

> Dense fog this morning but soon lifted and the sharpshooters commenced. In the evening brisk shelling through the Gap from both sides. We have been expecting an assault all day. About 8 miles off to the left could see Sherman's supply trains moving towards Resaca. The train seemed miles in length. As dark was setting in, the Federals tried to force back our skirmishers in front of Stewart but failed. Had quite a fight—all of which we could plainly see. The evening cold and damp.

As the Red River slowly rose behind the dam constructed near the rapids upstream from Alexandria, La., the ironclads U.S.S. *Mound City*, *Carondelet*, and *Pittsburg* were hauled across the upper falls above the obstructions by thousands of soldiers pulling on ropes. As the banks were lined with spectators, the gunboats, with all hatches battened down, lurched through the gap and into safe water below the rapids. The sluice was closed to build more water level.

May 12 (Thursday)

At Spottsylvania Court House the Federals charged Lee's prepared lines in wave after wave in one of the costliest battles of the war. The "Bloody Angle" claimed about 6800 Union and 5000 Confederate casualties in killed and wounded alone. Another 4000 Confederates were captured. The loss was far greater for the South because of the attrition. These Confederate veterans could not be replaced easily, while the North had seemingly endless manpower. Grant was accused of butchery in the Northern papers, but Lee now had nearly 10,000 fewer men in his immediate army.

Sheridan was moving towards the James and Ben Butler's army, having to fight nearly every mile of the way. Butler was still stuck at City Point and Bermuda Hundred, being contained by Beauregard.

The fabled "Cavalier" JEB Stuart was dead, having succumbed to his wounds received at Yellow Tavern on the 10th. In the concept of death in that century, Stuart was said to have "died well." Richmond went into mourning.

In Georgia, Sherman's troops had passed Snake Creek Gap and were approaching Resaca, where Johnston's army had moved from Dalton.

Jackman, Pvt., "The Orphan Brigade," Resaca, Ga.:

> Cold wind from the east which, being elevated as we are, has a full sweep at us. The enemy commenced moving from our front this morning, to our left, and have kept it up all day. Though thousands have gone, they can hardly be missed from our front. The supply train noticed yesterday still moving towards Resaca and sharpshooting and shelling kept up all day by both sides. Late this evening they commenced putting batteries in front of us as though they intended to shell us out.
>
> Half past 9 P.M. we fell in and marched 5 miles to Dug Gap to our left where we halted about midnight and lay down to sleep. We were allowed to rest about an hour and a half, or two hours, then we marched towards Resaca, distance 10 miles. At daylight we came up with Cleburne who was fortified on the side of the road. We passed him and halted in line of battle until he passed us then we moved and about noon we halted when in 3 or 4 miles of Resaca and I had a good nap. Late in the evening we moved to the left of the road and a ditch. Worked on fortifications all night. We were held in reserve to the balance of the division. Had a good night's sleep.

From Paris, France, Flag Officer Barron, CSN, wrote Secretary Mallory in Richmond that:

> To-day I have heard indirectly and confidentially that the *Alabama* may be expected in a European port on any day. Ship and captain both requiring to be docked. Capt. Semmes' health has begun to fail, and he feels that rest is needful to him.... There are numbers of fine young officers here who are panting for active duty on their proper element, and will cheerfully relieve their brother officers....

May 13 (Friday)

Grant had failed to break Lee's lines at Spottsylvania C.H. Grant now moved around to his own left with Warren's corps in the lead. This sidestepping movement would characterize the campaign. Sheridan moved to join Ben Butler's army on the Peninsula. Butler was at Drewry's Bluff wasting time and giving Beauregard time enough to entrench, typical of Butler.

At Resaca, Joe Johnston's army took up positions and awaited Sherman's arrival.

The Red River expedition's naval support was finally freed from the rapids above Alexandria, La., when the last three ships of Admiral Porter's river fleet passed over the rapids and into the river below, joining the remainder of the fleet. Troops were immediately loaded and the fleet went downriver. The ingenuity and dedication of Lt. Col. Joseph Bailey played the deciding role in the escape of the fleet

Bailey, born in Ohio in 1825, was raised in Illinois, where he studied civil engineering. He became a lumberman in Wisconsin in 1847. On July 2, 1861, he entered the Federal service as a captain in the 4th Wisconsin Infantry, serving most of the time in the area of Louisiana and Mississippi. On the Red River expedition, Bailey was serving as the Chief Engineer for the XIX Corps when he suggested building the coffer dams which saved the fleet. In recognition of his efforts, he was brevetted a brigadier general on June 7, 1864, and awarded a THANKS OF CONGRESS citation. He later served with distinction at Mobile, for which he was brevetted as a major general. After the war he became Sheriff of Vernon County, Mo. He was killed on March 21, 1867, at age 42 by two bushwhackers he had arrested.

Admiral Porter wrote Secretary Welles of Bailey's performance:

> The water had fallen so low that I had no hope or expectation of getting the vessels out this season, and as the army had made arrangements to evacuate the country I saw nothing before me but the destruction of the best part of the Mississippi squadron.... Words are inadequate to express the admiration I feel for the abilities of Lt. Col. Bailey. This is without a doubt the best engineering feat ever performed.... He has saved to the Union a valuable fleet, worth nearly $2,000,000....

Poor old Ft. Sumter was in for another pounding as the Federal guns would land another 1140 rounds on that pile of rubble over the next four days.

May 14 (Saturday)

Sherman arrived at Resaca and immediately ordered probing attacks, especially on the flanks, of Johnston's positions. The main attack would wait.

Jackman, Pvt., "The Orphan Brigade," Battle of Resaca, Ga.:

> Early, ordered further to the left. Just before we fell in, rations of whiskey were issued and some of the boys got so tippsey they could hardly march, in fact, some got so bad off they had to be helped along. When we got to the position...our regiment first commenced fortifying where 2d Ky. afterwards took position; but afterwards we moved to the works partly constructed by Tyler's brigade which was to lie in reserve. The works commenced were only piles of rail and logs, not capable of standing shells, as we got tools and commenced ditching. By 10 A.M. we had pretty good works and just in time for about that hour our skirmishers (Co. A) were driven in, the men skirmishing beautifully. Soon after, two lines of battle burst out of the woods in front of us and standards up, on the charge. We soon commenced "saluting" them, so did Slocum's battery on our left, and they retired. A more vigorous charge was made at the same time on the right of the brigade, there being several lines, and they came up within 50 paces of the works before being repulsed. The day has passed without our regiment being charged again. Several charges have been made on the right of our brigade and in front of Hinderman during the day. In the evening the roar of musketry to our right was quite loud. We have been kept close by the sharpshooters today having nothing to protect us but our works. The enemy is in the edge of the woods three or four hundred yards off while we lie in an open field. We could not get out after water until after dark. The artillery has been playing the wilds with us. Several batteries are in our front on a favorable hill for them and have kept up a shelling all day. Slocum's pieces being unprotected, he has been unable to fire much—the sharpshooters as well as their batteries being against him. Capt. Slocum and gunner would occasionally slip up from behind the hill, the Capt. loading the piece himself and the gunner would fire it, then they would both take shelter behind the ridge. Immediately a shower of shells would come flying and would mow down the trees about his guns but to say not a gun was injured. In the evening a battery to our right opened an enfilading fire on the left of our regiment. Company "A" suffered as they had to be out on the skirmish line in the morning and did not have an opportunity to strengthen their works. Lieut. M. Clian of that company was badly wounded the first shot and called for the infirmary corps but had hardly ceased when the second shot came, killing him instantly and three men (privates France, King and Edmonson) besides wounding several. The fire was kept up sometimes wounding several others but killing no more. Company "A" was on the left of the regiment and across the ravine from me and I was looking at the company (which was lying in rank behind the ill constructed works) at the time. The second enfilading shot struck and I saw the men tossed about like chaff. Seg't Wickliffe, Company C, was killed early in the action by a sharpshooter. The 4th and 2d regiments have been enfiladed all day by the middle battery and have lost many killed and wounded. At night strengthening our works—worked all night.

In a very heavy rain, the troops of Grant's corps moved to their left and "sidled" off around Lee's right flank to the southeast.

In the Shenandoah Valley, Federal Gen. Franz Sigel, with about 6500 men, had moved south "up the valley," faced only by Imboden's cavalry. Meantime, Major Gen. John Cabell Breckinridge had entered the valley and was going north with about 5000 troops.

May 15 (Sunday)

The Mississippi River fleet evacuating the army of Nathaniel Banks from the abortive Red River expedition neared the confluence of the Red and Mississippi rivers, where they met more resistance from the Confederate artillery and riflemen in that area. Acting Lt. Thomas B. Gregory, U.S.S. *St. Clair*, took his 200-ton stern-wheeler into action at Eunice's Bluff, La., trading fire with the shore batteries until the troop transports passed safely behind him and continued downriver. The unexpected level of the Mississippi itself caused a backwater into the Red River as far up as Alexandria, which provided a great lift to the fleet on their way downriver.

At Resaca, Ga., Sherman again decided that Johnston's positions were too strong for a frontal assault and started another flanking movement. In this one, Hood's and Hooker's corps mixed it up for a fierce set-to, and Hood's Confederates were driven back. There was heavy fighting along the Oostenaula River south of Resaca, with Sherman sending both cavalry and infantry to force the decision. Johnston, afraid of being outflanked, evacuated his positions during the night, burning the bridge over the Oostenaula and withdrawing towards Calhoun and Adairsville.

Jackman, Pvt., "The Orphan Brigade," retreat from Resaca, Ga.:

> We look more like standing a siege this morning. Our left companies, over the ravine, have thrown up traverses, impregnable to either shell or solid shot, which will protect them from enfilading fires. Slocum has thrown up works for his battery and the 2d and 4th have made traverses to protect them against the enfilade. Slocum opened early but too great odds against him. Two of his pieces were cut down by shot passing through the embrasures. Sharpshooting all day. Had several men wounded by stray minies coming across from the right. The sun has been very hot and we have had no protection from its rays. As twilight was coming in, I left the works to go after water thinking it too dark to be seen but I was discovered and had a shower of minies put after me. At last darkness came and a line of skirmishers was sent a short distance over the works to watch the movements of the enemy. The Federal skirmishers also advanced out onto the fields and we had a conversation, at long range, with them. We found them to be Kentuckians, Rousseau's old legion. They enquired for several men in our regiment. We have not been assaulted today. All the fighting was to our right. Sometimes the musketry would roar like they were having pretty hot works. Cleburne and Cheatham to our left have not been engaged yet. At 9 P.M. the signal gun fired and we commenced falling back. The moon was shining bright and while moving back from the works, company at a time, the men were ordered to hold their guns in front of them so the reflection could not be seen by the enemy. The skirmishers were left before the works. We moved with the utmost silence. Our brigade got separated from the division before we got into town and we started to move on the railroad but halted and went back and took the dirt road. Having lost time, we had to doublequick. Before we got to the bridge the Federals opened artillery all around the line and the skirmishers on both sides opened a brisk fire. Times looked a little squally then; but the firing soon ceased and we continued our march. The roads being crowded with troops, we did not get to Calhoun, 7 miles distant, until about daylight.

In a battle that would have its anniversary celebrated every year at Virginia Military Institute in Lexington, Va., for more than 125 years, the Confederate army under Major Gen. John C. Breckinridge defeated the Union army under Major Gen. Franz Sigel at New Market, Va. Sigel had about 6500 troops. Breckinridge had about 5000 Confederate infantry and a makeshift gathering of everyone he could get his hands on, including 247 students from VMI, who were mostly young boys. When the smoke cleared, Sigel had retreated, suffering about 831 casualties. The Confederate casualties were about 577, including 10 killed and 47 wounded among the cadets.

Sheridan was frustrated in his attempts to reach Butler's army on the Peninsula, so he took the day and rested at Haxall's Landing on the James River. At Drewry's Bluff, Butler was still getting ready for his assault. Grant's army was on the move to the southeast, making little contact with Lee's troops.

May 16 (Monday)

Sherman's army was still on the move with little contact with the Confederate forces. Heavy rains were making the roads miserable for marching.

Jackman, Pvt., "The Orphan Brigade," Calhoun, Ga.:

> Rested, in line of battle, until noon when we fell in and moved out on the Addairsville road. Soon we were turned back and had to double quick through town out on the Snake Creek and formed line of battle. The skirmishers of the Federal Corps which had crossed the river were driven in and our lines were being formed to advance and "take that Corps in out of the wet" when an order came to Gen'l Hardee stopping the move north. Sherman with his main army was passing too close down the Calhoun road. Night came on without our fighting, or further fighting, save light skirmishing. Tonight we have large fires kindled and I anticipate a good nights rest. We may move though before morning. The enemy came into Calhoun about sundown.

The cleanup was progressing at New Market Battlefield, with most of the public buildings and many of the private homes in the area filled with wounded. The dead were being collected for burial or transportation to their homes in the South.

In a dense early-morning fog, Beauregard attacked Ben Butler at Drewry's Bluff and nearly did him in. Butler had about 16,000 men, Beauregard about 18,000. Beauregard had audacity, Butler had a bad case of the "slows." Had the characteristics been reversed, Butler could have caused irreparable damage to the Confederacy and could possibly have ended the war by threatening Richmond enough to cause Lee to retreat to defend the city. This was his second blunder—the first was when he failed to take Petersburg on his first movement up the Peninsula. The battle, which accomplished little except killing soldiers, cost the North 4160 casualties; the South, 2506. The incompetence of the generals in the North was never demonstrated more clearly than at Drewry's Bluff.

May 17 (Tuesday)

Withdrawing from Calhoun, Ga., Joe Johnston's Army of Tennessee held briefly at Adairsville with Gen. George Thomas in front and McPherson and Schofield coming around both flanks. Johnston hurried his retreat to escape the box.

Jackman, Pvt., "The Orphan Brigade," Adairsville, Ga.:

> At 2 o'clock A.M. fell in and marched for Addairsville, 12 or 15 miles. The sun rose clear and we had nice marching before it got too hot. The country between Addairsville and Calhoun is beautiful. The forest trees looked like Kentucky and large fields of clover are on either side of the road. About noon we stacked arms near town for a rest. At 1 P.M. the rain poured down in torrents for nearly an hour. The enemy was pressing Cheatham about two miles back on the road at 2 o'clock. We fell in and marched back to his support. We formed line of battle to the left of the railroad and to the rear of Cheatham. There were four or five lines of battle and we being in the rear line had nothing to do but shift from right to left, or vice versa, as action required while the front lines were fortifying "like smoke." "Old Pat's" division was there also, in fact all of Hardee's corps and part of Polk's corps having kept the Cassville road, 2 divisions of Polk's Corps had joined us at Resaca. Batteries shelled at long range but none of the shells reached us. Maney's brigade of Cheatham's division had quite a fight at the "octagon house" on the road late in the afternoon. Night has now come on, have fires kindled, and (as Dr. B. says) have had "spirits" issued which the boys appreciate after being exposed to inclement weather.
>
> At 10 P.M., fell in and marched through Addairsville towards Kingston. The night was dark, the road muddy and crowded with troops. We would march probably a few steps, then halt a moment—not long enough to sit down to rest. We were until after daylight marching 10 or 12 miles. Once while standing in the road, one of the men who had his gun slung across his back went to sleep and fell back against me, his gun near breaking my nose.

Grant and Lee were fairly quiet except for slight movements of troops. On the Peninsula, Ben Butler had placed himself in a position where he could go almost nowhere. His threat to Richmond was negated. Sheridan gave up his attempt to reach Butler and headed home to Grant.

May 18 (Wednesday)

Another attack on the new Confederate lines at Spottsylvania C.H. did little other than create more casualties. Grant moved further south and east.

Beauregard had just about completed his "cork in the bottle" on Butler's army at Bermuda Hundred. Some action occurred at Foster's Plantation and at City Point, where the James and Appomattox Rivers meet.

Day, Pvt., Co. B, 25th Massachusetts Volunteer Infantry, on the sick list, City Point, Va.:

> Since the affair over the railroad, I have been on the sick list and have suffered severely with chills and fever and from other causes. I am not yet able to do much and I fear I shall not be able to go on many more excursions with the boys. The regiment has been out nearly every day, and has suffered loss of more than 200 men killed, wounded, and prisoners. In the fight at Drury's Bluff two mornings ago, we lost heavily, some 150 men being killed, wounded or taken prisoners. Heckman's brigade was almost annihilated. He was taken prisoner together with Capt. Begler, who lost four pieces of his battery, and Col. Lee with nearly the whole of the 27th Massachusetts regiment, besides a good many officers and men of the 23d Massachusetts and 9th New Jersey.

The Union Army of the Tennessee still followed Joe Johnston's Army of Tennessee from Adairsville to the Cassville-Kingston area, where fighting occurred as the Union forces converged. President Davis expressed his disappointment over Johnston's retreat from Resaca.

Jackman, Pvt., "The Orphan Brigade," Cass Station, Ga.:

> Rested in Kingston a while in the morning, then fell in and marched 3 miles towards Cass station. The day very hot. We stacked arms and I went to a creek to take a bath. All quiet the balance of the day. I slept well at night.

The huge Confederate ram, C.S.S. *Tennessee*, was finally floated over the Dog River Bar and out into Mobile Bay. Admiral Buchanan's efforts had paid off in getting the ship built and downriver.

May 19 (Thursday)

Lee, attempting to find out if Grant was moving to his right, ordered Richard Ewell to demonstrate against the Union line at Spottsylvania C.H., which brought on a severe fight which lasted most of the day—again, accomplishing nothing except more casualties. Grant was moving towards the Po River to the southeast. For the several battles which made up the whole of Spottsylvania, the Federals lost about 17,500 out of nearly 110,000 engaged. The South's losses were never accurately recorded but could be estimated roughly at 6000 from a total engaged of about 50,000. Grant could afford the loss, Lee could not.

Arnold, Pvt., 49th Pennsylvania Volunteers, Spottsylvania C.H., Va.:

> 6th Corps, 1st Division
> Verginia Neare Portsevania Court house
> May the 19 day 1864
> Dear wife and family
>
> It is with pleasure that I seat myself to drop a few lines to informe you that I am enjoying good and perfect health and hope you are enjoying the same blessing Futher I let you know that I and John Stahl left distribution camp the 4 day of this month on the 5 day wee arrived at mine run ware the battle commenst got thare the fight had already commenst and our Regeiment was in the fight so we could not get to our Regeiment on Friday morning the provost marshal said wee could not get to our Regeiment at preasand wee should go the the hose bittle and help to attend to the wonded our help was needed as much there as on the field so wee went there o it was a auful site to see the wonded come in by loads some had thare legs shot off and some thare armes some ware shot in thare heads and a grate many ware only slitely wonded I was looking to see some of our boys coming inn wonded but the had the luck not to get wonded our Regeiment was in the center the dident get a very bad ingagement the hardest fighting was on the right wing so wee remained at the hose bittle till Sonday morning then wee goined our Regeiment and

ware hapy to meet our company on the same eaving ware formed into line of battle and remained in line of battle till Tuesday eaving then wee were ordered forward to make a charge on the Rebels entrenchments which was on a hill so wee ware marched to the edge of the field ware Rebs ware on top of the hill and formed two lines of battle and laid about one hour thare then the orders ware given forward march and as soon as wee got a little wais up the hill then the bullets came as thick as hale but we ran up the hill to thare entrenchments just as quick as wee could and charged on them with our bayonets but I can tell you the skedadeled as fast as the could 6 or 8 thousand threw down thare armes and gave up fighting and fell in our hands as prisoners but is was a hard fight it was in that fight that our Col and lieutenant Col ware shot and our Capt Kephart and our orderly John Griner and a grate many of our company wonded James Swartz Jacob Steffen ware wonded and Edwin Shrauder I guess he is dead I went see him but was sin lying and the blood runing out of his mouth and nose and William Herrold he is either ded or a prisner wee havent herd anything of him since the fight Dear wife I have often thought about since I left home for I know that you havent got any money I cant see how you get along but you must do the best you can I hope I can send you some money before long I want you to write to mee and give mee all the news from home you must excuse mee for not writeing oftener for I hadent time to write often but I hope fighting will soon be over for a while we have bin marching and fighting ever scince wee are out here wee had some hard times since we are out her but all I wish is to stay well and keep my life to meet you againe I would have a grate elle more to write but havent time wen you have red this letter give it to John Steep I guess I must close for this time give my best respects to inquiring friends I wonder if Solomon Arnold couldent loaned the money for a few weeks I fell veary sory about him being disapointed by god nose I cant help it Deare wife dont trouble yourself about mee I think to wee all will be till falle All I here talk say the are will end this somer one way or the other and I hope that God may help that it may come to pass Dear wife kiss all the little ones for mee and tell them that papy will come home till falle now I will close for this time and write soon and often and tell franklin oves to write often to mee I will write to all my friends the first oppertunity I get tell all to excuse me for not writeing for instead I havent time now I will close for this time write soon so much from you sinsear husband and friend

In Georgia, Johnston realized that Sherman's army was now split and he was determined to attack it piecemeal. He sent Hood to attack the Federals, but Hood, wrongly believing that the Federals were on his flank and at his rear, fell back on the defensive. Johnston then withdrew into defensive positions south and east of Cassville. Sherman came closer and opened with his artillery. That evening, both Hood and Polk, thinking they could not hold the position, convinced Johnston to fall back, Hardee being the only dissenting voice. Johnston headed towards Cartersville and the Etowah River, followed closely by Sherman.

Jackman, Pvt., "The Orphan Brigade," Cassville, Ga.:

At noon a battle order was read to the troops from Gen'l Johnston, Commander-in-Chief, stating the time had come to decide matters by a general battle. The order was "Napoleonic" and elicited loud cheers from the troops. They seemed anxious to fight. Soon after the order was read, we fell in and marched out to form lines. Our first position was in advance of the main line as afterward formed to give battle. We had only a few shells thrown at us. Cleburne at the same time was over on the left of the R.R. and his men marched right up to a Federal battery before they knew it, thinking it one of our own. Granbury had to get back in a hurry. After we had worked a while our division marched off by the flank towards Cassville. We marched about the town first in line of battle, tearing down fences, etc., then moved around to the left to support Cleburne. The evening was very hot and we suffered much from heat.

Gen'l Johnston passed us late in the afternoon soon after arriving in rear of Cleburne and the boys cheered him loudly which seemed to please the General very much. Soon after "Old Pat" came along and the boys commenced cheering him. He told them he liked to see them in good spirits but that they ought not yell so loud, that it would cause our lines to [be] shelled. About sundown, drew rations. Tonight a heavy detail from the regiment to construct works to our left. I shall now try for some sleep as there will be no rest for the weary tomorrow. All looking for a big fight.

May 20 (Friday)

Gen. Nathaniel Banks's army today crossed the Atchafalaya River near Simmesport, La., on a bridge designed by Lt. Col. Bailey, made of steamboats anchored side-by-side. The Red River campaign was closed.

In Georgia, Johnston passed through Cartersville, crossed the Etowah River, and took up strong defensive positions at Allatoona Pass. Schofield's corps followed closely through Cartersville.

Jackman, Pvt., "The Orphan Brigade," Etowah Iron Works, Ga.:

> At 2 A.M. waked up and we marched down the railroad 7 miles to Cartersville on the Etowah, where we arrived at daylight. We were in an old field near the bridge until noon, before we crossed. The sun was very hot and the time was not pleasantly spent. We crossed on a pontoon bridge. About 2 miles from the river we turned to the right and bivouacked on a high hill at the base of which, on the railroad is the Etowah Iron Works. These hills are composed, almost entirely, of iron ore. Here we found our wagon train & I immediately took a bath and changed my cloths. Tis said the reason we did not fight at Cassville was Hood and Polk declaimed they could not hold their position.

In Virginia, Meade was ordered to go to his left and cross the Mattapony River. Lee, onto Grant's movements, began his shift to the right. Butler was still bottled up at Bermuda Hundred.

May 22 (Sunday)

At Mobile Bay, Admiral Farragut waited for his counterpart, Admiral Buchanan, to send forth the ironclads to do battle with wooden ships.

In Virginia, Lee's Confederates reached Hanover Junction, just north of Richmond, only a short time before Grant's blue columns arrived from Guiney's Station. Lee had the advantage of interior lines and therefore less distance to move.

Johnston's Army of Tennessee was located near Allatoona on the Chattanooga-Atlanta railroad in fairly strong defensive positions. Sherman again ordered a move around Johnston's left flank, going towards Dallas, Ga.

May 23 (Monday)

Sherman moved his entire army across the Etowah River and headed towards Dallas, Ga., Johnston, having little choice with his left flank turned again, prepared to move towards that same location.

Jackman, Pvt., "The Orphan Brigade," towards Dallas, Ga.:

> At 11 A.M. moved out on the road towards Dallas. The road was blocked up by troops, we were until sundown marching 8 miles. Having to stand up in the road seems more tiresome than rapid marching. Had a shower of rain in the evening—before that, very hot.

At Hanover Junction near the North Anna River, Lee awaited the arrival of Grant and the Army of the Potomac. Late in the afternoon the first of the Federals crossed the North Anna with Warren's Fifth Corps leading. About 6 P.M., A.P. Hill hit Warren's corps, made some initial gains, and then was stopped. Wright's corps was crossing the river and would arrive the next morning to help Warren. Hancock's Second Corps attacked near Old Chesterfield on the north side of the river. Lee's opportunity to attack Meade's Army of the Potomac piecemeal was lost because of Lee's indisposition and lack of coordination.

May 24 (Tuesday)

On the North Anna River near Hanover Junction, Meade's Sixth Corps moved to the right of the Fifth Corps and held. Hancock's corps, the Second, crossed at the Chesterfield Bridge further east. Burnside's Ninth Corps also crossed the river. The Army of the Potomac was now divided into three parts by the bend in the North Anna River and Lee's protruding line. Sheridan rejoined the army at this time. Lee waited within his position for the *axe* to fall.

In Georgia, Confederate Gen. Joseph Wheeler and his cavalry were loose in Sherman's rear, attacking wagon trains and creating havoc. Johnston realized that Sherman was around his left flank again and ordered his army towards Dallas via New Hope Church, which was even closer to Atlanta. This would lengthen Sherman's supply line and contract Johnston's, which was based in Atlanta.

Jackman, Pvt., "The Orphan Brigade," towards Dallas, Ga.:

At 2 A.M. on the road. After marching 5 miles towards Dallas our brigade was formed in line of battle across a road coming in from towards the river. Went with company on the skirmish line. We had a most lazy time all day. After taking a good nap, I finished the day reading Miss Evans' new novel "Micaria." Showery during the day. Continuous cannonading in front. Late the enemy came out on the main Dallas road and Tyler had quite a skirmish. About sundown we were taken off skirmish and joined the regiment which had marched back to New Hope Church. Marched 5 miles after dark and stopped in 2 miles of Dallas. Rained nearly all night and I slept on three fence rails placed side-by-side, one end of the rails resting up against the fence to give inclination so the water would run off. Did not sleep very well.

Barber, Cpl., Co. D, 15th Illinois Volunteer Infantry, Huntsville, Ala.:

...I cannot leave Huntsville without telling my readers what a beautiful city it is. It seemed like a paradise situated in a wild country. Its cottages were neat and tasty and closely entwined with ivy. The streets were deeply shaded, making it a nice, secluded spot. In one edge of the village was one of the largest springs of pure water in the United States. It gushed from the foot of a rock one hundred feet high. A deep basin formed a reservoir. A stream of considerable magnitude ran from this spring and it furnished water for the whole city.

The morning we were ordered to march, the regiment was consolidated into three companies, A, F, I and J forming one, called Company A; B and G formed another, called Company B; K, H, C and D forming the other, called Company C. This last order took us by surprise. We were dumfounded, indignant. It was the deepest wrong that had yet been done us. It was utterly lacking in faith. We re-enlisted with the understanding that we were to retain our company organization and have the privilege of electing our own officers.... Officers were forced upon us who were obnoxious to us.... Not one of Company D's officers remained....

The Union Navy came to Ben Butler's rescue when at Wilson's Wharf on the James River, Va., the wooden steamer U.S.S. *Dawn*, Acting Lt. Simmons, used naval guns to compel Confederates to desist in their attack on a Union position. Other Union ships also moved in to assist.

May 25 (Wednesday)

At New Hope Church, Ga., in the middle of a fierce thunderstorm, Hooker's corps drove against Hood's corps along Pumpkin Vine Creek. This location, about twenty-six miles north and east of Atlanta, would be the scene of the struggle for Atlanta until about June 4th.

Jackman, Pvt., "The Orphan Brigade," towards Dallas, Ga.:

All serene this morning, both on point of weather and warfare. At noon moved halfmile nearer town and bivouacked near a good spring. About sundown the musketry roared terribly towards our right. [Afterward learned that the enemy charged Stuart near New Hope Church and was repulsed with heavy loss]. Set in raining about dark. Adjt. C., Johnnie G. and myself made a "fly" out of a blanket which kept off the rain. Slept very well.

On the morning of the 25th, after we had stacked arms, went out "bear" hunting; but having failed in finding a "bear," brought in a sheep. They caught the sheep with salt. W., though a Jew, is death on swine. He kills more hogs than any man in the regiment....

On the North Anna River near Hanover Junction the confrontation was a stalemate. Grant would not assault the strong Confederate positions and Lee was too ill to conduct an offensive operation against Grant's divided army.

Five sailors from the U.S.S. *Mattahesett*, Capt. M. Smith, took a boat and two 100-pound torpedoes up the Middle River near Plymouth, N.C., in an attempt to sink the ironclad C.S.S. *Albemarle*. Two of the men, Charles Baldwin and John W. Lloyd, then swam across the Roanoke River with a towline which was used to pull the torpedoes over to the Plymouth side of the river. Baldwin was to swim down and place a torpedo on each side of the *Albemarle's* bow. Across the river, Alexander Crawford would then explode the torpedoes after

Baldwin was clear. Baldwin, however, was discovered when just a few yards from the ironclad and the mission was aborted. John W. Lloyd cut the guidelines to the torpedoes and swam back across the river to where the fourth member of the party, John Laverty, was stationed on watch. These two then made their way to where Benjamin Lloyd was waiting with the dinghy the five had used to come upriver and the three of them returned to the *Mattahesett.* Baldwin and Crawford returned to the ship four days later, on the 29th, completely exhausted. All five of these men were awarded the Medal of Honor for their exploit.

May 26 (Thursday)

Grant finally decided that it was futile to attack Lee's position at North Anna and began moving towards Hanovertown, south and east around Lee's right flank, Sheridan's cavalry leading the advance. They would move 18 miles before halting.

At New Hope Church, Ga., McPherson moved up to the general area of the church as Sherman's advance corps. The entire army moved forward slowly, skirmishing nearly all the time, and the Rebels waited. Both sides entrenched.

Jackman, Pvt., "The Orphan Brigade," Battle of Dallas, Ga.:

> At daylight the 9th and 5th Ky. moved to the left of the division and commenced fortifying. The morning was very hot. At noon before we got the works done, received orders to quit work. 1 P.M. the two regiments moved to the right of Finley and we immediately set to work completing the works which were nothing more than piles of rotten logs. We had not quite finished our defenses—just before sundown—when our skirmishers commenced firing. The minies whistled over us until darkness came on. Shells were also thrown pretty freely.
>
> When night came, the regiment was deployed in the works single file and two or three yards apart. The other regiments (2d and 4th) had been here all day fortifying. At night they were extended around further to the right and we had to fill up the interval by deploying. Soon after dark I rolled up in my blanket and lay down to sleep. Once the skirmishers in front commenced firing and we were all up in a moment. The firing soon stopped and we again went to sleep.

Admiral D.D. Porter was exhausted and his health was failing after many months of effort on the Mississippi River. With the Red River campaign completed, he returned to Cairo, Ill., and reported his status to Secretary Welles.

Off Mobile Bay, Admiral Farragut watched the Confederates busily laying torpedoes in the harbor entrances. He wrote Rear Admiral Bailey at Key West:

> I can see his boats very industriously laying down torpedoes, so I judge that he is quite as much afraid of our going in as we are of his coming out; but I have come to the conclusion to fight the devil with fire, and therefore shall attach a torpedo to the bow of each ship, and see how it will work on the rebels—if they can stand blowing up any better than we can.

In the Shenandoah Valley, Union Gen. David Hunter headed his 16,000 troops from the area of Strasburg and Cedar Creek towards Staunton, opposed by "Grumble" Jones, who had about 8500 Confederates.

May 27 (Friday)

Sheridan's cavalry trotted into Hanovertown, Va., south of the Pamunkey River, passed through the town and scouted the area south for Confederates. What fighting occurred involved Sheridan's cavalry, now reorganized after Sheridan took command from Gen. Gregg. Lee, outflanked again, began moving to get between Grant and Richmond.

In the vicinity of New Hope Church, Ga., Otis O. Howard's corps attacked the Confederates at Pickett's Mills through heavily wooded country and was repulsed after heavy losses.

Jackman, Pvt., "The Orphan Brigade," Battle of Dallas, Ga.:

> A little before day our regiment moved around to the right and just as daylight came we advanced up the hill expecting to have a hard fight; but Co. H, in front, as skirmishers found only a skirmish line which fell back after a little firing. Our regiment immediately commenced fortifying on top of the hill. I went with Company B on a skirmish to the right. Not being fairly light yet and seeing a line of battle advancing across a field, we first thought the soldiers Federals, but the troops proved to be Vaughn's brigade, Cheatham's

division. Cheatham's division advanced and took possession of a range of hills and commenced fortifying. They only had to drive off a heavy skirmish line which though fired briskly as they went back inflicting considerable loss to the Confederates. About 10 o'clock we marched back to our position on the right of Finley but had hardly gotten in the trenches when we were ordered back to the hill to the right again. We have been lying here all evening, the minies and shells continually flying over us. Tonight the boys are digging trenches but I do not see the need for Vaughn is in front of us on a fortified line.

May 28 (Saturday)

Lee rushed south and east and finally got back in front of Grant's army at Cold Harbor. Grant's forces were crossing at Hanovertown with heavy cavalry contact on the Pamunkey and Totopotomoy rivers.

The Confederates under Hardee took heavy casualties when Johnston ordered a reconnaissance in force against McPherson near Dallas, Ga.

Jackman, Pvt., "The Orphan Brigade," Battle of Dallas, Ga.:

> Before daylight clothing was issued to the regiment. At dawn we move to a position and occupy the works which had been constructed by Vaughn or Maney's brigade. All of Cheatham's division having moved to the right. The hill upon which we are now stationed is very steep and rugged at its terminus, on the right gradually sloping off to the left of the regiment being down nearly in a valley or a brake across the hill. We are 300 feet above the level. A. and myself are fortified about the top of the hill. The Federals sharpshooters are very close to us and keep a stream of bullets coming over the hill all the time. There were some old smooth-bore muskets by the Tenn. troops, also a box of buck-and-ball cartridges and our boys have been trying to see who could shoot the largest loads out of them directing the fire down through the woods at the Federal sharpshooters. Some have shot a handful of buckshot and several balls in a single load. Sharpshooting kept up briskly from both sides. We think the Federal sharpshooters are "terribly" inconvenient and they have the same opinion of ours. We captured one of them and he told Gen'l Bates that our sharpshooting is excellent but that our artillery is "not worth a damn."... About 4 P.M. the boys got to their places and were ordered to hold themselves in readiness to go over the works and advance on the enemy at the signal. We took off all extra baggage so that we would not be encumbered in anyway and waited the word. Soon the musketry and artillery commenced to roar in the valley to our left and front and the mingling yells of our boys charging was plainly heard. The firing lasted only a few minutes, then became perfectly silent—we knew the division had been driven back for soon after our neighbors commenced cheering all around the lines. Later. Have just heard the result of the charges. The division was ordered to advance at the firing of a signal gun on the left. The guns were not heard but by mistake the troops advanced. An order was given Gen'l Bates countermanding the move and aides were immediately sent to the brigade commanders with the order. Tyler's got the order before that brigade got under fire—Finley's before it near the enemy works—but our brigade did not receive the order until it had advanced on the works under a heavy fire of musketry and artillery. The brigade, alone, was charging the 15th Army Corps, strongly entrenched. Of course the brigade would have been compelled to fall back had the order not reached them. The 4th suffered most, being on the left flank—(the regiment was reversed)—was subject to a flank fire from the troops which would have been employed by Finley's brigade. A battery also enfiladed the regiment. The brigade is terribly cut up. Our regiment was not to go forward until the balance of the brigade swung around in line with it, and failing to do so, we did not advance. The boys think Gen'l Bates—"Old Grits" as they call him—went to Gen'l Hardee and got permission to make the charge reporting that only a Federal skirmish line was in front of his division. The boys generally know what is in front and could have told Gen'l Bates better. "Grits" catches it from all sides and quarters. While the charge was being made, Orderly Seg't Chamberlain of Co. H was killed by a sharpshooter and several of our boys have been wounded in the same way today. Bright and clear tonight. Has been warm through the day.

May 29 (Sunday)

In Virginia, Lee waited at Cold Harbor preparing his lines. Grant was on the way to the next meeting, seeing little opposition.

At Good Hope Church and Dallas, Ga., Johnston opened his artillery against McPherson's corps with little damage to the Union troops. Most of the damage was done by sharpshooters and skirmishers.

Jackman, Pvt., "The Orphan Brigade," Battle of Dallas, Ga.:

> Have been lying around idle all day. The minies have been singing over our heads as usual from the Federal sharpshooters. The boys have been replying occasionally with the old musket before-mentioned. After dark received two letters from home by flag-of-truce. Having rolled myself in my blanket, I lay down on the side of the trench to sleep. About 10 o'clock at night I was aroused from my slumber by heavy volleys of musketry and the thunder of cannon. The firing broke out so suddenly that for some time I did not know where I was or what was going on. At last I got my eyes open and found my way to our "fort" where I found A. already. We looked over and could see a perfect sheet of flames coming over the enemy's works and the flash of cannon lit up the dark woods so we could see the cannoneers quite plain and the shell and grape came shrieking over the hill, mingled with the hissing minies. We thought we saw a line advancing up the hill and opened fire. We soon saw that the line was not advancing and commenced firing at the battery which did not seem to be very far off. We had 60 rounds of extra cartridges to carry and we thought this a good time to get rid of them. The battery over to our right threw shells over the hill, which looked very much like rockets flying in the air. Cleburne thought our division attacked and came to reinforce us—Gavan's brigade came up to support our left. His men said they were afraid our works would be taken before they got here and they "plunged" through creeks and brush to get here in time. All soon became quiet and we again went to sleep. We were waked two or three times during the night by the same kind of procedures on the part of our neighbors. Three or four solid shot passed through the works on the left of the regiment but, fortunately, no one was hurt. They could not have fired better in daylight. As to the cause of the firing, we are at a loss. Some say the Federal skirmishers got drunk and turned around so completely that they commenced firing on their own works and the lines, thinking we were charging, opened fire. Some of the Federal skirmishers did come over to our side thinking they were going back to their own lines. One of them came upon the works of the 2d Ky. and halloed out "Colonel, the Rebs are making it so hot out yonder I can't hold my posish." He found out too late his mistake and was captured. After the first firing was over, an officer was heard riding along the lines telling that 5000 Rebels had just been captured over on the left and cheer upon cheer was sent up by our neighbors. As the enemy fired at intervals during the night from their works I believe it was all done to draw our troops from the right. This is only my opinion however.

May 30 (Monday)

In Virginia, Grant's and Lee's forces finally met again north of the Chickahominy and not far from Richmond. Grant ordered probing attacks prior to a full-scale assault.

At New Hope Church and around Dallas, Ga., the lines remained much the same, with skirmishing and an occasional outburst of artillery.

Jackman, Pvt., "The Orphan Brigade," Battle of Dallas, Ga.:

> Early in the morning we march to the left leaving Gavan's brigade at our position. The works where we stopped being illy constructed, we commenced strengthening them up. Had not worked long when we were ordered to our old position Gavan being ordered away. Ferguson's Cavalry, dismounted, came to reinforce us. All quiet save the popping of the sharpshooters and the Federal bullets whizzing over our works. There will be a good lead mine down in the valley if we stay here much longer. The bullets are lying around on the ground now, thick as hailstones.

Gen. John Hunt Morgan, in an effort to ease the pressure on Johnston, took Private James Pleasant Gold and several thousand other cavalrymen, on a raid into Kentucky.

A deserter from the C.S.S. *Hampton* reached the Federal fleet in the James River and reported that three ironclads and six wooden gunboats, all armed with torpedoes, had passed the obstructions at Drewry's Bluff and were below Ft. Darling, awaiting an opportunity to attack. The ironclads were the C.S.S. *Virginia II*, Flag Officer John K. Mitchell, C.S.S. *Richmond*, Lt. William H. Parker

(Commandant of the Confederate Naval Academy), and the C.S.S. *Fredericksburg*, Commander Thomas R. Rootes.

May 31 (Tuesday)

Grant, at Cold Harbor, adjusted his lines to get around Lee's right flank, so Lee moved his lines. On May 1st, Grant had been north of the Rapidan and Lee had been quietly lying at Orange Court House. In less than thirty days, Grant was outside Richmond and had Lee so heavily engaged that Lee couldn't go anywhere.

In Georgia, Sherman too had moved quite a distance since early May, now knocking on the outside door of Atlanta.

Jackman, Pvt., "The Orphan Brigade," Battle of Dallas, Ga.:

> Some shelling over on the left this morning. At noon Stephen's brigade relieved us and our brigade moved to the left and took positions in the works first made by Tyler's brigade to the right of Slocum's battery—Cobb and Slocum have not moved from their first positions. We worked some in the evening improving the defenses which are not strong enough to resist shells. From experience, the boys don't like for shells to come through the works. Slocum has had two of his pieces disabled since he has been here. The two batteries have been dueling with two Federal batteries "across the way." The Federals have two, or more, 20 pound Parrotts in position. Cobb's and Slocum's batteries are composed of six Napoleons guns each....

The U.S.S. *Commodore Perry*, Acting Lt. Amos P. Foster, was hit six times while duelling with Confederate artillery on the James River.

In the North the upcoming Federal elections were being discussed more and more.

JUNE 1864

This was an increasingly alarming month for the Confederacy. Attacked on two fronts, Virginia and Georgia, the South's supply problems increased even with the "interior lines" so touted by the military experts. The Southern railroads were wearing down rapidly. Many of the important east-west trunk lines were in the hands of the Union, especially in Tennessee.

Casualty lists lengthened both North and South. The casualty notifications from May were now reaching the homes of the soldiers and the toll in morale was devastating. In Georgia, Gen. Joe Johnston had evacuated Dalton and had fallen back to New Hope Church. Lee, in Virginia, was held by Grant at Cold Harbor. One is reminded of Lincoln's quote, "One holds a leg while the other skins."

June 1 (Wednesday)

Ghosts seemed to rise over the old Seven Days' battlefields in the vicinity of Cold Harbor as the Union forces arrived to find the Confederates already in possession of the field and digging in rapidly. A sharp fight between the cavalry forces of Sheridan and the infantry of R.H. Anderson's corps livened up the morning with musketry and some cannonading. Altogether, the month was off to a brisk start. Anderson's troops attacked Sheridan's twice and were thrown back. Action occurred on both flanks of the lines until late afternoon without significant gains for either side.

Down in Georgia, the Federal cavalry under Stoneman captured the pass at Allatoona. This provided Sherman with his rail link to Chattanooga and ensured that his supply line would be open. The opposing forces clashed near New Hope Church.

Jackman, Pvt., "The Orphan Brigade," New Hope Church, Ga.:

> Everything very quiet this morning. Don't know what is the cause. As the morning advanced we found that the Federals had left our front during the night. I walked around their works which are very strong. Nothing left but beef bones and empty ammunition boxes. Some places the bushes in front of their works are literally mown down by minie balls—done on the night of the 28th of May I presume; and when our brigade charged on the 28th. Late in the afternoon the division fell in and marched 5 miles to the right—bivouacked near New Hope Church for the night. The evening was warm and the march quite tiresome.

In Virginia's Shenandoah Valley, the sparring continued between Confederate and Union forces with the Confederates falling back "up" the Valley. The Yankees were expected momentarily in Harrisonburg.

In Tennessee, Brig. Gen. S. D. Sturgis was about to take a tiger by the tail. He moved out of Memphis with 8000 cavalry and infantry towards Ripley, Miss., to find and destroy Nathan Bedford Forrest; The latter had been reported in the vicinity of Tupelo. This was not to be a quiet campaign—nor a lucky one. Confederate John Hunt Morgan had been active in Kentucky, where he fought an engagement near Pound Gap.

To add to the intelligence received from a deserter on May 30th about the Confederate ironclads coming down the James River, Archy Jenkins, a Negro from Richmond, confirmed that the ironclads and six wooden gunboats were below Drewry's Bluff at Ft. Darling. Jenkins also reported:

> They are putting two barges and a sloop lashed together, filled with shavings and pitch and with torpedoes, which they intend to set on fire, and when it reaches the fleet it will blow up and destroy the fleet.... They all say they know "they can whip you all; they are certain of it." They believe in their torpedoes in preference to everything.

On the Mississippi River near Columbia, Ark., Acting Master James C. Gipson, U.S.S. *Exchange*, was wounded during a fight with Confederate shore batteries:

> They waited until I had passed by the lower battery, when they opened a destructive crossfire. As I had just rounded a point of a sand bar, I could not back down, consequently there was no other alternative but run by the upper battery if possible.... I opened my port broadside guns, replying to theirs; but unfortunately the port engine was struck and disabled, causing her to work very slow, keeping us under fire about forty-five minutes. I had barely got out of range of their guns when the engine stopped entirely.... I immediately let go the anchor...expecting every moment they would move their battery above us and open again; but we succeeded in getting out, although pretty badly damaged.

June 2 (Thursday)

The second day of the Battle of Cold Harbor. Nothing seemed to be working right for Grant on this day. Problems of troop placement, ammunition resupply, and a tired army compounded normal situations and caused the delay of the attack until 5 P.M. The day had been very hot and was cooled somewhat by late-afternoon showers. The skirmishes fought during the morning and early afternoon had only further fatigued the troops. Once again the attack was postponed until morning.

Sherman moved his three armies northeast towards the railroad that linked Atlanta and Chattanooga. The Rebels dug in further along the New Hope Church line, with skirmishing at Ackworth and Raccoon Bottom.

Jackman, Pvt., "The Orphan Brigade," New Hope Church, Ga.:

> Early in the morning we moved a mile further to the right and formed in rear of Stahl's brigade. Some cannonading along the line and sharpshooting. At noon the rain poured down for an hour in torrents. We could do nothing but take it as it came. At 2 P.M. the division fell in and we marched 4 miles to the extreme right of the army. The cannon were thundering all along the line of march and the Federal shells were tearing through the woods about us. Our brigade stacked arms in an old field and as night came on I made me a bed out of three fence rails. Slept well. Clear again.

Federal Gen. David Hunter continued his campaign of devastation through the Shenandoah Valley, fighting a skirmish at Covington on the road to Lynchburg. He had some 16,000 men opposing about 8000 Confederates commanded by Gen. W.E. "Grumble" Jones. The long-awaited Yankees finally arrived in Harrisonburg.

June 3 (Friday)

Confederate Commander Thomas P. Pelot took a boat expedition of 130 officers and men on a raid in the early-morning hours off Ossabaw Island, Ga. The objective was the anchored U.S.S. *Water Witch*, a 380-ton screw steamer. The Rebels' boats were within 150 feet of the *Witch* when they were spotted and the alarm given. It was too late for the Union crew. The Confederates boarded and a wild melee ended with the capture of the ship and the death of Commander Pelot, along with five other attackers.

The ship was taken into the Vernon River and moored above the obstructions guarding Savannah. The *Witch* was later taken to Savannah to add to the city's defenses.

Federal cavalry entered Ackworth, Ga., as Sherman again outflanked Gen. Joe Johnston near New Hope Church. Johnston responded by moving yet again.

Jackman, Pvt., "The Orphan Brigade," New Hope Church, Ga.:

> At daylight we commenced fortifying. After working awhile, Maj. Cobb came and selected our position for Mahane's battery of our division. We then moved around to the right of the brigade and commenced a line of works through a peach orchard near a house—Gen'l Bate's HdQtrs. At noon ordered to stop work. In the afternoon the rain poured down. At night slept with G. under a dog fly. Stopped raining at dark.

In the Shenandoah Valley, Brig. Gen. W.W. Averell's Union cavalry left Bunger's Mills to join Major Gen. David "Black Dave" Hunter in the Staunton area.

At Cold Harbor the fighting opened at 4:30 A.M. with a charge all along the two armies' entrenchments. The Confederates, having had two days to prepare, were well fortified. The attack was a head-on crash against the Rebel lines, relying on the sheer weight of numbers to breach them. A few problems developed. The Federal lines were enfiladed and the slaughter was terrible. The Federal losses, killed and wounded, were about 7000 in one hour. Nearly 50,000 troops were in the assault out of a strength of about 117,000. The South lost about 1500 from a strength of some 60,000. About noon the attack was called off and the Army of the Potomac prepared to move to the left again.

In the assault at Cold Harbor, within five minutes nearly one-half of the 11th Connecticut Volunteer Regiment was killed or wounded. The flagstaff for the national colors was hit so many times it was shot completely in two. Undaunted, the Color Sergeant bound the staff with bits of harness from the horses of an artillery battery close by.

June 4 (Saturday)

In Georgia, Gen. Joe Johnston began to move his troops in a rainstorm from the area around New Hope Church to the vicinity of Pine Mountain. Not all the troops were moving rapidly.

Jackman, Pvt., "The Orphan Brigade," New Hope Church, Ga.:

> Before daylight, went with the company a mile in front as skirmishers. Lieut. E. and I took up quarters in a house, which had just been vacated by the family, in front of the skirmish line with the intention of setting it on fire in case the enemy advanced so it would not protect his sharpshooters. As there was a cavalry picket in front, we did not have to be very watchful so we kindled a fire and "lived at home."
>
> K. and W. killed a large pet hog belonging to the premises and while scalding the animal in the large pot at the spring, the old lady came after her pot and caught them in the act. After giving them a piece of her tongue, she reported them to Capt. S. in command of the brigade skirmishers. He immediately had them arrested. When the old lady had gone (being satisfied as the Capt. had promised to report the offenders to the "General") the culprits were turned loose and went on with their cooking. Part of the meat, after being cooked, went into Capt. S.'s haversack and it is not likely that the "bear hunters" will be reported.
>
> Rained at times during the day. At sundown relieved by Company D. When we got to the regiment the boys were drawing clothing. Set in raining at dark. Am under a barn shed by a fire. We have orders to march at 11 o'clock tonight. This morning, after Company B went on skirmishers, the remaining companies were ordered to complete the works but when nearly done, they had to move for a Parrott battery to be placed in position. The Colonel would not fortify anymore. He said he had given away for batteries long enough and that if a fight came off his reg't could simple take it "straight." I don't think I can sleep any tonight. I shall "smoke" over the fire until we have to march. Looks "awful" dark—rain pouring down.

June 5 (Sunday)

In the Shenandoah Valley of Virginia, Union Gen. David Hunter moved his forces towards Staunton, forcing the Confederate Military Department of Southwest Virginia to do battle at Piedmont. The

Confederate forces, under W.E. "Grumble" Jones, were defeated, Jones was killed, and Hunter's troops looted Staunton. The Confederates lost about 1600 men, 1000 of whom were taken as prisoners. Hunter was soon joined by Generals Crook and Averell at Staunton. Hunter's orders were to move on Lynchburg, a major rail terminus, and destroy the railroad. Hunter decided to do otherwise, although he was urged by both Crook and Averell to move on Lynchburg before the Rebels could reinforce that city. Hunter moved on to Lexington, Va.

In Georgia, Johnston had placed his troops on the line near Marietta. There was some minor skirmishing near Pine Mountain as Sherman shifted closer to the railroad.

Jackman, Pvt., "The Orphan Brigade," Pine Mountain, Ga.:

> Last night we fell in at 11 o'clock and marched to our present position near Pine Mountain. The distance we marched was only about 4 miles; but the muddiest and most disagreeable march I have made since the war. The night was dark as pitch. The rain pouring down. I could not see what kind of a country we marched through but it seemed one continual swamp the mud and water being from ankle to knee deep every step. Troops having preceded us, the mud was well worked up. I kept on my feet all the time but many of the boys fell down and would splash around splattering mud in every direction. When a fellow would fall, his more lucky comrades would yell out to him to "get up out of that mud. What are you doing down there?"
>
> About 2 o'clock we filed off to the left in an old field and stacked arms. I composed myself to sleep on a log and never waked until the sun was shining in my face. About noon, moved into the woods and formed in rear of Cheatham. All quiet in front. Gen'l Hardee stated the next morning that the march we made that night was the most disagreeable he had ever made.

At Cold Harbor the wounded and dead were stacked all over the field. Some of the wounded had been treated and sent back to Fredericksburg for further evacuation. The long siege of continuous fighting took its toll on the troops' mental and physical health. Grant petitioned Lee for a truce to remove the wounded and dead. Pending the agreement, both sides withheld their fire as comrades of the wounded recovered them from the field.

Arnold, Pvt., 49th Pennsylvania Volunteers, Cold Harbor, Va.:

> Virginia Chicohomey River
> 6th Corps, 1st Division
> June the 5 day 1864
>
> Dear wife and famly I will now enjoy this preasant oppertunity to write a few lines to informe you that I am enjoying good and perfect health at preseant time and hope you are enjoying the same good blessing futher I let you know that I received you kind and welcome letter yeasterday and was glad to here from home and learne that you ware all well I was sory to here that Jacob Keller was not yet weil but hope god will spare his life yet awhile I also feele sorry that I could not sent you some money yet the pay day is past for over a month ago But as long as wee are marching and fighting wee wont draw any money and it wouldent do to draw any money now for wee could not sent any home in any safety at preasant for the is not express from here but I hope wee will soon get into camp and get our money I know you would need it veary bad but I hope your friends will not lieve you suffer you must do the best you can I hope everything will come rite after all for all that Abel Herrold wouldent trust you that flower I ecspect the cause is becase he is a copper head and the cant any thing better be exspected of such a man as he is for that is coper head princiapels The time I boated for him I had to wait 18 months for 40 dollars of my pay and he wont trust 5 dollars for a couple of weeks you said I should lieve you know where James Swartz was wonded and where he is I do not know in what hose bittle he is he is some wares in the hose bittle he was slitely wonded in one of his arms in which arme I cannot tell but I know he is better off than iff he was with us he has no marching to do and no hardships to go through as wee have I take all his letters up that is sent to him iff I now ware he was I would sent them to him he wrote to write so a boddy now you also said I should lieve you know which of our lieytenant was wonded the is no one of them wonded I said our colonel and our lieutenant Col were boath killed the Col.s name was Culen and the lieutenant Col.s name

was Patrick Miles Isaac Fackrick was wonded last Friday in the arme also on the same day our major was wonded but only slitely this morning our orderly was wonded perty bad throug the neck wee have bin laying in the front line of battle ever since Friday morning but wee had good rifle pits the Rebs couldent hurt us much and wee couldent hurt them much for the ware entrenched as well as wee ware but the bullets are wistling all the time our Regeiment was releived this morning wee ar now in third line of battle and I hope wee will be kept out of the front for a while for wee bin in front our share already our company had 106 men and now wee have only about 42 yet but I still have bin saved yet sofar and hope god will spare my life that is my prayer and I feel confident that iff it is not gods will for mee to be shot the is no reb that can shoot mee in god I put all my trust and you must do the same and not trouble yourselfe the least bit about mee I am as safe here as I would be at home in refference about getting pigs I think it would be best if you could get them but as yuou think best perhaps after harvest you can get them cheper but try and plant the lot full of potatoes if you can get them I guess I will close for this time give my best respects to all enquiring friends in speashly to Mr. Oves famly Keller and Mr Stepp and tell them all to write to mee the have more time then I have if I could I would write to them all but indeed I havent time I only had my boots off three nites scince I have bin out here Often times wee do not get time to wash for two days but I look foreward with pleasure hopeing soon to get into camp for a while and then I will write all the news Write often to mee I love to here often from home and from old Chapman Tell Harriett Stroup I gave her best respects to the lieutenant he send his best respects to her I will close by remaineing you cinsear friend and husband

John. C. Arnold
To his Dear wife and famly Mary a. Arnold
write soon and take good care of Magor

June 6 (Monday)

Sherman shifted further around the Big Shanty and Raccoon Creek areas, causing some skirmishing with Johnston's forces near Pine Mountain. It was generally quiet as Johnston awaited Sherman's next move.

Jackman, Pvt., "The Orphan Brigade," Pine Mountain, Ga.:

> Cloudy morning. At noon we moved two miles and formed line on Pine Mountain. Digging all evening in trenches. Rained a heavy shower. Slept well at night.

In the Shenandoah Valley Gen. David Hunter's troops arrived at Staunton, just north of Lexington, although it was the wrong direction to get to Lynchburg, where he was supposed to be going. At Cold Harbor, the evacuation of the wounded continued. The dead lay where they had fallen.

June 8 (Wednesday)

At the Republican Convention in Baltimore, Lincoln was nominated for a second term. Andrew Johnson of Tennessee was named as his running mate, instead of Hannibal Hamlin of Maine.

In Georgia, Federal troops were wading through mud in their movement to the Western & Atlantic Railroad near Pine Mountain. Francis P. Blair, in bringing up his corps, left a goodly part of it along the railroad to guard that vital link to Chattanooga. Johnston awaited Sherman.

In the Shenandoah Valley, Generals Crook and Averell joined Hunter on Hunter's drive to Lynchburg. "Black Dave" now had about 18,000 troops at his command.

At Mt. Sterling, Ky., John Hunt Morgan captured the town and its Union garrison. Some of Morgan's men robbed the local bank of over $18,000, and Morgan's share of the blame for this was never fully established. It was during this operation that Private James Pleasant Gold was taken prisoner and evacuated from the town towards Lexington before Morgan fully took Mt. Sterling.

June 9 (Thursday)

Fighting flared up near Big Shanty in Georgia. Sherman was about to move against Johnston at Pine Mountain.

Lincoln, notified of his nomination, immediately called for a constitutional amendment to abolish slavery. This one would pass easily.

At Cold Harbor, Grant ordered the building of fortifications to cover his own movement to the left, towards Petersburg. Jeff Davis, ever the general, warned Lee of the impending movement.

In Kentucky, John Hunt Morgan moved from Mt. Sterling towards Lexington, 40 miles away.

June 10 (Friday)

Near Pine Mountain, Sherman moved his troops through mud and mire towards the Rebel works. This set off skirmishing at Ackworth, Lost Mountain, and several other points on the line.

Jackman, Pvt., "The Orphan Brigade," Pine Mountain, Ga.:

> Early could see our cavalry falling back, skirmishing. Raining at 8 A.M. Soon after while standing on the works, I saw the glitter of bayonets in a skirt of woods "over the way" and soon after the skirmish line of the enemy came yelling over the field in front. A moment after, the middle battery opened on the hill in front where our skirmish line is established and that was after the battery on the right opened on our hill, being a mile and an eighth off. First the shells fell short; but they soon got the range. The noise of the sharpshooters sound quite natural. Pine Mountain, and the hill in front, are covered with trees—the line of the Federals seen mostly through fields. As yet our artillery has kept quiet.
>
> At 6 P.M. went with the company on skirmish—a wing of the regiment being taken at a time—and our position was in front on the hill rather to the right of brigade. Had heavy showers of rain during the day and when night came on, my clothes wringing wet. Not being allowed any fire, and being cold, I slept none during the night. Our neighbors kept up such a noise too, bugling, rattling drums, and chopping, etc. no one could have slept in a feather bed in that neighborhood—a long night—but day at last comes.

Barber, Cpl., Co. C, 15th Illinois Volunteer Infantry, with Sherman in Georgia:

> There was scarcely two hours in the day but what troops were on the move. The rear never got into camp until past midnight, and then they would take the lead the next day and march before daylight. I remember distinctly on one occasion when the 15th was rear guard. It was two o'clock A.M. before we got into camp and the wagon that carried our knapsacks got lost and did not come up until an hour later. Then we found the knapsacks scattered all over. Some of the boys never found theirs. We camped one and one-half miles from water, so it was out of the question to make coffee that night. We lay down in our wet garments in a rain-storm, to get a few minutes' rest before resuming the march.
>
> At five o'clock A.M. we were again on the move, being minus coffee for breakfast. After this, when our regiment was rear guard, when night came, some of the boys would go ahead several miles, lie down and take a nap before the regiment came up, and as we moved very slowly, they sometimes slept several hours. When the regiment came up, they would fall in and someone else would go ahead, but we were always careful not to go beyond our camping ground. On one occasion, some of the mess, including Charlie, Roll and Sime Smith stopped and lay down in the exact spot where our regiment camped and they were in the right spot for our company. Our mess used the camp fire they built to cook our supper by. Scarcely a day passed but we lost at least a score of mules. If there had not been a drove of extra ones along, a portion of the train would had to have been abandoned.

In Mississippi, near a little town called Brice's Crossroads, south of Corinth, Gen. Sam D. Sturgis finally found Forrest. In the following fracas, the Federals lost their artillery, over 170 wagons with supplies and over 1500 prisoners to a much inferior force—Sturgis with 8000, Forrest with only about 3500. This particular action was one studied for years afterward as a classic in the use of cavalry. Sturgis fled towards Tennessee.

At Cold Harbor Grant moved towards the James River crossings. In the Valley, Hunter moved towards Lynchburg, opposed by Breckinridge.

In Kentucky, John Hunt Morgan's "merry men" entered Lexington with "a whoop and a holler," brushing aside the local resistance and burning the Federal depot and taking about 7000 horses. Almost immediately, Morgan sent a force on towards Georgetown, Ky., and another demonstrating towards Frankfort, the state capital.

June 11 (Saturday)

In the Shenandoah Valley, Gen. "Black Dave" Hunter's troops, after a brief skirmish, entered Lexington, Va. Hunter spent three days looting the town and destroying much of Virginia Military Institute, in addition to turning the main building of Washington College into a horse stable. He also raided the Arrington Depot near that city. His delay in reaching Lynchburg allowed time for Confederate Gen. Jubal Early to join John Breckinridge's forces at Lynchburg.

Skirmishing near Pine Mountain continued as Sherman jockeyed for the advantage.

Jackman, Pvt., "The Orphan Brigade," Pine Mountain, Ga.:

> Rained heavy showers during the day and it was a meany day. Later in the afternoon went out in front as vidette with two or three men of our regiment. With two men of the Texas Cavalry had some fun getting a party of Federal sharpshooters out of a house in front of us. After the Federals fell back across the field we had quite a little battle. One of the 4th Tenn. soldiers was wounded in the arm late in the afternoon, that is nearly sundown, and our Parrott battery opened on a line of the enemy advancing to fortify to our left and the Federal batteries opened on our main line. The firing was pretty regular for a while. At 6 P.M. relieved by one wing of the 4th. At night slept very well.

In Virginia, Sheridan took on both Wade Hampton and Fitzhugh Lee in cavalry actions near Charlottesville, at Trevilian Station. The edge went to the Federals, but Sheridan decided that he had an insufficient force, and he gave up trying to join Hunter in the Valley.

Capt. Raphael Semmes, C.S.S. *Alabama*, arrived at Cherbourg, France, for some badly needed repairs. Lt. Arthur Sinclair, an officer aboard the ship, recorded:

> We have cruised from the day of commission, August 24, 1862, to June 11, 1864, and during this time have visited two-thirds of the globe, experiencing all vicissitudes of climate and hardships attending constant cruising. We have had from first to last two hundred and thirteen officers and men on our payroll, and have lost not one by disease, and but one by accidental death.

This is a remarkable record for a ship of the 19th century when fresh provisions were not always available and scurvy was a constant companion. It showed the great care with which Semmes treated his crew. In England, the word of *Alabama's* arrival was passed to Capt. Winslow of the U.S.S. *Kearsarge.*

June 12 (Sunday)

All reasonably quiet along the lines in Georgia. Some fighting near Ackworth, but the main effort was to bring supplies from Chattanooga to the Union forces.

Jackman, Pvt., "The Orphan Brigade," Pine Mountain, Ga.:

> Sunday. Am lying around. All quiet save sharpshooters. Our division seems to be holding Sherman's troops in check while our main army is fortifying 2 miles to the rear of us and on Kennesaw Mountain.

The Army of the Potomac began its move across the James River in one of the most brilliant moves of the war. Pulling out of Cold Harbor, the troops raced to the previously situated pontoon bridges and were in position near Petersburg within record time. Warren's Corps was left behind to cover Grant's movement and to hold Lee's forces as long as possible.

At Trevilian Station, Sheridan unsuccessfully attacked the entrenchments of Wade Hampton. He gave it all up and went back to the Richmond area to rejoin Grant.

In Kentucky, Morgan was attacked by the Federals at Cynthiana and was severely beaten. He left the area, driving his captured horses, and moved towards Abingdon, Va., several hundred miles away, arriving there on June 20th.

In Mississippi, Sturgis retreated after his decisive defeat by Forrest at Brice's Crossroads. The Federal cavalry continued to be harassed by Forrest's cavalry.

Arnold, Pvt., 49th Pennsylvania Volunteers, Cold Harbor, Va.:

> Virginia Cole Harbor
> June 12 day 1864
>
> Dear wife and famly with the grateest pleashure it is that I wish to drop a few lines to lieve you know that I am well and hope you are all the same I just finished my diner for a little while ago I will tell you

what I had it was fresh beef coffee and crackers was the maine of all that was missing I dident taist any bread for 32 days I would give a most any thing for some bread iff I only could get some but I dont eck-spect any till wee will get in camp and I dont know when that will be but I hope before long I am tired of dose hard crackers I wish I mite never have to see any of them teeth dollars any more I will tell you what was the best I taisted scince I am in the army it was pickeled cabbage wee drew some last week but it mitey little each one of us got about three table spoons ful the same day wee got some beens and rice for the first time scince wee are in this stinken virginia fresh beef and hard tacks is our regeral boarding some times wee get pickeled pork but not veary often coffee and shugar wee get a noff I am tired of fresh beef I would almost as soon not see any I had two good meals of beens and have got one good mess yet I dident draw them all I traided meet and hard tacks on some of them Dear famly I wish I was at home to day and I would a liked to spend the Sunday at home much sooner I have spent it at home then here but I hope I may soon spend some of my Sundays at home againe wee are still yet at the same place that wee ware when I wrote last The Rebs are shelling us all day but the havent hert one man to day yet as fur as I know our men hante shelling any at all to day and I think it veary nice of them becaus it Sunday I wish you could be here and see our rifle pits and our little fortes and battereys &c it would asstonish you you said that I should tell you iff I had a blanked a gaine and I forgot it to lieve you know in the last letter yes mom I have all the blankeds I want I can tell with the truth that I could a got more blankeds then William G. Herrold could hall with his four horses Wy the ground was covered over with blankeds napsacks haversacks &c but wat was it I couldent cent them home no how to fix it so I had to lieve them lay and I guess when I could seend them home then I wont have the chance to get any Molly I want you to write a little oftener then you do I would like to here a little oftener from you and my little chatter boxes then I do Write soon and lieve mee know who all of the drafted men are a gowne to come down in dixey I wish it would a hit all coperheads that new Regeiment wee wanted to get in is now with us and was in one hard battle already so we are just as well off ware ee are as iff wee ware with them wee havent had any fighting scince wee left Could Harbour but some pirty had marching The have bin hard fighting here scince wee are here but our division wasent engaged The ninth Coure was doing the most fighting here Cannon adeing is all the time here and hard musketry fighting as bin here last Sunday wee had preaching here that was the first sermen I have herd scince I left Distribution camp iff we stay in camp wee will have preaching every Sunday wee drawed soft bread on last Sunday for the first time I can tell you it seemed to bee something new not haveing any for two month each man got a small loaf about a nough for two meals wen wee will get more I cant tell wee have sutlers here any body that hase got money here can buy any line of pickeled fruit and spices butter chees cakes tobacco &c Butter is celling for 75 cts per lb small cakes 3 cts a piece I dont buy anything for I havent any mon-ey and dont wen I will get any they say wee will draw two monthes wages one of dose days that would only bee 28 dolars I think the mite keep that just as well tu iff the dont want to all that is due but the is so maney reports likely wee will get all due to us I will come to a close for this time for the ink is all Write as soon as you get this letter and tell me how you are geting along I will close by remaineing your true husband

John. C. Arnold

(on a scrap of paper within the envelope)

I guess I must close for this time I wish you clould scend mee some envelopes and paper I hardly can get any any more it is veary scarce here we all pirty near out of paper stock iff it should hapen that I should not write for a while you must not trouble your selfe it mite hapen that wee get to some place that there mite be no maile then I couldent write when you write give mee all the news but all good ones kiss Grant Melly and Cally for mee and tell them to send some sweet kisses for mee I will cole by remaining you cinsear husband father friend and lover

John C. Arnold to Mary ann Arnold

June 13 (Monday)

Sherman waited for the weather to clear somewhat to begin his advance. All remained quiet along the lines, except for a skirmish at Burnt Hickory.

Jackman, Pvt., "The Orphan Brigade," Pine Mountain, Ga.:

Did not sleep any last night as the rain was pouring down and I had to sit by a fire all night with my blanket thrown over my head. Raining all day long—slacked up at night. Heard locomotive whistling at Big Shanty which is not very far above Kennesaw. Sherman is bringing the cars with him.

Lee finally got the drift of the movement of the Army of the Potomac from Cold Harbor and began to shift his troops rapidly to cover Richmond and Petersburg. Grant moved rapidly across the James River—Hancock's Corps reached the James in the late afternoon and awaited the crossing. Lee, not really understanding the drift of Grant's move, detached Early's Corps towards the Valley to stop Hunter.

Sturgis's command was back in Tennessee being pursued by Forrest; an ill-fated expedition if one was ever formed. In the Shenandoah Valley, "Black Dave" Hunter moved on towards Lynchburg with skirmishing near Buchanan, Va.

At Dover, England, the U.S.S. *Kearsarge*, Capt. Winslow, departed to blockade the C.S.S. *Alabama*, in Cherbourg Harbor, France.

June 14 (Tuesday)

At Pine Mountain the South would lose one of her most stalwart sons this day. Lt. Gen. Leonidas Polk, along with Generals Johnston and Hardee were watching the Federal movements in front of Pine Mountain when Polk was shot by a Federal cannon. The shot struck him in the chest, killing him instantly. His remains were evacuated from the battle area and sent to Atlanta.

Jackman, Pvt., "The Orphan Brigade," Pine Mountain, Ga.:

Cloudy early this morning but cleared up at 7 o'clock. The Adjt. and I having made a bed on a brushpile, "spliced blankets"; I slept well last night. The sun is shining bright which is calculated to make us feel lively after the long rainy spell. Enemy shelling to our right.

Was wounded a few minutes after making the notes, June 14th, and I did not write any more in my journal for nearly three months. I shall try and give an account of my hospital experience during the time named in a brief manner:

About 9 or 10 o'clock A.M., 14th, Capt. G. and I were sitting by the Col.'s fire a little to the rear of the regiment. For two days not a shell had been thrown at our position and when a shell came shrieking over the mountain to our left I remarked to the Captain that some General and his staff, no doubt, had ridden up to the crest of the hill and the Federal batteries were throwing shells at them. "Yes," said the Captain, "and I hope some of them will get shot. A general can't ride around the lines without a regiment of staff at his heels." About this time we heard the second shell strike—I thought it struck into the side of the hill; but it had struck Lt. Gen. Polk. Where he was killed was not a hundred yards from us but the trees were so thick we could not see from where we were what was going on; and we did not learn what had happened for some minutes.

Soon after an order came for a report to be sent to brigade HdQtr and I sat down to write it out. Several of the enemy batteries had opened fire but as we were a little under the hill I thought we were in no great danger from the shells which were flying over—in fact we had gotten so used to bombshells that we scarcely noticed them. I was only a few minutes writing the report and turned my head to ask the Colonel if I should sign his name to the paper and had bent over and was about finished signing the paper when suddenly everything got dark and I became unconscious. If I had been sitting erect when the fragment of shell struck me, I never would have known what hurt me. When I came to my senses, Dr. H., our Asst. Surg, and Capt. G. were lifting me up off the ground. I stood on my feet and not feeling any pain I could not imagine what was the matter. The first thought that entered my mind was that my head was gone. I put my hand up to ascertain whether my head was still on my shoulders. I did not hear the piece of shell coming and it was such a quick, sharp lick I did not feel it strike. The fragment probably weighed little more than a pound. It came like a minie ball. After glancing off my head it struck against a rock and bounced and struck Col. C. on the leg but did not hurt him severely. There were several sitting around close together and they said there was a sudden scattering of the staff.

After Dr. H. bound up my wound there was so little pain I thought it no use to go to the hospital—my head only felt a little dizzy—but the Dr. said I had better go to the field hospital and stay a day or two as I was not very well anyway. He wished to send his horse back and I rode him back to the field hospital. Dr. B. again dressed my wound putting a ligature on a vein that was cut. He would not let me eat anything at dinner and in the evening had me sent to Marietta. He told me that the wound would turn out to be more serious than I thought for after arriving at the Distributing hospital in Marietta my head got quite sore and painful.

At 9 o'clock P.M. took train for Atlanta. Gen'l Polk's remains were taken down on the same train. I slept on a bench at the distributing hospital in Atlanta the remainder of the night.

The Army of the Potomac crossed the James River on pontoon bridges and by boat in their rush to gain the railroad center of Petersburg, before Lee understood what was afoot.

Things were relatively quiet in the Valley, only a skirmish at New Glasgow. In Richmond, the Confederate Congress passed many new taxes on property and income.

The U.S.S. *Kearsarge*, Capt. Winslow, arrived off the port of Cherbourg, France, where the C.S.S. *Alabama*, Capt. Semmes, had put in three days before. While *Kearsarge* took up a blockading station off the port in international waters, Capt. Semmes recorded:

...My intention is to fight the *Kearsarge* as soon as I can make the necessary arrangements. I hope they will not detain me more than until tomorrow evening, or after the morrow morning at furthest. I beg she will not depart before I am ready to go out.

Capt. Semmes need not have feared that the *Kearsarge* would depart. Winslow had long awaited the coming engagement.

June 15 (Wednesday)

Old "Slow Trot" George Thomas moved his corps beyond Pine Mountain towards Kennesaw Mountain, with moderate fighting. Sherman pressed Johnston's lines. There was fighting up around Allatoona Pass.

Barber, Cpl., Co. C, 15th Illinois Volunteer Infantry, Allatoona Pass, Ga.:

About the 15th we arrived at Rome, Georgia, and were once more in communication with the main army which was thirty miles distant. We continued our march in the track of Sherman's army until we arrived at Allatoona Pass. Our brigade—second—was left here to garrison this important post. Sherman's army was now before Kennesaw mountain which loomed grandly up in the distance, eighteen miles.

...We camped at Allatoona only one week, when we were ordered to Etowah Bridge to repel an anticipated attack. We put the place in a state of defense and left the 45th Illinois there as a garrison. Then we were ordered back to the Pass. We took up a different position this time. On top of one of the highest mountains, we fortified ourselves. The whole rebel army could not have driven us from this position....

Jackman, Pvt., "The Orphan Brigade," in hospital, Newnan, Ga.:

The breakfast was tough beef, old bakers bread and coffee that had flies in it and I longed for the hardtack and cornbread which I had left at the front. Maj. C. having given me a letter of introduction to his aunt in Covington, 40 miles towards Augusta, I wished to go there but my name was put on the Newman list. At 10 A.M. the train left for Newman, Ga. and arrived there at noon. I was taken to Ward No. 1, Bragg Hospital, Dr. Goss of Bloomfield, Ky. in charge. The room in which I was placed—the Masonic Hall—had about 30 beds but few of them occupied and mostly by men from our brig. The room was clean as could be and the beds really comfortable. I had been dreading the hospital all the time (never having been in but one general hospital before which I did not like much) but I was agreeably disappointed at finding everything so nice. John J. Woolfolk of Ark., ward master; McNeely of Tenn., first nurse; Baldridge of Ark., second; and Smith of Ga., third—all clever gentlemen. "Crawf" McClarity of the 4th was in the room wounded, the only one I knew at first.

I immediately went to bed for a sleep and scarcely waked until the next morning. For several days after being in the hospital, I imagined I could hear the whizzing of minie bullets and the thunder of artillery, I had become so accustomed to such sounds.

Beauregard slammed the back door to Richmond at Petersburg. Through a series of missteps, misunderstood orders, and downright stupidity, the Federals just barely failed to take Petersburg. The "Creole" Beauregard did the South good service this day by blocking the Union forces from their goal of the railroads in Petersburg. It would be almost a year before Grant got there. Lee, however, was still being held on the defensive.

In Ohio, Clement L. Vallandigham returned from his exile in Canada to add to the election confusion in that state.

June 16 (Thursday)

Fighting continued around the Pine Mountain area as both sides adjusted their lines and jockeyed for position.

Jackman, Pvt., "The Orphan Brigade," in hospital, Newnan, Ga.:

> The next day after being in the hospital had to take medicine for something like intermittent fever—I had been unwell for a week or so. Several days before I got up. My head did not give me a great deal of pain at first but after being in the hospital perhaps a little more than a week my wound became inflamed and gangrene ensued which threw me in a high state of fever. Old Dr. Estell of Tenn, our ward surgeon, and who was seventy-five years of age and had been practicing surgery for more than fifty years soon got the gangrene out by applying nitric acid, iodine, etc. The fever still kept with me and the doctors thought I would "go up." Dr. E., about this time, took sick and Dr. Goss prescribed for the ward. He immediately commenced giving me medicine to reduce my system. In about a week the fever left but I was so weak I could not get up and had to keep to my bed for sometime. While in this condition a force of Federal cavalry came to Moore's bridge on the Chattahoochee about 10 miles from town and threatened a raid on the place. The evacuation commenced about dark. All the hospital rangers able to walk cleared out. There were two left in my room, besides myself, not able to move. Smith, one of the nurses, and Watson, the ward clerk, were left with us. The citizens all left too. A moving mass of carriages, carts, wagons, "lowing herds," horses, sheep, goats, and people moved through the streets. Soon the town was left in a manner desolate. The night wore away and no raid came as the day advanced and though the raiding column was reported in four miles of town at daylight, yet they did not come. Late in the evening all of the refugees came back and matters went on as usual.
>
> Nothing took place again of interest until McCooks raid came to Newman about the last of July. I was then able to walk about on the street a little. That morning I was standing on the corner and saw the advance of the raid dash down towards the railroad depot. Gen'l Roddy's brigade happened to be at the depot on a train and saved the town. The raid went around the place, was surrounded by Wheeler 4 miles beyond, and the most of the force captured. A good many wounded were brought in town of both sides. We could hear the small arms quite distinctly which sounded very natural. There was but little artillery firing. There was great confusion in town all day. The streets were blocked up with cavalry for a time. Prisoners were brought in by squads for several days after the fight. The old citizens often brought in prisoners which they guarded very closely while in charge.

Pulling all but a few troops from the Bermuda Hundred lines, Beauregard reinforced the Petersburg line against the onrushing Federals. There were severe setbacks on both sides as the fighting continued. In the Valley, Hunter was holding Lynchburg under siege with Breckinridge defending and "Old Jube" Early's troops hurrying to assist.

At Cherbourg, France, Capt. Semmes, C.S.S. *Alabama*, wrote Flag Officer Barron in Paris:

> The position of *Alabama* here has been somewhat changed since I wrote you. The enemy's steamer *Kearsarge*, having appeared off this port, and being but very little heavier, if any in her armament than myself, I have deemed it my duty to go out and engage her. I have therefore withdrawn for the present my application to go into dock, and am engaged in coaling ship.

June 17 (Friday)

Heavy skirmishing continued around Petersburg. Lee was finally convinced that Grant intended to invest Petersburg and sent the remainder of the Army of Northern Virginia to Petersburg's defenses.

In a series of sharp engagements, the forces of Confederate Generals Early and Breckinridge repulsed all attempts of Union Gen. Hunter to take Lynchburg, Va. Hunter's troops, low on ammunition and food, retreated in a running fight with the Confederates. Both sides were exhausted by the fighting and things went pretty evenly until Early's cavalry launched an attack on the Union supply train at Hanging Rock, near Salem. In a very few minutes

Hunter lost nearly half of his remaining ammunition and food. Things were not looking good.

June 19 (Sunday)

Grant let his troops take a breather. Lee's troops dug in along the Petersburg line. Little fighting went on, for a change.

In Georgia, Sherman discovered that Johnston had pulled back, so Sherman advanced through the rain and mud again. Sherman always seemed to be fighting in the rain.

Generals Early and Breckinridge chased "Black Dave" down the Valley and over into western Virginia. This cleared the Shenandoah for the present time of any large Federal force.

The day the Union had waited for so long arrived at last—the C.S.S. *Alabama* had been brought to bay and a naval engagement between her and the U.S.S. *Kearsarge* off the coast at Cherbourg, France, would decide the fate of the Confederate raider. Capt. Semmes of the *Alabama* drew the scene before the battle:

> The day being Sunday and the weather fine, a large concourse of people—many having come all the way from Paris—collected on the heights above the town, in the upper stories of such of the houses as commanded a view of the sea, and on the walls and fortifications of the harbor. Several French luggers employed as pilot-boats went out, and also an English steam-yacht, called the *Deerhound*. Everything being in readiness between nine and ten o'clock, we got underway, and proceeded to sea, through the western entrance of the harbor; the *Couronne* [French ironclad] following us. As we emerged from behind the mole, we discovered the *Kearsarge* at a distance of between six and seven miles from the land. She had been apprised of our intention of coming out that morning, and was awaiting us.

The *Alabama* mounted eight guns to *Kearsarge*'s seven but Winslow had the advantage in weight of broadside, including two heavy XI-inch Dahlgren guns to Semmes's one VIII-inch gun. Two other advantages went to *Kearsarge*: her ammunition was newer and she was draped with heavy chains from topside to below the waterline. The *Alabama's* powder was old and had deteriorated during her long cruise. The *Alabama* had a crew of 149; *Kearsarge*, 163.

When the range got to about one and one half miles, the *Alabama* opened the contest with a broadside. Within minutes, the action was fierce, the ships firing starboard to starboard while steering in circles, the guns coming to bear as they passed each other. Semmes wanted to close with the *Kearsarge* and board her, but this could not be done. One shell from the *Alabama* lodged in the *Kearsarge*'s sternpost but failed to explode because of the age of the ammunition. While shot after shot crashed into and through the hull of the *Alabama*, her shot had little effect on the *Kearsarge* because of the chains hung over the latter ship's side.

After about one hour and ten minutes of heavy engagement, the *Alabama* was sinking, the enemy's shells having exploded in the side, and between decks, opening large holes through which the sea was rapidly pouring. Semmes hoped to reach the French coast but the water flooded the engine rooms, killing the fires. Semmes hauled his colors and surrendered.

The *Alabama* settled into the sea stern first, the bow high into the air and then sank into the English Channel to join the thousands of other ships that had gone down there over the centuries. Semmes and 13 of his crew were picked up by the *Deerhound* and taken to Southampton, England. The other crew members were picked up by the *Kearsarge* and French boats. The *Alabama* had captured and sunk 55 United States ships, all unarmed, worth over $4,500,000 and bonded 10 more with a value of $562,000 but this was her *first* big battle (she sank the *Hatteras* in an 11-minute battle off Galveston on January 11, 1863), and she lost. A great raider of ships, and a gallant fighter, her end brought rejoicing to the North. Semmes would return to the South and be promoted to Rear Admiral. Winslow would receive a vote of thanks from Congress and be promoted to Commodore.

June 20 (Monday)

Sherman's forces still pressed Johnston's lines near Kennesaw Mountain. There was some skirmishing around the area.

In the Petersburg area everyone who could handle a shovel was busy digging. The entrenchments were getting more complex and deeper. Lincoln left Washington to visit Grant on the James.

At New River, N.C., the iron screw steamer U.S.S. *Calypso,* Acting Master Frederick D. Stuart, along with the wooden side-wheeler U.S.S. *Nansemond,* Acting Ensign James H. Porter, transported Army troops to cut the Wilmington and Weldon Railroad. Unfortunately, the Confederates got wind of the operation and posted artillery batteries, which drove the Federal troops from the railroad. The Federals loaded on the transport under cover of the *Calypso's* guns.

In Illinois, Private James Pleasant Gold and the other prisoners taken during Morgan's raid on Kentucky arrived at the Federal prison, Rock Island Barracks, on the Mississippi between Illinois and Iowa, where he remained until May 1865, at which time he was released and he returned to Tennessee. Gold refused to take the oath of allegiance during his captivity, remaining a staunch Rebel. After the war Gold moved to Texas and eventually settled at the town of Santo, where he died on January 13, 1934, at the age of 89, one of the last surviving veterans of the war.

June 21 (Tuesday)

At Petersburg, Grant and Meade ordered a cavalry raid against the railroads and extended their lines to the left, an action that would continue until the siege was lifted. Grant and Lincoln visited aboard a steamer at City Point, and toured the lines on horseback.

Johnston, in Georgia, was feeling the pressure exerted by Sherman on the Confederate lines. To counteract, Johnston sent Hood from the Confederate right to the left flank of Johnston's line.

At Mobile Bay, Ala., Admiral Farragut pondered the tactical and strategic importance of the forthcoming battle for the Bay. Farragut viewed it as a battle between the old (wooden ships) and the new (ironclad ships). He wrote: "This question has to be settled, iron *versus* wood; and there never was a better chance to settle the question of the sea-going qualities of iron-clad ships."

June 22 (Wednesday)

To prevent the spreading of the Federal left flank, Lee sent A.P. Hill's corps to attack the Federals moving towards the Petersburg-Weldon (N.C.) railroad. Hill netted over 1700 prisoners and the Federal advance was halted. At White House, north of the James River, Sheridan looted a Confederate supply depot and headed north with nine hundred wagons, closely pursued by Wade Hampton.

Hood, in Georgia, arrived on the Confederate left flank, and made an attack at Zion Church, where the attack was broken up by the alerted Federals.

June 23 (Thursday)

In the Shenandoah Valley, Confederate Gen. Early's troops were in hot pursuit of Federal Gen. Hunter, looking for revenge for the burning and looting of the Valley. Hunter had retreated to the vicinity of Sweet Sulphur Springs on his way to West Virginia. He wanted to burn the famous hotel at that location, but was dissuaded by his staff. The Valley again belonged to the Confederates—at least temporarily. Hunter went on into West Virginia and the engagement was broken off. Relief supplies sent to Hunter finally reached him at Gauley Ferry, where his half-starved men engaged in fistfights over rations. Sheridan, with his immense captured wagon train, was still moving north and east. A cavalry raid was staged against the South Side Railroad near Petersburg.

In Georgia, the weather finally decided to cooperate, and the roads began drying out. Sherman started moving on Johnston.

On the Cape Fear River near Wilmington, N.C., Lt. Cushing, with Acting Ensign J.E. Jones, Acting Master's Mate Howorth and 15 men, all from the U.S.S. *Monticello,* went upriver in a boat to within three miles of Wilmington on reconnaissance to gain information on the ironclad C.S.S. *Raleigh,* not realizing that the *Raleigh* had been wrecked after an engagement on May 6th. Cushing's party rowed past the batteries guarding the western bar on the night of the 23rd and pulled safely to shore before daylight of the 24th, where they hid.

June 24 (Friday)

Sheridan's wagon train was attacked and his troops fell back in considerable confusion at St. Mary's Church, but they still retained the wagon train.

Lt. Cushing, USN, and his reconnaissance party were on the Cape Fear River near Wilmington, where they learned that the C.S.S. *Yadkin,* the 300-ton flagship of Flag Officer Lynch "mounted only two guns, did not seem to have many men." The ironclad sloop C.S.S. *North Carolina*, which was at anchor off Wilmington, "would not stand long against a monitor." Cushing reported that nine steamers passed them, three of them being fine, large blockade runners. Cushing also captured a fishing party and a mail courier, gaining valuable information on the obstructions in the harbor and fortifications. Cushing's party returned to the *Monticello* after dark, hotly pursued by Confederates in Wilmington Harbor. Three men, David Warren, coxswain, William Wright, yeoman, and John Sullivan, seaman, were singled out and awarded the Medal of Honor for their actions during this expedition.

June 25 (Saturday)

Things were heating up at Allatoona Pass in Georgia, as the Confederates pressed the Union defenders.

Barber, Cpl., Co. C, 15th Illinois Volunteer Infantry, Allatoona Pass, Ga.:

> The cloud of curling smoke which hung around the mountain and the hoarse, heavy notes of the artillery, plainly told us that our boys were still pushing bravely on, despite the rebel thunder and the fierce storm of iron ball rained down on them. It was the ambition of our gallant army to see our glorious flag floating from the highest peak of Kennesaw, where the rebel rag now waved.... Slowly, but surely, Sherman was weaving a web of fate which would place the rebel army in his power, but it was a fearful sacrifice. Charge after charge was made on the enemy's works. Close, fierce and deadly was the fighting.... We were soon summoned from our dizzy height on Allatoona mountain to repair immediately to Etowah as an attack was anticipated on the railroad bridge at that place.... This bridge was three hundred yards long and one hundred feet high, and it had just been completed. In seven days from the time that they commenced operations on the bridge, a train of cars passed over it. Such was the dispatch with which Sherman's engineers did their work. They had dimensions of every bridge from Chattanooga to Atlanta, and as fast as the rebels burned them and fell back, we would advance and rebuild, and the cars followed close in Sherman's wake. It was our duty to guard the railroad between Cartersville, one mile above us, and Allatoona Pass.

June 27 (Monday)

Yesterday, Sheridan finally got the captured wagon train he'd captured several days earlier into Union lines by crossing the James River and moving to the main Federal army.

Sherman's armies of the Cumberland and the Tennessee attacked the Rebel works at Big and Little Kennesaw Mountains in Georgia, with the Army of the Ohio attacking the Confederate left flank. The slaughter of Union troops was one of the worst yet in the west, with nearly 2000 killed or wounded. The attack failed to break the Rebel lines and many of the troops held on by their fingertips to the ground they had gained. This was a defensive victory for the Confederates, but it was a victory.

June 30 (Thursday)

In the Shenandoah Valley, Jubal Early and his troops left Staunton yesterday, going down the Valley towards Winchester. In Washington, Halleck got a little nervous. In Washington also, the Fugitive Slave Acts were repealed.

In Georgia, Sherman reinforced his supply line back to Chattanooga by posting troops all along the line. This was not only dangerous work, it could also be boring.

Barber, Cpl., Co. C, 15th Illinois Volunteer Infantry, Allatoona Pass, Ga.:

> At first we patrolled the railroad, but that got to be too dangerous business. Two of the 45th Illinois were shot dead only a few nights before by rebels in ambush, waiting for them. So we adopted the plan of stationing pickets at intervals along the railroad so that the videttes of each post could see each other. We took our position in the most concealed places and placed our videttes where they could see and not be seen. Then all night long we lay on our arms, scarcely moving and never speaking above a whisper lest it might betray our position. Ever and anon, the sharp crack of a rifle would ring out on the midnight air, which would cause us all to silently grasp our pieces and await the issue of events. In most instances, these were false alarms.
>
> ...We built us comfortable shanties on the bank

of the river; and despite our arduous duties, we enjoyed ourselves. The country abounded in whortleberries and notwithstanding the danger we incurred, we would go outside the lines to gather them. Some of our mess, No. 4, went out every day and we kept a supply constantly on hand, besides selling a good many. Milton would make berry pies and puddings, and with the other luxuries we procured, we lived pretty well....

The welcome news now came that our army held possession of Marietta and Kennesaw Mountain. By a sudden flank movement, Sherman had compelled Johnson to evacuate in hot haste. An unfortunate occurrence now happened to a party of our boys out foraging. They were surprised by a party of rebs and three were killed, one wounded, and one taken prisoner. ... Jack Gaynor of Company B was captured, but he happened to have a canteen of whisky with him and he got his guard drunk and effected his escape. Rollin, Milton and myself went out foraging one day. Four or five miles outside our lines we came to a deserted plantation. It was evident from the appearance of things that they had not been gone long. We found the garden in a thriving condition and we helped ourselves to all the vegetables we wanted. Amongst other things, we found raspberries. I also found a lot of fresh eggs and a sack of flour. After we got back, we cooked some of the flour and it made us all sick. It operated as an emetic on me. Some of the boys were sick several days. There were others in the regiment effected the same way. The flour had been poisoned.

In the Valley, Jubal Early and his troops arrived in New Market, making good time down the Valley. Halleck got more nervous in Washington.

Salmon P. Chase, Secretary of the Treasury and presidential hopeful, resigned yet again. He had done this so many times to Lincoln that Chase was absolutely shocked when Lincoln accepted the resignation. Lincoln had finally had enough of Chase's meddling and "back-parlor politickin'."

In the Gulf of Mexico off Mobile Bay, Admiral Farragut had requested that light-draft ironclads be provided for his assault on the Bay to cover the shoal areas which his larger ships could not venture into because of their deeper draft. Gideon Welles had requested such ships from Admiral D.D. Porter of the Mississippi River Squadron earlier and on this date Porter issued orders for the monitors U.S.S. *Winnebago* and *Chickasaw* to report to Admiral Farragut.

In all, the month ended with an upbeat note for the North. Grant was holding Lee at Petersburg, Sherman was forcing his way to Atlanta, and the war was progressing reasonably well for the North.

JULY 1864

Grant now had Lee by the leg and wouldn't let him go. Lee could not leave the entrenchments around Petersburg and do one of his famous "end runs" because he had neither the manpower nor the space. For all practical purposes, Lee's army was useless for offensive operations, and Lee was fully aware of it. In Georgia, Sherman and Johnston were doing the "Georgia reel" or "Southern sidestep." Johnston could not get loose from Sherman's constant pushing. Richmond was in dire straits and the food situation was worsening daily.

July 1 (Friday)

In Washington, the furor over the resignation of Salmon P. Chase, and Lincoln's speedy acceptance of it, finally died down, and Lincoln nominated Senator William Pitt Fessenden of Maine for the Cabinet position. Fessenden had long experience in the Finance Committee in the Senate and took the job reluctantly. Within a year the whole department would improve tremendously.

Throughout the South there was a shortage of skilled mechanical workers that seriously impeded the efforts of the weapons and machinery manufacturers. This had been true even before the war to some degree because the society of the South was mainly agricultural. The problem was further exacerbated by the conscription of many of the available mechanics when the "exemptions" were nullified. Commander Catesby ap R. Jones at the Naval Ordnance facility in Selma, Ala., had explained his problem carefully to Secretary of the Navy Mallory, who, in turn, wrote President Davis that the facility could not:

> ...make more than one gun in a week, whereas with a proper number of mechanics it could manufacture with carriages and equipments complete, three in a week, and in a few months one every day....

The C.S.S. *Florida*, Lt. Morris, captured the bark *Harriet Stevens* southwest of Bermuda, loaded with lumber, cement, and gum opium. The ship was burned, the opium was sent in with a blockade runner for use in the hospitals in the South.

Sherman was moving his troops around trying to find a hole and gain an advantage. There was light skirmishing at Howell's Ferry, Allatoona Gap, and at Lost Mountain.

Barber, Cpl., Co. C, 15th Illinois Volunteer Infantry, near Cartersville, Ga.:

> It had now been ascertained that some of the citizens who had professed Union sentiments had been engaged in plots to tear up the railroad, attack foraging parties, etc. and an order was issued to banish all citizens five miles outside our lines, under penalty of having their houses burned if not complying within a certain length of time. Severe as this order may seem, the circumstances justified it.

The Federal commander at First Manassas, Major Gen. Irvin McDowell, assumed command of the Department of the Pacific in San Francisco, a long way from the fighting.

July 2 (Saturday)

In Georgia, Gen. Joseph E. Johnston pulled his entire Confederate line back from the Kennesaw Mountains and to a line near Marietta, escaping being outflanked by Sherman. At Charleston Harbor, the Union forces occupied James Island, after brief resistance from the Confederate defenders.

In the Shenandoah Valley Jubal Early's Confederate force was nearing Winchester and the Potomac River. The ever-present Union garrison at Harpers Ferry was in danger of being captured yet again. There was skirmishing at Bolivar Heights.

The British steamer *Rouen* had a gutsy captain. The *Rouen* had just left Wilmington with a load of cotton when she was hailed by the U.S.S. *Keystone State*, Commander Crosby. The *Rouen* then threw all of the cotton overboard while pouring on all possible speed. The chase lasted four hours, during which Crosby fired 22 rounds at the *Rouen*, some falling very close and some exploding directly over the ship. In the end, the blockade runner was taken.

July 3 (Sunday)

The Confederate presence was back at Harpers Ferry when Gen. Jubal Early's Rebel force came down the Valley towards the Potomac. There was skirmishing at Leetown, Martinsburg, etc., as Sigel's Union troops evacuated across the Potomac at Shepherdstown, although Harpers Ferry was still held by the Federals. Washington was getting nervous.

In Charleston Harbor, Union forces landed to assault Ft. Johnson from Morris Island, but they were repulsed. The Stono River operation continued with the gunboats *Lehigh* and *Montauk* shelling both sides of the river as the small Union flotilla progressed upriver to cut the Charleston-Savannah rail link.

There was fighting again at Big Shanty and at Sweetwater Bridge, in Georgia, as Sherman moved past the Kennesaw Mountains towards Johnston's new line at Nickajack Creek. The dance continued.

July 4 (Monday)

Lincoln was beginning to expose his plan for reconstruction and the criticism was coming loud and long, especially from Republican abolitionist diehards.

At Harpers Ferry, Gen. Early's troops, preparing to crossing the Potomac, skirmished with the Federals at Patterson's Creek Bridge, South Branch Bridge, and other points. Washington was becoming more nervous.

Fighting continued on James Island in Charleston Harbor. The Union expedition up the Stono River near Charleston disembarked troops to capture shore batteries of artillery after the Confederate gunners had been chased away by naval gunfire. The ships continued upriver.

In Georgia, Gen. McPherson's Federals, on Sherman's right flank, were for the present closer to Atlanta than Confederate Gen. Joe Johnston was. Johnston pulled back, yet again, to prepared positions on the Chattahoochee River.

Barber, Cpl., Co. C, 15th Illinois Volunteer Infantry, Kennesaw Mountain, Ga.:

> The glorious Fourth now dawned upon us and we celebrated it as well as circumstances would permit. At the front it was celebrated by the firing of

cannon and musketry and the glittering of cold steel. It was no child's play there.... After leaving Kennesaw, the rebs made a stand at Chattahoochee River. They were now driven from that into their last stronghold around Atlanta. We were always within hearing of the fighting. At times could see the smoke of battle.... We now received marching orders and we hoped that it would be to the front. We were heartily tired of guarding communications in the rear.... Our hopes were doomed to disappointment. We halted at the foot of Kennesaw mountain near Marietta and went into camp.

July 5 (Tuesday)

Gen. Jubal Early decided that Harpers Ferry was too difficult to take (for the time being), so he crossed the Potomac at Shepherdstown into Maryland, causing skirmishing at Point of Rocks, Noland's Ferry, and other places on the river. Lincoln called for 24,000 militia from New York and Pennsylvania to help defend Washington. Lee believed that if Early put enough pressure on Washington, the Federals at Petersburg would leave to go to the relief of the capital and Lee could possibly escape Grant's hold on his army.

Sherman, with his right flank on the Chattahoochee River near Atlanta, pressed Joe Johnston closely. Skirmishing at Turner's Ferry, Howell's Ferry, and other points on the river, as Sherman looked for a weak spot in Johnston's lines.

In southwest Tennessee, at LaGrange, another Federal cavalry left in search of the elusive Nathan Bedford Forrest, this time under the command of Major Gen. Andrew Jackson Smith. Smith was different from Sturgis, who had tangled with Forrest the last time.

Andrew Jackson Smith, a Pennsylvania farm boy, was named after his father's commander at the Battle of New Orleans. He entered West Point in 1834, graduating as a 2nd Lt. of Dragoons in 1838, and was then assigned to the frontier to fight Indians. His service was all in the west, mostly under Grant and Sherman, who had great faith in him. Smith was one of only two generals to defeat Forrest. Smith stayed in the Army for four years after the war, resigning in 1869 for the job of Postmaster in St. Louis. He died on January 30, 1897, at the age of 82.

In New York, the New York *Tribune* editor Horace Greeley received a letter alleging that Confederate emissaries were in Canada with authority to negotiate peace. He asked Lincoln to consider investigating this situation.

July 6 (Wednesday)

Confederate Gen. Jubal Early's forces captured Hagerstown, Md., and were skirmishing at Big Cacapon Bridge in West Virginia and at Antietam, Md. Confederate cavalry commander John McCausland demanded $20,000 from the citizens of Hagerstown in retribution payment for "Black Dave" Hunter's burning and looting in the Shenandoah Valley.

Near Atlanta, Sherman and Johnston's forces were skirmishing at Nickajack Creek with some action around Allatoona. On the Stono River near Charleston, naval gunfire from the gunboats *Lehigh* and *Montauk* cleared Confederate riflemen out of their firing positions on Morris Island and the gunfire prevented them from building a fortification before the Federal troops could disembark and clear the area. The Federal flotilla returned downriver and the expedition ended on the 9th.

July 8 (Friday)

Major Gen. Schofield, on Sherman's left flank, crossed the Chattahoochee River at Soap Creek with little opposition. Johnston, surprised that his right flank was turned, evacuated his lines and withdrew to Peachtree Creek, closer to Atlanta. The "Georgia sidestep" dance was about over.

Barber, Cpl., Co. C, 15th Illinois Volunteer Infantry, Kennesaw Mountain, Ga.:

> Again the annoying and fatiguing duty of picketing and railroad guarding had to be performed. One picket post was stationed on top of the mountain. We stood picket two days here before being relieved. Sometimes we would go out five or six miles. It was blackberry season and we feasted on this delicious fruit to our heart's content.
>
> Marietta in time of peace was a model city. Its dwelling houses were so closely shaded by vines and shade trees as to be hardly visible. The yards and flower gardens were nicely laid out, the sidewalks nicely paved and shaded and everything bespoke comfort and elegance. The business part of town was nearly destroyed. A military college was situated here

and Gen. Sherman was at one time teacher in it and some of the Generals in the rebel army now fighting him were once his pupils at this institute.... Marietta was once a city of several thousand inhabitants and liquor was not permitted to be sold within its limits unless on a doctor's prescription. I suppose this was mainly to keep temptation away from the students attending military college.

The Third Division, Sixth Corps, Army of the Potomac, now in Baltimore, shook itself out and prepared to advance against Jubal Early's Confederate force now coming towards Washington. Major Gen. Lew Wallace gathered some scattered Federal forces near Frederick, Md., to oppose Early.

July 9 (Saturday)

Major Gen. Lew Wallace had collected some 6000 Federal troops—many of whom were raw recruits, some troops on leave, and anyone else handy—and faced Jubal Early's nearly 18,000 at Monocacy River between Frederick, Md., and Washington. The Union troops put up a stiff fight but finally broke, losing nearly 2000 casualties, about 1200 of whom were captured. Early's force suffered about 700 casualties. The advance of the Confederate army was not stopped, merely delayed by a day.

In Frederick, the Confederates imposed a levy of $200,000 on the city as retribution for the damage done in the Valley previously. The Rebel force continued towards Washington, where panic had set in among the citizens. Grant sent two divisions from the Sixth Corps at City Point, Va., by steamer to the capital.

At Petersburg, the hoped-for reaction of getting Grant to pull most of his men out of the trenches to defend Washington did not occur. Meade ordered further pressure on Lee's army and a probing action around Lee's right flank.

In Washington, Lincoln made an attempt to quiet Horace Greeley, editor of the New York *Tribune*, about alleged emissaries in Canada who wanted to talk peace. He told Greeley that he would talk to anyone who had a peace proposal, in writing, that included the restoration of the Union.

In Georgia, Joe Johnston, outflanked again, took his Army of Tennessee back to the very gates of Atlanta. President Davis, alarmed, sent Gen. Braxton Bragg to Atlanta to discuss Johnston's plans.

July 10 (Sunday)

Near Washington, Jubal Early's Confederates were now close to the city at Rockville and Gunpowder Bridge. Grant's two divisions from the Sixth Army Corps were en route to the city from City Point, Va.

In Virginia, Grant had established a huge supply point at City Point (now Hopewell) at the confluence of the James and Appomattox rivers. Rail lines were being laid around the perimeter of Petersburg.

Day, Pvt., Co. B, 25th Massachusetts Volunteer Infantry, 18th Corps Hospital, Point of Rocks:

I have been here a little more than a week and begin to feel a little rested. I have not written a letter for more than a month and about everything has been neglected. I hung around the regiment as long as Ass't Surgeon Hoyt would allow me to, and the first of the month he piled me into an ambulance and sent me here, saying I could have a much better celebration here than I could in the trenches. This was my first ride in an ambulance and I didn't enjoy it worth a cent. I have always had a strong aversion to that kind of conveyance and have always clung to the hope that I might be spared from it. My health began to fail early in the spring. I said nothing about it, thinking I should improve as the weather grew warmer, but instead of improving, I grew worse, until now I am unfit for anything. At first I was terribly afflicted with piles, then chills and fever, and now I have a confirmed liver complaint which no amount of blue mass, calomel or acids affect in the least unless it is to help it along. I reckon I can keep pretty quiet and can hold out till I get home I shall stand a chance to recover from it, but it will be a slow job.

In Georgia, Johnston had his back to Atlanta and Sherman laid his plans to invest the city. At Decatur, Ala., Major Gen. Lovell Harrison Rousseau began a cavalry raid against the railroads operating between Montgomery, Ala., and Columbus, Ga. It would be one of the most successful raids of the war.

Rousseau, a native Kentuckian, was born in 1818. After his father died, he worked his way into the practice of law, gaining admission to the bar in Bloomfield, Ind. He became a member of the Indiana Legislature in 1844. He served in the Mexican War as a Captain in the 2nd Indiana Infantry and returned to Indiana, where he was elected to the state senate, but he resigned and moved to Louisville, Ky. He fought at Shiloh with distinction as a Brigadier General and performed brilliantly at Perryville, where he was promoted to Major General. He returned to politics after the war, then returned to the army and served in Alaska. He died in New Orleans on January 7, 1869.

Barber, Cpl., Co. C, 15th Illinois Volunteer Infantry, Kennesaw Mountain, Ga.:

> There was to us one important event that happened that I have omitted to note and that was the consolidation of the 14th and 15th Illinois Volunteers into one battalion to be known as the 14th and 15th Veteran Battalion of Volunteer Infantry. This was done by order of Gen McPherson in pursuance of instructions from the War Department. This did not take us by surprise for we had long expected it and since it had become known that such a consolidation must take place, we were desirous that it should be with our brothers, the 14th. The whole battalion numbered only six hundred men, with six companies, three to each regiment. This organization took effect July 1st.
>
> ...The consolidation of the regiment had left a large surplus of non-commissioned officers, hence it was necessary to dispose of them in some way. It was given out that the excess was to be mustered out, and there were plenty who were willing to accept the sacrifice. In our Company C, there were fourteen corporals and eight sergeants. Six corporals and two sergeants had to be reduced. In the old organization I was first corporal. In the new I was second and Rollin fourth. Charlie Underwood was reduced. I was now offered a detail at headquarters as corporal of the guard, but declined to accept it, and got another person to go in my place....

July 11 (Monday)

At Silver Spring, Md., the Confederate forces under Gen. Jubal Early burned the home of Postmaster General Blair and threatened several of the forts surrounding the city. Early ordered an assault for the following day.

Meanwhile, in Washington, on the 6th Street wharves, the steamers carrying the veterans of the Sixth Army Corps, Army of the Potomac, were unloading troops such as the city had never seen. These were not the nattily dressed soldiers normally seen around town. These men were lean, dirty, somewhat ragged, and handled their muskets as if they knew exactly what to do with them. They filed off the steamers and formed long lines and struck off across the city with a swinging stride that had eaten up the miles on many a long and dusty road from Petersburg to Gettysburg. These were Grant's veterans of Cold Harbor, the Wilderness, and the Chickahominy, and they were not men to be trifled with. There was little straggling except for the occasional stop for a cold beer in a bar and then a run to catch up again. Old Jube Early, watching developments, spotted a long, low cloud of dust which indicated troops moving. But which troops? When they got to within range, Early could see they were not wearing the linen dusters and high-peaked caps of the local troops. These men wore the kepis such as he had encountered two days before when he had tangled with men from the Sixth Corps west of the city. To compound Early's problem, two divisions of the Nineteenth Corps from Grant's army arrived shortly after dark and unloaded, heading for the western defenses of the city.

At Ft. Stevens in Maryland, Lincoln and his wife paid a visit, where they witnessed Early's attack before Union soldiers ordered them away because of the danger. Lincoln seemed more curious than worried.

July 12 (Tuesday)

Early in the morning Jubal Early had second thoughts about assaulting the Washington forts, especially now that some "real" soldiers were there. He started pulling his troops away from Washington, leaving the skirmishers to mask the withdrawal. Major Gen. Wright, commander of the Sixth Corps, tried to get permission to send skirmishers out, but this was denied by the two ranking Major Generals present, both of whom had been eased out of combat command for poor performance, one at Chickamauga, the other at Port Hudson. Finally, in the late afternoon, Wright was given permission and he shook out a line of skirmishers about 6 P.M. and advanced them against Early's troops. The results were predictable. The firing increased and Lincoln, who had returned to Ft. Stevens, got his first real look at battle casualties immediately after they had been shot, with the blood still flowing from the wounds and the wounded in shock from the insult to their bodies. The firing continued until about 10 P.M., when it petered out and contact was broken. Early headed west to the Potomac crossings and Wright was content to stay in his breastworks and watch him go. The Confederates headed out, Generals Gordon and Breckinridge forming the rear guard and head of the retreating column.

During the early part of the action, Lincoln had gone up on the parapet and was looking over the top among the twittering and whirring of the minie balls when a young captain named Oliver Wendell Holmes, Jr., yelled at him, "Get down, you damn fool." Lincoln complied and sat with his back to the parapet, safe, but still able to hear the bullets murmuring overhead.

President Davis, greatly alarmed over Johnston's withdrawal to Atlanta, wrote Gen. Lee that "Johnston has failed.... It seems necessary to relieve him...."

July 13 (Wednesday)

At Washington, Major Gen. Wright, commander of the Sixth Corps of the Army of the Potomac, had gone to Grant for directions on chasing Jubal Early, who was retreating towards the Potomac and the crossing at Leesburg. Grant's directions, as usual, were forthright and immediate—pursue with both the Sixth and Nineteenth Corps. By evening, Wright would have nearly 15,000 troops on the chase, while the Washington generals were still debating.

Sherman sent his cavalry around Atlanta to wreck the railroads and generally create havoc while he crossed the Chattahoochee River, preparatory to the advance on the city.

President Davis, still worried over the situation in Atlanta, voiced his concern again to Lee about Johnston's movements and plans.

In northern Mississippi, Gen. Andrew Jackson Smith's cavalry was moving nearer to Forrest as the Confederates entered the city of Tupelo. Fighting was hot for a period of time at Camargo Cross Roads as the Confederates moved in for the attack against over 14,000 Federals. Smith took up a strong position on a low ridge and awaited results.

Admiral Farragut received information from Col. Albert J. Myer, USA, about the defenses of the harbor at Mobile, Ala. Col. Myer wrote:

> A line of piles driven under water extends from the shoal water near Fort Gaines, across Pelican Pass Channel, and to the edge of the main ship channel. One informant describes this obstruction as five rows of piles driven closely together. The other informant does not know how many are the piles or how closely driven.... From the western edge of the main ship channel, where the fixed obstructions terminate, a torpedo line extends eastward across the channel to a point differently estimated as at 400 yards and as at nearly one-half mile from Fort Morgan.

This "torpedo line" nearly caused Farragut's assault ships to turn back when they finally entered the harbor.

July 14 (Thursday)

Forrest was handed one of his two defeats today when he failed to rout Major Gen. Andrew Jackson Smith's Federal force at Harrisburg, near Tupelo, Miss. Smith's line repeatedly repulsed the Confederate assaults with heavy Rebel casualties. Of Smith's nearly 14,000 men, only 674 were lost by all causes, while the Confederate losses were about 1350 out of about 9500. It was a defeat for the South, but Forrest was not destroyed and was soon roaming the countryside again.

At White's Ford near Leesburg, Va., Jubal Early's Confederate force was back across the Potomac and safe for the time being. It was a near thing, however, since Gen. Horatio Wright's Federals were at Poolesville, Md., just north of the crossing. Wright would not pursue into Virginia.

Lincoln had moved back to the White House with his family during the scare of Early's raid and now he returned to the "summer White House" at the Soldier's Home, north of the city, where it was cooler.

The U.S.S. *Water Witch*, which had been captured by a daring raid by Confederate Commander Pelot on June 3rd, was now the C.S.S. *Water Witch*, and the target of a Union raid to destroy her. Acting Master George R. Durand, U.S.S. *Paul Jones*, took a landing party and, concealing themselves by day and moving at night, made their way to the anchorage of the *Witch*, only to be discovered and captured.

July 15 (Friday)

Near Leesburg, Va., Jubal Early's Confederate forces remained in the area, sorting themselves out after their thirsty attack on Washington.

At Tupelo, Miss., Major Gen. A.J. Smith kept his Federals waiting for another Confederate attack until midafternoon, when he pulled up stakes and headed back to Tennessee, closely followed, but not attacked, by Nathan Bedford Forrest's cavalry. This kept Forrest where Smith could watch him for a while and away from the railroad link carrying Sherman's supplies.

July 17 (Sunday)

President Davis, despairing of the loss of Atlanta, had reached a decision that Johnston would have to go. Consequently, he sent a message to Gen. Johnston:

> ...As you failed to arrest the advance of the enemy to the vicinity of Atlanta, far in the interior of Georgia, and express no confidence that you can defeat or repel him, you are hereby relieved from command....

The command of the Department and Army of Tennessee would go to John Bell Hood, one of the corps commanders. Johnston and Davis, ever on the outs since the war began, had differing viewpoints on the role of the senior general commanding. The command went from a wily fox (Johnston), who conserved his troops, to a "charge and smash 'em" brawler (Hood), who would destroy his own Army of Tennessee.

In Virginia, Early went westerly to Berryville at the bottom of the Valley, to find that "Black Dave" Hunter and Crook were there to contest his passage.

July 18 (Monday)

Two days ago, President Lincoln had sent his secretary John Hays to New York to determine if there was anything to the message from Greeley on the possibility of a "peace committee" in Canada authorized and willing to talk terms to end the war. Greeley, himself, traveled to Niagara Falls to meet with the group, only to find that they were not interested in restoring the Union, only finding terms for peace with independence for the South. Lincoln disregarded the effort.

At Atlanta, Gen. Joseph Eggleston Johnston turned over the command of the Army of Tennessee to Lt. Gen. John Bell Hood and left the city for North Carolina.

Admiral Farragut, at Mobile Bay, wrote of his plan for the assault on that formidable harbor:

> I propose to go in according to programme—fourteen vessels, two and two, as at Port Hudson; low steam; flood tide in the morning with a light southwest wind; ironclads on the eastern side, to attack the *Tennessee*, and gunboats to attack Rebel gunboats as soon as past the forts.

July 19 (Tuesday)

The Federals of "Black Dave" Hunter and Crook were looking for Jubal Early's Confederate force and found it near Berryville. A sharp fight took place at Berry's Ford, where Early threw in a number of troops against the advancing Federals. Early left the area and headed for Winchester.

At Atlanta, Major Gen. George Thomas and his Army of the Cumberland were located to the north of the city somewhat separated from the other two armies that made up Sherman's forces. Hood decided he would attack Thomas, hoping to defeat him before Federal help could arrive. He massed his forces for the assault the following day.

July 20 (Wednesday)

Hood attacked Thomas north of Atlanta. The attack began three hours late, but was intense for a period of time. Ultimately, it failed, with the Confederates taking dreadful losses. Thomas, with about 20,000, lost about 1800. Hood, with about the same number of men, suffered losses of nearly 4800. Nothing had been accomplished except that Hood had fewer men and had no way of replacing them. Sherman still faced him with an overwhelming force on almost three sides of the city, the only openings being to the south and southwest. Hood tried to blame the failure on Hardee, who, he said, was late and did not press the attack. Fruitless attacks and finding scapegoats were two of Hood's best traits.

Over around Harpers Ferry and the lower end of the Shenandoah Valley, the pressure on Jubal Early was getting stronger. There was a heavy and sharp fight at Stephenson's Depot north of Winchester, where Federal cavalry under William W. Averell took on a division of Confederates under Gen. Stephen D. Ramseur. Averell defeated them soundly; the Confederate cavalry brigade fled the field. Early withdrew further south up the Valley.

William Woods Averell, born in 1832, was an 1855 graduate of USMA, and was recovering from wounds received fighting Indians when the Civil War began. He began the war as a Colonel of the 3rd Pennsylvania Cavalry, fought well in the Peninsula campaign, and was promoted to Brigadier General of Volunteers. He fought less well during Antietam and Fredericksburg, but received credit for the cavalry battle at Kelly's Ford, the first Union large-scale cavalry victory over the South. Within two months he lost his command because of lack of performance at Chancellorsville, and he was sent to West Virginia, where he led several expeditions against the South, all successful. In 1864 he did well in the first part of the year, but when Sheridan came to the Valley to command, his performance was not up to Sheridan's expectations and Averell was relieved. He died at Bath, N.Y., on February 3, 1900.

Day, Pvt., Co. B, 25th Massachusetts Volunteer Infantry, 18th Corps Hospital, Point of Rocks:

> Thus far I have been unable to discover any charms in hospital life. With fair health, the active camp is far preferable. This hospital is divided into three departments. The first is the officers' ward, the second is the hospital for the wounded and very sick, and the third is the convalescent camp. The first two are in large hospital tents and are furnished with cots, mattresses and other necessary conveniences. In the third are more than 600 men, quartered under shelter tents. I am in this department.
>
> It is not supposed that there are any sick men here. They are all either dead beats or afflicted with laziness, and a draft is made from among them twice a week for the front. I had been here only four days when I was drawn, but Garland of Company C, who is an attache at Doctor Sadler's office, saw my name on the roll and scratched it off. Although there are none here supposed to be sick, there seems to be a singular fatality among them as we furnish about as large a quota every day for the little cemetery out here as they do from the sick hospital. But then in a population of 600 or more, three or four deaths a day is not surprising.
>
> I have been here three weeks and have been drafted four times, but with my friend Garland's help, I have escaped. I should be pleased to be back with the boys if I was only half well, but I reckon I shall not be troubled with any more drafts. Doctor Hoyt sent a man back the other day. The next morning he was sent up with a sharp note to Doctor Sadler saying that he didn't send men to the hospital that were fit for duty and didn't want them sent back until they were. That roused Doctor Sadler's ire and he says when Hoyt wants his men he can send for them.
>
> Doctor Sadler has the whole charge of the convalescent camp and has several young fellows, assistant surgeons so called, on his staff. Some of these fellows I should think had been nothing more than druggist's clerks at home, but by some hook or crook have been commissioned assistant surgeons and sent out here. Every morning all who are able in all the ten wards go up to be examined and prescribed for by these new-fledged doctors, and those not able to go seldom receive any medical attendance, but it is just as well and perhaps better that they do not go as the skill of these young doctors is exceedingly limited.... These assistants make the examinations and draft the men for the front, after which they are examined by Doctor Sadler and frequently a number of them will not be accepted, and the assistants oftentimes need not feel very much flattered by some remarks of the doctor.
>
> The convalescent camp holds it own in spite of all the drafts made on it. Recruits arrive daily and the drafts are made twice a week, sending back 50 or 100 at each draft. When a draft is made, one of the assistants comes into a ward and orders it turned out, and every man not down sick abed turns out. The ward-master forms them in single rank and the inspection begins. They commence on the right and go through the ward, making the same examinations and asking the same questions of every man in the ward. They feel the pulse and look at the tongue, and those are right they are booked for the front. They remind me of horse jockeys at Brighton examining horses. Some of the boys who are well enough but are in no hurry to go back, chew wild cherry or oak bark to fur their tongues and are thus exempted until Doctor Sadler gets hold of them, when they have to go. We get some recruits from the other hospital, for as soon as a sick or wounded man there is declared convalescent he is sent here.
>
> A good joke occurred one morning when one of them was drafted for the front. He had been slightly wounded in the leg and was getting around with a

crutch. When his ward was ordered out for draft he fell in with the rest and the doctor, not noticing the crutch, but finding his pulse and tongue all right, marked him as able-bodied. When Sadler inspected them he said to the fellow: "What are you here for?" "Going to the front, I suppose; there is where I am ticketed for." Sadler laughed and said: "I'll excuse you." Then turning to his assistant, remarked: "We are not yet so hard up for men as to want three-legged ones." The assistant looked as though he wished he was at home under his mother's best bed....

July 21 (Thursday)

It was extremely hot in Atlanta and Gen. Hardee's troops were sagging in their tracks as they took a long march of 15 miles south and then east to try and outflank Gen. James B. McPherson's Army of the Tennessee east of the city at Decatur. McPherson, meanwhile, had moved further west towards Atlanta, closing in on Hood. Major Gen. Francis P. Blair, Jr., one of McPherson's commanders, attacked Leggett's Hill successfully, despite valiant efforts by Confederate Gen. Patrick Cleburne's division. Blair had a full view of Atlanta from the top of the hill.

July 22 (Friday)

The Battle of Atlanta took place amid high temperatures that took a terrific toll on the contestants, both North and South. Hardee's corps, after a hot, long, night march, attacked the left flank of McPherson's corps located between Decatur and Atlanta without knowing that two Federal divisions had been moved into this location during the night. Confederate Gen. Cheatham's men fought fiercely, but in vain, on McPherson's front. The overall attack failed, with about 3700 Federal losses from nearly 30,000 engaged. Confederate losses were estimated to be from 7000 to 10,000, out of about 40,000 engaged. This was the second loss of 25 percent that Hood had had. Two tries, two failures. Neither time was he on the field in direct command. Major Gen. James Birdseye McPherson, USA, was killed, as was Major Gen. W.H.T. Walker, CSA. Hardee, again, was selected by Hood as the scapegoat. Union Major Gen. John A. "Blackjack" Logan assumed command of McPherson's Army of the Tennessee.

In the Shenandoah Valley, Federal forces were building up near Winchester, and Early had withdrawn towards Strasburg. Gen. Horatio Wright's Sixth Corps returned to the siege lines at Petersburg. Grant was trying to decide what to do about the Valley.

July 23 (Saturday)

In the Valley, Gen. Jubal Early had turned on Gen. "Black Dave" Hunter unexpectedly, and Early was coming down the Valley from Strasburg towards Kernstown, just south of Winchester. Major Gen. Crook went out to meet Early at Kernstown.

In Georgia, the armies of Sherman and Hood were busy tending the wounded and burying the dead after yesterday's fierce fighting. Little skirmishing was going on around Atlanta.

At Memphis, Union Gen. Andrew Jackson Smith and his troops returned after their engagement at Tupelo with Forrest and S.D. Lee.

July 24 (Sunday)

On the Valley Pike south of Kernstown, Jubal Early was heading north over the same ground that Jackson had fought over in 1862. Gen. John C. Breckinridge commanded on Early's right, with Gen. Ramseur's troops going around to the west to hit the Union right flank. Forcing the center after Breckinridge attacked the Union left, Early caused the Federal line to break and the footrace was on to Harpers Ferry yet again. Federal losses in matériel were high, and the loss in men was about 1200, mostly captured. Early followed at a leisurely pace.

In Georgia, the cleanup of the battlefield after the Battle of Atlanta continued. The wrangling and placement of blame also continued, Hood never being at fault—at least according to J.B. Hood.

July 25 (Monday)

In the Valley, after leaving Kernstown in hot retreat, the Federals got a chance to cool off when a heavy rainstorm began that made the roads a real mess. Early followed Crook's retreating Federals up the Valley Pike to Bunker Hill. Heavy skirmishing took place in the rain at Martinsburg, W. Va., and at Williamsport, Md.

Grant sent two cavalry divisions north of the James River to tear up railroads and make a pest of themselves, hoping to draw off some of Lee's army in pursuit.

In the quest to gain information on the C.S.S. *Albemarle*, Acting Master's Mate John Woodman and three other crewmen made a reconnaissance up the Roanoke River to Plymouth, N.C. Woodman would make three such visits over the next several months. He reported that:

> The town appeared very quiet; very few persons were moving about; I could hear the blacksmiths and carpenters at work in the town near the river...the ram was lying at the wharf near the steam sawmill.

At Mobile Bay, boats from the blockading ships off shore were entering the harbor at night and dismantling the torpedoes which had been installed to prevent the Union fleet from assaulting the harbor defenses. They found that many of the torpedoes were inoperative due to age and exposure to the water.

July 26 (Tuesday)

Sherman had sent Rousseau to destroy the rail link between Montgomery, Ala., and Columbus, Ga., earlier in the month. He now sent Gen. George Stoneman on a similar raid towards Macon, Ga., to destroy the railroads in that area.

In the Valley, Crook had crossed into Maryland, pursued by Early's infantry. Since there were no Federals to interfere, Early set his men to tearing up the Baltimore and Ohio Railroad near Martinsburg, W.Va.

The U.S.S. *Shokokon*, Acting Master Sheldon, was anchored at Turkey Bend on the James River and had placed pickets ashore when the ship was attacked by Confederate sharpshooters. The 710-ton double-ender replied with her naval guns—somewhat like swatting flies with a sledgehammer.

July 27 (Wednesday)

In Georgia, Sherman was setting up the siege of Atlanta and putting his cavalry to work tearing up track. Stoneman had gone to Macon. McCook would raid the Atlanta and West Point railroad to the southwest of the city. Garrard was sent towards South River. Major Gen. John "Blackjack" Logan was relieved of command of the Army of the Tennessee and the command was given to Major Gen. Otis O. Howard, a move very unpopular with some people. Joseph Hooker, currently a corps commander, felt that he outranked Howard and should have received the command, so Hooker resigned.

In the Shenandoah, Early had ripped up enough track to slow things down and now contemplated recrossing the Potomac and going back into Maryland.

At Petersburg, Hancock's large Second Corps, and Sheridan, with two divisions of cavalry, crossed the James and headed towards Richmond. This was a diversionary tactic to bring pressure on Lee and wear down the Confederate troops.

Admiral S.P. Lee sent the tugs *Belle*, *Martin*, and *Hoyt*, which had been fitted as torpedo boats, to Commander Macomb at New Bern, N.C., for use against ironclads in that area. The torpedoes were of the spar variety and were described as:

> This form of torpedo is intended to explode on impact, and to be placed on a pole or rod projecting not less than 15 feet, and if possible 20 feet, beyond the vessel using it. It contains 150 pounds of powder.

Admiral Bailey of the Key West Squadron wrote Secretary Welles about the current epidemic of yellow fever that was ravaging his crews:

> My worst fears have been more than realized, and for more than two months the disease has held its course without abatement and is now as virulent as at any time.... The mortality on the island I am told has reached as high as 12 to 15 in a day.... The squadron is much crippled....

A boat crew commanded by Lt. J.C. Watson, USN, made a daring daylight reconnaissance of the Mobile Bay channel, taking soundings of the outer channel and marking the outer limits of the torpedo field.

July 28 (Thursday)

Now that he had the cavalry running all over the landscape, Sherman sent infantry down the western border of Atlanta to extend his lines. Gen. O.O. Howard had moved from the eastern side of the city to the western and was sent south to disrupt the railroads south of this line. Hood sent Generals Stephen D. Lee and A.P. Stewart to counter Howard's move and they met in a sharp engagement at Ezra Church. Howard was in good defensive positions and easily held off the Confederate attacks, losing only about 600 as opposed to the Confederate losses of an estimated 5000. Hood could not stand losses such as this for a long period of time.

North of the James River, Hancock and Sheridan found that Lee had shifted some forces around and the Confederate lines were stronger than the Federals had believed. The expedition petered out and the Federals returned to their lines at Petersburg.

July 29 (Friday)

The Confederates again entered Maryland and the very tip of Pennsylvania. Jubal Early sent John McCausland across the Potomac west of Williamsport near Cave Spring while another cavalry unit demonstrated against Harpers Ferry. Skirmishing was reported at Hagerstown, Md., and Mercersburg, Pa. Panic again stalked the streets of the North.

At Petersburg, the mining operation for the Battle of the Crater was in progress.

In Georgia, Union cavalry met resistance as they attempted to destroy the railroads at Lovejoy's Station and Smith's Crossroads.

July 30 (Saturday)

For a month, or longer, the men of the 48th Pennsylvania, mostly coal miners, had been digging a tunnel 586 feet long under the siege lines at Petersburg and packed the tunnel with gunpowder. At about 4:45 A.M the powder was exploded, creating a hole 170 feet long, nearly 80 feet wide, and thirty feet deep in the Confederate entrenchments. About 280 Confederate soldiers died, never knowing what happened to them. The Federal assault began immediately thereafter, and by about 8:30 A.M. there were nearly 15,000 Union troops in the cratered area. Confederate Gen. Mahone's troops contained the Federals and around 2 P.M. the Federals pulled back. It cost 4000 Union killed to about 1500 Confederates. That *did not* count the wounded or injured.

During the Battle of the Crater, the 11th Connecticut Volunteer Regiment's Color Guard was decimated when a Rebel shell landed among the Guard. One of the Guard was killed, literally blown to pieces with his brains spattering the flagstaff and the national colors. Six of the other Guards were wounded.

Jubal Early's Confederates entered Chambersburg, Pa., and demanded $500,000 in currency or $100,000 in gold for ransom not to burn the town. The money was not available, so the town was burned and the Confederates moved towards McConnellsburg.

In Georgia, Sherman's cavalry were fighting all over the place—Macon, Clinton, Newnan, and Clear Creek.

A landing party from the U.S.S. *Potomska*, Acting Lt. Robert P. Swann, destroyed two Confederate saltworks on the Back River in Georgia. Coming out, the group was taken under fire by Confederate riflemen on the riverbank. Swann reported:

> Our arms, the Spencer rifles, saved us all from destruction, as the rapidity with which we fired caused the enemy to lie low, and their firing was after the first volley, very wild.... We fought them three-quarters of an hour, some of the time up to our knees in mud, trying to land and capture them, and some of the time in the water with the boats for a breastwork.

July 31 (Sunday)

The Confederate cavalry under McCausland, after burning Chambersburg, Pa., suddenly had to defend themselves against Gen. Averell's cavalry. At Hancock, Md., right over the Potomac from Berkeley Springs, W.Va. (then called Bath), Averell attacked McCausland, who hurriedly left towards Cumberland, Md., to the northwest.

In Georgia, action continued with the Federal cavalry doing the thing they did best—destroying property.

Barber, Cpl., Co. C, 15th Illinois Volunteer Infantry, Kennesaw Mountain, Ga.:

> The bloody battle of Peach Tree Creek, before Atlanta, was fought on the 21st and 22d of July. In that battle the country mourned the loss of one of its most illustrious defenders, the brave and noble McPherson. When his death became known to the army that he commanded, many brave and war-worn heroes wept like children. We loved him with a strong, deep love, a love which was born of his kindness to us and the bravery that he displayed on the field. Ohio might well be proud of him. It is said that Gen. Grant wept when he heard of his death.... The next day McPherson's body passed through Marietta on its way to his home in Ohio.

AUGUST 1864

Gen. Robert E. Lee had lost his mobility. No longer could he rely on movement to surprise the enemy and gain tactical advantage over long distances. Ulysses S. Grant had, in effect, nailed Lee's coattail to Petersburg's fortifications and kept the hammer. In Georgia, Hood was in much the same situation, although he would waste the lives of his men in fruitless attacks believing that he could defeat Sherman's men by sheer force of arms. There was still no light at the end of the tunnel—not yet.

August 1 (Monday)

Gen. Jubal Early's cavalry under McCausland's command had burned Chambersburg, Pa., and had returned to Hancock, Md., across the Potomac from Berkeley Springs, W.Va., pursued by Averell's cavalry, headed towards Cumberland, Md., upriver. McCausland was still in trouble, however, for the Federals were closing in rapidly.

At City Point, Grant had finally decided that a new commander was needed in the Valley, so he sent the one man in whom he had complete faith to do the job—Major Gen. Philip Sheridan. Sheridan was appointed commander of the Army of the Shenandoah and was sent to Harpers Ferry by the first train. His task was to rid the Valley of Jubal Early's threat once and for all.

Day, Pvt., Co. B, 25th Massachusetts Volunteer Infantry, 18th Corps Hospital, Point of Rocks, Va.:

> The ward next me on the left is a colored one, and contains from 60 to 80 men, according to recruits and drafts. Until recently they have been pretty much on their own hook, no one seeming to care for them. Some days ago Doctor Sadler asked me if I would take charge of them. I said I should like to do anything where I could be of use. He gave me my instructions and some blank reports and set me up in business. My duties are to attend roll-calls, surgeon's calls, keep an account of arrivals, discharges, desertions, deaths, march them up to the kitchen three times a day for rations and make my report to him every morning. Entering on the discharge of my duties, the first thing I did was to set them to work cleaning and fixing up their quarters so they would be more comfortable.
>
> A couple of hours' work showed a great improvement in the condition of things and while it was being done it gave me a chance to find out who among them were the worst off and need the most care and favors. A sick nigger is a curious institution and you can't tell so well about him as you can about a sick mule. He can put on the sickest look of anything I ever saw and appear as though he would die in seven minutes, but a nigger is never really sick but once, and is then sure to die. There is no more help for one than there is for a sick pig. I have three that are sick and I have no more faith in their getting well than I have that Gen. Lee will drive Gen. Grant from before Petersburg. Two of them are now unable to attend the surgeon's call in the morning and the other I expect will be in a few days. I have about 40 hobbling around with canes, spavined, ring-boned and foundered. The others are simply a little war-worn and tired.
>
> The kitchen is about 30 rods from the camp, and when I march them up there, there are so many lame ones they straggle the whole distance. Doctor Sadler called my attention to this and said he should like to see them march in a little better order. I replied: "Surgeon, come out in the morning and see the parade; you will see them marching a 28 inch step and closed up to 18 inches from stem to stern." He promised he would. The next morning at breakfast call I formed every one of those darkies that carried canes on the right, and the lamest I put at the head of the column, and gave them a send-off. It was a comical show, they marched at the rate of about one mile an hour, and those in the rear kept calling out to those in advance: "Why don ye goo long dar! Hurry up dar; shan get breakfas' fo' noon." They kept closed up better than they kept the step as the rear crowded the advance to push them along. We were cheered along the route as almost everybody was out to see the fun. We marched in review before the doctor and by the way he laughed and shook himself I thought he was well satisfied with the parade, at any rate he complimented me on my success when I carried in my morning report....

In Georgia, Sherman's artillery started warming up on the Confederates in Atlanta as the siege got off to a good start.

A Savannah newspaper published a notice from a Col. Gaulden, CSA, that a meeting was to be held at McIntosh C.H., Ga., for the organization of a coastal guard unit on August 2, 1864. A copy of this newspaper was read with much interest by Commander George M. Colvocoresses, U.S.S. *Saratoga*, who decided to attend the meeting. At night on Monday (August 1st) Colvocoresses led a party of 115 officers and men ashore, where they concealed the boats, went inland for a distance, and secreted themselves until the following day.

August 2 (Tuesday)

Back at Hancock, Md., Early's cavalry commander, McCausland, skirmished again with Averell's Federal cavalry as space for the Rebels to move got tighter.

At City Point, Va., the siege of Petersburg went on (and on). The buildup of troops, etc., was only a small part of the problem. As always, logistics was the key to success. Grant had developed extensive wharves, warehouses, and ammunition dumps at City Point to supply the Army. Huge bakeries were built to bake fresh bread for the troops and an intricate railway system was put in to deliver the supplies and matériel of war to the siege lines. The complex was far more than the South had any capability of providing at any point during the war. Those hated Yankee "mechanics and mudsills" knew how to support a war.

Today was the day of the scheduled meeting for the organization of the coastal guard unit at McIntosh C.H., Ga. When the meeting was called to order that evening, Commander Colvocoresses and 115 members of the crew of the U.S.S. *Saratoga* attended, after setting fire to the only bridge that could bring troops into the town. Colvocoresses then read to the meeting from the newspaper the order of Col. Gaulden, CSA, for their assembling, and regretting that the Colonel had failed to attend, he invited the entire meeting to go with him. All left and went to the place where the boats had been secreted.

In November 1863, the Confederacy purchased a steamer from the British, using private agents, which was later named the C.S.S. *Rappahannock*, and intended to be a commerce raider similar to the C.S.S. *Alabama*. Thinking the British might tie her up with red tape to prevent her release from port, the ship was run out of port at Sheerness into the English Channel on November 24, 1863, where she was joined by her officers and crew. She was scheduled to meet with the C.S.S. *Georgia* off the French coast, where she would take on guns and provisions and then head for the open seas. Unfortunately, going down channel she burned out the bearings on the main driveshafts and had to put into Calais, France, for repairs. The French then became intransigent about her leaving port and she idled for months at Calais. Finally, Flag Officer Barron, the senior Confederate naval representative in France, decided that the *Rappahannock* would never leave port, after he received a letter from the captain, Lt. Charles M. Faunteroy, to the effect that the latter had only 35 crew members and could not sail without more men. Barron replied:

> I agree with you in the absolute impossibility of navigating the ship with so small a complement as thirty-five, including yourself and officers. You will therefore proceed to pay off and discharge your officers and crew, keeping sufficient officers and men to look after the public property, and lay up the ship until we determine upon what course we shall pursue in regard to her.

August 3 (Wednesday)

Confederate Gen. McCausland was back across the Potomac with his cavalry force, and was with Gen. Early's command. Lincoln, very unhappy with the events in the Shenandoah Valley, told Grant that something had to be done immediately.

Commander George M. Colvocoresses and his guests from McIntosh C.H., Ga., arrived on board the U.S.S. *Saratoga*, where the 26 potential members of the coastal guard unit were provided accommodations and given an opportunity to reflect upon their future duties of guarding the coast. Col. Gaulden, CSA, who had organized the meeting, but did not attend and therefore missed his opportunity to be a guest of the United States Navy, published a letter in the Savannah *Republican* in which he regretted not being present when the Commander called, but

> as the Captain seems to be a reader of your paper, I take this opportunity to make my compliments to him and say that when he calls to see me again I shall be at home, and will try and give him a more respectful reception.

In preparation for the assault on Mobile Bay,

Federal Army troops landed on Dauphin Island and laid siege to Ft. Gaines, one of the forts guarding the entrance to the bay.

At Mobile Bay, Admiral Farragut was impatient to get on with the battle. Capt. Jenkins, the senior officer at Pensacola, received two letters from the Mobile area. The first, from Farragut's Fleet Captain, Percival Drayton, urgently requested that the ironclad monitor *Tecumseh* be sent to Mobile as soon as possible:

> If you can get the *Tecumseh* out to-morrow, do so; otherwise I am pretty certain that the admiral won't wait for her. Indeed, I think a very little persuasion would have taken him in to-day, and less to-morrow. The army are to land at once, and the admiral does not want to be thought remiss.

Farragut followed that with his own letter:

> I can lose no more days. I must go in day after to-morrow morning at daylight or a little after. It is a bad time, but when you do not take fortune at her offer you must take her as you can find her.

To further clear the entrance to Mobile Bay, Lt. J.C. Watson continued taking a boat crew into the bay at night under the guns of Confederate Ft. Morgan to deactivate and sink the Confederate torpedoes in the channel.

August 5 (Friday)

At long last, the battle for Mobile Bay was at hand. At about 6 A.M., Admiral Farragut took 18 ships, including four monitors, against the defenses of the Bay. The monitors *Tecumseh, Manhattan, Winnebago*, and *Chickasaw* were in column on the right side to take the brunt of the guns from Ft. Morgan, which they had to pass at close range. The smaller wooden ships were lashed to the port side of the larger wooden steamers, as was done during the passage of Port Hudson on the Mississippi.

A few minutes before 7 A.M., the guns of the *Tecumseh* opened fire on the fort and the firing became general. Admiral Buchanan, CSN, brought out the four Confederate ships to join battle. The heavy ram C.S.S. *Tennessee* with six large guns, the *Gaines* and *Morgan* with six smaller guns each, and the *Selma* with four guns, all hurried to engage the Union fleet. Commander Craven on the *Tecumseh* steered directly for the *Tennessee* to engage her, when the *Tecumseh* struck a torpedo and sank in seconds, losing 90 of the 114 men aboard, including the captain.

The heavy wooden steamer *Brooklyn* was to the left of the *Tecumseh* when the latter hit the torpedo, and the former started backing water to avoid the torpedoes, throwing the entire line of wooden ships into confusion. Farragut, lashed to the rigging of the *Hartford*, ordered: "Damn the torpedoes! Full speed ahead, Drayton! Hard astarboard; ring four bells! Eight bells! Sixteen bells!" The *Hartford* swept past the *Brooklyn* directly into the torpedoes, which were heard bumping along the hull of the ship, but none exploded. The Union fleet was into the Bay and headed for the Confederate ironclads.

The ram *Tennessee* tried unsuccessfully to ram *Hartford* and the ships became intermingled with each captain picking his own targets. Within a short time, the *Tennessee* was the only Rebel ship still fighting, the others either ran aground, were in a sinking condition, or surrendered. All of the Union ships then attacked the *Tennessee* by ramming, firing their guns, or anything else that they thought might be effective. Eventually, the damage was such that the *Tennessee* could no longer move, so the white flag was raised at about 10 A.M., and the naval part of the battle was over.

That afternoon, the ironclad *Chickasaw* fired into the rear of Ft. Powell at a range of 400 yards and compelled the evacuation of the fort, which was blown up that night. The remaining Confederate facilities in the bay area would be evacuated. The last major port on the Gulf coast was closed.

On the Potomac, Confederate forces once again crossed into Maryland, with skirmishing all around the area.

August 6 (Saturday)

Sherman was trying to cut the railroads south of Atlanta with his advance on Utoy Creek, where heavy fighting flared for the third day. The Federals finally outflanked the Confederate line, forcing the Southerners to fall back.

On the Potomac, Early's men were south of the river again, but things were due to change. Sheridan was coming to the Valley.

The C.S.S. *Albemarle* left Plymouth, N.C., and appeared at the mouth of the Roanoke River at about 4 A.M., and then stopped. Commander Harrell, U.S.S. *Chicopee*, reported:

> ...The ram made its appearance this morning at a few minutes before 4 A.M. It advanced as far as the mouth of the river and halted.... From the number of people in sight on the beach, no doubt it was expected that an engagement would ensue.... The ram is now lying in the river blowing off steam. I do not think, however, that she will advance. Should she do so, however, I will endeavor to draw her down towards the fleet. I shall now pay my respects to those gentlemen on the beach in the shape of a few shells.

At Wilmington, N.C., the C.S.S. *Tallahassee*, Commander John Taylor Wood, ran past the blockading fleet and went north to begin a raid on Northern commercial ships, destroying 30 ships in two weeks.

August 7 (Sunday)

Col. Charles D. Anderson, CSA, commander of Ft. Gaines at Mobile Bay, had been visited by the U.S.S. *Chickasaw* with a little bombardment yesterday. Today he proposed surrender to Admiral Farragut:

> Feeling my inability to maintain my present position longer than you may see fit to open upon me with your fleet, and feeling also the uselessness of entailing upon ourselves further destruction of life, I have the honor to propose the surrender of Fort Gaines, its garrison, stores, etc.

Major Gen. Philip H. Sheridan, at Halltown, Va., was assigned command of the new Middle Military Division, which included Washington, the Susquehanna, and West Virginia. His first, and main, task was to get Early out of the Valley.

August 8 (Monday)

At ten A.M., the Union flag was flying over Ft. Gaines, Mobile Bay, following the surrender of its garrison by Col. Charles D. Anderson, CSA.

At Atlanta, Gen. John Bell Hood was trying to fix the blame for everything that went wrong on Gen. William Hardee. Hood had problems relating to everyone.

August 9 (Tuesday)

Ft. Morgan at Mobile Bay had not surrendered, when Forts Powell and Gaines struck their colors. Brig. Gen. Richard L. Page, once a U.S. naval officer and more recently a Commander in the Confederate Navy, refused to surrender Ft. Morgan until he had no means of resistance. The Union army troops in the area prepared for a land assault and the naval ships under Farragut went into position to bombard the fort. The ships included the former Confederate ram *Tennessee*, which was towed into position so her guns could bear on the fort, and the bombardment began. At the end of the day, the *Tennessee* was towed back to her anchorage.

Richard Lucien Page was born in Clarke County, Va., on December 20, 1807. He became a midshipman in the U.S. Navy in 1824 and served all over the world, serving three years as ordnance officer at the Norfolk Navy Yard. He was friends with many of the other officers in the Navy, including Farragut and Dahlgren. When the war started, he resigned and returned to his native Virginia, where he was appointed as Commander and ordnance officer at Norfolk. He was promoted to Captain and later appointed as a Brigadier General and assigned to command the defenses of Mobile Bay. Refusing to surrender Ft. Morgan, the defenders withstood a two-week siege before being forced to surrender. Page was taken prisoner and held at Ft. Delaware until July 24, 1865. He returned to Norfolk, where he eventually became superintendent of schools. He died in Pennsylvania on August 9, 1901.

At City Point, Va., two Confederate members of the Torpedo Corps, John Maxwell and R.K. Dillard, carried a box through the Union sentry lines and down to the wharf, where dozens of Union ships were unloading supplies. Convincing a dock sentry that the box was to be delivered to the captain of an ammunition barge, they left the box on board and hurried out of the area. The box contained a clock mechanism and twelve pounds of gunpowder. When it exploded an hour later, it set off a chain reaction that blew pieces everywhere. Grant, back at City Point after his trip to Washington, wired Halleck:

> Five minutes ago an ordnance boat exploded, carrying lumber, grape, canister, and all kinds of shot over this point. Every part of the yard used as my headquarters is filled with splinters and fragments of shell.

At Halltown, Sheridan was organizing his staff and getting ready to begin his push towards Winchester. He would have another problem—Mosby was becoming more active.

In his effort to get south of Atlanta, Sherman gave his troops a breather from the extreme heat.

August 10 (Wednesday)

The soldiers and sailors stationed in Virginia's Tidewater region were constantly plagued by disease during the summer The cause of malaria was not then understood. The crews of the ironclads were especially vulnerable to sickness because of the heat inside the iron-covered vessels and the ships' poor ventilation. As an example, Flag Officer Mitchell, commanding the Confederate James River Squadron, wired Major Gen. George E. Pickett, area defense commander:

> Our crews are so much reduced in number from sickness that we shall have to discontinue our picket guard as Osborne's on James River to enable us to man our batteries, in order that we may act against the enemy. About one-third of the men are sick.

In the South, Confederate cavalry leader Joseph Wheeler left on a month-long raid against Sherman's supply lines in eastern Tennessee and north Georgia. Sherman's men got into a stiff scrap near Lovejoy's Station at Atlanta.

Jackman, Pvt., "The Orphan Brigade," in hospital, Macon, Ga.:

> The hospitals being broken up at Newman with other sick to be transferred to Macon, Ga., I took train for Atlanta at 10 o'clock A.M. During the afternoon we got to East Point, 7 miles from Atlanta, where the Macon and Western road branches off and had to lie over until dark. The brigade hospital being at East Point, I saw Dr. B. and several of the boys from regiment. The sharpshooters were "banging away" not very far off and the cannon were thundering and the shells crashing through the woods—all of which reminded me of old times. The train was very much crowded with wounded and sick and having learned our baggage was stored at Griffin, I got off the train at that place to get mine. I slept until morning on a pile of crossties. Got my baggage and took the nine o'clock train—passenger—for Macon where arrived at 1 P.M.
>
> That evening, J.L., first sergeant of company "B" and I went out to the Fair Grounds hospital 2 miles from depot on edge of Vineville which is a part of Macon. We were transported out in a wagon. The hospital was in tents and being crowded we had to take a tent without any beds in it. Our food was "awful." A day or two after, Dr. Fox of Ky., the steward, moved us into another ward.... I could now walk about considerably and Jimmie L. and I every evening took a walk through Vineville and sometimes as far as Macon....

Barber, Cpl., Co. C, 15th Illinois Volunteer Infantry, Ackworth, Ga.:

> We began to be very much annoyed now by scouting parties of rebel cavalry who would attack our forage trains and make raids upon the railroads. We were constantly kept on the move chasing them. Finally, we were ordered to Ackworth, a small village fourteen miles from Marietta, for scouting and picket duty. We took three days' rations. After scouring the country awhile, we returned, but had not been in camp twenty-four hours before we were ordered to return, prepared to stay a week or so. No sooner had we left before, than a band of rebel cavalry made a dash at the place and tore up some of the railroad track. We went back and took up our quarters in some of the vacant houses and established our picket line. One day a Union citizen came in and reported a large force of the enemy out about twenty-five miles.

August 11 (Thursday)

Gen. Jubal Early, faced with Sheridan's advance up the Valley, left Winchester and went towards Cedar Creek. Sheridan, using "Black Dave" Hunter's old troops, was not fully confident of them as yet, since they had no history of victory.

Having escaped from Wilmington, N.C., the C.S.S. *Tallahassee*, Commander John Taylor Wood, captured seven ships within 80 miles of Sandy Hook, N.J. All the ships were scuttled and burned except one, the *Carrol*, which was bonded and loaded with the passengers and crews from the other six ships and sent back to New York. Admiral Hiram Paulding at New York immediately wired Secretary Welles: "Pirate off Sandy Hook, capturing and burning." Within a few hours, three ships were out from New York looking for the raider and Welles had notified the Navy facilities at Hampton Roads, Philadelphia, and Boston to send more ships to catch the raider.

August 12 (Friday)

Off Sandy Hook, N.J., where the ships coming from New York Harbor entered the Atlantic, the Confederate raider C.S.S. *Tallahassee*, Commander John Taylor Wood, took six more ships, mostly loaded with lumber, and sent the crews and passengers back to New York on two of them, the *Suliote* and *Robert E. Packer*. He was about to become the hunted, rather than the hunter.

At Mobile Bay, the captured C.S.S. *Tennessee*, now manned by a Union crew, got up steam for the first time since her capture and the replacement of her smokestack.

August 13 (Saturday)

At Berryville, in the Shenandoah Valley, fighting erupted between Sheridan's Federals and Early's Rebel forces, as Sheridan moved up the Valley towards Cedar Creek.

The former C.S.S. *Tennessee*, now a Union gunboat, steamed down Mobile Bay to take her station for the bombardment of Ft. Morgan, which still had not surrendered.

Off New York, Commander John Taylor Wood captured and burned two more ships today, one loaded with coal. Meanwhile, the Board of Underwriters in New York was in a panic and demanding that Secretary Welles do *something* to counter this threat. Welles replied that all available ships were out in search for the raider.

August 15 (Monday)

The intrepid Commander John Taylor Wood, C.S.S. *Tallahassee*, had moved operations to the New England coast, capturing six more ships, of which five were burned and the remaining one loaded with the crews and passengers of the others, bonded, and sent to port.

In the Shenandoah Valley, Sheridan withdrew from Early's front at Cedar Creek, and headed back towards Winchester. For the time being he was giving up his advance until he could get his logistics worked out.

In Georgia, Sherman's force moved slowly to the southeast below Atlanta and the railroads. Fighting flared at Peachtree Road and other points. Joe Wheeler's Confederate cavalry raided the Union supply line on the railroads in Tennessee.

August 16 (Tuesday)

Commander John Taylor Wood, C.S.S. *Tallahassee*, captured and burned five more United States merchantmen off the coast of New England.

Commander Colvocoresses, U.S.S. *Saratoga*, returned to McIntosh C.H., Ga., with another raiding party, where he captured 100 prisoners, a quantity of small arms, and destroyed a saltworks and a bridge over the South Newport River on the main road to Savannah .

Grant's Federals were demonstrating towards Richmond again, creating noise and confusion, little else. Sheridan had pulled back from Early without detection, heading for Winchester.

August 17 (Wednesday)

On the James River below Richmond, Gen. Lee requested Confederate naval gunboat support to drive the Federals off Signal Hill, where they were entrenching. Lee wanted the hill for his own pickets. The ironclads C.S.S. *Virginia II*, Lt. Johnson, and C.S.S. *Richmond*, Lt. J.S. Maury, took the hill under fire and drove the Union troops off.

In the Valley, Early came out of his entrenchments and headed north towards Winchester. Sheridan's cavalry held the Confederates at Winchester, keeping Early from the main Confederate column.

The C.S.S. *Tallahassee*, Commander John Taylor Wood, was running short of coal, so she headed for Halifax, Nova Scotia, hoping to get coal at that place. En route, she captured and destroyed the schooners *North America* and *Josiah Achom* and released the brig *Neva* on bond.

August 18 (Thursday)

In the Valley, Sheridan moved further north towards the Potomac and Charles Town, W.Va., Gen. Early following towards Bunker Hill.

At Atlanta, Gen. Judson Kilpatrick began his four-day raid on Lovejoy's Station south of the city to destroy the Macon and Western Railroad. This raid would largely fail due to Confederate resistance. Schofield moved again against the Rebels at Utoy

Creek in another attempt to get south and east of Atlanta.

The Confederates were finding it impossible to cross the Mississippi with any large number of reinforcements from the Trans-Mississippi area. Gen. Richard Taylor, CSA, wrote Gen. E. Kirby Smith, CSA, of the difficulty:

> I have dispatched the War Department to the effect that I consider the crossing of any considerable body of troops impossible. Accurate observations have been made of the enemy's gunboats between Red River and Vicksburg, and from the strictness of the guard maintained no success can be anticipated.

At Halifax, Nova Scotia, the C.S.S. *Tallahassee* arrived and Commander Wood immediately requested recoaling. The U.S. Consul in Halifax wired Secretary Welles of the arrival and protested to the local authorities about the refueling. The Lieutenant Governor at Halifax refused to stop or interfere with the *Tallahassee*, allowing the refueling to continue. Meanwhile, Welles wired Lt. Commander George A. Stevens, U.S.S. *Pontoosuc*, which had just put into Eastport, Me., to continue to Halifax with all possible speed. Relenting somewhat, the Lieutenant Governor at Halifax told Commander Wood he could not load more than 100 tons of coal at that port.

In the Petersburg lines, Warren's Fifth Corps moved to the left flank of the Federal lines and occupied more than a mile of the railroad going to Weldon, N.C., which was one of the vital supply links for Richmond. Warren, after getting astride the railroad, turned towards Petersburg, fighting his way through densely wooded areas in a heavy rain. Confederate Gen. Henry Heth's division pressured the Federals enough to cause a halt for the night, at least.

In Richmond the sound of the guns could be distinctly heard both from the east and the south but their meaning was unclear.

August 19 (Friday)

South of Petersburg, things were quiet along the Weldon railroad (which Warren's Fifth Corps had taken yesterday) until late afternoon, when Confederate Gen. A.P. Hill's corps piled into the Yankees with a ferocious assault that drove the Federals back, but not off the railroad. Warren's troops held, but lost over 2500 captured, mostly from one division.

Gen. Jubal Early tried to advance against Sheridan on the Winchester Pike, but made little progress. Sherman, around Atlanta, was still pushing to take the railroad south of the city and to cut that supply line.

At Halifax, Nova Scotia, the C.S.S. *Tallahassee* finished loading coal—120 tons, 20 more than that authorized by the Lieutenant Governor—and sailed after dark.

August 20 (Saturday)

Gen. Judson Kilpatrick's cavalry were on the Macon and Western Railroad at Lovejoy's Station in Georgia smashing things and tearing up track.

Sheridan and Early were doing their "Virginia reel" out in the Valley, sparring around Berryville, Opequon Creek, and other points. At Petersburg, Warren and his Fifth Corps still held the Weldon Railroad south of the city.

Day, Pvt., Co. B, 25th Massachusetts Volunteer Infantry, 18th Corps Hospital, Point of Rocks, Va.:

> I have read a great deal in the papers of the Christian and Sanitary commissions, of the noble and humane work they were doing and the immense amount of money contributed for their support by the people throughout the north and west. I have taken a great interest in these commissions and have supposed they were a kind of auxiliary to the medical and surgical department of the army, carrying and dispensing some simple medicines, pouring in the balm of gilead and binding up gaping wounds, giving comfort and consolation to the sick, weary and distressed; but in all this, so far as my observation has gone, I find I have been laboring under a delusion.
>
> Since I have been here is the first I have ever seen of the workings of these commissions, and I have watched them with some interest and taken some pains to find out about them. Here is a branch of each located midway the convalescent camp and sick hospital and I find they are little else than sutler's shops, and poor ones at that. These places are said to furnish without money and without price to the inmates of this hospital and the boys in the trenches such little notions and necessities as we have been accustomed to buy of the sutlers, and in consequence of this no sutlers are allowed to locate anywhere in this vicinity. The boys are not supposed to be fooling

away their money to these thieving sutlers when our folks at home are willing to supply our little needs, free gratis for nothing. So when we happen to want a lemon or a pencil, a sheet of paper or a piece of tobacco, or whatever other little notion we require, all we have to do is to apply to one or the other commission and make known our wants; after answering all the questions they are pleased to ask, we are given a slice of lemon, a half sheet of paper, or a chew of tobacco. These are not wholesale establishments.

Fortunately for me I have stood in very little need of anything within their gift. I seldom solicit any favors and those are granted so grudgingly I almost despise the gift.... This is the first place I ever got into where I could neither buy, steal nor beg. I notice the officers fare a little better; they get in fair quantity almost anything they call for.... Sometimes a person calling for an article will be told they are out of it, but expect some when the team come up from the Point. In a little while after perhaps some officer will call for the same thing and get it....

The U.S.S. *Pontoosuc*, Lt. Commander Stevens, entered Halifax harbor looking for the C.S.S. *Tallahassee*, only to find that she had sailed the night before. Stevens had missed her by only seven hours. The U.S. Consul Jackson, at Halifax, told Stevens that he thought the raider was going into the Gulf of St. Lawrence to the north, so Stevens took off in pursuit. Meanwhile, the *Tallahassee* went back south, headed for Wilmington, N.C. En route, she captured and burned the brig *Roan*. This was to be her last prize in her short raiding cruise.

August 21 (Sunday)

There were many red faces in Memphis when Gen. Nathan Bedford Forrest and two thousand of his cavalry entered the city in the early-morning hours and nearly captured Federal Generals Hurlbut and Washburn in their beds. The Confederates held the city for a while and then left, going back to the countryside where they could roam freely, having no Federal opposition.

In the area of Harpers Ferry, Sheridan pulled back to Halltown and dug into good defensive positions, which Early refused to assault—a stalemate for a time.

South of Petersburg, Warren still held the Weldon Railroad despite the efforts of A.P. Hill's Confederates to dislodge the Federals. In extreme heat and occasional rain, the Rebels assaulted the Union lines heavily, but were repulsed. The rail link to Petersburg and Richmond was lost, and Lee knew it. In four days the Federals had suffered about 4500 casualties (mostly captured) out of about 20,000 engaged. Lee's losses were about 1600 out of 14,000. Grant could afford the loss, Lee couldn't, and things would only get worse. Grant, on the 18th, had again refused to exchange prisoners, believing that such an exchange would help the South in two ways: It would gain them fighting men, and it would relieve them of feeding Union prisoners.

August 23 (Tuesday)

Ft. Morgan, the last bastion at Mobile Bay, surrendered today after two weeks of heavy naval bombardment. The commander, Brigadier Gen. Page, recorded:

> My guns and powder had all been destroyed, my means of defense gone, the citadel, nearly the entire quartermaster stores, and a portion of the commissariat burned by the enemy's shells, it was evident the fort could hold out but a few hours longer under a renewed bombardment. The only question was: Hold it for this time, gain the eclat, and sustain the loss of life from the falling of the walls, or save life and capitulate?

In Georgia, the daring Commander George Colvocoresses, U.S.S. *Saratoga*, took another boat expedition ashore to capture an encampment at Bethel, Ga., near Savannah. This time the Confederates were alerted and fled.

South of Petersburg, Warren's Fifth Corps of infantry turned into destroyers of railroads as the Weldon Railroad was dismantled almost completely. There was some action by the Confederates on the road to Dinwiddie C.H., but little interference with the Federals' railroad destruction process.

August 25 (Thursday)

Commander John Taylor Wood, commander of the C.S.S. *Tallahassee*, and one of the most daring and lucky of the Confederate commanders, eluded the blockading squadron at Wilmington, N.C., and returned to his home port. On his most recent cruise, he had taken 31 U.S. commercial ships, destroying all but eight of them. His latest foray had caused intensified interest in the capture of the remaining Confederate raiders. Secretary Welles notified all naval activities to immediately report any intelligence which might bear on the raider's location.

In the Valley, Sheridan sat in his fortifications at Halltown while Early reentered Maryland at Williamsport and moved a force towards Shepherdstown.

In Georgia, Sherman began his advance to isolate Atlanta completely. He sent his blue columns to cut off the area south and east along the south side of the city towards Jonesborough.

Barber, Cpl., Co. C, 15th Illinois Volunteer Infantry, Ackworth, Ga.:

> Word was sent to Marietta, and Col. Logan, with the 32d Illinois, and Col. Rogers, with his command started out. They were to form a junction, about twenty miles out and attempt to surprise and capture the enemy, but, in an enemy's country, it was almost impossible to do it. They got word of our approach and hastily decamped. The forces joined about midnight. We had marched twenty miles since sundown without rest. We now started back for Marietta....
>
> We arrived at Marietta the next day about five o'clock P.M. having traveled fifty miles, without rest, through the scorching rays of an August sun. We were completely fagged out.... Hardly was our supper dispatched before an order came for us to get ready to march immediately, in light marching order, with three days' rations.... It was some relief to find out that we were to take the cars. The rebel, Gen. Forrest, had made a raid on the railroad near Dalton and was trying to capture that place. We were hurried forward to re-inforce it, but the next morning, when we arrived at Resaca, we learned that Forrest had been repulsed and was now making his way back. Our command of about three thousand was sent out to cut off his retreat. We marched rapidly until we arrived at the ford where we hoped to intercept him, but found that we were too late.... I came near being overpowered by the heat...a good supper and a bath in the river near by made a new man of me. At five o'clock the order came to countermarch.... We arrived in camp about two o'clock A.M. It is needless to say that we were in a condition to enjoy a good sleep. In thirty hours we had traveled fifty miles.
>
> Instead of going back to Marietta, as we anticipated, our regiment was ordered to halt at Ackworth and remain and garrison the place.... Our regiment was scattered along the railroad, Companies A and B at Big Shanty, D at Moon Station and C, K and E at Ackworth.... We converted the depot into a kind of fortress and barricaded the brick houses.... There were not two days in a week but what some of us were out on a scout. We usually marched thirty miles per day.... Scarcely a night passed but what attempts were made to tear up the track or a picket post was attacked. The country was alive with swarming bands of rebel cavalry, bent on mischief.
>
> One day while out scouting, a party of rebels came within one-half mile of camp and threw a train off the track by means of a shoe which the rebs had invented for the purpose. This shoe was made to fit the rail and as the wheel ran onto it, it ran off. It was a simple and ingenious contrivance and was much safer and easier than to try to tear up the track. We took possession of this shoe. This trick of the rebels causes us a great deal of trouble. We had to place our videttes so closely together that they could see the whole railroad.
>
> How we boys longed to get to the front. Most anything was more tolerable than this harassing life. We had only six hundred men to guard thirty miles of railroad which was lined with rebel scouting parties. Our boys at the front had now reached the goal of their ambition. Our flag now waved over the "Gate City of the South" and the rebel army, with ranks broken, was flying before our victorious army. By a bold flank movement, Sherman had marched to the rear of Atlanta and the enemy came out and met him at Jonesboro, thirty-five miles south of the city and they were utterly routed and scattered.... Gen. Hood gathered together what he could of his broken and disorganized army and halted at Newman, a place fifty miles to the west of Atlanta.... I was now detailed as color-bearer, but never had the opportunity to take my place.

South of Petersburg in the vicinity of Reams' Station, Va., Confederate A.P. Hill again attacked Warren's Fifth Corps with a reinforced corps. About 2000 Federals were captured, but little else was gained. Hill returned to the Confederate lines, Warren continued tearing up railroad.

August 27 (Saturday)

At Atlanta, Sherman was nearly ready to cut the final link into the city. Hood had not been able to provide much resistance to Sherman's buildup.

Admiral David Farragut at Mobile Bay was tired. He wrote Secretary of the Navy Welles asking to be relieved of his command:

> It is evident that the army has no men to spare for this place beyond those sufficient to keep up an alarm, and thereby make a diversion in favor of Gen. Sherman.... Now, I dislike to make a show of attack unless I can do something more than make a menace, but so long as I am able I am willing to do the bidding of the Department to the best of my abilities. I fear, however, my health is giving way. I have been down in this Gulf and the Caribbean Sea nearly five years out of six, with the exception of the short time at home last fall, and the last six months have been a severe drag on me, and I want rest, if it is to be had.

In October, Admiral Farragut would go north for a well-earned leave from his duties.

At Masonboro Inlet, N.C., a Union naval landing party went ashore and captured a quantity of rifles, ammunition, and provisions. The party was led by Acting Lt. Joseph B. Breck, U.S.S. *Niphon*, with crews from his ship and the U.S.S. *Monticello*, Acting Master Henry A. Phelon.

August 28 (Sunday)

Sherman was on the move around Atlanta. Major Gen. George Thomas's Army of the Cumberland reached the Atlanta and West Point Railroad at Red Oak, where some fighting occurred. Otis O. Howard's Army of the Tennessee was on the same railroad near Fairburn, and Schofield's Army of the Ohio was at nearby Mt. Gilead Church. Major Gen. H.W. Slocum manned the Union lines immediately around Atlanta. The city was almost sealed off.

In the Valley, Sheridan came out of his fortifications at Halltown and advanced towards Charles Town, W.Va., with light skirmishing.

August 30 (Tuesday)

The Democratic Convention meeting in Chicago today named former Major Gen. George B. McClellan as their choice for President, with Thomas H. Seymour, former governor of Connecticut, as Vice-President. The platform was essentially a "peace" platform.

The West Point-Atlanta rail link went by the boards today when Sherman's bluecoats occupied the line and continued their advance towards Jonesborough. Only the Atlanta-Macon rail link remained. Hood, trying to stop Sherman, sent Patrick Cleburne with Hood's old corps and the corps of S.D. Lee to head Sherman off before he got to Jonesborough—a futile exercise. Although Sherman's armies were separated, the combined strength of Cleburne and Lee could not successfully assail either of the Union armies.

In the Valley, Sheridan replaced "Black Dave" Hunter with Crook as the major commander in West Virginia. Sheridan then shifted his own advance towards Berryville and the Valley Pike.

August 31 (Wednesday)

George B. McClellan was formally nominated as Democratic Presidential candidate in Chicago, receiving 174 votes, the majority. The Ohio Copperhead, Clement L. Vallandigham, who had been expelled through the Union lines at Murfreesboro, Tenn., was back and attending the convention. He moved that the nomination of McClellan be made unanimous.

In the Valley, there was skirmishing around Martinsburg, W.Va., and on the Winchester Pike.

In the vicinity of Atlanta, Schofield's Army of the Ohio cut the last rail link to Atlanta when the Macon-Atlanta line was crossed between Jonesborough and Atlanta. Hood had sent Hardee to attack Otis O. Howard's Army of the Tennessee near Jonesborough. The Confederate attack was not pressed vigorously, and failed, the Southern losses heavy. With most of the Confederates south of the city trying to keep the rail lines open, Sherman told Slocum to try and enter the city, if possible.

Before entering the campaign, Sherman had organized and trained construction units that could lay track and build bridges almost as fast as they could be destroyed. Enormous stocks of rails, cars, engines, and other equipment were available to him in Tennessee to ensure that his rail link was maintained.

SEPTEMBER 1864

The presidential ballot was becoming crowded in the North. Lincoln, McClellan, and Frémont were all contesting for the privilege of serving. In the southeast around Atlanta there was little doubt that

Sherman would take the city before long. Hood's tactics of constant attack had decimated his own Confederate Army of Tennessee to a mere shadow of what it had been under Joe Johnston. That, plus the infighting between Hood and Hardee, created an unhealthy atmosphere. On the James River, Grant still held Lee immobile, and Grant gave no indication of letting go any time soon. Richmond's food supply was getting lower and prices were getting higher. In the North, abundant crops promised no lack of provisions for the Union Army.

September 1 (Thursday)

At the beginning of the war, the Southern plan for mounting its cavalry was for each man to supply his own mount. If the horse were killed, or otherwise lost, the soldier was given a thirty-day furlough to go home and get another horse. This had some obvious drawbacks, as pointed out by Maj. E.H. Ewing, Inspector of Field Transportation for the Confederate Army in the West:

> The policy adopted at the beginning of the war by the Government of making cavalrymen mount themselves is, in my opinion, the most extravagant to the Government, and has done more to demoralize the troops of this branch of the service than any other cause. When a soldier is dismounted...he is entitled to a furlough of thirty days to go home and remount himself. This makes every cavalry soldier, or at least all that desire to be, mere horse traders, selling their animals whenever they desire to go home. Many even go further than this; they steal every animal whether public or private, when it can be done with any show of success in retaining him for a few days, until they can sell or swap him. Some stations through which the army has passed have in this way been entirely swept of animals, thereby taking from the people their only means of support....

Atlanta was being evacuated and the munitions dumps and railroad yards were blown up by Hood's retreating Confederates. Fires broke out in the area of the explosions and little was done to extinguish them in the hurry to escape. Hood had failed gloriously in his task of holding the largest rail terminal in the South.

Meanwhile, Confederate general S.D. Lee's corps had been started back towards Atlanta and then held up by Hood at Rough and Ready. Hardee's corps was going against Howard's army and elements from both Thomas's army and Schofield's Army of the Ohio. The Battle of Jonesborough started about noon, and within a short time the Federals had decimated two Rebel brigades, although other Confederates held their ground. At dark Hardee pulled back to Lovejoy's Station to join with Hood and the remainder of the Army of Tennessee. At the end of the second day of fighting around Jonesborough, the Confederate army was ruined.

Barber, Sgt., Co. C, 15th Illinois Volunteer Infantry, Ackworth, Ga.:

> Most of the boys were now boarding with the inhabitants of the village, giving their rations for their board. Rollin and I were boarding with a lady, Mrs. Hunt, who's husband was in the employ of the Government, at Chattanooga, in the machine shop. He was a staunch Union man, but the rebels held him now as a prisoner....
>
> Great as was the danger we incurred, we would go out foraging. Some of our boys were captured by venturing too far. Roll and Milt went out a little way one day to get some beef. They had not gotten more than one mile from camp before they encountered some rebel cavalry who immediately gave them chase. They took to the woods in different directions and made pretty tall time for camp. They arrived about the same time, breathless. They were a little more cautious after this how they ventured out. We had a novel way of supplying ourselves with beef. Large droves of cattle were passing through every week for the front. When we would see a drove coming, some of the boys would slip out of the road a piece and when they came along, would select a nice fat one and hurry it out into the bushes until after the drove passed and then butcher it. This trick was played time and again.

In the Shenandoah Valley, Sheridan's army regrouped and advanced down the Valley Pike towards Winchester, with skirmishing going on at several points on the route.

September 2 (Friday)

On the Petersburg line, the Federals were again operating on the Weldon Railroad, securing more of that line and tearing up track. There was skirmishing at Yellow Tavern, south of Richmond, and other points.

Day, Pvt., Co. B, 25th Massachusetts Volunteer Infantry, Bermuda Hundred, Va.:

> About a week ago my brigade, Gen. Stannard commanding, left the trenches and was ordered into camp at Cobb's Hill; all the convalescents belonging to it were ordered to rejoin it. When I was about leaving, all my darkies gathered around me to give me their blessing and say their good-byes. They were earnest in their thanks for the kind treatment they had received and expressed their regrets at my leaving them.... I think I have been very successful with them in the little time I have had charge of them, having lost by death only three and I think there is small chance of any more of them dying at present, unless they should happen to be struck by lightning.
>
> Our brigade musters scarcely 1000 men for duty, and in a few weeks will be still further reduced by the expiration of the terms of service of those not re-enlisting. I learn that in a few days we go to New Bern, N.C. to relieve a full brigade which is ordered up here. Our old lines here are nothing more than skirmish lines on either side, with a few pickets between. There is no firing from either side and all is still and quiet as Sunday. The pickets keep up a truce between themselves, and although against orders, trading and communicating are carried on between them....

From Atlanta, to Chattanooga, to Nashville, to Louisville, to Washington, D.C., the telegraph lines hummed with the message from Sherman to President Lincoln: "Atlanta is ours, and fairly won!" Lincoln could have received no better present at this time. It confirmed his faith in his commanders and showed the doubters in the North that the war could be won.

Southeast of Atlanta, Hood was regrouping around Lovejoy's Station with the tattered remains of the Army of Tennessee and Major Gen. Slocum's corps actually entered the city. Sherman's men took a breather, and Sherman went to Atlanta to survey the city and to plan his next move. There was fighting along the rail link to Macon at Glass Ridge and Big Shanty, Ga.

There was considerable skirmishing at Darkesville and Bunker Hill in the Valley while Sheridan readied his offensive. Lee, feeling the shortage of troops at Petersburg, pressured Jubal Early to return Lee's loaned troops to the Army of Northern Virginia. Lee was also concerned about the diminishing strength of his army due to battle and disease, and the fact than few replacements were arriving.

September 3 (Saturday)

Sherman arrived in Atlanta and began planning for the next step. Hood, at Lovejoy's Station southeast of the city, regrouped, pulling his scattered remnants of units together and taking stock of what he had. President Davis was trying, in vain, to get troops from the governor of Georgia to assist Hood.

Sheridan, in the Valley, was moving up the Valley Pike with his now enlarged army. In response to Lee's direction, Early had detached R.H. Anderson's corps from his own army and sent it back to Petersburg. However, en route, Anderson's corps accidently ran into a corps of Sheridan's army, much to the surprise of both generals. A sharp fight then occurred that caused Early to rethink his decision about sending Anderson back to Lee.

In Washington, Lincoln was highly pleased with the fall of Mobile Bay and the capture of Atlanta, two victories at just the right time. Per Presidential Order, a 100-gun salute was to be fired at the Washington Navy Yard on September 5th, or to be fired upon receipt of the order, at every arsenal and navy yard in the United States in recognition "for the brilliant achievements of the fleet and land forces of the United States in the harbor of Mobile and in the reduction of Ft. Powell, Ft. Gaines, and Ft. Morgan...." Further, the President proclaimed that on the following Sunday thanksgiving should be given for Rear Admiral Farragut's victory at Mobile and for the capture of Atlanta by Gen. Sherman.

In February 1864, Union troops were ashore and in control of the port at Brownsville, Tex., and no blockading vessels were required. Therefore, the ships previously used for that purpose were sent to the Blockading Squadron off Mobile to assist there. On August 15th, Secretary of State Seward notified Secretary Welles that the Union troops were being withdrawn from Brownsville and that blockading ships would be required. On August 18th, Welles had directed Admiral Farragut to reinstate the blockade at Brownsville. However, due to the pressure of the upcoming battle for Mobile Bay, Farragut could not supply a ship at that time. On this day, September 3rd, Admiral Farragut reported to Welles that: "I am now increasing the blockading force off the coast of Texas, the recent operations here now enabling me to spare vessels for that purpose." Notification was sent to the senior naval commander off the coast of Texas to take appropriate action.

September 4 (Sunday)

Off Wilmington, N.C., the U.S.S. *Keystone State*, Commander Crosby, sighted the blockade-running steamer *Elsie*, which had just cleared the Wilmington channels with a load of cotton, but lost the steamer in the dark.

Sherman was in Atlanta and already the civilian authorities were arguing with him about who was responsible for the debris littering the streets, how they could feed the population left in the city, and who had control of law and order. Hood, southeast towards Macon, was still collecting his battered units, sorting them out and counting noses.

Jackman, Pvt., "The Orphan Brigade," Macon, Ga.:

> Went before Med. Ex. Board and got a furlough for 60 days. While getting to leave on furlough, I took too much exercise, getting my head in such a fix that I had to lie in bed....

A round of bombardment on Ft. Sumter lasting 60 days just ended, with 81 casualties on the little island fort after it had received 14,666 rounds of artillery and naval gunfire!

After the fight around Berryville between Anderson's and Sheridan's men, Early pulled his entire line back up the Valley.

September 5 (Monday)

Secretary of the Navy Gideon Welles, looking to a real winner, wrote Admiral David Farragut at Mobile asking that Farragut take command of the North Atlantic Blockading Squadron off Wilmington, N.C., and prepare the attack on that place, the last major port open to the Confederacy. This was done without the receipt of Farragut's letter of August 27th requesting relief from command for health reasons.

In the Valley, there was almost constant skirmishing between Sheridan's and Early's forces as each tried to find a hole in the line which could be exploited.

Miller, Lt., 1st Ohio Heavy Artillery, eastern Tennessee:

> Special courier arrived early this morning (before daylight) bringing the news that the detachments under the command of General Gillem had surprised the troops at General John H. Morgan's headquarters, and after a desperate encounter had captured General Morgan and Staff, besides a goodly number of prisoners, but that General Morgan was killed during the fight. The receipt of this important news caused general rejoicing among the citizens of Knoxville, and the stars and stripes could be seen flying over nearly every loyal residence; also bells were ringing all day, and every Union Tennessean felt that he was safe, for as a rule the mere mention of the name of "General Morgan, the Raider" sent a thrill of terror to the hearts of every loyal Tennessean. 80 Confederate prisoners were brought in at 9 o'clock this evening, which caused still greater excitement. Besides General Morgan's command there were Generals Wheeler and Forest, Confederate Cavalry, lurking around in Eastern Tennessee.

September 6 (Tuesday)

Day, Pvt., Co. B, 25th Massachusetts Volunteer Infantry, Portsmouth, Va.:

> On the 5th of this month the 23rd and 25th Massachusetts embarked on the steamer Winona from Bermuda Hundred bound for New Bern.... On the morning of the 6th we ran up to Portsmouth, taking our camp equipage and knapsacks aboard, and ran back into Hampton Roads and anchored. There was a heavy storm blowing outside and we lay at our anchorage all day the 7th.

Miller, Lt., 1st Ohio Heavy Artillery, eastern Tennessee.:

> General Gillem came to headquarters today and gave General Davis Tillson a detailed account of the capture and killing of the brave General Morgan of the Confederate Cavalry fame. I was present when

this interview took place. General Gillem said, "My command consisted of the 9th and 13th Regiments of Tennessee Cavalry, 10th Michigan Cavalry and a Battery of 6 Guns. Colonel John M. Miller commanding the Brigade. Our camp was located west and north of Greenville, near Bull's Gap. As Colonel Miller and myself were planning for the following days movements, a small boy about 11 or 12 years of age came to our headquarters and reported that a lot of Confederate soldiers were camped on the banks of Black Creek and that his father had sent him to tell the Yankee General. It was about 8 miles from our camp to Black Springs. The boy's statement was received with a due amount of allowance, and we informed the young lad that he must be mistaken, for there were no Confederate soldiers in the vicinity. The boy seemed to be quite excited, and when we doubted his statement he became apparently very much troubled, claiming that he had seen and visited their camp. We concluded there must be something in the boy's story, so we made our plans to capture the Confederate soldiers.

According to these plans the 13th Tennessee Cavalry, Lieutenant Colonel Ingerton commanding, was to start late at night on the old road towards Newport, Tenn., and march until it struck the Greenville road, then change its course towards Black Creek and surprise and capture the Confederates. It was the darkest night we ever saw, and to make it more hideous, it was accompanied by incessant thunder and lightening with heavy rain. I believe it never rained harder.

As the command reached the Greenville road, a Confederate courier could be seen between the flashes of lightning galloping down the road at full speed. He was captured and searched by our men, and a letter was found on his person from the Confederate General Vaughn, addressed to the Confederate General John H. Morgan, at the residence of Mrs. Williams, Greenville, Tenn. We must admit our nerves were a little unstrung for a moment, for we knew what it was to face so daring a General as John H. Morgan and his command. However, we changed our plans and determined to capture General Morgan if possible.

Lieutenant Colonel Ingerton then ordered his command to follow the main road until they reached Greenville. They arrived about 3:30 in the morning, just as it was becoming the break of day. Captain Wilcox and Lieutenant White, Company "G" of the 13th Cavalry, owing to their knowledge of the streets and alleys of Greenville, were to have charge of this, one of the most hazardous undertakings of the war.

When all was ready, Lieutenant White took a platoon of Company "G" and by a circuitous route reached the opposite side of Greenville and then, in true Indian style, marched direct to the Williams residence, capturing the guards outside with comparatively little resistance.

While Lieutenant White was performing this hazardous task, Captain Wilcox had taken the remainder of the Company and charged down the main road towards General Morgan's camp. Officers and men were yet asleep in their quarters and Captain Wilcox captured the Battery on the school house grounds, taking the guards as prisoners.

The Confederate army were greatly surprised and immediately began to fall into line of battle. Little did they surmise that a platoon of less than 20 Union soldiers had marched to their rear and surrounded the headquarters of their General. All this noise and consternation created by Captain Wilcox's command had its desired effect, for it directed the Confederates attention towards that part of the town.

About this time General Morgan, hearing the confusion, had stepped to the door of the Williams residence to see what was going on. Just previous to this Lieutenant White had been informed by a citizen in Greenville that General Morgan was in this house at the same time pointing to it and he then ordered his men to completely surround it. He had just marched around the house towards the garden when General Morgan stepped out. Before Morgan had time to rub his eyes, until they were fairly open, he was ordered to surrender. Up to this time no one knew it was General Morgan at the door, not even the members of his own staff, for he had passed out unnoticed. He had been in a great many tight places before and apparently at once decided to escape into the garden but there he ran against more of our men who again ordered him to surrender.

Morgan undoubtedly saw that his chances for escape were very slight for he drew his revolver and fired. Our men immediately returned the fire and with fatal effect. No further attention was given to the killing of this man, whom no one supposed to be General Morgan, and as soon as the shooting was done, our men proceeded to gather the prisoners who were in the house; these included all of General

Morgan's staff but two. General Morgan was nowhere to be found, and the members of his staff concluded he had, as usual, made good his escape.

As we marched the prisoners out, preparatory to taking them to the rear, the body of the dead soldier was discovered, for it was now quite light in the morning, when one of Morgan's staff cried out, "For God's sake, men, you have killed General Morgan." This was the first knowledge we had that the battle-scarred veteran, General John H. Morgan, had been killed.

It was the work of only a few moments to place his body crosswise in front of a rider, and with the prisoners, make a hasty retreat to the place where Colonel Miller was waiting with the brigade. Colonel Miller was greatly excited over the killing of General Morgan until he had been informed of his refusal to surrender, and of his firing the first shot. After hearing this, he ordered the body of the dead General to be placed on a wagon and returned, under a flag of truce, to the Confederate Army, Mrs. Williams assuming charge of the body after its arrival there. During this time Lieutenant Colonel Ingerton and the remainder of the 13th Tennessee Cavalry had marched to the assistance of Captain Wilcox, bringing in the prisoners numbering 75 to 80.

The report that General Morgan's body was mutilated in any way was not true. Our men might have taken his spurs and side arms. He was admired by both armies for his dauntless bravery. The killing of General Morgan struck deep into the heart of the Confederates.

Generals Wheeler and Forest decided to take Knoxville in revenge, but General Tillson ordered out the entire available force and blocked every street leading into Knoxville by chaining together more than 300 large army wagons besides using every other possible device at his command. In addition to the Union forces in Knoxville, there were 500 citizens enrolled; these drilled night and day, preparing for the reception of the Confederates, but about this time the Confederate army in Tennessee received orders to march south to intercept General Sherman's march to the sea so Knoxville was not molested farther.

September 7 (Wednesday)

Sherman took a rather unpopular stand and ordered the evacuation of the city of Atlanta—everyone other than his army was to leave. This included some 1600 people, comprising about 446 families who left, leaving their possessions and homes in the city. The mayor of Atlanta, Gen. Hood, and everyone else who could reach Sherman protested, to no avail. Sherman said he would have enough trouble feeding his own troops and would not feed the civilians. Those who wanted to go south, could go in that direction, all others could go north. He wrote:

> If the people raise a howl against my barbarity and cruelty, I will answer that war is war and not popularity-seeking.

September 8 (Thursday)

At Orange, N.J., Major Gen. George B. McClellan formally accepted the Democratic nomination for President.

At Andersonville prison in Georgia, an exchange of prisoners had been authorized, and the prison administration sorted out who would go, and who would stay. One of those chosen to go was Private S.J. Gibson, 103rd Pennsylvania Volunteers, who had been captured at Plymouth, N.C., on April 20, 1864, and had arrived at Andersonville, along with most of his unit, on Monday, May 2, 1864, slightly over four months previously. The exchange was tenuous because Grant had not authorized the exchange of prisoners for military reasons, believing it would help the South's manpower problems. The prisoners were notified to get their gear ready and to stand by.

Commander Melancthon B. Woolsey, USN, the senior commander off the Texas coast, notified Admiral David G. Farragut off Mobile:

> The *Kanawha* sailed hence last night with orders to blockade the Brazos Santiago [one of the points of approach to Brownsville]. She also bore orders to the *Aroostook* to blockade the Rio Grande.... The blockade of those places will be resumed from to-morrow morning (9th).

September 9 (Friday)

For some period, the Confederate government had owned its own blockade runners, which hauled government-owned cotton out of the ports and returned with government-owned stores of food, equipment, and munitions. There was also heavy reliance on the "commercial" aspect of the blockade running, which allowed the runners to bring in cargo for sale, *so long as at least 50 percent of it was of "necessities" or of military value.* Outgoing, these "commercial" runners were required to carry *at least 50 percent of their cargo of cotton from government-owned stocks,* on which the runners made little, or no, profit. As the war progressed, the press of getting more goods in became greater and the South resorted to assigning their naval officers to command blockade runners. There were many reasons for this, but the primary ones were: The Confederacy had few ships to occupy their officers, and many of the officers were eager for command at sea, even if it was a blockade runner, which was better than baking in an idle ironclad gunboat on some small river.

One of the most successful naval commanders the South had was Commander John Newland Maffitt, who had commanded the gunboat C.S.S. *Savannah,* the commerce raider C.S.S. *Florida,* and the ironclad C.S.S. *Albemarle.* He was assigned today to command the blockade runner *Owl.*

John N. Maffitt was truly a man of the sea. He was born at sea on February 22, 1819, the son of a seafaring man. His father later became a minister and did so poorly that John was adopted by his uncle, Dr. William Maffitt, who lived near Fayetteville, N.C. At age 13 John Maffitt became a midshipman in the U.S. Navy. In 1838 he was promoted and remained on sea duty until 1842, when he was assigned to the coastal survey of the east coast. For the next 15 years he conducted soundings of the various harbors and sea approaches along the coast, and became a known expert on the navigation of coastal waters. He resigned his commission on May 8, 1861, and was appointed a lieutenant in the Confederate Navy. He turned blockade running into an art form with his command of the *Owl,* primarily because of his daring and his knowledge of the coastal waters. After the war, Maffitt commanded a chartered British ship. He then commanded a Cuban ship used by the revolutionaries. He married for the third time in November 1870 and settled at his home called "The Moorings," near Wilmington. He wrote several books and magazine articles about his experiences during the war. He died on May 16, 1886.

Day, Pvt., Co. B, 25th Massachusetts Volunteer Infantry, en route to Hatteras, N.C.:

> On the morning of the 9th we received peremptory orders to pull up our mudhooks and start. Then ensued a sharp correspondence between our captain and someone in the fort, said to be Gen. Butler, and it certainly sounded a great deal like him. The captain objected.... Word came back that it made no difference about the owners or for what she was chartered, the boat was going to New Bern or go to pieces.... The captain said he...shouldn't take the responsibility for taking her out...word came back that he *would* take her out, or go into the fort wearing a ball and chain.... Toward night our consort, which was a sea-going boat, led off, we following after.... We found it rough going round Cape Henry...we encountered heavy swells and rollers and every little while a big roller would strike us under the port guard and make every timber in the old craft snap.... I remained awake the whole night watching our consort which kept ahead of us, and reckoned on my chance for a swim.

September 10 (Saturday)

The evening of the 9th, a mail steamer, the *Fawn,* had been seized by Confederates and burned on the Albemarle and Chesapeake Canal near Elizabeth City, N.C. Today, a landing party from the U.S.S. *Wyalusing,* Lt. Commander Earl English, landed at Elizabeth City and detained 29 of the leading citizens for interrogation. Upon questioning, it was learned that the raiding party was from the C.S.S. *Albemarle.*

Day, Pvt., Co. B, 25th Massachusetts Volunteer Infantry, New Bern, N.C.:

> We reached Hatteras inlet early on the morning of the 10th and landed at Fort Spinola on the south side of the Trent river at New Bern in the afternoon. After landing, we marched up into the camp of the 9th Vermont—a sick, ragged, dirty, lousy crowd. The Vermonters gathered wonderingly around us, extending us every sympathy and hospitality that lay in their power. The old regiment was divided off into three or four small companies, one of which under the command of Capt. Emory was sent out to Brice's creek about a mile from here to go into quarters and do some light picket duty. We have once more got ourselves cleaned up, our

hair trimmed and dress in clean whole clothing, and begin to look quite like ourselves again.

September 11 (Sunday)

At Andersonville prison in Georgia, Private S.J. Gibson, 103rd Pennsylvania Volunteers, among a group of 1380 prisoners, was packed 60 men to a railway car and sent from the prison. The heavily guarded train arrived at Macon at 2 A.M. the following morning, Augusta, Ga., at 4 P.M., and finally arrived at Charleston on the morning of September 12th.

In an all-day expedition commanded by Acting Lt. Wiggen, USN, the Union gained about 60,000 feet of lumber, an engine to run a sawmill, and some livestock. Wiggen embarked on the wooden sidewheeler U.S.S. *Stockdale*, Acting Master Spiro V. Bennis, which led the tinclad U.S.S. *Rudolph*, Acting Lt. George D. Upham, and the Army transport *Planter*, with a barge in tow, up the Fish River near Mobile Bay, where troops were landed. The loading of the lumber and engine took most of the day and dusk was falling when they started downriver. The Confederates along the river fired into the ships and felled trees into the river to stop the convoy. The gunboats returned the fire with their naval guns, and the *Rudolph*, in the lead, broke through the felled trees and all the boats went downriver to safety.

September 12 (Monday)

The "Virginia reel" played in the Valley by Sheridan and Early took a rest, much to the dismay of both Lincoln and Grant. Sheridan didn't seem to be able to get things moving.

Sherman began the second day of evacuation of the civilians from Atlanta amid curses, pleas, and threats coming from all sides. No relenting, however, all must go.

Jackman, Pvt., "The Orphan Brigade," Augusta, Ga.:

> When, though not really able to travel, I went to town in an ambulance and at 4 P.M. took train for Augusta, via Millin. I got on with some young ladies at the depot who gave me a nice dinner out of their basket and when the train was ready, I helped them into a car thereby getting a seat in the ladies coach. The train, in motion, did not agree well with my head. Thirty miles from the city my lady friends got off urging me to come to see them before I went back to the army. I gave a gentleman part of my seat. When nearly to Millin, and late at night, a young lady came in who could not find a seat, and as I liked her appearance, I woke my friend out of a gentle nap and the young lady was seated. She was going to Augusta to see her brother in hospital. We got to Millin at 12 o'clock at night and had to change cars. By being with a lady, I got into a ladies car again. Seeing a woman in distress, having several little children, and no one to assist her, I was employed in carrying children from one train to the other. I never saw such a jam of women in my life as was in that car. They kept crowding in at every station and kept up a perfect fighting and scratching. We got to Augusta at daylight. I took dinner with Lt. G..

The 1380 prisoners transferred from Andersonville prison for exchange included Private S.J. Gibson, 103rd Pennsylvania Volunteers. After a long train ride through Macon and Augusta, the prisoners arrived in Charleston, S.C., where they were unloaded and marched to the fairgrounds, which would be their home until October 1st. During their stay, Gibson would "celebrate" his sixth wedding anniversary (Sept. 16th), and his third anniversary of Union service (Sept. 23rd).

September 13 (Tuesday)

At Mobile Bay, one of the most dangerous jobs to be completed was the clearing of the torpedoes from the main channel. This was done by small boats entering the mine field and dismantling, then sinking, the torpedoes one-by-one. Why the use of the naval guns could not be employed was not stated. Admiral Farragut reported to Secretary Welles:

> This part of the channel is now believed to be clear, for, though beyond doubt many more were originally anchored here, report says they have sunk over one hundred to the bottom.

Despite all efforts, some of the torpedoes would be missed or would float down from other areas, and several Union ships would be sunk from these torpedoes over the months to come.

In the Valley, skirmishing, however light, showed that the armies of Sheridan and Early were not entirely asleep, as Lincoln was beginning to think. In Georgia, Sherman and Hood were into the third day of a ten-day armistice, and the third day of the evacuation of civilians from Atlanta.

September 14 (Wednesday)

In Atlanta the cleanup and clean-out continued. Sherman's troops were restoring the rail link to Chattanooga and the civilians in the city were still evacuating.

Jackman, Pvt., "The Orphan Brigade," Americus, Ga.:

> Took train for Warrenton, Ga., 50 miles towards Atlanta, on State road—5 miles from junction on Mayfield road. Got to W. at 1 P.M. and took dinner at the Warrenton Hotel. Staid all night at the same place.

In the Valley, Grant and Lincoln severly pressured Sheridan to do something about Early. Early was also being pressured by Lee to return R.H. Anderson's corp to the Army of Northern Virginia. Lee needed this corps badly to bolster his thinning ranks. Today, Early released Anderson to move his corps back to Petersburg.

September 15 (Thursday)

Secretary of the Navy Gideon Welles received a letter from Admiral David Farragut dated August 27th requesting that he be relieved of command for health reasons, having been on continuous service for over five years with only one period of leave. Welles had hoped that Farragut would lead the North Atlantic Blockading Squadron in the planning and assault on Wilmington, N.C. Upon receipt of Farragut's letter, Welles took action to appoint the other successful naval commander, Admiral D.D. Porter.

Things were quiet in the siege lines around Petersburg, so Grant left to talk with Sheridan about getting things moving in the Valley.

Day, Pvt., Co. B, 25th Massachusetts Volunteer Infantry, New Bern, N.C.:

> We are again on our old stamping grounds, but, alas, how changed! Only a small remnant now remains of that grand old regiment that left Worcester three years ago. They fill honored graves on half a hundred battlefields, they are inmates of every hospital from Boston to New Bern, and are wasting away in rebel prisons; a handful only remaining to tell the sad tale.... The whole south for the past three years has been singularly exempt from the scourge of yellow fever, but it has now broken out in New Bern and is raging to a great extent, 30 or 40 dying daily. It has not yet reached the camps outside the city and hopes are entertained that it will not.

The VicePresident of the Confederate States of America, A.H. Stephens, had left the Capitol in Richmond some time ago and remained absent. He and Davis did not get along or agree on most things.

September 16 (Friday)

At Verona, Miss., Nathan Bedford Forrest started out with about 4500 cavalry and mounted infantry to operate against Sherman's communications in northern Alabama and middle Tennessee. This particular expedition would last about a month. At Atlanta, the evacuation went on (and on).

Jackman, Pvt., "The Orphan Brigade," Americus, Ga.:

> Took train on southwest road for Americus at 8 A.M. and arrived at A. at 12 m. Went to Bragg Hospital.
>
> I again got in Ward No. 1, the same attendant being in charge save Baldridge and Smith. I also was placed in the Masonic Hall, a large room with nearly fifty beds in it, but there were few patients in the room. All the "rats" were glad to see me back again. My head was hurting me from loss of sleep, etc. and I went to bed.
>
> Americus is a town of about 3 or 4000 inhabitants. The business part of the town had lately been destroyed by fire. There are many fine residences in the suburbs. The town though while I was there looked much dilapidated—the effects of the war. The people generally were kind to the soldiers—bringing provisions to the sick, etc. The young ladies were "thick as hops" and as a general thing, very good looking. Being two hospitals in the place, a good many "rats" were about the streets.

With the loss of the C.S.S. *Alabama*, the South was looking for a new commerce raider as a replacement. Commander Bulloch, in Liverpool, England, wrote Confederate Secretary of the Navy Mallory:

> ...I have now the satisfaction to inform you of the purchase of a fine composite ship, built for the

Bombay trade, and just returned from her first voyage. She is 1,160 tons builder's measurement, classed A-1...frames, beams, etc., of iron, but planked from keel to gunwale with East Indian teak.... My broker has had her carefully examined by one of Lloyd's inspectors, who pronounced her a capital ship in every respect.... The log of the ship shows her to be a fast sailor under canvas, for with screw up she has made 330 miles in 24 hours by observation.

The ship being described was called the *Sea King*. She would soon be known as the Confederate raider of unarmed ships called the C.S.S. *Shenandoah*.

At Charles Town, W.Va., Sheridan and Grant met to discuss the situation in the Valley. Sheridan had now learned that R.H. Anderson's corps had departed for Petersburg and Richmond, weakening the Confederate forces.

On September 11th, Gen. Wade Hampton of South Carolina left the Confederate lines with his cavalry, and went on a beef roundup to feed the troops of Lee's army. At Coggin's Point, Va., Hampton's cavalry and Federal troops herding the cattle had a little fracas, with the Confederate "cowboys" making off with the beef. Hampton gained about 2400 head of cattle and 300 prisoners. By tomorrow, they would all be back in the Rebel lines at Petersburg.

September 17 (Saturday)

John Charles Frémont, "Pathfinder," businessman, Major General of Union forces, big spender from the West, and lately, Radical Republican presidential nominee withdrew his name from the ballot for the November elections. Frémont later said he withdrew to keep the Republicans from splitting the ticket and thereby giving the election to McClellan. Though this was suspect at the time, it may have been true.

Jubal Early, now weakened by the loss of R.H. Anderson's corps, moved down the Valley towards Martinsburg and the Baltimore and Ohio Railroad, which had been repaired after his last track-bending party. Early had about 12,000 men against Sheridan's nearly 40,000.

September 18 (Sunday)

In the Valley, Early sent a portion of his small force from Bunker Hill north to Martinsburg, where the Confederates drove in the Federal cavalry, and then pulled back to Bunker Hill. Sheridan ordered an advance up the Valley Pike, hoping to catch the separated elements of Early's force.

September 19 (Monday)

Things were finally moving in the Valley. Sheridan sent his 40,000 troops against Early's 12,000 north of Winchester, Va. The main force of Sheridan's infantry drove up the Valley Pike around Berryville and hit the Confederates hard. Confederate Gen. Robert E. Rodes was mortally wounded during the action that saw the Confederates drive into a gap in the Federal line. The Federals held and drove the Rebels back. The Union cavalry drove Gen. Breckinridge's division from north of the city to a new line east of Winchester. About 4:30, Sheridan ordered another advance, and Early withdrew up the Valley. Federal casualties were 4000 out of 40,000. Confederate losses were proportionately heavier, 3921 out of about 12,000. Early retreated with a much-weakened force.

The conscription business in the South, always a problem, was getting worse with the bad publicity it had received lately. The conscription bureau had now taken to defending itself to the Secretary of War and the President for its performance and against Gen. Braxton Bragg's allegations that it was corrupt and incompetent.

Out in Missouri, a desperate Gen. Sterling Price advanced into the state for the last time. Several times he had tried to regain the state for the Confederacy, but he had always failed.

There was high intrigue and deeds of daring on the Great Lakes. Near Sandusky, Ohio, the iron side-wheeler gunboat U.S.S. *Michigan*, Commander J.C. Carter, was assigned to guard the Confederate prisoners held at Johnson's Island. Capt. Charles H. Cole, CSA, a secret agent in the Lake Erie region, came up with the idea of capturing the *Michigan*, releasing the prisoners, and then embarking on guerrilla raids along the Lakes. He enlisted Acting Master John Yates Beall, CSN, and John Thompson, the Southern agent in Canada, in the plot. Cole was to get to know the officers and men on the *Michigan* and attempt to bribe them, while Beall would capture a steamer, approach the *Michigan*, and board her with his Confederate crew.

Beall and 19 of his men boarded the steamer

Philo Parsons as passengers and then seized the ship and took her to Middle Bass Island, en route from Detroit to Sandusky. While at Middle Bass Island, the *Philo Parsons* was approached by the steamer *Island Queen*, which Beall captured and burned. He then put the crew and passengers from both ships ashore and headed for Sandusky.

Meanwhile, Cole was attempting to bribe the crew of the *Michigan*. Commander Carter became suspicious and Carter had Cole and his assistant arrested. As Beall approached the *Michigan*, he did not receive the prearranged signals and he took the *Philo Parsons* to Sandwich, Canada, where the ship was stripped and burned and the crew dispersed.

September 20 (Tuesday)

In the Valley, Sheridan's troops chased Early's retreating columns through Middletown. Sheridan finally stopped when the Confederates were south of Strasburg on Fisher's Hill. The Federals entrenched north of the town. Early was later to remark that Sheridan missed a chance to annihilate him at Winchester.

At Atlanta, the Confederate cavalry under Wheeler was creating supply problems for Sherman. Wheeler had been tearing up track and stopping supplies for several days now. Forrest was loose and heading for middle Tennessee to do what he did best—create havoc.

Barber, Sgt., Co. C, 15th Illinois Volunteer Infantry, Ackworth, Ga.:

> One night, from my post on picket, I saw a squad of rebels skulking around. I told the boys not to fire for I thought it would not be prudent to disclose our position and bring down an overwhelming force upon us. It was hard to stand with loaded guns and see the rascals skulking about, but they did not come within good range of our guns and did not try to molest the railroad, therefore, I did not think it would be justified in alarming the camp by attacking them, but we kept a vigilant eye upon them until they disappeared.

Sterling Price moved through Missouri with 12,000 men, but only 8000 were armed. In Richmond, President Davis left for Georgia to discuss the current situation with local authorities.

September 21 (Wednesday)

In the Valley at Strasburg, Sheridan advanced on Early's fortifications on Fisher's Hill. There was fighting in the town of Strasburg, at Fisher's Hill, and at Front Royal. The fighting at Front Royal was to prevent the Federals from entering Luray Valley. After dark, Sheridan sent Gen. Crook with one of the Federal corps to the right and around the left flank of the Confederates, to a position of attack. The pressure on Early was building.

In middle Tennessee, Forrest was outside of Athens and threatening the city and its Federal garrison.

September 22 (Thursday)

Rear Admiral David Dixon Porter, USN, Commander of the Mississippi River Squadron, received a letter from Secretary of the Navy Gideon Welles concerning a new assignment. Welles wrote:

> Rear Admiral D.G. Farragut was assigned to the command of the North Atlantic Squadron on the 5th instant, but the necessity of rest on the part of that distinguished officer renders it necessary that he should come immediately North. You will, therefore, on receipt of this order consider yourself detached from the command of the Mississippi Squadron…and relieve Acting Rear Admiral Lee in command of the North Atlantic Blockading Squadron.

Admiral Porter, son of a distinguished U.S. naval officer and adopted brother of Admiral David G. Farragut, had more than distinguished himself in his command of the Mississippi Squadron with his attacks on Vicksburg and on the rivers flowing into the Mississippi. He was the obvious choice for this assignment.

At Fisher's Hill, Sheridan was poised to attack Early's diminished forces as soon as Crook got into position on Early's left flank. Late in the afternoon, Crook's Federals came boiling over the Rebel entrenchments, taking them in the rear and the flank. The Union troops in front attacked at the same time across the Tumbling Run ravine and up Fisher's Hill. During the melee, Confederate Lt. Col. Alexander Swift Pendleton, called "Sandie," was mortally wounded by a shot in the abdomen and died a short time later. The Union bluecoats chased the Confederates for four miles up the Valley before Early could get his lines together. Early lost 1235 men from his steadily diminishing force.

September 24 (Saturday)

In the Valley, Sheridan turned to burning crops, barns and anything else usable to the Confederacy, while he slowly advanced up the Valley towards Early. Smoke columns marked the progress of the blue-clad columns as they advanced. Early needed everything, but mostly men, and nothing was in sight.

Sterling Price attacked Fayette, Mo., with no great results.

Gen. Robert E. Lee wrote Secretary of War Seddon concerning the blockading of Wilmington, N.C.:

> Since the fitting out of the privateer *Tallahassee* and her cruise from the port of Wilmington, the enemy's fleet of blockaders off that coast has been very much increased, and the dangers of running the blockade rendered much greater. The question arises whether it is of more importance to us to obtain supplies through that port or to prey on the enemy's commerce by privateers sent from thence.... It might be well therefore, if practicable, to divert the enemy's attention from Wilmington Harbor and keep it open as long as possible as a port of entry. While it is open the energies...should be exerted...to get in two or three years' supplies so as to remove all apprehension on this score.

September 25 (Sunday)

Sheridan's army moved towards Staunton and Waynesborough, Va., destroying all in its path. Early was forced back to Brown's Pass in the Blue Ridge near Waynesborough. Tall columns of smoke were seen from horizon to horizon marking the Union army's passing.

Barber, Sgt., Co. C, 15th Illinois Volunteer Infantry, Ackworth, Ga.:

> We now had about thirty mounted men and they aided us materially in scouting and warning us of attacks. A picket post got nicely fooled one night. A party of horsemen was approaching and the sentinel challenged them. The leader said it was only Col. Rogers out on a scout. This threw the sentinel off his guard and he permitted them to approach. They were instantly surrounded and every man except one was captured. He lay concealed until nearly daylight, then came in and reported. It seems the rebel officer had had the Colonel's name from some rascally citizen, and so passed himself off for him until it was too late for the picket to escape. There was a whole regiment of rebels nearby. The next morning, bright and early, our whole command set out to try to overtake them. We pressed them so close that we came in sight of their rear guard. Sergeant Hooker chased down and captured one man by knocking him off his horse with his saber....
>
> There was a doctor and one lady in Ackworth, who were suspected of playing the spy. The doctor got passes to go out and in at pleasure to visit his patients, but I believe he was nothing more or less than a spy, although he professed to be a strong Union man. This lady, Jones by name, was a perfect virago. She made pretty free use of her tongue and abused us whenever opportunity would permit. The boys used to go to her house just to hear her rave at the Yanks.
>
> The Colonel and several of the boys thought it would be a nice thing to play a Yankee trick on her, and at the same time get some useful information out of her, so the Colonel procured a rebel Lieutenant's suit, and so disguised, presented himself at her house one night, after she had retired. The Colonel gave his name as Lieutenant—somebody—from Forrest's cavalry, and demanded to be admitted, as he had important information to communicate. Mrs. Jones rushed to the door to admit him. (It must be remembered that this Mrs. Jones was a young widow.) The Colonel told her that Forrest was out only a few miles, and that very night was going to attack and capture the place, and he wanted to know who were Union men and who were rebels, at the same time telling her that all Union men would be hung and their houses burned. She seized a pen and gave him the names of all the Union families in town. Amongst them were Mrs. Hunt's and Mrs. Crawford's.
>
> Before the Colonel came in, he had agreed with the boys on a signal and they were to rush in and capture him. After the Colonel had got all the information that he could, he commenced sparking her, and was progressing finely when a loud knock at the door suddenly interrupted their tete-a-tete. Hastily throwing some bed-quilts over the Colonel, she demanded to know who was there. "Soldiers after a rebel spy" was the prompt answer. "There has been no such person here" was the rejoinder, but they burst open the door and commenced search. The suppressed laugh of the Colonel betrayed his whereabouts, and he was dragged forth apparently much frightened.

The widow scolded, raved and begged of them to let him go, but all to no purpose. When fairly out of hearing the party laughed to their heart's content. It was not until several days after that she found out the trick that had been played on her, and if ever there was a mad woman, she was one.... We learned now that the rebel army had crossed the Chattahoochee and was making towards Rome.

About this time the Colonel and Adjutant were called to Atlanta; the former on a court martial and the latter on a visit. Capt. Kenyon of Company C was left in command. He put on more pomp and style than a Brigadier-General.... The last words the Colonel said to him were that if he were attacked by a superior force to fall back to Allatoona and save all the baggage, but self-conceited as he was, he chose to do as he pleased. The rebel army, instead of making for Rome, made directly for us. They attacked Big Shanty first, but not until they had killed and wounded twice their number and the rebel flag was planted on their works did our boys surrender. Equally firm was the resistance that they met at Moon Station.

September 26 (Monday)

In the Valley, Sheridan began his pullback after his cavalry had clashed with Early's around Port Republic, Weyer's Cave, and other points on the Valley Pike. Early was left to sort out his problems.

On the James River below Richmond, Union forces began digging a canal at Dutch Gap to bypass the Confederate obstructions at Trent's Reach. If completed, this canal would seriously threaten the Richmond area. The Confederate Navy considered using gunboats to prevent the completion.

Sterling Price and his Army of Missouri skirmished in Arcadia Valley and other points, then headed for St. Louis.

Three years ago on this date, John S. Jackman left his home in Kentucky to join the Confederate Army.

On the 24th, Gen. Lee had written to Secretary of the Navy Seddon concerning the use of the port of Wilmington, N.C. Today, the Army commander in Wilmington, Major Gen. Whiting, CSA, wrote to Gov. Zebulon Vance of North Carolina requesting that the C.S.S. *Tallahassee* and *Chickamauga* be retained in port:

> The Confederate steamers *Tallahassee* and *Chickamauga* are now nearly ready for sea, and will leave this port for the purpose of operating against the enemy's commerce. Should they leave on this service the few vessels they might destroy would be of little advantage to our cause, while it would excite the enemy to increase the number of the blockading squadron to such an extent as to render it almost impossible for vessels running the blockade to escape them.

September 27 (Tuesday)

Sterling Price was still skirmishing around Arcadia. At Ft. Davidson, Pilot Knob, Mo., Brig. Gen. Thomas Ewing evacuated the fort after holding Sterling Price off with only 1200 men. At Centralia, Mo., a small guerrilla force under the command of "Bloody Bill" Anderson, one of the more vicious of the Confederate guerrilla leaders, attacked the town. The force included such notables as George Todd and Frank and Jesse James. Twenty-four unarmed soldiers were murdered at Centralia, and when Federal troops came to rescue the town, they were ambushed, and 116 of them were killed.

At Smithville, N.C., the C.S.S. *North Carolina* sank at her pier because the bottom of the ironclad had been eaten out by worms. This made her virtually unusable, except as a stationary gun platform. This was the second ironclad to be used as such; the C.S.S. *Raleigh* had been beached on May 7th.

Acting Ensign Semon, USN, made his second trip by small boat to Masonboro Inlet and Wilmington on a dangerous and daring task to scout out the defenses and gain more information on the blockade runners.

Miller, Lt., 1st Ohio Heavy Artillery, eastern Tennessee:

> Our regiment and some cavalry and a section of a Tennessee battery move out from Bull's Gap as a part of an expedition having in view the destruction of the saltworks near Abington, Va.—about 75 miles east of Bull's Gap. The expedition is V-shaped. One column from Ky. through Pound Gap under Gen. Burbridge which was composed largely of colored troops. The other column was our own, and the point of the V was Saltville, Va.—a place where the Confederacy had made about all the salt it had during the war and a place that the yankees had never before tried to take....

Our Regt. was approaching Greenville, Tenn. going after the retreating rebel forces of Gen. Vaughn and Duke. Greenville was the home of the then Vice President Andrew Johnson, whose tin sign was seen by us as we passed through the town, "A. Johnson, Tailor."

September 28 (Wednesday)

A change of command took place on the Mississippi River and at the North Blockading Squadron off Wilmington, N.C. Admiral David Dixon Porter was leaving the Mississippi Squadron, to replace Admiral S.P. Lee off Wilmington. Lee would then come to the Mississippi Squadron and assume command. Admiral Porter, much admired by his men and the Army in the Mississippi Valley, wrote a farewell message to his officers and men:

> When I first assumed command of this squadron the Mississippi was in possession of the rebels from Memphis to New Orleans, a distance of 800 miles, and over 1,000 miles of tributaries were closed to us, embracing a territory larger than some of the kingdoms of Europe. Our commerce is now successfully, if not quietly, transported on the broad Mississippi from one end to the other, and the same may almost be said with regard to its tributaries.

Things were quiet on the Petersburg line, just the usual sniping and occasional shot on the picket line.

In Atlanta, the civilians had now been evacuated and the city was full of soldiers, very little action going on. Forrest was roaming around middle Tennessee.

In Missouri, Sterling Price continued his advance towards St. Louis.

September 29 (Thursday)

Gen. Forrest's cavalry engaged a Federal force near Lynchburg, Tenn., with light fighting, mostly maneuvering.

Miller, Lt., 1st Ohio Heavy Artillery, eastern Tennessee:

> Reached Carter Station and found the rebels intrenched at the head of a R.R. bridge and strongly fortified on the bluff on the opposite side of the river.... The fight opened and a hotly contested artillery duel continued all afternoon.... On our right down at the head of the bridge were intrenched some rebel sharp-shooters who annoyed us very much by constant firing at every man in sight...our men behaved well under fire. It is a great strain to be under the fire of the enemy and not be allowed to fire back.
>
> That night our two companies moved to the right and drove the rebel pickets away and worked, in a drenching rain, half the night trying to burn the bridge—the rebels occupying the other end of the bridge. We succeeded in partly destroying the bridge, in spite of the rain and put in the balance of the night fighting fleas in an old cooper shop where Tennessee hogs had slept before we routed them out to occupy their beds.

Acting Master John C. Braine, CSN, and a small party of Confederates overwhelmed the U.S. steamer *Roanoke* after she left Havana, Cuba, for New York. This was a major embarrassment for the Confederate government, because the steamer was seized coming from a neutral port. Braine had outlined his plan to Secretary of the Navy Mallory earlier and had received Mallory's blessing *providing that strict neutrality was observed.* Instead of boarding the steamer as a passenger in New York, he did it in Cuba, violating that country's neutrality. Braine sailed the ship to Bermuda, where he unsuccessfully tried to smuggle coal and supplies out to the ship. Braine offloaded the crew and passengers and burned the ship off that island. Braine was held by the British for a while and was then released.

In the Valley, Sheridan's troops and Early's Rebels engaged at Waynesborough, Va., with light contact. Sterling Price was at Leasburg and Harrison, Mo., on his way to St. Louis.

Two separate, yet related, actions occurred in the Petersburg area. Grant wanted to extend his left flank beyond the Weldon Railroad to encompass the South Side Railroad and the Appomattox River crossings. Near Peebles' Farm, Gen. George Meade and 16,000 Union troops began an operation that would last for four days without making major contact with Confederate forces.

Grant had also sent the Tenth and Eighteenth Corps north of the James River to keep Lee's army busy so the Confederates could not send reinforcements either to the South Side Railroad or to Jubal Early in the Valley. The Eighteenth Corps advanced rapidly and Gen. George Stannard's division took

Ft. Harrison, a major Confederate bastion in the defense line, and some of the surrounding entrenchments. The Confederates prepared to counterattack, with Lee personally directing the assaults.

September 30 (Friday)

Ft. Harrison, north of the James River, and on the Richmond defense line, was now in Union hands and, despite repeated counterattacks by the Confederate troops under Lee, would remain Union. The Confederacy now constructed new works to face Ft. Harrison and these new works were occupied rapidly.

South of Petersburg, Grant sent Meade to extend the Federal line to include the South Side Railroad and the crossings of the Appomattox River. There was considerable fighting and confusion at Peebles' Farm when Confederate general A.P. Hill drove his corps in between the two Federal corps of Warren and Parke. The Union line held and the two Union corps finally joined, causing the Confederates to spread their line a little thinner.

Late the evening before, the blockader U.S.S. *Niphon*, Acting Master Kemble, chased the British blockade-running steamer *Night Hawk* aground off Ft. Fisher, N.C., as the steamer attempted to run into New Inlet. Kemble sent a boat crew under the command of Acting Ensign Semon (the same man who had made the reconnaissance on the 27th) to board the *Hawk*. Semon boarded, removed the crew, and set the steamer afire while under fire from the guns of Ft. Fisher. The British master of the *Night Hawk* complained to the British Consul about his treatment and what he called "the premature burning of the vessel." This later became a subject of a diplomatic note about the mistreatment of the crew, etc. Semon was exonerated of all charges after a court of inquiry.

OCTOBER 1864

The autumn of the fourth year of the war brought good news for the North when Atlanta fell. The relative quiet along the Petersburg lines was also welcome. No great losses of Union troops had occurred in the Army of the Potomac for several weeks. Sherman seemed to have things in hand, despite the harassment of Forrest and Wheeler. Among the camps, the evenings were getting cooler, the mosquitoes had mostly disappeared, and the mornings were very brisk. The troops thought of winter camp.

October 1 (Saturday)

Forrest was loose in southeastern Tennessee and northern Alabama, cutting communications and capturing blockhouses. His main purpose was to make enough trouble to get Sherman's attention, so that the Union general would pull out of Georgia.

There was another Confederate general with the same idea. Hood's Army of Tennessee, a mere shadow of its former self, was now moving around south of Sherman at Atlanta, headed for Tennessee to get on Sherman's rail link with Chattanooga. Hardee was now gone from Hood's army, being assigned to command South Carolina, Georgia, and Florida.

Miller, 1st Ohio Heavy Artillery, eastern Tennessee:

> The rebels withdrew in the morning and were followed by our cavalry as far as Zollicoffer. At this time we learned that the Burbridge part of the expedition had been defeated and that if we advanced we would likely share the same fate. A retreat was ordered and by a rapid march of two days we were back in Bull's Gap (60 miles).

The British blockade runner *Condor*, with Confederate agent Mrs. Rose O'Neal Greenhow aboard, had almost cleared the area of New Inlet, N.C., when she was spotted and run aground by the U.S.S. *Niphon*, Acting Master Kemble. Mrs. Greenhow was carrying dispatches and a bag containing $2,000 in gold, the bag being around her neck. Fearing capture, she demanded that a boat take her ashore. During the attempt, the boat capsized, drowning her in the surf. The *Niphon* could not close with the grounded *Condor*, due to heavy fire from Ft. Fisher.

Off the coast of Texas, Capt. W.F. Brown, Confederate States Marine Corps, in company with Lt. Marcus J. Beebee, CSN, and a party of 10 sailors and marines, disguised themselves as passengers and boarded the steamer *Ike Davis*. Off Brazos they overwhelmed the crew and took the ship into Matagorda Bay, Tex., as a prize of war.

Sterling Price was making some (but not much) progress in Missouri towards his goal of regaining that state for the Confederacy.

Today, about 1000 former prisoners at Andersonville who had been moved to Charleston, S.C., and herded into the fairgrounds on September 12th, were moved by train to Florence, S.C., where a new stockade had been prepared for them. Among these prisoners was Private S.J. Gibson, 103rd Pennsylvania Volunteers, captured at Plymouth, N.C., on April 20, 1864. The departure from Andersonville was supposed to be for exchange of prisoners. However, Gen. Grant's new policy forbade the exchange on the grounds that it would help the South solve its manpower problems. The prisoners would remain at Florence until December 15, 1864.

October 2 (Sunday)

Things livened up at Big Shanty and at the Kennesaw Water Tank in Georgia, when Hood's Army of Tennessee reached Sherman's rail link with Chattanooga. The Confederates tore up the track of the Western & Atlantic Railroad and interrupted service on the line.

At Augusta, Ga., President Davis appointed Gen. P.G.T. Beauregard over the armies of Hood and Taylor in the west. Beauregard was not to interfere with tactical operations, except when he was personally on the field.

Jackman, Pvt., "The Orphan Brigade," Americus, Ga.:

> Sunday. Today my turn of service expired—three years. When I joined the army, I little thought the war would last so long.... The week past has been very dull. Out of books. Sometimes I would go to the Court House—a part of the hospital—and read old papers. The weather has been very hot which does not agree with me. The hospital fare is now very worse—will be better—so says Steward H..

Four days of mixed fighting around Peebles' Farm south and west of Petersburg had netted some prisoners on both sides, but gained little for the South. The Federals were still threatening the South Side Railroad.

In Missouri, Sterling Price was within 50 miles of St. Louis, but progress was slow.

Fighting in the Shenandoah Valley was limited to skirmishing at Bridgewater and Mt. Crawford, near Harrisonburg. A Federal expedition from Tennessee was under way against the salt-mine operations in southwest Virginia.

October 3 (Monday)

When the British steamer *Tasmanian* sailed from England for Havana, Cuba, it had aboard the famous (or infamous) former captain of the C.S.S. *Alabama*, Raphael Semmes, whose ship had been sunk in its first real combat by the U.S.S. *Kearsarge.* He hoped to return to Richmond and report to President Davis for another assignment.

In the area of Big Shanty, Ga., Gen. Hood's Confederate Army of Tennessee was astraddle the railroad linking Atlanta and Chattanooga and tearing up more track. Sherman was finally forced to pay some attention to both Hood and Forrest. Sherman began to send troops from Atlanta to cope with the problem. Gen. George H. Thomas had been sent to Nashville to organize the defenses in the event that Hood headed in that direction.

President Davis, arriving in Columbia, S.C., made a speech in which he said "...I see no chance for Sherman to escape from a defeat or a disgraceful retreat."

Jackman, Pvt., "The Orphan Brigade," Americus, Ga.:

> Great consternation among the "rats," the "ironclad" Med. Ex. Board from the army examined the attendants of the hospital and the convalescents, sending all who were able to pull a trigger to the front. The Board made nearly a clean sweep of the hospital. I witnessed the examination and it reminded me more of traders examining stock than anything else....

Barber, Sgt., Co. C, 15th Illinois Volunteer Infantry, Ackworth, Ga.:

> The evening of October 3d, they camped within one mile of Ackworth, their camp fires extending in a semi-circle around us. Some of us wanted to go out and reconnoitre but the Captain would not allow it; nevertheless, some did go out and reported a large rebel army with artillery, but the Captain would not believe it. He said it was a force of rebel cavalry and

they were trying to scare us. Contrary to the advice of all the other officers, he persisted in his foolish determination to remain. That night or early the next morning, he could have retreated to Allatoona and saved everything. All night long we lay on our arms in a drenching rain storm awaiting an attack. It seemed that the rebels were sure of their prey, but rather than alarm the garrison of Allatoona Pass, they would suffer us to escape.

Things were fairly quiet both at Petersburg and in the Valley, for a change. Lee's defenders kept diminishing, as they were wounded, killed, or taken prisoner. Desertions were on the rise also, as the men slipped through the pickets at night and went to the Union lines.

October 4 (Tuesday)

Sherman had finally taken full note of the situation near Big Shanty and Ackworth, Ga. He left one corps to hold Atlanta and took the rest up the rail line to discuss the situation with Hood. There was fighting at Ackworth and near Lost Mountain.

Barber, Sgt., Co. C, 15th Illinois Volunteer Infantry, Ackworth, Ga.:

> The morning of October 4th dawned bright and beautiful. The rain drops still hanging from the autumn foliage reflected in the bright rays of the morning sun, appeared like a sheen of silver, as if mocking at our calamity and rejoicing at the fate before us. Long before the rays of the sun tinged the eastern horizon, we were astir, watching with strained vision for the approach of the foe. We knew if Captain Kenyon persisted in his mad course, ere the sun set we would be prisoners in the hands of our foe, but with self-conceit and stupidity, which was wholly inexcusable, he bustled around giving us orders as though the fate of the nation depended upon the issue.
>
> As daylight began to approach and still the enemy remained quiet, Captain Kenyon said that if we were to get a fight out of those rebels, we would have to go out and meet them. So he sent out two companies, C and K to reconnoitre, and left the remaining company as reserve. We marched out a few rods and deployed in a line as skirmishers and cautiously advanced. I was sent with five men on the right to guard against a flank movement but keeping within hailing distance of the line, though quite concealed from it by intervening woods. We marched boldly up and drove in their light picket and marched up within full view of their camp. They were not yet astir. It seemed that General Loring, who commanded them, was in no haste to open the ball, so he allowed his men all the repose they could get, but our vehement attack soon roused them from their repose and some fell before our destructive fire before they had time to form their lines. When they were fully aroused, we saw a large army spread out before us. To oppose this host, we had barely one hundred and fifty men. Slowly and deliberately they formed their line. We could hear distinctly every order given. During the time, we made good use of our ammunition, well knowing that when they moved forward our time would be short.
>
> I now stole cautiously forward in advance of my men to get a better view of the position. A fierce yell now broke forth and I knew that the rebels were making a charge, and almost before I was aware of it, I was cut off from the command. Our boys were swept like chaff back to their quarters. I resolved to make the effort to regain them. In so doing, I had to pass the flank of the rebel line and cross an open space over the rise of a hill. I never expected to get over that hill safe. I rushed forward, casting side glances at the line of rebels. I saw a group in advance of the others, halt and fire at me. A shower of bullets rattled around me, two passing through my clothes. I made a desperate effort and got behind the cover of a house beyond, halted and discharged my gun into the advancing foe and then rejoined my comrades who were already sheltered by our frail defenses. Some took up a position in the depot, others around Mrs. Hunt's dwelling and the rest scattered to the brick houses that we had prepared for such emergencies. A portion of Company C took refuge in an old brick store whose walls projected several feet above the roof. On this roof about one dozen of us climbed and took our position. We made port holes through the brick and from there commenced a galling fire on every reb that came within range of our guns. Rollin and Milton were on picket. I did not know what had become of them until I saw them creeping around the corner of a house to get a crack at some rebels behind another house. I heard the simultaneous report of their guns and then saw them safely retreat to the other brick building. This set my mind at ease as regarded their safety.

The rebels did not seem disposed to attack us openly while in our fortresses, but they were not idle. They were rapidly surrounding us, the thick wood screening their movements from our view. Finally, to the east, where the country was more open, we saw a long line of troops emerge and a large force of cavalry march in our rear, but more fearful than all, a battery had been placed within easy range of our works and in fifteen minutes could level our defense to the earth, but with a reckless courage, we still fought on. Now was seen a horseman mounted on a white steed advancing towards us, waving a white flag. On the instant, the firing ceased, and we waited anxiously to know our fate. I took advantage of this temporary lull to retire to my quarters and fill my haversack with bread and canteen with water. Then I took a box of hard tack on my shoulders and started back. I meant to provide for a siege if it came to that. Just as I started back, the maddening shout rang out that we had been surrendered. I hastened back and found the other boys boiling over with rage at the manner in which they had been sold. A grand nephew of Patrick Henry, of revolutionary fame, bore in the flag of truce, accompanied with a demand for the surrender of the garrison with all stores. He gave three minutes for consideration and if the demand was not complied with, no mercy would be shown except to the sick and wounded. We could do nothing else but surrender. A useless sacrifice of blood would have been the result of a refusal. During the parley, Mrs. Hunt had secreted the Colonel's most valuable papers and the boys had entrusted her with their watches and other valuables, supposing that the rebels would take everything from us. She also concealed the mail bag which was filled with letters ready to mail. I had one directed to Let Eddy. After our forces got possession of our mail bag, some kind friend enclosed the letter in a note to Celestia, telling her that the writer of the letter had been captured.

The rebel army now began to pour in by the thousand. It was General Loring's division. We were fortunate indeed in falling into that humane officer's hands. After stacking our arms and delivering up our accoutrements and stores, he kindly permitted all to get their breakfast and such articles of clothing, etc., as we wished to take with us. He also ordered his men not to molest our private property without our consent but permitted them to purchase of us. This kindness was duly appreciated and we acted in a straightforward manner that won his confidence. This treatment was in striking contrast to that received by our comrades at Big Shanty and Moon Station. The rebels there stripped our boys of almost everything, even to their boots and hats, barely leaving them with their shirts and drawers. These wretches belonged to General French's division.

The 6th Mississippi infantry was detailed to guard us to General Hood's headquarters which was at Dallas. General Loring gave strict orders to have us kindly treated and recommended us to the favor of General Hood. We found the 6th Mississippi to be composed of a noble looking set of men. They were veteran soldiers and treated us civilly. As we marched by widow Jones', that detestable female rebel clapped her hands for very joy. Our little drummer boy, King, played a sharp trick. He went to Mr. Crawford's and donned a citizen's suit and passed himself off as their son, and the next day when our army marched through the place, he rejoined it. I will here mention that Company A and a part of Company B escaped. The rebels were now busy tearing up the railroad and filling up the cuts. Indeed, the night before, we could plainly hear them at work. As we marched past the place where we first made our attack, we counted no less than twelve newly made graves. We had only one man wounded. We were marched to General Stewart's headquarters at Big Shanty, and from there we marched toward Dallas. As we were marching along we could plainly see our signals flying from Kennesaw mountain. Right over the heads of the rebel army, that signal flag sent an order to Rome for re-inforcements to defend Allatoona Pass, and the consequence was that when the rebels attacked that stronghold the next day, they were bloodily repulsed. We went into camp that night late and within four miles of Hood's headquarters. Although a vigilant guard was kept over us, we were allowed a good many liberties. Early the next morning we were marched up to Hood's headquarters. We reluctantly parted with the 6th Mississippi here. We knew that we could not get into any better hands, but in all probability worse. I found amongst them some brother masons, and the strong bonds of fraternal love which permeates our order were held sacred by those arrayed in army against us. I have to acknowledge many kindnesses extended to me by the brothers.

Lt. Morris, C.S.S. *Florida*, took his ship into Bahia, Brazil, for provisions and coal. This commerce raider, formerly commanded by John Maffitt, had been very successful on its mission.

Sterling Price finally gave up the idea of taking St. Louis, never having come close enough to scare the populace. Things were reasonably quiet in the Richmond and Petersburg area, as well as in the Valley.

October 5 (Wednesday)

After all the trials and tribulations that beset Private Day of Massachusetts regarding his reenlistment, he had finally won his battle and was going home.

Day, Pvt., Co. B, 25th Massachusetts Volunteer Infantry, New Bern, N.C.:

> On the 5th of October, two days before the expiration of our term of service, an order came to Brice's creek ordering all those who were entitled to muster out to turn over to the proper authorities our arms and equipments and report at the railroad station near Fort Spinola. This was just after dinner. Capt. Emory sent to the pickets across the creek for all those who had not re-enlisted to report at quarters. In a few minutes we were all there; the captain read the order and the boys cheered. I was all ready to comply with the order, and bidding faithful Spitfire a long and final farewell, I handed it to the captain. It was soon found out what was up and for the next half hour the enemy was left to take care of themselves and all hands gathered at quarters to say their good-byes and see us off. We went aboard the cars at Fort Spinola and picked up others along the road, arriving at Morehead about dusk. There 15 officers and 248 enlisted men went aboard the steamer *Dudley Buck* and soon after were sailing out the harbor of Beaufort, leaving behind us the scenes of our triumphs and hardships.

The Confederates of Hood's Army of Tennessee were busily attacking the Union troops at Allatoona Pass. Brigadier Gen. John M. Corse refused the surrender demands of Confederate Major Gen. S.G. French; the latter had moved into position during the night. From atop Kennesaw Mountain to the southeast, Sherman could see the smoke of battle around Allatoona 18 miles away. The Confederates assaulted the Union garrison, but could not take the pass. The casualties were high from so small a force. The Federals lost 706 out of about 2000, the Confederates lost 799 out of about the same number. French received a report, later proven erroneous, that Major Gen. Jacob D. Cox was moving with a Union force to relieve Corse, so French pulled up stakes and left, leaving Corse in charge of the field.

Barber, Sgt., Co. C, 15th Illinois Volunteer Infantry, prisoner of war, Ackworth, Ga.:

> At Gen. Hood's headquarters, our names were registered and one day's rations were drawn, consisting of one pint of corn meal and a few ounces of raw beef without salt. We were not furnished anything to cook with. Indeed, the rebels did not have anything of the kind with them, so most of the boys made dough of their meal into mush and as good fortune would have it, we had a little salt also and we fared comparatively well. We now sold considerable of our baggage for which the rebels paid exorbitant prices in confederate money. For instance, for a good rubber such as cost three dollars, they would pay twenty-five. Milt, Roll, Alex and myself concluded not to part with these useful articles and it was well for us that we did not. We sold such things as we could dispense with. I sold my old canteen, knapsack and portfolio for twenty dollars of confederate scrip. My messmates, Roll, Milt and Alex sold enough so that we had about two hundred dollars in confederate money, and between us we had thirty dollars in greenbacks, and as the latter was eagerly sought for by the rebels, we felt that our condition could have been much worse. We found the rest of our battalion here and a sorry looking set they were. Some were minus boots, hats and coats but with a brave spirit they made light of it and we joked each other as freely as we would in our own camp.
>
> The 12th Tennessee Cavalry was now detailed to guard us, and with few exceptions, they treated us as kindly as the 6th Mississippi. We left Hood's headquarters about 3 o'clock P.M. and traveled until about 8 o'clock. During the day we heard heavy cannonading in the direction of Allatoona, and we knew that they were having a fierce fight there. We all felt deeply anxious to know the result of the engagement there. If they succeeded in capturing the place, it would be an irreparable loss to our army. Toward evening the sound of battle ceased, and to our anxious inquiries as to how the battle went, the rebels

remained silent, but their gloomy countenances told us just as plainly as words that they had been defeated. We passed through the whole rebel army, and as a general thing, we found them in high spirits. Their leaders had worked upon their minds and made them believe that victory and the destruction of Sherman's army was before them—that they could carry the war to the banks of the Ohio, and possibly invade the free states, but the bloody repulse at Allatoona rather chilled their ardor. They were out of rations and confidently expected to get the immense supply at that place, but that little band of three thousand men drove back in confusion two divisions of the rebel army, and they were forced to beat a hurried retreat to avoid a clash with Sherman's army, which was now closely pressing them. We firmly believed, and subsequent events justified the belief, that this was a trap laid by Sherman to compass the destruction of the rebel army.... We resumed our march at daylight. It had rained all night and nearly all day. We halted at 10 o'clock A.M. and drew two day's rations consisting of hard bread and bacon. Resumed the march at 12 o'clock M. The marching was very difficult on account of the mud. We camped at Villa Ricca, having marched over twenty-five miles during the day.

A boat expedition from the U.S.S. *Restless*, commanded by Acting Ensign Henry Eason, destroyed a large saltworks on St. Andrew's Bay, Fla., that contained 150 buildings used to house the compound, the machinery and the workers.

October 6 (Thursday)

In the Valley, George Armstrong Custer's cavalry was attacked by Confederate cavalry under Gen. Thomas L. Rosser at Brock's Gap. Custer commanded a part of the cavalry under Sheridan during the Valley campaign.

Forrest was active around Florence, Ala., and Sterling Price was still edging away from St. Louis, Mo.

Day, Pvt., Co. B, 25th Massachusetts Volunteer Infantry, at sea off North Carolina:

The next morning we were around Cape Lookout and out to sea. Pretty soon we saw the officers come up out of the cabin, they were talking among themselves and seemed to wear a troubled look. It was soon discovered there was a lot of citizens aboard coming down with yellow fever, and before noon one was brought up out of the cabin dead and laid in a boat that hung on the davits. The boys held an indignation meeting, declaring it was wrong and cruel on the part of the government or other authorities to allow these men to come aboard.... The captain disclaimed all knowledge of how they came aboard, but it was evident they were here and couldn't have got here without the knowledge and consent of somebody.

October 7 (Friday)

In a futile attempt to dislodge the bluecoats, Lee ordered an assault on the Union lines along the Darbytown and New Market roads. In Missouri, Sterling Price was in the vicinity of Jefferson City, the capital, skirmishing around the area.

In Tennessee, to counter raids by Forrest and other guerrilla bands, the Union commanders were placing blockhouses along the railroads to protect them. These blockhouses would prove to be only partially effective and require enormous amounts of manpower.

In Georgia, there was fighting at Dallas, as Sherman moved to counter Hood's cutting of the railroad.

Barber, Sgt., Co. C, 15th Illinois Volunteer Infantry, en route to prison camp, Ga.:

Resumed the march at daybreak. We camped that night on the south bank of the Chattahoochee, having marched over twenty miles. The rear of the rebel army was camped here. Gen. Beauregard passed during the evening....

On the 4th of the month the C.S.S. *Florida* had entered the port of Bahia, Brazil, for provisions and refueling. She had been closely watched by the U.S.S. *Wachusett*, Commander Napoleon Collins, who had been looking for this commerce raider for some months. Collins sent a message to Lt. Morris, captain of the *Florida*, essentially challenging him to a duel of ships outside the harbor, but Morris declined. The Brazilian authorities, not wanting the ships to fight in the harbor, exacted promises from both the U.S. Consul, Thomas Wilson, and Lt. Morris that no fighting would occur in Brazilian waters. Collins refused to allow the *Florida* to escape, and plans were made to attack her in the harbor. At 3 A.M., Collins pulled his anchor, sailed past the Brazilian gunboat anchored between him and the *Florida*, and rammed the raider on her starboard quarter. There was a very brief exchange of cannon fire and the Confederate ship was surrendered by Lt. Porter, who was in charge while Lt. Morris was ashore. The noise woke the harbor and Collins wasted no time in attaching a tow to the *Florida*, and Collins left the harbor under fire from the Brazilian harbor defenses. Collins towed the *Florida* to Hampton Roads, Va., where he arrived on November 12, 1864.

October 8 (Saturday)

Barber, Sgt., Co. C, 15th Illinois Volunteer Infantry, en route to prison camp, Georgia:

> During the night, the rebels took up their pontoon, marched at sunrise, arrived at Newman at 10 o'clock A.M. Here we drew two day's more rations. Newman is a small town on the West Point railroad. We were quartered here in the old court house and remained all night.
>
> During the day, Milton and I were drawn into a discussion with a violent rebel of the aristocratic sort. Our debate grew warm. Milton got his blood up and the guard interfered.... We indulged in the hope all along that a speedy exchange of prisoners would be made and we would be free soon. Had we known that we were going to Andersonville prison pen, we would not have gone so quietly along. We had some opportunities to try to effect our escape, but we thought that a failure would subject us all to more rigorous confinement, and if we succeeded, it would be worse for those that remained. So we desisted. Besides, our guard put us upon our honor and trusted us. A mason, one of the guard, allowed me to go out forty rods alone and fill some canteens.

Two ships sailed from England this date, the S.S. *Laurel* and the steamer *Sea King*. The *Sea King* was captained by G.H. Corbett, and was to rendezvous with the *Laurel* at Madeira. The *Laurel* had on board Lt. James I. Waddell, CSN, who, with most of the passengers aboard the *Sea King*, would comprise the crew of the *Sea King* when it was fitted and commissioned as the C.S.S. *Shenandoah*. The *Laurel* carried the guns and provisions which would be placed aboard the new *Shenandoah* at the rendezvous point on October 19th.

October 9 (Sunday)

At Tom's Brook, Va., in the lower Valley near Fisher's Hill, the site of Early's last fight with Sheridan, the cavalry of Gen. A.T.A. Torbet was sent against the Confederates, who had been harassing Sheridan's troops. Generals Custer's and Wesley Merritt's divisions attacked and chased the Confederate cavalry of Generals Thomas L. Rosser and L.L. Lomax for several miles back up the Valley, capturing 300 prisoners.

In Missouri, Sterling Price left the vicinity of the capital and moved towards Boonville. His campaign was losing steam *and* men.

Day, Pvt., Co. B, 25th Massachusetts Volunteer Infantry, New York Harbor, N.Y.:

> On the morning of the 9th we sighted Sandy Hook, and on getting nearer we could see quite a fleet of vessels lying there. This was the lower quarantine. We ran through this, arriving at the upper quarantine about 10 A.M. We were now in sight of New York and were buoyant in hope that we should soon be there. As we neared a big steamer lying in the middle of the channel we were hailed with "Steamer ahoy!" We slowed down and ran alongside. Some kind of official came to the middle gangway and said:
>
> "Where are you from?"
>
> "Beaufort, North Carolina."
>
> "Any sick aboard?"
>
> "Yes, sir."
>
> "Any deaths?"
>
> "Yes, sir."
>
> "How many days out?"
>
> "Four."
>
> "How many deaths?"
>
> "Four."
>
> "Four deaths in four days. About ship and go back to the Hook."
>
> Our hearts that a few moments before were buoyant with hope now sank within us.... We ran back to the Hook, and dropped anchor not far from a large hospital ship. After a little while we saw a gig lowered from the hospital ship; a man stepped in and was pulled alongside our boat; he climbed aboard and proved to be some kind of health officer. He looked us over and then looked over the boat. He signaled a tug alongside, he hustled out those citizens and put them aboard of it. He also took Samuel Champney of

company D, whom he found lying down, and took them all over to the hospital ship. We bade Sam good-bye...never saw him afterwards, and I have since learned that he died there....

Barber, Sgt., Co. C, 15th Illinois Volunteer Infantry, en route to prison camp, Georgia:

We took the cars at two o'clock A.M. for West Point. Arrived there at daylight. Here we parted with the 12th Tennessee Cavalry. I will here mention that at Newman I wrote home and entrusted my letter with Dr. Chafee. It was contrary to the rules to hold surgeons as prisoners. The doctor was going home by the way of Richmond, but as he never mailed the letter, our folks did not hear directly from me while a prisoner.

We now drew another day's rations and took up a line of march for Columbus in the charge of several companies of Alabama militia who treated us more like brutes than men. We halted at sundown and camped. Their insolence was hardly bearable, and we commenced secretly maturing plans for revenge and escape. It only wanted the sanction of our own officers to carry it into effect, but they would not countenance it. Possibly the rebels had an inkling of what was going on for they ceased their abuse. These were men who had never seen active service and they made much ado about their bravery, but they were the most despicable cowards imaginable. Could fifty of our men have got hold of arms, we would not have hesitated to have attacked the whole crew. As it was, they rode along with their pieces ready, fearing that we might attempt to escape. The commander of these brave Alabamians rejoiced in the name of Sir William Wallace. The boys put on the Sir just to excite his vanity. I will note one instance of his bravery. Some of the boys became footsore and weary. They marched us almost on the double quick and some could not keep up. This brave Alabamian would ride back, draw his revolver, flourish it over his head and threaten to shoot them if they did not keep up. One of our boys in Company C turned on him, drew his form up to its fullest extent, and with flashing eye bared his bosom and dared him to shoot. The valiant Captain was snubbed. He quailed beneath those flashing eyes.

October 10 (Monday)

In the Shenandoah Valley, Sheridan moved to a position straddling the Valley Pike near Cedar Creek and held, awaiting developments. Early was coming down the Valley.

Day, Pvt., Co. B, 25th Massachusetts Volunteer Infantry, New York Harbor, N.Y.:

The next morning when the gig was seen coming over, the call went over the boat: "All hands on deck; don't be caught lying down; all out on deck!" When he came aboard he found us all fooling and knocking off caps. He looked us over...then he looked the boat over and not finding any down, took his leave but if he could have looked through the side of the boat he would have seen half of us down by the time he was in his gig.

Capt. Denny of company K, who is in command of this detachment, and who is a genial, big-hearted man, said he would see what he could do for us. He went over to the hospital ship and a little while after we saw him on a tug going towards New York. I knew if there was may help for us, Capt. Denny was the man to do it....

In Georgia, Sherman's Union force made contact with Hood's Confederates along the supply line from Chattanooga—some heavy skirmishing.

Barber, Sgt., Co. C, 15th Illinois Volunteer Infantry, en route to prison camp, Georgia:

We were on the march again at early dawn and one hour before sunset the spires of the beautiful city of Columbus were in view. This was a place of some twelve thousand inhabitants and was noted for its extensive iron manufacturing works, they being the most extensive of any in the South. The place at this time was a military post and presented some signs of life. It lies on the Chattahoochee river and is a place of considerable importance. Our eager eyes took in everything, noting its defenses. We were sure that Gen. Sherman would ere long pay his compliments to this city. We were not mistaken. In less than two months after we were there, the federal flag waved over the city.

We were marched up before the commandant's headquarters for inspection where a gaping, eager crowd stared at us. They wanted to know where the rest of the prisoners were. They had read in their papers and heard by report that there were seven thousand prisoners expected. When they found out that there were only four hundred, they felt cheap enough. They inquired for Sherman. Some supposed that he was along. One man stepped out and pointed out a person of rather shabby appearance and said that he was Mr. Sherman. The crowd stared eagerly at him. We could not restrain a shout of laughter. These poor deluded beings did actually believe that Sherman was along. Their papers said that the was captured and of course they believed it. We were marched to the church green and rested awhile. Our valiant Alabamians were now relieved, and they returned, covered with imaginary laurels. It seemed as though the whole population of Columbus came out to gaze at us. The reigning belles, children and aged, and even the very dogs eyed us curiously. I suppose that they never saw a Yank before and they expected to see something like wild animals, but when they found out that we were veritable human beings, their wonder ceased and they seemed disposed to treat us kindly. We sent some of them to the bakery for us and they faithfully performed the errand and would not take a cent for their trouble.

A detachment of the 39th Alabama infantry now had us in charge. They were veteran soldiers and knew how to treat prisoners. In fact, in their presence, we almost forgot that we were prisoners. They allowed us a great deal of freedom and treated us with the most magnanimous kindness. We were quartered in an old cattle pen that night and a strict guard placed over us. They apprehended an attempt to escape. Early the next morning we took the cars as we hoped for Macon. We had a horrid dread of Andersonville. The inhuman treatment of prisoners received at that place had reached our ears, but when we came to the Junction and left the Macon road to our left, then we knew we were doomed for Andersonville. Our train moved slowly and we had plenty of opportunities to attempt to escape, and it seems now almost a wonder that we did not attempt it. The only reason I can give is that we did not fully realize our situation. Our guards treated us so kindly, we did not realize we would get into such fiendish hands as the rebel commandant of Andersonville, and here I will make a statement that is true and proved true in every instance, and that is, whenever we fell into the hands of veteran soldiers who had fought us bravely on the battle-field, we received all of the kind and considerate attention due a prisoner of war, but whenever we were in charge of militia or that class of persons who, too cowardly to take the field, enlisted in the home guard, we were treated in the most outrageous manner. Now let it be understood that most of the guard at Andersonville were these militia. There were a few veteran troops there.

On the Tennessee River, Federal gunboats, while landing Union troops, were ambushed by Confederate shore batteries at Eastport, Miss. The landing had just begun when the batteries took them in a deadly crossfire, immediately disabling Union transports *Aurora* and *Kenton*, which drifted off downstream out of control. Lt. King, U.S.S. *Key West*, commander of the expedition, ordered the U.S.S. *Undine* after the two transports, while King covered the reembarkation of the troops, and saw to it that the U.S.S. *City of Pekin* managed to escape.

October 11 (Tuesday)

The elections in the North were showing a strong Republican trend, with gains made in several congressional races and the reelection of Indiana Gov. Oliver P. Morton. Lincoln haunted the War Department telegraph office to get the election returns.

Day, Pvt., Co. B, 25th Massachusetts Volunteer Infantry, New York Harbor, N.Y.:

> Tuesday night came but no Denny, and the question "Where is Denny?" was oft repeated without an answer. I could but feel that the captain was working for us and no news was perhaps good news.

Federal troops moved northwest along the rail line, skirmishing as they advanced towards Flats Creek, Ga. Sherman began to concentrate his forces at Rome, Ga., to counter Hood, who was below the city.

Barber, Sgt., Co. C, 15th Illinois Volunteer Infantry, Andersonville Prison, Ga.:

> At 4 o'clock P.M. the Georgia Hell, which clutched in its iron grasp ten thousand Union soldiers, was seen in the distance. We were marched up to the commandant's headquarters, Captain Wirz, where a rigid search was performed before we were put inside the stockade. This devil in human shape, Wirz, I will briefly describe. Any man gifted with any

discernment would pronounce him a villain at first sight. I should judge that he was of German descent; five feet eight or nine inches high; sandy complexion, with a scowling look. On his upper jaw one tooth protruded, giving his other repulsive features a horrid expression. As he moved around amongst us, he spit out his vile abuse in the most disgusting manner, nearly every word an oath. It was evident that he had received instructions from his superiors in regard to our search else we would have fared differently. As it was they only took away our knapsacks, canteens, haversacks, knives, etc., and allowed us to keep all under twenty dollars in money. When his subordinate came to search me, I emptied my pockets before him. Amongst other things, I had a box of Brown's bronchial troches. I told the sergeant who was searching me (he appeared to be a nice fellow) that it was some cough medicine my mother had sent me for a severe cough. He thought that I would be allowed to keep them. Unfortunately, the captain happened to see them. He snatched them out of my hand, smelled of them, sniffed up his nose and then scattered them in the dirt at my feet. I never experienced a moment of such frenzied rage before in my life. If I had had a revolver I would have shot him on the spot, regardless of consequences, but a moment's sober thought convinced me how useless it would be to have remonstrated, for to have said one word would have been the signal for my death. We were powerless in the hands of a merciless foe. During the search Rollin picked up some of them, so I succeeded in breaking my cough. I firmly believe that it had not been for them I would have been added to the long list of victims whose bodies were left to rot in unknown and unmarked graves in this Southern hell. Rollin also had a box of homeopathic medicine which was taken from him.

About sundown we were marched to the outside gate of hell.... Its huge doors swung open to admit us and we were in the presence of—I do not know what to call them. It was evident that they were once human beings, but hunger, sickness, exposure and dirt had so transformed them that they more resembled walking skeletons, painted black. Our feelings cannot be described as we gazed on these poor human beings. Equally astonished were they to see us. I presume we appeared to them like heavenly visitants, so white did we appear in comparison with them. Almost the first cry that greeted our ears was "fresh fish," then eager questions as to where we came from, whether there was any prospect of exchange. How eagerly would they watch for the least gleam of hope!...How little you could realize the suffering and misery that your friends were experiencing in Southern prisons, confined in loathsome dungeons, or foul pens, starved, sick, meeting with nothing but injury and insult, with no ray of hope to illumine their path, no kind word to cheer, where death would seem an angel messenger to release them from their trouble....

Such squalid, filthy wretchedness, hunger, disease, nakedness and cold, I never saw before. Thirty-five thousand souls had been crowded into this pen, filling it completely. Poorly clad and worse fed, drinking filth and slime, from one hundred to three hundred of these passed into the gate of the eternal world daily.... The prison was surrounded by a double line of stockades, by palisades protruding ten or twelve feet above the surface of the earth. The palisades were pine logs from one foot to eighteen inches in thickness. On the outside of the inside stockade, platforms were erected for sentinels. In the daytime only every other stand was occupied. In the night it was doubled. Inside the stockade about twenty feet from its base, was erected what was called the "dead line" and a prisoner that even put a foot beyond that line sealed his death if the guard chose to shoot him. It is estimated that from two to five deaths occurred daily from this cause alone while the prison was so crowded. Subsequently, when a larger portion of the prisoners had been removed, our treatment was not so rigorous.... Before we entered Andersonville, the prisoners except about ten thousand, had been removed to other prisons and it had been enlarged to twenty-six acres, bringing the stream in the middle of the prison, and as the spring had broken out, we did not experience near as much suffering as the other prisoners did before a portion of them were removed, but our treatment would have put the wildest, untutored savage to the blush.

As soon as we got settled, we went to work renovating the camp and we produced a marked change in its appearance.... We had roll-call each morning. If one was found missing, our rations would be withheld until he was accounted for.... Our daily rations consisted of a piece of corn bread, about two and one-half inches square, one pint of beans, with pods, dirt and bugs all cooked together, and in lieu of these, some maggoty rice....We were not long in finding out the most favorably disposed guards and they would carry on a traffic with us on the sly, furnishing us with sweet potatoes, corn meal, etc. In this manner we managed to live.... There were some rebel sutlers who made money out of the prisoners. A sort of market street was established, and all times of the day the most avaricious were trying to speculate. Some would manage to get hold of a little flour and make a few biscuits, and for one biscuit, about two or three mouthfuls, they would charge ten cents in greenbacks or fifty cents in Confederate money.... A spoonful of salt would sell for fifty cents....

During the recent scare in Richmond the authorities had rounded up all able-bodied men on the streets and hustled them off to the front lines (actually about three miles outside of the city) without benefit of farewells to their families, and without acquiring additional clothing. This action was the subject of much controversy in Richmond, and was considered despotic. On the 10th, it was reported that many of these "involuntary soldiers" had deserted at the first opportunity.

October 12 (Wednesday)

Chief Justice of the Supreme Court Roger Brooke Taney died in Washington at age 89. Taney, born on a plantation in Maryland in 1777, was graduated from Dickinson College in 1795 and became a member of the bar in 1799. Politically active in Maryland, he took a special interest in the rights of blacks, either slave or free. He served as Andrew Jackson's Attorney General from 1831 to 1833, and as Secretary of the Treasury from 1833 to 1834. He was nominated for the Supreme Court in 1835 and confirmed as Chief Justice on March 15, 1836. His most famous written opinion concerned the Dred Scott case, brought before the Court in 1857.

Day, Pvt., Co. B, 25th Massachusetts Volunteer Infantry, New York Harbor, N.Y.:

Wednesday morning, the 12th, was a cold, bleak, cheerless morning and we were growing weaker every hour but all hands rallied on deck when that hospital fiend was seen coming. Noon came but no Denny. Where is Denny? What has happened to him? Can it be possible that he has deserted us? were questions that went unanswered. I said it was possible that something may have happened to him, but I *cannot* believe he has deserted us. He is not that kind of man, besides he would not miss taking us into Worcester for half the wealth of the city, but if he don't come tonight, we will send Captains Parkhurst and Emory to see what has become of him.

About 3 P.M. we sighted a large tug coming through the narrows, and soon after it headed towards our boat. Long before it got within hail we saw a man in the bow waving his cap. It was Capt. Denny. Deliverance had come and I reckon when that hospital doctor heard our cheers he must have thought we were not very badly affected with yellow fever. I had known Capt. Denny for several years before the war but cannot remember a time when I was so glad to see him as I was on that afternoon. The tug came alongside and we were not very long transferring ourselves aboard it and it was again heading for the city. We ran alongside the starboard side of the Norwich steamer and boarded her at the forward gangway and were hustled among the cotton bales and freight like so many lepers. We were not allowed abaft the forward gangway, and were not troubled with visitors...We cared nothing for that so long as we were going towards home....

Rear Admiral David Dixon Porter assumed command of the North Atlantic Blockading Squadron off Wilmington, N.C., this date, relieving Admiral S.P. Lee, who would assume command of the Mississippi River Squadron.

Sherman and Hood clashed near Resaca and Rome, Ga. In Richmond, the flap over the "recruiting" of men on the street still raged.

October 13 (Thursday)

In Maryland, voters adopted a new state constitution which abolished slavery, by only a majority of 375 votes—30,174 yeas, 29,779 nays.

West of Harpers Ferry, W.Va., Mosby and his men held up a Federal train which carried two paymasters, and the Confederates made off with $173,000. Mosby's men had torn up a section of the track, wrecking the train. After the robbery, the Confederates burned the train and departed for parts unknown.

In the Valley, there was skirmishing around Cedar Creek as the Confederates probed from their old lines at Fisher's Hill, against Sheridan's troops astraddle the Valley Pike.

Day, Pvt., Co. B, 25th Massachusetts Volunteer Infantry, Worcester, Mass.:

> We reached Norwich about 2 A.M. on the 13th and went aboard the cars, arriving at Worcester at 4 o'clock. At this hour Worcester people were still wrapt in the arms of Morpheus and of course we didn't meet with a very enthusiastic reception. Our little party formed on Foster street and noiselessly wended our way to the City Hall.... An hour after we received an invitation to go back to the depot refreshment room for lunch. This invitation was readily accepted and a famine was created in that refreshment room soon after our entrance.... After breakfast we returned to the hall to receive visitors among the first of whom was Col. Pickett who warmly welcomed us, shaking hands with all. We were right glad to see our colonel and learn that he was getting the better of his wounds received at Cold Harbor.
>
> At 8 o'clock the hall was filled and welcoming speeches were made by his Honor Mayor Lincoln and others.... Free tickets were furnished us on all the railroads and we were dismissed for a week or until our muster out. I arrived home at noon, agreeably surprising my family who were not expecting me for a week to come.

Hood's Confederate force took the railroad at Tunnell Hill, scene of much fighting earlier during the Battle of Missionary Ridge. They also occupied Dalton and Tilton, Ga., Sherman held Resaca.

Barber, Sgt., Co. C, 15th Illinois Volunteer Infantry, Andersonville Prison, Ga.:

> Arose early, washed a shirt, pair of socks and one pair of drawers and took a bath. The mortality of the camp is about twenty per day now. Rollin, Milton and Alex Killon are my messmates.

October 15 (Saturday)

In Missouri, Gen. Jo Shelby's Confederates, a part of Sterling Price's campaign, attacked Sedalia and captured the confused Federal garrison. The local militia made a poor showing during the engagement. There was also more fighting at Glasgow, Mo., and Price's men occupied the town of Paris.

The third daring reconnaissance of the Confederate positions at Plymouth, N.C., was completed by Acting Master's Mate Woodman, who reported that the C.S.S. *Albemarle* was still moored at the pier in the city and that efforts to raise the sunken U.S.S. *Southfield* had been abandoned.

October 17 (Monday)

John Bell Hood's Army of Tennessee moved from harassing Sherman's rail lines and went towards Gadsden, Ala., relieving some of the pressure on Sherman. The torn track would be replaced shortly, and the trains would be running again.

Barber, Sgt., Co. C, 15th Illinois Volunteer Infantry, Andersonville Prison, Ga.:

> Are gathering brick made of wet clay baked in the sun, for the purpose of building a small house for winter quarters.

In Missouri, Federal troops were closing in on Sterling Price's Confederates, from the front and from behind, near Lexington.

At Petersburg, Lt. Gen. James Longstreet returned to the Army of Northern Virginia after recovering from wounds received at the Wilderness in May.

October 19 (Wednesday)

Early this morning, while Sheridan was in Winchester looking at the town's defenses, Jubal Early's Confederates crept through the fog and surprised Sheridan's Eighth and Nineteenth Corps in an attack that sent the Federals flying down the Valley. Wright's Sixth Corps was the next victim of assault, but he held his ground fairly well for a period, falling back in an orderly fashion to north and west of Middletown. Many of the Confederates dallied in the evacuated Union camps to loot the tents and eat the breakfasts still on the cooking fires of the departed Yankees. At this point, Early had most of the artillery and ammunition and much of the equipment of Sheridan's whole force.

Sheridan arrived from Winchester at about 10:30 A.M., organized his force again, and attacked Early at about 4 in the afternoon. The Union attack was not expected and the troops were out to redeem themselves for running earlier that morning. Sheridan chased Early back to Fisher's Hill, with Confederate losses that reached about 2900, including Major Gen. Stephen D. Ramseur, out of a force of 18,000. Sheridan had lost nearly 5700 from a force of about 30,000. While Early was badly beaten, he still had proven that the Confederate Army was a dangerous adversary.

Today, a new commerce raider was born for the Confederacy. The fast steamer *Sea King* rendezvoused with the S.S. *Laurel* at Madeira, where the guns and provisions on the *Laurel* were transferred to the *Sea King* and the latter ship was recommissioned the C.S.S. *Shenandoah*. This raider was to become one of the most successful of those that sailed for the Confederate States, and would be the last ship to carry the Confederate flag.

Forrest led his cavalry from Corinth, Miss., towards Jackson, Tenn., on a raid in cooperation with Hood's advance through Alabama and into middle Tennessee. In Missouri, Sterling Price had pushed the Federals around Lexington into a pocket by the Little Blue River.

Barber, Sgt., Co. C, 15th Illinois Volunteer Infantry, Andersonville Prison, Ga.:

> We are having splendid weather; nights getting to be quite cold. Wrote a letter home according to the rules prescribed and sent it on its mission, trusting to the fate of war to reach its destination. Drew our back rations of bread this evening and the boys are feeling quite well. The number of deaths is decreasing.

The sailors of the South Atlantic Blockading Squadron, Admiral John Dahlgren, would not miss their chance to vote in the presidential elections due in November. Ballots had already been distributed to the fleet, and Dahlgren now sent Acting Master John K. Crosby, U.S.S. *Harvest Moon*, to "proceed with the U.S.S. *Harvest Moon* under your command to Savannah River, Warsaw, Ossabaw, Sapelo, and Doboy, and communicate with the vessels there, in order to collect the sailors' votes already distributed for that purpose. A number of ballots will be given you, in order to enable the men to vote."

A group of Confederates headed by Lt. Bennett H. Young, CSA, left Canada, crossing the United States border, and descended upon the town of St. Albans, Vt., where they robbed three banks of over $200,000. The citizens of the town rose up in protest and one was mortally wounded and several others hurt. The Confederates fled back across the border, where they were arrested. Only about $75,000 of the money was recovered.

October 20 (Thursday)

Today, Abraham Lincoln proclaimed that the last Thursday in November would be celebrated as Thanksgiving Day. It was to be a national holiday of "Thanksgiving and praise to our beneficent Father who dwelleth in the Heavens."

Sterling Price was nearly at the end of his rope in Missouri. His expected flood of recruits never materialized, and he now had Major Gen. Alfred Pleasanton's cavalry to his rear, Major Gen. Andrew Jackson Smith's infantry force on his left, the Missouri River on his right, and in front of him was Major Gen. Samuel Curtis. All of them, except the river, were hot for his blood.

In the Valley, fighting broke out as Early's stragglers fell back towards Fisher's Hill. Sheridan was getting his troops reorganized for an advance.

Day, Pvt., Co. B, 25th Massachusetts Volunteer Infantry, at home, Milford, Mass.:

> On the 20th of October we again met in Worcester for muster out and discharge papers. I was once more a free man, having been under the care and keeping of others a little more than thirty-seven months.
>
> Two months later we again met in Worcester to be paid off. This was to be our last meeting, henceforth we should travel in different paths and our meetings would be only by chance, if ever. Shaking hands and wishing each other all manner of good fortune, we said our good-byes and parted. I have been through it and have had a great experience. I shall have no regrets that I did not go and have brought back no sorrowing memories. I have done what I could do to preserve the union of the states. I have met the enemies of the country face to face, and done what I could to roll back the tide of rebellion, and if I have been of any little service to the country, I am glad of it.
>
> With all the officers of the regiment my relations have always been on the most amicable footing, and I am vain enough to believe that they will all bear me witness that I have always cheerfully obeyed all their commands and done all the duty required of me; that I have always treated them politely and shown them

all the respect due their rank. In my little sports and jokes I have shown no partiality, and I trust there is no one who bears any malice towards me on that account. I have brought from the field no resentments or animosities towards any, but shall always hold in pleasing remembrance all, both living and dead, with whom I have been associated.

Let him not boast who puts his armor on
Like him who lays it off, his battle done.

Barber, Sgt., Co. C, 15th Illinois Volunteer Infantry, Andersonville Prison, Ga.:

Was on fatigue this morning, filling up old wells. Some of the detail carried out the dead to the dead-house. It is very shocking to human feelings the way the dead are disposed of. They are piled up in a wagon like so much wood, taken to holes dug for them and piled in, with no respect for decency or humanity.

We are still working on our little house. The sides and one end are laid up two feet with brick. We are going to put on a mud roof. Will take several days to complete it. Its dimensions are six feet wide, seven feet long and four feet high. Four of us occupy this little building.... A few of us are allowed to go out once in awhile under strong guard for wood. Some of the boys have at such times attempted to escape, but the bloodhounds generally tracked them down and they were caught and brought back.... The accommodation for the sick is a little more humane than heretofore. A shed had been erected for their accommodation. A good portion of the prisoners belong to the Army of the Potomac....

October 22 (Saturday)

In Missouri, Sterling Price had turned on his attackers at Westport, and he was preparing to do battle.

Hood had moved from Gadsden to Guntersville, Ala., in his advance into Tennessee and towards Nashville. Upon arrival at Guntersville, he found the river too high to cross, so he continued west across Alabama.

Barber, Sgt., Co. C, 15th Illinois Volunteer Infantry, Andersonville Prison, Ga.:

Pleasant. Everything quiet. A poor soldier ended his suffering this evening within a few feet of us. The nights are quite cool and it causes untold suffering amongst the poorly clad soldiers who are without blankets, shoes or coats and some without any shelter.

October 23 (Sunday)

Just south of present day Kansas City, Sterling Price ordered Jo Shelby's Confederates to attack Curtis's Union forces, intending to rout them, and then to turn on Alfred Pleasanton's cavalry. Shelby's men attacked, and for nearly four hours the fighting raged back and forth. The Federals found a way around the Rebel left flank and attacked in a ferocious charge. Pleasanton, not waiting for Shelby to attack him, piled into the Rebels with his cavalry about midmorning, slamming head-on into Marmaduke's Confederate cavalry performing rear guard. The Rebel cavalry fled and Pleasanton then hit Shelby's rear and flank. The Confederates fled the field and withdrew south along the Missouri-Kansas line. The Missouri campaign of Sterling Price was over. There would be no more major battles west of the Mississippi.

Barber, Sgt., Co. C, 15th Illinois Volunteer Infantry, Andersonville Prison, Ga.:

Had a very poor night. The coldest we had had, but it is a very nice morning. In the past few days quite a number of soldiers have been brought back who tried to effect their escape. Some nearly reached our lines before being caught. One man in particular, by the name of Davis, of the 4th Iowa infantry, lived three weeks in a cave near the rebel army and within three miles of our lines. He was well fed and otherwise provided for by Negroes. This man used to live in Coral and worked for Mr. Bartholomew. Drew beans last night and rice the night before.... We have made some beer of corn meal and molasses to keep off scurvy. Its effects are very beneficial.... Milt baked some corn bread for dinner which was very good.

October 25 (Tuesday)

The pursuing Federals caught up with Sterling Price's fleeing columns near Mine Creek, Kans., and Pleasanton attacked with his full cavalry force, causing heavy damage to the Rebel wagon train. Shelby came back in support and in the ensuing fracas, the Rebels lost more of the wagons. The Confederates were finally forced to fall back, burn about a third of the remaining wagons, and continue south.

In northern Alabama and southern Tennessee, fighting broke out between Hood's Confederates and the Union forces manning the various outposts, as Hood moved west from Gadsden.

October 26 (Wednesday)

In one of the most daring operations of the war, Lt. William Barker Cushing, USN, and fourteen men went after the ironclad ram C.S.S. *Albemarle.* Cushing had designed, and then had built, two 32-foot steam picket launches, each fitted with a 14-foot spar to which was fitted a torpedo, and each had a 12-pound howitzer mounted in the bow. One of the boats had been lost to the Confederates on the night of October 8th, the other was to be used for the raid. The launch left at darkness for the *Albemarle,* but ran aground, and most of the night was spent getting her off and refloated. The attack was postponed until the night of the 27th.

At Decatur, Ala., Hood demonstrated against the Union force holding the town and then proceeded on west. In the west, Pleasanton gave up chasing Price and moved his Federal cavalry to Ft. Scott, Kans., Curtis continuing the pursuit. "Bloody Bill" Anderson was killed in an ambush set by Federal troops.

October 27 (Thursday)

In one of the last major actions before troops settled into winter quarters, the Federals took another stab at capturing the South Side Railroad. Two Union corps, Warren's and Hancock's, numbering nearly 17,000, were met by Confederates, at Hatcher's Run, under Heth and Mahone, with Hampton's cavalry thrown in for good measure. As a part of a diversion to the attack at Hatcher's Run, the Army of the James skirmished with the Confederates north of Petersburg, towards Richmond at Fair Oaks, and on the Darbytown Road. The Union troops attacked, the Rebels repulsed the attack, and everyone went home to settle in the thirty-five miles of trenches, redoubts, mudholes, and louse-ridden hovels for the winter.

In the same miserable weather that beset the troops in the siege lines at Petersburg, Lt. William B. Cushing, USN, and 14 men, including two veterans of such expeditions, Acting Master's Mate William L. Howorth and Acting Master's Mate John Woodman, ran up the Roanoke River in a steady rain and inky darkness in search of the ironclad ram C.S.S. *Albemarle.* Towed behind their steam launch was a cutter from the U.S.S. *Shamrock,* whose duty, as Cushing described it, "...was to dash aboard the *Southfield* at the first hail and prevent any rocket from being ignited." *Southfield* had been sunk by the *Albemarle* on April 19, 1864, about a mile below the present location of the *Albemarle.* With a heavy tarpaulin over the launch's engine to muffle the sound, Cushing's party moved upriver eight miles, keeping close to the bank and anticipating discovery and alarm at any moment. Luck was with them, and they passed within twenty feet of the *Southfield* without being detected. Cushing still hoped to board the *Albemarle* and capture her intact; however, as they approached the Confederate ram, an alert guard saw the dim form of the launch and challenged Cushing's party. Changing plans instantly, Cushing reported:

> ...Just as I was sheering in close to the wharf a hail came sharp and quick from the ironclad, in an instant repeated. I at once directed the cutter to cast off and go down to capture the guard left in our rear [aboard *Smithfield]*, and ordering all steam, sent the launch at the dark mountain of iron in front of us. A heavy fire at once opened upon us, not only from the ship, but from the men stationed on the shore, but this did not disable us and we neared them rapidly.

A large fire, sited to illuminate the scene, now blazed up onshore. Cushing discovered a large boom of protective logs surrounding the Confederate ram. Amid the growing light from the fire and the mounting small-arms fire, Cushing coolly turned the boat around in order to run at the obstructions at full speed. His report continued:

> As I turned the whole back of my coat was torn out by buck shot and the sole of my shoe was carried away. The fire was very severe. In the lull of the firing the Captain hailed us, again demanding what boat it was. All my men gave a comical answer and mine was a dose of canister which I sent amongst them from the howitzer, buzzing and singing against the iron ribs and into the mass of men standing fire-lit upon the shore.

According to Acting Ensign Thomas Gray, later captured, Cushing shouted: "Leave the ram, or I'll blow you to pieces." No response was heard, and Cushing ran through the hail of fire at full speed, his boat lurching over the log barrier. Cushing continued:

> The torpedo boom was lowered and by a vigorous pull I succeeded in diving the torpedo under the overhang and exploding it at the same time that the *Albemarle's* gun was fired. A shot seemed to go chasing through my boat, and a dense mass of water rushed in from the torpedo, filling the launch and completely disabling her.

The ironclad, a gaping hole in her port quarter, began to sink rapidly, and Lt. Warley, commanding the *Albemarle*, reported: "The water gained on us so fast that all exertions were fruitless, and the vessel went down in a few moments, merely leaving her shield and smokestack out."

Cushing found his own boat sinking, but refusing to surrender, he ordered his men to save themselves, and he started to swim for shore, virtually unharmed, although he had been the one to explode the torpedo. On the way to shore he tried to assist the gallant Woodman, who was injured, but Woodman drowned. Cushing finally pulled himself half out of the water and onto the riverbank, where he lay exhausted until morning. At dawn, he found himself near a Confederate picket station, where he managed to steal a skiff and row the eight miles downriver to the Sound, where he was picked up by the U.S.S. *Valley City*.

When news reached the squadron, rockets were set off and all hands called to "cheer ship." Admiral D.D. Porter's praise for Cushing and his men knew no bounds. Cushing was later promoted to Lt. Commander, and Edward J. Houghton, Cushing's old friend and adventurer, was awarded the Medal of Honor. The other members of the party were either killed or taken prisoner.

Barber, Sgt., Co. C, 15th Illinois Volunteer Infantry, Andersonville Prison, Ga.:

> The morning set in rainy. During the afternoon it rained very hard, completely destroying our mud roof, which proves to be a complete failure.... Some of our regiment have tried to escape within the past few days but all were caught and brought back. We have been talking of trying it but the ill success of the others discourages us. Caught a severe cold yesterday. Feel some better to-day. Prison fare is gradually reducing my strength. I am getting to be quite weak.

October 28 (Friday)

In Missouri, the race after Sterling Price was won by Gen. Curtis, who caught up with Price near a town called Newtonia, in southwest Missouri. Curtis immediately piled into the weak Confederate force which held him off until reinforcement came up on the Union side and tipped the scales in its favor, forcing Shelby's Confederates to withdraw. Curtis prepared to launch a new attack on the 29th.

In Alabama, Hood kept moving across the state, going west towards a crossing of the Tennessee. Sherman had turned his armies and headed back towards Atlanta, leaving Hood to Thomas at Nashville.

As Confederate forces under Gen. John Bell Hood neared the Tennessee River in their campaign to divert Sherman by invading Tennessee, the Union gunboats on the river became formidable obstacles in preventing the crossing of the Rebels and providing information on the Rebel whereabouts to Gen. George Thomas. Near Decatur, Ala., the paddle-wheeler U.S.S. *General Thomas* and the Army gunboat *Stone River* were passing when Confederate batteries ashore fired on the *General Thomas*, which sustained some damage. However, she ran past the batteries and turned, pouring a withering fire into the batteries. The *Stone River*, meanwhile, had begun firing on the batteries, catching the Rebels in a cross-fire that was deadly. Brigadier Gen. Robert Granger, commanding the Union troops in the area, saw the action:

> It was impossible for men to withstand this attack. They deserted their guns, a portion of them retreating to their main line, while many of them rushed down the bank and sought the protection of the trees at the water's edge. The guns of the boats, double-shotted with canister, were turned upon them at a distance of scarcely 300 yards, and poured in a terrible fire.

Barber, Sgt., Co. C, 15th Illinois Volunteer Infantry, Andersonville Prison, Ga.:

> Pleasant and cool. Considerable talk of our being sent to another prison at Millen, twenty miles from

Savannah.... Bought four quarts of sweet potatoes today for five dollars confederate scrip. Also bought two quarts of meal this evening for two dollars. It takes ten dollars confederate money as an equivalent for one dollar in greenbacks.

October 29 (Saturday)

Curtis, near Newtonia, Mo., was ready to attack Shelby and completely wipe out Sterling Price's Confederate force, when part of his own Union force was recalled to its headquarters, the Department of the Missouri, under Major Gen. Rosecrans. This made the remaining Union force too weak to attack on its own. Grant was appealed to and he ordered the pursuit of the Confederate force, but the Union forces were now scattered and couldn't be reassembled in time to do any good. Price was away free and clear.

Immediately after Cushing's return from blowing up the C.S.S. *Albemarle* on the 28th, Commander Macomb, commanding the naval forces in the Albemarle Sound, ordered an attack to be made on Plymouth, N.C.

On this day, Macomb steamed up the Roanoke River with six ships, the U.S.S. *Valley City* going up the Middle River to a point upstream from Plymouth. The remaining ships on the Roanoke River were nearing the site where the U.S.S. *Southfield* had been sunk, when they discovered that two schooners had been sunk as obstructions. They engaged the shore batteries at long range and then returned downriver to start up the Middle River.

Barber, Sgt., Co. C, 15th Illinois Volunteer Infantry, Andersonville Prison, Ga.:

> A little cloudy this morning. Market street is unusually active this morning. Notice articles for sale that I have not seen before, such as pies, radishes, apples, etc. The price of pies is one dollar and a half United States money.... Washed shirt and socks this afternoon.

October 30 (Sunday)

Near Plymouth, N.C., the Union gunboats from Albemarle Sound under Commander Macomb, USN, came up the Middle River to join the U.S.S. *Valley City* that had navigated this stretch yesterday. Macomb's force spent the entire day getting through the treacherous turns of the river, meanwhile engaging the shore batteries at Plymouth at long range.

Hood's Army of Tennessee arrived at Tuscumbia, Ala., and parts of it reached Florence, Ala., on the north bank of the Tennessee River. The Federals started gathering their major forces to trap and engage Hood's army.

On the Tennessee River near Johnsonville, Tenn. (the area around Ft. Henry), part of Nathan Bedford Forrest's cavalry was trying to get across the river, but Union gunboats were a problem. The U.S.S. *Undine*, Acting Master Bryant, had escorted the transport *Anna* to a point below Sandy Island when Bryant heard artillery fire from further downstream. Hurrying to investigate, the *Undine* was attacked near Paris Landing by a battery of several guns and muskets. While Bryant was engaged, the transport *Venus* came downriver, and disregarding Bryant's signal to stand off, went past the batteries and engaged them from below. About 20 minutes later, the transport *Cheeseman* came downriver and was disabled and captured. The *Undine* continued to duel with the artillery for nearly three hours, until her ammunition was exhausted and her engine disabled. Bryant hauled down his colors, but this was disregarded, and the firing continued, so he tried unsuccessfully to burn the ship. The *Undine* was taken intact as were the two transports. The transports, a great haul for Forrest, enabled him to move his troops across the river.

Barber, Sgt., Co. C, 15th Illinois Volunteer Infantry, Andersonville Prison, Ga.:

> Pleasant and warm. Six prisoners came in last evening, captured near Atlanta while out foraging. They report the capture of Petersburg and that Sherman was whipping Hood badly. Trains were expected through from Nashville the day they were captured. Only two deaths occurred in the hospital yesterday.

The new Confederate commerce raider C.S.S. *Shenandoah* took her first prize in the North Atlantic, due south of the Azores, the unarmed merchantman *Alina*. The ship was scuttled.

October 31 (Monday)

Hood arrived at Tuscumbia, Ala., and sent reinforcements across the Tennessee River at Florence. He still hoped that Sherman would follow him, although he had been informed that Sherman had turned back to Atlanta. Forrest set up his own "Confederate Navy" with the captured gunboat and transports his men had captured the day before.

Upstream from Plymouth, N.C., Commander Macomb and his Union gunboats got their act together and assaulted the defenses of the town. The fleet steamed up and engaged the Confederate guns and rifle pits at close range. During the battle, the U.S.S. *Commodore Hull* sustained heavy damage. Union guns detonated a large Confederate munitions dump that blew up, creating a tremendous explosion. Shortly thereafter, the Rebels began evacuating their fortifications. A landing party from the U.S.S. *Wyalusing* entered Ft. Williams, captured 37 prisoners, 22 cannon, a large quantity of stores, and 200 stand of arms. The Stars and Stripes again flew over Plymouth, N.C. For his action, Commander Macomb was praised highly by Admiral D.D. Porter, and Secretary Welles recommended and Congress approved his advancement ten numbers on the promotion list. The Albemarle Sound was again safe for the Union.

Barber, Sgt., Co. C, 15th Illinois Volunteer Infantry, Andersonville Prison, Ga.:

> ...The 1st and 2d detachment and two hundred of the third left this morning. We suppose that they are going to Millen, Ga., whither we expect to go as soon as transportation arrives. The reason for removing us, we are told, is for the purpose of repairing the stockade and putting up barracks for winter quarters. We may come back again. Three or four hundred carpenters remain on parole to work on barracks. This is a good place for a prison if it was properly laid out and accommodations made for the prisoners.

The commerce raider C.S.S. *Chickamauga*, Lt. Wilkinson, captured and burned the ships *Emily L. Hall*, loaded with sugar and molasses, and the *Shooting Star*, loaded with coal. The steamer *Albion Lincoln* happened by, bound for New York, and Wilkinson loaded all the crew and passengers from the two other ships aboard her. Wilkinson later wrote of transferring the prisoners:

> In truth, I was relieved from an awkward dilemma by the opportune capture of the *Albion Lincoln* for there was absolutely no place for a female aboard the *Chickamauga*. I do not doubt, however, that the redoubtable Mrs. Drinkwater [wife of the *Shooting Star's* Master] would have accommodated herself to the circumstances by turning me out of my own cabin. Heavens! what a tongue she wielded! The young officers of the *Chickamauga* relieved each other in boat duty to and fro and she routed every one of them ignominiously.

NOVEMBER 1864

The presidential elections rather than the war seemed to be on everyone's mind at the beginning of the month. However, the two were inseparable. Lincoln's stance was well known—restoration of the Union. McClellan's stand on this issue was not clear in the minds of many people, North and South, since he had never *really* said what he would do to restore the Union. The soldiers were voting in their units and the ballots were being taken to their home states for counting. Would these war-weary veterans vote Lincoln out of office in the middle of this war?

November 1 (Tuesday)

Nathan Bedford Forrest had captured a gunboat (*Undine*) and two transports (*Venus* and *Cheeseman*) on October 30th, and Forrest now went up the Tennessee River, his artillery following along the riverbanks. The goal was Johnsonville, Tenn., where the Union had a depot and a small garrison. Forrest wanted the depot, but he also wanted to get across the river.

Barber, Sgt., Co. C, 15th Illinois Volunteer Infantry, Andersonville Prison, Ga.:

> Weather still continues cloudy and cool. I made my first visit to the hospital to-day. Found it nearly deserted. They are removing all the sick to the hospital outside of the stockade. All that are able, return to their respective detachments. I think it is evident that they intend to clear the camp entirely of prisoners. There remain here now, besides the sick, four detachments, five hundred men in each, and two hundred in the fifth detachment.

In Missouri there was still action against guerrilla bands who constantly harassed the Union garrisons. However, with the retreat of Sterling Price and his army, the Sixteenth Army Corps of Major Gen. Andrew Jackson Smith was readied and sent to join

Major Gen. George H. Thomas at Nashville.

The Confederate States Navy's Surgeon in Charge, Office of Medicine and Surgery, Dr. W.A.W. Spotswood, was responsible for the procurement and maintenance of adequate medicinal supplies for the Confederate Navy. The continuing blockade created problems which he now addressed:

> It affords me much satisfaction to report that...an ample supply of medicines, instruments, and everything to meet the wants of the sick has been furnished up to the present time, but owing to the strict blockade of the seacoast...rendering it impossible to procure medical supplies from abroad, I feel there will necessarily be much difficulty in procuring many valuable articles soon required for the sick....

November 2 (Wednesday)

United States Secretary of State William Seward notified the mayor of New York of a plot to set fire to the city on election day (the 8th).

Barber, Sgt., Co. C, 15th Illinois Volunteer Infantry, Andersonville Prison, Ga.:

> Morning rainy and cold. Rained very hard during the night and our mud walls caved in completely, soaking our blankets with mud and water. We passed a rough night. For the past few days our rations have been cut down a little.

On October 30th, the Confederates under Nathan Bedford Forrest had captured a Union ironclad, the *Undine*, and two transports, the *Venus* and *Cheeseman*, near Ft. Henry on the Tennessee River. Today the weather was misty and overcast, making visibility poor, when two patrolling Union paddle-wheelers, the U.S.S. *Key West*, Acting Lt. King, and the U.S.S. *Tawah*, Acting Lt. Jason Goudy, spotted the *Undine* and *Venus*. A spirited chase ensued in which the *Venus* was recaptured and the *Undine* was damaged, but the latter escaped by outrunning the Union ships. Carrying her load of Confederate troops, the *Undine* ran under the Confederate guns near Ft. Henry. The Union boats did not follow.

November 4 (Friday)

Near Ft. Henry and Johnsonville on the Tennessee River, the Confederates again sent the captured *Undine* out to lure Acting Lt. King into the narrow channel between Reynoldsburg Island and the west bank of the river. This time, King accepted the challenge and took the paddle-wheeler gunboats U.S.S. *Key West*, *Tawah*, and *Elfin* after the *Undine*. The Confederates then burned the *Undine*, and opened with their shore batteries on the Union gunboats. Meanwhile, Lt. Commander Fitch, commanding the U.S.S. *Moose* and five other steamers, all transports, was brought under fire from the same shore batteries, part of which had been moved to bring the Federal depots at Reynoldsburg and the Union transports under fire. The fight raged for about an hour before King's three ships were disabled and he struck his colors. Most of the crews reached shore, where they burned Union supplies to prevent their use by the Rebels. Commander Fitch managed to get the *Moose* and the transports off to safety. Forrest was determined to stop river traffic and disrupt Gen. George Thomas's supply line.

Barber, Sgt., Co. C, 15th Illinois Volunteer Infantry, Andersonville Prison, Ga.:

> Very cold and cloudy. Rained a little during the night. Our rations were very scanty last evening. It is impossible to keep warm to-day unless bundled up in clothes or huddled around a warm fire.

Miller, 1st Ohio Heavy Artillery, eastern Tennessee:

> On this date the regiment moved west and distributed by companies along the R.R. at Cleveland, Charlestown, and Tyner's Station, Tenn.—part of the regiment still at Loudon.

November 5 (Saturday)

After the fracas between Nathan Bedford Forrest and the Union garrison at the depot at Johnsonville, Tenn., Forrest left to join Hood, going by way of Corinth, Miss. Forrest estimated that he had caused $6,700,000 worth of damage at the depot.

Barber, Sgt., Co. C, 15th Illinois Volunteer Infantry, Andersonville Prison, Ga.:

> Another day has passed and we still remain in this miserable pen, and get rations barely sufficient to sustain life. One year ago this evening, after nearly three years' absence, I crossed the threshold of home. Friends and plenty there surround me. How great a contrast now!....

Master John Y. Beall, CSN, was into another plot against the U.S.S. *Michigan*, Commander Carter, at Sandusky, Ohio. Beall had once before plotted to take over the *Michigan*, but the plot had failed when Carter smelled a rat and arrested the co-conspirators, Beall escaping. Now it seemed that Beall and a Southern sympathizer, Dr. James Bates, had purchased the steamer *Georgian* in Toronto, Canada, and plotted to capture the *Michigan* and to use both ships to attack the larger cities on Lake Erie. Strict surveillance by Union agents kept the plot from being fulfilled, and eventually the *Georgian* was put into dock on the Canadian side, and the ship was sold again.

The C.S.S. *Shenandoah*, Lt. Waddell, captured and burned the unarmed schooner *Charter Oak* at sea off the Cape Verde Islands, after taking off the crew, passengers, and a large quantity of fruit, vegetables, and other provisions.

November 7 (Monday)

In Richmond, the Second Session of the Second Congress of the Confederate States of America gathered for its meeting. It would also be its last. The message from President Davis was unduly optimistic in tone, playing down such things as the loss of Atlanta. He also sent a message to Gen. John Bell Hood urging him to beat Sherman, so Hood would have no obstruction on a Confederate march to the Ohio River.

Barber, Sgt., Co. C, 15th Illinois Volunteer Infantry, Andersonville Prison, Ga.:

> Cloudy and warm. We expect to move before to-morrow morning. Several of our boys scaled the stockade by means of ladders while the guard was warming by the fire and tried to escape, but the hounds were put upon their track at daylight and most of them have been brought back....

Acting Lt. Frederick S. Hill was placed in a rather awkward situation when he raided a house on the Arkansas side of the Mississippi River near Island No. 68, trying to capture some Confederate officers reported to be staying there. No men were present when he arrived at 2 A.M. However, the following morning, the mother of one of the Rebel officers showed Hill her permit to transport cotton up the Mississippi, and a request, officially endorsed by Major Gen. Cadwallader C. Washburn, USA, for gunboat protection. Hill reported:

> ...In the face of all these documents, as I was upon the spot and a steamer then at hand ready to take the cotton, I considered it proper to give her the required protection, although with a very bad grace. Permit me, Admiral, respectfully to call upon your attention to the anomaly of using every exertion to capture rebel officers at 2 A.M., whose cotton I am called upon to protect in its shipment to a market at 10 A.M. of the same day, thus affording them the means of supplying themselves with every comfort money can procure ere they return to their brother rebels in arms with Hood.

November 8 (Tuesday)

Abraham Lincoln was reelected President, and Andrew Johnson elected Vice President, by a 55 percent majority of the popular vote of the people of the United States. Lincoln-Johnson received 212 electoral votes to McClellan's 21. This same election saw a gain for the Republicans in the House of Representatives, increasing their majority and retaining their majority in the Senate. Although the people of the North were not happy with the bloodshed, they were interested in retaining the Union. Interestingly, the soldiers' vote was almost entirely for Lincoln. The war would continue.

The prisoners at Andersonville were aware of the significance of the day and conducted their own election.

Barber, Sgt., Co. C, 15th Illinois Volunteer Infantry, Andersonville Prison, Ga.:

> This day, fraught with so deep an interest to every American heart, dawned unpleasant and rainy. The great issue to be decided to-day will engross the whole attention of lovers of liberty and free government throughout the civilized world.... A vote was taken in our detachment. There were two hundred twenty-four votes cast. Lincoln received one hundred eighty-eight and McClellan thirty-six. Over one-half of the men did not vote. Our rations continue very scarce....

At Edenton, N.C., Acting Master Francis Josselyn, U.S.S. *Commodore Hull*, under orders from Commander Macomb, landed a party to break up a court session. Josselyn described his adventure:

> I landed with a detachment of men this afternoon at Edenton and adjourned *sine die* a county court which was in session in the court house at that place under so-called Confederate authority. This court, the first that has been held at Edenton since the breaking out of the war, the authorities had the impertinence to hold under my very guns.

November 9 (Wednesday)

There was much troop movement in Tennessee as the contestants set up the pawns for the next game. There was action at Shoal Creek near Florence, and some skirmishing near Ft. Henry. Gen. George Thomas's army buildup at Nashville was progressing.

At Kingston, Ga., a major decision had been made concerning Sherman's armies. Sherman would now emulate Grant's Vicksburg campaign when Grant crossed the Mississippi and plunged into the interior of Mississippi towards Jackson without long supply trains, living off the land.

First, the army had to be reorganized. The four corps were to be divided into two "wings," the left and right. The left wing would be commanded by Major Gen. Slocum, and would consist of the Fourteenth and Twentieth Corps. The right wing would contain the Fifteenth and Seventeenth Corps under Major Gen. Otis O. Howard.

Second, there would be no long "trains" in this army. The regiments would make do with one wagon each, the companies with none. Wagons would be reserved for ammunition and other "essentials," and all comforts were to be left behind. A liberal policy of acquiring draft animals, etc., en route was established, as was a policy for drawing rations from the local populace.

The March to the Sea was almost ready to begin.

Barber, Sgt., Co. C, 15th Illinois Volunteer Infantry, Andersonville Prison, Ga.:

> ...Traded off my scissors last evening for one pound of salt. Traded for four pounds more this evening and gave five dollars confederate money for it.

Jackman, Pvt., "The Orphan Brigade," Americus, Ga.:

> Beautiful day, which is welcome after the recent rains. The flowers continue to bloom here yet. Have been feeling bad for the last few days. With Capt. W. and Mr. S. rode 2 miles out in the country after breakfast. The ride made me feel better.

November 10 (Thursday)

In the Valley, Jubal Early's force was now so weak that it had little effect. Early was, however, still there trying. He made a demonstration north from the New Market area towards Sheridan.

In Tennessee, Forrest was moving slowly, towards Hood. Their juncture would provide a formidable force to face Thomas at Nashville.

Sherman continued his organization plans for his armies, preparing to move back to Atlanta.

Barber, Sgt., Co. C, 15th Illinois Volunteer Infantry, Andersonville Prison, Ga.:

> At eleven o'clock we received orders to get ready immediately and march to the depot. Seventy-eight were put in one car, which made it so full we could scarcely stand up. We remained in this condition twenty-four hours, but anything was a relief to get out of Andersonville. We were the last to leave. We drew one day's rations. During the night several of the boys jumped off the train and tried to escape. Only one succeeded.

November 11 (Friday)

In Georgia, Sherman ordered the railroads destroyed. At Rome, Ga., Union troops tore up the tracks, destroyed mills, foundries, etc., while the garrisons around Kingston were sent to pull up rails and send them back to Chattanooga for later use. There was more skirmishing in Tennessee.

The merchant steamer *Salvador* had sailed from Panama into the Pacific Ocean en route to California, when she was boarded by Union sailors from the U.S.S. *Lancaster*, Commander Henry K. Davenport, as soon as she cleared Panamanian territorial waters. The captain of the *Salvador* had alerted the Union Navy that an attempt was to be made to seize the ship and convert it into a commerce raider. A search of the baggage of the passengers revealed a cache of guns and ammunition, as well as a commission from Confederate Secretary of the Navy Mallory for the capture. The plotters, led by Acting Master Thomas E. Hogg, CSN, were taken into custody.

November 12 (Saturday)

In the Valley, Sheridan and Early sparred at Middletown and Cedar Creek, with light contact.

In Georgia, Sherman had sent his last message to Grant. Sherman's army was tearing Atlanta down except for the houses and churches. Sherman's force of 60,000 men and 5500 artillery was ready to march.

Barber, Sgt., Co. C, 15th Illinois Volunteer Infantry, prison camp near Millen, Ga.:

> Arrived at our new prison, five miles from Millen, at 3 P.M. Here we found the boys of our regiment who were captured a few days before we were. They were Houston, Lowell, Irvin and Shaffer. They had had hard usage and were looking thin, but had been in good health most of the time.... Our camp here is much more pleasant than it was at Andersonville or Sumter. It consists of an inclosure of about forty acres, surrounded by a single line of stockades. A splendid stream of pure water runs through the center. The ground is well adapted for a camp. It gently slopes from the east and west towards the stream. Below, at one side of the stockade, a privy is built over the stream, and all filth is thus carried away. At the upper portion of the stream we get water for cooking purposes, and a little below we do our washing.
>
> There are at present nine thousand prisoners here, all camped on the west side of the stream. They are divided into divisions of one thousand men each. Each division is divided into detachments of two hundred and fifty men. Each detachment is divided into messes, two of one hundred men each and one of fifty. Then these messes are divided to suit the taste of the soldiers. A rebel sergeant has charge of the division and one of our own sergeants charge of detachments, messes, etc., and draws his rations from division sergeant. Our rations to-day consist of beef, rice, beans and meal. We get double the amount of beef that we did at Camp Sumter, and of a great deal better quality. Our rations are drawn uncooked. We get one pint of meal to a man, which is sufficient to sustain life. We are bothered some for wood to cook with, but by digging up roots of stumps we manage to get along. We expect to be allowed after awhile to go out and bring in wood. This camp is named Lawton.
>
> An exchange of sick and wounded is going on now, and there is a prospect of a general exchange soon. Was on Market Street to-day. Noticed that they sold things a great deal higher than at Camp Sumter. Some of the rebel officials are in league with the sutler, and charge outrageously for everything.

The famous (or infamous) raider of United States commercial ships, the C.S.S. *Florida*, had been captured in Bahia, Brazil, on October 7th by Commander Napoleon Collins, U.S.S. *Wachusett*. Collins had entered the harbor in violation of international law and had rammed the *Florida*. In the ensuing fight, the *Florida* was surrendered to Collins, who then towed it out of harbor, past the Brazilian harbor defenses, who then fired on the *Wachusett*. Collins towed the *Florida* to Hampton Roads, Va., arriving on this date. She was later ordered returned to the Brazilian government, but before she could be sent, she mysteriously sank at Hampton Roads. Collins was court-martialed and ordered dismissed from the Naval Service. His only statement in his defense was "I respectfully request that it may be entered on the records of the court as my defense that the capture of the *Florida* was for the public good." Evidently Secretary of the Navy Gideon Welles agreed. He restored Collins to his command. The incident would not die, from an international viewpoint, and finally on July 23, 1866, a 21-gun salute as an *amende honorable* was fired by the U.S.S. *Nipsic* in Bahia harbor.

November 13 (Sunday)

In the Valley, Jubal Early's weak force was further weakened when parts of his troops were sent to Richmond to bolster Lee's shrinking army. Although not as famous as Jackson's Valley Campaign, Early's defense of the Valley was better conducted than Jackson's and Early faced a larger Federal force that was more experienced than it was in 1862. Jackson's campaign of 1862, while brilliantly executed, could not compare to the efforts made by Early, who had fought 72 engagements and marched nearly 1700 miles in a five-month span. The end of this campaign, however, was approaching.

Near the equator, in mid-Atlantic, the C.S.S. *Shenandoah,* Lt. Waddell, captured and bonded two ships yesterday, the *Kate Prince* and the *Adelaide.* Today, Waddell took the schooner *Lizzie M. Stacey,* with a load of pinesalt and iron, and burned her. Waddell reported that the *Lizzie*'s mate, an unabashed Irishman, told him:

> ...My hearty, if we'd had ten guns aboard her, you wouldn't have got us without a bit of a shindy, or if the breeze had been a bit stiffer, we'd given her the square sail, and all hell wouldn't have caught her.

Nichols, George W., Major, USA, Sherman's Hdqtrs., Atlanta, Ga.:

> Yesterday the last train of cars whirled rapidly past the troops moving south, speeding over bridges and into the woods as if they feared they might be left helpless in the deserted land. At Cartersville the last communications with the North were severed with the telegraph wire. It bore the message to Gen. Thomas, "All is well." And so we have cut adrift from our base of operations...launching out into uncertainty at the best, on a journey whose projected end only a few in command know.... Thirty days' rations and a new base: that time and those supplies will be exhausted in the most rapid march ere we can arrive at the nearest sea-coast; arrived there, what then?
>
> As for the soldiers, they do not stop to ask questions. Sherman says "Come," and that is the entire vocabulary to them.... Behind us we leave a track of smoke and flame. Half of Marietta was burned up—not by orders, however; for the command is that proper details shall be made to destroy all property which can ever be of use to the Rebel armies....
>
> Yesterday, as some of our men were marching toward the Chattahoochee River, they saw in the distance pillars of smoke rising along its banks—the bridges were in flames. Said one, hitching his musket on his shoulder in a free and easy way: "I say, Charley, I believe Sherman has set the river on fire." "Reckon not," replied the other with the indifference; "if he has, it's all right."... Atlanta is entirely deserted by human beings, excepting a few soldiers here and there. The houses are vacant; there is no trade or traffic of any kind; the streets are empty....

November 14 (Monday)

Work on the Dutch Gap Canal was proceeding well. When completed, the canal would permit the Union gunboats to bypass the obstructions at Trent's Reach on the James River and go up towards Richmond. The canal was a brainstorm of Federal Gen. Benjamin F. Butler. Butler's idea to cut across the neck of a sharp bend in the James River would result in a canal 522 feet long with a depth and width to handle large gunboats and steamers. The canal was started in August 1864 and was still not completed by the end of the year. The labor on the canal was done mostly by black Union troops who worked under sniper fire and fire from Confederate gunboats at Drewry's Bluff.

Federal cavalry under Gen. Judson Kilpatrick left Atlanta and headed towards Jonesborough and the southeast towards Savannah. Sherman's left wing, Maj. Gen. Slocum, went out to Decatur and Stone Mountain, where it demolished the railroad, bridges, and anything else of military value.

In Nashville, George H. Thomas was assembling his troops, and Schofield's two corps at Pulaski were positioned as a blocking force. Hood, near Florence, Ala., waited for Forrest to come up from Corinth, Miss., before Hood could enter Tennessee.

Barber, Sgt., Co. C, 15th Illinois Volunteer Infantry, prison camp near Millen, Ga.:

> ...Suffered with cold last night. Have had no chance yet to put up a shelter or bring in wood. We have drawn no rations to-day, and the pangs of hunger are sharpening our appetites to the keenest point.

McClellan, defeated in his race for President, resigned his commission as a Major General. The resignation was readily accepted by Lincoln. Sheridan was promoted to Major General in the Regular Army, ensuring his employment after the war.

November 15 (Tuesday)

Sherman's men destroyed what little of value was left in Atlanta, leaving an emotional scar that never healed.

Nichols, George W., Major, USA, Sherman's Hdqtrs., Atlanta, Ga.:

> A grand and awful spectacle is presented to the beholder in this beautiful city, now in flames. By

order, the chief engineer has destroyed powder and fire in all the store-houses, depot buildings, and machine shops. The heaven is one expanse of lurid fire; the air is filled with flying, burning cinders; buildings covering two hundred acres are in ruins or in flames; every insant there is the sharp detonation or the smothered booming sound of exploding shells and powder concealed in the buildings, and then the sparks and flame shoot away up into the black and red roof, scattering cinders far and wide.

These are the machine shops where have been forged and cast the Rebel cannon, shot and shell that have carried death to many a brave defender of our nation's honor.... The city, which, next to Richmond, has furnished more material for prosecuting the war than any other in the South, exists no more....

Barber, Sgt., Co. C, 15th Illinois Volunteer Infantry, prison camp near Millen, Ga.:

We were roused before sunrise and ordered to move over to the other side of the camp. Nearly one thousand sick and wounded leave here to-day for Savannah to be exchanged. We drew rations of sweet potatoes. Prisoners captured at Richmond one week ago report the capture of that place by Gen. Grant. Prisoners captured near Sherman's line within a few days report that three of his army corps have returned to Atlanta preparatory to a forward move to the Gulf, and left Gen. Thomas with forty thousand fresh troops to watch and take care of Hood.

November 16 (Wednesday)

Sherman left Atlanta in ruins, the economy wrecked, and the people without means of livelihood. He rode out with the Fourteenth Corps towards Lovejoy's Station. Skirmishing was light, mostly with local militia.

In lower Tennessee, the Federals at Pulaski waited for Hood to enter the state. Forrest had finally arrived, increasing Hood's force with a good cavalry arm. In eastern Tennessee, John C. Breckinridge's small force fought at Strawberry Plains before withdrawing back into southwestern Virginia. Not much had been accomplished at Strawberry Plains in the overall scheme of the war.

Barber, Sgt., Co. C, 15th Illinois Volunteer Infantry, prison camp near Millen, Ga.:

Removed back to our former camp last evening.... Drew sweet potatoes again to-day. Removed across the stream again this morning. Two car-loads of sick arrived last night from Andersonville. We have not had a chance to go out since we came in here, and we are greatly bothered to get wood to cook our rations. The sutlers ask such an enormous price for their articles that we cannot buy.

Jackman, Pvt., "The Orphan Brigade," Americus, Ga.:

My head has healed and the patients being transferred to other hospitals I applied to go to the front tho not able for duty. I did not care to go to another hospital. Evening rode out to Mrs. R.'s to tell them goodbye.

November 17 (Thursday)

Sherman, using four different routes, left the Atlanta area and moved towards Savannah, Federal cavalry screening the operations. The Confederate military in the area still were not aware of Sherman's intent, believing it would be a local move.

Jackman, Pvt., "The Orphan Brigade," Americus, Ga.:

Mrs. R. came and took me to the depot in her carriage. She also filled my haversack to overflowing with things good to eat. At 10 A.M. took train for Fort Valley. Had to lie over there until 10 at night then took train for Columbus, Ga. At daylight, 18th, changed cars at Columbus for Opelika, Ala. I staid with Capt. P., our old Quartermaster (now post Q.M. at the place) until evening then took train for West Point, Ga. Mr. H. and I slept in a car all night at West Point.

Barber, Sgt., Co. C, 15th Illinois Volunteer Infantry, prison camp near Millen, Ga.:

...Several car-loads of paroled rebel prisoners have passed through this place within a few days. Twenty-five hundred are reported to leave this camp to-morrow—mostly sick and wounded. Drew meal, rice, beef and salt this evening. Meal sells at ten cents a pint, rice sixty cents a quart, salt five cents a teaspoonful, sweet potatoes twenty dollars per bushel.

Went out to-day for the first time for wood. Roll and Alex went with me. Only thirty can go out at a time. Forty squads go out in a day. If one man fails to come back with the rest, the division to which he belongs does not go out again until he is brought back. A Dutch captain by the name of D.C. Vowles commands the prison. He is a harsh commander. The mortality of the camp averages about ten per day. My health continues good, though I am conscious of growing weakness.

November 18 (Friday)

Sherman was on the road to Savannah, travelling in two large columns, cutting a swath about 60 miles wide. Nothing was in his front except some scattered militia and weak military units.

Hood, after a delay caused by the weather, was ready to move into Tennessee, crossing at Florence, Ala.

Barber, Sgt., Co. C, 15th Illinois Volunteer Infantry, prison camp near Millen, Ga.:

The sick continue to leave daily. About three thousand have left. By paying the doctor a good sum, from twenty to fifty dollars in greenbacks, he will put a person on the sick list, and for this they will get out of prison. Those who are fortunate enough to have money and who are disposed to use it in this manner succeed in getting out, and many of the sick are actually crowded out to give place to those who have bought their freedom. The doctors are making quite a speculating game of it.

November 19 (Saturday)

Gov. Joseph Brown of Georgia had long been at loggerheads with the Confederate government about use of Georgia troops, often refusing to send conscripts from the state to the Confederate Army. On more than one occasion, Brown had refused to turn over to the central government muskets which had been produced in the state, reserving them for militia use.

Gov. Brown now called for every able-bodied man in the state to come forward to defend their homes from the deprivations of Sherman's marching columns. He got very little response from anyone; most were content to let Sherman's 60,000 men go where they pleased, since any small opposing force would be completely annihilated.

Barber, Sgt., Co. C, 15th Illinois Volunteer Infantry, prison camp near Millen, Ga.:

Rained last night. We put up our rubbers for shelter. Drew one-half ration of meal last night.... A load of beef heads was drawn into camp last night and the men eagerly secured them, although they smelled so strong that they would have turned our stomachs under ordinary circumstances. Soup was made of them. Rice, bean soup, biscuits, pies and corn dodgers were made and sold on Market Street at exorbitant prices. Alex sold his watch for twenty dollars in greenbacks and so we still had a little money to use in case of emergencies. Tommy Houston now bunks with us.

At Wilmington, N.C., the C.S.S. *Chickamauga*, Lt. Wilkinson, ran the blockade under cover of darkness and heavy fog, running into Masonboro Inlet (which would give him an easy access to the port) instead of New Inlet. He then had to wait until high tide to get over the bar. With dawn came the gunfire from the Union blockaders who thought the *Chickamauga* was a grounded blockade runner. Wilkinson then broke his colors from the mast and opened his guns, joined by the heavy guns on Ft. Fisher. The duel with the blockaders U.S.S. *Kansas*, *Wilderness*, *Cherokee*, and *Clematis* lasted for a period until *Chickamauga* could get water under her keel.

November 20 (Sunday)

The torpedo boat *Saint Patrick* was completed at Selma, Ala., and had been sent downriver to Mobile to act against the Union vessels in Mobile Bay. The boat, built by John P. Halligan, who was also her first commander, was described by Edward La Croix:

Length, about 30 feet; has water-tight compartments; can be sunk or raised as desired; is propelled by a very small engine, and will just stow in 5 men. It has some arrangement of machinery that times the explosions of torpedoes, to enable the operators to retire to a safe distance. The boat proves to be a good sailor on the river and has gone to Mobile to make last preparations for trying its efficacy on the Federal vessels.

November 21 (Monday)

Hood moved with about 30,000 infantry and over 8000 cavalry, including Forrest's, from Florence, Ala., to Tennessee. Hood's first objective was to get between Schofield at Pulaski and Thomas at Nashville and to try to defeat the Federals piecemeal.

Sherman took on Georgia state militia at Griswoldville and gave them a severe thumping. There was other fighting along the route of march, but nothing to slow it down.

Jackman, Pvt., "The Orphan Brigade," with the brigade, Ga.:

Rained all last night. Dr. B. advised me to return to hospital for a time yet. In morning, rode the Dr.'s horse to town through a pelting rain. Shortly after noon took train for West Point. Got off at La Grange. Slept at the depot all night and came near freezing as the weather turned very cold.

Barber, Sgt., Co. C, 15th Illinois Volunteer Infantry, Savannah, Ga.:

...All the sick have been removed. Just before dark this evening, very unexpectedly to me, Rollin's name and mine were called, with orders to get ready to march immediately. Roll afterward told me how it happened.

There had been a special call for two hundred fifty men to fill out the one thousand. Rollin saw the lieutenant, and he, recognizing him as a member of our fraternity, succeeded in getting his name on and vouched for me. He also tried to get Milton on. The lieutenant could not do it, but told Rollin that in less than one week all would leave and be exchanged, and so, under these circumstances, we parted in good spirits with our comrades. Milton followed us down to the bridge and stood until our names were called and we passed out. A sergeant Reed's name of our company was called and he was not there to answer it. Milton was strongly tempted to answer to it and pass out with us, but fear of detection restrained him. Besides, he expected to get out soon, anyway. Poor boy! Better would it have been for him had he acted upon the impulse of the moment and gone with us! Then he might have been spared the horrid fate that happened to him!

We passed out of the stockade up to headquarters where we were paroled. No guard now dogged our footsteps. We were free. The earth, the air, the very ground we trod on, seemed to echo our soul's deep gratitude. Never had the soul-stirring word freedom appeared to us in such beautiful relief as at this moment. Those of you who have ever passed weary, miserable days in prison can imagine our emotion as we shook the dust of prison from our feet and once more trod the earth free men.... We took the cars the same evening for Savannah. Arrived there at the break of day.... The city troops took us in charge and marched us to the river where we were to embark and proceed to our fleet near Fort Pulaski, at the mouth of the Savannah River. A strong Union sentiment prevailed at Savannah and the Union people would have fed us had they been allowed to. We did not start with rations, but Rollin and I managed to get hold of an ear of corn and we made this answer for food until we arrived at the fleet.

While we were passing through the city, a person dressed in the garb of a Federal soldier was seen to quickly take his place in our line. The guard supposing him to be one of us, did not take much notice of it, but it was a Union citizen of Savannah who adopted this method of escaping from the clutches of his enemies. It was raining quite hard.... Finally the rebel transport *Beauregard* loosed its moorings, steamed out into the stream and headed for our fleet.... About one o'clock P.M. we hove in sight of our fleet. I never saw a sight which awoke more ennobling feelings of pride and devotion in my bosom than when I again beheld our noble ensign floating over gallant ships which were soon to bear us back again to home and friends. Eyes that had long been strained to catch glimpses of the dear old flag, now grew misty with tears. Yes, soldiers who had faced death time and again with unfailing eye, now wept like children before that flag that had so often guided them on to victory.

At three o'clock P.M. we embarked on board one of our ships and passed entirely out of rebel hands. We had been in their power forty-seven days.

November 22 (Tuesday)

Slocum's left wing of Sherman's army entered the then-capital of Georgia, Milledgeville, ransacking the State House, throwing the archives and files on the floors, and generally making a real mess of things. Paper was said to be more than a foot deep in the state file rooms. It would take months to sort it all out, if indeed, it would ever get done. Sherman's famous "bummers" now came into their own. These foragers scoured the countryside for food, draft animals, wagons, carts, and anything that could be useful to an army on the march. Many people were left without food or even shelter as the Federals burned the crops and outbuildings on the plantations. State militia were ineffective against the Federal advance, being poorly equipped and worse led.

Barber, Sgt., Co. C, 15th Illinois Volunteer Infantry, at sea, en route to Annapolis, Md.:

> ...At four P.M. we weighed anchor and set sail for Chesapeake Bay.... When fairly out at sea, the wind increased to a strong gale. The ship rolled and tossed on waves mountain high and we all experienced that very disagreeable feeling of seasickness. Our long fasting with impure food that we had received in rebel prisons and our overtaxed stomachs which we filled after getting on board our fleet, made us remarkably fine subjects for seasickness. Soon there was not one but what was heaving up "Jonah," and that, with the gale, made a scene of great confusion.... I attempted to crawl out on deck and relieve myself. I went on all fours, and just as I stuck my head out of doors, a gust of wind took my hat off. The next morning when I got out, I found it filled with the essence of seasickness. I gave it a toss overboard and my unlucky hat found a watery bed.

In Tennessee, Schofield pulled back towards Columbia, with the Confederates in a position to flank him. Thomas waited at Nashville.

November 23 (Wednesday)

In Georgia, Sherman stayed overnight at Howell Cobb's plantation prior to entering Milledgeville; the Twentieth Corps was at Milledgeville. Gen. William Hardee had now taken command of the Confederate forces opposing Sherman.

Nichols, George W., Major, USA, Sherman's Hdqtrs., Cobb's Plantation, Ga.:

> ...General Sherman camped on one of the plantations of Howell Cobb. It was a coincidence that a Macon paper, containing Cobb's address to the Georgians as General Commanding, was received the same day. This plantation was the property of Cobb's wife, who was a Lamar. I do not know that Cobb ever claimed any great reputation as a man of piety or singular virtues, but I could not help contrasting the call upon his fellow-citizens to "rise and defend your liberties, homes, etc., from the step of the invader, to burn and destroy every thing in his front, and assail him on all sides," and all that, with his own conduct here, and the wretched condition of his Negroes and their quarters.
>
> We found his grainaries well filled with corn and wheat, part of which was distributed and eaten by our animals and men. A large supply of sirup made from sorghum...was stored in an out-house. This was also disposed of to the soldiers and the poor decrepit Negroes which this humane, liberty-loving major general left to die in this place a few days ago. Becoming alarmed, Cobb sent for, and removed, all the able-bodied mules, horses, cows, and slaves. He left here some fifty old men—cripples—and women and children, with nothing scarcely covering their nakedness, with little or no food, and without means of procuring it. We found them cowering over the fireplaces of their miserable huts, where the wind whirled through the crevices between the logs, frightened at the approach of the Yankees, who, they had been told, would kill them. A more forlorn, neglected set of human beings I never saw....

In Tennessee, Schofield hurried his two corps on the road to Columbia, running a footrace with Hood's infantry going to the same place. Hood wanted to get between Schofield and Thomas, who was waiting in Nashville.

Barber, Sgt., Co. C, 15th Illinois Volunteer Infantry, at sea, en route to Annapolis, Md.:

> The gale continued to blow all night. I passed a rough night of it..... Toward night the sea became more calm...our rations were furnished us cooked and we got plenty of them.

November 24 (Thursday)

In Tennessee, the footrace to Columbia was won

by Schofield's two corps, with Gen. Jacob D. Cox arriving just ahead of the Confederates. Forrest's cavalry, leading Hood's army, was repulsed by the strong Union infantry. Schofield also secured a bridge crossing on the Duck River on the road to Nashville.

Sherman arrived in Milledgeville while his columns continued to march with Hardee trying to figure out which road he was going to use. Hardee's defense was futile in the long run; he had not the troops to block even a single road, let alone the four used by Sherman.

November 25 (Friday)

In New York City rebel arsonists were arrested with incendiary chemical "bombs," and their plot to burn the city was foiled. They had managed to set fire to several hotels and to Barnum's Museum, but all was contained.

There was skirmishing between Sherman's men and Wheeler's cavalry in the vicinity of Sandersville, Ga., on Sherman's line of march. The Confederates contested all the way into the streets of Sandersville before giving way. Some Federal skirmishing took place with the ineffective Georgia militia. Most local militia units put up a token resistance and then scattered. While there was some harassment in the rear of the Union columns, the veteran troops handled that without trouble.

Nichols, George W., Major, USA, Sherman's Hdqtrs., Sandersville, Ga.:

> ...The army under General Howard was attempting to throw a pontoon across the Oconee at the Georgia Central Railroad bridge. Here they met a force under the command of General Wayne, which was composed of a portion of Wheeler's cavalry, militia, and a band of convicts who had been liberated from the penitentiary upon the condition that they would join the army. The most of these desperadoes have been taken prisoners, dressed in their state prison clothing. General Sherman has turned them loose, believing that Governor Brown had not got the full benefits of his liberality....

In Tennessee, the Federals on the Duck River crossing were digging in rapidly, expecting the Confederate force under Hood to arrive shortly.

Jackman, Pvt., "The Orphan Brigade," Montgomery, Ala.:

> The hospital being out of wood, we had a freezing time. Evening moved into Lt. O'C.'s room of our regiment. Nice little room. A Miss. Capt, Mo. Lt., and Ga. Lt, also Lt. O'C.—none very bad off. I don't like the place though and shall leave as soon as I can get away. This is too much like a penitentiary for me. The patients have passes to go out once a day—those able to walk. If one comes in after being out a few minutes, he could not get out again during the day.

November 26 (Saturday)

Sherman moved his wings forward from Sandersville, Ga., slowly waiting until the tail caught up.

Nichols, George W., Major, USA, Sherman's Hdqtrs., Oconee River, Ga.:

> We had been told that the country was very poor east of the Oconee, but our experience has been a delightful gastronomic contradiction of the statement. The cattle trains are getting so large that we find it difficult in driving them along. Thanksgiving-Day was very generally observed in the army, the troops scorning chickens in the plenitude of turkeys with which they had supplied themselves. Vegetables of all kinds, and in unlimited quantities, were at hand, and the soldiers gave thanks as soldiers may, and were merry as only soldiers can be.
>
> In addition to fowls, vegetables, and meats, many obtain a delicious sirup made from sorghum, which is cultivated on all the plantations.... The mills here and there furnish fresh supplies of flour and meal, and we hear little or nothing of "hard tack".... Our large droves of cattle are turned nightly into the immense fields of ungathered corn to eat their fill, while the grainaries are crowded to overflowing with both oats and corn....

At Columbia, Tenn., Hood finally arrived in front of Schofield's Duck River line and began to survey the problem of attacking Schofield.

Barber, Sgt., Co. C, 15th Illinois Volunteer Infantry, Annapolis, Md.:

> The ship anchored about midnight in the harbor of Annapolis. We disembarked at early dawn and

marched to the barracks outside the city.... In the evening we drew a complete suit of clothing, but before changing we were required to divest ourselves of every article of prison apparel, go into a bath room, prepared expressly for us, and thoroughly cleanse ourselves. We were also obliged to leave our prison apparel, but we did not care for that.

Our new suit was furnished us free gratis. Our boys practiced a little deception now, which under the circumstances, I think was justifiable. Those of our regiment who had not been captured, were now mounted and were bodyguard to General Smith, and as we desired a cavalry suit, we gave in our regiment as mounted infantry. After our change our transformation was complete. We looked like a different set of beings.

November 27 (Sunday)

Faulty intelligence from the cavalry caused Schofield to move all his men across the Duck River into the trenches dug on the north side at Columbia, Tenn. Schofield believed Hood was across the river and on the Union's flank.

At Waynesborough, Ga., the Federal and Rebel cavalry had a set-to for a couple of days, as Wheeler and Kilpatrick clashed. Sherman was moving again.

Barber, Sgt., Co. C, 15th Illinois Volunteer Infantry, Annapolis, Md.:

Arose early, after a good night's rest. Ate breakfast and then marched to the parole camp, three miles south of the city. It was a splendid camp, well and tastefully arranged, laid out in regular streets, excellent barracks, warm and well ventilated, with cook houses, etc.... Another boat-load of prisoners came in this morning.

The headquarters steamer *Greyhound*, belonging to Major Gen. Ben Butler, had just taken on board such personages as Butler himself, Major Gen. Schenck, and Rear Admiral D.D. Porter, and she steamed up the James River five or six miles when the boiler firebox blew up. Gen. Butler described it: "The furnace door blew open, and scattered coals throughout the room." Admiral Porter said: "We had left Bermuda Hundred five or six miles behind us when suddenly an explosion forward startled us, and in a moment large volumes of smoke poured out of the engine room." It was suspected that one of the Confederate "coal torpedoes" had been placed in the ship's coal hopper. These devices were metal, machined and painted to look like a lump of coal, and usually were filled with 5 to 10 pounds of powder. Once in the firebox, they exploded, usually, as in this case, destroying the ship. Admiral Porter added: "In devices for blowing up vessels the Confederates were far ahead of us, putting Yankee ingenuity to shame."

November 28 (Monday)

Forrest's cavalry crossed the Duck River in the evening, soon to be followed by more of Hood's men. The crossing was above the city of Columbia, Tenn., where Schofield's Federals were skirmishing with other elements of Hood's army.

Sherman's troops were meeting more scattered resistance as they advanced towards Savannah. Cavalry clashes were reported at Davisborough and Waynesborough. En route, the Federals were destroying the railroads.

Nichols, George W., Major, USA, Sherman's Hdqtrs., Tennile Station, Ga.:

The destruction of railroads in this campaign has been most thorough.... The method of destruction is simple, but very effective. Two ingenious instruments have been made for this purpose. One of them is a clasp, which locks under the rail. It has a ring on top, into which is inserted a long lever, and the rail is thus ripped from the sleepers. The sleepers are then piled in a heap and set on fire, the rails roasting in the flames until they bend by their own weight. When sufficiently heated, each rail is taken off by wrenches fitting closely over the ends, and by turning in opposite directions, it is so twisted that even a rolling-machine could not bring it back into shape. In this manner we have destroyed...the entire track of the Central Georgia line, from a point a few miles east of Macon to the station where I am now writing.

Barber, Sgt., Co. C, 15th Illinois Volunteer Infantry, Annapolis, Md.:

Arose early, answered to roll-call and then took breakfast, which consisted of soft bread, boiled bacon or beef and coffee. For dinner we had bread and bean soup. The sanitary commission has been busy all day distributing needful articles amongst the prisoners, such as thread, paper, envelopes, combs, etc. A large sutler's stand is also on the ground. A large wash house is near by which contains fifty tubs and other accommodations for washing clothes. The whole camp presents a neat and wholesome appearance, the streets being wide and kept perfectly clean. This camp will accommodate ten thousand soldiers, with good hospitals for the sick. ...All paroled prisoners would receive thirty days' furlough and two months pay as soon as the proper papers could be made out....

In the Valley, Confederate cavalry under Rosser raided west of Cumberland, Md., where they took some prisoners and stores of supplies.

November 29 (Tuesday)

A near-miracle occurred between Columbia's Duck River crossings and Spring Hill, Tenn. Forrest's cavalry had crossed the Duck River last evening and were skirmishing around Spring Hill by noon. Schofield was still on the Duck River line disengaging his troops and sending them north along the Pike between Columbia and Spring Hill. The Pike was being held open by Gen. David S. Stanley's Union troops. By some quirk, all of Schofield's men went up the Pike without being attacked by Hood's Confederates. The entire Federal force, wagon trains and all, escaped to take positions near Franklin.

Sherman, in an attempt to divert Hardee's attention towards Augusta, had sent Kilpatrick in that direction while Sherman continued his march. The objective was to get across the Ogeechee River on November 30th without major opposition. Kilpatrick was also aiming at the Confederate prison at Millen, Ga., and the possibility of freeing the Union prisoners there.

Nichols, George W., Major, USA, Sherman's Hdqtrs., Johnston Station, Ga.:

> ...All day long the army has been moving through magnificent pine-woods—the savannas of the South, as they are termed. I have never seen, and I can not conceive a more picturesque sight than the army winding along through these grand woods. The pines, destitute of branches, rise to a height of eighty or ninety feet, their tops being crowned with tufts of pure green. They are widely apart, so that frequently two trains of wagons and troops in double column march abreast. In the distance may be seen a troop of horsemen—some General and his staff—turning about here and there, their gay uniforms and red and white flags contrasting harmoniously with the bright yellow grass underneath and the deep evergreen. War has its romance and its pleasures, and nothing could be more delightful, nor can there be more beautiful subjects for the artist's pencil that a thousand sights which have met my eye for days past, and which can never be seen outside the army....
>
> The most pathetic scenes occur upon our line of march daily and hourly. Thousands of Negro women join our column, some carrying household goods, and many of them carrying children in their arms, while older boys and girls plod by their side. All these women and children are ordered back, heartrending though it may be to refuse them liberty. One begs that she may go to see her husband and children at Savannah. Long years ago she was forced from them and sold.... The other day a woman with a child in her arms was working her way along the teams and crowds of cattle and horsemen. An officer called to her kindly: "Where are you going, aunty?" She looked up into his face with a hopeful, beseeching look, and replied: "I'se gwine whar you'se gwine, massa."

A naval brigade consisting of 350 sailors and 150 Marines from the ships of the South Atlantic Blockading Squadron, Admiral John Dahlgren, landed at Boyd's Landing on the Broad River, under the command of Commander George H. Preble. The brigade had been organized at the suggestion of Major Gen. Foster to cut the Charleston-Savannah Railway and to establish contact with Gen. Sherman's forces, which were coming towards Savannah.

In Colorado Territory, citizens around Denver tired of being raided by the local Indians, who were becoming bolder because few Federal troops were there to contain them. About 40 miles from Ft. Lyon, over 500 Arapahoes and Cheyennes were peacefully living. They had insisted that they had not taken part in any of the recent raids. Col. J.M. Chivington left Denver with a force and killed all the Indians, men, women and children, in the camp. This disgraceful action became known as the Sand Creek Massacre.

November 30 (Wednesday)

Hood caught up with Schofield at Franklin, Tenn., where Schofield was dug in south of town.

Schofield was faced with the problem of repairing bridges to get his wagon trains up to Nashville, so while he waited, he would have to deal with Hood. Hood came swinging up the Pike from Columbia, swung his troops to the left and right, into line of battle, and attacked the well-fortified Yankees about 4 P.M. The Confederate line came in well, drove the Federals back to the Federals' second prepared line, and then pulled back. The casualties for the Rebels were very heavy—nearly 6300 out of a force of 27,000. Among the casualties were six Confederate generals: States Rights Gist, H.B. Granbury, John Adams, O.F. Strahl, and the incomparable Patrick Cleburne. John C. Carter was mortally wounded. The dead generals were all laid on the porch of a local house. Hood also lost 54 regimental commanders killed, wounded, or captured. His army was almost decimated. He now had fewer than 18,000 effective infantrymen.

Federal losses were about 2300 from nearly 27,000 engaged. At night, Schofield pulled his men out of Franklin and headed up the road to Nashville.

Sherman was across the Ogeechee River with no opposition. A major accomplishment when the Confederates could have contested the crossing, costing many Union casualties.

Nichols, George W., Major, USA, Sherman's Hdqtrs., Ogeechee River, Ga.:

> With the exception of the 15th Corps, our army is across the Ogeechee without fighting a battle.... I am more than ever convinced that, if General Sherman intends to take his army to the sea-board, it is his policy to avoid any contest which will delay him in the establishment of a new base of operations and supplies.... Macon, Augusta, Savannah, or Charleston are of no strategic value to us, except that they are filled with munitions of war, and that the two latter might be useful to us as a base of supplies, with the additional moral advantage which would result from their capture....
>
> We have heard to-day from Kilpatrick and from Millen.... It is with real grief that we hear he was unable to accomplish the release of our prisoners in the prison-pen at Millen. It appears that for some time past the Rebels have been removing our soldiers from Millen; the officers have been sent to Columbia, South Carolina, and the privates further south, somewhere on the Gulf railroad. We have had very little difficulty in crossing the Ogeechee....
>
> This evening I walked down to the river, where a striking and novel spectacle was visible. The fires of pitch pine were flaring up into the mist and darkness; figures of men and horses loomed out of the dense shadows in gigantic proportions; torch-lights were blinking and flashing away off in the forests; and the still air echoed and re-echoed with the cries of teamsters and the wild shouts of the soldiers. A long line of the troops marched across the foot-bridge, each soldier bearing a torch, and, as the column marched, the vivid light was reflected in quivering lines in the swift-running stream. Soon the fog, which here settles like a blanket over the swamps and forests of the river-bottoms, shut down upon the scene; and so dense and dark was it that torches were of but little use, and our men were directed here and there by the voice.
>
> "Jim, are you there?" shouted one.
>
> "Yes, I *am* here," was the impatient answer.
>
> "Well, then, go straight ahead."
>
> "Straight ahead! where in thunder *is* 'straight ahead'?"
>
> And so the troops shuffled upon and over each other, and finally blundered into their quarters for the night....

The naval brigade which landed yesterday at Boyd's Landing on the Broad River under the watchful eye of Admiral John Dahlgren and Major Gen. Foster were engaged in the battle for Honey Hill, after which they entrenched on the Grahamville Road, blocking Confederate use of that artery.

DECEMBER 1864

Although the Petersburg-Richmond area was quiet, there was action enough elsewhere. At Nashville, Hood was approaching from the south with his battered army, hoping for a miracle. Sherman was lost in the wilds of Georgia, or so it seemed, since no one had heard from him for a while, and was probably heading for Savannah.

On the political front things were still up in the air. Some were still calling for a negotiated settlement to the war, others opted to pursue it at all costs. In Richmond the picture looked gloomy.

December 1 (Thursday)

In Tennessee, Major Gen. Schofield entered the Union lines at Nashville after eluding Hood's forces at Spring Hill, Columbia, and Franklin, Tenn. Gen. George H. Thomas had formed his defenses for Nashville in a semicircle, with both flanks resting on the Cumberland River. Hood brought his much-reduced and weary army to the front of Thomas's defenses to survey the options. Hood could now attack Thomas, or bypass Nashville in a Confederate drive to the Ohio River, leaving Thomas in his rear, a dangerous situation for Hood.

Gen. Thomas had received some formidable help from the Navy for the defense of Nashville in the form of the gunboats U.S.S. *Neosho* and *Carondelet.* Thomas telegraphed Gen. Halleck in Washington:

> I have two ironclads here, with several gunboats, and Commander Fitch assures me that Hood can neither cross the Cumberland or blockade it. I therefore think it best to wait here until Wilson can equip all his cavalry.

Sherman's troops were approaching Millen, Ga., site of a prison camp for Union soldiers. The Union forces were also reported heading for Andersonville, to free the prisoners there.

Barber, Sgt., Co. C, 15th Illinois Volunteer Infantry, parole camp, Annapolis, Md.:

> Received two months pay this afternoon, thirty-six dollars. The officers of this camp labor day and night to get the soldiers' papers straightened out.

December 2 (Friday)

Hood arrived outside the fortifications of Nashville today and began establishing his own lines, conforming to Thomas's. Halleck, in Washington, ordered Thomas out of his defenses to attack Hood. Thomas waited for developments.

Sherman turned his ponderous blue columns from an eastward course towards Augusta to a more southerly direction, pivoting on Millen, Ga., and heading in six columns almost directly south. Until this time, Hardee had no idea of the direction of Sherman's march, except that it seemed towards Augusta. Prior to this, Kilpatrick's cavalry, accompanied by Gen. Davis, had screened Sherman's movements effectively. The advance was now on Savannah, down the peninsula formed by the Savannah and Ogeechee Rivers.

Barber, Sgt., Co. C, 15th Illinois Volunteer Infantry, parole camp, Annapolis, Md.:

> Made some purchases at the sutler's stand, including satchel, and foolscap paper stamped with a picture of the parole camp.

December 3 (Saturday)

Hood had now settled his positions around Nashville, sending Forrest's cavalry to probe the Union lines and to attempt a blockade of the river downstream from the city. Federal authorities in Washington pressured Thomas to attack Hood's inferior force. Thomas again awaited developments.

Sherman was in Millen, Ga., with the Seventeenth Corps. Sherman, looking upon the remains of the prisoner-of-war stockade at Millen, told his cavalry commander Judson Kilpatrick to completely destroy the railroads around Millen. The four corps of Sherman's army now began to converge towards Savannah, and Sherman cocked an ear to hear the sound of the sea.

Nichols, George W., Major, USA, Sherman's Hdqtrs., Millen, Ga.:

> ...During our brief stay in Millen, we saw another sight which fevered the blood of our brave boys. It was the hideous prison-pen used by the enemy for the confinement of Federal soldiers who had become prisoners of war. A space of ground about three hundred feet square, inclosed by a stockade, without any covering whatsoever, was the hole where thousands of our brave soldiers have been confined for months past, exposed to heavy dews, biting frosts, and pelting rains, without so much as a board or tent to protect them after the Rebels had stolen their clothing. Some of them had adopted the wretched alternative of digging holes in the ground, into which they crept at times. What wonder that we found the evidence that seven hundred and fifty men had died there! From what misery did death release them! I could realize it all when I saw this den, as I never could before, even when listening to the stories of prisoners who had

fled, escaping the villains who rushed after them in hot pursuit, and foiling the bloodhounds which had been put on their track. God certainly will visit the authors of all this crime with a terrible judgment.

The railroad which has received our immediate attention within the last week, is altogether the best I have seen in the state.... The station-houses are generally built of brick, in the most substantial manner, and are placed at distances of fifteen and twenty miles apart. They have been destroyed by our army all the way along from Macon. The extensive depot at Millen was a wooden structure of exceedingly graceful proportions. It was ignited in three places...the building burning slowly.... The scene was so striking that even the rank and file observed and made comments upon it themselves—a circumstance which may be counted as unusual, for the taste of conflagrations has been so cultivated of late in the army that any small affair of that kind attracts very little attention.... An Irishman, while engaged, a day or two ago, in the useful occupation of twisting rails, remarked: "When the war is over General Sherman will buy a coal-mine in Pennsylvania, and occupy his spare time with smoking cigars and destroying and rebuilding railroads."

With the increased pressure on Savannah from both Sherman and the blockading fleet, more thought was given to the railroad link from Savannah to Charleston. Capt. W.W. Hunter, CSN, wrote Lt. Joel S. Kennard, C.S.S. *Macon*:

> The Charleston and Savannah Railway Bridge at the Savannah River is a very important point to defend, and, should it become necessary, endeavor to be in position there to defend it. In order to do so, and also to patrol the Savannah River, watch carefully the state of the river, and do not be caught aground or be cut off from the position at the bridge.

December 4 (Sunday)

At Waynesborough, Ga., there was an engagement when Wheeler's cavalry attacked Union soldiers guarding other Federal troops who were tearing up the railroads. Kilpatrick's cavalry responded and there was an all-cavalry fracas for a time, until the Confederates were driven off.

Nichols, George W., Major, USA, Sherman's Hdqtrs., Millen, Ga.:

> ...General Sherman neither wishes to sacrifice life needlessly nor be detained.... Besides, our soldiers have tired of chickens, sweet potatoes, sorghum, etc., and have been promised oysters at the sea-side—oysters roasted, oysters fried, oysters stewed, oysters on the half shell, oysters in abundance, without money and without price. In short, the soldiers themselves don't wish to be delayed!
>
> We daily traverse immense corn-fields, each of which covers from one hundred to one thousand acres. These fields were once devoted to the cultivation of cotton, and it is surprising to see how the planters have carried out the wishes or orders of the Rebel Government; for cotton has given way to corn.... One thing is certain, that neither the West nor the East will draw any supplies from the counties in this state traversed by our army for a long time to come. Our work has been the next thing to annihilation.

At Nashville, Thomas still waited to attack Hood, although the Union general was strongly urged to do so by Lincoln and Grant. Hood's cavalry had become aggressive, especially Forrest. Commander Fitch, U.S.S. *Moose*, took the U.S.S. *Carondelet*, *Fairplay*, *Reindeer*, and *Silver Lake* to engage the Confederate shore batteries of Nathan Bedford Forrest in the area of Bell's Mills, Tenn. The Federal gunboats engaged the batteries, silenced them, and recaptured three small steamers taken by Forrest the day before. Many of the Union prisoners who had been taken with the steamers were also released.

Barber, Sgt., Co. C, 15th Illinois Volunteer Infantry, parole camp, Annapolis, Md.:

> My furlough was made out to-day. I am to report to Camp Chase, Columbus, Ohio, at its expiration. Will start for home to-morrow. I have not yet informed my folks of my release from prison. I intend to surprise them and rise up before them like one arisen from the dead.

At Mobile, Major Gen. Maury, CSA, wired Secretary of War Seddon that John P. Halligan, the designer and builder of the torpedo boat *Saint Patrick* had not used that boat and doubted that he ever would. Halligan had moved the boat from Selma, Ala., to use against Union ships in Mobile Bay.

December 5 (Monday)

In Tennessee, Hood sent Forrest's cavalry on a demonstration for three days towards Murfreesboro. The cavalry could not capture the town from the Union defenders, so they returned to Nashville.

Sherman, still on the march towards Savannah, wasn't getting much sleep. One of his officers, Major Henry Hitchcock, reported that he often saw Sherman around the camp in the early hours "...poking around the camp-fire...bare feet in slippers, red flannel drawers...woolen shirt, old dressing gown with blue cloth (½ cloak) cape." On the march he would often lay next to the road where the troops were marching and take a cat nap after rising at 3:30 or 4 A.M. He never wore boots, always low-cut shoes and only one spur.

Jackman, Pvt., "The Orphan Brigade," Montgomery, Ala.:

> Walked half a mile upriver to the boat yard to see how much exercise I could take. I stood the walk pretty well—my head got a little dizzy, but did not pain me. The news of the battle in Franklin in Tenn—of Cleburne, Stahl, etc. being killed. Fight took place on 30th I believe.

Major Gen. Maury, CSA, wrote Commodore Farrand, commander of the naval forces in Mobile:

> Every opportunity and facility having been afforded Mr. Halligan to enable him to use his boat against the enemy, and he evidently not being a proper man to conduct such an enterprise, please order a suitable officer of your command to take charge of the *Saint Patrick* at once and attack without unnecessary delay.

In January 1865, the torpedo boat was transferred to Maury's command.

In Washington, Secretary of the Navy Gideon Welles reported to the President that since March 1861 the Navy had grown from 42 ships to 671 ships, mounting 4600 guns. A total of 203 ships had been built for the Navy in that time, including 62 ironclads.

December 6 (Tuesday)

At Nashville, Thomas had received a telegram from an angry Grant directing him to attack Hood at once. Grant feared that Hood would slip past Thomas and head for the Ohio River. Thomas replied that he would attack at once without waiting for cavalry remounts.

The U.S.S. *Neosho*, Acting Lt. Howard, with Commander Fitch aboard, went down the Cumberland River from Nashville in company with the steamers U.S.S. *Fairplay*, *Silver Lake*, and *Moose* to engage Forrest's artillery batteries located at Bell's Mills. The *Neosho* engaged the batteries single-handedly, firing grape and canister into them at a range of 20 to 30 yards, scattering the gunners and sharpshooters of the Confederate force. In two and one-half hours of engagement, the *Neosho* was struck more than 100 times with no damage to the ship, although the Rebels did blast away all that was loose on the upper deck. Fitch then withdrew upstream, knowing that the lightly armed steamers would not be able to withstand the shelling. Late in the day, the *Neosho* returned to Bell's Mills with the *Carondelet* and, using different firing positions, managed to disable some of the Confederate guns.

Nichols, George W., Major, USA, Ogeechee Church, Ga.:

> For two days past the army has been concentrated at this point, which is the narrowest part of the peninsula. General Howard is still on the west side of the Ogeechee, but he is within supporting distance, and has ample means of crossing the river, should it be necessary, which is not at all probable....
>
> In the course of our march to-day, we came upon a fine stately mansion, situated in a pleasant region, and surrounded by beautiful grounds, which were carefully and tastefully arranged. On entering the house, we found the reverse of a beautiful picture. It was a scene of shocking confusion; articles of furniture, soiled and broken, were strewn about the floors; household utensils lay in ill-assorted heaps; crockery, shattered into pieces, was beyond the mender's art. This was the work, not of our soldiers, but of Wheeler's Rebel cavalry, who had been on picket duty at this place on the previous night. The Negroes left upon the place, who explained the cause of all this ruin, also told us that their master and mistress were hidden in the swamp, with sundry animals and articles of value. A party of our soldiers went in search of the fugitives, and found them in a dreadful state of

fright. The Negroes did not seem to sympathize with their late owners, and three of them discussed in my hearing the propriety of absconding....

A significant feature of this campaign, which has not before been mentioned in this diary, received a marked illustration yesterday. Except in a few instances, private residences have not been destroyed by the soldiers, but there has been at least one exception, for an excellent reason. Yesterday we passed the plantation of a Mr. Stubbs. The house, cotton-gin, press, corn-ricks, stables, everything that could burn was in flames, and in the door-yard lay the dead bodies of several bloodhounds, which had been used to track and pull down Negroes and our escaped prisoners. And wherever our army has passed, every thing in the shape of a dog has been killed. The soldiers and officers are determined that no more flying fugitives, white men or Negroes, shall be followed by hounds that come within reach of their powder and ball.

Barber, Sgt., Co. C, 15th Illinois Volunteer Infantry, Baltimore, Md.:

> Left camp at three P.M. Received our transportation and furloughs at Annapolis and embarked for Baltimore at six-fifty P.M. Arrived at the above named place per steamer at ten P.M. No trains will leave tonight. Put up at the Susquehanna House.

In Washington, Lincoln nominated Salmon P. Chase, the President's former Secretary of the Treasury and rival, to be Chief Justice of the Supreme Court. Lincoln's annual message to Congress was read.

December 7 (Wednesday)

At Nashville, Thomas had still not attacked Hood, and Grant informed Secretary of War Stanton that if Thomas did not attack promptly, Thomas should be removed from command. Forrest was at Murfreesboro engaged in some severe fighting trying to overwhelm the Federal garrison.

Sherman, getting closer to Savannah, was engaged in skirmishing all along his advance, but there were no heavy engagements.

Nichols, George W., Major, USA, outside Savannah, Ga.:

> The army has been advancing slowly and surely, but as cautiously as if a strong army were in our front.... From fifteen to twenty miles distant lies Savannah, a city which is probably in some perturbation at the certainty of our approach. If the Rebels intend fighting in defense of the city, the battle will be an assault of fortifications; for as yet we have only skirmished with parties of cavalry, and the enemy has not seen the head of our infantry column, and can only judge of our strength through injudicious publications in the newspapers at the North....

Barber, Sgt., Co. C, 15th Illinois Volunteer Infantry, en route home:

> Started this morning at ten o'clock via the Harrisburg and Pennsylvania railroad.... Passed through Pittsburgh. Got our vouchers for commutation of rations, while prisoners, cashed here at thirty-one cents per day....

December 8 (Thursday)

Sherman could now hear the sea, beckoning like a siren. His soldiers had to contend with "land torpedoes" which had been planted in the roads leading to Savannah. The Union army considered these devices as proper when used around fortifications, etc., because they were something to be expected. Their use on the roads was considered barbaric and "simple murder." Sherman, coming upon a young lieutenant whose foot had been blown off by one such device, went into a rage. Major Gen. Blair had ordered a group of Confederate prisoners to dig up the remaining torpedoes and the prisoners were deadly afraid to do so, understandably. They begged Sherman to interfere and he flatly refused, telling the Confederates that their people had planted them there to assassinate Union troops, rather than fighting them fairly, and they, the prisoners, must remove them; if *they* were blown up, he didn't care.

Nichols, George W., Major, USA, outside Savannah, Ga.:

> General Howard has just returned from a bold and successful movement. Fearing that we should detach a force for the purpose of destroying the Gulf Railroad, which they are using to its utmost capacity just now, the Rebels pushed a force across the Ogeechee. While this body was covered by a strong

river-side line, General Crose, of Allatoona memory, shoved his division between Little and Great Ogeechee, thirteen miles in advance of our main column, to the canal which runs from Ogeechee to the Savannah River. He bridged the canal, crossed it with his division, and now holds a position out of which Hood's whole army could not drive him. This bold step has forced the Rebels to evacuate the line of works stretching from river to river, and they have now fairly sought refuge within the fortifications of Savannah.

Grant, perturbed with Thomas, told Halleck: "If Thomas has not struck yet, he ought to be ordered to hand over his command to Schofield." Halleck, ever the buck passer, said that the decision to change commander was Grant's. Grant again urged Thomas to attack, Thomas replying that his cavalry would not be ready before the 11th.

Admiral Porter wrote to Lt. Commander Watmough, the latter off New Inlet, N.C., concerning a plan suggested by Major Gen. Ben Butler to explode a vessel laden with powder off Ft. Fisher, hoping to destroy the outer works and guns:

> I propose running a vessel drawing 8½ feet (as near to Fort Fisher as possible) with 350 tons of powder, and exploding her by running her upon the outside and opposite Fort Fisher. My calculations are that the explosion will wind up Fort Fisher and the works along the beach, and that we can open fire with the vessels without damage.

December 9 (Friday)

Skirmishing at Hatcher's Run below Petersburg for the second day. There was light contact.

Sherman's march to the sea was almost complete. He was on the outskirts of Savannah! Skirmishing took place on the Ogeechee Canal at Cuyler's Plantation and the Monteith Swamp.

Grant issued an order relieving Gen. Thomas of command at Nashville, replacing him with Schofield. Grant suspended the order when Thomas said that he planned to attack on the 10th, but a heavy storm with freezing rain had made movement impossible. Grant waited.

Jackman, Pvt., "The Orphan Brigade," Macon, Ga.:

> At 8 A.M. took passenger train for Columbus. Met with B. of the Texas Rangers. We "ranged" together at Newman. The time passed very pleasantly conversing about old times. After we passed Opelika, the rain came down very hard. Changed cars for Macon at Columbus a little after dark. Owing to a freight train getting off the tracks, we did not arrive at Macon until after daylight the next morning.

Torpedoes were a real problem on the Roanoke River for an expedition headed by Commander Macomb, USN. The U.S.S. *Otsego*, Lt. Commander Arnold, struck two torpedoes, one after the other, and the tug *Bazely* struck one when she came alongside to assist. The *Bazely* sank immediately, the *Otsego* had part of her guns above the water, so she was used as an artillery platform to protect the river while the remainder of the boats went upstream—dragging for torpedoes.

December 10 (Saturday)

There was more action around Petersburg and the Weldon Road as Grant kept the pot boiling.

In Nashville, the vicious storm that had coated everything with ice was still around, preventing any movement. Thomas and Grant both waited for an improvement.

Sherman was in front of Savannah, and his cavalry was probing the city's defenses. Gen. Hardee, with somewhat fewer than 18,000 men defending the city, had flooded the rice fields of the area, leaving only a few roads available for the approach. Sherman, after a reconnaissance, ordered investigation of Ft. McAllister, south of the city, guarding the Ogeechee River, as the obvious approach to the sea. While rations were not short, forage for the horses and other draft animals was quickly used up, and some source was required.

Nichols, George W., Major, USA, outside Savannah, Ga.:

> ...We have now connected our lines, so that the corps are within supporting distance of each other.... The necessity of open communication with the fleet is becoming apparent, for the army is rapidly consuming its supplies, and replenishment is vitally important. Away in the distance, across the rice fields, as far as the banks of the Ogeechee, our signal-officers are stationed, scanning the seaward horizon in search

of indications of the presence of the fleet, but thus far unsuccessfully. On the other side of the river, within cannon range, stand the frowning parapets of Fort McAllister, its ponderous guns and rebel garrison guarding the only avenue open to our approach.

This evening a movement of the greatest importance has begun. Hazen's division of the 15th Corps is marching to the other side of the river. Fort McAllister must be taken. To-morrow's sun will see the veterans whom Sherman led upon the heights of Missionary Ridge within striking distance of its walls. Warm words have been uttered by the Generals of the 15th and the 17th Corps because the second division has been assigned the honor of this expedition. The possibility of repulse, the fear of wounds and death, do not seem to be considered in this rivalry....

Confederate Flag Officer Hunter, commanding a three-ship flotilla, attempted to run the gunboats past the Federal batteries at Tweedside on the Savannah River to join in the Rebels' defense of Savannah. Trading fire with the shore batteries, C.S.S. *Macon*, Lt. Kennard, C.S.S. *Resolute*, Acting Master's Mate William D. Oliveira, and C.S.S. *Sampson*, Lt. William W. Carnes, found that their boats were no match for the larger batteries. The *Resolute* was disabled in the exchange of fire and was abandoned, later captured. Hunter then decided to run his remaining boats upriver to Augusta, Ga., having destroyed the railroad bridge over the Ogeechee River.

In Savannah Harbor, the C.S.S. *Savannah*, Commander Thomas W. Brent, was preparing to fight her way out of the harbor and go to Charleston. To do this, the torpedoes in the harbor had to be removed. After several attempts, this was found to be impossible in the time allowed, the moorings of the torpedoes being too deeply imbedded in the sand. Brent pondered his next move.

Jackman, Pvt., "The Orphan Brigade," Ft. Valley, Ga.:

Finding that all of Wheeler's command had moved towards Waynesboro, Ga. and all the railroads being torn up and not being able to walk much, I hardly knew what to do. I was late in the evening making arrangements to leave the next morning on a train of wagons for Mayfield, 60 miles from Macon, where I could go by rail to Waynesboro. When I met with Dr. Goss, who told me our dismounted men were encamped near Fort Valley, I was greatly relieved.

Barber, Sgt., Co. C, 15th Illinois Volunteer Infantry, at home, Riley, Illinois:

... Our pulses glow with a new life to be once more in our own loved land. We here found our names reported in the papers as paroled prisoners and were afraid that our folks had found out that we would soon be at home.

Took the twelve o'clock train and arrived at Marengo at three P.M. I saw Uncle Almon first, and he had to take the second look before he could make up his mind that it was I. I gave a hurried call at Levi's and uncle Lorenzo's and then in company with uncle Almon, started for Riley.

I now learned with deep regret that Manda and Ann had gone to Pennsylvania, and with pleasure that Cinda was married.... It was dusk or deep twilight when uncle Almon drove rapidly up to the house. All were gone except father. He was out doing the chores when I went up and spoke to him. He looked at me as though a vision were passing before him. When the truth flashed upon him, he was nearly overcome.... Being somewhat hungry, I was not long in finding the old, familiar cupboard, and when mother, Rose and Amory returned, they found me coolly devouring the remnant of a chicken pie. When mother saw me, she exclaimed "Oh, my God, here is Lucius!" Rose tried hard to keep from crying and appear unconcerned, but the boo-hoos had to come out. Amory, quiet and dignified as a prince, came forward.... I will pass briefly over my visit home, but soon, very soon, the time came for me to again launch forth on the troubled sea of civil strife.

December 11 (Sunday)

Sherman was busy laying siege to Savannah and obtaining a link to the sea, where the Union Navy waited. The Confederates had destroyed the bridge across the Ogeechee River to Ft. McAllister; the bridge had to be rebuilt. Sherman's troops fell to with a will and, using axes to fell trees and parts of dismantled houses, started rebuilding the 1000-foot bridge.

Commander Preble, commander of the naval brigade on the Broad River in South Carolina, found the Confederates to be using a unique "explosive ball" against his skirmishers:

It is a conical ball in shape, like an ordinary bullet. The pointed end is charged with a fulminate. The base of the ball separates from the conical end, and has a leaden standard or plunger. The explosion of the charge drives the base up, so as to flatten a thin disk of metal between it and the ball, the leaden plunger is driven against the fulminate, and it explodes the ball.... It seems to me that use of such a missile is an unnecessary addition to the barbarities of war.

In Tennessee, the weather was still foul. Thomas said he would move when it improved.

Jackman, Pvt., "The Orphan Brigade," Ft. Valley, Ga.:

Took train at 8 A.M. and soon ran down to Fort Valley. I walked out to camp about 4 miles being the longest walk taken for a long time.... There are about 250 men here, all dismounted, or their horses not able for duty, under command of Col. W. of our regiment. About 30 or 40 of our regiment are here—several from our company. Geo. P. had two truce letters for me from home....

December 12 (Monday)

Sherman was preparing for the assault on Ft. McAllister; the 1000-foot-long replacement bridge was almost complete.

Rear Admiral John Dahlgren wrote to his friend President Lincoln, reporting news that the country had eagerly awaited. Sherman was at Savannah! Dahlgren wrote:

I have the great satisfaction of conveying to you information of the arrival of General Sherman near Savannah, with his army in fine spirits.... This memorable event must be attended by still more memorable consequences, and I congratulate you most heartily on its occurrence.

Sherman would now use naval ships to resupply his army rather than rely on rail links.

In Tennessee, the weather was still icy, and no movement was possible on the roads. Again, both Grant and Thomas waited.

December 13 (Tuesday)

The attack on Ft. McAllister was made across the 1000-foot bridge by the Fifteenth Corps at about 5 P.M. Sherman and several officers had climbed atop a rice mill to watch the show. At his elevated platform, Sherman could see the sea; that long-sought goal was there!

As Sherman watched the Fifteenth Corps go into the attack, a man yelled, "A steamboat!" Sure enough, black smokestacks and the Union flag were seen coming upstream on the river. A signal flag on the steamer asked: "Who are you?" Sherman's signalman replied: "Gen. Sherman." The boat then asked: "Is Ft. McAllister taken yet?" Sherman replied: "No, but it will be in a minute."

Charles Ewing, Sherman's adopted brother, was travelling with Sherman and was watching the assault. As the troops broke out of the woods and headed for the fort's defenses, they suddenly disappeared, and Ewing thought they had all been killed. Braced for a failed assault, he was happily surprised to find that the Union troops had reappeared and were soon yelling and screaming from the top of the fort's parapets; the fort had been taken. Sherman's comment was: "It's my old division, I knew they'd do it!"

Nichols, George W., Major, USA, outside Savannah, Ga.:

...The sun was now fast going down behind a grove of water-oaks, and as the last rays gilded the earth, all eyes once more turned towards the Rebel fort. Suddenly white puffs of smoke shot out from the thick woods surrounding the line of works. Hazen was closing in, ready for the final rush of his column directly upon the fort. A warning answer came from the enemy in the roar of heavy artillery—and so the battle opened.... From out the encircling woods there came a long line of blue coats and bright bayonets, and the dear old flag was there, waving proudly in the breeze. Then the fort seemed alive with flame; quick, thick jets of fire shooting out from all its sides, while the white smoke first covered the place and then rolled away over the glacis. The line of blue moved steadily on; too slowly, as it seemed to us, for we exclaimed, "Why don't they dash forward?" but their measured step was unfaltering. Now the flag goes down, but the line does not halt. A moment longer, and the banner gleams again in the front.... Then the enemy's fire redoubled in rapidity and violence. The darting streams of fire alone told the position of the fort. The line of blue entered the enshrouding folds of smoke. The flag was at last dimly seen, and then it went out of sight altogether.

The firing ceased. The wind lifted the smoke. Crowds of men were visible on the parapets, fiercely fighting—but our flag was planted there. There were a few scattering musket-shots, and then the sounds of battle ceased. Then the bomb-proofs and parapets were alive with crowding swarms of our gallant men, who fired their pieces in the air as a *feu de joie*. Victory! The fort was won....

This evening we have enjoyed unrestricted opportunities of examining Fort McAllister. It is a large enclosure, with wide parapets, a deep ditch, and thickly-planted palisades, which latter are broken in several places where our men passed through. The dead and wounded are lying where they fell. Groups of soldiers are gathered here and there, laughing and talking of the proud deed that had been done....

The link to the sea was open and Savannah was doomed.

Rear Admiral David G. Farragut, hero of New Orleans and Mobile Bay, returned to New York, to the cheers of thousands, aboard the battle-scarred flagship U.S.S. *Hartford*.

Capt. Raphael Semmes had sailed from London to Bagdad, Mexico, arriving in November. He then made his way to the Mississippi River, where he crossed with his son, Major O.J. Semmes, on his way home to Mobile. He described his crossing of the river:

We reached the bank of the Mississippi just before dark. There were two of the enemy's gunboats anchored in the river, at a distance of about three miles apart.... The enemy had converted every sort of a water craft, into a ship of war, and now had them in such number, that he was enabled to police the river in its entire length, without the necessity of his boats being out of sight of each other's smoke.... Our boat was scarcely able to float the number that were packed into her.... As we shot within the shadows of the opposite bank, our conductor, before landing, gave a shrill whistle to ascertain whether all was right. The proper response came directly, from those who were to meet us, and in a moment more, we leaped on shore among friends.

The Union ships had gathered at Hampton Roads for the bombardment of Ft. Fisher, and today they departed for Wilmington to meet the powder ship *Louisiana*, which was being towed by the steamer U.S.S. *Sassacus*, Lt. Commander John L. Davis. The *Louisiana* was taken to Beaufort to "top off" her load of powder, some *350 tons of it*! Major Gen. Benjamin Butler, who conceived the idea, had talked Grant into letting him command the Army force which would assault the fort after the *Louisiana* blew up. So far in the war, Butler has done little right, no matter where he was. Maybe this would work.

At Nashville, the weather was still icy and everyone waited. Grant had ordered Gen. John Logan to Nashville to relieve Thomas if the latter did not attack when the weather cleared.

December 14 (Wednesday)

Gen. George Thomas, in Nashville, decided to attack Hood on the 15th, and so notified Grant.

Commander Fitch of the Mississippi Squadron took seven gunboats downriver from Nashville to support Thomas's troops by engaging the batteries of Forrest's cavalry along the river which anchored Forrest's left flank. Fitch described the action:

Acting Volunteer Lieutenant Howard then returned to where I was, just above their works, and reported but four guns in position. These I could easily have silenced and driven off, but our army had not yet sufficiently advanced to insure their capture. I therefore maneuvered around above them till the afternoon, when our cavalry had reached the desired position in the rear; the *Neosho* and *Carondelet* then moved down again and the rebels, finding the position they were in, had tried to remove the guns, but were too late; our cavalry closed in and took them with but little resistance.

The Union gunboats then engaged other batteries downriver, keeping them occupied until the Union cavalry could encircle and capture them.

Sherman spent a busy day visiting the fleet and Major Gen. Foster, commander of the Union Army troops in the area. The message was on its way north that Sherman was safe and on the coast.

It seemed obvious to Confederate Secretary of the Navy Mallory that Savannah would fall to Sherman. He wrote Flag Officer Hunter, commanding the naval forces in the Savannah area, that:

> Should the enemy get and hold Savannah, and you can do no further service there, you are expected to dispose of your squadron to the greatest injury to him and the greatest benefit to our country. If necessary to leave Savannah, your vessels, except the *Georgia*, may fight their way to Charleston. Under no circumstances should they be destroyed until every proper effort to save them shall have been exhausted.

Union gunboats from the South Atlantic Blockading Squadron supported Sherman's capture of Savannah by bombarding the forts defending the city's outer works. This continued until the forts were abandoned by the Rebel defenders on December 21st.

December 15 (Thursday)

The first day of the Battle of Nashville began when George H. Thomas's blue lines slowly edged their way through heavy fog and, with about 35,000 men, struck Hood's left. Hood's right flank was held in position by more Union forces. The Federal onslaught was almost irresistible, driving the gray-clad veterans more than a mile to the rear, where they held on the Franklin Pike, but barely. The weather was foul, with melting ice. Both lines were adjusted somewhat during the night.

Private S.J. Gibson, 103rd Pennsylvania Volunteers, was paroled at Florence, S.C. The prisoners, having been held in a local stockade since October 1st, were removed from the stockade in the middle of the night and held in an open field without blankets, food, or shelter. At about 4 P.M. 1000 prisoners were loaded on trains and departed for Charleston, S.C.

In recognition of the bravery of Lt. William B. Cushing, USN, President Lincoln sent a message to Congress:

> I most cordially recommend that Lieutenant William B. Cushing, U.S. Navy, receive a vote of thanks from Congress for his important, gallant, and perilous achievement in destroying the rebel ironclad steam *Albemarle* on the night of the 27th October, 1864, at Plymouth, North Carolina. The destruction of so formidable a vessel, which had resisted the continued attacks of a number of vessels on former occasions, is an important event touching our future naval and military operations, and would reflect honor on any officer, and redounds to the credit of this young officer and the few brave comrades who assisted in this successful and daring undertaking.

December 16 (Friday)

The second day of the Battle of Nashville was fought today. At 6 o'clock in a morning filled with rain and snow, Thomas's blue-clad troops moved into the assault. The Confederate right was pressed back and then held at the line of its main entrenchments. The Union cavalry got in behind Hood's left flank and the Confederates' rear was threatened. Late in the afternoon the Federals made their main assault and the firing became almost continuous for a time. The Confederate left caved in first, moving back, then the center folded and left the right to play rear guard. Thomas described the action as the Confederates being "hopelessly broken." The Confederate rear guard held off the pursuing Federals until late in the afternoon, when the entire line gave way and the Rebels fled the field. Hood lost most of his artillery and many of his wagons.

Thomas had engaged about 55,000 men and suffered 3600 casualties, mostly wounded (2562). Hood's force had a little over 20,000 men, and he lost 4500 captured and another 1500 killed and wounded. The Army of Tennessee was an army in name only, having been almost decimated by Hood's actions since he had taken command in Atlanta.

Thomas destroyed the last major threat to Kentucky and the Ohio River, and, in the process, he saved his own career.

Sherman was busy unloading supplies of ammunition and other necessities from the ships of the fleet. His troops bent willing backs to get the cargo off as fast as the ships could be docked on the Ogeechee River. Another, more precious, commodity, mail, was also aboard the steamers in anticipation of a Federal land-sea linkup.

Private S.J. Gibson, 103rd Pennsylvania Volunteers, arrived at Charleston, S.C., where he and the other prisoners were loaded onto Federal transport steamers, operating under a flag-of-truce, and taken to Port Royal.

Acting Master Charles A. Pettit, U.S.S. *Monticello*, preparatory to the assault on Ft. Fisher, took a small boat at night near the base of Ft. Caswell, one of the forts guarding Wilmington,

N.C., and removed several Confederate torpedoes and their firing apparatus.

December 17 (Saturday)

Federal cavalry under James H. Wilson, plus some infantry, chased Hood's retreating Confederates down the Pike towards Columbia, Tenn., where skirmishing broke out with Hood's rear guard at Franklin, Hollow Tree Gap, and West Harpeth River. The rear guard held Wilson until the rest of the Rebels made their escape.

At Savannah, Sherman was demanding that Hardee surrender his troops in Savannah. Hardee demurred, planning evacuation.

Jackman, Pvt., "The Orphan Brigade," Ft. Valley, Ga.:

> Over 50 men, being mounted ready for the front, started this morning. Pleasant day for winter. We have nothing to burn but pine wood and standing around the campfires so much—which have to be out in the open air—the smoke is making us as black as coal-heavers. We are living well. Have good fresh beef, fresh pork, flour, sorghum, rice and so on issued in abundance. We make the molasses into candy—have "candy pullings" among ourselves.

The group of prisoners containing Private S.J. Gibson, 103rd Pennsylvania Volunteers, arrived at Port Royal, S.C., where they were disembarked at Hilton Head for examination.

The U.S.S. *Louisiana*, Commander Rhind, had been loaded with 350 *tons* of gunpowder and was towed to the sea off Ft. Fisher, near Wilmington, N.C., to be used as a floating bomb against that fort. Admiral David Dixon Porter, commanding the North Atlantic Blockading Squadron, instructed Rhind.:

> Great risks have to be run, and there are chances that you may lose your life in this adventure; but the risk is worth the running, and when the importance of the object is to be considered and the fame to be gained by this novel undertaking, which is either to prove that forts on the water are useless or that rebels are proof against gunpowder.... I expect more good to our cause from a success in this instance than from an advance of all the armies in the field.

December 18 (Sunday)

Wilson's cavalry pursued Hood to Rutherford Creek near Columbia, Tenn. ,where the Federal chase was called off when Union forces found the stream flooded and impassable. As the news of the defeat at Nashville was telegraphed to North and South, all believed that a serious blow had been dealt the Confederacy, one which would aid greatly in its defeat.

Sherman waited quietly, resupplying his troops with new uniforms, etc., while Hardee, who had refused Sherman's demand for surrender yesterday, pondered his next move. Sherman wrote Grant that he wanted to drive for Raleigh, N.C., burning and tearing up track all the way, forcing the Confederates to evacuate Richmond. For an example he related the damage done in his march from Atlanta:

> I estimate one hundred million dollars, at least twenty millions of which has inured to our advantage, and the remainder is simple waste and destruction. This may seem a hard species of warfare, but it brings the sad realities of war home to those who have been directly or indirectly instrumental in involving us in its attendant calamities.

At Hampton Roads, Butler's force to assault Ft. Fisher at Wilmington, N.C., weighed anchor and sailed. Butler had taken time out from his Trent's Reach canal to pull enough political strings to get command of this expedition. Meanwhile, the U.S.S. *Sassacus*, Lt. Commander J.L. Davis, had towed the U.S.S. *Louisiana*, Commander Rhind, from Beaufort, S.C., where it had been loaded with 350 tons of gunpowder. The *Louisiana* was to be towed as close as possible to Ft. Fisher and then exploded, so that the blast could demolish the outer works of the fort and silence its guns. Immediately following the blast, the Army would land an assault force and storm the fort. The ships being in readiness, the *Louisiana* was now towed in towards the fort by the U.S.S. *Wilderness*, Acting Master Henry Arey, but the swells of the sea were too heavy for the troop-landing craft, so the ships turned back and the attack was postponed.

Private S.J. Gibson, 103rd Pennsylvania Volunteers, spent the day ashore on Hilton Head, S.C., taking a bath and cleaning up. Late in the afternoon the former prisoners were loaded aboard large steam transports and they sailed with the tide late at night.

December 19 (Monday)

The Federal cavalry and infantry were still unable to cross the swollen Rutherford Creek north of Columbia, Tenn., making Hood safe for the time being.

In the Valley, Sheridan, at Grant's order, sent 8000 cavalrymen under A.T.A. Torbert towards the Virginia Central Railroad and Gordonsville. This resulted in skirmishes at Gordonsville, Madison C.H., Liberty Mills, and other points. Torbert returned on the 23rd without having accomplished much.

Sherman's men, waiting for orders, had time to visit the seashore, some for the first time, and to eat their fill of oysters. They ate oyster soup, oyster stew, oysters on the half shell, roasted oysters, fried oysters and roasted goose stuffed with oysters.

On June 3rd, the Confederates had made a daring raid and had captured the U.S.S. *Water Witch* near Savannah, taking her up the Savannah River and renaming her the C.S.S. *Water Witch*. Since that time the ship had not been used, merely lying at anchor awaiting developments. With the capture of Savannah, the ship was destroyed to prevent her recapture.

December 20 (Tuesday)

Sherman's demand for surrender to Hardee was coolly refused. Hardee's refusal took some iron, since Hardee had only 9089 men for duty against Sherman's nearly 62,000. Sherman, however, did not want to waste men assaulting the city on the few roads left after Hardee flooded the rice fields. Hardee evacuated Savannah. He left at night on an ingenious bridge of rice-carrying rafts strung across the river, and he headed north. Behind him he left one of the premier cities of the South to the Union and an inventory of 250 cannon and siege guns, plus 40,000 bales of cotton. Little, if any, blood had been shed; there had been only the assault on Ft. McAllister, and one skirmish of any note.

Nichols, George W., Major, USA, Savannah, Ga.:

> ...The path by which Hardee escaped led through swamps which were previously considered impracticable. The Rebel general obtained knowledge of our movement through his spies, who swarmed in our camp.
>
> It was fortunate that our troops followed so quickly after the evacuation of the city by the enemy, for a mob had gathered in the streets, and were breaking into the stores and houses. They were with difficulty dispersed by the bayonets of our soldiers, and then, once more, order and confidence prevailed throughout the conquered city.... We had not been in occupation forty-eight hours before the transport steamer *Canonicus*, with General Foster on board, lay alongside a pier, and our new line of supplies was formed.

Wilson's cavalry and infantry following Hood's retreat through Tennessee had been stalled for two days by the high water of Rutherford Creek north of Columbia. Putting the axes to work, Wilson had a bridge built of floating "pontoon" logs, and he crossed his Union troops and pushed hard for Columbia.

Federal cavalry under Stoneman fought over the saltworks at Saltville in southwestern Virginia, near the Tennessee line, destroying the works and stopping production for months.

Commander Macomb, USN, had an expedition which kept running into torpedoes while going upriver towards Rainbow Bluffs, a strongly fortified position. Two of his vessels had been sunk on December 9th (U.S.S. *Otsego* and *Bazely*) and since then he had small boats dragging for torpedoes as he advanced. More than 40 torpedoes were found in some bends in the river. He continued upriver.

The paroled prisoners from Andersonville aboard the steamer transports spent Monday at sea passing Hatteras, near the place where Private S.J. Gibson, of the 103rd Pennsylvania Volunteers, had been captured on April 20th. Plymouth was back in Union hands at this time. The transports arrived at Hampton Roads in the late afternoon and sailed again that evening.

With some sadness, Admiral David G. Farragut, hero of New Orleans and Mobile, hauled down his Admiral's pennant from the mast of the U.S.S. *Hartford*, his flagship in both adventures, and turned the ship over to the Navy Yard for repairs. The ship and the man closed their Civil War careers.

December 21 (Wednesday)

Gen. John W. Geary's division of the Twentieth Corps led the march into Savannah, meeting no opposition. Sherman was disappointed that he had not bagged Hardee, but was not sorry for the lives saved in the process.

The U.S.S. *Winona*, Lt. Commander Dana, had been shelling Forts Beaulieu and Rosedew, which were part of the Savannah defenses, since December 14th. The log of the *Winona* recorded for this date: "At 10:05 saw the American Ensign flying on Ft. Beaulieu. Ships cheered; captain left in the gig and proceeded up to the fort."

Commander Thomas W. Brent, CSN, had tried, unsuccessfully, to remove the torpedoes in Savannah Harbor on December 10th so he could take the C.S.S. *Savannah* and other Confederate ships to Charleston, fighting his way out of the harbor. With Sherman in Savannah, it was only a question of time before Brent's ships would be in Union hands. On December 21, Brent ordered the destruction of the *Savannah*, *Isondiga*, *Firefly*, and the huge ironclad floating battery *Georgia*, to prevent their capture by the Union. This one act eliminated most of the Confederate naval force in Savannah.

Thomas's force chasing Hood was plagued by destroyed bridges, swollen streams, and increasingly weary troops. It had been almost five days since they left Nashville, and the men had been in the field in rain, snow, and slush enough to last them forever.

The cavalry of Stoneman at Saltville, Va., finished their destruction and departed.

Jackman, Pvt., "The Orphan Brigade," Ft. Valley, Ga.:

> Hard wind with rain last night. Today disagreeably cold. Lying in bed nearly all day to keep warm—to stand by a fire was to be smoked to death. Late in the evening the sun shone out white and cold. Masses of inky clouds about the heavens....

December 22 (Thursday)

Sherman returned from a visit to Port Royal to find that Hardee had left Savannah and that Union troops were in possession of the city. Entering the city, he found little war damage, except to the pride of the people. Sherman, at the urging of an aide, wrote President Lincoln a telegram to be sent at the first available station:

> I beg to present you as a Christmas gift, the city of Savannah, with one hundred and fifty heavy guns and plenty of ammunition, also about twenty-five thousand bales of cotton.

The Federals in pursuit of Hood's beaten Army of Tennessee found part of that army at Columbia, Tenn., and a little skirmishing developed. The weather was still cold and wet.

Private S.J. Gibson, of the 103rd Pennsylvania Volunteers had arrived at Annapolis, Md., late the 21st of December and had been immediately transferred to the "parole camp" outside the city for processing. Here the prisoners were given an opportunity to bathe, get haircuts, wash clothes, and be fed as much as they liked.

December 23 (Friday)

The Navy, not to be outdone by the Army's creation of the rank of Lieutenant. General, asked that Congress create the rank of Vice Admiral, which would be equivalent to Lieutenant General. Today, Lincoln signed a bill authorizing that rank, and it was conferred on Rear Admiral David G. Farragut; he became the first Vice Admiral in U.S. history, just as he had been the first Rear Admiral.

The fleet that sailed from Hampton Roads on Sunday the 18th had run into a very heavy storm off Hatteras and it had scattered. Today it reassembled off Wilmington—Major Gen. Benjamin F. Butler and 6500 troops. The assault on Ft. Fisher was set to begin.

The naval expedition going upriver towards Rainbow Bluff on the Roanoke River, N.C., had been clearing torpedoes, under sniper fire most of the time, as it advanced. The Army elements which were to assault the fortifications were late in arriving, and the Confederates had heavily reinforced their troops on the Bluff. The assault was called off and the gunboats headed downriver.

December 24 (Saturday)

Lincoln, at the White House, received Sherman's telegram from Savannah on Christmas Eve. His admiration of, and pride in, that red-headed general knew no bounds. Coming as it did following Thomas's victory at Nashville, it was the best Christmas of the war. Lincoln gave the news to the country as a present. The nation was ecstatic.

Sherman, in Savannah, found that he was besieged by women who wanted protection from those "Yankees." Confederate generals Hardee, Smith, and McLaws had left personal letters for Sherman asking his personal interest in the welfare of their families. The wife of Gen. A.P. Stewart, one of Hood's officers, asked Sherman for special assistance, which he gladly granted. A Mrs. Sarah Davenport won Sherman over immediately when she explained that she had three sons in the Union army, three in the Southern forces, and a son-in-law serving with Lee.

Sherman followed his usual policy of allowing the ministers of the local churches to pray for Jeff Davis, saying, "Yes, Jeff Davis and the devil both need it." Sherman also maintained the present political office-holders in office without interference, as long as they did nothing to damage the Union's war effort. He also ordered the opening of farmer's marketplaces throughout the city so that the people might find food. All of these things did much to offset the reputation he had developed on his march to the sea.

In Tennessee, the chase after Hood's army was just about to wind down. Hood had been losing men steadily as his retreat continued towards the Tennessee River. Rear Admiral S.P. Lee arrived with gunboats off Chickasaw, Ala., near Muscle Shoals on the Tennessee River, in an attempt to cut off Hood's retreat from Nashville. At Chickasaw, the gunboat U.S.S. *Fairy*, Acting Ensign Charles Swendson, destroyed a Confederate fort and magazine but the gunboat couldn't proceed upriver due to low water.

After days of delay, the U.S.S. *Louisiana*, loaded with 350 tons of gunpowder, was towed by the U.S.S. *Wilderness* to within 250 yards of Ft. Fisher, the major bastion guarding Wilmington, N.C. Commander Rhind and his volunteer crew set the time mechanism for 1:18 A.M., set a fire in the stern of the ship, and escaped to the *Wilderness* in small boats. The time fuse didn't work, but the fire did. When it reached the powder, the ship blew with a noise that was heard for miles. Ft. Fisher's commander, not shaken by the explosion, wrote in his diary: "A blockader got aground near the fort, set fire to herself and blew up." The Union troops had been held 12 miles away, anticipating that the blast might damage the transports. While the transports were brought up, the gunboats commenced a terrific bombardment of the fort. The transports did not arrive until late in the afternoon, so the assault was postponed. While some guns were dismounted on the fort, little damage was done to the earthworks, and the fort was still operational. The flotilla waited out the night.

Private S.J. Gibson, of the 103rd Pennsylvania Volunteers, having been processed at the "parole camp," had his pay brought up to date and was paid $36, representing two months' pay. He was given a train ticket, his discharge, and taken to the depot. He boarded the train on Christmas Eve after spending three years, three months in the Union Army; he had spent four months in the prison at Andersonville, Ga., and almost four months in other prison camps in Georgia and South Carolina before being exchanged. He arrived home late, but he was home.

December 25 (Sunday)

At 10:30 A.M. this morning, the gunboats of the Union fleet off Ft. Fisher opened again in a heavy bombardment. Gen. Ben Butler's troops landed north of the fort, near Flag Pond Battery. The naval gunfire kept the defenders pinned down while Butler put 2000 men ashore and, forming a line of battle, they advanced on the fort. Meanwhile, the Navy was attempting to force an entry at New Inlet, but found that a sandbar was blocking passage. Lt. Cushing, who had sunk the *Albemarle*, attempted marking the channel with buoys but he was driven back by heavy fire.

The assault troops approached the works in the late afternoon, but decided that the works were too strong for so small a force, so an order to withdraw was given. The weather got worse, with heavy seas running, and some 700 of the 2000 were left on the beach, covered by the fire of the U.S.S. *Santiago de Cuba*, which provided continuous support.

Lt. Aeneas Armstrong, CSN, was inside Ft. Fisher during the bombardment and described the scene:

> The whole interior of the fort, which consists of sand, merlons, etc., was as one eleven-inch shell bursting. You can now inspect the works and walk on nothing but iron.

Commander Macomb's expedition up the Roanoke River towards Rainbow Bluff had turned back, and today Macomb reached the point where the U.S.S. *Otsego* and *Bazely* had been sunk by torpedoes on December 9th. The two sunken ships were completely destroyed to prevent their being raised by the Confederates. The gunboats continued downriver.

Jackman, Pvt., "The Orphan Brigade," Ft. Valley, Ga.:

> For breakfast had fresh pork, biscuit, sweet potatoes, etc. Cool disagreeable morning. At noon cold rain commenced falling. Bad prospect for a Christmas dinner—can't cook in the rain. Slept all evening. Rain pouring down. Has been a most gloomy day—being the fourth birth day spent in the army. At night sat up late chatting around a smoky fire built under the sheds out of the rain....

Hood's beaten Army of Tennessee finally reached the Tennessee River at Bainbridge. There wouldn't be much of a Christmas for these weary men.

Sherman spent Christmas in Savannah,` thinking of his family, as did all his men.

December 26 (Monday)

John Bell Hood's bone-weary men finally crossed the Tennessee River at Bainbridge, and the Army of Tennessee, for all practical purposes, passed into history. The dream to reach the Ohio River and draw Sherman out of Georgia became a hazy memory, to be remembered as a montage of long, cold marches, colder nights, and periods of hellish gunfire.

Lincoln, deeply grateful for the victory at Savannah, wrote Sherman this day and sent the letter with Major Gen. John A. Logan, who was rejoining Sherman:

> MY DEAR GENERAL SHERMAN:
>
> Many, many thanks for your Christmas gift—the capture of Savannah.
>
> When you were about to leave Atlanta for the Atlantic coast, I was *anxious*, if not fearful; but feeling you were the better judge, and remembering that "nothing risked nothing gained," I did not interfere. Now the undertaking being a success, the honor is all yours, for I believe none of us went further than to acquiesce. And taking the work of General Thomas into the count, as it should be taken, it is indeed a great success....
>
> Please make my grateful acknowledgments to your whole army, officers and men.
>
> Yours very truly,
>
> A. LINCOLN.

Logan's arrival brought, for the first time, information on just how close George Thomas had come to ruining his own career. Grant had gone so far as to send Logan to Nashville with orders to relieve Thomas if he did not move against Hood as soon as practical. Logan arrived just as the ice was melting, and Thomas was getting ready to advance through the slush and freezing mud. Thomas did not know that Logan had the power to relieve him, and Logan did not tell him, keeping in the background and letting Thomas win his victory.

Sherman's problem at this time was that Grant wanted Sherman to fortify an enclave at Savannah and then take the remainder of his army to Virginia to reinforce the Army of the Potomac for the assault on Lee. Sherman fought this idea with every power he had, and Sherman finally convinced Grant that he could do better service by driving through the Carolinas, destroying as he had done in Georgia.

There was talk of promoting Sherman to the rank of Lieutenant General, equal to Grant's rank. To this Sherman responded:

> I will accept no commission that would tend to create a rivalry with Grant. I want him to hold what he has earned and got. I have all the rank I want. I would rather be an engineer of a railroad, than President of the United States. I have commanded a hundred thousand men in battle, and on the march, successfully and without confusion, and that is enough for reputation. Now, I want rest and peace, and they are only to be had through war.

Lt. Wilkinson, CSN, who had commanded the Confederate commerce raider C.S.S. *Tallahassee*, had run her into Wilmington, N.C., after a successful raid on the Northern coast. There the raider was renamed the *Chameleon*, and converted to a blockade runner. Amid the confusion attending the assault on Ft. Fisher, Wilkinson sailed the *Chameleon* out of the harbor for Bermuda. At that port he loaded provisions for the Confederate Army and returned to Wilmington in January, only to find that the port had fallen into Union hands.

December 27 (Tuesday)

The remnants of Hood's army entered Mississippi and went into camp. Hood would shortly be relieved of command.

Admiral S.P. Lee, USN, was with his gunboats on the Tennessee River near Florence, Ala., attempting to cut off Hood's retreat when the gunboats engaged and destroyed two Confederate artillery batteries. The water in the river was falling drastically, and the boats moved downriver towards Eastport.

Sherman rested and refitted in Savannah, planning his trip north through the Carolinas.

The last of the assault force that had landed to attack Ft. Fisher, Wilmington, N.C., was taken from the beach after two very cold days and nights. High wind and heavy seas had prevented the removal of the troops on Christmas day after the attack failed. The fort would have to wait for later. So much for Butler's brilliant idea. The Navy went back to blockading and Butler returned to Virginia, and his canal at Trent's Reach.

In a feat of derring-do, Ensign N.A. Blume, U.S.S. *Virginia*, took a boat crew and "cut out" the schooner *Belle*, which was loaded with cotton and at anchor in Galveston Harbor. Blume and his men boldly boarded the ship and sailed her out of harbor past the Confederate guard boat *Secompte*.

December 28 (Wednesday)

With the remnants of Hood's Army of Tennessee in Mississippi, there was little activity in that area.

News of the fiasco at Wilmington had not reached Washington, but Grant had been informed. He told Lincoln, "The Wilmington expedition has proven a gross and culpable failure..." and, though he did not name the culprit, Lincoln knew with certainty who was responsible.

Commander Macomb's expedition up the Roanoke River to Rainbow Bluffs returned to Plymouth, N.C., minus the Union vessels U.S.S. *Otsego* and *Bazely*, which had been sunk by torpedoes on December 9th and which had then been completely destroyed by Macomb on Christmas Day.

December 29 (Thursday)

The C.S.S. *Shenandoah*, Lt. Waddell, captured and destroyed the unarmed bark *Delphine* in the Indian Ocean. The *Delphine*, with a cargo of rice, was the last capture of the year and the ninth vessel destroyed in eight weeks.

December 30 (Friday)

At Wilmington, N.C., Admiral David D. Porter was unhappy with Major Gen. Butler's conduct during the attack on Ft. Fisher on Christmas Day, so he wrote his old friend Grant, urging Butler's removal from command and urging that a new assault force be organized. Grant's reply was immediate: "Please hold on where you are for a few days and I will endeavor to be back again with an increased force and without the former commander." Meanwhile, Porter's guns kept up the bombardment of the fort.

December 31 (Saturday)

In New York City, the merchants presented a gift of $50,000 in government bonds to the new Vice Admiral David G. Farragut, in appreciation of services rendered his country. This was a nice ending for the year for the hero of New Orleans and Mobile.

The year ended differently for 27 Union sailors in Charleston Harbor, when their picket boats were driven aground by high winds and they were captured by Confederate pickets.

The captain of the C.S.S. *Shenandoah*, Lt. Waddell, wrote in his journal:

> Thirty-first of December closed the year, the third since the war began. And how many of my boon companions are gone to that bourne from whence no traveler returns. They were full of hope, but not without fears, when we last parted.

1865

The South was teetering on the brink of collapse in this, the beginning of the final year of war. Gone were the bright hopes and dreams of an easy separation from the United States and present were the realities—Tennessee was gone with Hood's defeat at Nashville; Sherman was in Savannah and Atlanta lay in ruins; one serious attempt to close Wilmington had been made and another was sure to come. Peace initiatives were discussed, but nothing happened. Where, or even when, would it end?

January 1 (Sunday)

There was not much activity in the trenches around Petersburg and Richmond, except for soldiers trying to keep warm.

On the James River at Dutch Gap, Major Gen. Ben Butler had started digging a canal across Trent's Reach to bypass Confederate batteries commanding the river. Grant never had much faith in the project, but it kept Butler busy and out of Grant's hair. Butler had taken some time off in December 1864 to try his luck at capturing Ft. Fisher, near Wilmington, N.C., and, as usual, he had managed to fail at that task also. He came back to finish the canal. On this day, he exploded 12,000 pounds of powder under what was to be the last wall holding the water. The wall was to disappear, the water flow in, and a new route to Richmond was to be opened—courtesy of Ben Butler, and about 4000 Negro laborers.

The powder was set. The fuse lit. The powder exploded. Dirt flew in the air 40 to 50 feet and came back down in the same place it went up from. No water flowed, ergo, no canal. Butler quit the project and sent everyone back to their camps. The canal was later finished but never used.

Sherman was still in Savannah visiting the various commands, and especially the Navy offshore, who would supply him as he progressed north through the Carolinas. He planned for all his sick and wounded to be evacuated to the coast, where they would be placed on hospital ships and sent north for treatment. This was a much easier ride for the wounded and it eliminated the problem of moving the wounded with the slow-moving army.

After the fiasco on Christmas Day 1864, when Major Gen. Ben Butler's troops had been put ashore to assault Ft. Fisher at Wilmington, and had then been withdrawn immediately with only a halfhearted effort made, Admiral David D. Porter wrote to Grant asking that another expedition be organized, but that *another* commander be assigned. Grant immediately replied in the affirmative, and a new expedition was begun. Porter, to support the operation, began issuing orders for 66 warships to assemble off the Wilmington coast with, as he put it, "every shell that can be carried" for shore bombardment.

The U.S.S. *San Jacinto*, involved in the international affair in 1861, when Mason and Slidell were taken from the British ship *Trent* on their way to Europe as Confederate States Consuls, met an inglorious end when she ran aground at Green Turtle Bay, Abaco, in the Bahama Islands. Capt. Richard W. Meade, who had been assigned to the ship after the *Trent* affair, managed to salvage most of the armament, ammunition, rigging, cables, and even much of the copper bottom. The hulk was abandoned.

January 3 (Tuesday)

Grant assigned Major Gen. Alfred H. Terry to command the army element of the assault on Ft. Fisher, the main bastion guarding Wilmington, N.C. In his instructions to Terry, Grant said: "I have served with Admiral Porter and know that you can rely on his judgment and his nerve to undertake what he proposes. I would, therefore, defer to him as much as is consistent with your own responsibilities." Grant also notified Porter that Terry was coming as the commander of the army troops.

Alfred Howe Terry, a native of Connecticut, was 34 years old when the war began. He attended Yale Law School in 1848 and later became Clerk of the New Haven Superior Court from 1854 until the war began. He commanded the 2nd Connecticut at First Manassas and then recruited for the 7th Connecticut for three years. He was at the assault and capture of Port Royal, S.C., and Ft. Pulaski, Ga. He was promoted to Brigadier in April 1862, and was then assigned to command X Corps in Butler's Army of the James. He had participated in the Christmas Day fiasco at Wilmington, and had performed well there. For his work in the assault on Ft. Fisher he would receive THANKS OF CONGRESS, and a promotion to Major General of Volunteers. He was named a Brigadier in the Regular Army as of January 15, 1865, one of the few non-West Point graduates who served in the war ever to achieve that status. He ended the war as part of Schofield's Army of the Ohio, with Sherman in the Carolinas. After the war he went west and fought Indians, achieving Major General in the Regular Army in 1886 at age 59. He died in New Haven on December 16, 1890.

Sherman, in concert with Dahlgren, began moving some of his troops by transport from Savannah, Ga., to Beaufort, S.C., thereby flanking the Confederate troops between the two points. The U.S.S. *Harvest Moon* carried the first of these troops to Beaufort, saving a long, weary march.

January 4 (Wednesday)

Leaving nothing to chance in the planning of the assault on Ft. Fisher, Admiral D.D. Porter directed that all available sailors and Marines were to be formed into landing parties to hit the beach on the seaward side of Ft. Fisher, while the Army assaulted the landward side. The sailors, armed with cutlasses and pistols, were to be backed up by the Marines who would provide rifle fire, the sailors "boarding" the fort in the accustomed naval manner.

January 6 (Friday)

The passage of the Thirteenth Amendment of the Constitution was a matter of priority for Lincoln in this session of the U.S. Congress. Having failed passage before, this time it had passed the Senate and was before the House of Representatives. Lincoln was pressuring the House members to vote for its passage now, rather than wait to pass it on to the Thirty-Eighth Congress, which would meet in the autumn.

Grant, finally tired of Butler's fumbling and politicking, asked Lincoln to remove Butler from command of the Army of the James. Grant, rightly so, felt that there was no confidence in Butler's ability. Butler's latest failure was on January 2, at the canal at Trent's Reach near Drewry's Bluff on the James River. Immediately prior to that, he had demanded, by right of seniority, the command of the ill-fated campaign against Ft. Fisher in December 1864. That expedition was completely botched, all due to Butler's incompetence.

January 7 (Saturday)

Farragut, the hero of New Orleans and Mobile, visited President Lincoln at the White House, where he was warmly welcomed. Farragut was accompanied by Secretary Welles.

Lincoln, who had procrastinated before about Butler's removal from active duty, finally had his fill and, at Grant's request, relieved Butler from the active list, and the general would command no more. Controversial from beginning to end, Butler was a prime example of the political generals who permeated the beginning of the war—most of the others were long since gone. Major Gen. E.O.C. Ord was named as Butler's replacement.

At Savannah, Sherman wrote Admiral Dahlgren

about a projected route through the Carolinas. In particular, Sherman wanted contact with Admiral Porter to obtain information:

> ...I am not certain that there is a vessel in Port Royal from Admiral Porter or I would write him. If there be one to return to him I beg you to send this, with a request that I be advised as early as possible as to the condition of the railroad from Beaufort, N.C., back to New Bern, and so on, towards Goldsboro; also all maps and information of the country above New Bern; how many cars and locomotives are available to us on that road; whether there is good navigation from Beaufort, N.C., via Pamlico Sound, up Neuse River, etc. I want Admiral Porter to know that I expect to be ready to move on the 15th; that I have one head of column across Savannah River at this point; will soon have another at Port Royal Ferry, and expect to make another crossing at Sister's Ferry.... The more I think of the affair at Wilmington the more I feel ashamed of the army there; but Butler is at fault, and he alone. Admiral Porter fulfilled his share to admiration. I think the admiral will feel more confidence in my troops, as he saw us carry points on the Mississippi where he had silenced the fire. All will turn out for the best yet.

Jackman, Pvt., "The Orphan Brigade," en route to Augusta, Ga.:

> A little after daylight we took up our line of march. The dismounted men—over 1000—took the train at Fort Valley for Macon. The wagon train and the men with horses, moved by the direct dirt road—there are no pikes in the south—for the same place. A great many have to lead their horses and few have saddles. All the wagons of the brigade are along, being quite a train. We also have a drove of cattle with us.... When we started this morning was very cold—a cutting wind blowing. The Colonel stopped in Fort Valley to draw rations.... We marched 20 miles and camped. Put up a fly at night and made a log-heap in front—slept magnificently.

Barber, Sgt., Co. C, 15th Illinois Volunteer Infantry, Camp Chase, Columbus, Ohio:

> Arrived at Crestline at six o'clock A.M. Waited until afternoon before starting for Columbus. Arrived at... fifty minutes past two P.M. Reported at headquarters at Camp Chase and found out, much to our surprise, that we had been exchanged and would be sent forward to our command on Monday. This was a keen disappointment to me.... Our barracks here were cold and comfortless and poorly provided with the necessary accommodations for soldiers. The snow lay over one foot deep on the ground.

January 8 (Sunday)

The transports containing Major Gen. Terry's expeditionary force from Hampton Roads arrived off the coast of Beaufort, S.C.

Major Gen. John A. Logan, who had resigned from active command when Sherman relieved him to place a West Pointer in command of the XV Corps during the Battle of Atlanta, returned to Sherman's army and resumed command of his old corps.

Jackman, Pvt., "The Orphan Brigade," en route to Augusta, Ga.:

> A raw disagreeable day. Twelve miles brought us to Macon. We crossed the Ocmulgee and found the dismounted men camped on its banks below the city. Nearly night before the wagons got ferried over.

Barber, Sgt., Co. C, 15th Illinois Volunteer Infantry, Camp Chase, Columbus, Ohio:

> The weather is quite cold. Over seven thousand rebel prisoners are confined here and they are well and clothed. We were transferred to Tod barracks this morning and are now awaiting transportation to Nashville.

January 9 (Monday)

The passage of the Thirteenth Amendment was one vote closer when Democrat Moses Odell of New York came out in favor of its passage; he had formerly opposed it.

The spies were active along the Potomac, crossing the river in India-rubber rafts, in the vicinity of Port Tobacco, as Secretary Welles advised Commander F.A. Parker:

> These messengers, wear metal buttons, upon the inside of which dispatches are most minutely photographed, not perceptible to the naked eye, but are easily read by the aid of a powerful lens.

In Mississippi, John Bell Hood moved his battered army to Tupelo and went into camp. The shell of the Army of Tennessee required major refitting and rest.

Jackman, Pvt., "The Orphan Brigade," en route to Augusta, Ga.:

> Had to wait until 11 o'clock until we got forage over the river—have 5 days forage on wagons.... Pete and I footed it 6 miles towards Milledgeville through a cold rain. When we stopped to camp soon got our fly pitched and a fire made. Cooked supper. Rain poured down all night. Slept well.

January 10 (Tuesday)

Commander Bulloch, in London, wrote Secretary of the Navy Mallory, in Richmond, that the ship previously contracted for in France, and withheld from delivery by the French government, had been sold to the Danish government for use in the Schleswig-Holstein War. The European war ended abruptly, and the Danish government had refused to take delivery, although the ship was in Copenhagen. Bulloch bought the ship secretly, under the name *Sphinx*, and directed Capt. Thomas Jefferson Page, CSN, to take command of her in Copenhagen. The ironclad was to be renamed the C.S.S. *Stonewall* and was to be used to break the blockade at Wilmington and then to become a commerce raider. Page had sailed from Copenhagen on January 7th hoping to rendezvous with the blockade runner *City of Richmond*, at Belle Isle, Quiberon Bay, France. The *City of Richmond* carried armament and stores, as well as the officers and men for the *Stonewall*.

A raging storm off the coast of South Carolina made the lives of the men in the Union transports miserable, as they waited for the word to move for the assault on Ft. Fisher.

Jackman, Pvt., "The Orphan Brigade," en route to Augusta, Ga.:

> At daylight loaded up and moved out. I thought I would walk awhile. Had not been on the road long before it commenced thundering and soon after the heaviest shower of rain fell I ever saw. Got drenched to the skin. Three miles brought us to Griswoldville which is nearly all in ashes.... We passed the battlefield near Griswoldville which evidences quite a fight.... We have traveled 16 miles today. The dismounted men have to march....

Barber, Sgt., Co. C, 15th Illinois Volunteer Infantry, Cincinnati, Ohio:

> We marched to Kelton barracks to await further orders. This is a dirty and disagreeable place. The lower story is used as a prison in which to keep bounty jumpers and deserters. The upper story is used to receive recruits, convalescents, exchanged soldiers and furloughed men preparatory to sending them to their respective commands.
>
> We were kept in close confinement on account of so many trying to get away, and to the disgrace of the government officials, no discrimination was made between men or conditions. According to existing orders, we had no business to be detained and treated in this manner. In Chicago and other cities in the West, no one pretended to dispute our right to go and come at pleasure while within the limits of our furlough or while we were paroled prisoners.

January 11 (Wednesday)

In Missouri, the Constitutional Convention adopted a resolution abolishing slavery within the state.

Major Gen. Thomas L. Rosser, CSA, led a raid on Beverly, W.Va., that netted him 580 prisoners and tons of rations. Rosser had previously raided in the Cumberland, Md., area.

Thomas Lafayette Rosser was born in Campbell City, Va., on October 15, 1836, and moved with his family to Texas in 1849. He entered West Point, where he was an intimate friend of flamboyant George A. Custer. Two weeks before graduation, he resigned from West Point and returned to Virginia to serve as an artillery officer at First Manassas. Rosser was a handsome man, with dark, curly hair and fine features. He served brilliantly and won high praise during the Peninsula Campaign, and Stuart appointed him Colonel of the 5th Virginia Cavalry after Rosser had recovered from wounds received during that campaign. In September 1863, he was promoted to Brigadier General and assigned command of the Laurel Brigade (another signal honor). That brigade often clashed with the Federal troops of Rosser's old friend George A. Custer. Rosser served again with distinction under Early in the 1864 Valley campaign, and Rosser was promoted to Major General on November 1, 1864. He conducted several successful raids on Federal depots during late 1864 and into 1865. He was present at Appomattox when Lee surrendered, but managed to escape with two regiments of cavalry and fought on until May 2, 1865, when he was captured. After the war, he served as an engineer on the railroads in the west, renewing his friendship with Custer, whose troops often guarded the surveying parties on the railroad. When the Spanish-American War began, President McKinley commissioned him a Brigadier General of Volunteers and gave him command of a brigade. He died in Charlottesville, Va., on March 29, 1910.

In Richmond, President Davis was trying, without much luck, to gather all available troops to oppose Sherman's march through the Carolinas.

Jackman, Pvt., "The Orphan Brigade," Milledgeville, Ga.:

> Up hour and a half before day started at 7 o'clock. Cloudy most of the day, a cold wind blowing. "Marched" mostly in the wagon today. Fourteen miles brought us to Milledgeville and we camped one-half mile west of town. The Oconee river is so high the pontoon bridges taken up. We may have to stay here several days....

Barber, Sgt., Co. C, 15th Illinois Volunteer Infantry, Cincinnati, Ohio:

> Stormed hard all day. Barracks cold. Received orders this morning to be ready to start for New York City at eight o'clock in the evening. This order surprised us much as we were expecting to go to Nashville all the time.

January 12 (Thursday)

The largest American fleet ever to be assembled under one command sailed from Beaufort, S.C., up the Atlantic coast towards Wilmington and Ft. Fisher. The army forces under Major Gen. Terry had met with Admiral Porter's fleet, and the assault of Ft. Fisher was set. The armada arrived off the coast, and the Navy prepared for the bombardment, which was to be followed by the landing of 10,000 soldiers, sailors, and Marines.

The C.S.S. *Columbia*, a ram built in Charleston, ran aground while coming out of her dock. Great effort was expended in trying to refloat the ship so she could be used in defense of the city. The ram would be abandoned in mid-February and refloated by the Union Navy in April. The ship was described by Admiral Dahlgren as:

> ...209 feet long (extreme), beam 49 feet, has a casemate 65 feet long, pierced for six guns, one on each side and one at each of the four corners, pivots to point ahead or astern and to the side. She has two engines, high pressure, and plated on the casemates with 6 inches of iron in thickness, quite equal, it is believed, to the best of the kind built by the rebels.

President Davis, still mindful of the problems to be encountered with Sherman's advance, wrote Gen. Richard Taylor in the west that the remnants of Hood's army should be divided between his (Taylor's) command and the command to be named in the east. Troop shortages were plaguing everyone.

Jackman, Pvt., "The Orphan Brigade," Milledgeville, Ga.:

> Weather more moderate today. Lying about in the sunshine reading "Love After Marriage." Took a bath this morning and as all the ice was not yet melted, cold application. Wagons sent back to Gordon for rations.... G.P. and I sleep together. Sleep cold too. A moonlight night.

In the Congress at Washington, the debate on the Thirteenth Amendment to abolish slavery went on (and on).

January 13 (Friday)

The seeds of the idea of the Naval War College were planted in the mind of Lt. Commander Stephen B. Luce, U.S.S. *Pontiac*, when he was assigned to support Sherman in his crossing of the Savannah River at Sister's Ferry, Ga. The *Pontiac* continued covering Sherman's army on its approach along the coast to Charleston. Luce, who later would be instrumental in the founding of the Naval War College, said of his relationship with Sherman:

After hearing General Sherman's clear exposition of the military situation, the scales seemed to fall from my eyes.... It dawned on me that there were certain fundamental principles underlying military operations... principles of general application whether the operations were on land or at sea.

Early this morning off Wilmington, the U.S.S. *New Ironsides*, Commodore William Radford, led the monitors *Saugus*, *Canonicus*, *Monadnock*, and *Mahopac*, to within 1000 yards of Ft. Fisher and they opened with their naval guns. The defenders, 1500 men under Col. Lamb, replied with spirit, at least initially. The U.S.S. *Brooklyn*, Capt. Alden, led the heavy wooden-hulled ships into line behind the ironclads and the bombardment lasted all day and into the night. Major Gen. Terry, in command of the army forces, landed his 8000 men on a definite beachhead, out of range of the fort's guns. Admiral Porter said of the bombardment:

It was soon quite apparent that the iron vessels had the best of it; traverses began to disappear and the southern angle of Fort Fisher commenced to look very dilapidated.

In Mississippi, Lt. Gen. John Bell Hood resigned as commander of the Army of Tennessee, to be replaced by Lt. Gen. Richard Taylor, son of Zachary Taylor.

Jackman, Pvt., "The Orphan Brigade," Milledgeville, Ga.:

The Judge and I went into Milledgeville this morning. Visited the State House which we found all topsy-turvy. The desks overturned, the archives scattered over the floor—in some places the papers being on the floor a foot deep. This was done by Sherman's men. There are some splendid portraits in the Representative Hall and in the Senate Chamber which are in *status quo*. The arsenal standing in the State House yard was burned. We also visited the penitentiary which was also burned by Sherman's Army. With the exception of the arsenal and penitentiary and perhaps a little fencing, we could see no further indication of the destruction of property about the town. The railroad depot is in ashes and a bridge across a slough burned. We passed through the cemetery and saw a fine monument to the memory of a Mr. Jordan. The country between here and Macon is not as much torn up as I had expected to see. With the exception of one or two houses, only fences were burned. Griswoldville was the worst served—a large factory for making pistols being destroyed. I saw no dwellings had been burned in the village—that is, no signs of any having been burned, rather....

Barber, Sgt., Co. C, 15th Illinois Volunteer Infantry, Cleveland, Ohio:

Took dinner at the Soldier's Home where everything was nice and comfortable, and then took a stroll about the city. Started for Buffalo at three P.M.... Stopped at a small place in central New York and our squad had a nice time on a mill pond near by, where the village gentry was out enjoying a fine skate. On the same train were hundreds of recruits, but they were not permitted to step off the cars. We, being old soldiers and in a gang by ourselves, did just as we pleased. A Lieutenant was in charge of us, but he knew that he could trust us.

January 14 (Saturday)

Federal naval bombardment was pouring 100 shells per minute into Ft. Fisher. The Confederates had suffered 300 casualties and could not bury their dead because of the lethal shrapnel flying around. Only one gun on the land face of the fort was left in a serviceable condition, all the others had been dismounted by the incessant naval gunfire.

Meanwhile, Gen. Terry had prepared defensive works facing his approaches from Wilmington to protect his rear from a possible assault by the 6000 Rebel troops at Wilmington under Gen. Braxton Bragg. During the day, the C.S.S. *Chickamauga*, based at Wilmington, came down and fired on Terry's Union troops from her position on the Cape Fear River.

Terry visited Porter aboard the flagship *Malvern* to coordinate the attack for the following day. The plan called for 4000 of Terry's troops to hold the defensive line and the other 4000 to attack the land face of the fort in midafternoon. At the moment of Terry's attack, 2000 sailors and marines would assault the sea face of the fort on the northeast bastion.

The blockade runner *Lelia* foundered off the mouth of the Mersey River, England. In the mishap, Commander Arthur Sinclair, CSN, and Gunner P.C. Cuddy, both veterans of the C.S.S. *Alabama*, died. Commander Hunter Davidson, when he heard of the accident in February, commented: "What an awful thing the loss of the *Lelia.* To death in battle we become reconciled, for it is not unexpected and leaves its reward, but such a death for poor Sinclair, after forty-two years' service...."

Barber, Sgt., Co. C, 15th Illinois Volunteer Infantry, Governor's Island, New York City, N.Y.:

> Arrived at New York City at four A.M. Went to a Soldier's Home and got our breakfast and after a while reported to headquarters.
>
> In the forenoon of the same day, we went over on Governor's Island to Fort Columbus and Castle Williams with the promise that we would be immediately forwarded to our command. Had we known the treatment we were to receive there, we never would have gone over. The island itself is beautiful. Fort Columbus is situated in its center and mounts seventy guns of heavy caliber.
>
> Castle Williams, to which place we were assigned, is situated on the extreme west side of the island. It is an old structure of solid masonry, three stories high. It was commenced in 1807 and completed in 1811. It is built in a circle and access is gained to the different stories by means of winding stairs built in a turret. The entrance is secured by a large gate. The lower story is used principally as a store house and in case of necessity, twenty-five or thirty guns can be mounted in it. The second and third stories are divided into apartments connected with each other by arches large enough to move a heavy gun through. In each apartment is a heavy siege gun. I believe that the Castle mounted seventy-four guns.
>
> We were assigned quarters in the second story already crowded almost to suffocation. The upper story was used for rough cases, such as bounty jumpers and deserters. For the first few days, we were allowed the liberty of the island, but a murder was committed one night and some of the soldiers were suspected and all were confined within the Castle after that.

January 15 (Sunday)

After the constant crashing and exploding of shells within the confines of Ft. Fisher, the end of the bombardment at 3 P.M. must have been a deafening silence. The Confederate gunners, however, manned the guns that were left and began firing on the assaulting Federals. The naval landing force was the first target available, the Army troops having farther to come, and as the landing party crossed the beach the defenders' fire was point-blank, "ploughing lanes in the ranks." The naval landing force, under the command of Lt. Commander K. Randolph Breese, pressed the attack, with one group headed by Lt. Commander Thomas O. Selfridge reaching the top of the parapet and temporarily breaching the defenses, but it was driven back. Ensign Robley D. Evans—later to become a Rear Admiral with the sobriquet "Fighting Bob"—described the command problem of the assault: "All the officers, in their anxiety to be the first into the fort, had advanced to the heads of the columns, leaving no one to steady the men in behind; and it was in this way we were defeated, by the men breaking from the rear."

The Confederates were cheering upon the repulse of the naval force when they realized that Terry's forces had taken the western end of the fort in strength. A counterattack was immediately launched and hand-to-hand fighting soon ensued. Reinforcements rushing to the western end from other points of the fort now were hit by naval gunfire, firing with pinpoint accuracy and destroying the Confederate columns as they moved. Other ships fired on the riverbank behind the fort to prevent any reinforcements from that direction. Gen. Whiting was mortally wounded during the assault, and command was taken by Major James Reilly after Col. Lamb was hit in the hip by a bullet. Reilly fought doggedly and well but was overwhelmed by the onrushing Union troops and the naval gunfire. He was driven from the fort and surrendered his men later that night.

Union casualties were heavy, nearly 1000 killed or wounded, to about half that number for the Confederates. Col. Lamb, the gallant defender said of the assault:

> For the first time in the history of sieges the land defenses of the works were destroyed, not by any act of the besieging army, but by the concentrated fire, direct and enfilading, of an immense fleet poured into them without intermission, until torpedo wires were cut, palisades breached so they actually offered cover for assailants, and the slopes of the work were rendered practicable for assault.

The magnificent cooperation between Terry and Porter signalled the end to the last haven for blockade runners supplying the Confederacy. Admiral Porter wired Secretary Welles, "Fort Fisher is ours."

Barber, Sgt., Co. C, 15th Illinois Volunteer Infantry, Governor's Island, New York City, N.Y.:

> In our apartment were recruits, exchanged prisoners, furloughed men and rebel prisoners. The latter received the same rations and in every respect were treated with as much consideration as ourselves. It was very hard for us to submit to all the indignities heaped upon us here. Andersonville was still fresh in our minds and here were rebel prisoners put on an equality with us, though God knows our fare was an insult even to a prisoner.

January 16 (Monday)

Francis Preston Blair, Sr., had been in Richmond for several days to talk to President Davis informally about peace. While there, Davis gave him a letter for Lincoln. On his return, Blair went to the White House to talk to President Lincoln about his visit with Davis and gave him the letter. The letter spoke of peace negotiations *between the two nations*, not about reunification of the United States. Lincoln turned the offer down. Blair would return to Richmond for more talks, but nothing would come of them.

The Confederate Congress passed a resolution stating that Gen. Robert E. Lee should be given the command of *all* Confederate armies.

At Ft. Fisher, celebrating soldiers, sailors, and Marines were firing off their weapons when one shot accidentally set off a powder magazine which exploded, killing about 25, wounding nearly 70, and 13 men were never found.

Near Wilmington, Braxton Bragg ordered the destruction of the remaining forts guarding the port, this despite urgings from President Davis that Bragg attempt to retake Ft. Fisher. With Ft. Fisher lost, the port was effectively closed and there was no need for the Confederares to remain. As the munitions in the forts were blown up and the buildings fired, the Confederate garrisons moved towards Ft. Anderson. Admiral Porter wrote Capt. Godon: "... the death knell of another fort is booming in the distance. Ft. Caswell with its powerful batteries is in flames and being blown up, and thus is sealed the door through which this rebellion is fed."

At Clifton, Tenn., the Twenty-Third Army Corps, Major Gen. John M. Schofield commanding, embarked on troop transports to be taken by water to Cincinnati, Ohio, and then by train to Washington-Annapolis to board ocean transports for the area of Wilmington, N.C. Schofield would assault Wilmington and form a juncture with Sherman's advancing blue columns. Here was another example of Grant using his western generals in positions of great responsibility, in preference to those generals of the east.

In Richmond, Secretary Mallory was urging Flag Officer Mitchell of the James River Squadron to take action against Grant at City Point. Mallory maintained, and rightly so, that if Grant's supply line could be cut, the Union general would be forced to retire from in front of Petersburg. Mitchell promised to look into the situation.

Barber, Sgt., Co. C, 15th Illinois Volunteer Infantry, Governor's Island, New York City, N.Y.:

> Very cold and windy. Heard to-day from the rest of my comrades in rebel prisons by an escaped prisoner belonging to Company D of the regiment. We learned with deep regret that they were suffering horribly, even worse than at Andersonville. Instead of being paroled and sent home as they had been led to believe, they were sent to Florida and were kept moving from place to place, almost naked and nearly starved.

January 17 (Tuesday)

Sherman, delayed in his departure from Savannah, wrote Admiral Dahlgren:

> When we are known to be in rear of Charleston, about Branchville and Orangeburg, it will be well to watch if the enemy lets go of Charleston, in which case Foster will occupy it, otherwise the feint should be about Bull's Bay.... I will instruct Foster, when he knows I have got near Branchville, to make a landing of a small force at Bull's Bay, to threaten, and it may be occupy, the road from Mount Pleasant to Georgetown. This will make the enemy believe I design to turn down against Charleston and give me a good offing for Wilmington....

Rear Admiral Porter visited Ft. Fisher shortly after it was captured, and then wrote Secretary of the Navy Gideon Welles of his impression:

> I have since visited Fort Fisher and the adjoining works, and find their strength greatly beyond what I had conceived; an engineer might be excusable in saying they could not be captured except by regular siege. I wonder even now how it was done. The work…is really stronger than the Malakoff Tower, which defied so long the combined power of France and England, and yet it is captured by a handful of men under the fire of the guns of the fleet, and in seven hours after the attack commenced in earnest.… And no *Alabamas* or *Floridas, Chickamaugas*, or *Tallahassees* will ever fit out again from this port, and our merchant vessels very soon, I hope, will be enabled to pursue in safety their vocation.

Knowing that the blockade runners, unaware of the capture of Ft. Fisher, would attempt to run in to Wilmington, Admiral Porter ordered the signal lights on the Mound (a towering man-made hill used to hold a flaring light to signal that all was clear in the harbor). "…properly trimmed and lighted, as has been the custom with the rebels during the blockade. Have the lights lighted to-night and see that no vessel inside displays a light, and be ready to grab anyone that enters."

Jackman, Pvt., "The Orphan Brigade," en route to Augusta, Ga.:

> So cold last night did not sleep much.… Started at 8 A.M., crossed the Oconee on pontoon bridge. By 3 P.M. we had marched 11 miles.… I rode in a wagon nearly all day. One of my ankles very much swollen. The boys say I am taking "scratches" being among horses with that disease. The country we passed through today not torn up much. Had good supper of beef steak, etc. Sun warm in the evening—wind cool. Slept well—put up our fly.

January 18 (Wednesday)

Francis P. Blair, Sr., was going back to Richmond for further talks with President Davis. Lincoln, on the exit interview, gave Blair a letter to Davis in which he spelled out that he would be willing to talk to anyone about peace as it dealt with "our one common country." Therein lay the problem, Davis insisting that there were "two nations."

Lt. Commander William B. Cushing, USN (the destroyer of the C.S.S. *Albemarle*), now commanding the U.S.S. *Monticello*, landed at Ft. Caswell, near Wilmington, and hoisted the Stars and Stripes over that destroyed fortress, taking possession for the Union.

Jackman, Pvt., "The Orphan Brigade," Sparta, Ga.:

> Started at daylight. 12 miles brought us to Sparta, a nice little town. The country we have traveled through today looks fertile. Besides, there has been no raids here.… Camped 3 miles from town. Had sweet potatoes, etc. for supper. Bishop Pierce called at HdQtrs to see Parson Kavanaugh, nephew of Bishop Kavanaugh and Chap. of 6th Ky. There is no danger of the Parson's dying for having too much sense; and Captain E. says that the "Bishop's" call to see the Parson is something like the sentiment in the song "Let me kiss him for his Mother."

January 19 (Thursday)

Sherman's army was ordered to begin its march north from Savannah and Beaufort, S.C. The army moved in stages, not as one force. The objective was Goldsborough, N.C., on March 15th, less than 60 days away.

Lincoln asked Grant if there was a place in his "military family" for Lincoln's son Robert. Capt. Robert Lincoln was appointed as assistant adjutant general on Grant's staff shortly thereafter.

Gen. Lee, reluctantly, told President Davis that the general would take any assignment given him. However, he felt that if assigned as commander-in-chief, he would not be able to do any good. In essence, it was too late.

Lt. John Wilkinson, *Chameleon* (formerly the C.S.S. *Tallahassee*), had departed Wilmington on December 24, 1864, while the first assault on Ft. Fisher was going on, and he had sailed to Bermuda. Today he returned, loaded to the gunwales, and ran past the blockaders, much as he had done 21 other times, into the channel for the Cape Fear River, only to discover that the port had fallen to the Union. Turning, figuratively, on a dime, because of the twin screws of the ship, he sailed past the blockaders again and went south towards Charleston. Finding that port closed, he sailed for Liverpool, arriving there on April 9, 1865, the day Lee surrendered at Appomattox. He turned the ship over to Commander Bulloch.

January 20 (Friday)

Sherman's troops were moving, although Slocum's left wing was not making much movement because of heavy rains. The Union troops were anxious to reach South Carolina, considering it the birthplace of the rebellion, and they were eager to wreck the state.

The blockade-runners *Stag* and *Charlotte*, completely unaware that Ft. Fisher had fallen, and noting the light burning on the Mound, entered the port and anchored near the U.S.S. *Malvern*, flagship of Admiral D.D. Porter. They were immediately captured. The *Stag* was commanded by Lt. Richard H. Gayle, CSN, who had previously been captured aboard the blockade runner *Cornubia* in November 1863. Porter wrote: "I intrusted this duty of boarding the blockade runners to Lt. [Commander] Cushing, who performed it with his usual good luck and intelligence. They are very fast vessels and valuable prizes."

Off the coast of France, in Quiberon Bay, the blockade runner *City of Richmond*, loaded with the provisions, armament, and crew for the C.S.S. *Stonewall*, anchored and awaited the arrival of the latter ship.

Jackman, Pvt., "The Orphan Brigade," Thompson, Ga.:

> Moved out at 8 A.M. Warrenton looked about the same as when I was there last Sept. Has been raining all day. Walked nearly all the time. Have come 15 miles.... Stopped raining and we got supper—had turnips, sweet potatoes, etc.... Raining all night. Our fly leaked and I did not sleep well.

January 21 (Saturday)

Sherman's headquarters left Savannah for Beaufort, S.C., by steamer, with a stop at Hilton Head, S.C. For the troops, the heavy rains made slow going on the dirt roads common to this area.

Nichols, George W., Major, USA, outside Pocotaligo, S.C.:

> Last week the 17th Corps and two divisions of the 15th were moved by water from Thunderbolt round to Beaufort, and from there to the main land. Advancing towards the Charleston Railroad, they met the enemy, who fell back after a sharp skirmish. Our loss was light, and the troops went into camp under the fire of the Rebel batteries. The next day preparations were made for a detour which would have flanked the position. The Rebels did not wait for this, but evacuated their works, leaving three guns behind them; so we now occupy Pocotaligo, with a loss of ten men killed and wounded.... The 20th, 14th, and two divisions of the 15th Corps remained here; two divisions of the 20th crossed the rice lands opposite to the city and reached Hardeeville, opening communication with Howard at Pocotaligo. Then the rains fell in torrents, and a freshet came down the river, and there was from ten to fifteen feet of water where our wagon trains passed along safely a week ago. We have attempted to march up the river on this side, but the water covers all the roads, until they also are impassable.... It seems as if we must wait until the water runs off.

South of Richmond, on the James River, Flag Officer Mitchell had received yet another message from Secretary Mallory concerning a possible attack on the Union headquarters and supply depot at City Point. Mitchell decided that he would attempt to push past the obstructions the next day (22nd) and he wrote Gen. Lee of the impending movement, and asked Lee to visit him, or at least for an officer to coordinate the movements.

At Cincinnati, Ohio, Gen. Schofield's Twenty-Third Army Corps, late of Nashville and Clifton, Tenn., disembarked from steamer transports and directly boarded railcars destined for Washington, D.C., Alexandria, Va., and Annapolis, Md. The troops were en route to Wilmington, N.C., for the assault on that city.

Barber, Sgt., Co. C, 15th Illinois Volunteer Infantry, Governor's Island, New York City, N.Y.:

> Had my satchel and everything in it stolen last night. A thorough search proved futile to restore the property or apprehend the thief. I feel the loss more from the fact that my valuables and keepsakes were in

it, such as photographs. The wretch that would commit such a theft is hardly fit to live.

January 22 (Sunday)

Sherman's march along the coast included the areas along the railroad running to Branchville, S.C. Sherman notified Gen. Blair *not* to destroy the railroad, since it would possibly be needed later. Sherman gave all indications of heading towards Charleston.

At Trent's Reach on the James River, Flag Officer Mitchell's Confederate fleet could not move against the obstructions in the river due to heavy fog. He also had received no word that the torpedoes had been cleared from the river. Mitchell notified Major Gen. George E. Pickett that:

> To-morrow night, if the weather is sufficiently clear for the pilots to see their way, our movement will be made, and I will be glad to have your cooperation as agreed upon for to-night.

Jackman, Pvt., "The Orphan Brigade," en route to Augusta, Ga.:

> Started at 8 A.M. The next station below, all the dismounted men took cars for Augusta. I preferred staying with the wagons. Raining all day. Rode in wagon all the time. Came 19 miles. At Warrenton, some of the men *mutinied* declaring they would take the cars against the order of the Colonel. This morning he had the leaders arrested and is making them walk under a mounted guard. Slept well. Raining at night.

January 23 (Monday)

In Richmond, Davis signed an act creating the position of General-in-Chief of Confederate Armies, the position obviously intended for Robert E. Lee.

In Mississippi, Lt. Gen. Richard Taylor assumed command of the remainder of the Army of Tennessee, a motley collection, 17,700 men strong, many sick. John Bell Hood left for Richmond. Whatever men Taylor had, he would send most of them east to Gen. Joe Johnston in the Carolinas to try to stop Sherman. Johnston later reported that due to sickness, desertions, etc., he eventually received only about 5000. This left Taylor with a large piece of geography and few troops.

Flag Officer Mitchell sent his James River Squadron downriver to force the obstructions and attack City Point's large depot. The fleet sailed past the obstructions going downriver. The Federal ships, consisting of wooden vessels and only one ironclad, withdrew downriver. The formidable Confederate force consisted of the ironclads C.S.S. *Richmond*, Commander John McIntosh Kell, *Virginia No. 2*, Lt. John Dunnington, and the *Fredericksburg*, Lt. Francis E. Shepperd, with the gunboat *Drewry*, Lt. William H. Wall, and the torpedo boat *Scorpion*, Lt. Edward Lakin.

Almost immediately after passing the obstructions, the *Virginia No. 2* and the *Richmond* ran aground, to be followed by the *Drewry* and the *Scorpion*. All were brought under fire immediately by Federal shore batteries and mortars. The *Drewry* took a mortar hit which blew her magazines and destroyed the ship. The *Scorpion* was abandoned because of suspected damage from the explosion of the *Drewry*.

The Federal defense ships, led by the double-turreted monitor U.S.S. *Onondaga*, Commodore W.A. Parker, had moved downstream when the three Confederate ironclads appeared. Parker would be severely criticized for his action in withdrawing. The Confederates worked furiously to get the two ironclads refloated.

Jackman, Pvt., "The Orphan Brigade," Augusta, Ga.:

> When we started, I got in a wagon and rode awhile but Pete and I concluded to walk ahead of the train. We got to Augusta some time before the train got in as the roads were bad.... The city has just been flooded from the Savannah River and is the muddiest place I ever saw. Boats floated on the highest streets. Camped 2 miles out on the Waynesboro road. Have come over 17 miles today.

Barber, Sgt., Co. C, 15th Illinois Volunteer Infantry, Governor's Island, New York City, N.Y.:

> Rained all day. Yesterday came the inhuman order to keep us confined within the Castle, not even letting us go below. Our quarters now would shame a hog pen.... Confined within these loathsome walls are one thousand brave men, who on many bloody

battle-fields have attested their devotion to their country by shedding their blood, or suffering in rebel prison pens. Is this a crime for which we merit this outrageous treatment? Can this be the nation's gratitude? The patience of the soldiers is taxed to the utmost. It needs but a spark to ignite a flame which will sweep over this Castle and cover it with human gore. We get only one-fourth rations and those of the poorest quality. We have every reason to believe that the government officials on this island draw us full rations, but appropriate the greater part to fill up their purses. We have our pork raw, and as a consequence many have the dysentery. Our rooms are damp and filthy. The dirt is the accumulation of years and a hoe and spade will not remove it. We have a coal stove for each room, and the only place the smoke has for egress is through the port holes which are barely large enough for the cannon to protrude. The only light we get is through these holes. As a consequence, the air becomes fetid and unwholesome. The walls are damp and chilly. Disease is fast laying its icy chill on many a sufferer. We have borne up all along in hopes that every day would be our last on the island, but now forbearance ceased to be a virtue. We determined to apply for redress.

January 24 (Tuesday)

The Confederate Congress again offered to exchange prisoners, and this time Grant accepted. Many Union prisoners who were then suffering in Southern prison camps would shortly be home.

President Lincoln notified Vice President-Elect Andrew Johnson that he shouldn't be late for the inauguration on March 4th.

Major Gen. William Tecumseh Sherman's headquarters began to head north along the coast of South Carolina, having crossed the Savannah River. The Union Navy was providing support along the river at any point to which gunboats could ascend. Admiral Dahlgren was determined that no stone would be left unturned in the support of the drive northward.

Early this morning Commodore W.A. Parker, U.S.S. *Onondaga*, led the Federal defense vessels back up the James River to Trent's Reach to find out what had happened to the Confederate vessels which had attempted a run downriver yesterday. He found the C.S.S. *Richmond* and *Virginia No. 2* still aground and took them under fire with his 15-inch guns, damaging both Confederate ships. As soon as they could be refloated, the Rebel ironclads withdrew back upriver. This, the last Civil War battle between ironclads, ended with a Union victory and saved the City Point depot.

About 10 A.M., the C.S.S. *Stonewall*, Capt. T.J. Page, entered Quiberon Bay to meet the blockade runner *City of Richmond*, which was loaded with the provisions, armament, and crew for the *Stonewall*. Immediately the loading of the ironclad began. This would continue for four days.

January 25 (Wednesday)

Sherman was notified by Grant that Lee *would not* send any troops from Petersburg to bolster the Confederate forces in the Carolinas. Sherman's armies moved through a flooded countryside, the past four days having been nothing but rain.

One hundred eight days out of England, the C.S.S. *Shenandoah* put into Melbourne, Australia, for repairs and provisions. Lt. Waddell reported to Flag Officer Barron in Paris: "I am getting along boldly and cheerfully." Although the *Shenandoah* could handle a crew of 150, only 51 men were aboard.

The captain of the C.S.S. *Stonewall*, T.J. Page, wrote Secretary Mallory from off the coast of France that: "You must not expect too much of me; I fear that the power and effect of this vessel have been too much exaggerated. We will do our best."

The lights on the Mound at the Cape Fear River approach to Wilmington had been kept burning at the order of Admiral Porter, in the hope of luring more blockade runners into the net. Shortly after dawn, a boarding party from the U.S.S. *Tristram Shandy*, Acting Lt. Francis M. Green, swarmed aboard the steamer *Blenheim* just inside the bar at New Inlet, N.C. *Blenheim* had run past the blockaders, thinking that the port was still in Confederate hands. This was the third ship so captured.

Jackman, Pvt., "The Orphan Brigade," Waynesboro, Ga.:

A cold cloudy day. Have come 20 miles today. Camped 1/4 of a mile from Waynesboro. Walked nearly all the way. Am worn out—head aching. Hard looking country we have come through today. Waynesboro is a most desolate, woe-begone looking place

I have seen for some time. Some of the buildings were burned by the Federals—Wheeler had a fight with Kilpatrick here not long since.

Barber, Sgt., Co. C, 15th Illinois Volunteer Infantry, Governor's Island, New York City, N.Y.:

A petition has been sent to General Sherman, setting forth our grievances and asking for relief, which we have confidence will follow as soon as it reaches him. A copy of the petition was also sent to the New York *Herald* for publication. The language of the petition animadverted in the strongest terms upon the conduct of the government officials upon the island.

January 26 (Thursday)

Barber, Sgt., Co. C, 15th Illinois Volunteer Infantry, Governor's Island, New York City, N.Y.:

Very cold to-day. Yesterday a wife came to see her husband who was confined in the Castle with us. She was denied the privilege of seeing him. She could only approach as far as the gate. In his frenzy the outraged husband threw himself over the banister and broke his leg.

January 27 (Friday)

Sherman's army was now widely scattered and wet. The incessant rains had been a problem in both movement forward and supplies. The stationary positions used up the supplies fast and no foraging could be done. For better movement, Sherman again "stripped" the army of excess baggage.

Nichols, George W., Major, USA, Pocotaligo, S.C.:

In the outset of the campaign orders of a general character were issued. All sick, wounded, and incompetent soldiers were left behind. Transportation was reduced to the smallest possible space. The amount of hard bread, coffee, and salt, the number of wagons for the different headquarters and for each regiment and battery, and the size of the supply-train were specified. The number of officers to occupy a tent, and the kind of tent to be used, were also designated. Except for the uses of the adjutant's offices, the wall-tent, which we look back upon with tenderest gratitude, is forbidden, and two officers are permitted to share the "fly" which formerly was stretched over the wall tent. This will answer when the weather is pleasant, for with half a dozen blankets one can sleep comfortably in the open air; but let the wind blow and the rain fall, and comfort in your fly is an open question. But we manage to rig up boughs and water-proofs, which keep out some of the wind and a limited amount of water....

Wall-tents are not the only luxuries now forbidden. Chairs, camp-cots, trunks, and all unnecessary personal baggage, are thrown out without exception. No officer is permitted to take with him more horses than the regulations allow, and he is also restricted in the number of his servants. In truth, General Sherman has reduced the army to its simplest and most effective fighting and marching conditions.... In all these personal sacrifices General Sherman demands nothing of his soldiers which he does not himself share. His staff is smaller than that of any brigade commander in the army. He has fewer servants and horses than the military regulations allow; his baggage is reduced to the smallest possible limit; he sleeps in a fly-tent like the rest of us, rejecting the effeminacy of a house....

The torpedo boat *Scorpion*, which had been abandoned by the Confederates when they withdrew upriver from Trent's Reach, was recovered by a Federal crew in a launch from the U.S.S. *Eutaw*, commanded by Acting Ensign Thomas Morgan. Morgan found the *Scorpion* hard aground, and he immediately refloated her and took her downriver past the obstructions to the Union fleet. She was found to be little damaged. She was described as 46 feet long, 6 foot 3 inches abeam, midships, and drew 3 foot 9 inches of water.

Barber, Sgt., Co. C, 15th Illinois Volunteer Infantry, Governor's Island, New York City, N.Y.:

Last evening witnessed the perpetration of an outrageous act which came well nigh creating a scene of great confusion and danger. It was no less than an order for a portion of the soldiers to vacate their rooms and go out in the cold so as to give room to one hundred and fifty rebel prisoners who had arrived that evening. We protested, refused to obey the order and dared them to do their worst. Afterwards the order was rescinded and quiet was restored.

January 28 (Saturday)

On Quiberon Bay, France, the C.S.S. *Stonewall* had completed loading her armament, provisions, and crew from the blockade runner *City of Richmond*, and was prepared to sail, although she was short on coal. The two ships left the bay together, the *Stonewall* operating under sail to conserve fuel.

In December 1864, there had been a hassle about who would control the torpedo boat *Saint Patrick* at Mobile Bay. Major Gen. Maury, who commanded the defenses of the city, had tried unsuccessfully to get the builder, Halligan, to take the boat against the Union fleet. The problem was solved by giving the boat to the Confederate Army, which put Lt. John T. Walker, CSA, in charge. He took the boat out against the U.S.S. *Octorara*, Lt. Commander Lowe, but when Walker rammed the torpedo against the Federal ship, the torpedo did not fire. Despite being shot at from all angles, Walker managed to get the boat back safely.

Off Wilmington, N.C., Grant visited Admiral Porter to coordinate the next assault—Wilmington. Grant had troops en route from Tennessee, commanded by Gen. Schofield for this purpose.

In South Carolina, Sherman's men were still slogging through muddy roads as the rains continued, although the rains somewhat abated. Sherman prepared to cut loose from the coast and head towards Columbia, S.C.

January 29 (Sunday)

Sherman began to veer away from the coast, towards the interior of South Carolina. Word had reached Sherman that reinforcements were coming from George Thomas's army in Tennessee to him. Few knew that the reinforcements were destined for Wilmington and were already en route.

In the Petersburg lines, the soldiers, blue and gray, huddled against the cold. The major difference was that the Union men were better fed and could stand the cold better.

January 30 (Monday)

President Lincoln issued passes for the three Confederate Commissioners to enter Union lines at Ft. Monroe, Va. This had been the traditional point of entry for flag-of-truce boats, etc., going between the two opponents.

Sherman turned northwest and headed his avalanche of blue towards Columbia, S.C. This irresistible tide would smash South Carolina, where it had only "touched" Georgia.

Nichols, George W., Major, USA, Army of the Tennessee, S.C.:

> The actual invasion of South Carolina has begun.... The well-known sight of columns of black smoke meets our gaze again; this time houses are burning, and South Carolina has commenced to pay an instalment, long overdue, on her debt to justice and humanity. With the help of God, we will have principal and interest before we leave her borders. There is a terrible gladness in the realization of so many hopes and wishes. This cowardly traitor state, secure from harm, as she thought, in her central position, with hellish haste dragged her Southern sisters into the caldron of secession. Little did she dream that the hated flag would again wave over her soil; but this bright morning a thousand Union banners are floating in the breeze, and the ground trembles beneath the tramp of thousands of brave Northernmen, who know their mission, and will perform it to the end.

The Confederate ships C.S.S. *Stonewall*, Capt. T.J. Page, and the blockade runner *City of Richmond* had been out from Quiberon Bay, France, for two days when the steamer *Stonewall* signalled the *City of Richmond* that the steamer was running very short on coal and would put into Ferrol, Spain, for refueling. The *City of Richmond* sailed for Bermuda, the *Stonewall* for Spain.

January 31 (Tuesday)

At long last, the United States House of Representatives passed the Thirteenth Amendment, abolishing slavery by a vote of 119 to 56. It would be December 18, 1865, before two-thirds of the states approved the Amendment and it would become law.

President Davis proposed, and the Confederate Congress promptly approved, the appointment of Gen. Robert E. Lee as General-in-Chief of *all* Confederate Armies. It was too late to have any effect, most of the armies having melted away.

In Washington, Lincoln directed Secretary of State Seward to go to Ft. Monroe to treat with the "peace" committee from Richmond. The guidelines had not changed. *One* common country, not *two* as Davis had insisted.

Sherman continued his march towards Columbia, the smoke still rising from burning buildings, the troops building corduroy roads through the swamps, and the movement never stopping. What little resistance they met was outflanked and brushed aside.

Barber, Sgt., Co. C, 15th Illinois Volunteer Infantry, Governor's Island, New York City, N.Y.:

> We were relieved from our long and unpleasant confinement this morning. Our petition had the desired effect.

Two thousand of Sherman's men embarked on board the *Blackstone* and at three P.M. set sail for Hilton Head, S.C.

FEBRUARY 1865

February's cold, wintry breath was only partially responsible for the chill that settled in the South. Things were not going well for Richmond's government. First Wilmington, and then Charleston fell, the last hope of survival cut by Federal bayonets and naval guns. As Raphael Semmes said: "... the anaconda had, at last, wound his fatal folds on us." The blockade was complete.

While things were quiet at Petersburg and in Nashville, Sherman had left Savannah and started north towards Charleston along the coast, only to veer towards Columbia. Carolina was burning!

February 1 (Wednesday)

Illinois became the first state to ratify the Thirteenth Amendment. Earlier today, Lincoln wired Grant to: "Let nothing which is transpiring, change, hinder, or delay your Military movements, or plans," obviously referring to the "peace committee" going to Ft. Monroe from Richmond.

The former commerce raider C.S.S. *Tallahassee,* now called the *Chameleon,* Lt. Wilkinson, CSN, had nearly been caught in the net at Wilmington after Ft. Fisher fell. Wilkinson had run out of the harbor in December 1864 to Bermuda, where he loaded provisions for the Confederate Army and returned to the Cape Fear River believing the port of Wilmington still to be open. On January 19th, he ran past the blockade and discovered, in the nick of time, that the port was now in Union hands. Using his twin screws to the best of their capability, he turned in midriver and ran back to sea for Nassau, Bahamas, arriving there on January 30th. Today, he sailed from Nassau, evading the U.S.S. *Vanderbilt,* and he headed for Charleston.

Gen. Slocum, commanding Sherman's left wing, was having a hard time with flooded rivers and streams and getting his troops across the Savannah River at Sister's Ferry, despite the assistance of the Federal Navy. Gen. Howard, Sherman's right wing, encountered burned bridges and felled trees that presented few problems to Sherman's trained engineers and Pioneer battalions. They had plenty of experience with those obstacles before. Progress, though slow, was steady.

Gen. William Hardee had a makeshift group of soldiers to oppose Sherman's legions and, despite calls for help to the local governments, no reinforcements were in sight. The remnants of the Army of Tennessee were inbound, supposedly, but for the present, nothing. The best Hardee could do was to set his cavalry yapping at the heels and flanks of the blue army.

Nichols, George W., Major, USA, Hickory Hill, S.C.:

> The 15th Corps has reached Hickory Hill tonight, making a fine march of twenty miles from Pocotaligo. The roads are much better, for we have found higher ground in each mile of our march.... During the march to this point we have had opportunities of observing a barren agricultural region, and a population of "poor whites" whose brain is as arid as the land they occupy. The wealthy landholders, who formerly held this region by a sort of feudal tenure, have all run away on the approach of our troops, leaving a contingent remainder of ignorant, half-civilized people, whose ideas are limited, and whose knowledge of the English tongue is, to say the least, extremely imperfect. A family of this class I found in full and undisputed possession of the mansion of an escaped magnate (I came near writing the word convict). The head of this family was a weak creature, with pale face, light eyes, and bleached beard. His wife, a woman of about thirty years, was bowed,

crooked, and yellow. She carried in her arms a dirty boy about three years old. A frightened young girl of thirteen, the woman's stepdaughter, completed the number of the household. The man entered freely into conversation on the subject of the war. He seemed to understand but little of the great principles which were at stake in the conflict, and, in point of fact, it is an open question whether he knew what a principle meant; yet even his dull intellect took in two points, namely, that the success of the Rebels would certainly establish a bondage of his own class to the aristocrats of the South, and that our own victories would secure freedom to the slaves. The emancipation of the blacks, he thought, "would be a derned shame"; but he immediately added: "I don't pretend to understand these questions; I don't know much anyhow!" To this remark I mentally gave my hearty assent.

He continued: "The poor whites aren't allowed to live here in South Carolina; the rich folks allus charges us with sellin' things to the niggers; so they won't let us own land, but drives us about from place to place. I never owned a foot of land all my life, and I was born and raised in this state. It was only a little while ago they cau't a man a sellin' to the nigs, so they tarred and feathered him, and put him into Georgia across Sister's Ferry. They hate the sight of us poor whites."

"And yet," said I, "you are the class that are now furnishing the rank and file of their armies. How absurd that is!" The man answered with a vacant, listless stare, and the remark, "It mought be so."

Jackman, Pvt., "The Orphan Brigade," Mill Haven, Ga.:

Cold in the morning but as the day advanced, got pretty hot. Started at daylight for Mill Haven, 28 miles distant.... The country passed through covered with pines—thickly settled. Just as the sun was setting we got to the brigade. I had not been with the reg't before since last June. Was glad to see the boys. They like the cavalry very much. At night, the brigade had a battle with the "milish" camped close by using lighted pine-burs, or cones, for missiles. The boys charged the "milish" out of their camp and sacked it. They got hats, coats, saddle-blankets, etc. The battle lasted for some time and presented a beautiful sight. At times the air would be full of the blazing missiles, burning like turpentine-balls. Tired and slept well.

Sgt. Barber, still recuperating from Andersonville, and free of Governor's Island, sailed for Hilton Head, S.C.

In Richmond, President Davis accepted the resignation of Secretary of War Seddon, with reluctance, and under considerable pressure from the Confederate Congress.

February 2 (Thursday)

President Lincoln left Washington for Hampton Roads, Va., where the three Confederate commissioners had arrived yesterday evening by steamer. Rhode Island and Michigan became the second and third states to ratify the Thirteenth Amendment.

The weather in Virginia was so severe that the James River was freezing over, threatening Wilton Bridge, one of the communications links from Drewry's Bluff to Richmond. Flag Officer Mitchell of the James River Squadron sent the C.S.S. *Beaufort*, Lt. Joseph W. Alexander, to break up the ice and remain near the bridge to keep the ice from reforming.

Sherman's right wing, under Otis O. Howard, was now into the swamps, and the Confederate troops and the terrain were both delaying the advance. Heavy skirmishing was taking place along the crossings of the Salkehatchie River.

February 3 (Friday)

At Ft. Monroe, Va., the five men, representing North and South, sat in the salon of the steamer *River Queen* and discussed peace possibilities. Lincoln said that the national authority of the United States *must* be recognized within the rebellious states before anything else could even be considered. There was some talk of a "joint" operation against France in Mexico, but again Lincoln said this would mean recognizing the Confederacy as a separate government, and that this would not be done. Armistice was suggested. Lincoln said this was impossible until Federal authority was reestablished throughout the country. The Southern representatives said that this sounded like unconditional surrender, but Seward demurred, saying that the term had never been used. Lincoln indicated that his terms for reconstruction would be liberal, but he had no control over Congress in this matter. In all, it was a total bust for the Southern commissioners. There would be no peace for the South before surrender.

Maryland, New York, and West Virginia ratified the Thirteenth Amendment.

Sherman's Seventeenth Corps cleared the Confederates from Rivers' Bridge by crossing three miles of swamp, water sometimes up to their shoulders, and then outflanking the Rebels. From this point on the Salkehatchie River, the blue columns moved rapidly on towards Columbia.

Flag Officer William W. Hunter, CSN, had ordered the C.S.S. *Macon*, Lt. Joel S. Kennard, and C.S.S. *Sampson*, Lt. William W. Carnes, up the Savannah River towards Augusta when Sherman advanced upon the city of Savannah. The Rebel gunboats had now run out of water to float on. Hunter directed that the ammunition on the boats be turned over to the Confederate Army at Augusta.

A request to Admiral Dahlgren at Charleston from Brig. Gen. John P. Hatch, one of Sherman's commanders, concerned close support:

> If you can spare a tug or two launches, to cruise in upper Broad River during the stay of this command near here [Pocotaligo, S.C.], it would be of service to us. Night before last three of our boats were stolen, and I fear some scamps in the vicinity of Boyd's Neck or Bee's Creek are preparing to attempt to capture some of our transports.

Jackman, Pvt., "The Orphan Brigade," Sylvania, Ga.:

> The brigade moved for Sylvania across Briar Creek this morning. The Judge started with "Trojan" but Colonel W. turned him back.... The Judge and I took C. of Co. H into our mess—a disabled man, in the arm. We have for housekeeping—one canteen, one little tin bucket and one round gourd. We have to borrow from the Colonel a skillet to cook bread in. Drizzly day.

In the Wilmington, N.C., area, Grant requested that Admiral Porter maintain patrolling vessels on the coast while the transports carrying the Army Twenty-Third Corps made their passage to Wilmington. Porter readily complied.

The naval commanders preferred the use of the monitor-type gunboat when attacking fixed fortifications, because of the monitor's low silhouette and heavy guns. After the fall of Ft. Fisher, Porter had sent one of his two monitors to Charleston to assist Admiral Dahlgren. With the impending assault on Wilmington, Porter requested the return of the monitor—Dahlgren demurred and won his case by showing that the ship was needed more in Charleston. The crews of the monitors did not have the same love for the ships that the commanders did. One officer wrote:

> I will never again go to sea in a monitor. I have suffered more in mind and body since this affair commenced than I will suffer again if I can help it. No glory, no promotion can ever pay for it.

February 4 (Saturday)

Lt. Commander William Cushing, U.S.S. *Monticello*, took a boat expedition on a raid up Little River, S.C., near the North Carolina border. Cushing, the officer who sank the C.S.S. *Albemarle*, was no stranger to small-boat operations. Progressing as far as All Saints Parish, he captured a number of Confederate soldiers and a quantity of cotton. He then placed a guard on that town and remained overnight.

Sherman's whole front was now in motion, headed for Columbia. Slocum's problems getting across the flooded Savannah River had been solved, and he was making good time in the higher, less swampy, terrain. There was skirmishing at several points across the front. The smoke was still rising from the burned houses, barns, etc. President Davis, in Richmond, was discouraged and he placed Beauregard in charge of the defense of the Carolinas.

Barber, Sgt., Co. C, 15th Illinois Volunteer Infantry, Hilton Head, S.C.:

> Arrived at Hilton Head last evening. Are lying here awaiting further orders. The town, as far as can be seen from the boat, seems to be a small place of four or five thousand inhabitants.

February 5 (Sunday)

At City Point, Va., Grant sent the Second and Fifth Corps south and west, again extending the line that Lee would have to cover with his dwindling

Confederate forces. The objective was the railroads leading south, which supplied the Confederate Army and the Virginia civilians. The action was at Hatcher's Run and the Boydton Plank Road, where the Federals were virtually unopposed.

Sherman was still advancing on Columbia, with part of the Union forces on the road to Millersville and Buford, others on the road to Barnwell. The smoke still rose on the horizon.

Nichols, George W., Major, USA, inside South Carolina:

> The land improves as we advance into the interior. The region through which we are now traveling is rich in forage and supplies, and the army is once more reveling in the luxurious experiences of the Georgia campaign—turkeys, geese, ducks, chickens, nicely-cured hams, potatoes, honey, and abundance of other luxuries for the soldiers, and plenty of corn and fodder for the animals. The soil does not seem to be very prolific in Barnwell County, as it has a large proportion of sand, yet the planters, judging from their houses and the outbuildings, seem to have been wealthy. Nearly all these places are deserted, although here and there we find women and children, whom it is difficult to persuade they are not at once to be murdered. Wide-spreading columns of smoke continue to rise wherever our army goes.... It is grievous to see a beautiful woman, highly cultured and refined, standing in the gateway of her dismantled home, perhaps with an infant in her arms, while she calls upon some passing officers to protect her home from farther pillage; for the advance-guard, who have just been skirmishing with the enemy or some stragglers, have entered and helped themselves to what they needed or desired. No violence is done to the inmates, but household furniture is pushed about somewhat. The men of the house have all run away.... These people have one cry in common, now that they feel the bitterness of war. They pray God that it may cease upon any terms, any thing, any time, but give them peace. They say, with the most emphatic unanimity, that they never for a moment thought the war would come to South Carolina. Oh no, her sacred soil was forever to be free from the touch of the hated, despised Yankee! But here we are; and where our footsteps pass, fire, ashes, and desolation follow in the path....

Early in the morning, Lt. Commander Cushing roused his boat crews at All Saints Parish, S.C., on the Little River and spent the day burning $15,000 worth of cotton, being unable to take it downriver to the fleet. Again, he remained overnight.

The blockade-runner *Chameleon*, Lt. Wilkinson, CSN, arrived off Charleston from Nassau, Bahamas, loaded with provisions for the Confederate Army. She had nearly been caught at Wilmington on January 19th when she ran past the blockade there, coming in from Bermuda. Escaping, she ran for Nassau and learned that Charleston was still in Confederate hands, so, on the 1st she sailed for Charleston. When Wilkinson arrived off Charleston, he found that the number of blockading ships had increased so dramatically since the fall of Ft. Fisher that he could not get through while the tide was high. Wilkinson wrote:

> As this was the last night during that moon, when the bar could be crossed during the dark hours, the course of the *Chameleon* was again, and for the last time, shaped for Nassau. As we turned away from the land, our hearts sank within us, while the conviction forced itself upon us, that the cause for which so much blood had been shed, so many miseries bravely endured, and so many sacrifices cheerfully made, was about to perish at last!

Barber, Sgt., Co. C, 15th Illinois Volunteer Infantry, Pocotaligo, S.C.:

> Left Hilton Head for Pocotaligo Landing. Arrived in the afternoon.... The corps is forty miles from here and on the move. They had a severe fight on the 31st. Charged the rebels through a swamp, water waist deep, and drove them from their fortifications. Some of our wounded were drowned while crossing the stream.

The Confederate ironclad ram C.S.S. *Stonewall*, having been fitted with provisions and crew off France by the blockade runner *City of Richmond*, put into Ferrol, Spain, for refueling. This information was relayed to Commodore Thomas T. Craven, USN, U.S.S. *Niagara*, at Dover, England. Craven sailed for Spain to try to capture the *Stonewall*, or sink her.

February 6 (Monday)

At Hatcher's Run, south of Petersburg, the Federals ran into some resistance, and in the melee Brig. Gen. John Pegram, CSA, was killed. While the Federals held the Boydton Plank Road with little difficulty, the fighting at Hatcher's Run caused a short retreat for Warren's Fifth Corps when more Confederate troops arrived.

Sherman's columns were fighting for every ford and bridge on the numerous rivers bisecting their march route. The delays were usually neither long nor costly, but they were delays. Fighting took place on the Little Salkehatchie River, at Fishburn's Plantation, and near Barnwell, S.C. Most of the Confederates were outflanked, rather than taken head-on.

Early in the morning, Lt. Commander Cushing sent two boat crews up Little River, S.C., from All Saints Parish. The boats, under command of Acting Master Charles A. Pettit, advanced to Shallotte Inlet, N.C., where they surprised a small number of Confederate soldiers who were engaged in gathering provisions for Ft. Anderson, near Wilmington. Six prisoners were taken and the stores destroyed. All of the other troops in the area had been sent to Ft. Anderson, which was to be the major defense point for Wilmington. Pettit, with his crews and prisoners, returned downstream, where he rejoined Cushing. All the boats returned to the *Monticello.*

Major Gen. John Cabell Breckinridge was named Secretary of War in Davis's Cabinet, replacing James A. Seddon. Gen. Robert E. Lee assumed command of all Confederate Armies. Both appointments were too late to do any good.

February 7 (Tuesday)

Maine and Kansas approved the Thirteenth Amendment. In Delaware, the Amendment failed by one vote.

At Hatcher's Run, south and west of Petersburg, the Federals dug in to stay, stretching the Confederate lines to nearly 37 miles of fortifications. Lee had only about 46,000 men to man the trenches—not much over 1000 men per mile—very thin.

Sherman's advance had been slowed due to heavy rains and flooded countryside. Where possible, he was using transports to cross the rivers and flooded areas to keep up the momentum. He even considered returning to the coastal route, which included Charleston, to go up-country towards Wilmington. Sherman wrote Admiral Dahlgren:

> We are on the railroad at Midway [S.C.], and will break 50 miles from Edisto towards Augusta and then cross towards Columbia. Weather is bad and country full of water. This cause may force me to turn against Charleston. I have ordered Foster to move Hatch up to the Edisto about Jacksonboro and Willstown; also to make the lodgement at Bull's Bay. Watch Charleston closely. I think Jeff Davis will direct it to be abandoned, lest he lose its garrison as well as guns. We are all well, and the enemy retreats before us. Send word to New Bern that you have heard from me, and the probabilities are that high waters may force me to the coast before I reach North Carolina, but to keep Wilmington busy.

Acting Ensign George H. French, U.S.S. *Bienville*, took two cutters into Galveston Harbor at night, intending to board and destroy the blockade runner *Wren.* The current was very strong and daylight was approaching when French decided instead to board the two schooners *Pet* and *Annie Sophia*, both loaded with cotton. French sailed both schooners out of the harbor.

February 8 (Wednesday)

Massachusetts and Pennsylvania ratified the Thirteenth Amendment.

Confederate Flag Officer Barron, in Paris, France, received orders from Secretary Mallory to return home, his work done in Europe. Barron's main function had been to obtain and outfit vessels for the Confederacy and to send them to the South. In part, he had been successful. The problem now was how he would reenter the Confederacy. With Wilmington and Charleston closed, Texas seemed the only route open. The problem was solved when he resigned on February 28, 1865, and he remained in Europe.

At Ft. Fisher, N.C., the first of Major Gen. Schofield's XXIII Corps arrived from Tennessee for the assault on Wilmington.

Sherman's advance continued, the blue columns outflanking the Confederate positions, the Confederates withdrawing. In addition to the burning of houses and barns, the railroads were being demolished as the Federal army progressed. Fighting for the fords of the Edisto and South Edisto Rivers continued. An escaped Union prisoner from Florence, S.C., reported that the Union prisoners there were in desperate straits, very low on rations.

Barber, Sgt., Co. C, 15th Illinois Volunteer Infantry, Pocotaligo, S.C.:

> One hundred and twenty-five wounded men from our division came in to-day and were sent to Hilton Head.... Our force is augmenting daily by new recruits, exchanged prisoners, convalescents and furloughed men. There are now several thousand here. We are enjoying rich feasts now on oysters. We can gather them on the beach when the tide is out. There are several large beds of them near by.

February 9 (Thursday)

Virginia Unionists approved the Thirteenth Amendment. All was quiet along the Petersburg lines, the troops huddled against the snow and sleet.

Sherman was advanced along the north bank of the Edisto River towards Orangeburg, S.C., supported by naval gunboats on the river. At Ft. Fisher, N.C., more of Schofield's XXIII Corps arrived. The assault on Wilmington was building.

Jackman, Pvt., "The Orphan Brigade," Green's Cut, Ga.:

> Got orders to move for Green's Cut and marched 12 miles on the way. Cold cloudy day. Slept badly at night.

In Richmond, Lee took over as General-in-Chief, saying that no major command changes would be made at this time. Lee was fully aware of the manpower problems, so he proposed, and Davis approved, a pardon to deserters who would return to duty within 30 days.

February 10 (Friday)

Ohio and Missouri ratified the Thirteenth Amendment.

Capt. Raphael Semmes, late of the C.S.S. *Alabama,* was in Richmond, and had been nominated for the rank of Rear Admiral in the Confederate Provisional Navy. He was assigned to command the James River Squadron, replacing Commodore J.K. Mitchell, a step Semmes took most reluctantly, he and Mitchell being old friends.

At Wilmington, Major Gen. Schofield's plan called for a movement to outflank the Confederate Ft. Anderson by moving Federal troops on pontoon bridges, transported and emplaced by the Navy, and to cross the Myrtle Sound to the mainland of the peninsula behind the fort. While this action was taking place, the Navy was to provide close support and to bombard the fort. Admiral Porter directed:

> The object will be to get the gunboats in the rear of their intrenchments and cover the advance of our troops.... As the army come up, your fire will have to be very rapid, taking care not to fire into our own men.... Put yourself in full communication with the general commanding on the shore, and conform in all things to his wishes....

The 16 gunboats on the Cape Fear River were all to support Schofield's assault. The heavily armored monitor U.S.S. *Montauk* would provide the heavy guns to silence the batteries, the lighter gunboats would then rush in and fire grapeshot and canister against the Confederate emplacements, driving the gun crews away. Aimed fire would then dismount the Confederate guns.

Sherman's advance continued in good weather, making the roads easy. More smoke on the horizon. There was some action around Charleston, notably on James Island and at Johnson's Station.

Nichols, George W., Major, USA, Edisto River, S.C.:

> The crossing of the South Edisto was a feat worth mentioning somewhat in detail. It was Mower's fortune to have the lead. Upon the arrival of his division at the place known as Bennaker's Bridge, which he found burned, he was met with a sharp cannonading from the Rebels, who were in position on the other side. This was in the afternoon. He at once set to work to find means to cross the stream. A little lower down, by dint of wading and swimming, he managed to get into the water four pontoon boats. Upon these, about eight o'clock in the evening, just as the moon was rising, he crossed his division. This night attack was something the Rebels were not prepared for, accustomed as they are to the strange doings of the "Yankees." The moon rose above the

tree-tops in all her queenly splendor. Mower thought it was light enough to whip Rebels by. He was not well out of the swamp, and knew that the sooner he gained the high road the better. So, as we say in the army, he "went in," and the result was that the Rebels went out; that is, all who were not killed or captured. Our first step in the campaign is an accomplished fact....

Barber, Sgt., Co. C, 15th Illinois Volunteer Infantry, Pocotaligo, S.C.:

> The men belonging to the different corps were organized into companies to-day, my squad belonging to Company G, 17th army corps. Six hundred more soldiers arrived to-day. One thousand more are expected this evening. Heard to-day that Sherman had taken Branchville, S.C., and was marching on Columbia, the capital of the State. Yesterday the quartermaster of this post was shot by guerrillas while out a short distance from camp. Six of our men have been found hung and their bodies were outraged and mutilated in the most shameful manner. The country is swarming with guerrillas and cut-throats.

In another attempt to capture and destroy the Federal depot at City Point, and to cut the communications between Grant and Hampton Roads, Confederate Lt. Charles W. Read loaded four torpedo boats on wagons to take them across the narrow neck of land at Drewry's Bluff, where they would be put into the water. Read, with 100 officers and men, would then capture any passing Federal ships, arm the ships with torpedoes, and attack and sink the Union gunboats on the James River. The wagons were loaded, the men readied, and the overland trek began.

February 11 (Saturday)

The U.S.S. *Niagara*, Commodore Craven, arrived at Coruña, Spain, having been delayed by foul weather. Craven was in search of the C.S.S. *Stonewall*, a newly outfitted Confederate commerce raider, which had put into Ferrol, Spain, nine miles distant, for refueling. Craven requested assistance from the U.S.S. *Sacramento*, but found that she was in Lisbon, Portugal, repairing, and would not be available for ten days or more.

Sherman's troops were now in positions between the Confederates on the coast at Charleston and those in Augusta, Ga. In neither place did the South have sufficient men assembled to oppose Union forces successfully. There was fighting in the vicinity of Orangeburg, Aiken, and around Johnson's Station. President Davis wired Hardee that if the Confederate army could be gathered around Charleston, the Union army could be defeated—this at a time when Beauregard was counseling evacuation of Charleston to save the army. In South Carolina, the weather remained good, roads dry.

Seven Union gunboats engaged Confederate guns at Half Moon Battery on the coastal flank of the Cape Fear River, six miles below Ft. Fisher. The naval fire contained Gen. Hoke's Confederate division, while Schofield's XXIII Corps moved up the beach and behind the Rebel lines. Bad weather prevented the use of pontoon bridges, so Schofield withdrew his men to Ft. Fisher.

Robert Frederick Hoke was born at Lincolnton, N.C., on May 27, 1837. He attended the Kentucky Military Institute, and by age 17 he was managing the family cotton mill, ironworks, and other commercial enterprises. At the beginning of the war he entered the 1st North Carolina Infantry as a 2nd Lieutenant. He fought with distinction at Big Bethel and soon became major of the regiment, then was promoted to Lieutenant Colonel of the 33rd North Carolina. After the action at New Bern in March 1862, and the Peninsula Campaign, he was transferred to the 21st North Carolina, promoted to Colonel, and appointed commander of the regiment. He fought again with distinction at Second Manassas and Antietam, and for his action at Fredericksburg in January 1863, he was promoted to Brigadier General and given command of five North Carolina units. He was seriously wounded at Chancellorsville while holding the line atop Marye's Heights. The wound kept him out of Gettysburg. After recuperating, he commanded the troops that captured Plymouth, N.C., in April 1864. Serving under Bragg at Wilmington, N.C., in February 1865, he lost the battle for Ft. Anderson and withdrew to the interior. He later fought at Kinston and Bentonsville, N.C., where he surrendered on May 1, 1865. He returned home to his commercial enterprises and died in Raleigh on July 3, 1912.

Lt. Charles W. Read, CSN, continued overland with his four wagons and 100 men to the rendezvous point on the James River. The weather made it very slow going, little progress having been made since they left on the 10th.

February 12 (Sunday)

Lt. Charles W. Read, CSN, and his torpedo-boat-laden wagons and men moved through a sleet storm to a point only a few miles from their rendezvous with Lt. John Lewis, CSN, who had gone ahead to reconnoitre the area. Master W. Frank Shippey, one of Read's party, wrote that while the party sought shelter in an abandoned farmhouse,

> ...a young man in gray uniform came in and informed us that our plan had been betrayed, and that Lewis was at the ford to meet us, according to promise, but accompanied by a regiment of Federals lying in ambuscade and awaiting our arrival, when they were to give us a warm reception. Had it not been for the storm and our having to take shelter, we would have marched into the net spread for us....

Read then ordered the men and wagons to return on their route for about a mile and go into camp, and he left alone to confirm, or deny, the story of the young Confederate soldier.

At Orangeburg, S.C., the Union columns at first went around the town and started tearing up railroad track. As the main body of the column entered the town, the local drugstore was already on fire, with flames coming through the roof. The town was small, about 800 inhabitants, but there were plenty of churches, brokers' offices, etc., as well as many slave quarters around the major buildings. In a high wind, the dry wood crackled and the flames spread rapidly despite the attempt of Union troops to extinguish the blaze. About half the town burned before the flames could be controlled. Wade Hampton's cavalry was reported in Columbia.

Five blockade-runners, *Carolina, Dream, Chicora, Chameleon,* and *Owl,* were anchored at Nassau, Bahamas, all loaded with supplies for the Confederacy. A meeting was held by the captains of the ships and it was decided that all would make a run for Charleston Harbor, hoping that some would evade the Union blockaders. They sailed that night for Charleston and only the *Chicora,* Master John Rains, got through, the ship being the last to enter and leave that port before it was evacuated. Commander John Maffitt, *Owl,* evaded the blockaders and went to Galveston, Tex., where he ran in and unloaded his cargo. He then ran past the blockaders to Havana, Cuba, reaching there on May 9th. Refueling, he returned to Nassau, and finally to Liverpool, on July 14th. For him the war ended when he left Galveston.

At Ferrol, Spain, the C.S.S. *Stonewall,* Capt. Thomas Jefferson Page, and the U.S.S. *Niagara,* Commodore T.T. Craven, watched each other for signs of weakness. The *Niagara* was much too weak a ship to engage the *Stonewall* on her own. Craven described the armament of the ship:

> The *Stonewall,* is a very formidable vessel, about 175 feet long, brig-rigged, and completely clothed in iron plates of 5 inches in thickness. Under her topgallant forecastle is her casemated Armstrong 300-pounder rifled gun. In a turret abaft her mainmast are two 120-pounder rifled guns, and she has two smaller guns mounted in broadside. If as fast as reputed to be, in smooth water she ought to be more than a match for three such ships as the *Niagara....*

February 13 (Monday)

Sherman's army now approached the Congaree River, S.C., which the troops would cross on the 14th (Tuesday). Sherman had severed his supply line to the sea while at Augusta, Ga., and now relied on foraging. The weather remained good and clear. Progress of the columns was marked again by rising columns of black smoke as the troops burned the countryside.

Nichols, George W., Major, USA, Army of the Tennessee, S.C.:

> The magnificent spectacle of a fire in the woods was the striking episode of our march yesterday. The army moved through a tract of hilly country which was thickly clothed with pine forests. Many of the trees were dead, and all had been scraped in order to obtain the resinous substance which formed their fruit and life. Accidently, or otherwise, the dry leaves and pine cones had caught fire, which ignited these trees, and for miles the woods were on fire. It was grand and sometimes awful to see the flames flying over the ground like a frightened steed. As we approached one of these forests, filled with flames and

just down from Ft. Anderson. Major Gen. Schofield's XXIII Corps was readied for the assault and would be supported by naval gunboats.

February 17 (Friday)

Early in the morning, Major Gen. Jacob D. Cox, part of Schofield's XXIII Corps, advanced 8000 men north from Smithville towards Ft. Anderson. The Navy, in support, sent the monitor U.S.S. *Montauk*, Lt. Commander Edward E. Stone, and four gunboats to bombard the fort, and they silenced the fort's twelve guns. Since he had not been able to get the other monitor back from Admiral Dahlgren at Charleston, Admiral Porter used the same subterfuge he had used on the Mississippi River; he created a bogus monitor using a scow, timber, canvas, and paint. The fake monitor, dubbed "Old Bogey" by the sailors, was towed to the head of the bombardment line, where she received much attention from the Confederate gunners.

At Charleston, S.C., the gunboats U.S.S. *Pawnee, Sonoma, Ottawa, Winona, Potomska, Wando, J.S. Chambers*, and other vessels supported landings of Major Gen. Foster's soldiers at Bull's Bay. This was a diversionary tactic meant to tie down Confederate forces and keep them from Sherman's route of march. Its secondary mission was to put pressure on the city.

During the night, the Confederate defenses at Forts Moultrie, Sumter, Johnson, Beauregard, and Castle Pinckney were abandoned, and the Rebel troops marched north to join Lee. The defenses of Charleston were silenced after 567 continuous days of attack. Four Confederate ironclads were scuttled or blown up, the fifth, the C.S.S. *Columbia*, was found run aground and was later salvaged by the Union Navy. Several torpedo boats of the "David" class were also found, one of which was eventually taken to the U.S. Naval Academy and put on display. Several blockade runners were captured in port and several more were lured in by the same trick used at Wilmington—leaving the signal light burning.

Admiral Dahlgren wrote Admiral Porter: "You see by the date of this [February 18] that the Navy's occupation has given this pride of rebeldom to the Union flag, and thus the rebellion is shut out from the ocean and foreign sympathy." Lt. Wilkinson, former commander of the C.S.S. *Tallahassee*, learned of the fall of Charleston while in Nassau, and wrote: "This sad intelligence put an end to all our hopes...." The city that had most symbolized the spirit of the South was in Union hands.

At Columbia, the mayor and a delegation rode out to see Sherman and to surrender the city. As Union troops entered the city, the remnants of Hampton's cavalry departed, leaving cotton bales still smoldering. It has been a bone of contention since as to how the fire had started—evidence points to bales of cotton being fired by Hampton's retreating horsemen; however, many in the city believed that the fire had been set by the Yankees. At any rate, burning bales of cotton were found and thought to have been extinguished. The troops found the liquor supply and were greeted warmly by the freed Union prisoners and the Negro population. Sherman's Provost Guards were soon busy arresting drunken soldiers. Several of the latter held a mock session of the State Legislature in the State House. The colors of the 8th Missouri Volunteers, having been the first to fly at Ft. Donelson, been riddled by Rebel bullets at Shiloh, carried into Vicksburg, flown over Kennesaw Mountain and Ft. McAllister were now hoisted over the state capitol in Columbia.

Sherman set up headquarters in one of the quieter streets of the town and retired. The high winds evidently fanned the flames of the cotton back to life and bits of burning cotton spread over the city like a blanket, starting new fires blocks from the source. Sherman had his Union troops out fighting the fires, but the high winds prevented containment. Wade Hampton's home, one of the finest in Columbia, was burned, along with many others. For more than 100 years the burning of Columbia would be cited by the South as an example of Northern excess during the war.

With Charleston empty of defenders and Columbia in flames, this was, indeed, a day of retribution for the North against South Carolina.

February 18 (Saturday)

In Charleston, S.C., the evacuation continued all night, and at about 9 A.M. the Union troops of Brig. Gen. Alexander Schimmelfennig entered the city. Shortly after, the mayor surrendered the city to the Union commander amid the ruins of what once had been a beautiful city. A few fires were set to burn cotton and military stores and the Union bands played "Hail, Columbia" to the delight of the local Negroes. Charleston had, indeed, fallen!

Commodore John R. Tucker, CSN, after scuttling the Confederate gunboats at Charleston, took charge of the remaining naval forces in the area, loaded them on trains, and set out for Wilmington. He got as far as Whiteville, S.C., when he learned that the rail line had been cut, and that Wilmington was in danger of evacuation. Tucker then unloaded his sailors and struck out cross-country on a 125-mile march to Fayetteville, N.C.

At Wilmington, the naval gunfire had silenced the guns at Ft. Anderson, the Confederates had evacuated their defensive positions, and had fallen back to Town Creek. At the same time, the Confederates who had dug in at Sugar Loaf Hill, on the east bank of the river, withdrew to Ft. Strong, some three miles south of Wilmington. The Union drive was working well.

At Columbia, the fine weather continued, and the fires were mostly burned out. The local residents were poking about in the ashes and cursing the Yankees. Sherman set about destroying the depots, railroads, and anything of military value. About 4000 rifles, complete, and another 6000, partially complete, were destroyed along with 10,000 rounds of artillery ammunition, 500,000 rounds of rifle ammunition, and a vast amount of cavalry equippage. The powder magazines were full, and, in destroying these, an accident caused the death of twenty Union soldiers when one of the magazines exploded. Twenty boxcars, nineteen locomotives, and other railroad machinery was destroyed, including 650 sets of car wheels. Mills and factories along the Congaree River were destroyed and their smokestacks either blown up or holed severely. The troops not engaged in the destruction were outside the city in camps, awaiting orders to march north.

Barber, Sgt., Co. C, 15th Illinois Volunteer Infantry, Pocotaligo, S.C.:

> Pleasant. Am not feeling very well. Have a severe cold. Washed a shirt and pair of drawers this morning. We are out of rations but expect to draw this evening or to-morrow. We are almost shut out from communication with the outside world. I have not seen a daily paper in a long time.

At Melbourne, Australia, the C.S.S. *Shenandoah*, Lt. Waddell, completed repairs and set sail. When the pilot was dropped off, 42 men were found aboard as stowaways. Thirty-six of them signed on as sailors, the remainder as Marines, having been recruited for the ship in Melbourne.

February 19 (Sunday)

At Columbia, S.C., Sherman's troops were completing their destruction of the mills, factories, etc., that might be of some military use. Outside the city, the blue columns left the camps and began moving into the advance marching columns, going north. The next major stop would be Fayetteville.

Nichols, George W., Major, USA, Columbia, S.C.:

> ...Columbia will have bitter cause to remember the visit of Sherman's army.... It is not alone in the property that has been destroyed—the buildings, bridges, mills, railroads, material of every description—nor in the loss of the slaves, who, within the last few days, have joined us by hundreds and thousands.... It is in the crushing downfall of their inordinate vanity, their arrogant pride, that the rebels will feel the effects of the visit of our army. Their fancied, unapproachable, invincible security has been ruthlessly overthrown. Their boastings, threatenings, and denunciations have passed by us like the idle wind.... I know that thousands of South Carolina's sons are in the army of the rebellion; but she has already lost her best blood there. Those who remain have no homes. The Hamptons, Barnwells, Simses, Rhetts, Singletons, Prestons, have no homes. The ancient homesteads where were gathered sacred associations, the heritages of many generations, are swept away. When first these men became traitors, they lost honor....

In the Wilmington area, Ft. Anderson had been evacuated, the Confederates withdrawing towards the city at Ft. Strong. Admiral Porter's gunboats steamed up the river seven miles to Big Island shallows and the point where there began the obstructions formed of piles driven into the river. While the gunboats engaged the batteries of Ft. Strong, boat crews worked clearing the torpedoes from the channel.

The Confederate steamer *A.H. Schultz*, used as a flag-of-truce boat between Richmond and the

Varina vicinity on the James River, and as a transport by the Southern forces south of Richmond, struck one of the torpedoes previously laid by Lt. Beverley Kennon of the Confederate Torpedo Service, and the steamer sank. The ship had just completed the delivery of 400 Union prisoners to Varina, and was returning empty, there being no Confederate prisoners to bring back.

February 20 (Monday)

At Wilmington, N.C., the Federal boat crews sweeping for torpedoes in the Cape Fear River channels were kept very busy. The Confederates released 200 floating torpedoes during the night, causing much consternation as they floated into the boats clearing the channel, some destroying the small boats, others striking the steamers and doing great damage. Casualties from the torpedoes were slight, but they were worrisome.

Sherman's columns left Columbia, passing through a fertile country for about five miles. They then passed into the area of hills with stunted pines, the sandy soil almost barren. A large train of refugees consisting of several hundred white people followed the army as it left. There were many reasons for the exodus. Some left to escape starvation, some to escape conscription, some to escape persecution. All were a bother to the Union army and they made many demands for protection, provisions, etc., which could not be met. Sherman ordered them expelled from the columns.

February 21 (Tuesday)

In Wilmington, the Confederate Army was destroying its stores, sending huge columns of black smoke into the air. Gen. Bragg had ordered the city evacuated in the face of the Union advance.

During the initial landings for the assault on Ft. Anderson, a bogus monitor-type ironclad had been rigged using an old scow, timber, canvas, and black paint. This bogus ironclad had been named "Old Bogey" by the sailors who towed her around. Now, with the torpedoes coming downriver, "Old Bogey" was called into service again. She was pushed across the river into the path of the torpedoes. One observer described the action:

> Johnny Reb let off his torpedoes without effect on it, and the old thing sailed across the river and grounded in the flank and rear of the enemy's lines on the eastern bank, whereupon they fell back in the night. She now occupies the most advanced position of the line, and Battery Lee has been banging away at her, and probably wondering why she does not answer. Last night after half a days fighting, the rebs sent down about 50 torpedoes; but although "Old Bogey" took no notice of them, they kept the rest of us pretty lively as long as the ebb tide ran.

Admiral Porter's gunboats closed with Ft. Strong and kept up a rapid fire as Schofield's XXIII Corps moved up both sides of the river in the assault.

Sherman was moving on the most direct route to the North Carolina border. Now the country was improving, becoming more cultivated, with more houses to be seen (and burned). The Confederates were burning cotton, even small amounts, to keep it away from Sherman. One Union observer noted: "How do they imagine we are going to take it [the cotton] out of the country?"

Nichols, George W., Major, USA, Winnsboro, S.C.:

> This place is northwest of the Rebel capital, and the 20th Corps, which first reached it, has made the march from Columbia in two days, thoroughly destroying the track of the South Carolina Railroad as it moved.... The 20th Corps arrived early this morning, just in time to prevent the spread of a conflagration which, starting in the central part of the city, threatened to destroy every thing in its path. Several regiments were engaged in this work, and especial efforts were unsuccessfully made to save the house of a brother of Governor Aiken. As it was, only a few buildings were burned, to the unbounded gratitude of the thousands of inhabitants, many of whom are refugees from Vicksburg, Nashville, Atlanta, Savannah, Charleston, and later, Columbia. I am thus particular in mentioning the names of these places, for, as Mrs. Aiken told me, "They never expected a Yankee army would come here."...

Jackman, Pvt., "The Orphan Brigade," Graniteville, S.C.:

> The brigade marched toward Columbia. Not being able to stand the service, I...got on the cars and came back to Graniteville, S.C....

February 22 (Wednesday)

Kentucky rejected the Thirteenth Amendment.

The Confederates evacuated Wilmington, N.C., sending much of the military stores on the railroad towards Richmond. What remained was destroyed. After the evacuation of Ft. Strong, the Federal gunboats steamed upriver to Wilmington, which was already occupied by Brig. Gen. Terry's troops, Gen. Bragg having evacuated the city. Wilmington had fallen and Admiral Porter wrote Secretary of the Navy Gideon Welles:

> I have the honor to inform you that Wilmington has been evacuated and is in possession of our troops.... I had the pleasure of placing the flag on Fort Strong, and at 12 o'clock noon today shall fire a thirty-five guns salute this being the anniversary of Washington's birthday.

It was now official. Gen. Joseph E. Johnston was assigned as commander of all Confederate forces in South Carolina, Georgia, Florida, Tennessee, and those concentrating in North Carolina. Gen. Beauregard, in ill health, was told to report to Johnston for orders.

Sherman was skirmishing at Camden and on the Wateree River north of Columbia. The railroads on the route of march were a special target of Sherman's destroyers. The Twentieth Corps reached Rocky Mount, S.C., and waited for the crossing of the Catawba River. Sherman feinted towards Charlotte, N.C., and then aimed his main drive towards Goldsborough and a linkup with Schofield.

Jackman, Pvt., "The Orphan Brigade," Graniteville, S.C.:

> Moved camp above the factory. Established ourselves on the margin of the pond which is very large and clear as crystal. There are two sheets of water connected, of considerable size—nearly two miles in length. This factory is for the manufactory of sheeting, etc. Works 350 looms and 500 operatives—mostly women. The town is regularly built—houses mostly swiss cottages, or built on that plan, and are occupied by the operatives; it is a "manufacturer's" town. Above, on the same stream, is another manufactory called Vancluse—3 miles from here. It is owned by the same company. The country around here is very poor—nothing but sand-hills. We made a shelter for ourselves by putting up fence rails and spreading blankets over them.

February 23 (Thursday)

Admiral Dahlgren sent Capt. Henry S. Stellwagen, U.S.S. *Pawnee*, with a squadron of gunboats to occupy Georgetown, S.C., and to establish a link with Sherman's route from Columbia, S.C., to Fayetteville, N.C. Ft. White, at the entrance to Georgetown Bay, was evacuated upon the approach of the Federal gunboats. The fort was then occupied by U.S. marines.

Things were turning nasty in South Carolina. Not only had heavy rains begun midafternoon, but on the 22nd, two of Sherman's men had been found murdered—their heads crushed by heavy blows. That day, reports of more such findings were circulating. The *Official Records (OR)* cited a report of Gen. Judson Kilpatrick's:

> An infantry lieutenant and seven men murdered yesterday by the Eighth Texas Cavalry after they had surrendered. We found their bodies all together and mutilated, with paper on their breasts, saying "Death to foragers." Eighteen of my men were killed yesterday and some had their throats cut.... I have sent Wheeler word that I intend to hang eighteen of his men, and if the cowardly act is repeated, will burn every house along my line of march.... I have a number of prisoners, and shall take a fearful revenge.

Sherman's orders to Major Gen. Otis O. Howard, also cited in the *Official Records*, show his determination to take life for life:

> Now it is clearly our war right to subsist our army on the enemy.... I contend if the enemy fails to defend his country we may rightfully appropriate what we want. If our foragers act under mine, yours, or other proper orders they must be protected. I have ordered Kilpatrick to select of his prisoners man for man, shoot them, and leave them by the roadside labeled, so that our enemy will see that for every man he executes he takes the life of one of his own. I want the foragers, however, to be kept within reasonable bounds for the sake of discipline. I will not protect them when they enter dwellings and commit wanton

waste.... If any of your foragers are murdered, take life for life, leaving a record in each case.

February 24 (Friday)

At Ft. White, S.C., Capt. H.S. Stellwagen sent two of his squadron under the command of Ensign Allen K. Noyes up the Pee Dee River to accept the surrender of Georgetown, S.C. Arriving at Georgetown with the U.S.S. *Catalpa* and *Mingoe*, Noyes led a party ashore and received the surrender of the town, while a small party climbed to the city hall dome and ran up the Stars and Stripes. A small party of Confederate horsemen came rushing into town to protest the flag-raising with guns, so more Federal sailors were landed and the guerrillas were driven off. The town was later garrisoned by five companies of U.S. Marines.

In South Carolina, heavy rains held up Sherman's advance, little ground was gained. The countryside east of the Catawba River was now sandy, the roads poor, the country covered with pine forests which were being harvested for turpentine. Many of the civilian population were evacuating, bag and baggage.

Nichols, George W., Major, USA, Sherman's Hdqtrs., Catawba River, S.C.:

Within the last week Rebel cavalry have committed atrocities upon our foragers which make the horrors of a battle-field tender mercies in comparison. In one instance a courier was found hanged by the roadside, with a paper attached to his person bearing the words, "Death to all foragers." In another instance three men were found shot, with a similar notice upon their persons. Yesterday, our cavalry, in the direction of Chesterville, found in a ravine twenty-one of our infantry soldiers lying dead, with their throats cut, but no notice given as a reason for the frightful murders.... There is but one course to be taken in this matter—retaliation, and that fourfold. General Sherman has given General Kilpatrick orders to hang and shoot prisoners who fall into his hands to any extent he considers necessary. Shame on Beauregard, Hampton, and Butler! Has the blood of their patriot fathers become so corrupted that the sons are cowardly assassins?...

Union troops at Wilmington were preparing for movement into the interior of North Carolina and the linkup with Sherman.

Secretary of the Navy Gideon Welles, with an eye to the end of the war, took steps to cut back the huge Federal fleet now that all the major ports were in Union hands. He directed that the Gulf Squadrons and those on the Atlantic coast:

...send North such purchased vessels as appear by surveys to require very extensive repairs... and those no longer required. These will probably be sold or laid up. You will also send home any stores that are not required. Further requisition must be carefully examined before approval, and the commanders of squadrons are expected to use every possible exertion and care to reduce the expenses of their squadrons.

February 25 (Saturday)

The Confederates took the C.S.S. *Chickamauga* up the Cape Fear River to just below Indian Wells, N.C., and scuttled her in a position to obstruct the river. The flow of the stream swept the ironclad to where it was parallel with the bank, causing no obstruction.

Sherman's columns were halted for the time being. Weather and roads were bad and a time had come to "close up the column" and make it more compact. There were problems with the "bummers" (foragers) even within, and between, the commands. Judson Kilpatrick, who was usually in front or on the flanks of the armies, had occasion to pass foragers from other commands through his own. In a letter cited in the *Official Records*, he tells of some of his problems:

Stragglers and foraging parties of the Twentieth Corps were here yesterday, eight miles from their command, committing acts most disgraceful. This house [Kilpatrick's headquarters] was pillaged at 10 A.M. yesterday by men of the Twentieth Army Corps. I have allowed foragers from the left wing to pass through my lines, and even assisted them. Yesterday a detail sent out by Major Dunbar, my quartermaster, captured ten mules and four horses for his wagon train. An officer of the Twentieth Army Corps arrested them and took mules and horses away. I shall now allow no foraging parties to pass through or out of my lines, and I shall dismount and seize all horses ridden

> by infantrymen who enter my column. This I shall continue to do, unless otherwise ordered by you or until my people are treated with that same respect and courtesy I feel their conduct and services demand. I also call your attention to the fact that foraging parties burned sufficient forage on this road to have fed my entire command.

Gen. Joseph Eggleston Johnston, at Charlotte, N.C., assumed command of the troops in South Carolina, Georgia, and Florida. Upon examination of the troop strength and state, he notified Lee that, in his opinion, his force was entirely too weak to take on Sherman and that it should be consolidated with Bragg's in North Carolina.

Jackman, Pvt., "The Orphan Brigade," Graniteville, S.C.:

> Cloudy. Took a bath in the pond. Evening, the Judge and I went through the factory. Some very handsome girls at work here. The factory runs by both water and steam power. They weave 13,000 yards of cloth daily. I never heard such a fuss and clatter.

February 26 (Sunday)

Sherman's Twentieth Corps moved to Hanging Rock, S.C., the remainder of Sherman's armies moving more slowly in the rain, although it was clearing in some areas. The Army of the Tennessee was in the Kershaw district and having a hard time with rising water, although the rain had stopped.

Nichols, George W., Major, USA, Sherman's Hdqtrs., Lancaster, S.C.:

> This morning opened with mists and fog, obscuring the sun's rays, while now and then the humid atmosphere condensed into drops of rain. The horsemen dashing through the woods of low pine-trees shook off the moisture which had gathered upon the delicate spindles in beautiful drops of diamonds and pearls, and the gray mists swept over the hills and into the valleys, completely enveloping the long trains.... The district of Lancaster is not only much more beautiful, in an artistic sense, than any we have seen in South Carolina—stretching away for miles in gentle undulations, and dotted with low pine-trees, which seem like spots of green upon a carpet of red and gold—but the land is more prolific. Wheat, corn, oats, cotton, and fruits grow in abundance, the barns and hay-ricks yielding a plentiful supply for all our needs...Not only is there a surfeit of rails, but some of the fences are built of boards, the first instance in our experience in this campaign of such extravagance in farm life. The soldiers, with a good taste which does them infinite credit, have appropriated the boards for building material. To be sure, it is only for a night, but one of the articles in a soldier's creed is to make himself comfortable while he can....

At Wilmington, Schofield was preparing for his move inland, refitting troops and evacuating the sick and wounded by hospital ship.

February 27 (Monday)

Commodore Tucker and his 350 stalwart Confederate sailors had walked the 125 miles to Fayetteville, where Lt. Commander Rochelle's naval detachment joined them. Tucker took the entire group to Richmond, and then to Drewry's Bluff, to man the guns controlling the river.

Sherman was still moving through to Fayetteville.

In the Shenandoah Valley, Sheridan was back with about ten thousand cavalry and was opposed by Jubal Early and two weak Confederate brigades. Grant had directed that the Virginia Central Railroad and the James River Canal be destroyed. Lynchburg was to have its railroads, etc., destroyed, and its military stores burned.

February 28 (Tuesday)

Sherman's armies were near the North Carolina line at Rocky Mount and Cheraw, S.C., where skirmishes occurred. Johnston, at Charlotte, was trying to scrape the bottom of the barrel to get a force to oppose Sherman.

Rear Admiral Dahlgren was leaving for Charleston from Georgetown Bay and gave his instructions to Capt. Henry Stellwagen, U.S.S. *Pawnee*, before leaving:

> I leave here for Charleston, and you remain the senior officer. The only object in occupying the place, as I do, is to facilitate communication with General Sherman, if he desires it here, or by the Santee.... Keep up information from the Santee by a courier over the Santee road or by water.... Let parties be pushed out by land and water, to feel the rebel positions, and drive back his scouts and pickets.

MARCH 1865

Thoughts were increasingly of peace and how the reconstruction of the nation would be accomplished. It was obvious that the South was losing the war and that the end could not be far off. The only army of any size was located at Petersburg, and it was tied down by the tenacious and formidable Union Army of the Potomac. Few options were left.

March 1 (Wednesday)

In the Shenandoah Valley, the thunder of cavalry could be heard again as Sheridan's hard-riding bluecoats pounded up the Valley in pursuit of Jubal Early's two battered brigades. In Washington, news of the passage of the Thirteenth Amendment by Wisconsin was offset by its rejection by New Jersey.

Sherman's Army of the Tennessee, right wing, spent the day getting across a river at Kelley's Bridge. Gen. Blair's corps made little progress, Howard's wing corduroying roads as it went.

Admiral Dahlgren went back to Georgetown, S.C., up the coast from Charleston, to visit the naval forces at that location and to "inspect" Ft. White, which controlled the bay. Remaining overnight, Dahlgren, in his flagship *Harvest Moon*, was in his cabin awaiting breakfast as the ship sailed for Charleston. The ship struck a torpedo and, in Dahlgren's words:

> Suddenly, without warning, came a crashing sound, a heavy shock, the partition between the cabin and wardroom was shattered and driven in toward me, while all loose articles in the cabin flew in different directions.... A torpedo had been struck by the poor old *Harvest Moon*, and she was sinking.

Five minutes later the ship was gone. Only one life was lost, and the Admiral had nothing but the uniform he was wearing.

March 2 (Thursday)

Gen. Lee wrote a message to Gen. Grant, proposing a meeting to attempt resolving the present "unhappy difficulties" by a military convention. Grant demurred, saying he had no authority to hold such a conference, there must have been something misunderstood. Dealing with the South in such a manner would, in effect, be a recognition of it as a sovereign military force—a separate nation's military power. This was the same ploy used at the "peace committee" meeting with Lincoln at Hampton Roads, when Confederate Vice President Stephens suggested that the North and South jointly throw Napoleon III out of Mexico.

At Waynesborough, Va., the last battle of any significance in the Valley was fought between Federal cavalry and Confederate infantry. The remnants of Jubal Early's brigades were overwhelmed by a charge of 5000 cavalry led by Gen. George A. Custer. While Early escaped with his staff, Custer captured 200 wagons, seventeen flags, and well over 1000 prisoners. The ghosts of Cross Keys, McDowell, Winchester, and Kernstown must have cringed. The Valley was lost.

Sherman was moving slowing through a country of pine barrens and wire grass, the armies making only 10 to 15 miles per day. The Twentieth Corps neared the North Carolina border.

In early January 1865, a Confederate naval force of one officer and eight sailors was organized in Richmond, equipped with torpedoes, and sent by rail to Bristol, Tenn. There a boat was obtained and fitted with the torpedoes. The boat was then launched into the Holston River and went down to the Tennessee River, where they hoped to sink Union vessels. At Kingston, Tenn., a group of local Unionists captured the boat and crew. The torpedoes were destroyed and the crew was sent north to prison camps.

The Confederacy had purchased a high-speed steamer in England for use as a blockade runner. This ship, the *Bat*, was captured in October 1864 and sold to the U.S. government at a prize court in December for $150,000. Because of her speed, she was being used as a courier ship between City Point and Washington, D.C.

March 3 (Friday)

The Thirty-Eighth Congress would officially adjourn at 8 A.M. tomorrow, but tonight much work needed to be done. One major item was the act establishing the Bureau for the Relief of Freedmen and Refugees—to be known as the Freedman's Bureau. This bureaucratic body would provide the basis for support of the Negro, both economically and politically, for the next 20 years. It would initially provide food, clothing, and other assistance. Later, it would be used to build schools, establish secondary learning institutions, and provide a political base for Negro elected officials.

Sherman was at Cheraw, S.C. (immediately across the North Carolina border), where large amounts of ammunition and other munitions were captured in the depot. Cheraw, an old town of about 2000, had wide streets, well shaded, with the houses well kept. One observer noted that the streets were full of Confederate cavalry, which cleared immediately upon the firing of a few rounds of artillery. The Union infantry skirmishers entering the town would approach a house, knock out the windows on one end, enter the house and fire at the Confederates from the windows at the other end. Before long, the gray infantry left across the bridge on the Pee Dee and fired the turpentine and resin barrels on the bridge, destroying it.

The Cape Fear River was the scene of much activity as the Federals worked to clear the Confederate torpedoes and make the river safe for steamers. With Sherman's line of march following the coast towards Wilmington and Goldsborough, N.C., communication routes for supplies would be needed for his large armies.

In the Valley, the guards along the long column of Confederate prisoners from Early's command were attacked several times as they headed north. Sheridan approached Charlottesville, heading back to join Grant with most of the cavalry. Early was inbound to Richmond.

March 4 (Saturday)

It was Inauguration Day in Washington. Vice President Andrew Johnson of Tennessee took the oath of office prior to President Lincoln, as tradition demanded. He had been drinking, and his acceptance speech was slurred and almost incoherent. The feeling of peace was in the air and Lincoln would see it through. The city was in a gayer mood than it had been four years ago, when war was looming on the horizon. Lincoln's inaugural address would be remembered for its brevity and eloquence, especially the closing, which began: "With malice toward none; with charity for all; with firmness in the right, as God gives us to see the right...."

Admiral Samuel P. Lee, now commanding the Mississippi River Squadron from New Orleans, received a request from Major Gen. E.R.S. Canby, now at Mobile Bay, for mortar boats to be used during the assault on the forts guarding the city. The boats were sent from Mound City, Ill.

The rising water on the James River presented an opportunity for the Confederate ironclads at Drewry's Bluff to pass the downriver obstructions and raid the Union depot at City Point. Conversely, the rising water gave the Union the same opportunity to pass the obstructions and to attack the Confederate ironclads. Grant, sensing this, wired Secretary Welles from City Point, "The James River is very high, and will continue so as long as the weather of the past week lasts. It would be well to have at once all the ironclads that it is intended should come here."

Within minutes of receiving Grant's telegram, Secretary Welles ordered Capt. Oliver S. Glisson, senior naval officer at Hampton Roads, to direct a steamer to go to Wilmington and to send the ironclad monitor *Montauk* to City Point and then the steamer was to continue on to Charleston and to notify Admiral Dahlgren to send two ironclads from Charleston to City Point.

Sherman's Army of the Tennessee was building a pontoon bridge across the Pee Dee River at Cheraw, S.C., having put a brigade over the river to hold the bridgehead. Realizing it was Inauguration Day, many of the troops were celebrating by firing off captured ammunition. Others raided a wine cellar.

Nichols, George W., Major, USA, Sherman's Hdqtrs., Cheraw, S.C.:

> One of the wealthiest citizens in [Cheraw] is a Mr. McFarland, whose interests in blockade running has, it is said, been very profitable for him. I hear that a liberal use has been made of his choice wines. Many a bumper was filled there yesterday to the health of Mr. Lincoln, and confusion to South Carolina.

Barber, Sgt., Co. C, 15th Illinois Volunteer Infantry, Pocotaligo, S.C.:

> Cloudy and some rain. Received New York papers yesterday of the 24th of February. It was a rich treat to us. We had been four weeks without seeing any papers from the North.... Charleston and Wilm-

ington had fallen, and the dear old flag once more floats over Sumter, in ruins though it be. Sherman's campaign through Georgia to the sea, and through the Carolinas into Virginia, is proving to be one continual series of brilliant successes, on a scale so magnificent that history scarcely furnishes a parallel....

March 5 (Sunday)

At Hampton Roads, Capt. Oliver S. Glisson received Secretary Welles's telegram and took immediate action:

> Your telegram was received this morning at fifteen minutes after midnight; blowing a gale of wind at the time. U.S.S. *Aries* sailed at daylight this morning. The monitors are expected every moment from Cape Fear, and I shall send them up the river immediately.

One monitor, U.S.S. *Sangamon*, arrived at Hampton Roads in the afternoon and was dispatched upriver immediately. Three more monitors arrived within several days.

Sherman's men were crossing the Pee Dee and moving slowly towards Fayetteville. Schofield was still at Wilmington.

Nichols, George W., Major, USA, Sherman's Hdqtrs., Cheraw, S.C.:

> Our ordnance officers have sometimes been puzzled in the effort to destroy the powder and fixed ammunition which we captured. The Rebels are criminally careless in the way they leave it about, stored in all sorts of places and in all kinds of buildings. Either in their extreme haste they packed it into any place which was handy, or they were determined to blow up the town. Thirty-six hundred barrels of this powder were just outside of the town, stored in a sort of arsenal; but another large lot was packed into a building near the depot, which the Rebels set on fire before we arrived. Trains of powder were laid from the depot to this store, and it seems wonderful that it was not ignited and hundreds of lives of non-combatants lost....

March 6 (Monday)

Sherman's scouts had determined that the Confederate force at Florence, S.C., was too strong for less than a major attack, and Sherman did not want to be sidetracked from Fayetteville. Most of the Federal troops crossed the Pee Dee River and entered North Carolina. At Cheraw, a large explosion killed one man and injured five. The explosion was investigated and the report sent to the Fifteenth Corps. The report, taken from the *Official Record*, is as follows:

> The explosion was caused by ignition of a large quantity of rebel ammunition which had been found in the town of Cheraw and hauled out and thrown in a deep ravine lying between the town and the pontoon bridge. The ammunition consisted of loaded shells and loose powder. The bottom of the ravine to the depth of four or five feet was filled with it, and powder was scattered on the banks of the ravine, and for several rods from the edge of the ravine. While the brigade was halting, having stacked arms to await the passage of the train, of which it was the rear guard, some of the men at a distance of several rods from the edge of the ravine are reported to have applied fire to some small cakes of powder found on the ground. The fire immediately ran to the edge of the ravine, down the bank, and exploded the immense pile of ammunition in the bottom of the ravine. One man of this brigade was killed and 1 Officer and 4 men wounded. After diligent inquiry I am unable to ascertain the names of the men who set fire to the powder, but I have no doubt they were ignorant, as I was myself, that any explosive material was in the ravine.

To attest to the strength of the boats used by the naval forces, Acting Ensign Charles H. Hanson, U.S.S. *Jonquil*, was working near Charleston, clearing the Ashley River of torpedoes and obstructions, when his ship was damaged, but he was able to resume operations the following day. Hanson reported:

> I hooked on to the log which had the fourth one [torpedo] on, but the log came up with the end, not having the torpedo on. I hoisted it to the bows of the steamer and started for shore. On shoaling the water, the torpedo being down struck the bottom and exploded directly under and about amidships of the steamer. Its force was so great as to raise the boilers 5 inches from their bed and knocked nine men overboard and completely flooded the vessel.

Barber, Sgt., Co. C, 15th Illinois Volunteer Infantry, Pocotaligo, S.C.:

> Am on picket to-day. My post is on the main road leading to Pocotaligo and contrabands are coming in by the score. Two mounted darkies came in on splendid animals, and reported a small force of rebels out about three miles. I did not care so much about the rebs as I did the horses, so I sent them to headquarters, under guard, and they soon came back minus the horses....

March 7 (Tuesday)

As Sherman's columns moved north in North Carolina, their train of Negroes grew larger. They were constantly underfoot and they were always in the wrong place. Sherman's commanders were getting very short-tempered with the situation. The roads were finally drying out and progress was good, after several days of constant rain.

Nichols, George W., Major, USA, Sherman's Hdqtrs., across the Pee Dee River, S.C.:

> The four grand columns of infantry are all south of Kilpatrick, covering a strip of country forty miles in width. All the corps commanders report abundance of forage and supplies, and the numerous streams which empty into the Pedee have excellent water-power, with flour-mills situated at points convienent for the army—a providential circumstance, for several divisions have exhausted their stores of hard bread. All these mills were in operation yesterday, and will not rest until this evening. They will grind corn enough to last for a week, then, perhaps, we shall reach tide-water again.
>
> To-day has been sunny and bright; the roads have been dry (in truth we have seen dust rising over the moving column for the first time since we left Savannah); the gentle wind from the east has come to us laden with fragrant perfume of pine and cedar, and all have journeyed on as happy and contented as mortals can be, and as glad as only men have a right to be who have plodded on so many dreary days through heavy mud and pitiless rain. The refugees, and especially the Negroes, expand in this sunlight like flowers, if I may use such a simile when speaking of such dusky subjects. Their exuberant laughter may be heard for a long distance as they journey on, sometimes riding in their queer go-carts, with curious nondescript rigging, or puffing and sweating under a load of blankets, pots, etc....

On the North Carolina coast it was decided that New Bern was actually the best of several ports for use to resupply Sherman's army. Gen. Jacob Cox was sent there with a large force to organize the town and get the railroad to Goldsborough rebuilt.

Lt. Commander Hooker had ascended the Rappahannock River with a flotilla of four ships yesterday to conduct a raid. The Army units were landed at Hamilton's Crossing, six miles downriver from Fredericksburg, where they burned and destroyed a railroad bridge, the railway depot, a portion of the track, cut the telegraph line and carried off the telegraphic equipment, destroyed by burning 18 cars loaded with tobacco and 10 others, captured a quantity of mules, took 30 to 40 prisoners, and captured a quantity of mail with valuable information in it.

The U.S. Congress got the full range of Rear Admiral David Dixon Porter's anger when he addressed that body and scorched the walls with salty comments about Generals Butler and Banks, both of whom he had had the misfortune to serve with. His next stop was City Point to see his old friend Ulysses S. Grant, and to discuss the coming spring campaign.

March 8 (Wednesday)

Sherman's columns were mostly in North Carolina, having travelled 350 miles across South Carolina. The Fifteenth Corps was at Laurel Hill, the Seventeenth in advance of the Fifteenth, with Slocum's left wing to the west. Sherman directed that Slocum be the one to capture Fayetteville.

Nichols, George W., Major, USA, Sherman's Hdqtrs., Laurel Hill, N.C.:

> The line which divides South and North Carolina was passed by the army this morning.... The real difference between the two regions lies in the fact that the plantation owners work with their own hands, and do not think they degrade themselves thereby. For the first time since we bade farewell to salt water I have to-day seen an attempt to manure land. The

> army has passed through thirteen miles or more of splendidly-managed farms; the corn and cotton fields are nicely plowed and farrowed; the fences are in capital order; the barns are well-built; the dwelling houses are clean, and there is that air of thrift which shows that the owner takes a personal interest in the management of affairs....

Gen. Jacob D. Cox, commanding the buildup at New Bern, was attacked by elements of Braxton Bragg's Confederates coming from Wilmington. During the attack, near Kinston, N.C., some of the Federal troops broke, but the remainder held and fought off the Rebels. Bragg's force was not really strong enough to sustain an attack for long.

March 9 (Thursday)

Vermont ratified the Thirteenth Amendment to the Constitution. Lincoln, in Washington, accepted the resignation of John P. Usher as Secretary of the Interior.

Fighting continued between Bragg's Confederates and Jacob Cox's Federals near Kinston, N.C.

At Monroe's Crossroads, N.C., the cavalry of Wade Hampton and Joe Wheeler attacked the unsuspecting Federals of Judson Kilpatrick and totally surprised them, almost catching Kilpatrick in his bed. Kilpatrick fled, some say without his pants, giving the name to the affair "The Battle for Kilpatrick's Pants." Kilpatrick rallied his men, counterattacked, and severely beat Hampton's Legion.

Sherman's Fifteenth Corps was at Randallsville, N.C. Believing that Schofield was at Wilmington, Sherman sent scouts to make contact. In his *Memoirs*, Sherman wrote:

> I traveled with the Fifteenth Corps and on the 8th of March reached Laurel Hill, N.C. Satisfied that our troops were at Wilmington, I determined to send a message there; I called for my man, Corp. [James] Pike, whom I had rescued [from the prison] at Columbia, and instructed him in disguise to work his way to Cape Fear River, secure a boat, and float down to Wilmington to convey a letter, and to report our approach. I also called on General Howard for another volunteer, and he brought me a very clever young sergeant, who is now [1875] a commissioned officer in the regular army. Each of these got off during the night by separate routes....

March 10 (Friday)

Sherman's army approached Fayetteville, N.C., in rain and on muddy roads. Movement was very slow. The soil was very sandy and made necessary the corduroying of the roads to get the wagons over them. Quite often the logs used for the corduroying would sink after one or two wagons passed. If wagons strayed off the roads, they would sink to their beds, with little hope of getting out.

As Sherman approached Fayetteville, the clearing of the Cape Fear River became of prime importance. The river was reported to have parts where "the stream is very narrow and tortuous, with a strong current." In some instances, progress could only be made using hawsers to haul the boats upriver, and then the paddle wheels were fouled with debris and the smokestacks were damaged from trees. It was also noted that "the *Chickamauga* is sunk across the stream at Indian Wells, with a chain just below. Her two guns are on a bluff on the western bank of the river."

At Kinston, N.C., Bragg, finding that he could not dislodge Cox, broke off the engagement and went to Goldsborough to join Johnston's force.

In Richmond, Lee proposed putting the legislation on using Negro troops into force immediately. However, the Confederate Congress was still debating it in its House of Representatives.

March 11 (Saturday)

Sherman's armies nearly surrounded the town of Fayetteville, N.C., waiting to go in. Scouts sent in were met with firing from Confederate cavalry, which was soon dispersed, the cavalry leaving town by the bridges over the Cape Fear River. The old U.S. Arsenal at Fayetteville, destination of the rifle-making machinery removed from Harpers Ferry in 1861 by Stonewall Jackson, was occupied and would be destroyed. Sherman's messengers to Schofield had reached Wilmington, and Union boats were on their way upriver to Fayetteville.

An expedition consisting of the steamer U.S.S. *Eolus*, and boat crews from the U.S.S. *Maratanza*, *Lenapee*, and *Nyack* under the command of Lt. Commander George W. Young, proceeded up the Cape Fear River towards Fayetteville, N.C., making Devil's Bend the first night.

In Virginia, Sheridan's cavalry, coming in from defeating Early in the Valley, were outside of Richmond at Goochland Court House, causing a scare in the Confederate capital.

March 12 (Sunday)

Sherman's men fell to with a will to destroy the Arsenal and other military facilities in Fayetteville, N.C., a town of about 3000 inhabitants. A Confederate steamer had been captured below the city on the Cape Fear River, and this would be loaded with Negroes and refugees, and then sent to Wilmington.

Nichols, George W., Major, USA, Sherman's Hdqtrs., Fayetteville, N.C.:

> Again we have made a capture of much greater importance than was at first supposed. The magnificent arsenal which our government built here contains millions of dollars' worth of machinery and material. The Rebels have used the work-shops in this city for the manufacture of guns, fixed ammunition, gun-carriages, etc., to a much larger extent than was supposed.... Here are stored vast amounts of well-seasoned woods, weapons in all stages of completion, thousands of muskets; in short, every description of machinery and tools requisite for the manufacture and repairs of material of war.... We shall destroy it utterly....

Sherman's letters to Gen. Terry at Wilmington are in the *Official Record*:

> I want you to send me all the shoes, stockings, drawers, sugar, coffee, and flour you can spare; finish the loads with oats or corn. Have the boats escorted and them run at night at any risk.
>
> Gen. Howard just reports that he has secured one of the enemy's steam-boats below the city, and General Slocum will try to secure two known to be above, and we will load them with refugees, white and black, that have clung to our skirts, impeded our movements, and consumed our food.... I must rid my army of from 20,000 to 30,000 useless mouths, as many to go to Cape Fear as possible, and balance will go in vehicles, and captured horses via Clinton to Wilmington.

The U.S.S. *Eolus* and the boat crews under Lt. Commander Young spent last night at Devil's Bend on the Cape Fear River and continued today to Fayetteville, N.C., where contact was made with Gen. Sherman's columns, just arrived at that city. Communication to the sea was open.

March 13 (Monday)

In Richmond, the Confederate Congress finally passed legislation to use Negro troops in the Southern army. Lee acted promptly on this, and by the end of the month Negro troops were seen in Confederate uniform in Richmond.

Sheridan's cavalry, en route to Grant at Petersburg, skirmished at Beaver Dam Station outside Richmond.

At Fayetteville, N.C., the destruction went on, Sherman's men tearing the place apart while waiting for the supplies to come up from Wilmington. A steamer and two gunboats arrived at the city from Wilmington, carrying a staff officer (from Gen. Terry) who was critical of Sherman's method of operations—but not to Sherman.

An intelligence report reaching Commander Macomb, commander of the Union ships in the North Carolina Sounds, stated:

> A deserter from a North Carolina regiment came on board the [Army steamer] *Ella May* yesterday morning. He states that the whole rebel force under Bragg (estimated by him at 40,000) had evacuated Kinston, moving towards Goldsboro, but that Hoke's division returned when he left. The ironclad [*Neuse*] is afloat and ready for service; has two guns, draws 9 feet. No pontoon was found on the Neuse. If you can send me a torpedo launch at once he may have an opportunity of destroying the ironclad. The bridge (railroad) at Kinston has been destroyed by the enemy.

The troops being withdrawn were part of the consolidation effort of Gen. Joseph E. Johnston to get sufficient troops to oppose Sherman's large force. As the Confederate troops were withdrawn, the Federals immediately took their places, occupying Kinston with no opposition. The Confederates destroyed the ironclad *Neuse* to prevent her capture.

The four-boat flotilla under Lt. Commander Hooker had gone downriver from Fredericksburg where it had destroyed the depot, railroad, etc. The flotilla stopped at Tappahannock, Va., on the south bank of the river. A Federal landing party destroyed eight boats, including a large flatboat used as a ferry. They used naval gunfire to destroy the bridge connecting the town with abandoned Ft. Lowry. During their stay they were taken under fire by Confederate rifled artillery and cavalry. The returned fire emptied some saddles.

March 14 (Tuesday)

Sheridan was at the South Anna Bridge on his way back to Grant at Petersburg. Lee, in Richmond, was hoping that Johnston could strike either Sherman or Schofield before the two Federals united. Maybe the Federals could be defeated piecemeal.

The Customs Officer at St. Mary's had cleared the schooner *Champanero* and endorsed the accuracy of its manifest. Acting Lt. Sylvanus Nickerson, U.S.S. *Wyandank*, stopped the schooner off Inigoes Creek in Chesapeake Bay for inspection. He found that more than one half of the cargo was not manifested, including a large quantity of gunpowder. He also found that the customs official who had signed the manifest had $4000 worth of liquor and other merchandise aboard. The official was later visited by his superiors in the Customs Service.

Sherman's armies at Fayetteville were cleaning the army of sick animals, replacing them with captured stock. Sick and wounded men were being sent to Wilmington by steamer to be sent north to hospitals. The remainder of the Negroes and refugees was sent to Wilmington, under escort, to further lighten the load. Some supplies had come up, mostly sugar, coffee, and several thousand pairs of shoes—still not enough to fill the needs. Uniforms were desperately needed, some of the men being in rags.

Gen. Jacob D. Cox's troops occupied Kinston, N.C., and pushed on towards Goldsborough with little opposition.

March 15 (Wednesday)

Sheridan was now at Hanover C.H., heading towards the James River to link up with Grant.

Sherman was again on the move, northeast towards Goldsborough, N.C. Kilpatrick, in front of Slocum's left wing, was skirmishing with Johnston's rear guard units as the Union advance was made. The armies were travelling light again, after shedding the Negroes and refugees. One observer, watching a column of about 7000 Negroes and refugees pass, commented that it looked like "a flock of black sheep," the majority being women and children, with a mixture of men. The Confederate Army was now overburdened with generals of all grades, more than were needed for an army three times the size.

March 16 (Thursday)

Slocum, commanding Sherman's left wing, attacked Hardee's force four miles south of Averasborough, N.C., turning Hardee's right flank and causing the Confederate to withdraw. Late in the afternoon, word came to Hardee that Slocum's men were on his left flank, so during the night, in the middle of a storm, Hardee withdrew and marched towards Smithfield. The remainder of Sherman's armies was moving on bottomless roads and through water about two feet deep where the creeks had overflowed. Every crossing, again, was contested by a burned bridge and a small Confederate force that was flanked out of position by Union forces wading the stream, and the whole thing was done over again at the next stream.

March 17 (Friday)

After the fighting yesterday in front of Slocum, skirmishing continued in front of Sherman's march route as the Union force got closer to Goldsborough. The columns were not quite so long, having closed up during the day yesterday, with the vanguard being slowed by bad roads and the necessity of building bridges.

In the fighting yesterday around Averasborough, Confederate Col. Alfred Rhett, who had commanded Ft. Sumter for a period, was captured by an aide on Gen. Kilpatrick's staff.

Nichols, George W., Major, USA, Army of the Tennessee, Averasborough, N.C.:

> Kilpatrick, who has the advance, ran into a strong body of Rebel infantry this afternoon, and skirmished with them until night came on. He captured several prisoners, among them Colonel Rhett, son of the noted Robert Barnwell Rhett, one of the "first family" names of which South Carolina is so proud. From the conversation of this Rebel colonel, I judge him to be quite as impracticable a person as any of his class. He seemed most troubled about the way in which he was captured. Some of Kilpatrick's fast riders got inside his

> skirmish line, and one of them, without any sort of regard for the feelings of a South Carolina aristocrat, put a pistol to the colonel's head and informed him in a quiet but very decided manner that if he didn't come along he'd "make a hole through him!" The colonel came; but he is a disgusted man. From what I know of the sentiments of Kilpatrick's men, I make no doubt that they would have had but little scruple in cutting off one branch of the family tree of the Rhetts if the surrender had not been prompt.

At Mobile, Ala., Major Gen. E.R.S. Canby began moving his 32,000 men against the Mobile defenses. One force moved from Pensacola, the other from Mobile Point and up the east side of the bay. Brig. Gen. R.L. Gibson had only 2800 Confederates to defend the city, but they were in some strong forts.

March 18 (Saturday)

The left wing of Sherman's armies, the two corps under Slocum, were just south of Bentonville, N.C., on this warm and clear day. Opposite Slocum was Lt. Gen. Wade Hampton's cavalry, opposing Kilpatrick, whose cavalry was in front of Slocum. Sherman's right wing, commanded by Howard, was south and east of Bentonville, facing Goldsborough. Johnston's 20,000 faced 30,000 Federals and Johnston was going to try and beat the Federal army piecemeal, having no chance at all facing Sherman's full army, including Schofield, of about 100,000. The Battle of Bentonville opened today when Hampton's cavalry began a skirmish with the advance Federal units near Benton's Cross Roads.

At Mobile, Ala., a column of 1700 Federals left Dauphin Island and started up the west side of Mobile Bay as a diversion to draw off some of the Confederates in Mobile. The main thrust was to be on the east side of the bay.

March 19 (Sunday)

Sherman, who had been travelling with Slocum on the left wing, left early in the morning for Howard's right wing as the Federals began their advance. As they advanced, they ran head-on into Johnston's prepared positions south of Bentonville, N.C. Slocum pressed his advance, but Johnston wouldn't budge, and by midafternoon Slocum entrenched, not knowing as yet what he faced.

On the Confederate side there was a delay in attacking, and when they did go crashing into the Federal line, the progress was slow. No problems were met with the first Federal line, but Gen. Jefferson C. Davis, USA, rallied his men, who withstood the attack until more units could be brought up. The fighting, which included three separate assaults on the Federal line, lasted until dark, when both sides pulled back and reinforced their positions.

Meanwhile, Sherman, having arrived at Howard's right wing, thought the fight less severe than it was and held Howard's troops in their forward positions. In the evening, couriers from Slocum's headquarters arrived to tell Sherman of the battle and of the current situation.

Sheridan, in Virginia, had reached White House on the Pamunkey River after tearing up the Virginia Central Railroad and the James River Canal. He was almost back in Grant's backyard.

Jackman, Pvt., "The Orphan Brigade," Graniteville, S.C.:

> This was the last note I made in my journal. The old book made of damaged quartermaster blanks. I shall have to write the balance from memory.
>
> Our dismounted men continued camped at Graniteville until about the middle of April. Our mess continued at the depot.... We fared well at the depot. Our rations we had cooked at Mr. Pollaty's near the depot—he and lady being very clever.... We became acquainted with the telegraph operators—old soldiers—in the office and could have the latest news.
>
> Time passed a little monotonously.... The Judge was a great source of fun. He was no longer bothered with "Trojan." Old "Trojan" was honorably discharged from service and retired to the fields of Georgia to draw the plow—he had helped whirl the cannon along on many a field and the old veteran bore the marks of hostile missiles. He had served in two arms of the service—artillery and cavalry.
>
> My lady friend from Augusta often came out on the road and I was always remembered by a bundle of something nice to eat.

March 20 (Monday)

Early in the morning, the men of Howard's right wing moved towards Bentonville to join the fight against Johnston's Confederate force. The roads were dry and fast, the troops moving easily. Shortly after starting they ran into a body of Confederate cavalry, which delayed them only briefly. As the columns closed up, the cavalry was driven as fast as the infantry could march, until the Federals came up to the main lines and formed to Slocum's right. The battlefield was a quicksand flat that, while no water was showing, had a high water table that made the ground unable to support artillery or wagons. The ground offered little cover for either force. By late afternoon, Sherman's entire army was facing Johnston and overlapping the Confederate flanks. Things quieted down for the evening.

In Tennessee, Major Gen. George Stoneman, USA, led 4000 Union cavalrymen on a destruction mission from Jonesborough towards western North Carolina. This mission was in support of Sherman's drive through North Carolina.

Gen. Canby's column from Pensacola departed for Mobile to add weight to the Federal assault.

The C.S.S. *Albemarle*, sunk by Lt. Cushing in a daring raid on October 27, 1864, was raised at Plymouth, N.C., on the Roanoke River by Commander Macomb, U.S.S. *Shamrock*. The *Albemarle* had been the deciding factor in Brig. Gen. Hoke's capture of Plymouth earlier in 1864.

March 21 (Tuesday)

At Ferrol, Spain, the C.S.S. *Stonewall*, Capt. Thomas J. Page, had been detained for several weeks getting fuel and minor repairs. Today, the *Stonewall* headed for the ocean, but turned back because of high seas and foul weather. She was being watched closely by the U.S.S. *Niagara*.

At Bentonville, N.C., Sherman kept the pressure on Johnston's line while Major Gen. J.A. Mower moved around the Confederate left and threatened Mill Creek Bridge, which was on Johnston's retreat line. Some heavy fighting resulted, with the Federal advance being checked. This was the last fighting of the Battle of Bentonville, which was the last major battle of the war in North Carolina. Johnston withdrew, upon getting reports that Schofield had taken Goldsborough. The North lost over 1500 casualties, mostly wounded; the South, 2600, mostly prisoners.

At Mobile, Canby awaited the arrival of the Federal troops from Pensacola.

March 22 (Wednesday)

The Commandant of the Washington Navy Yard was notified to have the U.S.S. *Bat* ready to convoy the *River Queen*, with President Lincoln aboard, to City Point on the James River. Sherman was coming up from North Carolina, via Wilmington, for a meeting with Grant and Lincoln.

In Tennessee, Brevet Major Gen. James H. Wilson moved from the Tennessee River with 13,500 cavalry and headed towards Selma, Ala., one of the few Confederate naval and manufacturing centers left in the South.

James Harrison Wilson was born near Shawneetown, Ill., on September 2, 1837, graduating sixth in his class at West Point in 1860. His first assignments were all engineering and staff positions until 1862, when he was transferred to Grant's army in the west. Wilson and Grant formed a solid friendship that led to Wilson being promoted to staff lieutenant colonel and assigned as the inspector general of the Army of the Tennessee. Promoted to Brigadier General on October 30, 1863, after the Vicksburg campaign, Wilson stayed with Grant through the Chattanooga campaign and then through the winter of 1863-64. When Grant came east, he offered Wilson the 3rd Cavalry Division in the Army of the Potomac. Wilson served well in that capacity under Sheridan. In the fall of 1864, after doing well in the Shenandoah Valley with Sheridan, Wilson was transferred back west to Sherman's command (with the rank of brevet major general). Wilson reorganized Sherman's cavalry there and he was with Gen. George H. Thomas at the Battle of Nashville. He spent the three months that followed equipping and training his men, and then he moved against Nathan Bedford Forrest at Selma, Ala.

At Bentonville, N.C., skirmishers reported that Johnston's fortifications were abandoned. Sherman ordered that no advance was to be made beyond Mill Creek below Bentonville until things could be sorted out. After a period of reconnaissance, Sherman ordered Slocum's left wing towards Goldsborough, the right wing to move the next day. The roads were bad and the movement slow.

Schofield was at Goldsborough, and Terry at Cox's Bridge, both prepared to move on Johnston when Sherman gave the word.

March 23 (Thursday)

At Ferrol, Spain, Capt. T.J. Page again tried to get the C.S.S. *Stonewall* out of the harbor, but found the seas too rough for the ship. He decided to off-load 40 tons of coal to lighten the ship. The U.S.S. *Niagara* was still watching.

In North Carolina, Johnston placed his army across the paths to Raleigh and Weldon, both routes Sherman was expected to take. It also put Johnston in position for a linkup with Lee if the Army of Northern Virginia somehow escaped Grant and came to North Carolina.

Sherman joined Schofield and Terry at Goldsborough. The combined armies now totalled more than 100,000 and completely dominated the military situation in the area. Sherman, now linked to his supply line to the sea, would reclothe his army and give them rest before continuing his drive on Johnston and on to Virginia.

Nichols, George W., Major, USA, Sherman's Hdqtrs., Goldsborough, N.C.:

> General Schofield is in Goldsboro'. Our army will at once be moved into position in the vicinity of this place to refit for the next campaign; not only to be reclothed, but to gain the repose it needs. Mind, as well as body, requires rest after the fatigues of rapid campaigns like these. These ragged, bareheaded, shoeless, brave, jolly fellows of Sherman's legions, too, want covering for their naked limbs.

Wilson's large cavalry force moved slowly through northern Alabama to meet Nathan B. Forrest.

March 24 (Friday)

The heavily armed Confederate ironclad C.S.S. *Stonewall*, Capt. T.J. Page, sailed from Ferrol, Spain, after two abortive attempts to leave. She challenged the two wooden Union frigates U.S.S. *Niagara* and *Sacramento* under command of Commodore T.T. Craven. Craven explained to Secretary Welles:

> At this time the odds in her favor were too great and too certain, in my humble judgment, to admit of the slightest hope of being able to inflict upon her even the most trifling injury, whereas, if we had gone out, the *Niagara* would most undoubtedly have been easily and promptly destroyed. So thoroughly a one-sided combat I did not consider myself called upon to engage in.

Craven would later be court-martialed for not engaging the *Stonewall.* Sitting as President of the Court was Vice Admiral David G. Farragut and sitting as a member of the Court was Commodore John A. Winslow, the destroyer of the C.S.S. *Alabama.* Craven was sentenced to two years suspension on leave pay. Welles, refusing what he called a "paid vacation," restored him to active duty.

In the lines at Petersburg, the Confederates were preparing an attack on Ft. Stedman. If they could break the line there, they could attack City Point, and that attack would require Grant to shorten his lines, which, in turn, would allow Lee to evacuate and join Gen. Joe Johnston in North Carolina. Major Gen. John B. Gordon had been assigned to lead the Confederate force in the attack. The attack, scheduled for tomorrow, would have President Lincoln as an observer. Lincoln arrived at City Point aboard the *River Queen.*

In North Carolina, the refitting of Sherman's ragged troops went along, all the supplies needed having been brought up to Goldsborough by Schofield. The troops, as they entered Goldsborough, presented a somewhat picturesque sight.

Nichols, George W., Major, USA, Sherman's Hdqtrs., Goldsborough, N.C.:

> The army is marching through the city to the designated camping-grounds, where it will for the present remain. As the troops passed through, we found food for infinite merriment in the motley crowd of "bummers." These fellows were mounted upon all sorts of animals, and were clad in every description of costume; while many were so scantily dressed that they would hardly have been permitted to proceed up Broadway without interruption. Hundreds of wagons, of patterns not recognized in army regulations, carts, buggies, barouches, hacks, wheelbarrows, all sorts of vehicles, were loaded down with bacon, meal, corn, oats, and fodder, all gathered in the rich country through which the "bummers" had marched during the day. Quartermaster Meigs should have been here to see the funny additions made to his department.

Canby, at Mobile, was advancing his positions for the assaults on the various forts defending the city, while Wilson's cavalry continued towards Selma, Ala., north of Mobile.

March 25 (Saturday)

At Grant's request, Admiral Porter sent gunboats up the Appomattox River to the pontoon bridges to guard them against an expected attack by Gen. Lee. At the same time, the U.S.S. *Wilderness* was sent up the Chickahominy River to contact Gen. Sheridan for dispatches.

At three o'clock this morning a group of Confederates appeared at Ft. Stedman, a major Union bastion in the siege lines, and announced themselves as deserters. An hour later, 4 A.M., Gen. Gordon threw his troops against the Union strongpoint and completely overwhelmed it, surprising the garrison and the line for nearly a mile. The Confederates swarmed over the defenses, and some selected units headed for City Point. There was not enough weight behind the attack and it faltered, giving the Federals time to regroup and drive the Confederates back to their own lines. The Rebels still held Ft. Stedman. At about 7:30 A.M., the Union sent a division against Ft. Stedman, and the Confederates were routed back to their own lines. The Union line was whole again. Grant lost about 1500 in casualties; Lee, about 4000, many more than he could spare. The line quieted again.

The expected assault at Mobile Bay got under way, with Gen. Canby coming up to Spanish Fort on the east side of the bay. Brig. Gen. R.L. Gibson's 2800 men had little hope of holding against Canby's 32,000 without some immediate help—and none was in sight.

Grant and Lincoln were conferring at City Point. Lincoln took the railroad to the Petersburg lines, where he walked over the battlefield at Ft. Stedman.

March 26 (Sunday)

Sheridan's cavalry crossed the James River and headed towards Grant's position at Petersburg. This provided Grant with about 15,000 aggressive cavalry, and an even more aggressive commander. Lincoln was on hand to watch the long lines of blue cavalry cross the river and move on west. Sheridan remained at City Point to confer with Grant on further movements, and Lincoln watched the troops review.

Lee was getting ready to evacuate Petersburg and move west, hoping to join with Johnston in North Carolina

At Mobile Bay, the Federals began their approach to Spanish Fort, which provoked heavy skirmishing.

March 27 (Monday)

Secretary Welles ordered the U.S.S. *Wyoming*, Commander John P. Bankhead, at Baltimore, to sail in search of the C.S.S. *Shenandoah*, Lt. Waddell, which had left Melbourne, Australia, five weeks before. The U.S.S. *Wachusett* and *Iroquois* were also on the chase for Waddell.

Capt. T.J. Page, C.S.S. *Stonewall*, wrote Commander Bulloch in England that Page would sail from Lisbon, Portugal, to Tenerife, and then to Nassau. The U.S.S. *Niagara* and *Sacramento* arrived in Lisbon in the evening, but were unable to sail after the *Stonewall* for 24 hours after her departure, per international law.

A flotilla under Rear Admiral Thatcher began the assault on the city of Mobile, Ala., in cooperation with the troops under Gen. Canby. The current objective was Spanish Fort near the mouth of the Blakely River, which was thickly sown with torpedoes. During the torpedo-clearing operations, over 150 torpedoes were removed, but some remained undetected, sinking three Union ships in five days.

At City Point, Sherman arrived from North Carolina, taking a fast steamer from Wilmington. Admiral Porter also came in from Wilmington for the conference with the President. Upon arrival, both Sherman and Porter called on the President and spent the evening socializing.

March 28 (Tuesday)

At City Point, most of the major players in the game were present for a conference. President Lincoln, Generals Grant and Sherman, and Admiral D.D. Porter all attended the conference aboard the *River Queen.* Lincoln stressed his desire to bring the war to a speedy close and with as little loss of life as possible. A rather lenient policy was to be followed at the end of hostilities. When the conference closed, Porter sent Sherman back to New Bern, N.C., aboard the fast steamer U.S.S. *Bat.* Sherman was to rejoin his troops, which were located only 125 miles straight-line distance from City Point.

The double-ender monitor (having a turret on each end of the ship), U.S.S. *Milwaukee*, Lt. Commander James H. Gillis, struck a torpedo in the

Blakely River at Mobile Bay. She sank stern first, allowing time for the crew to evacuate with most of their possessions.

In western North Carolina, Stoneman's cavalry was moving slowly down the railroad into the interior of the state, clearing pockets of resistance and meeting many strong Union supporters along the way.

Wilson, in Alabama, had a skirmish at Elyton on his way to Selma and an "appointment" with Forrest.

March 29 (Wednesday)

Lincoln remained at City Point with Grant, awaiting developments. Sherman returned to North Carolina to begin his drive on Raleigh.

At Mobile Bay, the U.S.S. *Osage*, Lt. Commander William M. Gamble, got underway and was trying to avoid the U.S.S. *Winnebago*, which was drifting in a strong breeze. The *Osage* struck a torpedo and sank with four dead and eight wounded by the explosion.

At Petersburg, the Appomattox campaign began with the movement of Grant's army to the southwest and Sheridan's large cavalry force towards Dinwiddie C.H. Lee, trying to defend more than 30 miles of entrenchments, was running out of men for the battles. The whole purpose of the Union movement was to force Lee out of his entrenchments and into the open, where he could be defeated by the larger Union force.

March 30 (Thursday)

Amid pouring rain, Sheridan was getting his troops, cavalry and infantry, organized for the push on the Confederate right flank. The rain, which turned the dirt roads to slop, delayed the advance. There was some skirmishing at Hatcher's Run and near Five Forks. Gen. Humphreys pushed his Second Corps up to the Rebel works at Hatcher's Run, while Warren's Fifth Corps moved on Gravelly Run. Lee's lines were getting weaker as he concentrated his forces southwest of Petersburg to protect the South Side Railroad.

The daring Lt. Charles W. Read, CSN, found the ram C.S.S. *William H. Webb* in the Red River, La., with no guns aboard, few crewmen, no fuel, no small arms, and a few cutlasses. He immediately fueled the ship, mounted a 30-pound Parrott rifle (obtained from Gen. Kirby Smith) and prepared to take the ship out of the Red River, down the Mississippi, and to the open sea.

In Alabama, Wilson's cavalry skirmished with Forrest's troops at Montevallo, their first contact. In Mobile, the assault on Spanish Fort continued.

March 31 (Friday)

As the rain ended southwest of Petersburg, Sheridan put in motion his large force of cavalry and infantry towards Dinwiddie C.H., on the Confederate right flank. Lee had about 10,000 men against more than 50,000 Federals on the western Confederate lines. The Confederates initially drove Sheridan back, but not for long. At night, Pickett realized that Warren's Fifth Corps and Sheridan's mix of cavalry and infantry was too strong for him, so he withdrew to Five Forks. Humphrey's Second Corps repulsed an attack at Hatcher's Run and held without difficulty.

In Alabama, Wilson's cavalry destroyed iron furnaces and collieries at Montevallo and skirmished with Forrest's troopers at Six Mile Creek. Union troops were in the towns around Mobile and drawing the noose tighter around the forts.

Master John C. Braine, CSN, was up to his tricks again. This time he boarded the *St. Mary's*, a 115-ton schooner out of St. Mary's, Md., with a raiding party, and captured the ship off the Patuxent River in Chesapeake Bay. The ruse the Rebels used was to come alongside in a yawl saying that their craft was sinking. The *St. Mary's* was taken to sea, where the New York-bound schooner *J.B. Spafford* was captured and released after the *St. Mary's* crew was placed aboard and the Confederates robbed the crew of the *Spafford* of their personal effects. Braine's original destination was St. Mark's in Florida, but he next put into Nassau.

APRIL 1865

April began with the leafing of the trees in Virginia and the smell of the earth awakening. Deeper in the ravaged South, those remaining in the path of Sherman's "bummers" looked forward to a lean and hungry spring, until a crop could be harvested. Both armies were tired, bloodied, and weary of the whole idea of battle. Most of the soldiers only looked forward to the end of the conflict and their return home.

At Mobile, Ala., Major Gen. Canby had Spanish Fort under siege and the city only awaited the sure outcome—surrender. Sherman was back in North

Carolina after his visit to City Point, and he was ready to continue the offensive against Johnston's army.

Grant, encouraged by Sheridan's success over the past few days, ordered an all-out assault on Lee's right flank, hoping to smash through Lee's lines.

April 1 (Saturday)

Today, Lee's right flank finally caved in under overwhelming numbers. Grant ordered an assault on the lines for the following morning, and all night the artillery thundered in preparation. Ft. Sedgewick's heavy guns belched forth to sustain its name of "Fort Hell." Lee withdrew from Petersburg during the night.

Jefferson Davis wrote Gen. Lee that the Confederate President had made little progress raising Negro troops and that the distrust in both military and civil circles was embarrassing.

Mrs. Lincoln returned to Washington aboard the *River Queen*, and the President transferred to Admiral Porter's flagship, the *Malvern*. Upon retiring, the President found that his "bunk was too short and he was compelled to fold his legs the first night." Porter, hearing this, had the ship's carpenter do a remodeling job on the morning of the 2nd to lengthen and widen the bunk. On the morning of the 3rd, Lincoln reported to breakfast with the story that he had shrunk "six inches in length and about a foot sideways."

Newspaper accounts:

Petersburg, Va.: It is believed that the enemy is still at Dinwiddie Court House. Thursday afternoon General Fitz Lee attacked and dislodged a division of Sheridan's cavalry from a position it had taken between the plank road and Southside Railroad, and drove the Yankees some distance.... Our lines are secure against all attacks of the enemy. On the whole, all goes well with us, and ere long we hope to be able to chronicle a glorious victory for our arms and a crushing defeat to the enemy.

Richmond, Va.: The weather is cool and pleasant. Excited couriers have arrived from off the line of the Southside Railroad and report the Yankees are fighting their way through our lines, and their numbers as so great that we cannot much longer hold Petersburg.

The numbers of Virginians reported absent from their regiments without leave, will, this morning, exceed fifty thousand. What can this mean?... News reaches us to-night that General Pickett has lost control of his troops at Five Forks, and that the Yankees are gradually moving towards Richmond. It seems that our troops have become discouraged and are easily confused. The Yankee assault on Pickett's Division has completely demoralized it, if reports are true.

April 2 (Sunday)

At 4:40 A.M., the Federals advanced in a heavy fog against the Petersburg lines. Little resistance was met; in some cases the Confederate battle line simply vanished. Along the Boydton Plank Road near Hatcher's Run, Lt. Gen. Ambrose Powell Hill, one of Lee's best generals, was killed. Lee notified Davis that "I think it is absolutely necessary that we should abandon our position tonight...." Lee ordered the evacuation of Petersburg and designated Amelia Court House, 40 miles west, as the concentration point for all units.

At 11 P.M. President Davis and the Cabinet evacuated Richmond, Mrs. Davis and her party having already gone. Richmond became a study in chaos. Many tried to leave the city, jamming the roads and railroad stations, while others decided to stay and face the enemy. Many openly wept in the streets. At the local state prison, inmates overpowered the guards and escaped to begin looting before leaving the city. Confederate Secretary of the Navy Mallory directed that the James River Squadron be blown up and the officers and men be transferred to Gen. Lee's forces, which were evacuating the capital. Mallory left Richmond in the party with President Davis and the Cabinet. Rear Admiral Semmes, CSN, outfitted his men with arms and field equipment, and then had the crews of the C.S.S. *Virginia No. 2*, *Fredericksburg*, and *Richmond* burn and sink their ships south of Richmond, near Drewry's Bluff. Semmes then loaded his men aboard wooden ships and returned to Richmond, watching the explosions of the ironclads left at Drewry's Bluff. Upon arriving at Richmond, the wooden ships were fired and set adrift in the James River. The naval crews, lacking transportation west, found a locomotive and several cars which carried them to Danville. Semmes was appointed a Brigadier General in the Confederate Army and given the task of defending Danville, a command he held until Lee's surrender at Appomattox.

At Selma, Ala., the mighty Nathan Bedford Forrest had finally been beaten. This "wizard of the saddle" was finally overcome by superior numbers and a lack of maneuvering space. Forrest and some of his men escaped, leaving the Federals with 2700 prisoners, 40 guns, and a large store of supplies.

April 3 (Monday)

Petersburg had fallen, and steps were being taken to evacuate all stores and troops from Richmond. At the Richmond Arsenal on the James River, the officer-in-charge issued orders for all fires to be extinguished, all gas lights to be turned off, and everyone to leave the premises. Between 5 and 6 A.M. he toured the facility and told the sentries not to allow anyone in the buildings. An hour later, explosions rocked the area as someone set fire to the buildings and the explosions destroyed the arsenal. At the time there were about 25,000 rounds of artillery ammunition in the arsenal. Some ammunition had been dumped in the river, but the labor required was too much and this idea was abandoned.

The Confederate government and the army set fire to the business district of Richmond, the bridges, military stores that could not be evacuated, and the tobacco warehouses. By the time the Federals arrived the fires were fairly out of control, despite their efforts.

All but 10 of the 60 midshipmen of the Confederate Naval Academy, under the command of Lt. William Harwar Parker, were assigned to escort the archives of the government and the specie and bullion of the treasury from Richmond to Danville. This assignment continued during the later moves to Charlotte, N.C., Washington, Ga., Augusta, Ga., and on to Abbeville, S.C. The remaining ten midshipmen of the Academy, commanded by Lt. James W. Billups, CSN, were charged with the firing and scuttling of the C.S.S. *Patrick Henry*, the Academy's training ship.

Federal troops entered Richmond. Major Atherton H. Stevens, Jr., of Massachusetts raised the first Union flag over the Capitol building. Negroes swarmed into the streets, laughing and shouting. Major Gen. Godfrey Weitzel accepted the surrender of the city at 8:15 A.M. at the City Hall. Richmond, although ablaze, was fairly won.

In Petersburg, Union troops entered the city. No mass destruction occurred here, things being quite orderly. President Lincoln, after a conference with Gen. Grant, reviewed the troops passing through the city.

The Union naval crews along the coast were busy sweeping the rivers for torpedoes (mines), especially the James River approaches to Richmond. This was done using ships' boats working as a team during a sweep. To facilitate operations, the banks of the river(s) were patrolled looking for anchor wires for the mines. When found, the wires were cut and the mines either dragged to shore or blown up.

Union newspaper accounts:

> *Washington, D.C.*: The news of the fall of Richmond came upon the Capital shortly after breakfast, and while all were awaiting official bulletins that should announce the renewal of the fighting. It ran from mouth to mouth and from street to street, till within ten minutes the whole town was out, and for a wonder Washington was in a state of old-fashioned excitement such as it has not experienced since the memorable second Bull Run battle....
>
> *Boston, Mass.*: Bells are pealing, salutes firing, and flags flying everywhere, and our citizens are in the highest state of jubilee over the fall of Richmond.

April 4 (Tuesday)

Today, escorted by a small naval party of ten men, President Lincoln and Rear Admiral Porter entered Richmond about noon, landing one block above the infamous Libby Prison. The President and escort walked to the Confederate White House, where Lincoln toured the former home of Jefferson Davis, taking time to sit at his desk. The President returned to Admiral Porter's flagship, the U.S.S. *Malvern*, for the night.

Lee retreated towards Amelia Court House, with Sheridan in hot pursuit. Sheridan's cavalry occupied Jetersville on the Danville Railroad south and west of Amelia Court House, thereby blocking the use of the railroad by the Confederates.

President Davis was in Danville on his way south. In Alabama, Tuscaloosa was lost to Brig. Gen. James H. Wilson's cavalry.

Commodore John R. Tucker, CSN, commanding the Naval Brigade at Drewry's Bluff, was not notified that Richmond was being evacuated, his first clue being the burning of the Confederate ironclads on the James River near the Bluff. Using his initiative, he joined his brigade to that of Major Gen. Custis Lee's division of Ewell's corps, and marched west with that unit.

At the siege of Mobile, a battery of three 30-pounder Parrott rifles, manned by seamen and commanded by Lt. Commander Gillis, were landed on the banks of the Blakely River to support the action against Spanish Fort.

Union newspaper accounts:

Washington, D.C.: Mrs. Lincoln received a dispatch from the President to-day, dated as follows: "From Jefferson Davis's late residence at Richmond."

New York City: This morning's Tribune contains the following editorial: RICHMOND IS OURS!... It might have been ours long ago. It could have been taken with little loss by the tens of thousands whom Gen. Scott persistently held idle and useless around Washington throughout May and June, 1861. It might easily have been taken by McClellan in the spring of 1862, had that illustrious professor of the art How Not To Do It really and zealously tried. It might have been taken, but was not, for God's time had not yet come. At last, that time *has* come, and millions joyfully echo "RICHMOND IS OURS!"

April 5 (Wednesday)

Lee and the Army of Northern Virginia arrived at Amelia Court House to find that the expected supplies were not there. Sheridan's cavalry was to Lee's front at Jetersville, and the Danville Railroad to Farmville was not usable to bring supplies from Lynchburg. Sheridan, restrained by Meade, waited.

In Richmond, Lincoln came back to the city to confer with John A. Campbell and to make a statement that peace was possible only through the reestablishment of Federal authority throughout the South. Lincoln returned to City Point, where he learned that Secretary of State Seward had been injured in a carriage accident that day.

April 6 (Thursday)

On this day the 1st Maine Heavy Artillery Regiment, serving as infantry skirmishers in the advance of the 2nd Army Corps, made seven distinct charges against the defenses of Lee's retreating columns. During this day they captured 47 wagons, three artillery pieces, two battle flags and 350 prisoners.

Lt. Gen. Richard S. Ewell's entire corps was captured today at the Battle of Saylor's Creek—the last battle between the fabled Army of Northern Virginia and the Army of the Potomac. The last to surrender was the Naval Brigade from Drewry's Bluff, commanded by Commodore John R. Tucker, CSN, who gave his sword in surrender to Lt. Gen. J. Warren Keifer. Years later, Keifer returned the sword to Tucker.

Lt. Commander Ramsay, USN, reported to Admiral Porter of finding several large mines in the James River near Chaffin's Bluff. One such device contained 1700 pounds of powder, one 1400 pounds, and two 850 pounds each.

Union newspaper accounts:

Washington, D.C.: The War Department has been perfectly inundated with applications for passes to visit Richmond, from parties having friends or property there, curiosity seekers and tobacco or cotton speculators....

To-day's City Point boat brought up the band of the Fourteenth Virginia. They numbered twenty-seven pieces, and deserted to us last Sunday. They have been playing "Yankee Doodle," "Star Spangled Banner" and the like in our streets to their own and our citizens' extreme delight.

The hospital steamer *State of Maine* arrived at Alexandria this evening with six hundred wounded Union soldiers. Two other vessels similarly freighted have arrived here to-day.

New York City: The steamers *Decatur* and *Jersey Blue* arrived at Ft. Monroe on April 2d, from Newbern, N.C., with an aggregate of eight hundred Rebel prisoners and about two hundred refugees. The condition of these refugees is of the most distressing nature, many of them being incumbered with numerous children, barefooted, ragged and half-starved. They were taken charge of by the Provost-Marshal and will be sent north in a few days....

April 7 (Friday)

Grant wrote Lee, "The result of the last week must convince you of the hopelessness of further resistance on the part of the Army of Northern Virginia in this struggle. I feel that it is so, and regard it as my duty to shift from myself the responsibility of any further effusion of blood, by asking of you the surrender of that portion of the C.S. Army known as the Army of

Northern Virginia." Lee declined politely, but asked "the terms you will offer on condition of its [the Army of Northern Virginia] surrender."

At Farmville, Va., the Confederates crossed the Appomattox River against resistance by Federal troops, and continued to retreat west on the north bank of the river. Having obtained rations at Farmville, Lee's troops were in better shape, although they had been delayed. Lincoln told Grant, "Gen. Sheridan says, 'If the thing is pressed I think Lee will surrender.' Let the *thing* be pressed."

In Alabama, Nathan Bedford Forrest's troops skirmished with Wilson's cavalry near Stockton. Canby's troops at Mobile scouted towards the city.

Barber, Sgt., Co. C, 15th Illinois Volunteer Infantry, Pocotaligo, S.C.:

> Detachment of 15th corps has come back to Pocotaligo. The whole command expect to march to Beaufort soon and take transportation to Morehead City, N.C., and from there join Sherman's army at Goldsboro.... We will rejoice when we leave this sickly place. It has been one continual series of harassing alarms resulting in forced marches by night and day, in rain or shine....

April 8 (Saturday)

Spanish Fort and Ft. Alexis, the two key defenders of Mobile, surrendered on this date. The fate of Mobile was sealed.

In Virginia, the road to Lynchburg, passing through Appomattox Court House, was filled with Lee's legions. Trailing closely behind was Meade's Army of the Potomac and the relentless Grant. Sheridan was to the south and in front of Lee, between him and Lynchburg. Lee refused a general engagement with Meade regardless of the unremitting skirmishing between the two armies. Sheridan had seized the supplies at Appomattox intended for Lee, along with the supply trains from Lynchburg. Grant was at Farmville and received the letter from Lee of the previous day. Grant replied, "Peace being my great desire, there is but one condition I would insist upon, namely that the men and officers surrendered shall be disqualified from taking up arms again against the Government of the United States until properly exchanged." Lee replied later in the afternoon that "I did not intend to propose the surrender of the Army of Northern Virginia, but to ask the terms of your proposition." Lee still indicated a willingness to talk to Grant.

In the evening Lee held a final council of war. It was decided to try a breakthrough to Johnston.

Barber, Sgt., Co. C, 15th Illinois Volunteer Infantry, Pocotaligo, S.C.:

> There was a mutiny in the detachment of the 15th corps to-day occasioned by Colonel Henry arresting and tying up hand and foot a soldier belonging to said corps for disobeying orders by firing off his gun without leave. A squad of twenty men marched up to headquarters and the sergeant in command boldly walked up to Colonel. Henry and demanded the prisoner's release. Colonel Henry then went to the door and ordered the others to stack arms which they refused to do. Colonel Henry then drew his revolver and told them he would shoot every one unless they obeyed. So the twenty men were cowed by the determined manner of the Colonel. They were all immediately arrested.
>
> The detachment was in a blaze of excitement and soon over four hundred armed men were at Colonel Henry's headquarters, bent on releasing the prisoners. Colonel Henry sent orders for the detachment of the 17th corps to arm themselves and prepare to enforce his order. We obeyed the order but mentally resolved that we would never shed the blood of our brother soldiers. A better feeling began to prevail now. Col. Henry released all except the ringleader. He had his trial and was sentenced to be shot. I never learned whether the sentence was carried into effect.

In Charlotte, N.C., Lt. William H. Parker, CSN, and his cadets arrived with the archives and treasury of the Confederacy. On learning of a strong Union force nearby, Parker decided to move his charges further south. He added all local uniformed personnel from the Navy Yard to his force, bringing its strength to about 150 men. The President's lady, Varina Davis, arrived in Charlotte, and Parker suggested she join his command for protection.

Union newspaper accounts:

> *Richmond, Va.*: All the hospitals of Richmond have been taken possession of by the military authorities and are used for the care and comfort equally of the Union and Confederate sick and wounded. A

number of Confederate surgeons left in the city have been paroled to attend to the Confederate sick and wounded. More than half of General Pickett's Division has been brought in or captured, and the country between Richmond and Amelia county is said to be full of Confederate soldiers, nearly all of them Virginians, making their way to their homes. The Castle is used as a receptacle for citizen prisoners, of whom quite a number are gathered there.

April 9 (Sunday)

Generals Lee and Grant met at Appomattox Court House for the purpose of the surrender of the Army of Northern Virginia. After the surrender in the McLean house, Lee returned to his disheartened troops, and Grant notified Washington of his action. Lincoln, returning to Washington from City Point, learned of the surrender that evening when he landed at Washington. The celebration was riotous throughout the North, as the news reached the cities and hamlets that had endured four long years of war.

At Mobile, Canby's troops attacked Ft. Blakely after the fall of Spanish Fort. The fort fell without much resistance. Only two forts remained to guard Mobile—Huger and Tracy.

Barber, Sgt., Co. C, 15th Illinois Volunteer Infantry, Port Royal Ferry, S.C.:

Marched at precisely nine o'clock this morning. The boys are all jubilant at leaving this sickly and disagreeable place and at the prospect of soon joining our comrades.... When we arrived at Gardner's Corners, the first telegraph station, we learned that Richmond was taken....

Union newspaper accounts:

Mobile, Ala.: Spanish Fort. and Fort Blakely were captured to-day. We secured seven hundred prisoners at Fort Blakely and five thousand at Spanish Fort, with a large amount of guns and ordnance stores. Our troops have entered Mobile and are this evening in full possession....

Washington, D.C.: Three companies of Mosby's guerrillas disbanded on Wednesday last at Culpeper Court House, and dispersed for their homes. Mosby has less than three hundred men left, mostly operating on a neck of land running down Cynia Creek and Fredericksburg.

April 10 (Monday)

At Appomattox Court House, the Union forces, working with their Confederate counterparts, began preparing the lists of troops for parole. Jefferson Davis left Danville, Va., for Greensborough, N.C., by train, hoping to escape the Union cavalry under Stoneman, which was coming from the west. Sherman's army went on the road again, heading north.

With a saddened heart, Lee prepared his famous General Order No. 9, which disbanded the Army of Northern Virginia, knowing that he had no choice.

Union newspaper account:

Chattanooga, Tenn.: To-day, at ten o'clock, the gratifying news that Lee has surrendered was received at General Steedman's headquarters, creating the wildest excitement. As the news spread the men gathered in crowds and rent the air with the most vociferous cheers. The Twenty-ninth Indiana was ordered to "fall in" without arms, and then followed a regimental "three times three" that would have done your heart good to hear. At noon the forts that crown the crests of the hills about town fired a salute of one hundred guns, the whistles of the locomotives and machine shops screamed, while everybody feels good.

April 11 (Tuesday)

Sherman, moving towards Raleigh, N.C., upon entering Smithfield, learned of Lee's surrender. The Union troops cheered themselves hoarse.

Davis arrived at Greensborough, N.C., with his Cabinet, including John Cabell Breckingridge, former Vice President of the United States, and currently Confederate Secretary of War.

Barber, Sgt., Co. C, 15th Illinois Volunteer Infantry, Cape Fear River, N.C.:

Sailed last night at eleven P.M. Beautiful weather and smooth sailing; nevertheless I was seasick, which was owing to the poor state my stomach was in by living in the sickly camp of Pocotaligo so long. We passed Charleston harbor during the day and on the same evening arrived at the mouth of the Cape Fear River where we now lie.... We have learned by official information that Richmond is captured with twelve thousand prisoners and five hundred pieces of artillery.

Lt. William H. Parker, CSN, added the First Lady of the Confederacy to the archives and the treasury of the Confederacy to be guarded. They departed Charlotte, N.C., heading south.

In Mobile, the last two forts offering resistance, Forts Tracy and Huger, surrendered, and the Confederate troops retreated through the city heading north, pursued by ironclads in the bay. The Confederates sunk or burned all remaining vessels before departure.

Union newspaper account:

Appomattox C.H., Va.: Near the Appomattox, and at the point where Sheridan and Wright achieved their brilliant success of Friday, lay the ruins of army wagons, ambulances, forges, caissons, and the *debris* generally of the Rebel army. On the white canvas cover of an army wagon some wag, possibly a good-natured Johnny, had written in glaring capitals, "WE UNS HAVE FOUND THE LAST DITCH." From the scene presented in the gorge referred to one might very easily believe that it was the long-vaunted "last ditch" of the expiring "Confederacy."

April 12 (Wednesday)

The Mayor of Mobile met the Union military commanders and surrendered the city to prevent it from being destroyed by the ironclad fleet in the bay. The long campaign was over.

Gen. Wilson's cavalry occupied Montgomery, Ala. Sherman advanced towards Raleigh. Stoneman, coming from east Tennessee, entered Salisbury, N.C., on his way to link up with Sherman.

At Appomattox Court House, the formal surrender ceremony took place. Confederate troops marched between two lines of Union troops to lay down their arms and colors. The Federals showed their respect for their former foes, and they watched with a twinge of sadness.

At Greensborough, N.C., Davis met with Gen. Joseph E. Johnston and the Confederate Cabinet. Davis indicated that the Union would not negotiate; only full surrender would be allowed. Johnston was authorized to meet with Sherman.

Union newspaper accounts:

Richmond, Va.: Mrs. General Lee is seriously indisposed. A negro guard was placed in front of the home she is occupying, but on it being represented the color of the guards was an insult to Mrs. Lee, they were withdrawn and white guards substituted.

Fairfax Station, Va.: Colonel Gamble, commanding the Union forces at this point, received a message from the Rebel General Mosby, in which he says he does not care about Lee's surrender, and that he is determined to fight so long as he has a man left.

Fifth Army Corps, near Appomattox C.H., Va.: General Longstreet's entire corps marched from their camps and formed in line in front of the First Division of this corps and stacked their arms, flags, &c., when they slowly and sorrowfully returned to their camp. It is a sight that cannot be pictured properly to those who have not witnessed it. General Longstreet wore a smile on his face while General Gordon's expression was very different. General Pendleton disliked to give up Lee's artillery, but did so.

Mobile, Ala.: The Stars and Stripes were hoisted on Batteries Porter and Mackintosh at half past ten this morning. The most prominent church steeple also had our flag placed on it at half past two o'clock. General Granger's forces are now in full possession of this city.

April 13 (Thursday)

Sherman entered Raleigh, N.C., in a pouring rain, and Johnston rejoined his army to await developments. In Washington, Stanton ordered a stop to the conscription of troops and the further purchase of war materials. Grant was in Washington to confer with Lincoln and the Cabinet.

Commander Macomb reported from the North Carolina Sounds that on the Roanoke River "the rebels have evacuated Weldon, burning the bridge, destroying the ram at Edward's Ferry, and throwing the guns at Rainbow Bluff into the river. Except for torpedoes, the river is therefore clear for navigation. The floating battery, as I informed you in my No. 144, has got adrift from Halifax and been blown up by one of their own torpedoes."

Union newspaper account:

Raleigh, N.C.: Evidently one of our opponents has had what they call "His fill of it." The following letter picked up on our entrance here states the case, and does it in a very pointed manner. The letter is given exactly as it was written:

deers sister libby: i hev conkludid that the dam fulishnes uv tryin to lick shurmin Had better be stoped. we have bin gettin nuthin but hell & lots uv it ever sinse we saw the day yankys & i am tirde uv it. shurmin has a lots of pimps that dont care a dam what they doo. and its no use tryin to whip em. if we dont get hell when shurmin starts agin i miss my gess. if i cood git home ide tri dam hard to get thare. my old horse is plaid out or ide trie to go now. maibee ile start to nite fur ime dam tired uv this war fur nuthin. if the dam yankees Havent got thair yit its a dam wunder. Thair thicker an lise on a hen and a dam site ornraier. youre brother jim.

Raleigh, N.C.: The capital of North Carolina was entered and occupied this morning by the Union troops, and the Stars and Stripes waved from the ample dome of the State House.

April 14 (Friday)

Today, Major Gen. Robert Anderson, who had surrendered Ft. Sumter on April 14, 1861, raised the same flag that he had lowered on that date over the fort four long, bloody, weary years before.

At 10 P.M. in Washington, D.C., John Wilkes Booth entered the Presidential box at Ford's Theater and shot Lincoln in the back of the head. Booth leaped to the stage and escaped through the side door of the theatre.

In North Carolina, Sherman's army moved towards Durham Station in a driving rain. Confederate Gen. Joseph E. Johnston wrote Sherman asking for a "temporary suspension of hostilities," with Sherman replying that he was amenable, providing Johnston kept his troops in their present positions.

April 15 (Saturday)

At 7:22 A.M. this date President Lincoln died of the wound inflicted to his head. After being shot, he had been carried across the street from the theatre to a private home. The national mourning would be deep and lasting. Booth was still at large, having arrived at the home of Dr. Samuel Mudd in rural Maryland. The Cabinet asked Vice President Andrew Johnson to take the oath of office as President.

In North Carolina, President Davis departed Greensborough, heading south with a cavalry escort.

April 16 (Sunday)

The North went into deep mourning for the fallen President. The North was joined, in most places, by the South. In Washington, Johnson assumed office as President. Mrs. Lincoln was prostrate with grief. Booth arrived at the home of Samuel Cox at Rich Hill in southern Maryland.

Secretary of the Navy Gideon Welles directed that all ships sailing down Chesapeake Bay be searched, as well as all ships leaving any port in the vicinity. All suspicious persons were to be arrested and sent to the Washington Navy Yard for questioning.

In the deep South, Gen. Wilson's cavalry captured West Point and Columbus, Ga., with little resistance. President Davis's party arrived at Lexington, N.C.

Jackman, Pvt., "The Orphan Brigade," Graniteville, S.C.:

> About the middle of April the dismounted men were ordered to Columbia, S.C.... Not being able to stand a march in warm weather, I made an application for a furlough which Capt. H., Asst Adj General of our brigade took to Augusta himself to have approved but Gen'l Young had left for Columbia. The "Old Guard" (who was also not able to march) and I were detailed to take the brig. archives—and of the regiments—to Washington, Ga. We performed this going to a hospital. We were to stay at W. until further orders. We remained at Graniteville two or three days after the com'd had marched....

April 17 (Monday)

In Washington, the slain President's body was taken to the East Room of the White House, where it would lie in state. Booth and his travelling companion, David Herold, were in the vicinity of Port Tobacco, Md., seeking transportation across the Potomac River.

By direction of the Navy Department, a gun would be fired every thirty minutes from sunrise to sunset on this date to honor the fallen Lincoln. Further, all flags on ships and at naval installations would be flown at half-staff until after the President's funeral, and all naval officers were to wear crepe mourning badges for a period of six months.

In North Carolina, Generals Sherman and Johnston met at the Bennett House, close by Durham Station, to discuss the surrender of all Confederate forces east of the Mississippi. President Davis's party approached Salisbury, N.C., en route to Charlotte.

At Columbus, Ga., Major Gen. George H. Thomas reported that the city had been captured and "the rebel ram *Jackson*, nearly ready for sea, and carrying six 7-inch guns, fell into our hands and was destroyed, as well as the navy yard, foundries, the arsenal and armory, sword and pistol factory." Columbus had been a major shipbuilding site for the Confederacy.

Lt. William H. Parker, CSN, arrived at Washington, Ga., with the archives and treasury of the Confederacy, as well as with the Confederate President's wife and party.

Jackman, Pvt., "The Orphan Brigade," Washington, Ga.:

> On the 17th day of April the "Old Guard" and I took train for Augusta in the morning having in charge several boxes of books, papers, etc. Before starting or on way to Augusta, one of our "telegraph" friends told me that some very bad news had come over the wires, but would not tell me what it was. At 7 o'clock P.M. we took passenger train for Barnett, 58 miles up towards Atlanta.... We got off at Barnett about 2 o'clock at night and slept in a freight car until morning. Barnett is only a station at the junction of the Washington road. We had to lie over until 2 P.M. the 18th.
>
> Gen'l Hood came down on the train from Washington and took the up train for Atlanta at 12 M. He must of know of Lee's surrender for he looked very "blue." At 2 A.M. the train left for Washington, and being only 18 miles to run, we soon got there. We immediately went to the building where a detail from our brigade was making saddles. We remained with the detail all the time.... I amused myself by writing most of the time. Wrote the first 6 months of my journal from memory and copied from my little memorandum books the notes of each day so far as right after Mar 30th 1862....
>
> At last the news came of the surrender of Johnston. We knew then that we had "gone up." One evening the 8th Texas Cavalry—"The Rangers"—came through town making their way west of the Chattahoochee. They "charged" the corn depot at the Court House for forage. They then got the straggling soldiers into a Q.M.'s department and they threw out writing paper, thread, buttons, etc. in the streets by the wagon load. The little negroes and citizens soon had wheel-barrows in the ground to take the plunder home. After the "Rangers" had gone, the Q.M. had a guard to stop the pillage. The guards were chasing the little negroes about for some time on the streets making them "shell out" the stolen goods.
>
> The next day Ferguson's brigade came through and they "charged" around considerable but all the government stores were about gone before they came in. At the depot were piles of ammunition which the little boys and citizens carried away as much as they could haul. I expected to see the depot blown up by carelessness.

Newspaper accounts:

> *Army of the Potomac, Burkesville Station, Va.:*... The announcement of the assassination of Mr. Lincoln and Mr. Seward and his son was received throughout this army with the utmost sorrow. Every man seemed to think it the greatest calamity that could have possibly happened just at this time....
>
> *Winchester, Va.*: Mosby surrendered his force to Gen. Chapman at Berryville to-day. The terms of surrender were the same as those accorded Gen. Lee and his army.

April 18 (Tuesday)

In North Carolina, Sherman and Johnston signed an "agreement" on an armistice that would be very controversial. For all practical purposes, fighting had ceased in both Virginia and North Carolina.

In Washington, Lincoln lay in state at the White House. Vice Admiral Farragut wrote to his wife: "All the people in the city are going to see the President in state. I go tomorrow as one of the pall bearers."

Newspaper account:

> *Raleigh, N.C.*: After a two days' conference between Major Gen. Sherman and Major Gen. Joseph E. Johnston, commanding the Rebel forces east of the Mississippi River, with the concurrence of Jefferson Davis, and in the presence and with the advice of Gen. John C. Breckenridge, the whole remaining Rebel army from the Potomac to the Rio Grande has been surrendered to the forces of the United States.... Gen. Johnston expresses deep and apparently sincere sorrow and much concern at the assassination of President Lincoln, in which he was

joined by each Confederate officer present. Gen. Johnston regards it as the most terrible blow yet inflicted upon the Confederate cause and the Southern people, and seems deeply to deplore the event, coming as it does upon the close of this great struggle.

April 19 (Wednesday)

Amid tolling bells and the booming of the minute guns in Washington, Lincoln's funeral was held and the body moved in a procession to the Rotunda of the Capitol, where it would be viewed by thousands of mourners.

From Cairo, Ill., the U.S.S. *Lexington*, Acting Lt. William Flye, transported Col. John T. Sprague, Gen. John Pope's Chief of Staff, down the Mississippi and then up the Red River to meet Confederate Gen. Kirby Smith to discuss the surrender of the Confederate forces west of the Mississippi.

President Davis's party arrived at Charlotte, N.C., where it would remain until the 26th. Gen. Wade Hampton of South Carolina suggested to Davis that the presidential party move west of the Mississippi and continue the fight. Nothing was done about this.

Newspaper account:

Washington, D.C.: The great and solemn pageant of removing the remains of the Nation's revered and beloved Chief from the White House to the Capitol is closed. Never was such a scene witnessed where each and every one of the vast throng moved in silent sadness, as if bearing the burden of a personal bereavement....

April 20 (Thursday)

Gen. James H. Wilson's cavalry took Macon, Ga. Arkansas ratified the Thirteenth Amendment.

In Washington, the body of the President was prepared for shipment to Illinois, where it would be interred.

April 21 (Friday)

The President's funeral train left Washington on a circuitous route to Illinois.

Barber, Sgt., Co. C, 15th Illinois Volunteer Infantry, near Goldsboro, N.C.:

Marched at half past five. The news came today that President Lincoln, Secretary Seward and son have been assassinated, resulting in the President's death and severely wounding the others. And now, while the nation is rejoicing with unspeakable joy at its deliverance, it is suddenly plunged into the deepest sorrow by the most brutal murder of its loved chief.

We are now continually passing paroled men from Lee's army on their way to their homes, or to where their homes were. Many found blackened ruins instead, and kindred and friends gone, they knew not whither. Oh, how much misery treason and rebellion have brought upon our land!

Camped on the river three miles from Goldsboro. Colonel Hall is here with seven hundred recruits for the 14th Regiment, and Colonel Rogers is at Raleigh with seven hundred for the 15th. The old organization is to be resumed. All the veterans are justly indignant at this usurpation of their right and their honor and reputation....

Newspaper account:

Fauquier, Va.: *Mosby's Farewell Address*: "Soldiers: I have summoned you together for the last time. The vision we have cherished for a free and independent country has vanished, and that country is now the spoil of a conqueror. I disband your organization in preference to surrendering to our enemies. I am no longer your commander. After an association of more than two eventful years, I part from you with a just pride in the fame of your achievements, and grateful recollections of your generous kindness to myself; and now at this moment of bidding you a final adieu, accept the assurance of my unchanging confidence and regard. Farewell."

April 22 (Saturday)

In rural southern Maryland, Booth and Herold crossed the Potomac, headed south. The train carrying Lincoln's body reached Philadelphia, arriving from Harrisburg.

Secretary of the Navy Welles notified the ships in the Potomac that John W. Booth had been seen near Bryantown on April 15th, and that all boats were to be searched to obtain his capture.

Barber, Sgt., Co. C, 15th Illinois Volunteer Infantry, near Goldsboro, N.C.:

> Marched at seven A.M. towards Goldsboro and turned off on the Raleigh road. Went into camp at nine A.M. to draw rations. To-day I received the startling and sorrowful intelligence that Milton had escaped from prison, been home, returned to the army and been captured by a band of rebel cavalry while out foraging and brutally murdered in company with four of his comrades. One escaped and brought the news to camp. In consequence of this intelligence, my spirits are much depressed to-day. I have a faint hope that the information is incorrect. I will soon know....

April 23 (Sunday)

Secretary Welles ordered the ships on the Mississippi to search all vessels for President Jefferson Davis and his party to prevent their escape west. Rear Admiral S. P. Lee, commander of the Mississippi Squadron, took immediate action to put the search operation into effect.

At 8:30 P.M., Lt. Read took his ship, the C.S.S. *Webb*, out of the mouth of the Red River into a startled flotilla of Union ships in the Mississippi. The ship, painted all white, took off down the Mississippi at full steam and managed to elude the pursuing vessels. Other ships involved in the chase reported that the *Webb* was doing 25 knots on the river.

Newspaper accounts:

> *Vicksburg, Miss.*: Eight thousand Andersonville prisoners are here getting ready to return to their homes.
>
> *Knoxville, Tenn.*: Among the trophies of Stoneman's expedition are twelve battle flags and banners, one old United States flag found in the house of a loyal citizen of Salisbury. The poisonous pen, where many unfortunate Union prisoners pined their lives away, was burned to the ground. A few Union prisoners were found, skeletons of their former selves. Almost all of them died on the way to Knoxville. They preferred rather to die under the Stars and Stripes than to be left in the loathsome hospitals of Salisbury.

April 24 (Monday)

At Port Conway, Va., Booth and Herold crossed the Rappahannock in their escape from Federal troops. Lincoln's body was now at New York, where it lay in state.

In North Carolina, Grant met Sherman and told him that his (Sherman's) terms given to Johnston were not acceptable to President Johnson. Johnston was to be notified that unless he surrendered unconditionally within 48 hours, hostilities would be resumed.

In Augusta, Ga., Lt. William H. Parker, guardian of the Confederacy archives and treasury, learned that the surrender terms offered to Johnston by Sherman had been rejected by the Federal Government. So, gathering his escort and charges, he departed for Abbeville, S.C., thinking that that would be the most likely place to join President Davis.

The C.S.S. *Webb*, having shaken all pursuers, hoisted the Union flag to half-mast and roared past New Orleans at about midnight going full steam. Federal gunboats fired on her and hit her three times without serious damage. She continued on downriver towards the Gulf.

Newspaper accounts:

> *Selma, Ala.*: From the *Daily Rebel*: The people of the North are now reaping the natural and inevitable harvest of crime growing out of the demoralization incident to a state of war. The last dispatches exhibit a most shocking and horrible state of society. The President and his Prime Minister killed by assassins, and the new President and the Secretary of War murdered by a mob which has obtained and holds possession of the Capital of the Nation. Other cities sacked and a great popular revolution against the rulers impending. While their armies are devastating our land, their own downtrodden populace, infuriated by tyranny and driven to despair by want, bursts the bonds of law, and a reign of terror and of ruin is established.
>
> That Nation which prided itself upon its strength and prosperity, finds three different Presidents occupying its Executive Chair within a space of a single month, two of whom were murdered; discord and anarchy riding rampant and ruling the hour. Perhaps they may yet find it necessary to recall the armies they have sent to these States to ruin us to restore order and law among themselves. God grant it.
>
> *Chattanooga, Tenn.*: The Atlanta papers know of the assassination of President Lincoln, but make no comment. They deny the surrender of Lee's Army, and say he was all right on the 16th inst.

April 25 (Tuesday)

Near Bowling Green, Va., Federal cavalry closed in on Booth and Herold at a farm north of the city.

In North Carolina, Johnston asked Sherman to renew negotiations concerning the fate of the Confederate troops under Johnston's command.

Near Washington, Ga., Lt. William H. Parker met Mrs. Jefferson Davis and her party, which was proceeding to Florida with a small escort. Mrs. Davis having no information on the whereabouts of her husband, Parker proceeded to Abbeville, S.C.

In the early hours of this day, the C.S.S. *Webb* finally reached the end of her rope. About 25 miles south of New Orleans, she met the U.S.S. *Richmond* and was then caught. The crew ran the Confederate ship aground and burned her before taking to the swamps and bayous in boats. Within hours they were captured and taken to New Orleans. The crew was later paroled and sent home. The dashing Lt. Read became a river pilot on the Mississippi after the war.

Barber, Sgt., Co. C, 15th Illinois Volunteer Infantry, near Raleigh, N.C.:

> Marched at seven A.M. Arrived at Raleigh at twelve M. The corps moved from Raleigh at eight o'clock A.M. in pursuit of Johnson [General Joseph Johnston]. Hostilities were resumed to-day at seven A.M. We rested awhile at Raleigh and then set out to join the corps, which we overtook twelve miles from Raleigh. Then each soldier reported to his proper command. I am now with the mounted squad but have not yet got a horse. I found here about fifty of my old comrades of the 14th and 15th veteran battalion and several boys whom I had left in prison.

April 26 (Wednesday)

At about 2 A.M. Federal troops surrounded a tobacco barn located on the Garrett farm north of Bowling Green, Va., where Booth and Herold had taken refuge. The commander of the troops, Lt. Col. Everton Conger, called for their surrender. Booth refused; Herold accepted and left the barn. After a standoff of a few hours, Conger ordered the barn set afire to drive Booth out. While the barn was burning, Sgt. Boston Corbett shot Booth, wounding him mortally. Booth died shortly thereafter, on the porch of the Garrett house.

In North Carolina, Johnston and Sherman met to finalize the surrender of all Confederate forces east of the Mississippi. The terms were the same as those signed by Grant and Lee.

Also in North Carolina, President Davis met with his Cabinet in Charlotte and they agreed to try to escape to west of the Mississippi. The Confederate Attorney General, George Davis, left the presidential party and returned to his home.

April 27 (Tuesday)

The body of John Wilkes Booth, the assassin of President Lincoln, and the captured David E. Herold were delivered aboard the U.S.S. *Montauk* anchored in the Anacostia River near the Washington Navy Yard. An autopsy was performed on Booth's body and positive identification was made. The corpse was then taken to the Washington Arsenal (present site of Ft. McNair), and there buried in a gun box near the Old Capital Prison. Herold was kept aboard the *Montauk*, along with the other suspected conspirators.

On the Mississippi River another tragedy unfolded. The steamer *Sultana* blew up north of Memphis, killing 1450 of the 2000 passengers. All but 50 of the dead were former prisoners of war on their way home. The cause of the explosion was never determined. A sad ending for so many who had endured so much.

President Davis, who had now reached South Carolina, lost another Cabinet member—Treasury Secretary G.A. Trenholm, who resigned because of ill health and returned home.

En route to Illinois, Lincoln's funeral train made stops at both Rochester and Buffalo, New York.

April 28 (Wednesday)

Sherman departed North Carolina for Savannah, Ga., to attend to matters there. Mrs. Davis was in Abbeville, S.C., with her escort. Grant had returned to Washington.

In Cleveland, Ohio, the body of Lincoln was viewed by over 50,000 people.

April 29 (Thursday)

Lincoln's funeral train arrived in Columbus, Ohio. President Davis reached Yorkville, S.C., continuing south.

Lt. William H. Parker, CSN, escorting the

archives and treasury of the Confederacy, arrived at Abbeville, S.C., with his band of about 150 men. He placed his cargo aboard railcars and posted guards. A locomotive was kept immediately ready in case there was a need to flee.

On the Cumberland River near Eddyville, Ky., the U.S.S. *Moose*, Acting Master W.C. Coulson, surprised a Confederate raiding party of about 200 led by Major Hopkins of Brig. Gen. Abram Burford's command. The *Moose*, with her main battery, sank two boats loaded with troops and then put a landing party ashore to engage the remaining Confederates. The landing party killed or wounded about 20 men, captured 6, and took 22 horses.

April 30 (Friday)

The Lincoln train reached Indianapolis. The eight conspirators in the Lincoln assassination were transferred by boat to the Old Capital Prison for detention and trial. The old prison building is gone, but the building in which the trial was held still stands and is used for government housing.

Outside Mobile, Federal Gen. Canby met Confederate Gen. Richard Taylor to discuss the surrender of all troops in Alabama and Mississippi.

In North Carolina, Sherman's army was on the march north to Washington, D.C. The government requested 50 bakers each from Baltimore, Philadelphia and New York to help with the rations for the troops expected to arrive shortly.

MAY 1865

It was now three weeks since Lee and Grant met at Appomattox Court House in Virginia to set in motion the disbanding of the Confederate States Army. Much had changed in this short period of time. A new President was at the helm, the smoke had cleared from the battlefields, and the troops were on their way home. A fresh breeze was blowing.

May 1 (Monday)

The assassinated President Lincoln lay in state in Chicago, en route to Springfield for burial. Thousands of mourners filed past the bier for a final look at the man who had so changed the direction of the nation.

In Washington, President Andrew Johnson named nine army officers to head the military tribunal which would sit in judgment on the accused conspirators of the assassination. This was to be a strictly military trial, it having been ruled that the conspirators would not be tried in a civil court.

On the roads of Virginia and North Carolina, long blue lines of Federal troops marched towards Washington and home. The step seemed more sprightly, somehow, heading home.

Newspaper account:

> *Sherman's Troops, Fairport, N.C.*: Another fine day for marching, starting at five in the morning, by three o'clock in the afternoon the troops were in camp at Fairport, having marched twenty-two miles without experiencing more than usual fatigue, owing to the excellence of the roads....

The C.S.S. *Shenandoah*, Lt. Waddell, unaware that the war was over, had ranged to the Bering Sea in search of whalers since leaving Lea Harbor, Ponape, Caroline Islands.

May 2 (Tuesday)

In Alabama, Major Gen. E.R.S. Canby notified Grant that the forces under Confederate Gen. Richard Taylor were ready to surrender—one less army in the field.

Confederate Naval Lt. William Harwar Parker, with his 150-man naval escort, met the fleeing President Davis at Abbeville, S.C. Parker transferred his cargo of archives and bullion to Davis's escort commander, Brig. Gen. Basil Duke, and then disbanded his men. At this point he directed his midshipmen to "report by letter to the Hon. Secretary of the Navy as soon as practicable," after they had visited their home.

Later this same day Parker advised Davis to abandon his large escort for a smaller troop of men, which would be able to move faster. Davis left for Washington, Ga.

Barber, Sgt., Co. C, 15th Illinois Volunteer Infantry, to Petersburg, Va.:

> Marched at six o'clock. Went eighteen miles and camped for the night. Passed Forest Dale yesterday. It was a splendid looking place. A college is situated here. Drew clothing to-night. The country is broken and barren.

Newspaper accounts:

Twentieth Army Corps, near Williamston, N.C.: It is painful to be obliged to record the lawless conduct of our soldiers at any time, particularly it is so when that conduct is utterly without extenuation. Despite the stringent orders issued in regard to the peaceable behavior of our troops upon their march to Richmond, some of the soldiers both of the Army of Georgia and the Army of [the] Tennessee have been permitted to straggle from their commands, and have committed depredations upon the inhabitants much to be deplored. It would seem that the roving spirits fostered by army life cannot at once be chastened into a domestic one by the white-winged angel of peace....

Robertson County, Tex.: Brig. Gen. William P. Hardeman's Brigade assembled in mass this evening, and, with General Hardeman in the chair, resolved, among other things, that in spite of the reverses to the cis-Mississippi armies, they would not abandon the struggle until the right of self-government is fully established....

May 3 (Wednesday)

In Illinois, the funeral train carrying President Lincoln had finally reached its destination at Springfield. The country lawyer who had risen to such fame and had suffered so much for the Union was home at last.

President Davis and his escort crossed the Savannah River and moved to Washington, Ga. Confederate Secretary of State Judah Benjamin resigned his post and left the presidential party, headed for England.

Confederate Secretary of the Navy Mallory resigned from the Confederate cabinet citing the needs of his family. Davis, with regret, accepted the resignation and Mallory departed for LaGrange, Ga., where his family was waiting.

Federal Secretary of the Navy Gideon Welles directed that the Potomac flotilla be reduced by half in light of the lessened need for ships in that area.

Jackman, Pvt., "The Orphan Brigade," Washington, Ga.:

I believe it was in the afternoon of May 3d "Uncle Jeff" rode into town escorted by Company B of the 2d Ky. Cavalry—Geo. Duke's old regiment. He had on a broad-brimmed light colored felt hat which had a wide stripe of black around the crown and the brim turned down. He wore a gray coat without any gold lace on it (but it was cut in a military style) and he had a pair of gray pants which stuffed in a pair of cavalry boots. I had never seen him dressed in this style before, but I knew him the moment I saw him. He dismounted at the old bank-building in the public square near where we were staying. Nearly all of his Cabinet were with him. Dr. ———, the banker entertained him. Many citizens called on the President.

The next morning Gen'l Bragg came into town and about 9 A.M. he and the President rode away alone going back towards Abbeville—or started out that street at least. The Cabinet here left the President, or they separated rather, and the Confederate government ceased to exist.

That afternoon Gen'l Breckinridge, Secretary of War, came to town and staid all night at the same place Pres. Davis had lodged. Before leaving town he sent an order to Duke's brigade which had passed through in the morning to surrender, that the department had been surrendered by Johnston. This was the last order as such by the authority of the Confederate government. The following morning Breckinridge left town and in the evening a company of Federal cavalry came in and took charge of affairs.

Newspaper account:

Fifth Army Corps, Richmond, Va.: The old pine woods south of Manchester are luminous to-night with the camp fires of the returning veterans of the Fifth Army Corps. To-morrow they will be gratified with their first view of the city for which they so long and so nobly battled. Their first view did I say? No, for in the long column are scores to whom the town will only serve to bring back to memory the long days and longer nights of privation and suffering endured in the former prison dens of the enemy. Following the Fifth will march the Second Corps, both on their way to Alexandria, where they will enjoy for a season the rest and relaxation to which they are so eminently entitled by their arduous service in the field. The battle fields of Cold Harbor, North Anna, Spottsylvania and Fredericksburg will probably be passed on their way to their point of destination.

May 4 (Thursday)

Amid much pomp and ceremony, the remains of the sixteenth President of the United States, Abraham Lincoln, were interred at Springfield.

President Davis and his escort continued south through Georgia, seeking a way to escape west.

At the small town of Citronelle, Ala., forty miles from Mobile, Gen. Dick Taylor officially surrendered his forces to Gen. Canby, thereby writing the final chapter to the defense of Mobile.

At Bermuda, the C.S.S. *Ajax* arrived from Nassau, ignorant of the fact that the Confederacy had collapsed. Lt. Low attempted to get armaments for the ship but he was refused, the local Governor, W.G. Hanley, stating that "she wants nothing but armament to be in a position to take the seas as a privateer."

Barber, Sgt., Co. C, 15th Illinois Volunteer Infantry, to Petersburg, Va.:

> Marched at seven A.M. Marched fifteen miles and went into camp. Are waiting for pontoons to be laid to cross the Roanoke River.... A scouting party from the 1st brigade found ten pieces of artillery and a large amount of ammunition secreted in the woods.

Newspaper account:

> *Citronville, Ala.*: "Lieutenant General Taylor has this day surrendered to me with the forces under his command, on substantially the same terms as those accepted by General Lee. E.R.S. Canby."

May 5 (Friday)

Sherman's troops continued northward, looking forward to the final Grand Review in Washington. The countryside seemed filled with soldiers moving in all directions. The paroled Rebels were heading home by any means at their disposal, slowly at times, and with sadness.

Barber, Sgt., Co. C, 15th Illinois Volunteer Infantry, to Petersburg, Va.:

> Marched at three A.M. Crossed Roanoke River at 5 A.M. Crossed the state line from North Carolina into Virginia at six A.M. Marched twelve miles farther and halted for the men to make coffee, and so we took our first lunch in the State of Virginia.... It is now forty-five miles to Petersburg....

Newspaper accounts:

> *Twentieth Army Corps, Near the Big Nottoway River, Va.*: As the army nears Richmond it begins to grow impatient. Home becomes near and more vivid in the mind's eye, and hearts beat more longingly for the loved ones at home. The soldiers eagerly discuss the prospects of their early muster out of the service, and universally hope that they will not be detained any longer than is absolutely necessary....
>
> *Sixteenth Army Corps, Montgomery, Ala.*: We arrived here from Blakely, opposite Mobile, on the 25th of April, marching by way of Greenville. The distance is one hundred and eighty miles; time of marching, thirteen days, including one day of rest at Greenville. Major General Grierson, with a cavalry command, passed us at Greenville, striking out to Americus, Ga. He has been heard from at Eufaula, Ala., where Governor Watts had taken up his abode and located the fugitive seat of [the] Government of Alabama.
>
> The first half of the march from Blakely was through pine woods—*barrens* the country is called, the soil being light, but by no means barren—with very few clearings or settlers. A few families of Creek half-breeds, and of the "poor white trash," were the only inhabitants of the country. For two days before we reached Greenville, and from Greenville to Montgomery, the country is well settled and cultivated.
>
> No Union army has passed through the country before us, and the people were greatly excited and terrified. The wealthy planters tried to hide their stock and supplies, but in vain. The mules and loads of bacon were dragged out of the swamps and hiding places, to replenish our scant commissary supplies, and to replace worn-out animals in the train. The negroes hailed us as deliverers. They thronged the highways, almost impeding our march. I have heard the number that came into Montgomery with the corps estimated as high as five thousand. In many cases we advised them to stay with their old masters, but they said "No da was going to be free," and their old masters had treated them too cruelly. One old man seventy-eight years old, born in the North and a free man, had been kidnapped at the age of fifteen and had been held in slavery *sixty-three* years. He said this was the first chance he had had in all these

long years of slavery to regain his liberty, and he was bound to avail himself of it; he wouldn't risk staying with his old master and take the chance of being made free by the laws....

May 6 (Saturday)

The War Department, in accordance with an Executive Order, named Major Gen. David Hunter to head the commission to try the assassination conspirators. Brig. Gen. Joseph Holt was named judge advocate of the commission.

In Georgia, President Davis continued moving south, reaching the town of Sandersville.

Jackman, Pvt., "The Orphan Brigade," Washington, Ga.:

The next evening, May 6th, the brigade came to Washington. As they marched through the streets coming in from one direction, all armed and their flags flying, they passed the 13th Tenn. Federal Cavalry coming from the opposite direction. It looked strange not to see them commence shooting at each other. I worked until ten o'clock at night getting up the proper papers for the regiment to be paroled. The Federal Provost Marshal worked nearly all night paroling us.... The next day all the brigade was paroled and we "broke up housekeeping." Each fellow being allowed to wander off as his inclinations led him, with his horse, saddle and bridle.

Newspaper account:

Vicksburg, Miss.: The Vicksburg *Herald* extra of this date give additional official information confirmatory of the surrender of Gen. Dick Taylor and command to Gen. Canby on the 4th. This makes almost a clean sweep of the Rebel troops in arms east of the Mississippi river.... Up to to-day about four thousand Rebel prisoners of war have been received at this city (Vicksburg) for delivery to the Rebel Bureau of Exchange....

May 7 (Sunday)

Barber, Sgt., Co. C, 15th Illinois Volunteer Infantry, Petersburg, Va.:

Marched at five A.M. Moved 12 miles and halted for rest and refreshments. After dinner moved to within two miles of Petersburg and went into camp. For the past day we have been on the tramping and fighting ground of the Potomac army. All along the road is strewed evidence of severe fighting. Our present camping ground is dotted as far as the eye can reach with spots where was camped the vast Army of the Potomac, the brave but unfortunate army which has fought so bravely, suffered so much and accomplished so little. From the Potomac across the Rappahannok to beyond the James River, their bodies lie slumbering in an unbroken sleep, never more to waken to active life, but the cause for which they sacrificed their lives will live and grow, until its splendor eclipses the whole world....

May 8 (Monday)

In Alabama, Gen. Canby's appointed officers completed the parole of Gen. Dick Taylor's Confederate force. The Rebels began the long trek home. Throughout the South the paroled Confederate troops were finding it difficult to get home, due to the condition of the railroads. In most cases the tracks had to be rebuilt before they could be used, or at least extensive repairs were required. Timetables were unheard of at this time.

Jackman, Pvt., "The Orphan Brigade," White Plains, Ga.:

I went to Augusta and a few days after nearly all the regiment met there. We expected to go around by water *via* Savannah but we gave out such a trip and all started up by Atlanta. Not being able to travel much, I got off the train with a friend at Union Point near Greensburg, Ga. and went out near White Plains to stay until the railroad repairs were completed from Atlanta to Chattanooga. We stopped with Mr. Wright, a clever old planter (and old Mrs. W. was a very kind old lady) about 2 miles from the Plains. Here we staid until the later part of the month amusing ourselves fishing and other sports were gotten up for our entertainment....

Newspaper accounts:

Army of Tennessee, Petersburg, Va.: At eight o'clock this morning, Major General [O.O.] Howard and staff, commanding the Army of the Tennessee, took position in front of Jarrett's Hotel for the purpose of reviewing the Seventeenth Corps, Major General Frank Blair commanding, as they marched through Petersburg on their way to Richmond and Alexandria.... More than two-thirds of the men comprising the Army of the Tennessee are veteran troops, who have marched through the greater portion of the so-called Southern Confederacy, and there are but few regiments in the command who have not marched upward of six thousand miles, incredible as it may appear, since their first enlistment and muster into the service....

Richmond, Va.: Dick Turner, the noted turnkey of Libby Prison, is securely locked up in the most dismal, subterranean dungeon of that place of torture. There is no pity felt for him in Richmond. He is as pale as leprosy, his beard whitening, his deficient teeth ajar and his eyes full of terror. He is now as mean and cringing in his behavior as, in power he was insolent and cruel. When turnkey, he shot men dead with a revolver, who came to the windows for air and light, kicked and knocked down others, and took delight in augmenting the untold miseries of the poor prisoners under his charge. He has heard, in his loathsome cell, that the soldiers have decreed his death so soon as they are fully assured of his identity, and his pleadings for mercy are presented to all who come near him; but he pleads to hearts of stone.

May 9 (Tuesday)

In an effort to bring Virginia back into the Union as rapidly as possible, President Andrew Johnson recognized Francis H. Pierpont as Governor.

In Arkansas, Brig. Gen. M. Jeff Thompson was considering surrender of his Rebel forces.

In Washington, D.C., at the Old Capital Prison, the trial of the assassination conspirators began.

In Georgia, President Davis met his wife on the Oconee River near Dublin. This was their first meeting since Varina and the children were sent from Richmond before its fall.

Newspaper accounts:

Petersburg, Va.: The Seventeenth and Fifteenth Corps of Sherman's Army—dusty and tired infantry columns, mounted officers, cavalry battalions, martial bands in full blast, fluttering banners, rattling artillery trains, and rumbling army wagons—have been passing through Petersburg all day, bound for Manchester, opposite Richmond, and thence to Alexandria, by way of the battle-fields of last spring....

Raleigh, N.C., Paroling Johnston's Army: The whole number of officers and men paroled proves to have been twenty-nine thousand nine hundred and twenty-four. The officers mentioned personally signed their own parole, and also the muster rolls of their respective commands. Before doing this, however, they were careful to have an inspection of the men actually present, refusing to be held for a large number who were borne on the rolls, but who had absented themselves....

Upon opening the paroling office at Greenborough, General Hartsuff observed a Confederate officer who had been standing near the door from a very early hour. He pressed in eagerly and first signed the following to a parole already written out in his own hand: "Rear Admiral and Brigadier General, C.S.N. and C.S.A., R. Semmes."

The wasting effects of war were never more apparent than in this Southern army, as may be seen by an inspection of these muster-rolls. The following are a few sample cases:

The Forty-sixth North Carolina Volunteers had three officers, three noncommissioned officers and eight men—total fourteen.

The Forty-seventh North Carolina Volunteers had two officers, two noncommissioned officers and three men—total seven.

The Forty-eighth North Carolina Volunteers had three officers, three noncommissioned officers and fourteen men—total twenty.

It required nine regiments of North Carolina troops to make a battalion of sixty-one officers and men. The original number of these regiments was, maximum, one thousand men each....

May 10 (Wednesday)

Today, President Andrew Johnson officially declared that armed resistance to the Federal Government was at an end.

In Spencer County, Ky., the infamous William Clarke Quantrill was fatally wounded near Taylorsville, and was removed to Louisville for treatment, where he later died. This effectively closed a long and bloody chapter of guerrilla warfare motivated more by criminal than patriotic instincts. The legacy of Quantrill's band of marauders would long haunt the hills of Missouri.

Near Irwinville, Ga., the Fourth Michigan Cavalry surprised the Jefferson Davis party early in the morning and captured the former President and his escort.

Barber, Sgt., Co. C, 15th Illinois Volunteer Infantry, Richmond, Va.:

> Visited Richmond to-day. Went through Libby Prison and inspected every room accessible to visitors. Went to Castle Thunder, also to the State Capitol used during the Rebellion as capital of the confederacy..... Richmond is a splendid looking city. Saw Gen. Lee today. Also visited Jeff Davis' and Lee's city residences.

Newspaper account:

> *Tallahassee, Fla.*: The Rebel troops in Florida, with all the public property, surrendered to McCook today. The number of troops paroled and already reported is 7200, and will, doubtless, reach 8000 when the returns are complete....

May 11 (Thursday)

In Havana, Cuba, the C.S.S. *Stonewall* arrived from Europe. Learning of the location of the Confederate raider, Admiral Cornelius K. Stribling dispatched a squadron led by the U.S.S. *Powhatan* and commanded by Commander Reed Werden, to cruise off Havana and engage the ram if she left port. Meanwhile, Capt. Thomas J. Page, commander of the *Stonewall*, learning of the surrender of the South, delivered the ship to the Governor General of Cuba and in turn received $16,000—the amount of money Page needed to pay off the officers and crew. The ship was later turned over to the United States and then later sold to Japan. Page and his crew returned home.

In Arkansas, Brig. Gen. M. Jeff Thompson surrendered the remainder of his force, ending a short but distinguished career.

May 13 (Saturday)

In Texas, Gen. E. Kirby Smith met with the Confederate governors of Arkansas, Louisiana, Missouri, and a representative from Texas to discuss the situation. Gen. Jo Shelby and others, determined to pursue the war, threatened Smith with arrest if he suggested surrender.

In the North Pacific, the C.S.S. *Shenandoah*, Lieutanant Waddell, headed into the whaling zone, while the merchants and shipowners in New England beat on the door of Secretary Welles for him to do something about stopping the raider.

May 14 (Sunday)

Barber, Sgt., Co. C, 15th Illinois Volunteer Infantry, en route to Alexandria, Va.:

> The roads are very bad. Marched ten miles and went into camp. In passing the defenses of Richmond, I confess that I saw nothing that seemed very formidable, but what could have been easily overcome if military movements were properly directed, but perhaps on the other part of the line the works are stronger. Passed near the battle-ground of the Wilderness and Spottsylvania Court House. We are treading the ground now that the army of the Potomac has marched over time and again, sometimes in victory, and sometimes in defeat.

May 16 (Tuesday)

Jefferson Davis and the officials of the late Confederate Government, captured at Irwinville, Ga., on May 10, were taken down the Savannah River to Port Royal, where they boarded the *William P. Clyde*, Master John L. Kelly, for Hampton Roads, Va. The *Clyde* was escorted by the U.S.S. *Tuscarora*, Commander James M. Frailey, to Virginia.

Barber, Sgt., Co. C, 15th Illinois Volunteer Infantry, en route to Alexandria, Va.:

> Marched at four A.M. Passed through Fredericksburg and crossed the Rappahannok about noon. The town showed evidence of severe fighting, nearly all the houses being perforated with bullets, shells or cannon balls. On the north side of the river the country is more open, and for several miles scarcely any woods are to be seen, the land rolling and soil sandy....

May 17 (Wednesday)

Major Gen. Philip H. Sheridan was today

assigned to command west of the Mississippi and south of the Arkansas rivers—a very large territory. The appointment did not sit too well with some from the South.

May 20 (Saturday)

Former Confederate Secretary of the Navy Mallory was arrested at the home of Benjamin H. Hill in LaGrange, Ga. He was charged with "treason and with organizing and setting on foot piratical expeditions." He was sent to Ft. Lafayette in New York, where he remained until his parole in March 1866.

Barber, Sgt., Co. C, 15th Illinois Volunteer Infantry, Alexandria, Va.:

> Went to the city to-day. The streets were crowded with soldiers from both armies. There was a disposition amongst some to blackguard each other. Alexandria is a city of ten thousand inhabitants and business is very lively, consequent upon so large an army being there. There are over two hundred thousand troops camped in and around it....

May 21 (Sunday)

The C.S.S. *Shenandoah*, Lt. Waddell, entered the Sea of Okhotsk, looking for Yankee whalers.

May 22 (Monday)

President Johnson removed the blockade from most major Southern ports. Former President Davis was imprisoned at Ft. Monroe, Va.

In Albemarle Sound, N.C., Commander Macomb's picket boats seized the steamers *Skirwan*, *Cotton Plant*, *Fisher*, and *Egypt Mills*, near Halifax on the Roanoke River.

Newspaper account:

> *Fort Monroe, Va.*: At one o'clock this afternoon the steamer *Silas B. Pierce* left Baltimore wharf at this place with Brevet Major General Miles, accompanied by other officers of prominence, and proceeded immediately to the steamer *William P. Clyde*, at anchor in the stream, with Jeff. Davis and remainder of the Rebel party on board. An hour, perhaps sufficient to give departing Rebels time to take a long farewell of friends and dear ones, was awarded them.... In a short time after the *Pierce* reached the wharf the prisoners began to land. Such were the arrangements strictly enforced by the military authorities, that no person was allowed to approach the wharf where the prisoners landed except at a distance of over five hundred yards. As the prisoners marched up the wharf, preceded by a guard of their captors of the Fourth Michigan cavalry, the tall, spare form of Jeff. Davis, dressed in grey clothes and wearing a light felt hat, could be easily discerned.... Mrs. Davis and her four children, her brother and sister and the wife of Clement C. Clay remain on board the steamer *Clyde*; and, it is thought, will be sent south this evening, as orders have been received from the War Department prohibiting them from going north. The parting between Jeff. Davis and his family is described to have been of an extremely affecting nature, during which the feelings of the once ambitious and desperate Rebel leader were completely overcome....

May 23 (Tuesday)

Today the Army of the Potomac, after four long years of suffering defeat and then final victory over its old adversary, Gen. Robert E. Lee, marched in its last parade down Pennslyvania Avenue in Washington, D.C. The Grand Review, on its first day, contained seemingly endless lines of blue infantry and artillery and a constant clatter of cavalry as that proud army had its last hurrah. For most it was a day of unbounding joy. For others, it seemed that the ghosts of the thousands of fallen sat sadly in the reviewing stands unable to let the moment go without remembrance.

Jackman, Pvt., "The Orphan Brigade," en route home:

> At last, about the latter part of May, learning the railroad between Atlanta and Chattanooga was about done, we bade our friends good-bye and in a carriage came to Union Point, 12 miles, to take the cars. At 1 P.M. the train for Atlanta came along and we "bounced" it. Eight miles above, at Greensburg, our two other companions came aboard. We got to the ruins of Atlanta late at night and slept under a shade tree until morning.
>
> The next day, finding 60 miles or more of the road not completed, we bargained with a Federal, who had two wagons under his charge, going through to Resaca, to take us over the road. We left Atlanta at

1 P.M. Atlanta looked desolate having been burned since I had last seen it. We camped at Marietta at night. The town was also in ruins.

The next day we came as far as Acworth. The day after we passed through Cartersville, on the Etowah, and Cassville, which was in complete ruins. In the evening we got to Addairsville and took the train for Dalton. The road had just been finished to A-ville and we came up on the construction train. The employees seemed disposed to show us favor. We bivouacked near the depot at Dalton for the night—got there about 10 o'clock P.M.. Cold night. Last time I slept on the ground.

The next morning the train, which was flat cars, left for Chattanooga. Got into Chattanooga at noon. Being quite a number of Confeds along, we could not get transportation that day. At night we put up at the Soldiers Home, "Yank" and "Confed" eating out of the same platter and cracking jokes at each other as though they had never met in many a mortal combat.

The next evening we took train for Nashville and by daylight, or a little after the next morning we were in that city.

Barber, Sgt., Co. C, 15th Illinois Volunteer Infantry, Washington, D.C.:

Cleared off pleasant during the night. Moved camp to-day to the south side of the Potomac in full view of the city of Washington. The Capitol towers up majestically above all the other buildings. We can see the White House, War Department, Washington Monument, and Smithsonian....

To-day the army of the Potomac was reviewed by Grant, Meade, President, Secretary of War and other high government officials. The army was dressed in its gayest suit. The soldiers appeared splendid, showing the effects of good discipline and good living. Their step was elastic and guided by a strict military gait, quite different from the free step of Sherman's army.

To-morrow Sherman's army appears upon the stage. Thousands of visitors from all parts of the United States are flocking to the Capital to witness these grand reviews, the largest and most brilliant ever known. The interest is enhanced greatly from the fact that the two rival armies are just fresh from the victorious fields....

May 24 (Wednesday)

It was the second, and last, day of the Grand Review in Washington. Today the men who marched six thousand miles and gained fame as Sherman's "Bummers" would have their day. This was a different army from the one that had marched the day before. The midwesterners, and most were from that area, had a longer stride that seemed to eat the distance. Their formations were less formal and their uniforms were certainly more ragged. But the hit of the parade was the inclusion of goats, sheep, cattle, chickens, wagons, carts, and all the other "equippage" of the "Bummers" that were in the parade. Sherman's men took pride in being a hard-marching, hard-fighting, independent lot.

Sgt. Barber describes his feelings about the Grand Review. He and his comrades of Sherman's Army would today participate in one of the most splendid parades ever held in Washington. Every veteran who marched in this parade never forgot the feeling of pride, patriotism, and comradeship that pervaded the air this day.

Barber, Sgt., Co. C, 15th Illinois Volunteer Infantry, Washington, D.C.:

The eventful 24th of May dawned bright and beautiful. The heart of every veteran in Sherman's Army beat high in anticipation of the events of the day. We could not doubt our success. The eye of our matchless leader was upon us.... Our regiments of recruits were divided off into companies of twenty files each, and veterans placed in each company as right and left guide. The remainder of the veterans did not join us. They were too proud to mingle on this occasion with men who had never smelled gunpowder. We only went at the request of our Colonel to act as guides, so as to make the regiment appear as well as possible. Rollin and I were right and left guide in one company.

Early in the morning the army commenced crossing Long Bridge and moved towards the Capitol grounds, the 14th and 20th Corps in advance. By ten A.M. we were all massed on the grounds south of the Capitol, and prepared to march in review. At the command to move, seventy-five thousand men in column, with bands playing, drums beating, and colors flying, in exact order and time to the music, marched down Pennsylvania Avenue, saluting our President and commanders as we passed the reviewing stand. For six long hours the steady tramp, tramp, tramp of Sherman's heroes echoed along Pennsylvania Avenue. The shouts of the multitude rent the air. Garlands of flowers were strewed in our pathway, and blessings showered upon us. Though our attire was not as gay as the Potomac Army, yet we excelled them in appearance. We wore the hard, bronzed visage of war incident upon a march of a thousand miles, fighting day after day, bridging rivers, corduroying swamps that before were deemed impassible. I do not wish to detract from the just merits of the Potomac Army, but the press and public bear me out in saying that Sherman's Army bore off the palm. We marched five miles north and went into camp. This is to be our camp while we remain here....

May 25 (Thursday)

In Mobile, Ala., an explosion in a warehouse containing surrendered Confederate ammunition caused a serious fire, threw shrapnel three quarters of a mile, and caused damage estimated at five million dollars. Federal Navy Quartermaster John Cooper who "at the risk of being blown to pieces by exploding shells" entered the fire and carried a wounded man to safety on his back was awarded the Medal of Honor for the second time—his first award being for actions on board the U.S.S. *Brooklyn* in the same area of Mobile in 1864.

Newspaper accounts:

New Orleans, La.: Rebel deserters and escaped prisoners of the Thirty-third Iowa Regiment just arrived from Texas, report that the Union prisoners confined at Tyler, Tex., were allowed to escape in large numbers, the guards saying that, when they are all gone, they will have nothing to do, and then can go home. The interior of Texas is in a terribly disorganized condition. A telegraph line is to be constructed from San Antonio to Austin to Matamoras.

Boston, Mass.: The United States gunboat *Tuscarora*, from Fort Monroe, with Alexander H. Stephens and Postmaster Reegan on board, arrived below this port this morning, and anchored in the Narrows. The Rebel party will be lodged in Fort Warren to-day.

May 26 (Friday)

Today in New Orleans Confederate Lt. Gen. Simon Bolivar Buckner, who surrendered Ft. Donelson to Grant in February 1862, met representatives of Major Gen. Canby to surrender the last significant army of the Confederacy. Gen. Jo Shelby, refusing to surrender, would take some of his men and go to Mexico.

May 27 (Saturday)

President Johnson ordered that most political prisoners held by military authorities be released.

In Annapolis, Lt. Commander Luce arrived with the U.S.S. *Pontiac* from Charleston, S.C. Aboard were a torpedo boat and several torpedoes of various types sent to the Naval Academy by Rear Admiral Dahlgren for display in the museum. In Dahlgren's opinion, Confederate torpedo warfare was "most troublesome" to the Union naval forces, and Secretary Gideon Welles stated that "torpedoes have been more destructive of our naval vessels than all other means combined."

May 29 (Monday)

General amnesty and pardon was granted (with a few exceptions) by President Johnson to all persons who directly, or indirectly, participated in "the existing rebellion."

Jackman, Pvt., "The Orphan Brigade," home at last:

This was May 29th. We were all marched—not under guard—to the Provost Marshal's office and there informed that the Kentuckians could not go home unless first taking the amnesty oath and we were "galvanized." I did not care to wait for government transportation by water, so that evening, at 3 o'clock I took the train for Louisville having to pay my passage and at 7 o'clock at night got off at Bardstown Junction. Rather than wait until the following evening for the train, I immediately started on foot up the railroad and got home about 10 A.M. the 30th of May, having been absent 3 years, 8 months, and 4 days.

May 30 (Tuesday)

Barber, Sgt., Co. C, 15th Illinois Volunteer Infantry, Washington, D.C.:

Warm and pleasant. Went to Washington to-day and visited the Capitol.... The most sacred relic I saw was the original Declaration of Independence with the original signatures attached. The marble statue of Tecumseh represented in the agonies of death is splendid.... I next visited the Patent Office where equal admiration enchained me. Here are laid up in the archives of the nation many ancient relics of our country. Here Washington's personal and military effects are deposited.... Here is Franklin's original printing press and the coat that Jackson wore at the battle of New Orleans... a model of all patents ever issued at the Patent Office... I next visited the Treasury and War Department and White House, each of which was full of interest to a stranger.... I intend to visit the Smithsonian Institution and Mt. Vernon next. The talk is now that we will be sent to Louisville soon and from there to our respective States to be mustered out.

EPILOGUE

It was done. The South had been defeated, the Union restored, and it was time to go home to other pursuits and to get on with life.

At the camps outside Washington, in neighboring Virginia and Maryland, the last muster rolls of the Union troops who had participated in the Grand Review were prepared by the company 1st Sergeants and attested to by the Commanding Officers. Discharge papers were prepared, accounts settled, and the soldiers began their journey home, for the first time in a long time unencumbered by muskets and cartridge boxes. A cadre remained to complete the housekeeping—compiling the records, preparing them for storage, etc., work that would go on for months.

But the war didn't just end with the Grand Review. Many armed troops were still in the field, and much was to be done to gather these men in and effect their surrender. This epilogue summarizes the final stages of the war.

JUNE 1865

The political prisoners held at various facilities around the country were released and sent home. Some had been incarcerated for up to two years.

The British government officially withdrew belligerency rights from the Confederate government.

In Galveston, Tex., Confederate Gen. E. Kirby Smith officially surrendered, accepting the terms outlined in New Orleans on May 26th. On June 3rd, the Southern naval forces on the Red River officially surrendered.

President Andrew Johnson appointed provisional governors to the various states of the late Confederacy.

The C.S.S. *Shenandoah*, Lt. Waddell, captured 19 whalers in the Bering Sea off Alaska during this month, all unaware that the war was over.

On the last day of June, the Lincoln conspirators were found guilty by the military court.

Sgt. Lucius Barber, Co. D, 15th Illinois Volunteer Infantry, had reenlisted for a period of three years on his last reenlistment, believing that he would be discharged at the end of the war. Many of the soldiers whose terms expired in 1863 and 1864 believed as Barber did.

Barber, since the Grand Review, had been sightseeing in Washington and resting up after his long march from South Carolina. On June 8th, Barber left Washington for Illinois, passing through Harpers Ferry on the Baltimore and Ohio Railroad to Parkersburg, W.Va., where he boarded the steamer *G.R. Gilman* on the 10th. With many stops along the way, he passed Cincinnati on the 12th, and arrived in Louisville with his unit on the 15th. On the 20th he was paid up to date, receiving $369.00.

On the 21st, Barber's unit was on the march again, this time for St. Louis, boarding the steamer *Camilla* at Louisville. The reaction to this unexpected event was rather angry:

> Marched at 5 A.M. Took the transport *Camilla* for St. Louis. Are just shoving off from shore and slowly dropping down stream. This sudden move still remains a mystery to us. Some think we are going to be mustered out. Some think that we are going to

> some distant post to do garrison duty. We veterans cannot believe that the government will be guilty of so great an injustice as still keeping us in the service after we have so faithfully performed our part of the contract.

The government, considering that they had at least another year to go on their enlistments, was going to put them to work on the frontier. This was finally disclosed to the troops on June 25th, at which time the reaction became even angrier:

> At St. Louis. Our astonishment and anger knew no bounds when we found that we were to be sent to the frontier to fight Indians. Our brigade commander, General Stolbrand, was the author of this outrage. The recruits had no reason to complain as they were bound to service one year if their services were required, but we had fulfilled our part with the government to the very letter. Symptoms of mutiny began to manifest itself. A large number of the veterans took French leave, determined not to go. To quiet the tumult, orders were issued to grant furloughs—twenty per cent of all enlisted men, but about ninety per cent were given to the veterans. I obtained a furlough without the asking....

Sgt. Barber went to Pennsylvania to attend a wedding at Titusville, where he arrived on the 29th.

JULY 1865

On a hot and humid summer day, July 7th, the assassination conspirators were hanged at the Old Capital Prison in Washington.

Sgt. Barber, arriving at home in Illinois from the wedding in Pennsylvania, found that he and his friend Rollin had received papers from their Company Commander which might be useful in getting them mustered out.

On July 24th, Hillery Boss in Illinois wrote a letter to the parents of Julius Allen in North Carolina concerning the death of the Allens' son. Allen, originally from Salisbury, N.C., had been in Asheville, N.C., at the beginning of the war and had walked almost all the way to Illinois to enlist in the Union Army. He had served with the 10th Illinois Cavalry in the western campaigns, but never returned to Illinois. The letter stated that "he got drowned in the Mississippi river. I suppose his body was not recovered. To my knowledge, he was drowned between the 26th of April, 1863 and June 12, 1863."

On the 27th of July, Barber was really no closer to solving the problem of getting mustered out than he had been.

> We went to Springfield to see if we could not procure our discharge, but did not succeed. I went to Colonel Oaks, chief mustering officer for the State, and presented my descriptive list, but my furlough ordered me to report back to the regiment and he could do nothing for us. I then went to Adjutant-General Hayne and he told me to go to the commandant of the post and if I could induce him to give me an order for a discharge, I would be all right, but he would not do it, so I had no other resource left but to go back to the regiment or return home. I chose the latter alternative, and in company with five of my comrades, I returned on the evening train. I helped father do his harvesting and then Rollin and I started for the regiment.

SEPTEMBER 1865

At long last, Barber, our final protagonist, was mustered out after many trials and tribulations dealing with the bureaucracy.

September 1

> Arrived back at Ft. Leavenworth about the 1st of September, and preparations were immediately made to muster us out. I assisted in making out our company's rolls. I had now been promoted to 3d sergeant.

September 15

> We were mustered out about the middle of the month and the next day started for Springfield for our pay and final discharge. Our progress over the Hannibal and St. Joseph railroad was very tedious and slow. There was hardly a mile of the track but what had been disturbed by guerrillas during the war and it was not yet repaired.

September 30

> On the 30th day of September we received our final pay and discharge. I had worn the livery of Uncle

Sam for four years, five months and twenty-seven days.... it is with a thankful heart and intense joy that I lay aside the honorable title of *Soldier* and once more enjoy the proud title of *American Citizen*, a subject of the best and truest government on God's earth. Before leaving for home, in company with several of my comrades, I paid a parting visit to the tomb of Lincoln at Oak Ridge Cemetery. We passed within the enclosure and registered our names beside hundreds of thousands of others who had been there before us. We then went to the grated opening of the sepulchre and took one last lingering look at the narrow resting place where sleeps all that is mortal of Lincoln, whose noble heart and mind had guided us through all the dark and bloody years of our Nation's struggle for existence....

Sgt. Lucius W. Barber recorded the mileage he had travelled during his life in the Union Army. In total it came to an incredible 10,897 miles. Lucius Barber died in Riley, Illinois, on March 12th, 1872, at the age of 32 years and 9 months. He succumbed to consumption, believed to have been contracted while a prisoner at Andersonville.

NOVEMBER 1865

On November 6th, the C.S.S. *Shenandoah*, Lt. Waddell, surrendered to British officials at Liverpool, England. The ship would be stripped of its armament and used as a merchant vessel. At the time it was finally sunk, in 1879, it was owned by the Sultan of Zanzibar. Waddell, realizing on August 2nd that the South had lost the war and also believing that his actions in sinking so many merchant ships after the war ended had made him an outlaw, disguised the ship and sailed the 17,000 miles to England. He later returned to the United States.

On November 10th, the infamous Capt. Henry Wirz, former commander of Andersonville Prison, was hanged after a military-commission trial in Washington.

APRIL 1866

President Johnson officially declared that the war was over and the insurrection was at an end.

For most of our protagonists, the closing of the war wrote a final chapter of a great adventure which would be relived time and time again until, at last, the final bugle sounding "Taps" was played over the last survivor. The mists of memory would gradually cloud the scenes of bloody combat until they were as if in a dream, real, but unreal, in their vivid flashes of remembrance. The old men the veterans were to become would recount their stories to thousands of wide-eyed children for two generations. They would meet in reunions to relive the glory and remember the dead. They are, Blue and Gray, a part of the American heritage forever.

INDEX

B

C

D

H

I

M

N

Q

R

S

T

Y

Z

ABOUT THE AUTHOR

ROBERT E. DENNEY served with the U.S. Marines in China and on Guam. In 1950 he entered the Army, serving in the Korean and Vietnam Wars. He was wounded in action in Korea and was awarded the Silver Star, Bronze Star with "V" device, and Purple Heart. Graduating from the Warrant Officer's Flight Program in 1956 as a helicopter pilot, he went on to become an Assistant Project Officer for the testing of low-level navigation systems for helicopters. For his performance during these tests, he was awarded the Army Commendation Medal. For various actions in Vietnam, he was awarded the Distinguished Flying Cross, Bronze Star (OLC), several Air Medals, and another Purple Heart. On retirement in 1967 as a major in the Signal Corps, Denney pursued his lifelong interest in the Civil War, an avocation which he attributed to the influence of a high-school history teacher who in the early 1940s "peppered his American History classes with tales he remembered [from his youth] as told by the veterans, and stories of rural Indiana in the late 1800s." A computer systems consultant, Denney is married, has four children and three grandsons, and is a past president of the Civil War Round Table of Washington, D.C.